Reference Guide to

ENGLISH LITERATURE

SECOND EDITION

VOLUME 3

St. James Reference Guides

American Literature

English Literature, 3 vols.

World Literature, 2 vols. (in preparation)

Reference Guide to

ENGLISH LITERATURE

SECOND EDITION

Volume 3
Works
Title Index

EDITOR
D. L. KIRKPATRICK

St J

ST. JAMES PRESS
CHICAGO AND LONDON

For information, write:
ST. JAMES PRESS
233 East Ontario Street
Chicago, Illinois 60611
U.S.A.

or

2–6 Boundary Row
London SE1 8HP
England.

British Library Cataloguing in Publication Data
Reference guide to English literature.—2nd ed.
I. Kirkpatrick, D.L. (Daniel Lane), 1949–
820.3

ISBN 1-55862-150-4

Library of Congress Catalog Card Number: 91–61857

Earlier versions of most of the entries in volumes 1 and 2 were published in *Great Writers of the English Language*, 3 vols., 1978, and in a different format in the *Reference Guide to English Literature*, first edition, 1984.

CONTENTS

ALPHABETICAL LIST OF WORKS

Absalom and Achitophel, poem by John Dryden, 1681
Adam Bede, novel by George Eliot, 1859
The Admirable Crichton, play by J.M. Barrie, 1902
Adonais, poem by Percy Bysshe Shelley, 1821
The Advancement of Learning, prose by Francis Bacon, 1605
The Age of Anxiety, poem by W.H. Auden, 1947
"Air and Angels," poem by John Donne, 1633
The Alchemist, play by Ben Jonson, 1610
The Alexandria Quartet, novels by Lawrence Durrell, 1957–60
Alice's Adventures in Wonderland and *Through the Looking-Glass*, fiction by Lewis Carroll, 1865 and 1871
All for Love, play by John Dryden, 1677
All's Well That Ends Well, play by William Shakespeare, 1602(?)
"The Altar," poem by George Herbert, 1633
The Ambassadors, novel by Henry James, 1903
Amelia, novel by Henry Fielding, 1751
Amoretti, poems by Edmund Spenser, 1595
Ancrene Riwle or *Ancrene Wisse*, prose, late 12th–early 13th century
The Angel in the House, poems by Coventry Patmore, 1854–62
The Anglo-Saxon Chronicle, prose, 9th century–12th century
Animal Farm, novel by George Orwell, 1945
Anne of Green Gables, novel by L.M. Montgomery, 1908
The Anniversaries, poems by John Donne, 1611 and 1612
Antony and Cleopatra, play by William Shakespeare, 1606(?)
Apologia pro Vita Sua, prose by John Henry Newman, 1864
Arcadia, prose by Sir Philip Sidney, 1590
Arden of Faversham, play, c.1587–92
Areopagitica, prose by John Milton, 1644
"As kingfishers catch fire," poem by Gerard Manley Hopkins, written c.1877
As You Like It, play by William Shakespeare, 1600(?)
The Ascent of F6, play by W.H. Auden and Christopher Isherwood, 1936
Astrophel and Stella, poems by Sir Philip Sidney, 1591
At Swim-Two-Birds, novel by Flann O'Brien, 1939
"At the Bay," story by Katherine Mansfield, 1922
Atalanta in Calydon, play by Algernon Charles Swinburne, 1865
Aurora Leigh, poem by Elizabeth Barrett Browning, 1857
The Autobiography of Leigh Hunt, prose by Leigh Hunt, 1850
Autumn Journal, poem by Louis MacNeice, 1939

Barnaby Rudge, novel by Charles Dickens, 1841
Barrack-Room Ballads, poems by Rudyard Kipling, 1892
Barsetshire series, novels by Anthony Trollope, 1855–67
Bartholomew Fair, play by Ben Jonson, 1614
"Batter my heart" (Holy Sonnet 14), poem by John Donne, 1633 (written c. 1609)
The Battle of Maldon, poem, 11th century
"A Beautiful Young Nymph Going to Bed," poem by Jonathan Swift, 1734
The Beaux' Stratagem, play by George Farquhar, 1707
The Beggar's Opera, play by John Gay, 1728
A Bend in the River, novel by V.S. Naipaul, 1979
Beowulf, poem, 8th century
The Berlin Stories, fiction by Christopher Isherwood, 1935–49
"Bermudas," poem by Andrew Marvell, 1681 (written c. 1653)
Biographia Literaria, prose by Samuel Taylor Coleridge, 1817
The Birthday Party, play by Harold Pinter, 1958
Bleak House, novel by Charles Dickens, 1853
The Book of Common Prayer, liturgy, 1549 (and later editions)
The Book of Margery Kempe, prose by Margery Kempe, 1432–36(?)
The Book of the Duchess, poem by Geoffrey Chaucer, c.1370
Brave New World, novel by Aldous Huxley, 1932
Brideshead Revisited, novel by Evelyn Waugh, 1945
Brighton Rock, novel by Graham Greene, 1938
The Browning Version, play by Terence Rattigan, 1948
Brut, prose, c.1400
Bussy D'Ambois, play by George Chapman, 1604

Caedmon's *Hymn*, poem, c.657–80
Caleb Williams, novel by William Godwin, 1794
The Canterbury Tales, poetry and prose by Geoffrey Chaucer, wrriten from c.1387
Capricornia, novel by Xavier Herbert, 1938
The Castle of Indolence, poem by James Thomson, 1748
The Castle of Otranto, novel by Horace Walpole, 1764
The Castle of Perseverance, play, early 15th century
Castle Rackrent, novel by Maria Edgeworth, 1800
The Changeling, play by Thomas Middleton and William Rowley, 1622
A Chaste Maid in Cheapside, play by Thomas Middleton, c.1613
Childe Harold's Pilgrimage, poem by Lord Byron, 1812–18
"Childe Roland to the Dark Tower Came," poem by Robert Browning, 1855
Children of the Ghetto, novel by Israel Zangwill, 1892
"Christabel," poem by Samuel Taylor Coleridge, 1816
A Christmas Carol, story by Charles Dickens, 1843
The Chronicles of England, Scotland, and Ireland, prose by Raphael Holinshed and others, 1577; revised edition, 1587
Cider with Rosie, prose by Laurie Lee, 1959
"The City of Dreadful Night," poem by James Thomson (B.V.), 1880
The Clandestine Marriage, play by George Colman the Elder and David Garrick, 1766
Clarissa, novel by Samuel Richardson, 1747–48
Cleanness, poem by the Gawain Poet, late 14th century
The Cloister and the Hearth, novel by Charles Reade, 1861
The Cloud of Unknowing, prose, c.1370
The Comedy of Errors, play by William Shakespeare, 1594(?)

The Compleat Angler, prose by Izaak Walton, 1653
Comus, play by John Milton, 1634
Confessio Amantis, poetry by John Gower, 1390
Confessions of an English Opium Eater, prose by Thomas De Quincey, 1822
The Conscious Lovers, play by Sir Richard Steele, 1722
The Conservationist, novel by Nadine Gordimer, 1974
Cooper's Hill, poem by Sir John Denham, 1642
"Corinna's Going a-Maying," poem by Robert Herrick, 1648
Coriolanus, play by William Shakespeare, 1606(?)
The Country Parson, prose by George Herbert, 1652
The Country-Wife, play by William Wycherley, 1675
Cranford, novel by Elizabeth Gaskell, 1853
Cry, The Beloved Country, novel by Alan Paton, 1948
Culture and Anarchy, prose by Matthew Arnold, 1869
Cymbeline, play by William Shakespeare, 1609(?)

A Dance to the Music of Time, 12 novels by Anthony Powell, 1951–75
Daniel Deronda, novel by George Eliot, 1876
"The Daughters of the Late Colonel," story by Katherine Mansfield, 1922
David Copperfield, novel by Charles Dickens, 1850
De Profundis, prose by Oscar Wilde, 1905
"The Dead," story by James Joyce, 1914
The Death of the Heart, novel by Elizabeth Bowen, 1938
The Defence of Poesy, prose by Sir Philip Sidney, 1595
"A Defence of Poetry," prose by Percy Bysshe Shelley, 1840 (written 1821)
Delia, poems by Samuel Daniel, 1592
The Deptford Trilogy, novels by Robertson Davies, 1970–75
The Deserted Village, poem by Oliver Goldsmith, 1770
The Devils, play by John Whiting, 1961
A Dictionary of the English Language, work by Samuel Johnson, 1755
Doctor Faustus, play by Christopher Marlowe, 1594
Dr. Jekyll and Mr. Hyde, story of Robert Louis Stevenson, 1886
Dombey and Son, novel by Charles Dickens, 1848
Don Juan, poem by Lord Byron, 1819–24
The Double-Dealer, play by William Congreve, 1693
Douglas, play by John Home, 1756
"Dover Beach," poem by Matthew Arnold, 1867
Dracula, novel by Bram Stoker, 1897
The Dream of the Rood, poem, in 10th century manuscript
Dream on Monkey Mountain, play by Derek Walcott, 1967
A Drunk Man Looks at the Thistle, poem by Hugh MacDiarmid, 1926
The Duchess of Malfi, play by John Webster, 1614
The Dunciad, poem by Alexander Pope, 1728–43

East Lynne, novel by Ellen Price Wood, 1861
"Easter 1916," poem by William Butler Yeats, 1916
Eastward Ho, play by George Chapman, Ben Jonson, and John Marston, 1605
Edward II, play by Christopher Marlowe, 1592(?)
The Egoist, novel by George Meredith, 1879
An Elegy Written in a Country Churchyard, poem by Thomas Gray, 1751
Emma, novel by Jane Austen, 1815
The End of the Affair, novel by Graham Greene, 1951
Endgame, play by Samuel Beckett, 1958
Endymion, play by John Lyly, 1588
English Bards and Scotch Reviewers, poem by Lord Byron, 1809
Epicoene, play by Ben Jonson, 1609
Epithalamion, poem by Edmund Spenser, 1595
Erewhon, novel by Samuel Butler, 1872
An Essay Concerning Human Understanding, prose by John Locke, 1690
An Essay on Criticism, poem by Alexander Pope, 1711
An Essay on Man, poem by Alexander Pope, 1733–34
An Essay on the Principle of Population, prose by Thomas Malthus, 1798
Essays, prose by Francis Bacon, 1597
The Essays of Elia, prose by Charles Lamb, 1823–33
Euphues, prose by John Lyly, 1578
"The Eve of St Agnes," poem by John Keats, 1820
Evelina, novel by Fanny Burney, 1778
Every Man in His Humour, play by Ben Jonson, 1598
Everyman, play, c.1510–35
The Exeter Book, manuscript of poetry, 10th century

The Faerie Queene, poem by Edmund Spenser, 1590–96
The Fair Maid of the West, play by Thomas Heywood, part 1, before 1610; part 2, 1630(?)
Fair Stood the Wind for France, novel by H.E. Bates, 1944
Fanny Hill, novel by John Cleland, 1748–49
Father and Son, prose by Edmund Gosse, 1907
Felix Holt, novel by George Eliot, 1866
The Female Quixote, novel by Charlotte Lennox, 1752
Finnegans Wake, novel by James Joyce, 1939
For the Term of His Natural Life, novel by Marcus Clarke, 1874
"The force that through the green fuse drives the flower," poem by Dylan Thomas, 1934
The Forsyte Saga, fiction by John Galsworthy, 1906–21
The Fortunes of Richard Mahony, novel by Henry Handel Richardson, 1917–29
Four Quartets, poems by T.S. Eliot, 1943
"Fra Lippo Lippi," poem by Robert Browning, 1855
Frankenstein, novel by Mary Shelley, 1818
The French Revolution, prose by Thomas Carlyle, 1837
Friar Bacon and Friar Bungay, play by Robert Greene, 1589(?)
"The Function of Criticism at the Present Time," prose by Matthew Arnold, 1865

Gammer Gurton's Needle, play, c.1550–60
"The Garden," poem by Andrew Marvell, 1681 (written c.1650–52)
Gitanjali, poems by Rabindranath Tagore, 1912
The Go-Between, novel by L.P. Hartley, 1953
Goblin Market, poem by Christina Rossetti, 1862
The Golden Bowl, novel by Henry James, 1904
The Golden Notebook, novel by Doris Lessing, 1962
The Good Companions, novel by J.B. Priestley, 1929
The Good Soldier, novel by Ford Madox Ford, 1915
Gorboduc, play by Thomas Sackville and Thomas Norton, 1562
Great Expectations, novel by Charles Dickens, 1861
Green Mansions, novel by W.H. Hudson, 1904
"Guests of the Nation," story by Frank O'Connor, 1931
Gulliver's Travels, fiction by Jonathan Swift, 1726

Hamlet, play by William Shakespeare, 1601(?)
A Handful of Dust, novel by Evelyn Waugh, 1934
Handley Cross, novel by R.S. Surtees, 1843
The Handmaid's Tale, novel by Margaret Atwood, 1985
Hard Times, novel by Charles Dickens, 1854
Havelok, poem, late 13th century
"The Haystack in the Floods," poem by William Morris, 1858
"Heart of Darkness," story by Joseph Conrad, 1902

The Heart of Mid-Lothian, novel by Sir Walter Scott, 1818
The Heart of the Matter, novel by Graham Greene, 1948
Heartbreak House, play by Bernard Shaw, 1919
Henry IV, part 1, play by William Shakespeare, 1596–97(?)
Henry IV, part 2, play by William Shakespeare, 1597–98(?)
Henry V, play by William Shakespeare, 1599
Henry VI, parts 1–3, plays by William Shakespeare, 1591–92(?)
Henry VIII, play by William Shakespeare and John Fletcher, 1613
Henry Esmond, novel by William Makepeace Thackeray, 1852
Hero and Leander, poem by Christopher Marlowe, 1598
Hindle Wakes, play by Stanley Houghton, 1912
The History of England, prose by Thomas Babington Macaulay, 1848–61
The History of the World, prose by Sir Walter Ralegh, 1614
Hobson's Choice, play by Harold Brighouse, 1915
"Holy Willie's Prayer," poem by Robert Burns, 1799 (written 1785)
The Homecoming, play by Harold Pinter, 1965
The Honest Whore, play by Thomas Dekker and Thomas Middleton, 1604
"An Horatian Ode upon Cromwell's Return from Ireland," poem by Andrew Marvell, 1681 (written 1650)
The Horse's Mouth, novel by Joyce Cary, 1944
The Hostage, play by Brendan Behan, 1958
"The Hound of Heaven," poem by Francis Thompson, 1893
The Hound of the Baskervilles, novel by Arthur Conan Doyle, 1902
The House of Fame, poem by Geoffrey Chaucer, written c.1379
The House of Life, poems by Dante Gabriel Rossetti, 1870 and 1881
Howards End, novel by E.M. Forster, 1910
Humphry Clinker, novel by Tobias Smollett, 1771
Hyde Park, play by James Shirley, 1632

I, Claudius and *Claudius the God*, novels by Robert Graves, 1934
"I Hid My Love," poem by John Clare, written late 1840's
Idylls of the King, poems by Alfred, Lord Tennyson, from 1859
Imaginary Conversations, prose by Walter Savage Landor, 1824–29 and 1853
The Importance of Being Earnest, play by Oscar Wilde, 1895
In Memoriam, poem by Alfred, Lord Tennyson, 1850
"Intimations of Immortality from Recollections of Early Childhood," poem by William Wordsworth, 1807
Iolanthe, opera by W.S. Gilbert, music by Arthur Sullivan, 1882

Jane Eyre, novel by Charlotte Brontë, 1847
Joseph Andrews, novel by Henry Fielding, 1742
A Journal of the Plague Year, fiction by Daniel Defoe, 1722
Journey's End, play by R.C. Sherriff, 1928
Jude the Obscure, novel by Thomas Hardy, 1895
Julius Caesar, play by William Shakespeare, 1599
The Jungle Books, stories by Rudyard Kipling, 1894–95
Juno and the Paycock, play by Sean O'Casey, 1924

Kim, novel by Rudyard Kipling, 1901
King John, play by William Shakespeare, 1594–96(?)
King Lear, play by William Shakespeare, 1605
King Solomon's Mines, novel by H. Rider Haggard, 1885
"Kinship," poem by Seamus Heaney, 1975
The Knight of the Burning Pestle, play by Francis Beaumont, c.1607
Krapp's Last Tape, play by Samuel Beckett, 1958
"Kubla Khan," poem by Samuel Taylor Coleridge, 1816 (written 1797)

Lady Audley's Secret, novel by Mary Elizabeth Braddon, 1862
Lady Chatterley's Lover, novel by D.H. Lawrence, 1928 (and later versions)
"The Lady of Shalott," poem by Alfred, Lord Tennyson, 1832
The Lady's Not for Burning, play by Christopher Fry, 1948
"The Lake Isle of Innisfree," poem by William Butler Yeats, 1890
Lalla Rookh, poetry and prose by Thomas Moore, 1817
"L'Allegro" and "Il Penseroso," poems by John Milton, 1645 (written c.1631)
Lament for the Makaris, poem by William Dunbar, 1505–08
"Lamia," poem by John Keats, 1820
Lavengro, fiction by George Borrow, 1851
Lays of Ancient Rome, poems by Thomas Babington Macaulay, 1842
Leviathan, prose by Thomas Hobbes, 1651
The Life of Samuel Johnson, prose by James Boswell, 1791
Little Dorrit, novel by Charles Dickens, 1857
The Lives of the English Poets, prose by Samuel Johnson, 1779–81
The London Merchant, play by George Lillo, 1731
Look Back in Anger, play by John Osborne, 1956
Lord Jim, novel by Joseph Conrad, 1900
Lord of the Flies, novel by William Golding, 1954
The Lord of the Rings, novels by J.R.R. Tolkien, 1954–55
Lorna Doone, novel by R.D. Blackmore, 1869
"The Love Song of J. Alfred Prufrock," poem by T.S. Eliot, 1917
"Lovers of the Lake," story by Sean O'Faolain, 1957
Love's Labour's Lost, play by William Shakespeare, 1594(?)
Lucky Jim, novel by Kingsley Amis, 1954
Lycidas, poem by John Milton, 1638

Macbeth, play by William Shakespeare, 1606
Mac Flecknoe, poem by John Dryden, 1682
The Madras House, play by Harley Granville Barker, 1910
The Maid's Tragedy, play by Francis Beaumont and John Fletcher, before 1611
Major Barbara, play by Bernard Shaw, 1905
The Malcontent, play by John Marston, 1602–03(?)
Man and Superman, play by Bernard Shaw, 1903
The Man of Feeling, novel by Henry Mackenzie, 1771
The Man of Mode, play by Sir George Etherege, 1676
The Man Who Died, novella by D.H. Lawrence, 1929
The Man Who Loved Children, novel by Christina Stead, 1940
Mansfield Park, novel by Jane Austen, 1814
Marius the Epicurean, novel by Walter Pater, 1885
The Marriage of Heaven and Hell, prose and poetry by William Blake, 1793(?)
Martin Chuzzlewit, novel by Charles Dickens, 1844
Martin Marprelate pamphlets, 7 prose tracts, 1588–89
Mary Barton, novel by Elizabeth Gaskell, 1848
Maud, poem by Alfred, Lord Tennyson, 1855
The Mayor of Casterbridge, novel by Thomas Hardy, 1886
Measure for Measure, play by William Shakespeare, 1604(?)
Melmoth the Wanderer, novel by Charles Robert Maturin, 1820

The Merchant of Venice, play by William Shakespeare, 1596(?)
The Merry Wives of Windsor, play by William Shakespeare, 1597
Middlemarch, novel by George Eliot, 1872
A Midsummer Night's Dream, play by William Shakespeare, 1595(?)
The Mill on the Floss, novel by George Eliot, 1860
Milton, poem by William Blake, 1804–08(?)
The Mirror for Magistrates, poetry, 1559 (and later revisions)
Mr. Perrin and Mr. Traill, novel by Hugh Walpole, 1911
Mrs. Dalloway, novel by Virginia Woolf, 1925
Mrs. Warren's Profession, play by Bernard Shaw, 1898
Modern Love, poem by George Meredith, 1862
Modern Painters, prose by John Ruskin, 1843–60
A Modest Proposal, prose by Jonathan Swift, 1729
Moll Flanders, fiction by Daniel Defoe, 1722
Molloy, *Malone Dies*, and *The Unnamable*, novels by Samuel Beckett, 1955–58
The Monk, novel by Matthew Gregory Lewis, 1796
"The Monkey's Paw," story by W.W. Jacobs, 1902
Morte Arthure (Alliterative), poem, late 14th century
"Mountain Lion," poem by D.H. Lawrence, 1923
Mucedorus, play, 1598
Much Ado about Nothing, play by William Shakespeare, 1598(?)
Murder in the Cathedral, play by T.S. Eliot, 1935
"My First Acquaintance with Poets," prose by William Hazlitt, 1823
"My Last Duchess," poem by Robert Browning, 1842
The Mysteries of Udolpho, novel by Ann Radcliffe, 1794
The Mystery of Edwin Drood, novel by Charles Dickens, 1870

New Grub Street, novel by George Gissing, 1891
A New Way to Pay Old Debts, play by Philip Massinger, 1625(?)
News from Nowhere, fiction by William Morris, 1890
Nightmare Abbey, fiction by Thomas Love Peacock, 1818
Night-Thoughts, poem by Edward Young, 1742–46
Nineteen Eighty-Four, novel by George Orwell, 1949
North and South, novel by Elizabeth Gaskell, 1855
Northanger Abbey, novel by Jane Austen, 1817
Nostromo, novel by Joseph Conrad, 1904

Ode on a Distant Prospect of Eton College, poem by Thomas Gray, 1747
"Ode on a Grecian Urn," poem by John Keats, 1820
"Ode on Melancholy," poem by John Keats, 1820
"Ode to a Nightingale," poem by John Keats, 1820
"Ode to the West Wind," poem by Percy Bysshe Shelley, 1820
Of Dramatic Poesy, prose by John Dryden, 1668
The Old Curiosity Shop, novel by Charles Dickens, 1841
"Old Man's Story," story by Frank Sargeson, 1940
Old Mortality, novel by Sir Walter Scott, 1816
The Old Wives Tale, play by George Peele, 1591–94(?)
The Old Wives' Tale, novel by Arnold Bennett, 1908
Oliver Twist, novel by Charles Dickens, 1838
On Liberty, prose by John Stuart Mill, 1859
"On the Move," poem by Thom Gunn, 1957
"On the Wounds of Our Crucified Lord," poem by Richard Crashaw, 1646
Orchestra, poem by Sir John Davies, 1596
The Ordeal of Richard Feverel, novel by George Meredith, 1859
The Origin of Species, prose by Charles Darwin, 1859 (6 revisions, 1860–76)
Oroonoko, novel by Aphra Behn, 1688
Ossian, poems by James Macpherson, 1760–63
Othello, play by William Shakespeare, 1604(?)
Our Mutual Friend, novel by Charles Dickens, 1865
The Owl and the Nightingale, poem, late 12th–early 13th century
"The Owl and the Pussy-Cat," poem by Edward Lear, 1870
Owls Do Cry, novel by Janet Frame, 1957

The Painter of Signs, novel by R.K. Narayan, 1976
Palliser series, 6 novels by Anthony Trollope, 1864–80
Pamela, novel by Samuel Richardson, 1740–41
Paradise Lost, poem by John Milton, 1667
Paradise Regained, poem by John Milton, 1671
The Parliament of Fowls, poem by Geoffrey Chaucer, c.1380
A Passage to India, novel by E.M. Forster, 1924
Patience, poem by the Gawain Poet, late 14th century
Pearl, poem by the Gawain Poet, late 14th century
"The Pearl," poem by George Herbert, 1633
Pericles, play by William Shakespeare and George Wilkins, 1608(?)
Persuasion, novel by Jane Austen, 1817
Peter Pan, play by J.M. Barrie, 1904
The Pickwick Papers, novel by Charles Dickens, 1837
The Picture of Dorian Gray, novel by Oscar Wilde, 1891
Pig Island Letters, poems by James K. Baxter, 1966
Pilgrimage, novel by Dorothy Richardson, 1915–38
The Pilgrim's Progress, fiction by John Bunyan, 1678 and 1684
The Plain-Dealer, play by William Wycherley, 1676
The Playboy of the Western World, play by J.M. Synge, 1907
The Pleasures of Imagination, poem by Mark Akenside, 1744; revised edition, 1772
The Plough and the Stars, play by Sean O'Casey, 1926
"Poems of 1912–13," poems by Thomas Hardy, 1914
The Portrait of a Lady, novel by Henry James, 1881
A Portrait of the Artist as a Young Man, novel by James Joyce, 1916
Preface to *Lyrical Ballads*, prose by William Wordsworth, 1800
The Prelude, poem by William Wordsworth, 1850 (written from 1798)
Pride and Prejudice, novel by Jane Austen, 1813
The Prime of Miss Jean Brodie, novel by Muriel Spark, 1961
The Prisoner of Zenda, novel by Anthony Hope, 1894
Private Lives, play by Noël Coward, 1930
The Private Memoirs and Confessions of a Justified Sinner, novel by James Hogg, 1824
The Private Papers of Henry Ryecroft, fiction by George Gissing, 1903
Prometheus Unbound, play by Percy Bysshe Shelley, 1820
The Provoked Wife, play by Sir John Vanbrugh, 1697
The Provost, novel by John Galt, 1822
Purgatory, play by William Butler Yeats, 1938
Pygmalion, play by Bernard Shaw, 1914

"R. Alcona to J. Brenzaida" ("Remembrance"), poem by Emily Brontë, 1846
"Rain," story by W. Somerset Maugham, 1921
The Rainbow, novel by D.H. Lawrence, 1915
Ralph Roister Doister, play by Nicholas Udall, 1553(?)
The Rambler, periodical edited by Samuel Johnson, 1750–52 and *The Idler*, series of essays by Samuel Johnson, 1758–60

The Rape of Lucrece, poem by William Shakespeare, 1594
The Rape of the Lock, poem by Alexander Pope, 1714
Rasselas, fiction by Samuel Johnson, 1759
Rebecca, novel by Daphne du Maurier, 1938
The Recruiting Officer, play by George Farquhar, 1706
Redgauntlet, novel by Sir Walter Scott, 1824
The Relapse, play by Sir John Vanbrugh, 1696
Religio Medici, prose by Sir Thomas Browne, 1642
The Renaissance, prose by Walter Pater, 1873 (and later revisions)
The Return of the Native, novel by Thomas Hardy, 1878
Revelations of Divine Love, prose by Julian (Juliana) of Norwich, written c.1373 and c.1393
The Revenger's Tragedy, play by Thomas Middleton or Cyril Tourneur, c.1606
Richard II, play by William Shakespeare, 1595–96(?)
Richard III, play by William Shakespeare, 1592(?)
Riders to the Sea, play by J.M. Synge, 1904
The Rights of Man, prose by Thomas Paine, 1791–92
"The Rime of the Ancient Mariner," poem by Samuel Taylor Coleridge, 1798
The Ring and the Book, poem by Robert Browning, 1868–69
The Rival Queens, play by Nathaniel Lee, 1677
The Rivals, play by Richard Brinsley Sheridan, 1775
The Road, play by Wole Soyinka, 1965
Robinson Crusoe, fiction by Daniel Defoe, 1719
Roderick Random, novel by Tobias Smollett, 1748
Romeo and Juliet, play by William Shakespeare, 1594–95(?)
Rosalynde, fiction by Thomas Lodge, 1590
Rosencrantz and Guildenstern Are Dead, play by Tom Stoppard, 1966
The Rover, play by Aphra Behn, 1677
Rubáiyát of Omar Khayyám, poems by Edward FitzGerald, 1859 (and later revisions)
Rural Rides, prose by William Cobbett, 1830

"Sailing to Byzantium," poem by William Butler Yeats, 1928
Saint Joan, play by Bernard Shaw, 1923
Salome, play by Oscar Wilde, 1894
Samson Agonistes, play by John Milton, 1671
Sartor Resartus, fiction by Thomas Carlyle, 1836
A Satire Against Reason and Mankind, poem by John Wilmot, Earl of Rochester, 1679
Saved, play by Edward Bond, 1965
Scenes of Clerical Life, stories by George Eliot, 1858
The School for Scandal, play by Richard Brinsley Sheridan, 1777
The Sea, The Sea, novel by Iris Murdoch, 1978
The Seafarer, poem, in 10th-century manuscript
The Seasons, poem by James Thomson, 1726–30
"The Second Coming," poem by William Butler Yeats, 1920
The Second Mrs. Tanqueray, play by Arthur Wing Pinero, 1893
The Second Shepherds' Play, play by the Wakefield Master, 15th century
The Secret Agent, novel by Joseph Conrad, 1907
"The Secret Sharer," story by Joseph Conrad, 1912
Sense and Sensibility, novel by Jane Austen, 1811
A Sentimental Journey Through France and Italy, novel by Laurence Sterne, 1768
Serjeant Musgrave's Dance, play by John Arden, 1959
The Shaughraun, play by Dion Boucicault, 1874
She Stoops to Conquer, play by Oliver Goldsmith, 1773
The Shepheardes Calender, poems by Edmund Spenser, 1579
"The Shield of Achilles," poem by W.H. Auden, 1955
Shirley, novel by Charlotte Brontë, 1849
The Shoemaker's Holiday, play by Thomas Dekker, 1599
A Shropshire Lad, poems by A.E. Housman, 1896
Silas Marner, novel by George Eliot, 1861
Sinister Street, novel by Compton Mackenzie, 1913–14
Sir Charles Grandison, novel by Samuel Richardson, 1753–54
Sir Gawain and the Green Knight, poem by the Gawain Poet, late 14th century
Sir Orfeo, poem, early 14th century
Sir Thomas More, play by Anthony Munday, William Shakespeare, and others, written c.1593–1601
Sizwe Bansi Is Dead, play by Athol Fugard, 1972
Sketches by Boz, fiction by Charles Dickens, 1836
A Song to David, poem by Christopher Smart, 1763
Songs of Innocence and of Experience, poems by William Blake, 1794
Sonnets 33–35 and 71–74, poems by William Shakespeare, 1609 (possibly written 1590's)
Sonnets from the Portuguese, poems by Elizabeth Barrett Browning, 1850
Sons and Lovers, novel by D.H. Lawrence, 1913
The Spanish Tragedy, play by Thomas Kyd, 1589(?)
"Spelt from Sibyl's Leaves," poem by Gerard Manley Hopkins, written 1884
The Spoils of Poynton, novella by Henry James, 1897
The Stones of Venice, prose by John Ruskin, 1851–53
The Story of an African Farm, novel by Olive Schreiner, 1883
"Strange Meeting," poem by Wilfred Owen, written 1918
Strife, play by John Galsworthy, 1909
Sublime and Beautiful, prose by Edmund Burke, 1757; revised edition, 1759
Such Is Life, fiction by Joseph Furphy, 1903
Summer Lightning, novel by P.G. Wodehouse, 1929
Sunshine Sketches of a Little Town, fiction by Stephen Leacock, 1912

A Tale of a Tub, fiction by Jonathan Swift, 1704
A Tale of Two Cities, novel by Charles Dickens, 1859
"Tam o' Shanter," poem by Robert Burns, 1791
Tamburlaine the Great, play by Christopher Marlowe, 1587(?)
The Taming of the Shrew, play by William Shakespeare, 1594
The Task, poem by William Cowper, 1785
The Tatler, periodical edited by Sir Richard Steele, 1709–11, and *The Spectator*, periodical edited by Joseph Addison and Sir Richard Steele, 1711–12
The Tempest, play by William Shakespeare, 1611
Tess of the d'Urbervilles, novel by Thomas Hardy, 1891
The Testament of Cresseid, poem by Robert Henryson, c.1465–90
Testament of Youth, prose by Vera Brittain, 1933
"They flee from me," poem by Sir Thomas Wyatt, 1557
Things Fall Apart, novel by Chinua Achebe, 1958
Three Men in a Boat, novel by Jerome K. Jerome, 1889
The Time Machine, novel by H.G. Wells, 1895
Timon of Athens, play by William Shakespeare, 1607(?)
"Tintern Abbey," poem by William Wordsworth, 1798
'Tis Pity She's a Whore, play by John Ford, 1629–33(?)
Titus Andronicus, play by William Shakespeare, 1594
"To a Skylark," poem by Percy Bysshe Shelley, 1820
"To Autumn," poem by John Keats, 1820
"To His Coy Mistress," poem by Andrew Marvell, 1681
"To Penshurst," poem by Ben Jonson, 1616

CHRONOLOGICAL LIST OF WORKS

Caedmon's *Hymn*, poem, c.657–80
Beowulf, poem, 8th century
The Anglo-Saxon Chronicle, prose, 9th century–12th century
The Exeter Book, manuscript of poetry, 10th century
The Seafarer, poem, in 10th-century manuscript
Wulf and Eadwacer, poem, possibly mid-10th century
The Dream of the Rood, poem, in 10th century manuscript
The Battle of Maldon, poem, 11th century
Ancrene Riwle or *Ancrene Wisse*, prose, late 12th–early 13th century
The Owl and the Nightingale, poem, late 12th–early 13th century
Havelok, poem, late 13th century
Sir Orfeo, poem, early 14th century
Morte Arthure (Alliterative), poem, late 14th century
The Book of the Duchess, poem by Geoffrey Chaucer, c.1370
The Cloud of Unknowing, prose, c.1370
Revelations of Divine Love, prose by Julian (Juliana) of Norwich, written c.1373 and c.1393
Cleanness, poem by the Gawain Poet, late 14th century
Patience, poem by the Gawain Poet, late 14th century
Pearl, poem by the Gawain Poet, late 14th century
Sir Gawain and the Green Knight, poem by the Gawain Poet, late 14th century
The House of Fame, poem by Geoffrey Chaucer, written c.1379
The Parliament of Fowls, poem by Geoffrey Chaucer, c.1380
Troilus and Criseyde, poem by Geoffrey Chaucer, c.1385
The Canterbury Tales, poetry and prose by Geoffrey Chaucer, written from c.1387
Confessio Amantis, poetry by John Gower, 1390
Brut, prose, c.1400
The Castle of Perseverance, play, early 15th century
The Book of Margery Kempe, prose by Margery Kempe, 1432–36(?)
The Second Shepherds' Play, play by the Wakefield Master, 15th century
The Testament of Cresseid, poem by Robert Henryson, c.1465–90
"The Twa Corbies," ballad, possibly 15th century
Lament for the Makaris, poem by William Dunbar, 1505–08
Everyman, play, c.1510–35
Utopia, prose by Sir Thomas More, 1516
The Book of Common Prayer, liturgy, 1549 (and later editions)
Gammer Gurton's Needle, play, c.1550–60
Ralph Roister Doister, play by Nicholas Udall, 1553(?)
"They flee from me," poem by Sir Thomas Wyatt, 1557
Tottel's Miscellany, collection of poems, 1557
The Mirror for Magistrates, poetry, 1559 (and later revisions)
Gorboduc, play by Thomas Sackville and Thomas Norton, 1562
The Chronicles of England, Scotland, and Ireland, prose by Raphael Holinshed and others, 1577; revised edition, 1587
Euphues, prose by John Lyly, 1578
The Shepheardes Calender, poems by Edmund Spenser, 1579
Arden of Faversham, play, c.1587–92
Tamburlaine the Great, play by Christopher Marlowe, 1587(?)
Endymion, play by John Lyly, 1588
Martin Marprelate pamphlets, 7 prose tracts, 1588–89
Friar Bacon and Friar Bungay, play by Robert Greene, 1589(?)
The Spanish Tragedy, play by Thomas Kyd, 1589(?)
Arcadia, prose by Sir Philip Sidney, 1590
Rosalynde, fiction by Thomas Lodge, 1590
The Faerie Queene, poem by Edmund Spenser, 1590–96
Astrophel and Stella, poems by Sir Philip Sidney, 1591
Henry VI, parts 1–3, plays by William Shakespeare, 1591–92(?)
The Old Wives Tale, play by George Peele, 1591–94(?)
Delia, poems by Samuel Daniel, 1592
Edward II, play by Christopher Marlowe, 1592(?)
Richard III, play by William Shakespeare, 1592(?)
Sir Thomas More, play by Anthony Munday, William Shakespeare, and others, written c. 1593–1601
Venus and Adonis, poem by William Shakespeare, 1593
Doctor Faustus, play by Christopher Marlowe, 1594
King John, play by William Shakespeare, 1594–96(?)
Love's Labour's Lost, play by William Shakespeare, 1594(?)
Romeo and Juliet, play by William Shakespeare, 1594–95(?)
The Comedy of Errors, play by William Shakespeare, 1594(?)
The Rape of Lucrece, poem by William Shakespeare, 1594
The Taming of the Shrew, play by William Shakespeare, 1594
The Two Gentlemen of Verona, play by William Shakespeare, 1594(?)
The Unfortunate Traveller, fiction by Thomas Nashe, 1594
Titus Andronicus, play by William Shakespeare, 1594
A Midsummer Night's Dream, play by William Shakespeare, 1595(?)
Amoretti, poems by Edmund Spenser, 1595
Epithalamion, poem by Edmund Spenser, 1595
Richard II, play by William Shakespeare, 1595–96(?)
The Defence of Poesy, prose by Sir Philip Sidney, 1595
Henry IV, part 1, play by William Shakespeare, 1596–97(?)
Orchestra, poem by Sir John Davies, 1596
The Merchant of Venice, play by William Shakespeare, 1596(?)
Essays, prose by Francis Bacon, 1597
Henry IV, part 2, play by William Shakespeare, 1597–98(?)

The Merry Wives of Windsor, play by William Shakespeare, 1597
Every Man in His Humour, play by Ben Jonson, 1598
Hero and Leander, poem by Christopher Marlowe, 1598
Mucedorus, play, 1598
Much Ado about Nothing, play by William Shakespeare, 1598(?)
Henry V, play by William Shakespeare, 1599
Julius Caesar, play by William Shakespeare, 1599
The Shoemaker's Holiday, play by Thomas Dekker, 1599
As You Like It, play by William Shakespeare, 1600(?)
Hamlet, play by William Shakespeare, 1601(?)
Twelfth Night, play by William Shakespeare, 1601–02(?)
All's Well That Ends Well, play by William Shakespeare, 1602(?)
The Malcontent, play by John Marston, 1602–03(?)
Troilus and Cressida, play by William Shakespeare, 1602(?)
A Woman Killed with Kindness, play by Thomas Heywood, 1603
Bussy D'Ambois, play by George Chapman, 1604
Measure for Measure, play by William Shakespeare, 1604(?)
Othello, play by William Shakespeare, 1604(?)
The Honest Whore, play by Thomas Dekker and Thomas Middleton, 1604
Eastward Ho, play by George Chapman, Ben Jonson, and John Marston, 1605
King Lear, play by William Shakespeare, 1605
The Advancement of Learning, prose by Francis Bacon, 1605
Volpone, play by Ben Jonson, 1605–06
Antony and Cleopatra, play by William Shakespeare, 1606(?)
Coriolanus, play by William Shakespeare, 1606(?)
Macbeth, play by William Shakespeare, 1606
The Revenger's Tragedy, play by Thomas Middleton or Cyril Tourneur, c.1606
The Knight of the Burning Pestle, play by Francis Beaumont, c.1607
Timon of Athens, play by William Shakespeare, 1607(?)
Pericles, play by William Shakespeare and George Wilkins, 1608(?)
"Batter my heart" (Holy Sonnet 14), poem by John Donne, 1633 (written c. 1609)
Cymbeline, play by William Shakespeare, 1609(?)
Epicoene, play by Ben Jonson, 1609
Sonnets 33–35 and 71–74, poems by William Shakespeare, 1609 (possibly written 1590's)
The Alchemist, play by Ben Jonson, 1610
The Fair Maid of the West, play by Thomas Heywood, part 1, before 1610; part 2, 1630(?)
The Winter's Tale, play by William Shakespeare, 1610(?)
The Anniversaries, poems by John Donne, 1611 and 1612
The Maid's Tragedy, play by Francis Beaumont and John Fletcher, before 1611
The Tempest, play by William Shakespeare, 1611
"A Valediction: Forbidding Mourning," poem by John Donne, 1633 (written 1612)
The White Devil, play by John Webster, 1612
A Chaste Maid in Cheapside, play by Thomas Middleton, c.1613
Henry VIII, play by William Shakespeare and John Fletcher, 1613
The Two Noble Kinsmen, play by William Shakespeare and John Fletcher, 1613
Bartholomew Fair, play by Ben Jonson, 1614
The Duchess of Malfi, play by John Webster, 1614
The History of the World, prose by Sir Walter Ralegh, 1614
"To Penshurst," poem by Ben Jonson, 1616
The Changeling, play by Thomas Middleton and William Rowley, 1622
A New Way to Pay Old Debts, play by Philip Massinger, 1625(?)
Women Beware Women, play by Thomas Middleton, 1625–27(?)
'Tis Pity She's a Whore, play by John Ford, 1629–33(?)
"L'Allegro" and "Il Penseroso," poems by John Milton, 1645 (written c.1631)
Hyde Park, play by James Shirley, 1632
"Air and Angels," poem by John Donne, 1633
"The Altar," poem by George Herbert, 1633
"The Pearl," poem by George Herbert, 1633
Comus, play by John Milton, 1634
Lycidas, poem by John Milton, 1638
Cooper's Hill, poem by Sir John Denham, 1642
Religio Medici, prose by Sir Thomas Browne, 1642
Areopagitica, prose by John Milton, 1644
"On the Wounds of Our Crucified Lord," poem by Richard Crashaw, 1646
"Corinna's Going a-Maying," poem by Robert Herrick, 1648
"An Horatian Ode upon Cromwell's Return from Ireland," poem by Andrew Marvell, 1681 (written 1650)
"The Garden," poem by Andrew Marvell, 1681 (written c.1650–52)
"The World," poem by Henry Vaughan, 1650
Leviathan, prose by Thomas Hobbes, 1651
The Country Parson, prose by George Herbert, 1652
"Bermudas," poem by Andrew Marvell, 1681 (written c. 1653)
The Compleat Angler, prose by Izaak Walton, 1653
Paradise Lost, poem by John Milton, 1667
Of Dramatic Poesy, prose by John Dryden, 1668
Paradise Regained, poem by John Milton, 1671
Samson Agonistes, play by John Milton, 1671
The Country-Wife, play by William Wycherley, 1675
The Man of Mode, play by Sir George Etherege, 1676
The Plain-Dealer, play by William Wycherley, 1676
All for Love, play by John Dryden, 1677
The Rival Queens, play by Nathaniel Lee, 1677
The Rover, play by Aphra Behn, 1677
The Pilgrim's Progress, fiction by John Bunyan, 1678 and 1684
A Satire Against Reason and Mankind, poem by John Wilmot, Earl of Rochester, 1679
Absalom and Achitophel, poem by John Dryden, 1681
"To His Coy Mistress," poem by Andrew Marvell, 1681
Mac Flecknoe, poem by John Dryden, 1682
Venice Preserved, play by Thomas Otway, 1682
Oroonoko, novel by Aphra Behn, 1688
An Essay Concerning Human Understanding, prose by John Locke, 1690
The Double-Dealer, play by William Congreve, 1693
The Relapse, play by Sir John Vanbrugh, 1696
The Provoked Wife, play by Sir John Vanbrugh, 1697
The Way of the World, play by William Congreve, 1700
A Tale of a Tub, fiction by Jonathan Swift, 1704
The Recruiting Officer, play by George Farquhar, 1706
The Beaux' Stratagem, play by George Farquhar, 1707
The Tatler, periodical edited by Sir Richard Steele, 1709–11,
An Essay on Criticism, poem by Alexander Pope, 1711
The Spectator, periodical edited by Joseph Addison and Sir Richard Steele, 1711–12
The Rape of the Lock, poem by Alexander Pope, 1714
Trivia, poem by John Gay, 1716

Robinson Crusoe, fiction by Daniel Defoe, 1719
A Journal of the Plague Year, fiction by Daniel Defoe, 1722
Moll Flanders, fiction by Daniel Defoe, 1722
The Conscious Lovers, play by Sir Richard Steele, 1722
Gulliver's Travels, fiction by Jonathan Swift, 1726
The Seasons, poem by James Thomson, 1726–30
The Beggar's Opera, play by John Gay, 1728
The Dunciad, poem by Alexander Pope, 1728–43
A Modest Proposal, prose by Jonathan Swift, 1729
The London Merchant, play by George Lillo, 1731
An Essay on Man, poem by Alexander Pope, 1733–34
"A Beautiful Young Nymph Going to Bed," poem by Jonathan Swift, 1734
Pamela, novel by Samuel Richardson, 1740–41
Joseph Andrews, novel by Henry Fielding, 1742
Night-Thoughts, poem by Edward Young, 1742–46
The Pleasures of Imagination, poem by Mark Akenside, 1744; revised edition, 1772
Clarissa, novel by Samuel Richardson, 1747–48
Ode on a Distant Prospect of Eton College, poem by Thomas Gray, 1747
Fanny Hill, novel by John Cleland, 1748–49
Roderick Random, novel by Tobias Smollett, 1748
The Castle of Indolence, poem by James Thomson, 1748
The Vanity of Human Wishes, poem by Samuel Johnson, 1749
Tom Jones, novel by Henry Fielding, 1749
The Rambler, periodical edited by Samuel Johnson, 1750–52
Amelia, novel by Henry Fielding, 1751
An Elegy Written in a Country Churchyard, poem by Thomas Gray, 1751
The Female Quixote, novel by Charlotte Lennox, 1752
Sir Charles Grandison, novel by Samuel Richardson, 1753–54
A Dictionary of the English Language, work by Samuel Johnson, 1755
Douglas, play by John Home, 1756
Sublime and Beautiful, prose by Edmund Burke, 1757; revised edition, 1759
The Idler, series of essays by Samuel Johnson, 1758–60
Rasselas, fiction by Samuel Johnson, 1759
Tristram Shandy, novel by Laurence Sterne, 1759–67
Ossian, poems by James Macpherson, 1760–63
A Song to David, poem by Christopher Smart, 1763
The Castle of Otranto, novel by Horace Walpole, 1764
The Clandestine Marriage, play by George Colman the Elder and David Garrick, 1766
The Vicar of Wakefield, novel by Oliver Goldsmith, 1766
A Sentimental Journey Through France and Italy, novel by Laurence Sterne, 1768
The Deserted Village, poem by Oliver Goldsmith, 1770
Humphry Clinker, novel by Tobias Smollett, 1771
The Man of Feeling, novel by Henry Mackenzie, 1771
She Stoops to Conquer, play by Oliver Goldsmith, 1773
The Rivals, play by Richard Brinsley Sheridan, 1775
The Wealth of Nations, prose by Adam Smith, 1776
The School for Scandal, play by Richard Brinsley Sheridan, 1777
Evelina, novel by Fanny Burney, 1778
The Lives of the English Poets, prose by Samuel Johnson, 1779–81
The Village, poem by George Crabbe, 1783
"Holy Willie's Prayer," poem by Robert Burns, 1799 (written 1785)
The Task, poem by William Cowper, 1785
Vathek, novel by William Beckford, 1786
"Tam o' Shanter," poem by Robert Burns, 1791
The Life of Samuel Johnson, prose by James Boswell, 1791
The Rights of Man, prose by Thomas Paine, 1791–92
Wild Oats, play by John O'Keeffe, 1791
A Vindication of the Rights of Woman, prose by Mary Wollstonecraft, 1792
The Marriage of Heaven and Hell, prose and poetry by William Blake, 1793(?)
Caleb Williams, novel by William Godwin, 1794
Songs of Innocence and of Experience, poems by William Blake, 1794
The Mysteries of Udolpho, novel by Ann Radcliffe, 1794
The Monk, novel by Matthew Gregory Lewis, 1796
"Kubla Khan," poem by Samuel Taylor Coleridge, 1816 (written 1797)
An Essay on the Principle of Population, prose by Thomas Malthus, 1798
"The Rime of the Ancient Mariner," poem by Samuel Taylor Coleridge, 1798
"Tintern Abbey," poem by William Wordsworth, 1798
Castle Rackrent, novel by Maria Edgeworth, 1800
Preface to *Lyrical Ballads*, prose by William Wordsworth, 1800
Milton, poem by William Blake, 1804–08(?)
"Intimations of Immortality from Recollections of Early Childhood," poem by William Wordsworth, 1807
English Bards and Scotch Reviewers, poem by Lord Byron, 1809
Sense and Sensibility, novel by Jane Austen, 1811
Childe Harold's Pilgrimage, poem by Lord Byron, 1812–18
Pride and Prejudice, novel by Jane Austen, 1813
Mansfield Park, novel by Jane Austen, 1814
Emma, novel by Jane Austen, 1815
"Christabel," poem by Samuel Taylor Coleridge, 1816
Old Mortality, novel by Sir Walter Scott, 1816
Biographia Literaria, prose by Samuel Taylor Coleridge, 1817
Lalla Rookh, poetry and prose by Thomas Moore, 1817
Northanger Abbey, novel by Jane Austen, 1817
Persuasion, novel by Jane Austen, 1817
Frankenstein, novel by Mary Shelley, 1818
Nightmare Abbey, fiction by Thomas Love Peacock, 1818
The Heart of Mid-Lothian, novel by Sir Walter Scott, 1818
Don Juan, poem by Lord Byron, 1819–24
"Lamia," poem by John Keats, 1820
Melmoth the Wanderer, novel by Charles Robert Maturin, 1820
"Ode on a Grecian Urn," poem by John Keats, 1820
"Ode on Melancholy," poem by John Keats, 1820
"Ode to a Nightingale," poem by John Keats, 1820
"Ode to the West Wind," poem by Percy Bysshe Shelley, 1820
Prometheus Unbound, play by Percy Bysshe Shelley, 1820
"The Eve of St Agnes," poem by John Keats, 1820
"To a Skylark," poem by Percy Bysshe Shelley, 1820
"To Autumn," poem by John Keats, 1820
Adonais, poem by Percy Bysshe Shelley, 1821
"A Defence of Poetry," prose by Percy Bysshe Shelley, 1840 (written 1821)
Confessions of an English Opium Eater, prose by Thomas De Quincey, 1822
The Provost, novel by John Galt, 1822
The Vision of Judgement, poem by Lord Byron, 1822
"My First Acquaintance with Poets," prose by William Hazlitt, 1823
The Essays of Elia, prose by Charles Lamb, 1823–33
Imaginary Conversations, prose by Walter Savage Landor, 1824–29 and 1853

Redgauntlet, novel by Sir Walter Scott, 1824
The Private Memoirs and Confessions of a Justified Sinner, novel by James Hogg, 1824
Rural Rides, prose by William Cobbett, 1830
"The Lady of Shalott," poem by Alfred, Lord Tennyson, 1832
Tracts for the Times, prose by John Henry Newman and others, 1833–41
Sartor Resartus, fiction by Thomas Carlyle, 1836
Sketches by Boz, fiction by Charles Dickens, 1836
The French Revolution, prose by Thomas Carlyle, 1837
The Pickwick Papers, novel by Charles Dickens, 1837
Oliver Twist, novel by Charles Dickens, 1838
Barnaby Rudge, novel by Charles Dickens, 1841
The Old Curiosity Shop, novel by Charles Dickens, 1841
Lays of Ancient Rome, poems by Thomas Babington Macaulay, 1842
"My Last Duchess," poem by Robert Browning, 1842
A Christmas Carol, story by Charles Dickens, 1843
Handley Cross, novel by R.S. Surtees, 1843
Modern Painters, prose by John Ruskin, 1843–60
Martin Chuzzlewit, novel by Charles Dickens, 1844
"R. Alcona to J. Brenzaida" ("Remembrance"), poem by Emily Brontë, 1846
"I Hid My Love," poem by John Clare, written late 1840's
Jane Eyre, novel by Charlotte Brontë, 1847
Wuthering Heights, novel by Emily Brontë, 1847
Dombey and Son, novel by Charles Dickens, 1848
Mary Barton, novel by Elizabeth Gaskell, 1848
The History of England, prose by Thomas Babington Macaulay, 1848–61
Vanity Fair, novel by William Makepeace Thackeray, 1848
Shirley, novel by Charlotte Brontë, 1849
David Copperfield, novel by Charles Dickens, 1850
In Memoriam, poem by Alfred, Lord Tennyson, 1850
Sonnets from the Portuguese, poems by Elizabeth Barrett Browning, 1850
The Autobiography of Leigh Hunt, prose by Leigh Hunt, 1850
The Prelude, poem by William Wordsworth, 1850 (written from 1798)
Lavengro, fiction by George Borrow, 1851
The Stones of Venice, prose by John Ruskin, 1851–53
Henry Esmond, novel by William Makepeace Thackeray, 1852
Bleak House, novel by Charles Dickens, 1853
Cranford, novel by Elizabeth Gaskell, 1853
Villette, novel by Charlotte Brontë, 1853
Hard Times, novel by Charles Dickens, 1854
The Angel in the House, poems by Coventry Patmore, 1854–62
Barsetshire series, novels by Anthony Trollope, 1855–67
"Childe Roland to the Dark Tower Came," poem by Robert Browning, 1855
"Fra Lippo Lippi," poem by Robert Browning, 1855
Maud, poem by Alfred, Lord Tennyson, 1855
North and South, novel by Elizabeth Gaskell, 1855
Aurora Leigh, poem by Elizabeth Barrett Browning, 1857
Little Dorrit, novel by Charles Dickens, 1857
Tom Brown's School Days, novel by Thomas Hughes, 1857
Scenes of Clerical Life, stories by George Eliot, 1858
"The Haystack in the Floods," poem by William Morris, 1858
A Tale of Two Cities, novel by Charles Dickens, 1859
Adam Bede, novel by George Eliot, 1859
Idylls of the King, poems by Alfred, Lord Tennyson, from 1859
On Liberty, prose by John Stuart Mill, 1859
Rubáiyát of Omar Khayyám, poems by Edward FitzGerald, 1859 (and later revisions)
The Ordeal of Richard Feverel, novel by George Meredith, 1859
The Origin of Species, prose by Charles Darwin, 1859 (6 revisions, 1860–76)
The Mill on the Floss, novel by George Eliot, 1860
The Woman in White, novel by Wilkie Collins, 1860
East Lynne, novel by Ellen Price Wood, 1861
Great Expectations, novel by Charles Dickens, 1861
Silas Marner, novel by George Eliot, 1861
The Cloister and the Hearth, novel by Charles Reade, 1861
Goblin Market, poem by Christina Rossetti, 1862
Lady Audley's Secret, novel by Mary Elizabeth Braddon, 1862
Modern Love, poem by George Meredith, 1862
The Water-Babies, novel by Charles Kingsley, 1863
Apologia pro Vita Sua, prose by John Henry Newman, 1864
Palliser series, 6 novels by Anthony Trollope, 1864–80
Uncle Silas, novel by Sheridan Le Fanu, 1864
Alice's Adventures in Wonderland, fiction by Lewis Carroll, 1865
Atalanta in Calydon, play by Algernon Charles Swinburne, 1865
Our Mutual Friend, novel by Charles Dickens, 1865
"The Function of Criticism at the Present Time," prose by Matthew Arnold, 1865
Felix Holt, novel by George Eliot, 1866
"Dover Beach," poem by Matthew Arnold, 1867
The Ring and the Book, poem by Robert Browning, 1868–69
Culture and Anarchy, prose by Matthew Arnold, 1869
Lorna Doone, novel by R.D. Blackmore, 1869
The House of Life, poems by Dante Gabriel Rossetti, 1870 and 1881
The Mystery of Edwin Drood, novel by Charles Dickens, 1870
"The Owl and the Pussy-Cat," poem by Edward Lear, 1870
Through the Looking-Glass, fiction by Lewis Carroll, 1871
Erewhon, novel by Samuel Butler, 1872
Middlemarch, novel by George Eliot, 1872
The Renaissance, prose by Walter Pater, 1873 (and later revisions)
For the Term of His Natural Life, novel by Marcus Clarke, 1874
The Shaughraun, play by Dion Boucicault, 1874
"The Wreck of the Deutschland," poem by Gerard Manley Hopkins, written 1875–76
Daniel Deronda, novel by George Eliot, 1876
"As kingfishers catch fire," poem by Gerard Manley Hopkins, written c.1877
"The Windhover," poem by Gerard Manley Hopkins, written 1877
The Return of the Native, novel by Thomas Hardy, 1878
The Egoist, novel by George Meredith, 1879
"The City of Dreadful Night," poem by James Thomson (B.V.), 1880
The Portrait of a Lady, novel by Henry James, 1881
Iolanthe, opera by W.S. Gilbert, music by Arthur Sullivan, 1882
The Story of an African Farm, novel by Olive Schreiner, 1883
Treasure Island, novel by Robert Louis Stevenson, 1883
"Spelt from Sibyl's Leaves," poem by Gerard Manley Hopkins, written 1884
King Solomon's Mines, novel by H. Rider Haggard, 1885

Marius the Epicurean, novel by Walter Pater, 1885
Dr. Jekyll and Mr. Hyde, story of Robert Louis Stevenson, 1886
The Mayor of Casterbridge, novel by Thomas Hardy, 1886
Travels in Arabia Deserta, prose by Charles Montagu Doughty, 1888
Three Men in a Boat, novel by Jerome K. Jerome, 1889
News from Nowhere, fiction by William Morris, 1890
"The Lake Isle of Innisfree," poem by William Butler Yeats, 1890
New Grub Street, novel by George Gissing, 1891
Tess of the d'Urbervilles, novel by Thomas Hardy, 1891
The Picture of Dorian Gray, novel by Oscar Wilde, 1891
Barrack-Room Ballads, poems by Rudyard Kipling, 1892
Children of the Ghetto, novel by Israel Zangwill, 1892
"The Hound of Heaven," poem by Francis Thompson, 1893
The Second Mrs. Tanqueray, play by Arthur Wing Pinero, 1893
Salome, play by Oscar Wilde, 1894
The Jungle Books, stories by Rudyard Kipling, 1894–95
The Prisoner of Zenda, novel by Anthony Hope, 1894
Trilby, novel by George du Maurier, 1894
Jude the Obscure, novel by Thomas Hardy, 1895
The Importance of Being Earnest, play by Oscar Wilde, 1895
The Time Machine, novel by H.G. Wells, 1895
A Shropshire Lad, poems by A.E. Housman, 1896
Dracula, novel by Bram Stoker, 1897
The Spoils of Poynton, novella by Henry James, 1897
Mrs. Warren's Profession, play by Bernard Shaw, 1898
The Turn of the Screw, story by Henry James, 1898
"Trinket's Colt," story by Somerville and Ross, 1899
Lord Jim, novel by Joseph Conrad, 1900
Kim, novel by Rudyard Kipling, 1901
"Water Them Geraniums," story by Henry Lawson, 1901
"Heart of Darkness," story by Joseph Conrad, 1902
The Admirable Crichton, play by J.M. Barrie, 1902
The Hound of the Baskervilles, novel by Arthur Conan Doyle, 1902
"The Monkey's Paw," story by W.W. Jacobs, 1902
The Wings of the Dove, novel by Henry James, 1902
Man and Superman, play by Bernard Shaw, 1903
Such Is Life, fiction by Joseph Furphy, 1903
The Ambassadors, novel by Henry James, 1903
The Private Papers of Henry Ryecroft, fiction by George Gissing, 1903
The Way of All Flesh, novel by Samuel Butler, 1903
Green Mansions, novel by W.H. Hudson, 1904
Nostromo, novel by Joseph Conrad, 1904
Peter Pan, play by J.M. Barrie, 1904
Riders to the Sea, play by J.M. Synge, 1904
The Golden Bowl, novel by Henry James, 1904
De Profundis, prose by Oscar Wilde, 1905
Major Barbara, play by Bernard Shaw, 1905
The Forsyte Saga, fiction by John Galsworthy, 1906–21
Father and Son, prose by Edmund Gosse, 1907
The Playboy of the Western World, play by J.M. Synge, 1907
The Secret Agent, novel by Joseph Conrad, 1907
Anne of Green Gables, novel by L.M. Montgomery, 1908
The Old Wives' Tale, novel by Arnold Bennett, 1908
The Wind in the Willows, fiction by Kenneth Grahame, 1908
Tono-Bungay, novel by H.G. Wells, 1908
Strife, play by John Galsworthy, 1909
Howards End, novel by E.M. Forster, 1910
The Madras House, play by Harley Granville Barker, 1910
Mr. Perrin and Mr. Traill, novel by Hugh Walpole, 1911
Zuleika Dobson, novel by Max Beerbohm, 1911
Gitanjali, poems by Rabindranath Tagore, 1912
Hindle Wakes, play by Stanley Houghton, 1912
Sunshine Sketches of a Little Town, fiction by Stephen Leacock, 1912
"The Secret Sharer," story by Joseph Conrad, 1912
Sinister Street, novel by Compton Mackenzie, 1913–14
Sons and Lovers, novel by D.H. Lawrence, 1913
"Poems of 1912–13," poems by Thomas Hardy, 1914
Pygmalion, play by Bernard Shaw, 1914
"The Dead," story by James Joyce, 1914
Hobson's Choice, play by Harold Brighouse, 1915
Pilgrimage, novel by Dorothy Richardson, 1915–38
The Good Soldier, novel by Ford Madox Ford, 1915
The Rainbow, novel by D.H. Lawrence, 1915
A Portrait of the Artist as a Young Man, novel by James Joyce, 1916
"Easter 1916," poem by William Butler Yeats, 1916
The Fortunes of Richard Mahony, novel by Henry Handel Richardson, 1917–29
"The Love Song of J. Alfred Prufrock," poem by T.S. Eliot, 1917
"Strange Meeting," poem by Wilfred Owen, written 1918
Heartbreak House, play by Bernard Shaw, 1919
"Tradition and the Individual Talent," prose by T.S. Eliot, 1919
Valmouth, novel by Ronald Firbank, 1919
"The Second Coming," poem by William Butler Yeats, 1920
Women in Love, novel by D.H. Lawrence, 1920
"Rain," story by W. Somerset Maugham, 1921
"At the Bay," story by Katherine Mansfield, 1922
"The Daughters of the Late Colonel," story by Katherine Mansfield, 1922
The Waste Land, poem by T.S. Eliot, 1922
Ulysses, novel by James Joyce, 1922
"Mountain Lion," poem by D.H. Lawrence, 1923
Saint Joan, play by Bernard Shaw, 1923
A Passage to India, novel by E.M. Forster, 1924
Juno and the Paycock, play by Sean O'Casey, 1924
A Vision, prose by William Butler Yeats, 1925
Mrs. Dalloway, novel by Virginia Woolf, 1925
A Drunk Man Looks at the Thistle, poem by Hugh MacDiarmid, 1926
The Plough and the Stars, play by Sean O'Casey, 1926
Winnie-the-Pooh, fiction by A.A. Milne, 1926
To the Lighthouse, novel by Virginia Woolf, 1927
The House at Pooh Corner, fiction by A.A. Milne, 1928
Journey's End, play by R.C. Sherriff, 1928
Lady Chatterley's Lover, novel by D.H. Lawrence, 1928 (and later versions)
"Sailing to Byzantium," poem by William Butler Yeats, 1928
Summer Lightning, novel by P.G. Wodehouse, 1929
The Good Companions, novel by J.B. Priestley, 1929
The Man Who Died, novella by D.H. Lawrence, 1929
Private Lives, play by Noël Coward, 1930
"Guests of the Nation," story by Frank O'Connor, 1931
The Waves, novel by Virginia Woolf, 1931
Brave New World, novel by Aldous Huxley, 1932
Testament of Youth, prose by Vera Brittain, 1933
"Ulysses," poem by Robert Graves, 1933
A Handful of Dust, novel by Evelyn Waugh, 1934
I, Claudius and *Claudius the God*, novels by Robert Graves, 1934
"The force that through the green fuse drives the flower," poem by Dylan Thomas, 1934
Murder in the Cathedral, play by T.S. Eliot, 1935

The Berlin Stories, fiction by Christopher Isherwood, 1935–49
The Ascent of F6, play by W.H. Auden and Christopher Isherwood, 1936
Brighton Rock, novel by Graham Greene, 1938
Capricornia, novel by Xavier Herbert, 1938
Purgatory, play by William Butler Yeats, 1938
Rebecca, novel by Daphne du Maurier, 1938
The Death of the Heart, novel by Elizabeth Bowen, 1938
At Swim-Two-Birds, novel by Flann O'Brien, 1939
Autumn Journal, poem by Louis MacNeice, 1939
Finnegans Wake, novel by James Joyce, 1939
"Old Man's Story," story by Frank Sargeson, 1940
The Man Who Loved Children, novel by Christina Stead, 1940
Four Quartets, poems by T.S. Eliot, 1943
Fair Stood the Wind for France, novel by H.E. Bates, 1944
The Horse's Mouth, novel by Joyce Cary, 1944
Animal Farm, novel by George Orwell, 1945
Brideshead Revisited, novel by Evelyn Waugh, 1945
The Age of Anxiety, poem by W.H. Auden, 1947
Under the Volcano, novel by Malcolm Lowry, 1947
Cry, The Beloved Country, novel by Alan Paton, 1948
The Browning Version, play by Terence Rattigan, 1948
The Heart of the Matter, novel by Graham Greene, 1948
The Lady's Not for Burning, play by Christopher Fry, 1948
Nineteen Eighty-Four, novel by George Orwell, 1949
A Dance to the Music of Time, 12 novels by Anthony Powell, 1951–75
The End of the Affair, novel by Graham Greene, 1951
The Go-Between, novel by L.P. Hartley, 1953
Lord of the Flies, novel by William Golding, 1954
Lucky Jim, novel by Kingsley Amis, 1954
The Lord of the Rings, novels by J.R.R. Tolkien, 1954–55
Under Milk Wood, radio play by Dylan Thomas, 1954
Waiting for Godot, play by Samuel Beckett, 1954
Molloy, *Malone Dies*, and *The Unnamable*, novels by Samuel Beckett, 1955–58
"The Shield of Achilles," poem by W.H. Auden, 1955
Look Back in Anger, play by John Osborne, 1956
"Lovers of the Lake," story by Sean O'Faolain, 1957
"On the Move," poem by Thom Gunn, 1957
Owls Do Cry, novel by Janet Frame, 1957
The Alexandria Quartet, novels by Lawrence Durrell, 1957–60
Voss, novel by Patrick White, 1957
Endgame, play by Samuel Beckett, 1958
Krapp's Last Tape, play by Samuel Beckett, 1958
The Birthday Party, play by Harold Pinter, 1958
The Hostage, play by Brendan Behan, 1958
Things Fall Apart, novel by Chinua Achebe, 1958
Cider with Rosie, prose by Laurie Lee, 1959
Serjeant Musgrave's Dance, play by John Arden, 1959
The Devils, play by John Whiting, 1961
The Prime of Miss Jean Brodie, novel by Muriel Spark, 1961
"Wodwo," poem by Ted Hughes, 1961
The Golden Notebook, novel by Doris Lessing, 1962
"The Whitsun Weddings," poem by Philip Larkin, 1964
Saved, play by Edward Bond, 1965
The Homecoming, play by Harold Pinter, 1965
The Road, play by Wole Soyinka, 1965
Pig Island Letters, poems by James K. Baxter, 1966
Rosencrantz and Guildenstern Are Dead, play by Tom Stoppard, 1966
Wide Sargasso Sea, novel by Jean Rhys, 1966
Dream on Monkey Mountain, play by Derek Walcott, 1967
What the Butler Saw, play by Joe Orton, 1969
The Deptford Trilogy, novels by Robertson Davies, 1970–75
The Vivisector, novel by Patrick White, 1970
Sizwe Bansi Is Dead, play by Athol Fugard, 1972
The Conservationist, novel by Nadine Gordimer, 1974
Travesties, play by Tom Stoppard, 1974
"Kinship," poem by Seamus Heaney, 1975
"The Wedding," story by V.S. Pritchett, 1975
The Painter of Signs, novel by R.K. Narayan, 1976
The Sea, The Sea, novel by Iris Murdoch, 1978
A Bend in the River, novel by V.S. Naipaul, 1979
The Handmaid's Tale, novel by Margaret Atwood, 1985

WORKS

A

ABSALOM AND ACHITOPHEL.
Poem by John Dryden, 1681.

In 1681, England was in the throes of the Exclusion Crisis, the attempt by the Whigs to exclude Charles II's brother, the Catholic James, Duke of York, from the succession to the throne, and replace him with the Protestant Duke of Monmouth, Charles's illegitimate son. The leader of the Whigs, the Earl of Shaftesbury, was to be tried for high treason on 24 November. On 17 November, *Absalom and Achitophel* was published. John Dryden as poet laureate, almost certainly at Charles's personal request, was attempting to influence public opinion at this crucial moment, and in particular to occupy the middle ground, to sway "the more Moderate sort" as he calls them in his preface. His poem then must eschew extremism and violent satire, and be reasonable, subtle, persuasive, and authoritative. Or to be more exact, it must give that impression.

Achieving authority over the reader is always a satirist's first and most difficult task. Dryden achieves it through biblical allegory. He retells the events of II Samuel 13–18, where King David's illegitimate son Absalom rebels against his father under the guidance of the unscrupulous politician Achitophel, exploiting the close parallel with events in 1681. Every biblical figure has a contemporary equivalent, the most important being: David and Charles; Absalom—Monmouth; Achitophel—Shaftesbury; Zimri—Duke of Buckingham, Shaftesbury's lieutenant; Shimei—Slingsby Bethel, sheriff of London, who will pack the jury at Shaftesbury's trial; Corah—Titus Oates, the witness (or inventor) of the Popish Plot; Barzillai—Duke of Ormonde, Lord Lieutenant of Ireland; Hushai—Laurence Hyde, leader of the Tories. On a further allegorical level, signalled by references to Milton's *Paradise Lost*, the threesome of David/Charles, Absalom/Monmouth, and Achitophel/Shaftesbury represents God, Adam, and Satan. In the Eden of England, the Whigs are serpents, and their cause is Satanic.

Also, Charles is "God-like." This concept, as well as being related to the Divine Right of Kings, which was precisely what the Whigs were challenging, is exploited by Dryden to solve two problems, the beginning and ending of the poem. He has to start with an explanation of who Monmouth is, and yet not discredit the king. The masterly opening sentence, 10 lines long, iambic for nine lines until the trochee in the first foot of line 10 gives us the main verb, extensively alliterative, moves from reference to Old Testament polygamy to identifying Charles's sexual generosity with the creative generosity of God, as the king "wide as his Command / Scatter'd his Maker's Image through the Land." At the end, Dryden obviously cannot continue to follow the biblical story, which finishes with Absalom's death in battle, so Charles makes a speech, "God-like" both before and after, receiving explicit divine approval. There is a risk of anti-climax here, as Samuel Johnson complained, but the technique reflects Dryden's "reasonable" approach. A speech is better than a civil war.

In the heart of the poem, Dryden displays an extraordinary range of satirical devices, such as ironic narrative, the unwittingly self-damning speech, and direct address to the reader, as well as extensive imagery, particularly that of disease; but the most notable sections, in terms of both satirical and poetic effect, are the portraits. The Achitophel portrait is a masterpiece of couplet writing, exploiting the rhyme words and the caesura, with the reinforcement of alliteration, to achieve lines at once perfectly balanced and vigorously energetic: "Restless, unfixt in Principles and Place, / In power unpleas'd, impatient of Disgrace . . . / In Friendship False, Implacable in Hate, / Resolv'd to Ruine or to Rule the State." The effect is reinforced by imagery, particularly the highly original development of the "ship of state" idea, and, in a favourite device of Dryden's, clinched by a memorable generalisation: "Great Wits are sure to Madness near ally'd; / And thin Partitions do their Bounds divide."

The Zimri portrait, which Dryden thought the finest, uses ironic understatement and another favourite device, the list, to expose its victim: "But, in the course of one revolving Moon, / Was Chymist, Fidler, States-Man and Buffoon." Shimei, the religious hypocrite, is exposed in superb fashion by manipulating biblical quotations virtually to enact Shimei's own manipulation of biblical values: "Did wisely from Expensive Sins refrain, / And never broke the Sabbath, but for Gain." In these portraits, along with those of Absalom, Corah, and the balancing, positive portraits of the loyalists, such as Barzillai, we see at their clearest those qualities in Dryden which Pope so rightly praised: "The varying verse, the full-resounding line, / The long majestic march, and energy divine."

—P.E. Hewison

ADAM BEDE.
Novel by George Eliot, 1859.

Appearing in 1859, an *annus mirabilis* of Victorian publication, alongside *A Tale of Two Cities*, *The Virginians*, Meredith's *The Ordeal of Richard Feverel*, Tennyson's *Idylls of the King*, Mill's *On Liberty*, *Omar Khayyam*, *The Origin of Species*, and other notable works, this first novel was a runaway success and established George Eliot "at once among the masters of the art" (the *Times*, 12 April 1859). It was the novel of the year, acclaimed by reviewers as "enlarging the scope of fiction" (Michael Wolff in *1859: Entering an Age of Crisis*, 1959). Eliot first intended it for her *Scenes of Clerical Life* but decided that its potentialities exceeded that series' short-story/nouvelle length. The public excitement about it led to renewed speculation about the identity of "George Eliot" and soon her incognito was destroyed.

The basic plot of the humbly-born pretty girl caught between a decent faithful lover from her own class and a more glamorous but unprincipled rich admirer (wicked baronet, squire, "gentleman," industrial magnate) was very familiar in contemporary drama and fiction (Mary/Jem/Carson in Gaskell's *Mary Barton*, Emily/Ham/Steerforth in *David Copperfield*) but Eliot's treatment of it was characteristically original. Not only does the girl fail to escape intact in time from this imbroglio but instead, tragically and realistically, becomes pregnant, lets her baby die and is sentenced to death for infanticide; but also the characters and motives of the girl and her seducer are explored with uncommon intelligence, inwardness, sagacity, and sympathy (which does not inhibit firm moral judgment). Henry James, in 1866, regarded the girl, Hetty Sorrel, as Eliot's most successful female figure. Adam Bede, her humble carpenter lover, has been less admired as a creation, though at a non-literary level his depiction was much praised by an old friend of the author's father: "That's Robert [Evans], that's Robert to the life!"

Adam, as George Eliot recorded, has some of her father's qualities (steady, proud craftsmanship, upright character):

> "Adam . . . by no means a marvellous man . . . was not an average man. Yet such men are reared here and there in every generation of our peasant artisans—with an inheritance of affections nurtured by a simple family life of common need and common industry, and an inheritance of faculties trained in skilful courageous labour."

The novel's climactic event—the girl's conviction for infanticide—came from family memory too. Eliot's Methodist preacher aunt Mrs. Samuel Evans had accompanied a lass during her final night in a condemned cell and on her way to the scaffold and had received her confession to killing her child. This incident implied a seducer and, given the fictional conventions of the day, another (socially humbler but morally superior) lover. To marry the latter off to the estimable Methodist lady, Dinah Morris, after a decent interval, was as predictable as the girl's last-minute reprieve at the scaffold ("a horseman cleaving the crowd at full gallop . . . it is Arthur Donnithorne [the seducer], carrying in his hand a hard-won release from death"). These later events and developments carry less conviction than the rest of the narrative where, as Eliot puts it in her famous chapter 17 manifesto, she is "dreading nothing, indeed, but falsity, which, in spite of one's best efforts, there is reason to dread. Falsehood is so easy, truth so difficult." Her later succumbing to temptation does not, however, negate the very substantial merits of the body of her "simple story," appropriately prefixed by an epigraph from Wordsworth, promising "Clear images. . . . Of nature's unambitious undergrowth" and "something more than brotherly forgiveness" for those who went astray.

"Our supreme novel of pastoral life," V.S. Pritchett has called it, though he was irritated by what he regarded as failures in its presentation of sexuality. Eliot certainly fulfilled her promise to her publisher (17 October 1857) that it would be "a country story—full of the breath of cows and the scent of hay." Memories of rural Warwickshire ("Loamshire") were backed by typically scholarly research into events before her lifetime (the action begins in 1799 and ends in 1807). This related especially to Methodist activities, here depicted with uncommon understanding and respect. The well-named village of Hayslope with its manor and parsonage, farms, workshops, and places of assembly, is presented in loving and convincing detail. Mrs. Poyser, the kindly but redoubtable farmer's wife who is Hetty's and Dinah's aunt, became a legendary figure overnight (quoted in Parliament soon after publication date) for her fluent forthright folk-wisdom vigorously expressed in bucolic imagery—"I'm not one o' those as can see the cat i' the dairy, an' wonder what she's come after" (though, followed immediately by "I aren't like a bird-clapper, forced to make a rattle when the wind blows on me," this trick of speech can become mechanical).

The narrator, a more sophisticated and better informed Mrs. Poyser, is equally liberal with tough-minded generalizations—"Our deeds determine us, as much as we determine our deeds," "that fuller life which had come to him from his acquaintance with deep sorrow"—and with sharp assessments of individuals ("Yes, the actions of a little trivial soul like Hetty's, struggling amidst the serious, sad destinies of a human being *are* strange"). Opinions differ on how fully and fairly Eliot "sympathises"—trademark word—with pretty but simple ("shallow") minded Hetty and high-minded grey-clad Dinah. But Hetty's foolish dreams of marrying the heir to the manor and becoming a "lady" with a plentiful wardrobe, and her lone sufferings before and after childbirth, are splendidly rendered, as is the process whereby the fundamentally decent but wobbly-conscienced Arthur allows himself to continue seeing Hetty and eventually to seduce her and to lose the respect of Adam (whom he much values) and eventually of the whole village (Hetty's trial coincides with his coming into his inheritance).

As often in Eliot elements of the conventional happy ending—the novel's penultimate chapter is entitled "Marriage Bells"—are balanced by severer fates: death for Hetty as she was due for release, disappointment for Adam's brother Seth, who had unsuccessfully courted Dinah and is provided with no alternative mate, and disgrace for Arthur, though he is finally granted a purgatorial illness after which he may be largely forgiven (a frequent dénouement device in fiction of the period).

—Philip Collins

THE ADMIRABLE CRICHTON.
Play by J.M. Barrie, 1902.

The Admirable Crichton was first staged at the Duke of York's Theatre in 1902, with H.B. Irving, son of Sir Henry, in the title role. Together with *Quality Street*, which opened at the Vaudeville Theatre in the same year, it established J.M. Barrie as a substantial force in the British theatre. It is, in effect, a parable play which lacks the courage of its own convictions.

The Earl of Loam, a widower with three nubile daughters, cherishes liberal ideas. Once each month, to the chagrin above all of his "perfect" butler Crichton, he insists that his family and associates should entertain the servants in one of Loam House's several reception rooms. The ordeal over, the family prepares for a cruise on the Earl's yacht and Crichton is prevailed upon to go with them, together with the timid "between" maid, Tweeny, who idolises him. Act Two transports the company to a desert island in the Pacific. The yacht has just been wrecked, but Crichton is already exhibiting the resourcefulness of a "natural" leader and Tweeny the talents of a lieutenant. It is a patterning out of the Act One dispute between Lord Loam and Crichton: "Can't you see, Crichton, that our divisions into classes are artificial, that if we were to return to Nature . . . all would be equal. . . ." "The divisions into classes, my lord, are not artificial. They are the natural outcome of a civilised society. There must always be a master and servants in all civilised communities. . . .” In the new civilisation of the desert island, Crichton, “naturally,” becomes King, selecting as his “consort,” towards the end of Act Three, the former Lady Mary (now plain Polly), who is the eldest and most athletic of the Earl’s daughters. They have been two years on the island by then, and Crichton has licked the puny aristocrats into shape. But the celebrations that follow Crichton’s majestic proposal to Polly are interrupted by the arrival of a ship and, in a scene that slips uneasily between the heroic and the mock-heroic, Crichton fires the beacon. Act Four returns the company to Loam House, Crichton to his place and the daughters to their “appropriate” fiancés. After his experiences on the island, Lord Loam thinks of “going over to the Tories.” Having salvaged the family honour by concealing the truth, Crichton takes his leave of Lady Mary.

It is a disappointingly complacent conclusion to a play that frequently cross-refers to Oscar Wilde’s *The Importance of Being Earnest*. But, unlike Wilde’s sparkling satire of Victorian values, Barrie’s ironies are more or less confined to the stage directions. There we learn the vapid truth about the Hon. Ernest Woolley, who will end the play engaged to Lady Agatha: “Probably Ernest’s great moment is when he wakes of a morning and realises that he really is Ernest, for we must all wish to be that which is our ideal”; there Barrie explains that “it would not be good taste to describe Crichton, who is only a servant” and that Loam House has “several famous paintings on the wall, of which you may say ‘Jolly thing that,’ without losing caste as knowing too much”; there, after the Earl of Loam’s egalitarian speech, the lineless page-boy cheers “and has the one moment of prominence in his life. He grows up, marries and has children, but is never really heard of again.” It seems not to have occurred to the original audience, certainly not to H.B. Irving, and perhaps not even to Barrie, that Crichton’s behaviour on the island is that of a fascistic despot. It is a beguiling possibility that the play owed some of its London success to the fact that the actor who created the utterly charmless Crichton believed him to be charming. But it is not easy to exonerate Barrie for his pallid imitation of Lady Bracknell in the person of Lady Brocklehurst, nor for asking us to tolerate the impending marriage of the lively Lady Mary to Lady Brocklehurst’s inert son, whom Barrie has already hit off in a stage direction as “nothing save for his rank. You could pick him up by the handful any day in Piccadilly or Holborn, buying socks—or selling them.” For all its theatrical verve, *The Admirable Crichton* is no great advance on Tom Robertson’s *Caste* (1867).

—Peter Thomson

ADONAIS.
Poem by Percy Bysshe Shelley, 1821.

Adonais was written from April to June 1821, and printed in July, in grief and anger over the death of the 26-year-old John Keats. Keats died in Rome on 23 February of tuberculosis, induced, Percy Bysshe Shelley claimed, by the shock of an anonymous attack on *Endymion* in the *Quarterly Review*. Shelley rebuked the critic and exalted Keats in an adaptation of the pastoral elegy, as the Greek elegist Moschus had complimented the poet Bion by imitating his “Lament for Adonis,” thus initiating the identification of a dead poet with the beautiful young man slain by a boar, mourned by his lover the nature goddess Aphrodite, and restored to new life in some form. Shelley elaborates and spiritualizes the myth, creating the name “Adonais” by combining “Adonis” with the loftier “Adonai” (Hebrew for “Lord”). He substitutes the Aphrodite Urania of Plato’s *Symposium*, goddess of heavenly love, for Bion’s Cyprian Aphrodite, goddess of earthly love. Urania is also muse of astronomy, giving Shelley altitude to move from the earth-bound fertility myth skyward as, in the most sustained figure of speech in the poem, poets rise above the mere earthly to become eternal stars, Keats the “Vesper” (planet Venus) of the “throng” (line 414). Urania was Milton’s “Heavenly Muse” in *Paradise Lost* and so inspirer of the highest poetry, as she was also for Dante and Spenser. By combining the earthly and heavenly Venuses in his Urania, Shelley hoped to run the gamut from earthly grief to sublime spiritual consolation.

Urania is a presence in the poem from stanza 2 through at least stanza 34 and, as the planet Venus, is in some sense present right to the end. Whereas Bion has Aphrodite wake immediately to the poet-mourner’s call and rush off to the wounded Adonis, Shelley expands and elaborates. Whereas the classical poets address the Hours (seasons), Shelley addresses one Hour, which he makes last for most of the poem, the hour in which Urania (Keats’s muse and audience) becomes slowly aware of his death, responds to it with frantic grief, and finally accepts it. It is the hour of the setting of a sun and the rising of a star. Corruption waits at the door of the death chamber but does not dare “to deface / So fair a prey, till darkness . . .” (lines 70–71). During this timeless interval the only mourners are abstractions, Keats’s “quick Dreams” (line 73), his emotions (stanza 13), his subjects in nature (stanzas 14–17). Finally the poet-speaker himself mourns the death of the individual amid the recurrence of nature (stanzas 18–22). Only with the coming of Urania (stanzas 23–29) when she rises “like an autumnal Night, that springs / Out of the East, and follows wild and drear / The golden Day” and clasps Adonis so that for a moment “life’s pale light / Flashed through those limbs” to fade as “Death . . . met her vain caress,” only then is the moment of Adonais’s physical death completed.

The 29-stanza timeless interval of death over, the real people, time-bound mortals, contemporary poets—Byron, Moore, Shelley himself, Leigh Hunt (stanzas 30–35) join the procession of mourners. In their presence and with their implied approval, the poet-speaker denounces the insensitive critic (stanzas 36–38) and contrasts his “cold embers” with Adonais’s “pure spirit” which “shall flow / Back to the burning fountain whence it came, / A portion of the Eternal, which must glow / Through time and change, unquenchably the same. . . .”

Thus Adonais’s apotheosis begins. His sun is set, his star rises, as Urania has explained in the stanza which, in the poem’s structure, marks Adonais’s setting: “The sun comes forth, . . . / He sets . . .: / A godlike mind soars forth, . . ./ It sinks, the swarms that dimmed or shared its light / Leave to its kindred lamps the spirit’s awful night” (stanza 29).

The themes of mortality, of the critic’s “Envy and calumny,” of the mourning of nature for the individual, are reworked in stanzas 40–44 and everything is reversed—“’tis Death is dead, not he.” Adonais has “outsoared . . . Envy and calumny” and is free of the “world’s slow stain.” Earth is left bare to “the joyous stars.” Adonais’s being is withdrawn to that of the “one Spirit” whose “plastic stress / Sweeps through the dull dense world" "bursting . . . into the Heaven's light." The confidence of stanza 4 is now triumphantly reaffirmed: "The splendours of the firmament of time / May be eclipsed, but are extinguished not." Adonais's sun has set only to rise as the star Vesper, and in the final stanzas of the poem there is a true reversal of the light imagery. The clouds of mortality are consumed (line 486) and "Life, like a dome of many-coloured glass," no longer "Stains the white radiance of Eternity . . ." (lines 462–63). Thus the "Fond wretch" who is addressed in stanzas 47–52 is urged to know himself and Keats by darting his "spirit's light / Beyond all worlds," then back to the point of earth.

"Or go to Rome. . . ." Rome is "at once the Paradise / The grave, the city, and the wilderness." This image is a magnificent expansion of the earlier very beautiful one in which Keats's unused dream is "Lost Angel of a ruined Paradise" (line 88). The ruined paradise of Keats's individual brain is expanded into the ruined paradise of Rome, example of the grand failure of all human endeavor. A paradise (garden, brain, or city) is the earthy locus of beauty. It is "in her Paradise" (line 14) that Urania heard Keats's poems and it is "Out of her secret Paradise she sped" (line 208) toward Rome at his death. It is an example of the "highly wrought" art of Shelley's *Adonais* that Urania's "secret Paradise" of the individual genius becomes the eternal city, made eternal only by such genius. Urania and her paradise have not been dropped from the poem but subsumed under the paradise of the ultimate classical city. The dead brain of Adonais and the dead city (though with a newly kindled "light of laughing flowers") are relics of the genius which escapes to eternity.

—David R. Clark

THE ADVANCEMENT OF LEARNING.
(*Of the Proficience and Advancement of Learning.*)
Prose by Francis Bacon, 1605.

Francis Bacon, lawyer and courtier to Elizabeth I and to her successor King James, was torn all his life between a desire to fulfil a major role in public affairs and an even more ambitious desire to "take all knowledge to be my province" and create a definitive philosophy for his times. Essentially a man of the Renaissance, a Marlovian personality of bounding aspirations, he looked beyond England towards a European audience and for this reason wrote most of his philosophical treatises in Latin, believing (as Milton did) that this would ensure him a permanent audience.

The Advancement of Learning is the exception. It was published in English in 1605 and did not appear in its Latin version *De Augmentis Scientiarum* until 1623. The *Advancement* has a twofold importance. It is the only book Bacon published in English that expresses his significant views on what was to become later known as the scientific method of inductive thinking based on observation of the natural world; and second it was in its time the supreme example of a new way of writing English prose. Bacon was not to know that his Latin works would within a century be virtually unread, while his English *Advancement* would become a founding text for the scientific revolution of the late 17th century.

The *Advancement* is made up of two books. The first book examines the objections that have been made in the past to "learning" (the nearest modern equivalent to which is "scientific study"). He begins with the religious objections and adopts the Renaissance humanist attitude that learning and religion do not conflict. Indeed one of his main tenets in the *Advancement* is that divine knowledge (and hence faith) are outside the province of "learning." He then works through a series of other objections and proceeds to discuss and (discard) the "vanities" to which learned men have been subject and which have brought learning itself into disrepute. Book I concludes eloquently: "the monuments of wit and learning are more durable than the monuments of power or of hands."

The function of Book I was, in Bacon's opening words, "to clear the way and as it were to make silence." Having thus prepared the ground, Bacon in Book II examines the scope and nature of human learning in a closely argued consideration of the whole intellectual world of the 16th century. The contents and coherent methodology of Book II could best be illustrated by a tree-diagram of the topics and arguments presented (a handy analysis can be found in the preface to the Everyman edition of the *Advancement*).

A detailed account lies beyond the limits of this entry. One of Bacon's major propositions is the clear separation of theology ("placed and exempted from examination of reason") and of human truth, which is capable of examination by observation followed by rational induction. "Learning" can thus be applied to the physical world and men can contemplate "things as they are, without superstition or imposture, error or confusion." Bacon did not found a school of philosophers, but the attitudes of the *Advancement* were adopted by the early members of the Royal Society, who regarded him as a founding father.

The other quality of the *Advancement* is its prose style. During the early part of the English Renaissance the authority of the Latin orator Cicero was profound, and most writers of "serious" English prose evolved a comparable prose of considerable elaboration with a sentence structure of great length made up of intricately patterned subordinate clauses. Examples of such "periodic" sentences can be found readily in the prose of Elyot, Milton, Hooker, and Browne.

Bacon viewed this prose style with distaste. He wrote of it in Book II: "This grew speedily to an excess; for men began to hunt more after words than matter; more after the choiceness of the phrase, and the round and clean composition of the sentence, and the sweet falling of the clauses, and the varying and illustration of their works with tropes and figures, than after the weight of matter, worth of subject, soundness of argument, life of invention or depth of judgement."

Bacon replaced Ciceronianism with a new way of writing. He had already used the short gnomic sentence of the Roman philosopher Seneca as the basis for the earliest (1597) version of his *Essays*. In the *Advancement* of 1605 he used the terse sentence structures of both Seneca and Tacitus as the model for a new kind of English fitted for philosophical exposition. Both in ideas and in style *The Advancement of Learning* is a key text, heralding the modern world.

—Ian A. Gordon

THE AGE OF ANXIETY.
Poem by W.H. Auden, 1947.

Although *The Age of Anxiety* won the Pulitzer prize in 1948, it has never stood very high in critical esteem. Panned by such American disciples of W.H. Auden as Delmore Schwartz and Randall Jarrell, the poem has generally been received in terms similar to those of G.S. Fraser in a contemporary review: "enormous technical development seems, for the time being, to have outrun [Auden's] development as a person; he is a skilled craftsman . . . but a less sensitive and alert observer . . . than he was in the 1930's. . . . As a kind of ruthless and obstinate exercise in pure technical skill, *The Age of Anxiety* is a striking poem. What it lacks is alertness to living idioms and current urgencies." Nevertheless, if this poem finally falls short of the high standard set by Auden's greatest writing, it contains many fine poems and passages, and its experimental exuberance, even daring, contests the claim that Auden's talent is here tired and waning. A fairer assessment would be that offered by John Fuller in what remains one of the best short accounts of it, in *A Reader's Guide to W.H. Auden*: "*The Age of Anxiety* is rich not only in noble despair, but in a kind of inner glee and inventive response to the conditions of life. . . ."

The urgencies of its wartime genesis, which provides theme and starting point of the poem, do seem at times a little remote from its timeless allegorical framework and dense periphrastic *textuality*—a textuality signified by its subtitle, "A Baroque Eclogue." Not only is this poem cast in that most artificial of discourses, the pastoral, but it is also an eclogue in the elaborate mannered style of that most artificial of artistic periods, the Baroque, an age of secondary spiritual and creative activity, in which a surface convolution and complexity of style often mask an inner emptiness and lack of conviction. Nevertheless, the form is appropriate to its theme and setting. Allegorical narratives such as *Piers Plowman*, which provided a model for Auden's unrhymed three-stress alliterative lines, reflect the medieval world-vision of a God-given cosmos underwriting an unchangeable social and political order. Baroque art flourished in the apparently settled imperial autocracies of Europe in the 17th and 18th centuries. The pastoral eclogue, which emerged in the Alexandrian cultural metropolis of an empire whose military priorities had marginalised culture, expressed the futility of an urbane elite which could only play at experience. Such a world-outlook, Auden was to argue in his essay on C.P. Cavafy, links our own age of the *Pax Americana* with this earlier period, for both are epochs where the individual is "politically powerless, and in it, therefore, politics are regarded with cynical amusement." In the supposedly "self-governing" kingdoms of such empires "everyone knows that the rulers are puppets," in reality merely satellites of a power which is elsewhere, so that their subjects ask "why should they care what name their master bears?"

The momentous events between July 1944, when *The Age of Anxiety* was begun (a month after the D-Day landings in Normandy, with the Allies advancing on all fronts) and November 1946, when it was completed (a year after Hiroshima and the surrender of Japan), might seem quite at odds with such settled epochs. But in fact the poem expresses the powerlessness and passivity felt by men and women reduced to depersonalised ciphers, massacred in anonymous multitudes, generic victims of a world war that has become a universal cosmic force. This is a time, in the words of the "Prologue":

> When the historical process breaks down and armies organize with their embossed debates the ensuing void which they can never consecrate, when necessity is associated with horror and freedom with boredom . . . when everybody is reduced to the anxious status of a shady character or a displaced person, when even the most prudent become worshippers of chance, and when, in comparison to the universal disorder of the world outside, his Bohemia seems as cosy and respectable as a suburban villa.

The poem's democratic collision of registers, placing bureaucratic circumlocution, high-flown philosophising or scientific erudition up against racy demotic in a way which subverts and relativises all discourses, is in keeping with the poem's desperate anxiety about the absence of an absolute value on which to found morality and action. Language is *not* the same as the real: it spins baroque fantasies and pastoral narratives out of its material ground, but, in the end, it is brought down, humbled, shorn of pretensions, by the resistance of the actual.

If the poem dethrones our grandiose illusions at the level of linguistic style, it does so equally in the thrust of its narrative. Four strangers, two older men, Malin, an officer in the Canadian Air Force, and Quant, an Irish shipping-clerk, Emble, a youthful recruit to the U.S. Navy, and a woman, Rosetta, a buyer for a New York department store whose origins are English and Jewish, sit apart in a wartime bar on, appropriately, All Souls' Night. They are brought together by the news bulletin of beach-heads, battles, and negotiations to realise that, despite their diverse personal memories, they share a common world of grief and loss in which, in the words of the common refrain to their separate reminiscences—"Many have perished; more will"—and the dead return in memory and prospect alike. In the second section of the poem, "The Seven Ages," each recounts a different version of the seven Shakespearian ages which, outside wartime, they might all hope to have in common. The "state of semi-intoxication" into which they sink enables them, briefly, "to establish a rapport in which communication of thoughts and feelings is so accurate and instantaneous that they appear to function as a single organism." This empathy leads, in the third section, "The Seven Stages," to a tipsy tour of an allegorical landscape in the shape of the maternal body. Warned against hubris by the physical constraints and limitations of their human condition, revealed in their explorations of a terrain by turns delightfully, comically, or disgustingly corporeal (echoes of *Gulliver's Travels* add a twist to the text), they come, at the end of this section, to what seems like a disabling revelation:

> Graven on all things,
> Inscribed on skies, escarpments, trees,
> Notepaper, neckties, napkin rings,
> Brickwalls and barns, or branded into
> The livid limbs of lambs and men,
> Is the same symbol, the signature
> Of reluctant allegiance to a lost cause.

This lost cause is lamented in the next section ("The Dirge") as an imaginary patriarch, god or hero, "some semi-divine stranger with superhuman powers, some Gilgamesh or Napoleon, some Solon or Sherlock Holmes . . .," who, long or lately, has always died or disappeared. In this undiscriminating amalgam of foundation myths, "The didactic digit and dreaded voice" of the compound father-figure "imposed peace on the pullulating / Primordial mess," giving shape and purpose to human life. Now, however, in the demythologizing of the world, he has finally died, "Our lost dad, / Our colossal father." And, they ask, "Who will dust / The cobwebbed kingdoms now?"

As the tired wanderers retire to Rosetta's apartment for a late-night private party, they each in secret resolve "to banish such gloomy reflections and become, or at least appear, carefree and cheerful." This distinction, between becoming and appearing, is central to the last two sections of the poem. These "seven stages" are those through which the body passes in life. But the word "stages" also indicates the theatricality of the human endeavour: each is a stage upon which man struts and frets his hour. This theatricality, which had previously suggested that human life was a sham, becomes now the improbable ground of redemption.

The artificiality of the poem is part of its originality and relevance. Like the semi-dramatic long poems which preceded it, "The Sea and the Mirror," a "Commentary" on Shakespeare's *Tempest*, and *For the Time Being* (subtitled "A Christmas Oratorio"), this poem adopts a deliberately estranging artifice and defamiliarisation derived from that opera which had increasingly become a passion of Auden's in his New York exile. (The poem has been staged on several occasions, and was performed as a ballet by Jerome Robbins in 1950. It also provided the inspiration for Leonard Bernstein's Second Symphony.) This quasi-operatic staginess is part of its meaning. As the world-weary, apparently middle-aged unnamed narrator comments, at the beginning of the penultimate section, "The Masque": "[O]nly animals who are below civilization and the angels who are beyond it can be sincere. Human beings are, necessarily, actors who cannot become something before they have first pretended to be it; and they can be divided, not into the hypocritical and the sincere, but into the sane who know they are acting and the mad who do not." In a masque individuals don a persona, a mask of assumed identity, in order to participate in what in the end is a theatrical masquerade of encounters for which they cannot be held responsible in "real life." Rosetta and Emble drunkenly pretend to each other and themselves that they might fall in love, while the other two pretend they are enthusiastic parties to their union (the homosexual Malin is in fact himself interested in Emble, while Quant fancies Rosetta). Instead Emble passes out on the bed while Rosetta shows the others to the elevator, and she reflects to the sleeping form that when he wakes "You'll be glad you didn't," for such an encounter would only have led, sooner rather than later, to mutual disenchantment.

But this is not necessarily a cause for cynicism. Rosetta expresses towards the sleeping youth the same rueful, affectionate kindness expressed in the poem "Lay your sleeping head, my love." This "kindness" to one's own kind, as subjects of a nature a later poem was to call "Dame Kind," unites all four characters. They had gone to Rosetta's flat feeling "it was time that something happened" and determined "to do their best to see that it did. Had they been perfectly honest with themselves, they would have had to admit that they were tired and wanted to go home alone to bed." But that they pretended otherwise was due not only to "vanity, the fear of getting too old to want fun or too ugly to get it, but also to unselfishness, the fear of spoiling the fun for others." The grand passions may be self-deceiving delusions, but such "kindness," despite all the contrary evidence of a world at war, is a real and for the later Auden an increasingly important positive to set against the paranoid viciousness of a deranged and fallen existence, a sign that humankind is redeemable, and worthy of the attentions of a forgiving Christian God. It is this God, growing out of and transforming Rosetta's Judaic God of exile and vengeance, that the "Epilogue" celebrates, as all four lives disperse into their separateness and solitude. The poem's artificiality invites us to consider the staginess of our lives, in this larger religious perspective, not to dismiss the human with contempt, but to recognise its limitations and absurdities as the ground for redemption. We must refuse to exalt ourselves at the expense of others, for we are weak and dishonest and venal just like them. But we can find in Christian empathy and shared humility that solidarity which, in the 1930's Auden had sought in communism.

The theology behind this poem is that Christian existentialism, deriving from Kierkegaard, which Auden had learnt from his friend Reinhold Niebuhr, the Christian socialist who had helped him overcome his disenchantments with communism, dissuaded him from pacifism, and provided a potent spiritual influence in these middle years. In Niebuhr's words in *The Nature and Destiny of Man*, "man, being both free and bound, both limited and limitless, is anxious. Anxiety is the inevitable concomitant of the paradox of freedom and finiteness in which man is involved. Anxiety is the internal precondition of sin. It is the inevitable spiritual state of man. In a review in the *New Republic* on 15 May 1944, just before he started writing the poem, Auden defined "The basic human problem" as "man's anxiety in time; e.g., his present anxiety over himself in relation to his past and his parents (Freud), his present anxiety over himself in relation to his future and his neighbours (Marx), his present anxiety over himself in relation to eternity and God (Kierkegaard)." The allegorical framework of the poem allows Auden to explore the various levels at which this anxiety is manifest, in man's physical, social-economic, psychological, and spiritual being—at the level of nature, society, personal life, and religion.

—Stan Smith

AIR AND ANGELS.
Poem by John Donne, 1633.

The more than 50 love poems which make up John Donne's *Songs and Sonnets* provide many dramatically compelling episodes, real or imagined, with many recurrent ideas but practically no narrative linkage from one poem to the next. This remains true even when the haphazard order of the early editions is replaced by so careful a rearrangement as that in the edition by Helen Gardner (1965), which separates early poems from later ones on a basis mostly of theme and stanza form. Here "Air and Angels" appears beside other intensely thoughtful poems assignable to the period beginning in 1602 when Donne's worldly ambitions seemed to have been blasted by his marriage, and when also he seems to have extended his reading into Neoplatonic love theory.

The poem is a lover's address to his lady in which he tells her the story of his progress from early benightedness to his present enlightenment in love. From the beginning, he says, it was she who was the real object of his desire even when he was in love with others and had not yet seen her or even heard of her:

> Twice or thrice had I loved thee
> Before I knew thy face or name;
> So in a voice, so in a shapeless flame,
> Angels affect us oft, and worshipped be.

A similar thought appears less cryptically in "The Good-morrow":

> If ever any beauty I did see

Which I desired, and got, 'twas but a dream of them.

These first intimations of love, he continues, are like the manifestations of the angels who "affect" (that is, love) us—often a mere voice or flame which still moves us to worship. So Abraham twice heard an angelic voice (Genesis 22), and the Angel of the Lord confronted Moses in a flame (Exodus 3).

The next stage in the lover's progress came when he met the lady but even in her lovely presence could see only "some lovely glorious nothing" because he still lacked understanding. Faced with this dilemma, he reasoned that love is the child of the soul; the soul can do nothing unless it takes "limbs of flesh"; and since love cannot be more "subtle" than its parent soul it must similarly find some fit embodiment. The solution, it seemed, was to think of love as taking for a body the very body of the beloved, in whose beauty it could contentedly fix itself. But on further thought, beginning with the second stanza, he saw that this idea would not do. If love were a ship, the effort to provide ballast and make it go more steadily would in fact overload the light vessel; a cargo of all the lady's beauty would sink "admiration" (wonder) itself. And there was a further consideration in the very nature of physical beauty, which is not something single but rather a collection of many beautiful parts. Love could not properly "inhere" in "nothing" (as at the first uncomprehending meeting with the lady) nor in "things / Extreme and scattering bright" such as the lady's every hair would be. To inhere is to belong to the intrinsic nature of something. To find a perfect embodiment of his love the lover must turn again, as in the first stanza, to an analogy with the way in which angels manifest themselves, not by mere voice or flame this time but in their full angelic presence. An angel, being pure spirit, is invisible, but can become visible by assuming a body created of air, "not pure as it, yet pure"; and in just this way the lover can find a fit embodiment for his love in the answering love of the lady: "thy love must be my love's sphere." In this analogy, which may also be read as a plea and an expression of gratitude for the lady's love, the lover has found fulfilment of his quest for understanding.

An anachronistic reading of the final lines has left some modern readers unhappy with what they take to be a gratuitous aspersion on women's love:

Just so much disparity
As is 'twixt air and angel's purity
'Twixt women's love and men's will ever be.

It is true that Donne, like his contemporaries, thinks hierarchically, but he surely has nothing bad to say here about women's love, or about air, for that matter. His main point is not the disparity but the smallness of the disparity, at least for the purposes of the present poem. He ends two other poems with a similar minimizing of differences; thus "The Ecstasy" concludes with the assurance of "small change, when we're to bodies gone," and in "The Flea" the lady's apparent triumph after killing the flea is countered with another "just so much" denoting "very little"; "Just so much honour, when thou yieldst to me, / Will waste, as this flea's death took life from thee."

Donne's treatment of reciprocity in love might be compared with Leone Ebreo's definition of perfect love (in *Dialoghi di Amore*, 1535) as a transformation of the lover into the beloved; it is one of the books Donne seems likely to have read. The theory of angelic bodies is expounded by Thomas Aquinas (*Summa Theologiae*, I, li, 2), who says the angels can assume bodies of condensed air, as in a cloud; this power, which God has given them so that they may help men, points figuratively to the Incarnation.

—Rhodes Dunlap

THE ALCHEMIST.
Play by Ben Jonson, 1610.

The Alchemist is one of Ben Jonson's comic masterpieces. In many ways it exemplifies his artistic theory. The play, however, is far from formulaic: it has proved slippery for critics.

No other of Jonson's comedies follows as precisely the classical unities. The play is confined to one day, in fact, approximately to the length of performance time. Its setting is not simply one city, but one place, immediately inside and immediately outside the main door of Lovewit's house. And the plot is a remarkably constructed "entire and perfect action," to use Jonson's own description of the ideal.

Jonson also espoused comedy that held up a glass to the audience. The characters in *The Alchemist* represent different common types of Jacobean Londoners. The play is highly topical: its idiomatic language and many contemporary references can be difficult for today's audiences. The setting is the fashionable section of London called Blackfriars, the very location of the theatre where the play most likely was first performed. It is set probably at the very time of its first production, 1610, the year of an outbreak of the plague in London.

In the play, the plague has forced Lovewit to flee London and leave his house in the hands of his butler, Jeremy. Jeremy as Face and two other rogues, Subtle and Dol Common, have set themselves up to fleece numerous clients. The primary fiction is that Subtle is an alchemist. Their clients come for various purposes. A lawyer's clerk wants an attendant spirit to help him gamble, a tobacconist wants advice about his shop, a country youth wants to learn how "to quarrel," and, most important, Sir Epicure Mammon and a Puritan group want the philosopher's stone—the ultimate goal of alchemy, the essence by which all nature can be transformed into its perfection, base metals into gold, even age into youth. To the house also come a highly desirable rich young widow and Surly, Mammon's friend, who understands immediately that this is a "nest of villains."

The success of the rogues depends on their orchestrating and controlling the inside world and the entry of the outside. Characters are continually arriving, leaving, being maneuvered so they don't meet others. The rogues carefully assume different identities depending on whom they are conning. Dol Common plays the Queen of Faery and a lord's mad sister. Face is Captain and the Alchemist's Assistant, as well as the butler. Subtle has only one alternate identity—the Alchemist—but he "subtly" adjusts that character as necessary.

The climax occurs in Act IV with two events—one showing the rogues' masterful planning and the other their mastery of improvisation. There is an explosion in the laboratory. The philosopher's stone, supposedly near to completion, is destroyed, the "saintly" Alchemist falls in a swoon—all because of Mammon's unchaste attentions (or so he is led to believe) to a lord's mad sister. This is immediately followed by the entrance of Surly who has disguised himself as a Spanish gentleman and who comes close to unmasking the rogues' villainy. But the rogues in an extraordinary choreography of manipulation turn everything to their advantage.

The busyness of all the entrances, exits, different identities, is focused and clarified by the constancy of the stage itself. Through the whole play, one stage door—likely the center one—with a window beside it, used to see who is arriving, remains Lovewit's front door. That door represents the demarcation of inside and outside the house, and it is the visual focus for the audience's sense of the outside pressing, seeking entry. The play's climax leads into its turning point. Abruptly, the frequent use of that center door stops. To the consternation of Face, Subtle, and Dol, what they feared had happened in the very first scene, now actually happens. Lovewit has returned and is standing outside with a group of neighbors. The outside world beats on the door; entrance is demanded. The front door stays closed until the conclusion of the play, when, significantly, it is opened by Lovewit himself.

Jonson believed that comedy should "teach" as well as entertain. It should hold up to the viewer his imperfections. *The Alchemist* is obviously satiric. The gulled characters are not innocents. Their culpability is clear. Mammon makes no claim to the purity necessary for attaining the philosopher's stone. He is using the supposedly saintly Alchemist. The "godly" Puritan Ananias has no qualms about cheating orphans whose parents were not Puritans. The central metaphor is alchemy, defined by Jonson as a false science, a con game. There is no philosopher's stone, no elixir. The mysteries of alchemy are a ruse to fleece the greedy. The concept underlying alchemy that nature is perfectable, the Renaissance idea of humanity's limitlessness, is not illusion, but self-serving delusion.

That, however, does not quite sum up the impact of the play. Our knowledge of Mammon's self-centered greed does not cancel out his rhapsody on his utopian future. The rogues' immorality does not dispel our admiration for their vitality, intelligence, ingenuity. In contrast, the "good" characters are unimpressive. The widow Pliant is so "pliant" she seems without integrity, and Surly's desire to unmask the rogues becomes linked to his wanting the widow for himself. Mammon and the other gulls are punished, but do not change. Subtle and Dol are kicked out, but only to continue their chicanery elsewhere. Most important, the arrival of Lovewit, the turning point in the play, does not lead to a cleansing of his house. When Lovewit enters his home, guided by Face, he becomes part of the redesigned, but nonetheless still manipulating inside world. The stolen goods and the widow becomes his. Surly is out-faced, as unable as the others to perceive that the butler is the rogue Face. His is a surly wit, ultimately unsuccessful—the contrast to Lovewit.

Some critics have seen the ending as ironic, a bleak vision of humanity. Others have focused on the play's wit and humor and have seen it finally as affirming. Jonson's play is rich enough to sustain a complex variety of interpretations.

—Susan T. Viguers

THE ALEXANDRIA QUARTET
(includes *Justine*, *Balthazar*, *Mountolive*, *Clea*).
Novels by Lawrence Durrell, 1957–60.

Lawrence Durrell wrote *The Alexandria Quartet*, often considered his masterpiece, in several periods of intense energy; but the idea and plan had been long gestating. As early as 1937 he referred to his proposed "Book of the Dead," as he called it. Originally intending the setting for Athens before and during World War II, he changed it to Alexandria because Egypt offered an even older past and a more varied population. He meant for his city to represent the world. What Durrell was writing was a highly experimental novel, in many ways a kind of palimpsest "where different sorts of truth are thrown down one upon the other, the one obliterating or perhaps supplementing another."

Narrated by a young writer, Darley, with the help of many other voices, the *Quartet* involves "an investigation of modern love"—but love mixed with both mystery and political ferment. It is also the story of an artist's learning his craft, an intellectual journey which, in turn, is abstracted into a philosophical quest for both self- and soul-knowledge. Durrell's great interest in form permeates its structure. In *Justine* Darley, quoting another author, explains his method: "*I would set my own book free to dream.*" Accordingly, what at first seems a random gathering of poignant memories in the words of a struggling writer actually conceals Durrell's master plan: "Our common actions in reality are simply the sackcloth covering which hides the cloth-of-gold—the meaning of the pattern." Thus Durrell's form is shown to exist behind Darley's formlessness.

Shifting tone and point of view are among Durrell's most dazzling stratagems. The second volume, *Balthazar*, "a 'sibling,' not 'sequel,'" is a realistic and comic reappraisal, as viewed by others, of the romantic first volume. The third, *Mountolive*, "a straight naturalistic novel," written omnisciently, exposes the inner political "truth" behind the romance. But the fourth volume, *Clea*, again in Darley's voice, but now classical in its clarity, reveals a deeper poetic reality and completes Darley's journey to illumination.

Central to the *Quartet* is its concept of space-time. The first three parts present the story in varied perspective, while only the fourth moves forward in time. This idea, "based on the relativity proposition," is integral to the *Quartet*'s structure and to Durrell's design—to escape from the tradition of linear novels set in a Newtonian time frame. Durrell believes that fiction should reflect the understanding of its own age.

Just as Durrell incorporates Einsteinian thought, so he turns to the new psychology. "Freud torpedoed the idea of the stable ego," he says; and, in his characterization, he seeks to realize some of Freud's and Jung's revolutionary ideas. Above all, Durrell is trying, as Justine suggests, "for a multi-dimensional effect in character, a sort of prism-sightedness." As a result his people do not present reliable, clear-cut portraits but are ever-changing, prismatic, and many-layered, revealing archetypes within as well as outer masks.

The *Quartet* radiates in space from the city's center, the Soma of Alexander, and even as it portrays the current scene it refers back through symbolic layering to the ancient "white city": "A marriage of past and present with the flying multiplicity of the future racing towards one." Thus Durrell, through an allusive use of history and myth, recreates the city of Cleopatra, whose image, as conceived by Shakespeare, is revealed in Justine. In his mythic resonances he goes even beyond Alexander to Isis and Osiris. And, as he evokes the modern and the mythic city, he recalls the philosophic city, center of many creeds, and considers the Alexandrian dichotomy of "extreme sensuality and intellectual asceticism." He parallels to the visions of early Christianity modern Jewish and Coptic aspirations to find their own heavenly cities. Finally the medieval Grail quest is seen to lie symbolically within the modern waste land, to be achieved through finding what Durrell calls the "heraldic universe," related to both western and eastern metaphysical ideals.

This search for understanding appears, too, in hints and allusions to the Tarot, the occult card deck, which shows the Magus or initiate, aided by the Fool, moving through the passages of life to join in the Dance of the World. This relationship is realized most fully in the character of the great novelist, Pursewarden, who mocks Darley as "Brother Ass" but urges him forward creatively. Pursewarden's style, totally different from the neophyte narrator's, is cryptic, terse, cynical, tender; and it is through his voice that Durrell himself characteristically speaks.

The *Quartet* is, in one aspect, a kind of poem that achieves its lyrical effects through symbolism, imagery, and leitmotif. Most haunting of all is the mystic strain of music—repeated at crucial moments throughout—that the dying Antony is said to have heard. The voice of Cavafy, "the old poet of the city," is also sounded and echoed in Durrell's prose. And Alexandrian festivals and processions wind through the pages, their wild music apotheosizing flesh and spirit as they celebrate saints' days or erupt into carnival.

Major critical charges levelled at the *Quartet* attack its exotic setting, heightened characterization, and over-luxuriant prose. Durrell responds that he emulates his beloved Elizabethans and that his critics are "disconcerted by my changes of tone, by the mixture of poetry, meditation, humour, and *grand guignol*." He strives to evoke the spirit of place in the Mediterranean lands he knows and loves. He sees his characters as psychological beings informed by eternal presences behind and within them. And he admits that language is at once his bane and crowning achievement. In the *Quartet* it changes color throughout as the romantic, wordy Darley gradually chastens himself ("Fine writing!" he scoffs at an overwritten paragraph) and progresses painfully but finally to control and artisthood. As E.M. Forster says about the "Prophetic" novelist, "he proposes to sing, and the strangeness of song arising in the halls of fiction is bound to give us a shock."

The Alexandria Quartet has been called a literary sport. Certainly it stands alone, though related to "Prophetic" works like *Moby-Dick* and *Wuthering Heights*. It is, however, very much of its time, modern like the works of Joyce, Lawrence, and Eliot in its use of myth, diffusion of character, and layering through reference and allusion. Even more surely, though, it is postmodern like the novels of Nabokov, Pynchon, and Fowles in its new understanding of time and "reality," unorthodox mockery, and fabulous, self-reflexive nature. For this combination alone it seems guaranteed a place in literary history. Yet, all told, it transcends genre and school and remains of itself an extraordinary and enduring achievement.

—Carol Peirce

ALICE'S ADVENTURES IN WONDERLAND and **THROUGH THE LOOKING-GLASS.**
Fiction by Lewis Carroll, 1865 and 1871.

Apart from their literary qualities, the resilience of Lewis Carroll's Alice books lies in the fact that they seem open to an extraordinary range of different interpretations. To name but a few, occultists, Christians, and Zen Buddhists, as well as psychoanalysts, politicians, and social commentators of various schools find expression and enhancement of their beliefs in Alice's world of logic and topsy-turvydom. *Alice's Adventures in Wonderland* and *Through the Looking-Glass* fluctuate between sharply observed truths and sheer nonsense, and it is this strange amalgam that has made the books so intriguing now for over a century and a quarter.

It is no exaggeration to say that the publication of *Alice's Adventures in Wonderland* in 1865 represented a revolution in juvenile fiction, although its influence can hardly be charted in a logical or linear manner. Rather we have to say with Alice that "Things flow about so here . . .," and be prepared to go sometimes forwards and sometimes back; to dart and swoop and dive into widely diverse moods. The open-mindedness of the books is suggested by Carroll's own comments on them: "In a desperate attempt to strike out some new line of fairy lore I had sent my heroine straight down a rabbit-hole to begin with, without the least idea what was to happen afterwards."

Before *Alice's Adventures in Wonderland* almost all of the books designed for children were heavily oppressive. In turgid and often gruesome tales young readers were warned of dreadful retributions that awaited them if they departed from the straight and terribly narrow paths of unquestioning obedience to their elders, and to the accepted religious and social mores. But Alice, candid and extroverted, was a new type of heroine whose exploits were unashamedly motivated by curiosity, something which mid-Victorian parents rarely encouraged in their offspring. When Carroll sent Alice into Wonderland he demanded the recognition of childhood as an adventure to be enjoyed and not (in the traditions of earlier books) a grim training-ground for adult (or after-) life.

Writing about Alice Liddell and her sisters in the boat on the celebrated July afternoon in 1862 when he began telling the story, Carroll describes "the three eager faces, hungry for news of fairyland." There is, however, a robustness about the magic that he created for them. Alice moves through a world of wit as well as wonder, where there is a sense of goblins without gossamer, of magic without mawkishness. The fairyland of folk-literature is suddenly no longer far away. Alice may say that "There's no use trying . . . one can't believe impossible things," but in the books she can and does; and reading them, so do we.

She has, of course, to cope with transformations of situation and experience which come thick and fast, and sometimes frustratingly. She deals successfully with challenging circumstances simply by being true to herself, by turns happy, irritated, sympathetic, or impatient. She is prompted by an uninflated desire for information, and seeks the reality of every situation—without reward or retribution. Events in the books endorse this. There are no prizes—except her own thimble—and no punishments. But there is a sense of freedom. For instance, Carroll's parodying of the didactic nursery verses which were so often inflicted on Victorian children, represents a challenge to adult authority which must have made heady reading for children accustomed to strong social restraints.

Freedom is also symbolised by the gardens in the books, which come at the end of quests. They are places of self-discovery, where liberty and order are, at least for brief moments in the books, correctly balanced. "How she longed to get out of that dark hall, and wander about among those beds of bright flowers and those cool fountains," Carroll writes in *Alice's Adventures in Wonderland*, bringing into immediate and pictorial focus the average child's sense of claustrophobia at being confined indoors when the garden offers a golden invitation to adventure. Alice is constantly attracted by her idyllic through-the-door glimpses of the Wonderland garden, and she tries again and again to get into it, but is hampered by her changing size. When at last she succeeds she does so simply by opening the door and being the right size to pass through it, in the apparently haphazard but actually logical fashion of many Carrollian situations. Despite the fact that this garden contains negative elements like the chaotic croquet game and the Queen of Hearts bawling out sentences of execution, while that of *Through the Looking-Glass* has its tetchily self-defensive Live Flowers, the image of the sunlit, beautiful, and expansive garden persists. The chess-board garden of *Through the Looking-Glass* even opens out to represent the whole world.

Carroll had profound insight into and empathy with the mind of the child. It is no accident that the most famous small girl in literature was created by him, nor that she has had a profound effect on story-book heroines from the time of her origination to the present day. It can be argued that many celebrated writers (E. Nesbit, John Masefield, Kenneth Grahame, C.S. Lewis, and P.L. Travers, for example) whose fantasy is rooted in realism, and who successfully recapitulate the child's capacity for wonder, have probably drawn inspiration from the Alice books. Of these stories Andrew Lang wrote that they "suggest so much more than they say." They were certainly the first children's books to blend nonsense with enquiry, and fact with fantasy; to exploit the dream not only as a device for magical adventure but to suggest intriguingly different levels of experience. Many of us could say just as Alice's creator did, that

> Still she haunts me, phantomwise,
> Alice moving under skies
> Never seen by waking eyes.

Never seen, but indelibly drawn on the imagination.

—Mary Cadogan

ALL FOR LOVE.
Play by John Dryden, 1677.

When John Dryden stated in his preface to *All for Love* that he had "gained the confidence to try myself in this bow of Ulysses amongst the crowd of suitors," he was admitting, on the one hand, that neither he nor any of the other playwrights who had treated the death of Antony and Cleopatra could aspire to emulate the mighty Shakespeare's version. For as he had said earlier in his essay *Of Dramatic Poesy*, Shakespeare was the "man who of all Modern, and perhaps Ancient Poets, had the largest and most comprehensive soul." Yet Dryden wished to take his "own measures at aiming at the mark" and unblushingly admitted, on the other hand, "that by imitating him I have excelled myself throughout the play."

Dryden defines the art of imitation in his preface to *Ovid's Epistles* (1680) as "an endeavour of a later poet to write like one who has written before him on the same subject; that is, not to translate his words, or to be confined to his sense, but only to set him as a pattern, and to write, as he supposes that author would have done, had he lived in our age." This is precisely what Dryden did with Shakespeare.

Since early in the 19th century, it has been fashionable in critical circles to compare *All for Love* with *Antony and Cleopatra* to assess the literary worth of Dryden's finest play. Such comparisons reveal the striking difference in the scope, nature, and language of the two plays, but do little else than prove Shakespeare the superior poet. Given that, *All for Love* is best judged as an outstanding example of English neoclassical drama, not simply as a Restoration version of Shakespeare's genius. Dryden, whose great admiration for Shakespeare's plays was somewhat tempered by his unease regarding their "irregular" nature, created a drama in which, as he states in his preface, "the action is so much one that it is the only of the kind without episode or underplot; every scene in the tragedy conducing to the main design, and every act concluding with a turn of it."

His workmanship in this regard is superb. Unlike *Antony and Cleopatra*, which covers the last 11 years in the lives of the tragic lovers and moves from Rome to Alexandria, *All for Love* takes place only in and around the Temple of Isis in Alexandria and restricts itself to action as near to the catastrophe as Dryden can fashion, the last day in their lives. Dryden confines the action to Antony's struggle between his passionate love for Cleopatra, and his desire to live the life of a highly respected Roman general. The action is not complicated or diluted by subplots, although the deaths of Antony and Cleopatra are brought about by the lies of Cleopatra's eunuch, Alexas. All five acts are shaped around Antony's heroic wrestling with his own soul, and each builds to an emotional resolution, or "turn," reflecting the whip-saw torment that grips him.

Act I, in which the honorable and faithful Ventidius implores Antony to forsake Cleopatra, closes with Antony's resolve to leave the woman who "deserves / More worlds than I can lose" and return to the battlefield. Act II closes with Antony's decision to return to her arms: "I'll not be pleased with less than Cleopatra." Act III ends with yet another resolution, Antony's pledge to abandon Cleopatra and return to his wife and children. Act IV continues the structural symmetry: Antony's mistaken jealousy of Cleopatra and Dolabella once again causes him to forsake her.

Act V climaxes with the catastrophe, the double suicide. Each act, then, is highly charged emotionally and is structured symmetrically: complication, confrontation, resolution. Duty, honor, friendship, family are all dashed by Antony's towering love for Cleopatra, and hers for him.

To achieve the proper emotional intensity and avoid the bombastic rhetoric that marked his heroic dramas like *The Conquest of Granada* and *Aureng-Zebe*, Dryden abandoned the heroic couplet and adopted blank verse, again "in Imitation of Shakespeare's Stile," as the title page of the first edition has it. Even more, the play echoes much of Shakespeare's language. Linguistic and figurative allusions from many Shakespearean plays abound in *All for Love*. But Dryden clothes these allusions in the dress of his own imagery. For example, in Act III Cleopatra in her galley "so charmed all hearts, that gazing crowds / Stood panting on the shore, and wanted breath / To give their welcome voice." Here, the allusion to the Enobarbus speech in *Antony and Cleopatra* is unmistakable, but Dryden stamps the description with his own effective poetry.

Instead of the 34 characters in Shakespeare, Dryden has 12, including Antony's children, who say almost nothing. Of the 12, Antony is by far the most complex and fascinating. Occasionally histrionic, sometimes acquiescent, often vacillating, when with Cleopatra he displays little of his erstwhile greatness; yet with Ventidius he shows flashes of his former self, now "unsinewed" by his overwhelming passion for Cleopatra. Ventidius and Alexas reflect these two extremes of Antony's character: the honorable Roman general possesses integrity and strength; the self-serving eunuch is cowardly and weak. As for Cleopatra, although lacking the "infinite variety" of Shakespeare's queen, she is a striking figure of obsession: "But I have loved with such transcendent passion, / I soared at first quite out of reason's view."

All for Love is far from an inferior version of *Antony and Cleopatra*: it is unquestionably Dryden's best work of dramatic literature. Indeed, some critics over the years have even argued that *All for Love* is better drama that Shakespeare's play. Such claims do not hold up under the scrutiny of comparison, but that they are made is a tribute to the most outstanding literary figure of the Restoration period.

—Gilbert P. Prince, Jr.

ALL'S WELL THAT ENDS WELL.
Play by William Shakespeare, 1602(?).

All's Well That Ends Well is one of three works often called "problem" plays (the other two are *Measure for Measure* and *Troilus and Cressida*) and is usually dated between 1601 and 1604, when William Shakespeare was writing his first great tragedies. Part of the difficulty these three plays raise is generic. Both *Measure for Measure* and *All's Well* are comedies in the sense that they end with promises of marriage and love. Yet in *All's Well* Shakespeare explores aspects of human experience, such as the desire to marry across class boundaries, selfish self-service, and lust, that strain his comic medium. While these difficulties are not new to Shakespearean comedy, in *All's Well* instead of relegating such problems to minor characters, as in the earlier festive plays, we encounter them in Bertram, the Count of Rossillion, and Helena.

Helena, like Portia, Rosalind, and Viola, drives much of the play's plot. But her methods for overcoming the barriers to marriage and the quality of the final reconciliation she constructs, more than these other heroines, are subjects for debate. On the one hand, the folktale origins of *All's Well* cast Helena as a generous virgin whose cure of the King shows "a heavenly effect in an earthly actor." When Helena persuades France to venture her cure, she repeatedly links herself to the power of heaven. Conversely, when considering how to win Bertram, Helena states, "Our remedies oft in ourselves do lie, which we ascribe to heaven," as though the individual will should act on its own, without much dependence on providential help. Her pursuit of Bertram, though she is guilt-ridden over the class difference that may make her unworthy of a count, has been called "too self-regarding." It is not so much the bed trick itself, a well-known convention, which is troubling, but rather the control of Bertram which Helena exercises. Strangely, though she asserts absolute love for him, she also must have an acute understanding of his weaknesses: Helena knows Bertram will try to bed Diana at the price of a valued family heirloom, a ring passed down through six generations. For most of the last scene, Helena, though off stage, orchestrates her rebirth in a manner that leads Bertram to lie repeatedly to the King. In Shakespeare's direct source for *All's Well*, Painter's translation of Boccaccio's *Decameron* Day 3, Story 9, there is no embarrassing exposure of the count.

Of course, it is Bertram's refusal to bed Helena, his disregard of the King's order to forego the wars, and his challenge for her "to get the ring upon my finger" as well as bear his child, that invite her efforts. Bertram's distate for Helena has been explained as immaturity. In addition, the aristocracy was alarmed by the expansion of social mobility during Shakespeare's age. Perhaps Bertram's initial horror at a marriage that may "corrupt" his blood ("A poor physician's daughter my wife?") is understandable in these terms. And yet, if this is forgivable, his behavior at the news of Helena's supposed death and his lies in the last scene are less so. As M.C. Bradbrook writes, "The Elizabethan code of honor supposed a gentleman to be absolutely incapable of a lie. To give the lie was the deadliest of all insults and could not be wiped out except in blood. Alone among Shakespeare's heroes Bertram is guilty of the lie."

In one sense, Bertram's difficulties spring from his inability to understand the service he owes to others (he fails to serve his King and his mother when he flees) or the service others offer to him (he forgoes Helena's pledge of service to follow Parolles). While the wise fool Lavatch jests about an answer that "will serve all men," Bertram chooses the answer that serves only himself (and serves badly) when he follows the braggart soldier. After Parolles' exposure as a coward, he undergoes a transformation and later pledges humble domestic service to Lafew. Yet we do not know whether Bertram, after his own exposure, can make a true pledge of service to Helena. Bertram and the King offer a conditional "if" in their last remarks, as though both are hedging their bets on the eventual outcome. We should add that even the best service in the play is somehow tainted; Helena only thinks of saving the King as a means to win Bertram, and later Diana, as Helena notes repeatedly, will receive "over pay and pay again" for her help. The fool's remarks on inevitable cuckoldry, masturbation, and venereal disease, as well as Parolles' anatomizing of Bertram's and the other lords' low behavior (though we cannot entirely trust his comments) describe a world where few care about anything but themselves.

A notable contrast to this is the support both the Countess and King give to Helena and to the marriage. In Shakespeare's earlier comedies, the older generation were barriers to love; here the difficulties are clearly within Bertram and, to the extent one argues that her behavior is unnecessarily manipulative, in Helena also. But *All's Well* does not give adequate voice to these internal layers of personality which lead to the troubling behavior of both characters, and thus the resolution of these difficulties remains in doubt. We are unsure how well Helena and Bertram understand themselves and are ready to accommodate honestly the needs of others. While there are some reasons to be comforted by the conclusion, this is a different world from Shakespeare's festive comedies, a world influenced by the tragedies written at this time, tragedies where the difficulties between men and women as well as problems with class and service, to no surprise, can be much more directly confronted. We could say that *All's Well* concludes pregnant with human problems that receive a full birth in the tragedies. As Lavatch paradoxically describes the Countess' health to Helena, in *All's Well* the action and resolution leaves us feeling both "very well" and "not well."

—Chris Roark

THE ALTAR.
Poem by George Herbert, 1633.

The reader of George Herbert's *The Temple* finds himself engaged in something like a holy quest or pilgrimage. Rather than being admitted at once to what Herbert calls the mystical repast of "The Church," the pilgrim must be made ready at "The Church-porch," where he undergoes a course of versified instruction extending to many gnomic stanzas. Thus taught and purified, he can respond to a welcome inscribed at the threshold, where another inscription sternly forbids all "prophaneness" to enter. Then, passing into the large collection of poems which make up "The Church," he comes to the first of these poems, which is "The Altar."

As its title suggests, "The Altar" is a poem about sacrifice and dedication. *The Temple* has already been dedicated at the front of the volume in a short poem which offers the poet's first fruits to God. What is dedicated in "The Altar" is the poet's heart. A heart can be like an altar in that both can be made of stone; both, too, can be broken and both can be made whole again. The opening couplet presents this parallel in a way appropriate to spiritual autobiography; the broken heart has been cemented with tears. In the lines that follow, the images of altar, heart, and stone gain further meaning in relation to a biblical context. Speaking from Sinai (Exodus 20:25) God commanded that, "if thou wilt make me an altar of stone, thou shalt not build it of hewn stone: for if thou lift up thy tool upon it, thou hast polluted it." The poet's stone altar, even in its broken state, conforms to this injunction, having been touched by no hand but God's; only God's power can cleave such a stone or such a heart. With this perception the poem reaches its midpoint; the remaining half, a mirror image of the first in the pattern of long and short lines, incorporates another biblical passage, Christ's words (Luke 19:40) to the Pharisees who asked him to rebuke his disciples for proclaiming the heavenly King: "I tell you that, if these should hold their peace, the stones would immediately cry out." So if the poet should fall silent every segment of his hard heart, joined in "this form," would still be heard. The poem ends with two prayers; it asks that "thy blessed sacrifice" may be the poet's own, and that "this Altar" may be sanctified as God's.

Herbert's poems often echo one another even when separated by many pages, but it is possible to see "The Altar" as the first in a more closely linked sequence of 12 poems written against a dramatic background of the Passion and ending with "Easter Wings." In "The Sacrifice," which is the second poem, Christ calls from the cross to ask, "Was ever grief like mine?" Then in the succeeding poems the poet grapples with the question of whether any sacrifice on his part can fully emulate or repay Christ's sacrifice for him. Clearly he cannot win such a contest, and he may well complain of the unequal odds—"though I die for thee, I am behind"—but with Christ's aid he can overcome "the man who once against thee fought"; he freely receives from the dying Lord a new "lease" or covenant of redemption; and in the end he shares Christ's victory: "Rise heart; thy Lord is risen."

"The Altar" is a pattern poem, with long and short lines laid out on the page to create the shape of a classical altar, broad at the top and base and narrower in the supporting shaft. In Herbert's only other pattern poem, "Easter Wings," the two shaped stanzas are displayed on facing pages as though from the shoulders of the two angels at Christ's sepulchre. Such patterning has a long history, there being pattern poems, including altars and wings, preserved in the *Greek Anthology*, and modern investigators have catalogued several versified altars in English before Herbert. Puttenham's *The Art of English Poesy* (1589) values this kind of "ocular representation" for "briefness and subtlety of device" but thinks of it primarily as a pastime for the "delicate wits" of ladies at court. Whatever the degree of seriousness involved, the vogue of pattern poems, which never lacked detractors, soon fell into total disrepute. Davenant (*A Discourse upon Gondibert*, 1650) explains that it is foolish for a writer to seek glory from the needless difficulty of patterning his lines; Dryden (*Mac Flecknoe*, 1682) is simply contemptuous; Addison, surveying "false wit" in its many forms, begins with the pattern poem and singles out "Mr. Herbert" among offending "poets of the last age" (*Spectator* 58, 1711). It is perhaps no coincidence that when the poem itself ceased to appeal as a visual emblem it began to need external illustration. In the edition of 1674 there is an engraving of a Christian altar with the poem printed under the canopy; an engraving for the poem in 1703 placed a heart on the altar; an engraving used in 1809 shows a Communion table with the sacred vessels. But to depict Herbert's symbolic altar as a Communion table is to misdirect the reader. Whether the Communion table might be referred to as an altar was in Herbert's time a matter of controversy; he seems never to have used the word in this sense, and "The Altar" has little in common with his poem "The H. Communion." And here we may look again at "The Altar" as a pattern poem in which the shape on the printed page may, more than in most pattern poems, help to direct and confirm our understanding.

—Rhodes Dunlap

THE AMBASSADORS.
Novel by Henry James, 1903.

The Ambassadors was the first written of Henry James's three late "major phase" novels. James himself regarded it "as, frankly, quite the best, 'all round,' of my productions" (Preface). After the shorter "experimental" fiction of the 1890's, experimenting with technique and treating English themes, James returns here to a large-scale novel treating the theme of international confrontation with which he originally established his reputation. His middle-aged hero, Lambert Strether, is a recognizable Jamesian type sometimes referred to as "the poor sensitive gentleman," who combines sensibility, integrity, and a capacity for growth, with naivety and relative powerlessness in worldly terms. Strether is the first of the ambassadors designated in the title, and the novel concerns the gradual evolution of his insights and attitudes.

He arrives in Europe from Woollett, Massachusetts, as the representative of his patron and provisional fiancée, Mrs. Newsome, assuming that it is his unequivocal duty to rescue her son Chad from a French mistress and from the dissipations of Paris. But he discovers an immensely improved and civilized Chad, and a lady, Madame de Vionnet, whose gentility is unquestionable and whose sophistication and grace both captivate and intimidate Strether himself. Strether's gradual awakening to the pleasures, beauty, style, and nuance of Paris is epitomized in the first of the two great recognition scenes of the novel, that of the sculptor Gloriani's garden party in Book V. Here Madame de Vionnet makes her first appearance in her representative character of *femme du monde*, accompanied by her exquisite young daughter Jeanne, as quintessential *jeune fille*. Strether must now speculate anew on what holds Chad in Paris. Moreover, he is overwhelmed by the sense of his own social ineptitude, middle age, and lost opportunities, and this sense culminates in the speech which James designates in his Preface as the origin of the novel, Strether's enjoinder to a young man present to "Live all you can; it's a mistake not to."

In this ecstatic embrace of Parisian possibilities Strether finds himself altogether at odds with the Woollett point of view, and by the end of Book VI, the exact midpoint of the novel, he reverses his original position. It would be wrong for Chad to desert a world and a person who have recreated him as a civilized man. Hence the need for Mrs. Newsome to despatch the second ambassador alluded to in the title, her thin-lipped, humorless, narrowly judgmental daughter, Sarah Pocock, accompanied by Sarah's husband Jim, who thinks that Paris is the Folies Bergère. The arrival of the Pocock ménage therefore sets off the imaginative distance Strether has traversed, his spiritual evolution from the moralistic Woollett pole of values toward the aesthetic Parisian pole of values. But the structure of the novel was devised by James as that of an hourglass, and its second half now reverses the first. Having cast all his allegiance with Madame de Vionnet and Paris, and effectively resigned his Woollett ambassadorship, Strether is now gradually subjected to a more intimate view of Paris, the seamy underside of his own original impression. Chad, he discovers, is superficially refined but not intrinsically changed and is, therefore, susceptible to the bait of a pretty girl back home and an advertising career in Woollett. Madame de Vionnet and not Jeanne fears for the loss of him. In the second great recognition scene of the novel, in Book XI, Strether accidentally discovers Chad and Madame de Vionnet boating together in the countryside during a weekend excursion and must recognize, after all, that this is the old Parisian story of an adulterous love affair. This moment of discovery indisposes his moral stomach and he must retreat to Woollett to maintain his own integrity, yet his vision of a richer, more beautiful life in Paris and his own affection and pity for Madame de Vionnet have unfitted him for Woollett, too.

The Ambassadors is representative of James in this sort of unresolved, bleak ending in which loss figures largely; in its counterpointing of aesthetic and moral values, sophistication and naivety, against one another in association with European and American points of view; and in its suggestion that the fusion of aesthetic and moral sensibility exists as an ideal bought at great price by his supersubtle protagonists. *The Ambassadors* is also representative in technique, for example in its architectonic crafting, manifest in the hourglass structure and in the counterbalancing of the recognition scenes in Books V and XI, and also in its dramatization of intense inward subjective experience. To this end James utilizes functional characters ("*ficelles*") such as Maria Gostrey, a Europeanized American resident in Paris, and Waymarsh, a staunch New Englander and Mrs. Newsome's spy, to engage and challenge Strether and thereby to draw out and dramatize his states of mind. Likewise, settings and symbolic metaphors project character and mental attitudes, for the story is primarily one of inward evolution rather than outer events.

—Jean Frantz Blackall

AMELIA.
Novel by Henry Fielding, 1751.

Amelia is Henry Fielding's last novel is his most sombre work. His view of humanity may have darkened after he was commissioned as a justice of the peace in 1748 when he began his campaign of attack upon crime and corruption in London. Failing health and the chastening responsibilities of public office possibly affected him, and caused the preoccupation with failed relationships and human weakness which so heavily load the plot of *Amelia*.

Fielding's earlier novels are mainly structured around a journey undertaken by the hero, and are principally set in the countryside: *Amelia* is London-based, and, furthermore, within a restricted area of London, for William Booth, its hero, is a bankrupt, and must live within the verge of the court to escape arrest for debt. A sense of restraint and imprisonment runs as a leitmotif throughout the work. Gone too is the picaresque stringing together of incidents which characterise the earlier novels. *Amelia* is much more consciously structured. Although it employs retrospect and flashback, it is essentially the story of a consecutive portion of the domestic life of Booth and his wife, Amelia.

Amelia is not a conventional love story culminating at the moment where hero and heroine marry. The Booths have been wed for some time, and Fielding concentrates upon the tensions and vicissitudes caused by the feckless irresponsibility and weakness of Booth as husband and as father. His domestic shortcomings are many and serious. He commits adultery, gambles away the family's income, deceives his wife as to his motives and whereabouts, and is led with distressing ease into acts which strain domestic harmony. Amelia bears all this with long suffering patience. From early on in the book she has known of and already forgiven Booth's sexual lapse with the vampish Miss Mathews. The reader is unaware that Amelia has this knowledge, as Booth himself is, and the novel is given a curious jolt when Amelia finally reveals her cognisance of an adultery which Booth has spent so much time twisting and fibbing to conceal. The reader can only feel a sense of exasperation that so much plotting has apparently been set up merely to delude him. Yet that exasperation is exactly what Fielding is striving to inculcate. It permeates everything that happens in the book. The sense of constraint, limitation, and lack of freedom is universal.

Equally pervasive is the sense of human relationships being fallible and untrustworthy. Virtually every person with whom the Booths come into contact lets them down. Miss Mathews —an old flame of Booth's—bails him out when he is penniless in Newgate but this kindly act is vitiated by her calculating seduction of Booth, and the subsequent threats of blackmail with which she hounds him throughout the novel.

The landlady with whom the Booths lodge, Mrs. Ellison, at first appears a benevolent friend and mentor. But she turns out to be procuress to the anonymous and infamous "noble Lord" who spends the whole book attempting to seduce Amelia, having already succeeded in debauching her friend, the unfortunate Mrs. Bennet, whom he infects with syphilis. After Mr. Bennet's death she marries Sergeant Atkinson, the novel's one uncomplicatedly good character. Yet our sense of trust in Mrs. Bennet/Atkinson is undercut when she takes to drink and is revealed as something of a sharp-tongued shrew and self-opinionated bluestocking.

Booth's army friends, Colonels James and Bath, both betray him or let him down. Other casual acquaintances lead him astray, delude him, or take advantage; his naive trust is forever being deflated.

Fielding's earlier novels introduce a kindly overseer whose benevolence suffuses the denouement of the plot. This role is given in *Amelia*, to Dr. Harrison, a polemical and judgemental parson. While he certainly does assist the Booths, he is by no means universally good-tempered and readily forgiving. Nor is Fielding above satirising Harrison's sermonising morality.

The social realism of the book is reinforced by Fielding eschewing his earlier habit of using "humorous" names for his characters: Thwackem, Booby, Allworthy. In *Amelia* the names are everyday ones. This change of tactic reinforces the new tone of earnestness and melancholy which suffuses the book.

Critics are divided about how far Fielding intended *Amelia* as experimental, or how far it is the work of an ailing, disillusioned, and tired author. While the novel is uneasy reading it is also extremely challenging. Its conclusion is perhaps unconvincing; Booth and Amelia leave London, their debts now paid after the discovery that Amelia has for long been cheated of an inheritance by rascally lawyers. The melding of realism and theatricality is uneasy to say the least, and Booth's conversion to wisdom and rectitude through the reading of Barrow's sermons while in jail is far from psychologically convincing. Fielding may well have intended this anticlimactic ending, however, as though suggesting that the uncomfortably vitiated relationships he has shown can only be meliorated by the artifice of fiction, not by the logic of life.

Read thus, as a book charting the fallibility of domestic relationships, and the near-saintly quality of forgiveness necessary to counteract it; as a catalogue of the predictable unpredictability of trust, friendship, and professional probity, *Amelia* is both a brave and a chastening experiment.

—T. Bareham

AMORETTI.
Poems by Edmund Spenser, 1595.

Edmund Spenser's pursuit of permanence in a world of mutability is the dominant theme of his poetic works, and his sonnet sequence the *Amoretti* is no exception. The *Amoretti* is unique among sonnet sequences of the period in its being addressed to a woman who was to become the poet's wife (Elizabeth Boyle), and in its culminating in marriage, as celebrated in the *Epithalamion* with which it was published in 1595. Consequently there is considerable pressure to read the sonnets as a poetic diary, as an historically accurate record of a private courtship. Such an approach, however, is not so much erroneous as insufficient. Unlike other sonnet sequences of the period which "escaped into print" without the poet's authorization—Samuel Daniel's *Delia*, Philip Sidney's *Astrophel and Stella*, and Shakespeare's *Sonnets*, for instance—Spenser published the *Amoretti* almost immediately after composing it. It was, therefore, a thoroughly public performance (as Spenser himself acknowledges in sonnet 85), and it is the message it addresses to its reading public (of which we are members) that most concerns us. That message is not the poet's private declaration of love for Elizabeth Boyle, but rather love's place in the universe. In the *Amoretti*, Spenser celebrates human love as the only possible still point in a universe of mutability.

The clearest and most consistent articulation of this insight appears in Spenser's recurrent comparison between the "little paine" of frustrated courtship and the "endlesse pleasure" or "eternal blisse" of the eventually reciprocal love (sonnets 6, 26, 51, 63). Although the *Amoretti* (like other sonnet sequences) devotes much of its attention to the frustrations of unrequited love, those same frustrations are simultaneously diminished by the larger awareness of "eternal blisse" in which they are consistently located. The gift of eternity which the beloved's love affords the poet-lover is reciprocated by the poet's own immortalizing verses: "my verse your vertues rare shall eternize" (sonnet 75, see also sonnets 27 and 69). This reciprocity is made explicit in sonnet 49: "so shall you live by giving life to me" (see also sonnet 82).

The immortality sought, and offered, in the *Amoretti*, however, is a thoroughly secular one. Although the poet employs religious terminology to celebrate his beloved as "my sweete Saynt" and "goddesse" (sonnet 22), as "divine" and "celestiall" (sonnet 45), as "of the brood of Angels hevenly borne: / and with the crew of blessed Saynts upbrought" (sonnet 61), it is a mistake to reduce the character of the beloved to a symbol of God or Christ. She remains Elizabeth Boyle, soon to be Mrs. Spenser. The spiritual component of the *Amoretti* is not to be found in neoplatonic transcendence of earthly love but in the sanctity of human love as embodied in *holy* matrimony.

The beloved's association with Christ is made explicit in sonnet 68 (the "Easter sonnet") and the two preceding sonnets. In sonnet 66, the poet compares the beloved's humble acquiescence to his suit with Christ's acceptance of mortality, asking "why did ye stoup unto so lowly state?"; and in sonnet 67, the beloved, like Christ, offers herself as a sacrifice "with her owne goodwill." In sonnet 68, however, Christ himself is addressed, and the final lines do not conflate Christ and Elizabeth but distinguish between them as model and aspirant: "So let us love, deare love, lyke as we ought, / love is the lesson which the Lord us taught." In sonnet 72, Spenser goes even further to distinguish between heavenly and earthly love, concluding that earthly love is sufficient for the human heart: "Hart need not with none other happiness, / but here on earth to have such hevens blisse." In the *Amoretti*, the beloved is identified *with* Christ but not *as* Christ. "Eternal blisse" is available only through mutual love.

While other sonnet sequences of the period dramatize the poet-lover's unfailing dedication to the beloved in the face of her intransigence, demonstrating the energy and anxiety of unrequited courtship as a means of courtly self-advertisement, such conventional expectations are immediately subverted in the *Amoretti* by Spenser's confident expectation of ultimate reward. Although the *Amoretti* contains its share of the obligatory "cruel fair" sonnets, the anxiety that normally accompanies such awareness of the beloved's paradoxical nature is defused by Spenser's declared acknowledgement of the difficulties inevitably attendant upon courtship. Such difficulties are even celebrated as harbingers of future felicity. As early as sonnet 6, Spenser says, "love . . . the harder wonne, the firmer will abide."

This same confidence characterizes Spenser's occasional criticism of the beloved's "pride." Although he condemns her "cruel pride" (sonnet 47), he is more intent on deploying such conventional reproaches to acknowledge her legitimate claims, since such pride ultimately reflects positively on their mutual love: "Most happy she that most assured doth rest, / but he most happy who such one loves best" (sonnet 59). This is not a conclusion the poet only gradually arrives at through love's difficult tutorial; it is an ongoing debate throughout the sonnet sequence. As early as sonnet 5, the poet declares "Such pride is praise, such portliness is honor," and as late as sonnet 81 he is still deploring "that cloud of pride, which oft doth dark / her goodly light." But most references to her pride in the *Amoretti* seek to justify it, not condemn it. Like everything else in Spenser's sonnet sequence, "self-assurance" is shared equally by the lovers. This mutual self-assurance contributes a calm cheerfulness to the *Amoretti* unknown to any other sonnet sequence of the period. Although the lover follows convention in deploring the beloved's "cruelty" and begging for "mercy," there is a comfortable awareness in the poems that he is merely playing a "part" (sonnets 18 and 54). It is revealing that the *Amoretti* contains many more references to smiles and laughter than to tears.

There are a number of small cruxes in the *Amoretti* that have attracted a disproportionate amount of critical attention, but they can only receive passing mention here. There is, for instance, the case of the duplicate sonnets—35 and 83. The ease with which authorial self-consciousness is deconstructed by modern critics allows for all manner of explanations for the duplication, but it remains a dilemma. Sonnet 58 has the curious heading, "By her that is most assured to her self," which some readers have interpreted as meaning that the sonnet was written by, or at least represents the sentiments of, Elizabeth Boyle. Such a reading, however, founders on the concluding couplet, unless the poet has suddenly become a "proud fayre" himself. The final three sonnets, which mourn the beloved's absence, have created problems for some readers and generated a great deal of critical speculation, but no one has offered a satisfying analysis of Spenser's choice of conclusions. The most intriguing of the narrow-focus approaches to the *Amoretti* is perhaps the "calendrical" analysis which assigns each sonnet to a single specific day in Spenser's courtship. Such analyses are occasionally insightful, frequently ingenious, but almost inevitably procrustean in their emphasis on structure as meaning. The poetic depths of the *Amoretti* demand a critical approach that opens it up to more global interpretations rather than imposing structural limitations, as intriguing as they may be.

—Derek B. Alwes

THE ANATOMY OF MELANCHOLY.
See the Writers entry on **BURTON, Robert.**

ANCRENE RIWLE or **ANCRENE WISSE.**
Prose, late 12th–early 13th century.

Editions and Translations

Ancrene Riwle, translated by Mary Salu. 1956.
Ancrene Wisse, parts 6 and 7, edited by Geoffrey Shepherd. 1959.
Ancrene Wisse: The English Text of the Ancrene Riwle, edited by J.R.R. Tolkien. 1962.
Introduction and Part 1, edited and translated by Robert W. Ackerman and Roger Dahood. 1984.

Critical Studies: *The English Mystics* by David Knowles, 1927; *Studies in the Dialect and Vocabulary of the Ancrene Riwle* by Arne Zettersten, 1965; *Structure and Imagery in Ancrene Wisse* by Janet Grayson, 1974; *The Origins of Ancrene Wisse* by E.J. Dobson, 1976; *The Solitary Self: Individuality in the Ancrene Wisse* by Linda Georgianna, 1981; "The Rule of the Body: The Feminine Spirituality of the *Ancrene Wisse*" by Elizabeth Robertson, in *Seeking the Woman in Late Medieval and Renaissance Writings* edited by Sheila Fisher and Janet E. Halley, 1989.

Ancrene Riwle is the title given by a 19th-century editor to a prose work of religious instruction which survives in a number of manuscripts; it is sometimes known as *Ancrene Wisse* ("guide" or "rule" for anchoresses), a name given to it in one important medieval manuscript, now in the library of Corpus Christi College, Cambridge. It also exists in French and Latin versions. There has been considerable discussion concerning its origin. It was probably written in the late 12th or the early 13th century in the west of England. It has been suggested that it is connected with the Augustinian abbey of Wigmore in Herefordshire (and indeed that it was written by a secular canon there, Brian of Lingen, for his three sisters), but this remains uncertain. Originally written for three sisters, it was later adapted for a wider community and seems to have retained its popularity until the end of the Middle Ages.

The bulk of the work consists of an "inner rule," a guide to the spiritual life of contemplation, divided into sections discussing prayer and devotions, the outward and inward senses, temptations, confession, penance, and love. This is framed by an "outer rule," a brief final (and—to the modern reader—entertaining) section of notes concerning the anchoresses' domestic arrangements and manner of life—"you must not keep any animal except a cat," "you must sleep in a gown belted at the waist, but loosely enough to allow the thickness of your hand between," "let your shoes be soft, roomy and warm in winter." The author combines learning and reason (reflected in the way he uses scholastic distinctions, gives a spiritual exposition of the etymologies of biblical names, or elaborates an allegorical interpretation) with an emotional devotion to the humanity of Christ. It is all marked by moderation, humanity ("man is gentle by nature"), and an absence of the extreme ascetic harshness sometimes found in this kind of medieval literature—"a sweet and gentle heart is always best. I would rather you suffered a hard word well than a hard hair-shirt."

The *Ancrene Riwle* has an important place in the history of English prose for the sheer excellence of its writing as well as for its early date. It gives an immediate impression of simplicity and directness, but this is the product of art, since it soon becomes obvious that the writer is using the resources and the techniques of rhetoric—in particular, balanced phrases, patterned repetitions, and rhetorical questions—with ease. The author achieves a remarkable vividness—by the use of homely proverbs which are quoted alongside scriptural and patristic tags ("without hope the heart would break," or, more satirically, "from mill and from cheaping [market], from smithy and from anchoresses' house one hears tidings"), or by the use of colloquial turns of phrase (people tie knots in their belts to remind them of things, people say of a generous man that he has holes in his hands). He gives us snatches of speech or imagines the inner flow of thought—when a person will think suspiciously about her neighbours: "Look how they are talking about me, the two of them . . . sitting there together"—or that one of his charges will argue with him: "'But, dear master,'" someone may say, is it then so excessively evil to peep out?'" It is, he answers, recalling Eve who leaped after her eye had leapt "from the eye to the apple, from the apple in paradise down to the earth, and from earth to hell. . . ." The beginning and root of all this misery was, he says, a light glance. His imagination is a powerfully visual one: in his account of the Seven Deadly Sins, the wrathful man "juggles with knives in front of the devil," "he plays with swords, balancing them with the sharp point upon his tongue"; the slothful man "lies sleeping in the devil's bosom, his dear darling, and the devil puts his mouth to his ear and whispers to him all he wishes to"; the greedy glutton is the devil's manciple, who "comes before his lord besmutted and besmeared, a dish in one hand, a bowl in the other" with confused speech, and an unsteady walk—"behold his great belly: and the devil laughs." He loves metaphors and images—true anchoresses are like birds because they leave the earth and fly up towards heaven; they are "indeed birds of heaven, flying high up, or sitting and singing in happiness on the green boughs"—or similitudes, which often turn into minature allegories. He will tell little stories, like that Christ the "lover-knight," who loved a lady who was oppressed by her enemies, besieged in an earthen castle, and her land all laid waste, so much that in spite of her hard-heartedness he delivered her from her enemies and was himself tortured and slain. The end of all this is instruction, but it is instruction delivered with liveliness, wit, and feeling.

—Douglas Gray

THE ANGEL IN THE HOUSE.
Poems by Coventry Patmore, 1854–62.

The Victorian verse-novel with contemporary scene and theme (Tennyson's *Maud*, Clough's "Amours de Voyage," Meredith's *Modern Love*, *The Angel and the House*) is part of a larger phenomenon. With the passing of Keats, Byron, and Shelley, all dead by 1824, English poetry and painting ceased to draw on classical themes and Mediterranean vistas. From the 1840's onwards—the new great age—the English house, great, large, or small, with its current life within, began to dominate fiction, poetry, and painting. Reasons enough can be found: the new royal domesticity, the industrial metamorphoses that changed the whole ways of living. But the facts are evident in the work of every main artist and writer. One curious effect was that (while novelists often seem unconscious poets), the poets used their medium for fiction, from ballad length to novel.

Coventry Patmore's *The Angel in the House* is a prime example. First published in 1854 (there were later sections), it was a huge bestseller on both sides of the Atlantic; some quarter of a million copies were sold in the poet's lifetime. Why the success? Why the disappearance? The clues should be in the work itself.

The plot is simple enough. Felix Vaughn the narrator, young, handsome, gentleman landowner and amateur poet (details conveyed obliquely, as they should be) returns from a six-year absence to his home, an ancestral estate in the west of England. He calls on old friends at Sarum Close, the Dean of the cathedral and his three daughters. These three were scarcely more than children when he left; now they were young ladies: Mildred, the youngest, still a teasing sprite; Mary, pretty for all her bookishness. And Honoria, the oldest?

How changed! In shape no slender Grace
But Venus, milder than the dove. . . .

She is no child but a woman, mysterious, desirable.

Felix, obsessed (like the author) by the idea of love ("I never went to Ball or Fete / Or Show, but in pursuit express / Of my predestinated mate") is convinced that here is the end of his search. The Dean cheerfully gives consent for the young man's wooing. But how can he win her? Both have endless leisure and no occupation. Any rapid move can chill the temperature. In episodes ("Cantos") each with a philosophic Prelude, the course is traced: the picnic, the dance, the fears and misunderstandings, the wedding day itself (acutely observed)—and the joy of marriage.

The metre of the poem, an easy prancing four-iambic line throughout, with abab, cdcd rhyming, might seem casually chosen. It was not. (Indeed, it is hard to think of *The Angel* running to any other tune.) Patmore was always concerned with form; his later works—not always happily—show his continual wish for experiment. The choice for his verse-novel, he told Gosse, was "of set purpose." "It was a swift and jocund measure, full of laughter and gaiety, suitable, not to pathetic themes but to a song of chaste love, fortunate marriage." It had been, he added, "continually used by poets for erotic poetry, on account of its joyous air." The "measure" has more range than this suggests. It reflects the lover's philosophising, his thwarted sullenness too, as at dawn, "on Avon's misty flats the herds / Expected comfortless the day." But most characteristic are such passages as this:

Good Mrs. Fife,
To my, "the Dean, is he at home?"
Said, "No, sir; but Miss Honor is;"
And straight, not asking if I'd come,
Announced me, "Mr. Felix, Miss,"
To Mildred in the Study. There
We talk'd, she working. We agreed
The day was fine; the Fancy-Fair
Successful; "Did I ever read
De Genlis? . . ."

or the much-quoted sand shoe verse:

I, while the shop-girl fitted on
The sand shoes, look'd where, down the bay,
The sea glow'd with a shrouded sun.
"I'm ready, Felix, will you pay?"
That was my first expense for this
Sweet Stranger, now my three days' Wife.
How light the touches are that kiss
The music from the chords of life!

The mingling of the near-banal with the near-profound is intentional; it is the keynote of the book. But how far does it work? "This laureate of the tea table," commented Gosse, "with his hum drum stories of girls that smell of bread and butter, was in his heart the most visionary of the mystics." "He has no conception," wrote the Patmore contributor to the *Dictionary of National Biography* of 1901, "of the sublime in other men's writings or of the ridiculous in his own." Both have a truth. What George Herbert could do, Patmore could not.

Certainly, *The Angel in the House* can be greatly enjoyed today, as a sub-Trollopean period piece, as "wit-writing of an extremely competent and felicitous kind" (Herbert Read), even as a curiously sensual experience. For the reader is increasingly compelled to share the lover's vexed and restless dreams, his growing fever at the minuscule pace of the courtship. (Well, without it, where would the story be?) The poem will always be a happy private discovery.

Such approaches would not have pleased the poet. For him, the gravitas of the piece was deeply important. Even before the finding and marrying of his perfect wife (he was then 24), he had planned to write a work on love, to be the "poem of the age." He did: it was. But the age was brief. Certainly he had more acclaim in his day than another, greater poet of marriage, one who also used in many lyrics the image of the house. But Browning, who wrote of equal opposites in the game or war of love, is still wholly viable today. Patmore's marriage poem, happy and summery as it was, stays fixed within its time.

The Angel herself, with her "rapture of submission" ("And all the wisdom that she has / Is to love him for being wise") could be the problem. Her secret, Felix observes obscurely, "is mine, but let the darkness guard / Myst'ries that light would more perplex." A strange utterance. No—Honoria has as little common with the Jane Austen heroine of a few decades earlier as with any of a century later. She is essential to the poem, but she is also immovable, and makes the poem so. Tennyson declared that women ought to erect a statue to Patmore. But Tennyson, too, had little understanding of women.

Patmore was no mean poet: his mind was adventurous, but he could not take criticism and—technique apart—imposed none on himself. He has his devotees today, and they include considerable names in poetry and scholarship. But his apologists are too often drawn by the Catholic-sensual-mystical aroma of his later work and not by qualities that would bring him readers today.

—Naomi Lewis

THE ANGLO-SAXON CHRONICLE.
Prose, 9th century–12th century.

Manuscript versions

- A *Parker Chronicle*, Corpus Christi College Cambridge 173 (late 9th c.)
- B British Library, Cotton Tiberius A. vi. (late 10th c.)
- C British Library, Cotton Tiberius B. i (mid 11th c.)
- D British Library, Cotton Tiberius B. iv (late 11th c.)
- E *Peterborough Chronicle*, Bodleian Library Laud Misc. 636 (early 12th c.)
- F British Library, Cotton Domitian viii (late 11th or early 12th c.)
- G British Library, Cotton Otho B. xi (early 11th c.)
- H British Library, Cotton Domitian ix f. 9 (a 12th c. fragment)
- β British Library, Cotton Tiberius A. iii f. 178 (a fragment originally appended to B)

Editions and Translations

Two of the Saxon Chronicles Parallel, with Supplementary Extracts from the Others, edited by Charles Plummer. 2 vols., 1892–99.

The Anglo-Saxon Chronicle, translated by G.N. Garmonsway. 1953.

The Anglo-Saxon Chronicle: A Revised Translation, edited and translated by Dorothy Whitelock, David Douglas, and Susie Tucker. 1961.

The Anglo-Saxon Chronicle: A Collaborative Edition, edited by David Dumville and Simon Keynes. 1983–

Critical Studies: "Anglo-Saxon Royal Genealogies" by Kenneth Sisam, in *Proceedings of the British Academy*, 1953; "The Narrative Mode of *The Anglo-Saxon Chronicle* Before the Conquest" by Cecily Clark, in *England Before the Conquest* edited by Peter Clemoes and Kathleen Hughes, 1971; *Historical Writing in England c. 550 to c. 1307* by Antonia Gransden, 1974; articles by Janet Bately and Peter Clemoes, in *Leeds Studies in English*, new series 16, 1985.

Ever since Charles Plummer's thorough and valuable scholarly edition, *Two of the Saxon Chronicles Parallel*, appeared in 1892 and 1899, anyone interested in the extraordinary phenomenon of English chronicles recorded in the vernacular before the 13th century has been obliged to choose whether to study *The Anglo-Saxon Chronicle* as a single text with variants in different manuscripts or as a complexly interrelated group of chronicle*s*. The series of editions currently being published as *The Anglo-Saxon Chronicle: A Collaborative Edition* makes a clear statement that the seven manuscripts (listed above) are not *one* chronicle.

Study of the *Chronicles* is made yet more complex by the reality that no one manuscript version limits itself to one genre. *The Anglo-Saxon Chronicles*, like Latin chronicles, derive from the early habit of noting important events for a year in the margin of an Easter table and run the gamut from chronicle (a chronological arrangment of important events that occurred during a particular year in a separate manuscript) to history (texts that include comment, interpretation, evaluation of the events) and to literature, both in some of the prose entries which are evidence of a fine tradition of vernacular, literary prose in England before the Norman conquest and in the poems that are included in some of the *Chronicles*.

The earliest chronicle manuscript that has survived (MS A, or the *Parker Chronicle*) was probably begun late in the 9th century. The entries from the preface and for individual years from 60 B.C. up to 891 are often referred to as "the common stock" because the details are shared by MSS B, C, D, E, and G; however, no other manuscript has an identical preface except the fragment β, which very likely was formerly appended to MS B. The Peterborough Chronicle (MS E), which includes the latest entries, continues to the coronation of Henry II in 1154. Between the 9th and 12th centuries manuscripts moved around from one part of England to another, picking up new entries and changing in focus.

This 9th-century historical project of vernacular chronicles may have resulted from King Alfred's campaign to increase literacy and learning by translating or having translated important documents from Latin to English. Some scholars see the pre-892 chronicle entries and their preface in MSS A and fragment β as part of a propaganda campaign to support Alfred and his successors in their indomitable attempt to defend their people and land from the onslaughts of the Vikings and increase and consolidate their territory, restricting the Danes to the Danelaw and living side-by-side with them in lawful peace.

The entries in all the manuscript versions begin to be longer and more complex after the fall of Rome, when the English people could no longer depend on Rome to maintain order and safety. Indeed many of the years before 449, when Hengist and Horsa (with their following of Angles, Saxons, and Jutes) were invited to England to assist the Britons but then stayed on to wrest the land away from the Britons, are "barren" annal numbers—the year is recorded but with no information for that year. However, from mid-century on, the entries seem to be written as events occurred or to be copies of entries written at the time of the events. MS A ceases to be the best source of information. For instance, Cnut's conquest of England (1017) resulting from the inept leadership of both Ethelred and Edmund and Cnut's reign are recounted in the most detail in MSS D and E. The different manuscripts emphasize different parts of English history. They not only include long, detailed passages in prose; they also include one of the great poems in Old English, *The Battle of Brunanburh* as the entry for 937 (included in MSS A, C, D, E, and F).

MS E or the Peterborough Chronicle shares with MSS D and F a preface taken from Book I, chapter I, of Bede's *Ecclesiastical History of the English People*, the other main source of information about early English history. (Bede's history, composed in Latin, was translated into Old English at about the same time that the earliest versions of the Chronicles were compiled.) This preface describes England, lists the languages of its inhabitants, and recounts the collaboration between Picts and Scots (the Irish) that led to the overthrow of the Britons. Perhaps by the 12th century, when MS E seems to have been copied, less need to articulate the legitimacy of Alfred's reign was felt. MS E is particularly noted for its account of later English history, the years preceding Cnut's conquest, through the civil war between Stephen and Matilda (Maud), to Stephen's death and the coronation of Henry II in London just before Christmas in 1154. Fragment H also includes entries for the 12th century, but they are distinct from the details in E.

All the manuscripts except F begin the annals proper in 60 B.C., informing the reader of Rome's first, unsuccessful attempt to subjugate the Britons. Then the entries begin with 1 A.D. and continue, providing a brief history of Christianity. MS F differs from all the other manuscripts, partly because it is a bilingual text, with entries in both Old English and Latin, also because its entries after the preface begin in the year 47, stating that Mark the Evangelist began to write his gospel then in Egypt, and because MS F seems throughout more concerned with continental Christian history than any other Anglo-Saxon chronicle.

The seven recensions (and two fragments) extant offer different views and emphasize different events; however, some of the manuscripts share details in a way that allows us to see important relationships among them. For instance, MS G, a late copy of A, preserves some entries that were erased from A by the scribe of F, who viewed additions from an archetype of E to be more important than the earlier history recorded in A. Fortunately Laurence Nowell made a transcript of G before G was nearly completely destroyed by the fire in the Cotton library in 1731. MS A provides valuable information about events up to the year 920 but is increasingly cryptic in its accounts of later years. After 1001 all entries are probably added by the scribe of F. MSS B and C share many entries, and D and E, often referred to as the northern recensions, are similar until 1031, when their entries begin to vary considerably. MS D continues its northern emphasis, while E moves south to Canterbury, where it is an important basis for MS F.

Another shared characteristic of the *Chronicles*, including the preface to MS A and the fragment β, is the illustration of a closely woven Germanic-pagan and Christian-Roman texture of the culture of medieval England. The descent from the Germanic god/hero Woden (and even the god's predecessors) of Alfred, Edward the Elder, and Athelstan as well as other notable leaders in Anglo-Saxon days is intertwined with the ecclesiastical ties between the English peoples and Christian Rome and other embryonic continental nations.

The Anglo-Saxon Chronicles contain a wealth of information for historians, students of literature, and archeologists, who often find material in this early record that helps them understand otherwise meaningless artefacts or confirm hypotheses about them. It, like Latin chronicles, allows a reader to see early England through first- and second-hand reports. The use of the vernacular, however, gives a sense of a text for the people, not just the educated elite. The choice of vernacular gives great strength to the chroniclers' accounts of determined attempts to unify England and the equally moving though more poignant accounts of disasters such as those that characterized the reign of Ethelred the Unready.

—Phyllis Rugg Brown

ANIMAL FARM.
Novel by George Orwell, 1945.

Most directly *Animal Farm* is an allegory of Stalinism, growing out of the Russian Revolution of 1917. It is cast as a beast fable, thus giving the reader some distance from the specific political events. George Orwell's use of the fable form helps the reader go beyond the details of one revolution and examine the elements of human nature which produce a Stalin and enable him to seize power. The novel is thus lifted above the particularities of polemic and presents a perspective on universals.

Orwell does, however, set his fable in the familiar events of current history. Old Major, a venerable pig on the Jones farm, is regarded as the wise patriarch by the other animals. He has had a strange dream and calls the other animals together to talk about their condition of misery. Old Major uses a Hobbesian figure when he declares: "Let us face it, our lives are miserable, laborious, and short." And he also speaks in Marxist terms when he declares that Man is the problem. "Only get rid of Man, and the produce of our labor would be our own. Almost overnight we could be rich and free. What then must we do? Why, work night and day, body and soul, for the overthrow of the human race! That is my message to you, comrades. Rebellion!"

It is simplistic, emotion-freighted exhortation, rousing the illiterate, simple, common animals. The challenge catches fire and, as in all revolutions, the planning begins in euphoria and hope. No voice is raised to ask pertinent questions or call for considered deliberation. Along with the euphoria, idealism also possesses everyone. The appearance of rats at the meeting raises a question: "Are rats comrades?" A democratic vote results in a ringing "Yes!" And Old Major proclaims, "No animal must ever tyrannize over his own kind. Weak or strong, clever or simple, we are all brothers. All animals are equal!"

It was, however, generally recognized that the pigs were the cleverest of the animals, so the work of organizing for the Rebellion fell naturally to them, especially to three who took over leadership: Napoleon and Snowball, the two boars of the farm, and Squealer. These three elaborated Old Major's teaching into a complete system of thought: Animalism. A code of equality, austerity, and hard work was proclaimed and encoded in The Seven Commandments—"an unalterable law."

All the animals were energized with great enthusiasm which they expressed through Old Major's rallying hymn, "Beasts of England." Orwell gives it some of the same power as Blake's great patriotic quatrain: "I will not cease from Mental Fight / Nor will my sword sleep in my hand / 'Til we have built Jerusalem / In England's green and pleasant land."

The Rebellion comes sooner than had been expected and the successful animals join together with a will to build the New Jerusalem. And to symbolize the new day the name of the farm is changed from Manor Farm to Animal Farm.

Very soon, however, under the leadership of Napoleon, the techniques and hypocricies of tyranny begin to appear. First, there is a strong emphasis on ceremony and ritual. A regular Sunday morning meeting is set up where Napoleon gives an inspirational address. Slogans are recited in unison. A favorite is their great affirmation: "Four legs good—two legs bad!" When a counter-attack by farmer Jones is beaten off, the great occasion is proclaimed "The Battle of the Cowshed," and military decorations created including "Animal Hero-First Class" and "Animal Hero-Second Class." Napoleon awards both of these to himself.

Very soon comes the discrediting of co-leader Snowball. Snowball is the idealist, constantly wanting to consider the welfare of all the animals while Napoleon is the pragmatist, ready to be brutal to achieve his purposes. So the technique of the "big lie" and contrived evidence results in Snowball's being driven out of Animal Farm, leaving Napoleon in sole command. And the discredited Snowball is blamed whenever problems arise. Orwell is paralleling the conflict in Russia between Trotsky and Stalin with Stalin the winner.

Another recognizable technique: revision of the past. The Seven Commandments—"unalterable law"—are revised one by one to suit Napoleon's purposes. Also the democratic meetings are changed to assemblies where Napoleon issues his orders. The workers are often puzzled but they absorb everything they are told and thus become perfect subjects for manipulation.

The most blatant and most effective techniques used by Napoleon are the show trials, the abject confessions, and the summary executions. Orwell does not include an explanation of this epidemic of confessions, but a reasonable conclusion is that the rampant climate of Machiavellian fear paralyzes the judgment, generates irrational guilt, and creates a kind of hysterical contagion of confession, in the hope that this will earn safety. We have in these scenes a parallel of the infamous Moscow treason trials of 1936–38.

Other techniques include optimistic reports that things are better than ever before; creation of a Mystique of the Leader; discarding of even loyal supporters when they can no longer be useful. The sale of Boxer to the glue factory when he is too ill to work any more is a case in point.

Hypocrisies are numerous, for special privileges for the pigs are decreed and then justified through Squealer's Doublespeak. And revisions of the Seven Commandments are continually made to suit Napoleon's personal wishes. The final cynical attitude of all tyrannies is expressed in the ultimate distillation of the Seven Commandments into one: "All Animals are equal, but some animals are more equal than others."

At the end of the novel the common animals realize what they have never been able to understand: the pigs are the same as their human masters were. Instead of gaining freedom they have only exchanged one set of masters for another. The vision with which they began has been corrupted. They have experienced a kind of rite of passage to sad knowledge—events have come full circle and the common animals now know the irony of expectations.

Orwell's fable illuminates his satirical theme: man's vulnerability to man's greed for power. His allegory is a clear statement verified by history.

—Paul H. Robb

ANNE OF GREEN GABLES.
Novel by L.M. Montgomery, 1908.

The characterization of Anne Shirley has often been hailed as a triumph of psychological realism in turn of the century children's literature, and, in fact, a study of L.M. Montgomery's accomplishment does confirm her achievement, even while we see the boundaries of acceptable child behaviour that she refused to cross.

Long before the publication of *Anne of Green Gables*, Montgomery had jotted down an idea for a story involving the botched adoption of a child by an elderly brother and sister. Asked to come up with a serial for children, she resurrected the premise, piling episode upon episode until she had a finished novel. The situation reveals Montgomery's sleight of hand with realistic characterization: Anne is initially perceived as undesirable, the "wrong" child, not because of any inherent flaw or fault of character, but because she is a girl when Marilla and Matthew had wanted to adopt a boy. Once the decision is made to keep her, the novel must continually juxtapose Anne's sprightly nature and talent for innocent misadventure against Marilla's rigidity and the horrified amusement of the community.

Members of the community include a cross-section of turn-of-the-century society of Prince Edward Island; the minister, the school teacher, the farming families move through the novel, and Anne manages to exasperate, impress, and ultimately touch them all. The qualities in her that Marilla sees as faults—her honesty of speech, her lively and persistently vocal imagination, and her capacity for abrupt and dizzying mood changes, set her apart from other more docile little girls and have endeared her to generations of readers.

Yet, no reader could be scandalized by Anne's nature or conduct. Despite her succession of foster homes, Anne is uncorrupted by bitterness or slyness; eager to love and be loved, she hungers for a best friend, becomes the dominant social and intellectual force of the Avonlea school, and returns Matthew and Marilla's cautious investment of care and affection tenfold, transforming the emotional aridity of Green Gables to a paradise of blossoms and blooming potential.

Her mishaps stem from impulsiveness and imagination, never from any taint of viciousness or manifestation of the unlovely survival skills that an unwanted child might well exhibit. In fact, Anne's good qualities clearly outweigh her imperfections. She is depicted as generous and loyal with friends, resourceful and courageous in crisis, ardent and introspective in her interior life. Montgomery creates in Anne a variation of the ugly duckling; seen at first as physically unprepossessing, she becomes a beauty, her once-despised red hair an auburn crown, while her intelligence and imagination, initially seen as contributing to her oddness and dilatory behaviour ultimately secure her a prestigious university scholarship.

The reader who seeks the roots of 20th century psychological realism in children's literature in *Anne of Green Gables* would be well advised to turn his or her attention to the characters with whom Anne interacts. Marilla Cuthbert's asperity makes her the perfect foil for Anne's verbal pyrotechnics, while Rachel Lynde combines warm-heartedness with the most appalling talent for speaking her thoughts, regardless of the feelings of her hearers. Josie Pye, Anne's fellow scholar and bête noire is refreshingly nasty, and when she dares Anne to walk the ridge pole of Barry's kitchen roof, with predictably painful results for Anne, she comes as close to positive evil as Montgomery is able to depict within the nature of a child.

It is innocence unsullied by experience that chiefly characterizes Montgomery's tone. The loveliness of the setting, which Anne alone seems to appreciate, the romantic resolution of every conflict in which she becomes embroiled, and above all the thematic resonances of the rescue of Anne by Matthew and Marilla and their subsequent redemption from sterility, all proclaim Montgomery's gentle optimism. If, in the years which separate us from her perspective, it has become impossible for us to share this comforting outlook we can at least celebrate it in this, her most famous and best realized work for children.

—Judith N. Mitchell

THE ANNIVERSARIES
(includes *An Anatomy of the World* and *Of the Progress of the Soul*).
Poems by John Donne, 1611 and 1612.

John Donne's *The Anniversaries* were poems written in consecutive years (1611 and 1612) ostensibly to commemorate the death of 14-year-old Elizabeth Drury, daughter of Sir Robert Drury, a wealthy landowner, courtier, and soldier. The poet never met Elizabeth Drury, and his reasons for writing the first poem are unknown, though what is documented of common acquaintances between Donne and Robert Drury suggest the *First Anniversary* (entitled *An Anatomy of the World*) was commissioned. Following the writing of the first poem, Donne accompanied the Drury family abroad and in France wrote the second work (*Of the Progress of the Soul*).

The Anniversaries are part of only a handful of poems published during Donne's lifetime—thus they lack the problems with text and dating that characterize Donne's other poetry. Donne, similar to Milton in *Lycidas*, does not detail particularities of the deceased's life, but offers a meditation on human existence spurred by feelings of lost human potential which accompany the death of someone young. The first poem contains some of the elements of elegy defined as a sustained lament on death; like *Lycidas*, the *Anatomy* charges others with negligence, remarks that all mourn the death, comments on current corrupt conditions, and offers a closing consolation with thoughts of life after death. The second poem concentrates less on a corrupt world and more on the soul's escape to heaven. Both poems celebrate the power of the poet to depict an ideal.

Yet Donne's method for doing these things, especially his scathing comment on the fallen, or, indeed, "dead" world juxtaposed with an extreme idealization of "the idea of a woman," his own reported phrase for the poem's subject, is fraught with contradictions that grow out of both poems' hyperbolic statements, resulting in much critical debate regarding *The Anniversaries'* achievement. Especially in the *First Anniversary*, the dead Elizabeth Drury is rendered as the unrecoverable source of "all" beauty, proportion, color, and right understanding; though a figure of absolute piety to Donne, she arguably displaces God as the source of order in the world. As one scholar remarks, "The main problem with *The Anniversaries* is that they are unable to support the weight of their own hyperbole. They collapse under their own exaggerated burden of praise." The sense of time in the first poem is also confusing. If the living Elizabeth Drury does "glue all virtues," and is the world's source of "form" and "frame," how did a golden world exist previously? If from the dead carcass of the old world a new world is being created, why does the poem go on to emphasize the world's present condition (the word "now" is used six times) as hopeless and unalterable? How could Elizabeth Drury be both the source of all perfection and order, but at the same time destroyed by a corrupt world?

To solve these problems and thus argue for the *Anatomy*'s value, or to explain its failure, critics have variously tried to define who or what Elizabeth Drury could stand for (some examples are Christ, the Logos, *Sapientia*) or emphasized the influence of various rhetorical forms, such as meditation and celebration. Yet in the effort to argue for the poem's coherence or failure, these interpretations, while often useful for understanding structure, can subvert or dismiss as faulty the essential power generated by the problems noted above. Part of the *First Anniversary*'s concern, in addition to offering Elizabeth Drury as an image of order to contrast with the world's decay, is to assert how the poet is uniquely able to proceed through an acute understanding of the elegiac medium to create this image. In the effort to "emprison" the memory of Elizabeth Drury or "the idea of a woman" by establishing her extreme and holy difference from the world, and thus also partially defeat death though poetry, Donne revitalizes elegy with hyperbole that leads to unresolved contradictions so "that the world should have notice of this." Thus the poet challenges generations of readers to make sense of the colliding relationship between the extreme praise of Elizabeth Drury and the debased world this figure stands against, or otherwise respond to the energy this conflict generates, insuring his subject an audience through time. In this sense, Donne the poet is, like his depiction of Elizabeth Drury, a creator offering order, though not an order we can easily grasp, in a corrupt world. The poem which prefaces the *First Anniversary*, "To the Praise of the Dead, and the Anatomy," whose author is unknown, also suggests this.

On the other hand, while asserting his unique power as a poet, Donne is acutely aware that he too "thinks he hath got / to be a phoenix." The poems are ostensibly addressed to a wider public—yet we sense also the characteristic private mode of metaphysical poetry in which Donne struggles with himself, realizing that in the process of establishing distinctions between his perception of public falsity and his own private integrity he necessarily becomes implicated in the very conditions he strives to define and transcend. The narrator's use of the pronouns "our," "we," and "us" show Donne's consciousness of his close connection to the fallen public world. *Of the Progress of the Soul* strives to "forget this world" as Donne turns to address his own soul, and thus leaves behind many of the problems encountered in the first poem. And yet here too, Donne, while in the "ecstasy" of this progress, still understands he is an "author" in the world who must ask his soul, "When wilt thou shake off this pedantery, / Of being taught by sense and fantasy." Generally regarded as more successful than the first poem, *The Progress* shows how Donne strives to transcend a corrupt world, and yet still remains fascinated by it. We could call both poems complex explorations of the contrasting and simultaneous processes of the soul's putrefaction and purification.

—Chris Roark

ANTONY AND CLEOPATRA.
Play by William Shakespeare, 1606(?).

William Shakespeare's most expansive tragedy in terms of its geographical range—Rome, Athens, Alexandria—nonetheless provides an intense focus on its two protagonists; its chronological range is also expansive, covering the ten years from 40 B.C. to 30 B.C., the year of both Antony's and Cleopatra's deaths. To confine these elements into a 5-act structure and the 2-hour traffic of the stage required a telescoping of events; stage action, consequently, has been reduced to 12 days with the passage of time between events somewhat casually suggested within the dialogue. The original printing did not mark act divisions nor any of the numerous scenes that modern editors have indicated according to the principle that each clearing of the stage introduces a new scene; a Jacobean audience would thus have more readily sensed the fluid action propelling events to their tragic end than do modern readers.

The primary locales of Alexandria and Rome become character coordinates of the two protagonists, the "Egyptian fetters" of the entrancing queen contrasting with the noble virtues of a Roman hero. In abstract terms the conflict is between pleasure and honour, love and world empire, but there is nothing abstract in Shakespeare's delineation of his two main characters. They are presented in concrete terms, exhibiting the emotional variability that marks the altogether human qualities of their relationship.

The opening lines of the play denigrate both protagonists; according to a Roman view their admired military leader—the triple pillar of the world—is enslaved, not to the acknowledged Queen of Egypt, but to a strumpet, a mere gipsy; in a bitter mood, even Antony calls her "triple-turned whore," recalling her earlier love affairs with Julius Caesar and the son of Pompey the Great. Yet Shakespeare has contrived to present Cleopatra in all her infinite variety—coquettish, even at times shrewish, but still a noble empress, descended of many royal kings. This volatility of mood and demeanor the bluff Enobarbus captures in his marvellous description of her in Act II, a description which is impressively verified by the dramatic action.

Antony is presented as torn between political-military concerns and the powerful attractions of Alexandrian life; at times he seems indecisive, even vacillating as, at the battle of Actium, he surrenders his military advantage to follow the fleeing Cleopatra "like a doting mallard." Despite his flaws, he emerges as an individual of great human warmth and magnanimity. "For his bounty," as Cleopatra says, "There was no winter in't: an autumn it was / That grew the more by reaping."

The plot is simplicity itself: Antony, one of the triumvirate who with Lepidus and Octavius Caesar rule Rome, is neglecting his duties for "lascivious wassails" in Alexandria. When the political situation with Octavius becomes strained, he returns to Rome where, in order to tie an "unslippable knot" between them, he marries Octavia, an irreproachable matron of a "holy, cold, and still" deportment, the dearly loved sister of Octavius. To celebrate this renewed political alliance, the three leaders feast and drink aboard Pompey's galley; here one of Pompey's allies suggests that the galley cables be cut as well as the throats of the three competitors; here Lepidus, a "third part of the world" is carried off in a drunken stupor, while the others disport themselves, dancing the Egyptian bacchanals. This Roman scene of revelry is counterpoised to Antony's heady Alexandrian indulgences.

Antony and Octavia take up residence in Athens, but after a new dissension develops with Octavius, she returns to Rome and Antony departs for Egypt. When war follows, despite his "absolute soldiership" by land, Antony agrees to fight at sea because Caesar dares him to it, with the result that the entire Egyptian fleet turns tail at Actium, and Cleopatra, who has insisted on being present, also turns tail, to be followed by Antony.

Utterly disgraced in his own mind, he dismisses his followers, providing them with a ship laden with gold, and he forgives Cleopatra. He then sues Caesar for permission to live in Athens a private man, his messenger on this occasion a mere schoolmaster whereas "not many moons gone by" he had "superfluous kings for messengers." When his suit is refused, he offers to settle the war "sword against sword"; at this Enobarbus observes that Octavius has even subdued his judgement in thinking that his rival would hazard his present advantage. On seeing Octavius' messenger kissing Cleopatra's hand, Antony orders him whipped, vehemently charging her with her past life: she was "half-blasted" ere he knew her, "a morsel cold upon / Dead Caesar's trencher." Again he forgives her. Before what proves to be his last battle, he plans one more "gawdy night." At his farewells, his servants weep.

Meanwhile some of his followers desert, including Enobarbus; on learning this, Antony sends his treasure after him with "gentle adieus and greetings"—an act which induces such grief in Enobarbus over his desertion that he seeks out a ditch in which to die. In spite of one successful sally, the following day Antony sees the Egyptian fleet once again desert; again he rages at Cleopatra, who seeks refuge in her monument; then she sends word that she has slain herself, the name "Antony" being the last word she uttered. At this he, too, resolves on death and asks Eros, his freed bondservant, to hold the sword; instead Eros turns it on himself. Stirred by this act, Antony falls on his own sword, a wound that will prove mortal but not immediately. When a messenger from Cleopatra announces that she is not dead, he is carried to her monument; fearing to open it, she hoists him aloft with the help of her two waiting women. At his death, she resolves to do what's brave, what's noble, "after the high Roman fashion."

Given two protagonists, Shakespeare was faced with the necessity of a double catastrophe, a dramaturgical problem that he handled with consummate skill—Act IV belonging to Antony's demise; Act V to Cleopatra's but with no diminution of dramatic tension. Learning of Antony's death, Caesar and his Romans are moved but nonetheless proceed to palter with Cleopatra with the intent of taking her to Rome in triumph. Following a splendid encomium of Antony, she palters with them, calling on her treasurer to present her true worth; instead he reveals that she has kept back as much as is reported. The intent of this scene is differently interpreted, some viewing it as Cleopatra's means of deceiving Caesar about her real intention, in accord with Shakespeare's source; others as conduct that accords with her opportunistic nature.

Once certain that Caesar is untrustworthy, Cleopatra calls for her queenly robes and crown, determined now to join Antony. A rustic, earlier summoned, brings her the basket of figs and the asps she applies to her breast and arm. Finding Cleopatra and her two gentlewomen dead, Caesar comments that she looks as if she would catch another Antony "in her strong toil of grace." He directs that the two be buried together: "No grave upon the earth shall clip in it / A pair so famous."

The poetry of this play is truly dramatic in that its sole function is to reveal character; except for Enobarbus' description of Cleopatra on her barge, there are no set passages. Yet there are an enormous number of images that echo and re-echo throughout the play as well as a great variety of styles, ranging from the colloquial to the opulent to a stunning simplicity. The text first appeared in the Folio (1623) where it is labelled a tragedy, but it is of a different sort from Shakespeare's other tragedies. With Act IV and the death of Antony we are made aware of the tragic waste proper to the genre, yet with Act V we feel the death of Cleopatra not as a waste but as a triumph.

Shakespeare's source is the *Parallel Lives* by Plutarch, a first-century Greek rhetorician and philosopher. Extremely popular in the Renaissance, this work focuses on the heroic deeds of great men (whether flawed or not), their characters revealed through action and the telling anecdote. In 1579 Sir Thomas North produced a vigorous and colourful translation (reprinted in 1595 and frequently thereafter), and "The Life of Antony" together with the "Comparison of Demetrius [King of Macedonia] and Antony" provided Shakespeare with all the necessary historical material. Above all, the range of North's language allowed the playwright to appropriate much of the prose into his poetry, as with Enobarbus' description of Cleopatra. Indeed North's Plutarch was a great stimulus to the playwright, who plundered it not only for *Antony and Cleopatra* but also for *Julius Caesar* and *Coriolanus* and in part for *Timon of Athens* and *A Midsummer's Night Dream*.

—Elizabeth Story Donno

APOLOGIA PRO VITA SUA.
Prose by John Henry Newman, 1864.

Like all John Henry Newman's major works, except *An Essay in Aid of a Grammar of Assent*, the *Apologia pro Vita Sua* was written to meet a particular occasion. At the end of 1863, he read a review by Charles Kingsley of Froude's *History of England*, which included the words: "Truth for its own sake has never been a virtue with the Roman clergy. Father Newman informs us that it need not, and on the whole ought not, to be." When Newman pointed out that he had never thought and never said such a thing, it was Kingsley's obvious duty to withdraw and apologize. Instead, he shuffled, blustered, and introduced new and irrelevant points; convinced, apparently, that in Protestant England anti-Catholic prejudice was so strong that any libel would wash, and the normal decencies of public debate need not apply. He proved to be mistaken.

The particular stimulus that made Newman write the history of the Oxford Movement, and the story of his own conversion to Catholicism at this time, and in response to this challenge, was a fortunate one. It enabled him to combine an intimate personal story with a chivalrous concern for the reputation of his fellow Catholics; and it induced him to face a difficult question: why had others seen that the inevitable goal of his Anglo-Catholicism was conversion to Rome so long before he had seen it himself? Also, the sympathy excited in his old friends who were still Anglicans by these absurd accusations secured for him the loan of hundreds of his old letters. Thus, the book, as well as being eloquent and deeply felt, is also extremely well-documented and accurate. Lastly, Newman's need to write with extraordinary speed (with the possible exception of *Waverley*, this work is the most rapidly written of all lengthy classic works in our literature) endowed the *Apologia* with a unity of feeling which fused at great heat materials that might have seemed intractable because of the mass of detail and the high abstraction of the theological argument.

Kingsley was a paradoxical opponent. He was a stupid, gifted man. His contribution to the novel, though perhaps minor, is fresh and original. As a public figure he was an effective, though sometimes crude, controversialist for the causes he favoured. As tutor to the Prince of Wales, and friend of the Queen, he was, grotesquely, appointed professor of history at Cambridge, an appointment whose blatant favouritism seemed to smack more of the 18th century than the 19th. Yet his attitudes and controversial methods when dealing with Catholics were very near to those of that traditional popular "No Popery" party, which Newman had satirized so brilliantly a few years before. As a clergyman of the Church of England, he was a gentleman by law. He could not be ignored as a gutter Protestant even if he behaved like one.

One theme of the *Apologia* is honesty, which was simple, because Newman knew he was honest, and his readers, if not hopelessly prejudiced, knew it too. Why else should a middle-aged man abandon his life-work, his friends, and the university he loved, to begin life again among strangers? But the other theme is complex and difficult, the theme of continuity and change. Newman felt the need to reconcile an essential consistency of life with startling reversals of opinion. At 15 he had been a Calvinist, at 35 a convinced Anglican, at 44 a Catholic. He submitted to the papacy, which he had once imagined to bear the mark of anti-Christ. He is able to show that, unlike some of his colleagues in the Oxford Movement (Keble, for instance), he had been committed to the Anglican Church only because he believed it to be the true heir of the undivided primitive Church. Since that primitive Church had certainly not been either Protestant or Erastian, he had to suppose that the Protestantism and Erastianism of the Church of England was only an appearance or a removable corruption, not of its essence. Quite early in the Movement, while he still had no doubts about Anglicanism, he had mooted the possibility that Anglo-Catholicism was only a paper system, not a real religion, shaping souls and nations. This paper system had to be made real. The bishops to whose authority he looked with reverence must stand up for it. The Protestant appearance of the 39 Articles, which every clergyman had to sign, had to be explained away. But the bishops were united in the view that they had no authority (one bishop amused Newman by admitting that he did not know whether he believed in Apostolic Succession or not) except from the Crown. Tract 90, in which Newman tried to reinterpret the

Articles in a Catholic sense, was generally received as a unfair blow at Protestant and insular traditions.

At the same time Newman's study of the early Church began to sap the foundations of his anti-Catholic prejudices. The phrase of St. Augustine, "securus iudicat orbis terrarum," rang in his ears, and brought home to him the impossibility of justifying schism on Catholic principles. The pain of his Anglican deathbed at Littlemore was intense, but appears in the book masked by reticence. Indeed, a mark of the whole work is deep feeling under strong literary control. There is nothing emotional in his prose style here. In the last section, describing the position of his mind since 1845, he is able to state his middle position on controversies within the Catholic church upon the nature and limits of authority, combining an unshakeable belief in the necessity of dogma with a robust defence of the liberty of theological enquiry.

—A.O.J. Cockshut

ARCADIA.
Old Arcadia, written 1577–81.
New Arcadia, written 1582–84.
Prose by Sir Philip Sidney, 1590; revised edition, 1593.

Sir Philip Sidney's *Arcadia* was written in response to a sudden upsurge in the popularity of prose fiction with a strong psychological orientation. Sparked off during the 16th century by the publication and translation into several European languages of novels from the Greek and Roman empires, the taste for this new fashion grew rapidly. Action-packed chivalric narratives of the middle ages based on the heroism of crusaders, knights of the Round Table, and magical fairylands, came to be rivalled, and later outstripped by, this earlier and more character-centred prose fiction.

The ancient novel features the mental anxieties suffered by idealised young people, forcibly separated from those they love but trying desperately to reunite. Exotic Asian, Middle Eastern, and North African settings, oracles, and the symbolic use of architecture, costume, and jewellery, are complemented by elegant and rhythmic prose styles adopted by rhetorically trained authors to beautify their works.

Sidney's *Arcadia* appears to be the earliest full-scale attempt during the European Renaissance to revive this sophisticated style and form. It had been kept alive during the middle ages in the mainly verse Byzantine novels. Sidney's neoclassicism also governs the shape of the plot: after many complex difficulties the miseries of the central characters take an abrupt and unexpected shift towards a happy resolution.

Modelled on the ancient novels of the greatest artistic merit, Achilles Tatius's *Clitophon and Leucippe*, Longus's *Daphnis and Chloe*, Apuleius's *Golden Ass*, and Heliodorus's *Aethiopika*, from the second, third, and fourth centuries, the *Arcadia* blends into its classical matrix a well-known plot outline from the predominantly 15th-century *Amadís de Gaula*. This popular chivalric prose romance lies behind Sidney's central story: Prince Musidorus of Thessalia disguises himself as a shepherd to court the Arcadian Princess Pamela, while his cousin, the Macedonian Prince Pyrocles, transforms himself into an Amazon warrior to initiate a relationship with Pamela's younger sister, Philoclea.

Pyrocles deceives the ageing Arcadian ruler, Basilius, whose response to a foreboding oracle has been to divorce himself and his family from the civilizing restraints of the court. They are all bored. Basilius's erotic obsession with Pyrocles is mild in relation to the emotional upheaval of his young wife Gynecia. Her sexual awareness, heightened by the isolation of the countryside, instinctively recognises a potential lover. Gynecia is not only driven to physical illness from the stress of her passion; she exposes herself and ignominiously pleads with Pyrocles for relief, while her jealousy forces her to consider murdering Philoclea, whom she regards as a rival.

The effect of love on the human psyche is one of Sidney's primary interests. Rivalry and jealousy are recurrent themes. When Sidney revised and restructured his novel between 1582 and 1584, creating the distinction between the *Old Arcadia* and the *New Arcadia*, this aspect was further accentuated by adding the character Amphialus. Knocked out of the succession to the throne of Arcadia through the death of his father and the birth of the princesses, Amphialus is encouraged by his vengeful mother Cecropia to develop and consummate an excessive and unsavoury passion for his first cousin Philoclea.

In the new Book III, which is where the unfinished *New Arcadia* ends, Cecropia kidnaps the princesses and their ostensibly female companion, the Amazon Pyrocles, in order to feed Amphialus's reticent lust and one way or another secure the monarchy. Amphialus holds back, governed by conscience and the chivalric codes of honour, believing that the pageantry of bloody single combat will win Philoclea's favour. Obsessed with idealized abstractions, he remains oblivious to the tortures to which Philoclea and her sister are subjected by Cecropia. His medieval ideals are out of step with reality; his understanding of women, young and old, negligible.

Two themes, one-on-one armed combat and the treatment of women, are introduced by Sidney into the earlier version but more fully developed here. In mounted battle with the sword, concepts of virtue and correct chivalric behaviour are tested against the personalities and capabilities of the male characters. Sidney fulfils the didactic purposes of literature by instructing his readers in the arts of military horsemanship, symbolic costumes, and pictorial devices. These become integrated into the literary symbolism of the plot. The treatment of women is far more complex.

Evidently Sidney recognized the inadequacy of the coarsely humorous posture adopted in the *Old Arcadia*. The chief herdsman Dametas's strident relationship with his wife Miso, who mentally and physically abuses him, encourages him to transfer his aggression in an anti-chivalric manner. Dametas boasts that he has hit the disguised Pyrocles with the blunt end of his bill-hook, made "her" cry, and because of this has taken pity on her. Basilius with equal insensitivity wholeheartedly approves. In the revision, Dametas is too cowardly to strike the Amazon.

Basilius's mistrust and over-protectiveness of his wife and daughters is accentuated near the beginning of both works by Philanax's letter of advice. As women's minds resist containment, he recommends lack of restraint as the best course to win their cooperation. The *New Arcadia* elaborates upon this theme in Parthenia's rejecting her enforced engagement to Demagoras, his brutal disfiguring of her face, and her happy marriage to Argalus. Pamphilus's infidelity to a string of fiancés seems as nothing compared with Cecropia's torture and whipping of Philoclea, and her encouragement to Amphialus to rape her (or her sister Pamela if he prefers). Then, after Cecropia dies and Amphialus is wounded, all three kidnapped prisoners become objects of sexual desire to Anaxius, Lycurgus, and Zoilus.

Pamela's Christianity coupled with Argalus's and Musidorus's chivalric idealism lends a thread of hope to these ordeals, which Pyrocles appears to be ending when the *New Arcadia* breaks off. He has killed Zoilus and Lycurgus, and has Anaxius well engaged in single combat with the sword. Such free bloodletting remains characteristic of Renaissance imitations of Homer and Virgil. It goes with the subject of war, which in the *New Arcadia* is inextricably entwined with love and politics. Sidney's heroes defend monarchy as their preferred system of government, and actively overthrow it if it becomes oppressive or irresponsible. Their present inactive posture as lovers is ironically ambiguous.

The plot of both versions is predicted by an oracle to end with the marriage of the princes and princesses, after the apparent death of Basilius and the occupation of his throne by a foreign power. This is fulfilled in the completed *Old Arcadia* but not in the *New*, which was left unfinished. When Sidney altered his serio-comic *Old Arcadia* into an epic form, the predominantly pastoral tone of the *Old Arcadia*, adapted from the *Diana* of Montemayor, was reduced, and the Eclogues separating each of the five Books or Acts substantially incorporated into the prose of the new Books I and II.

The idea of separating the Books with Eclogues comes from Sannazaro's *Arcadia*. The poems they contain constitute the bulk of Sidney's surviving verse. Inspired shepherds join the court figures in verse-based discussions related to the central themes: politics, idealisation of women, love, and marriage. Other than the disguised Pyrocles, women take no active part. The narrative background in the first two Eclogues describes the princes' development of their chivalric prowess through defending oppressed women. During the process of revision this prose and many of the poems from all four Eclogues were placed in the body of the expanded *New Arcadia*. The piecemeal remains of the Eclogues, left in ruins by Sidney, were reconstituted by editors after his death, and printed between the Books.

The nature of the revision, which consists of two redeveloped Books, and one entirely new, is indicated by alterations to Sidney's persona, Philisides. In the *Old Arcadia* he is a cynical and melancholy shepherd. In a series of poems he describes his falling in love, Mira's beauty, and her rejection of him. He engages in a debate on youth and age, and in a beast fable recounts the development of tyranny. This he learned from Hubert Languet, statesman and Sidney's mentor during the years of his continental education.

Sidney develops an implicit link between Philisides and the character Pyrocles, whom he clearly favours. In the *Old Arcadia* Philisides's erotic description of Mira is recalled by Pyrocles when he is in bed with Philoclea. Philisides of the *New Arcadia* is a shepherd who makes a sudden transition into a fully trained knight. The design of his armour and his entourage reflect his pastoral origins, and he is reported by Pyrocles to be in love with a lady of the court, his "star." Pyrocles is privy to intimate knowledge of this episode in Philisides's life.

This autobiographical interlude reflects the author's own developing interest in pageantry and the symbolism which could be tacitly conveyed in architecture, costume, and jewellery. It typifies the heroic tone of the revised work with its equally ornate sentence structures, and demonstrates a strong affinity with the art of the ancient novel.

—Victor Skretkowicz

ARDEN OF FAVERSHAM.
Play, c. 1587–92.

Editions

The Tragedy of Master Arden of Faversham, edited by M.L. Wine. 1973.
Arden of Faversham, edited by Martin White. 1982.

Critical Studies: *The Shakespeare Apocrypha* edited by C.F. Tucker Brooke, 1908; *English Domestic or Homiletic Tragedy* by Henry Hitch Adams, 1943; "Theme and Imagery in *Arden of Faversham*" by Sarah Youngblood, in *Studies in English Literature*, 3, Spring 1963; "The Imagery of Tragic Melodrama in *Arden of Faversham*" by Max Bluestone, in *Drama Survey*, 5, 1966; *Arden of Faversham: A Study of the Play* by Anita Holt, 1970; *Domestic Drama: A Survey of the Origins, Antecedents, and Nature of the Domestic Play in England 1500–1640* by Andrew Clark, 2 vols., 1975; "Alice Arden's Crime" by Catherine Belsey, in *Renaissance Drama*, 13, 1982; "Man's House as His Castle in *Arden of Faversham*" by Lena Cowen Orlin, in *Medieval and Renaissance Drama in English*, 2, 1985.

Arden of Feversham (the original spelling), the earliest and best of the Elizabethan domestic homiletic tragedies, was entered on the Stationers' Register on 3 April 1592, though it may have been performed as early as 1587. The same year (1592) appeared the first edition, in quarto, with a title-page reading: "THE LAMENTABLE AND TRVE TRAGEDIE OF M. ARDEN OF FEVERSHAM IN KENT. Who was most wickedlye murdered, by the meanes of his disloyall and wanton wyfe, who for the loue she bare to one Mosbie, hyred two desperat ruffins Blackwill and Shakbag, to kill him. Wherin is shewed the great mallice and discimulation of a wicked woman, the vnsatiable desire of filthie lust and the shamefull end of all murderers." Two other quartos appeared during the Elizabethan-Jacobean era, in 1599 and 1633. Edward Jacob, a Faversham antiquary, first attributed the play to Shakespeare in 1770; it has also been attributed to Kyd and/or to Marlowe, but it remains anonymous, though generally considered the best play of the Shakespeare apocrypha. No external evidence links it with Shakespeare; only the internal evidence of its powerful blank verse lines and complex psychological characterization suggest his possible authorship, strongly enough that M.L. Wine, in the best scholarly edition of the play (1973), concludes that internal evidence "at least qualifies it for the apocryphal works."

The murder upon which *Arden of Feversham* is based occurred in Faversham, Kent, on 15 February 1551, and is described in detail in Holinshed's *Chronicles*, in five great folio pages, double-columned and closely printed. The problem in interpreting the play is complicated by the fact that all three quartos are imperfect and appear to be distant from authorial intent.

Arden of Feversham is one of the few examples of an unsentimental Elizabethan domestic homiletic tragedy. It has those traits which were to come to mark such tragedies: commoners for its main characters, a domestic setting with personal and family relationships as its background, an historical contemporary event as its subject, an ethical level of interpretation, occasional non-integral moralizing, emphasis on the macabre, a familiar directness of style, a centering of plot interest on the individual scene rather than on the single climax. In these traits, it stands in opposition to most of the dominant tendencies of mainstream romantic Elizabethan tragedy.

It is its preference for the incremental repetition of episode rather than for Aristotelian architectonics which most marks *Arden of Feversham*. Its powerful stage effect is due partly to this use of recurrent scenes: six attempts to murder Arden fail before the seventh succeeds. The failures seem almost providential, as if the intended victim is being given chance after chance to save himself by freeing himself of his two besetting vices: avarice and uxoriousness.

When the play opens, Alice Arden and Mosby are already adulterous lovers plotting Arden's murder. Alice enlists the aid of Michael and Clarke by promising each of them Susan, her maid and Mosby's sister, in return for his aid in the murder. Greene appears, swearing revenge on Arden for stealing his lands, and is added to the conspirators. He in turn hires Black Will and Shakebag, two professional killers, and the roster of would-be murderers is complete early in the play. Most of its remainder is devoted to six attempts of the conspirators to murder Arden, whose escapes teach him nothing. After the fifth of these attempts, Arden meets Dick Reede, a sailor whose land he has appropriated, and scorns his plea to return the land to Reede's needy wife and children. Reede curses him:

> That plot of ground which thou detains from me—
> I speak it in an agony of spirit—
> Be ruinous and fatal unto thee!
> Either there be butchered by thy dearest friends,
> Or else be brought for men to wonder at. . . .

Reede's curse is not long in being fulfilled. After one more abortive incident, Black Will pulls Arden down with a strangling towel in his own house (while he is playing at tables—backgammon—with Mosby), and he is stabbed to death by Mosby, Shakebag, and Alice. The murderers drag his body out behind the abbey, to the grounds which Reede had accursed. But they earlier had allowed Arden to be seen entering the house; they cannot clean the blood from the floor; they leave a trail of footprints in the snow (which stops and fails to cover up the prints); they leave Alice's towel and knife by the body, the rushes from her floor on his slippers. Finally, his wounds begin to bleed afresh in the presence of his guilty wife. Penitent, she confesses; most of the guilty are captured and sentenced to death. Arden's friend Franklin speaks the epilogue, telling what became of the other characters.

Arden of Feversham is remarkable in a number of ways. Its psychological characterization is complex and dark. There are no thoroughly good characters in the play; even Franklin is gullible and flawed and opportunistic; the victim Arden is unsympathetic, ambitious, hard-hearted except that he is uxoriously fond of Alice, that Kentish village Clytemnestra. But neither is there an unrelieved villain in the piece. Alice and Mosby have recurrent moments of repentance, regret, self- and mutual reproach; Michael, the servant willing to kill his master for gain and for Susan, relents more than once and cries out "O, mistress!" when Alice actually stabs Arden; even the professional killers, Black Will and Shakebag, have redeeming trivialities, ineptitudes, humannesses.

The play is also notable for its naturalism—of speech, of environmental minutiae, of characterization. The two characters not in Holinshed, the apprentice and the ferryman, add local color, convincing small Kentish commoner detail. As a whole, the play is a melodrama, but incident by incident it is convincing.

Although it has some prose and some heroic couplets, *Arden of Feversham* is metrically extraordinary only in its passages of blank verse, often charged and metaphorical, put into the mouths of characters for whom it is sometimes surprising. Shakebag and Black Will both have astonishingly eloquent speeches, as one in which Shakebag equates the blackness of night to their evil purpose. And the anonymous playwright knows Shakespeare's trick of letting a character, after an ornate metaphorical passage, suddenly say something direct and plain and monosyllabic: "Love is a god, and marriage is but words," says Alice, early in the play, and Mosby, later having doubts about his liaison with this woman, grieves, "My golden time was when I had no gold" and, later in the same soliloquy, "'Tis fearful sleeping in a serpent's bed. . . ." Alice looks at herself and knows that she might, repentant, turn once again to be "honest Arden's wife" but can never again be "Arden's honest wife." She sums up the reason to murder her husband, "Nay he must leave to live that we may love." But after he is slain, she looks at his bleeding body and implores him

> Rise up, sweet Arden, and enjoy thy love,
> And frown not on me when we meet in heaven;
> In heaven I love thee though on earth I did not.

Arden of Feversham is often described as homiletic, moral, didactic, but it is a strange didacticism. Except for the title page, it preaches very little. Even Franklin's epilogue draws no maxim but simply tells of the fates of the other characters, making no judgments or expostulations. It is not plain what judgments could be made. The innocent Bradshaw and the half-innocent Susan (an accessory only after the fact) are executed along with the guilty; the guilty Clarke escapes. If Providence has preserved Arden through six attempts on his life, why does it fail him during the seventh? His appropriation of Reede's lands was no worse than his appropriation of Greene's, before the play began. For every character who speaks a moral line, there is another who dismisses it. (When Will and Shakebag fall upon Arden and Franklin, and Shakebag and Mosby are wounded, Will says of Arden, "doubtless, he is preserved by miracle." But earlier, when Greene had declared similarly after an aborted murder attempt that "The Lord of Heaven hath preserved him," it is Will himself who had retorted, "The Lord of Heaven a fig! The Lord Cheyne hath preserved him. . . .") Arden's prophetic strangulation dream of his own murder foretells the manner of his death; Reede's curse foretells the disposal of his body, on the spot where no grass will grow for two years afterwards. But both portents suggest an inescapable doom rather than exhort toward improved behavior.

Arden of Feversham has held the stage for the past four centuries. George Lillo wrote another version of the same plot in the 18th century, one which saw numerous performances and printings. In its compounding of high imagery and blunt speech, of melodrama and stark realism, of social climbers who spurn and hate the rungs by which they have climbed, it seems peculiarly modern. Its fusing of mayhem, realism, and low comedy suggests O'Casey or the later Synge or Pinter. It gives us a world without heroes, in which ambitious individualistic greed is the prime mover. The world of *Arden of Feversham* is violent, libidinous, threatening. Things fall apart; the center cannot hold.

—Frances Mayhew Rippy

AREOPAGITICA.
Prose by John Milton, 1644.

In his *Life* of John Milton (1779) Samuel Johnson contended that the poet "had formed his style by a perverse and pedantic principle. He was desirous to use English words with a foreign idiom. This in all his prose is discovered and condemned. . . ." The tendency which Johnson noted (which is also true of Milton's poetry) does not impair one's enjoyment of *Paradise Lost* or *Samson Agonistes* because in both instances the subject matter seems to call for a certain remoteness from the familiarity of everyday usage. But in the case of Milton's prose, it has to be admitted that the modes of expression adopted are likely to cause difficulties. Readers accustomed to the dignified urbanity of Dryden or the raciness of Defoe find the unorthodox grammatical constructions and elaborate sentence patterns irritating and bizarre. Milton's vocabulary contains many unfamiliar elements, and his punctuation is distinctly archaic. This kind of prose is clearly not intended to be a vehicle for sequential exposition or meditative reflection; the reader must be vigilant in the extreme if he is not to lose the thread of discourse. As for rhythm and musicality, Milton appears to care little for qualities which other authors have striven hard to achieve; there are few passages in his prose which could be regarded as conforming to the demands of "decorum."

But if they lack mellifluousness, Milton's writings exhibit a certain muscular power, derived in part from the author's readiness to take up issues which invited polemical utterance. A high proportion of all Milton wrote was the outcome of the violent controversies characteristic of a period when highly partisan authors engaged in shameless calumny and insulting exchanges. This was only to be expected in an age when political and religious altercation was rife throughout England. *Areopagitica* is only one item in a vast flood of pamphlets composed by men anxious to advance the rival claims of factions all aiming to influence public opinion in respect of causes now largely forgotten. Milton called his tract a "speech," and it is indeed modelled on an oration by the Greek political theorist Isocrates (436–338 B.C.). As it stands it is hardly suitable for oral delivery; yet Milton—addressing himself to an assembly such as met on the Athenian hill of Areopagus—adopts a truly "forensic" manner in order to arouse a passionate response. Throughout his works he shows himself to be a staunch advocate of individual liberty; in *The Ready and Easy Way to Establish a Free Commonwealth . . .* (1660) he writes: "The whole freedom of man consists either in spiritual or civil liberty . . .," and then goes on to say that freedom of conscience is more likely to be attainable in a "free commonwealth" than under "kingship" because the republican system of government is "most magnanimous, most fearless, and confident of its own fair proceedings." When *Areopagitica* was written England was still a monarchy, the king being largely antipathetic to the anti-prelatical posture adopted by such men as Milton. When in 1643 it was proposed as a measure of public safety that all books issued from English presses should appear only under licence, Milton saw this as a serious infringement of liberty. The repressive intentions behind the decree in question were serious enough; but in the long run any such enactment must have the effect of undermining the position of those who dissented from High Anglican principles. *Areopagitica* is therefore an extended plea that the "Lords and Commons" should rescind the order which would prohibit the unfettered dissemination of opinion through the written word.

With hindsight it would be possible to argue that Milton over-stated his case, and that his anxieties were unjustified since in practice the eventualities he foresaw could never have been realised. This does not alter the fact that his vigorous manifesto "spoke to the condition" of a fair section of the English people in the 1640's, and that many of his contentions are still applicable today. It is impossible to *précis Areopagitica* adequately, though the main thrust of Milton's thinking is clear. He sees censorship as originating with the enemies of Protestantism. He admits that it is prudent to institute some kind of surveillance over the public press, though not in what he takes to be the extreme form now advocated. The view that every single item emanating from the printing houses must submit to examination before being offered to scrutiny is fallacious; one man's notion of what is morally objectionable may be widely at variance with that of someone else equally well qualified to act as official licenser. In any case, the very suggestion that the public at large is incapable of distinguishing for itself between wholesome literature and obnoxious "libels" is an affront to the intelligence of those who, like Milton, contend that God gave man free will and along with it the ability to choose between good and evil. "That which purifies is trial," he insists; unless men undergo experience of whatever is contrary to virtue, they are unprepared for the proper exercise of moral responsibility. It is at this point that Milton anticipates a splendid passage in *Paradise Lost* (III.9) in which he tells us that the Almighty made Adam "Sufficient to have stood, though free to fall." Assuming that man *is* a reasonable creature, it follows that he must be allowed access to as wide a range of ideas as possible; only in this way can he gain a fair conception of Truth. The suppression of free communication is thus an insult to both God and man; even in its post-lapsarian state humanity does not deserve to be kept in ignorance simply to comply with the will of an arbitrary legislator.

One striking feature of *Areopagitica* is the skill with which Milton manages to develop several themes concurrently, so that his work becomes at once a defence of free speech, a critique of Catholicism, and an apologia for the untrammelled exercise of the creative imagination. The eloquent paragraph near the beginning in which the author speaks of the "potency of life" contained in books, and the "living intellect that bred them" is no mere purple patch but an assertion which carries strong personal conviction. And the varieties of tone employed—from the highly charged rhetoric of "Methinks I see in my mind a noble and puissant nation rousing herself like a strong man . . ." to the satirical banter in which Milton points out that "if we think to regulate printing, thereby to rectify manners, we must regulate all recreations and pastimes"—indicate how short-sighted it is to stigmatise Milton's attitudes as narrowly "puritanical." His *Areopagitica*, though provoked by a set of circumstances peculiar to 17th-century England, offers a classic discussion of matters which still have universal significance.

—E.D. Mackerness

AS KINGFISHERS CATCH FIRE.
Poem by Gerard Manley Hopkins, written c. 1877.

Robert Bridges, who edited the posthumous publication of Gerard Manley Hopkins's poems, drew this poem from an undated manuscript among the papers that he obtained after the poet's death in 1889. Its comparatively conventional versification and positive mood suggest that it was composed in Hopkins's middle period, after he had become familiar with the thought of the medieval philosopher Duns Scotus in 1872 and before the despair of his last years descended on him.

The two parts of the sonnet make three different, but related assertions. The octave proclaims the individuality of things, declaring that each object retains and proclaims its particularity in the range of creation, in the way that the plucked string of a musical instrument or a bell will give forth consistent sounds. The sestet then continues, "I say more," declaring first that the particular is an aspect of the general, and then that the specific quality of "grace" found in the good actions of men is an aspect of Christ, as men are seen by God.

The sonnet links Hopkins's theory of "inscape" with his theology, and reflects the influence of Duns Scotus, whom Hopkins admired. "Inscape" is a term coined by Hopkins which has passed into general usage; while he never defined it, it seems to mean the unique essence of objects or poems as it is exhibited in their external pattern or design. Hopkins looked for this quality in natural objects like trees and clouds, and also sought to achieve it in his poetry. When in this sonnet he declares that "Each mortal thing does one thing and the same," that "*myself* it speaks and spells," he is emphasizing the element of individuality which gives every object its dignity and significance.

Bridges called this a "Scotist" sonnet because it seems to echo a concept similar to "inscape" which Hopkins had found in the work of Duns Scotus. Scotus distinguishes those aspects of a thing which belong to its species or general class from its individuality, which he calls "haeccitas," or "thisness," a term that corresponded, Hopkins thought, with the inscape his poetry both celebrates and illustrates.

This poem exhibits in conservative form some of the departures from convention that mark Hopkins's later poems. The insistent alliteration and interior rhymes emphasize the auditory element, which Hopkins thought important in poetry, and also link words with a common significance. In this way, "stones" and "string" parallel each other in meaning, as well as in sound, for both objects illustrate selfhood through the sounds they make. In a number of places, including the first line, the poet has provided accents to indicate deviations from the normal stress pattern, an unorthodox practice that was to become much more common in his later poetry. The tendency to neologism and grammatical displacement that characterizes Hopkins's later style also appears, in somewhat tentative form, with "roundy" and "goings." Perhaps the most significant of these is the verb "selves," which is drawn from Hopkins's thinking about personal identity. In one of his meditations, he wrote that his most powerful intuition was his sense of the difference between his own being and everything else and he consistently used the verb "selving" for this process of self-recognition. In his sonnet each object of the world "selves," that is to say proclaims its individuality and announces its special purpose in coming into the world.

The significance of this vision of the world is double for the poet. First, it provides him with particulars that can be celebrated in the imagery and music of poetry. Second, and for the priest Hopkins more important, it implies that from God's point of view, the just actions of men display a nature that is continuous with that of Christ.

—Jacob Korg

AS YOU LIKE IT.
Play by William Shakespeare, 1600(?).

As You Like It, William Shakespeare's happiest comedy and most complete excursion into pastoral, derives closely from Thomas Lodge's popular novel *Rosalynde* (1590). The play begins violently, Orlando, youngest son of Sir Rowland de Boys, complaining that his elder brother, Oliver, has not discharged their father's will and given him a fitting education and upbringing, although sending his other brother, Jaques, to university. Oliver plots Orlando's death in a wrestling match at the court of the villainous Frederick, who has usurped the dukedom of his brother, Duke Senior. Orlando, however, wins the contest, and falls in love with Frederick's niece, Rosalind, kept at court as a companion to the usurper's daughter, Celia. When Frederick banishes Rosalind in a mad fury, both cousins leave, with Touchstone the clown, to seek the exiled Duke Senior in the Forest of Arden. For protection, Celia disguises herself as a poor woman, Aliena, and Rosalind, being taller, dresses as a man, Ganymede, with "a swashing and a martial outside," though a "woman's fear" may lie hidden in her heart.

In Arden they find the old shepherd Corin, the infatuated Silvius pining for the disdainful shepherdess Phebe, and extravagant verses to Rosalind hung on trees. Discovering the lovesick writer is Orlando, fled to Arden with his old servant, Adam, Rosalind, herself "fathom deep" in love, offers a cure: he shall woo Ganymede as if "he" were Rosalind (as indeed "he" is). The great central scenes sparkle with humour as Rosalind uses her disguise both to encourage Orlando's declarations of love and to defeat him in combats of wit in ways not ordinarily available to a woman.

Complications ensue when Phebe falls in love with Ganymede, despite "his" warnings that her passion is futile. Meanwhile the more fleshly Touchstone woos the plain but honest Audrey. These love-games are observed by the courtier Jaques (not to be confused with Jaques de Boys), whose fashionably melancholy pose and cynical wit provide a darker shade in the generally light tones of Arden. Though clever, Jaques (whose name puns on "jakes," an Elizabethan word for a lavatory) is frequently put down: the pessimism of his famous speech on the seven ages of man), for example, is immediately shown to be false by Orlando's care for Adam.

Oliver comes to the forest to murder Orlando, but his hatred changes to love when Orlando saves him from a snake and a lioness. Orlando's arm is torn in the struggle and he sends Oliver with a bloodstained handkerchief to find Ganymede, "the youth he calls his Rosalind"; while Celia and Oliver fall in love at first sight, Rosalind faints on receiving the bloody handkerchief, reviving to assure Oliver she merely pretends.

When Orlando tells Ganymede that Oliver and Aliena are to marry next day before Duke Senior, Ganymede, claiming magic powers, promises Orlando will also marry Rosalind. In the last scene, Hymen, god of marriage, enters with the cousins, now undisguised; Rosalind gives herself first to her father, then to Orlando, Oliver and Celia join hands, Phebe accepts the patient Silvius, and Touchstone and Audrey "press in . . . amongst the rest of the country copulatives." Jaques de Boys brings news that Duke Frederick, invading Arden with an army to kill Duke Senior, has been converted to a religious life by a hermit at the forest edge. The exiles are able to return to court. Only Jaques stays, to enjoy talking with the repentant Frederick. The other characters join in a symbolically harmonious dance, then Rosalind steps forward to speak an epilogue in which, for the only time, Shakespeare allows the boy actor (males took women's roles in the English theatre until 1660) to tell the audience directly that he is a male playing a female part, thus drawing particular attention to the play's comedy of ambiguous gender.

Although *As You Like It* was first printed in the 1623 folio edition of Shakespeare's plays, there is no clear evidence of early performances, the first recorded being at Drury Lane on 20 December 1740, with music by Thomas Arne; it has been popular ever since. Actresses giving especial distinction to the brilliant Rosalind, the longest female role in Shakespeare's comedies, second in length only to Cleopatra in all his works, have been Hannah Pritchard, Margaret Woffington, and Dorothy Jordan in the 18th century, Helena Faucit, Ada Rehan and Mary Anderson in the 19th; in the 20th Athene Seyler, Peggy Ashcroft, Edith Evans, Vanessa Redgrave, and Juliet Stevenson in England and Julia Marlowe, Margaret Anglin, and Katharine Hepburn in the U.S.

The play's five complete songs include "It Was a Lover and His Lass," and while the comedy's prevailing tone is light-hearted, it comments seriously on such issues as love (is it "a madness," as Rosalind claims?), power, double standards, family relationships, and the literary genres of romance, pastoral, and drama itself. The 18th century interpreted the play boisterously, the 19th sentimentalized it, and the late 20th century found it broader and bawdier, more complex, and even funnier than previously suspected.

—Alan Brissenden

THE ASCENT OF F6.
Play by W.H. Auden and Christopher Isherwood, 1936.

What some critics consider the best of the Auden-Isherwood collaborations, and others a failure, is a dramatic fable that (like Dante, who is discussed in the first scene) must be read on different levels to be grasped fully. On the surface it tells of a British expedition to climb F6, a "terrifying fang of rock and ice" reminiscent of both K-2 and Everest, on which all the climbers but one perish. As a political fable it dramatizes the ways power corrupts. F6 is on the frontier between British and Ostnian (=German) Sudoland; a local legend says that the mountain's first conqueror will rule over both Sudolands for a thousand years. On this level F6 stands for the heroic challenges desired by youth, to which vested interests, for their own purposes, send them to die. As a psychological fable it embodies the dialectic of strength and weakness in the human soul, the quest to ascertain the value of the egoistic will, and the ambiguity of the maternal principle. Finally, as a tragedy it reënacts the fated destruction of conscious good that has become enmeshed with evil, on the stage of the world.

The least successful of these levels is the psychological. Auden's and Isherwood's interest in Jung and Freud appears both in an ambivalent mother-figure (Mrs. Ransom) and in the ceremonies at the monastery on F6, which utilize Jung's *Commentary on the Tibetan Book of the Dead*. The handling of Mrs. Ransom is problematical. That the protagonist Michael Ransom is persuaded to undertake the expedition not by his politician brother, nor by representatives of the press and British womanhood, but by his mother, is interesting; that the climax of the play—after significant political and existential questions have been broached—is the revelation that the legendary Demon at the top of the Haunted Mountain is Mrs. Ransom "as a young mother," however, is merely bathetic. It risks evoking not Jung's maternal archetype but Philip Wylie's hatred of "Momism." (The authors acknowledged that they "never got that ending right.")

Michael Ransom is the focus of interest; writers on the play commonly see his development, or attempt to develop, from weakness towards strength as the centre of the play. But this, like the expressionist ending, does not really come off, partly because the playwrights try to define him in terms of literary analogues and real-life models. His opening soliloquy, which refers to another heroic adventurer, Ulysses, as "a crook speaking to crooks," sets the pattern (and the debunking tone). On F6, addressing the skull and enduring the storm, he faintly echoes Hamlet and Lear. Isherwood said that Ransom was based on T.E. Lawrence (though he and Auden seem not to have agreed on what this meant), while certain features of the expedition recall Mallory on Everest and Scott in the Antarctic. The intent was presumably to achieve a certain resonance, but the result is pastiche. Ransom's most striking characteristic, from the first scene on Pillar Rock where he soliloquizes over "the stupid peasants . . . making their stupid children" to his death-wish near the summit of F6, is misanthropy. Remarks such as "happy the foetus that miscarries" and "all we do is evil" indicate a deep-seated hatred and rejection of life in this brilliant and successful 28-year-old.

Nor is his outlook unique in the play. Mr. and Mrs. A., the Everycouple who comment antiphonally on the expedition's progress, live a kind of suburban death-in-life that they describe in dull flat verse redolent of early T.S. Eliot.

> I have eaten a scrappy lunch from a plate on my knee.
> I have spoken with acquaintances in the Stores;
> Under our treble gossip heard the menacing throb of our
> hearts,

intones Mrs. A., and her husband wonders. "Shall we be like this when we are dead?" What they ask is "something to live for." Yearning for heroes, they are initially delighted by reports of Ransom's success, but even this soon palls ("Turn off the wireless; we are tired of descriptions of travel; / We are bored by the exploits of amazing heroes"). A dead climber seems to them well out of it. The Chorus too is infected with despair, evoking images of ruin in the tones of Old Testament prophets: "let the eye of the traveller consider this country and weep, / For toads croak in the cisterns." Although they concede grudgingly that "Love finally is great, / Greater than all," they add, "large the hate, / Far larger than Man can ever estimate." This is apropos of Mrs. Ransom *qua* Demon, with her dead son on her lap atop F6.

The desiccated mood of the A's' damaged lives and Ransom's vision of Dante "in his private desert" appears in Auden's other work of the period. Images of barrenness recur frequently in poems such as "The Journey," "As I walked out one evening," "In Memory of W.B. Yeats" and "Journey to Iceland" (and in *Letters from Iceland*, with Louis MacNeice). Auden's summary of the symbolic associations of the desert in *The Enchafèd Flood* is helpful: it is the end of life, a place of purgation and "actualised triviality," yet also "an image of modern civilization" and (like the mountains) a place of freedom. With the drying out of the human spirit, landscape—especially in its great and barren forms—takes on increased importance as setting and allegory; becomes, in fact, a "*paysage moralisé*." "Upon the mountains of my fear I climb," Auden wrote in "Two Climbs." Mountains become magic mirrors; "F6 has shown me what I am," says the dying Ransom. In "Mountains" (1954), Auden would acknowledge the attraction of mountains as "a fine refuge" from noisome humanity—exactly the rationale Ransom gives for climbing.

—Richard Bevis

ASTROPHEL AND STELLA.
Poems by Sir Philip Sidney, 1591.

The 108 sonnets and 11 songs of Sir Philip Sidney's *Astrophel and Stella* (*Astrophil and Stella* in William A. Ringler's 1962 edition of the *Poems*) make up one of the earliest, and the most influential, of Elizabethan sonnet sequences. To them was largely due a vogue which during the next 20 years drew from every notable English poet a collection of sonnets utilising Petrarchan conventions to recount in the first person the course of a (frequently unhappy) love affair. Such innovative poets as John Donne in his *Songs and Sonets* and George Herbert in *The Temple* would define their own poetic agenda through imitation and parody of Sidney's.

The sonnets, in a form which combines a classical octave (abba abba) with an English sestet (cdcdee), tell of the unsuccessful wooing of Stella ("Star") by Astrophel ("Star-lover"). Their account bears some relation to biographical fact. Several sonnets identify Astrophel with Sidney: there is, for example, an allusion to his father's governorship of Ireland (in sonnet 30), to the Sidney coat of arms (in sonnet 65), and play on the name "Philip" (in sonnet 83). When, in sonnet 13, Stella's face is described as Cupid's shield, its "roses gueuls . . . borne in silver field" recall the Devereux coat of arms. In 1576, shortly before his death, Walter Devereux, 1st Earl of Essex, had expressed the wish that his daughter Penelope, then aged 13, should marry Sidney, then aged 21. Two years later, Sidney's uncle, Robert Dudley, 1st Earl of Leicester, married the widowed Countess of Essex. In January 1581 she journeyed to London to present Penelope at court. Within two months Penelope was engaged to Robert Rich, 3rd Baron Rich, afterwards Earl of Warwick. They married in November. There is play on the word "rich" in sonnets 24 and 35, and in 37, describing "Towardes *Aurora's* Court a Nymph . . . / Rich in all beauties" who "Hath no misfortune, but that Rich she is"; and from both sonnet 78, line 14, and song viii, line 10, it is clear that Stella is married. In sonnet 33 Astrophel laments the fact that she whom he might have enjoyed is now lost to another. Sidney himself withdrew from court late in 1581 and it was probably during the following months of retreat that *Astrophel and Stella* was written.

Biography, however, intrudes only fitfully and teasingly in a sonnet sequence (witness the case of Shakespeare and his "dark lady"), for it is neither a narrative nor a biographical genre. The facts of Sidney's experience appear only in a highly selective and tendentious form in *Astrophel and Stella*, which is vague about the beginning, course, and outcome of the relationship, and omits all circumstantial detail concerning both Sidney and Penelope Devereux. Certainly, the sonnets themselves were no part of any wooing that may have occurred. Although many are apparently addressed to Stella herself, there would be little point in inviting her to guess her own name (sonnet 37) and Sidney would hardly have confessed to her that, despite his disavowals, his aim is sexual conquest (sonnet 69). And as Stella is not the true addressee of the sonnets, so she is hardly their subject. The love-affair provides the context, and the figure of the suffering lover the vehicle, for an examination of those rational and courtly images of human nature inscribed by the cultural and philosophical discourses of the Renaissance. It is the predicament of Astrophel, whose moral and courtly identity is threatened by the passionate and irresistible desires which overwhelm him, which is the true focus.

Astrophel and Stella, that is to say, is to be read neither as history nor as a versified diary. This is as we should expect from Sidney's own *Defence of Poetry*, which argues that poetry is superior to history precisely because the poet, "disdayning to be tied" to reality, "dooth growe in effect another nature, in making things either better than Nature bringeth forth, or, quite anewe, forms such as never were in Nature." Unconstrained by the need for literal accuracy, the poet may rework fact into more searching and affecting images than any provided by mere biography. Sidney and his experience are transmuted through artistry into the fiction of Astrophel and Stella, a fiction which may be biographically misleading but which is imaginatively authentic: in sonnet 45 Astrophel, dejected by the realization that Stella is more affected by "a fable . . . / Of Lovers" than by his plight, implores her to "thinke . . . that you in me do reed / Of Lover's ruine some sad Tragedie: / I am not I, pitie the tale of me."

How to create such a moving fiction thus becomes a matter of pressing concern which is canvassed in many sonnets. Indeed, the first sonnet is about neither love nor Stella; rather, it explores the predicament of the poet unable to turn received conventions to his purpose. In that sonnet, and again in sonnet 6, Sidney surveys the rhetorical resources available to the Renaissance poet, apparently to reject them all in favour of plain statement. However, his exemplary recapitulation of Petrarchan diction, pastoral, classical allusion, figures, and tropes, shows him to be master of them all; the rejection of rhetoric is itself a rhetorical strategy. Though Sidney can mock the role of the poet with cacophonous incredulity ("Some do I hear of Poets' furie tell / But (God wot) wot not what they meane by it" [sonnet 74]), such ironies are but one of the means by which he makes poetry itself the true subject of this most rhetorically sophisticated and self-reflexive of Renaissance sonnet sequences.

—N.H. Keeble

AT SWIM-TWO-BIRDS.
Novel by Flann O'Brien, 1939.

At Swim-Two-Birds is, as its creator said, a very "queer" book and he did not like it all. Its plot, if that is not too structured a term, centres round the activities, thoughts, reading matter, and "spare-time literary activities" of an unnamed student at University College, Dublin in the 1930's. The student lives with his uncle whom he despises for his occupation, his traditional piety, and his interest in the Gaelic League. He attends college desultorily being more interested in billiards and in the rowdy meeting of the Literary and Historical Debating Society than in his studies. He fancies himself as a "cold and hostile" personality, is interested in promulgating theories about modern literature and sees his offensive smell, drunkenness, sloth, and sordid lifestyle as marks of the true writer. Most of his time is spent prostrate on his bed writing a book about a Dublin publican called Trellis who is himself writing a book about sin for which he borrows, hires, or steals most of the characters from other fictions. Some come from cowboy romances, one, Finn MacCool, from Irish legend, others come from folklore or from "realistic" novels. He has to create only two original characters for whom there are no suitable existing models. One is his villain, John Furriskey, the other his heroine, Sheila Lamont. Furriskey, however, does not find that the role of villain suits him. Sheila Lamont is so beautiful that Trellis rapes her and the son she bears before dying of shame, is found to have inherited his father's literary gifts and is persuaded by the others characters in Trellis's book to write a book about Trellis in which he can be brought to trial and punished for mistreating his characters and forcing them to act out of character for the sake of the plot.

The book is structured around 10 "Biographical Reminiscences" in which the student, in first-person narrative, keeps the reader up to date with events in his life, with his reading (which includes letters from bookmakers, old school textbooks, synopses of poems, encyclopedias, and biographies), with the progress of his book and the aesthetic principles on which it is based, with the progress of Trellis's book and the increasingly independent lives led by Trellis's characters who delight in telling stories which are themselves versions of older Irish tales. The *Táin Bó Cuailnge* appears as the story of the Circle N raid, told in the style of a cowboy adventure. Finn MacCool tells the story of Mad King Sweeney, Shanahan and Lamont tell tales of jumping Sergeant Craddock and of Jem Casey, Poet of the Pick and Bard of Booterstown, whose poem "A Pint of Plain is Your Only Man" is held to have more "permanence" than the story of Sweeney.

Trellis's characters also talk endlessly. Shanahan, Lamont, and Furriskey converse intelligently on illnesses, on methods of reading a gas metre, and on the history of the papacy. The Pooka MacPhellimey and the Good Fairy have a multi-clause colloquy incorporating speculations as to whether the Pooka's wife is a kangaroo, the virtues of odd and even numbers, and the exponential consequences of the mating of angels and humans. Within the "realistic" frame novel, the student and his friends also talk—about the benefits of sleep, God, the merits of the Penny Catechism, drink, and poetry. Almost every character in the book has ideas about literature.

At Swim-Two-Birds is said to have been shortened by Niall Sheridan without any apparent damage to its plot or structure. It has three different openings and as many endings, one of which appears to be entirely unrelated to anything that has gone before. The first page announces "Chapter 1"; it never gets to chapter 2. On page 96 there is a "synopsis of the plot for the benefit of new readers."

In this novel within a novel within a novel a multiplicity of different literary styles, both Irish and English, are juxtaposed and an episode given in one style will often be repeated in another, quite different, one. Since realism exists side by side with fantasy—modern Dublin becomes the wild west and ancient Ireland intrudes into the world of the 1930's solely through the modulation of style—attention is focussed on the inseparability of form and content. Often the result of this juxtaposition is to give equal primacy to pulp fiction and to the most elevated style of 18th-century biography, for example. Overall, however, the effect is to undercut the claims of literary "realism" to mirror the world.

Much of the impetus for the book appears to have come from O'Brien's impulses towards parody and satire. It owes much to the example of *Tristram Shandy*, and to the formal experiments of Aldous Huxley and James Branch Cabell. Formally, it is an "anti-novel," a postmodern fiction, structured so as to call into question all the conventions of the traditional novel, especially those of mimesis and of character creation. Intentionally, it sets out to parody the writings of James Joyce, stylistically and in the despicable character of the narrator who is a comic version of Stephen Dedalus. More positively, *At Swim-Two-Birds* is a fantasy which undercuts realism, highlights the limitations of that style, in order to give primacy to the imagination, and to propose that the proper purpose of literature is to use language to transcend the mundane and the painful and to articulate the spirit.

The title is taken from Swim-Two-Birds or *Snamh da En*, a place on the river Shannon, where Sweeney, in one of the main interpolated tales, lands in his crazed flight through Ireland. Sweeney, isolated, in pain, mad, and deprived; half tormented flesh, half soaring spirit; half man, half bird, "a huddle between the earth and heaven," out of his pain and misery composes poems of praise of the beauty around him. Ultimately, in spite of the proliferation of style, character, and mode, Sweeney is the book's most compelling image and the one which unites its apparently disparate themes into a single one. That theme is the assertion that there is not a conflict between reality and imagination, but that reality is expressed, can only be expressed in imaginative terms and that imagination is as real an aspect of existence as the stream of "buff coloured puke" which covers the man who had been discoursing about Rousseau.

—Anne Clune

AT THE BAY.
Story by Katherine Mansfield, 1922.

Katherine Mansfield's stories of late Victorian life in New Zealand have often been praised for their supposed "unity," and sometimes faulted in the same terms. To one critic (Ian Gordon) they are "unified by the selecting eye of a great prose artist"; to another (John Bayley) they are "all too unified." Either way, such remarks echo Edgar Allan Poe's formulaic pronouncements, according to which the short story form is dependent on "unity of effect or impression," and they have many parallels in commentaries on many other works of fiction. But their frequent application to Mansfield's stories is noteworthy here because it obscures the achievement of her most distinctive work, exemplified by "At the Bay."

Discussing this story, C.A. Hankin comments: "The pervasive motifs of the sun and sea (or water) provide a unifying framework." Only on the surface is that true. While imagery representing the natural environment does indeed recur in "At the Bay," it is deployed in such a way as to suggest the very opposite of unity. Mansfield's narrative method makes *division* both emphatic and problematic, creating a form that corresponds to putative divisions between the natural and social worlds, and to real divisions within social structures. As the dozen numbered sections of this story move to and fro between various locations and family members, the arbitrary selectiveness of narration itself is underlined, for shifts in focus do not always coincide with the sectional breaks. The same is true of Mansfield's other major New Zealand story, "Prelude," a companion piece to "At the Bay": each comprises 12 marked beginnings and the same number of endings, as if to signal that for whatever is packed into any part of it there must be innumerable omissions.

While "At the Bay" follows in its structure a seemingly natural temporal unity—the span of a single day—its multiple starting and finishing points declare implicitly that any particular sequential arrangement is factitious. Furthermore, its very language calls all demarcation lines into question. Thus the opening passage accentuates misty indistinctness, obscuring two boundaries in particular: the margin between sea and land, and the one between domesticated area and surrounding bush. The indeterminacy of categorical differences, foreshadowed here, is a pervasive motif throughout the story, and continues to be specifically linked with uncertainties of voice and focus. Although the title indicates a kind of placement, "At the Bay" turns out not to be an innocent phrase. What is this liminal world where different categories, and different story-fragments, come into restless proximity?

It is not a world of clear-cut and consequential actions. Early parts of the story are teasingly uneventful, moving in a discontinuous manner from one lightly limned scene to another as if merely to collocate sketches of a particular social microcosm: an upper-middle-class household near Wellington in colonial New Zealand. But the story goes on to acknowledge discreetly the partiality of its representations, to show that the *real* can be rendered textually only insofar as particular social constraints and compensatory strategies are exemplified in the positions from which a story is told and from which it permits responses. What people may tell or do at the bay depends very much on the position each occupies vis-à-vis its lines of demarcation. Yet even the natural margins continue to seem as unstable as they did at the beginning of the story. This is especially so later, in section 7, where the sea is imagined as merging with the life of the land and incorporating the houses. The shoreline becomes a place of mysterious mirrorings, transpositions: boundaries dissolve and change is insidious. What this troubled marginality means in individual terms is clear in section 5, where Beryl, down on the beach, meets the sinister Mrs. Kember, who is notorious for declining to abide by conventional distinctions. Her husband Harry is reported to be similarly outrageous: "How did he live? Of course there were stories, but such stories! They simply couldn't be told. The women he'd been seen with, the places he'd been seen in . . . but nothing was ever certain, nothing definite." The Kembers' transgressions simultaneously generate and curtail stories, because in such a constricted cultural environment there is an appetite for gossip and yet only certain things are fully tellable. To Beryl, this indefinite quality of the Kembers is disturbing; they remind her of non-human creatures, and resemble one another in a way that confuses gender dichotomies.

Such unstable categories provide a context, even a plausible rationale, for narratorial shifts. If the language of the text can hardly distinguish human from animal, or the-bay-as-settlement from the-bay-as-unsettling-wilderness, then by the same token a teller's authority to tell becomes very precarious, very partial. Neither "natural" nor "cultural" is itself a homogeneous category; and the lines that sometimes seem to separate them may also turn out to be indistinct. Far from providing secure reference points or sources of value for any human exchange, they seem to confound the desire for meaning. This is underlined in the final section of "At the Bay." Beryl is at the window of her bedroom at night time, and her narcissistic fantasies materialise in the person of Harry Kember, prowling past. In response to his invitation, she steps over the window sill—but stops short of the garden's edge; the tall fuchsia bush, which falls "over the fence in a shower" and has "a little pit of darkness beneath," is too sinister in its sexual allure. And what options, anyway, would she have beyond the boundaries of her home? Her own earlier jibe about the servant girl Alice has turned back on her own situation: where could a girl like that go in a place like this? The question is no less specifically social in its implications for remaining rhetorical. So it is too with the question that Harry Kember flings out when she retreats: "Then why in God's name did you come?' . . . Nobody answered him." The story ends, as it had begun, with the indecipherable murmur of the sea.

—Ian Reid

ATALANTA IN CALYDON.
Play by Algernon Charles Swinburne, 1865.

This verse drama belongs to the tradition of unperformable dramatic works favoured by romanticism and its heirs. It bears some similarity to Byron's efforts in this direction (*Manfred* of 1817 or *Cain* of 1821) and is related to Arnold's *Merope* of 1858 as well as to successors such as Hardy's *Famous Tragedy of the Queen of Cornwall* of 1923. It is, however, more closely modelled on Greek tragedy than many such plays having, for instance, a strict unity of time, place, and action as well as a classical plot taken from Homer, Ovid, and elsewhere. It was not Algernon Charles Swinburne's only attempt at this form and can be compared with his *Erechtheus* of 1876.

Swinburne borrows the whole structure of his play from the Greek drama: he uses a chorus to comment on the action, restricts himself to a few principal characters, and makes no attempt to promote any realism in the piece. The play opens with a prayer to Artemis by the chief Huntsman of King Oeneus of Calydon and this is followed by a hymn to the same goddess (the famous Chorus "When the hounds of spring are on winter's traces"). Oeneus's queen, Althaea, then laments her lot and tells us of the prophecy that her son, Meleager, will die if the brand she rescued from the fire at his birth is ever allowed to be burnt up. A boar hunt is announced and the kings and heroes gather to take the field against the great Boar that has been ravaging Calydon. The Chorus indulges in a polemic against love (Aphrodite) for bringing such pain to earth and there is an abrasive exchange between Atalanta and Althaea's two brothers (Meleager's uncles) who have turned up for the hunt and are worried that the holy virgin, Atalanta, dedicated as she is to Artemis, will steal some of their thunder.

While the Chorus rather astonishingly sing of "The supreme evil, God" the hunt takes place off-stage and a huntsman returns to tell the story of the slaying of the boar by the combined assaults of Atalanta, Althaea's brothers, Meleager, and others. But soon another messenger arrives to tell of the sequel. Meleager has insisted on presenting the boar's head to Atalanta, with whom he has fallen in love, and has as a result been attacked by Althaea's brothers both of whom he has managed to kill. This news destroys Althaea who casts the brand into the fire thereby bringing about the slow death of Meleager. We watch him dying, Atalanta returns home, and the play ends.

The action, as in some of the Greek plays, is not very dramatic. Everything depends on the psychological interest generated by the speeches and choruses and on the confrontations of Althaea with bad news. Swinburne was a great poet in the sense that he could produce fluent melodies in English without apparent effort. But immediate perspicuity is rarely his strong point and a lot of *Atalanta* has a cloud of incomprehensibility hanging over it. In addition, although he borrows from Shakespeare (as well as from Milton and Wordsworth) the basic blank verse line of much English epic and dramatic poetry, he proves virtually unable to handle it. Much of the play is rather wooden and opaque and many of the speeches are written in an unsuccessful version of Shakespearian blank verse that cramps the sense of what is being said without rising to the wonderful music of which Swinburne is capable.

In the choruses, on the other hand, we find Swinburne at his best and most characteristic. Obviously this is so in the opening chorus, so often anthologised, but the later choruses, where the poet permits himself rhyme and a rhythm other than that of rather lame iambic pentameters, are also worth reading and a relief after the stretches of often pointless blank verse. Here is the first stanza of another chorus, also sometimes found in anthologies:

> Before the beginning of years
>   There came to the making of man
> Time, with a gift of tears;
>   Grief, with a glass that ran;
> Pleasure, with pain for leaven;
>   Summer, with flowers that fell;
> Remembrance fallen from heaven,
>   And madness risen from hell;
> Strength, without hands to smite;
>   Love that endures for a breath:
> Night, the shadow of light,
>   And life, the shadow of death.

The powerful rhythm of this sort of verse, together with its tendency to romantic overstatement, tearful antitheses, and a rather satisfying pessimism give it a lush yet effective quality that is not present in the dull blank-verse passages. If there is any discernible theme or purpose in *Atalanta* it is to be found in these choruses. In the stanza quoted, for instance, the oppositions and paradoxes (pleasure and pain, life and death) stress the Greek tragic view, very evident in Sophocles, that the play manifests overall—resignation, submission to Fate, a kind of qualified despair.

The climaxes of the play thus become the moments of tragic philosophy couched in Swinburne's swinging rhythms. It is Sophocles mediated through Schopenhauer and Hardy: love brings pain and ruin (in the chorus to Aphrodite "We have seen thee, O Love") and the Gods are the "supreme evil," "cruel" where men are "piteous," so "we are all against thee, against thee, O God most high." Here the voice of the Victorian crisis of faith begins to break through the somewhat vacuous surface of the play. *Atalanta in Calydon* is unactable and it is also virtually unreadable today. Only the astonishing strength of Swinburne's music-making in the choruses preserves it from oblivion.

—Lance St. John Butler

AURORA LEIGH.
Poem by Elizabeth Barrett Browning, 1857.

In a letter to Robert Browning in 1845, Elizabeth Barrett described her intention to write "a sort of novel-poem . . . running into the midst of our conventions." In 1857 Chapman and Hall published *Aurora Leigh*, an epic poem in blank verse concerning the making of a woman poet. Not only in its polemical discussion of gender, but also in its revision of literary forms, its relocation of sites of poetic authority, and its representation of contemporary social issues, *Aurora Leigh* challenged literary and cultural conventions and articulated a sustained critique of Victorian patriarchy.

The narrative itself is self-consciously indebted to the fiction of other 19th-century women writers. The portrait of Marian Erle owes much to Elizabeth Gaskell's *Ruth*. Aurora's story strategically exploits the cultural relativism of Mme. de Staël's *Corinne*, while the dénouement carries a manifest echo of the equalising resolution of *Jane Eyre*. Though the narrative is at times clumsy and unconvincing, *Aurora Leigh* firmly inserts itself within a tradition of women's writing as surely as it redirects this influence into the lofty citadel of the masculine epic, indiscriminatingly mixing domestic detail with philosophical longueurs, drawing-room society with aesthetic discussion, social critique with lyric meditation. This medley of fragmented and competing formal tones is aptly conveyed by Virginia Woolf's comment that the poem's "ungainly" discourse "overwhelms and bewilders" and points to the transgression of conventional literary codes that *Aurora Leigh* enacts.

This disruption of formal convention is combined with a redefinition of the "legitimate" content of poetry. Aurora protests against the Victorian tendency to look to the past for poetic inspiration, insisting that the poet's "sole work is to represent the age." Browning's unrefined *Weltanschauung* permits her to intervene poetically into contemporary ideological debates on class conflict, morality and, not least, the fraught issue of male-female relations. *Aurora Leigh* has been described as the most violent and complete exposition of the "woman question" in mid-Victorian literature, protesting as it does against the limitations of female education and the socialization of women while presenting a model of independence and autonomy. Aurora's development as a poet is seen as conditional upon her initial rejection of Romney's marriage proposal in favour of vocational and artistic independence. This process involves problematic negotiations with traditional figures of poetic authority, yet ultimately Aurora finds her muse in the unconventional guise of the "fallen" woman, Marian Erle, who tacitly fosters Aurora's development towards that point at which a mature poetics can emerge.

Throughout her passage towards literary recognition, Aurora wrestles with patriarchal definitions of femininity and the obstacles and assumptions placed in the path of aspiring women writers. "[A] good book / And you, a woman!," Vincent Carrington incredulously exclaims. Yet *Aurora Leigh* is notable for the self-confidence of its proclamations, its unequivocal seizing of the right to a public voice, and its claim that not only can women legitimately be poets, but that they may also extend the boundaries of what is considered poetic.

Although *Aurora Leigh* was a sensational success, some reviewers protested against its "coarse" elements, its inclusion of topics deemed unsuitable for poetic representation. There is a link between the poem's critical reception and the "woman question," since it was the treatment of prostitution, rape, and illegitimacy to which reviewers objected. Although Marian Erle is initially seen as a victim she becomes increasingly self-determining and resistant to Victorian definitions of womanhood. She expresses no shame with regard to her fatherless son and when Romney desires to make her respectable through marriage, she rejects his proposal and with it the cultural construction of the "fallen woman" and single mother: "We . . . never call him fatherless / Who has God and his mother"; ". . . I'm clean. Ay, clean as Marian Erle!" But although Marian's story seems to speak of the empowerment of a working-class woman, it is rather her embourgeoisement which allows such an outcome. "Nowhere in the literature of the mid-century is the bourgeois rejection of working-class consciousness more glaring than in *Aurora Leigh*" writes Cora Kaplan, exposing the problematic gulf between Browning's "feminist" concerns and the class-bound ideologies in which her text is wrapped. The representation of the poor graphically displays middle-class fear and hostility: "Those, faces? 'twas as if you had stirred up hell / To heave its lowest dreg-fiends uppermost / In fiery swirls of slime." Marian might be saved, but the rest of her class are damned. Reformist attempts to improve social conditions are presented as futile. Romney's philanthropic efforts backfire when the subjects of his charity turn against him and destroy his property, and Aurora's elitist interpretation that this justifies her argument that liberation comes through art rather than politics marks the moment in the text where the discourses of sex and class most dramatically collide.

In affirming the legitimacy of a fixed social hierarchy *Aurora Leigh* is complicit with the dominant ideology of the period—that conservative timidity on the reform question which extends from Burke to Carlyle. The poem's transgressions are nonetheless considerable, and its exploration of the issues surrounding female creativity are unparalleled in the poetry of the period. *Aurora Leigh* is now considered Browning's major work, signifying her poetic maturity as well as her commitment to the consolidation of a female poetic tradition.

—Kathryn Burlinson

THE AUTOBIOGRAPHY OF LEIGH HUNT.
Prose by Leigh Hunt, 1850; revised edition, 1859.

The history of Britain in the first half of the 19th century is plush with literary grandeur, and the fame of most of the writers who made it resplendent has not been tarnished by time. Coleridge, Wordsworth, Lamb, Hazlitt, de Quincey, Southey, Byron, Shelley, Austen, Keats, Cobbett, Scott, Dickens, Thackeray—the list is long, but had it been compiled by a contemporary one name would have been added, without hesitation in the earlier decades if with some misgivings as mid-century drew near: that of Leigh Hunt. Today Hunt has slipped almost to the status of a footnote to the lives of others greater than himself, his personality mislaid behind caricature (Dickens's scabrous—and ungrateful—representation of him as Harold Skimpole in *Bleak House*), his unique editoral contribution to letters seldom acknowledged, his own vast and diverse creative production, the fruits of almost 50 years of continuous activity, held from oblivion only by two poems still much favoured by anthologists: "Jenny Kissed Me" and "Abou ben Adhem," and by the *Autobiography*.

The *Autobiography* survives in part, of course, by reason of Hunt's centrality to the literary life of his time. He knew every one of these outstanding representatives of the age (with, it seems, the solitary and surprising exception of Jane Austen). To many he was a close friend, to some editor-in-chief, to others pioneering editorial patron. He welcomed to the pages of his journals the essays of Charles Lamb. His own poetry was the inspiration and the model for Keats's neophyte verses, he published Keats's first mature poem, found a publisher for his first collection, stood by him as friend, ally, and adviser for the rest of Keats's short life, and for the remaining 38 years of his own life continued as the poet's most vehement and most vocal advocate. With remarkable critical shrewdness he had heralded not only Keats but also Shelley as destined for greatness before ever they had proved themselves by much publication. With Shelley and Byron as collaborators Hunt planned a journal (the *Liberal*) and he was their companion in Italy during their last months. He encouraged the young Dickens. He used his considerable influence to help secure, first for Southey and later for Tennyson, the office of Poet Laureate, and this though he coveted the appointment, though he needed, and needed desperately, the financial benefits which would follow in its wake, and though much informed and influential opinion considered him to be the obvious candidate.

All those still-resonant names are in the *Autobiography*, their bearers vividly and for the most part affectionately recalled, and with them many now lost to memory as well as some—Macaulay, Mary Shelley and Hunt's schoolfriend, Thomas Barnes, "the Editor who put thunder into the voice of the *Times*"—who must have been included in any roll-call of luminaries compiled by a contemporary.

The *Autobiography* is in many ways an unbiographical work. The author tells something of his ancestry and early childhood; there are two lively and affectionate chapters on his school-days, which stand well even in comparison with the reminiscences of Hunt's immediate predecessors at Christ's Hospital, Coleridge and Lamb (two of the greatest autobiographers of all time), but for the rest of his private life there is little. Hunt elides the financial worries which dogged him throughout his adult years, says almost nothing about his children, and even his slatternly wife Marianne, at once the curse and the blessing of his life and perhaps also the prime cause of his money-problems, appears only occasionally and then *in passim*.

It is, therefore, principally as source-book—perhaps the richest of all—for enlightenment about London's literary world that the work is most valuable and most valued, and as such primarily for the earlier decades, the years when Hunt was central and seminal. (The second half of his life Hunt crammed into little more than one-tenth of his text.) But there are other reasons for holding the *Autobiography* in high esteem and of them all the most cogent that it is a superb demonstration—indeed one of the finest in all literature—of the craft of a rarely competent practitioner at work with scissors and paste.

The *Autobiography* appeared first, in three volumes, in June 1850, and was savaged by the reviewers. In the early months of 1859 Hunt revised and compressed the work, added a valedictory chapter, "Life Drawing Towards Its Close" and wrote also a reply to Skimpole, which he withdrew just before he died, on 28 August. The book was seen through the press by his son, Thornton, was published in December of the same year, and was greeted with applause by all the critics, even Dickens. (It is on this, the 1859 version, that the standard modern edition, edited by J.E. Morpurgo is based.)

But this work was far from being Hunt's first venture into autobiography. In 1828 he had published *Lord Byron and Some of His Contemporaries*, an uncharacteristically venomous book, for the most part designed to poison the memory of Byron, whom Hunt reviled for betraying their friendship. Even this book was not free of self-plagiarism. Much that was not about Byron or Shelley Hunt took without amendment from his own previously-published articles and character sketches. When he came to prepare the *Autobiography* proper he set about this business of recycling his journalistic past with even more deliberation and in the 1859 version only six of the 24 chapters are virginal: the first two, "The Author's Progenitors" and "Childhood," and the last four, covering the second half of his life. Many, and substantial, passages in the intervening 16 chapters are immediately recognisable as adaptations of earlier writings. Even more Hunt lifted verbatim either from *Lord Byron and Some of His Contemporaries* or from contributions to his own periodicals originally published between 1812 and 1823. Yet such was the quality of Hunt's craft that the seams do not show. The *Autobiography* reads as a newly-created narrative, flowing and elegant. And such was his artistry that it was in truth a new book. Whereas *Lord Byron and Some of His Contemporaries* is evil-tempered the later work is generally good-humoured and gracious. Whereas the 1828 book has one villain, Lord Byron, as central and all-pervasive character, and though in the *Autobiography* still Byron is not given a halo, the focus of the author's attention has shifted to a hero, Percy Bysshe Shelley.

—J.E. Morpurgo

AUTUMN JOURNAL.
Poem by Louis MacNeice, 1939.

Historically, the focal point of *Autumn Journal* is the end of the year 1938; "the Czechs / Go down and without fighting" and war with Germany is near certain. Considering his political views in the years preceding 1938, Louis MacNeice would have had little difficulty in stringing together a long chorus of variations on "I told you so." What he did instead was to write a long, meditative poem, combining private events with public; one of the literary models for *Autumn Journal* is surely Yeats's "Meditations in Time of Civil War."

In a foreword to *Autumn Journal* MacNeice characterises his journal form (one that he had used previously in his travel book *I Crossed the Minch*): "In a journal or a personal letter a man writes what he feels at the moment." MacNeice's concept of "honesty," an attribute he consciously strove for in *Autumn Journal*, is bound tightly to the spontaneity that this definition implies. But this spontaneity is not Wordsworthian naturalness, rather it seems an increasingly desperate race against time to lay down even a particular, personal truth before the events and actions of the outside worldhave time to work on and corrupt it. Complicating this, there is MacNeice's "admission" of imbalance and "over-statements," and the self-contradiction that "spontaneity" reveals. Yet the poetic self that "narrates" *Autumn Journal* is coherent both in voice and in philosophical characteristic.

Autumn Journal's devices for cohesion are many and various. The verse form in the 24 sections is held by the strand of an "abcb" rhyme scheme, while rhythm becomes all important in, for example, section VIII, in which the lilt of the first lines ("Sun shines easy, sun shines gay / On bug-house, warehouse, brewery, market") eases off, becomes revised in the motion of a car journey, then re-energises more harshly in a tumbling crescendo inherent to its political anger and hard-nosed irony ("Glory to God for Munich": compare "Glory to God in the Lowest," section II). The following section (IX) seems almost embarrassed at the vitality of its predecessor and comforts itself, along with the poet, with being "back to normal," "Back to the even tenor of the usual day." Linking of sections is achieved in other ways, ranging from the simple use of "And" to begin a section, to the irony of section XVIII, which begins "looking north," section XVI having been on the subject of Ireland (predominantly Northern Ireland, MacNeice's birthplace).

A recurrent motif in *Autumn Journal* is the "river" (often Heraclitean in descent—"no river is a river which does not flow," section I), which becomes a fluid metaphor (in two senses), being repeatedly adapted until the poem seems saturated: the rain in London (section VII); in section XVII the poet is in the bath! References to rivers in the classics (Lethe, Styx), lead to the poem's final river image, in section XXIV, where there is a river "to be crossed, however deep." The phrase "the die is cast" used here (notably from Caesar on the banks of the Rubicon) places the end of the poem, with the strength of fortitude it has gained, on the brink of war.

However *Autumn Journal* does not end with resolution. The final line "And the equation will come out at last" concretises hope and belief, not certainty: the word "will" is repeated from the previous line and its double use, its over-emphasis, undermines its firmness. Doubts and, more pressingly, fears still remain. MacNeice fears and detests propaganda ("a monologue / Is the death of language"); while the "blank invective" of the newspapers in pre-Civil War Spain was a "lark," in Ireland (XVI) there is "Free speech nipped in the bud," and in the classics, on which MacNeice was a lecturer, "free speech shivered on the pikes of Macedonia" (section IX). MacNeice's vitriol against Ireland and the classics (and Oxford) are explicable in themselves for the reasons he cites, but the "over-stated" fury with which he condemns them can be linked to the analogous loss of "free speech" (and hence any role for "honest" poetry) in a contemporary war. The problem MacNeice foresees is to stay silent while the anti-Nazi forces, in order to beat the Nazis "must model ourselves upon the enemy / A howling radio for our paraclete." His reasons for turning the poem to memories of school in section X, prompted by term "again beginning," become clear when he charts the development of "the critic jailed in the mind" which would, "husky long from silence, murmur gently / That there is something rotten in the state." This "critic" has its origins in "a whisper in books" that "Would challenge the code, or a censored memory." The loss of "free speech," the disappearance of the right, necessity, or appropriateness of criticism, and the abuse of language exemplified in the Hitlerian voice ("Hitler yells on the wireless"), all amount to a threat not only to political and linguistic liberty, but to poetry.

Despite the apprehensions of *Autumn Journal*, World War II did not enforce a poetic silence: it did necessitate a change in voice and tone, and *Autumn Journal* is both culminatory in terms of 1930's poetry and an attempt to probe towards a new way of approaching the writing of war poetry. It has anger, scepticism, sarcasm, and doubt, tempered by an abiding belief in "the human animal's endless courage."

—Colin Graham

B

BARNABY RUDGE.
Novel by Charles Dickens, 1841.

Barnaby Rudge was Charles Dickens's first attempt to combine historical fact and romantic fiction. Manifestly a flawed and patchy work it nonetheless has real merits, and embodies ideas and interests seminal to an understanding of Dickens's art. The story centres around the Gordon riots which seriously threatened national peace and stability in 1780. These were headed by Lord George Gordon; the intention was to bring public pressure to bear upon Parliament to repeal the Act of 1778 for the relief of Roman Catholics. For about a week London was out of the control of the forces of law; Newgate Prison was sacked and the inmates set loose. The nation felt itself close to the brink of mob rule.

Dickens portrays Gordon as a weak, easily led figure, under the tutelage of his paranoid and insidious secretary Gashford. The lawlessness fomented in Gordon's name is the more powerfully felt for this disturbing suggestion that its motivations are not actually related to the nominal cause of popular indignation. Around this quasi-historical plot-centre Dickens builds a series of characters and relationships which echo the theme of disruption and anarchy. And, as so often in later and more mature novels, he situates these characters in domestic environments which symbolise their emotional condition.

At the Maypole Inn at Chigwell live landlord John Willet, and his son Joe. Old Willet makes Joe's life a misery by bullying him, putting him down in public, and generally treating the amiable Joe as though he were a child. Eventually this humiliation becomes too much for young Willet who makes his escape by joining the army.

Close by the Maypole stands The Warren, home of the Catholic Haredale family. Gloomy, and mysterious, the outward opposite of the Maypole Inn, the house was, 22 years previously, the scene of the brutal murder of its owner, Reuben Haredale. The perpetrator of this crime was never apprehended, but the mutilated and unidentifiable body supposedly of Haredale's steward, Rudge, was found, while the gardener disappeared. The murdered man's daughter Emma now lives at The Warren with her uncle, Geoffrey. The gloomy seclusion of their lives, tainted by the murder, is compounded both by the social disadvantages of their Catholicism, and by the fact that Emma has contracted an "unsuitable" attachment for young Edward Chester. A deadly enmity subsists between Haredale and Edward's father, the latter being a heartless, dandified, and ruthless sybarite—partly modelled on the real life Lord Chesterfield. Here, then, Dickens sketches another series of disrupted domestic relationships, veering towards anarchy.

The wife of the supposedly murdered steward Rudge now lives in retired widowhood, flinching from the public gaze, and devoting herself entirely to the well-being of her mentally inadequate son, Barnaby—yet another disturbed and unnatural domestic menage. Barnaby's near idiocy frees him to wander in and out of all strands of the plot, and Dickens uses him as a constant reminder of the inter-relationships of crime, innocence, nature, and voluntary will.

Central to the story is the personality and household of Gabriel Varden, the extrovert and fatherly locksmith. Varden's daughter Dolly is the object of Joe Willet's unavailing affections, for Dolly is self-centred and vain. The story partly concerns her education through suffering and experience, so that she will eventually be a fit mate for the stalwart Joe.

Despite Varden's unremitting cheerfulness, not even his household is peaceful. His wife, egged on by her sycophantic maidservant Miggs, takes fits of ultra-Protestant piety. The household is further riven by the antics of Varden's apprentice, Simon Tappertit. Barely five feet high, but with an overweening sense of self-importance, Tappertit is nominal head of a ludicrous guild of apprentice revolutionaries. With great insight and skill Dickens weaves his plot to involve these comic anarchists in the deadly serious underworld plotting which existed during the Gordon riots. Tappertit is thus thrown into the maelstrom cheek by jowl with the sinister Dennis, the public hangman who sports his own brand of fascinatingly paranoid anarchy, and with Hugh, part-time ostler at the Maypole, and joyful participant in the riots, since as a rootless and houseless outsider he feels no sense of allegiance to any social centre.

The riots are eventually quashed, and the two love plots resolved happily. The murder mystery is resolved—steward Rudge (who escaped detection by mutilating the gardener's body and leaving it to be found in his own clothes), was the murderer. He then later returned to blackmail his unfortunate wife, and to drive her and Barnaby from pillar to post and deny them any domestic peace. Barnaby, who has innocently become implicated with the revolutionaries, is in danger of being hanged, but gains a last-minute reprieve. Numerous ancillary coincidences further complicate this typically intricate Dickens plot.

Despite its melodrama and sentimentality, *Barnaby Rudge* is probably under-estimated. Its convoluted relationships do convey a sense of inexorable destiny, and the concept of making all the plots hinge upon the theme of anarchy and disruption through deployment of domestic leitmotifs is effective. The riot scenes are charged with a wonderful energy and with a real insight into the disparate causes of civil disorder. There is, for all its simplistic handling, a ghastly prescience in Dickens's descriptions of the way in which religion can be used as a stalking horse to foment civil unrest in the community.

—T. Bareham

BARRACK-ROOM BALLADS.
Poems by Rudyard Kipling, 1892.

The 23-year-old Rudyard Kipling who came to London in late 1889 from India, where he had already become a successful journalist, rapidly achieved success as a writer. His short stories of Indian life immediately attracted attention, as did the poems about British soldiers which he came to call by the evocative title "barrack-room ballads"—Wordsworth and Coleridge's *Lyrical Ballads* had challenged conventional expectations in 1798, and Kipling did the same nearly a hundred years later with poems about a way of life seldom commemorated before in literature. 13 of these poems were brought together in the literary weekly the *Scots Observer* in the first part of 1890, and soon became widely known, their subject matter and tone of voice taking them far beyond the literary world. Thus when Kipling published a volume with these poems and a few others as *Barrack-Room Ballads and Other Verses* in 1892, he was launching one of the most successful volumes of poetry ever published in English. Charles Carrington, in his excellent introduction to his 1973 edition, states that: "for thirty or forty years it was the most popular book of verse in the English-speaking world, as popular in America as in England."

This extraordinary success was achieved by the way in which Kipling made his poems accessible to readers with no specifically literary background. He seemed to be speaking—very unusually for an English poet—both for and to the common man. The language in which he wrote created this intimacy—it is a language which we can believe to be spoken by actual soldiers, in most of the poems a modified version of Cockney. The speaker of the poems is, however, not a single person—he may be Irish, as in "Belts," or from a higher social class, as in "Gentlemen-Rankers"—but he is always part of the culture of the barrack-room, of the private soldiers who carried out the harsh work of Imperialism for low pay and little respect. The poem simply called "Tommy" is an excellent example of how Kipling can build up a challenging picture of contemporary British attitudes and behaviour from the experiences of a simple speaker—in this case a soldier, Tommy, who is excluded by society from its usual pleasures (soldiers in uniform were not served in public houses, the public was censorious about their drunkenness and immorality) until military force is needed, when he is treated quite differently:

> Then its Tommy this, an' Tommy that,
>   an "Tommy, 'ow's yer soul?"
> But it's "Thin red line of 'eroes" when
>   the drums begin to roll.

The hypocrisy of a society which at once valued its Empire and despised the men who fought to create and maintain it is perfectly caught. In these poems Kipling is always on the side of the common soldier, whom he nevertheless refuses to sentimentalize.

Thus the poems show both the patriotism of the soldiers, their devotion to "The Widow at Windsor," Queen Victoria, in the poem of that name, and their less admirable characteristics which are readily explicable in terms of the grim circumstances of their lives: "Belts" deals with fighting between an Irish and an English regiment in which a soldier is killed; "Cells" with a man who cannot resist the drink which leads him to fighting and punishment; "Loot" with the activity of its title, which is implied to be commonplace though forbidden; and most powerfully of all, "Danny Deever" recounts in a dialogue between a recent recruit and a Colour Sergeant the hanging of a soldier for shooting one of his comrades: "Ho! the young recruits are shakin', an' they'll want their beer today, / After hanging' Danny Deever in the mornin'." / Other poems deal more directly with military campaigns, and well before the more celebrated poetry of World War I reveal the fatigue and grimness of it, though poems like "Screw-Guns" also celebrate the devastating effects of fire-power. Two of the best known, "Gunga Din" and "Fuzzy-Wuzzy," pay tribute to men of other races, the former as a servant of the regiment, the latter as fearless enemies. "Mandalay," which became a popular song, is the nostalgic memory of an ex-soldier now in drizzling London of the exotic landscape of Burma and a girl he had known there. It makes a striking contrast with "Troopin," in which the men are looking forward to returning to England and leaving the army after their six hard years of service: "The Colonel an' the regiment an' all who've got to stay, / Gawd's mercy strike 'em gentle—Whoop! we're goin' 'ome today." *Barrack-Room Ballads* created a new mode, revealing much more about how Imperialism really worked than had been made evident before, and in terms to which a wide variety of readers could respond. It is an achievement to respect and enjoy.

—Peter Faulkner

BARSETSHIRE SERIES.
Novels by Anthony Trollope, 1855–67.

Six of Anthony Trollope's 47 novels—*The Warden* (1855), *Barchester Towers* (1857), *Doctor Thorne* (1858), *Framley Parsonage* (1861), *The Small House at Allington* (1864), and *The Last Chronicle of Barset* (1867)—were republished in 1878 as *The Chronicles of Barsetshire*. Except for *The Small House at Allington*, whose locale is slightly westerly, these works are set in the south of England in a Trollopian cathedral town called Barchester and its surrounding Barsetshire.

It was the Barsetshire novels that established Trollope's reputation. They were not consecutive, but 4th, 5th, 7th, 10th, 13th, and 18th among his novels in order of publication. Nor did Trollope plan them as a series, although *Barchester Towers* was written as a sequel to *The Warden*, and the title of *The Last Chronicle of Barset* explicitly declared the author's purpose. Trollope intended "that the stories should go forth to the public as being in all respects separate, the sequence being only in the Author's mind."

Still, the Barsetshire novels are a coherent series. They are unified not only by their common setting, but also by recurrent characters and a consistent contrast between the values of London and Barsetshire. Each of the six explores the intricacies and difficulties of courtship, and all but *Doctor Thorne* and *The Small House at Allington* probe the social, political, and economic lives of the Barsetshire Anglican clergy, and even these two offer insights into the subject. Their lengths and modes of publication vary: *The Warden* was issued in a single volume; *The Small House at Allington* and *The Last Chronicle of Barset* (the longest of the six novels) were extensive two-volume works; the others came out in three-volume format. As Trollope's reputation developed, serial publication of his fiction became feasible. Before being published as books, *Framley Parsonage* and *The Small House at Allington* appeared in the *Cornhill*, and *The Last Chronicle of Barset* was offered experimentally in sixpenny numbers.

The Warden is an essay in balance, a demonstration of Trollopian sympathy for contending values. The story revolves around a time-honored though lawful clerical abuse, which results in the proceeds of an endowment of a home for the aged going largely to its warden (administrator) rather than to its beneficiaries. Trollope satirizes Dickensian indignation and Carlylean rant, as he speculates on how these contemporary reformers would have aimed at so broad a target. He recognizes the impropriety of the situation and the intolerability of its continuance, yet he sympathizes with the inoffensive and compassionate warden, Rev. Septimus Harding, the victim of a newspaper's crusade. Perhaps Trollope's depiction of the love of John Bold, the principled and likable physician who uncovers the situation, and Harding's daughter Eleanor seems artificial, but the conflict in *The Warden* between Anglican autonomy, as personified in Archdeacon Theophilus Grantly, the warden's son-in-law, and secular reform is realism itself: a fictional skirmish (with a historical basis) in the larger battle of the Oxford Movement.

The sequel, *Barchester Towers*, is a comedy of manners. Characters are broadly drawn in a sometimes unseemly battle between the high and low church factions in the see of Barchester. Although Trollope's interest in the controversy attendant to the Oxford Movement seems confined to its political, social, ecclesiological, and ritual implications, he was well aware of the various schools of contemporary Anglican thought. His characterizations show that he realized that high church advocates included ritualists, the "high and dry," and traditionalists, and that low church sympathizers had latitudinarians, Sabbatarians, and anti-Catholics within their ranks. But these subtleties are casualties of his comedy. The Tory highs are gentlemen, and their wives are ladies; the Whig lows are either henpecked like Bishop Proudie or unscrupulous like Rev. Obadiah Slope, and the pattern wife, Mrs. Proudie, is a domineering and self-aggrandizing woman, who inflates her role as a bishop's helpmate. Some refreshing minor characters—notably an absentee vicar, Dr. Stanhope, and his family; the Thornes of Ullathorne, a lovable if absurdly reactionary bachelor squire and his spinster sister; the De Courcys, pretentious county nobility; and the Lookalofts, a socially aspiring farmer's family—contribute to the popularity of *Barchester Towers*, perhaps over the years the most read of Trollope's books.

While *Barchester Towers* may be the perennial favorite, the best-selling Trollope novel during the author's lifetime was *Doctor Thorne*. It was not promoted as another Barchester chronicle; at that time Trollope "had taught [himself] to believe that few novels written in continuation . . . had been successful. Even Scott, even Thackeray had failed to renew a great interest. Fielding and Dickens never ventured the attempt." Accordingly, few of the familiar characters of the earlier novels are prominent in *Doctor Thorne*, but its success induced Trollope to complete the series. The principal figures are not the clergy of Barsetshire, but its laity: the once affluent Greshams; the noble but objectionable De Courcys; the self-made Scatcherds; the linament queen, Miss Martha Dunstable; Dr. Thomas Thorne, a county physician and apothecary and distant relative of the Ullathorne branch; and his niece, Mary. The Thornes are effectively drawn, and although Trollope did not think them especially memorable, generations of readers have dissented. As to plot, Trollope so minimized its importance that he cheerfully admitted in his autobiography that it was his brother who devised the plot of *Doctor Thorne*, which Trollope thought good. Perhaps Trollope was right in thinking this intricate plot, involving a concealed identity, a timely if improbable death, a fortunate bequest, and a fairy-tale marriage, was responsible for the novel's success, yet a modern reader might find it contrived. The book is more romance than novel, and it is the titular character who as *deus ex machina* controls the action.

Framley Parsonage is in some respects a *Bildungsroman*, in which two Barsetshires, east and west, emerge. As in *The Warden* and *Barchester Towers*, Trollope focuses on clergymen, but with a significant difference. In the earlier novels, the chapter, the diocese, and clerical politics predominated; in *Framley Parsonage* the subject is the belated education of Mark Robarts, a likeable and essentially decent young parish priest, whose way had previously been paved. Familiar figures—Rev. Harding, Dr. Grantly and his family, Miss Dunstable, Dr. Thorne, Mary Gresham (née Thorne), the Proudies, and others—reappear, but the major characters are new. Politics, more secular than ecclesiastical, are not as integral to the fiction as in the first two Barsetshire chronicles. East Barsetshire, under Archdeacon Grantly, the rejuvenated Greshams, and especially Lady Lufton, a firm, upright, and generous widow, is Tory and high church. West Barsetshire, dominated by the Duke of Omnium, whose wealth is legendary, and the De Courcys, is Whig territory and from motives less religious than political encamps with the low church faction. *Framley Parsonage*, whose author described the story as "thoroughly English" with "no heroism and no villainy" and "much Church, but more love-making," was the novel that made Trollope an English household name.

When Trollope first contemplated the "republication of those tales which are occupied with the fictitious county of Barsetshire," he omitted *The Small House at Allington*. However, his publisher and friends prevailed, and it was included. Trollope's objections may have been rooted in a geographical precision that few readers would share, yet they might agree with him in noting a difference between the four earlier Barsetshire chronicles and *The Small House at Allington*. Unlike them it is not a patent morality. The good people are not immediately rewarded, and the bad, although not unscathed, seem at first to be only lightly punished. Lily Dale, her cousin Bernard Dale, and John Eames are disappointed in their loves, and the genuine benevolence of Squire Dale to his nieces and sister-in-law is misunderstood and often rebuffed. On the other hand, the physical, financial, and social indignities inflicted on the renegade Adolphus Crosbie appear mild, and the heartless De Courcys experience only alienation (although readers of *The Last Chronicle of Barset* are told of Lady Alexandrina's unexplained demise, a death that seems more convenient than retributive). Nonetheless, when the ultimate happiness of the characters is weighed, the scales of justice balance. The fates of the characters are plausible, a tribute to Trollope's mature powers of characterization.

Trollope's favorite among the Barsetshire novels was *The Last Chronicle of Barset*. In fact, he referred to it in both his correspondence and his autobiography as the best of all his novels. Among 20th-century critics there is no consensus. Perhaps too many earlier Barsetshire characters, e.g., Lily Dale, John Eames, Adolphus Crosbie, the Grantly family, and Rev. Harding, reappear in the novel simply for final disposition; the consequence is a needlessly long book. The main plot, whose fabric is a check for £20 that Rev. Josiah Crawley (whom the reader met in *Framley Parsonage*) may or may not have stolen, seems threadbare. However, it raises a perplexing question for the modern reader: is one morally responsible for an illegal act that s/he did not intentionally commit? And Crawley himself—a proud, poverty-stricken, archaic, and humorless scholar of unimpeachable integrity, equally unsparing of others and himself—is one of Trollope's finest characterizations.

Trollope liked *The Chronicles of Barsetshire* well enough to present a copy in 1879 to Winchester College, which he had attended a half century earlier. Modern taste agrees: the six volumes were reissued in 1989 in a uniform clothbound format, a tribute to their continuing popularity as the most widely read fictional series written in English before the present century.

—Daniel Rutenberg

BARTHOLOMEW FAIR.
Play by Ben Jonson, 1614.

Ben Jonson's *Bartholomew Fair*, like *Volpone* and *The Alchemist*, depends for its dramatic structure on the clash between two worlds, each possessing different values, attitudes, and modes of discourse. Unlike the two earlier plays, however, this festive production concludes with an almost Shakespearean comedic closure wherein both sides agree to reconcile their differences in a communal banquet. The external structure of the text is simple: Act I introduces the censorious outsiders whose innate longing for the delights of the Fair is equalled only by their moral condemnation of the enormities that occur therein. The rest of the action takes place in the Fair itself and finds the visitors being systematically humiliated, exposed, and ultimately converted from their authoritarian (and in some cases hypocritical) attitudes to a genuine acceptance of the fallen, yet natural, flesh-and-blood urges that the Fair people embody.

In Act I, then, we meet Littlewit (significantly a proctor and thus associated with Law), whose fatuous superficiality is exposed in his hunt for "quirks and quiblins," a delight in trivial punning that confirms the semiotic indications of his surname. Wasp, a classic example of choleric imbalance, is also in a position of authority (over his imbecile ward, Cokes) and equally mono-dimensional in acting out the allegorical implications of his name ("turd in your teeth"). The two self-professed Puritans, Dame Purecraft (another ominous nominal warning) and her spiritual brother Zeal-of-the-Land Busy, embody a different kind of authority, the Law of Puritan religion with its hatred for the allurements of the senses and its repressive Old Testament mode of discourse (hilariously parodied by Jonson: "Verily, for the disease of longing it is a disease, a carnal disease, or appetite, incident to women; and as it is carnal and incident, it is natural, very natural. . . ." All these characters are examples of a discrepancy between their paternalistic authoritarian functions and intrinsic personal inadequacies. It is this discrepancy that the vibrant, anarchic, heteroglottic world of the Fair is about to expose.

A hint of this development is given towards the end of Act I when Busy is revealed as a hypocrite, his overt strictures on carnal longings devastatingly undermined by his being discovered "fast by the teeth in the cold turkey pie in the cupboard." The principal voice of oppression is not heard, however, until the beginning of Act II, where, now in the Fair itself, we encounter Adam Overdo, a justice of the peace, preaching against the criminal enormities of the Fair folk and at the same time revealing the gap between his professional function and his personal incompetence: "Thus must we do, though, that wake for the public good . . . a while agone, they made me, yea me, to mistake an honest zealous pursuivant for a seminary." The comparison to Junius Brutus (who sacrificed his children in the name of the Law) reinforces Adam's self-image as upholder of rigorous justice and ironically reveals to the audience his lack of basic human sympathy.

The rest of the play is organised so as to fling these repressive law-givers into collision with the lawless Fair people, to drown paternalistic discourse in the anarchic Rabelaisian heteroglossia of the Bartholomewites who "know no better ware than they have, nor better customers than come," but at least possess self-awareness and an indomitable urge to survive. The etiolated values of the outsiders (which they all conceive in terms of *art*—verbal, rhetorical, even physical as in Overdo's disguise) will be opposed by the essentially *natural* drives of the denizens of the Fair—with dramatically deflationary results for the former party.

At the centre of the Fair sits Ursula, a kind of female Falstaff, a primal "mother o' the pigs," whose tent provides for all the basic needs of the body, food and sex, "pig and punk," though to Adam she is "the very womb and bed of enormity." Around her constellate a gang of picaresque criminals whose illegal activities we nonetheless find it hard to condemn outright since in the first place they are driven by the simple necessity of survival and, second (as in *Volpone* and *The Alchemist*), they prey off people who, for all their upright pretensions, are much stupider than they are. It is hardly surprising, then, that in this catalytic atmosphere Overdo mistakes a pickpocket for a decent gentleman; Wasp attempts to exert his authority and ends up paradoxically the victim of the authority of others when he is put in the stocks; Mistress Littlewit, seduced by Whit's vision of the life of a lady of fashion, becomes a "mistress o' the game," and Mrs. Overdo promptly follows suit. Only Cokes seems totally at home in the Fair, "my fair," and he, significantly, is presented as a "cosset"—immature enough, that is, to love the tawdry delights of the urban pastoral world he has entered: indeed it requires only a series of "strippings" (he loses his silver, his gold, his clothes, his licence, and finally his fiancée) to render him one with the Fair folk. As the appurtenances of "civilisation" and the law-regulated world drop away, Cokes becomes assimilated to the carnivalesque order of St. Bartholomew.

It requires more dramatic means to force the other outsiders to acknowledge their own frailties and the incompleteness of the authoritarian order they represent. There is no space in this article to chart the methods whereby Jonson manoeuvres Dame Purecraft into admitting that for seven years she has been "a wilful holy widow, only to draw feasts and gifts from [her] entangled suitors"; or how, similarly, Zeal-of-the-Land Busy is finally confuted by a puppet in a play (itself a subversive parody of authorised discourse) and compelled to admit that "the cause hath failed" him and that he is "changed, and will become a beholder with you." Wasp too must eventually conclude that "the date of my authority is out," and articulate one of the major moral lessons of the play: "I must think no longer to reign, my government is at an end. He that will correct another must want fault in himself." Even the sanctimonious Overdo is driven to concede that "compassion may become a justice," and ultimately to acknowledge the frailties of his wife and himself as he submits to Quarlous's admonition: "remember you are but Adam, flesh and blood! you have your frailty, forget your other name of Overdo, and invite us all to supper." And that is exactly what happens: the outsiders, humbled into a new self-awareness, affirm their solidarity with the (unchanged) Fair folk in a communal feast.

Jonson, however, is in no way glamourising the fair world: certainly it presents a forbidden object of desire to the outsiders, a land of Cockaigne releasing the primal urges that their legalistic, licence-dominated existence has repressed. But its occupants are (ethically) criminals, and Jonson doesn't let us forget this. Indeed the whole text could be seen as a debate on the two (equally valorised) meanings of the word "licence"—one both pastoral and anarchic ("se piace, ei lice"), the other paternal and legalistic ("have you got a licence to do that?"). The marriage licence is in this sense the symbol of Grace Wellborn's subjection to the mandates of patriarchal law. This ambivalence is foregrounded in the discourse of the madman Trouble-All, who also makes us realise that we are dealing here with a binary opposition in which neither term is prioritised—both extremes are insufficient. We need laws (but the law-givers must be honest); we need carnival—pig and punk—but the Lenten power of authority is essential to restrain it from going too far. Hence the sense of temporariness and provisionality that undercuts the festive conclusion to the text (Adam even reverts to legalistic Latin in the penultimate lines): a balance has been reached, but the tension remains. Jonson has problematised fascinatingly for us the insoluble dilemma of culture—how do we harmonise the potentially life-denying but necessary power structures of law, religion, family, patriarchy with the primal, but possibly anarchic, urges of childhood, food, sex, survival, and Carnival? If *Volpone* forced an unwelcome ethical conclusion on us, and *The Alchemist*, by opting for an aesthetic solution, proved simply that crime pays, *Bartholomew Fair* offers no such single answer, and is perhaps for that the greater play.

—A.W. Lyle

BATTER MY HEART (Holy Sonnet 14).
Poem by John Donne, 1633 (written c. 1609).

John Donne wrote 19 Holy Sonnets, most of them probably between 1609 and 1611. These years seem to have been a time of spiritual crisis for Donne, as well as part of a larger cultural crisis for England. In 1602 he had been dismissed from his post as secretary to Sir Thomas Egerton, Elizabeth's lord keeper, on account of his unauthorised marriage the previous year. And between then and his ordination in 1615, his life was one of unemployment, isolation, and alienation from the court, which, in the early years of the 17th century, was the centre of English life. At the same time, the characteristic changes of the period were gathering head: the shift from a feudal to a capitalist economy, the growth of puritanism, the rise of science, the increasing rift between Parliament and crown. It was a critical development registered in Donne's two *Anniversaries*, published in 1611 and 1612.

The Holy Sonnets, then, represent a turning to God at a moment of personal and cultural crisis. Holy Sonnet 14 begins with a forceful, even aggressive, assertiveness, of a kind found in the love poems: in "The Canonisation," for instance. Here, however, the person addressed is not the reader, or a woman, but God. "Batter my heart, three-personed God," says Donne. "For," he adds, using an unusually homely metaphor of a tinker mending pots, "you / As yet but knock, breathe, shine, and seek to mend." Something more violent is demanded. "That I may rise, and stand," he goes on, immediately and characteristically alert to paradox, "o'erthrow me"; and, moving on to another unusually commonplace image, "bend / Your force, to break, blow, burn, and make me new," like a blacksmith, the lines gaining a sense of enormous force from their enjambment and from the alliteration and emphasis on the packed, brief verbs in line 4.

Although the emotion is violent, it is also carefully contained within the sonnet form, in a way typical of the Holy Sonnet, where Donne can be seen using the form to control the experience being expressed: in this poem, the desperate need for some sort of inner renewal. The initial plea, therefore, presented in the guise of a succession of commands, is contained within the first quatrain. And the move to the second quatrain marks both a shift in tone and a transition of thought. "I," explains Donne, changing to political imagery, "like an usurped town, to another due, / Labour to admit you"—to admit God, his rightful ruler—"but oh, to no end." The attempt is fruitless, because "Reason your viceroy in me"—God's deputy in him—"me should defend, / But is captived, and proves weak or untrue." In the face of the rapidly and radically altering world of 1609, in which he plays no part, Donne is helpless.

So far Donne has used the Italian sonnet form, as he does in all the Holy Sonnets. And with the explanation of his need for renewal completed in the second quatrain, not without stress but more calmly and rationally than the expression of emotion in the first, he turns the poem, in the manner of the Italian sonnet, between the octave and the sestet in the direction of the desired resolution: again, in a way representative of the Holy Sonnets as a whole. "Yet," he declares, foregrounding the turn, "dearly I love you, and would be loved fain." The need for renewal is a need to be loved, to be wanted. But he is committed to a world that does not want him, and which in fact threatens to destroy him: "But am betrothed unto your enemy," to Satan. And Donne picks up the sexual imagery. As the sense of stress returns to the writing, the imperatives recur. "Divorce me," he orders God, with an audacity characteristic of these poems, "untie, or break that knot again": untie or break the bond of marriage to the devil. "Take me to you," he cries: hold me. Then a sudden intensification of sentiment, as the desperation of the first quatrain returns, and the metaphor changes again: "imprison me."

At the end of what is, in effect, the third quatrain of the poem, the emotion breaks through the form. And the thought carries over into the concluding couplet. As in all the Holy Sonnets, Donne combines the Italian with the English sonnet form, in order to attain the possibility of a resolution of sentiment in the English sonnet's final rhyme. The enjambment between lines 12 and 13 creates a feeling of suspense and anticipation. And the resolution arrived at is one of absolute submission to an external authority. It is expressed, once more, in terms of paradox. At first, by using a political metaphor: "for I / Except you enthral me, never shall be free." Unless God enslaves him, he will never achieve any kind of freedom. Then by a return to sexual metaphor: "Nor ever chaste, except you ravish me." He will never achieve any purity of life, any authenticity, unless God rapes him, somehow takes him by force.

The theology of the poem is typically protestant. Salvation cannot be achieved. It can only come from God. And the Holy Sonnets stand at the source of a distinctive tradition of religious poetry in the 17th century. It is a tradition one can see in the work of Donne's younger contemporary, George Herbert; in that of Henry Vaughan, in the middle years of the century; and, in the later part of the century, in the work of Thomas Traherne.

—William Zunder

THE BATTLE OF MALDON.
Poem, 11th century.

Edition

The Battle of Maldon, edited by D.G. Scragg. 1981.

Critical Studies: *English and Norse Documents Relating to the Reign of Ethelred the Unready* by Margaret Ashdown, 1930; *Die Battle of Maldon als historisches und literarisches Zeugnis* by Helmut Gneuss, 1976; *Modes of Interpretation in Old English Literature* edited by Phyllis Rugg Brown and others, 1986.

The Battle of Maldon is a late Old English narrative poem concerned with a calamitous encounter near Maldon in Essex on 10 or 11 August 991, when a band of Viking invaders (from Denmark, and already triumphant at Ipswich and beyond) routed a southeastern English army (part household retinue, part provincial levy) led by Ealdorman Byrhtnoth of Essex. The spare details of *The Anglo-Saxon Chronicle* pick out what was historically significant about this confrontation—that the Vikings won, as they had done before that year up and down the coastline of southeast England, and that Byrhtnoth was killed. But out of this local and accustomed disaster the unknown poet of *Maldon* created an enduring and popular literary work: a heroic poem about loyalty, and about the shared experience of battle and defeat, and a subtle piece of contemporary political irony which pointedly recalls the ancient Germanic battle ethic and the heroic manner of traditional literature at a time of demoralization and appeasement—the late 10th-century reign of the directionless Ethelred "Unræd." Central to the theme of *Maldon* are the tribal values of the Germanic *comitatus* where the generous, protective, and reliable leader gains undying loyalty in return.

The text of the poem, occupying 325 metrically alliterating lines, some of them irregular, is incomplete. The original manuscript was part of a compilation lost in a fire in 1731. Fortunately, a transcript made some years earlier by one David Casley (not as once thought John Elphinstone) survives. This shows the poem as already incomplete when copied, and since the poem occupied six manuscript leaves in the original compilation, it can be presumed that the first and last leaves of an eight leaf quire had become lost. That would indicate that 50 or so lines may be missing from both the beginning and end of the poem. The surviving poem suffers very little from its incomplete state: its essence is still there.

Maldon is no blow-by-blow battle narrative: it is not a versified historical chronicle. The poem is instead a series of vignettes, clearly reflecting the progress of the battle but focussed on the attitude and experience of individual warriors, first in the exchanges prior to the fighting, and then in the conventionalized speeches by which, at the height of the battle, various English warriors avow their commitment to avenge their now-fallen leader. This episodic organization gives the poem a clear linear development where each self-contained stage is fully foregrounded.

The stages of the poem show Byrhtnoth encouraging and arranging his men; then the approach of a Viking messenger offering peace for booty, and Byrhtnoth's defiant refusal; the brief success of the landward English in pinning the Vikings down on the island they have strategically occupied; Byrhtnoth's pivotal decision to allow the Vikings across the causeway separating the forces; the joining of battle; the wounding of Byrhtnoth, who kills his assailant but is then himself mortally wounded. Byrhtnoth's death is the prelude to contrasting developments in the second half of the poem. There is, at first, the flight of Godric and his cowardly brothers, but then comes the resistance of the most experienced and trusty members of Byrhtnoth's household army who in turn, in variously conventional speeches, and then in action, signal their determination to fight to the death or avenge their dead leader. The climax of the poem is the speech of the senior warrior Byrhtwold, whose opening words emphatically and memorably express the paradoxical interdependence of moral resolution and physical strength:

Hige sceal þe heardra heorte þe cenre
Mod sceal þe mare þe ure mægen lytlað

(Thought must be the harder, heart the keener, spirit must be the greater, as our strength lessens).

The style of the poem is direct and uncluttered. Individual speeches may involve rhetorical or emphatic contrivance, but otherwise the diction avoids prolixity and typically chooses ordinary prosaic devices rather than a traditional compounded and figurative complexity. What is notable in the poem, linguistically, is a deal of irony and verbally indirect wit.

Traditional criticism saw *Maldon* as composed, if not with a journalistic contemporaneity, at least sometime in the 990's by someone well-informed about what had occurred and familiar with those involved, and who meant the poem as an obituary tribute to the English dead. But more recent views put the composition of the poem anything from 30 to 50 years later than the battle, either because of the absence from the poem of a chronicler's historical concern, or because of signs of Scandinavian linguistic influence, or because of plausible but unproved links with early 11th-century sources. Essentially, *Maldon* is poetry before it is history, and its values are artistic rather than documentary. Nevertheless, a poem with its central idealistic themes—valour, incorruptible resolution, unyielding loyalty—clearly would have had a timely significance in the context of a decade marked by uncertain national leadership and by the practical demoralizing realism involved in paying Danegeld.

—Norman Macleod

A BEAUTIFUL YOUNG NYMPH GOING TO BED.
Poem by Jonathan Swift, 1734.

Jonathan Swift's "A Beautiful Young Nymph Going to Bed" appeared in small-pamphlet form in 1734 along with two other now widely anthologized poems, "Strephon and Chloe" and "Cassinus and Peter." Commonly referred to as "excremental," all three rely on Swiftian coarseness to satirize women as repugnant and, in the case of "Strephon and Chloe" and "Cassinus and Peter," men as deluded by romantic misconceptions of women. All three are typical of Swift's poetry in that the language is simple, the imagery bold, the tone humorous, and the intent didactic. But in "A Beautiful Young Nymph" his satire moves from the obvious to the more complex, a scheme not typical of his poetry.

The dramatic situation is simple enough: Corinna, a bedraggled London prostitute, returns to her fourth-floor room at midnight and carefully removes her wig, a glass eye, eyebrows, corset, and various other artifices that disguise her venereal-plagued body. She attends to her "chancres, issues, running sores" before painfully climbing into bed. Once asleep, she dreams of her life as a prostitute with all its attendant miseries. Upon waking, she discovers that her glass eye is missing, a rat and pigeon have stolen some of her medicinal aids, her cat has "on her plumpers pissed," and her dog has filled her wig with fleas. The poem ends with a moral tag, as do many of Swift's poems: once Corinna is able to reassemble herself, "Who sees, will spew; who smells, be poisoned."

On the obvious level—and this is so in "Strephon and Chloe" and "Cassinus and Peter" as well—Swift holds contempt for the traditional practice in poetry of elevating women, of presenting them as objects of goddess-like physical attraction, to him a false beauty that masked reality and ignored bodily functions. He felt that the entire pastoral tradition and its offshoots fed this myopic, dishonest portrayal. Although no defender of women, Swift attacks the popular misconceptions of them by parody. Here, his prostitute is named Corinna, a derivative of "kore," the Greek word for young maiden; her squalid room is her "bower"; and she is a "lovely goddess" for whose services "no shepherd sighs in vain." This glaring discrepancy between appearance and reality ridicules the pastoral tradition while it mocks her physical repugnance.

Undeniably, Swift's dismantling of Corinna, his emphasis on her physical decay caused by syphilis, is Juvenalian. He was intolerant of fornication and never failed to attack those involved in it, male and female. But he was also fully aware of social and economic conditions contributing to the perpetuation of the hapless, as his poem describing London, "A Description of a City Shower," and his famous essay about the Irish famine, *A Modest Proposal*, well exemplify. On another level then, 18th-century London also becomes an object of this satire. Corinna's fitful dreams transport her to a series of unpleasant experiences: first to Bridewell, the correctional house known for its harsh treatment of prostitutes and penniless women; then to the "compter," the city prison where inmates were jammed together in filthy quarters; next, she finds herself bullied by a "faithless" pimp in a cheap tavern before being arrested and sent to Jamaica with other felons; also, after encountering "watchmen, constables and duns," she dreams of the religious organizations that do not denounce her publicly as long as "she pays them all in kind." Swift in no way exonerates Corinna. He means it when he says that just the sight of her can induce vomiting and that her smell is poisonous. But his sharp denunciation is softened somewhat because Corinna is a victim of an unenlightened and hypocritical society.

Humor plays an important role in much of Swift's poetry, and "A Beautiful Young Nymph" is no exception. Corinna's plight notwithstanding, her sitting on a rickety three-legged chair to remove her wig, glass eye, false teeth, and such, presents a comical picture. Likewise, the next morning when she finds fleas in her wig and cat urine on her "plumpers," the scene is similarly intended to be comical. Yet Swift's intention extends beyond the comic, and here his satire reaches a new, disturbing, level.

The chuckling reader, sharing Swift's scorn for prostitution, the pastoral tradition, and a benighted society that promotes immorality, now realizes the strong possibility that the satire may also be aimed in his direction. He has, after all, found amusement at the expense of one who must suffer the unceasing "anguish, toil, and pain / Of gathering herself up again." Earlier phrases in the poem that heretofore seemed out of place in Juvenalian satire—like "gentlest touch" and "sad disaster"—begin to take on a new dimension. Swift was too skillful a poet to lose control of his tone and jeopardize the unity of his poem by inadvertently including such sentiments, as some critics maintain. These hints at pathos, far from compromising the artistic success of "A Beautiful Young Nymph," add to it. For in satirizing a character who deserves contempt, Swift subtly turns the reader's harsh glance upon himself.

—Gilbert P. Prince, Jr.

THE BEAUX' STRATAGEM.
Play by George Farquhar, 1707.

Most critics agree that *The Beaux' Stratagem* is the best of George Farquhar's plays. It was also performed more often than any other play written by the Restoration comic dramatists. Its obvious appeal can be attributed to a number of factors. Farquhar was an actor as well as a professional playwright, and *The Beaux' Stratagem* has all the marks of a writer who relied on experience and knowledge of public taste rather than inherited theories or rules to please audiences. The play moves rapidly, from its opening stage direction ("Enter Bonniface, running") to the end, and the plot is original, simple, and less episodic than those of most comedies. The play does not strive to be too good for its audience, nor does it pose as something written quickly to display wit. It is a transitional work that shares many of the characteristics of the earlier Restoration comedy of manners and some of the traits of the emerging moral or sentimental comedy, but differs significantly from both types. It might best be classed as "laughing comedy," a precursor of the type that would later be perfected by Goldsmith and Sheridan. There is less wit, more "humor," and more stage action in *The Beaux' Stratagem* than in most Restoration manners comedies, and the laughter is generally less malicious and more sympathetic. On the other hand, the play's worldliness, boisterousness, and natural, flowing dialogue, which Pope called "pert and low," distinguish it from genteel or morally exemplary comedy. *The Beaux' Stratagem* is a highly amusing comedy, but it is not merely entertaining; Farquhar combines comic liveliness with an examination of human values and such serious social problems as repressive divorce laws.

The Beaux' Stratagem is set at an inn and at a country house in Lichfield, and concerns the efforts of two young London rakes to recoup the fortunes they have spent in self-indulgent pursuits. Archer and Aimwell journey into the country with the intent of tricking an heiress into marriage. They succeed when Lady Bountiful's daughter, Dorinda, agrees to marry Aimwell, but Aimwell falls in love with her, cannot carry out the deception, and reveals that he is penniless. Archer, disguised as Aimwell's servant, dallies with Mrs. Sullen, who is married to Lady Bountiful's brutish son, and also pursues Cherry, the innkeeper's daughter. The cast also includes an Irish chaplain, a French count, highwaymen, and assorted others who afford Farquhar the opportunity to exercise his considerable skill in developing amusing character-types. The play ends with Dorinda's acceptance of Aimwell after it is revealed that the latter has inherited the family fortune, and with Mrs. Sullen's separation from her husband, although she is not free to marry Archer.

The Beaux' Stratagem resembles earlier Restoration comedies in that the action of the play derives from sexual intrigue, the two leading males are unreformed rakes who do not repent having spent their youth in the pursuit of pleasure and who have profited from experience, and the typical Restoration couple who engage in intrigue and a battle of wits is present in Archer and Mrs. Sullen. However, Farquhar alters the formula significantly. Although the play's language suggests the usual Restoration amorality or licentiousness and sexual intrigue is at the center of the play, nothing really happens. Mrs. Sullen escapes Archer's advances, as does Cherry, and even tells Dorinda that although she may talk freely, she will not "go a step beyond the bounds of honor." This pattern is repeated throughout the play; Farquhar's characters may sound like Restoration rakes, but they are prevented from acting on the libertine sentiments they profess. Moreover, Farquhar distinguishes between Aimwell and Archer. The latter is the more consummate Restoration hero—witty, sophisticated, sexually adept, his reason in control of his senses—whereas Aimwell becomes a genuinely reformed rake whose love for Dorinda leads him to reveal his impoverished condition. He is converted by her "goodness" and she is won by his honesty. Hence conventional virtue triumphs in scenes resembling those in sentimental comedy.

If the Dorinda-Aimwell relationship ends happily in marriage, that between Mrs. Sullen and Archer does not. In his portrait of the Sullens' marriage, Farquhar addresses a serious social problem—the rigidity of English divorce laws that do not allow completely incompatible couples to dissolve their marriages. The play contains numerous ideas and even whole sentences from Milton's *The Doctrine and Discipline of Divorce*, all of which argue for the liberalization of divorce laws. The conclusion of the play asserts that mutual consent is sufficient "to set you free," but it was not in Farquhar's day. Mrs. Sullen is separated from her husband and regains her fortune, but she cannot marry Archer. Hence her future choice is between loneliness and adultery. Farquhar is not an active reformer nor is *The Beaux' Stratagem* a problem play, but he provides adequate argumentation and sufficient evidence of human suffering in his portrayal of the very appealing Mrs. Sullen to give his essentially comic play serious undertones.

The world of earlier Restoration comedies of manners is that of modish London society. The country is almost invariably portrayed negatively, and those associated with it are generally comic butts whose ignorance of the manners and mores of fashionable society and whose boorish manners and bumpkinish pursuits make them fair game for ridicule. The behavioral standard is that of the city wit in these plays, but there is a shift of values in *The Beaux' Stratagem*. Despite conversations in the play that argue for the superiority of city delights, Farquhar is aware of the charms of country life. Moreover, Lady Bountiful's country house becomes a kind of locus of goodness; not only are the sick healed there, but the deserving are rewarded and honesty made triumphant. Certainly country humors are laughed at and the boorish country squire criticized, but Farquhar provides a more balanced portrait of the country than do his immediate predecessors.

—James S. Malek

THE BEGGAR'S OPERA.
Play by John Gay, 1728.

The Beggar's Opera was first performed at Lincoln's Inn Fields theatre in London on 29 January 1728. John Gay had been writing plays for some 15 years and he produced three more, including a less successful sequel to the *Opera* called *Polly*, before his death in December 1732. This was by far the greatest hit of his dramatic career and indeed it was arguably the most popular new play seen on the London stage in the entire century. There were a record 62 performances before the first season closed in June 1728. As early as 20 March Gay could report to his friend Swift that he had earned between seven and eight hundred pounds from the play: its promoter John Rich, the manager at Lincoln's Inn Fields, cleared more like four thousand pounds.

Not only did the work survive as one of the most performed items in the repertoire for generations to come—it equally inaugurated a hugely popular form, that of ballad opera. Numerous imitations of the genre which Gay had invented appeared over the next quarter of a century, with at least 22 examples in the single year 1733. Few of these have held the stage, although Charles Johnson's *The Village Opera* (1729) and some of the variants devised by Henry Fielding in the early 1730's enjoyed some appeal at the box-office and some notoriety. But none ever matched the spectacular success of the original work.

The central device is that of supplying new words to familar tunes: most of these are folksongs or well-known broadside ballads, but a few of the 69 items come from recent opera or other "serious" musical sources. The airs were arranged by Johann Christoph Pepusch, a German musician resident in London, who also composed an overture. At the heart of the play's effects is this regular use of point "numbers," which do not so much interrupt the action as freeze the narrative in order to draw out social and political implications, while diversifying the texture of the piece by calling up the previous associations of the tune in question. The original cast were actors who could sing, rather than singers (an especially vivid impact was made by Lavinia Fenton, up till then fairly obscure, in the role of Polly Peachum). However there is enough musical content for front-line professional singers to have made numerous outstanding interpretations of the central roles.

The ostensible hero is the highwayman Macheath, charming, feckless, and debonair. But he is outwitted both as a criminal and as a lover, and the real power belongs to the thief-taker and fence Peachum and the Newgate jailer Lockit. It is the daughters of these two men, Polly Peachum and Lucy Lockit, who compete for the heart of Macheath, and who help to humanize what is in many respects a bleak story with moments of tenderness and dignity. Peachum is supported by his tough and prudential wife. Surrounding the principal characters are two parallel groups of low-life figures. Macheath's gang is made up of an assortment of mostly hapless rogues, who delight in picturesque names pointing ominously to their dismal career and prospects—Jemmy Twitcher, Matt of the Mint (a refuge for debtors and outlaws), Harry Paddington (an allusion to the site of the Tyburn gallows). Against them are ranged the women of the town, garnished with equally fanciful cognomens—Diana Trapes, Betty Doxy, and Jenny Diver (this last a slang term for pickpocket). Both groups employ a racy argot full of criminal "cant," deliciously exploited by Gay to show the correspondence between the openly professed attitudes of the poor and the hidden motives of their betters.

The play is framed by scenes involving a beggar, the presumed author of the entertainment, and an actor. In the opening sequence we have little more than a conventional introduction, but a fine irony is introduced at the end, where the beggar's desire to follow strict poetic justice with the hanging of Macheath is averted by the intervention of the actor. A general dance is substituted as Macheath survives and links arms with Polly. This conclusion has a complex function, like many other elements in the design; it satirizes popular taste, it makes fun of the accustomed *deus ex machina*, it suggests the ease of deathbed repentance, and it hints at the possibilities of subverting justice when a popular clamour is raised. But it also makes for a resounding and cheerful closure, which is in key with a kind of cheerful resilience which has pervaded the action, even when the events in themselves have been gloomy and the situation unappetizing.

Peachum is the key figure in the design. On one level he certainly matches the real-life criminal boss Jonathan Wild, who had been hanged in 1725 after a brief period as the godfather of London crime. (Fielding was to write his own satirical account of Wild in 1743.) But Wild had before this come to be identified with the prime minister Robert Walpole, seen as the gang boss of the ministerial mafia. There is debate as to the precise extent of political allusion within the text, but it is clear that from the beginning audiences made the Peachum-Wild-Walpole equation without any reserve. It may be added that one title for a song Pepusch used in the overture was "Walpole."

The work, then, is dramatically involved and linguistically allusive. It draws on the world of Italian opera, though the greatest figure in that realm, Handel, seems to escape without injury. It adumbrates the whole criminal environment, not just that of Wild but also that of other prominent jailbirds such as the escape-artist Jack Sheppard. It attacks people in high places, quite apart from Walpole, and consistently suggests that the basic strategies of the court and of the underworld are indistinguishable. Finally, there is a pervasive link to other literature of the age. Swift may have given Gay the idea of a "Newgate pastoral," and the dramatist's erstwhile collaborator Pope took on some of the same targets in *The Dunciad*, published within weeks of the triumphant premiere of the *Opera*. It is a rich and resourceful play, which has continued to stimulate audiences in regular revivals down to the present day. It did not need Bertolt Brecht's 20th-century recension, *The Threepenny Opera* (1928), with its spikily evocative music by Kurt Weill, to breathe life back into the play. Gay's own *Opera* is the first and only surviving member of its species, but one such masterpiece is enough to dignify the genre.

—Pat Rogers

A BEND IN THE RIVER.
Novel by V.S. Naipaul, 1979.

Paul Theroux wrote of his subject in *V.S. Naipaul* (1972) that "he may be the only writer today in whom there are no echoes of influences." Strangely, a few years later (1979) Naipaul published *A Bend in the River*, the whole of which seems a reworking of Conrad's "Heart of Darkness" from the perspective of a post-colonial Kurtz. The vision of an outsider in the heart of Africa itself creates interest. But Salim, a trader of Indian ancestry, is also a keenly intelligent observer. The differences from Conrad are striking: Salim survives, for example, his decadence not being all-consuming. But like Kurtz he is there to exploit the land and the people, and his stay at the bend in the river which he has made his home ends only after he has been caught illegally trading in elephant tusks.

Salim enters the upper reaches of the Congo not by going upstream (Western European style), but through the traditional and ancient slave-trading route from the east coast of Africa. The time is the present, and in part the novel chronicles the problems of living through revolutionary changes and depicts the harsh reality for ordinary people behind the rhetoric of "Radicalization" and "Nationalization." The narrator is a keen observer of society, astutely aware of ironies brought out by cross-cultural contacts—and conflicts—but this is not essentially a social novel.

That is so in part because the action of the story is presented so impressionistically—as a sequence of epiphanies or highly charged moments rather than in a tautly structured plot. The technique respects, just as it reflects, the integrity of the central consciousness of the narrator. But it also results in a limited vision, most obvious in the partial portraits given of other characters and the sudden surprise revelations concerning them or their motives. Even Yvette, Salim's lover, is presented somewhat tangentially—an approach artistically effective, but suggesting a certain myopia. In the final meeting of the narrator and his (basically) loyal servant Metty, the narrator confesses that he should have given Metty some money before leaving, but did not see the need: "I never thought of it. I never thought of you in that way." Clearly his vision and his conduct are functionally related—and both seem lacking.

For the narrator is a rather conventional existential hero, displaced from his own culture, an outsider in the one he adopts. He does find that status sometimes protective socially, just as he senses that not being bound by traditions, as in other Naipaul novels, is a decided advantage. Yet he is also more than a mere survivor. He is uncompromisingly independent and realistic, an entrepreneur, not a visionary, but a dispassionately honest reporter. His final wisdom is simply grim: "The world is what it is; men who are nothing, who allow themselves to become nothing, have no place in it."

That vision seems shared by Naipaul and more than anything else makes the book in its own darkness comparable to Conrad's. Although possibly influenced by the African politics and racism it depicts, the vision seems more fundamentally tragic, a darkly pessimistic view of human nature and man's fate. Naipaul employs physical darkness symbolically, much as Conrad did, not merely as a sign of the unknown or of the mysterious at the heart of Africa, but as an emblem of the condition (maybe even the heart) of man. In the closing passage of the novel, the narrator is leaving by boat during yet another incipient coup or retaliatory strike by the dictatorial government. Suddenly darkness falls, the boat is attacked, and in the fighting a passenger barge attached earlier to the steamboat breaks away. "The searchlight lit up the barge passengers, who, behind bars and wire guards, as yet scarcely seemed to understand that they were adrift." Then all is dark and the novel ends. Such seems to be the human condition. One can sympathetically respond, "The Horror!"

A complementary symbol in the novel is the water hyacinths. A constant presence, they represent some sort of primal force in nature, its fecundity and capacity for renewal, its total indifference to the individual. We learn that the hyacinths, like the people living along the river, have not always been so abundant, and that clumps of the hyacinths, displaced from the shore, drift downstream. It seems frighteningly appropriate that the people in the lost barge at the end are last seen adrift among the hyacinths at the edge of the river. Nature, it seems, will have its way, rather aloof to the human dramas that the novel chronicles—whether these be petty squabbles among associates or outright bloodbaths.

A dark and somber novel, *A Bend in the River* ingeniously rebuilds on Conrad's design without taking issue with Conrad's dark conclusions. The chief limitation of the novel is part of its design. The conflict of cultures in Africa is explored through an alienated vision that never can give us anything but a partial picture. The meticulously reported details, brilliant though they may be, can mask the inevitably narrow constraints of the outsider's perspective.

—Harold Farwell

BEOWULF.
Poem, 8th century.

Editions and Translations

De Danorum Rebus Gestis Seculis III et IV Poema Danicum Dialecto Anglosaxonica, edited by Grim. Johnson Thorkelin. 1815.
Beowulf and the Fight at Finnsburg, edited by Fr. Klaeber. 1922; revised edition, 1950.
Beowulf and the Finnsburg Fragment, edited by C.L. Wrenn. 1953; revised edition, by W.F. Bolton, 1973.
Beowulf: A New Prose Translation, translated by E. Talbot Donaldson. 1966; edited by Joseph F. Tuso, 1975.
Beowulf: A Verse Translation, translated by M.J. Alexander. 1973.
Beowulf, edited and translated by Michael Swanton. 1978.
A Readable Beowulf, translated by Stanley B. Greenfield. 1982.
Beowulf, translated by Ruth P.M. Lehmann. 1988.

Bibliography: *Beowulf Scholarship: An Annotated Bibliography* by Douglas D. Short, 1980.

Critical Studies: *Beowulf: An Introduction* by R.W. Chambers, 1921, revised edition (with supplement by C.L. Wrenn), 1959; *Beowulf: The Monsters and the Critics* by J.R.R. Tolkien, 1937; *The Audience of Beowulf* by Dorothy Whitelock, 1951; *The Art of Beowulf* by Arthur G. Brodeur, 1959; *An Anthology of Beowulf Criticism* edited by L.E. Nicholson, 1963; *The Structure of Beowulf* by Kenneth Sisam, 1965; *A Reading of Beowulf* by Edward B. Irving, 1968; *Beowulf and Its Analogues* by G.N. Garmonsway and J. Simpson, 1968; *Beowulf* by T.A. Shippey, 1978; *Alcuin and Beowulf: An Eighth-Century View* by W.F. Bolton, 1979; *Beowulf and the Tenth Century* by Wilhelm G. Busse, 1981; *The Dating of Beowulf* edited by Colin Chase, 1981; *Beowulf: The Poem and Its Tradition* by John D. Niles, 1983; *Reading Beowulf: An Introduction to the Poem, Its Background, and Its Style* by J.D.A. Ogilvy and Donald C. Baker, 1983; *The Hero in the Earthly City: A Reading of Beowulf* by Bernard F. Huppé, 1984; *Beowulf and the Appositive Style* by Fred C. Robinson, 1985; *Beowulf and Christianity* by Mary A. Parker, 1987; *Rereading Beowulf* by Edward B. Irving, Jr., 1989; *Beowulf* by George Clark, 1990.

The *Beowulf* poet is anonymous, but most scholars have placed him north of the Thames, in the Anglian kingdoms in the early or middle 8th century, and have supposed him to be a Christian nobleman or ecclesiastic, since the poem has some Christian and aristocratic colouring. The Northumbria of the age of Bede (died 735) and the Mercia ruled by Offa from 757 to 796 have suggested themselves as the milieux where such a monumental court poem might have been composed and appreciated. The language of the poem supports such a provenance, though the Late West Saxon form in which it survives (in a unique manuscript of about the year 1000, now in the British Library) overlies the largely Anglian language of its composition.

We know less about the *Beowulf* poet than we do about Homer, since we lack even his (or her) name, but it is proper to think of a *Beowulf* poet rather than of the author of *Beowulf*, since the monster-slaying story and its associated historical material seem to have been in circulation long before the poem achieved its literary form of 3,182 Old English verses. The name of Beowulf the Geat does not appear elsewhere, but his king, Hygelac, is recorded by Bishop Gregory of Tours as having died in a raid on the Franks in 521. The setting of the poem is southern Scandinavian, and the historical and legendary characters, such as Offa the Angle and Hrothgar the Dane, belong to the heroic age of migration, before the Angles had fully settled in Britain, a land which is not mentioned in the poem.

The *Beowulf* poet seems to have inherited not only his matter but also his medium of composition (and his world-view) from his Germanic ancestors. The language and style of *Beowulf* are shaped by the traditions of public, oral-formulaic verse composition, and recitations are described several times in the poem. Christianity and literacy, however, also contribute to *Beowulf*, which portrays a heroic world from a post-heroic and even elegiac viewpoint. The poem achieves a profound synthesis between these pre-Christian and Christian traditions, and its Anglian redactor may have been a "unifier" (a meaning of the Greek *Homēros*) as well as a creator.

The story of Beowulf, who slew monsters in his youth and a dragon in his last fight, is set in a world of heroic feuds between the tribes of the Baltic and North Seas. After his death his own people will be over-run by their neighbours; the seeds of the destruction of heroic civilisations are seen to be contained in the heroic code itself, where magnanimity and courage are accompanied by the duty of revenge. The monster Grendel and his mother, who terrorise the Danes, are the descendants of Cain, the first murderer; Tolkien interprets them as embodiments of evil. Human heroic society is portrayed in the ceremonious and hospitable court of Hrothgar at his hall, Heorot, where a poet sings of the creation of the world; Grendel attacks Heorot at night, and devours the bodies of the sleeping Danes: "Night's table-laughter turned to morning's/lamentation."

A young Geat, Beowulf, comes to Heorot to rid it of Grendel. Beowulf is an exemplary hero, loyal, generous, brave, courteous, and gentle, though of immense bear-like strength, and above the common motive of revenge. He heeds Hrothgar's warnings against pride and complacency in his youthful successes, but falls in old age against the dragon who ravages the Geat countryside after his hoard has been robbed of a golden cup. Some recent critics have developed Christian interpretations of the poem in which the hero is doomed by the limitations of his paganism; but the emphasis of the ending is clearly admiring:

Then the warriors rode around the barrow,
twelve of them in all, athelings' sons.
They recited a dirge to declare their grief,
spoke of the man, mourned their King.
They praised his manhood and the prowess of his hands,
they raised his name; it is right a man
should be lavish in honouring his lord and friend,
should love him in his heart when the leading-forth
from the house of flesh befalls him at last.
This was the manner of the mourning of the men of the
Geats,
sharers in the feast, at the fall of their lord:
they said that he was of all the world's kings
the gentlest of men, and the most gracious,
the kindest to his people, the keenest for fame.

Beowulf is the longest Old English poem, and easily the most considerable piece of literature in English before the reign of Richard II. It has a grave and profound understanding of life and has poetic merits of the highest sort; it is a work of art of mature complexity and balance.

—M.J. Alexander

THE BERLIN STORIES
(includes *Mr. Norris Changes Trains*, *Sally Bowles*, *Goodbye to Berlin*).
Fiction by Christopher Isherwood, 1935–39.

The Berlin Stories established Christopher Isherwood's reputation as the most important novelist of the Auden generation and they provide an unsurpassed portrait of Berlin in the turbulent years of Hitler's rise to power. Consisting of two novels, *Mr. Norris Changes Trains* (published in the U.S. as *The Last of Mr. Norris*) and *Goodbye to Berlin* (which incorporates several separately published stories, including *Sally Bowles*), *The Berlin Stories* evokes a mythic city of sexual and political excitement only to expose the loneliness and despair that lie beneath its enticing veneer. The two novels are quite distinct, but in each Isherwood masters a unique voice, creates some of the most memorable characters in modern fiction, and movingly depicts a city in the process of internal decay. As explorations of the ways in which public and private concerns intersect, they are politically engaged. The brooding spectre of Nazism hovers in the background, finally to impinge even on characters as indifferent to politics as the landlady Fraulein Schroeder and the innocently naughty cabaret singer Sally Bowles.

In *The Berlin Stories*, Isherwood perfects his naive, first-person narration. The narrators—William Bradshaw in *Mr. Norris Changes Trains* and Christopher Isherwood in *Goodbye to Berlin*—bear the author's own names. (Isherwood was christened Christopher William Bradshaw Isherwood.) But these narrators should not be equated with Isherwood himself. Their passivity, lack of commitment, and failure to perceive the irony of their relationships with the characters in the books they narrate serve to differentiate them from the author. The narrator of *Goodbye to Berlin* may be "a camera with its shutter open, quite passive, recording, not thinking," but the author is the activist director who decides where to point the camera and who creates an ironic perspective by placing the reader in positions of intellectual and moral superiority to the passive narrators.

Mr. Norris Changes Trains is a moral fable disguised as light comedy. It opens in 1930 when William Bradshaw, a young English writer, encounters Arthur Norris, an aging adventurer who introduces him to other members of the Berlin demimonde; it concludes in 1933, when Hitler comes to power. The key to the novel's absorbing interest resides in the mysterious charm of the lovable but dangerous Mr. Norris. Bradshaw's continuing susceptibility to Norris's charm—his romanticization of him as "a most amazing old crook"—is at the heart of the novel's political lesson that private failures yield public consequences. Although Bradshaw fails to perceive it, Norris is actually a small-scale, comic version of Hitler. The attentive reader ultimately corrects Bradshaw's misperceptions and gullibility, but only after having fallen prey to the identical misjudgments. The effect of this irony is not only to condemn Bradshaw's naivety and passivity, but also to force the reader toward compassionate understanding, both for Bradshaw and for the German people, who have naively and gullibly embraced Hitler.

Isherwood described *Goodbye to Berlin* as a "loosely connected sequence of diaries and sketches." But this description fails to do justice to the artful symmetry of the novel, which achieves unity as the result of two structural principles. One involves the deliberate balancing of economic, sexual, social, cultural, and political polarities in its various sections and among its disparate characters. Beneath such oppositions as rich and poor, homosexual and heterosexual, Jew and Gentile, Communist and Nazi is a shared reality of the deadened spirit that unites everyone in the book, even as it makes real integration impossible. The other source of unity is the continuing and developing presence of the narrator. His inability to connect meaningfully with any of the polarized characters, despite his open sympathy for them all, mirrors the state of Berlin itself. His personal failure to achieve intimacy is symptomatic of the social disease that blights the city and that culminates in the spiritual death represented by Hitler's triumph.

Goodbye to Berlin is a dynamic portrait of an inhibited young man, preoccupied with the ghosts of the past and the fears of the future, belatedly maturing in a world that is dying. But the novel is also a political study. Private loneliness and individual failures of commitment, personal isolations and particular distortions of reality all contribute to the public tragedy of fascism. It contains no public figures and no explicit ideology, but *Goodbye to Berlin* is among the most significant political novels of its day.

The Berlin Stories is an elegy for a dying city. Compassionate, understated, and ironic, the novels domesticate the tragedy of the fall of the Weimar Republic by focusing on social and political outcasts on the periphery of the public arena. Depicting Berlin in all its squalor and poverty, loneliness and despair, they capture the fullness of a society on the brink of disaster. The Berlin of Herr Issyvoo, Frl. Schroeder, Sally Bowles, Baron von Pregnitz, the Landauers and the Nowaks, and Mr. Norris has been extended, in altered—and distorted—form, into the popular imagination through stage and film adaptations. But Isherwood's original Berlin stories remain the most authentic and indelible portrait of the "cold and cruel and dead" city that "glowed so brightly and invitingly in the night sky above the plains."

—Claude J. Summers

BERMUDAS.
Poem by Andrew Marvell, 1681 (written c. 1653).

"Bermudas" probably dates from the period beginning in July 1653 when Andrew Marvell went to live with John Oxenbridge, a fellow of Eton College, as the tutor to Cromwell's ward William Dutton. Oxenbridge, who had visited the Bermudas twice, was an exuberant Puritan like the singers in the poem, and had been expelled from his Oxford tutorship by Archbishop Laud in 1634. At the Restoration, also like the Puritans in this poem, Oxenbridge sought religious freedom from the re-established Anglican prelacy by emigrating to the Americas, dying in Boston. However, one of the most fashionable Cavalier poets of the time, Edmund Waller, also wrote a charming mock-heroic poem set in the Bermudas, called "The Battle of the Summer Islands" (1645), humorously celebrating the islanders' struggles with two beached whales, which are perhaps recalled by Marvell's "huge Sea-Monsters." Waller also praises the oranges and ambergis mentioned by Marvell. Earlier still, in *The Tempest*, Shakespeare had borrowed from accounts of the Bermudas from the various Virginia Voyages such as those of Sir George Summers (and later of Captain Henry Smith), as both the other poets probably also did, in order to evoke a magical island where storms and other tribulations seem little more than illusions. Like Homer, Tasso, Spenser, and many other poets, Shakespeare's play also exploits the European myths of various enchanted islands spread far across the Atlantic, which had also inspired Columbus. For example, the botanical imagery in the poems of Waller and Marvell recalls the Golden Apples of the Hesperides which are specifically mentioned by Waller, but these apples also match an even more deeply rooted tradition, evoked by the impression Marvell gives that the New World has preserved remnants of the unfallen condition of the Garden of Eden, in which Nature is still spontaneously productive and benevolent. The island fowls are sent through the air for human advantage by a benevolent deity rather as were the ravens who brought nourishment to the Old Testament prophet Elijah.

The poem's fascination thus derives from many of the most powerful traditions of landscape poetry in the western world, and it is at least as archetypal in its effects as "To His Coy Mistress." However, unlike that poem, "Bermudas" deftly reconciles traditional literary effects of opulence and luxury with a sense that there is a divine sanction for the Puritan settlers to enjoy the islands' natural bounty without the guilt of pagan self-indulgence or risk of the lethargy that threatens in "The Garden," or even the questioning of vocation that disturbs the relaxed mood of "Upon Appleton House." "Bermudas" reads like a pendant or resolution of the temptations and anxieties expressed in the two earlier poems, which in turn probably reflect Marvell's previous stay at Appleton as tutor to Mary Fairfax (1650–52), where General Fairfax had withdrawn deep into Yorkshire, fleeing from the political centre of activity in London. The mood of "Bermudas" was surely established after Marvell's return to Eton placed him once more in the vicinity of London. It is still serene yet powerfully affirmative in ways prefiguring the dawning professional career of Marvell in 1653, when he was first proposed as assistant Latin secretary, to aid Milton's labours for the Commonwealth, an appointment finally made in 1657, which led to an influential career as a parliamentarian, representing the port city of Hull.

In this poem's affirmative mood Marvell illustrates the curious blend of Puritan decorum and Platonic mysticism which the University of Cambridge induced in so many of its graduates during this century, through the influence and teaching of the Cambridge Platonists. The nature poetry of Vaughan shares this confidence in the religious symbolism of the natural world. The idyllic mood also appears in such French poets as Saint-Amant and Théophile de Viau, two Anglophiles who both visited England and were also both Huguenots (at least initially). They created similar landscape lyrics to Marvell's, such as *L'Autonne des Canaries* of the former and the latter's *La Maison de Sylvie*, from both of which Marvell probably borrowed (he returned to France about this time with his pupil, William Dutton). Marvell's playfulness in "Bermudas" and in many of his other poems is also found in the kind of sceptical libertinism which these writers adopted in their rural retreats, fleeing the stresses of the contemporary religious confrontations. However, unlike their verses, Marvell's poem displays the resolution to sustain the autonomous political career upon which he duly launched himself as boldly as the Puritan adventurers whom he visualises assimilating themselves to the New World of the Bermudas.

—Hugh M. Richmond

BIOGRAPHIA LITERARIA.
Prose by Samuel Taylor Coleridge, 1817.

Composed in 1815 and published in 1817, *Biographia Literaria* includes intellectual autobiography, philosophy, literary theory, and an extended analysis of Wordsworth's poetry. It is widely recognised as one of the most important critical works in English because it bases a comprehensive theory of imagination and a substantial body of practical criticism on a general philosophy of the human mind.

The starting point of Samuel Taylor Coleridge's philosophy is a rejection of 18th-century empiricism, derived from Locke's concept of the mind as the passive recipient of sense impressions, and an attack on Hartley's associationism, which reduced all mental activity to a mechanical process of association. Drawing heavily on Kant and Schelling, Coleridge reexamines the entire concept of the relationship between the mind and the world, or between subject and object. Without retreating into solipsism or the subjective idealism of Berkeley, he views the mind as active in perception since it reshapes the external world so as to endow it with meaning. This creativity in cognition Coleridge names the primary imagination. It is common to all human beings and an image of God's own creativity; it is "the living Power and prime Agent of all human Perception and a repetition in the finite mind of the eternal act of creation in the infinite I AM."

Like the primary imagination, the secondary or artistic imagination recreates by shaping diverse materials into a significant whole. Its chief manifestation is its reconciliation of opposites, for it blends emotion and order, judgment and enthusiasm, art and nature, matter and manner. It differs, however, from primary imagination in that it is initiated by a conscious act of will, thus rendering judgment and volition an important aspect of poetry. By reconciling opposites the imagination shapes the poem into an organic unity in which the various parts are interdependent. Following the organicism of A.W. Schlegel, Coleridge sees the poem as developing in accordance with the requirements of its own nature. Like a plant's, its form is determined by the force within since "the *rules* of the IMAGINATION are themselves the very powers of growth and production." In such a unity all the parts—ideas, subject, diction, images, metre—"mutually support and explain each other," and are essential to the central harmony. This shaping or esemplastic power of imagination separates it from fancy, which is associative and aggregative, rearranging the flux of experience and images into new but arbitrary combinations.

From these central principles emerge several other ideas concerning poetry and the poet. One is the insistence that poetry should be ideal, that is, it should divest its subjects of accidental trappings and fuse the universal with the particular. Another fundamental is the connection of poetry with pleasure and with philosophy. A poem proposes "for its *immediate* object pleasure, not truth"; this communication of pleasure enables the poet to hold the attention of his readers and so ultimately increases their moral awareness. But because pleasure leads to appreciation of truth, poetry and philosophy are integrally involved, and Coleridge asserts that "no man was ever yet a great poet, without being at the same time a profound philosopher." Finally imagination is linked with passion, and the two operate jointly as a "blending, *fusing* power."

In these principles Coleridge transforms neo-classicism. The doctrines of universality and pleasure are basics of neo-classical theory, as is the stress on good sense and precision, standards which, Coleridge says, were inculcated in him by his teacher, James Bowyer. Yet the gulf between a neo-classical criticism of rules and Coleridge's understanding of the dynamic power of imagination is reflected in his summation: "GOOD SENSE is the BODY of poetic genius, FANCY its DRAPERY, MOTION its LIFE, and IMAGINATION the SOUL that is everywhere, and in each; and forms all into one graceful and intelligent whole."

The purpose of Coleridge's theorising was, as he explained in his opening paragraph, to determine the true nature of poetic diction and to establish the distinctive poetic character of Wordsworth. Responding to Wordsworth's earlier account of *Lyrical Ballads*, he described the composition as a double experiment: Wordsworth was to arouse the reader's sympathy by giving "the charm of novelty to things of every day," while Coleridge was to depict the strange and supernatural in such a way as to produce a "willing suspension of disbelief," which would make the unfamiliar credible. Although Coleridge refers to a wide range of authors, notably Shakespeare, the chapters on Wordsworth most clearly demonstrate his critical perceptiveness and his ability to base specific criticism in philosophical principles. He disagrees sharply with Wordsworth's theory of imagination, which he felt relied too heavily on Hartley's associationism and underestimated the shaping, modifying power of imagination. Similarly he rejects Wordsworth's theories of diction, maintaining that the language of poetry differs from that of prose and that the best model for the poet is the language not of the rustic or the ordinary person but of the impassioned philosopher. In discussing Wordsworth's practice, Coleridge adopts the neo-classical method of listing defects and excellences, but he relates the evaluations to his theories of imagination. Wordsworth's defects include inconstancy of style, obstructing imaginative synthesis, and a minute particularity of detail, which precludes the fusion of the universal and the particular. His beauties, on the other hand, comprise purity and appropriateness of language, weight of thought, truth of images, union of thought and feeling, and above all "the gift of IMAGINATION in the highest and strictest sense of the word," a gift which gave Wordsworth the potential for producing the first great philosophical poem.

Biographia Literaria is the most complete single source of Coleridge's literary theory and criticism. The result of more than 15 years' thinking about the mind, the imagination, and literature, it is remarkable for both its firm grasp of generalities and its judicious estimation of particulars. It establishes Coleridge at the centre of the English romantic movement, and it effected a permanent shift in the entire direction of English literary criticism.

—Muriel Mellown

THE BIRTHDAY PARTY.
Play by Harold Pinter, 1958.

The Birthday Party has been interpreted variously as a parable about death, "The Establishment," the assimilated Jewish artist, betrayals, relationships with women, relationships between parents and children, and as a study of political or emotional violence. As a play dealing with that same faceless menace stalking through the tragicomedy of Beckett and Ionesco, *The Birthday Party* is at one and the same time "all of the above" and "none of the above."

Like all Harold Pinter's early plays, *The Birthday Party* is built upon a pattern of arrival and departure, in which someone who thinks (or hopes) himself to be secure loses his place of safety, is "cast out" by mysterious intruders whose arrival seems menacing and whose departure completes the action of the play. Stanley Webber, lodger at Meg and Petey's bed and breakfast in an unidentified seaside town, suddenly changes his manner when Meg mentions that "two gentlemen" will be coming to stay for a couple of nights. All the hilarious banter and teasing that opened the play (Stanley's calling the stale breakfast "succulent" and Meg's inane flirtatious misunderstanding, "You shouldn't say that word to a married woman") gives way to some unspecified dread. Stanley goes through a series of ploys to stave off the threatening arrival: first, denial ("I don't believe it"); then logic ("Why didn't they come last night, if they were coming?"); assertion of superiority ("I once gave a concert . . . They were all there that night"); and finally temporary displacement of his fear onto another, as he becomes the aggressor, Meg his victim. In a terse exchange he drives the foolish 60-year-old woman into breathless terror: his question ("Have you heard the latest?") and his points of information ("They're coming today," They're coming in a van," "They've got a wheelbarrow in that van") are punctuated by her breathless monosyllabic replies ("No," "Who?" "What?") culminating in his menacing assertion that "They're looking for someone" and her horrified denial. Neither Stanley's earlier fear nor the fear he generates in Meg is explained, but the audience sees that the characters themselves understand the source of their own terror and, without knowing specifically why, finds the play's hilarity darkened.

Although this sense of impending menace builds throughout the play, it is regularly interrupted by some other mood. For example, in Act II, as Stanley and McCann circle each other after Stan has kicked Goldberg in the stomach, Meg enters in her evening dress, playing the drum she had earlier given Stan for his birthday; serious violence is quickly replaced by silliness. But then, resuming in the game of blind man's buff, menace seems even more pervasive, more inescapable than before.

Each of the three acts ends with a particularly violent moment. Act I, in which the fearful visitors arrive, ends with Stanley beating his toy drum in a frenzy, "savage and possessed." Act II, in which the birthday party itself occurs, ends with Stanley trying to strangle Meg and assault LuLu. Act III, in which Stanley is reduced to blind, speechless submission, ends with the most fearful event of all: a violence so effective that it is quiet, Stanley taken passively from his place of refuge, Petey afraid to object, Meg utterly unable to see that anything untoward has happened. "They" have indeed come, "looking for someone," found him, and taken him away—as Stanley and even Meg knew they would.

Everyone in the play knows what is going on. And so does the audience. Pinter, like Beckett in *Waiting for Godot*, is writing in that distinctive 20th-century genre, tragicomedy: aptly characterized by Alfonso Sastre as "that mysterious situation before which, horrified, we laugh." The mystery of the situation need not be solved: it is the dark presence Beckett's Krapp senses over his shoulder (*Krapp's Last Tape*), the meaningless meaning that maddens Ionesco's professor (*The Lesson*), the haunting threat that frightens so many of Pinter's other characters (as different as vulgar Rose in *The Room* and cultured Edward in *A Slight Ache*). *Not* knowing specifically, or not admitting, what this threat is constitutes part of the force of the horror, both for the characters in the play and for the audience witnessing the fear those characters feel while at the same time trying to push away any sense of its own fear. Coming to the theatre to be entertained, to *watch* the fate of others, the audience laughs at Meg's silliness, Stan's wit, McCann's parody of a tough guy, Goldberg's nostalgic memories; it puzzles over the word play (especially in the interrogation scenes) and the "symbolism" (such as Stanley's broken glasses), and feels the touch of vicarious horror which the various acts of violence produce. But this play double-crosses the audience by destroying its exempt status: the laughter that distances horror here becomes acknowledgement of recognition, of understanding. The control gained by intellectual activity ("Who are the two men? Where did Stanley come from?") is belied by the fact that the "mysterious situation" is both inexplicable and endlessly explicable. Pinter lets his audience witness Stanley's loss then, in the midst of laughter, makes them face their own, whatever nameless terror awaits each one: seaside resorts are not havens of endless safety, and neither is the theatre. *The Birthday Party* is "about" the opposite of what its title implies.

—Kristin Morrison

BLEAK HOUSE.
Novel by Charles Dickens, 1853.

Charles Dickens began *Bleak House* in November 1851, little more than a year after the completion of *David Copperfield*. As a serial it quickly became a considerable popular and commercial success: in a letter written on 8 May 1852 he described it as "a most enormous success, all the prestige of Copperfield (which was very great) falling upon it, and raising its circulation above all my other books." In the preface (dated August 1853) to the first edition in volume form, he declares, "I believe I have never had so many readers as in this book." In recent times it has been one of the most widely discussed of all Dickens's novels.

Technically, *Bleak House* represents a striking experiment that Dickens was never to repeat. In its predecessor, *David Copperfield*, he had used the first-person, autobiographical method; in the novel before that, *Dombey and Son*, the more traditional third-person mode of narrative. In *Bleak House* he combines these two methods, alternating between an anonymous and omniscient third-person narrator (as in the opening chapter) and the heroine, Esther Summerson, who, like Jane Eyre a few years earlier, tells her own story in the first person (as in chapter 3). Although they alternate irregularly, the novel as a whole is almost exactly equally divided between these two contrasting voices, and there is evidence in the manuscript that Dickens took particular pains to differentiate between them stylistically. To a large extent they introduce different characters and cover different areas of the narrative, though there is some overlap between their roles.

The novel opens in the November of an unspecified year (the story as a whole is vague, and even inconsistent, in matters of chronology): the scene is London, specifically Lincoln's Inn Hall, where the Lord Chancellor presides over the Court of Chancery, notorious at the time for its inefficiency and delays. It quickly becomes clear that the fog brilliantly evoked on the opening page is not just a piece of scene-painting but a powerful symbol for legal obfuscation and confusion. An important element of the plot is to turn upon a protracted law-suit concerning a disputed will; lawyers and hangers-on of the legal system are numerous among the characters, and, as T.W. Hill has noted, "the London scenes are nearly all within a half-mile radius of Chancery Lane."

Chancery was very much in the news when Dickens began his novel: John Butt has referred to "the interest which everyone was taking in chancery that year [1851]," and on the very first day of the year the *Times* had published a leading article on the subject. A Chancery Reform Association had been formed, and as early as 7 December 1850 Dickens had published in his own magazine *Household Words* an article "The Martyrs of Chancery," the title of which sums up a significant aspect of the novel. Chancery is, however, only one example of the topicality of this richly topical book, which touches the contemporary scene at many points. The following list is illustrative rather than exhaustive.

The philanthropic Mrs. Jellyby is a vehicle for Dickens's satire on idealistic schemes such as the disastrous Niger expedition of 1841—"telescopic philanthropy," in Dickens's phrase, because problems at home are ignored while the gaze is fixed on distant objectives. Jo the crossing-sweeper seems to be based on one George Ruby, a boy who gave evidence at the Guildhall in a case reported in Dickens's monthly supplement to *Household Words* in 1850. Inspector Bucket, who has been called the first detective in English fiction, is a member of a brand-new profession (the detective branch had been introduced only in the previous decade) and may be more particularly based on an acquaintance of Dickens's, Inspector

Charles Field, whom he had already depicted as "Inspector Wield" in articles in *Household Words*. Hortense, the lady's maid who becomes a murderess, owes something to Maria Manning, who, with her husband, was executed for murder in 1849 (Dickens attended the execution).

As these instances suggest, Dickens has incorporated many topical allusions within an imaginative design and social vision of great complexity. For contemporary readers there would have been many points at which the novel brought to mind something they had encountered in the newspapers, in a satirical magazine such as *Punch*, or within their own recent memories. John Butt, who in *Dickens at Work* has analysed the topicality of the novel in detail, declares that it "began as a tract for the times," but reminds us also that Dickens turned this mass of detail into an organic whole that has universal and lasting power. Its great theme is the inter-relatedness of all men and women: no matter what social level they occupy, what calling they pursue, or where they live, they are—or should be—"members one of another." Responsibility and its opposite, indifference, are two of the great motivating forces for the characters, Jarndyce and Woodcourt (for example) illustrating the former, Skimpole and Chadband the latter. The interweaving of plots and subplots dramatizes hidden connections, most obviously in the mystery of Esther's parentage. And the infectious disease (both a contemporary fact and a symbol) shows by its spreading from the slums to the middle-class world of Esther that social classes cannot be segregated as if they belonged to different species. With its incomparable mingling of satire, comedy, melodrama, and pathos, its memorable characters, and powerful sense of place, *Bleak House* is the work of a great novelist in mid-career and at the very height of his powers.

—Norman Page

THE BOOK OF COMMON PRAYER.
Liturgy, 1549, 1552, 1559, 1662.

Critical Studies: *English Prayer Books* by Stanley Morison, 1943, revised edition, 1945, 1949; *The Shape of the Liturgy* by G. Dix, 1945; *Notable Editions of the Prayer Book* by J.F. Gerrard, 1949; *The Booke of Common Prayer of the Church of England: Its Making and Revisions 1549–1661* by E.C. Ratcliff, 1949; *Our Literary Heritage and the Book of Common Prayer* by Kemp Malone, 1950; *The Language of the Book of Common Prayer* by S. Brook, 1965; *A History of Anglican Liturgy* by G.J. Cumming, 1969, revised edition, 1982; "Communion and Commonweal: The Book of Common Prayer" by John E. Booty, in *The Godly Kingdom of Tudor England* edited by Booty, 1981.

The Book of Common Prayer, the product of the English Reformation and the work mainly of Thomas Cranmer, has moulded the minds and language of generations of Englishmen until its current supersession by the mean and vulgar Alternative Services Book. It originated in a twofold need to correct English worship from the errors of Rome in the 16th century and at the same time to present that worship in the native rather than the Latin tongue.

As early as 1538 the Injuctions of that year had required every incumbent to read the Lord's Prayer, the Creed and the Ten Commandments in English so that their congregations might learn them by degrees, and in the same year the English Bible was set up in every church. By 1543 it was ordered that a chapter of the New Testament should be read at both Matins and Evensong, while a year later the Litany was commanded to be said in English.

With the accession of Edward VI (1547) a short form of service in English was inserted in the Latin Mass in 1548, and a year later the first English Prayer Book was produced. It was a compromise between the more extreme Reformers and the conservatives, prominent amongst whom was Bishop Stephen Gardiner, whose claim to be able to interpret the 1549 Book consonantly with Roman beliefs led to Cranmer's more radical Second Prayer Book (1552). This, however, had hardly come into use when the young Edward VI died and Mary succeeded and restored the Roman supremacy. Mary died in 1558 and Elizabeth imposed the 1559 settlement, largely but not exclusively restoring the 1552 Book.

As his statement "Concerning the Service of the Church" makes clear, Cranmer sought to simplify and bring uniformity into the structure and language of the liturgy. He conflated and reduced the several daily offices of the medieval church into the familiar forms of Morning and Evening Prayer, and into these services he introduced the regular cycle of the psalms and, more importantly, Bible reading. He wished to combine instruction with worship.

The most important changes, however, related to what the 1549 Book called "The Supper of the Lord and the Holy Communion, commonly called the Mass" because around this centred the principal controversies of the Reformation—whether Christ is actually present in the bread and wine, whether these are changed by the action of the priest, whether by themselves they are automatically effectual for anyone who partakes of them, whether the mass is a propitiatory sacrifice. All this Cranmer rejected, relying on the Reformation stress on the biblical doctrine of individual justification by faith. The service thus became not the sacrifice of a mass with the need for continual repetition but a communion of the people constantly reminded of what Christ had done for them, "(by His one oblation of Himself once offered) a full, perfect, and sufficient sacrifice, oblation, and satisfaction, for the sins of the whole world."

To achieve his aim Cranmer adapted and transformed the Latin mass, changing several ceremonies and details of priestly dress. Small but crucial changes of language were also introduced as, for example, in 1549 the supersession of the words of the Latin mass that the bread and wine "may be *made* unto us the Body and Blood" by "they may *be* unto us the Body and Blood." By 1552 Cranmer had gone further with such changes as replacing the first part of the present words of administration: "The body (blood) of our Lord Jesus Christ which was given (shed) for thee" with the second part "Take and eat (Drink) this in remembrance that Christ died (Christ's blood was shed) for thee . . ." There were many other changes in 1552, but these were the most important. The alterations of 1559 were not extensive, but they did include the combination of the two forms of administration mentioned above.

No less than its doctrines has the language of the Prayer Book unconsciously but deeply influenced the English character. In the careful structure particularly of Morning and Evening Prayer with its succession of penitence, praise, instruction, and prayer is to be found the well-known pattern of Cranmer's style with its balance and repetitions, its homely but vivid analogies and its simple but telling phrases to be found in such collects as those for Advent Sunday and Ash Wednesday but perhaps most memorably in the General

Confession in such sentences as "We have erred and strayed from thy ways like lost sheep" and "We have left undone those things which we ought to have done; And we have done those things which we ought not to have done."

It is little wonder that in the 1662 revision which has been used since that date there is little new and little altered from what Cranmer had produced a century before.

—Arthur Pollard

THE BOOK OF MARGERY KEMPE.
Prose by Margery Kempe (1373?–1440?), 1432–36(?).

Editions and Translations

The Book of Margery Kempe, edited by S.B. Meech and Hope Emily Allen. 1940.
The Book of Margery Kempe, translated by B.A. Windeatt, Jr. 1985.

Critical Studies: *The English Mystics*, 1927, and *The English Mystical Tradition*, 1961, both by David Knowles; *English Mystics of the Fourteenth Century* by T.W. Coleman, 1938; *Kempe, Genius and Mystic* by Katharine Cholmeley, 1947; *Kempe: An Example of the English Pastoral Tradition* by M. Thornton, 1960; *Middle English Prose Style: Kempe and Julian of Norwich* by Robert K. Stone, 1970; *On Julian of Norwich, and In Defence of Kempe* by E.I. Watkin, 1979; *The Middle English Mystics* by Wolfgang Riehle, 1981; *Mystic and Pilgrim: The Book and the World of Kempe* by Clarissa W. Atkinson, 1983; *Mysticism: Medieval and Modern* edited by Valerie M. Lagorio, 1986; "A Very Material Mysticism: The Medieval Mysticism of Kempe" by Sarah Beckwith, in *Medieval Literature* edited by David Aers, 1986; "*The Book of Margery Kempe*: The Marginal Woman's Quest for Literary Authority" by Karma Lochrie, in *Journal of Medieval and Renaissance Studies*, Spring 1986.

The Book of Margery Kempe exists in a single manuscript. It is written in a Norfolk dialect and dates from around the middle of the 15th century. The original work, of which the manuscript is a copy, was produced in the 1430's, and consists of Margery Kempe's account of her life and her religious experiences as she reported them to two separate scribes. The second of these was a priest who revised the work of the first, described as an Englishman living in Germany.

These details serve first to remind us of Margery's illiteracy which entailed that her female, somewhat subversive religious experiences should be mediated by a male priest, just as her knowledge of religious works was subject to similar controls. Secondly, they emphasise the close connection of Lynn, Margery's birthplace, with the Low Countries and with Germany. The account of her experiences, unique in English, is less surprising when placed within a continental tradition of female and lay mysticism, and is slanted to establish her as a mystic so that recollections of individual, specific events merge with accounts of the more conventional manifestations of spiritual feeling.

Margery, the daughter of John of Brunham, a mayor of Lynn, was born about 1373 (the year of the death of St. Bridget of Sweden, a saint whom she attempted to emulate) and married John Kempe around 1393. Although she had 14 children by him, and she describes him with some condescension as pleasant and easy and on the whole supportive in many of her numerous predicaments, bourgeois family life seems to have been a sphere in which she felt less than comfortable. Her first movement toward religion occurred during a breakdown after the difficult birth of her first child when she feared for her life, and the failure of the business enterprises she undertook further confirmed her in her spiritual pursuits. On what has been calculated as 23 June 1413 she induced her husband to join with her in a vow of chastity. In return she undertook to pay his debts.

Her religion as it is described in the book is affective, emotional, and public, and seems to have met with a mixed response from those who encountered it. Not surprisingly, perhaps, her "holy tears," her noisy transports of emotion during church services were not universally welcomed, and the loss of friends is a recurrent motif in the life. Also noticeable is the attempt to imbue events with miraculous significance, and an emphasis on visions in which Margery figures prominently as helpmeet to the Holy Family. The visions culminate in her account of her mystical marriage to the Godhead in the Apostles' Church in Rome which seems to have taken place in 1414.

Margery presents herself as a Wife of Bath figure in the early years of her conversion, obsessed with her finery and with the impression she made in church. To the reader, her fasting and the pure white garments she later adopted, supposedly in accordance with divine command, suggest perhaps a change in style rather than of heart. As one reads of her pilgrimages, more numerous and more adequately documented than those of the Wife, one has a sense of life imitating art. After her vow of chastity she describes journeys to the Holy Land and Italy, and to Compostella via Bristol. Her travels are full of incident as she is abused by her fellow pilgrims for preaching too much (they suggest that her husband should have governed her better), and finally left behind to make her own way along the pilgrim routes, supported by chance acquaintances she met on the way. In Rome she met St. Bridget's servant, and back in England was accused at Leicester of being a Lollard. Thereafter she and her husband had to travel to one ecclesiastical court after another—Beverley, York, Canterbury—in order to clear her name. In her sixties she accompanied her widowed daughter-in-law back to Germany and probably went to Aachen, another site of pilgrimage.

While one might question the status of the work as a religious document it provides a fascinating insight into the way in which religion was a means by which a powerful woman could create her own individual sphere of activity and achieve considerable freedom. That the theologically orthodox Margery should be accused of Lollardy illuminates the important role of women in such heterodox movements, as well as in such continental movements as the Via Moderna. Finally, Margery's travels, and the influence of continental writers on this unlearned woman remind us that in the later Middle Ages England was very much a part of Europe.

—Anne Samson

THE BOOK OF THE DUCHESS.
Poem by Geoffrey Chaucer, c. 1370.

The first and most moving of Geoffrey Chaucer's dream visions is an elegy for Blanche, Duchess of Lancaster, the first wife of John of Gaunt. Like other elegies, it confronts the difficulty of offering comfort in words. In doing so, it becomes an exploration of eloquence and its limits.

Rich to the point of bafflement in varied materials and contrasting tones, it is almost an anthology of poetry. Before falling asleep, the narrator reads Ovid's story of Ceyx and Alcione, the tale of a queen grieving at the death of her beloved husband. He dreams that he wakes in a room decorated with the *Roman de la Rose*, the most popular of all medieval love poems. The *Roman* contributes to the spring landscape, alive with birdsong, in which the dreamer finds an unnamed Man in Black, himself a poet. When first seen, this figure is sitting alone, reciting a desolate complaint against Death, who has taken his "lady swete." In the conversation that follows, he amplifies the lyric, running through a repertory of poetical set-pieces: a series of antitheses in the form "My song is turned to pleynynge, / And al my laughter to wepynge," an allegory about playing chess with Fortune who took his queen, a narrative account of wooing the fair lady White, a blazon of her beauty.

All this poetic activity is, in some ways, unsuccessful. Three times the Man in Black charges the dreamer with failure to understand. Frustration leads to trying new ways of communicating what he has lost. Wooing the lady, too, was at first a series of failures; he describes three attempts to persuade her of his true and faithful love before she granted him the gift of her mercy.

By casting the elegy as a dream vision, Chaucer tactfully solves the problem of how to address consolation to John of Gaunt. As the Man in Black, it is the bereaved husband who praises Blanche and mourns her death. The free associations and fluid transitions of dream experience have other advantages. Apparently haphazard, full of comedy as well as grief, the poem is nonetheless firmly and subtly constructed.

Allusions to French poems which a courtly audience would instantly recognize permeate the dream vision, and Chaucer's most economical effects depend on recognizing how he alters his sources. In the *Jugement dou roy de Behaigne*, by Guillaume de Machaut, a lady whose beloved is dead and a knight whose lady is unfaithful compete in unhappiness. Both tell autobiographical stories of love and loss; the king of Bohemia, who resolves the debate, rules that suffering from love scorned or betrayed is worse than the sorrow of death. Implied in *The Book of the Duchess* is such a contrast between the melancholy of the narrator, who hints at unrequited love, and that of the Man in Black, who recalls delighted reciprocal affection. His opening lyric imitates the lament of Machaut's lady, but while her story is told chronologically, Chaucer organizes *The Book of the Duchess* so that it moves back in time to the first song composed by the lover during the period of courtship. The first of the poems within the poem concentrates on self-absorbed grief: "I have of sorwe so gret won / That joye gete I never non." The development of the narrative is a recovery of earlier joy; the second poem within the poem begins with the lines "Lord, hyt makesth myn herte lyght, / Whan I thenke on that swete wyght." The measure of his loss is the measure of that joyful perfection.

In *The Book of the Duchess* as in his later poetry, Chaucer works through indirection. He leaves for the reader the task of seeing the symmetries between the preliminary story of Ceyx and Alcione and that of the Man in Black and his fair White. A reader may be expected to remember that music, poetry, hunting, companionship, nature were all seen as remedies for melancholy. The aristocratic hunt which frames the conversation between the dreamer and the Man in Black is presented as part of a spring landscape; at the end, there is no need to stress the pun on hart and heart in "al was doon, / For that tyme, the hert-hunting."

—Kay Gilliland Stevenson

BRAVE NEW WORLD.
Novel by Aldous Huxley, 1932.

Aldous Huxley was fascinated throughout his career by the the idea of Utopia, the society in which change has settled down into a stasis of perfection. In his last novel, *Island*, he saw it as a benign perfection in a peaceful and ecologically aware society guided by mystics. But in his much better known *Brave New World*, published three decades before in 1932, he saw it as a malign society controlled by technocrats whose aim is complete happiness, but in whose hands happiness is equated with the total absence of freedom.

Brave New World is both a fantasy about the future and a satire on present trends. And in both roles it carries conviction because of the expert and convincing handling of detail to create a plausible world. It is England 600 years ahead, and Huxley has been wise enough not to change it beyond recognition. It is the country we know and a different world, and this paradox sustains our attention.

The society of the future is a parody of Plato's republic, with a small group of World Controllers ruling five castes of subjects, divided not merely socially but biologically, since they have been conditioned to their future tasks in the bottles where they were bred. To preserve happiness, the World Controllers discard everything that might provoke either thought or passion.

> The world's stable now [says Mustapha Mond, Controller for England]. People are happy; they get what they want, and they never want what they can't get. They're well off; they're safe; they're never ill; they're not afraid of death; they're blissfully ignorant of passion and old age; they're plagued with no mothers or fathers; they've got no wives, or children, or lovers to feel strongly about; they're so conditioned that they practically can't help behaving as they ought to behave.

There is no need for violent or overt repression. Men are so conditioned from the time the spermatazoon enters the egg in the Hatchery that there is little chance of their breaking into rebellion; if they do become discontented there are always drugs to waft them into the heavens of restorative illusion. Thus the Controllers are able to govern with a softly firm hand; the police use whiffs of anaesthetic instead of truncheons, and those over-brilliant individuals who do not fit the established pattern are allowed to indulge their heretical notions in the intellectual quarantine of exile.

The daily lives of the conditioned inhabitants of the brave new world are passed in a carefully regulated pattern of production and consumption. Since it was found that too much leisure created restlessness, scientists are discouraged from devising labour-saving inventions, and the working day is followed by gregarious pleasures so organised that elaborate machinery is needed and maximum consumption is encouraged. Complete freedom of sexual behaviour, plus the availability of drugs, provide release from all ordinary frustrations. The abolition of viviparous birth has made families and all other permanent attachments unnecessary; individuals have become merely cells, each occupying his special position in the carefully differentiated fabric of society.

All this would not make a novel of its own. Huxley brings it to life by showing the hidden perils of any attempt at a perfect society. The higher castes, the Alphas and Betas, cannot be as closely conditioned as the worker castes, because their tasks involve intelligence and the occasional need to use judgment, and even the best conditioning is not foolproof. So we get individualists like the stunted Bernard Marx who has a heretical longing for solitude, like Lenina Crowne who is inclined to remain too constant in her attachments, like Helmholtz Watson who secretly writes forbidden poems about the self instead of slogans for the state.

The crisis in the life of these three misfits is provoked by a journey into unfamiliarity. Bernard takes Lenina on a trip to the reservation for primitive people. There they discover a woman from their own society who was lost years ago and since then has lived and brought up a normally born child among the Indians. The young man—John—is not only a savage; he has also acquired a copy of Shakespeare, which, with the mixed heathen-Christian native cults, has enriched his language and shaped his outlook. In our sense he is far more "cultured," if not more "civilized," than the Utopians.

Bernard brings the savage back to London, where he creates a sensation by his baroque behavior and Elizabethan speech. On Bernard and Helmholtz he has the effect of crystallizing their sense of difference from society, while Lenina lapses into an old-fashioned attachment to the savage, who meanwhile has conceived a romantic attachment to her.

Bernard, Helmholtz, and the savage create a minor rebellion by interrupting a distribution of soma (a drug) to the workers. Bernard and Helmholtz are exiled to join those who have shown themselves unreliable (the real intellectual élite of the brave new world). The savage is forbidden to join them, because the Controllers wish to continue the experiment of subjecting him to "civilization." Since he cannot go home, the savage tries to hide out in the Surrey countryside, but Utopia's equivalent of newshounds discover him, and the fervent pleasure-seekers of the brave new world, hearing that he is flogging himself like a Mexican penitent, descend on him in their helicopters. Lenina is foremost among them. There is a great orgy in which he first whips and then possesses her. The next day, revolted by Utopia and his surrender to its seductions, he hangs himself. It is the savage who alone, since he is the only character conscious of the nature of tragedy, can embody the tragic possibilities of man's future.

—George Woodcock

BRIDESHEAD REVISITED.
Novel by Evelyn Waugh, 1945.

It is often said that Evelyn Waugh's novels fall into two groups, those up to *Put Out More Flags* (1942), and those from *Brideshead Revisited* (1945) onwards. In this division, the early novels are classified as "social satire," and the later ones are seen as more "serious," bleak expressions of despair at the state of postwar Britain. However, Waugh himself objected to this type of categorization, arguing that the society which he depicted in his early novels was too lacking in any fundamental values or beliefs to provide a satirist with the necessary fixed point of reference. There was, consequently, he argued, a continuity rather than a disjunction in his literary work; from beginning to end he was presenting a portrait of meaningless lives, of insulated coteries surrounded by a bigger world of horror and brutality, of the enormous gap between what is presented as romantic or heroic and the chaotic charade of muddle, accident and posturing which is the reality.

There are, clearly, elements of pure social comedy in *Brideshead Revisited*, especially in the accounts of the attempt to convert the barbarian Rex Mottram to Catholicism and of the cultured viciousness of the warfare between Charles Ryder and his father. Throughout, Waugh shows his intense awareness of social gradation and snobbery and of the cliquishness of English Catholics. All this is familiar Waugh territory from the earliest novels onwards. Yet, Waugh makes it clear that his purpose in this novel was intensely serious. As stated directly in a note on the inside flap of the dust jacket of the first edition and as echoed in the voice of the narrator ("My theme is memory, that winged host that soared about me . . .") his theme is no less than the creation of a modern *Paradise Lost*:

> . . . *Brideshead Revisited* is *not* meant to be funny. There are passages of buffoonery, but the general theme is at once romantic and eschatological. It is ambitious, perhaps intolerably presumptuous; nothing less than an attempt to trace the workings of the divine purpose in a pagan world. . . . I have given my hero . . . a hope, not, indeed, that anything but disaster lies ahead, but that the human spirit, redeemed, can survive all disasters.

The structure of the novel, a Prologue and Epilogue set in the midst of the aimless comfortless manoeuverings of troops during World War II, surrounding a retrospective, nostalgic look at the world of pre-war Britain, emphasises the bleakness of the world presented. The modern world is symbolised by Hooper who looks "scarcely human" and who inhabits a world which is as grey and colourless as the world of Winston Smith in *Nineteen Eighty-Four* and is in sharp contrast to the traditional, aristocratic world of Brideshead and the idyllically represented world of Oxford where "leaf and flower and bird and sun-lit stone and shadow seem all to proclaim the glory of God." Both the world of Brideshead and of Oxford have been irretrievably lost as the novel opens and all that is left to the narrator, Charles Ryder, is memory and a bitter acceptance that this has all been the divine purpose.

The first of the two sections, "Et in Arcadia Ego," makes clear that the beauty and joy which the young men experience, and their sense of escape from the oppression of family, are illusory. The central image is of the human skull resting in a bowl of roses which "bore the motto *Et in Arcadia ego*" inscribed on its forehead and which is perceived to be a truer reflection of the saliencies of existence than the opulent furnishings of Ryder's room. Throughout the text there are constant reminders of religion, "It was this cloistral hush which gave our laughter its resonance. . . ." It is clear that Ryder's attraction to Sebastian is not merely because Sebastian is the "forerunner" for Julia, but because, through

Sebastian and the dangerous "charm" of Brideshead and its inhabitants, Ryder will be drawn away from his agnosticism and led to acknowledge a divine purpose in the world and the way in which people, no matter how unwillingly and with no matter how much suffering, are foredoomed to respond to it ("In St Aldgate's I passed a crocodile of choir boys, in starched collars and peculiar caps . . . So through a world of piety I made my way to Sebastian").

The importance of the title of the second section, "A Twitch upon the Thread," is made clear by Cordelia:

> Anyhow, the family haven't been very constant, have they? There's him gone and Sebastian gone and Julia gone. But God won't let them go for long, you know. I wonder if you remember the story mummy read us . . . Father Brown said something like "I caught him" (the thief) "with an unseen hook and an invisible line which is long enough to let him wander to the ends of the world and still bring him back with a twitch upon the thread."

The second section details how Lord Marchmain is brought, despite his irregular life, to make a "good" death, how Sebastian, in spite of his attempts to escape "Mother Church," ends up as a kind of lay saint in a monastery in north Africa, and of how Julia, the most "pagan" of them all is made to relinquish her love for Ryder and her hope for a future with him because ultimately she needs God more than she needs Charles. "I can't shut myself out from His mercy. That is what it would mean; starting a life with you, without Him." She cannot, by divorcing Rex Mottram "set up a rival good to God's." In the end, then, the "twitch on the thread" brings them all back to God and, it is implied, brings also Charles, through loss and pain, to an awareness that he has found a "small red flame . . . burning anew among the old stones" of the *art nouveau* chapel at Brideshead.

The author's intention, then, is clear. The question that has constantly been asked, however, is whether it has been realized. Much depends on the reader experiencing the "charm" of the Marchmains and the importance to them of their Catholicism. Yet the primary spokespersons for Catholicism are the priggish, absurd, Brideshead, the nunlike Cordelia, and the destructive yet "saintly" Lady Marchmain. The "Divine Purpose" itself appears, in retrospect, to be a life-denying, joyless, and dehumanising force which destroys the individual and renders them, since much has been fore-ordained, incapable of a truly free choice. In many ways, then, the choices that are made do not seem compelling or even necessary and, for all the care that has been expended on imagery and allusion, the novel fails to cohere into a satisfactory whole.

—Anne Clune

BRIGHTON ROCK.
Novel by Graham Greene, 1938.

Before this novel, Graham Greene was known principally for his thrillers. In *Brighton Rock* Greene does not abandon the thriller formula but adds a new dimension: evil confronted by religious belief. Greene casts this religious element in terms of Catholic teaching. His focus, however, is not Catholicism, but rather the broader question of the importance of religious belief, or non-belief, in the life of his characters.

The plot of *Brighton Rock* centers around Pinkie Brown's murder of Hale, an informer who had betrayed Kite, the leader of a protection racket mob, to his rivals. Kite was murdered. After Hale's death the story follows the efforts of young Pinkie, now successor to the murdered Kite, to escape detection as the revenge killer. A part of his strategy is to marry Rose, a young waitress. Pinkie despises this plain girl, but marries her because a wife cannot testify against her husband. Rose is flattered by the attentions of this boy who has something of a reputation as being "in the know." The religious conflict is set up because both Pinkie and Rose have been raised as Catholics. Pinkie, ambitious to achieve the luxury and voluptuous life style of Colleoni, a rival protection racketeer, has rejected his Catholic teaching. Rose, on the other hand, has kept her faith, and feels deeply the teaching of the church about salvation and damnation. She becomes increasingly aware of Pinkie's guilt and evil but holds to her belief that no matter what he has done he can be saved through confession and repentance. She gets little response, however, from Pinkie, who says that confession and repentance are important only when you're dying: "Just call a priest."

The main theme of *Brighton Rock* is the implacable opposition of good and evil. Greene puts this opposition in terms of allegory with Rose as absolute goodness in conflict with Pinkie as absolute evil. Further, he casts the conflict in mythic terms. Pinkie has the "ageless eyes of evil, the eyes which had never been young stared with grey contempt into the eyes which had only just begun to learn a thing or two." Pinkie's cold, calculating evil is described as reptilian, an allusion to the serpent in the Garden of Eden. This immature adolescent presented as an emissary of Satan—"credo in unum Satanum"—embraces "an essence he does not himself understand." Pinkie epitomizes evil as a malevolent force—as a fact of human existence.

One of the chilling things about Pinkie's evil is his ordinariness. His evil is all involved in achieving a grubby ambition and escaping the consequences of his trickery and bullying; it is based on greed and meanness of spirit. This ordinariness means that there is no escape from a continual confrontation with evil.

Pinkie is convinced that for his safety he must get rid of Rose, but his associate, Dallow, refuses to go along with any more killings. "But suppose she killed herself?" At first mention and out of context this seems a flaw in the writing. Who would even consider such an agreement, especially if one is a devout Catholic? But Greene has skillfully developed Rose's devotion to Pinkie: she holds to her hope that he can be reclaimed for the church. Acknowledging to herself that suicide would be a mortal sin, she does not openly refuse. She clings to her hope that some way out will be found. Greene's account of the struggle in Rose's mind as she and Pinkie drive to the cliff, where the pact is to be carried out, is a superb example of his skill in building suspense and tension.

Pinkie, of course, has no intention of abiding by his part of the pact. He is, nevertheless, destroyed by one of his own favorite instruments of cruel enforcement, vitriol, splashed into his eyes and face by the crash of a policeman's baton on the glass bottle. When, in agony, he runs over the edge of the cliff into the sea, the poetic justice is clear.

Pinkie is brought to this civil justice by his nemesis, Ida Arnold, who pursues him to his death. But this does not address the question posed by Greene regarding the conflict of good and evil. Ida represents a this-worldly judging of right and wrong. These are relative concepts set in a particular time and place—they are subject to change. But for Greene, good and evil are eternal cosmic forces in conflict, universal and unchanging, which finally focus on questions of salvation and damnation. Non-religious Ida does not know what a mortal sin is, but, convinced that she knows the difference between right and wrong, she pursues Pinkie relentlessly. However, in *Brighton Rock* Greene is underscoring the religious view of evil: the Fall and the concept of sin. Sin, unconfessed and unrepented, leads to damnation. And damnation goes far beyond civil justice.

The struggle between good and evil in this novel is not resolved. Even after Pinkie's death, Rose still has much of his evil to face. She will never be able to forget his urging of the suicide pact, and she has yet to hear Pinkie's vicious recording made on their wedding day where his deep hatred of her is poured out. Also she is tormented by the uncertainty of Pinkie's state of grace. On her way back from Pinkie's funeral Rose stops for consolation from her priest. She declares that Pinkie was a Catholic and knew what he was doing, so he must have died in mortal sin. The priest points to the teaching of the church that salvation is possible even at the very last moment. In explaining this he says, "You can't conceive, my child, nor can I, nor anyone . . . the appalling . . . strangeness of the mercy of God." The priest offers this in the hope of quieting the tormenting uncertainty in Rose's mind about the damnation of Pinkie. But it fails. Rose is left without the intended consolation.

—Paul H. Robb

THE BROWNING VERSION.
Play by Terence Rattigan, 1948.

This beautifully crafted short play was later filmed, with fine performances from Michael Redgrave as Andrew Crocker-Harris and Jean Kent as his frustrated and angry wife. The subtle manipulation of our sympathies was lost, however, in the filmed version, which extended the original script and sentimentalised it. Millie Crocker-Harris says, of the young man who is to take her husband's place, "Still, I bet when he leaves this place it won't be without a pension. It'll be roses, roses all the way, and tears and cheers and goodbye, Mr. Chips." She is telling her husband that he is no Mr. Chips, but the film, unable to tolerate the play's truthful, downbeat ending, turns him into just that, although such an ending goes against the grain of this poignant little drama.

The Browning Version recounts the serial humiliations of the retiring "Crock" (the name is no accident), once a brilliant classical scholar, but a failure as a teacher. He is leaving his post for health reasons and going to a less well-paid job in a school of inferior standing. It is implied that this job will be less taxing, though why should it be? The subtext is that Crocker-Harris is being pushed out as ineffectual. Unlike a popular master who left after being injured playing rugby against the school, he is to receive no pension. The rules had been broken for the rugger-player, but the governors refuse to make an exception for him.

Those who have seen the film will not quickly forget Jean Kent's desperate question as to this pension: "Do we get it?" she hisses through clenched teeth. Equally unforgettable is her look, on receiving the negative reply, of baffled rage and disappointment, or her smirk as she mentions her uncle, "Sir William Bartop, you know."

Millie despises her husband and we learn she is unfaithful to him. Her current lover, Frank Hunter, seeing the contemptuous way she tells her husband what she sees as home truths when she is actually making malicious attacks, abandons her. It emerges that it was Millie who seduced Frank and that though she is passionately obsessed with him, he has never loved her at all. Eventually we learn, in a delicately modulated series of revelations, that Andrew knows, that he has always known of her lovers over the years because with all her faults she never lies, and that the sexual failure has been Andrew's. Although the initial love between the couple has turned to "bitter hatred," he forbears reproach and defends himself merely with self-defensive irony and scrupulous courtesy.

The climax of his misery is discovering his own nickname: "the Himmler of the lower fifth." This wounds him deeply because, unlike his wife's adulteries, he was unaware of it.

The hypocritical headmaster asks him to make his retirement speech earlier than that of a popular master who is also leaving, and Crocker-Harris agrees. He unburdens himself to Frank Hunter, the lover who has rejected Millie and who is clumsily trying to become matey with the man he has cuckolded. Crocker-Harris's choice of confidant is a measure of his desperation.

"The Crock's" self-respect is restored, however, by a gift from a pupil, the Robert Browning translation of Aeschylus's drama of adultery followed by murder, the *Agamemnon*. The pupil, Taplow, is giving up classics for science. (The science master says, "We get all the slackers," for in those days the best students were expected to do classics and the weaker ones to make do with science.) But Taplow has shown, by his own inventive approach to translation, that he is sensitive and imaginative. We feel he is a loss to the classical forms. Crocker-Harris breaks down at this unaccustomed kindness and despises himself for letting slip his careful control. But this small love-offering restores some of his battered self-respect and encourages the worm to turn: he announces to the headmaster that he will not, after all, allow himself to be manoeuvred: he doesn't care if his valediction is going to be an anti-climax. The play ends with the Crocker-Harrises sitting down at table together, having decided to separate.

The tacked-on ending of the film which showed him giving an emotional speech, cheered to the echo by the boys who loved him really, was a desecration of a play which explores, with tight dry irony, character and motivation, in a domestic tragedy of adultery which parallels the *Agamemnon* but whose outcome is less bloody.

—Valerie Grosvenor Myer

THE BRUCE.
See the Writers entry on **BARBOUR, John**.

BRUT.
Prose, c. 1400.

Edition

Brut; or, The Chronicles of England, edited by F.W.D. Brie. 2 vols., 1906–08.

Critical Studies: *English Historical Literature in the Fifteenth Century* by C.L. Kingsford, 1913; *Populäre Englische Chroniken des 15. Jahrhunderts* by F.-J. Starke, 1935; *Historical Writing in England* by Antonia Gransden, vol. 2, 1982.

The *Brut* is a long chronicle which tells the story of Britain from its founding and its conquest by Brutus ("a wonder fair man, and a strong, and a huge of his age, and of glad cheer and semblaunt, and . . . wel beloved among his people"), the descendant of Aeneas. The account up to 1333 was translated (anonymously, probably c. 1400) from a version of the Anglo-Norman *Brut*, which was based on Geoffrey of Monmouth's 12th-century *Historia Regum Britanniae*; a series of continuations carries the story on to 1461. It was immensely popular, surviving in over 160 manuscripts, was printed by Caxton (1480) and by his successors; as the first printed history of England it influenced later chroniclers and indeed the whole view of the English past in the later 15th and the 16th centuries.

It is not only an important source for our knowledge of events in the later Middle Ages, but is also a work of some literary significance. The style is usually direct, and sometimes vivid: "the Scots had that day no more foison ne might against the Englishmen than twenty sheep should have against five wolves." And there are little anecdotes (a number of which provide material for later history plays): Henry IV smitten down by infirmity just as he hoped to set forth on his expedition to the Holy Land, and asking his chamberlain what he called the chamber in which he was lying, and at the answer "Jerusalem," recalling the prohecy which said that he should die in Jerusalem. One version has an elaborate account of the misspent youth of the Prince of Wales who "intended greatly to riot, and drew to wild company," and of his subsequent conversion and dismissal of his companions. And we have the French ambassadors bringing their present of tennis balls for the young king Henry V. The great "gunstones" that the king causes to be made come into their own when he besieges Harfleur: there "he played at tennis" with those inside the town; "when they should [=had to] play, they sang 'weilaway' and 'allas' that any such tennis-balls were made, and cursed all those that war began, and the time that they were born." The rhythmical movement of this sentence, and the hints of rhyme, indicate that here the chronicle is using one of the ballads or poems in circulation which celebrated this victorious campaign. This is done elsewhere in descriptions of battles and sieges, like those of Rouen (where in some manuscripts the whole poem, attributed to one John Page, is quoted) or of Calais in 1436.

The events of Henry V's reign are described with considerable vigour and dramatic imagination. At Agincourt, when the king sees "the multitude and number of his enemies," "with a meek heart and a good spirit" he lifted up his hands in prayer to God; he encourages his army to make ready "for he would rather be dead that day in battle or in field than be taken of his enemies; for he would never put the realm of England to no ransom for his person," and he gives instructions for the soldiers to take a wooden stake, and sharpen it at both ends so that it can be put in the ground "aslope" to prevent the French "over-riding" them (meanwhile the French are lighting many great fires, making "much revel with hunting," and gambling on the next day's proceeds). Like the poems on the battle, the chronicle makes good use of direct speech. In the morning the king asks what time of day it is, and he is told that it is prime, he speaks to his men: "'Then,' said our king, 'now is good time, for all England prayeth for us; and therefore be of good cheer, and let us go to our journey [= day's work].' And then he said with an high voice: 'In the name of Almighty God and Saint George, avaunt banner! and Saint George, this day thyn help!'" It does not have Shakespeare's eloquence, but the spirit is very similar. And there are accounts of domestic matters: the doings of "Lollards and false traitors," and the rebellion of Sir John Oldcastle; the public penance of Eleanor Cobham, accused of witchcraft; storms and bad weather, like the great frost of 1436–37 which "grieved the people wonder sore; and much people died in that time, for cold and for scarcity of wood and coal. And tender herbs were slain with this frost." The *Brut* deserved its popularity.

—Douglas Gray

BUSSY D'AMBOIS.
Play by George Chapman, 1604.

George Chapman's tragic masterpiece, *Bussy D'Ambois*, has had the most successful stage history of any of his plays. The plot is based on the actual career of an historical figure, Louis de Clermont d'Amboise, Seigneur de Bussy, a flamboyant soldier and courtier in the time of Henri III of France. Chapman's depiction of Bussy is influenced by the Marlovian hero, an ambitious, aspiring virtual superman whose heroic achievements end in ultimate tragedy. Bussy's ambition, however, is neither for military nor intellectual prowess but rather for total excellence and independence. He does not seek to master all knowledge, like Doctor Faustus, nor does he seek to conquer the world, like Tamburlaine, but he seeks instead to achieve complete self-sufficiency through his own physical and moral superiority. It is Bussy's tragedy that he lives in a world where the complex forces of politics, the inescapable authority of the monarch, and the unruly passions of other individuals all conspire to destroy his self-image. Bussy asserts his individualistic credo before the King who is dismayed by the violent and adulterous activities of this brash new courtier: "Who to himself is law, no law doth need, / Offends no law, and is a king indeed." These stirring words appeal to audiences and readers but in the world of political reality they can only eventuate in the downfall of the speaker.

Chapman's strong poetic line in this play is by no means limited to the speeches of its fiery hero. The dialogue is rich in both imagery and idea. Many of the images associated with Bussy, although spoken by others, relate to fire and stars. Candles and meteors flame in the dark, and the ghost appears as a "sudden flash." The eulogy for Bussy at the end of the play foresees his future in the heavens: "Look up and see thy spirit made a star." Bussy's own dying words draw on the same image but turned to stress the tragic loss, for he sees himself as "a falling star, / That silently glanc'd, that like a thunderbolt / Look'd to have struck and shook the firmament."

Along with the imagery, the rhetoric of idea is also strong in the play. Many speeches deal with philosophical issues, such as fate and free will, the nature of human destiny, the role of authority in human society, and the purpose of Nature. Throughout many of these set speeches, often spoken out of character, a strain of pessimism dominates. Monsieur, a Machiavellian villain, voices a negative view of Nature. Being spoken by a villain, the words are suspect, but they are so forcefully expressed as to have an impact, and as a set speech, they are not specifically related to the actions of the moment.

> Now shall we see that Nature hath no end
> In her great works responsive to their worths;
> That she, that makes so many eyes and souls
> To see and foresee, is stark blind herself.

Supremely pessimistic is Bussy's summary comment on life. Unable to accept the fact of his own impending death, when he is mortally wounded, he laments the dependence of supposedly divine spirit on mere flesh. Since he must die, "let my death / Define life nothing but a courtier's breath. / Nothing is made of nought, of all things made, / Their abstract being a dream but of a shade."

In spite of the gloomy mood of the play, however, there is much in the way of sensational action to make it lively. There are scenes of torture and murder, a warning ghost, and an especially spectacular invocation and appearance of a devil. Although Bussy dominates the play, it is not merely by poetry and rhetoric. In an early scene he single-handedly kills three courtiers in a duel (actually reported, not staged), he arranges an affair with a married Countess, meeting her by following a secret passage in the dead of night, and he engages in the summoning up of a devil.

The sense of tragedy is real, for Bussy's death, although inevitable, evokes pity and fear. His death confirms his bleak view of human nature: "Man is a torch borne in the wind; a dream / But of a shadow, summ'd with all his substance."

The sequel, *The Revenge of Bussy D'Ambois*, is a highly original work but not nearly so effective as a tragic drama. The hero of this play is Clermont, the brother of Bussy, who is called upon by the ghost of the latter to seek revenge for his death. Clermont is an entirely different personality. Not at all the swashbuckling, defiant, individualistic courtier, Clermont is a stoic, a quietly philosophical man who has no interest in worldly power. Throughout the play his patience, poise, and nobility make him a striking contrast to his brother, a passionate adventurer.

In this play Chapman is rejecting the conventions of the popular revenge play. Clermont accepts the ghost's charge with reluctance and displays no eagerness to accomplish the deed. When he finally confronts his brother's murderer, he forces him to fight but rather than killing him strikes him down, then forgives him. His rejection of blood revenge is Chapman's protest against the conventional image of the revenger. Furthermore, whereas the usual stage avenger died as a result of the intrigue involved in planning the revenge, Clermont dies by choice as a matter of stoic principle. Shortly after his generous forgiveness of the man responsible for his brother's death, he learns that his close friend and patron, the Duke of Guise, has been slain at the King's command. Rather than stay alive in a world where such atrocities take place, Clermont chooses to commit suicide.

Chapman thought highly of this play, as it embodies his own ideal of the Senecan stoical hero. The language is lofty, with many long philosophical and ethical speeches, often out of character. Unlike its predecessor, however, *The Revenge of Bussy D'Ambois* does not have much theatrical appeal. Not only does the play lack sensational scenes, there is essentially no action at all, not even on the psychological level. Clermont is already an idealized figure in his author's view so that there is no need to portray him as either developing or experiencing inner conflict. The elegant language is for the most part static. This play represents Chapman as the inspired student of classical philosophy rather than as a theatrically motivated dramatist.

—Charlotte Spivack

C

CAEDMON'S HYMN.
Poem, c. 657–80.

Editions and Translations

The Caedmon Poems, translated by C.W. Kennedy. 1916.
The Manuscripts of Caedmon's Hymn and Bede's Death Song, edited by E. van K. Dobbie. 1937.

Critical Studies: "The Poetry of Caedmon" by C.L. Wrenn, in *Essential Articles for the Study of Old English Poetry* edited by J.B. Bessinger and S.J. Kahrl, 1968; "Orality and the Developing Text of Caedmon's *Hymn*" by Katherine O'Brien O'Keefe, in *Speculum*, January 1987.

Caedmon's *Hymn*, well-crafted as it is, owes its fame and significance more to the circumstances of its composition and to its position in the English canon than to intrinsic merit. Dating from the mid-7th century, the verse appears in an unprecedented (except for Bede's Death Song) 17 manuscripts, two of them the oldest Anglo-Saxon records in existence, and in all versions of Bede's *Ecclesiastical History of the English People*. This song of the Creation, supposedly of miraculous making, is believed to be the first example of Old English Christian poetry; indeed, with the possible exception of a few charms and *Widsith* fragments, it represents the earliest extant Anglo-Saxon literature.

Just as the *Ecclesiastical History* alone preserves the text of Caedmon's *Hymn*, so does Bede offer the only account of its author and composition. Caedmon, he tells us, was an uneducated herdsman in an abbey's employ, so unskilled in song that he fled the meadhall whenever the communal harp neared him. On one such occasion, he retired to the stables, fell asleep, and dreamed of a strange man who commanded, "Caedmon, sing me something!" He replied that he could not. The admonition repeated, along with the suggestion to "sing the beginning of creatures," Caedmon composed the hymn, which he remembered upon waking. He took his story to the abbess and thereafter proved able to render in song any religious tale told him. He later became a monk and, apparently, a celebrated poet, although the *Hymn* is the only work which can be attributed to him with any confidence.

Bede's account is suspect, not only on the basis of its many analogues in both English and continental literature, but also on that of the poem's formal excellence. The author may indeed have been illiterate, but Caedmon's *Hymn* betrays a familiarity with and an expertise in most conventions of the Old English poetic. Its alliterative and stress patterns are remarkably regular; in only nine lines it offers seven different appellations for the deity, admirably illustrating the Anglo-Saxon technique of emphasizing a major idea by restating it with controlled lexical variation. Most impressive, however, is Caedmon's adaptation of his culture's heroic archetypes to his Christian theme. God, cast in the mould of the ideal earthly ruler, is "glorious" and "mighty" and acts as the guardian of his realm (*heofon-rices weard*, "Heaven-kingdom's ward") and the protector of his people (*mann-cynnes weard*, "mankind's ward"). Accordingly, the poem evinces in the creation of heaven and earth the construction of a meadhall for warrior-dependents:

He aerest scop   ielda bearnum
heofan to hrofe   halig scieppend
þa middan-geard   mann-cynnes weard
ece dryhten   aefter teode
firum foldan . . .

(He first shaped   for the children of men
heaven as a roof,   holy shaper,
then middle-earth   mankind's ward,
eternal Lord,   after created
earth for men . . .)

Moreover, in creating his hymn, Caedmon casts himself as God's *scop*, the king's poet whose first responsibility lies in "praising" the "might" and "works" of his patron.

This expression of Christian concepts in heroic terms and in alliterative verse is believed to be the first attempt to do so in Anglo-Saxon literature and lays the foundation for what we now term the "Caedmonian school." The poem, however, exhibits other noteworthy features. The story of its composition, although not the verse itself, foreshadows the dream vision genre of late Anglo-Saxon and medieval times (e.g., *The Dream of the Rood*, *Pearl*, and Chaucer's *The Book of the Duchess* and *The House of Fame*), and, possibly, suggests an early classical influence on the native tradition. More interesting evidence for this conclusion is to be found in the poem's suggestion of stanzaic form. The most commonly accepted division is succinctly expressed by John C. Pope, in his introductory *Seven Old English Poems* (1981):

> The first four lines, celebrating God's divine powers and the unspecified wonders of the Creation, introduce him as the guardian of the heavenly kingdom. The next four direct attention to his care for the human race and call him the guardian of mankind. The two sets of four are marked and balanced by the one repeated epithet, *ece Dryhten*, in lines 4 and 8. The ninth line partly offsets this symmetry because it is technically a mere variation of the statement in lines 7 and 8 and to this extent differentiates the second part from the first. But the closing epithet, *Frea aelmihtig*, harks back to the magnificence of God as he is described in the first section.

It is, however, possible to observe a different stanzaic pattern, one which matches the content equally well and which in addition takes into account other formal patterns. Only three lines (1, 5, and 7) begin on an unstressed syllable, and each alliterates only twice. Moreover, this division coincides with the frequently noted progressive movement of the poem, for each of these lines contains a time marker which helps to define the content of its section. The first line immediately leads us into a present-tense celebration of God the Creator with "*Now* we shall praise . . ." This ends when line 5 relates that "He *first* shaped . . . heaven," evoking the earliest act of Creation and establishing the primacy of "heavens-kingdom" over "middle-earth." Finally, line 7 tells us that God "then" went on to create the world for men. The hierarchy of God-heaven/man-earth is, in the manner which Pope suggests, reconfirmed by the final reference to "God Almighty."

Among the multiplicity of manuscripts containing Caedmon's *Hymn* we find surprising textual consistency. Sources (in which the hymn appears in both the Northumbrian and West Saxon dialects) date from every century ranging from the 8th to the 15th and include both the original Latin and the Alfredian vernacular translation of Bede's work. Nonetheless, except for variant spelling and word forms, the sole difference between them lies in line 5b, where the manuscripts are almost evenly divided (nine vs. eight) between "children of earth" (*eordan*) and "children of men" (*ylda*). However, even this discrepancy is of little import in either the interpretation of the poem or the analysis of its stylistics, for neither the sense of God's protectorship, nor the alliteration, nor the stress pattern is disturbed.

The straightforward nature of Caedmon's *Hymn* offers meager grist for the interpretive mill and only slightly more to scholars of the language. Nevertheless, with the poet's tight control of formal conventions it remains a model for students of Anglo-Saxon literature, and this, combined with its primary position in English Christian poetry, secures it a place of double significance in the canon.

—Gwendolyn Morgan

CALEB WILLIAMS.
(*Things as They Are; or, The Adventures of Caleb Williams.*)
Novel by William Godwin, 1794.

William Godwin's *Things as They Are; or, The Adventures of Caleb Williams*—or *Caleb Williams* as it is generally called—has been hailed as the first real detective novel, and also as a precursor of the 20th-century novel of guilt and pursuit. Certainly at the time of its publication (1794), it made an extraordinary impression. As the later critic H.N. Brailsford once said, "it is the one great work of fiction in our language which owes its existence to the fruitful union of the revolutionary and the romantic movements. It spoke to its own day as Hugo's *Les Misérables* and Tolstoy's *Resurrection* did to later generations."

Caleb Williams spoke to its time partly because it was, among other things, a pioneer propaganda novel, and because it combined a kind of social realism, contained in its claim to present "Things as They Are," with a fashionable gothic preoccupation with the extravagant and the extreme.

Godwin wrote it after he had published his famous political treatise, *An Enquiry Concerning the Principles of Political Justice*, in 1793. *Political Justice*, with the attack on the very idea of government that made it the first great anarchist treatise, was received with equally wide praise and vituperation, and Godwin, who had already written some undistinguished and unsuccessful fictions, decided to take advantage of his notoriety to produce a novel embodying many of the ideas contained in his theoretical treatises. He wrote *Caleb Williams* quickly, in time to be published in 1794, when it became even more popular than *Political Justice*.

The principal theme of Caleb Williams, a theme which was repeated in all of Godwin's five later novels, is that of the crushing of the individual by the forces of organized society. In each novel we find in the central character a victim, often of physical coercion by his immediate neighbours and always of the legal and moral conventions of the society around him. His life is a flight in which he seeks a state of peace where he can escape the evils that prey upon men whenever "positive institution" rules in place of the natural law. He is the symbol of man frustrated by force and prejudice, and in his fate is portrayed that of mankind while it continues to live without reason. As Godwin put it in his preface to *Caleb Williams*, he proposed "to comprehend, as far as the progressive nature of a single story would allow, a general review of the modes of domestic and unrecorded despotism, by which man becomes the destroyer."

The plot of *Caleb Williams* is in itself simple in form, and the strength of the book is built up mostly in the detail with which Godwin depicts the injustices of human society.

A feud arises between two country gentlemen, Tyrrel, a coarse bully, and Falkland, a cultured man who had imbibed all the "poison of chivalry." Tyrrel humiliates Falkland in a quarrel, and is murdered by his rival who allows two innocent yeomen to be hanged in his place. Caleb Williams, Falkland's secretary, discovers his master's secret, and is kept silent by threats. Eventually he tries to escape from Falkland's service, but is caught and cleverly framed, so that he goes to prison on a capital charge of stealing jewellery that had been secreted among his possessions. After several attempts, he escapes and joins a gang of thieves, whose nobility of action is used admirably to accentuate the corruption of law-abiding society. He then flees to London, where he is detected and brought to trial, but his master, fearful of exposure, does not appear, and he is set free. His liberty is in fact an illusion, for wherever he goes his enemy's agents follow, stimulating the prejudices of the people among whom he lives, so that he becomes an outcast everywhere. Eventually, Williams is persecuted to the end of his endurance and resolves to expose his master. He and Falkland are brought face to face, and in a dramatic scene in which Caleb speaks with a sincerity that moves all beholders, Falkland, a dying man, confesses and praises his accuser.

Into this somewhat improbable story Godwin contrives to work all the principal ideas of *Political Justice*, and to expose all the major injustices of his day. He describes eloquently how the landlords in those times of the great enclosures were destroying the peasants. His indictment of the prison system was made all the more formidable by his personal indignation over the sufferings many of his fellow radicals underwent in England even while he was writing *Caleb Williams*. From these partial tyrannies he demonstrates the general tryanny by which the great in wealth and position enslave the minds and dwarf the lives of their weaker neighbours.

The plot and the characters are alike marred by the heavy didacticism of the novel, which helped to make it popular in the early 1790's but equally unpopular when the political climate changed and England moved into a highly conservative and reactionary period during the Napoleonic wars. It remained largely unread for a century and a half until, in the mid-20th century, it was recognized as an ancestor of both the political fiction of writers like Malraux, Orwell, and Silone that gained popularity during the 1930's and of the line of pursuit novels represented on one level by Kafka and on another by Graham Greene in which the structure of the gothic novel which Godwin had adapted was revived again.

—George Woodcock

THE CANTERBURY TALES.
Poetry and prose by Geoffrey Chaucer, written from c. 1387.

The Canterbury Tales by Geoffrey Chaucer, was—or were—mostly written between about 1387 and some time in the 1390's. It was his last work before his death in 1400, which is clearly foreseen in the conclusion (see Derek Brewer, *An Introduction to Chaucer*, 1984). The tales include romances, comic bawdy tales, religious tales of several sorts, and serious prose tracts. The whole is prefaced by *The General Prologue*. This is a series of character sketches of the tale-tellers, who are as varied as their tales, and are represented as 29 pilgrims about to set out from London to Canterbury. The tales fall into groups which are little dramas of their own. The variety of *The Canterbury Tales* forbids definitive summing up, or claims for overall thematic or structural unity, or for the attribution to the poet of any single point of view. Critical comment must base itself on this extraordinary openness, which yet allows for "closed" tales within the whole. Another paradox is the conjunction of a clear-flowing style, readily understood at the most literal narrative level, with an extraordinary depth of meaning and implication.

A principal source of the combination of so many apparently contradictory elements is the mixture in *The Canterbury Tales* of spoken and written styles, with the very different attitudes of mind which they imply.

The spoken, or oral, style, implies the poet's presence among a known group. It was still natural in Chaucer's day. He was close to the oral narrative tradition and imitates it in all his verse narratives. An oral style has marked characteristics based on the need to convey meaning clearly and immediately, usually to an audience familiar with traditional phrases and stories. It is "popular" and "warm." It uses formulas and set phrases, often becoming proverbial and sententious. It is repetitious, though with variation, and consequently verbose. It uses puns and jingles in wordplay, is extravagant in expression and exaggerates for effect. Characters and events are large and simple in outline. These characteristics mark traditional oral styles from the Bible and Homer to Shakespeare. They create clear strong effects of beauty, pathos, or farce, or solemnity, and allow them to be juxtaposed—witness the pathos and flippancy juxtaposed together in the account of Arcite's death in *The Knight's Tale* (I, 2743–2852; all references are to *The Riverside Chaucer*, 1987). The sententious commonplaces on death with which this passage concludes should be taken "straight," as true and appropriate, typical of the oral style, not ironical, for that would be pointless.

Yet Chaucer often *is* ironical, partly because his poetry is highly literate despite the many oral characteristics of his style. From his earliest works like *The Book of the Duchess* he had laid the oral style upon the foundation of other written texts. Literacy involves the assumption of a reader deprived of the author's presence, tone of voice, gestures. We are so used to this situation that we take it for granted and forget the implications. An author who expects to be *read* by a solitary reader rather than heard by a listening group has to build everything into his text, including himself and (in a sense) his audience, who are turned from a listening group to a solitary reader. The literate text is thus more fictional, more precise, more varied in vocabulary than the oral experience. Both writer and reader can turn the page back to refresh their memories. They can bind cause and effect more firmly together, because inconsistencies and inconsequence are more glaring on the written page. Greater realism is more possible for the writer, and more desired by the reader. Chaucer has orality and literacy deeply interwoven.

The oral and the literate aspects of Chaucer's genius were reinforced by the ubiquitous influence of rhetoric taught in schools. Rhetoric analyzes figures of speech so as to enable a writer to re-create them. Its origins were in the ancient Roman courts of law, to instruct a pleader how to combine emotion with logical argument, by the use of various patterns of words which could be labelled and taught. The use of such figures of speech could be mere trivial adornment and Chaucer, like Shakespeare, could mock the artificiality of rhetoric, but rhetoric encouraged variety and resourcefulness in the use of language and influenced Chaucer profoundly. It is part of his self-consciousness.

Rhetoric taught Chaucer how to vary his language from high to low, rich to plain, according to subject-matter and the effect he wishes to achieve. An example of high style occurs when he paradoxically praises Griselda's humility even when she was in her high estate:

> No wonder is, for in hire grete estaat
> Hire goost was evere in pleyn humylitee;
> No tendre mouth, noon herte delicaat,
> No pompe, no semblant of roialtee,
> But ful of pacient benyngnytee,
> Discreet and prideless, ay honurable,
> And to hire housebonde evere meke and stable,
> (IV, 925–31).

Contrast this with the occasion when Absolon in *The Miller's Tale* has given Alison the indescribable kiss: "Tehee! quod she, and clapte the wyndow to" (I, 3740). Chaucer's range is from magnificent to simple, learned to gross and plain, from smooth narrative to vivid jerky dialogue, from literate to oral.

He can be flippant, magnificent, pathetic by turns, but also curiously neutral or "toneless," leaving us to guess quite what he means, or how he means it. Thus he says of the Monk in *The General Prologue*, whom he is showing to be very unclerical and whom he treats with some irony, "And I seyde his opinion was good" (I, 183). What are we to make of this? More obviously playfully he says in *The Nun's Priest's Tale* "I kan noon harm of no womman divyne" (VII, 3266) where "divyne" may be an adjective "divine," still leaving the line ambiguous, or a verb "guess," equally ambiguous. But the style itself seems clear and simple, despite its depths. *The Canterbury Tales*, being stories, are based on a straightforward, easily understood narrative style, which allows room for description, dialogue, commentary, rhetorical adornment. The pace of narrative varies from leisurely description of splendid scenes, as in *The Knight's Tale*, to rapid farce, as at the end of *The Reeve's Tale*. Metaphor and simile are brief, and of the kind common to ordinary speech, often traditional, as in the "hot and cold" of love, or "cold care."

Chaucer's narrative style is often of that traditional kind called "paratactic." Many of his most telling episodes, serious or comic, are built on a series of phrases connected simply with "ands," such as the setting adrift of Constance after the murder of her husband (II, 438–45), or the hilarious fight in the bedroom in *The Reeve's Tale* (I, 4292–4307). Chaucer is not however in any way limited to the paratactic, oral style. He learnt to manage a long sentence, beautifully spaced out, the product of an intensely literate mind and much reading. The most famous example is the superb opening sentence of *The General Prologue*, with its swoop from the heavens to the earth. The ability to control long powerful sentences in verse is another part of Chaucer's greatness.

He developed metre by the same mixture of orality and literacy. He combines the stress-patterns of the spoken word with the precise syllable-counting and regulated stress of literacy. He had discovered the 10- (or 11-) syllable, five-stress line before he wrote *The Canterbury Tales*. The great breakthrough is in *The General Prologue* to *The Canterbury Tales* for which he uses the wonderfully flexible 10-syllable, five-stress couplet, with its moveable inner pause. In such narrative verse Chaucer remains unrivalled until Marlowe and Shakespeare. In *The Canterbury Tales*, he also uses other metres, sometimes in stanzaic form, with magnificent control. Chaucer's verse *must* be read as scanning regularly, though not monotonously, by sounding in many words the final *-e*, a relic in the language of earlier fuller inflections. Not to follow the scansion deprives the reader of the varied pleasures of the music of the verse.

Chaucer creates in his poems a strong sense of the activity of the storyteller. He personalises his storytelling, and gives us a vivid, though intermittent, sense of communication with a real person who is genial, sceptical, amusing, sometimes sentimental, capable of seeing several different points of view. He is inclined to characterise himself in a deferential, self-deprecatory way, though the humility is more apparent than real. Chaucer exploits the use of the self in his earlier poems as vigorously as his French master Machaut with a continuously developing subtlety and light self-mockery. In *The Canterbury Tales* he goes further. He still begins with himself, and after the springtime opening tells us that he met a mixed group of pilgrims, gathered at the Tabard Inn in Southwark to make their pilgrimage. He then in *The General Prologue* gives remarkable sketches of each person. Description of a person was a well-recognised formula in medieval rhetoric. Chaucer's originality and new depth is to describe them as seen by his own partly fictionalised self in the poem and to break up the formal description into arbitrary concrete detail. His apparently objective associative method is terse and realistic. He then weaves into the visual impression, with the same apparent casualness, various observations relating to the character's moral quality, activities, whole life.

How did he think of such a variety of persons? He could well have had in mind the descriptions of precedence given in courtesy books (which give social instruction) and which refer to descending social ranks, and which thus provide one frame. Another frame is the very ancient division of society into the three orders of Warriors, Clergy, Labourers, into which he inserted the new mercantile classes. For much actual detail he also used the traditional descriptions of the various classes of society in what is called Estates Satire (as described by Jill Mann in her classic study *Chaucer and Medieval Estates Satire*, 1973). A few of the characters, probably the Reeve, the Man of Law, the Shipman, for example, and certainly the Host of the Tabard Inn, were intended to be recognisable persons, drawn from life. It is a profound innovation that all the characters are described with reference to their functions, their work, though all, good or bad, are described as the very best of their kind.

Only the Knight, the Clerk, the Parson, and the Ploughman, with the Knight's son and yeoman, representing the ancient three orders, are portrayed with full approval, reflecting Chaucer's fundamentally traditionalist and courtly outlook. The rest, many of them clergy, are treated with varying degrees of satire. The elegant Prioress is lightly mocked. The Pardoner who exploits the simple with bogus relics, is described much more sarcastically.

The gallery of characters Chaucer creates in *The General Prologue*, including, beside those mentioned, others such as the irrepressible Wife of Bath, the coarse ebullient Miller, the drunken Cook, constitutes one of the most remarkable poems in English. The descriptions are amazingly fresh and direct, seeming effortlessly casual, yet under this bright surface is an extraordinary richness of implication explored by many critics and scholars. There is irony in the presentation of some characters, such as the unwarrantably worldly but still rather splendid Monk, but satire and irony coexist with a genial acceptance unusual in satirists.

Apart from characters and his own experience Chaucer had another great resource, the body of European traditional stories. There was a huge reservoir of stories, oral and written, of all kinds, whose patterns were often familiar. Characters could be fitted to, or invented for, favourite stories, which could be retold with a fresh slant. Before he started *The Canterbury Tales* Chaucer had already written the stories that became *The Knight's Tale* and *The Second Nun's Tale*, but there were many others, learned and popular, that he was drawn to tell again. The pleasure in a traditional story comes from knowing it already at least in type or outline, and then hearing or reading it in a new setting, perhaps with fresh characterisation, even a modified plot. What persists is the general underlying structure to which new circumstances are added. Chaucer had been particularly attracted to courtly romance, of which *The Knight's Tale*, based on a long poem, *Teseida*, by Boccaccio, is the grand example in *The Canterbury Tales*. He was also attracted to religious tales of devotion and of suffering bravely borne, usually in a courtly setting, of which *The Man of Law's Tale* of Constance, and *The Clerk's Tale* of Patient Griselda are examples. They are the religious equivalent of courtly secular romance. In every case he vastly enriched the earlier version he was working on.

As *The Canterbury Tales* developed he was further attracted to examples of the international comic tale. They were equally a courtly taste, for all their bawdiness. They show cunningly comic dirty tricks played on each other by the lower classes, bourgeois merchants or artisans, well-to-do village folk, and the like. They are not so much opposite as complementary to courtly romance. The juxtaposition in *The Canterbury Tales* of *The Knight's Tale*, *The Miller's Tale*, and *The Reeve's Tale*, all in one single group with *The General Prologue*, is the classic illustration of this complementarity of refined love with bawdy knockabout farce. Each tale appeals to the same audience with a typical "gothic" mixture of sentiment and comedy. Realism decorates fantasy. Learning and rhetoric deepen the simple oral narrative structure.

This first group is also an example of the progressive expansive movement of the general concept of *The Canterbury Tales*. Not even the portraits of *The General Prologue* are quite static, for their apparent arbitrariness makes them living and dynamic.

When the tales begin to be told, one tale answers another. The Miller's gives a provincial parody of chivalric love. The Miller's story, which mocks an old carpenter, provokes the Reeve, who is by original trade a carpenter, to tell an equally comic internationally known tale at the expense of a Miller. The character of the Miller in *The Reeve's Tale* is Chaucer's own adaptation of the central figure in the traditional tale, and the realistic Oxford and Cambridge settings of the

Miller's and *Reeve's Tales* are similarly Chaucer's own additions to plots which in other versions have quite different European settings.

The drama born of the clash and interplay of stories has only a touch of superficial characterisation here. The tales are not realistic dramatic monologues. We soon forget the tellers and enjoy the generally Chaucerian raciness and attitude. Chaucer went further, however, so that some later tales are clearly not merely in keeping with their tellers but have a point which arises out of the nature of the tellers. This is most clearly so with the Wife of Bath whose own character as given in *The General Prologue* grew under Chaucer's delighted contemplation. She is given a long monologue as prologue to her tale, defending women by making paradoxical use of the age-old tradition of clerical anti-feminism. This is a splendidly dramatic comic yet sympathetic monologue. The Pardoner's prologue is self-revelatory in a different way and equally comic, though in his case he is sharply satirised.

The drama of character is not consistent and should not be exaggerated. Chaucer uses a variety of methods. *The Canterbury Tales* itself seems to be on the move, as it were, yet the reader experienced in traditional literature is never at a loss to understand the level of meaning, and will not demand consistency and uniformity where none is meant or needed.

The underlying theme of the pilgrimage is an example of how Chaucer can raise or lower the reader's consciousness of a particular effect at suitable times. The pilgrimage is used as the fictional pretext for gathering the characters and stories together. Then the delightfully realistic vignettes of episodes of pure realism between some stories, with their references to real places, Rochester, Boughton-under-Blee, Bob-up-and-down, occasionally remind us of the journey, the time of day, and the interplay of character. These scenes are purely secular and there is no hint of allegory. But a pilgrimage is primarily a religious activity which offers a model not only for a person's secular life seen as a journey but also for the progress of the soul. In the prologue to *The Parson's Tale* the Parson sounds this note too: "To shewe yow the wey, in this viage / Of thilke parfit glorious pilgrymage / That highte Jerusalem celestial" (X, 49–41). It is a mistake to interpret the *whole* of *The Canterbury Tales* from this religious perspective. The religious dimension is shown here from a clerical point of view. It corresponds, as Derek Pearsall notes (in his excellent *The Canterbury Tales*, 1985) to the famous opening of *The General Prologue*, which from a more secular point of view evokes the springtime when all nature revives and people long to go on pilgrimage. Chaucer gives us the whole span of existence from Heaven to the mud on the road. But the religious idea of pilgrimage is not evoked in the rich intermediary series of tales between beginning and end.

Although the pilgrimage form of *The Canterbury Tales* should be recognised, and the realistic drama involving some of the tellers heightens the significance of the individual tales, Chaucer did not attach too much importance to any overall frame. If you do not like the story that is coming, he says in the prologue to *The Miller's Tale*, "Turne over the leef and chese another tale" (I, 3177). Here he is fully literate and thinking for the moment only of a varied collection of miscellaneous tales in a book. This particular remark is part of a jesting yet enigmatic refusal to take responsibility for the tale, typical of the traditional storyteller. The same passage also remarks on the obligation to report faithfully and literally what was said, which reflects the interests of literacy. Chaucer both declines moral responsibility and claims (ironically here, for sure) to be under another duty, that of accurate realistic reporting. The reader is still free—and it is very much a reader who is in mind. As usual an apparently simple passage, easy to understand, with an easy relationship between poet and reader, has subtle ambivalences and many implications.

Of the wealth of stories only a few examples can be given. Chivalric romance is the most typical of high secular medieval fiction. Its essence is a romantic love story, with exciting adventures, and a happy ending. It is focussed on that most interesting and vivid period of human life, adolescence, or, in medieval terms, young adulthood, and represents a kind of coming of age. It is set in idealised but realistic courtly surroundings. Chaucer seems impressed not only with the beauty of love but with its pain and pathos, with the problems of love, and with the consequent philosophical meditations.

In *The Knight's Tale* the underlying current of feeling is expressed by the dying Arcite, one of the two young men who love and fight for Emily: "What is this world? What asketh men to have? / Now with his love, now in his colde grave / Allone, withouten any compaignye" (I, 2777–9).

The poem has several extended passages of philosophical meditation, based on Boethius' *Consolation of Philosophy*, not much to modern taste, and superficial in some critic's eyes, but essential to deep appreciation of the variety of life portrayed. These are matched by some vigorous descriptions of a tournament and fighting, rare in Chaucer, who is not normally interested in fighting. There are also learned but vivid descriptions of the temples of the pagan gods. Chaucer presents the gods as rhetorically colourful portrayals of the planets which bear their names, Mars, Venus, and Saturn. The stars were thought to have real influence on human affairs, so there is an undercurrent of implied material causation of events, more subtle and complex than might seem at first reading. A modified optimism emerges from the structure of the tale in so far as the gentler of the two young warrior-heroes, Palamon, eventually wins the beloved Emily. The characters are stylised, but the narrative is richly varied, and *The Knight's Tale* would probably have been judged the winner of the competition in storytelling, had Chaucer pursued his original plan to the end.

The Franklin's Tale should be briefly noted here as nearer to romance than anything else. The story, called by the Franklin a "Breton lay" is set in the pagan past and concerns the rash promise, made by a beautiful woman anxious for her husband's safety in his absence, that she will "give her love," i.e., sleep with, a young squire, desperately in love with her, provided he can remove the rocks in the sea which threaten her husband's safe return. Although artificially set up, as in a folk-tale, the paradox has obvious roots in human feelings. Chaucer allows the various aspects of the dilemma to be worked out by a display of generosity by all three main characters and a fourth, a learned magician. The ultimate "message" is that it is dangerous to interfere with the course of nature, and that there are links between the natural and moral world which we do ill to disturb, as the heroine, Dorigen, for good, natural, but misconceived reasons, wishes to disturb. It is a tale of great moral perception and humanity, as well as a wealth of learning lightly carried.

The religious tales are similar to romance in portraying feeling, though of a different kind, and Chaucer had a special affinity for them. They are distinguished by the central position given to women and by what we may call women's values, faithfulness, gentle love, endurance of suffering. (Even the portrait of the Knight in *The General Prologue*, while commending his military virtues without irony, had emphasised his gentleness, courtesy, generosity.) So it is with the hero Troilus, in the earlier poem *Troilus and Criseyde*. These values, which conquer without aggressiveness, seem to be those that Chaucer most cherishes. Even *The Wife of*

Bath's Tale, another courtly folk-tale, essentially a romance, teaches with a touch of learning these "women's values."

The religious tales are virtually saints' lives, that baggy popular late-medieval genre, but Chaucer's are of immense superiority, being far more intellectual, artistic, and genuinely religious than the vast majority of actual saints' lives. They are *The Man of Law's Tale* of Constance, whose name reveals her special virtue, twice cast adrift at sea, the second time with her baby son; *The Clerk's Tale* of Griselda, the humble village girl whose patience triumphs over harsh testing by her husband, the Marquis. This is a profoundly Christian tale, which is nevertheless followed by a mocking, brilliantly versified epilogue in a characteristically Chaucerian shift of perspective. *The Pardoner's Tale*, which is preceded by the Pardoner's remarkable confessional prologue, is in essence another folk-tale, in this case of self-destructive deceit. *The Prioress's Tale* tells of a little Christian boy murdered by Jews in Syria (there were effectively no Jews in England in the 14th century). Here the pathos of the mother's suffering, most touchingly rendered, is matched by the cruelty of punishment imposed on the Jews and the miraculous triumph of the little martyr's celebration of the Mother of Christ. *The Monk's Tale*, a series of brief "tragedies," is stopped by the Knight as too gloomy, but has among narratives of the falls of great men the affecting story of the death of Hugelino of Pisa and his three sons in prison, adapted from Dante. *The Second Nun's Tale* (probably written a good deal earlier), is about Saint Cecilia. *The Parson's Tale* is not a tale at all, but a long prose meditation on Penitence. It is mainly a translation which rather heavily emphasises some of the Christian values which are implicit in all the tales. It leads naturally into the Retractions, in which Chaucer, in his own person, "revokes," that is, condemns, all his secular work, including those tales in *The Canterbury Tales* "that sownen [tend] into synne" (X, 1086), which has usually given critics some distress, but is not to be glossed over. Chaucer meant it seriously and thus provides yet another shift of perspective.

It is typical of Chaucer that the devotional tales of great beauty are matched by the same number of comic tales, some rather bawdy. Chaucer calls them "churls' tales," but they are part of the body of internationally popular medieval comic tales. *The Miller's* and *Reeve's* Tales have been mentioned. *The Shipman's Tale* is similar, told at the expense of a simple merchant. *The Merchant's Tale* with an ironical prologue has been found bitter by some, but is rather an example of wry, middle-aged, unillusioned humour characteristic of the medieval popular comic tale. Not all the comic tales are about sex, though all are told with brilliant rhetorical bravura. Friar and Summoner deride each other's professions. Most brilliant, perhaps, is *The Nun's Priest's Tale*, telling, with much digression, the fable of the cock and the fox. It is the tale where Chaucer most obviously plays with the self-contained "truth" of stories.

Very typical of Chaucer is the story he attributes to himself as one of the pilgrims. Within the fiction it is the worst tale of all, a silly, English chivalric romance in the old-fashioned jog-trot metre. Thus he mocks himself. Outside the fiction, in reality, it is a brilliantly comic genial burlesque of old-fashioned romance, and perhaps also of certain unfashionable Flemish knights. When stopped by the Host the pilgrim-Chaucer tells a long prose "tale," the *Melibee*, which is rather more a treatise than a tale, perfectly serious, on Chaucer's favourite values of forbearance and peacefulness. The juxtaposition of *Thopas* and *Melibee*, comedy and forbearance, self-mockery which nevertheless suggests, without arrogance, perfect self-awareness and an unabashed self-confidence, represents, though it by no means sums up, that rich variety of *The Canterbury Tales*, forever marked by Dryden's immortal phrase, "Here is God's plenty."

—Derek Brewer

CAPRICORNIA.
Novel by Xavier Herbert, 1938.

Capricornia is the major and best-known novel by the overtly "nationalistic" Australian novelist Xavier Herbert. When it was published in 1938 it represented a breakthrough in Australian writing. Much of the best Australian fiction of the present century has been done by authors like Patrick White, Randolph Stow, and Eleanor Dark who, though consciously Australian in attitudes and choice of material and theme, write for an extended public. They have normally published their books in London and do not feel in any way divorced from the main body of English fiction.

Herbert is in many ways the odd-man-out among Australian novelists, pursuing all his life a determinedly independent line. He never belonged to Australian literary circles, which are concentrated in the major cities, but wrote by choice in the remote outback. He claimed that writing for him was merely a sideline to a life of rugged outdoor activity, including learning to fly when he was over 50; and (though in fact a compulsive writer) perpetuated this image some years ago when he was interviewed on Australian television. Instead of appearing at the typewriter in the conventional book-lined study, he insisted on giving his interview running outdoors, the camera and recording equipment being mounted on the rear of a truck moving ahead of him. What the viewer experienced was an inexhaustible talker pounding along an empty outback road that stretched to a distant horizon. It would not suit the image of White or Stow but it captured the essential Xavier Herbert.

He was born in a small town in Western Australia, its inhabitants partly European, partly Aboriginal. He qualified as a pharmacist and moved to Melbourne to study medicine, but he gave up both ("my true study, I decided, was life") and the remainder of that life saw him in dozens of outdoor jobs all over Australia, many in the Northern Territory, which provided the scene for *Capricornia*. During these wander-years he wrote assiduously in local papers. In 1930 he sailed for London and there settled down to the first draft of *Capricornia*, said to be a million words. No London publisher would touch it, though Jonathan Cape was prepared to consider a shorter version, cutting out what was "offensively Australian." Herbert, disappointed, and sick of the "awful climate" returned to Australia in 1932.

It was to be six more years before *Capricornia* was published. There were complicated negotiations with various Sydney firms and much revision of the manuscript but the book finally came out in 1938. A single advance copy had been lodged for a competition for "the best novel published, or accepted for publication in Australia in 1937." It won the award, and other awards followed. There were five Australian editions in the following five years and a London edition in 1939.

Capricornia is a vast and sprawling novel. It has a cast of more than a hundred characters, introduced (as in a Dickens novel) by a list of its dramatis personae. It is packed with incident and violence; what "plot" it has is simply the sum of the lives of the people involved (Herbert called the novel, with heavy irony, a "botch"). Yet it has unity of impact. He portrays European man and his struggle to come to terms with a hostile environment, displacing a native race that had always accepted it. Herbert has an almost mystic feeling for what he calls "The Spirit of the Land," to which he is profoundly attached.

Certain characters in the novel stand out as clear symbols: the Shillingsworth brothers, one who accepts what is around him, one who flees it to become a nomad, and one who opts for civilisation "Down South"; above all the central character of Norman, son of one of the brothers and of an Aboriginal girl, who straddles uneasily the two worlds from which he is derived. The novel can be read at one level as propaganda; Herbert is savage on the relationships between white settlers and Aborigines. The whole book is eloquent and impressive, its writing reminiscent of the prose-poetry of Whitman.

—Ian A. Gordon

THE CASTLE OF INDOLENCE.
Poem by James Thomson, 1748.

The Scottish poet James Thomson won fame, a sinecure and a pension from the British government for his four-part meditative and descriptive poem in Miltonic blank verse, *The Seasons*, published in collected form in 1730. He settled comfortably into his villa at Richmond, in the Thames valley, enjoying a life-stlye that led William Hazlitt, in his *Lectures on the English Poets*, to observe that: "Thomson, the kind-hearted Thomson, was the most indolent of mortals and of poets." Though Hazlitt added: "But he was also one of the best both of mortals and of poets." *The Castle of Indolence* arose, according to Patrick Murdoch, Thomson's earliest biographer, as "little more than a few detached stanzas in the way of raillery on himself, and on some of his friends, who would reproach him with indolence, while he thought them at least as indolent as himself. But he very soon saw that the subject deserved to be treated more seriously, and in a form fitted to carrying one of the most important moral lessons."

In a letter to his friend William Paterson, dated April 1748, the poet wrote: "Now that I am prating of myself, know that, after fourteen or fifteen years, *The Castle of Indolence* comes abroad in a fortnight . . ."

Thomson probably began to work on the poem before he settled at Richmond in 1736 and worked at it during most of his stay there. The first quarto edition was followed in the same year by a second octavo edition, for which Thomson made some corrections. A few weeks later, the poet was dead.

The poem itself is couched in two Cantos, written in Spenserian stanzas within which Thomson makes a half-hearted attempt to introduce some archaic Spenserian words. Some, such as Moe for more, Ne for nor, Noyance for harm and the intrusion of the letter y, such as in Yborn, Ycleped and Ymotten, to gain an extra syllable, do not present the reader with halting problems. Others, such as Glaive (a sword), Losel (idle fellow), Prick'd (rode) and Transmewed (transformed), may drive him to a glossary. Thomson, a Roxburghshire son of the manse, was educated at Edinburgh University, and so also used a number of Scots words, including Certes (certainly), Atween (between), Lea (a meadow), Mell (mingle), Muchel—usually spelled Muckle—(much), Sicher (sure), and Stound (misfortune).

The first part of the poem both captures something of Spenser's manner and movement, but also achieves a lulling sense of drowsiness, echoed a century later by Tennyson's "The Lotus-Eaters." The first Canto, by far the more successful of the two, describes how the wizard Indolence entices weary passers-by, including some of Thomson's friends, into the Castle, with a sleepy song.

> Come ye, who still the cumbrous load of life
> Push hard up hill; but as the furthest steep
> You trust to gain, and put an end to strife,
> Down thunders back the stone with mighty sweep
> And hurls your labours to the valley deep,
> Forever vain: come . . .

Thomson does not precisely locate the Castle for us, but from the lulling sounds of an English high-Summer, no doubt it was not unlike his own Thames valley, where there:

> Was nought around but images of rest:
> Sleep-soothing groves, and quiet lawns between;
> And flowery beds that slumberous influence kest,
> From poppies breath'd; and beds of pleasant green,
> Where never yet was creeping creature seen.
> Meantime, unnumber'd glittering streamlets play'd
> And hurl'd everywhere their waters sheen;
> That, as they bicker'd through the sunny glade,
> Though restless still themselves, a lulling murmur made.

The inside of the Castle is also described, with flickers of wit that was apparently a feature of the poet's conversation.

> Soft quilts on quilts, on carpets carpets spread,
> And couches stretch around in seemly band;
> And endless pillows rise to prop the head;
> So that each room was one full-swelling bed.

Among the guests who have been identified from among Thomson's friends are the actor James Quin, referred to as "Esopus of the age," George Lyttelton, one-time secretary to the Prince of Wales and the owner of Hagley Park estate and who is said to have written a few lines of one of the stanzas, and the Reverend Patrick Murdoch, the "little, round, fat oily man of God." There is a beautiful description of a poet (in stanzas 57 to 59) believed by some to refer to Paterson, who wrote stiff verse-tragedies (as, indeed, did Thomson), but whom others think depicts the poet William Collins, who took lodgings in Richmond to be near Thomson. The vaguely medical stanzas 74 and 65, incidentally, were written by another of Thomson's friends, the Roxburghshire-born doctor John Armstrong, author of *The Art of Preserving Health*, in heroic couplets, and, also in heroic couplets, a poem on sexual technique, *The Economy of Love*.

The second Canto of *The Castle of Indolence* describes how the knight Sir Industry gets to hear of the castle's existence and resolves to rescue those in the wizard's power. This gives full rein to the Calvinistic work ethic latent in every Scot. With Thomson, it takes the form of a versified moral discourse on the excellent progress made by industry and the arts in Britain; a moral but dull theme more extensively treated in Thomson's long five-part poem of 1735–36, *Liberty*.

It is thus for the dreamy music-making and the verbal magic distilled by the first canto that *The Castle of Indolence* is still enjoyed more than two centuries after it first appeared.

—Maurice Lindsay

THE CASTLE OF OTRANTO.
Novel by Horace Walpole, 1764.

What recent scholars have come to call "The Age of Sensibility" was driven by a group of mid-century poets intensely interested in expanding the "aesthetic" range of writing beyond the rational control of "civility" that the Augustans had built up like protective clothing. Horace Walpole knew this protective power and civility well because his father had been Prime Minister during the zenith of Alexander Pope's dominance over a literature that surely represented "modern" civilization—even though much of Pope's power in writing came from the depiction of the cracks in that dominance. But writers of the Age of Sensibility wanted something else; the weight of civilized clothing had become too heavy to wear comfortably. Walpole's friend Thomas Gray broke away most effectively in verse with his poem "The Bard," which Walpole printed on his private press in 1757. Walpole's own wonderfully imaginative novel *The Castle of Otranto* broke the hold of Augustan control equally effectively for narrative—so much so that it started a whole new genre, or vogue, in prose fiction. This first gothic novel, indeed, conveys a similar message to the opening lines of Gray's poem: "Ruin seize thee, ruthless King! / Confusion on thy banners wait;" and the ruthless king is in part Walpole's strong father, in part the whole classical tradition of rational, genre writing, of civility that had nurtured Walpole.

The success of Walpole's strange, confused story about the crushing weight of clothing, such as the giant helmet and the glove which figure prominently in the plot, indicates how ready the reading public was for the "confusions" of the unconscious and the mysteries of the Middle Ages even at this time of Enlightenment. Walpole himself said he wrote the story in a feverish heat of rapid writing after dreaming he had been confronted by a "gigantic hand in armour," and this sounds much like the crushing fate of young Conrad at the start of the story. In fact, Walpole had been pushing himself with overwork in the rational game of politics for his family because a part of him always believed in the crushing responsibility of civilization. The tale of terror he put down in haste was his momentary escape.

The gothic, or medieval, setting for the novel had already been imaged in Walpole's own elaborate restoration of his country house at Strawberry Hill (very near Pope's Twickenham house) as a medieval castle. Somehow around the turn of the century Whig legends of British liberty, in the traditions of the Glorious Revolution, had become associated with the rugged structures and supposed individualism of feudal lords. So even though Walpole himself was far from rugged like his Whig father and was very "civilized" and classically educated, he associated his "Whiggism" and love of liberty with these rough structures and had his "castle" built of lath, plaster, and stucco. It is no wonder that he dreamed feverishly and sensed that the whole structure would tumble down.

In the novel, it is inevitable that the strong man, Manfred, will fall. He is doomed by the equivalent of original sin, a hidden mystery from the far past of his paternity. But as the ruling prince of Otranto, Manfred makes the effort to be a "modern" and effective politician, like Walpole's own powerful father. Manfred's plan is to make a clever second marriage with the youthful Isabella (Walpole had had a young stepmother) in order to insure the survival of his political power. Instead, he inadvertently murders his own daughter, Matilda, just as the haunting "sin" of the family had caused the death of young Conrad his son. In other words, Manfred and his family cannot escape the sinister presence of the past. Ancient family portraits come alive. The castle itself moves to wreck all "modern" planning. The story is, indeed, a nightmare to balance against and to challenge all notions of Whig optimism. The young Matilda and her brother offer the only hope for intercession; just before she dies she places her father's large hand into the hand of her true mother. This represents Walpole himself trying to modify the oppressive "civility" of the practical politics he knew so well. But the young people in the novel, of course, die young. Walpole himself and his literary creation, with its strange awkward style that is so non-Augustan and its vivid, peculiarly modern symbolism, live on to remind us of the healing role of dreams and of the continual, evolutionary tendency in literature to spawn new genres.

—Donald M. Hassler

THE CASTLE OF PERSEVERANCE.
Play, early 15th century.

Editions

In *The Macro Plays*, edited by Mark Eccles. 1969.
In *The Macro Plays*, edited by David Bevington. 1972.
In *Four Morality Plays*, edited by Peter Happé. 1979.

Critical Studies: "Stage Directions in *The Castell of Perseverance*" by J. Willis, in *Modern Language Review*, 51, 1956; *The Medieval Theatre in the Round: A Study of the Staging of The Castle of Perseverance and Related Matters* by Richard Southern, 1957, revised edition, 1975; "The Allegory of Feudal Acquisition in *The Castle of Perseverance*" by Milla P. Riggio, in *Allegory, Myth, and Symbol* edited by Morton W. Bloomfield, 1981; *Strangers and Pilgrims: From the Castle of Perseverance to King Lear* by Edgar T. Schell, 1983; "The Virtue of Perseverance" by Richard Proudfoot, in *Aspects of Early English Drama* edited by Paula Neuss, 1983; *Homo, Memento Finis: The Iconography of Just Judgement in Medieval Art and Drama* by David Bevington, 1985; "Penitence and Parody in *The Castle of Perseverance*" by Frances J. Hildahl, in *Early Drama to 1600* edited by Albert H. Tricomi, 1987; "Coveytyse Copbord Schal Be at the Ende of the Castel Be the Beddys Feet: Staging the Death of Mankind in *The Castle of Perseverance*" by Alan J. Fletcher, in *English Studies*, August 1987; "Covetousness, Contrition, and the Town in *The Castle of Perseverance*" by S.E. Holbrook, in *Fifteenth-Century Studies*, vol. 13, 1988.

The Castle of Perseverance is a late medieval religious morality, with a cast list of personified abstractions in opposing, balanced groups. It opens with the World (Mundus), the

Devil (Belyal), and Flesh (Caro), each in turn on his own booth-stage, boasting of his powers and of his determination to destroy Mankind (Humanum Genus). Mankind is "born" – naked and weak, wavering between the contradictory paths of advice given him by the Good and Bad Angels. He eventually opts to follow the Bad Angel who introduces him to Pleasure (Voluptas) and Folly (Stulticia). They quickly lead him to World and, in return for giving total allegiance to worldly ways, Mankind is sumptuously dressed and then passed to Covetous (Avaricia) to be briefed on how to acquire worldly wealth, and then to the rest of the Seven Deadly Sins.

Meanwhile, the Good Angel and the Seven Virtues agree to help the Good Angel part Mankind from the Deadly Sins; they lead him to safety in the Castle of Perseverance. War is declared, six of the Deadly Sins attack the Castle, and Virtues hurl down scalding ammunition – roses, symbolic of Christ's passion. The forces of good seem to be winning, but Covetous quietly circles the Castle and, with honeyed, silken words, wheedles Mankind out of the Castle by pointing out that he needs money in his old age (Mankind ages throughout the play). The Virtues are powerless to prevent Mankind's departure from the Castle; he has free will and cannot be constrained. Death (Mors) then appears, kills Mankind, and the Bad Angel carries off his soul, after his unsuccessful appeals to the Good Angel.

The Four Daughters of God now appear. Mercy (Misericordia) has heard her name called and with her sisters Peace (Pax), Truth (Veritas), and Justice (Justicia), has come to investigate. They debate the fate of Mankind's soul but cannot come to an agreement, so decide to place their case before God the Father whose booth-stage now opens, revealing him sitting in majesty. After listening to the Daughters, God declares in favour of Mercy and orders Mankind's soul to be retrieved from Hell; his soul is brought up to share God's heavenly abode. The play closes with the actor playing God stepping out of his role saying: "Thus endeth our games./To save you from sinning,/Ever at the beginning/Think on your last ending," and the action is completed with a *Te Deum*.

The Castle of Perseverance is the most complete surviving early religious English morality play (*The Pride of Life* predates it but is seriously incomplete). Although two leaves of the unique manuscript of *Castle* are missing (with a consequent loss of some 200 lines) this is not a serious lapse in a play of 3,649 lines, especially when a quite detailed plot is given in its *Banns* (even though it is thought these *Banns* are a later addition to the play and do not quite square with the play itself; the *Banns* indicate that Mankind's soul is saved through the intercession of the Blessed Virgin Mary).

With typical, personified abstractions as characters, and with the usual morality structure of fall and redemption, this play is of the "full scope" morality genre depicting the birth, life, death, and salvation of its protagonist Mankind. It promotes the sacraments of the church, extols the way of Christian virtue, comments on the unexpected and inexorable advent of Death, and emphasises that God's mercy is infinite. Although undeniably verbose, the play is theatrically entertaining, by turns amusing and serious, didactic and spectacular.

The manuscript contains notes and a sketch depicting the play's staging which constitutes a valuable addition to our understanding of the production of medieval theatre. *The Castle of Perseverance* was written to be performed in a circular, open space with five perimeter stages and a central stage (representing the Castle built high on stilts). The audience is located between the stages on the perimeter and kept out of the central acting area (the "place" or *plateau*). The action flows between these six stages across and around the "place." The cast is large, with 33 speaking characters, and minimal opportunities for doubling up. The play is a very active one with lots of opportunities for colourful costume, spectacle, and pyrotechnics.

Like all medieval drama *The Castle of Perseverance* is written in verse of strong rhythm and abundant alliteration but of surprising flexibility. Its main form is a 13-line stanza: ababababcdddc, which is particularly effective even though characters never speak less than a full stanza. The language (Middle English) is a variety of East Midlands dialect, possibly of Norfolk. Stage directions and names of characters are in Latin. Although there are a number of female characters, in accordance with medieval theatre practice all parts would have been played by males. There is no evidence as to who originally created or performed the play, which in presentation would have lasted up to four hours. From the *Banns* it is evident that the play was expected to be performed at different locations in the region, although to achieve this a large, affluent company with a high degree of organisation would have been necessary.

In the 20th century the play (in a reduced form) has been produced occasionally, although not professionally, and not until 1974 was it given a full-scale open air performance in accordance with the original staging plan – at Culham College, Abingdon. In 1979 it was also staged at the University of Toronto. Both productions proved beyond question the play's highly effective theatrical potential. It is to be regretted that the scale of *The Castle of Perseverance* militates against its frequent revival. It deserves to be better known.

—Philip S. Cook

CASTLE RACKRENT.
Novel by Maria Edgeworth, 1800.

Castle Rackrent is a historical account of the fall of the House of Rackrent told in the form of a memoir written by Thady Quirk, an ancient retainer. What he does not know personally about the family, he has learned from a still lively oral tradition. Remembering his grandfather's stories, Thady recalls how Sir Patrick O'Shaughlin inherited the Castle Rackrent estate on condition that he change his name from O'Shaughlin to Rackrent. Undoubtedly, this name change signals the family's conversion from the old Catholic faith, circumscribed throughout the 18th century by penal legislation, to ascendancy Protestantism, thus it also announces their ability to partake of all the privileges of professional advancement and financial aggrandizement that membership in the establishment confers. One of the sharpest ironies in Thady's narrative is that, despite their comprehensive political and economic advantages, the Rackrents come to such spectacular grief.

Whatever Sir Patrick's early religious opportunism, it has long been forgotten; his reign is remembered as a kind of Golden Age of community entertainment. Moving from legend to living memory, Thady details directly his service to Sir Murtagh, Sir Kit, and Sir Condy, and in the process, although he does not perceive it, he records the abuses of the

Protestant ascendancy. Sir Murtagh marries into the family of Skinflints, and, to advance the Rackrent fortunes, husband and wife implement a policy of miserliness buttressed by legal intimidation, the combination of which drains their tenants and, in some cases, their neighbours of their money, their labour, and, occasionally, their lives. More extravagant than Sir Murtaugh, Sir Kit abandons his responsibilities to his tenants and to his estate for the pleasures of dissipation, brutalizing his wife and terrorizing the neighbourhood until he is killed. Sir Condy is a throwback to the glory days of Sir Patrick. An easy-going man, he likes drinking parties and all-night carousing. Unable to restrain his wife's lavish spending, he ignores it, allowing her to squander what little remains of the Rackrent fortune.

Although each generation of Rackrent landlords is characterized by its own idiosyncracies, the four generations are linked by a nearly suicidal self-indulgence, an abbreviated moral imagination, and a vast social irresponsibility. As Thady's narrative progresses through these four generations, the old feudal notion that land ownership involves a mutuality of interest between landlord and tenant loses force. Still present in Sir Patrick's and Sir Murtaugh's day, this idea of the land gives way to a newer view of land as a commodity to be bought, sold, or rented for the sole benefit of the landlord, a view shared by Sir Kit and Sir Condy. Unfortunately, Sir Kit and Sir Condy lack the necessary skills to turn land into money. By the time Sir Condy dies, the Rackrent fortune has disappeared, and the Rackrent holdings have been transferred to Jason Quirk, Thady's son and one of Sir Condy's agents. Thus, Thady's memoir of the decline of the ascendancy is also a record of the emergence of a new monied class.

Jason Quirk, born into the old feudal world of retainers and masters, is, nonetheless, the embodiment of this new class. By education he has removed himself from the old ways. A shrewd lawyer and hard-nosed land agent, Jason manages, by using a variety of sharp practices and by receiving inside knowledge from his father, to gain control of the Rackrent land. In the hindsight realization that almost every Rackrent loss is a Quirk gain, Thady's detached and non-judgemental treatment of even some of the most outrageous Rackrent behaviour, such as when Sir Kit incarcerates his wife for over five years, now seems rooted in something more complicated than simple-minded loyalty to the Rackrents. Although Thady may believe he is "honest," there are indications that Thady's intimate knowledge of the Rackrents' affairs has allowed Jason to make the right bid at the right time. In other words, Thady is not above manipulating events for the benefit of his son. Thady's narrative suggests that it is not difficult tolerating the weaknesses and abuses of one's masters when their fortunes are passing into the coffers of one's own family.

Thady's manuscript is annotated by an anonymous editor who, fascinated himself by the strange behaviour and customs of the Irish, believes the English audience to whom the work is directed will also find much of interest. To facilitate their understanding, the editor contributes about 20 footnotes, some of which are short glosses of words the editor believes the reader will not recognize. "Gossoon" he tells us comes from the French "garcon"; "childer" is an Irish variation of "children." Other notes are long and erudite. The editor also attaches a brief four paragraph end-note with some observations about the state of Ireland, and a "Glossary," ostensibly of terms, but actually a commentary on the idiosyncracies of the Irish.

The effect of this editorial superstructure on the narrative, at least in the first instance, is to endow Thady's narrative with the authenticity of a historical document. More important, the editor offers his own ideas for the improvement of Ireland. From the editor's point of view, if the "few gentlemen of education" who reside there were to take themselves to England thereby making space for "the introduction of British manufacturers," conditions might improve. The implementation of such ideas, would, of course, seriously undermine the scope not only of the old landed aristrocracy, but of the newly-arrived, indigenous middle-class Quirks. The final irony in Thady's record of the fall of the Rackrents and the rise of the Quirks is that the events described may be only one stage of an ongoing process by which the social and economic arrangements of Ireland are continually destabilized.

—Bernice Schrank

THE CHANGELING.
Play by Thomas Middleton and William Rowley, 1622.

Although first printed only in 1653, *The Changeling* had been licensed for performance in 1622. It is generally agreed that the tragic main plot is Thomas Middleton's and that the comic subplot is the work of William Rowley, who may also have been responsible for the first and last scenes of the play. (For discussion of the text see N.W. Bawcutt's 1958 Revels edition.)

The comic subplot is a slight thing, catering to the Jacobean taste for bawdy, clowning, and the antics of madness. Disconcertingly, it includes the title part: the literal "changeling" is Antonio who feigns insanity so that, admitted to an asylum, he may tempt Isabella to be false to her husband Alibius, the asylum-keeper. The parallels between this situation and that which occurs in the main plot subvert the pretensions of the main plot, alerting us to the lustfulness there rarely explicit, and pointing up the kinship between sexual passion and madness. Despite this ironic relationship, made explicit in V.iii.196–215, which lists, besides the case of Antonio, a series of changes involving characters in the main plot, the subplot is of no dramatic originality compared to the main plot.

This has been long admired for the psychological accuracy of its depiction of the relationship between De Flores and Beatrice-Joanna. *The Changeling* by and large eschews the more spectacular and bloodthirsty effects of Jacobean stagecraft; it relies rather upon the creation of an intensely claustrophobic atmosphere through concentration upon one relationship which develops to a tragic culmination in a single location through a short space of time. The play is in this respect a species of domestic tragedy, closer to *Othello* than to other Jacobean revenge tragedies.

The play centres upon two great scenes, II.ii and III.iv. In the first, Beatrice, through sudden infatuation for Alsemero, arranges for a servant, De Flores, to murder Alonso, the man her father intends she should marry. Beatrice has an excessive and irrational loathing for De Flores which, in its intensity, betrays an unacknowledge desire ("Women have chid themselves abed to men" observes De Flores). Despite her contempt for him, De Flores is himself subject to a no less obsessive infatuation with Beatrice ("I can as well be hanged as refrain seeing her"). Beatrice, self-centredly complacent, hires De Flores with no appreciation either of her own complicity or his motivation. She supposes that his passionate willingness to take on the murder may be answered by gold; but he expects sexual gratification: when assured "Thy regard shall be precious," he replies, "That I have thought on / . . . the thought ravishes!" The linguistic, psychological, and thematic ironies multiply, as, prevented by their preconceptions from attending to the other, each misconstrues what is being said and grows increasingly pleased with the prospect they believe is promised.

When, following the murder, Beatrice comes to pay De Flores off, she is quite at a loss to understand his dissatisfaction or his expectations. As the truth dawns upon her in III.iv she is, despite her horror and revulsion, compelled by the relentless logic of her situation to submit. Her assumption of moral as well as of social superiority is destroyed by De Flores: "Why, are not you as guilty, in, I'm sure, / As deep as I? And we should stick together. . . ." To her incredulous exclamation "Why, 'tis impossible thou canst be so wicked, / . . . To make his death the murderer of my honour?" he calmly replies: "Push, you forget yourself! / A woman dipped in blood, and talk of modesty?"

There is little about Beatrice to attract sympathy or respect. She has none of the impressive vitality of a character like Webster's equally vicious Vittoria Corombona in *The White Devil*. Nevertheless, when finally she admits to De Flores "I'm forced to love thee now, / 'Cause thou provid'st so carefully for my honour," Beatrice's choice of the word "honour" illustrates that she is as much the victim of a patriarchal culture as she is a culpable perpetrator of criminal acts. She is more concerned with her "honour" than with her innocence because, in a society which permits her only the role of a wife, to lose her reputation would be to lose her very identity. The play begins with Beatrice being passed from father to husband, without regard for her own desires. There is no legitimate way in which she can assert her "will" (a key word in the play), and so, though she does contrive a situation which enables her to marry the man she (rather than her father) chooses, there is a price to pay: she is trapped in an adulterous liaison with De Flores. This makes her vulnerable to ostracism and disgrace, for, as an insubordinate act which repudiates the authority of the husband, androcentrism deems infidelity in a woman intolerable. It is fear that she will be spurned as a whore which lies behind Beatrice's concern for her "honour." At the end of the play she will confess to murder rather than be thought guilty of adultery. She still insists "I am true unto your bed." Even were this true, it is unlikely it would be credited, for Beatrice is surrounded by the suspicion that women are naturally as sexually voracious as Diaphanta, a virgin supplied in Beatrice's place on her wedding-night, proves to be when she will not leave Alsemero's bed. We may put down De Flores' "some women are odd feeders" to his warped sensibility, but patriarchy's pervasive fear of uncontrolled female sexuality appears in Alsemero's readiness to believe allegations against his bride and in the paraphernalia of the virginity test which occupies much of Act IV. Virginity would prove that Beatrice is Alsemero's possession alone. It is Beatrice's tragedy that in a woman, wilfulness is inevitably transgressive: "Would creation / . . . Had formed me man. / . . . 'tis the soul of freedom!"

—N.H. Keeble

A CHASTE MAID IN CHEAPSIDE.
Play by Thomas Middleton, c. 1613.

Thomas Middleton's last and most successful "citizen comedy" fuses localised references to London life onto the conventions of Latin comedy—testy parents, disobedient children, and scheming servants. It attacks familiar targets—the city's materialism and vulgarity—stimulating the audience's well-known prejudices against merchants, social climbers, parasites, pedants, and Puritans.

The bustle of the town is captured by crowding the scene with water-men, police informers, idle passers-by, and citizens hurrying home with their baskets of shopping. The play opens in a London street with "*a shop being discovered*." It has a naturalistic scene of a lying-in ("*a bed thrust out upon the stage*") with rowdy visitors chattering over the new-born, fingering and evaluating the presents, eating and drinking whatever is offered them until they fall off their "low stools." A staged funeral service, described in an elaborate stage direction, closely mimics the real thing. There are constant reminders that the action takes place in contemporary London, with Westminster, Holborn, St. Paul's, Bow, Greenwich, and Barn Elms nearby.

So the audience identifies easily with the setting; at the pretended funeral of Touchwood Junior and Moll, "such throngs" come, a "pair of lovers / Had never more spectators." The spectators in the theatre and the actors on stage gawking around the coffins become as one.

The characters have the typical anxieties and obsessions of Jacobean citizenry. Maudline, wife of Yellowhammer the goldsmith and bossy mother of Moll, the "chaste maid," combines snobbish longing for what is above her—her daughter should be "fit for a knight's bed"—with equally snobbish scorn for those beneath her—"You dance like a plumber's daughter." She has a parvenue's delight in her elegant life-style, and an affected vocabulary that surprises even her husband: "Nay, the city cannot hold you, wife, but you must needs fetch words from Westminster." He in turn proudly displays his understanding of his aristocratic customers, "You gentlemen are mad wags," and tries to make his dim-witted son fit in among the gentlemen-commoners at university by sending him a silver spoon to eat with in hall.

The Yellowhammers' social climbing and their mercenary ethics, driving them to plan fine marriages for their children, are subjects for Middleton's satire. The tyrant father of Latin comedy got the action going, but had little interest as a character. The Yellowhammers behave as they do because of their carefully drawn flaws. Their actions have a psychological plausibility to which the audience can respond with legitimate moral disapprobation. Middleton's attack is unremitting—in the final act, believing Moll dead, they still think only of status and money; they plan to leave town to avoid embarrassment before the neighbors, and they hasten their second plot to marry their son Tim to the "rich Brecknock gentlewoman." They are inept snobs, however; they cannot recognise that this "gentlewoman" is no more than a disguised whore.

The plot of *A Chaste Maid* is complex but neatly managed. The aptly-named Sir Walter Whorehound inherits only if Sir Oliver and Lady Kix remain childless. Sir Walter keeps Allwit in luxury to maintain access to Mistress Allwit's bed—a long-standing arrangement that has produced seven children. Now Sir Walter courts Moll Yellowhammer, who loves Touchwood Junior. The comedy consists of Touchwood Junior's attempts to elope with Moll, to persuade his notoriously fecund brother to get Lady Kix with child, and to set Sir Walter and the Allwits at odds. He succeeds in all; the bankrupt Sir Walter is led off to gaol, and the Allwits and the Yellowhammers are discomforted.

Throughout, the play contrasts avarice and honesty—honesty being defined by unaffected conjugal love. Touchwood Senior and his wife, and Sir Oliver and Lady Kix are devoted despite their contrasting problems—Touchwood's ever-increasing family and Kix's sterility. Touchwood Junior and Moll are attractive lovers headed for happy marriage. In contrast, Allwit thinks only of money and sees his wife as a mere commodity. His satisfaction with Sir Walter's unusual patronage is expressed in terms chillingly mercenary and expedient. He need not labour for his modish wife's extravagances, and her healthy children give him status while costing him neither worry nor money. He does not care that his servants scorn him—Sir Walter assumes all the domestic problems: "when the strings / Of his heart frets, I feed."

Feeding and food are central images. The action takes place during Lent, but the voracious gossips at the lying-in and the greedy citizens seeking out illicit supplies of meat to break their fast suggest the self-indulgence and hypocrisy of mercantile London. Contrasting barrenness and fertility is also a major theme, extending from a moving portrayal of Lady Kix's longings to earthy jokes about pregnancy, childbirth, and the dampness of babies. But this theme is not clearly moralised. The deplorable Sir Walter and the amiable Touchwood Senior are equally prolific; the sympathetic Sir Oliver and the mean-spirited Allwit are equally childless.

—Richard Morton

CHILDE HAROLD'S PILGRIMAGE.
Poem by Lord Byron, 1812–18.

Cantos 1 and 2 of *Childe Harold's Pilgrimage* were published in March 1812; canto 3 appeared in 1816, and canto 4 in 1818. Written during Lord Byron's European travels, the poem derives its substance and unity from the description of places visited and from the central figure of Childe Harold, in the later cantos subsumed into the poet himself. It owed its immense success to the fact that it crystallized the romantic spirit as that spirit was understood by the educated, liberal audience of the time. More forcibly than any previous work it reflects the prevalent longing for excitement, attraction to external nature, admiration of the lonely, rebellious hero, and hatred of tyranny.

Cantos 1 and 2, while undeniably inferior to the later cantos, captured the imagination of contemporary readers by their flamboyant statement of romantic attitudes, concerns, and political trends. Recounting Byron's travels between 1809 and 1811 through Portugal, Spain, Greece, and Albania, they depict an exotic landscape endowed with the interest of recent political and military events during the Peninsular War and with the glamour of the East. The observer of this landscape, Childe Harold, is the first and most striking representation of the Byronic hero. Labouring under a sense of guilt at some mysterious sin, he is alternately melancholy and bitter, cynical and resigned, proud and remorseful. Above all, he is isolated, cut off by his passions and sufferings, so that his restless wanderings come to embody the undefined and unsatisfied aspirations of the romantic soul. As Byron traces his hero's journeyings, he voices ideas which express both the spirit of the age and his own reactions to the hectic, fluctuating scenes around him. Thus in describing the sites of Spanish resistance to the invading French he declares his hatred of oppression, and while recalling the former splendour of Greece he deplores her present subjection. Already too he sees in nature a refuge from the pervasive evidence of human woes. These were the topics to be more fully developed in the succeeding cantos.

Canto 3 records Byron's journey across Belgium, down the Rhine, and into Switzerland. Although it initially resurrects the figure of Harold, the Childe is soon dismissed, and the poet himself emerges as the hero. The brooding solitude of Harold now gives way to an aloof defiance of society and a resolute assumption of superior romantic genius made more intense by Byron's direct references to his personal sufferings and wrongs. The two great subjects of canto 3 are the battlefield of Waterloo and the magnificent natural scenery. Description of Waterloo leads Byron to expound on characteristic themes: the vicissitudes of earthly existence, the transiency of joy, the evils of injustice, and the futility of war. But the chief interest lies in the attitude to nature. Through Shelley, Byron had come briefly to adopt a Wordsworthian stance, and here he sees nature not just as a refuge from the cold indifference of society but as a life form which is fused with and a part of his own being. Yet unlike Wordsworth, even now Byron often found in nature not so much a mystical communion as a symbol of his own mind, the "loftiest peaks most wrapt in clouds and snow" (stanza 45) betokening the grand isolation of the romantic genius.

In canto 4 the focus shifts from nature to human creations, to literature, sculpture, and architecture. Having by now completely abandoned the fictitious Harold, Byron describes his journey from Venice through Ferrara and Florence to Rome. The literary associations of these cities, which recalled Tasso, Petrarch, Dante, and Ariosto, lead him to affirm the power of literature to create a life more vital and beautiful than the world of dreary routine. In the depiction of Rome, however, the emphasis changes, and the architecture of Rome, especially its crumbling ruins, illustrates the theme of grandeur and inevitable decay. Since the 18th century ruins had been commonly seen as emblems of mortality, but Byron moves beyond the standard theme to suggest that the lost glory of Rome mirrors the failure of all human efforts and ideals, and while meditating on the vanity of ambition and the passing of tyrants, he graphically presents in Rome an image of all the falsity, the uncertainty, the thwarted aspirations, and unfulfilled hopes which beset human beings. In a world characterised by misery and insecurity the only permanence is to be found in the written word and in the creations of human thought. Here the poet finds his own consolation and justification, recognising that "there is that within me which shall tire / Torture and Time, and breathe when I expire" (stanza 137). In canto 4 the poet's Promethean defiance and despairing energy do not merely embody the essence of the romantic hero but also provide a possible response to the universal human predicament.

The style of the poem is well matched to the subject, for Byron adapted the Spenserian stanza to his own purposes. Although in the first two cantos he followed the consciously archaic style of 18th-century imitators of Spenser such as James Thomson, in the later cantos he endowed the stanza with a new speed and flexibility. The run-on lines move vigorously, reproducing the impetuous rush of images and ideas in a manner very different from the slow, stately movement of Spenser, and they build to a declamatory climax in the alexandrine. The eloquent rhetoric, with its apostrophes, exclamations, questions, parallels, and hyperboles, corresponds to the public orientation of a poem dealing with history and politics, while at the same time the note of passion and drama reinforces the image of the solitary, questing hero.

Childe Harold's Pilgrimage is the work in which Byron most fully expresses his own ardent romanticism and the spirit of the time. And yet in its final depiction of desolation and mutability the poem also suggests a world of shifting uncertainty which is peculiarly modern. In this respect *Childe Harold's Pilgrimage* anticipates in serious terms a vision of life which would soon be given a comic, but far more subtle, shape in *Don Juan*.

—Muriel Mellown

CHILDE ROLAND TO THE DARK TOWER CAME.
Poem by Robert Browning, 1855.

Robert Browning did not employ his usual methods in writing this poem. "Childe Roland,'" he said, "came upon me as a kind of dream. I had to write it, then and there, and I finished it the same day, I believe. But it was simply that I had to do it. I did not know then what I meant beyond that, and I'm sure I don't know now." The place and time of composition are uncertain. Browning is quoted as saying both that it was written in Paris early in January 1852, and in Florence the following year.

As might be expected, this burst of spontaneous creation produced a poem that is sharply different from Browning's other work. Like Coleridge's "Kubla Khan," which was also written in a dream-like state, it contains imagery that is both enigmatic and intensely suggestive, echoes literary memories, and establishes a threatening nightmare atmosphere, while lacking ultimate coherence. It resembles Browning's favorite form of the dramatic monologue, since it is spoken by a single character, but there is no auditor.

The "childe" or apprentice to knighthood who is the narrator, already convinced that he will fail in an undefined quest that has lasted many years, begins his story by saying that he followed the directions of an evil, crippled figure, taking a road that he knew would lead to the mysterious Dark Tower and his destruction. The country he traverses is consistently sterile and ugly, and its grotesque, sharply-defined features bring agonizing images to his mind. He encounters an old blind horse, a rusty wheel that seems to be an instrument of torture, and a black bird that he takes as an omen of death. He tries to draw encouragement from memories, but only recalls the treachery of his dead comrades who have left him as the only survivor to pursue a foredoomed quest.

His arrival at the tower is thoroughly ambiguous; it is the goal he has been seeking, but it seems to threaten rather than to satisfy. On the one hand, a vision of his comrades wrapped in "a sheet of flame" rises on the surrounding hills, and he blows his horn "dauntless"; on the other, the tower and its setting are sinister, and the knight compares his discovery of it to a ship driven on a reef in a storm. The narrative ends abruptly in this moment of ambiguous resolution by repeating the title in its last line.

The poem is said to have numerous sources. Some of these were, of course, deliberately chosen. The title is a line from a speech of Edgar during the time he is playing the role of the mad Poor Tom in *King Lear*, and the fifth and sixth stanzas, beginning "As when a sick man very near to death / Seems dead indeed. . . ." is a paraphrase of a passage from John Donne's "A Valediction: Forbidding Mourning." But a great deal of the material seems to have arisen from Browning's unconscious recollections as he composed rapidly and almost unthinkingly, in a manner resembling automatic writing. The poem contains echoes from children's stories and Arthurian romances, from Dante's *Inferno*, Bunyan's *Pilgrim's Progress*. Shelley's "Julian and Maddalo," a story by Edgar Allan Poe, and numerous other works. A major source is a chapter called "Of Things Deformed and Broken, Falsely Called Painter-Like" from *The Art of Painting* by Gerard de Lairesse, a book that Browning knew well. The poem's major images and themes, such as the waste land, the tower, the shipwreck, and failure are parts of Browning's poetic repertory, and their meaning here can be somewhat clarified by their appearance in other poems.

Browning, when asked whether the poem meant that "he that endureth to the end shall be saved," agreed to that interpretation. But since he left the question of its meaning nearly entirely open, critics have swarmed into the gap, and provided numerous interpretations in spite of Browning's denial that the poem was intended to be an allegory. The most interesting of these see the narrative as a psychological allegory, dramatizing the trial of a soul through landscape imagery symbolizing such emotions as hatred, guilt, isolation or the fear of death or failure. The knight's journey has been interpreted as an exploration of the self, an artist's awareness of his failure, an exposure of the sterility of the romantic epic, a condemnation of warfare, and an allegory of industrialism. The tower itself may be a symbol of death, failure, or disllusionment. The poem's ambiguity, disjunctive structure, and failure to project a coherent meaning have been convincingly related to the processes of Freud's dream-work, whose purpose is that of concealing meaning.

Critical disagreement about the poem is especially notable with regard to the last lines:

> And yet
> Dauntless the slug-horn to my lips I set
> And blew, "*Childe Roland to the Dark Tower came.*"

The knight may be expressing triumph at reaching his goal, and is blowing his horn to summon the enemy that lurks inside the tower to combat. This conclusion has been seen as a moment of rebirth following the initiation ordeal of his journey. But more common are the pessimistic interpretations which find the knight acknowledging final failure because he has discovered the ugly truth of his inadequacy at last, or is confronting death. Perhaps the most attractive view sees the poem as a variant of Browning's theme of "apparent failure." The knight may have failed in his external striving, but he has won an inner victory through endurance and self-discipline.

—Jacob Korg

CHILDREN OF THE GHETTO.
Novel by Israel Zangwill, 1892.

Children of the Ghetto: *Being Pictures of a Peculiar People*, probably Israel Zangwill's most popular work, was published in three volumes in 1892 as a commission of the Jewish Publication Society of America. Divided into two parts,

Children of the Ghetto and *Grandchildren of the Ghetto*, the novel provides a panoramic view of Jewish life in 19th-century London. Troubled by the often virulent anti-Semitism of Victorian England and the reductive popular images of Jews—"a mixture of Fagin, Shylock, Rothschild, and the characters of the American comic papers" (according to an article by Bernard Winehouse)—Zangwill set out to create credible Jewish characters and to reveal the religious conflict and poverty that divided the Jewish community as well as the family solidarity and religious tradition that bound it together. The result is an uneven, unconventional, yet strangely memorable novel.

Applying the term "novel" to *Children of the Ghetto* is in itself problematic: from the time of its publication the work was criticized for its loose, episodic structure. That it was later adapted for both stage and movie screen is not surprising given the fact that *Children of the Ghetto* contains a number of highly dramatic self-contained scenes; but it is also flawed by sometimes clumsy plot shifts and awkward coincidences. Defenders of the novel have argued that its structure is thematic and that the story of Esther Ansell gives the plot unity.

The novel does, however, provide a vivid portrait of the poverty and religious identity crises faced by London Jews. In the memorable opening scene, Esther Ansell, the novel's protagonist, joins a crowd of impoverished people waiting at a soup kitchen for a meager allotment of soup and bread. With a piercing irony reminiscent of Dickens, Zangwill contrasts the self-congratulating public officials at the soup kitchen with their underfed, destitute clients. Esther's childhood experiences of poverty and social injustice later cause a crisis in her religious faith. Other characters likewise find their beliefs challenged or undermined by the foreign yet often alluring English culture: some Anglicize their names and conceal their origins; others discover the difficulty of preserving family unity and religious tradition. In one of the novel's most touching scenes, Moses Ansell goes to the deathbed of his charity-educated son, Benjamin, but almost until the moment of death child and father cannot communicate because the son has forgotten Yiddish and the father does not speak English. Other "children of the ghetto" strain against strict, and to them, incomprehensible, religious rules: Hannah Samuels, daughter of a pious rabbi, is barred from marrying the man she loves in a Jewish ceremony because of a technicality in rabbinical law. Torn by conflicting allegiances, she finally sacrifices personal happiness but with great emotional cost; her rejected fiancé converts to Christianity.

Just as Zangwill creates a variety of characters, he speaks in varied tones. In contrast to the somber scenes of ghetto poverty are the reappearances of the self-promoting, absurdly vain poet Melchitzdek Pinchas. Also targets of sometimes biting comedy are the organizers of the *Flag of Judah*, a Jewish newspaper whose beleaguered editor, Raphael Leon, cannot print even an obituary without unwittingly provoking internal squabbling, and those nouveau riche Jews who in attempting to become more English than the English themselves compromise their religious beliefs and in fact deny their heritage.

The same humorous touches that leaven the novel's somber depiction of urban poverty drew the fire of some Jewish critics, who felt Zangwill was abetting anti-Jewish prejudice by showing some Jews in an unflattering light. Other readers complained of unfamiliar language in the novel, so that Zangwill reluctantly appended a Yiddish/Hebrew glossary to later editions. Zangwill was especially disappointed by negative reactions from the Jewish community, though he ironically predicted these reactions in describing the outcry following the publication of Esther Ansell's novel, *Mordecai Josephs*, whose satiric view of London Jews outrages the well-to-do Anglo-Jews among whom she has come to live. Esther, who to some extent represents Zangwill, discovers that she cannot reconcile her contrary experiences: the desperately poor child of the ghetto is taken under the protection of a fashionable family; her unease with this latter life is manifested in her pseudonymously written novel. The suffering she has witnessed in the ghetto undermines her faith, and it is only after returning to live in the ghetto that she can find reconciliation. The ending of the novel suggests that questioning, intelligent Esther will marry the idealistic and devout Raphael Leon and thus offers hope for the future.

Children of the Ghetto is an uneven book, marred by preachiness, authorial intrusion, and speechifying characters. But by creating credible Jewish characters and revealing the complex dilemmas faced by Anglo-Jews, Zangwill's novel was crucial in transforming the portrayal of Jews in English literature.

—Mary Fitzgerald-Hoyt

CHRISTABEL.
Poem by Samuel Taylor Coleridge, 1816.

"Christabel," an unfinished narrative poem by Samuel Taylor Coleridge written in 1797–1801, has been popular ever since its first publication in a pamphlet of 1816. Its mode of supernatural, mediaevalized romance has had major as well as minor heirs. Critics and anthologists have ranked it slightly below "The Rime of the Ancient Mariner" and "Kubla Khan." Coleridge's preface claimed originality in the loose, four-stress accentual versification. The lines rhyme chiefly but not altogether in couplets. Such tumbling verse lends to the macabre a naive and comic air. Although Parts I and II were written in different years and differ in effect, atmosphere is throughout more significant than action and situation.

The maiden Christabel, at midnight near an old oak on the baronial estate of her father, Sir Leoline, prays for her lover who is far away. In this chill hour she encounters a damsel dressed in white silk who claims to have been abandoned under the oak by one of five warriors who abducted her from her noble father's manor. She gives her name as Geraldine (rhyming with "a noble line"). The poem is often said to show the inability of innocence to defeat evil. It is true that the maiden offers to share her bed in polite wording that invites the stranger "to share your couch with me." Conduct more dubious follows. When Geraldine swoons at the gate, Christabel lifts her (like a bride) over the threshold; urging silence lest Sir Leoline be awakened, she ignores a series of symbolic warnings that evil is present. Such warnings as Geraldine's verbal repulse of the ghost of Christabel's mother are evident to the reader, if not to Christabel, as Christian clues to demonic possession.

Abed, the maiden beholds on the bosom next to her "a sight to dream of, not to tell." According to one manuscript insertion, she witnessed flesh "dark & rough as the Sea-Wolf's hide." Geraldine, from her malformed bosom, her serpentine eye, and her oppressive influence, has been identified by critics as demonic witch, lamia, and vampire. Geraldine herself refers to the mark of her shame; repeatedly the narrator declares her force malign and contagious.

From private knowledge before the poem was published, reviewers familiar with the current gothic iconography of rape and sexual nightmare denounced the obscenity of an embrace seen either as lesbian or, with less obvious warrant, as the lover's illicit return in feminine guise. Geraldine can be interpreted as having moments of revulsion, and her assurance to Christabel that the angels above love her lacks the ironic language needed for clear evidence of hypocrisy. If Christabel must be taken as "devoid of guile and sin" (line 599), nothing in the unfinished poem incontestably proves Geraldine other than a woman of limited guilt acting under possession similar to that she imposes on Christabel. The psychic energy transferred from Geraldine may be a first stage in Christabel's growth from venomous initiation.

Part I is sprinkled with such general paraphernalia of the supernatural as a hooting owl and the Catholicized appeals of the narrator to "Jesu, Maria." In Part II Coleridge accepted the more severe challenge of depicting witchery by daylight. Place-names and legends soon pepper the poem with evidence that he had now read up on the Lake District, toured it, and found an unsettling love there.

Christabel awakens with a sense of unidentified sin. When Sir Leoline hears from Geraldine that she is the daughter of Lord Roland de Vaux of Tryermaine, dear friend of his youth but long estranged, he embraces her with tears. Christabel witnesses the embrace with a shudder of dread. Sir Leoline's retainer Bard Bracy reports his dream of a gentle dove in the coils of a bright green snake. Dramatic irony is apparent to every reader in Sir Leoline's deduction that the dove is Geraldine and the snake her abductors. Vowing to challenge and punish the culprits in a tournament, he dispatches Bracy to assure Lord Roland of renewed friendship and Geraldine's safety.

Christabel in a trance returns Geraldine's look of malice and dread with such hatred as innocence can muster. Freed from the trance, she prays at the feet of her father, by the soul of her mother, that he send away this woman. In a raging sense of dishonour, the Baron—ending Part II—escorts their guest from the room. The conclusion of Part II is a lyrical effusion on the tendency of fathers to express excess love in words of unmeant bitterness.

No Part III ever followed. Self-identification of the poet with Christabel, or self-division between Christabel and Geraldine, possibly accounts for Coleridge's inability to go forward. A close friend and the poet's son Derwent each gave, as from the poet, an account of the planned continuation. The differing accounts agree on a happy ending to Christabel's sacrificial ordeal for the benefit of her absent lover. Few readers and no critics have been able to reconcile these cheerful accounts with the depths of psychic division the extant portions convey.

—Carl Woodring

A CHRISTMAS CAROL.
Story by Charles Dickens, 1843.

Though Charles Dickens wrote five "Christmas books," the first, *A Christmas Carol*, is the most memorable. The name of its protagonist, Scrooge, has become part of the English language, and this story of the transformation of a miserly, hard-hearted misanthrope to a kindly philanthropist is, though not the author's artistic masterpiece, perhaps his most widely-known work. Wildly popular during Dickens's lifetime, *A Christmas Carol* in later years has been imitated, parodied, and retold through recording, film, and even animation.

A Christmas Carol was written relatively early in Dickens's career and consequently lacks the complexity of his later work. At the same time, the story encapsulates Dickens's lifelong social concerns and his struggling belief that his country's ills could be ameliorated by individual changes of heart.

The story's narrator has been described by Michael Slater as "a jolly, kind-hearted bachelor uncle seated across the hearth from his hearers on some festive domestic occasion." Yet though the tone is genial and laced with wry humor, Dickens seeks to expose the serious plight of the poor in 1840's England. Scrooge is a "squeezing, wrenching, grasping, scraping, clutching, covetous old sinner," the proprietor of a London counting house. As he so often does in later works, Dickens characterizes his protagonist through physiognomy and domestic setting. Scrooge is raspy-voiced, sharp-featured, and cold; his dwelling is remote, cheerless, and uncomfortable. The story begins on Christmas Eve, and Scrooge's miserliness and misanthropy are quickly established by his rudeness to his kind-hearted nephew, Fred, his bullying of his underpaid clerk, Bob Cratchit, and his dismissal of two men seeking contributions for the needy. Scrooge is a firm supporter of the Poor Law of 1834, a law Dickens abhorred. Scrooge believes, as in Dickens's eyes did the framers of the Poor Law, that the poor were responsible for their plight and that the workhouses were a viable solution for the destitute. Using the sort of Malthusian reasoning that Dickens detested, Scrooge asserts that the death of poor people is no real tragedy as it reduces the "surplus population." Scrooge views the poor as a nebulous mass of social irritation, not as suffering individuals, and the crux of Scrooge's transformation is his final ability to overcome his bigotry and see the poor as "fellow-passengers to the grave, and not another race of creatures bound on other journeys."

Scrooge is visited by four spirits: his former partner, Jacob Marley, and the Ghosts of Christmas Past, Present, and Yet to Come. Marley, who in life was so like Scrooge that people used their names interchangeably, reveals to Scrooge the everlasting torment of the unrepentant sinner: he wanders the earth weighed down by a heavy chain loaded with ledgers, cash-boxes, and all the other accoutrements of his trade. In death he has learned compassion, but the real source of his suffering is that though he now has the desire to help the needy he no longer has the ability to do so. He warns the incredulous Scrooge that such will be his own fate if he does not reform. Scrooge's next three ghostly visitors help to effect this transformation.

Like Marley, the ghosts' appearances bespeak their essences: Christmas Past seems at once young and old, symbolizing the chronological distance of the past but the freshness of memory. The Ghost of Christmas Present is large, genial, hearty, and surrounded by succulent Yuletide foods as well as the symbolic greenery of the season. The Ghost of Christmas Yet to Come is shrouded in a dark robe reflective of the mysterious future. Voiceless and sexless, its only bodily manifestation is a relentlessly pointing hand.

Through the three spirits we discover that Scrooge was once a loving, open-hearted man whose natural affections were thwarted by an unhappy childhood and a burgeoning desire for wealth. Greed caused him to lose a loving fiancée and the joys of fatherhood. And through the memories summoned by the Ghost of Christmas Past, Scrooge realizes that though he was kindly treated by his employer, Mr. Fezziwig, he has himself been a cruel and stingy employer.

The Ghosts of Christmas Present and Yet to Come demonstrate to Scrooge that the poorest of people can celebrate Christmas with joy and magnanimity and give him an ominous warning of what will transpire if he does not change: Tiny Tim Cratchit, whose frailty and gentleness have touched the miser's heart, will die if his family's poverty continues; Scrooge himself will die in obscurity regretted by no one and exploited even in death by avaricious servants.

When Scrooge awakens to discover that he has not died and is in fact being given a second chance at life he is a changed man who immediately embarks on acts of charity. And as the narrator informs us, Scrooge learns to celebrate and cherish Christmas: his charity forestalls the death of Tiny Tim, and he becomes "as good a friend, as good a master, and as good a man, as the good old city knew . . ."

What Dickens urges in *A Christmas Carol*, as he urges in all his works of social criticism, is that the transformation of society can be effected by the change of heart of the individual. The story contains Dickensian foibles—characters occasionally verging on caricature, impossibly virtuous children, and sentimentalization of the poor—but also Dickensian triumphs: vivid renderings of 1840's London, wry humor, and the impassioned exposure of social evils. *A Christmas Carol* contains the seeds of Dickens's later masterpieces: social criticism, the importance of domestic harmony, the responsibility of the empowered toward the powerless. But the Dickens of *A Christmas Carol* is still optimistic enough to argue the ability of the individual to transform a corrupt society; in later works that belief seems increasingly shaken.

—Mary Fitzgerald-Hoyt

THE CHRONICLES OF ENGLAND, SCOTLAND, AND IRELAND.
Prose by Raphael Holinshed (d. 1580?) and others, 1577; revised edition, 1587.

Critical Studies: *Shakespeare's Holinshed: The Chronicle and the Historical Plays Compared* by W.G. Boswell-Stone, 1896; *Holinshed's Chronicle as Used in Shakespeare's Plays* edited by Allardyce Nicoll and Josephine Nicoll, 1927; *The Book Called Holinshed's Chronicle: An Account of Its Inception, Purpose, Contributors, Contents, Publication, Revision, and Influence on William Shakespeare* by Stephen Booth, 1968; "Some Aspects of Shakespeare's Holinshed," in *Huntington Library Quarterly*, 1987, and "Abraham Fleming: A Learned Corrector in 1586–1587," in *Studies in Bibliography*, 42, 1989, both by Elizabeth Story Donno.

The first, together with the second enlarged, edition of this compendium of British history and topography is, as it were, a relic of a more grandiose project—a "universal cosmography" which was to include an account of every nation in the world. Its progenitor was a refugee printer who after 25 years of research, not surprisingly, left the task unfinished at his death in 1573. His assistant Raphael Holinshed then took over as editor (as well as giving his name in popular usage to the two editions), and the earlier grand project was restricted "merely" to the history and description of England, Scotland, and Ireland from the time they were inhabited down to 1576.

A timely syndicate of publishers undertook to publish the work in 1577 in two folio volumes, amply illustrated with woodcuts. Under the scrutiny of the Privy Council, however, some portions of the text were deemed improper from a political-social perspective so that a few passages were expurgated, their paucity a tribute to the skill of the compilers, and compilers they were. For during the 16th century, a history was largely an aggregate of earlier printed materials, with later information extending it to the time of publication. Thus for the account of Henry VIII, Holinshed had recourse to Edward Hall's *Union of the two noble . . . Families of Lancaster and York* and for his own later histories (published in 1580, 1592), John Stow simply appropriated his earlier contributions to the 1587 *Chronicles*.

This second edition, amounting, according to estimate, to 3.5 million words, brought the history up to date to 1586. It, too, came under government scrutiny, particularly for events of the most recent decade of Elizabeth's reign, and sale of copies was delayed until the censors, appointed by the Privy Council, had had a chance to review the text. The result this time was multiple excisions, so carefully carried out that few uncensored copies exist. Even the title page was altered; the original had carried the statement "*cum privilegio regiae majestatis*," that is, with the queen's permission to publish. Significantly, this was deleted and replaced by a Latin motto.

An instance of alteration of recent affairs was the toning down of the extravagant receptions that the Earl of Leicester had received on taking command of the English forces aiding the Low Countries in 1586, the intent here, apparently, being to highlight his military rather than his ceremonial activities. A perhaps concomitant change related to his favorite nephew, Sir Philip Sidney, who had lost his life in the fighting at Zutphen. Sidney is remembered today for his courtly writings—sonnets, criticism, and pastoral romance—all published posthumously. The censors excised the reference to the *Arcadia*, perhaps wishing as in the previous instance, to emphasize his military stature. Abraham Fleming, a Cambridge graduate and a "learned correctior," that is, proofreader, had the task of reckoning with the excisions, splicing the resultant texts, and compiling the indices—a most useful feature of the work—"sweating mightily" in the process, as one of his co-authors put it.

Though including a good bit of local trivia (e.g., monstrous births), the thematic emphasis of the *Chronicles* is a nationalistic one within a providential context: the English state under divine auspices. Historical critics have consequently looked to these materials for understanding the dominant ideas of the period, particularly as they were reflected in literary works. Thus Shakespeare turned to Holinshed (and Hall) in his English history plays as well as for *Macbeth* and *Cymbeline*. That he had recourse to the 1587 edition is shown by his appropriation of certain words found only in that edition.

Among the several contributors—Holinshed (d. 1580?), Richard Stanyhurst, and John Hooker *alias* Vowell (for the Irish material), Francis Thynne (for recent history of the Scots), Stow (for recent history of England)—the one with an important claim to originality is William Harrison. His *Description of Britain* and the *Description of England* in three books is the first topographical survey of the country, though by his own admission he seldom moved more than 40 miles from his rural parish in Essex; he had, however traveled through many reams of documents. The result is a valuable accounting of social history, with chapters on the universities, on English dogs, on inns and thoroughfares, on food and diet, including his wife's recipe for brewing beer, and many other topics.

Harrison was also a humanist scholar, so he, too, looked to classical sources like Pausanias and Strabo, to continental geographers like Sebastian Münster and Abraham Ortelius as well as to English monastic records. But within the wide-ranging compass of his survey, written in a pungent conversational style, he manages to convey a distinct sense of his own personality. On the one hand he looks at the period as a culmination of what has gone on before—as a builder Henry VIII was not inferior to the Emperor Hadrian; Queen Elizabeth's court is among the most renowned in Europe. On the other hand, he grumbles about increasing costs and the effect of wealth on the social order. He appreciates the stately residences that were being built (to the impoverishment of the builders), but he wryly comments that when their houses were built of willow, then England had oaken men. In recounting the punishments meted out to malefactors, his tone is factual: "Rogues are burned through the ears . . . Heretics are burned quick; harlots and their mates by carting, ducking, and doing of open penance." But, he adds, since this is regarded by some as no punishment at all or very little, he would wish a sharper law for adultery and fornication. "For what great smart is it to be turned out of an hot sheet into a cold or after a little washing in the water to be let loose again to their former trades?"

Since a proofsheet of a 16th-century work is a rarity, it is a matter of note that proofsheets of the *Chronicles* are now in the Huntington Library. The corrections are finicky, relating mainly to the aesthetics of the printed text, but they amount to an estimated 8,000 changes and so illustrate the care expended on this national record. As his signatures and standard motto indicate, they were made under Fleming's supervision, and the proof volumes no doubt were preserved by him as a testimony to his manifold labours.

—Elizabeth Story Donno

CIDER WITH ROSIE.
Prose by Laurie Lee, 1959.

Cider with Rosie is not so much a straightforward childhood autobiography as a series of essays on the author's upbringing and early memories in a remote Cotswold village in the 1920's: "that generation which saw, by chance, the end of a thousand years' life." The final paragraph describes the development of Laurie Lee's first poetic attempts. The book is observably the work of a poet, not always in a strictly favourable sense; there are undoubted purple passages, parts that strike one as padded poeticising. But these tend to be soon forgotten among the wealth of fascinating atmosphere and reminiscence which *Cider with Rosie* contains. In retrospect, it is the tales and anecdotes of childhood and village life which stick in the memory.

Lee came to the village of Slad, four miles from the Gloucestershire town of Stroud, at the age of three. His father had left his mother in charge of her own three children (of whom Laurie was one), together with four of his children by a previous marriage. Despite Mrs. Lee's hopes, he never returned. Meanwhile the family lived an odd, warm, hand-to-mouth existence under her care. Mrs. Lee is the book's dominant character, disorganised but affectionate, infuriating yet lovable. Some of the most memorable passages concern her recollections of life in service in great houses at the turn of the century. Her hungry family await their supper as she describes the grandeur of a fine table laid for a grand dinner party: "Meanwhile Mother would have completely forgotten our soup, which then boiled over, and put out the fire." The exquisite story of the Indian prince, "with jewels in his beard," who bowed and stood courteously aside to allow a terrified young servant illicitly to enter the privy reserved for gentry, exemplifies her concept of perfect manners: "So I held up my head, and went in, and sat down. Just like that. I felt like a Queen. . . ." Descriptions of her organising (or, rather, disorganising) a picnic, and of riding her borrowed bicycle downhill to Stroud, where she had to be caught by a specially briefed shop assistant as she had no idea how to stop it herself, stay in the mind also.

An author's note warns that "some of the facts may be distorted by time." Occasionally, one suspects, there may be some fudging to hide actual identities. This is particularly the case in the memorable story of the boastful returned emigrant murdered in revenge for his contempt by a group of village youths "soon after the First World War." None was ever caught as the village closed ranks to protect them, and they grew to be respectable family men. "They are all dead now anyway," Lee concludes this section; but it seems unlikely that they should all have died by the early 1950's, none having lived to much above their late fifties or early sixties.

Among other bits of atmosphere from a skilfully recaptured vanished world may be instanced the rote learning of nine years' compulsory schooling, parodied as "One God is King, one King is George . . ."; the unquestioning attendance of the entire village at church every Sunday morning, together with the existence of a benign, sentimental, absent-minded Squire who always slept throughout the service except when woken "with a loud 'God damn!' . . . when a visiting preacher took some rhetorical flight"; and, of course, the accounts of colourful neighbours and village characters.

The title refers to the incident which effectively ended the author's childhood: his inebriation and seduction under a haycart by a village hoyden, who later "married a soldier and I lost her for ever."

—Michael Grosvenor Myer

THE CITY OF DREADFUL NIGHT.
Poem by James Thomson (B.V.), 1880.

"The City of Dreadful Night" is one of the most powerful evocations of the nightmare of modern life between the "darkling plain" of Arnold's "Dover Beach" and Eliot's *The Waste Land*. James Thomson was so poor and little-regarded in his own day that this poem could be published at first only on the cheap, smudgy pages of Charles Bradlaugh's republican, atheistical journal the *National Reformer*, where it appeared in 1874, cut up arbitrarily into four instalments, to meet the editor's and printer's convenience. Book publication followed in 1880.

Thomson's imaginary City of Dreadful Night is an image that evokes the condition of solitary man in urban surroundings (the "lonely crowd") while at the same time it performs its chief function in objectifying the poet's own religious despair and sense of psychological disintegration. Arnold had known that the inescapable city was a breeding ground for "this strange disease of modern life": Thomson displays the ravages of this disease, not as "sick hurry and divided aims," but, more sensationally, as the divided selves and the "Infections of incurable despair" of a series of terrifying nightmare figures.

The first section of Thomson's poem describes the geography of the City of Dreadful Night: its great river, causeways, bridges, street-lamps, and houses "dark and still as tombs," where all are asleep or dead, save for a few isolated wanderers. It is a palpably realized place and it is also the hell of Thomson's own insomniac consciousness:

> The City is of Night, but not of Sleep;
> There sweet sleep is not for the weary brain;
> The pitiless hours like years and ages creep,
> A night seems termless hell. This dreadful strain
> Of thought and consciousness which never ceases,
> Or which some moments' stupor but increases,
> This, worse than woe, makes wretches there insane.

In the second section we find a shadowlike, frail creature, who visits, in turn, the church where Faith died, the villa where Love died, and the squalid little house where Hope died. The poet, who is another wanderer in these streets, asks how life may continue when faith, love, and hope are dead; he is told that human life is like the works of a clock which continue to function when the hands and dial that gave them purpose have been torn away.

In the fourth section a John the Baptist-figure, preaching in an empty square, tells how he came through an accursed desert, among flames and dragons and "A Sabbath of the Serpents," a desert compared with which "Hell is mild / And piteous," where he saw his better self, corpselike, carried off by his dead mistress, leaving his other, "viler" self to stride in on fear and anger into the City. A dead mistress recurs in section x, which contains the luxurious lament of a necrophiliac in a great mansion. In section xviii the poet meets a deformed, bestial, crawling figure, who is trying to retrace the path of his life and become "An infant cradled on its mother's knee": an infant who would scream "if it saw this loathsome present Me." In its objectification of neuroses "The City of Dreadful Night" is nothing if not a despairing work of what Mario Praz would call "the Romantic Agony."

The intellectual message underlying these symbolic figures and settings is one of unrelieved pessimism. In section vi the poet overhears a dialogue between two hopeless men, who had attempted to escape from the City by entering Hell itself, but had been refused entrance to that place because they lacked the admission fee, which is Hope. In another dialogue, overheard in section viii, one speaker curses the God who is viler even than man, because he condemns man to so much suffering, but the other speaker replies that there is no God. In section xii the poet enters the great cathedral of the City, along with kings, authors, clowns, magistrates, and drunkards, each of whom, as he enters, summarizes his career and gives a password: "I wake from daydreams to this real night." There (section xiv) they hear a Messiah preaching:

> Good tidings of great joy for you, for all:
> There is no God; no Fiend with names divine
> Made us and tortures us . . .
> I find no hint throughout the Universe
> Of good or ill, of blessing or of curse;
> I find alone Necessity Supreme

In section xx we are told how two statues face one another on the front of the cathedral: one a sphinx, the other a winged angel with hands on the cross-hilt of a naked sword. There is a crash as the angel's wings fall off, transforming him into a warrior leaning on his sword, but, with another clatter, the sword lies broken. This is a grimly ironic parody of the Positivists' view of intellectual history: the angel (theism), the warrior (science), and the unarmed man (nihilism), fall in turn before the sphinx Necessity.

The last section (xxi) describes a great bronze statue on a hill overlooking the City: it is the City's titanic "Patroness and Queen," modelled evidently upon Albrecht Dürer's "Melancolia." The City-dwellers "often gaze up to her there: / The strong to drink new strength of iron endurance, / The weak new terrors; all, renewed assurance / And confirmation of the old despair."

—A.J. Sambrook

THE CLANDESTINE MARRIAGE.
Play by George Colman the Elder and David Garrick, 1766.

The product of a joint effort by David Garrick and George Colman the Elder, *The Clandestine Marriage* opened on 20 February 1766. The combination was fortuitous, combining the actor's feeling for the stage with the playwright's view from the audience. Both authors were experienced theatre men, and both agreed that action on the stage took precedence over the written word. The approach reduces the value of the witty line in favor of comic situation, as the history of the work suggests, for although the play became a part of the regular repertory almost at once, it has proved to be more popular with audiences than with readers.

The authors claimed they had drawn their inspiration from Hogarth's *Marriage à la Mode*, but the connection is minimal and confined to the comic subplot of Sir John and Miss Sterling. In its entirety, the work unites three elements of late 18th-century drama: the sentimental, the rising middle class, and theatrical effectiveness. These are not isolated elements but reflections of the time, for they can be found in the taste for "graveyard" poetry, gothic novels, and highly charged melodrama.

The central plot, the unhappy situation of the young couple, Lovewell and Fanny, is pure sentiment, although it also suggests the sense of practicality that accompanied this kind of romance. Fear of being be cast off penniless has prevented them from revealing their secret marriage, a fear that proves well founded when the inevitable revelation occurs. The audience would have been well aware that the pair could also be prosecuted, since clandestine marriages had been against the law since 1748. The helpless victims, caught in a net of false values and pretensions, evoke the same kind of sympathy as Richardson's heroines, a sympathy that increases with the complex misunderstandings that threaten to overwhelm them.

One of the usual hallmarks of sentimental drama is in its positive attitude toward the middle class. *The Clandestine*

Marriage, however, makes it a target for ridicule. Mr. Sterling is no country gentleman but a direct descendant of Molière's *Bourgeois Gentilhomme*. Having made a fortune in trade, he tries to imitate the upper classes, and he wants to buy a titled husband for his daughter. His efforts are hampered by his complete lack of taste, and in his house, furniture, and gardens, he has substituted external show for elegant style. His sister, Mrs. Heidelberg, holds the same values, to which are added malice and affected manners that make her even more ridiculous. She has an apt pupil in her elder niece, and their contempt for Fanny not only adds to the heroine's sufferings but reveals their own moral poverty. It is a satirical picture of the newly affluent class at the beginning of the Industrial Revolution.

The upper class is more gently treated but does not escape unscathed. Fifty years earlier, Lord Ogleby might have been a Lord Foppington, but here he is only the wreckage of a former beau who requires matutinal medicines and massages before he can face the day. Ridiculous he may be, with his eye for the ladies and his old-fashioned gallantries, but his judgment of women is sound, for he is immediately attracted to Fanny. He is, moreover, without malice. Once he learns the truth, his true nobility comes to the surface, and he lends his assistance to the lovers. His nephew, Sir John Melvil, is also shown as less than admirable in his desire for a loveless but wealthy match, but his good sense in preferring Fanny over her sister and his graciousness in ceding her to Lovewell redeems him. Although the aristocracy may act foolishly at times, their essential morality is never in question.

The sense of theatre permeates all. The minor characters offer a range of personalities from servants like the simple, garrulous Betty and the libidinous Brush to the Latin-spouting Sergeant Flower. Each makes a particular contribution to the plot, and none is brought on simply for a specialty act or to add atmosphere. Visual effects are important; costumes denote character as the overdecorated Miss Sterling makes a strong contrast to Fanny's simplicity, while the scenes themselves are varied as they shift rapidly to different parts of the house and gardens. Misunderstandings abound, each complicating the plot until it appears impossible to unravel, yet the audience is aware of the truth at all times, and however much they pity the two lovers, no concern for a satisfactory ending is allowed to dim the humor.

In keeping with the principles of sentimental drama, the recompense of virtue takes a material form, and true love is properly rewarded through the magnanimity of Lord Ogleby and the reluctant benevolence of Sterling: Lovewell retains his position and Fanny her inheritance, with the residual implication that Sir John and Miss Sterling will continue on their loveless "Marriage à la Mode" path, a fate both deserve.

The Clandestine Marriage foreshadows no great theatrical movement but rather is a prime example of late sentimental drama with less of the tearful and more of the comedy than most. It preaches no lesson but that of virtue fortuitously requited. As a theatre piece, it is masterfully written and plays well even in the 20th century, but it is seldom performed. Even in its own day, its appeal was soon eclipsed by the brilliant comedies of Richard Brinsley Sheridan that followed within a decade.

—Helene Wickham Koon

CLARISSA.
Novel by Samuel Richardson, 1747–48.

Clarissa is great in several senses. It is immensely long: its 900,000 words makes it roughly twice the length of *War and Peace* and well over twice as long as *Tom Jones*, *Vanity Fair*, *Bleak House*, *Middlemarch*, and *Ulysses*. Its artistry is also extraordinary: generally considered the finest epistolary novel ever written, it is one of three fully-achieved 18th-century novels (along with *Tom Jones* and *Tristram Shandy*) that together showed what could be done within that new genre. Its innovations are thus of the greatest import: its psychological analysis deepened and its spiritual conflict widened the range of English fiction; its accuracy as social reporting (for instance, in presenting the position of women) established realism as the dominant mode in the new genre; Richardson's subtle management of structure, symbol, and point of view opened up whole new dimensions of fictional technique; furthermore, although virtually all 18th-century English novels and most subsequent ones are comic in form and vision, *Clarissa* is a stark and unqualified tragedy. Its influence has also been immense: on the domestic realism of Burney, Austen, and George Eliot; on later novels in letters such as Goethe's *Young Werther* and Laclos's *Liaisons Dangereuses*; on the gothic novel; on the Satanic hero-villain found in so much literature of the romantic movement; and on the tragic fiction of Hardy, James, and Conrad.

This greatness all rests on a slight plot of the kind Richardson would have found in now-forgotten women novelists of his day. Eighteen-year-old Clarissa Harlowe, beautiful, perceptive, and idealistic, the younger daughter in a family of ambitious country gentry, is torn between two suitors: Robert Lovelace (pronounced "loveless"), a dashing aristocrat who is Clarissa's male counterpart in force of personality, and Mr. Solmes, an obsequious miser whose pursuit of Clarissa has been encouraged by her family for dynastic reasons. Clarissa detests Solmes; she prefers Lovelace to all men, and unknown to herself loves him—but is unwilling to admit her love because of his reputation for sexual immorality. Her family, led by her greedy brother James and her envious older sister Arabella, attempt to force Clarissa to marry Solmes by browbeating her, punishing her, and finally by keeping her prisoner in her room and threatening a forced marriage. Through a secret correspondence, Lovelace appeals to Clarissa to allow him to rescue her; she wavers, and when she grants him a secret meeting, he makes it appear that their meeting has been discovered and tricks the terrified girl into eloping with him.

Clarissa's fate is set once she leaves her father's house. Events follow one another with swift inexorability. Disowned and disinherited by her family, Clarissa is induced by Lovelace to move to London, where he settles her in apparently respectable lodgings with a widow and her two nieces. In reality, however, the house is an elegant brothel, the widow is a madam, and the nieces and servants are prostitutes whom Lovelace has himself seduced and brought to their trade. The setting epitomizes Lovelace's conception of women—that beneath their decorous surface they are in essence sexual beings—and gives him the perfect opportunity to prove himself right. He proposes marriage to Clarissa, but meanwhile sets about tempting or surprising her into yielding her virginity. She resists his advances indignantly; in desperation, he rapes Clarissa while she is drugged. Clarissa, far from being tamed as Lovelace expects, falls into a dazed stupor, then fits of madness, and finally, after her reason is restored, into ever-increasing illness. The rape has destroyed her will to live. Though she subsequently escapes from

Lovelace's power, it is only so that she can die a peaceful death among strangers, still disowned by her family, still refusing to accept the now-remorseful Lovelace's offer of marriage as reparation. The novel ends with Lovelace's death some weeks later in a duel with Clarissa's cousin, Colonel Morden.

These events are reported as they happen in letters to and from the main personages. Of the approximately 600 letters, some 180 are from Clarissa to her closest friend, the shrewd and tart-tongued Anna Howe, and some 170 are from Lovelace to his somewhat older and soberer fellow rake, John Belford. Anna writes some 60 letters to Clarissa; Belford, who comes to befriend Clarissa after her escape and presides over her death, writes some 80 letters. Some 25 characters surrounding the central foursome write the 100 or so remaining letters. These figures immediately point to *Clarissa*'s immeasurable advance upon Richardson's one previous novel, *Pamela*, which consisted almost entirely of letters from the virtuous young serving-girl Pamela and gave very little direct access to the thoughts of Mr. B., her rakish master and eventual husband. This disposition of letters also suggests some striking facts: Clarissa and Lovelace are paired, equal but opposite, at the heart of the novel, towering above the other characters; Anna and Belford in their different ways serve as normal foils to each protagonist; the mental gap between Clarissa and Lovelace is poignantly embodied in the fact that both explain themselves only to their respective confidants (there are only a handful of letters between Clarissa and Lovelace). Furthermore, these parallel correspondences create a subtlety not found in *Pamela*, since a single scene is often recounted by first one, and then the other, of the two protagonists—and the stresses and omissions in each account are thereby highlighted.

The novel's format thus focusses upon the characters' minds, not the events which spring from those minds. And, strangely enough, the minds of Clarissa and Lovelace mirror each other in many ways. Each rebels against the prevailing values of society, values embodied in the Harlowes. Each is highly intelligent and articulate; each lives through his or her writing, so that experience only seems real to each when it has been confessed, re-enacted, analysed in letters. Each has the grandeur that comes from uncompromising allegiance to an abstract conception of life—for Clarissa, the Christian morality forgotten by all (even the novel's clergymen) except her childhood nurse, Mrs. Norton, and for Lovelace, the rake's code of stratagem, seduction, and mastery (Lovelace writes to Belford at one point, "If I give up my contrivances, I shall be but a common man").

Most important of all, however, Clarissa and Lovelace are inwardly divided: each loves the other against his or her will. Clarissa clearly is attracted by Lovelace's handsome person, his energy and flair, his disdain for Harlowe values, his single-minded devotion to her, his willingness to be reformed by her—and yet she cannot bring herself to acknowledge to herself or to Lovelace her feelings. Insisting again and again that she will not bestow her love upon an unworthy man, she reveals that she has already done so. One main result of the rape, in fact, is that it forces Clarissa to admit and take responsibility for her love. Lovelace is similarly divided. He is drawn to Clarissa by the very things in her that threaten his identity: her purity, her intransigent integrity, her candour, her noble conception of personal relations, her evident love for him, her vulnerability. After the elopement and before the rape, Lovelace several times finds himself professing his sincere love and proposing immediate marriage—in contradiction to his own careful plans. But he, too, stung by her rejections, renounces his love. Each murders the loving self within, and in doing so each murders the other. Just before the elopement, Clarissa dreams that Lovelace stabs her and throws her into a grave; late in the book, Lovelace dreams that, as he attempts to clasp Clarissa to him, she eludes his embrace and vanishes into the heavens, leaving him falling into a bottomless hole. The symmetry is maintained to the end: the two deaths are in their different ways willed and embraced, suicides as well as murders.

Such patterning gives Richardson's immense novel a satisfying structure. Even more prominent than the parallels between Clarissa and Lovelace are those between Lovelace and the Harlowes, and especially Clarissa's brother James. One obsessed with money and status, the other with sexual possession, both are obsessed; both imprison and torment Clarissa in order to break her to their will; both seek to turn Clarissa into a prostitute; both become uncontrolled sadists as the experience of administering torture increases their appetite for it; both only cease tormenting when Clarissa escapes from their power. Unity is also provided by some other obvious patterns: the opening pages recount the duel between Lovelace and James Harlowe, while the final pages present the duel of Lovelace and another Harlowe, Colonel Morden; the opening section of the novel deals with Clarissa's refusal to marry Solmes and the final section with her refusal to marry Lovelace. Furthermore, the narrative is punctuated by irreversible turning-points: the elopement, the rape, Clarissa's escape from Lovelace. At the exact midpoint of the novel, between elopement and rape, occurs a scene that is as crucial as any: Lovelace arranges for a fire to break out in their London lodgings in the middle of the night and invades Clarissa's room, ostensibly to rescue her but really to attack her when she is surprised, alarmed, and semi-naked. Lovelace ends up sparing the near-hysterical Clarissa, but from this point on she is undivided in her scorn for him and in her determination to escape from him, while Lovelace from here on can no longer believe that Clarissa can be won by anything short of violence.

Richardson is equally deft in his handling of point of view. In this respect, the novel falls into three parts. In the long first section, up to the elopement, Clarissa's point of view dominates: of just over 100 letters, only four are written by Lovelace (three to Belford, an exposition of all that Clarissa does not understand about her predicament, and a brief note to her). As a result, the reader is, like Clarissa, imprisoned within Clarissa's mind and shares her growing claustrophobia; the few glimpses we have of Lovelace guarantee that he seems as appealing an alternative to us as he does to Clarissa. After the elopement, point of view again mirrors the course of events. Like Clarissa, we move ever more fully into Lovelace's compulsive world; the climactic section from the fire-scene to Clarissa's escape, a stretch of more than 300 pages, contains only one letter from Clarissa. In the final section of the novel, there are surprisingly few letters from Clarissa herself; her turning away from this world and preparation for the next is narrated almost entirely by Belford, thereby guaranteeing that the novel's tragic and spiritual dimensions retain their mystery. Lovelace's death is presented through a coda of letters to and and from him, concluding with a terse account of the duel by his French valet, who does not even know who Clarissa is. His end is thus equally remote and mysterious: is it, as he thinks, expiation or simply self-extinction or a final assertion of his need to dramatise himself and control events?

Despite its artistry, its fascinating characters, its tragic vision of wasted excellence, its insights into evil and sexual antagonism, its devastating presentation of the costs to both sexes of the female code of dependence and innocence—

despite all these things, *Clarissa* has been more admired than read, and more read in abridgements to about one-quarter of its length than in its entirety. It remains, nevertheless, one of the truly great works of English literature.

—Bruce Stovel

CLEANNESS.
Poem by the Gawain Poet, late 14th century.

Cleanness is one of four great poems of the late 14th century written in English, probably by the same unknown author, in the alliterative metre; that is, in lines of four stresses and a number of unstressed syllables, three of the four stresses usually beginning with the same letter. The style is a richly poetic diction based on the dialect of Derbyshire. The other poems are *Sir Gawain and the Green Knight*, *Pearl*, and *Patience*.

The poet begins by retelling the parable of the Wedding Feast in which dirty clothes symbolize sin, as told in the Bible, Matthew 22 and Luke 14. He then tells the story of the Flood with remarkable vividness (from Genesis 6), then equally dramatically the destruction of Sodom and Gomorrah (from Genesis 19), and finally the disaster that befell after Belshazzar's blasphemous feast (from Daniel 4 and 5). Some of these episodes had been linked in the Second Epistle of II Peter in connection with sexual impurity and more generally unrighteousness and rebelliousness towards God. But the full sequence is the poet's own.

The poet enriches the biblical stories with a wealth of further allusion and realistic detail of a purely 14th-century kind. The narratives are full of zest for life and a passionate intensity for goodness. The style is dense and witty. There is no doubt that for this poet the centre *can* hold.

Appreciation of this passionate poem must first depend on an act of the historical imagination. We must accept what is unfamiliar in the late 20th century, namely the biblical and until recently normal belief in Christendom that sexuality is the spiritual and material core of the human being and that promiscuous or perverted sexuality is bad. Sexuality when distorted therefore becomes a metaphor and a leading example of all sin. The poet is as earnest, didactic, and passionate as D.H. Lawrence, but in the service of totally opposite though traditional values. Those values include proper use of sex which he describes as God's greatest gift "like the bliss of paradise"; a zestful appreciation of material beauty as in the ornate description of Belshazzar's feast; obedience to God; and a powerful sympathy for condemned humanity, as in the description of families, friends, and lovers drowning in the Flood. The poet's descriptions may verge on the lurid but he can equally well compass the courtliness of Abraham entertaining the angels (based on Genesis 18) as the appalling desert created by the destruction of Sodom and Gomorrah.

The method of the poem is to select and link together biblical passages and mould them into the poet's own terms. Geoffrey Shepherd in "The Nature of Alliterative Poetry in Late Medieval England" (*Middle English Literature*, 1989) has shown how such poetry consists of a series of scenes regarded as mental "illuminations" derived from a mixture of reading and real life, then meditated deeply upon. They become crucial to a view of life and conduct, then rich in multiple significance which demands the poet's utterance. These marvels described with concrete detail become both medium and message. They are not allegories, for the poet's argument is incarnate in the very scenes themselves, though he makes explicit moral comment too. This is the poetry of the illuminated memory characteristic of other great 14th-century alliterative poems like *Piers Plowman*.

The style is complex, with concrete words sometimes forced into unusual meanings, but also forceful, descriptive without much metaphor, as if the poet were standing by and commenting on what he sees. Out of all this emerges a complex feeling for what "cleanness" is, namely a proper appreciation of the good of the world and a proper orientation, based on love and fear, towards God.

—Derek Brewer

THE CLOISTER AND THE HEARTH.
Novel by Charles Reade, 1861.

"I will never attempt an old world story again. Good Heavens! How often have I been stuck? Henceforth I shall remember the advice *soyez de votre siècle*." It is not surprising that Charles Reade wished never again to endure the toil that went into his great 15th-century novel *The Cloister and the Hearth*. Years earlier he had set out his theory and practice in writing fiction: facts, facts; research, research. "The plan will, I see, cost me undeniable labour. I propose never to guess where I can know." Facts were essential to the Reade approach, but never more so than in this huge foray into bygone history.

Why then did he choose so demanding a theme? There were reasons enough. For one thing, any informing item could trigger a plot: a book about hermits, his co-writing of a play, *The First Printer*. More immediate was the fact that in 1859 Bradbury and Evans had commissioned Reade to write the opening serial for their new magazine *Once a Week*. Dickens had just left these publishers to start his own weekly *All the Year Round* and was speeding it off with *A Tale of Two Cities*. Possible Bradbury and Evans had suggested a theme from history; probably Reade wished to outmatch his novelist rival in his own field. There was one even deeper prompting. The whole plot hinges on the required celibacy of the clergy—to Reade, "an invention truly fiendish." For Gerard's case mirrored his own. As a fellow of Magdalen College, Oxford, he was prohibited from marriage.

It should be said that there is an earlier, shorter version of the novel: "A Good Fight." After several instalments of the serial, Reade found that his text was being tampered with. The editors claimed the right to alter: Reade replied, in effect, not when a work carried the author's name. The connection broke. Reade wrote a quick happy ending and set to work on the novel as we know it now. It was published in 1861 and is still in print, an immense, eventful, picaresque, vividly documented trudge (with extraordinary interludes) through 15th-century Holland, Germany, France, and Rome. It is also a love story—a less stark version of the Heloise-Abelard story. Gerard and Margaret, the much divided pair who reflect the title's conflicts, also have roots in fact. Their son, in time, and beyond the story's range, will become the great humanist scholar Erasmus. Gerard, artistically gifted, is one of the nine children of a Dutch cloth merchant. He works for the monks as a scribe and painter, and is clearly destined for the Church. Among his siblings are two villainous brothers, a saintly little crippled girl Kate, and a dwarf, fearsomely strong and agile and a creature of mischief: best to have as an ally. All are operative in the plot. Encouraged by an elderly patron, sister of the painter Van Eyck and herself a painter, Gerard takes the road to Rotterdam where there is a contest of the arts. He wins a prize for his calligraphy and the promise of a benefice when his training is completed. He becomes a priest.

But the good news is also bad. For on his journey he has met the girl Margaret with her frail elderly father, and they are at once drawn to each other. In the course of time (tracks lost, refound, no lack of event) the furious cloth merchant learns of his son's (so far blameless) attachment—a ruin to his prospects!—and has him arrested and locked in a high tower. This allows for one of Reade's great escape scenes. Gerard is pursued; the wedding is stopped at the altar, but he and Margaret have already gone through a betrothal ceremony, maybe or maybe not of legal worth. Now, advised by the Dame Van Eyck, Gerard starts for Italy where his work will be valued; with money he can return to Margaret to live as man and wife. So starts another colourful journey. But all his plans are destroyed when a letter, the work of his evil brothers, announces, falsely, the news of Margaret's death. A period of reckless debauchery does not comfort him, and he is persuaded to try the Church. A dire choice! Meanwhile, Margaret gives birth to Gerard-Erasmus, and wins over the hostile grandparents—helped not a little by the betrothal evidence: a nice Victorian touch. She discovers Gerard at last (now Brother Clement) living as a hermit in a cave. The child provides a bridge. But how can cloister really unite with hearth? It is the novelist's hardest problem.

The labour of research (he listed 79 source books) gave Reade occasional doubts about its final worth. "But surely," he concluded, "this *must* be the right method." Swinburne—often at his sanest in the role of the critic—confirmed this view. He greatly admired Reade's skill in transmuting his material into creative narrative. Some of the detail will stay in the reader's mind for years: how the Van Eycks prepared their paints, how roses were preserved for the winter, the role of the scribe—and the ominous coming of the printer, the horrible entertainments and penalties (a man is broken on the wheel), facts about food, clothes, inns and taverns, laws, weapons, musical instruments, gypsy cant, much else. All are intrinsic to the whole.

But facts, *per se*, were not all. Reade voiced the view that the "weakness" of most historical novels was that "characters look forward instead of back and are before their age." An interesting observation. But how far did he himself "look back"? His accounts of squalor, violence, and cruelty were set down with determined realism, but Gerard's instinctive distaste for all these was not typically medieval. Violence itself was entirely permissible in a Victorian novel where overt sex was not. Gerard's "debauchery" phase is both briefly and vaguely dealt with. Margaret's pregnancy, even, may cause some readers to glance back at the chronicle; has something been overlooked? But it is the sentimental baby passages, near the end, when the little Erasmus prattles in toddler-talk to his withdrawn father, that Reade really drops his own standards. But such a lapse need not be dwelt upon, it does not diminish the whole.

Reade began as a playwright, and the theatre man's hand can still be seen in this novel—the cliff-hanging episodes (*how* can Gerard escape this time?), the period characters (dwarf, bawd, soldier, beggar), the forged letter, the stolen title deed, weirdly discovered. Yet for all this, something of the living past can be caught within its pages: the smells, the cruelties, the slow, anguished pace of time, so unlike our own. No, it is not the dream world of Morris or Burne-Jones. The parts may be uneven but the whole is a monument: a Victorian monument, but no less remarkable for that.

—Naomi Lewis

THE CLOUD OF UNKNOWING.
Prose, c. 1370.

Editions and Translations

The Cloud of Unknowing and The Book of Privy Counselling, edited by Phyllis Hodgson. 1944; revised edition, 1958.
The Cloud of Unknowing, translated by Ira Progroff. 1957.
The Cloud of Unknowing, translated by Clifton Wolters. 1961.

Critical Studies: *Sense and Thought: A Study in Mysticism* by Greta Hort, 1936; *The English Religious Heritage* by Conrad Pepler, 1958; *English Spirituality* by M. Thornton, 1963; *Three 14th-Century English Mystics* by Phyllis Hodgson, 1967; *This Transcending God: The Teaching of the Author of The Cloud of Unknowing* by Constantino Sarmiento Nieva, 1971; *Scattering and Oneing: A Study of Conflict in the Works of the Author of The Cloud of Unknowing* by R.W. Englert, 1983; *The Negative Language of the Dionysian School of Mystical Theology: An Approach to The Cloud of Unknowing* by Rosemary Ann Lees, 1983; article by Maureen Fries, in *An Introduction to the Medieval Mystics of Europe* edited by Paul E. Szarmach, 1984; article by John C. Hirsch, in *Middle English Prose* edited by A.S.G. Edwards, 1984; article by William Provost, in *Medieval Women Writers* edited by Katharina M. Wilson, 1984; "Mystical Experience in the *Cloud* Literature" by Robert K. Forman, in *The Medieval Mystical Tradition in England* edited by Marion Glasscoe, 1987.

Medieval spirituality offered two ways of coming to a "knowing" of God in private contemplation or meditation. The first of these, with which we associate the elaborate and systematic iconography of the cathedral or, on a miniature scale, illustrated books of "Hours," is the "way of images." In spiritual writing this was the fashion of 13th-century Franciscan lyrics (e.g., "Stond wel moder under rode"), which focus the reader's attention on the Passion of Christ, the Sorrows of his mother Mary, or the physical Cross itself. But another way of dealing with the inexpressible heights of mystical knowing is the "negative way" (*via negativa*), the "way without images." In this type of devotional writing, it is not a "positive" regimen of visualization which expedites a higher experience of the love of Christ, but a renunciation of all such *tangibilia* as encumbrance—in effect a kind a naivety to be transcended by the soul mature enough to contemplate God directly as "spirit." This negative way of mysticism finds its chief expression in English spiritual literature of the late Middle Ages in the (appropriately) anonymous *The Cloud of Unknowing*.

The same anonymous author is responsible for Middle English translations of some of the works of Dionysius (Pseudo-Dionysius) the Areopagite, a 6th-century mystic greatly influenced by neoplatonism. The best known of these are *Deonise Hid Diuinite* (a version of Dionysius' *Mystica Theologia*) and *The Boke of Privy Counselling*. He also made a free translation of the mystical treatise of Richard of St. Victory known as *Benjamin Minor*. While *The Cloud of Unknowing* is perhaps somewhat less intensely speculative than most of these works, it clearly owes substantially to their influence. It is a distinctly affective work, setting out to describe for one who would pursue the *via negativa* the purgative and illuminative stages by which the soul might ascend to its desired union with God. Thus, the author of *The Cloud* paradoxically affirms that while God is *ultimately* unknowable—utterly beyond our limited, finite categories of thinking about him—he is not *absolutely* unknowable. That is, he can be reached—"known" and communed with by love. While this kind of knowledge as love has become possible for us only because Christ revealed it to us on the Cross, nevertheless it cannot be attained in its fullness in a state of analytical consciousness—the realm of reason and the senses. Perfect oneness with God is finally divorced from all analytical reasoning, all analogy.

The Cloud of Unknowing reveals its neoplatonic ancestry in yet another way—its teaching of an "art of recollection." This recollection can only commence when there is a "forgetting" of intervening dross in the memory. The novitiate in mystical prayer must endure a "dark night of the senses" in which the "cloud of forgetting" obscures all manner of conscious thought, even as the "cloud of unknowing" conceals God himself. This first "night" lasts for whatever amount of time God deems necessary—expedition is not subject to manipulation by technique—is sometimes accompanied and sometimes succeeded by a "night of the spirit" during which the soul realizes its own worthlessness before God, and the dross of egotism is also purged away. At this point and only at this point can God be loved entirely for himself, and not merely for his gifts and blessings, the creature comforts of our mortal existence. This "dark night of the soul" is a trying experience indeed, because even understanding is taken away, and there is in its place only a desperate hunger for God which expresses itself as a "groaning and travailling in pain." Here the inherent incapacity of language for the subject begins to be apparent; his language of yearning for birth images the excruciating pressure for transition to a stage where the writer's soul is to be relieved by "touches of God," a deep if intermittent sense of God's reaching out and directly caressing the soul which loves it. This is a prelude to the state of spiritual marriage which is the consummation of the soul's *anagogicus mos*, its upward leading journey. The ultimate state of consummation is called by the author of *The Cloud* "a love that is pure and perfect."

The Cloud of Unknowing is consistent about its characterization of true spiritual ecstasy to the degree that it laments and suspects as counterfeit most of the "manifestations" associated with popular charismatic expression: tongues, loss of physical self-control, apparent madness, and self-proclaimed visionary profundity are all to be eschewed; rather to be preferred is "a modest expression . . . sobriety, quietness, and . . . a genuine happiness." Some demonstrative behaviour arises, he says, merely through spiritual ignorance and a lack of maturity. But some of it is actually antagonistic to the Spirit, a deception of the foolish by "the fiend" who also inspires some persons to self-righteous declamations against sin and self-appointed guardianships of "the law of God." Such people tyrannize spiritually, saying they have been "moved to do so by fervent charity, and by the love of God that is in their hearts. But they lie. It is the fire of hell which is welling up in their minds and imaginations."

The pathway and destination recommended in *The Cloud* is thus found to bear a subsequent practical aspect in the life of the Christian in the world. On the one hand, it enables a distinguishing and avoiding of false religiosity, the "hypocritical bleating" of those who do not have a true knowledge of God. On the other, it grants to the person who has been successful in the work of contemplation a gracious self-transcendence. Therefore, the author exhorts,

> seek to get this gift by grace; for whoever really has it will be well able to control both himself and his possession by virtue of it. It gives him discernment, when he needs it, to read people's needs and characters. It gives him the knack of being at home with everyone he talks to, habitual sinner or not, without sinning himself . . . to the astonishment of the onlooker, and with a magnetic effect on others, drawing them by grace to the same spiritual work that he practises.
>
> His face and his words are full of spiritual wisdom, fervent and fruitful, assured and free from falsehood, far from feigned and affected hypocrites.
>
> (translation by Clifton Wolters, 1961)

This concluding *apropos* aptly ties the special experience of the Christian mystic of the *via negativa* back to the ordinary Christian community at large, wherein by his true humility the mystical contemplative is now able, ironically, to "image" positively the character of Christ.

—David Lyle Jeffrey

THE COMEDY OF ERRORS.
Play by William Shakespeare, 1594(?).

Increasingly seen as a remarkably well-constructed, sophisticated combination of literary and dramatic materials drawn from diverse sources, and as anticipating in a number of ways many of his later comedies and romances, William Shakespeare's *The Comedy of Errors*, while it has always been a hit on the stage, used to be dismissed by critics as apprentice work. Deemed facile, farcical, lightweight, with no interesting characters, no deep meanings, no memorable poetry, the play hardly had a chance in a critical tradition which attached high value to those elements, which rated the tragedies above the comedies anyway, and romantic, poetical comedy above mere farce and clownage. The play was labelled "farce" at least as early as Coleridge's day, and there it has remained, one of Shakespeare's slightest and earliest plays, perhaps the very first. He was soon to leave behind such schoolboy stuff, mere crowd-pleasing frivolity, and begin to write real comedies. This dismissiveness regarding *The Comedy of Errors* is less prevalent nowadays. Recent analysis of the canon and chronology of Shakespeare's works, notably by the Oxford Shakespeare editorial team, would place *Errors* in 1594, the year of its earliest recorded performance, later than *The Two Gentlemen of Verona* and *The Taming of the Shrew* among the comedies, later also than the *Henry VI* trilogy and *Richard III*. It would thus be roughly contemporary with the major narrative poems, and with *Love's Labour's Lost* and *A Midsummer Night's Dream*.

A main reason for the traditional positioning of *Errors* so near the beginning of Shakespeare's career as a dramatist is its evident debt to Roman comedy, especially Plautus's *Menaechmi* and *Amphitryo*. Shakespeare, it was argued, was drawing upon his knowledge of Roman drama gained at school, where Plautus and Terence were among the staples of the curriculum; later in his career, when he knew more and had read more widely, he would no longer need to do so. It is a curious argument at best and Shakespeare continued to draw upon classical works that he may first have read at school throughout his career. In any case, there is more in this play than Roman comedy at second hand. Furthermore, his choice of a classical source may have been made deliberately, with the venue for the play's first performance, or even a specific commission in mind. Records for the Gray's Inn Revels at Christmas, 1594, refer to a play of "errors" like "Plautus his *Menaechmi*" as part of the evening's entertainment; the unusual brevity of the comedy and its overtly classical structure and plot (part of it) suggest that it may have been composed for the occasion and its audience of classically-educated lawyers and law students and their friends, a sort of coterie play with literary allusions and a complicated plot, and a good measure of hilarity.

Whatever the occasion, Shakespeare complicated Plautus's plot even further, by giving the servant of a Syracusan gentleman, as well as the gentleman himself, an identical twin brother. This pair, master and servant, after years of searching, arrive in Ephesus (where Shakespeare chose to set his play, rather than in Plautus's Epidamnus, thus giving it biblical as well as classical resonances). There, unknown to them, live their long-lost respective twins, also master and man. The strangers are immediately mistaken for the local pair, and the Syracusan Antipholus meets the local servant Dromio, mistaking him for his own man; the error is soon repeated in reverse, and the confusion spreads to the family and friends of the Ephesian Antipholus and to the townspeople in general. The visitors become panic-stricken, convinced they are surrounded by witches and devils and that they are going mad, and take refuge in a convent. The local pair, mistaken for the oddly-behaving strangers, are adjudged to be mad and are incarcerated.

But the comedy of identical twins will inevitably end once both sets appear on stage at the same time; such a plot has its own mechanism. But Shakespeare framed that plot with another, drawn from a different genre, that of narrative romance. The play opens with an old man, Egeon, arrested in Ephesus as a citizen of an enemy state, Syracuse, and given the remainder of the day to try to find the money to pay his ransom; if he fails he must be executed at sundown. Before setting off "hopeless and helpless," Egeon tells his long story of wandering and searching. It is a typical romance tale, told in the first person, of shipwreck and separation, the loss of his wife and one of the infant twins with another twin, one of two boys born in the same place at the same time as Egeon's sons, the departure from his home in Syracuse years later of the surviving Antipholus and Dromio to seek news of their lost brothers, and now his own despairing search for the former pair. The threat of doom hangs over the intervening action, and we are reminded frequently of the time of day and thus of the passing of the hours until five o'clock, the hour of execution. Egeon disappears at the end of the first scene and does not reappear until well into the last one; no sooner has he left than Antipholus and Dromio of Syracuse arrive on the scene: the two plots are thus linked immediately, with the father and the son for whom he is searching both in Ephesus. Egeon must of course first meet the wrong pair, the Ephesian ones, who have never known him, and suffer the anguish of their denial of any acquaintance with him when he makes a last, desperate appeal for rescue even as he is being led to execution. Shakespeare makes the suspense last for 200 lines before bringing on the Syracusan pair.

The surprises do not end there. Utterly improbably—and thus utterly typically in the world of romance—the abbess of the convent where the Syracusan Antipholus and Dromio had taken refuge turns out to be Emilia, Egeon's long-lost wife, mother to the Antipholus twins, who had been separated from one of them and the other Dromio after the storm. The family is reunited: husband with wife, parents with children, brothers with brothers. The language of rebirth echoes throughout the scene and, with the moving moments of recognition, given an almost ritualistic solemnity by Shakespeare, the scene anticipates those in his later romances. Almost forgotten in the general rejoicing (Egeon is of course pardoned and freed) are the reconciliation of Antipholus of Ephesus with his wife Adriana and the new couple of the other Antipholus and Adriana's sister Luciana.

This masterful combination of the classical legend of Apollonius of Tyre, the main source of the Egeon plot and known to Shakespeare in John Gower's *Confessio Amantis*, with Roman comedy is typical of his mixing of genres in his dramatic works. The old romance, which he also knew as the story of Pericles, remained in his mind: he returned to it in *Pericles* some years later. And he returned to the comedy of identical twins with the romance motifs of shipwreck and separation in *Twelfth Night*. But *The Comedy of Errors*, with its deft handling of so many dramatic techniques and comic devices, its use of blank verse, rhyme, doggerel, and prose, its confident blending of diverse kinds of source material, does more than look ahead to later achievements. It is itself a masterpiece in miniature, the shortest but not the least of Shakespeare's plays, worthy of its now secure place as a keystone in his dramatic oeuvre.

—Charles W. Whitworth

THE COMPLAINT. See **NIGHT-THOUGHTS**.

THE COMPLEAT ANGLER.
Prose by Izaak Walton, 1653 (and later revisions).

The original edition of *The Compleat Angler* appeared anonymously in 1653, its subtitle begin *The Contemplative Man's Recreation*. It was a small volume, small enough to be slipped into a fisherman's pocket, and few copies have survived. Designed as much to give pleasure as to provide good advice—as the prefatory remarks make clear—the book was well received, and Izaak Walton put his name to the second edition (1655). This was much enlarged and elaborated, so that the revised treatise, with its moral disquisitions and passages of conscious fine writing, was even less of a handbook than the first version.

It had always included poems and songs, and the framework had always been a dialogue, interspersed with snatches of narrative and digressions. Now there are three speakers in the opening scene—a huntsman (Venator), a falconer (Auceps), and an angler (Piscator), instead of Viator and Piscator in the 1653 version. The falconer, having argued the merits of his sport, goes off to practice it; but the huntsman joins Piscator in a leisurely four-day fishing trip along the river Lea, sampling the rural pleasures around Tottenham, Hoddesdon, Amwell, and Ware. The experienced angler constitutes himself Venator's mentor, instructing his "scholar" about the habits of various fresh-water fish, what bait to use, how to cook them.

Piscator also disseminates much curious lore about natural history, and extols the spiritual benefits of the sport that encourages contemplation and patience. The fact that no fewer than four of the twelve Apostles were fishermen is a telling argument in favour of angling. But Piscator's piety does not inhibit his enjoyment of good food and drink or the singing of catches at an ale-house. Walton, a devout Anglican and convinced royalist, wrote *The Compleat Angler* during the Protectorate, and the tone of the book owes much to his idealisation of the good old days.

Walton continued to revise and expand the book. The fifth edition (1676), the last to appear in his lifetime, was entitled *The Universal Angler*. It incorporated an essay on fly-fishing by his angling friend Charles Cotton, and *The Experienced Angler* by Sir Henry Venables. Walton was always modest about his own expertise, and acknowledged his indebtedness to Thomas Barker, whose handbook *The Art of Angling* came out in 1651, and was reprinted as *Barkers Delight* four times before the end of the decade. Walton could scarcely have foreseen that his celebration of his favourite pastime would become his chief claim to literary fame.

The writing of *The Compleat Angler* had itself been a pastime—"the recreation of a recreation." Walton had already published two lives of distinguished men whom he had known, John Donne and Sir Henry Wotton. He was to produce three more brief biographies: George Herbert, Richard Hooker, and Richard Sanderson. Walton was a pioneer in the art of biography. His *Lives* were justly admired in his own lifetime, and are still regarded as little masterpieces. Samuel Johnson, who had a high regard for Walton as a biographer, persuaded Moses Brown to reprint *The Compleat Angler* in 1750, but it was not until the 19th century that its vogue was established.

Almost 300 editions have been published since Charles Lamb, writing to Coleridge in 1796, epitomised its charm: "It breathes the very spirit of innocence, purity and simplicity of heart; there are many choice old verses interspersed in it; it would sweeten a man's temper at any time to read it." How can one account for this belated literary success? Walton's devotees over the past two centuries have certainly included many anglers; but Lamb was no fisherman, and what he singled out for praise is the book's idyllic quality. Even when it first appeared, it was old-fashioned, the testimony of an elderly man to the simple pleasures that had stood him in good stead all his life long. Essentially it is a book that communicates happiness. Walton is known to have been a man with an unusual gift for friendship. He was on excellent terms with people whose social status and education were much more distinguished than his own. And *The Compleat Angler* is a conspicuously friendly book, its language lively and varied, its attitude welcoming, its temper serene.

In Winchester Cathedral there is a commemorative window depicting "honest Izaak" with fishing rod and book, and the motto "Study to be quiet." Posterity has invested Walton with a homely kind of sanctity, and *The Compleat Angler* still evokes an uncommon degree of affection. It is what the Elizabethans might have called a Handful of Pleasant Delights. Diversified with poems and fanciful digressions, it has some of the qualities of a pastoral. Maudlin the milkmaid sings Marlowe's "Come live with me and be my love"; her mother counters it with Ralegh's sober reply. Walton introduces this episode to conjure up a vision of English country life too good to be true even for the first readers of *The Compleat Angler*; but his is not a courtly version of pastoral. Angling is a sport enjoyable by anyone who can afford fishing tackle, and Walton often refers to the brotherhood of those who practice it. The unpretentiousness of *The Compleat Angler* is one clue to its enduring popularity.

—Margaret Bottrall

COMUS.
Play by John Milton, 1634.

Originally nameless in the first printed edition of 1637, this masque or celebration takes the form of a pastoral drama mixed with songs and dances. *Comus* was written for performance on the Feastday of St. Michael: 29 September 1634, at Ludlow Castle on the Welsh border, to honour the inauguration as the lord president of Wales of John Egerton, Earl of Bridgewater. John Milton was aware that Ben Jonson had written two masques for the Stuart court on similar subjects: *Pleasure Reconciled with Virtue*, about the relationship of relaxation to good works as reflected in the labours of Hercules, and *For the Honour of Wales*, about the Welsh and English, a topic appropriate to the title of Prince Charles as Prince of Wales. Milton had also himself previously written an elegantly brief pastoral masque called *Arcades* for Lord Egerton, honouring his stepmother, the Countess Dowager of Derby.

Like most masques Milton's makes open use of its specific occasion and makes direct allusions to its intended audience, using the three Egerton children as performers. The young daughter, Lady Alice Egerton, played the heroine who loses her way after parting from her two brothers in a wood, where she is captured by an evil spirit who seeks to corrupt her. As lord president, the Earl was responsible for keeping the peace in the wild environment of Wales and its borders. Moreover, St. Michael traditionally headed the angelic forces that overthrew the rebel angels led against Heaven by Satan. St. Michael's feastday is still closely associated with harvest festivals celebrating the successful completion of crop-gathering, which often risk becoming orgies of self-indulgence in the benefits of Nature. The plot of *Comus* therefore deals appropriately with subversive forces incarnated in the anti-masque of bestial figures led by Comus, supposedly an offspring of the witch Circe from Homer's *Odyssey*. His magic also shares some of the sinister aura of the Druids associated with ancient, celtic Wales, and it can only be finally neutralised by the white magic of Sabrina (the murdered infant daughter of the ancient British ruler Locrine) whose name survives in corrupted form in that of the River Severn. The river flows near to Ludlow on the Welsh borders, and Sabrina was drowned in it by a jealous stepmother. Sabrina is invoked by a celestial Spirit attending on the children—a part acted by Henry Lawes, the childrens' music teacher, who also wrote the masque's music. (Lawes' music for the songs has survived and has been performed and recorded: it displays considerable expressive powers, for which Milton lauds Lawes both in the masque itself and in the sonnet he later addressed to him.)

Despite its occasional lack of dramatic tension, the masque represents the culmination of the earlier poetical career of Milton, as the longest and most complex poem he produced at this time. It has the characteristics of his other earlier writings: the verse is fluent and melodious, and its predominant values are idealistic and sophisticated. Much of the dialogue between the brothers and the Attendant Spirit is formal and abstract as befits the youthful performers, who show little anxiety about the fate of their missing sister. The captive Lady remains firm and unmoved despite intimidation. Many sections of the masque present a kind of Platonic mysticism about the superiority of virtue to worldly difficulties which is appropriate to its youthful characters' naive and elitist point of view, but this confidence is also reinforced by their Attendant Spirit.

By contrast, the subversive genius of Comus dynamically reflects the darker side of Milton's own sensibility: the arguments for enjoying the sensual resources afforded by Nature are powerfully expressed. Comus echoes Satan tempting Eve in the medieval biblical plays as well as Renaissance versions of the theme of seduction, including Shakespeare's Richard of Gloucester in his courtship of Lady Anne. Comus also anticipates Milton's own compelling Satan in *Paradise Lost*. The power of Comus is seen in the Lady's physical paralysis while under his influence, coupled with his final escape from defeat through the incompetence of the virtuous Brothers, who must depend on the unexpected magic of Sabrina, the murdered bastard daughter of the pagan Locrine. Such effects all indicate that the world of the masque ultimately eludes narrowly positive definitions. This implicit rejection of the self-sufficiency of human virtue matches Milton's own puritanism rather more than the masque's overtly philosophical tone suggests. Milton endows Comus with hedonistic arguments to make the most of this world that cannot easily be refuted, and which indeed Milton treats as plausible choices for the alienated students described later in *Of Education*. G. Wilson Knight praises these speeches of Comus, in which he sees Milton "dramatising a conflict in his own mind" (*The Burning Oracle*, 1939).

It is no wonder that the originally anonymous masque now invariably goes under the name of the evil spirit who is its most memorable character. The innocent virtue of the Lady successfully resists the arguments of Comus, but she is unable to free herself without Sabrina's springwater, which many identify with Christian baptism. Yet Comus himself symbolically escapes to renew his assaults on virtue, through the Brothers' incompetence. Thus evil is presented as not to be overthrown by humanity, even if aided by celestial powers. Thereby the masque not only discreetly admonishes the new lord president of Wales of the difficulty of his responsibilities in dealing with the challenge of an alien culture, it also reminds its spectators of the universal difficulty in protecting innocence from its own incompetence. The masque prefigures in miniature the tragic re-enactment of similar concerns on a cosmic scale in *Paradise Lost*.

—Hugh M. Richmond

CONFESSIO AMANTIS.
Poetry by John Gower, 1390.

John Gower's *Confessio Amantis*, completed and twice revised in the early 1390's, incorporates over 100 stories into the framing narrative of a lover's confession to a priest named Genius. Gower organizes these exempla into a structure derived from the penitential treatises. Priest of Venus as well as orthodox confessor, Genius examines Amans' conscience to ascertain his sins against love. Adapting the model of confessional manuals, like Robert Mannyng's *Handlyng Synne*, Gower arranges the narratives in Books 1 through 6 according to the divisions of the deadly sins of pride, envy, wrath, sloth, avarice, and gluttony.

This organizational pattern is suspended, however, in Book 7, which concerns the education of Alexander, and in Book 8, which consists of only one tale, the Greek romance of Apollonius of Tyre, and the conclusion to Amans' confession. The prologue to the *Confessio Amantis* also complicates the narrative of the lover's examination of conscience because it is a Juvenalian satire on 14th-century society. The abrupt change from the traditional public topoi of the three estates and the golden age in the prologue to the focus on the individual lover's private confession in the succeeding 8 books has raised questions about the unity of the *Confessio Amantis* and the clarity of Gower's plan.

Perhaps Gower's revisions provide the best clue to his purpose. The first recension of the poem, finished in 1390, includes in the prologue Gower's account of his meeting with Richard II on the Thames during which the king commanded him to compose a new work. However, by the time of the third recension of the prologue, completed in the 16th year of Richard's reign (June 1392 to June 1393), Gower revised his claim that he wrote "A bok for king Richardes sake" to the assertion that the *Confessio Amantis* is "A bok for Engelondes sake." In this final version Gower also moved the dedication to Henry Lancaster which had originally appeared in a Latin epilogue into the prologue. Gower's explicit concern with social problems in the prologue as well as his dedication of the poem to royalty suggest that he regarded the *Confessio Amantis* as a mirror for princes, a collection of exempla for the education of the ruling class.

Such a conception of the genre of the *Confessio Amantis* accounts for the transition from the satire of the prologue to the confession of Amans through the rest of the poem. Near the end of the prologue, Gower declares that the social problems of his time result from the disorder in the individual caused by sin.

> The man, as telleth the clergie,
> Is as a world in his partie,
> And whan this litel world mistorneth,
> The grete world al overtorneth.

This analogy between the macrocosm and the microcosm, the public and the private, justifies Amans' confession in Books 1 through 8 and clarifies Gower's purpose in the *Confessio Amantis*, for, he believes, only if individuals rule themselves well, can the nation be properly governed.

Likewise, a recognition that Gower's poem is a mirror for princes solves the problem raised by the apparent inappropriateness of the Genius' account of the education of Alexander the Great in Book 7. Aristotle's instruction of his pupil in the theoretical disciplines of theology, physics, and mathematics, in rhetoric, and in practical matters of ethics, economics, and politics, constitutes for Gower the kind of education needed to govern well.

Genius' discussion of chastity as the fifth and final topic under policy in Book 7 also partially compensates for Gower's failure to concentrate on lust in this book as his organizational plan seems to demand. Perhaps the best explanation of his omission of a book devoted to the seventh deadly sin, however, involves his characterization of Genius. Modeled after characters of the same name in Alain de Lille's *Complaint of Nature* and Jean de Meun's *Roman de la Rose*, Gower's Genius is both an orthodox priest and a priest of Venus. Through the confessor's dual responsibilities, Gower distinguishes between a procreative or good Venus and a lecherous or evil one. By having his confessor repudiate in Book 5 the lustful Venus who rules Jean de Meun's priest, Gower restores Genius to his duties in Alain's poem as a priest of Nature. In the concluding book of the *Confessio Amantis*, Amans, finally acknowledging his old age, realizes that his love is lustful rather than natural; as a result of Genius' instruction, his reason regains control of his desire.

Although the prudish Man of Law in *The Canterbury Tales* berates him for including several narratives about incest in the *Confessio Amantis*, Gower undoubtedly deserves the epithet "moral" by which Chaucer addressed him in Book 5 of *Troilus and Criseyde*.

—Denise N. Baker

CONFESSIONS OF AN ENGLISH OPIUM EATER.
Prose by Thomas De Quincey, 1822; revised edition, 1856.

Written at the age of 36, *Confessions of an English Opium Eater* was Thomas De Quincey's first published work and is now his main claim to fame. The original version was published in the *London Magazine* in 1821 and republished, with minor changes, in book form in 1822. A revised version, twice the length of the original and generally regarded as its artistic inferior, was published in 1856.

The title of De Quincey's masterpiece misleadingly promises sensationalism and exoticism; its publication date also erroneously suggests connections with the later Romantics, Byron and Keats. The overall impression, however, is more of a prose segment of Wordsworth's *The Prelude*. A major part of *Confessions* is autobiography, objectively observed and presented. Almost the entire first half of the 1822 version narrates De Quincey's life from his school days to the start of his association with opium, the aim being to explain the underlying causes for his drug use and to provide a background to the dreams he describes later. The second part, "The Pleasures of Opium," outlines the circumstances, in 1804 at the age of 19 and in his early days at university, in which De Quincey first took the drug. He describes the effects it initially had upon him and rebuts common misconceptions that the occasional use of opium produces intoxication, followed by an equivalent decline into depression and a general torpor. The remaining third of the book, "Introduction to the Pains of Opium," briefly sketches De Quincey's development from an occasional to a daily drug user and then describes at greater length the dreams that tormented him as his physical and mental condition declined.

Confessions is a curious mixture of styles and seemingly confused purposes. To the modern reader the book seldom delivers what it promises. The glamorous title almost immediately leads to disappointment. We quickly discover that De Quincey did not eat opium but drank the rather less sensational laudanum tincture which was as widely available and commonplace as aspirin today. More seriously, 40 years on from the publication of Rousseau's startlingly frank *Confessions*, even contemporary readers might have expected greater revelations and deeper psychological exploration. De Quincey seems painfully aware, as his introduction states, that "nothing is more revolting to English feelings than the spectacle of a human being obtruding on our notice his moral ulcers or scars." He therefore presents the book as an "interesting record . . . in a considerable degree useful and instructive." At two crucial moments, when De Quincey moves from being an occasional or recreational drug user to developing a large daily habit, and again when he commits himself to breaking the habit, he skims tantalisingly over both his motives and his experiences. He blandly states "that at the time I began to take opium daily I could not have done otherwise." The reason he gives is that in the summer of 1813 he "suffered much in bodily health from distress of mind connected with a very melancholy event." He avoids expanding on this event stating that it was "no ways related to the subject now before me" and begs the reader not to criticise him for "his own forbearance and regard for your comfort." But criticise we must, for even contemporary readers must have hungered for an attempt at explanation in a work aiming to be instructive. The closest we get to psychological or medical exploration is much earlier in the work when he records that "it was not for the purpose of creating pleasure, but of mitigating pain in the severest degree that I first began to use opium as an article of daily diet." At the end of the book De Quincey repeats the evasion by skipping over any examination of how and why he broke the habit. He reaches a point when he "concluded that I must die if I continued the opium." He succeeds in "diminishing the opium" despite experiencing "the torments of a man passing out of one mode of existence into another." Frustratingly, the nature of these torments is omitted as are "the motives external to myself" which enabled him to fight his way through them.

De Quincey's other aims for the book show similar inconsistencies and his ambiguous attitude to the drug. He states that one of the aims of the book is to warn the opium eater of the physical and psychological dangers of the habit but succeeds in conveying a predominantly favourable impression of it. Paradoxically, his attempt to correct some popular misconceptions about opium use are contradicted later by his descriptions of his own experiences as a heavy user. Indeed many of the effects he ascribes to opium now seem, in the light of modern knowledge, to be more the product of his own state of mind.

The weaknesses in theme and purpose are, however, counterbalanced by a highly conscious, polished yet apparently effortless style which at times bursts into brilliant flashes of an "impassioned prose" which fluently and lucidly expresses strong emotion. De Quincey demonstrates an extraordinary literary power in capturing the mysterious quality of his dream visions but devotes only one tenth of the book to them. Untimely digressions, though less intrusive than in later works, help to create a disjointed overall effect. Nevertheless, De Quincey's achievement in observing the connections and significances to the unconscious mind of apparently incidental events in daily life and in childhood memories represented, in its time, something new and remarkable in English literature, anticipating Dickens, Joyce, and Woolf.

—Jamie Lane

THE CONSCIOUS LOVERS.
Play by Sir Richard Steele, 1722.

The Conscious Lovers, Sir Richard Steele's last play, loosely derived from Terence's *Andria*, is considered one of the finest examples of sentimental comedy. Drury Lane's managers had originally been reluctant to produce it because the tone seemed too serious for comedy, without, according to Colley Cibber "one laughing line" in it. Steele, too ill to revise, turned the task over to Cibber, who added the characters of Tom and Phillis, and on 7 November 1722, it opened to an unusually long run of 18 consecutive performances, with eight more before the end of the season.

Sentimental drama, based on Shaftesbury's philosophy that true happiness results from benevolence was, in part, a reaction against the intellectual Restoration comedy which had been supported by court aristocrats of previous generations, in part, the result of a change from court patronage to a broader spectrum where the sole common bond was that of feeling or "sentiment." The mode was ideal for a moral reformer like Steele, allowing him to demonstrate (and, by implication, teach) virtuous conduct by playing upon the emotions.

The Conscious Lovers is a kind of moral exemplum, but Steele covers the bare skeleton with flesh of his own age and illustrates his moral views in social terms: the duty of children to their parents, the obligations of friendship, the evils of arranged marriages, and the dangers of excessive jealousy. As in his earlier plays *The Lying Lover* and *The Funeral* Steele's idealized central characters are tested by acute distress and then, as virtue wins over seemingly impossible odds, richly rewarded.

The Shaftesburian premise that man is essentially good precludes innate villainy, so that evil must come from external causes or from mistakes in judgment rather than from flaws of character. Both of these elements are present in *The Conscious Lovers*; the troubles of Bevil Jr. and Indiana are not of their making but stem from the situation in which they find themselves. Bevil is torn between his love for Indiana and his duty to his father's plan that he marry Lucinda; Indiana is a helpless victim of circumstances that have left her orphaned and penniless—the epitome of the pathetic heroine. Parallel with them is the secondary pair of lovers, Myrtle and Lucinda, whose difficulties are exacerbated as much by Myrtle's immoderate jealousy as by the marriage being forced on Lucinda.

Bevil Jr. is the personification of Steele's "Christian Hero" —benevolent, compassionate, and admirable, particularly in that quality so prized by the day, filial piety. His generosity to Indiana began with benevolence that demanded no return except her happiness, but once it develops into love, he is faced with a conflict between his own desires and his duty to his father. The gentle Indiana is his counterpart, bearing her afflictions with noble resignation, deferential to her elders, refusing to believe Bevil has ulterior designs on her honor. Steele presents the pair as models rather than the norm, and offers the worldly interpretation of Bevil's actions through the eyes of Indiana's aunt, Isabella. Even when she finally understands, she can only exclaim, "they are made for one another as much as Adam and Eve were, for there is no other of their kind but themselves."

The treatment of the secondary couple is lighter, but the underlying message is equally moral. Myrtle must learn to control his unreasonable jealousy, and Lucinda must be saved from an arranged and loveless marriage. The heavy morality is lightened by comic scenes involving less sympathetic characters who also serve as examples of improper behavior: Lucinda's snobbish bourgeois mother Mrs. Sealand, the coxcomb Cimberton, and the two servants Tom and Phillis, whose attempts to imitate the airs and manners of their betters are a satire of contemporary society.

One of the ways in which sentimental comedy differs markedly from the Restoration mode is in its sympathetic treatment of the older generation. Bevil Sr., Mr. Sealand, and Isabella are honest, sincere, and morally upright. The two fathers arrange the marriage between Bevil Jr. and Lucinda in the belief that it is an ideal match, Isabella's only care is for her niece's welfare. None of them places social or financial status above the happiness of the young, and their approval of the change in wedding plans puts a moral seal on the action.

Steele claimed the play "was writ for the sake of the scene of the fourth act," in which Bevil Jr. persuades Myrtle that a duel is not the way to resolve their differences. Steele had long opposed duelling and, in *The Conscious Lovers*, found a means to demonstrate his principles in highly charged terms. It is, perhaps, the best representation of his thesis that "a play has the effect of example and precept" in correcting evil habits. It also reveals the weakness of the sentimental mode, for the didactic message, however excellent, does not contain the dramatic impact of physical confrontation.

It would be fallacious to assign the influence of sentimental drama entirely to Steele, but certainly *The Conscious Lovers* incorporates all the main elements of a style that gradually came to dominate the theatre. That the Age of Reason had a taste for such drama is not an anomaly but a correlation to the emphasis on intellect. A serious if improbable plot, exemplary hero, pathetic heroine, good-natured characters with middle-class values and, above all, morality presented in emotional terms not only appealed to a large segment of the 18th-century public but adapted well to the changing societies of the next two centuries.

—Helene Wickham Koon

THE CONSERVATIONIST.
Novel by Nadine Gordimer, 1974.

The Conservationist, Nadine Gordimer's story of an African farm, exposes the colonialist biases of her predecessors Olive Schreiner and Karen Blixen (Isak Dinesen), through the self-incriminating interior monologue of its central character, Mehring, a pig-iron industrialist whose international entrepreneurial activities contrast with his weekend pose as would-be farmer and conservationist. Despite his origins in Namibia, Mehring is a thoroughly representative South African type, his story offering a classic example of the "complicity plot." In this masterplot of recent South African fiction individual whites seek lives of relative harmlessness, separation, and privacy, only to find themselves unable to maintain any such separate peace. In *The Conservationist* the return of the politically repressed is symbolized by the slow rising to the surface of an imperfectly buried black body, accompanied by the repossession of the land by blacks, in symbolic and politically proleptic terms. Influenced by the

Black Consciousness movement, which emphasised a return to black cultural roots and traditions, Gordimer employs Zulu myth to create a buried logic of fictional events, a subtext which slowly comes to obliterate the social text of public culture. The major events on the farm—drought, the dead man, the attack on Solomon for debt, fire, the spirit-possession of Phineas's wife, flood, and finally reburial of the black body as the cycle of the seasons completes itself—are specifically related to patterns of Zulu myth, as represented in the novel by interpolated quotations from Henry Callaway's *The Religious System of the Amazulu* (1878). Thus the attack on Solomon connects with the non-payment of a cultural debt to the "Amatongo" (ancestors) in the cursory burial of a black brother. Rainmaking practices, mediumship, and spirit-possession articulate a different set of values to those of white society. In addition the feminine empowerment of these black cultural practices contrasts with the masculine colonialism and latent sexual fascism of Mehring's world. Phineas's wife's spirit-possession shapes the life of her surrounding community, whereas the white female characters are almost without exception sexually exploited and repressed. The point is dramatised in Mehring's airborne molestation of his flight-neighbour, a young girl, in a scene in which the identification of woman and land allows sexual guilt to function as a surrogate for colonial lusts.

It may be objected that the mythological anchoring of the novel involves resorting to an archaic and pre-industrial basis for African values, rendering the tale both apolitical and ahistorical. Gordimer is, however, careful to demystify the content of religious symbols as such, concentrating upon their potential power as carriers of political change. Thus, when floods follow the activities of the rainmakers, the weather comes from the Mozambique channel, near the Portuguese territory which was soon to claim its independence. The regeneration of the land by fire and flood, a mock-apocalypse, offers a vision of Africa without the white man, as Mehring's labourers take over the farm in his enforced absence. When the black body is reburied the reader learns that "he had come back," invoking the African National Congress rallying cry "Afrika! Mayibue!" ("Africa! May it come back!"). The refusal to address political issues is more properly that of Mehring, a thoroughly modernist character through whose consciousness the entire narrative is filtered. Mehring's colonialism extends to the whole of reality. His interior monologue creates the impression of consciousness functioning in a void, dissociated from the world about him. Just as his relationship with the young girl involved surreptitious contact beneath a pretence of physical separation, so his society is presented as a set of circumscribed codes and worlds which communicate only crudely, underhandedly or with violence. Mehring's wilful refusal to recognise his place in history, his botched attempts to communicate across the race and class lines, and his solipsistic blindness to events in the black community culminate (in a highly ambiguous ending) in a mock death and final abandonment of his claims. As a result *The Conservationist* offers a prophetic image of a different South African future, in the best tradition of the visionary political novel. In formal terms, Gordimer throws into sharp relief the connections between conventional representations of realism and the imposition of colonial structures on the land and landscape of Africa. By rendering an internal reality (Mehring's) progressively divorced from the reality outside it, and ultimately replaced by an alternative social text, Gordimer refuses to grant final narrative or political authority to her white centre of consciousness, and avoids translating events into the realism of a materialist society. Modernist Mehring is "dis-placed," in more than one sense, in favour of a socially-led aesthetic in which conservation equates with community and possession with prophecy.

—Judie Newman

COOPER'S HILL.
Poem by Sir John Denham, 1642 (and later revisions).

Cooper's Hill, Sir John Denham's best known poem, was first published during the early period of the Civil War. A revised version appeared in 1655, and the final version in Denham's *Poems and Translations* of 1668. It is this final version which became one of the most read and admired poems during the later 17th and 18th centuries. Its fame was twofold: as the prime work of one of the reformers of poetic numbers, doing much to establish the heroic couplet as one of poetry's main forms, and as the progenitor of a vast corpus of topographical poems. Pope acknowledged both factors. His *An Essay on Criticism* praises "the Easie Vigor of a Line, / Where Denham's Strength, and Waller's Sweetness join"; and his own loco-descriptive poem, *Windsor-Forest*, affirms that "On Cooper's Hill eternal Wreaths shall grow, / While lasts the Mountain, or while Thames shall flow."

Cooper's Hill is also a political poem in its praise of Stuart royalism, and it is this aspect which modern criticism has stressed. The key to the poem's success, however, is the way in which the political and moral meaning is made to inhere in landscape. It is Denham's method of description and the poem's careful structure which allow the poet's visual experience to shape the meaning. Landscape is more than an emblem to be read and interpreted: it is the natural manifestation of an ideal which the poet seeks to re-create in equivalent verbal terms.

The poem opens by asserting the value of contemporary landscape. Poets make their subjects, so it is up to the writer to make of Cooper's Hill (near Egham in Surrey) a modern Parnassus. From the summit, the poet then surveys the prospect, his eye lighting first on the far distance where the towering mass of St. Paul's Cathedral appears to be either "a proud / Aspiring mountain, or descending cloud," while the city of London at its foot "seems at this distance but a darker cloud." The grandeur and stability of the cathedral establish its value as contrasted with the unattractive city. Having clarified a visual conflict, Denham elaborates it in political terms, associating cathedral with monarchy (James I began and Charles I completed repair work on St. Paul's) and city with its blind businessmen. This, then, is the poem's method: description fixes the essential qualities of the scene, and reflection relates them to contemporary issues.

The poet next dwells on the hill of Windsor with its "easie and unforc't ascent." The sight is one of harmony and moderation, nature itself indicating that order lies in avoidance of extremes. Windsor's royal associations, both past and present, form the subject of Denham's development of the scene and make it a politically relevant contrast to the city of London. His reflections on monarchy are halted when his eye catches sight of St. Anne's Hill, upon which stood the Benedictine Chertsey Abbey now reduced to "dismal heaps." Destruction here contrasts with the creativity noted at St. Paul's, and the rage and extremism which caused that destruction with the moderation of Windsor's hill. The despoliation of the abbey was the work of Henry VIII, so that royalism, too, can be taken to destructive extremes in the "Name of Zeal." The poet's appeal for a temperate region as a refuge is answered by the most famous passage in the poem, Denham's description of the River Thames winding below Cooper's Hill (visually, then, we are moving towards the foreground). Nature here asserts its beauty, order, and beneficent creativity. The climax of the account comes in the much-imitated "Thames couplets," where the poet exclaims his wish to make his own poem flow like the river, "Though deep, yet clear, though gentle, yet not dull, / Strong without rage, without ore-flowing full." The balanced structure of these lines is the culmination of a stylistic feature which Denham employs earlier in the poem (e.g., St. Paul's as "Secure, whilst thee the best of Poets sings, / Preserv'd from ruine by the best of Poets sings"). Just as the landscape represents an ideal of harmony, so Denham seeks to make his poem stylistically balanced so that it also comes to represent the ideal it recommends. Poem and landscape become as one expression.

The poet's view now embraces a whole section of landscape rather than an individual feature, as if stepping back to perceive a panorama. This broad view he sees as uniting opposites, such as "the steep horrid roughness of the Wood" and "the gentle calmness of the flood," into a harmonized entity. Variety and harmony can co-exist, reflecting the divine creation of order out of discord and implying the possibility of social harmony. Past realization of this ideal and present failure to realize it are suggested by Denham's account of two chases on the slopes of Cooper's Hill. A stag hunt on Egham Mead represents current political uncertainties (the editor of the 1655, post-regicide, edition speaks of "that excellent Allegory of the Royall Stag"), whereas an earlier pursuit of liberty by arbitrary power ended on the same Runnymede where Magna Carta sealed a harmonious resolution by which "Kings give liberty, and subjects love." Both oppressive kings and rapacious subjects have since threatened this peace, both running "to the same extreams." The lesson lies in the landscape: a river forced from its natural course will flood the land. This image, retained for the very last lines of the poem in the 1655 and 1668 editions, acts as a warning to observe the order and moderation which the landscape declares, if we have eyes to see.

—W.B. Hutchings

CORINNA'S GOING A-MAYING.
Poem by Robert Herrick, 1648.

Robert Herrick's "Corinna's Going a-Maying," the only text of which is found in the *Hesperides* of 1648, is one of the finest Caroline lyrics, deceptive only in an elegance of diction which can cause the reader to miss its substantial content.

A celebration of the first of May as the beginning of spring goes back to before the coming of Christianity to western Europe. The 4th-century poem *Pervigilium Veneris* (The Vigil of Venus) which appears to be one of Herrick's sources, already contains the same elements as Herrick's poem: a ritual excursion into the woods and fields to celebrate the coming of spring and the first days of love and courtship after the constrictions of the winter. In the Middle Ages the May celebrations continued, being ritualised in aristocratic circles into elaborate May-games. They continue today, in such forms as the May morning carol in Oxford and the dance and procession of the "Padstow 'Oss" in Cornwall.

At the time when Herrick was writing (this poem is conjectured to date from the 1630's) such annual communal celebrations were becoming the focus of considerable political and religious debate: the Puritan, ultimately Parliamentary, party disapproved of these markers in the year as reminiscent of either pagan festivals or of the sacramental calendar of the Catholic and Anglican churches. Those who could subsequently be described, as attitudes hardened, as "Cavaliers" or royalists on the other hand took pleasure in such recreations, seeing them as harmless and socially unifying.

Herrick, throughout the *Hesperides*, devotes many poems of celebration to the annual festive year, both within the church and outside it, delighting in this reminiscence of antiquity which enables him to write poems of ritual and (in all senses) pastoral celebration just as if he were a Greek or Roman poet.

As well as marking an occasion in the year, this is a poem about love and the transience of pleasure, a theme common to almost all cultures, but one which occurs literally times without number in the works of the Caroline lyrists. In his concluding stanza Herrick makes reference to the most celebrated classical precedent, Catullus' "Vivamus mea Lesbia atque amemus . . .," a poem which received a particularly fine translation from the early 17th-century poet Thomas Campion, whose version is echoed in Herrick's conclusion.

Throughout the poem, Herrick uses clearly sacramental imagery: this is a ritual, equated with religious ritual in such words as "Mattens," "Hymnes," "profanation." The poem concerns itself with moments of transformation: flowers into votaries, natural things into adornments for Corinna, the decorated and garlanded streets into a simulacrum of the fields, the single into the married and, finally, the living (gently, inevitably) into those who will join the dead. Herrick does not use this final transformation simply as an argument to persuade his Corinna into surrender (as does, most notably, Marvell's "To His Coy Mistress"): he and his Corinna simply join the public ceremony as anticipated, but they do so in the consciousness of their mortality and the transience of pleasure.

The nexus of classical and biblical allusions in the last stanza could be called a collection of commonplaces. It is interesting to note, however, that the same tissue of allusions, and in much the same order occur in that great Caroline meditation on transience, Burton's *The Anatomy of Melancholy* (section 3.4.2.1.; 1638 edition, p. 684), a reminder of the serious substance of what might appear to be an elegant, if conventional, poem.

—Peter Davidson

CORIOLANUS.
Play by William Shakespeare, 1606(?).

Coriolanus is William Shakespeare's last and most bitter study of Rome's implicit glory; an Elizabethan stereotype from which he was a vehement dissenter. The earlier Roman plays examine the monomania, the selfishness, and the paranoia which underlie the eternal power-struggle that torments the city. Rome comprises a series of factions each claiming its goal is stability. This is never achieved, for the factions comprise self-seekers, ideologues, monomaniacs, cynics. At its close *Julius Caesar* may *imply* that the Augustan ideal is about to bear fruit in the victory of Octavius Caesar. But Shakespeare challenges this "official" view of history. The cold-fish Octavius is dominated by the sybaritic but charismatic Antony. And while Egypt is enervatingly decadent in *Antony and Cleopatra*, Augustan Rome is icy, mechanical, and soulless.

Coriolanus is governed by this sense of the unattainable ideal of "Elizabethan" Rome. It plunges us into the turbulence of hunger riots in the streets of pre-imperial Rome—a community alienated and riven by irreconcilable schisms; a world hagridden by its factions, each equally mindless. There is bread a-plenty, but the patricians will not distribute it to the common people: "What authority surfeits on would relieve us . . ." complains the First Citizen, and—without ever being refuted by the other side—predicates a city state where the upper classes "suffer us to famish, and their storehouses cramm'd with grain; make edicts for usury, to support usurers; repeal daily any wholesome act established against the rich, and provide more piercing statutes daily to chain up and restrain the poor. . . ."

We recognise, however, not only patrician intransigence and oppression; as in all such power-struggles, the plebeians are themselves led by petty demagogues lacking intelligence, foresight, or public spirit. Part of the play's desperate timelessness comprises its foreshadowing of 20th-century predicaments. The question of true equity in civic government is closely addressed, but as always with Shakespeare, while the questions are formulated with disturbing clarity, there are no answers.

Civil malaise is only a part of the problem *Coriolanus* presents. Their neighbours, the Volsces, are threatening war—or so the Roman patricians maintain. But not the least terrifying part of the tragi-farce of Rome is that a valid cause for these hostilities is never presented.

This is the background, but the play of course is named after the Roman general who leads the patrician cause—Caius Marcius—later accorded the battle honour of the title Coriolanus. Of all Shakespeare's tragic protagonists he is the least charismatic—indicating his total lack of higher imagination. He never utters a single speech which is memorable save for the general negative and vituperative tone it conveys. The entire play is without an anthologisable excerpt.

We see Marcius first as enemy of the people, scorning and denigrating the avowedly shifty and turbulent plebeians. And we learn that another bout of motiveless Roman-Volscian hostilities is in train. With characteristic insight Shakespeare then shows us the domestic life of the great Roman general's household. We learn that this colossus of the battlefield comes from a totally matriarchal background. Coriolanus' mother Volumnia is a frightening study of rampant matriarchalism—another modern echo in this prophetic and gloomy play.

The core of the action juxtaposes civic turbulence and battlefield success for the Romans. Coriolanus, monomaniacal, brave, but pathologically foolhardy, wins the day—though significantly his fellow Romans never make him general of their army. Much to the chagrin of Aufidius, the drab Volscian rival to Coriolanus, the city of Corioli falls. Returning in triumph, Coriolanus (as he is now called), seeks to become consul in Rome. But Brutus and Sicinius, the tribunes of the people, deliberately foment unrest, and persuade the mob of Coriolanus' unsuitability for office because of his pride. At the public ceremony where he must beg the popular vote Coriolanus is goaded by the demagogue-driven populace. He loses his temper, insults the citizens, is arrested and exiled. "I banish you," he cries as he leaves Rome, lucky to escape with his life.

He seeks Aufidius, and in a terrible fit of destructive pique, begs the privilege of fighting against his own country. Made aware of this, the Romans panic and send Coriolanus' mother and wife to beg him off as the Volscian army approaches. Their pleas are successful, he reneges upon his bargain, and refuses to sack Rome. Upon his return to Corioli he is arraigned by the opportunist Aufidius, arrested, and perfunctorily assassinated.

Its bitterness, its deliberately unresonant speech, its gloomy view of noble "manly" aspirations assuredly make *Coriolanus* one of Shakespeare's most trenchant and intelligent plays, but these very qualities preclude popular appeal. Equally disturbing is the play's applicability to our own world; the recognition of how little progress we have made since Shakespeare portrayed so clearly the horror, absurdity, and aridity of the world of military boyscouts and civic ostriches.

—T. Bareham

THE COUNTRY PARSON.
Prose by George Herbert, 1652.

George Herbert when he died in 1633 was not yet 40. He had been in priest's orders for less than three years, and his English works were still in manuscript. His poems he sent on his deathbed to his friend Nicholas Ferrar of Little Gidding, who had them printed in the following year under the title *The Temple*. His prose treatise was also entrusted to a member of the Ferrar entourage, but for some unknown reason it was not published till 1652, when it was included in *Herbert's Remains*. That it was intended to supplement the poems is suggested by its title, *A Priest to the Temple*; but its scope is indicated by the sub-title, *The Country Parson His Character, and Rule of Holy Life*. It is as *The Country Parson* that the book is generally known. Izaak Walton in his *Life* of Herbert used no other name.

At the time of its publication the Church of England, under the Cromwellian dispensation, was in eclipse. *The Book of Common Prayer* was proscribed and many faithful pastors dispossessed. The editor, who contributed a valuable "Prefatory View of the Life of Mr. George Herbert" did not disclose his own identity until the treatise was reprinted in 1671, when he congratulated himself on his temerity in issuing the original edition "in that day when Violence was at its height." In the 1671 preface he revealed himself as Dr. Barnabas Oley, a Cambridge divine who had suffered under the Protectorate for his strong royalist sympathies. Reinstated and promoted at the Restoration, he specially commends Herbert's book to the younger clergy as a reminder of "what a Halcyonian Calm, a Blessed Time of Peace, this Church of England had for many years, above all the Churches in the World beside." Walton, writing in 1670, also looks back nostalgically to what seemed an idyllic period, suffusing Herbert at Bemerton in a sanctified radiance.

Yet *The Country Parson* itself is concerned with actualities. It was written during the brief period when Herbert's daily endeavour was to strengthen the hold of the established church on the hearts and minds of his parishioners. His own preface tells how he came to set down "the Form and Character of a true Pastor, that I may have a mark to aim at, which also I will set as high as I can, since he shoots higher that threatens the Moon, than he that aims at a Tree."

The word "Character," emphasised on the title page by large capitals, links the book with other 17th-century essays epitomising the typical characteristics of a chosen model. But Herbert's book is nourished by firsthand experience. It is a series of reflections on the different aspects of his calling, and gives the impression of a work in progress. It surveys the opportunities afforded to a country parson to become a "deputy of Christ," and is not an idealising fantasy. Those called to the cure of souls could still profit from Herbert's spiritual wisdom and shrewd assessment of human foibles—though the breakdown of the traditional parochial system in the countryside makes the relationship between pastor and flock postulated by Herbert seem quite archaic.

Nowadays the majority of readers of *The Country Parson* will be those who already are attracted to Herbert's poems. For them, the book illuminates both his personality and his art. The chapters on The Parson Preaching and The Parson Catechising particularly throw light on his poetic methods. His fondness for parables, his homely imagery, his forthright diction, are all related to the axiom "People by what they understand are best led to what they understand not." He recommends familiar language and everyday comparisons because they were habitually used by Christ himself. And *The Country Parson* is written in an admirably lively and straightforward style.

Herbert does not minimise the difficulties encountered in a rural parish—squalid dwellings, ignorance, obstinacy, arrogance on the part of the well-to-do—but the reiterated note is one of joy: "His parish is all his joy and thought." Sunday is his "day of joy," "the pulpit is his joy and his throne." Some of the Bemerton poems, notably "The Cross," witness to the fact that Herbert did suffer anxieties and frustrations in his chosen calling, but chiefly on account of the ill-health that thwarted his desire for total dedication to the service of Jesus his Master. *The Country Parson* is explicitly not autobiographical, yet the priest it portrays is recognisably George Herbert. He is comfortably circumstanced, highly educated, at ease with people of whatever social background. More significantly, he is a man of holiness.

Lord Herbert of Cherbury recorded that his younger brother, in his latter years, was esteemed by his neighbours as "little less than sainted." Nicholas Ferrar testified that Herbert's faithful discharge of his pastoral duties made him "justly a companion to the primitive Saints." *The Country Parson* is irradiated by Herbert's reverence for all that is holy and his beautiful courtesy towards his fellows. He wrote it that he might have a mark to aim at, but only a man who had already attained a measure of sanctity could have set down his ideals with such single-hearted sincerity.

—Margaret Bottrall

THE COUNTRY-WIFE.
Play by William Wycherley, 1675.

It is likely that William Wycherley's *The Country-Wife* was first performed by the King's Company on 12 January 1675 with a second, and penultimate, production for that year recorded three days later. Its publication was entered in the Term Catalogues in May and the title page of the 1675 edition included a quotation from Horace which implies that the play met with so poor a reception on account of its modernity. Certainly the play has a contemporary flavour, with its references to specific London settings. On the other hand, the hinge of the play's action, Horner's feigned impotence, is as old as the plot of Terence's *Eunuchus*, although other details of the plotting, notably the tricks with letters and with disguise, are more closely indebted to Wycherley's great French contemporary, Molière.

In addition to the antiquity of its plot one might claim that the play's broad theme, that of the relationship between the sexes, is as ancient as recorded comedy. More specifically this theme here embraces the problems both of winning and of keeping a wife which had regularly lent themselves to the plotting of romantic and satiric comedy respectively. As earlier 17th-century dramatists had done, Wycherley with *The Country-Wife* explored the merits and disadvantages of trust in courtship and marriage and, concomitantly, the destructive effects of the sexual jealousy which is uppermost in the mind of many of his characters most of the time. What was most contemporary, however, was the playing of this theme with the role of the ingénue at its centre.

Clearly the Restoration was fascinated by the state of innocence, by the effects of experience on it, and by its transition to knowledge and sophistication; nowhere was this fascination explored more diversely than by playwrights exploiting the potential of young professional actresses. Those who played the role of ingénue, in various modes, were talented (Moll Davis's dancing was admired by Pepys) and attractive (the legs of several were displayed in breeches parts). Mrs. Boutell, the original Mrs. Pinchwife, is described in Betterton's *History of the Stage*, as not tall and with a childish look; she generally acted "the young innocent lady whom all the heroes are mad in love with." With Mrs. Pinchwife this role married well with another preoccupation of 17th-century comedy, the vulnerabilities of those bred in unsophisticated ignorance but operating in an alien play world of codes and manners. In comedy the incomer is usually male, a pretender to wit and one to be gulled out of his fortune and prospects; he is likely to be a countryman loose in the shark-tank of the metropolis. Mrs. Pinchwife expresses the essence of both roles: the artless ignorance of the child, with the stupidity of the country gull, here relying on the maid Lucy to direct her actions and on the rake Horner to save her by a lie.

Although these are clearly the play's main interests, earlier moral criticism of Restoration comedy focussed on Horner, culminating with Macaulay for whom English literature reached its nadir with the "skunk" Wycherley. Much 20th-century criticism has adopted other approaches, although nearly always one finds that moral considerations are implicit. Of course, for contemporary theorists moral social purpose was paramount and, indeed, Wycherley gestured at this in the epilogue, warning men not to imagine that they could get away with behaving like Horner.

Horner is indeed a witty strategist, but for the plot to work itself out while maintaining Mrs. Pinchwife's lascivious ineptitude Wycherley needed a much cleverer strategist, one to think quickly and use advantageously the circumstances that arose. Not unlike Molière, he chose a true outsider, a female servant, barely acknowledged by the other characters, her reward unspecified by Horner at the end. From Act III the maid Lucy operates as clear-sighted commentator on others' actions, as pragmatist beside Alithea's foolish and self-deceiving promise to Sparkish, and as one who can stage-manage for Horner when his own scenario gets out of hand. In addition she has a witty way with words; she questions meanings, offers *doubles entendres*, and plays on romantic susceptibilities. Above all, as a commentator, she can speak in aphorisms, offering what might be seen as the sentimental germ at the moral core of the play, "Can there be greater cheat or wrong done to a man than to give him your person without your heart?" In these terms she exposes the whole plot as cheat and wrong. Where Wycherley had trouble was in providing a motive for her actions; we are to understand merely that Lucy's wish to see Alithea suitably matched is behind all she does. Certainly the part was thought sufficiently important to be given to Mrs. Corey, a versatile and well-known actress.

Lucy's wit serves also to highlight the deficiencies of other would-be plot manipulators. Sir Jasper organising his women, Horner with his lie and his farcical china-store, Harcourt with the "languages" he can speak, Pinchwife's desperate ploys. All are at odds, all seeking selfish ends and the postures of all are more or less deceiving, from Horner's sexual status to Sparkish's faith in Alithea; even Harcourt devotedly pursues Alithea disguised as a clergyman.

The exposure of a parasite society, operating by deception, is a deeply serious matter, but *The Country-Wife* is still a very entertaining play. One might suggest that some of the disguises are stock, but that variations on them should have been refreshing to the original audiences: Harcourt's "divine" language, the attentions of Horner to Pinchwife's pretty "brother-in-law" and the "real" seduction taking place offstage. It seems strange that in 1675 a play which is such a clever blending of the old with such modern elements as these, should not have been more popular than Wycherley's epigraph implies.

—Barbara A. Murray

CRANFORD.
Novel by Elizabeth Gaskell, 1853.

> In the first place, Cranford is in possession of the Amazons.

Cranford is often seen as the quintessential Elizabeth Gaskell text—a simple, charming, tale of life in a small English village. As a result, much conventional critical commentary on *Cranford* unproblematically asserts the ironic status of the opening line. The Cranford ladies—genteel and delicate—are "simply" the inverse of the mythically fierce female warriors. Feminist theory, however, now offers a new way to explore the Cranford community of women, one that examines the Victorian gender ideology which structures their presentation.

One such examination focusses on the relation of women to language in the text. There appear to be two "models" of language, public and private, access to which is structured upon gendered lines. The public language is exemplified by Deborah Jenkyns and her love for Samuel Johnson. In essence, this type of language is gendered masculine. Not only is Johnson its originator, but the rector is its propagator, and Deborah ensures that it remains at the centre of Cranford's language. The characteristics of this language can be ascertained by collating the evidence which the language of the rector, Mr. Smith, and others provide. Mr. Smith's letter to Mary, the narrator of *Cranford*, confines itself to the communication of apparently impersonal facts: there is rain, trade is stagnant, and business rumours are disagreeable. The rector's letters are similarly impersonal. They appear not to be addressed to his wife at all, and provide none of the personal, domestic information which she requires from him. Deborah Jenkyns's letters confirm the impersonal, "public" nature of this masculine language. They are letters from which "Anyone might profit," and are compared to Hester Chapone's published *Letters on the Improvement of the Mind* (1773).

The residents of Cranford appear to share Deborah's enthusiasm for masculine language. Their obsession with nomenclature, the "proper" form of address, suggests an interest in an impersonal use of language which establishes public status. The discussion on how to address Lady Glenmire; the preference for naming Sam Brown "the signor" because "it sounded so much better"; and the overall tendency to transform names from the personal to the formal, suggests that the Cranford women use and delight in "masculine" language. Mary, however, finds such language unsatisfactory, dull and lifeless. Her disapproval of this public, "masculine" language parallels her disapproval, couched in comic terms, of Cranfordian propriety and elegant economy. Mary cites a number of occasions on which adherence to propriety necessitates the public disavowal of what is a personal pleasure, be it oranges, an evening's magical entertainment, or a visit to an old lover.

But of course, reading *Cranford* one is struck not only by the constraint of these women's lives, but also the vitality and spontaneity. If the Cranford women are concerned with nomenclature, they are also prodigious and imaginative storytellers. Not only does the imparter of news partake of an exalted status in Cranford, but there is a constant exchange of stories. More importantly, the status of the Cranfordian women as "storytellers" is significantly different from their status as users of masculine language. Whenever women in Cranford espouse masculine language and the rules of propriety which mimic its impersonality, they are essentially ridiculous creatures, all "swimming courtesy," bowing acceptance, and polite speech. As storytellers, however, women retain a dignity which overrides any impression of ridiculousness, a dignity achieved primarily by the personal nature of storytelling in Cranford. Though the stories of the cat who swallowed the lace, and the cow in the flannel suit are comic, the storytellers are not ridiculous in their telling.

Cranford explores the fragmented speaking status of women who accept the authority of a public, masculine discourse, while revelling in a creative, vital, "private" discourse of their own. Specifically, Mary Smith, the narrator of *Cranford*, concentrates on the change of status which the women undergo when they alter their method of communication. Her interest in this "other," personal language is seen in her eager willingness to listen to the tales of Miss Pole, Miss Barker, and Miss Matty. But Mary does with these tales something which the Cranford women would never think of doing: she publishes them. What the women deem a "private" incident to be related when propriety can be momentarily banished, is brought into the public realm of discourse—taking its place with the rector's sermons, Mrs. Chapone's letters, and Samuel Johnson in the published, public world. By doing so, Mary attempts to confer the same "authority" and "validity" which such public discourse possesses upon the private discourse which resides behind the "proper" sphere of the Cranford spinsters.

For readers sensitive to the depiction of types of language in *Cranford*, the opening sentence is no longer simply ironic. By asserting the validity of a language which stresses creativity, equality, and the personal, Mary attempts to banish the fragmented female self created by the split between the "public" female sphere—the domestic, restricted sphere of the Cranford spinsters—and the "private" or hidden sphere of their storytelling. She confers retrospectively a unification of self upon Cranford women which, as speakers/users of both masculine and creative languages, they lack. By "publishing" their private speech and in effect making them speak, Mary attempts to fashion the women of Cranford into "amazons," women who step out of the boundaries of a female "proper" sphere by speaking with a voice not contained by the domestic sphere which constrains them.

—Susan Hamilton

CRY, THE BELOVED COUNTRY.
Novel by Alan Paton, 1948.

When Alan Paton's *Cry, The Beloved Country* appeared in 1948 it was compared favourably with Harriet Beecher Stowe's *Uncle Tom's Cabin* and praised for its lack of bias in presenting "a calm and clear statement, in human terms, of South Africa." Since then several black writers, most notably Ngugi wa Thiong'o, have questioned Paton's realism and identified his central black character, the Zulu parson Stephen Kumalo, as a product of the white imagination. Valued on its first appearance as a revealing record of the South African social and racial situation in a brief period after the end of World War II and for many years the world's window on South Africa, it is now widely regarded as a work of liberal paternalism, its Christian sense of a common humanity tragically mocked by the movement of recent history. Such an ideological reading does not do complete justice to the moral intensity which shapes the novel nor to the lyric "singing" with which Paton celebrates the Natal countryside, witnessed most memorably in the famous opening, "There is a lovely road that runs from Ixopo into the hills. . . ."

Paton was driven by two impulses, the one to constructive social work, the other to be a writer. The first of these impelled him to write about his own observations of the social and moral disintegration of South Africa, the drift of young men to Johannesburg and the consequent problem of urbanisation and growing frustration and crime within the townships, above all the crime of man's inhumanity to man. It is this desire to write, as Paton put it, "books that would stab South Africa in the conscience" that leads to the novel's apparent realism, parts of it being written in a conversational discourse borrowed from seemingly "real life" situations that Paton himself had experienced. One of the white priests, Father Vincent, is based on Father Trevor Huddleston and there was an actual gold-find at Odendaalsrust as described in Paton's fictional account. The writer, however, shapes the impulse of the social reformer into an apocalyptic vision of the struggle between good and evil, a story of reconciliation and ultimately of regeneration after suffering.

Paton begins with the repeated motif of the father's quest for a son. The Reverend Stephen Kumalo's journey to find Absalom in the maelstrom of Johannesburg is paralleled by the search of the white farmer, James Jarvis, for his son Arthur, not in the sense of pursuing an errant son but in order to understand what kind of man Arthur is, representing as he does the younger generation of liberal whites for whom the status quo is a burden on the conscience. The murder of Arthur by Absalom functions in a similar way to that of Henry Carson in an earlier "liberal" text, Elizabeth Gaskell's *Mary Barton*. In both, the incident illustrates moral disintegration as a result of hardship, both writers offer a warning of incipient violence to a complacent readership, and both finally use the event to lead to a redemptive vision of Christian forgiveness and reconciliation. Paton ends the novel with the Reverend Kumalo returning to his village, his son in prison awaiting execution, taking with him Absalom's pregnant girlfriend and striking up a friendship with the young son of the murdered Arthur Jarvis.

Cry, The Beloved Country is not then a work of realism but a novel with a message and it thus invites the usual questions relating to the way life is expressed in art: does Paton's "message" make sense and satisfy on the imaginative evidence supplied by the text? The presentation of the black characters is a useful test-case. Characters in general in this novel are not defined psychologically but ethically. Stephen Kumalo is cast in the mould of what has been known pejoratively since Stowe's novel as an "Uncle Tom" character. He remains the suffering Christlike figure from beginning to end, full of humility, always bewildered. Even after his bitter experiences in the city he can still address Jarvis's little grandson as *inkosana*, little master. He clearly represents the older generation of Africans who behave with self-effacement and it is a bold gesture on Paton's part to have Kumalo contemplate his own stereotypical nature, "He was too old for new and disturbing thoughts. A white man's dog, that is what they called him and his kind."

In contrast, the "bad" black man is not poor Absalom, the wayward son who like his biblical namesake torments his father and then repents, but Stephen's brother John Kumalo, a new type of politicised African who has outgrown both the old tribal formation and the more recent social control of missionary Christianity. A new urban society is being forged in Johannesburg, John says, which is looking for new values and new forms of social organisation and it is the ruthless silencing by Paton of the rising tide of black consciousness articulated through John Kumalo that is with hindsight so revealing. John's powerful oratory is presented as being deeply suspect, his smile is cunning and knowing, and most damning is the statement that he wishes to avoid prison because there "no applause" will reach him. Paton undercuts John's political solution to social crisis with numerous instances of white philanthropy like that of James Jarvis at the end of the novel. It is from this source that change will come, not from people like John Kumalo.

Human nature then is falsified by the creation of characters who, as Es'kia Mphahlele has pointed out, groan under the weight of Paton's sermon. When the book was written, the ANC Youth, among them Nelson Mandela, were putting forward arguments that sounded very like those of John Kumalo. Though Paton makes a concerted effort to transcend politics in favour of Christian redemption, history has proved that in the case of Nelson Mandela there *is* applause in prison.

—Phyllis M. Pollard

CULTURE AND ANARCHY.
Prose by Matthew Arnold, 1869.

Two features of Matthew Arnold's complex nature are specially relevant to a fair evaluation of *Culture and Anarchy*, perhaps now his most celebrated work in prose. Long experience of education had taught him how little people remember of what they are told. So, although perhaps more by nature inclined to the witty, allusive Oxford style of speech and writing, whenever he had something to say that he thought of real importance, he adopted what Chesterton was to call the style of the patient master of the idiot school, endlessly repeating his points, and embodying them in easily-remembered maxims and slogans. Hence, the over-simplifications involved in the use of words like "hebraize" and "philistine." And he was, in Halifax's sense, a "trimmer," one who tried to correct rather than to follow the dominant tendencies of the age, and the presuppositions of his audience. Thus a hasty reader might suppose that he was all for what he called Hellenism as against Hebraism. But the man who said that conduct was three-fourths of life could never be a believer in the power of intellect without conscience, or a butterfly of aestheticism.

Perhaps the most unsatisfactory of his constantly repeated stock terms is *culture*. It is by no means persuasive, and may become irritating, to substitute the words "Culture says . . ." for the more honest "In my opinion. . . ." "Culture" may be a word of many meanings, but one of the things it can never be is a spokesman of an ultimate authority.

The words "hellenize" and "hebraize" Arnold took from Heine; and they, too, may be open to some objection. In the first place, he grossly overrates the continuity between Judaism and Christianity, and treats the latter as a mere appendage to the former. He abstracts the moral element from the Christian system, and almost makes it the whole; considering the high praise he always awards to Newman, it is strange how little he really seems to learn from the latter about the doctrinal, prophetic, and sacramental aspects of the church. "Hellenism" is a somewhat more satisfactory term, though again, by abstracting one element, this time the intellectual, from a complex literary culture, he presents us with Greeks without their pagan superstitions. Did he ever brood on the *Bacchae* of Euripides?

However, all this is merely rhetoric, designed to enforce the proposition that the English middle classes are too much concerned with duty, narrowly conceived, and too little with knowledge and beauty. This brings us to his analysis of the English class system. Once again, he sacrifices exactness and subtlety for the sake of a memorable simplicity. In the face of the endless varieties and contrasts of the middle class, as revealed by Dickens, Trollope, and Eliot, it is unhelpful to label them all Philistines. Two omissions are especially notable here. Arnold is writing in one of the great classic ages of English literature, achieved mainly by members of the despised middle class; one would never think so from reading his text. And he omits altogether the very important class to which he himself, like his father, belonged—the class that later became know as the meritocracy. Its importance was already great and growing, and soon Gladstone's first administration would set the seal on its triumph by opening the Civil Service to intellectual competition and abolishing Purchase in the Army. Because he has no word for this class, Arnold wryly pretends to include it with the Philistines. Though every reader will know that he is ironical when he pretends to include himself among them, the unanswered question still remains, "What class do you belong to then?" The meritocracy has many faults, but philistinism, in Arnold's sense, is certainly not among them.

His trimming is seen again in his treatment of liberalism. He always maintained that he was a liberal himself, sometimes adding "of the future." But his critique of the actual liberalism of his day is both savage and frequently very funny. His humour is at is best in reducing liberal nostrums to ridiculous bathos; as if marrying your deceased wife's sister or ordering your dinner intelligibly in Paris would do anything to alleviate the condition of the slums or improve the laws. Behind the fun is the fear of what he calls "anarchy." He made a great deal of comparatively trivial incidents like the removal of the Hyde Park railings. He was influenced by his French and German friendships; he admired the tradition of strong central government in France and Prussia; indeed he may be said to have been dazzled by this tradition, when he actually presents as wisdom the extraordinary idea that conscription is a civilizing influence. Twenty-four hours in a barrack-room would have cured this delusion. He idealizes the state, without seriously asking himself who is to control it, and what are to be the safeguards against tyranny. Here, too, perhaps, he might defend himself on the plea of being a trimmer. Perhaps in the England of the 1860's there was more danger that the power of the state would prove too weak than that it would prove too strong.

One notable feature of his method of writing he shares with other Victorian sages, such as Carlyle and Ruskin. He combines, often in a startling and eloquent way, extreme topicality, quoting often from newspapers and political speeches, with long historical perspectives and the application to events of high abstract principles. Perhaps in his time the most persuasive feature of his writing was this: the reader was aware of a man who seemed to have the world's history and literature at his finger-tips, while he made witty and telling comments on the passing events of the day. At the same time he protested eloquently against English insularity and unreal self-satisfaction.

—A.O.J. Cockshut

CYMBELINE.
Play by William Shakespeare, 1609(?).

Cymbeline belongs to the group of plays usually labelled the late comedies or romances which William Shakespeare wrote at the end of his career as a dramatist. It was probably written after *Pericles* and *The Winter's Tale* but before *The Tempest*, and it is printed as the final play in the First Folio of 1623 where it is classified as a tragedy. In fact it could be seen as falling into Polonius's catch-all category of "tragical-comical-historical-pastoral," and it mixes times and places as freely as it mixes genres, ranging between ancient Britain and Jacobean England, classical Rome and Renaissance Italy. While it attracted the disapproval of neoclassical critics such as Samuel Johnson, who famously denounced its "unresisting imbecility," it was surprisingly popular on stage in the 18th and 19th centuries, partly because of widespread enthusiasm for its heroine Imogen, described by Swinburne as "the immortal godhead of womanhood."

While the historical narrative of Cymbeline, legendary king of Britain, is taken (like that of *King Lear*) from Holinshed, and the love story of his daughter Imogen ultimately comes from Boccaccio, the complicated plot seems deliberately to recapitulate a number of elements in Shakespeare's own earlier plays: the jealousy of Imogen's husband Posthumus, engineered by Iachimo, recalls *Othello*; Imogen's flight from the court to rural Wales and her adoption of male disguise recalls Rosalind in *As You Like It*; her consumption of a drug which induces a death-like trance recalls Juliet; the roles of the wicked Queen and her oafish, would-be rapist son Cloten recall those of Tamora and her sons in *Titus Andronicus*; the motif of the King's long-lost sons recalls the missing children and siblings of *The Comedy of Errors* and *Twelfth Night* (as well as those of *Pericles* and *The Winter's Tale*); the nationalistic Britain-against-Rome rhetoric recalls *King John*.

Moreover, *Cymbeline* not only recapitulates but celebrates the joys of narrative. It combines the self-conscious naivety of fairy-tale coincidence and deliberately artless exposition with an extraordinarily complex manipulation of multiple plots and multiple levels of awareness on the part of both characters and audience. Its long-drawn-out climax, in which some two dozen separate misunderstandings are cleared up, is one of the most elaborate final scenes in the entire canon; frequently abbreviated on stage in the past (and brilliantly rewritten by George Bernard Shaw), it has only recently been acknowledged as an enjoyable and highly theatrical masterpiece.

In addition to its narrative complexity, *Cymbeline* is written in an unusually difficult and convoluted style. It takes the mannered, elliptical syntax shared by the other late comedies to an extreme, setting up considerable barriers for the actor or reader. Sentences seem to lose their way, changing direction in mid-stream or disintegrating into strings of loosely connected parentheses. It is not at all easy to say why Shakespeare should have chosen to write in this way at this stage in his career, except for a desire to experiment in the medium he had mastered so well: he seems to want to push the language itself beyond its normal limits.

Some of the most interesting modern critics of *Cymbeline* have read it from a psychoanalytical viewpoint. It is certainly a drama which explores family relationships as a fundamental aspect of individual identity. Characters have to escape from the claustrophobic, even incestuous aspects of their families (Imogen resists her father's desire to marry her to "his wife's sole son"), but they also have to recover and come to terms with their pasts. There is a dream-like quality to several of the play's episodes and one character, Posthumus, actually experiences an on-stage dream in which the god Jupiter and his own deceased parents and brothers appear to him. Pervasive metaphors of confinement and bondage, fragmentation and mutilation, underline the darker side of the family thematic.

By way of contrast, a completely different strain in recent criticism emphasizes the historical, even topical, significance of the play as a text which reflects contemporary Stuart politics and in particular James I's vision of the union of the kingdoms of England and Scotland. Shakespeare uses the word "Britain" 26 times in the entire canon, 23 of those instances being in *Cymbeline*, indicating at least an awareness of the union issue. Such a reading also helps to explain the odd ending of the political plot whereby Cymbeline, having won the war he has fought against Rome to avoid paying tribute, nevertheless agrees to pay anyway. The vision at the end is thus one of harmony between nations as well as between individuals.

—Ann Thompson

D

A DANCE TO THE MUSIC OF TIME.
12 novels by Anthony Powell, 1951–75.

Generally considered Anthony Powell's outstanding achievement, *A Dance to the Music of Time* charts over 50 years of English life in the 20th century. Powell takes his title and central metaphor from Nicolas Poussin's painting in the Wallace Collection, noting in his memoirs that the four figures in the picture represent the Seasons "dancing to Time's tune" (*Faces in My Time*). The opening of the series elaborates the nature of this dance, enacted by characters like the Seasons, "moving hand in hand in intricate measure . . . or breaking into seemingly meaningless gyrations, while partners disappear only to reappear again, once more giving pattern to the spectacle: unable to control the melody, unable, perhaps, to control the steps of the dance."

Often referred to as a social history, the series (set mainly within intersecting circles of fashionable and Bohemian society) contains hundreds of characters, closely observed by Nicholas Jenkins, the first-person narrator representing a generation whose youth was shadowed by the first war, adulthood disrupted by the second, and later life dampened by the postwar climate. Because the novel is rich in amusing characters and incidents, readers may forget the underlying seriousness with which Powell pictures individual and societal changes, unfolding a story both comic and melancholy. Illustration of this combination comes from the memorable Widmerpool, whose will to succeed invests him with formidable powers despite something fundamentally absurd in his makeup. The butt of jokes while at school, he ends as he began, striving doggedly to advance, a humorous figure, yet a dark and damaging one.

Variations on Poussin's metaphor come from other paintings and painters, both invented and real, used to describe and develop character. Jenkin's schoolfriend Stringham, for instance, is presented physically and temperamentally by reference to 16th-century portraiture, Veronese's Alexander, and the faces in Elizabethan miniatures. Even when direct allusions to painting are absent, Powell's presentation of characters is highly pictorial. John Bayley has shown that the infamous Widmerpool "is built up from a sequence of pictures, vignettes, glimpses, as if done by a series of brilliant artists and photographers."

Like the dancers in his opening section, Powell's characters are often "partnered"—seen in relation to others for purposes of comparison. Pairs such as schoolfriends Stringham and Templer, literary hustlers Quiggin and Members, eccentric Americans Gwinnet and Glober, get closely examined by Jenkins, as do "paired" approaches to life: "conflicts and compromises between the imagination and the will, reason and feeling, power and sensuality." The steps Powell's dancers take will be largely determined by which of these approaches dominates.

Powell also uses the Seasons to structure stages in the life of Jenkins and his contemporaries, the 12 volumes comprising four trilogies or seasons: Spring (school, university, sexual initiation); Summer (work, marriage); Autumn (the war years); Winter (postwar England). Perceived patterns and complicated connections among characters preoccupy the observant and reflective Jenkins (himself a writer) with characters living and dead invoked in the final volume by the narrator (now sixtyish and quite ruminative) who finally, however, acknowledges a "wintry silence" in which "Even the formal measure of the Seasons seemed suspended."

The total effect is of an intricately patterned world in which Jenkins, paradoxically, fails to discern much larger meaning—despite feeling that "some pattern common to all" must exist. No comforting spiritual perspectives emerge: those characters who possess "transcendental gifts" are decidedly sinister. Affirmed are the undramatic but quietly admirable qualities of Jenkins himself—tolerance, compassion, interest in and respect for his fellow creatures, despite the difficulty of understanding either individual or collective patterns of behavior.

Critical opinion is divided about the use Powell makes of Jenkins. For some, his character is insufficiently engaging, too weak to carry a lengthy series, his privileged background limiting insight, his reserved personality seeming passive. Others (see Robert K. Morris and John Russell) find Jenkins a wise interpreter of humanity, whose strengths infuse the series. In addition, the complexity of the first-person narration lends readers a sense of knowing characters well, even though Jenkins lacks access to their inner consciousness and must rely on what they choose to reveal, usually on public or social occasions. Jenkins establishes his reliability by adjusting his impressions of those around him, recounting youthful misconceptions, adding mature reconsiderations, with readers tantalized by the possibility, until the series's end, of further revision of individual histories.

Inevitably, the sequence has been compared with works of other serial novelists of this century, especially Proust, Waugh, and Snow, whose series also contain elements of social history. Yet Powell's achievement is distinctive: his narrator, as Russell notes (*Anthony Powell: A Quintet, Sextet, and War*), is more outward looking, less self-absorbed, than in Proust's; Powell's vision is more humane than Waugh's; his language more allusive, more charged with implication, than Snow's.

—Joanne H. Edmonds

DANIEL DERONDA.
Novel by George Eliot, 1876.

Daniel Deronda, published in 1876, is George Eliot's last novel. It is a departure from her previous work in several respects. Set much closer to its own time than her previous fiction, it breaks with conventional time structure by opening in the middle of the action and then going back to the beginning. But perhaps the most significant change from the earlier fiction is that there is a break from the kind of realism that is the dominant mode of novels such as *Adam Bede* or *Middlemarch* in favour of a fictional mode that brings together the realist and romance traditions of the novel.

One reason for this is that romantic themes dominate this novel. Several of the characters are egotists on a romantic scale and virtually all of the major characters search in various ways for a sense of identity that will give meaning to their lives. As the novel's epigraph makes clear, the self is vulnerable to dangerous forces if no secure identity is achieved: "Let thy chief terror be of thine own soul." The novel's implied solution to alienation, the excesses of egotism, the threat of the demonic, is also romantic: the discovery of a tribal consciousness in which the individual can identify with an ideal which creates an organic relationship between self and world. The main proponent of this idea is the Jewish visionary and proto-Zionist, Mordecai, whose aim is to "Revive the organic centre: let the unity of Israel which has made the growth and form of its religion be an outward reality." He provides Daniel Deronda with the "ideal task" he has always longed for.

The structure of the novel is based on the conflict within the romantic tradition between egotism and organicism. As Mordecai is the novel's most committed representative of organicist thinking, Deronda's mother, the Princess Halm-Eberstein, is the most extreme romantic egotist. She has rebelled against her Jewish race and religion and cast off constraints such as motherhood in order to achieve total self-realisation as an opera singer. Almost all the major characters are drawn either to some form of romantic egotism or to Mordecai's organicist ideal of a tribal consciousness. The conflict is exemplified by the two main characters, Gwendolen Harleth and Daniel Deronda. In the opposition between their personalities and the relationship that develops between them, the structure of the novel is worked out.

Gwendolen Harleth is one of Eliot's most complex and interesting psychological studies. Whereas the princess could find an outlet in art for the demonic forces in her nature, Gwendolen, possessing similar egotistic tendencies, has no such form of sublimation, and the demonic side of her self makes her capable of murder as a response to the frustrations of her life. Pressured by material circumstances into the necessity of marrying for money, she performs an egotistic act that proves to be radically self-alienating: she chooses to marry Grandcourt—a man who lived for passion when he was young but who now lives only for the sadistic pleasure of making people submit to his will—even though previously she had spontaneously felt it would be wrong to injure Mrs. Glasher, Grandcourt's mistress by whom he has several children. The struggle of wills that takes place between Gwendolen and Grandcourt is one of the most powerful elements in the novel.

Whereas Gwendolen's life shows the dangers of egotistic assertion, Deronda suffers from such a degree of self-consciousness that the danger for him is that he will become cut off from any centre of self. Instead of acting to dominate the world by force of ego like the novel's assertive egotists, Deronda reacts self-consciously to experience and shrinks from any commitment that demands any exposure of his personality. Though one of Eliot's most ambitious characterisations, Deronda is, at best, only partially successful in artistic terms. The 19th-century novel, with its dominant narrator, lacked the technical means to give dramatic life to such introverted, intellectual characters, and only the later development of techniques such as interior monologue and stream of consciousness made it possible to give this type of character dramatic credibility. With Deronda the narrator's discourse tends to dominate the character so much that he fails to take on an independent life.

But Deronda remains one of Eliot's most interesting characterisations at a philosophical level. Though he finally embraces Mordecai's vision there is no indication that he accepts it in a metaphysical sense. Whereas Mordecai believes fervently in his prophecy that someone will come to carry on his work and that Deronda is that man and must therefore be a Jew, Deronda retains his scepticism but refuses to undermine Mordecai's faith by rationalistic questioning. Through his relationship with both Mordecai and Mirah, Mordecai's sister, Deronda discovers the partiality that relativistic thinking had previously made impossible for him. But though he identifies with Mordecai's vision, he knows he must be a Jew by race if he is to devote his life to it.

That Deronda should turn out to be a Jew is open to criticism as a blatant contrivance, but in a novel in which gambling is an important theme Deronda's going along with Mordecai's conviction that he is a Jew is best seen as a gamble on Deronda's part. Deronda has little expectation that Mordecai is right and is prepared to console him if he is wrong. Furthermore, Deronda will not be a Jew in the same way that Mordecai and Mirah are: rather it is a role he has consciously chosen to play even though he is determined to commit his whole being to it. But in choosing to fulfil that role he must disappoint Gwendolen and leave her in the interests of his own higher ideal. It is another innovatory feature of this novel that it is one of the most open-ended in Victorian fiction, with Gwendolen's future problematic and Deronda's success in carrying forward Mordecai's visionary hope unknown.

—K.M. Newton

THE DAUGHTERS OF THE LATE COLONEL.
Story by Katherine Mansfield, 1922.

Katherine Mansfield herself described this work, in a letter to William Gerhardie, as "the only story that satisfies me to any extent." It is one of her "12 cell" stories, divided into 12 sections with no immediately obvious reason for the divisions as they do not indicate a shift in time or place, though they sometimes indicate a flashback. It is about a commonplace situation, as most of Mansfield's stories are, this time about the complex emotions, thoughts, and impulses elicited in his daughters by the death of father which was obviously expected, timely, and in no way tragic.

The title suggests the social milieu of the story; "the late colonel" is a phrase that reminds the reader of genteel conversations in private hotels, and the daughters are defined only in relation to their father and his status. The story opens in an informal, colloquial style as if the reader is dropping in on an already familiar situation, with the evasiveness of the opening phrase "The week after" suggesting that the daughters can only mention their father's death euphemistically. There is a tension in them between clichéd expectation and reality: they weep over replying to letters of condolence but also want to giggle like liberated children. The tone is an unexpected blend of comedy and pathos.

As the story develops, the idea that the sisters find the ordinary business of life intractable is established; they have always been tyrannised over in the past and cannot now take authority. The nature of their irresolute, confused minds is hinted at by the structure of the story: the second part begins "Another thing" but it is not clear what the first thing was. Two new tyrants who temporarily take father's place are characterised differently: Nurse Andrews by her pretentious attempt at an accent she cannot master, and Kate by the violence of her actions ("snatched away," "slapped down," "stalked off"). The point of view is mostly that of the sisters, as when they remember father's last moments and the way in which he expired. Cyclops fashion, opening one eye. "How much easier to tell people about it, if he had only opened both! But no—one eye only." Again they are preoccupied by their social difficulties, but underlying that is a wonderful suppressed urge to laugh. Their subconscious desires surface for the reader in the following passage, where Josephine rejects the idea of "a little Communion," genteelly proffered by the vicar who is significantly wearing kid gloves, and tells him she wants an inexpensive funeral. "'At the same time, I should like'—'A good one that will last,' thought dreamy Constantia." They eventually confront their dead father in the sixth section, when to Josephine's horror Constantia locks "the huge glittering wardrobe" in which they both feel father is lurking, thereby sealing his position in his coffin. It reminds her sister of the time that "Constantia had pushed Benny into the round pond," implying that both were gestures of defiance against oppressive males, and an assertion of Constantia's own identity.

The next two sections are retrospective and provide the only male view of the two sisters, as a pair of grotesque maiden aunts; for the first time the reader feels some sympathy with the late colonel as his daughters subject him to a comic and trite conversation about meringues. At the same time a clear picture of the tyrannical colonel waving his stick emerges, and the daughters' struggle to maintain appearances in straitened circumstances is again hinted at. Kate's banging and slamming takes the place of the dead father's thumping stick, but the sisters cannot decide to dismiss her.

In the final section of the story a new possibility is suggested. In the organ-grinder's music the sisters hear the cheerful refrain, "A week since father died"; the unspeakable is formulated and the sun comes out, in contrast to the earlier cold or excessive heat in the colonel's bedroom. The tone changes to one of tremulous hope as the sun touches the sisters and they speculate about how their lives might be different: "The rest had been looking after father and at the same time keeping out of father's way. But now? But now?" Constantia feels that life with father "all seemed to have happened in a kind of tunnel. It wasn't real . . . What did it all lead to? Now? Now?" But when they try to speak to each other of the future a cloud covers the sun and the vision of what might be is engulfed by habit and the dominance of the past. Mansfield writes of the conclusion in another letter to Gerhardie: "All was meant, of course, to lead up to that last paragraph, when my two flowerless ones turned with that timid gesture, to the sun. Perhaps *now* . . . ' And after that, it seemed to me, they died as surely as Father was dead."

—Angela Smith

DAVID COPPERFIELD.
Novel by Charles Dickens, 1850.

The success of Charlotte Brontë's *Jane Eyre* (1847) had created a fashion for autobiographical narratives, and *David Copperfield* is the first of Charles Dickens's two major novels to employ the first-person method throughout (the other is *Great Expectations*). Its full title—*The Personal History, Experience, and Observations of David Copperfield the Younger* . . . —is reminiscent of such 18th century novels as *Tom Jones*, in which the structure is derived from the adventures and relationships of the hero, and Dickens's novel begins with David's birth and keeps him firmly in sight throughout, the large cast of characters being seen primarily in terms of their contacts with him. Dickens was startled when it was pointed out to him that he had given his protagonist his own initials reversed, and while the personal element in the book must not be exaggerated there is no doubt that some of David's childhood experiences correspond closely to those of Dickens himself. The fragment of autobiography that he had written in or about 1847 (not published until after his death) is reproduced almost verbatim in the early part of the novel, and in a more pervasive way it has been suggested that David's relationships with various women (his mother, his nurse Peggotty, his first wife Dora, and his second wife Agnes) may be seen in terms of Dickens's own relationship with his mother, his wife Kate, and his sister-in-law Georgina Hogarth.

The novel was begun in February 1849 and completed in October 1850: for much of the time, therefore, composition and publication proceeded hand in hand. From the outset it was very popular with Dickens's readers, and came to be regarded by many as his masterpiece. Dickens himself described it as his "favourite child."

While the subject of the novel is the young David Copperfield, from infancy onwards, the narrator is the middle-aged David, a professional novelist widowed and remarried, and a sadder and wiser man than in the periods of childhood and youth with which the story is largely concerned. Dickens thus exploits a double perspective on his hero's experiences: we see simultaneously the young David confronting the world and his older self reflecting and commenting on the follies and errors of his own earlier life. This perspective, like the novel's concern with the emerging self and the influences of upbringing and education, is part of the romantic tradition of autobiography, and it is a happy coincidence that this novel appeared in volume form in the same year as the long autobiographical poem *The Prelude* by the great poet of memory, Wordsworth.

Graham Greene and many others have paid tribute to the extraordinarily brilliant and sensitive rendering of the child's world in the early chapters, from the happiness of David's earliest years as the spoiled child of a household dominated by adoring women to the misery that follows the arrival of his stepfather, his schooldays, and his employment at a factory bearing a very strong resemblance to the blacking-factory that so marked the consciousness of the young Dickens. Dickens's mother and nurse, who symbolically share the same name (Clara), represent two sides of female nature as Dickens perceived it, the one sexually attractive but weak, pettish, and incompetent, the other maternal, dependable, and domesticated. This sets the pattern for the rest of the book, much of which is concerned with exploring the hero's relationships with the opposite sex. Aunt Betsey, who rescues him from destitution and neglect, is grotesquely unfeminine but serves as a fairy godmother or substitute mother; Little Em'ly, later seduced by Steerforth, is like a reincarnation of David's mother; Dora, his first wife, is also sexually desirable but weak-natured and a hopeless housekeeper; only in Agnes does David find a merging of the qualities that go to make the perfect wife. Michael Slater and other recent critics have seen in the novel an expression, perhaps largely unconscious, of Dickens's deepest feelings towards women.

David Copperfield is notable for the richness and variety of its characterization and contains some of Dickens's most familiar figures, many of them imprinted on the visual imagination of readers by the brilliant illustrations executed by "Phiz" (Hablot K. Browne), the novelist's most loyal illustrator. Among them only a handful can be mentioned here. Mr. Micawber is partly a portrait of the novelist's father, the improvident John Dickens. Martha is a somewhat melodramatic study in the "fallen woman" or prostitute who is susceptible to reform—a form of charitable work in which Dickens had a strong practical interest. The emigration of Mr. Peggotty and a number of other characters to Australia reflects another of Dickens's current concerns, with "family colonization." Uriah Heep is one of the most celebrated of Dickens's villains, and a different, more genteel kind of villainy is represented by Steerforth, who owes something to romantic stereotypes associated with such figures as Byron and Shelley.

Stylistically, *David Copperfield* differs markedly from the novels that precede and follow it, and must have been very consciously an experiment on Dickens's part in creating a distinctive tone of voice quite unlike that of the usual Dickensian narrator, less rhetorical and given to bold contrasts, more intimate and confidential, as befits a novel of memory. At the same time it should not be forgotten that the David who narrates his own story is supposed to be a professional novelist, and he shows not only a very sharp eye for idiosyncrasies of appearance, behaviour and speech, but a willingness to produce a set-piece of writing when occasion demands. The storm scene in which Steerforth is drowned, for instance, was praised by Tolstoy and others.

Like many novels that are held together by the continuous presence of a central hero, *David Copperfield* is somewhat episodic in nature and lacks the intricate structure of plots and subplots of either its immediate predecessor *Dombey and Son* or its successor *Bleak House*. Its great strength lies in characterization, in control of tone, and in the presentation, especially in the early chapters, of unforgettable episodes that have something of the quality of Wordsworthian "spots of time."

—Norman Page

DE PROFUNDIS.
Prose by Oscar Wilde, 1905 (and later editions).

Aside from the autobiographical implications of its being a "love letter" to Alfred Douglas—the "dear Bosie" of Oscar Wilde's homosexual life—*De Profundis* on strictly literary merits stands as the noble work of a suffering and remorseful man. In this Wilde strives not to repudiate the sins of the past but to accommodate himself to them in the present growth toward enlightenment.

Written in Reading Gaol near the end of his two years of confinement for homosexual practices, the small book, a prose poem, begins with the "twilight" of the present humiliation and the suffering with the loss of his children. Out of the depths of his infamy, Wilde has grown to appreciate simple gestures of sympathy and to realize that in these gestures he treads holy ground. He acknowledges the previous life of passion, greed, and appetite, and knows that he has abused the rare artistic gifts the gods had given him; he knows he has irreparably blighted the lives of those close to him. Out of humility he resolves to free himself of bitterness toward the world.

Morality, religion, and reason as the world knows them do not help him, and his personal experience must redefine them for him. Morality must govern not what one has done but what one becomes; reason reveals the injustice of the laws that convicted him; and the physical facts of prison must be transformed into spiritual exercises. Spiritual growth is the "becoming" of Wilde's morality; he does not wish to deny his past life but—having built a reputation for epigrams—"To regret one's own experience is to arrest one's own development." The opposite of *de profundis* is shallowness, the refusal to accept the consequences of one's deeds.

Growing out of melancholy and a former decision to commit suicide on leaving prison, Wilde now desires to cheer his friends by sharing their sorrow. He finds sorrow and suffering to be the experience of love, by which humanity reaches perfection. With art still his life and his goal, he finds truth in art expressed in the indivisible body and soul, "the soul made incarnate; the body instinct with spirit." Prison normally turns the heart to stone, and rebellion closes up the soul; but humility accepts experience, and love is the artist's sense of beauty that reveals body and soul.

While the 1890's argued the human versus the divine Christ, Wilde finds the poet in the human Christ, who occupies fully one-fourth of *De Profundis*. Christ likened man's soul to a tiny seed, a handful of leaven, a pearl; the supreme individualist, like the artist, Christ saw no difference between the lives of others and his own. The supreme romanticist, he knew that eternal love is given to the eternally unworthy. His morality is sympathy, with the woman taken in sin and with the ignorant, in whose mind "there is always room for a great idea." He warred against the Philistines, and would not consider the conversation of a publican into a Pharisee a great achievement. For Him, the moment of repentance is the means to alter the past and the moment of initiation.

Out of the depths, Wilde realizes that prison is not an ending but a beginning. Having been jeered mercilessly, he knows now that mocking a soul in pain is "a dreadful thing." He mistakenly took action against his adversary, the Marquess of Queensberry (the father of Alfred Douglas), and appealed to society for help and protection; and society, appalled at Wilde's mode of life, took action against him. To his former mean companions, he acted as a snakecharmer, and he would not now have a friend deceived into believing he was innocent. If the truth is painful, lies are worse. Others, mechanical people who wear the mask of respectable achievement, are those who pile the faggots that burn a saint, but the saint looks on the face of God. Although cynicism is delightful for the intellect, nothing is ever revealed to the cynic.

To God, the past, present, and future are one moment; and now that the future is lost to Wilde, he may, on leaving prison, be able to teach people the meaning of sorrow and its beauty. He is weary of the formerly-vaunted articulate and ends seeking only the mystical—in art, in life, and in nature.

To reduce this message to autobiographical importunity violates and invalidates its beauty. To dismiss it because Oscar Wilde, after release from prison, returned to companionship with "Bosie" implies that moments of greatness must be discounted if they are not sustained. Prison procedures at first forbade Wilde any writing materials and then required submission of each day's effort, which somewhat diminishes the continuity. Nevertheless, the book progresses by means of several stages of realizations brought out of the depths, as its title indicates, from reviewing the past and rising to the altered thinking that imprisonment has brought.

—Grace Eckley

THE DEAD.
Story by James Joyce, 1914.

"The Dead," written during 1906 and 1907, forms an important link between the earlier, shorter fiction of *Dubliners*, where it is the final story, and James Joyce's three later novels. The narrative is a revealing transitional work because it maintains some thematic preoccupations common to all his fiction and prefigures some later techniques, but it is a polished and elaborate lyrical work as well. In it Joyce displays his mastery of using precise detail for evocative effect. The tightly knit components of the story dramatize the problems of defining identity, central to Joyce's narratives, because external elements operate as correlatives for suggesting latent possibilities of an intuitive or spiritual nature. In this way the story transcends its mimetic surfaces and moves towards an ambivalent, paradoxical, and yet unifying symbolism that make it a prime example of modernist art.

The ostensible structure for the story is provided by the brief chronology of events set in Dublin at the turn of the century. They cover only the evening and early hours of a day and the next morning during the Epiphany festival: Gabriel Conroy and his wife, Gretta, arrive for the annual feast hosted by his aunts, mingle with the guests, partake of a banquet at which Gabriel gives a speech, and retire to a hotel room in order to avoid an inconvenient journey home. Beneath such minimal action exist the real structural dynamics of the story's rich design: the complex series of images and allusions, unified through Gabriel's subjectivity and given meaning through interlocking associations and repetitions. These patterns may initially appear as oblique or disjointed because they often lack conventional causal relationships, and they tend to acquire significance depending upon the degree of recognition and emphases accorded to them by the reader. Consequently, different significances are possible, but many images and allusions are drawn from Joyce's direct experiences in Dublin and cluster around specific nationalistic, religious, or musical references. Under scrutiny these invariably connect with one another to form patterns, often suggesting motifs related to death or decay and, conversely, rebirth or resurrection.

One example of such a pattern is the archetypal shape given Gabriel's journey towards self-definition. The pattern of journeys would include Gabriel and Gretta's journey to the party, for instance, as well as several discussions of past and projected journeys, Miss Ivor's references about a journey to the west of Ireland, the journey to the hotel, and Gabriel's ambivalent "journey westward" in the final paragraph. References to the east, west, and circular directions connected with such journeys support and compound possibilities of meaning created within the specific context of the story and also help suggest more broadly ranging mythic implications. The image of the snow, especially, permeates and unifies the story and provides a final medium for crystallizing and—paradoxically—transcending Gabriel's tremulous quest for selfhood.

Distinct stages in the story develop with increasing intensity Gabriel's uneasy preoccupation with the connections between Ireland and himself. Shifts in point of view allow for specificity and distance at the same time, giving different perspectives to Gabriel's character and developing the aura of ritual initiation connected with the interior journey of this middle-aged Irishman. These techniques foreshadow the developments in point of view and the mythic subtext of Joyce's later fiction. Equally subtle is the series of associations that undercuts Gabriel's complacent notions of himself: Lily's deflation of his fatuous romanticism; Miss Ivor's imputations about his national loyalties; the repeated undeniable connections between him and a country he regards as primitive; and his own grandiose speechmaking, ironically reflective, that deprecates the new "thought-tormented" generation.

The claim that much of Joyce's artistry depends on suggestion and implication is well supported by the story's culminating scene in the hotel room. Here Gabriel's egoistically developed passion for Gretta is devastatingly undercut when she reveals that, instead of reciprocating his feeling, she has been thinking of a youthful companion, Michael Furey, who she thinks "died for me." Gabriel's juxtaposition and eventual reluctant identification with the absent Michael Furey allow him to glimpse for the first time his own true self and give him an understanding of the force of real love. Finally, as he fades into sleep, other visions of death and of the dead return him spiritually to the Ireland he has been trying to avoid and cause him to relinquish his former sense of himself, suggesting a truer bond with humanity. In this fashion, the details of the story both disappear and coalesce, much like different combinations of parts to a puzzle, to generate levels of irony and interpretive possibility. Above all else, the story demonstrates Joyce's ability to invest common events with an uncommon significance and to make an intensely private experience universally emblematic.

—Thomas Loe

THE DEATH OF THE HEART.
Novel by Elizabeth Bowen, 1938.

As its title invites, *The Death of the Heart* has been misread as a rather sentimental account of a 16-year-old girl's loss of innocence in a valueless, if not corrupt, upper-middle-class pre-war London. But in no one of Bowen's previous novels has her complex inheritance of the subtle and ambiguous morality of Henry James and Jane Austen been clearer. For the author is at least as concerned with the devastating effect of aggressive innocence on a social world more vulnerable than venial. "Illusions are art, for the feeling person," says the novel's narrator, "and it is by art that we live, if we do." So from the first chapter, the unedited immediacy of the artless Portia Quayne's diary threatens the more sophisticated arts of deception by which her elders protect themselves and manipulate others. In each of the three sections of the novel Portia confronts, with varying success, the World, the Flesh, and the Devil.

Portia's first world is financially stable but emotionally occluded: temporarily adopted by her half-brother Thomas after the death first of her father (cast out by the other Quaynes because of his unsuitable second marriage to Portia's mother), then of her mother (with whom she had been living a vagabond existence in cheap continental hotels), she uneasily shares their Regency house in the Outer Circle of Regent's Park. Tolerated by Thomas, whose mind is usually benignly elsewhere, Portia is actively resented by his wife Anna, who discovers by secretly reading Portia's diary the full extent of the girl's ability to expose a woman who has cut feeling from her own life (her conversations with Thomas echo those of the Game of Chess section of *The Waste Land*), and carries on a coldly intellectual flirtation with the homosexual novelist St. Quentin Miller. Their narratives of Portia's life—spoken to one another—insist on her power to disrupt, while the Quayne's independent-minded housekeeper Matchett provides Portia with a family history that is severe but sympathetic (in her upright protectiveness she plays Michael to St. Quentin's Satan).

In the realm of the Flesh—Portia's visit to the "unedited" sea-side bungalow ("Waikiki") of Anna's former governess—Portia is visited by, then betrayed by the novel's least sympathetic "innocent," Eddie—employee of Thomas, protégé of Anna—who trades his identity for anonymity and impersonation. Though Eddie has appeared to be her ally in being as manipulated as she in the world of Windsor Terrace (at Oxford, "he was taken up, played about with, taken down, let down, finally sent down"), he mocks her naive pleasure in the pastoral, vulgar vitality of Seale-on-Sea and cruelly betrays Portia's dependence on him by holding hands with Daphne Heccomb, her hostess' teen-age daughter, in the cinema ("Eddie's fingers kept up a kneading movement; her thumb alertly twitched at the joint"). When Portia discovers to her surprise that Waikiki can accept sexual license only as long as it remains unspoken, Portia begins to learn that by subjecting itself to some sort of pattern the romantic will can adjust itself to reality. The narrator, as often in the novel, is more articulate about this than Portia can be:

> Pictures would not be hung plumb over the centres of fireplaces or wallpapers pasted on with such precision that their seams make no break in the pattern if life were really not possible to adjudicate for. These things are what we mean when we speak of civilisation: they remind us how exceedingly seldom the unseemly or unforeseeable rears its head. . . . Only outside disaster is irreparable. At least there would be dinner at any minute; at least she could wash her hands with Vinolia soap.

Portia returns from "The Flesh" of self-discovery at Waikiki to "The Devil" of further betrayal in London—in particular, to St. Quentin's disclosure, for Portia's education, that he and Anna have been discussing her diary, and to his defense of such deceptions as "simply our little way of keeping ourselves going. We must live, though you may not see the necessity." To hear this, and to learn moreover that Anna and Eddie have been making fun of his weekend at Waikiki, become "two allied betrayals" that have "push[ed] up to full growth, like a double tree," and Portia flees—first, to Eddie's bleak flat with its "anti-moral colour," and then, when he rejects her because "we've got to live in the world," to the Karachi Hotel, residence of Major Brutt, an innocent friend of Anna's former lover, "whose thought could puzzle out nothing," and who has turned up in London looking for a job only to discover that "makes of men date, like makes of cars." Here, in the confrontation of the two innocents, is the ultimate death of the heart, where the power of innocence ends with its entrance into consciousness.

Matchett, sent to retrieve Portia and return her to Windsor Terrace, does so accompanied by a narrator whose language is now more lyric than satiric:

> In gardens outside London roses would burn on, with all gone in the dusk. Fatigue but a sort of joy would open in all hearts, for summer is the height and fullness of living. Already the dusk smelled strong. In this premature night of clouds, the sky was warm, the buildings seemed to expand. The fingers on the piano halted, struck true notes, found their way to a chord.

This evocation of seasonal renewal in harmony with the notes of music reminds the reader that it is an art that has enabled each successful character to survive in a world where "one is empowered to live fully; occasion does not offer"—as Bowen says in a contemporaneous short story. St. Quentin obviously has his novels, Lillian (Portia's schoolmate) her memories of a lesbian affair with a cello mistress, Matchett a submission to stern morality, Major Brutt his daily ritual, the Heccombs their pseudogentility. Anna's coldness of heart is more a denial of life than a saving organization of it, and Eddie's anonymity is not a saving art but destructive fragmentation, resulting in "a lasting state of hysteria." In arguing for a stay against confusion and chaos, the narrator (and presumably the author) is nearly of the Devil's party:

> Happy that few of us are aware of the world until we are already in league with it. Childish fantasy, like the sheath over the bud, not only protects but curbs the terrible budding spirit, protects not only innocence from the world but the world from the power of innocence.

This was, in fact, the last of Bowen's novels in which a narrative voice was allowed anything like this authority (though its confidence is, of course, implicitly criticized by the fragments of Portia's diary). In the world of her next novel, *The Heat of the Day* (1949), acknowledged as one of the finest English novels about London in the Blitz, the "irreparable" outside disaster makes such security in the arts of civilization and the conventions of the novel far more problematic.

—William W. Heath

DECLINE AND FALL OF THE ROMAN EMPIRE, The History of the. See the Writers entry on **GIBBON, Edward.**

THE DEFENCE OF POESY (The Defence of Poetry).
Prose by Sir Philip Sidney, 1595.

Sir Philip Sidney's *The Defence of Poesy* is the most frequently published of his works and the only one regularly read by non-specialists. This popularity (in both senses of the word) is no doubt attributable both to the essay's witty and urbane tone which makes it such a pleasure to read and to its epigrammatic richness, the famous aphorisms that resonate in the imagination and have captured the essence of poetry for a wide range of readers over the years. Sidney's familiar depictions of the poet continue to ring true after more than 400 years:

> Only the poet, disdaining to be tied to any such subjection, lifted up with the vigour of his invention, doth grow in effect another nature . . . he goeth hand in hand with nature, not enclosed within the narrow warrants of her gifts but freely ranging only within the zodiac of his own wit.
> . . . with a tale forsooth he cometh unto you, with a tale which holdeth children from play, and old men from the chimney corner.
> . . . the poet, he nothing affirms, and therefore never lieth.

Literary critics have also been attracted by the essay's aphoristic quality and have often concentrated on tracing the many classical allusions that Sidney skillfully weaves into the smooth stylistic surface of his work. Such a piecemeal appreciation of Sidney's essay, however, fails to capture the total effect of the *Defence*. Sidney's wit and urbanity, his mastery of classical sources, his compelling articulation of familiar themes, and his famous *sprezzatura* (the skill of making difficult things look easy) all serve to obscure the ambivalence and contradictions which energize the work as a whole.

Although Sidney ridicules philosophers for "wrangling" over "whether the contemplative or the active life do excell," this is precisely the question that resonates throughout the *Defence*, and Sidney's interest in this question is not merely academic, it is personal and urgent. It is important to remember that Sidney wrote the *Defence* during a period of increasing frustration with Queen Elizabeth's refusal to employ him in a political capacity. The *Defence*, therefore, like Sidney's other works, stands as a comment upon and a response to that frustration. As a result, the essay is not simply a defence of poetry but a defence of Sidney himself as well.

Sidney's intimate involvement in his argument must have been a source of discomfort to him, because he uses a number of means to distance himself personally from his theoretical project. He repeatedly declares the impersonal focus of his argument: "I speak of the art, and not the artificer." He subordinates the contemplative to the active life: "the ending end of all earthly learning being virtuous action." And he places poetry in a large cultural framework, celebrating the historical benefits of poetry to earlier civilizations, calling it "the first light-giver to ignorance," the passport "into the gates of popular judgements," "the food for the tenderest stomachs," "a medicine of cherries." At other times, however, he identifies himself personally and acknowledges his courtly audience. Like Sidney himself, poetry has a dual identity—politically sanctioned oratory and self-authorized private vision—but Sidney is unable to accept the full implications of such conflicting alternatives because they represent his own difficult choice of careers. As a result, the alternatives stand in distinct, unameliorated contrast.

Ever since O.B. Hardison, Jr.'s, seminal essay, "The Two Voices of Sidney's *Apology for Poetry*" (*English Literary Renaissance*, 2, 1972), much scholarship has been devoted to exploring the essay's contradictory nature and to determining Sidney's success or failure in reconciling the contradictions. Most readers discover an inconsistency between the early remarks on the poet's freedom and power and the later stylistic constraints recommended in the "digression" on contemporary English poetry, labelling one "romantic" and the other "neoclassical" or distinguishing between Icarean and Daedalean impulses. The responses to this perceived inconsistency range from Hardison's conclusion that the two parts were written at different times in Sidney's career to various attempts to impose a "unity" on the dialectical nature of the essay.

Such attempts, however, disregard the fact that Sidney himself was a mix of contradictions, especially in his attitudes toward his writing. He was always simultaneously a poet and a politician, and the place of poetry and politics in his life was the underlying theme of all his works. In the *Defence* he adopts the voices of both the self-empowered creator of fictions and the politically sanctioned patron of letters. But these do not represent two different Sidneys; they represent the dual perspective inspiring the *Defence* as a whole. In between the paean to the poet's power and the precepts of the patron, in between Icarus and Daedalus, in between the son and the father, in between poetry and politics, lies Sidney's many-voiced attempt to reconcile the dichotomy which polarized his brief life. Readers of *The Defence of Poesy* must listen for the anxious and passionate undertone of the essay in order not to be misled by the competing voices or merely beguiled by the seductive stylistic surface.

—Derek B. Alwes

A DEFENCE OF POETRY.
Prose by Percy Bysshe Shelley, 1840 (written 1821).

"A poet in our times is a semi-barbarian in a civilized community," wrote Thomas Love Peacock half in jest in *The Four Ages of Poetry* (1820). Peacock's friend Percy Bysshe Shelley responded with one of the most serious and eloquent assertions of the moral and social role of poetry in English prose. For Shelley, poets in 19th-century England as in any other time or place were "the unacknowledged legislators of the world."

"A Defence of Poetry" is the result of years of thinking on the subject and incorporates passages from Shelley's earlier critical writings. In it, Shelley argues that poetry is essentially moral, and more effective morally than any work of ethics. While ethical writings appeal to the reason, poetry works through the sympathetic imagination, awakening the mind to the reality and beauty of the world beyond the self. While it is possible for reason to operate merely in the service of self-interest, imagination intrinsically leads beyond the self. The imagination for Shelley is essentially an extender of consciousness. The greatest poets have a powerful moral effect because they stir the imagination beyond solipsism. More overtly moral poets are necessarily less morally effective because they depend on reason rather than imagination; among such great but over-didactic poets Shelley includes Spenser, Euripides, and Tasso.

For Shelley, the imagination operates morally in the same way as love in directing the attention outwards: "the great secret of morals is love; or a going out of our own nature, and an identification of ourselves with the beautiful which exists in thought, action, or person not our own." Shelley's emphasis on the moral value and beauty of love—"that sublimest victory over sensuality and force"—reflects in part his veneration of Plato whose great dialogue on love, *The Symposium*, Shelley had translated and whom he honours in "A Defence of Poetry" as a great poet because "the truth and splendour of his imagery and the melody of his language are the most intense that it is possible to conceive." For Shelley, Dante is the great celebrator of love in the modern world as Plato is in the ancient world. In particular he admires the *Paradiso* because of its conception of love as the moving force behind the universe; he sees it as "the most glorious imagination in modern poetry."

Dante's work, like Milton's, will, according to Shelley, outlast the Christian faith that nourished them both. Shelley respected Jesus as an "extraordinary person" and looked on Christianity as "the exoteric expression of the esoteric doctrines of the poetry and wisdom of antiquity"; he also looked on this stage of its history as brief and Jesus's teachings as "quickly distorted." Essentially Christianity for Shelley was one transitory myth like any other:

> The *Divina Commedia* and *Paradise Lost* have conferred upon modern mythology a systematic form; and when time and change shall have added one more superstition to the mass of those which have arisen and decayed upon the earth, commentators will be learnedly employed in elucidating the religion of ancestral Europe, only not utterly forgotten because it will have been stamped with the eternity of genius.

Shelley's religious and political views were equally notorious in his own times. His political commitment is reflected in his concept of the function of poetry in industrial society. He argues that scientific and technological improvements have led to greater inequalities in society, a greater contrast between "luxury and want," because imaginative growth in industrial society has not kept pace with scientific growth, so that the rich use the tools of the new knowledge merely to further their own interests and exploit the poor more skilfully. He regards "poetry, and the principle of self, of which money is the visible incarnation" as "the god and Mammon of the world," essentially at odds. His political ideals colour his discussion of *Paradise Lost*, where his hatred of tyranny, and his love of the strength that opposes tyranny lead him (like Blake and Byron) to see Satan as morally superior to Milton's God.

In many ways in "A Defence of Poetry" Shelley is the heir of Wordsworth and Coleridge. His treatment of the imagination is certainly very close to that of Coleridge whose *Biographia Literaria* he had read soon after it appeared in 1817. He stresses that the imagination operates and creates through synthesis, by creating new combinations of perceptions. Like his great predecessors he is also very much aware of the deadening effect of familiarity on the consciousness, and the healing role of the imagination in this regard. He argues that the imagination "purges from our inward sight the film of familiarity," or, using a variation of the image, that it "lifts the veil from the hidden beauty of the world."

Throughout his literary career Shelley was profoundly interested in the nature of inspiration. Here he writes of poetic creation as having little to do with the will: "the mind in creation is as a fading coal," he writes, and again, "when composition begins, inspiration is already on the decline, and the most glorious poetry that has ever been communicated to the world is probably a feeble shadow of the original conception of the poet." The labour necessary to the poet is merely a matter of making the original inspiration intelligible.

"A Defence of Poetry" is perhaps in some ways Shelley's most powerful treatment of the role of the poet. The figure of the poet in some of his poems is tainted with his interest in his own image and his own sufferings. In this work, however, any such tendency is lost or subsumed in the power and conviction of his argument.

—June Sturrock

DELIA.
Poems by Samuel Daniel, 1592.

Samuel Daniel's first published poems, 28 sonnets, appeared in Thomas Newman's unauthorized edition of Sidney's *Astrophel and Stella* in 1591. In the following year he, himself, issued a collection of 50 sonnets, *Delia*, revising 23 from Newman's edition, together with a long narrative poem, *The Complaint of Rosamond*. He dedicated this collection to Sidney's sister, Mary, Countess of Pembroke, with the following conventional disclaimer:

> Right Honorable, although I rather desired to keep in the private passions of my youth, from the multitude, as things uttered to my self, and consecrated to silence: yet feeling I was betrayed by the indiscretion of a greedy Printer, and had some of my secrets betrayed to the world, uncorrected . . . I am forced to publish that which I never meant.

Thus, whether he liked it or not, Daniel's career as a poet was auspiciously launched through his association with the Sidneys, and by 1594 his collection had swelled to 60 poems. Other revised editions appeared in 1595, 1598, and 1601, the last revised extensively.

Because Newman's edition inaugurated the fashion of sonneteering in the 1590's, both Daniel's and Sidney's cycles, as different as they are from one another, were highly influential. Sidney experimented with a variety of forms, presenting a dramatized "voice" in a broad range of attitudes (exuberance, sorrow, self-recrimination, humor), using a flexible verse line sometimes end-stopped but frequently open, reflecting the attitude of his speaker. Daniel confined himself to the English or Shakespearean form, which had been introduced by Surrey decades earlier, and with little exception (some *carpe diem* sonnets and those on his verses as monuments) his "voice" is unrelievedly that of the lamenting Petrarchan lover. While he is not nearly so interesting as Sidney, he demonstrated a level of competence unattained by anyone else at that time, Sidney and Spenser excepted. Despite his four-square approach to the sonnet form (units of thought invariably conform to the structure of three quatrains and a couplet), his iambic lines are rarely heavy and he is capable of creating interesting tensions between the metrical norm and natural speech patterns: "False Hope prolongs my certain grief, / Traitor to me, and faithful to my Love" (Sonnet 25). He understands the strength of the basically monosyllabic line (which he must have learned from Sidney) as in Sonnet 30 on the theme of his projected "lover's-death,"

> If any ask me why so soon I came,
> I'll hide her sin and say it was my lot:

In life and death I'll tender her good name,
My life nor death shall never be her blot.

From time to time he can nicely correlate the flow of his line to his thought and imagery: "Whils't by thy eyes pursu'd, my poor heart flew / Into the sacred refuge of thy breast" (Sonnet 31), and he is capable of achieving functional sound effects, as in his most accomplished sonnet, "Care charmer Sleep" (Sonnet 54), which also illustrates all of the strengths mentioned above.

Without any sort of narrative thread, the *Delia* sonnets seem all of a piece through the sameness of the generalized lamenting voice, and a kind of artistic unity is achieved through Daniel's practice of linking sonnets either by extending a conceit or, more commonly, by opening with a phrase or line from the ending of a previous sonnet (see Sonnets 6–7, 9–10, 34–35, 39–42, 43–44, 50–51).

The meditative sonnets on *carpe diem* and on the immortality of his verses in the face of destructive time are consistently among his better pieces, and lines like the following have raised the question of Shakespeare's indebtedness to Daniel:

Though the error of my youth in them appear,
Suffice they show I liv'd and lov'd this dear.
(Sonnet 55)

These colors with thy fading are not spent,
These may remain when thou and I shall perish.
(Sonnet 42)

For had she not been fair and thus unkind
Then had no finger pointed at my lightness.
(Sonnet 7)

We can assume that Daniel's original 28 sonnets, from which the above lines have been taken, had been circulating for some time before 1591, and although Shakespeare's *Sonnets* cannot be dated, the likelihood is that Daniel's preceded Shakespeare's. If so, in choosing the English sonnet as his form and creating a more reflective rather than dramatic voice, not to mention using the device of linking sonnets together, Shakespeare looked to Daniel not to Sidney. For this and for the several very effective pieces in the cycle, *Delia* remains a significant literary document.

—Frank Fabry

THE DEPTFORD TRILOGY
(includes *Fifth Business*, *The Manticore*, *World of Wonders*).
Novels by Robertson Davies, 1970–75.

The Deptford Trilogy's re-publication in one 863-page volume is in keeping with Robertson Davies's reputation as the author of blockbusters with class; it also makes narrative and thematic sense. Deptford is a fictional village in southwestern Ontario. *Fifth Business* begins there, with the stone that Percy "Boy" Staunton puts in the snowball that mistakenly strikes Mrs. Dempster; *World of Wonders* ends with the revelation of who put the same stone in Staunton's mouth before his suicide, or murder, 60 years later. The dénouement takes the form of a conversation in a large bed at the Savoy Hotel, between Magnus Eisengrim, the world's greatest illusionist (inside Mrs. Dempster at the time of the accident, but soon to emerge); Dunstan Ramsay, a retired schoolmaster who is an authority on saints (at whom the snowball had been aimed); and Liselotte Naegeli, a wealthy and deformed Swiss aristocrat (sometime mistress to them both). It is long way, and a long time, from Deptford, but the *Trilogy* is all a "continual reminder of the consequences that can follow a single action."

Fifth Business is Ramsay's memoir. It describes Deptford's charity, and brutality, to Mrs. Dempster, who never recovers her wits after the accident and the premature birth of her son Paul; the scholarship that is the fruit of Ramsay's conviction that Mrs. Dempster, as the author of three miracles, is a saint; his lifelong friendship with "Boy" Staunton; and occasional meetings with the adult Paul Dempster, who runs away from Deptford as a child. Paul Dempster has become Magnus Eisengrim, the magician; the novel ends with the Liselotte, as the voice of the Brazen Head, pronouncing on Staunton's death in a highly elliptical fashion, at the climax of Eisengrim's performance. Ramsay—cranky, romantic, and tight with a penny—is a good narrator, but not an omniscient one: the next two novels move back and forth within the same framework of events.

If *The Deptford Trilogy* is central to Davies's three novel-trilogies, *The Manticore* is the centre of *Deptford*, and central to *The Manticore* is the analysis, in Zurich, of David Staunton, the alcoholic son of the Boy, whose public persona, or mask, has shattered in the face of the Brazen Head. Davies's interest in Jung informs the entire trilogy (and has been the focus of one critical study). Other novelists have used analyst-psychiatrists, and more particularly the buried memories they elicit, as propellors to the plot. But Davies chooses to shape almost the whole novel in the form of conversations between Staunton and Dr. von Haller, and the notes that the analysand makes between sessions. As a technical device, it provides a commodious vehicle for Davies to do what he does best: write dialogue that is to a great extent concerned with the imparting of a craft. Staunton saw nothing nasty in the woodshed; but, as the reader is by now learning to predict, a fine intellect and conventional Canadian upbringing cannot shield him from the realization that, as Davies told an audience in 1968, throughout our lives "we move through a throng of Sleeping Princesses, Belles Dames sans Merci . . . Ogres . . . Sagacious Animal Helpers and Servers, yes and Heroes and Heroines." Staunton joins Ramsay, Liselotte, and Eisengrim at the end of the novel in a fine catharsis, filled with shit and the numinous; we do not, unfortunately, meet him again.

Eisengrim attributes his success to modern man's "concealed longing for romance and marvels"; Davies could say the same. But his popularity must also be attributed to the way in which Davies satisfies the novel-reader's perdurable longing for exculpation in the form of knowledge, for information. *The Deptford Trilogy*, while not as overtly pedagogic as *The Cornish Trilogy*, still provides much fascinating stuff on the work of genealogists, rich men, hagiographers, actors, and Jungian analysts. They are all, in their way, historians of a special kind. First, they are storytellers. Good as Davies is at differentiating his characters by the *way* they say things, none of them ever says anything ill-considered or fatuous, except at the most trivial level. This means that the author's favorite positions can be advanced in a way that is remarkably forthright, but with emphases differing according to each character's experience—which, with Davies, often means expertise—and projections. Second, these are "historians" of psychological, or mythic, as opposed to literal or historical truth. The two may, of course, be identical: for example, Davies has a special place in the affections of anglophone Canadians for his constant reassurances that, however "cold and cautious" we appear, inside we are a "mass of intuition and dark intimation." However, more often we are asked to accept that "myth and fairy-tales are nothing less than the distilled truth about what we call 'real life'" (from the same lecture); taking his cue from Oscar Wilde, Davies makes clear in *World of Wonders* that art, or illusion, is also distilled truth, which is often more credible than "real life." The book opens with an assembly of artists collaborating on a film about Houdini, in which Eisengrim stars. Partly in an attempt to stop their quarrelling, it is suggested that Eisengrim tell the story of his own long life since leaving Deptford as Paul Dempster. The account of how he triumphs over a childhood filled with sexual and every other kind of exploitation and humiliation, to become the fortunate man who can not only change his name but rewrite his history, is not an edifying one. It is suggested more than once that he could not have done it without a complete innocence of books.

—Christine Stevenson

THE DESERTED VILLAGE.
Poem by Oliver Goldsmith, 1770.

In *The Deserted Village*, first published in May 1770, Oliver Goldsmith returns to a subject first treated in his essay "The Revolution in Low Life" (1762), which gave a detailed account of an emparking enclosure which, Goldsmith claimed, occurred the previous summer about 50 miles from London, when the inhabitants of nearly 100 houses were evicted because "a Merchant of immense fortune in London, who had lately purchased the estate on which they lived, intended to lay the whole out in a seat of pleasure for himself." In *The Traveller* (1764) he made a more generalized protest: "Have we not seen at pleasure's lordly call, / The smiling long-frequented village fall?"

Finally, in his account of the desertion of Auburn, Goldsmith established the myth of rural catastrophe in its familiar form. The myth rests upon the clear fact that villages were being destroyed to make way for rich men's pleasure grounds. Castle Howard, Cirencester Park, Crichel, Harewood, Holkham, Houghton, Kedleston, Mereworth, Milton Abbas, Normanton, Nuneham Courtenay, Shottesbrooke, Stowe, and Wimpole were among the gardens that ate up villages in the 18th century. These landscape gardens sought to give physical shape to great landowners' conceptions—derived from classical pastoral direct, or at one remove through the paintings of Claude Lorraine—of Arcadia, the Vale of Tempe, the Golden Age. But for Goldsmith the laying out of such pleasure grounds signalled the destruction of another Arcadia or Golden Age, the joy, virtue, and independence of a community of happy husbandmen. The desertion of the village is Goldsmith's occasion for an attack upon "luxury" and the excessive power of trading interests, and so the poem is a tract for the times, but Burke was correct in describing it as a pastoral.

The opening of *The Deserted Village* describes "Sweet Auburn, loveliest village of the plain" as it was before its destruction. Though it has features of a workaday English village,

> The sheltered cot, the cultivated farm,
> The never failing brook, the busy mill,
> The decent church that topt the neighbouring hill,
> The hawthorn bush, with seats beneath the shade,

Auburn is pastorally idealized as "Dear lovely bowers of innocence and ease." This description, in which the words "sweet" and "charms" are often repeated, is suddenly cut short to make way for a more graphic description of the present ruinous condition of Auburn:

> No more thy glassy brook reflects the day,
> But choaked with sedges, works its weedy way.
> Along thy glades, a solitary guest.
> The hollow sounding bittern guards its nest.

This is more closely observed than the account of the unspoiled village, but is not without overtones of the pastoral convention that nature should mourn human misfortune.

Between unspoiled and ruined Auburn there is a shift in mood from the sentimental to the pathetic; at line 51 there is a more abrupt shift to the sternly prophetic: "Ill fares the land, to hastening ills a prey, / Where wealth accumulates, and men decay." These moods continue to alternate throughout the poem. The destruction of Auburn is a symptom of national social, economic, and moral malaise, but, to the extent that Auburn was the place where the poet spent his childhood and where he wished to retire, its destruction images the poet's own sense of alienation. The scenes of Auburn throughout are suffused with the pastoral singer's own feelings: "Remembrance wakes with all her busy train, / Swells at my breast, and turns the past to pain." This couplet introduces a "retirement" passage where the subjective element becomes insistent, and rises to an emotional climax with the image of the poet as a hunted hare; for the singer sees not only the object of his sorrow but himself in a suitable attitude before it. He is the sentimentalist who withdraws into himself to contemplate his own feelings, but he also looks outwards in a purposeful manner. The main public theme of the poem is introduced with the words:

> Ye friends to truth, ye statesmen who survey
> The rich man's joys encrease, the poor's decay,
> 'Tis yours to judge, how wide the limits stand
> Between a splendid and an happy land.

The pastoral theme of virtue in humble rural life is proclaimed in references to the villagers collectively and is elaborated in sketches of individuals, one of whom, the solitary, dispossessed, sad matron, is a stock character of humanitarian literature (though she may also be that common enough figure—the poor decrepit man or woman housed by a depopulating landlord in order to prevent his being obliged to pay towards the support of the poor in the next parish). The contrasts that provide an intellectual framework for the poem are those of pastoral: nature against art, country against city, and frugality against luxury.

—A.J. Sambrook

THE DEVILS.
Play by John Whiting, 1961.

A public relations pamphlet on the Royal Shakespeare Company's productions in the early 1960's describes *The Devils* as "a dark, sarcastic, sensuous tragedy, uneven but at best superb." The last drama John Whiting completed before his death in 1963, it grew from Peter Hall's request for a historical play the company could stage at the Aldwych with a large cast and period costumes. After considering Rolfe's *Hadrian VII*, Whiting decided to adapt Aldous Huxley's *The Devils of Loudun*.

A great deal of simplification was necessary to compress Huxley's study of hysteria and demonic possession in early 17th-century France into a coherent play, and Whiting focuses even more closely than Huxley on Urban Grandier, the priest of Loudun, and on the nuns and political figures who accused and condemned him. He excludes most of the psychological theorizing and frequent references to other examples of possession and public hysteria that enrich Huxley's book, but vivifies the thoughts and reactions of people ranging from an invented sewerman to the perceptive Prince Henri de Condé. While some critics disliked the play, saying the characters lacked depth, others felt it was a successful modern evocation of the spirit of Jacobean tragedy, and drew parallels with the work of John Webster.

Like many early 17th-century English tragedies, *The Devils* is panoramic. It covers the years from 1623 to 1634 in a quick succession of short scenes on a relatively bare stage. Its focus, while not on a king or prince, is on a talented, outstanding, physically attractive priest with the potential to rise high in the church, but with the flaws of pride and sensuality. Like his Jacobean forerunners, Whiting does not shy from physically repelling scenes. The play begins on a grimly realistic note, with a corpse hanging from the municipal gallows and the somewhat choric sewerman working in a drain and commenting on the body. Sister Jeanne, hunchbacked Prioress of St. Ursula's convent, must later act demonic possession, and the nuns must writhe through an exorcism at the climax of the second act. Near the end, the audience, though innured to television violence, is shocked by the torture of Grandier in an effort to force a confession, and horrified by the sight of the physically broken man collapsing on smashed legs at the convent door.

Like the chronicle histories of Shakespeare, *The Devils* portrays real figures, bringing them to life through invented dialogue, soliloquies, and comments by others. Certain events are selected and highlighted, and other scenes are created to give coherence and shape to the story. The language and point of view, however, are modern. Whiting avoids archaic language except for occasional Latin passages that convey a sense of ritual. Some of the purported devils are clipped and sarcastic. The Prince sounds effete. Father Mignon, the old priest who becomes confessor and instigator, is more formal when "deeply disturbed by this sudden cessation of diabolical manifestations." The Sewerman's idiom is terse and comparatively vulgar. All speak in prose, though some of the language is highly imaged and metaphoric, and most of the speeches are short with the exception of the soliloquies. While Whiting avoids archaisms, he also eschews slang that would make the characters seem displaced 20th-century Londoners.

The point of view is also modern. Existentialistic and nihilistic concerns are expressed that go beyond any early 17th-century crisis of faith. There is a satirical overtone as exorcists and accusers pontificate about a demonic possession that is obviously faked. At the same time, there is a keen psychological awareness of the power of suggestion, of fixation on the idea of a person, of the spread of hysteria, and of the seductiveness of suddenly becoming the center of attention. Grandier and Jeanne both indulge in self-analysis that their originals might not have been able to voice.

Structurally, the play moves back and forth among the groups that gradually join against Grandier, who has offended all. Churchmen resent his sensuousness and ability to attract congregations; the Public Prosecutor thinks of his daughter, impregnated and abandoned by Grandier; the chemist and surgeon resent his jibes; Jeanne is probably dismayed when he refuses to become confessor to the convent; central political forces dislike his stance in favor of keeping the town walls. In a period when people believed in demonic possession, all realize that Jeanne's cries of "Grandier" can be used to destroy him and show the church ever-vigilant against the Devil. The great public accusation and exorcism of the second act, with a crowd in holiday mood, is almost foiled by the skeptical Prince, and we feel disgust at the opportunism of the churchmen.

The final act, although distressing in its torture scenes, also becomes a kind of affirmation, for it shows Grandier's strength in the face of his fears. The ultimate irony comes when the broken, stripped man is taken to the convent and for the first time sees the women who have accused him. At this moment, too, Jeanne sees in him a beauty that seems unrelated to the perfumed, elegant beauty he exhibited in the first act.

The Devils is part of a long line of plays about possession. Around 1590, Marlowe showed Faustus selling his soul and ultimately going to hell. In the 1950's, the Salem witch trials were put to allegorical use by Arthur Miller to comment on the accusations of communism then sweeping the U.S. Whiting resembles Miller in focussing on hysterical females who have become the center of attention and gained a new power. He differs, however, in surrounding protagonist and antagonist with a whole range of figures and forces that turn a sensual fascination into a battle of wills, threatening to make Jeanne and Grandier into pawns. At the end, the audience may think of Grandier as a martyr, but the Sewerman denies any religious significance. People are hunting his charred relics as charms, though Jeanne still calls his name.

—Frances A. Shirley

THE DIARY OF A NOBODY. See the Writers entry on **GROSSMITH, George**.

A DICTIONARY OF THE ENGLISH LANGUAGE.
Work by Samuel Johnson, 1755.

When, in *The Plan of a Dictionary of the English Language*, Samuel Johnson asserts that he intends to assemble a dictionary "by which the pronunciation of our language may be fixed, and its attainment facilitated; by which its purity may be preserved, its use ascertained, and its duration lengthened," he places his dictionary in the tradition of the dictionaries of the French and Italian academies. Even though he compiled his English dictionary without the financial and scholarly support lavished on those other great enterprises of Enlightenment codification—he received £1575 and had the assistance of only six copyists—he set out to prescribe comprehensive standards of usage for the English language. Earlier dictionaries of English words were inadequate, limited in many cases to obscure (and spurious) words of foreign origin. Indeed, Johnson differed from all of his English predecessors in his plan to assemble a comprehensive list of English words—simple or obscure, technical as well as common—through a survey of "the boundless chaos of living speech." His dictionary is based not on other word lists, but on his reading of writers in English from the Elizabethan period to the Restoration. In the preface, he describes the English language as an untended garden that has run to "wild exuberance"; as lexicographer, his task was empirical: to "reduce" this exuberance to method—to establish orthography, etymology, and meaning—through "experience" and "analogy."

However, while Johnson clearly sets out in the *Dictionary* to discern a rational order in this dimension of human experience, and to establish rational principles for future linguistic behavior, it is essential to recognize that the *Dictionary* also reflects his knowledge of the ultimate futility of such a project. It has as much in common with his ironic vision of human accomplishment in *The Vanity of Human Wishes*, *the Rambler*, and *Rasselas* as it does with the ambitious dictionaries and encyclopedias of the Enlightenment. In particular, the *Dictionary* is evidence of the limitations of scholarly diligence and rational scrutiny, and of the elusiveness and inscrutability of language itself. Although Johnson's original intention was to admit only those words which he could document as words used by English writers, he does include some words which can be found only in dictionaries "because they may perhaps exist, though they have escaped my notice"; similarly, he omits many words specific to sciences and crafts, for "it had been a hopeless labour to glean up words by courting living information, and contesting with the sullenness of one, and the roughness of another": a lexicographer cannot in the end construct a definitive word list.

Johnson's dramatization of his limitations as solitary lexicographer is remarkable throughout the dictionary. He frequently presents himself in the first person, expressing uncertainty about etymologies or definitions, or disagreeing with his sources. Perhaps the most frequent reason for rejecting words is that they are "cant," or "peculiar to some certain class or body of men." However, it is clear that the basis for these judgments is in many cases personal; words are "cant," "low," or even "ludicrous" or "bad" because they seem so from Johnson's perspective. Johnson believed that the definitions, or, as he styled them, "explanations," would open him to censure; he expresses frustration at the difficulty in defining simple words, common verbs like "run," particles, and expletives. Indeed, it is by quirky definitions like the one for "oats," or the convoluted and latinate definition of "network," that the work is often characterized. (However, it is difficult to generalize about some 40,000 definitions. Many are merely synonyms, those for obscure or technical words are often borrowed from other sources, and some are masterpieces of Johnsonian abstraction.) Finally, Johnson seems to confirm the presence of his personna in this reference work by inserting personal references (see the entry for "lich") and jokes about lexicographers (see the entry for "grubstreet").

Johnson had to retreat from his original intention of including for each word a series of quotations which would represent a history of its use by English writers; for most words, only one illustration is offered. However, the effect of these illustrations is to demonstrate the tendency of language to become metaphoric, and of words to change subtly in use. Johnson does not quote uncritically; he points out when a writer like Spenser has taken liberties in using a word, or when he considers a word used by Dryden to be inadmissible. But because the use of words by English authors is a primary basis for including them in the dictionary, many of the definitions which he lists are figurative; this is especially evident in the many definitions based on Shakespeare's usages. In the preface to the *Dictionary*, Johnson describes the process by which words pass from "primitive" to "remote and accidental signification," and concludes that it is impossible to determine all meanings in the "exuberance of signification which many words have obtained." The literary illustrations, necessarily epigrammatic because of their brevity, are in addition often irreverent, or subversive of the very word illustrated. For example, for "lexicon," Johnson quotes Milton's statement that if a linguist "had not studied the solid things in [languages] as well as the words and *lexicons*, yet he were nothing so much to be esteemed a learned man as any yeoman competently wise in his mother dialect." For "impregnate" he quotes a passage from Browne's *Vulgar Errors* to the effect that hermaphrodites cannot impregnate themselves. Taken as a whole, the illustrations reveal a world of verbal irony and distorted social order.

Near the end of the preface to the *Dictionary*, Johnson concludes that neither he nor the French and Italian academies can preserve language from change; that mutability is as intrinsic to language as are "folly, vanity, and affectation" to the world. He speculates that the language of a "barbaric and secluded" nation might be preserved, but that any nation "polished by arts and classed by subordination, where one part of the community is sustained and accommodated by the labour of the other" cannot sustain a language unaltered with the passage of time. Words from both the world of trade and the cultivated sciences creep into the language and take on general significance. His initial dream of delineating and prescribing a "common" language has given way to the recognition that the English language is comprised of a diversity of languages, that all men—including lexicographers—are to an extent linguistically isolated by class, education, and interests. Rather than a work which preserves the English language for perpetuity, the dictionary displays the process by which tradesmen, great writers, and the mediating lexicographer himself alter—and create—meaning.

—Sara B. Varhus

DOCTOR FAUSTUS.
Play by Christopher Marlowe, produced 1594; published versions 1604 and 1616.

Johann Faust was a wandering German scholar and magus who lived c.1488–c.1541. His alleged pact with the devil had been treated in several publications before the first full-length narrative of "the celebrated conjuror and master of black magic" Dr. John Faust and "how he sold himself to the Devil" appeared in German in 1587. It was translated into English by

"P.F." as *The History of the Damnable Life and Deserved Death of Doctor John Faustus*. This work was Christopher Marlowe's chief source. If the earliest known copy, from 1592, is of the first edition, then Marlowe's play (whose first recorded performance was in 1594) must have been written during the year before his death in May 1593; but some scholars argue for a date earlier in his career, c.1588–89.

The text of this blank verse and prose drama is problematic. The first edition of 1604 (the A Text) omits much of the comic subplot which first appeared in the longer text (the B Text) published in 1616. Earlier editors (e.g., C.F. Tucker Brooke in 1910) supposed that the A Text was the more authentic, but in his parallel-text edition of 1950 W.W. Greg demonstrated that the B Text actually antedated the A Text, which was an imperfect memorial reconstruction of it, probably by a group of players wishing to acquire a copy for performance. More recent editors have therefore preferred the B Text (e.g., J.B. Steane's Penguin edition of *The Complete Plays*, 1969), although some have produced a composite text (e.g., John D. Jump's Revels edition of 1962, which is the edition here cited). Matters are further complicated by the fact, generally agreed, that the comic subplot is not the work of Marlowe but of a collaborator, probably Samuel Rowley.

Faustus's opening soliloquy traces the history of his commitment to that audacious pansophical quest which is characteristic of one side of Renaissance culture. Having mastered all scholarly disciplines his frustration at the limitations of his knowledge and power ("Yet are thou still but Faustus, and a man"), and his ambition, which "Stretcheth as far as doth the mind of man," now finally lead him to necromancy. Faustus thus takes his place beside Marlowe's other aspiring and individualistic protagonists (who are perhaps recalled in the opening lines of the first Chorus), but in no other of his plays is Marlowe's examination of the fallibility of human nature and the fallaciousness of its pretensions to omnipotence so searching. In its scepticism about human motivation and its comic subversion of apparently grandly idealistic schemes to benefit humankind it is perhaps the first example of the sensibility characteristic of the modern period.

It is Faustus's tragedy that his aims, though perhaps intrinsically admirable, so consume him as to blind him to his actual case. He believes he controls the devils though told by Mephostophilis, whom he has summoned, that "I am a servant to great Lucifer / And may not follow thee without his leave"; he believes he has chosen the more powerful supernatural allies, though Mephostophilis acknowledges God's supremacy; he dismisses hell as a fable despite Mephostophilis's admission that he endures eternal torment. Mephostophilis's truthfulness is unexpected, but he has no need to deceive Faustus: Faustus is self-deceived. This telling dramatic irony is enforced by the counterpointing of Faustus's deeds in the comic subplot which equates his achievements with the ability to perform a few conjuring tricks. Faustus is doomed by his single-minded obsession with power and dominion, not by any external agency.

It is this which renders mistaken any suggestion that *Doctor Faustus* is an anti-Christian play, a kind of humanistic plea for liberation of the human spirit from the constraints of Christian doctrine. Faustus is not predestined to damnation by a malignant deity determined to prevent legitimate human achievement. It is repeatedly demonstrated that the devils have no power over Faustus which he does not himself grant them. The allegorical Good and Evil Angels (one of several devices from the old morality plays employed by Marlowe) represent the possibility of repentance, a possibility made more dramatically poignant by the figure of the Old Man who sees "an angel hovers o'er thy head / And with a vial full of precious grace / Offers to pour the same into thy soul." Against him the devils are powerless. Faustus is himself aware that "Hell strives with grace for conquest in my breast," and in his final soliloquy, one of the most powerful in all Renaissance drama, he sees "where Christs blood streams in the firmament." Faustus is doomed not by a Christian doctrine which cannot tolerate his activities but by an unconstrained and obsessive lust for "a world . . . / Of power, of honour, of omnipotence" which is insatiable and implacable. The apparatus of conjuring and devils is less a representation of an external supernatural force than it is an image of Faustus's self-enslavement, his self-created destiny.

Although Faustus dominates the play its import extends beyond his personal predicament. His ambition to achieve unfettered mastery over "All things that move between the quiet poles" was, even as Marlowe wrote, being given scientific validity by Francis Bacon and would soon recognise in technology and science more reliable means than magic for its attainment. In Faustus's desire to "Ransack the ocean for orient pearl, / And search all corners of the new found world / For pleasant fruits and princely delicates" *Doctor Faustus* is presciently aware that a civilisation founded upon the presumption that nature is a resource which may be endlessly exploited will share Faustus's fate.

—N.H. Keeble

DR. JEKYLL AND MR. HYDE.
(*Strange Case of Dr. Jekyll and Mr. Hyde.*)
Story by Robert Louis Stevenson, 1886.

Rarely does the title of a short story become proverbial in common speech. Yet when Robert Louis Stevenson's *Strange Case of Dr. Jekyll and Mr. Hyde* was published, its impact was so great that phrases such as "a Jekyll and Hyde character," meaning someone alternately agreeable and unpleasant, or even "a Jekyll and Hyde policy," meaning one with a mixture of good and bad points in it, came rapidly into general use and were immediately understood.

As often happens, the proverbial reference is based on a simplification of the original, amounting in this instance almost to a misreading. Stevenson's Jekyll and Hyde are not one person but two, not a single individual compounded like common humanity of both good and evil traits, with the one or the other in the ascendant at any given moment. Duality of virtue and vice in one person there certainly is, in the character of Jekyll, the baser side of whose nature is fascinated by Hyde. But the latter is a distinct and separate person from the Doctor, and furthermore an individual of entirely unalloyed evil.

Herein lies the book's startling originality. Stevenson is concerned to portray more than the conflicts of a self-justifying occasional sinner. He presents in the persona of Hyde the principle of evil itself in a pure and unadulterated form. The intensity with which he achieved this accounts no doubt for the strength of the story's impact on the public.

The plot may be summarised as follows. Jekyll is a respected and wealthy physician, a bachelor of mature years who, like many of his Victorian counterparts, has long been accustomed to the discreet indulgence of his sexual appetite —pleasures which Stevenson in a letter about the story declared to have no harm in them apart from some hypocrisy in the commission. Experimenting in his laboratory, Jekyll stumbles on a chemical compound which completely transforms both his physical and his moral being. Jekyll is replaced by Hyde, a diabolical young man exulting in his wickedness and sensuality. Another draught of the compound, and Hyde is replaced by the older, on the whole well-doing, Jekyll. Hyde's brutal behaviour during his nocturnal forays, and some mysterious connection with the Doctor, come to the notice of Jekyll's friend and solicitor, Utterson, who holds Jekyll's will naming Hyde as his heir. Finally Hyde commits a violent murder using Jekyll's walking stick as the weapon, and disappears from his rooms. Utterson calls on Jekyll, who shakenly declares that Hyde will never be heard of again; he himself will have no more to do with him. Over two months later, Jekyll suddenly refuses to receive visitors. Utterson consults Dr. Lanyon, another old friend and physician, whom he finds in a state of terminal shock and who refuses to hear mention of Jekyll's name. Finally, when Jekyll locks himself into his laboratory and his servants fear for his health and sanity, Utterson and the butler break in, to find not the Doctor but the body of Hyde, who has committed suicide.

The theme of this macabre tale was suggested by a nightmare, which Stevenson wrote up the next day as a horror story rather in the manner of Poe. He then started afresh, completing the draft of a new extended treatment in only three days. This, with minor alterations in one further revision, is the text as we now have it.

The construction of the narrative, with its shifting viewpoints—we are introduced to Hyde in a scene of horrifying brutality reported by a minor character who reappears only once, fleetingly and unimportantly, halfway through the book—and with its recourse to Lanyon's and Jekyll's written statements finally to elucidate the mystery, falls short of Jamesian ideals of fiction. But the work remains a tour de force nonetheless. The pace of the narration, the deft way in which details supporting both the action and its unravelling are interwoven throughout the narrative, and the economy with which the story's terrifying atmosphere is created, combine to form a work of extraordinary psychological depth and powerful impact.

The principal characters are well-to-do professional men—lawyers and doctors, pillars of society, and men of the world. Yet around them, and in the mean streets abutting on the squares and crescents where they live their respectable lives, there lurks an underworld of menace, violence, and evil.

Stevenson sketches this with a sure hand, using murky London fogs, clear frost-rimed nights, and brilliant moonlight as visual contrasts for scenes such as Hyde, like some automaton, trampling heedlessly over a small child, or again in a burst of incandescent rage battering a white-haired gentleman with such force that his bones were audibly shattered and his body jumped on the roadway.

As a counterpoint to these sharply focused images of violence, the delineation of Utterson's character is equally economical and graphic; unsmiling, unsentimental, austere, but tolerant of the peccadilloes of others, and inclined always to help rather than to reprove; a man of complete probity and conscience in matters of trust.

The theme of *Dr. Jekyll and Mr. Hyde*—the notion of evil and the frailty of conscience—coincides here with Stevenson's imaginative treatment and literary craftsmanship to form a work of remarkable power; so much so, particularly as the pace quickens with Jekyll's desperate attempts to replace the failing supply of his drug, that the reader is swept forward without questioning the premises of the allegory or the credibility of this strange but realistic tale. The book went rapidly through several editions in the months after its publication, and remains today an outstanding example of the long short story or novella.

A final note on pronunciation: Stevenson, like Gertrude Jekyll the garden designer, pronounced the name to rhyme with treacle.

—Stewart F. Sanderson

DOMBEY AND SON.
(*Dealings with the Firm of Dombey and Son.*)
Novel by Charles Dickens, 1848.

In 1846 Charles Dickens was travelling abroad when he began to write *Dombey and Son*. It was a turning-point in his career. His last book, *Martin Chuzzlewit*, had sold less than any of his previous books; some thought he was losing both inspiration and reputation, though he himself considered *Martin Chuzzlewit* his best book to date. He was becoming weary, perhaps, of the fantastic exuberance of farce and melodrama which had succeeded so brilliantly in his earliest books. He had tended, up to now, to push his stories back in time. *Martin Chuzzlewit*, like its predecessors, and like some of its successors into the 1860's, is full of coach journeys, though the railway age had begun. Now for the first time, from his foreign vantage-point, Dickens began to assimilate into his art his impressions of the contemporary world. The railways are the most obvious and impressive feature; but it is true also of subtler aspects. From one point of view the book is a meditation on the relation between a merchant class, conscious of a new authority and influence in the country, and a hereditary ruling class, unsure whether power was beginning to slip away. This theme would be developed further a few years later in *Bleak House*. Mr. Dombey is not an aristocrat, but in many ways he tries to behave like one. The books title and Dombey's incessant brooding on his heir show that he thinks of his business as an aristocrat thinks of a landed estate, a sacred trust passed to him by his ancestors to be preserved intact for his descendants. But, in the dynamic world of the 1840's, this traditionalism may be the road to commercial ruin, as it is here. Then, the commercial man does not feel an entire inner confidence in playing an aristocratic part. Hence, Dombey's tendency to be taken in by disreputable but imposing representatives of a higher class: Major Bagstock, Mrs. Skewton, and Edith.

In his brilliant treatment of the railways, Dickens shows both the excitement of newness, and the extraordinary sensation of travelling at high speed for the first time in human history, and, at the same time, the rapid habituation to novelty so that "there was even railway time observed in clocks, as if the sun itself had given in." And at the time of Carker's death, the train seems to be endowed with the sombre qualities of an avenging angel. An altogether subtler effect is achieved in the meeting of Dombey with Toodle, whose wife has suckled the motherless Paul Dombey is seriously displeased because Toodle wears a sign of mourning for his (Dombey's) dead son. His pride, his grief, his class sensibility are all alike outraged at this plebeian sympathy.

The whole book shows a new inwardness in the depiction of thoughts and feelings. Dombey, Paul, and Florence are all brooders and waiters. Dombey is waiting for his son to grow up, Paul is waiting to die, Florence is waiting for the precious, ungraspable prize of her father's love. Dombey's coldness to his daughter is intensified by jealousy at Paul's obvious preference for her over himself. Matching this new inwardness is a pervasive symbolism, never before obtrusive in the author's work. The sea, boisterously and literally present in the Brighton scenes, is also the image of the inner voice and of the mystery of life; so, in the first chapter, Mrs. Dombey, clinging to the "spar" of Florence, moves into the "dark and unknown sea that rolls round all the world"; the dying Paul sees the moving shadows on the bedroom wall as waves carrying him away, while Mr. Feeder, Blimber's assistant, "plainly hears the waves informing him . . . that Doctor Blimber will give up the business." Mrs. Skewton, being all outside and no inside, is "deaf to the waves that are hoarse with the repetition of their mystery."

Dickens had not, of course, completely abandoned melodrama, represented, for instance, by Edith's strange elopement with Carker, followed by her rejection of him, and by Dombey's attempted suicide. But he combines it with a new mature and intelligent understanding of things, shown, for instance, in the brilliant comedy of Blimber's academy, and the thought-provoking contrast with the Charitable Grinders. He had already, in *Oliver Twist* and *The Old Curiosity Shop*, won immense popularity by his studies of childhood; the absence of children from *Martin Chuzzlewit* may have been a reason for its comparative unpopularity. But Florence and Paul show an immense literary advance on Little Nell, and prepare the way for *David Copperfield*. Perhaps, oversimplifying a little, we may say that *Dombey and Son* is the point in Dickens's career when the master entertainer became a truly great novelist.

—A.O.J. Cockshut

DON JUAN.
Poem by Lord Byron, 1819–24.

Written between July 1818 and May 1823, the 16 cantos of *Don Juan* represent the culmination of Lord Byron's mature poetic style. The poem breaks off abruptly at canto 17, stanza 14, giving no hint as to what future Byron envisaged for his hero. This indefiniteness and lack of closure epitomize the quality of the whole, for the poem may be regarded as a modern epic which presents in its form and events, in the character of Juan, and in the ever-present figure of the narrator a world of uncertainties and relativities, a world of the absurd.

Although many influences may be cited, the form of *Don Juan* defies categorization. One of Byron's greatest debts was to the Italian romances, especially Pulci's *Morgante Maggiore* (1483), which, like Byron's poem, combines the serious and the comic in a free-ranging *ottava rima* stanza. John Hookham Frere in *The Monks and the Giants* (1817) was the first to adapt the Italian tone to English, and Byron acknowledged Frere as the model for *Beppo*, his own first attempt at the style. But the mode of *Don Juan* is not easily pinned down. The classical epic, the mock epic, neoclassical satire, the burlesque of Butler's *Hudibras*, the picaresque novel, the gothic novel, all contribute to its distinctive manner. Byron himself described the work both as an epic and a satire, but perhaps most significantly he wrote to Douglas Kinnaird on 26 October 1818, "Is it not *life*, is it not *the thing*?" As the remark suggests, in *Don Juan* he set out to capture the realities of life as he saw it, in all its shifting variety and inconsistency.

The events give an epic panorama of the modern world. The narrative begins with Juan's love for Julia, wife of Don Alfonso of Seville. Thereafter it recounts his adventures as he travels from one level of experience to another: shipwreck on the voyage from Seville; a romantic idyll with Haidée on a Greek island; enslavement by Haidée's pirate father, Lambro; sale to the Turkish sultana, Gulbeyaz; escape from the harem and involvement in the Siege of Ismail; service for Catherine the Great of Russia; and finally entrance into English aristocratic society and a possible romance with the coquettish Duchess of Fitz-Fulke. The narrative thus attains an epic quality in its scope, its traditional subjects of love and war, and its mingling of fiction with historical events and personages. *Don Juan*, however, is a distinctly modern epic in that it crystallizes the modern spirit with its rejection of romantic illusion, for in this poem love often comes to an abrupt and undignified end and danger brings out not the best but the worst in human beings.

Byron's deflation of human ideals and pretensions establishes a fallen world of disappointments and uncertainties. Juan seeks a paradise which constantly eludes him. His love for Julia proves a false paradise which dissolves into farce when Alfonso searches Julia's bedroom. With Haidée he seems to find a true paradise, but this romance ends precipitately with the reappearance of Lambro. Thereafter no hope of paradise is possible as Juan encounters the evils of war, the tyranny of Catherine, and the hypocrisies of English society. If Aurora Raby, the heroine of the English cantos, was to open up another chance at perfect love, she is displaced, at the point where the poem breaks off, by the sensual and frivolous Duchess. In this fallen world there are no absolutes and no fixed values; both the events and the characters are ambivalent. Julia is self-deceiving but sincere. Haidée's love depends upon her pirate father and eventually destroys her. Gulbeyaz loves Juan but orders his death. Catherine favours him, but with her he succumbs to near fatal illness. Aurora is virtuous but enigmatic.

In this uncertain world Juan is an appropriate hero. The opposite of the legendary Spanish libertine, he is a passive outsider. Unsure of himself and of those around him, he is adrift in a world that he cannot comprehend or control. From beginning to end he is at the mercy of external forces and—ironically in view of the legend—of women, who all in their different ways prove stronger than he. Moreover, he is the victim of impulses within his own personality. His declarations of love for Julia are cut short by seasickness, and his love for Haidée is superseded by his interest in the ladies of the harem. His best efforts come to nought, and his search for personal identity is never concluded. At the end of the poem, when the supposed ghost's cowl drops to reveal the Duchess's mocking face, he is once more confronted with mysteries which preclude his realisation of himself or of the external world.

If Juan represents the plight of human beings in a confused and confusing world, the narrator suggests the best response to such a world. Throughout the work, he remains the one constant, dominating and unifying the whole. A complex and shifting personality, who both is and is not Byron, he is a sophisticated observer, who views the world with cynical amusement, yet as he talks on, fluently and garrulously, he displays a warm sympathy for the foibles of humanity. While he laughs at the delusions of Juan and Julia, he recognises the charm of first love. While he savagely attacks the barbarism evoked by the shipwreck, he sees the gentle self-denial of a father caring for his dying son. While he exposes the folly and brutality of the Siege, he admires the courage of the old Khan fighting to the end. And despite his witty disillusion, he assumes an essentially moral stance as he opposes injustice and sympathises with the poor, the weak, and the victims of society. Finally he reveals that pity, humour, and compassionate acceptance are the only way to counter a chaotic and uncontrollable world. The perspective of the narrator is ultimately the perspective of the poem. It is through the interaction of narrative and narrator that Byron has created a work which is epic in scope, modern in spirit, and one of the great comedies of English literature.

—Muriel Mellown

THE DOUBLE-DEALER.
Play by William Congreve, 1693.

The Double-Dealer, the second of William Congreve's four comedies, was the least successful (though it has enjoyed several 20th-century revivals). Audiences of 1693, uncomfortable with the way *The Double-Dealer* overflowed the boundaries of social comedy into tragicomedy or some other kind of hybrid, tolerated it, but no more. If they sensed that the young author was turning away from the style for which he was already known, they were right: the play is experimental in ways that Congreve would return to, more successfully, in *The Way of the World*. His novel *Incognita* and first comedy, *The Old Bachelor*, are baroque: sprawling casts and plots, luxuriant rhetoric, masses of energy and intrigue. *The Double-Dealer* is scaled down; Congreve keeps a smaller, more aristocratic cast penned in a suburban house for a few hours, being "resolved to preserve the three unities of the drama" and write a "true and regular comedy." Critics debate how well he succeeded—it is difficult to find "unity of action" in the three triangular intrigues—but the real question is why Congreve would move away from popular modes towards a purer neoclassicism. A likely answer is the appeal of a style championed by prestigious English and French critics to literary ambition.

The centre of the play's action and interest is its title-character, Maskwell, a manipulative factotum who schemes to supplant his "friend" Mellefont in Lord Touchwood's will and Cynthia's marriage-bed, if not her affections. "Double dealer" would have suggested an inversion of Manly in Wycherley's prestigious satire *The Plain-Dealer*, but more broadly Maskwell links the Elizabethan Machiavel (Iago) to the 18th-century villain (Fielding's Blifil), and he has an ancestor in Terence. For one critic, Maskwell images an actual Restoration commoner who schemed against Marlborough (*The Cultivated Stance* by William Van Voris); for others he is the Vice in a morality play or Satan himself (*An Approach to Congreve* by Audrey L. Williams). Maskwell is surrounded by diabolic imagery, and does resemble Iago in how nearly he just tells his victims the truth and lets their own pettiness or vice do the rest.

But Congreve mismanages this potential. He has Mellefont ignore a direct warning against Maskwell in the first scene, turning the audience's attention to the former's credulity. Then the soliloquies in which Maskwell announces his villainy are awkward and melodramatic (especially compared to Iago's), and that in which he deliberately misleads Lord Touchwood is a bald violation of Congreve's own rule: "if he supposes anyone to be by, when he talks to himself, it is monstrous and ridiculous to the last degree" ("Epistle Dedicatory"). The power of Iago's diabolism comes from his persuasive subtlety and vague sense of grievance; Maskwell is too *simply* ambitious, so his victims seem fools, leaving the play without a hero.

Maskwell and Congreve succeed better in demonstrating that we must sometimes veil ourselves and our purposes in this world; by the end Mellefont and Lord Touchwood, tired of being dupes, have donned parson's robes to spy on Maskwell. The play's women do not need to learn this lesson, though: they already know how to dissemble. Long before he sees the advantage of disguise, Mellefont has a notion that women "are most truly themselves in a vizor mask." If most of the men are foolish, most of the women are vicious; the Ladies Touchwood, Plyant, and Froth all have adulterous intrigues. Only Cynthia is clever and *good*, counterbalancing Maskwell. Unfortunately she does not meet her match in this respect; Mellefont cannot sing his part of the duet. He never makes good on his promise to "give [her] a very evident demonstration of his wit" by "undermining" Lady Touchwood, nor does he have a duel of wits with Cynthia: they agree to "marry for love" in mid-play. Audiences' expectations may have been violated in this regard, too.

Bonamy Dobrée once observed that in his first three comedies Congreve was "at war with himself," not having found his "real style"; "The light-hearted atmosphere was not really natural to him. . . . " This may be so, yet the play's lightest components are quite successful. The bumbling, frustrated Plyants and Froths, and the vacuous Brisk ("This is all very surprising, let me perish"), at least have considerable entertainment value. There are the beginnings of a Scandal Club that Congreve and later Sheridan would develop, with Cynthia playing the moral ingenue, and even a Mr. Sneer. It is in the darker intrigues of the principals, and in the jarring shifts between the two modes, that Congreve stumbles. Influenced, perhaps, by the contemporary popularity of *chiaroscuro* in painting, he tried to juxtapose sharply different tonal masses, which, at 23, he could not control. Seven years later, in *The Way of the World*, he softened the contrasts to avoid this disjunctiveness.

In his Dedication, Congreve says he "designed the moral first, and to that moral I invented the fable." The procedure cannot be recommended on the evidence of *The Double-Dealer*. Few critics if any have found Lord Touchwood's closing moral—"Let secret villainy . . . be warned": treachery destroys itself—adequate, or been able to see how the Plyants' and Froths' two-thirds of the plot support it, or to discover another. Of course authors are notoriously unreliable analysts of their own work; Congreve is presumably testifying to his discomfort with the frivolity of the prevailing comic style, and his ambition to transcend it. The *dramatic* problem with the moral tag is that it gives a lame conclusion to a weak final scene in which the exposed Maskwell does not speak—not even, like Iago, to announce his future silence. This is a disappointing finale for abilities such as Maskwell has shown. We feel that Congreve owed him—and us—a fuller denouement.

—Richard Bevis

DOUGLAS.
Play by John Home, 1756.

The most famous of John Home's six tragedies, *Douglas* achieved instant success when first performed in Edinburgh and London, and became the subject of a heated theological and literary controversy that led to Home's resignation of his ministry in the Church of Scotland. The church controversy and an ensuing pamphlet war, coupled with Home's blatant appeal to Scottish national pride, undoubtedly contributed to the play's initial box office appeal, but *Douglas* became a part of the standard repertory because it is one of the 18th century's best blank-verse tragedies.

Home's historical importance lies chiefly in his experimentation with various tragic modes and unusual themes and subject matter and in his achievements in poetic language. Despite differences in type, Home's plays share several general characteristics. All are written in fairly regular blank verse, and all seek to evoke pathos as a primary audience response while eschewing sentimentalism and didacticism. Home draws most of his subject matter from native British material, but often chooses remote settings to enhance the romantic and exotic aspects of his plays. In Home's best work, he establishes a melancholy mood and a sense of timelessness in which man's fate is played out on a stage that is part of the natural order and beyond the control of any individual. *Douglas*'s strengths (and weaknesses) are particularly illuminating of Home's achievement as a playwright.

Douglas is often regarded as the first romantic tragedy and has also been called the most complete precursor of gothic drama, largely because of the play's emphasis on the natural world and on Lady Randolph's psyche, and the presence of dark woods, mistaken identities, a concealed marriage, and an aura of mystery and secrecy. In contrast to the drawing rooms of many contemporary plays, the world of *Douglas* is depicted as part of the natural order that transcends individuals. Nature, consisting chiefly of caves, cliffs, mountains, and woods, is virtually a living presence in the play.

Although the play is entitled *Douglas*, its protagonist is really Lady Randolph. The action of the play is simple, dealing with the untimely death of the valiant young Douglas and the subsequent suicide of his mother, Lady Randolph. Interest focuses on the shifting states of mind of Lady Randolph, from her melancholy reflections in the opening scene to her despair at the end. Incidents in the play function chiefly to deepen the audience's interest in Lady Randolph's psychological complexity, to increase gradually its sympathy for her, and to maximize the emotional impact of her suicide. In contrast, Douglas's character is simple and uncomplicated; brave, honest, naive, he seeks fame through military exploits, and his premature death functions chiefly to increase Lady Randolph's grief.

The play strives primarily to achieve what the epilogue calls "celestial melancholy" by focusing on tragic irony and to evoke pity by focusing on Lady Randolph's frustrated maternal love. At the heart of the play lies a contrast between Lady Randolph's past suffering and her present though temporary happiness, which changes to despair after Douglas's death. Lady Randolph's introverted nature and her passion for her son have encouraged Freudian readings of the play that stress Lady Randolph's Oedipal stirrings, her "Byronic" self-pity, suggestions of incest, and the play's twilight world of the psyche (the "landscape of romance"). Indeed, Lady Randolph is remote from daily life; for her, ordinary social exchanges are less real than the inner workings of her mind, and time has become so meaningless that years and hours are indistinguishable. Throughout the play, Home associates Lady Randolph with the most solitary forms of nature, and uses her isolation and introspection to introduce and develop the play's principal themes.

Chief among these is the role of providence in men's lives. Lady Randolph's faith in a beneficent providence gradually erodes; by the end of the play, she doubts the existence of a divine will and commits suicide. Home's intent is not to call divine wisdom into doubt; rather, *Douglas* provides an instance of the demands of art triumphing over the writer's personal beliefs. Home skillfully develops Lady Randolph's reflections on providence to increase the audience's pity for her. The primary ends of his play are well-served by her increasing awareness, resulting from constant questioning and personal experience, of a malignant destiny that overwhelms her earlier confidence in divine justice. The final self-portrait of this woman who is essentially outside time and place as an object on whom "Omnipotence displays itself" to awe mankind is both powerful and moving.

In the 18th century, *Douglas* was criticized for lacking a "moral." Certainly it is free from the didacticism characteristic of many contemporary tragedies, which may help account for its long popularity. However, the absence of moral choices in the play reduces its potential to achieve genuinely tragic effects. But Home's intent was not to write a classical tragedy. Instead, he opted for less conventional choices—pathos, romance, tragic irony—that appealed to the tastes of mid-century audiences, which generally responded enthusiastically both to the subject matter and to the fluid, poetic language of *Douglas*.

—James S. Malek

DOVER BEACH.
Poem by Matthew Arnold, 1867.

"Dover Beach," perhaps Matthew Arnold's best-known poem, was composed well before its publication in his 1867 volume *New Poems*, possibly as early as 1851. It is the fullest expression of its author's religious doubt and a classic text of Victorian anxiety in the face of lost faith. It is not coincidental that it was probably written soon after the publication of that epic of Victorian doubt, Tennyson's *In Memoriam* of 1850, and contemporaneously with the agnostic poetry of Arnold's friend Arthur Hugh Clough. It can usefully be set alongside Arnold's "Stanzas from the Grande Chartreuse," also from the 1867 volume, in which the poet characterises himself and his generation as "Wandering between two worlds, / One dead, the other powerless to be born."

In "Dover Beach" the dead world evoked is that of medieval Christendom when the sea of faith lay round "earth's shore" like the folded garment in a medieval picture ("like the folds of a bright girdle furl'd"). That was a snug and safe world in contrast to the present, the "here" where the ignorant armies clash. In his later work on the possibility of a renewed Christianity (*St. Paul and Protestantism* of 1870 or *Literature and Dogma* of 1873 for instance) Arnold will say something about the new world and how it might be born, but in "Dover Beach" the only bulwark against lost faith is love.

The poem opens with the peace that can be shared with a loved one: "Come to the window, sweet is the night air!" All is idyllic until we reach the words that describe the sea: "grating roar," "suck" and "fling" are not entirely peaceful in tone. The note struck is softened in the lines that follow but it is picked up again in the "sadness" of the last line of this first stanza.

In a manner quite typical of Victorian modes of writing "Dover Beach" moves from the convincingly realistic to the absolutely symbolic while hardly appearing to shift gear. Thus this *is* the beach at Dover; we hear the sounds of the Channel and feel the summer evening; over on the French side we can see the lighthouse. Yet all this leads into quite other and larger considerations—for the noise of the waves reminds Arnold that Sophocles wrote about the sea in the early days of western civilisation and it made him think of "human misery." So the present poet, too, thinks of the misery that is his own. Why, on a lovely night with his "love" beside him, should he be miserable? His answer is that it is "a thought" that destroys his peace of mind: "we / Find also in the sound a thought, / Hearing it by this distant northern sea." For the problem is *intellectual*, too much thinking has undermined the deep security needed for the full enjoyment of a scene such as this.

We have to adopt some such reading as this of the word "thought" if the poem is not to seem strangely broken-backed between the second and third stanzas. Careful reading will show that strictly there is no point of definite connection between the two halves of the poem beyond the general notion of waves on the shore, yet we make the connection easily enough: the sea reminds Arnold of Sophocles on sadness, it also provides him with an image (one of his favourite kind concerning water) for the loss of faith, that fundamentally intellectual problem of Arnold's time. Instead of, say, welcoming the new intellectual liberation of the times, it is the old security that he laments. The rhetoric of the poem rises to a new level in the third stanza. The rather soft, slow cadences of the first two stanzas are replaced by a prophetic, elegiac music: the "melancholy, long, withdrawing roar" sounds marvellously apt for the tide going out (on a rougher night than this) but is, of course, applied to the waning of the beautiful certainties of faith. Suddenly, we notice, it has become winter—the sea "roars," the night wind blows, the beach no longer offers us "pebbles" or the "cadence slow" of little waves but becomes instead the "vast," "drear," and "naked" "edges" and "shingles" of the entire world.

Once the style has risen to these heights Arnold launches into an exhortation and a bitter aside which are quite at variance with the poem's opening. No mention has been made of infidelity yet the plea is for the lover's truth. The poem has been about the sea and yet now the poet looks landward where, as when the quiet channel conjured up a terrible roar, an apparently beautiful new land is in reality ("really") devoid of joy, love, light, and other good things including, notably, certitude. What has been lost are hope, charity, and, above all, faith. The poem ends with the powerful, louring image of the "darkling plain" and the "ignorant armies" clashing by night. Victorian melancholy strikes no gloomier note.

—Lance St. John Butler

DRACULA.
Novel by Bram Stoker, 1897.

When Bram Stoker wrote *Dracula* in 1897 he was able to draw upon a century-long tradition of interest in vampirism, firmly associated with the exotic fantasies of romanticism and with the theme of seduction and evil. By 1913 the book was in its 10th edition. After its first stage production in 1930 the sales of the book doubled and by the 1930's the first vampire films began to emerge. With the extraordinary number of subsequent films produced this century, Dracula has become a 20th-century myth of unparalleled resonance.

Stoker's text has been the focus of renewed critical interest in the last few decades, as the subject of a plethora of critical readings and interpretations: Marxist, Freudian, feminist, and Darwinian. As fantasy, drawing on one of the most ancient Eastern European superstitions, it invites and stimulates such diverse and interesting speculations.

Those familiar with the film myth of Dracula are often surprised by the density and literary quality of Stoker's text. Film versions are rarely loyal to it to any degree. It insists, like so many fantastic texts, on its own authenticity. In the tradition of Wilkie Collins it claims authenticity by narrating events through the diaries and letters of the characters involved. But Stoker goes much further than Collins by mobilising almost any form of information: ship's logs translated from the original Russian, newspaper cuttings, doctors' reports, telegrams, memoranda, even transcribed verbal accounts from a phonograph.

The text needs contemporary testimony to provide a scientific account of the movements, habits, and history of the central threat of the novel—Dracula—and it relies on the constant production of such information. Van Helsing (a Dutch Catholic "scientist"), the principle vampire hunter, supported by his team of assistants—Seward (a medical man specialising in the treatment of the insane), Godalming (an aristocrat), Harker (a lawyer), and Quincey Morris (an American), insist on a flow of information within the band of hunters. "Good women tell all their lives," Van Helsing tells Mina. *Dracula* is a confessional novel: without confession there would be no text.

The central action of the novel is defensive. Dracula is planning to invade England, to create an empire of "semi-demons." Harker travels to Transylvania as lawyer to the Count and it is in this opening "gothic" section of the novel that we are first introduced to the vampire superstition and its Eastern European origins. The second section of the novel jolts us back to England and the domestic complacency of the central characters. In the background, unseen, Dracula is invading the country. Invasion stories of many kinds were reaching a peak around the turn of the century, exacerbated by real fears of political instability in Europe. *Dracula*, for all its gothic and fantastic characteristics, dramatises this fear.

Lucy Westenra, the innocent and beautiful young heroine, is the first victim of the invading Count. Van Helsing is brought in to study the strangely anaemic state of the fading heroine. With Mina Harker, the heroine with a "man's brain," the defenders band together to protect England from the advancing threat, now identified by Van Helsing as vampirism. They are too late to save Lucy despite a series of major blood transfusions from four men. Now dead, but Undead, she stalks Highgate cemetery preying on young children, and she must be staked in a violent and ritualistic ceremony which critics have identified as a kind of gang rape. The novel is packed with scenes of erotic power which have invited sexual readings in the late 20th century, but which went apparently unnoticed by the novel's 19th-century audience.

It has been observed that the vampire hunters not only doubt their own sanity (much of the novel takes place in a lunatic asylum) but actually mirror the sadism and violence of Dracula. The instability of narrators and the problematising of vision are characteristics of fantastic literature from Poe onwards, as is the compulsion to exorcise the demonic "other": the Not-I. The band of vampire hunters enact many sadistic rituals, such as the staking of Lucy, in the name of the protection of the Empire.

Dracula is a novel which insists on protecting (and patrolling) women as much as it insists on patrolling the Empire. The men are forever placing protective circles of Holy Wafer and garlic flowers around the women. Dracula will invade through any gap. It is a novel which expresses fears of Dracula's effect upon women—their sexualisation. While the central threat of the novel is the seducing Dracula, the novel is populated with *female* vampires—four of the five central female characters are vampires. Dracula attacks only women.

The novel forms part of a late 19th-century genre which David Punter has identified as decadent gothic. The four great novels of this genre are Stevenson's *Dr. Jekyll and Mr. Hyde*, Wilde's *The Picture of Dorian Gray*, Stoker's *Dracula* and Wells's *The Island of Dr. Moreau*. All these novels enact fears of regression and degeneration stimulated by the discoveries of evolutionary theory. All are concerned in some ways with "the liberation of repressed desires." Dracula can be seen as the beast within, so precariously contained. He must be tracked down and eliminated. While the novel moves towards his final elimination—he crumbles into dust once staked—the hunters do not observe the elaborate rituals of staking. The ending is ambiguous: Mina (who has herself sucked Dracula's blood) gives birth to a child on the anniversary of Dracula's death—a male child who bears the names of all the band of men involved in the tracking of Dracula. Moreover, the hunters are thrown back again on their own uncertainty. They are left with their only record of the dramatic events as a "mass of typewriting."

—Rebecca Stott

THE DREAM OF THE ROOD.
Poem, in 10th-century manuscript.

Editions and Translations

The Dream of the Rood, edited by Bruce Dickins and A.S.C. Ross. 1934; revised edition, 1963.
The Dream of the Rood, edited by Michael Swanton. 1970; revised edition, 1987.

Critical Studies: "*The Dream of the Rood*: Patterns of Transformation" by L.H. Leiter, in *Old English Poetry: Fifteen Essays* edited by R.P. Creed, 1967; "*The Dream of the Rood* as Prosopopoeia" by M. Schlauch, in *Essential Articles for the Study of Old English Poetry* edited by J.B. Bessinger and S.J. Kahrl, 1968; "*The Dream of the Rood* and Liturgical Drama" by Julia Bolton Holloway, in *Comparative Drama*, Spring 1984; "Crucifixion Witnesses, or, Dramatic Interaction in *The Dream of the Rood*" by Edward B. Irving, Jr., in *Modes of Interpretation in Old English Literature* edited by Phyllis Rugg Brown and others, 1986; *The Message and the Structure of the Dream of the Rood* by Paavo Rissanen, 1987.

The Dream of the Rood (i.e., Cross) is the modern title of a 156-line poem in the West Saxon dialect, surviving in the Anglo-Saxon Vercelli manuscript. It has sometimes been attributed, though without any good reason, to the poet Cynewulf. The poem is an extremely sensitive and imaginative treatment of Christ's Passion, though, in the absence of others on the same subject, it is impossible to know to what extent the approach is unusual or unique.

The poem is the earliest dream vision in English. The narrator begins by describing how one night he dreams that he sees a spectacular Cross, venerated by the whole of creation. Through the golden trappings, however, he perceives puzzling signs of an earlier struggle, for the Cross seems to alternate from being at one moment decked with jewels and at the next wet with blood. Then, for what is the main part of the poem, the Cross speaks directly of its experiences, from the time when it was a growing tree in the forest, through the horror of being fashioned into the unwilling instrument of Christ's torment, until now it stands proudly as an object of devotion throughout the world. The dreamer is instructed to tell others what he has seen. He reflects upon the comfort the Cross can bring and looks forward to the fulfilment of its promise of everlasting life.

A remarkable feature of the poem is its exploration of the many paradoxes inherent in the Crucifixion. There is a careful balancing of the effects of triumph and suffering, reflected in the terms used for the Cross—"victory tree," "tree of glory," and "shining beacon" alongside "slayer" and "gallows." The dreamer, too, is paradoxically both a sinner, whose shame is heightened by the shining presence of the Cross, and a prophet of the Redemption. Equally striking is the portrayal of Christ himself, who is both Man and God, suffering mortal agony while at the same time rising above it.

This ambivalence seems also to have a liturgical connection, being linked to the shame of Good Friday and the rejoicing associated with Easter Day. Liturgical links have also influenced the vocabulary, some of which appears to originate in Latin hymnody. When formulating his descriptions the poet may have envisaged actual jewelled wooden crosses of the time—e.g., in details such as the five gems representing the five wounds. In describing the cross as "changing in garments and colours" he may have in mind the practice of shrouding ecclesiastical crosses before Easter or of substituting for the red cross of Lent a jewelled cross on Easter Day to symbolise the glory of the Redemption.

The portrayal of Christ owes something to non-Christian heroic literature. He is called a "young hero" and hastens to ascend the Cross like one eager to join battle. He strips himself like a man preparing for a trial of strength. His heroism and fortitude are deliberately set against his passivity and willingness to submit to suffering and degradation. The personified Cross also contributes to this aspect of the poem, being cast in the role of a faithful retainer whose natural instinct is to defend his lord rather than inflict pain upon him. Several times the Cross says that it could have felled the enemies, or broken, or bowed down, but that it dared not act against his command. By sharing Christ's anguish in this way the cross is now rewarded: "On me the Son of God suffered for a while; / therefore glorious I now tower beneath the heavens. . . . " The use of a speaking personification (*prosopopoeia*) is a brilliant device in this context, for it enables the Cross to act as a surrogate for Christ, sharing his pain (and even bleeding as he did) as well as his glory. The Cross is also used to communicate the brutality and shame, speaking emotionally and passionately while Christ himself maintains a dignified silence. This use of *prosopopoeia* may be a brilliant invention of the poet: however, the device is not uncommon in Old English literature, for example in a number of the riddles of the Exeter Book, where the subjects (e.g. horn, sword) describe themselves with tantalising ambiguity and challenge the reader or listener to identify them.

Some of those parts of the poem in which the Cross speaks are found in the Northumbrian dialect, carved in runes in the margins of the east and west faces of the stone cross at Ruthwell, near Dumfries, in Scotland, which dates from c.700. It is unclear whether the Ruthwell version is an abridgement and adaptation of a longer poem like that of the Vercelli manuscript or whether the surviving poem is an elaboration of a shorter one, like that of the inscription. Two lines of the Cross's words, which may be adapted from a similar poem, are also found on a silver plate attached to a small reliquary cross now in Brussels.

—G.A. Lester

DREAM ON MONKEY MOUNTAIN.
Play by Derek Walcott, 1967.

Dream on Monkey Mountain, Derek Walcott's most acclaimed play, was first performed in Toronto in 1967 and won an Obie Award in 1971. Experimental in technique—as its author described it, "The play is a dream, one that exists as much in the given minds of its principal characters as in that of its writer, and as such, it is illogical, derivative, contradictory"—*Dream on Monkey Mountain* blends West Indian folklore and English literary allusions, dream and waking reality, Creole patois and British English, dance and song, to explore frequent Walcottian themes: the evils of colonialism and the difficult search for personal and national identity.

The protagonist, Makak, or monkey, is jailed for his disorderly behavior at a local bar. He reveals to his fellow prisoners, Tigre and Souris, and to his captor, Corporal Lestrade, that his lonely, self-deprecating life has been transformed by the vision of a white goddess, who so inspires him that he no longer feels old, ugly, and ashamed, but rather empowered, connected to his African heritage.

Prisoners and cells vanish, and Makak is awakened by Moustique, a lame man whom he has befriended and made a partner in his charcoal business. Makak relates to him his vision of the goddess: "She say I should not live so anymore, here in the forest, frighten of people because I think I ugly. She say that I come from the family of lions and kings." Reminiscent of Don Quixote and Sancho Panza, the charcoal-burner and the incredulous Moustique set out with their decrepit donkey to find Africa, and on their journey Makak achieves the status of a savior in the surrounding countryside when he cures a dying man. Pragmatic Moustique sees in Makak's healing power a way of making money, and his impersonation of Makak—accompanied with demands for remuneration—so angers the crowd that they beat him to death with the Corporal's acquiescence.

In part 2, the setting once again the cells of the three prisoners, Tigre incites Makak to attack the Corporal and thus secure their release.

> How else can you prove your name is lion, unless you do one bloody, golden, dazzling thing, eh? And who stand in your way but your dear friend, Corporal Lestrade the straddler, neither one thing nor the next, neither milk, coal, neither day nor night, neither lion nor monkey, but a mulatto, a foot-licking servant of marble law? He cause Moustique to die.

Makak stabs Lestrade, who does not die but vows to recapture the prisoners, now joined in Makak's quest for Africa. Through Souris and the pursuing Lestrade, Walcott exposes the evil committed in the name of empire. Frightened Souris declares, "When I was a little boy, living in darkness, I was so afraid, it was as if I was sinking, drowning in a grave, and me and the darkness was the same, and God was like a big white man I was afraid of. . . . And that is what they teach me since I was small. To be black like coal, and to dream of milk. To love God, and obey the white man." Lestrade, a mulatto with unflinching allegiance to the English, has become a monstrosity, his language peppered with racial slurs and English idiom. But Lestrade undergoes a transformation: throwing off his clothes like Lear, he swears allegiance to Makak and his African dream: "Too late have I loved thee, Africa of my mind, *sero te amavi*, to cite Saint Augustine who they say was black. I jeered thee because I hated half of myself, my eclipse." Makak, however, prophesies internecine war, tribe killing tribe, a prediction realized when Lestrade kills Tigre.

In scene 3 a reluctant Makak is enthroned as a tribal king, and Basil, the figure of Death, joins Lestrade's fanatical damning of all whites, from Shakespeare to Al Jolson. A resurrected Moustique appears, warning Makak of the dangers of his new followers: "Once you loved the moon, now a night will come when, because it white, from your deep hatred you will want it destroyed." But Makak follows Lestrade's instructions and beheads his white goddess.

The epilogue once again returns to the cells, where Lestrade is once again a cruel captor, Makak a tired old man. But Makak now acknowledges his true name, Felix Hobain, and returns to Monkey Mountain with Moustique, having reached a new serenity and sense of self. As he stated earlier in the play, "What power can crawl on the bottom of the sea, or swim in the ocean of air above us? The mind, the mind. Now, come with me, the mind can bring the dead to life, it can go back, back, deep into time. It can make a man a king, it can make him a beast."

Dream on Monkey Mountain is a vibrant play that captures brilliantly the shifting perceptions of dream yet also speaks realistically to the experience of black people living in the wake of oppressive colonialism. In fact, the play may be read allegorically as a microcosm of black history, particularly black nationalism in the 1960's. Makak, self-hating yet visionary, achieves self-acceptance not by journeying to Africa nor by responding in kind to violence and bigotry, but by turning inward and going home. *Dream on Monkey Mountain* speaks particularly to the West Indian experience, for as Walcott stated in a 1977 interview:

> The fact is that every West Indian has been severed from a continent, whether he is Indian, Chinese, Portuguese, or black. To have the population induced into a mass nostalgia to be somewhere else seemed to me to be as ennobling as wishing that the whole population was in Brooklyn, or Brixton. . . . The reality is that one has to build in the West Indies.

Makak, according to Robert D. Hamner, ". . . determines to establish himself on his mountain and fulfill his chosen destiny—neither white nor black, but a West Indian with a home, a job, and self-esteem." Other critics have read the play's ending more pessimistically, asserting that although

Makak undergoes internal change, he remains an impoverished charcoal-burner in an oppressive society.

—Mary Fitzgerald-Hoyt

A DRUNK MAN LOOKS AT THE THISTLE.
Poem by Hugh MacDiarmid, 1926.

Hugh MacDiarmid's long poem *A Drunk Man Looks at the Thistle* was published in 1926, the same year as his second collection of Scots lyrics *Penny Wheep* and the year after *Sangschaw*. 1926 might therefore be considered as much of a landmark in Scottish letters as 1786, the year when Burns's Kilmarnock *Poems* appeared.

MacDiarmid's three books have some features in common. Together, they mark his movement from Georgian English into a form of Scots strengthened by his re-incorporation of some vivid words and expressions that had dropped out of use—"dictionary dredging," hostile contemporary critics called it, though no dictionary was ever dredged to better purpose—and his discovery of an individual poetic voice. They also reflect his concern with current political, psychological, and metaphysical thinking, already deployed in his early prose book of "psychological studies," *Annals of the Five Senses*.

Using the romantic device of detachment which the condition of drunkenness allows the self, MacDiarmid examines the state of Scotland and the shortcomings of the Scots (with a devastatingly accurate frankness never before voiced). He then moves on to a consideration in philosophical terms of human life in relation to the magnitude of the universe, returning, in the end, to the inevitable point of the poet's origin, the self.

In the course of this wide-ranging intellectual journey, the poet is much concerned with various forms of duality. At the most basic physical level he observes:

It's queer the thochts a kittled
  cull [tickled testicle
Can lowse or splairgin' glit
  annul [release splashing slime
Man's spreit is wi' his ingangs
  twined [spirit internal organs
In ways that he can ne'er unwind. [mixed

Symbolically, there are several contrasting dualities. The contrasting nature of the thistle, which provides both thistledown and thorns, for example; and the relationship between the sea-serpent of Celtic mythology and women. There is obvious use made, too, of Christian symbolism, and of the fact that both whisky and moonlight change the surface appearance of things. The unbridgable gap between human achievement and human possibility, the search for the seamless garment or the perfect song (though music was an area where MacDiarmid had no real knowledge at all) provide the raison d'etre of the whole metaphysical poetic journey.

Satirical, descriptive, or witty sections carry forward the examination of these and other contrasts in the search for wholeness of spirit. These passages are interspersed with lyrical reflective interludes, often of intense power and beauty. In the end, the quest proves unattainable.

For ilka thing a man can be or think or dae
Aye leaves a million mair unbeen, unthoucht, undune,
Till his puir warped performance is,
To a' that micht ha' been, a thistle to the mune.

It is Mortality itsel'—the mortal coil,
Mockin Perfection, Man afore the Throne o' God
He yet has bigged himself, Man torn in twa [built
And glorious in the lift and grisly on the sod! . . . [sky

According to the composer Francis George Scott, the poet's one-time English teacher at Langholm Academy, and thereafter almost a life-long friend (MacDiarmid chose to quarrel with the senile Scott towards the end of the composer's long life), the older man played a part in the structuring of the poem. In a letter to the present writer (quoted in my book *Francis George Scott and the Scottish Renaissance*, 1980), Scott "outlined the plans and supplied the title of the poem during a rainy hike and a night in Glen Cloris Hotel. Christopher usually wrote his poems in snatches: he never had any sense of form and after some months of scribbling on the back of envelopes and odd bits of paper, he sent to Glasgow an urgent call for me to come for a weekend"—the poet was then working as a journalist in Montrose—"and see (the mess) he'd been making of my bright ideas, as Blackwood's"—the publisher of the three books—"were asking for MS and there was *no* MS."

Some, including MacDiarmid's biographer, Alan Bold, have sought to minimalise Scott's influence on the construction of the poem, but Scott was a truthful man and an enthusiastic admirer of his former pupil's three great books. When MacDiarmid's first *Collected Poems* appeared in 1962, the poet broke up *A Drunk Man Looks at the Thistle* into a series of separately-titled pieces, an act of dismemberment David Daiches persuaded him to abandon for the second edition. This shows that a sense of construction, with the exception of a very few later poems (notably the magnificent poem in English "On a Raised Beach"), is hardly a feature of MacDiarmid's work, and lends some substance to the probability of Scott's story.

Not that it matters. MacDiarmid had used the title for fragments published in the Glasgow *Herald* some time before. It may have been that Scott saw the appositeness of the already-used title to the new whole. In conception and execution, however, the poem is wholly MacDiarmid's own; a masterpiece of the first order which it is impossible to analyse in detail, or define in summary, in the space available here. It is certainly one of the greatest poems ever produced by a Scottish poet and arguably one of the finest long poems produced by any 20th-century European writer.

—Maurice Lindsay

THE DUCHESS OF MALFI.
Play by John Webster, 1614.

The Duchess of Malfi's emotional power and theatrical potency, first defined by Charles Lamb and A.C. Swinburne, derives from its persuasive dramatic realism and its tirelessly intelligent and complex poetry.

The plot follows an account in William Painter's *Palace of Pleasure* (1567) based on true events in early 16th-century Italy. Two powerful brothers, Ferdinand, Duke of Calabria, and the Cardinal, are determined that their widowed sister, the Duchess, shall not remarry. They set Bosola, a malcontent courtier, to spy on her. She secretly marries her steward, Antonio Bologna, and bears him several children. Bosola betrays her and, on instructions, imprisons her, torments her with false news of Antonio's death and with a grisly display of mad folk, and finally has her killed, together with two of her children and her maid Cariola. Ferdinand, repentant after the fact, runs mad. In a grim final sequence of confusion and revenge, Ferdinand, the Cardinal, Bosola, and Antonio die, and it is left to the Duchess's young son to restore an orderly society.

At every turn in this dark action, the characters identify their fears, their rage, or their despair in language startling in its specific physical immediacy and its general moral pessimism: "We are merely the stars' tennis-balls, struck and banded / Which way please them." The events and the language—equally painful—mark Webster's characteristic awareness of human impotence before evil and malignant fate.

Critics have observed many ambiguities and inconsistencies. There is no convincing reason for the brothers' prohibition of the Duchess's remarriage, nor do they justify her murder as an appropriate consequence of her actions. That a marriage and the birth of three children should remain secret is highly unlikely. A child of the Duchess's first marriage is mentioned (III.iii.70), then ignored. An elaborately presented horoscope does not come true. Antonio and the Duchess flee in different directions for no clear reason.

Some theatrical problems have been noted. The crucial moment of the Duchess's banishment is relegated to part of a dumb show. Act V, subsequent to the Duchess's death, may seem anti-climactic: a hectic series of accidents and random killings.

But such inconsistencies may be validated; Webster's realism depends on his recognition that his characters' intense emotions create around them, as if by passionate magnetism, a field of irrational behaviour and fatal consequence. Ferdinand's sexually explicit ravings against his sister—"Are you stark mad?" asks the Cardinal—his extravagant grief and his collapse into lycanthropia cannot be rationally explained, but Webster's language gives his actions a potent, frightening plausibility.

The malcontent Bosola is ambiguous; a reputedly skilled intelligencer who cannot solve the simple mystery of the Duchess's marriage and who finally stabs Antonio by mistake, he is conscience-stricken and ashamed, even while he undertakes the brutal murders. Yet his ceaseless and insightful self-analysis is convincing and even extenuating.

The events of Act V may be seen not as anti-climactic, but as the unavoidable results of Machiavellian policies which, after the Duchess's murder, must be played out in a sequence of lesser acts—ignoble, grotesque, but still inevitable. Webster finds an apt symbol of inflexible fate when an "ECHO *from the* Duchess' *grave*" prompts Antonio and his friend Delio by ironic repetition.

Webster is dramatising an historical event which English audiences would believe only possible in the intolerant and disorderly society of 16th-century Italy, with its dissolute churchmen, corrupt courtiers, and crazed nobility. The opening contrasts the court of Italy with that of France, where the "judicious king" has sought to "reduce both state and people / To a fix'd order." Two pilgrims, the only outsiders in the play, express their opinions with equally judicious balance:

> Here's a strange turn of state! Who would have thought
> So great a lady would have match'd herself
> Unto so mean a person? yet the cardinal
> Bears himself much too cruel.

Their comments remind the audience that a world does exist outside the malevolent environment of the action. The obvious lapse of time in the Duchess's marriage between the scenes similarly draws attention to a period of presumed tranquillity and domestic love. The moment at which chaos and horror descend on the Duchess and Antonio is precisely marked. Antonio and Cariola tiptoe from the Duchess's bedroom, leaving her alone. As she continues talking, Ferdinand enters *solus*, showing her a poinard when, thinking Antonio is silent behind her, she queries, "Have you lost your tongue?" The Duchess's instant recognition that the inevitable discovery has come to pass is brilliantly expressed:

> Tis welcome:
> For know, whether I am doom'd to live or die.
> I can do both like a prince.

These contrasts between an attainable harmony in a time or a place outside the confines of the tragic setting and the necessary chaos within that setting, are mirrored by the contrasts in the Duchess's character. She begins the play by assuring her brothers that she will never remarry, but without a pause in the action proceeds to the dangerous wooing of Antonio: "If all my royal kindred / Lay in my way unto this marriage, / I'd make them my low footsteps." Recognising her "dangerous venture," she undertakes, "through frights, and threat'nings," the commitment which Cariola sees as a "fearful madness." Though full of "noble virtue" and a model of sweet and pious behaviour, her "tetchiness and most vulturous eating of the apricocks" when pregnant are hardly evidences of nobility. After the birth of three children, she still lies to Ferdinand: "when I choose / A husband, I will marry for your honour." Moments later, in conversation with Antonio and Cariola, she is "merry," holding that "Love mix't with fear is sweetest." She can organise Antonio's escape with good sense and dispatch, but is trapped by her thoughtless and misplaced trust in Bosola. She meets her torments and death with grandeur—"I am Duchess of Malfi still." Some critics have suggested that these inconsistencies are flaws in characterisation. By turns deceitful and impassioned, playful and fearful, practical and naive, haughty and petulant, her character may indeed not be consistent, but her frailties and strengths are recognisably human responses to the terrible world into which she is thrust.

—Richard Morton

THE DUNCIAD.
Poem by Alexander Pope, 1728–43.

From October 1713, when he issued proposals for a translation of Homer's *Iliad*, Alexander Pope's main attentions were taken up by translation and editorial work. It was not until the publication of his edition of Shakespeare in 1725 and of the final volume of the *Odyssey* in 1726 that original poetry again took centre stage in his work. The three-book *Dunciad* of 1728 marked this return, and also signalled a major reorientation of his poetry from that of 1709–14. Pope had become embroiled in the petty world of literary and critical warfare, initiated by rival versions of the *Iliad* and sustained by the publication in 1726 of Lewis Theobald's *Shakespeare Restored*, in which the incompetence of Pope's edition was exposed. The beginnings of *The Dunciad* may lie earlier, but Pope's decision to make Theobald his king of the dunces fixes this as the crucial date.

The poem is partly in the mock-heroic mode whose significant earlier examples are Boileau's *Le Lutrin* (1674–83) and Pope's own *The Rape of the Lock* (1714). This form is to be distinguished from burlesque: as Boileau puts it in his prefatory address to the 1674 publication of the first four *chants* of *Le Lutrin*, in burlesque "Didon et Enée parlaient comme des harengères et des crocheteurs" ("Dido and Aeneas spoke like fishwives and picklocks"), whereas in this new type of poem "une horlogère et un horloger parlent comme Didon et Enée" ("clockmakers speak like Dido and Aeneas"). In one, the subject matter of epic is burlesqued by being made to use inappropriately low language; in the other, the socially or conventionally low ape the language and manner of epic. *The Dunciad*, like Dryden's *Mac Flecknoe* earlier, mixes the two methods. Elements of burlesque are present, particularly the scatological games of book two, where events such as the urinating contest operate as a degraded version of epic games, dirt literally and metaphorically fouling the dunces who produce it. These elements constitute *The Dunciad*'s vitriolic vision of a contemporary society peopled by a motley but largely indistinguishable collection of writers, critics, and editors whose Dulness lies in the way in which they degrade true literature by their production of cultural filth.

The seriousness of the poem, however, derives mainly from its presentation of the Grub Street hacks' presumptions of grandeur. Settle's prophetic vision in book 3 is not just a parody of the vision of the future of Rome unfolded by Anchises to Aeneas in the sixth book of the *Aeneid*: its depiction of the success of Dulness and her disciples is that of a cultural event as significant as that defined by Virgil. Through the parallel we recognize that the low have taken over the forms and world of the great. The poem begins with a couplet which sums up this central idea: "Books and the Man I sing, the first who brings / The Smithfield Muses to the Ear of Kings." Geographical and cultural distance collapses, so that the properties of Bartholomew Fair are adopted by royal patronage and thus become official, national art. That this matters depends upon our taking poetry and writing in general as serious indicators of the values of a civilization. When Pope places the line, "E'er Pallas issued from the Thund'rer's head" alongside "In eldest time, e'er mortals writ or read," he is drawing a parallel between the act of using language and the birth of knowledge. Without a sustained creative use of language, we regress to the cultural anarchy of Dulness, "Daughter of Chaos and eternal Night." Such a regression to a state of ignorance is the subject of the finale of Settle's vision.

The four-book *Dunciad* "celebrates" the achievement of this vision. *The Dunciad Variorum*, with its spoof notes perhaps supplied by a number of Scriblerian hands but, in all probability, mostly the work of Pope himself, had already extended the poem's range to take in the mechanical, heavy products of editorial pedantry. But it was with the new fourth book of 1742 that the major extension was made. Music, philosophy, natural history, antiquarianism, the fashionable Grand Tour are all sucked into Dulness's vortex, their representatives entering indiscriminately the throng of her train. Most significantly, education takes its place in the figure of the notorious Dr. Busby, former headmaster of Westminster School, whose stated aim is to repress his pupils' creativity by separating words from meaning, turning language into mere breath by confining thought and making words an imprisoning, rather than liberating, medium. By this means, the new generation is enabled to achieve the reality of the poem's central oxymoron, the "uncreating word" of chaos. Pope's transference of this apocalyptic passage from the end of book 3 to the conclusion of book 4 in the revised version signals (as does his alteration of the line, "And universal Darkness covers all," to "And Universal Darkness buries all") the completion of the task. That Colley Cibber, George II's poet laureate, replaces Theobald as the poem's hero confirms the successful movement of the Smithfield Muses to the ear of kings.

—W.B. Hutchings

E

EAST LYNNE.
Novel by Ellen Price Wood (Mrs. Henry Wood; 1814–87), 1861.

Critical Studies: *Memorials to Wood* by C.W. Wood, 1894; *Victorian Wallflowers* by Malcolm Elwin, 1934; *The Maniac in the Cellar: Sensation Novels of the 1860's* by Winifred Hughes, 1980; "The 'Sin' of Isabel Vane: *East Lynne* and Victorian Sexuality" by Gail Walker, in *Heroines of Popular Culture* edited by Pat Browne, 1987.

Ellen Price [Mrs. Henry] Wood's *East Lynne* was first published in the *New Monthly Magazine* in January 1861. It became, along with such novels as Braddon's *Lady Audley's Secret* (1862) and Collins's *The Woman in White* (1860), one of the best-selling sensation novels of the Victorian period, as well as a hugely successful play in both England and the U.S. The story of the temptation and punishment of the aristocratic Lady Isabel Vane who leaves her middle-class lawyer husband and their children in a jealous rage, and returns a disfigured, unclaimed woman only to die, nursing her children and observing her re-wed husband, in her guise as governess, was one of the most widely read of its day.

Despite its importance to our understanding of Victorian popular culture, *East Lynne* has received little critical attention. Elaine Showalter's brief discussion of the novel in *A Literature of Their Own* (1977) suggests that *East Lynne*, like other sensation novels by women writers, tapped the female frustrations of the Victorian period. Specifically, she suggests that *East Lynne* explores the sexual and emotional frustration of women who find themselves constructed by the Victorian institution of marriage as passive, asexual, dependent beings. Showalter detects a sympathetic treatment of the married woman's frustration in *East Lynne*, despite the relentless punishments which Isabel Vane endures for her inability to fulfill adequately her wifely duties. Suggesting that the severity of Isabel Vane's punishments in *East Lynne* are the ideologically necessary "deterrent[s]" for the understandable temptation of flight from such a repressed existence, Showalter explores the novel in terms of its representation of Victorian marriage. Similarly, Sally Mitchell emphasizes *East Lynne*'s place within the tradition of women's sensation novels, and explores the repressed "shared assumptions" or cultural values about women's role in marriage in her introduction to a recent reissue of the novel. Both critics are, in the short space allotted them, superficially attentive to the construction of femininity in the text.

But the intersection of class with the constructions of gender that structure *East Lynne* require more critical attention. *East Lynne* opens with an essentially clichéd image: the gouty, dissipated Earl of Mount Severn, father to Isabel Vane, finds it necessary in his penury to sell the only piece of property he owns that might have provided for his soon-to-be orphaned daughter. But the text carefully points to what should be, despite her incipient poverty, Isabel's saving grace: she has been reared by an "admirable," "judicious" governess. Mary Poovey's work in *Uneven Developments* (1988) explores the importance of the governess in Victorian fiction. Noting the peaking interest in the "plight of the governess" during the 1840's, Poovey reconstructs the ideological function of the governess figure in Victorian culture. She suggests that the governess figure played an ideological role in mediating anxieties about eroding economic, political, and sexual roles. At the same time, however, she points to the contradictions in the governess figure itself, contradictions which indicated that "the very figure who theoretically should have defended the naturalness of separate spheres threatened to collapse the difference between them." She notes too that the governess was "meant to police the emergence of undue assertiveness or sexuality in her maturing charges and that she was expected not to display willfulness or desires herself."

Isabel Vane—once the epitome of Victorian womanhood, now a fallen woman—becomes the governess to her own children as a direct result of sexual "willfulness" and "desire." The presentation of her ability to enter East Lynne, where she was once wife and mother, is structured by the anxieties Poovey posits as underscoring the construction of the governess figure. When the governess Vine is discovered on her deathbed to be the Lady Isabel Vane, both Archibald Carlyle and his wife Barbara's responses are structured by anxiety about the "sexual" threat to domestic happiness which the governess / fallen woman / wife represents. Archibald's "first clear thought . . . was, that he must be a man of two wives," an anxiety which the text formally undermines by Archibald's previous decision to divorce Isabel when she leaves him (the recent divorce law passed in 1857 is integral to the plot). Barbara Carlyle's response to the unveiling of Isabel Vane confirms the sexual anxiety which the governess figure embodies. Her "first confused thoughts" are also of bigamy and, importantly, of the loss of her husband's love which the discovery of Isabel's identity seems to mean for her.

It can be argued that these "first thoughts" testify to the sexual threat that the governess represented in Victorian culture. Despite her middle-class status, the governess is forced by financial circumstance to be paid for those duties which were perceived as "naturally" those of woman, and so assumed the sexually dubious status that accompanied all paid work for Victorian women. Importantly, *East Lynne* works in two ways to displace the sexual threat which Isabel Vine, the governess, presents to the middle-class Carlyle household. Archibald's response to his newly-discovered "wife" is quickly restructured to emphasize her role as mother to their children. Though he "suffer[s] his lips to rest upon hers" before she dies, this kiss is bestowed paternally, both as "father" to Isabel's "mother" and as God the Father in whose name Carlyle forgives his fallen wife. Equally important, however, is Isabel's class status. Poovey's work makes clear that it is middle-class Victorian culture that constructed the governess as both an ideal and threatening figure. Isabel Vane is an aristocrat. Sally Mitchell notes that Isabel is "totally unlike typical aristocratic women." But it is precisely by making the typically middle-class governess figure an upper-class figure that the text works to displace the sexual anxiety which that figure represents. Isabel's fall from sexual and moral grace restructures the governess figure in class terms which seek to displace its sexual threat. Without such restructuring, the questions which the governess figure raises about the nature of feminine sexuality would overwhelm *East Lynne* and make impossible the confirmation of middle-class marriage and culture which closes the text.

—Susan Hamilton

EASTER 1916.
Poem by William Butler Yeats, 1916.

As its closing lines indicate, William Butler Yeats's "Easter 1916" was written to commemorate the militant nationalists who took arms, declared an Irish Republic, occupied public buildings and factories in central Dublin and held them against British forces to whom they eventually surrendered, after which the leaders and a random selection of other participants were executed. The poem takes as its point of address to these events the general air of surprise with which they were met in Ireland. Although those named in the poem were known as nationalist activists, the sudden outbreak of hostilities took Crown and country by surprise.

The poem reflects on this entirely unanticipated turn of events in specific detail and in broad terms. The line, "For England may keep faith," refers to the state of juridical relations between England and Ireland at the time of the Easter Rising. The long-held ambition of contemporary Irish political activity was not violent rebellion but constitutional reform, an ambition described as Home Rule, or internal self-government by an Irish parliament independent of the Crown. This ambition had been realised with the passing of the Home Rule Bill of 1914, implementation of whose provisions was, however, deferred by mutual consent of English and Irish parliamentarians until the end of World War I. And in broader terms, the poem registers the seismic shift in emphasis to which Irish reality had been subjected. One of the utter changes to which the poem's refrain draws attention is the substitution of militant rhetoric with heroic action. The poem's use of a refrain maintains an air of amazement, of musing over and questioning the events and personalities which are its subject by repeating the poet's recognition of a *fait accompli* rather than, for example, expressing his desire for an explanation of events. This device cunningly provides "Easter 1916" with dramatic tension and a sense of build-up. And in addition to unifying the poem's wide range of material and approach, tension and build-up act as effective reminders of Yeats's power as a public poet, a ratifying witness to the drama of history, and a celebrant of the heroic conceived of as self-sacrifice. (These elements of Yeats's significance as a poet are consolidated in his later poems on the Irish Civil War, for which "Easter 1916" is an instructive rehearsal.)

Typically of Yeats, his emphasis is on the actual personages in the forefront of the rebellion, rather than on their politics, or their social vision (particularly relevant in the case of the socialist James Connolly). The poem's first stanza renders irrelevant social class as a criterion for evaluating and appreciating the participants. Once class has been disposed of, the poem finds itself free, in the second stanza, to laud the individual attainments of, for example, Padraic Pearse and Thomas MacDonagh, two teachers who were evidently capable of rising above themselves. Conversely, those who had fallen from social grace—Constance Markievicz and John MacBride—are, if not entirely restored to their former status, raised to a higher standing in the poet's mind for having identified with the heroic deeds of the day.

Once the cast of characters and the scenario have been assembled the poem is able to interrogate the principle of single-mindedness which seems to have animated the participants' ideal (what the poem calls "their dream"). In contrast to the relatively unadorned language and basically urban setting of the opening pair of stanzas, the language of the interrogation is obviously poetic—being, for the most part, metaphorical—while the setting (in the third stanza) and ambience (in the fourth) revert to one of the poet's most familiar tropes, nature. Just as there is a strong, though perhaps unobtrusive, distinction made in the first and second stanzas between social class and individual personality, in the third and fourth stanzas the distinction is suggested between the pace of natural life and the rebels' state of mind. Such interplay between the stanzas contributes to a sense of the poem's dynamics, a further appreciation of which may be derived from considering "Easter 1916" as a poem in two parts. One part consists of the two opening stanzas and is basically expository, while the other part, consisting of the two final stanzas, is essentially reflective. The dialogue between the these two parts constitutes not only the totality of the poem but a description of Yeats's artistic intention in "Easter 1916," which is, as ever, to assimilate the matter of Ireland to poetic utterance, on this occasion in an elegy which will outlast the lives it hymns by authenticating their reputations' honour.

It should be noted, however, that the poem explicitly rejects its metaphorical approach with the doom-laden line in the fourth stanza, "No, no, not night but death." From that point, Yeats's emphasis is firmly placed on the undeniable reality, the "terrible beauty," to which the poem attempts to give tongue. When the poet declares, "I write it out in a verse," he is drawing attention not only to his work's occasion but to the fitness of poetry to preserve and commemorate that occasion's ethos. Thus, Yeats reminds us, art becomes history's counterweight, poetic energy accepts and vindicates in a spirit of tragic joy the rebels' transformative power.

—George O'Brien

EASTWARD HO.
Play by George Chapman, Ben Jonson, and John Marston, 1605.

Eastward Ho, as its generous-minded prologue states, was written in response to the deserved success of *Westward Ho*, a comedy by Thomas Dekker and John Webster (1604). It was first performed at the Blackfriars playhouse by boy actors, the Children of Her Majesty's Revels, and resembles other plays for the boys' companies in containing topical satire, of which more mention will be made later. It belongs to the dramatic type known as citizen comedy, and is set in contemporary London.

The central character is William Touchstone, a city goldsmith. He has two apprentices, the idle embezzling

Quicksilver and the industrious honest Golding, and two daughters, the vain and socially ambitious Gertrude and the sensible and modest Mildred. Gertrude is marrying a knight, Sir Petronel Flash, who claims to have a castle in the country: though her mother approves of the marriage, her father does not, and resolves to add no dowry to the legacy of land that she has inherited from her grandmother. After the wedding feast Quicksilver behaves with drunken impudence to Touchstone, who discharges him. He also discharges Golding, setting him up in business and giving him Mildred as his wife. Quicksilver lodges at the old usurer Security's house, where he keeps a mistress, the puritanically named Sindefy; he now arranges to exploit the Flashes by engineering the sale of Gertrude's inheritance to Security for ready money, which Sir Petronel needs because, having none of his own, he plans to desert his wife and emigrate to Virginia. Sindefy is presented to Gertrude as a country gentleman's daughter and becomes her waiting-woman, and with Mistress Touchstone they set off eastward to Sir Petronel's supposed castle as soon as Gertrude has been tricked into signing away her land. Sir Petronel, who that evening is to receive the cash and meet his fellow-adventurers at the Anchor Inn in Billingsgate, is scheming to take Security's young wife Winifred with him to Virginia, and makes Security himself an instrument of his scheme by pretending that it is the wife of the lawyer Bramble (who had drawn the conveyance for Gertrude's land) that he means to abduct. After a carouse, the Virginia party take boat downstream to their ship, careless of tide and tempest; Security returns to his house, discovers his wife's absence, and pursues them in another boat. All are overset in the Thames. Winifred, having obtained dry clothes, is reunited with Security at the Anchor, and persuades him that she had left their house in order to search for him. The adventurers are likewise washed ashore, Sir Petronel mistaking the Isle of Dogs for France, and he and Quicksilver are brought before Golding—who has been promoted with meteoric speed to civic office—and committed to prison on suspicion of felony, whither Security is soon sent to join them. Touchstone, their accuser, is obdurate until Golding by a stratagem lures him to the prison, where he is moved to compassion by the penitence of all three, and everything ends happily, Gertrude too having learned her lesson from her wild-goose chase.

Apart from the gulling of Security—derived from a story by Masuccio—the plot is original. Chapman is currently credited with the middle scenes, Jonson with the dénouement, and Marston with the exposition, though all three are thought to have had a hand in the shipwreck sequence. The coherence of the play, in spirit as well as in narrative structure, is remarkable in a tripartite collaboration, and critics have observed that *Eastward Ho* is free from the respective obscurity, pedantry, and vulgarity of which its three authors are sometimes capable. It is also free from moralistic heaviness. Though its design recalls the 16th-century moral plays in which up-dated versions of the Prodigal Son parable are dramatized in the manner of Terence, and in which the careers of good and bad children are contrasted in dire symmetry, its mood is light-hearted and its style extravagant: Touchstone tells Golding, "Let them behold the melancholy of a magistrate, and taste the fury of a citizen in office." However, to find a simply inverted morality, with Golding and Mildred contemptible in their uprightness, would be as wrong as to find nothing but simple didacticism. Touchstone, whose name both fits his trade and proclaims his sound judgement, is not, as Anthony Trollope thought, finally taken in by a mock repentance; but Quicksilver's truly penitent ballad is a joyous Jonsonian parody (the highwayman of the original, 1576, had once cut off a horse's head at a blow, and Quicksilver aspires to "cut off the horse-head of Sin"). Nearly all the characters' names, as usual, are appropriate (a petronel is a large horse-pistol), and the local colour is strong. Proverbs abound. There are topical allusions to the theatre: Quicksilver quotes lines from plays, and a footman called Hamlet makes a brief appearance.

Topical allusions to the Scots got the authors into trouble. James I (VI of Scotland) had succeeded Elizabeth I in 1603. Talking of the Virginia voyage (itself a topical aspect of the play), Captain Seagull wishes that a hundred thousand Scots would go, "for we are all one countrymen now, ye know, and we should find ten times more comfort of them there than we do here." James's selling of knighthoods is also glanced at, and even his accent mocked, when a gentleman says of the stranded Sir Petronel "I ken the man weel; he's one of my thirty-pound knights." Chapman and Jonson were committed to prison, but soon released. Some years later (January 1614) the play actually received a court performance, no doubt suitably cut, before the King himself.

—T.W. Craik

EDWARD II.
Play by Christopher Marlowe, 1592(?).

With *Edward II* the customary problems of chronology and textual corruption that dog evaluation of Christopher Marlowe's works are exacerbated by critical uneasiness before the homosexual content of the play. Despite Harry Levin's warning in *The Overreacher* that to ignore the homoeroticism of *Edward II* "as most of its critics discreetly tend to do, is to distort the meaning of the play," modern critics have found it difficult to come to terms with the meaning of Edward's love for his two "minions," Gaveston and Spencer.

The critical tradition has dealt more readily with Marlowe's deft compression of 23 years of chronicle history from the major source, Holinshed. Irving Ribner places the play within the developing genre of the historical play and examines the fused genre of historical tragedy as "a tragedy that probes the political and moral implications of the king's suffering." He places Marlowe within the category of the classical and Italian humanist historians who evaluate history not as providential, but "as the actions of men who bring about their own success or failure entirely by their own ability to cope with events."

Marlowe condenses the 23 years of Edward II's reign—a miserable tale of poor harvests, cattle murrain, civil strife, and foreign war that takes 24 folio pages in Holinshed—into a fast-moving narrative that seems to record the events of a single year. Marlowe structures the drama around the *de casibus* pattern—sequentially Gaveston, Edward, and finally Mortimer fall from high estate in the inexorable movement of fortune's wheel.

The play begins with Edward's accession and his recall of Gaveston from banishment. Gaveston's triumph is marked by the imprisonment of one of his enemies, the Bishop of Coventry. Yet that action allies the Church with the dissident nobility who insist that Edward banish Gaveston to Ireland. Edward forces his queen, Isabella, to plead for Gaveston's return, a plan agreed to by Mortimer because it offers readier opportunity for assassination of the king's favorite. The first three acts document Gaveston's reunion with Edward that only too swiftly ends in battle between Edward and his peers and Gaveston's execution. Edward is denied even the opportunity to see Gaveston once more before his death. At the center of the play, in Act III.ii., Edward swears bloody vengeance on the rebel lords and rallies around him loyal servants and Spencer, his new favorite. Edward defeats the rebels and orders their execution. Fatally, his enemy Mortimer escapes to France with Edward's brother, Kent, who is appalled by the execution of the rebel peers. They join Isabella, Edward's wife and Mortimer's mistress. The queen returns to England and defeats her husband in the name of her son. Her adultery with Mortimer disgusts Kent, who turns again and supports his brother, but too late. Edward is betrayed and taken. The final act details Edward's degradation. Forced to resign the crown, he is imprisoned, half-starved, and forcibly shaved in puddle water. Kent's attempt to rescue his brother is forestalled and Mortimer orders Edward's murder with an ambiguously punctuated message. Lightborn kills Edward in a grotesque parody of homosexual intercourse, with anal penetration by a red hot poker. Edward dies with an agonized scream. Yet Mortimer's triumph is brief, for Edward's son immediately exposes and punishes his father's murderer.

Particular critical discretion surrounds the murder of Edward. Despite William Empson's identification of the parody of homosexual intercourse in 1946, F.P. Wilson, finding "too much horror" in the death scene argues that the omission of overt stage directions indicates that the red hot poker prepared by Matrevis is never used. That position is challenged by Clifford Leech, among others. "There can, I think, be no doubt that Marlowe intended the mode of killing to be that narrated in Holinshed and clearly indicated by Lightborn in his talk with the jailors at the beginning of the scene." The reading of implied stage directions clearly indicates the preparation of a red-hot spit, a table, and featherbed—all implements for a parody of homosexual intercourse.

Jennifer Brady, drawing on the insights of contemporary gay studies, constructs a persuasive analysis of *Edward II* by making the death scene central to her analysis. She argues that "Edward is remade into the anal sodomite of nightmare" in a rehearsing of a masculinist culture's horror before homosexual desire. She emphasizes the significance of the masques planned by Gaveston for the king as "a profusion of erotic stimuli, a world without sharp gender differentiation" that oppose the barons' masculinist hierarchies. She argues that the homosocial community of love created by Gaveston and the king profoundly challenges the barons' rigid hierarchies of birth. Certainly, the barons' horror before Gaveston's elevation turns on questions of rank; "disparagement" their crucial concern. Once a conventional heterosexist reading is abandoned, the sentimentality that surrounds interpretation of the queen's position is exposed. The queen is no pathetic victim of Edward, but an adulterous woman unscrupulously used by Mortimer to mask his assault on the homosocial community of Edward and Gaveston. Analysis from the perspective of gay studies may lead to a fuller re-evaluation of all of Marlowe's works for his percipient scrutiny of the hierarchies—political, religious, and familial—that rest on the institution of heterosexuality.

—Karen Robertson

THE EGOIST.
Novel by George Meredith, 1879.

George Meredith was stylistically the most eccentric of the late Victorian novelists and this has undoubtedly had a negative effect on his literary reputation. But *The Egoist* survives to show that he could write with vivacity and wit, and tackle an important theme—that of what would now be termed "male chauvinism." The central character in the novel, Sir Willoughby Patterne, is—as his name suggests—the very pattern of masculine complacency. A youngish man of wealth and good fortune, it seems reasonable to him to condescend to his less wealthy neighbours, including Mr. Dale and his sweet daughter, Laetitia. Meredith uses his characters' names to suggest their inner natures: Laetitia Dale is very much the Victorian heroine, charming, intelligent, respectful to men. With her Sir Willoughby can maintain a sentimental friendship which survives the lowered estimation of women which he develops as the result of the sudden withdrawal of Miss Durham, to whom he is engaged at the start of the book.

Nevertheless, Sir Willoughby is susceptible to the charms of livelier women than Laetitia (which we may believe Miss Durham to have been). When the learned Dr. Middleton brings his lively daughter Clara to Patterne Hall, the scene is set for high comedy: the theatrical metaphor is highly relevant. Meredith had given his lecture, "On the Idea of *Comedy* and the Uses of the Comic Spirit" only two years earlier, in which he had claimed that "Comedy is the fountain of sound sense," that "there will never be civilization where comedy is not possible; and that comes of some degree of social equality of the sexes," and that "the test of true Comedy is that it awakens thoughtful laughter." In *The Egoist* he deliberately writes a comedy of manners in the form of a novel—an unusual but in this case highly successful combination, though his explanation of it in the overwritten "Prelude" may put some readers off.

As in classic comedy, the audience can foresee much of what will happen. Sir Willoughby is drawn to Clara Middleton, and reveals his extravagant egotism in a series of what he sees as light-hearted conversations with her. But Clara is the antitype to Laetitia: she is intelligent, independent (in so far as a young Victorian girl can be), cheeky to her pontificating suitor, and physically energetic (she enjoys the company of the young boy Crossjay Patterne, and even races him across the fields). She begins to feel the dangerous force and power of Sir Willoughby's egoism. When she attempts to withdraw from the relationship, he bribes her father, hedonist as well as scholar (a character based on Meredith's father-in-law, the novelist Thomas Love Peacock), with a bottle of old port. The two men thus decide the young woman's fate. Fortunately Clara has the energy to fight back (and is helped by the author's comic strategy). First she tries to run away, but this would have caused a scandal and she is dissuaded from it by a man she respects, the austere young intellectual Vernon Whitford (based on Leslie Stephen) whom Sir Willoughby employs as a secretary and enjoys patronizing. Clara is reassured by knowing she has the support of Whitford and of another guest, the worldly and witty Colonel de Craye, but still Sir Willoughby insists on upholding the engagement. The situation is well poised between male authority and female determination, and Clara's escape is achieved only after a series of comic events such as that in which the boy Crossjay is hidden under a coverlet in a room in which Sir Willoughby—by now sure that he will lose Clara, but anxious to keep face by being seen as having dismissed *her*—is proposing to the long-suffering Laetitia, who quite unexpectedly refuses to be used in this way. The comic twists and turns work on the side of Clara, and although Laetitia does finally accept Sir Willoughby, it is on her own terms. The final chapter, "Upon Which the Curtain Falls," gives us a complete resolution.

By now Clara has discovered that her real love is for the unworldly, dependable, intelligent Vernon, and they go off to celebrate their marriage with a walking-tour of the Alps. This is a symbol of their relationship, associated with nature rather than the stifling conventions of Patterne Hall. Although some feminist critics like Kate Millett, who writes enthusiastically about the novel in *Sexual Politics*, regret Clara's taking a male partner at all, for many readers the new relationship seems positive and authentic in a way that none of Sir Willoughby's are, and provides an appropriate conclusion to this most entertaining novel of sexual politics.

—Peter Faulkner

AN ELEGY WRITTEN IN A COUNTRY CHURCHYARD.
Poem by Thomas Gray, 1751.

Thomas Gray, writing in the mid-18th century, could be seen as a transitional poet, looking both back to the essentially urban Augustan writers of the earlier part of the century and on to the nature-based, Romantic poets of the end of the century.

The Augustans were characterised in part by artificiality and by their use of an escapist, pastoral myth of the countryside for the projection of cosmological, social, political, international, and aesthetic principles. Nature was transformed into a suitable vehicle for the expression of these ideas.

With Gray, the process is, in part, reversed, and his poetry is more a statement of how the landscape affects the poet, than the poet's manipulation of the landscape. This is not to say that Gray's involvement with the landscape is in any sense complete, or that the subjective elements blot out any historic or aesthetic qualities. Indeed, Gray's dilemma, when he is faced with the contrasting merits of a country and town life in the "Elegy," demonstrates clearly that he is very much concerned with historical and aesthetic categories.

Although the scenes Gray chooses for the settings of his poems condition his melancholic response, he is constantly removed from those scenes, both in time and space as, for example, the title, *Ode on a Distant Prospect of Eton College* and its opening line, "Ye distant spires, ye antique towers" suggest.

Again, in the "Elegy," the first four stanzas are devoted to a distancing of the surroundings and *departure* is the immediate impact of the first line. Time is distanced, for day is seen as parting, accompanied by the inevitable death and doom-like connotations of "curfew," "tolls," and "knell." Life too, both animal and human, "wind" and "plod" into the distance. And the poet, the observer of these various departures, is superfluous to their existence. The syntax of the following line is vital: "And leaves the world to darkness and to me." For, by including the preposition "to" a second time, Gray has created an ambiguity in that he has, in a sense, separated himself from even that darkness. His solitude is complete.

The second stanza continues the process of isolation: this time, that of the senses. "Now fades the glimmering landscape on the sight." Sound diminishes. "And drowsy tinklings lull the distant folds." Distance and the vacuum of the silent air are intensified by the touch of realistic detail of the beetle. The beetle continues to drone, but again there is distance implied (of what relevance is Gray to a beetle?). The gothic imagery of the third stanza is again distanced. If Gray does not identify with the pastoral elements of the first stanzas, neither does he with this wilder form of nature. Once again, Gray is dissociating himself from another literary tradition, this time that of the sublime. The adjective "yonder," which distances the tower, and the concept of the tower itself, made more inaccessible through the presence of ivy, are seen as removed from the poet as is the owl independent of man. In the fourth stanza, the graves, too, are distanced by deities. They lie "Beneath *those* rugged elms, *that* yew-tree's shade." And the graves, "narrow cells," are distanced by eternity. The contrast of the following stanzas only emphasises the sense of melancholy and solitude of the poet himself. Of course, they also stand in direct contrast to the state of death ("No more . . . For them no more . . . "), but the fact remains that such homely comforts are not for the poetic persona.

From these stanzas alone, it is clear that Gray is not seeing himself in terms of "Everyman" or "microcosm." He has, through careful phrasing and choice of adjectives and prepositions, prepared a background altogether removed, in time and space and mood, from himself. So far, Gray has concentrated upon his separation from country people: in the following stanzas he concentrates upon the rich. In stanza 8 Gray distances himself from the rich by lecturing them upon their attitude to the poor. At a first glance, it may appear that Gray is simply defending the poor. The conventional abbey-sculpture figures—Memory, Honour, Knowledge, are also seen as Ambition, Grandeur, Flattery, Luxury, and Pride. But the situation is more complicated than this. It is not simply a case of upholding the virtues of the poor at the expense of the rich. Rather, Gray displays ironic and overlapping attitudes towards them both. Cleanth Brooks has pointed out the irony implicit in the choice of "annals" for the poor (see his essay on Gray in *The Well-Wrought Urn*).

There is ambiguity, too, in stanza 15. Besides insisting, on the surface, upon the possible virtues of these potential Hampdens, Miltons, and Cromwells, the converse possibility is also an integral part of the comment. There is a hint of the ridiculous in the idea of the "village Hampden," "with daunted breast," withstanding "the little tyrant of the fields," the "mute, inglorious Milton" and the Cromwell "guiltless of his country's blood." A further irony is implicit in the choice of the adjective "animated" in relation to the busts in the cemetery (again see Brooks for a detailed account of this). In stanza 20, the contrasts are again brought together to give perspective to the rustic churchyard and humanity to the abbey.

The ironies and ambiguities emphasise and bring together three important strands which run throughout the "Elegy." The political and religious implications are quite apparent—Death is the great leveller, and so it is pointless to strive after ambition and power. The ambiguities present in the poem also stress that on a purely material level, there is not such a clear distinction between rich and poor as may be apparent. The third strand is the pervading sense of the *separateness* of the poet. He is the poet-observer, content to take part in neither of the two worlds. Gray's perceptions concerning the two groups are limited. His reactions are stylised and conventional. As Wordsworth later pointed out, a peasant's hearth may not always blaze, and crops may fail. And stanza 7 has once again almost the air of Jonson's "To Penshurst," where nature is pleased to be of service to man. This is, essentially, a version of the idealised, pastoral vision. His attitude towards the rich is also generalised and was probably heavily conditioned in its imagery and phrasing by Richard West's "Monody on the Death of Queen Caroline" or Dart's "Westminster Abbey."

Gray is, essentially, in a position of indecision. Neither existence will satisfy him. He has rejected the shortcomings of the rich, and has withdrawn from this way of life. But the tension is that if Gray takes up a country existence instead, he must give up his claim to fame. The consolations he produces through his ironies, ambiguities, and levelling perspectives do not satisfy this desire (stanza 22). The answer is, in short, to take the best of both worlds. He will have his epitaph in the country churchyard. This is not exactly a conscious or true alternative, but rather a compromise. Gray is still in a state of indecision.

Neither does he *choose* melancholy: rather, if we look carefully at the epitaph we find that "melancholy marked him for her own." The mid-18th century was taking on a new, fashionable meaning, implying a heightened sensibility that does not consist solely in solitary walking and gloominess, but in socially and aesthetically advanced modes of behaviour.

Gray's role is essentially passive. The images of distance and movement away from the poet in the opening stanzas take on a more definite emphasis. It is not Gray who is actively withdrawn: he is static, passive, and indecisive. The movement, the distancing, is external. The dusk, the transition between night and day, both echoes his state of mind and provides a perfect setting for it. Gray's attitude is basically urban, as his own personal dilemma in the "Elegy" and his idealised vision of a country hearth show. But he differs from Pope in that his expression is less settled, more subjective and affected to a certain extent by his surroundings. And yet, because of his lack of involvement with his surroundings, his stance is not that of the Romantics.

Finally, it remains to be said that the epitaph is problematised by the uncertainty as to exactly who is speaking. Is it Gray (or the poet into whom he projects himself) or the "hoary-headed swain" or some person unknown? The question has puzzled scholars over the centuries and there is no clear answer. Again, this could be seen as a co-relative of the lack of commitment or indecision on Gray's part that we have been tracing throughout the text.

—Anne Katherine Monaghan

EMMA.
Novel by Jane Austen, 1815.

Discussing *Emma* for the *Quarterly Review* in 1816, Sir Walter Scott, one of the few contemporaries to appreciate Jane Austen's merits, remarked: "*Emma* has even less story than either of the preceding novels" (ie., *Pride and Prejudice* and *Mansfield Park*). In a novelist famed for not dealing in the sensational, *Emma* seems the quintessence of her social comedy: in its original three-volume form, the first covers the misunderstandings of Harriet Smith and Mr. Elton, which impinge on Emma; as Mr. Elton is removed to Bath, the second introduces Jane Fairfax and Frank Churchill, with further effects on Emma, and then removes Frank, introducing Mrs. Elton towards the end; in the third volume, Frank returns, there are the ball at the Crown, the Strawberry-picking at Mr. Knightley's and the visit to Box Hill, with complication followed by resolution. The novel contains no obvious wickedness such as seduction or adultery; the social and financial range of the characters is narrow even for Austen; and the setting is restricted to the surroundings of Highbury—we never accompany the few significant journeys. Within this claustrophobic world, unusually fine discriminations are required by reader and heroine alike.

In personal terms, the novel charts the process of self-discovery of the meddling "imaginist" heroine, whose assertive self-confidence based on family wealth and social position is modified through a series of misunderstandings, reversals, and painful clarifications to a greater understanding of her relative standing. Emma's apparent dominance in Highbury is reflected in a narration which is often conducted from her point of view and offers as seemingly authorial judgment what is in fact closer to her reported thought. Like Emma, the reader is deceived by the Frank Churchill-Jane Fairfax complication, although by that stage in the novel Austen has taught us to distance ourselves somewhat from the heroine. Through a series of small episodes such as Emma's portrait-painting, we see established a hierarchy of judgments in which Emma is plainly more perceptive than the romantic Harriet or the fatuous Mr. Elton, yet blind to aspects of her own exploitative relationship with them which Mr. Knightley unsuccessfully invites her to recognise. On any true view of this society, Mr. Knightley, magistrate, farmer, descendant of an ancient local family, and "gentleman" in the best senses, ought to be at its centre: that he does not initially seem so is due to the mistaken values and perceptions offered through the heroine. Within the novel, there are different sets of values expressed in the abstract nouns so characteristic of Austen. In her resentment of Mr. Elton in Chapter 16, Emma refers to "connection, rank, fortune, consequence" as partly explaining his inferiority. These external factors based on money, property, social position, reflect a snobbery that runs through the novel; but Emma also damns him (and, ironically, herself to some extent) in terms of more personal qualities: "perception, consideration, delicacy, elegancies of mind." Her first reaction is that Mrs. Elton possesses "ease, but not elegance," whereas she thinks of Jane Fairfax, brought up with "every advantage of discipline and culture," as "remarkably elegant."

In its miniature dramas, the novel plays the values of money, power, and social position against those of the human heart and mind. The moneyed drones who exploit their social inferiors—Mr. Woodhouse, Emma, Mrs. Elton—are set against Mr. Knightley's good-humoured social responsibility or Jane Fairfax's condemnation, despite her talents, to the "governess trade." Comparison and parody are vital methods by which Austen aids our indirect judgment: Mrs. Elton's glaring snobbery is all too competitive a version of the heroine's own, while Emma's complacent assessment of Miss Bates as a fellow-spinster in Chapter 10 is based on the security of her own material position, from which she later thoughtlessly exercises the wit which incurs Mr. Knightley's rebuke. Within this society, talent and position bring the responsibility of restraint, while social or emotional problems often centre on the difficulty of continued living among those associated with hurt or embarrassment: hence Emma's relief on her own and Harriet's account at Mr. Elton's departure for Bath, or her remorse at hurting the vulnerable Miss Bates; her need for final joyful expression of her feelings for Mr. Knightley conflicts with her regard for the deceived Harriet. In this narrow world, hell can indeed be other people, and so much of the comedy depends on concealment or misunderstanding (as between Emma and Harriet about both Mr.

Elton and Mr. Knightley) within a society with strict codes of behaviour and emotional decorum. To minimise the rubs of social life, the adoption of a mask and mutual accommodation through mild hypocrisy may be desirable. The self-deceiving Emma regards the central Fairfax-Churchill concealment as "a system of hypocrisy and deceit—espionage and treachery." For them, concealment is the means to liberation and happiness, though Mr. Knightley praises to Emma "the beauty of truth and sincerity in all our dealings with each other"; and she finally resolves, under the tutelage of this favourite-uncle-cum-husband, to "repress" her imagination which has hitherto been her principal means of self-expression. Harriet's revelation in Chapter 47 about her love for Mr. Knightley provokes in Emma the crucial self-revelation of her love for him, which has been overlaid with romantic games and interference in the lives of others.

Within her famous "miniature" scope, Austen offers a suggestive analysis of the social and economic basis of her society, while charting with great delicacy the moral and intellectual growth of the heroine who is further from its centre than she thinks. The lightness of touch shown in the characterisation through dialogue places Mr. Woodhouse, Mrs. Elton, Miss Bates in relation to the novel's themes and elicits their contributions to the plot without boring the reader. George Knightley remains at a slight distance from us, as from Emma, but in him personal qualities and social position coincide to embody the traditional English hero, whose essential restraint reflects the novel's own best qualities.

—Ian McGowan

THE END OF THE AFFAIR.
Novel by Graham Greene, 1951.

Graham Greene's *The End of the Affair* in some ways straddles his own distinction between the serious novel and the entertainment: it explores, rather selfconsciously, the role of the novelist (its protagonist and main narrator, Bendrix) in a world where the question of God's omnipotence and omniscience (reflected as intervention in the lives of people and of nations) is problematic. Yet at the same time it is a rather sentimental love story (of Bendrix's affair with Sarah, unfulfilled wife of the civil servant Henry), a mystery (the condition of Bendrix's survival after a V-1 bomb hits his Clapham Common flat in June 1944, Sarah's secret "lover" alluded to in her purloined diaries, a comically incompetent inquiry agent and his son), and a "plot" with the identity of plotter undetermined. Like other novels of London during the war (Elizabeth Bowen's *The Heat of the Day*, Henry Green's *Caught*), the vulnerability of the traditional novelist's London extends to the role of the narrator: how to tell a story when its scene is disappearing.

The "facts" of this story come from the unreliable recollections of the very self-interested Bendrix and the (unintentionally) ambiguous diaries of his lover, Sarah Miles. He "investigates"; she expresses. She believes, and dies; he denies, hates, and survives. Does his hatred of the pact between Sarah and God that he finally uncovers (that if he survives the bombing, Sarah will give him up) become an inverse form of belief? Does her loving attempt to find a justification for disbelief by becoming the protégé of a "professional" atheist constitute love or infidelity—toward Bendrix, or God? Greene's reluctance to invest his own authorial confidence either in Bendrix's cynicism or Sarah's acceptance echoes his contemporaneous insistence in *Why Do I Write?* (an exchange of views with Bowen and V.S. Pritchett in 1948) on the writer's (especially the Roman Catholic writer's) essential *disloyalty*, the analog of the soldier's loyalty. But as Greene implies in *The End of the Affair*, the novelist—perhaps more often than other people—does have to decide between coincidence and miracle: the purely gratuitous conjunction of events in a contingent universe; and the possible existence of an over-riding intelligence who constructs and orders all narratives. It is a tribute to Greene's honest disloyalty in this book that he is able to negotiate lawless roads (the oxymoronic title of his nonfiction book about Mexico), but that the uncertainties of the novel do not defeat the reader's interest in the end of the story. In fact, the "story" has two endings: the first is Sarah's dying statement that "I've fallen into belief like I fell into love"; the second, after her funeral, is Bendrix's rather begrudging acceptance of his obligation to Sarah's widower Henry, and his final "prayer": "I'm too tired and old to learn to love. Leave me alone forever."

—William W. Heath

ENDGAME.
Play by Samuel Beckett, 1958 (as *Fin de partie*, 1957).

A comic / tragic mime for human puppets treating a depleted universe at the apocalyptic end of its tether, *Endgame* is quintessential Beckett. Typically, this play is impoverished in every sense, but dauntingly rich in implications and effects. It has been noted that Samuel Beckett tends, no matter what his medium, to eliminate everything inessential, but in the process, he manages to introduce a multitude of mysteries. In *Endgame* he finds ways to imprint on the tabula rasa of experience small signs that expand in our consciousness.

The set for *Endgame* is a case in point, as are its cast and action. The curtain opens on a sparely furnished box with two small curtained windows located like eye holes to the left and right backstage, a door leading to the kitchen offstage, a picture turned face to the wall, Hamm's throne / chair on castors center stage, two "ashbins." Mourning is implied by the ponderous bulk of Hamm and the two cans being initially draped in sheets, the curtained windows, the reversed picture. As critics have plausibly noted, the set resembles the interior of a skull with two eye holes lidded but looking out on a double desert, land and sea, a terminal emptiness. The characters of *Endgame* are on the very edge of mortality in the wake of an unspecified catastrophe. Since little is made of the loss, we must assume that the catastrophe is a thing of the distant past, if catastrophe it was and not simply the gradual wearing away of substance. The play is played by and around a remnant of four reluctant survivors. It is about diminution and ending, a topic handled with the wit of a mortician in the shadow of a possible death.

None of this should be very entertaining. On its surface it is all patently antitheatrical. In fact, by using and abusing all the tricks of the trade: by slyly inserting small nuggets of humor, by using a purified plot, setting, cast, and action to suggest parallel systems of significance, Beckett has created an engrossing dramatic event, a mystery play for our times.

The play has four characters and two invisible supernumeraries (a small boy reportedly seen from one of the windows and an old lady, perhaps dead). The principals are the master, Hamm, the servant / son Clov, and the two canned progenitors, Magg and Nell, jack-in-the-box figures for a forgotten past who pop up periodically from their ashbins. It has been noted that all the names can mean nail (coffin nail or unresponsive thing?), though both the character and the name of the imperious Hamm seem more appropriately to suggest a hammer. Name games in Beckett are always open-ended. The Shakespearean allusions, like the Dantean or biblical ones, justify a host of related readings. Is this a post-deluge or a pre-Judgement world; is this yet another version of Hell; are we reconstituting Shakespearean plots . . . ?

Endgame's action, like that of the similarly spartan *Waiting for Godot*, is essentially devoted to killing time without performing significant actions. Beckett was profoundly aware that nothing could be funnier, more senseless, more pathetic than human existence, a life sentence that defies both words and images. The excuses we make up to explain and justify that existence are worthy topics for mockery and disdain. They are Beckett's ultimate subject matter, just as ritual and farce are his favorite modes. No wonder this play is decked in the trappings of low-quality theatrical or music hall farce, no wonder all of its protagonists remind us of clowns and fools. Every bit of mime and slapstick is played slow motion; even the stichomythic dialogue is laced with pauses; the gags are sick jokes deflating conventional values; and the actions are formulaic and ritualistic in their absurdity.

Nothing if not consistent, *Endgame* (the word refers to the terminal move in chess) is a play that eschews conventional action. Like the famous chess game Beckett's Murphy plays with the catatonic Mr. Endon in *Murphy*, the game in which neither party's men make contact with the opponent, little progress is made during the drama toward either check or mate. The tone is set by Clov's opening mime, the meticulous and reiterated climbing up and down a ladder to look through the windows to see if anything has changed. This metaphor for view is matched by Hamm, whose blindness and immobility make his commanding presence, his whimsical commands, cruel wit, and childish petulance emblematic of impotent power and a darkly absurd destiny.

It is Hamm, the chess king, who, powerless, controls the action by dominating center stage as his pawn, Clov, more or less willingly does his will: fetching his toy dog; covering and uncovering Nagg and Nell, his parents; promising to provide him with painkillers; staring at the outer waste. Such is the infertile ground on which Beckett scatters seeds of solace, unrelieved suspense, a handful of narratives, some pointless parables worthy of the action. Add to that the irreverent dialogue, and the crabbed presence of Nagg and Nell with their mock-syrupy reminiscences of an occluded past and you have the "substance" of this play whose appeal derives not from that substance but from Beckett's ingenious but unlabored engagement with it. For ultimately, it is to the splendor of his treatment, the orchestration of dialogue, pauses and movement, and the inscription of erased conventions that *Endgame* owes its success.

By stripping his action of everything that might be deemed inessential, the author has opened his play up to the director, the actor, and the reader. Predictably, critics, like biblical exegetes, have found multitudes of meanings, erecting systems of reading based on philosophy, Shakespeare, history, psychoanalysis, etc. Beckett, having made this inevitable, abhorred the results, but then, such readings, if carried far enough, all tend to self-destruct, leaving the play as open and as evocative as before, as individual in its impact and echoes. It is in the nature of such theatre that every reader reads his own play and that interpretations, though not necessarily wrong, are beside the mark or only way stations. One might say, as Beckett himself said of Joyce's *Finnegans Wake*, that *Endgame* is about itself.

—David Hayman

ENDYMION.
Play by John Lyly, 1588.

At one time, *Endymion* and John Lyly's other dramatic works, because they were court plays, were viewed as allegorical representations of specific court intrigues. Today there is general agreement that these plays, and especially *Endymion*, should not be read as disguised references either to particular intrigues or to the roles of court personages in these intrigues. This particular play should be read as a dramatic work that exhibits both Lyly's masterful command of traditional components of a court *performance* and his verbal, syntactic, and structural virtuosity.

By 1588 Lyly had experience as a court dramatist, and he here manages a convergence of humanist, courtly, and dramatic traditions, manipulating the Endymion myth to make it in style and matter appropriate to the occasion. Presented before the queen and her court on Candlemas night, 1588, *Endymion* lays claim to being the most noteworthy of Lyly's plays. Like his other writing for court presentation, this play is careful to refer to the queen with persistent admiration. However, this play is curiously crafted so that it makes that admiration a central, as well as decorous, component of the theme.

The title refers clearly to the classical myth in which the shepherd Endymion is loved by the moon. As the passive object of celestial love, in one version of this myth, Endymion is cast into sleep by the moon. In another version, he lies down to sleep and while asleep is kissed by the moon. In this version, Endymion is enthralled by the dreams the moon has given him and upon awaking begs Zeus to allow him immortality so that he may return to sleep forever and never leave those enthralling dreams.

The presentation of Lyly's *Endymion* to the queen and her court is itself the gesture of a humanist courtier. The use of the moon as allegorical representation of the queen and of Cynthia as personification of moon and monarch was a familiar device in the Court of Elizabeth I (used, for example, by Ralegh and by Spenser). The joining of this device with the classical myth of the moon goddess and the beloved youth would ready this courtly audience for some allegorical treatment of love in the relationship of subject and sovereign. This relationship was a serious humanist concern, and the audience would be alert to observe how Lyly fashioned *Endymion* for the queen. In fact, how the fashioning was managed would be part of the diversion, for Elizabeth I would not tolerate an allegorical presentation that seemed in any way to counsel her, and it would be unthinkable to present a character representing queenship if that character were to be represented as amorously captivated by a subject.

What we see in this work is perhaps the most impressive demonstration of Lyly's adeptness at independent use of a classical source and romantic elements to create a play that moves harmoniously and with diverting tact to its conclusion.

Although brief and seemingly ingenuous, the prologue allows us to see an essential quality of this play as a courtly diversion. One major source of its power to entertain is its continual diverting of meaning, playing with the sophisticated expectations of its audience to seem to develop one meaning while suggesting another, sometimes contradictory or paradoxical, possibility. In the case of this prologue, the reference to "chimera" along with the notation that interpretation of such a fiction was forbidden links up with the insistence that this play is not possibly anything but absolutely itself, and the result is immediately to remind the audience of the traditions of allusiveness of courtly plays. The untrustworthiness of this sort of disavowal is meant to be obvious to a sophisticated audience, and this intentional obviousness of the untrustworthy stance initiates a sense of shared play between audience and performance.

In place of a developing complication of conflict, the five-act structure through which the scenes and characters are presented provides a sequence of narrative situations and parallel levels of characters. This "situational" mode of presentation allows time and opportunity for the masque-like unfolding of scenes, humanistic debate among characters, and the evocation of allegorical implications (Peter Saccio, *The Court Comedies of John Lyly*, 1969).

The refashioned Endymion that Lyly offered his audience through this "situational" mode is made the enamored lover of an unreachable moon. Almost immediately features of the moon are introduced that reveal her centrality to the rhythms and well-being of the earth. The mythic casting of Endymion into sleep is now an act of vengeance of Tellus, a gentlewoman who represents (at some points) the level of earth-bound affections and processes spurned by Endymion in his adoration of Cynthia. At the central point in the play, preceding Act 3, Lyly utilizes the dream of the mythic Endymion by presenting a dumb-show dream allegory experienced by the sleeping Endymion. In Act 3 itself, Cynthia enters the play, to help resurrect her enchanted courtier, and in the last half of the play, Cynthia's kiss is the means by which Endymion's bewitchment is lifted. Here the drama focuses upon Cynthia and her court as representative of Elizabeth and her court, presenting the sovereign functioning as the instrument of a renewing justice and mercy.

In the central third act, the comically fantastic braggart, Sir Tophas, is employed to parody Endymion's exalted love, bewitchment into sleep, and his allegorized dream. In one facet of this parody, Sir Tophas self-servingly interprets *his* dream owl's bird call, "twit." This centrally located parodic interlude provides a lighthearted undercutting of the sort of elaborate allegorical interpretation which the second half of the play invites. Throughout, Lyly controls the whole so that all the strands of *Endymion* are woven into a coherent conclusion in which concord and romantic reconciliation prevail under Cynthia's reign and the reawakened Endymion's "honorable respect" for his queen may be sanctioned and "christened love."

Endymion's dialogue, the substance out of which this play of allegory is woven, constitutes a rhetorical exploration that focuses on the relationship of courtier and sovereign, the roles of friendship and of love, and the nature of justice and mercy as fundamental manifestations of a sovereign's rule. The rhetorical explorations in *Endymion* do not operate as demonstrations of truths, but they do contribute to a sense of the human experience of inquiry (and perhaps wonder) in what Carter A. Daniel called "a fathomlessly deep play."

—Richard Haber

ENGLISH BARDS AND SCOTCH REVIEWERS.
Poem by Lord Byron, 1809.

Like most reviewers and many satirists, George Gordon, Lord Byron resented criticism, but liked to mete it out in full measure to others. What David Daiches calls "a life of self conscious dissipation in England" throughout 1809 was followed by a two-year European journey and *Childe Harold's Pilgrimage*. Before Byron left England, however, he had produced and published anonymously (though no one doubted the identity of the author), *English Bards and Scotch Reviewers*, an attack upon amateur and professional writers and critics who had annoyed him.

The poem came out in March 1809, but the text usually favoured today is that of the fifth edition of 1812, suppressed after it appeared. It is couched in heroic couplets after the manner of Pope though, to quote Daiches again, "far less cunningly wrought and carried on by a negligent energy Byron was to learn to harness more effectively."

The trouble is that the majority of the poetasters attacked, while they may or may not have been gnats around the poet's ear in their lifetime, are now utterly and totally forgotten. Those who are remembered did not, for the most part, merit the treatment they receive.

The raison d'etre for the poem is the curious situation whereby in the early decades of the 19th century Scots editors running Scots periodicals exercised widespread influence among, so to say, the "opinion-formers" of the whole of Britain. This state of affairs was an outcome of the intellectual dominance of the academic world exercised by Edinburgh during its "Athens of the North" phase in the late 18th century; an upsurge that produced David Hume, Adam Smith, the historian William Robertson, the mathematician Colin Maclaurin, William Smellie's *Encyclopaedia Britannica*, and many others, and which included the poet Burns. It was an energy that lasted until about 1832, the year of Scott's death, latterly manifesting itself through periodicals such as the *Edinburgh Review* and the *Quarterly Review*, both of which Byron's enemy Francis, later Lord Jeffrey, edited in turn. Jeffrey, who sneered at the arrival of the Lakeland poets, was even credited by some with hastening the death of Keats by a hostile review in the *Quarterly*, leading Byron to observe in *Don Juan*: "Tis strange the mind, that fiery particle, / Should let itself be snuffed out by an article." Byron's poem thus serves the triple purpose of attacking Jeffrey, demolishing popular poetasters of the day and scoring off his serious rivals.

Who today knows or cares anything about "hoarse Fitzgerald," a versifier fond of declaiming his verses in pubs; the Honourable George Lamb, whose sister was later to become to Byron an infatuated nuisance; "grovelling Stott," a versifier who wrote for the *Morning Post* as "Hafiz"; "Hibernian Strangford," a peer whose *Translations from Camoens*, the Portuguese writer, enjoyed brief renown; the prosperous dilettante William Hagley, author of *The Triumphs of*

Temper; "Sepulchral Gordon," the totally talentless author of *Sabbath Walks* and *Biblical Lectures*; Reverend William Lisle Bowles, an undistinguished Oxford sonneteer; the amateur playwright Sir Lumley Skeffington; or " . . . Amos Cottle-Phoebus what a name / To fill the speaking trump of future fame"? Who is interested in the parade of literary peers set up before us in order to be knocked down?

Among those attacked whose names have survived in various degrees is "Little," a pseudonym used by Thomas Moore, with whom in earlier days Byron had been friendly. Thomas Campbell, author of "The Pleasures of Hope," gets off comparatively lightly, as does "Monk" Lewis, the author of gothic horror novels. Not so Wordsworth, Coleridge, Southey, and Scott. "Simple Wordsworth," "Vulgar Wordsworth," is called:

> The meanest object of the lowly group
> Whose verse of all but childish prattle void,
> Seems blessed harmony to Lamb or Lloyd.

—while Wordsworth's verse:

> . . . both by precept and example shows
> That prose is verse and verse is merely prose,
> Convincing all, by demonstration plain
> Poetic souls delight in prose insane.

Coleridge, " . . . To turgid ode and tumid stanza dear" also comes under Byron's lash: "Though themes of innocence amuse him best / Yet still Obscurity's a welcome guest." Of all the Lakers Southey fares the worst; author of dull epics, of which *Thalaba* is probably the only one now known at all; a *Life of Nelson*; and, in his miscellany *The Doctor*, of the children's tale "The Three Bears." "Oh Southey! Southey! cease thy varied song! / A bard may chaunt too often and too long . . . "

The attack that Byron lived most to regret was that upon Sir Walter Scott, whom he later visited at Abbotsford and came to revere. As the creator of "The golden-crested haughty Marmion," Byron asked of Scott: "And thinkest thou, Scott! by vain conceit perchance / On public taste to foist thy stale romance." Lamenting an age when: " . . . Milton, Dryden Pope, alike forgot, / Resign their hallowed Bays to Walter Scott."

The central focus-point of Byron's attack is, of course, Jeffrey, that "Self constituted Judge of Poesy." Byron likens him to the famous English hanging judge of the same name:

> Health to immortal Jeffrey! once in name
> England could boast a judge almost the same;
> In soul so like, so merciful, yet just,
> Some think that Satan has resigned his trust,
> And given the Spirit to the world again
> To sentence Letters as he sentenced men.

While Jeffrey's aristocratic or titled supporters may be attacked, Jeffrey himself remains secure:

> For long as Albion's heedless sons submit,
> Or Scottish taste decides on English wit,
> So long shall last thy unmolested reign,
> Nor any dare to take thy name in vain.

Byron, however, concludes that he is now:

> . . . so callous grown, so changed since youth,
> I've learned to think, and sternly speak the truth;
> Learned to deride the critics starch decree
> And break him on the wheel he meant for me.

This Byron did. Jeffrey is now quite unread, but not so the poet. *English Bards and Scotch Reviewers*, though an excellent example of the proverbial hammer applied to a collection of mostly very small nuts, is an occasional poem still readable with pleasure today for its spirited wit rather than for the critical scattering of the cracked shells of tiny reputations it originally brought about.

—Maurice Lindsay

EPICOENE.
Play by Ben Jonson, 1609.

A careful assessment in Dryden's *Of Dramatic Poesy* (1668) calls Ben Jonson, for the honour of England, "the most learned and judicious writer which any theatre ever had," and finds in *Epicoene* "the pattern of a perfect play." This posthumous accolade from a classically minded critic would hardly have surprised Jonson, who was never lacking in confidence. And there was similarly high contemporary praise; Latin verses by John Donne, printed with *Volpone* in 1607, see Jonson's genius and industry as creating timeless classics, guided by the ancient examples and going beyond them to something new.

Epicoene was first acted in 1609 by the Children of Her Majesty's Revels in the "private" Whitefriars Theatre, where the performances would have taken place indoors by artificial light. The boy actors had already appeared in other plays by Jonson, and he later told Drummond that he gave instruction to one of the boys in Latin poetry. The prose work which they were now to perform was the first of Jonson's comedies to have a London setting. Strictly observing the classical unities, it offers a single action which takes place in a small area of the city in one day. A hater of noise named Morose, who carries his eccentricity to fantastic extremes, has disinherited his nephew, Sir Dauphine Eugenie, on unjust suspicion of complicity in some noisy practical jokes, and to confirm his spite he has decided to be married and beget an heir. But first he must find a sufficiently quiet bride, and the wonderfully quiet Mistress Epicoene, who lodges nearby, seems a likely choice. Actually Epicoene has been placed there and instructed as to behaviour by Dauphine; but Dauphine's impetuous friend Truewit, ignorant of this, tries to prevent the marriage by bursting in on Morose with dire warnings about wives and women generally. Morose thinks that Truewit has been sent by Dauphine, and in a fit of rage he resolves to marry Epicoene at once. No sooner is the marriage ceremony complete, however, than the supposed paragon of silence bursts into shrill railing. This happens in the third act, and the rest of the play is a carnival of noise and absurdity. Finally Dauphine offers to show his despairing uncle a way out of the marriage in exchange for a modest allowance and a restoration of his rights as heir, and when the offer is accepted he pulls off Epicoene's wig and declares the marriage invalid because the supposed bride is really a boy. "Now," he tells Morose, "you may go in and rest; be as private as you will, sir. I'll not trouble you till you trouble me with your funeral, which I care not how soon it come." This heartless speech has troubled some editors and directors, who accordingly specify an exit for Morose before the concluding sentence; but the play as a whole, which mocks unrelentingly at the foibles of the minor characters, does not suggest that Jonson would have seen a need for such compunction.

Jonson's literary debts in *Epicoene* help to document his boast to Drummond that he was "better versed and knew more in Greek and Latin than all the poets in England." His skilful use of the many borrowings show him not only learned but in total control of his learning; as *Of Dramatic Poesy* puts it, these borrowings are not thefts but conquests. For the plot of *Epicoene* he remembered a hater of noise in a Greek declamation by the 4th-century rhetorician Libanius, where a quiet citizen, called Morosus in the Latin translation, is driven desperate by a loud and talkative wife and asks official sanction to take hemlock. The second main element in the plot, that of a marriage trick with a disguised male as bride, appears in the *Casina* of Plautus. For some of the witty dialogue Jonson draws happily on the *Ars Amatoria* of Ovid, and for Truewit's warning to Morose against marriage he finds ammunition in Juvenal's sixth satire. Even the genial prologue contains echoes of Terence and Martial, and a splendid song, "Still to be neat," which is performed in the play as the work of Dauphine's friend Clerimont, recreates a lyric from the *Anthologia Latina*. Besides these unmistakable Greek and Latin sources, it has been argued that Jonson knew Pietro Aretino's comedy *Il Marescalco*, where the bride is a disguised page.

At the first production of *Epicoene* there was trouble with the authorities, and Jonson wrote a second prologue indignantly denying the charge of offensive topicality. No more happy was his memory of a scoffing set of verses which somebody left on the stage to the effect that "the play was well named 'The Silent Woman'; there was never one man to say Plaudite to it." But thereafter *Epicoene* achieved success with many kinds of audience by its finely crafted combination of comedy of humours, comedy of manners, and sheer slapstick. There was a revival at court in 1636, a year before Jonson's death; in 1667 Pepys noted that there was "more wit in it than in ten new plays"; the role of Epicoene provided a successful vehicle, perhaps surprisingly, for Sarah Siddons and other famous actresses; and later still, when Stefan Zweig adapted the play as a libretto for Richard Strauss's *Die schweigsame Frau* (1935), the composer declared it the best text for comic opera since *Figaro*.

—Rhodes Dunlap

EPITHALAMION.
Poem by Edmund Spenser, 1595.

Edmund Spenser's *Epithalamion* or marriage hymn (*epi*, before + *thalamos*, bridal chamber) was written to celebrate his marriage to Elizabeth Boyle, on 11 June 1594, in Ireland. It has been called "Spenser's highest achievement" (Ernest de Selincourt). It is modelled on classical epithalamia, which retain elements of ancient customs: invoking the gods, dressing the bride, bringing her from her home in torch-lit procession, banqueting, preparing the bridal chamber and bringing the bride into it, all accompanied by the cry of "Hymen io Hymen" and by songs and dancing. Though steeped in tradition, Spenser's poem stands alone. He makes himself, the bridegroom, be the proud singer of his own epithalamion. Then he celebrates the actual date of his wedding, "Barnaby the bright," St. Barnabas's day, the longest day (and, unfortunately for newly-wed lovers, the shortest night) of the year.

It is a very homely poem, echoing not just the time but the place of Spenser's marriage. The refrain "The woods shall to me answer and my Eccho ring" changes slightly as the utterance of each particular stanza echoes in the "woods" near Spenser's Kilcolman castle. There is great pride of locality. The "Nymphes" are those of Irish "rivers" and "forrests" and "of the sea that neighbours" his bride's home. The "trouts and pikes" of Mulla (the nearby river Awbeg) "all others doo excell." The "rushy lake, / Where none doo fishes take" and the "hoary mountayne," which is Galtymore, overlooking the valley of Aherlow in Tipperary, are particular references. The lark, thrush, mavis, ouzell, and ruddock are familiar birds of Ireland and Britain. The "merry Musick" of "The pipe, the tabor, and the trembling Croud" are specifically Irish. The "Pouke," who is not Shakespeare's mischievous Puck, remained a really threatening evil spirit in Ireland. The "Quyre of Frogs still croking" which "Make us to wish theyr choking," thought a fault by C.S. Lewis, is an in-joke for Spenser's wife and friends, goes with the "rushy lake," and firmly anchors the poem to its setting.

Enid Welsford has shown that day and poem fall into four periods divided by the risings of the sun, the evening star, and the moon. Furthermore Spenser resounds his "owne loves prayses" by firmly associating her with each of these heavenly bodies, thus enhancing her luminous ever-presence in the poem. The dawn is associated with the bride's waking, as Spenser assembles the muses and nymphs at her chamber door, there to await the rising of the sun and the coming forth of the bride. When she appears Spenser identifies her with both sun and moon by echoing Psalm 19:5, where the sun "commeth forth as a bridegroome out of his chamber, and rejoyceth like a mightie man to runne his race" but switching the comparison to bride and moon: "Loe where she comes along with portly pace, / Lyke Phoebe from her chamber of the East, / Arysing forth to run her mighty race, / Clad all in white, that seemes a virgin best." Thus when the moon illuminates the marriage chamber at the hour of consummation she becomes a stand-in for the bride and future mother who in emotional and spiritual terms is the true light of that room.

With the same magnanimity of style Spenser substitutes Hesperus, the evening star, for Phosphor, the morning star, when describing the opening of his bride's eyes at sunrise: "My love is now awake out of her dreames, / and her fayre eyes like stars that dimmed were / With darksome cloud, now shew theyr goodly beams / More bright than Hesperus his head doth rere." Thus when Hesperus later appears at the proper time, Spenser can subtly suggest an analogy to his bride's eyes—without offending her modesty—when that "Fayre child of beauty" looks "chearefully" on the preparations for the wedding night and "seemst to laugh atweene thy twinkling light / As joying in the sight. . . . " Through rich, subtle interconnections, then, Spenser suggests that his bride is sun, moon, and star of his wedding day. Yet with these identifications we have not reached the limit to which, it is claimed, Spenser went to make "this one day" his and his bride's own.

According to the hypothesis of A. Kent Hieatt, the 24 stanzas of the poem (23 plus the envoy) stand for the hours of this day and the 365 long lines for the days of the year. Since 24 will not go into 365, the stanzas cannot be identical in length, and *Epithalamion* is Spenser's only poem in which the stanzas vary. They are long stanzas (appropriately suggesting the love canzone of Petrarch). Each of the 23 full stanzas has 15 or 16 long lines in groups divided (except in two instances) by three short lines. The short lines vaguely suggest quarter-hours as their minor chimes lead up to the emphatic "ring," the rhyme at the end of each stanza (hour). The total of short lines, 68, is the total of the seasons, months, and weeks. 15 or 16 is the number of days the sun lingers in each of the sidereal hours, and the Hours who wait on the bride (as on no other character in Spenser) stand for these as well as for the diurnal hours. At the end of Stanza 23 there have been only 359 long lines, and this total is brought up to 365 by the six long lines of the envoy. This arrangement symbolizes the fact that when the celestial sphere has completed 360° the solar sphere (in the Ptolomaic system) has completed only 359°, the sun's lag creating the annual variety of 365 unique days. Spenser's sources calculated that on 11 June in the latitude of southern Ireland there are 16 and one-quarter hours of daylight and seven and three-quarters of dark. Therefore, Spenser places the words "Now night is come" one-quarter of the way through Stanza 17, and with that stanza the refrain changes to the pattern "The woods no more shall answere, nor your echo ring."

Did Spenser expect readers to grasp his numerological intent, or was this arrangement merely a self-imposed poetic discipline? Whatever his expectation, readers ignorant of the numerology have praised for four centuries the triumphant art with which Spenser exalts his marriage day.

—David R. Clark

EREWHON.
Novel by Samuel Butler, 1872.

Erewhon is the first of Samuel Butler's three fictional works, and the best known, except for *The Way of All Flesh*, published after his death. The third is *Erewhon Revisited*, a sequel to the first. From the many volumes of his collected works, it is apparent that his greatest gifts were his powers of observation and his interest in examining ideas and presenting new theories on many varied subjects. Although both an artist and a musician, he was not a particularly talented creative writer of imaginative literature, but was especially influential, nonetheless, upon George Bernard Shaw for his iconoclasm, and particularly annoying to Darwin for the same reason.

Erewhon belongs to the genre of Utopian literature which, through the creation of a fictitious country where perfection ostensibly exists, tends to satirize contemporary life. Butler, however, by his reversal of everything in Nowhere, including the title, names, ideas, and way of life, introduces double-edged irony directed not only at the religious, scientific, and economic concepts in 19th-century Britain, but also at the Erewhonians who have gone to the opposite extremes. The result is a shattering of both points of view and a challenge for total reappraisal.

The nucleus of the work emerged from two articles submitted to the Christchurch *Press*—"Darwin among the Machines," in 1863, when Butler had a sheep station in New Zealand, and "Lucubratio Ebria," in 1865, after he had returned to England. In 1869, Frederick Napier Broome, formerly a neighbor in New Zealand, suggested rewriting the articles for a book, which Butler then did.

The first five chapters are based, to a large extent, upon Butler's own explorations for new grasslands to lease, and the scenic descriptions are graphic, credible, and exciting as the nameless narrator and Chowbok (Kahabuka), a rum-addicted Maori chief and nominal Christian, who worked on the same station as the narrator, search for waste lands. Chowbok, however, deserts as they approach an area of tribal taboo, where the narrator proceeds on alone until he is confronted by a number of gigantic statues with malevolent expressions and hollow heads which emit fearful sounds from the wind. On the other side of the pass, he sees a landscape based more on the alpine regions of Italy.

He finds himself in a land of beautiful women and handsome men, living in manner resembling that of the 12th or 13th century. Machines are outlawed, though some parts can be seen in museums. For a time, he is jailed and provided with a tutor to teach him the language, though he learns more of it from Yram, the beautiful daughter of the jailer, than from the teacher. After three months he is sent to live with Mr. Nosnibor, is granted a pension to live on, and is to have audience with the King and Queen.

He hopes he has found the 10 lost tribes of Israel and that he may convert them, but first he must endeavor to learn their beliefs. He discovers that the ill, the poor, and the ugly are treated as criminals, tried, and imprisoned; while thieves, embezzlers, and other moral defectives are sent to hospital or placed under the care of straighteners and receive commiserations from friends. Next, he visits a Personal Bereavement Court where he finds a man who has lost his wife, another who has been swindled by his guardian, and one with tuberculosis all tried and punished for their misfortunes. Then he describes the attitude of the Erewhonians toward death, which they consider simply as a bugbear, and their burial customs, which consist of cremation, the scattering of ashes over some favored spot, and the sculpting of a statue of the deceased while still alive, the latter custom falling into desuetude because of the inordinate number cluttering up the country.

Each of these laws, customs, and mores receives separate treatment in the book and is discussed at length in expository fashion, first with respect to Erewhonian society, then, ironically, to English or Italian or Maori society, giving instances where yellow fever victims are punished by quarantine, or morally reprehensible people are respected and loved, or those suffering irreparable misfortune are descended upon in droves and pillaged of all property. Though the double-edged irony is challenging, the extended exposition often makes for heavy going.

The story periodically returns to life with the Nosnibors, where the narrator falls in love with Arowhena, but cannot marry her because she has an unmarried older sister Zulora. He and Arowhena agree to flee the country if he can devise an escape plan.

Interspersed between this thought and the deed, are the largest sections of the work—one on the Musical Banks, a quasi-religious, quasi-commercial institution, established for worship of the goddess Ydgrun (though the gods the Erewhonians actually worship are personifications of human qualities, and they believe in the world of the unborn and the necessity for the document called a birth formula absolving parents from all responsibility in the matter); another on the Colleges of Unreason which are dedicated to a study of hypothetics; and the longest, on the Book of the Machines, partially translated by the narrator, giving the history of the civil war between the machinists and the anti-machinists when the latter feared that machines would acquire a consciousness and supersede man. One of the concepts referred to here, that machines represent an extension of man himself in the process of evolution and that unconscious memory is inherited, was the basis of Butler's rift with Darwin. Along with the alienation from machines, philosophers convinced the Erewhonians that both animals and vegetables have rights, and were it not for a certain amount of evasion and hypocrisy, the race would have become extinct for lack of food.

Out of curiosity the Queen permits the narrator materials and machine-minded antiquarians to enable him to build a balloon. He smuggles Arowhena aboard, escapes over the Pacific, is rescued off South America, transfers to a wool ship from Melbourne to London, turns to writing for an income, and plots a scheme for converting the Erewhonians by removing them in a gunboat on their one navigable river to the Queensland sugar plantations and placing them with good Christian families, an ironical thrust at the Polynesian labor trade.

—Wesley D. Sweetser

AN ESSAY CONCERNING HUMAN UNDERSTANDING.
Prose by John Locke, 1690 (and later revisions).

John Locke's object in *An Essay Concerning Human Understanding* is "to enquire into the Original, Certainty, and Extent of humane knowledge; together, with the Grounds and Degrees of Belief, Opinion, and Assent."

The objects of human understanding are termed by him "ideas": an idea is an intermediate object between the knowing mind and some ultimate object of perception. Such ideas include sense-data, memories, and more abstract conceptions; but Locke habitually refers to them all, whether sensory or conjectural, as "pictures." At one point he takes the *camera obscura* as a model for the way in which such pictures are painted in the mind: "methinks the *Understanding* is not much unlike a Closet wholly shut from light, with only some little openings left, to let in external visible Resemblances, or *Ideas* of things without." The dominant metaphor of ideas as pictures reinforces Locke's demonstration that our simple ideas are principally derived from sight, the most comprehensive of our senses and the chief intermediary between matter and mind.

Locke begins his *Essay* by refuting the hypothesis, shared by ancient Stoics and modern Cartesians, that certain notions are innate in the mind. In its place he puts forward the theory advanced earlier by Aristotle and Bacon (those least mystical of philosophers), that the mind is a *tabula rasa* at birth, and acquires all ideas by experience. The powers by which external objects produce ideas in the mind are called by Locke qualities; of these he distinguishes two kinds, primary and secondary. Primary qualities are "Solidity, Extension, Figure, Motion or Rest, and Number." Secondary qualities "in truth are nothing in the Objects themselves, but Powers to produce various Sensations in us by their *primary Qualities*. . . . as Colours, Sounds, Tastes, etc." Primary qualities would exist if no one perceived them; secondary qualities are inconceivable without perception. Even though our ideas of secondary qualities, unlike our ideas of primary qualities, are not exact resemblances of "the thing in itself," Locke does not regard secondary qualities as subjective.

Locke refers to the mind metaphorically as a *camera obscura*, but he speaks also of ideas being admitted through the senses and the nerves, "which are the Conduits, to convey them from without to their Audience in the Brain, the Mind's Presence-room." This presence-room metaphor implies that the understanding has the active role of a ruler or judge. In Locke's view the mind is both passive and active. It is passive like a *camera obscura* when it receives simple ideas from sensation and reflection (this passiveness, coupled with the notion of the *tabula rasa*, is a warrant for the reality of the external world); but the mind is active when exerting its power over simple ideas in order to combine them into complex ideas, or to relate them to one another, or to abstract from them. Such activity is not always deliberate: as Locke shows in his influential chapter on the association of ideas (Book 3, chapter 33), the mind may combine ideas just as powerfully by chance as by volition. This was Mrs. Shandy's case, as Sterne indicates with his reference to "the sagacious Locke, who certainly understood the nature of these things better than most men" (*Tristram Shandy*).

Though the number of complex ideas is infinite, they may all be categorized as substances, modes, or relations. Ideas of substances are such natural combinations of simple ideas as are taken to represent distinct particular kinds of things: for instance, the idea of a swan is "white Colour, long Neck, red Beak, black Legs, and whole Feet, and all these of a certain size, with a power of swimming in the Water, and making a certain kind of Noise, and, perhaps, to a Man, who has long observed those kind of Birds, some other Properties." Nevertheless, the abstract idea of pure substance, the "Substratum" in which duly united simple ideas subsist, remains a problem: "all our *Ideas* of the several sorts of Substances, are nothing but Collections of simple *Ideas*, with a Supposition of something, to which they belong, and in which they subsist; though of this supposed something, we have no clear distinct *Idea* at all." Whereas substances, by definition, subsist by themselves, modes do not. Modes are attributes of substances, such as the complex ideas signified by the words *piety, triangle, gratitude, beauty, justice, theft*, and so on. Relation "consists in the consideration and comparing one *Idea* with another."

Knowledge of objects by sensation was, however, placed by Locke in the lowest of three degrees of certainty. In the second degree he placed "demonstration," by which we know "the Existence of a GOD" (the indefinite article is revealing). In the highest degree, following Descartes, he placed "intuition," by which we know our own existence: "In every Act of Sensation, Reasoning, or Thinking, we are conscious to our selves of our own Being; and in this Matter, come not short of the highest degree of *Certainty*." For Locke, though, "our selves" are no more, or less, substantial than our states of consciousness: "*Socrates* waking and sleeping is not the same person . . . *Self* is that conscious thinking thing (whatever Substance, made up of whether Spiritual, or Material, Simple, or Compounded, it matters not) which is sensible, or conscious of Pleasure and Pain, capable of Happiness or Misery, and so is concern'd for it *self*, as far as that consciousness extends." The parenthesis might disconcert orthodox Christians, but the notion of the self constantly being remade as it becomes conscious of next sensations was to become one of the intellectual foundations of the 18th-century sentimental novel.

—A.J. Sambrook

AN ESSAY ON CRITICISM.
Poem by Alexander Pope, 1711.

An Essay on Criticism is Alexander Pope's first major work, published when he was only 23 years old, yet it is a poem of great maturity both in technique and in substance. It stands in a long tradition of treatises on reading and criticism, and throughout recalls ideas found in poets and commentators from the ancient Greek writers pseudo-Longinus and Aristotle to the minor Restoration authors Roscommon and Sheffield. Though formally a discussion of the nature of criticism, Pope's poem also deals substantially with the art of poetry, and as a whole constitutes a meditation on the interrelations of the critical and creative as they affect both the artist and the would-be critic. The flexibility of the essay form allows Pope to include argument, satire, exhortation, historical description, and even a hymn of praise, for the classical poets' indestructible glory.

But what is most remarkable about *An Essay on Criticism* is the ease and assurance of Pope's verse. This is no dreary collection of precepts, but a dazzling display of poetic artistry in a highly concentrated form. One sign of Pope's imaginative fecundity is the number of pithy lines which have since become proverbial: "To Err is *Humane*; to Forgive, *Divine*," "For *Fools* rush in where *Angels* fear to tread," "A *little Learning* is a dang'rous Thing." Moreover Pope himself espouses the principles he expounds in his own verse. With apparently effortless ease he exemplifies, for example, the principle that "the Sound must seem an *Eccho* to the *Sense*," in a *tour de force* of auditory mimesis:

Soft is the Strain when *Zephyr* gently blows,
And the *smooth Stream* in *smoother Numbers* flows;
But when loud Surges lash the sounding *Shore*,
The *hoarse, rough Verse* shou'd like the *Torrent* roar.

Above all, Pope's graceful, elegant, witty verse produces the opposite effect from those treatises he castigates as "dryly plain, without Invention's Aid." The *Essay* is no "*dull Receit*," and if Pope is offering a prescription, it is in terms which are kept suggestively loose, and to the perceptive reader subtle and subtly interrelated.

The vitality of the poem's verse arises from Pope's inward engagement with his subject, a subject of crucial importance now as then. At bottom, Pope is dealing with the nature of Truth and Reason. The good critic or judge will be not only a good thinker, but a person committed to the cause of Truth: "Tis not enough, Taste, Judgement, Learning, join; / In all you speak, let Truth and Candor shine." The issue is ultimately a moral one, not merely aesthetic. The "*never-failing Vice of Fools*" is Pride; poetasters refuse to recognise true poets out of Envy. Truth and Reason thus flow not from learning (which will not eradicate bad faith) but, in the end, from an individual's own better nature. This is but one component of the complex of ideas Pope gathers under the general heading "Nature" in the *Essay*. Nature is the source of all true judgement, a "*clear, unchang'd*, and *Universal Light*"; its uncovering and just representation is also what the greatest poets achieve. The study of the ancient poets, and of the laws of poetry, are of fundamental importance, but these activities are only means to the end of representing Nature, "the working of the whole," by showing it "to Advantage drest" in its clearest and most expressive form. The rules of good writing, or the poetic art in general, are no more than systematically expressed perceptions about Nature's own characteristics. The true critic, therefore, is the man whose heart and mind are equally at one with Nature; for only thus will he be capable of reading a poem "With the same Spirit that its Author *writ*." Ultimately, however, no summary of the poem's ideas can do it justice, especially since these ideas are very often neither new nor meant to be so. The uniqueness of *An Essay on Criticism* lies not in its qualities as a theoretical treatise, but in its profoundly effective poetry.

—Stuart Gillespie

AN ESSAY ON MAN.
Poem by Alexander Pope, 1733–34.

Attacks on the first *Dunciad* (1728) as ill-natured and negative perhaps induced Alexander Pope to execute the project he had been meditating for years: a great moral poem, heading a series of "ethical epistles." The classic apology for satire—that it attacks deviations from an implied ideal or norm of conduct—gave way then to the need to state that ideal. In letters Pope described his desire "to contribute to some honest and moral purposes in writing on human life and manners." The poem is usually described as a theodicy or justification of God, but it is equally a psychology, a sociology, a teleology, and an ethics. In every respect, however, it is didactic poetry, and its once-great repute waned with the popularity of its species. It has been called self-contradictory, superficial and / or unoriginal, although the old idea that Pope "just" versified his friend Viscount Bolingbroke's prose, at least, has now given way to a realization that both men drew on a broad spectrum of classical, Renaissance, and contemporary thought. Pope used, among others, Plato, Aristotle, Lucretius, Vergil, Pascal, Newton, and Archbishop King's *On the Origin of Evil* (1702).

The first of the four epistles sets out the theology of "Optimism," drawn from Latitudinarian preaching and philosophers such as Leibniz and Shaftesbury, with whom it blends Locke, Mandeville, and Milton ("justify the ways of God to men" becomes "vindicate the ways of God to Man"). Pope is seeking a consensus, a lowest common denominator of ancient and modern religious thought, but the argument is not logically rigourous. "Of God above, or Man below," he asks, "What can we reason, but from what we know?" The passage implies that we cannot know metaphysical truths, yet Pope proceeds on the basis of assumptions about God:

Of Systems possible, if 'tis confest
That Wisdom infinite must form the best,
Where all must full or not coherent be,
And all that rises, rise in due degree;
Then, in the scale of reas'ning life, 'tis plain
There must be, somewhere, such a rank as Man;

And all the question (wrangle e'er so long)
Is only this, if God has plac'd him wrong?

If the rule of an omniscient God over the Great Chain of Being is simply a given—Pope never undertakes to "prove" their existence—then the rest of Epistle I is a pseudo-argument: its conclusions are implicit in its premises. Most modern scholars stress the hierarchical features of the system, its balance and fixed order, the conservative political implications at every level. (Basil Willey dubbed it "cosmic Toryism.")

But what "if 'tis *not* confest?" Is Pope quietly admitting how provisional, or consensual, the scheme is? *Only* if we "confess" the assumptions of lines 44–46 will we finally have to agree that "Whatever IS, is RIGHT" (the program's most sharply criticized deduction, beginning with thinkers as diverse as Voltaire and Johnson). If we take that option and skip directly to Epistle II, Pope himself seems to adopt the anti-metaphysical line ("Know then thyself, presume not God to scan"), although we still encounter the Great Chain of Being, which assumes God.

The famous passage on human contradictions that opens Epistle II, however, does not depend on our accepting the Chain as theology; it merely uses it as an image. If we have another understanding of why humanity "hangs between" higher and lower impulses, "The glory, jest and riddle of the world," fine: Pope's catalog of paradoxes remains one of the great statements of the human condition. Here he has been beforehand with the deconstructionists, depicting us as composed of opposites that check and countercheck, so that every assertion must be qualified. As in the Chain we are inspired by the cherubim and dragged down by the goats, so in the individual psyche we are led upward by reason and abased by passion. The desideratum is balance, and passion is stronger than reason, so the moralist advises, "Reason still use," but notes gloomily, "What Reason weaves, by passion is undone." At times the two may work together, like horse and rider, to produce our strongest virtues.

Some critics have found the shifting roles of reason and passion, self-love and virtue, problematical. Surely that is Pope's point about the human condition, and just as surely it is self-expressive. (He once described the poem to Swift as "an investigation of my own territories.") The objectionable lines on the supposed happiness of beggars and cripples (II, 263–71), which Johnson rightly savaged, are explicable only as a fiction Pope found personally necessary. As Dryden said of Divine Right, "That Kings can do no wrong we must believe."

Pope's sociology derives from his cosmology. As partial evil was shown to be (really) universal good (I, 292), so private good is identified with general good (III, 318). The problem here is that Pope, by subsuming private good and evil in the universal, which he defines as good, seems to argue that selfishness and tyranny do not exist. The distinctions between real and ideal, "is" and "should be," are blurred, and we must often remind ourselves that the poetry transcends the philosophy. Epistle IV is less open to criticism, being mainly a compendium of ethical advice from the classical and Judaeo-Christian traditions. At the end, for example, we are back to Socrates and Delphi: "all our knowledge is, OURSELVES TO KNOW."

An Essay on Man is historically useful as a summary of some European intellectual trends of the time: the reaction against metaphysics, the rationalization of social hierarchies, deism, Optimism, secularism, etc. Its studied avoidance of a specifically Christian interpretation of existence made it controversial at the time, and its internal tensions—viewed as symptomatic of the period—still generate critical interest. "A mighty maze! but not without a plan," it "hangs between" belief and doubt, both a "general map of man" and an inner exploration.

—Richard Bevis

AN ESSAY ON THE PRINCIPLE OF POPULATION.
Prose by Thomas Malthus (1766–1834), 1798; revised edition, 1803.

Critical Studies: *A Reply to the Essay on Population by Malthus* by William Hazlitt, 1807; *Of Population: An Answer to Mr. Malthus's Essay* by William Godwin, 1820; *Malthus and His Work* by James Bonar, 1885; *The Malthusian Controversy* by Kenneth Smith, 1951; *Introduction to Malthus* edited by D.V. Glass, 1953; *Hungry Generations: The Nineteenth-Century Case Against Malthusianism* by H.A. Boner, 1955; *Must Men Starve? The Malthusian Controversy* by Jacob Oser, 1956; *Homage to Malthus* by Jane Nickerson, 1975; *"Population" Malthus: His Life and Times* by Patricia James, 1979; *Malthus* by William Petersen, 1979; *Malthus Past and Present* edited by J. Dupâquier and others, 1983; *Malthus: Critical Assessments* edited by John Cunningham Wood, 4 vols., 1986; *Malthus and His Time* edited by Michael Turner, 1986; *Malthus* by Donald Winch, 1987.

Although most educated people have heard of Thomas Malthus and his theory on population, probably few really understand exactly what he says in *An Essay on the Principle of Population*. Published in 1798, Malthus's essay hummed the umbra's note at a time when the perfectability of man was a widely held view. Indeed, the essay itself grew out of discussions that Malthus had with his father on that subject. Arguing that human population increases geometrically while food production increases arithmetically, Malthus so convinced his father of the substance and originality of his argument that the latter encouraged his son to publish his ideas.

In his essay Malthus reminds the reader early on that to his knowledge, no one "has supposed that on this earth man will ultimately be able to live without food." Nor is it likely in the forseeable future that the passion that draws men and women together sexually will dwindle. Thus it was obvious to Malthus that "unconquerable difficulties" stood in the way of man's struggle for perfectability. A population that unchecked will double itself every 25 years against a food supply that increases at a much lower rate reflects an inequality that would only lead to general misery and vice. Not doubting the talents nor the candor of Godwin and Condorcet, both strong advocates for the perfectability of man, Malthus does question their neglect of the above basic postulates that to him so obviously militated against that hoped for perfection.

The constant movement towards greater population, which Malthus saw even in the most vicious societies, increases the number of people before the necessary means of subsistence are increased. As food is thus divided among more and more people, many are reduced to severe distress. The value of labor is decreased, but the cost of food rises. The result is a decline in marriages and the size of families. Because labor is cheap, however, the landowner cultivates more—and soon an equilibrium is once more reached, but only to be upset again by an increasing birthrate. And so is repeated an oscillation that Malthus says often goes unnoticed because the "histories of mankind that we possess are histories only of the higher classes." And even though, according to Malthus, it is these higher classes that contrive "to prolong a season of distress among the poor, yet no possible form of society could prevent the almost constant action of misery upon a great part of mankind, if in a state of inequality, and upon all, if all were equal."

For Malthus it was incomprehensible that anyone could refute the truth of his position, clearly and solidly based as it was. A population cannot increase without necessary subsistence. A population with necessary subsistence will increase. The superior power of population cannot be checked without causing misery and / or vice. Malthus goes on to say that facts—for example the rapid growth of the English colonies in America—show "that population increases exactly in the proportion that the two great checks to it, misery and vice, are removed, and that there is not a greater criterion of the happiness and innocence of a people than the rapidity of their increase."

The question, of course, is whether there is indeed a correlation between the proclivity for man to reproduce and the ability of the earth to sustain a constantly increasing population. In short, is Malthus's theory irrefutable? Some have dismissed his ideas as nothing more than a restatement of the obvious in an exaggerated mode. Malthus himself said, "It is probable that, having found the bow bent too much one way, I was induced to bend it too much the other in order to make it straight." And there may be some truth in the view that his ideas were readily accepted by higher circles of society because they relieved them of any responsibility for the working poor. But at the same time his argument provided grist for the Darwinian hypothesis that man reaches his greatest level of existence through a constant struggle and competition. Antony Flew sees Malthus's main achievement as practical in nature, an achievement that has "brought questions of national population and individual family size within the sphere of morality and prudence, of policy and decision." And indeed if these questions were ever relevant to society, they surely are today. Malthus's plea was for regulation and direction of the principle of population and of the passions of mankind—not their extinction, or even diminution. The goal of man's perfection is fine, but the happiness of the journey toward that elusive goal is even better.

—Wilton Eckley

ESSAYS.
Prose by Francis Bacon, 1597; revised edition, 1612, 1625.

When Shakespeare in *Lucrece* wrote "Who fears a sentence or an old man's saw?" he was using two terms now grown obsolete: "saw" (a moral saying) and "sentence" (a maxim). They were at that time near-synonyms—a "saw" was a saying, in proverbial and colloquial language, while a "sentence" was written, and was an established literary form.

Any short and well-expressed maxim was a "sentence." (Polonius offered a whole set of them to Laertes in *Hamlet*.) The term sentence has, and had, other meanings, judicial and grammatical. Where the obsolete sense of "moralising maxim" (still present in the adjective "sententious") is intended in this entry, this usage will be distinguished from modern usages by the use of quotation marks (i.e., "sentence").

"Sentence" was an anglicised form of the Latin *sententia*, an aphorism or maxim. It was a regular practice during the Renaissance for writers to make collections in their commonplace books of striking quotations of such *sententiae* or "sentences." Francis Bacon, a man of the late Renaissance, was no exception. The difference was that he wrote his own. A jurist of distinction and a great writer on scientific method, who was to publish in 1605 his important treatise *The Advancement of Learning*, he was in the habit of summarising his reflections, in the form of short epigrammatic notes, written in a taut prose style that he had learned from the Latin authors Seneca and Tacitus, whose succinct styles were coming into vogue, displacing the older use of long-winded Ciceronian periodic sentences.

In 1597 he published a small collection of his "sentences." Borrowing the name (but not the discursive form) from Montaigne he called his book *Essays*, adding the subtitles *Religious Meditations* and *Places of Perswasion and Disswasion*. ("Place" is an old word, now obsolete, for a short isolated piece of writing, i.e. a "sentence.") Bacon's *Essays* tend to be read now in the form appearing in his later editions, particularly that of 1625. Modern reprints of the original 1597 edition do not reproduce the important punctuation, where each short "sentence" is separated off from contiguous "sentences" by the paragraph indicator ¶.

Bacon's first *Essays* were a collection of discrete epigrammatic "sentences" all relating to a central theme. Readers with access to the World's Classics' edition of the *Essays* can find the 1597 form (though not the important paragraph signals) in its appendix. The 1597 collection of "sentences," which comprise the opening essay "Of Studie," is in sharp contrast to the later and better-known 1625 version "Of Studies."

Bacon in 1612 published an enlarged edition, increasing the number of essays from 10 to 38, and in 1625 the number was increased to 58. Not only was the number of essays increased. He rewrote the early essays in a more fluent form, linking up each step in his presentation. The final result was a meditation on a set theme—usually on affairs of state ("Of Great Place", "Of Seditions and Troubles", "Of Judicature") or on moral topics ("Of Usury", "Of Vain-Glory", "Of Revenge") but occasionally on more private themes (the rewritten "Of Studies", "Of Building", "Of Gardens").

It was not the essay as written by Montaigne; even less was it the essay later written by writers like Hazlitt or Lamb or present-day columnists. Indeed, though Bacon introduced the essay into literary practice, the form he created has had no followers. In spite of the more fluent construction of the essays in his final edition, they remain firmly a collection of "sentences," powerfully expressed epigrammatic pronouncements on set topics. "Reading maketh a full man, conference a ready man, and writing an exacte man." So Bacon wrote in his 1597 collection of "sentences" "Of Studie." Precisely the same "sentence" in precisely the same words occurs in the 1625 expanded form of the essay "Of Studies." Bacon had no intention of throwing away any of his early "sentences" and in his later additional essays he found he had established a mode he had no intention of discarding.

The result is that Bacon's *Essays* are a great source of "quotations." Any dictionary of quotations bristles with sayings from Bacon, all apposite, all eminently quotable, the rhetoric of each "sentence" skilful and forceful. For the few who read Bacon's *Essays* there are hundreds who know or have heard of him in quotation. Such is the continuing power of the "sentence." He subtitled his 1625 edition *Counsels, Civil and Moral*; nobody reads his *Essays* for civil or moral counsel. But he provides memorable epigraphs for the chapter headings of innumerable books. His "sentences" live on.

—Ian A. Gordon

THE ESSAYS OF ELIA.
Prose by Charles Lamb, 1823–33.

Charles Lamb's *Elia* essays appeared in the *London Magazine* from 1820 onwards. In 1823 he collected and republished them and in 1833, the year before he died, a second series appeared. More than Lamb himself may have realized, the creation of Elia as his personal artistic voice redressed the tragedy of 22 September 1796, a day of primal horror when his sister Mary, in a fit of insanity, killed their mother and destroyed the Lamb family. Throughout the rest of his life, Lamb was faced with those memories, with Mary's periodic relapses, with his own history of precarious mental health, and with deep-seated personal and career disillusionments. Through Elia, he came to terms with his inner turmoil and composed works that are among the most appealing of the English romantic essays. The first of these essays celebrated the past glory of the South Sea House, indirectly commemorating the centenary of the South Sea Bubble, a financial scheme or hoax that had ruined thousands. Lamb's fascination with illusion (or imagination) and reality—with past and present; innocence and guilt; word and meaning; imperfection and ideality; emptiness and plenitude—provide the fundamental contrasts around which all of his essays are organized. His compositions juxtapose or blend disparate themes and images that neither simple chronology nor logical sequence alone can connect suitably. Somewhat like the discursive poetic meditations of William Wordsworth's romantic verse, Lamb's essays are less formally artistic than works in the classical tradition; they digress, play with the readers' expectations, and sometimes trail off in unfinished propositions.

Elia's textual identity is a function of Lamb's losses and imperfections employed against themselves to present with humor and pathos such subjects as institutions and their odd personages ("South-Sea House," "Old Benchers"), eccentric friends ("Two Races of Men," "Mrs. Battle's Opinions on Whist," "Amicus Redivivus"), poignant childhood memories ("Witches and Other Night-fears," "Christ's Hospital," "Blakesmoor"), personal incidents ("My First Play," "Superannuated Man"), fantasies or whimsical dreams ("A Dissertation on Roast Pig," "Dream Children"), and meditations on books, the minor arts, or life ("Oxford in Vacation," "Old China," "New Year's Eve"). Lamb stated that his pseudonym was borrowed from an Italian co-worker at the South Sea House, his first place of employment 30 years before (Lamb was later employed for many years as a clerk at the prominent East India House). Apart from its anagrammatic significance ("a lie"), Elia is the Italian form of Elijah, the biblical prophet whose passionate declaration of divine intention is ironically diminished in the tranquil, bookish life of his skeptical and little-known namesake, the clerk Elia. Lamb thus satirizes the romantic tendency to see the role of the writer as a visionary seer. Elijah, like the judge Samuel described as appearing from the dead in "Witches and Other Night-fears," was covered with a mantle, symbol of his office. Lamb will assume this mantle ironically, not as the prophetic, priestly seer but as the prosaic essayist.

Mary's frenzy, in which she killed her mother, potentially threatening to reappear in Lamb himself, is epitomized by the rising up of the old man covered with a mantle. This figure becomes for the Elia persona a dark double, the threat of an incoherent inspiration, refracted throughout the essays in a text of interlocking images. Motifs of pictures punctured, of the seductive opening of books and stage curtains, and of the transgression of boundaries and breaching of facades of all kinds express Lamb's aversion to a profane curiosity or visionary intoxication that tears away the mantle of life-in-time. Seeking, with seer-like intensity, to evoke some transcendent ideal, the persona only converts the present into a shroud covering the corpse of a dead past. Whenever the demonic old man threatens to rise up, Lamb swiftly turns as an antidote to the variety, the scintillation, and the familiar vesture of common life.

The physical and social facade presented in Elia's essays becomes the ultimate reality accessible to man:

> I am in love with this green earth; the face of town and country; the unspeakable rural solitudes, and the sweet security of streets[;] . . . sun, and sky, and breeze, and solitary walks, and summer holidays, and the greenness of fields, and the delicious juices of meats and fishes, and society, and the cheerful glass, and candle-light, and fire-side conversations, and innocent vanities, and jests, and *irony itself* ("New Year's Eve").

This catalogue of delights is deceptively simple: its alliteration, personification ("face" of town and country), sudden novelty of diction ("unspeakable"), oxymoron ("innocent vanities"), and the final intellectualized joy of "*irony*" following the more concrete delights (itself pointing up the irony of elevating the material to an almost spiritual plane) indicate a careful, but hidden control of language and theme. Perhaps the finest of all the Elia essays is "Old China," in which the freedom and agelessness of the "old" porcelain teacup figures contrasts with the very real and painful ageing of Elia and his sister Bridget (a Mary Lamb-figure). Bridget argues that youth and vitality made life more worthwhile previously than at present in their more affluent declining years. In youth, the purchase of books was a sacrifice but meaningful; now that Elia can go into the bookseller's "and buy a wilderness of Lionardos," it no longer means as much. The pun on Leonardo da Vinci's name is pure Lamb: "Here be Lions" always marked the wilderness of the Renaissance cartographers. Elia and Bridget may have tamed the wilderness of youth but by maturing have lost the excitement of fresh exploration. Elia, however, argues that he and his sister at tea frame the porcelain fantasia on their cups with a richer perspective: "And now do just look at that merry little Chinese waiter holding an umbrella, big enough for a bed-tester, over the head of that pretty insipid half-Madonnaish chit of a lady in that very blue summer-house." This blue and merry world with the vivacious and pretty lady may possess qualities that Bridget and Mary Lamb lack; but Elia implies that perhaps Bridget and Mary have surpassed the "chit" by their more human emotional depth and perspective that comes only with time and the loss of youth. This awareness, too, is as much a part of the green earth's reality as sun, sky, and irony.

—Gerald Monsman

EUPHUES.
Prose by John Lyly, 1578.

No other prose work of the English Renaissance shares the power of John Lyly's *Euphues* to dazzle us with its rhetorical display and ingenuity even while it seriously challenges and questions that very rhetoric. In fact, the two most vexing concerns of humanism—the capacities of man and the efficacies of a humanist education—are directly addressed throughout *Euphues*. "If nature canne no waye resist the furye of affection," one of the characters asks, "howe shall it be stayed by wisdome?" The question is an urgent one for Lucilla, whose name means "little light," for her life is especially troublesome and undirected and she finds that humanist rhetoric has so many different techniques at its instant command that she can be powerfully persuasive on any issue she likes and take any position she wants. She loves Euphues, but to pledge herself to him means breaking a prior pledge to Philautus, and this in turn makes any future pledge of hers suspect. What is she to do? When she learns further, as the other characters all will in turn, that she can only think, reason, and understand by using concepts conveyed in such words capable of treason, she finds her whole world collapses into a kind of doublethink or, worse, into falsehood, fabrication, and superficiality—into inauthenticity.

Such an inquiry penetrates humanism to its very core, and by the grandson of the first great humanist educator, William Lily, the friend of Thomas More and the author of the grammar school textbook under Henry VIII. But in tracing his prodigal characters as they hoard, spend, enrich, or cheapen their world through language, Lily suggests that the world itself is always a wider schoolroom where we cannot avoid learning, and the questions that learning poses for us. Thus Lily's grand fiction reverses that of an author like Castiglione who argues that style—that *sprezzatura*—can create through a society of manners a world of high polish, a true civilization. Instead, Lyly would examine that polish with a tough scrutiny that asks just what substance lies behind style. His own prose style is a primary instance. At first it seems impenetrable, and then, as we grow accustomed to it, we find it repetitive and cloying. It is based in absolute balance—balance of ideas, of syntax, and of sounds. But the style itself both constitutes Lyly's story and complicates and critiques it. Because the more we study the structure of incidents and sentences in *Euphues*, the more we discover that they break in half and pull in opposite directions. What the first half of an incident, a speech, or a sentence constructs, the second half always inverses, and thus challenges through destruction: we seem to be left with zero sum. The style is only superficially polished; it is fundamentally—or it can be—nihilistic. Style, then, is another way in which *Euphues* questions at some fundamental level the way men think and speak and know their being—or don't know what they think they know. In fact, the name Euphues is taken from a word Lyly knew from another humanist educator—Roger Ascham—who in his book *The Schoolmaster* (1570) noted that *euphues* denoted a quick wit—a mind which learned something swiftly but did not retain it. Such men, says Ascham—who was himself the tutor of Elizabeth I—make good poets but not wise orators: they can do fancy tricks with language but their understanding is (consequently) shallow. In a way which is remarkably modern Lyly uses *style* to convey *meaning*: style and matter, manner and meaning are reversible, identical, *indivisible*.

These are important recognitions to bring to a story which is, after all, nothing more than the old tale of the prodigal son who through his mistakes learns to mend his ways. Euphues is betrayed by what is superficial, just as those who see deep meaning in Euphues's rich array of proverbs and classical allusions and the use of unnatural natural history are betrayed by the dazzling surfaces of his style. We must realize that logic, not rhetoric, the use of reason (as orators employ it) and not sounds (as poets use), is what leads to truth and understanding. Lyly's story, then, tests language and learning in Eubulus's schoolroom with what actually happens to Euphues in the world itself; and the clear meaning of *Euphues* is that learning untested by experience is not true learning at all. This, too, might seem to be only the story of the prodigal son revisited, but Lyly has accomplished far more than that. In his own dazzling accomplishment by which he tests humanist ideas and principles by using humanism's own methods, he also writes one of the most important fictions of maturation or coming of age, one of the most popular *Bildungsromane*, of the English Renaissance.

—Arthur F. Kinney

THE EVE OF ST. AGNES.
Poem by John Keats, 1820.

"The Eve of St. Agnes," a narrative poem drafted by John Keats during a brief vacation from London in 1819, was published the next year in his great volume *Lamia, Isabella, The Eve of St. Agnes, and Other Poems*. The legendary tale of young love advances like the frames of a film through 42 richly sensuous Spenserian stanzas. In each stanza, eight pictorial lines of iambic pentameter are completed with firm closure by a longer Alexandrine.

Set more claustrally within its mediaeval manor than Coleridge's similar "Christabel," the poem even in summary evokes Shakespeare's *Romeo and Juliet*. On St. Agnes's Eve, Porphyro ventures into the mansion of revelling family enemies to woo their virgin Madeline. The ancient nurse Angela protests with strong words Porphyro's design for viewing and winning Madeline in her chamber, but upon his promise to do nothing blameworthy she provides everything necessary for his scheme. The reader has been told, and Angela confirms, that Madeline is conforming to the folk rituals of St. Agnes's Eve by going supperless to bed in order to dream of a visit in the middle of the night from her future husband. A stanza excised by the publishers told of delicious viands the lover would provide for her palate.

In the paradise of Madeline's chamber, Porphyro provides the prescribed delicacies, strums on her lute the ancient tune "La belle dame sans mercy," and wraps his arm about the undressed body of his sleeping prize. He so creates in actuality the substance of her dream that she wakes in piteous fear of accomplished disaster. Assuring her that the wind and sleet outside are "an elfin-storm," he draws her hastily out of the manor and across the icy moors toward his own estate. "And they are gone: ay, ages long ago / These lovers fled away into the storm."

The story is negligible only in comparison with the memorable phrasing and the masterly structure. The poem opens in the bitter chill of an old-time 20 January. Owl and hare are cold. With numb fingers the barefoot Beadsman pities the sculptured dead, icy in "purgatorial rails," as he shuffles toward the chapel to pray for the family's ancestors. The Beadman is as good as dead—more decidedly than Angela a "churchyard thing." He is flattered to tears by the "argent revelry" in the warmed hall beyond the chapel. These, says the poet of the chill and the revellers, "let us wish away." Warmth increases in intensity until at the center of the poem it achieves the maiden's chamber and then the heat of Porphyro's embrace. With the silver trumpets silent and the house asleep, the lovers glide like phantoms past the drunken porter and into the cold night. The poem ends as it began; nightmares of the baron and his guests presage chill and death. Angela and the Beadsman died long ago.

Imagery supports and enforces the structure. Silver revelry is a fragile barrier to protect white from red. Encountering the crimson of passion, innocence pales almost to the frost of death. Porphyro's stratagem "came like a full-blown rose," flushing his brow and bringing "purple riot" to his heart. Through the casement window—which Keats, with much effort of rewriting, made triple-arched—the wintry moon "threw warm gules on Madeline's fair breast." Rose-bloom fell on her hands before she slept in blanched linen as though "a rose should shut, and be a bud again." Her silver cross belongs to a realm of silence that excludes the "festive clarion"; the moon fades to a silver twilight as Porphyro loads the bedside table with candied quince and lucent syrups. After praying as a hermit on pilgrimage to Madeline as a wingless angel deserving heaven, "Into her dream he melted, as the rose / Blendeth its odour with the violet."

Into this vivid tapestry is woven a pattern of enchantment, elves, and magicians, the appropriation of Christian emblems and rituals by Porphyro and Merlin. Madeline herself is trapped in the pagan conversion of *Agnus Dei* into *Agnes Dies*. The revelry, like shadows of old romance haunting the brain, is background to a contrived actuality that encloses one dream within another. Angela says Porphyro must be liege-lord of fays to venture thus into a den of fanged wolves. Porphyro imagines Madeline enchanted by fairies pacing her coverlet. He peers breathlessly as her falling attire half hides her "like a mermaid in sea-weed." Most crucially there is the storm, granted by the poetic voice and the love-inflamed protagonist to be fierce, but declared by Porphyro "an elfin-storm from faery land" because it will allow escape from the "bloated wassaillers."

Debate among scholars over Keats's sources for the poem may reflect a complexity in his own sense of poetic ancestry and influenced creativity. The influence-minded Robert Gittings, without rejecting Shakespeare, Spenser, Coleridge, or Radcliffe, proposes also a collection of French romances, Lasinio's engravings of the frescoes in the Campo Santo at Pisa, the tombs and windows of Chichester cathedral, and a carnal affair with one Isabella Jones.

Readers for more than a century admired the poem as a fairy-tale contrasting the elders in the final stanza who dreamed of witch, demon, and coffin-worm—and died long ago—with the lovers who fled into the open and lived happily ever after. Recent sensibilities have found truth in the chill and death of the opening and close: sleet is cold, moors are wide, and death comes to all. It has been proposed that Porphyro hoodwinks Madeline. It is distinctly Keatsian to regard the supernatural, in "The Eve of St. Agnes" and elsewhere, as a human way of relishing a life of the senses.

—Carl Woodring

EVELINA.
Novel by Fanny Burney, 1778.

As its earliest reviews pointed out, the content as well as the style of Fanny Burney's first novel *Evelina* made it obviously suitable as family entertainment. (Burney's father, to whom the book is dedicated, and her sisters, once in the secret of its anonymous authorship, certainly found entertainment in reading it to each other and—even better—to those not yet in the know, including the second Mrs. Burney.) Told in a series of letters between a beautiful and innocent girl, making her début in the fashionable world, and the wise old guardian, Mr. Villars, who has brought her up in seclusion, Evelina's story offered amusing lessons on how (and how not) to behave in polite society, as well as satirical observations on that society's shortcomings. Evelina's faltering progress through London's plays, operas, balls, and pleasure-gardens is not just a social education, though; it is also a search for recognition and love. Until Evelina's real father, Sir John Belmont, acknowledges his marriage to her mother, Caroline Evelyn, and Evelina's identity as his daughter, she remains an anomaly, "a girl of obscure birth, whose only dowry is her beauty," unmarriageable to anyone of her rightful class, but unfitted by her genteel education to marry outside it. Her name itself—Evelina Anville—is a fiction, a coded reference to her apparently illegitimate state, the mother's maiden name feminized and scrambled in anagram. Belmont's denial means that, both linguistically and socially, Evelina is "nobody."

Evelina's ignorance of social forms involves her in frequent blunders and embarrassments, earning her the antagonism of the sneering fop Lovel, whom she accidentally snubs at a dance, but also attracting the attention of the gentle and considerate Lord Orville, whom she eventually marries. Much misunderstood, Evelina often finds herself unable to move or speak, hardly able to stand, blushing, crying, and fainting through embarrassment, fear, or vexation. Her experience of London society is a physically violent one, even in comparatively public places; she is pulled, tugged, grabbed, detained, and even kidnapped. The violence increases once she is reluctantly handed over by Villars to her bullying maternal grandmother, Madame Duval, who drags Evelina into the rough-and-tumble world of her vulgar cousins the Branghtons. Evelina finds herself on the wrong side of town, in an intensified version of every teenager's nightmare, unable to escape from her appallingly embarrassing family.

Evelina herself, struggling with the complexities of her situation, complains to her suitor Lord Orville that "I hardly know myself to whom I most belong," but her mother's relations obviously aren't the answer. Returning to Berry Hill, Villars's country home, dejected by her experiences and by a temporary misunderstanding of Orville's intentions, Evelina is sent to the spa of Bristol Hotwells to recover her health and discover her real family. It is Evelina's striking resemblance to her wronged mother—the "certificate of your birth . . . which you carry in your countenance," as Villars calls it—which determines Belmont's final, painful acknowledgement, in a passionate scene which moved contemporary readers (including Burney's own father) to tears. But Evelina Belmont does not enjoy her new name for long; she signs only one of her letters with it before she marries Lord Orville and sets off to honeymoon at Berry Hill, eagerly anticipating her reunion with Villars, "the Parent my heart acknowledges."

Critics have noted a discrepancy between the stammering, often speechless girl Evelina appears to be in the scenes she presents and the confidence of her narrative voice. Certainly Evelina as narrator has a sharp eye not only for her own discomfiture through ignorance of social rules, but for the foibles of others at all levels from the empty-headed gambler Lord Merton, setting up a race between two old women so he can bet on it, down to Samuel Johnson's favourite character in the novel, the impossibly conceited "Holborn Beau" Mr. Smith, convinced that every woman he meets is angling to marry him.

Much of Burney's comedy in *Evelina* is dependent on class and social convention; Mr. Smith is much funnier because he doesn't understand correct gentlemanly behaviour but still thinks he is a gentleman, just as Madame Duval and the Branghtons are comical because they don't know how to behave at the opera (and dreadful because they insist on dragging Evelina along with them). The coarse and hearty Captain Mirvan provides a rougher, more antisocial humour, with his nautical oaths and his violent practical jokes: Madame Duval is kidnapped, bound, and thrown into a ditch, while the foppishly dressed monkey Captain Mirvan introduces as Lovel's brother nearly bites Lovel's ear off (the comic climax of the book).

Contemporary readers' enjoyment of this cruel and boisterous streak in Burney's comedy seems as strange now as their ecstatic reaction to the sentimental melodrama of Evelina's scenes with her father; certainly these elements make it difficult to read *Evelina* as the delicate and sensitive comedy of 18th-century manners some critics have thought it. Evelina's marriage to the completely unthreatening paragon Lord Orville (whose character clearly owes much to Richardson's Sir Charles Grandison) is a muted business, overshadowed by Villars's joyful anticipation of his deathbed blessing to Evelina, "closing these joy-streaming eyes in her presence, and breathing my last faint sighs in her loved arms!" There is passion in *Evelina*, but—appropriately enough—the novel keeps it, too, in the family.

—Caroline Gonda

EVERY MAN IN HIS HUMOUR.
Play by Ben Jonson, 1598.

Along with Shakespeare, Ben Jonson shines as one of the brightest stars writing for the Elizabethan and Jacobean stage. *Every Man in His Humour* launched Jonson's playwriting career in 1598 in impressive fashion. The Lord Chamberlain's company, of which Shakespeare was part owner, first staged *Every Man In His Humour* with such noticeable success that Jonson's reputation was securely established. *Every Man in His Humour* is significant in dramatic history for two principal reasons: the play laid the groundwork for comic realism on the English stage, and it codified and popularized the comedy of humours. The "humours" concept, which reaches back to quasi-medical theories of the ancients, hypothesized that man contained four distinct bodily fluids which determine his physical health and temperament. An imbalance of the fluids—or "humours" —would tilt the personality of the person toward a specific eccentricity associated with the excessive element. For instance, an excess of "blood" (one of the four humours) meant that the person would be sanguine, or exuberant; excessive "phlegm" led to a sluggish constitution; too much "black bile" led to melancholy; and a surplus of "yellow bile" meant the person would be choleric or easily angered. Elizabethan psychology lent support to the long-standing notions concerning the humours, but it was Jonson with *Every Man in His Humour* who extended those theories into workable characters in drama—a fact to be explored later.

Every Man in His Humour revives certain key features from classical drama, particularly from Plautus' comedies. Like those plays, *Every Man in His Humour* centers on a love plot involving a well-born young man (Edward Knowell) seeking the hand of a girl of lesser birth (Bridget). But, in Northrop Frye's terms, young Knowell encounters a blocking figure in courting Bridget, in this instance, his well-intentioned but overly solicitous father. A generational conflict takes shape when the older Knowell intercepts a letter to his son from Wellbred, a young city playboy, who invites Edward Knowell into London for a siege of wine, women, and song. Jonson's loose plot thus involves the spying father following his son into the big, evil city in a vain attempt to spare the lad from potentially disastrous mishaps—such as an ill-advised marriage. Jonson borrows another device from classical drama, the clever trickster who assists the youthful lover in his amorous quest. Brainworm is the elder Knowell's servant, but he chooses to ally himself with the younger Knowell. Throughout the comedy, Brainworm assumes various disguises that help keep Knowell from catching up with his son until the marriage is safely concluded. Then—again using Frye's pattern—a new society is formulated around the young couple to revitalize the total community.

Ultimately, boy will get girl, and parents will have to accept it. Meanwhile, laughs abound as both old Knowell and Edward Knowell experience comical adventures in the city. Jonson's unique strength with comical realism emerges in the expansive portrait he paints of life in the London of his day. As it originally was written and performed in 1598, *Every Man in His Humour* was set in Florence, and all the characters carried Italian names. Even so, English audiences recognized themselves in Jonson's portraits of London citizens. To make even surer of the connection, however, Jonson recast the comedy in 1612, setting the action in London and renaming the characters as unmistakably English personages. Moreover, all the characters display humours which both contribute to the plot complications and to the overall fun of the play.

Old Knowell's name, for example, suggests that he believes he knows it all so that, not surprisingly, he is quick with *sententiae* for everyone he meets in the play. The crafty servant who helps his young master, Brainworm, carries a name that describes his special attribute, his braininess in concocting devices to throw old Knowell off the track. Jonson's purview in *Every Man in His Humour* includes fascinating eccentrics from all social classes, as well. Edward's bride, Mistress Bridget, is sister to the London merchant Thomas Kitely, who proves to be an insanely jealous husband, hence exhibiting excess yellow bile. And like a kite—a preying hawk—Kitely is eternally watching over his spouse in the belief that she is cuckolding him. Kitely's employee, a cashier named Thomas Cash, is kept perpetually on the run, spying on Dame Kitely on behalf of his boss. George Downright is described as a "plain squire," and he too is ever on the lookout for immoral city behaviour. Eventually his choleric temperament (again, a surplus of yellow bile) leads him to beat up on some of the city fops.

And fops appear in profusion in *Every Man in His Humour*. Jonson plays no favourites, introducing Edward's cousin Master Stephen as a country gull, while Master Matthew serves as city fool. Stephen goes into town to pick up sophisticated city mannerisms, and Matthew is a foolish poetaster who steals verses to pawn off as his own. Captain Bobadill is a combination of the classical braggart soldier—overflowing with bravado and bluster—and a phlegmatic "Paul's Man"—that is, an unemployed idler seen loafing around the city's popular meeting spots. Jonson generates great laughter when the innocents, Stephen and Matthew, turn to the craven Bobadill for lessons on how to become roisterers. Then, too, Jonson sketches in Oliver Cob and his wife Tib, lower-class water-bearers in London who become caught up in the tricks and disguises masterminded by Brainworm and Edward. Finally, the charades and misunderstandings in the plot are unravelled in the courtroom of Justice Clement. A bit zany in his own right, Justice Clement realizes that young Knowell simply desires to have his lady. At play's end Clement convinces the elder Knowell to accept the situation.

In contrast to Shakespeare's romantic comedies, *Every Man in His Humour* remains satiric in tone, dedicated (as Jonson writes in the prologue to the 1612 version) to "deeds and language such as men do use: / And persons such as comedy would choose / When she would show an image of the times, / And sport with human follies, not with crimes."

—C.J. Gianakaris

EVERYMAN.
Play, c.1510–35.

Editions

Elckerlijk and Everyman, edited by Henri Logemann. 1892.
Everyman, edited by A.C. Cawley. 1961.
The Summoning of Everyman, edited by Geoffrey Cooper and Christopher Wortham. 1980.
Three Late Medieval Morality Plays, edited by G.A. Lester. 1981.

Critical Studies: "Is *Elckerlijc* Prior to *Everyman*?" by E.R. Tigg, in *Journal of English and Germanic Philology*, 38, 1939; *Everyman: A Comparative Study of Texts and Sources* by Henry de Vocht, 1947; "*Everyman*: A Structural Analysis" by Thomas F. Van Laan, in *Publications of the Modern Language Association*, 78, 1963.

Everyman survives in two complete early editions and two fragments. These are dated c.1510–35, though some scholars have estimated the original to have been published as early as c.1495. The play's main source is the late 15th-century Flemish play *Elckerlijc*. The English dramatist has drawn on this extensively but not slavishly, elaborating the rather stilted verse of the original to produce more natural-sounding lines of varying length arranged in a wide variety of verse forms. There are more than 100 imperfect rhymes, some probably the result of textual corruption. Surprisingly, though, the resultant style is well suited to expressing strong emotion, and has been often admired.

Morality plays, which were popular in Britain in the 15th and 16th centuries, dramatise a spiritual crisis in the life of a character representing all human kind. This crisis is depicted externally as a conflict between personified abstractions or social types signifying good and evil, who try to influence the central figure for the better or for the worse. The ethical values are those of the medieval church, and the main theme is that God's mercy is always available to those who repent, no matter how abominable the sin. *Everyman* portrays a human being's struggle to raise himself to a state of grace so that he may die a holy death, confident in the expectation of everlasting life. Because the action is confined narrowly to the last phase of life, it is unlike the other moralities, some of which depict life from the cradle to the grave. The broader time-span normally gives playwrights the opportunity to show fallen man indulging in all sorts of wicked pursuits, to the great amusement of the audience. The dramatist of *Everyman* forfeits this opportunity for bawdy humour, but gains instead a spine-chilling seriousness.

The narrative framework can be traced to the eastern folktale of the Faithful Friend, which was well-known in medieval times and was sometimes used as an exemplary story by preachers. It tells of a man who is summoned to appear before the king. When he approaches his friends for support he finds that those whom he has loved and trusted soon desert him, whereas the one to whom he has given least regard agrees to accompany him, plead for him, and stick by him to the last. The adaptation of this basic story to include the strong theme of death and the need to prepare for it is typical of the 15th century, in which the fascinated revulsion for the subject is reflected in poetry, prose, art, and ecclesiastical monuments.

The play begins with God, who makes an impassioned complaint that Everyman (i.e. "every man" or "every human being") is living a life of sin and that the time has come for him to be summoned to give account of himself. He therefore sends his messenger, Death, who "arrests" Everyman by touching him with his dart. Whereas this would normally signify the moment of death, after which repentance is too late, dramatic convention requires that Everyman be given some time to put his affairs in order (otherwise, presumably, there would be no play). So Death goes away with the assurance that he will soon return. Everyman's first thought is to look for help from those he has loved in life—Fellowship, Kindred, Cousin, and Goods. As these make their excuses he falls increasingly into despair. As a last resort he turns to his Good Deeds, but finds her weakened by his neglect. Good Deeds, however, directs him to her sister Knowledge (i.e., "acknowledgement of one's sins" and possibly also "understanding"), and the process of Everyman's regeneration begins with the receipt of the sacrament of Penance. As he scourges himself his Good Deeds arise revivified from the ground. He is joined by four more friends—Discretion, Strength, Beauty, and Five Wits—who wait until he has received extreme unction from a priest, and then set out with him on the journey to the grave. However, at the graveside, where Death probably reappears but does not speak, his four new friends desert him, symbolising the fact that physical attributes are of no help at the moment of most need. Good

Deeds alone accompanies Everyman into the grave, above which his soul is then shown being welcomed in heaven by an angel.

Structurally the play is divided into two balanced parts, the false friends of the first part contrasting with the true friends of the second. This balance extends to details such as the pairing of Goods, immobilised by excess, and Good Deeds, helpless through neglect. Everyman's desperate cries for help in the first part are set against his measured prayers in the second, his fear of the passing of time against his later eagerness to proceed "without tarrying," and his expressions of pain against his rejoicing in the self-imposed suffering which he now knows to be the means by which all pain will ultimately be overcome.

—G.A. Lester

THE EXETER BOOK.
Manuscript of poetry, 10th century.

Editions and Translations

The Anglo-Saxon Poetic Records, vol. 3, edited by G.P. Krapp and E. van K. Dobbie. 1936.
Anglo-Saxon Poetry, translated by S.A.J. Bradley. 1982.

Critical Studies: introductions by R.W. Chambers, Max Förster, and Robin Flower to *The Exeter Book of Old English Poetry* (facsimile), 1933; article by Kathleen M. Dexter, in *Leofric of Exeter*, 1972.

The Exeter Book, almost certainly referred to in the list of Bishop Leofric's donations to Exeter Cathedral as "·i· mycel Englisc boc be ge-hwilcu*m* þingu*m* on leodwisan ge-worht" (one great English book written in poetry about various things), ranks among the most important surviving artifacts of Anglo-Saxon culture. Only three other manuscript collections of Anglo-Saxon verse are extant (the Junius Manuscript, the Vercelli Book, and Cotton Vitellius A. xv., also called the *Beowulf* manuscript), and none contains the Exeter Book's variety of genre and style: religious narrative verse, secular verse representing early Germanic culture (*Widsith* and *Deor*), elegiac and wisdom poems, and riddles. We have no other instance of a bishop acquiring such an eclectic manuscript and at his death (1072) donating it (among other gifts, including land, church furniture, vestments, and 66 manuscripts, 11 of which are not ecclesiastic) to a cathedral library.

The provenance of the Exeter Book in itself is emblematic of late Anglo-Saxon culture's mixture of cosmopolitan sophistication and the day-to-day lack of security. Leofric, probably not English-born and certainly educated in Lotharingia (the modern-day Low Countries), was appointed Bishop of Crediton by Edward the Confessor as a reward for his service as "the king's chancellor" (at that time head secretary of the royal household). Appointment of foreign clergy to high-ranking episcopal positions in England, rather than being unusual and solely characteristic of Edward's predispositions after his exile on the continent, was precedented by, for instance, Alfred's appointment of the Saxon Grimbald to an important post and Canute's appointment of Duduc, either a Saxon or a Lotharingian, Bishop of Wells. Later Leofric became first Bishop of Exeter when Edward the Confessor approved the removal of the episcopal seat to the better-protected Exeter after depredations of pirates proved Crediton unsafe. Because Leofric, with his continental roots, included the Exeter Book among his donations to Exeter, he is responsible for the survival of literature that shows us some of the richness, sophistication, and diversity of Anglo-Saxon culture that would otherwise be unknown to us.

Most scholars (the important exception is Robin Flower) agree that the Exeter Book is the work of a single scribe who meticulously copied miscellaneous poetry into the codex. Another scribe seems to have inserted a few corrections, and some time before the 16th century eight folio leaves were appended to the beginning of the Exeter Book proper. These leaves, the first of which is blank and unnumbered, contain one of two extant copies of an Anglo-Saxon list of Leofric's donations to Exeter, a Latin abstract of the list, and records of other gifts to the cathedral. Perhaps most important, however, are copies of 32 legal documents, often written with spellings that provide rich evidence about the transition from Old English to Middle English between the second half of the 11th century, when Leofric died, and the second quarter of the 12th century, during the reign of Henry I, when the dates for the last legal transactions occur. In addition to their philological interest, these documents provide important information about 12th-century legal practices, especially manumission.

The poetry of the Exeter Book, though not all of equal interest to a 20th-century reader, includes some of the most frequently anthologized and translated Old English poems, such as *The Wanderer*, *The Seafarer*, and *The Phoenix*, as well as a variety of examples of hagiographic poetry (*Guthlac* A and B and *Juliana*), didactic or homiletic verse (*The Gifts of Men*, *Vainglory*, *The Fortunes of Men*, *The Order of the World*, and *Judgment Day* I), shorter religious poems ("The Descent into Hell," "Alms-Giving," "Pharaoh," "The Lord's Prayer" I, and "Homiletic Fragment" II), Anglo-Saxon versions of the Latin Physiologus tradition ("The Panther," "The Whale," and "The Partridge"), wisdom verse ("Maxims" I), 91 or 94 riddles, depending on how the editors understand the text, as well as other poems more difficult to classify generically (*The Ruin*, *Widsith*, *Deor*, *The Riming Poem*, *Wulf and Eadwacer*, *The Wife's Lament*, *The Husband's Message*). The dates of the poems vary widely as does authorship. Only one author has been identified with any certainty: Cynewulf's runic signature closes both *Christ* II and *Juliana*.

The Exeter Book now consists of 131 parchment leaves. Before the eight preliminary leaves were bound with the volume of poetry, the book was damaged at front and back and several leaves were lost. The greatest damage was inflicted either by fire or corrosive liquid on the final 14 folios. The loss of at least eight interior leaves results for certain in a gap of one leaf in *Christ* II and *Guthlac* A, a fragmentary ending to *Guthlac* B and beginning to *Azarias*, two gaps in the text of *Juliana*, another in "The Partridge," a probable missing ending to Riddle 20, and a missing end to Riddle 40 and beginning to Riddle 41. In addition the first poem, *Christ* I, lacks a beginning; some critics, notably A.S. Cook, believe leaves are also missing at the end of the manuscript, though Max Förster, Frederick Tupper, Krapp and Dobbie, and Williamson all treat the final riddle as complete. Many scholars believe that the scribe of the Exeter Book worked from a pre-existing compilation since the stately quality of the manuscript shows little sign of being a "first draft." Another possible explanation for the unusually large writing and wide margins is its intended use as a school text. Others believe that the apparently random order, especially of the last sections of the manuscript, suggests that the scribe added poems as they became available to him. The beginning of the manuscript is consistent in treating the beginnings of poems with a line of capitals. (Despite this consistency, early editors used their own judgment rather than manuscript evidence, thus treating the three *Christ* poems at the beginning of the manuscript as one poem, treating *Guthlac* A and B as one poem, and treating the end of *Christ* III as the beginning of *Guthlac* A.) The first letter of a subsection is often given a large, ornate capital, with the rest of the word or a few of the letters sometimes in small capitals. As the manuscript progresses, there is less distinction between major divisions separating poems and minor divisions within poems.

There are many editions of the Exeter Book and translations of individual poems. Most notable is the superb facsimile *The Exeter Book of Old English Poetry: With Introductory Chapters by R.W. Chambers, Max Förster and Robin Flower*, which in some instances, assisted by ultraviolet light, provides clearer readings even than the manuscript itself now offers to the naked eye. The introductory chapters contain a mine of information that is nearly always reliable as well as texts from the appended eight leaves and, for instance, a Middle English version of the Donations of Leofric (Exeter Charter no. 2570).

—Phyllis Rugg Brown

F

THE FAERIE QUEENE.
Poem by Edmund Spenser, 1590–96.

The Faerie Queene, the great work which engaged Edmund Spenser during his years of semi-exile in Ireland, is the supreme expression of Elizabethan court poetry. No English poem of comparable literary stature has appealed, for widely different reasons, to so many later poets or proved so elusive to critical definition. Milton admired its author as "a better teacher than Scotus or Aquinas." Keats, Shelley, and Byron used the Spenserian stanza to varied effect, and Wordsworth spoke of "Sweet Spenser, moving through his clouded heaven / With the moon's beauty and the moon's soft pace." The variety of these responses suggests the difficulty which faces any attempt to define the nature of Spenser's achievement by confining it to any limiting critical formula.

The difficulty does not arise from any failure on the poet's part to state his purpose. In a letter to Sir Walter Ralegh, prefixed to the 1590 edition of the first three Books, Spenser said that "the general end . . . of all the book is to fashion a gentleman or noble person in virtue and gentle discipline." He also pointed to the influence of previous writers—Homer, Virgil, Ariosto, and Tasso—"by example of which excellent poets I labour to portray in Arthur, before he was king, the image of a brave knight, perfected in the twelve private moral virtues." He goes on to say that these virtues are "the purpose of these first twelve books, which if I find to be well accepted, I may be perhaps encouraged to frame the other part of politic virtues in his person, after that he came to be king." Finally, he states that "In that Faery Queen I mean glory in my general intention, but in my particular I conceive the most excellent and glorious person of our sovereign the Queen, and her kingdom in Fairy Land."

The application to the poem of this plan, which seems to envisage a work four times as long as the huge fragment actually completed, is fraught with difficulties. Most obviously, we have only six books and what seems to be the fragment of a seventh, published for the first time as "Two Cantos of Mutability" after the poet's death. Further, it is possible to find a certain completeness in the poem as it stands. A plan could be discerned in which Book I, dedicated to the adventures of the Knight of the Red Cross representing Holiness in search of the truth to be found in unity, might be linked to Book VI, in which the exploits of Sir Calidore, embodying the virtue of Courtesy, show holiness in action in the ideal courtly world. Similarly Book II, which presents in Sir Guyon the virtue of Temperance, might be linked to Book V, where the adventures of Sir Artegall show the same virtue engaged in advancing the values of Justice in a difficult public world. According to this plan Books III and IV, dealing with the stories of Britomart and of Cambel and Triamond, would constitute the turning-point of the whole conception. The two Books are united by the presence in them of the female knight Britomart, who represents in the third Book the virtue of Chastity, but who is linked in the fourth with Friendship to stress the fact, centrally important for Spenser's work, that the traditional virtue finds its fulfilment, not in ascetic denial of the flesh or withdrawal from the world, but in the socially central and creative relationship of marriage. If this possible scheme has any validity, the two Cantos on Mutability would constitute less the fragment of a seventh Book than a kind of coda placing the whole project in a philosophic context which turns on the relationship between the human world of temporal vicissitude and the timeless order of spiritual reality. This, in the last stanza of the work, is "that same time when no more Change shall be"; for, though it is true that "all that moveth, doth in Change delight," the poet asks us, as his final word, to join him in looking beyond this truth to a state in which "all shall rest eternally / With Him that is the God of Sabboath height," as he addresses the final source of all reality: "O that great Sabboath God, grant me that Sabboath's sight."

The scheme just outlined is, like any other that we might propose, tentative and uncertain. What is certain is that Spenser in writing his poem set out to rival or surpass the practitioners of the Arthurian epic as cultivated in Italy, more particularly by Ariosto in his *Orlando Furioso*. It would be difficult, however, to think of two poems more different in feeling and intention. Ariosto is essentially a narrator, who delights in his ability to keep an endless flow of incident moving and who projects upon his fantastic world the light of a pervasive comic irony. The effect of Spenser's poem is at once less consistent and more closely tied to the moral vision which has gone to its making.

These influences grow into rich complexity as the poem unfolds. In Book I the Red Cross Knight, representing the Holiness which is the source of all virtue, is accompanied by Una, who is Truth made manifest in unity. The pair proceed through a series of trials which correspond to the temptations of doctrinal error and the moral ills occasioned by it. The development of the allegory, however, is not one of simple correspondence. The Red Cross Knight, besides representing Holiness, is also Everyman in pursuit of that virtue and in need of the help of Grace and the possession of Truth to arrive at his goal. Similarly, in Book II, we are asked to see Sir Guyon both as representing the virtue of Temperance, a compound of equanimity, prudence, and self-control, and as a figure once again of Everyman who overcomes a variety of ills by arriving at a reasonable relationship between body and soul.

Up to this point the reader of the poem can feel that he is following a pattern of allegorical meanings which correspond to the development of the narrative. Already, however, submission to the poetry elicits a more complex response. This becomes apparent, for example, at the end of Book II, in the long description of the Bower of Bliss and of the witch Acrasia, the personified temptation at its heart. The poetry requires us both to respond to the real force of the passions called forth by Acrasia and to maintain a firm moral judgement in their regard. Words and phrases which stress the languor and artificiality which underlie the surface attraction are interwoven with others which relate to a more positive human perception. Spenser's aim is not to present a pre-established contrast between virtue and vice, but to embody the conflicting pressures which play upon real human experience. The resolution of the conflict is to be moral and life-affirming, but it will not be arrived at by prejudging the issues at stake.

Similarly in the allegorical scheme of the third and fourth Books Britomart, representing Chastity, emerges with the force of a real, breathing person. Her adventures concern an exploration of the meaning of real human love, conveyed through contrast and interaction with a series of other feminine figures—Amoret, Belphoebe, and Florimel—who represent varying facets of this moving force in the lives of men and women. In Book III Britomart affirms triumphantly the traditional virtue of Chastity. In Book IV, ostensibly dedicated to Cambel and Triamond in embodiment of male friendship, the exploration of love, its true sense and meaning, continues as Britomart is first involved in combat with Artegall and finally submits to the natural force of love.

Spenser's presentation of love in these two Books combines Platonic elements with traditional notions of courtly love, separating in the latter a true ideal from its barren and enslaving shadow. The ideal of chastity represented is not simply one of virginity defended against the assaults of the world, but rather of its natural fulfilment against a background of life-affirming acceptance eloquently declared in the apotheosis of Venus in her temple:

Great Venus, Queene of beautie and of grace,
  The joy of Gods and men, that under skie
  Dost fayrest shine, and most adorne thy place,
  That with thy smyling looke doest pacifie
  The raging seas, and makst the stormes to flie;
  Thee goddesse, thee the winds, the clouds do feare,
  And when thou spredst thy mantle forth on hie,
  The waters play and pleasant lands appeare,
And heavens laugh, and al the world shews joyous
    cheere . . .

So all the world by thee at first was made,
  And dayly yet thou doest the same repayre:
  Ne ought on earth that merry is and glad,
  Ne ought on earth that lovely is and fayre,
  But thou the same for pleasure didst prepayre.
  Thou art the root of all that joyous is,
  Great God of men and women, queene of th'ayre,
  Mother of laughter, and welspring of blisse,
O graunt that of my love at last I may not misse.

Representing in part a development from Chaucer's Boethian celebration of the creative power of love in his *Troilus and Criseyde*, the passage points to the principle of life which brings together the various strands of this great and protean poem.

Book V, dealing with the adventures of Sir Artegall, comes to most modern readers as a disappointment. The sense in the later cantos of a ruthlessness which seems to reflect the poet's experiences in Ireland acts as a chilling factor which even understanding of the importance for a Renaissance mind of the concept of Justice as a necessary defence against the threat of chaos can hardly overcome. Book VI, devoted to Sir Calidore and the courtly ideal of Courtesy, is less single-minded and more attractive. The virtue celebrated is a development of the medieval conception of "gentillesse" in accordance with the Platonizing philosophy which inspired such works as Castiglione's *Courtier*. The Book abounds in passages of delicate and sometimes nostalgic beauty, the expression of an ideal of courtly perfection which stands in contrast to the often sad realities of human evil and inadequacy. The shadow of the Blatant Beast, representing the envy and slander which were so rife in Renaissance courts and which no knightly pursuit of personal glory or the tenuous refinements of courtly love could eliminate or contain, lies across the delicate poetry which is perhaps more present here than anywhere in Spenser's work.

In a single passage, towards the end of the Book, this poetry reaches what may be its highest point of perfection. As Sir Calidore, imaginatively transformed into "the Elfin Knight," approaches a place "whose plesaunce did appeare / To passe all others, on the earth which were," he is made aware of the "merry sound" of a "shrill pipe" and of "many feete fast thumping th' hollow ground":

  There he a troupe of Ladies dauncing found
  Full merrily, and making gladfull glee,
And in the midst a Shepheard piping he did see.

The magic quality of the spectacle moves the knight to awe. Remaining under cover of the wood, he surrenders himself to contemplation of the dance:

All they without were raunged in a ring,
  And daunced round; but in the midst of them
  Three other Ladies did both daunce and sing,
  The whilest the rest them round about did hemme,
  And like a girlonde did in compasse stemme;
  And in the midst of these same three, was placed
  Another Damsell, as a precious gemme,
  Admidst a ring most richly well enchased,
That with her goodly presence all the rest much graced.

The vision granted to him is that of the Graces, "daughters of delight" and "handmaides of Venus"; but even this beauty is subsidiary to that of the "faire one / That in the midst was placed paramount": the figure at the heart of the dance "to whom that shepheard pypt alone." This is the culminating point of the vision, leading to the introduction into it of "poor Colin Clout," the poet himself ("who knowes not Colin Clout?"), the humble and yet proud witness of this transfiguring splendour:

  Pype jolly shepheard, pype there now apace
  Unto thy love, that made thee low to lout:
  Thy love is present there with thee in place,
Thy love is ther advaunst to be another Grace.

In the face of poetry of this order the attempt to extract from Spenser's enormous poem simple allegorical correspondences becomes irrelevant. The moral purposes declared in the letter to Ralegh no doubt provided him with the starting-point for a work that was certainly intended to advance deeply held moral convictions; but, as we read, we find our awareness of the moral framework giving way to a surrender to the poetry: not merely to its sensual qualities or to the lulling fascination of sound, but to the imaginative content involved in its world of fiction. The poem, indeed, proceeds by a progressive liberation from the trammels of moralizing allegory. As its end approaches Spenser unites all the rich strands at his disposal to achieve compelling moments of magic vision which answer to the deep-seated humanity of his purpose. Placing himself, with the true artist's mixture of humility and proper pride, in the figure of his Colin Clout at the periphery of a dance of entranced imaginative quality, he has found an image which expresses superbly the unifying and transforming imagination which finally animates his poem.

—Derek A. Traversi

THE FAIR MAID OF THE WEST.
Play by Thomas Heywood, part 1, before 1610; part 2, 1630(?).

Thomas Heywood's *The Fair Maid of the West* part 1 was first performed between 1597 and 1610 by Queen Anne's Company; part 2 was first performed, probably shortly after a revival of part 1, by Queen Henrietta's Men, 1630–31. Parts 1 and 2 were played before the king and queen at Hampton Court, and first printed in 1631.

Romantic narratives of sea voyages, exotic courts, pirates, and parted lovers were widely popular, the best known, Sidney's *Arcadia*, being the source for several plays. While these stories were exciting, they remained fantasies—as distant from reality as their settings and times were from Elizabethan England. Thomas Heywood's two-part play *The Fair Maid of the West* has the excitement of conventional romance, but sets it within a realistic framework. Bourgeois patriotism—focused on Queen Elizabeth, the bravery of west country sailors, and the invincibility of the English abroad—informs the play. Protestant virtues of business acumen and skill in a trade are as crucial as romantic virtues of fidelity and valour.

Part 1's unshakeable good humour disarms its obvious racism; its earthy geniality makes light of sexual harassment, bloodshed, slavery, and castration. Part 2 is grimmer, the central characters less assured and debonair.

The "fair maid" of the title, Bess Bridges, is a tavern wench in Plymouth; her beauty, wit, chastity, and ability to handle obstreperous customers attract celebrity and numerous wooers. She loves the gentleman-adventurer Spencer, who only holds back from marriage because of the social gap between them. When a fatal duel forces him to flee the country, he endows her with his possessions, including a tavern in Foy, Cornwall. So successful is her business here that she is worth several thousand pounds by the time she hears the false news of Spencer's death in Spain. Desperate in her grief, she furnishes a man-of-war, *The Negro*, and with her tavern staff and some ex-wooers goes, in male costume, buccaneering through the Mediterranean. Astounding adventures and near encounters with the wandering Spencer follow, until they meet again and marry in Morocco at the court of Mullisheg, King of Fez—which Heywood conveniently relocates on the seacoast. In part 2 the adventures continue, until the married pair are reunited at the court of a somewhat bewildered Duke of Florence.

Although a Chorus is required to narrate sea battles and the like, the staging is lively throughout, contrasting glamorous court rituals and Bess's triumphant costumes with the realistic portrayal of squabbling sailors and tavern life. Part 1 opens in Plymouth during the bustling preparations to repeat the success of Essex's recent (1597) expedition, which has "put heart / Into the English; they are all on fire / To purchase from the Spaniard." Heywood convincingly presents a busy town, with everyone in haste, with crowded taverns, overworked servants and uncertain tempers: "The gentlemen fling pots, pottles, drawers, and all downstairs. The whole house is in an uproar."

While the other adventurers, such as Captain Goodlack, "seek abroad for pillage," "tis for honour" that Spencer sails. He cannot acknowledge his love for Bess—"One of your birth and breeding thus to dote / Upon a tanner's daughter!" However, his flight and Bess's expedition upset the normal order; the distance between the daughter of a tradesman and the son of aristocracy is obliterated, or even reversed. Bess proves her nobility of spirit by rebuffing those who presume on her humble status; she proves her financial worth by her dazzling business success. She has power as mistress of a ship and crew, and she comes to foreign courts as either a conqueror or an ambassador:

> Know, King of Fez, my followers want no gold,
> I only came to see thee for my pleasure
> And show thee what these say thou never saw'st,
> A woman born in England.

Mullisheg recognises that "There's virtue in [Bess's] name"; "The mighty empress of the maiden-isle . . . is she not titled so?" He loads her with wealth and status: "Here seat thee, maid of England, like a Queen." Not surprisingly, Spencer, who has turned up in Fez, is eager to get married at once.

Throughout part 1 the English win gold from the Spaniards by plunder and from the Moroccans by their reputation and courtly arts; gold valorises Bess in the eyes of her countrymen and her foreign hosts—she is, after all, a "girl worth gold." In part 2, this innocuous delight in riches is shaded with moral ambiguities. Mullisheg is now devoured by lust for Bess and tries to suborn her crew, promising to "make these English strangers swim in gold." Similarly, his Queen tries to bribe her way to Spencer's love. Bess, Spencer, and the crew plan a subterfuge to escape from this suddenly threatening court. Later accident leaves them penniless on the Italian coast; they no longer swagger, but, rather touchingly, worry about supporting each other, the comic servant Clem getting a job as a tapster and promising, "as long as I have either credit, wages, or any coin i'th world, you shall not want." The glamour of wealth has faded; Roughman, the coarsest of Bess's followers, attacks the bandit-chief, "not for gain of gold [there is a large reward], yet for he injur'd *Bess*." Bess accepts the Duke's largesse only "After many compliments, circumstances, / Modest refusals, sometimes with repulse."

Part 1 has an attractive, swashbuckling bravado; part 2 shows a less confident society—the moral rhetoric is turgid, suspicion replaces trust, and the characters are fearful rather than irrepressible. At the extremes of Heywood's long career, part 1 and part 2 are products of different worlds.

—Richard Morton

FAIR STOOD THE WIND FOR FRANCE.
Novel by H.E. Bates, 1944.

Fair Stood the Wind for France stands as one of the most popular and successful novels (especially after its recent resuscitation by television serialisation) published by H.E. Bates, a prolific writer in both the novel and short-story forms. Bates is best known as a writer of short stories, and *Fair Stood the Wind for France* reflects his strength in this medium. Not a long novel, the book is nonetheless densely packed, and brings the reader to a warm understanding of, and involvement with, the young couple at the centre of the story.

Bates's title for this tale of love developing amid the harsh realities of war is taken from the poem "Agincourt." The allusion points up the shared theme of the English at war on the European continent, and more particularly the adventures of English fighting men in France, long the bitterest enemy of the English. Here, though, this enmity is put to one side: the common foe is the occupying power in France, Nazi Germany.

However, past antagonisms, exacerbated by the all-too-recent humiliation of the French armed forces, still surface as the narrative develops. Considerable tension is created for the story's principals by the ever-present fear of betrayal by French collaborators. Equally, the francophobia of one of the Englishmen threatens his party's safety at various junctures. In this way Bates avoids the creation of a eulogy to the alliance, and realises a more true and complex picture, through the adventures of ordinary characters in extraordinary circumstances.

Essentially the plot is simple; the crew of an English Wellington bomber is stranded in occupied France when an engine failure forces them to crash-land. Although the landing is a violent one, only the skipper of the plane, Franklin, receives any injury, his forearm being seriously gashed on impact. Having abandoned their aircraft, the crew sets out with the objective of reaching the Spanish border, and possible return from Spain to England. Franklin's injury forces them to seek assistance from a small French family, who operate a watermill. This introduces Françoise, daughter of the miller, who becomes the heroine of the story, with Franklin as the hero.

The heart of the book revolves around Franklin's period in the hands of the mill family. His crew variously depart, aided by false papers provided by the French, and he is ultimately left alone, unable to travel because of illness caused by his wound. His arm has to be amputated, with two local doctors bravely performing the operation at night to avoid discovery by the Germans. Throughout his period at the mill his relationship with Françoise grows. Love blossoms between them even as events around them turn blacker.

Tragedy befalls the family, as one of the doctors who treated Franklin, a close friend of the miller, is shot by the Germans, along with many other hostages, in retaliation for local riots. Shortly after, the miller takes Franklin's revolver and shoots himself, unable any longer to bear the misery and suffering of the occupation.

At this point Françoise takes the decisive step, as her love for Franklin becomes her main hope for the future, and threats to his continued stay at the mill mount. She insists that she will help him to make his journey through the unoccupied portion of France, and thence into Spain. They travel first by boat, and later by bicycle, to reach Marseilles, in Vichy France. Here their situation is threatened as much by the Vichy authorities as it was previously by the Germans.

The risks grow as Franklin searches for an English priest so that they can be married. Instead he finds O'Connor, one of his crew, who has reached Marseilles independently, and joins them in hiding, and two elderly British ladies who assist them in getting papers to continue their journey into Spain. Travelling by train, all three reach the Spanish border, where O'Connor is killed by French gendarmes. He has sacrificed himself in a deliberate attempt to distract the gendarmes' attention by running from the train, when it appears that Françoise is to be arrested for carrying false papers. In the confusion Françoise is able to rejoin Franklin and they escape into Spain. One is left to imagine what their future holds.

Published in 1944, *Fair Stood the Wind for France* reflected Bates's own wartime experience as a squadron leader in the Royal Air Force. Like the films of its period the book firmly sets out to reinforce popular determination to defeat the enemy, and to lend substance to the common cause taken with Free French forces and the French resistance movement. English and French are seen as warm human beings between whom friendship and love can prosper. Like the best wartime films the book is considerably more than propaganda, and its artistic value has survived the test of time.

Throughout his writing career, Bates returned to his love of the countryside, whether that of his native England or, as here, the heartland of France (and more exotic locations in some of his later works). In *Fair Stood the Wind for France* country life provides the backdrop to the action, and most of the characters are very much at home in the country. Marshland and forest, vineyard and river, towns and villages, all are woven into the story, even though, for most of the book, we have no clear knowledge of where exactly the events are taking place. This warmth in portraying a place is mirrored in the warmth of the development of Bates's characters. None is especially deeply drawn, but they are real, they feel, they relate to each other and to the circumstances in which they are living.

Here then is a work, not necessarily the best, or even the most characteristic of the writer, but one which reflects clearly his worth as a novelist, the themes which preoccupy him, and the strengths and limitations of his style. It is not challenging and disturbing in the manner of Graham Greene, it lacks the biting social comment achieved at his best by Evelyn Waugh, nor is there any innovation or development in the form of the novel. Nonetheless it is an intensely English book, written to reflect the experience of typical men and women, written with humanity and understanding. Though it lacks the vigorous element of humour which makes other works by Bates so entertaining, it has the powerful feeling for and sense of life which is perhaps the greatest strength of his writing.

—Andrew Parker

FANNY HILL.
(*Memoirs of a Woman of Pleasure.*)
Novel by John Cleland, 1748–49.

Drafted while he was a young soldier in India, John Cleland's *Memoirs of a Woman of Pleasure* was published in two volumes (November 1748; February 1749) while he was in London's Fleet prison having been arrested for debt. In late 1749 Cleland and his publisher were arrested for publishing an obscene work, and upon his release Cleland set about preparing an expurgated text which appeared in March 1750 under the title *Memoirs of Fanny Hill.*

While not an epistolary novel like Richardson's *Pamela* (1740) or *Clarissa* (1747–48), the *Memoirs* does have an epistolary frame, its two volumes comprising one long letter each addressed by Fanny to an unidentified "Madam" who has, apparently, requested her life story as an exemplum of vice turned to virtue. Since, however, *madam* is slang for *whore* and *brothel keeper*, we may suspect a joke: Fanny writes of her initiation and life of prostitution to one who is herself already initiated. Her letters are parodies of the traditional mode of polite female correspondence revealing to the female addressee what the male authorial mind regards as the secret preoccupations of the female mind. They are, in fact, an act of male appropriation, the taking-over of woman's voice in order to titillate a readership that will consist largely (but not of course solely) of males.

Yet Cleland is no mere pornographer and voyeur. Part of his reason for writing the *Memoirs* in the form he did was to attack the Richardson of *Pamela*. Even though such an attack was by then stale (Eliza Haywood's *Anti-Pamela* had concentrated on prostitution, and Fielding had exploited the obvious crudities of *Pamela* in *Shamela* and *Joseph Andrews*, including the opportunism implied in its subtitle, *Virtue Rewarded*, which he had read as recommending coquetry until your wealthy lover, unable to tolerate sexual deprivation any longer, agreed to marry you and bestow all his property on you), it still had relevance: Fanny begins by telling us how she was told "how several maids out of the country had made themselves and all their kin for ever . . . by preserving their VARTUE" and marrying their masters (*Vartue* comes from Richardson's subtitle via Fielding's *Shamela*). Cleland is poking an ironic finger at Fielding, too, however. Fanny's name (Frances Hill) recalls Fanny Andrews, the virtuous alternative to Pamela offered as the heroine of *Joseph Andrews*. One suspects that Cleland, with astute allusive awareness, is implying that he is one of the very few males among his contemporaries who actually has the courage of his sexual convictions: Richardson's *Pamela* is an act of authorial self-deception and hypocrisy; robust Henry Fielding, who has as big a libido as anyone, produces in *Joseph Andrews* a moralistic anti-*Pamela* whose full-blooded hero and heroine refuse to do anything except embrace until they are married. Cleland, on the other hand, uses the *Memoirs* to demonstrate that if the century's new genre is indeed the medium for the exploration of private history and is the modern form of romance, then we had better be honest about our private thoughts. And so Fanny Hill lifts the veil of hypocrisy and prudery by literally translating *mons veneris*.

Cleland's novel is, of course, a fantasy: not so much in the obvious sense that it confronts us with male members that are almost uniformly prodigious, but in the more insidious sense that it turns Hogarth's *Harlot's Progress* (and the real-life histories that underlay it) into fairy tale. This young country girl, also appropriated by a bawd, doesn't fall into the hands of successively exploitative masters until she ends up in Bridewell and dies of venereal disease. Instead, apart from one convenient miscarriage, she fulfils a male fantasy of the perpetually exploitable and rejuvenating female body. And, as her name suggests, her text records the autobiography of the genital mound rejoicing in its infinite capacity orgasmically to rewrite and re-present itself.

The *Memoirs* is indebted to a literary tradition that embraces Ovid's *Amores*, Donne's *Elegies*, and the libertine literature of the 17th century. Yet its echoes of Milton's *Paradise Lost* (as when Fanny spies on Mrs. Brown and her lover and on the homosexual youths, and in doing so imitates Satan spying on Adam and Eve in *Paradise Lost*, IV) imply, too, that Cleland's exploration of the female genitalia in terms of landscape (moss, tendrils, etc.) recalls Milton's description of paradise in terms of the female body which itself echoes Spenser's anatomical presentation of the Garden of Adonis in *Faerie Queene*, III. vi. Moreover, such reminiscences also suggest that Fanny's sexual liberation, her freedom from disease and childbirth pains, represent a rejection of God's edict in Genesis 3 that humanity should fall into mortality and that woman should be cursed with the agonies and sorrow of childbirth. That the *Memoirs* rewards this level of allusive attention from the reader is confirmed by the subtlety of its mythological underpinning: for example, the way in which Fanny is sexually initiated through the lesbian embraces of Phoebe (the moon goddess of the separatist feminist life); the way Phoebe's body fails, after Fanny has watched Polly at work with her male lover, to be anything other than a tantalising "shadow" of what Fanny now requires (thereby evoking the Narcissus myth with its notion of shadowy impalpability rather than sexual reality); and the way Fanny becomes Venus to her lover, Charles's, Adonis, so that her long separation from him mimes the mythological Venus's separation from Adonis through death, and her reunion re-enacts Adonis's regeneration as a vegetation god. When, in their first idyll together, Fanny leans over the sleeping youth, examining his "vernal freshness," for example, *vernal* carries its etymological meaning of *springlike* (Adonis was a spring god), and the tableau as a whole recalls the poses of Spenser's Acrasia over Verdant and his Venus over Adonis (*Faerie Queene*, II.xii and III.vi respectively). And we should perhaps remember in this connection that *Pleasure* (as in the novel's title) translates *Eden*, which was itself regarded as etymologically related to *Adon-is*.

This degree of linguistic alertness—Cleland was to become an etymologist—is apparent throughout, whether through puns or through the virtuosity with which Cleland finds periphrases for the penis and the act of love. Unlike one of its prototypes, *L'Ecole des Filles* (1655), the *Memoirs* contains not one explicitly sexual or obscene word but, rather, a multitude of metaphorical elaborations.

Feminist criticism has rightly moved from celebrating the *Memoirs* as a text of female liberation to interrogating Cleland's transvestite pose as he inhabits Fanny's body and takes over her voice. Maybe it is now time to say that the novel is not actually interested in female desire at all except in so far as the imagining of it enables the male author to fantasise over the male sexual organ. Cleland died unmarried and censured as a sodomite; and the linguistic ingenuity of the *Memoirs* focuses on penis and scrotum, not the female genitalia. This, I think, makes the novel one of the most technically interesting—because of its methodological indirectness—homoerotic texts in English.

—Douglas Brooks-Davies

FATHER AND SON.
Prose by Edmund Gosse, 1907.

Although he covered acres of paper in his life's work as poet, critic, and biographer (not to mention novelist and playwright), Edmund Gosse's reputation endures because of this one rather slim autobiographical volume that he published anonymously in 1907. The title of *Father and Son: A Study of Two Temperaments* makes its subject, predicated upon ideological difference, explicit: Gosse is here confronting his opposition to, and rejection of, the beliefs by which his father had lived. Put thus baldly, the book sounds conventional enough—a kind of re-run of Samuel Butler's *The Way of All Flesh* (1903). What makes it exceptional is the way

Gosse turns the work away from autobiographical narrative into autobiographical novel, a text in which structure and image are articulated into a brilliantly cohesive whole.

Gosse's father, Philip, Plymouth Brother and naturalist, had died in 1888. Within two years the son had written his biography. *Father and Son* revisits the father, then, 17 seventeen years after he had been officially memorialised, slanting the perceptions this time in the son's favour. It also revisits Gosse's dead mother Emily (she had died of cancer in 1857 when Gosse was seven). Her omission from *Father and Son*'s title may well, indeed, register the most significant feature of the work; for it testifies that, above all, it is an elegy for her absence, a testament to the emptiness of those two male lives without the bounding female third.

Apart from the title, the main thematic clue to the work is Darwinism. In the opening paragraph, the words *struggle* and *survivor* are both Darwinian code words, the former being embodied in the title of Darwin's *On the Origin of Species by Means of Natural Selection; or, The Preservation of Favoured Races in the Struggle for Life*. The bitter joke implied by Gosse here becomes evident as the narrative progresses, for the opposition between father and son focuses in the end round the topic of evolution. Philip takes a firmly fundamentalist line with regard to scripture: he is a naturalist who believes in the literal truth of the Genesis creation account. His inability to modify his ideas—from the fixity to the mutability of species—develops, as the text proceeds, into a metaphor for his character and the son's difference from him. One of the most heart-rending moments in this connection occurs when the son describes the father's anxious expectation of public reaction to his major (just pre-*Origin*) attempt to reconcile geology and Genesis, *Omphalos*, 1857. Its title alluded to Philip's belief that, at God's instantaneous creation of the universe, Adam was created as the archetype of all men as they are, with a navel. He awaits reviews and applause down in Devon, where he has had a new house built away from the loneliness of a London without Emily, who had recently died. What he receives instead is mockery and rejection, and the son watches, cheek pressed to the window, as his father storms round "the red ploughed field" of their unmade garden, angry, sad, and solitary. The very humanity of the son's recollection of the moment is itself memorable. What makes it superb writing—and *Father and Son* is full of such passages—is the way it takes on metaphorical life, engaging as it does the mythic regions in which the father walks but from which the son separates himself (hence the distancing and dividing window): the father believes in Genesis, so the characteristically red Devon soil reminds us that the meaning of *Adam* in Hebrew is *red earth*; the field is *going* to be their garden (echoes of paradise, the primal garden), but it isn't yet (so the text raises the question: can Philip not even now see that geology tells us that there were always things prior—even, maybe, to paradise?); while on the very page in which all this is described Gosse quotes from the work of another diehard puritan, Milton's *Paradise Lost*. Finally, *Omphalos* itself, in naming the navel, reminds Gosse as author, and us as readers, of the navel's biological function as the sign of our original bonding with, and severance from, our mothers; so that it recalls Emily's absence, standing, like *Father and Son*'s title, as an emblem of Gosse's deepest anguish.

For the fact is that, although Emily shared her husband's puritanism, she managed to offer Edmund the freedom of imaginative liberty because, as a young woman, she had written a secret commonplace book which she had subsequently discontinued and kept locked away. When he discovers it years later, Edmund speculates "Was my mother intended by nature to be a novelist?" The book is the record of the richness of her private inner life which, as *Father and Son* interprets it, her religion silenced. In becoming an imaginative writer himself, Gosse sees himself as living out his mother's lost self and, in doing so, repudiating his father, whose attitude to imaginative writing, though it becomes more liberal as Edmund grows older, is generally hostile and uncomprehending.

It is a sign of *Father and Son*'s richness that almost every detail takes on symbolic weight: for example, the son's first clever remark, at the age of four, that a skeleton was "a man with the meat off," which sets the scene for the text's subsequent preoccupation with death and bones, as well as neatly looking back to the infant "flash of memory" of a greyhound slipping into the room where he has been left alone in his highchair and loping off with a leg of mutton, which in turn anticipates his dying mother's journey home from her doctor "a day or two before Christmas, while . . . the butchers were shouting outside their forests of carcases." Or consider the moment of the son's baptism in chapter 8 when the pool is revealed as "a dark square" and he feels "as small as one of our microscopical specimens," so that the pool becomes equated with the rock pools and aquaria in which Philip found and kept his best sea creatures.

With the evolution debate as one of its central metaphors, *Father and Son* offers us one of the most compelling glimpses available of the impact of Lyell, Darwin, and the other evolutionists on their contemporaries. Its mark of excellence is that it privatises that debate, seeing it as an image of the right to, as well as need for, independence from the straitjacket of parental possessiveness. But its main fascination lies in the way its narrative develops in the dead Emily's favour, idealising her as a ghost floating free of religious intolerance and inspiring her son in his break for physical freedom (his arrival in London in the epilogue) and his lifetime's work as an imaginative writer. This most patriarchally titled of texts, in other words, is in fact the record of the son's Oedipal rejection of his father and his (symbolic) embracing of his mother.

—Douglas Brooks-Davies

FELIX HOLT.
Novel by George Eliot, 1866.

Felix Holt, one of George Eliot's best, and perhaps her most underrated novel, represented a partial return to the form and style of the early books, *Adam Bede* and *The Mill on the Floss*, which had established her reputation. In between had come two works less typical of her genius, *Silas Marner*, with its strong element of moral fable, and *Romola*, a somewhat heavy-footed excursion into Walter Scott's territory. Now she returned, as she was to do again in *Middlemarch*, to the period of the Reform Bill of 1832, and her own precocious perceptions as a girl of 12. She had seen then, at Nuneaton, election riots in which a man was killed, a charge against the crowd by the Scots Greys and bribery on a great scale. By a fortunate coincidence Reform was at once historical and topical, for it was the period of controversy leading up to the much more radical Reform Bill of 1867, introduced by the Tory government of Derby and Disraeli. Fears of public disorder were strongly felt in some quarters, as any reader of Arnold's *Culture and Anarchy* or of Carlyle's "Shooting Niagara" can easily see. Although her hero is a radical, and stated to be so on the title-page, the strong conservative strain in Eliot's thought is apparent both in the text, and in the essay, purporting to be written by Felix Holt, which she published a little after the Bill had become an Act. The essay is studded with warning phrases like: "It is constantly the task of practical wisdom not to say 'This is good, and I will have it', but to say 'This is the less of two unavoidable evils, and I will bear it.' " The essay reinforces the lesson given in the text of the novel by the crowd scene, where the innocent Felix, trying to divert angry men from mob violence, finds himself plausibly accused of having incited it.

Of the three leading radical figures in the book, Felix is too idealistic to be effective, a sort of plebeian John Stuart Mill, Harold Transome is a haughty aristocrat, a radical in the Byron tradition, who will pay anyone rather than admit his claim to equality, and Johnson is thoroughly corrupt. The liberal idealism that was soon to be harnessed to the enormous practical abilities of Gladstone is conspicuous by absence.

But the political theme is only one of three leading ones. The strongest, in a literary point of view, is the study of the long-drawn and bitter consequences of the ancient adultery of Harold's mother and his unknown father in the flesh, the lawyer, Jermyn. The well-worn story of the guilty secret, familiar to mid-Victorian readers from the character of Lady Dedlock in Dickens's *Bleak House* and from other examples, is here revivified in some of the most penetrating and poignant chapters Eliot ever wrote. She uses Dantesque imagery, and especially, the story of Paolo and Francesca, to universalize her theme; by a wise choice, stress is placed less upon the revelation of the old secret than on the irremediable effect of the past on the present. The sadness of an old woman, once beautiful and still proud, in her obsession with a son who neglects her and must condemn her when he discovers the story of his parentage is powerfully conveyed. Her sinister, cynical servant, Denner, is an effective counterweight, like an exaggerated emblem of her own dark broodings. This powerfully sad, static picture is transformed into a sudden and memorable climax in chapter 42, where Jermyn, afraid that his financial misdealings will be known to Transome, actually his son, but still treating him as an insignificant employee, pleads with Mrs. Transome to reveal the intolerable truth. When he asks if it would not be right for Transome to know who his father was, we have the fine comment: "Some of the most terrible irony of the human lot is this of a deep truth coming to be uttered by lips that have no right to it." This is followed by the brief, sharp recognition scene.

The third story, that of the Lyon family, is less satisfactory on the whole. Mysterious and complicated plots are not Eliot's forte; and the train of circumstances by which the Independent minister's daughter, Esther Lyon, becomes the heiress of the Transome estate is bound to seem laboured. But there are strengths here too. Lyon himself is one of the subtlest and tenderest of the series of Evangelical portraits in her work. The way his everyday language is shaped by his preaching style and by constant reading of the Bible is wholly convincing; and in his confrontation with Felix we have an emblem, deliberately fashioned or not, of the author's view of the new agnostic creed taking over the moral insights of religion. For Esther, Felix becomes a mentor, leading her to higher values, and enabling her to reject the false glitter of the Transome world. Discipleship leads to marriage, a mistake, or an error of taste, from which the author showed that she had learnt when, in *Daniel Deronda*, the hero is sexually indifferent to his disciple Gwendolen. Esther does not seem to be conceived with perfect exactness as the kind of girl capable of such a renunciation. She is too worldly and frivolous; a character more in the mould of the later creation, Dorothea Brooke, might have been appropriate here.

Like all Eliot's best work, *Felix Holt* is notable for deep and fascinating depictions of a vanishing social order, and for touches of sharp humour, as in chapter 7, when Lady Debarry's curiosity about Harold Transome's mysterious marriage in the East ludicrously conflicts with her tradition of aristocratic courtesy and detachment.

—A.O.J. Cockshut

THE FEMALE QUIXOTE.
Novel by Charlotte Lennox, 1752.

Written during the author's early twenties, *The Female Quixote* is Charlotte Lennox's second novel and best-known work. At a time when the realistic novel is increasingly being defined by its practitioners and defenders in opposition to the so-called absurdities of romance, Lennox imitates and adapts Cervantes's *Don Quixote* (1605) to create the story of a quixotic heroine, Arabella, who mistakenly believes that 18th-century England is like the world described in the 17th-century French romances of La Calprenede and Madeleine de Scudery. Her isolated upbringing accounts for her delusion and allows for a loose plot concerning her gradual introduction to the outside world, with visits to Bath and London in the later sections. Arabella's confrontations with reality make for a series of comic incidents in which mockery is aimed in more than one direction: at the heroine's stubborn belief that men are ready to die of love for her, so that she translates a servant trying to steal fish into a disguised nobleman about to drown himself; and at frivolous fashionable society, represented by Miss Glanville and various young gentlemen, which has no true learning to correct Arabella's false ideas and cannot share or understand her real, and romance-induced, nobility of mind and respect for other women.

The novel's central issue—women's power, or lack of it, in contemporary society—is addressed through the continual struggle between Arabella and her companions over history and its interpretation. Arabella's romances, centring on heroines continually in danger of ravishment, may not be historical but they express the psychological truth of their readers' fears and desires: desires for significance, fears of being reduced to men's victims. Arabella's reading compensates for her real-life powerlessness: informed by her father that she is to marry her cousin Glanville, she still thinks herself a heroine in control of her destiny. Her self-image takes on some reality when, after her father's death, Glanville decides "to accommodate himself, as much as possible, to her Taste, and to endeavour to gain her Heart by a Behaviour most agreeable to her." He becomes a hero against his will, rescuing his lady from dangers, entering sword-fights on her behalf, and wounding his rival, Sir George. Yet it is Sir George who reads romances and pretends that they are true, deceiving Arabella for his own ends. The hero steadfastly refuses to read romances himself. His knowledge of history, derived from that male prerogative, a classical education, tells him that women have never been to the wars like men, or if they did, Thalestris, Queen of the Amazons, was killed at the siege of

Troy. Arabella's history, learned from the woman-centred and sometimes woman-authored versions of recent romances, is one in which women once ruled by battle and now do so through the power of love and their own unimpeachable chastity.

Cleopatra, Queen of Egypt, is central to the novel's gendered struggle over meaning. To Arabella she is mainly important as the mother of the heroine of the same name in La Calprenede's romance, and she is a virtuous woman secretly married to Julius Caesar, or at least unfortunately deceived into believing so. Glanville dismisses Cleopatra as a Gypsy; another gentleman, more crudely, calls her a whore. The men's version of Cleopatra is as much a product of desire and the will to power as is Arabella's, and its tendency is to deny women any action, except degraded sexual action, in the history which the men claim to be synonymous with truth. Tellingly, the man who defines the Queen of Egypt as a whore is a sinister figure. Meeting Arabella on one of her flights from imaginary danger, he offers her his chaise, "being extremely glad at having so beautiful a Creature in his Power." He is a real ravisher in a world which, the heroine's mentors keep telling her, is too well-ordered nowadays to contain any.

The men's interpretations and actions encouraged the reader to doubt the narrative view that male history is true, Arabella's a mere romantic fiction. Ostensibly, though, Lennox endorses, not quite unequivocally, 18th-century realism and its attendant assumptions about female subordination. A wise Countess begins to educate Arabella in the boring life of obedience and calm marriage which 18th-century moralists claim to be the whole of reality for any virtuous woman. Her gentle teaching of womanly duty is interrupted by a demonstration of it when she is called away to nurse her mother, and Arabella's reform is left to men. She is finally convinced of the fictionality of her histories by the arguments of a clergyman modelled on Samuel Johnson, who may even have written this section himself. For good measure, "the Doctor" praises Samuel Richardson as a proof that "Truth is not always injured by Fiction." With these authorities behind her Lennox has a clear claim to be no silly female romancer but a moral writer of the new, truthful novel: a woman authorised, by her acceptance of modern, male-dominated reality, to be its historian.

Yet 18th-century novels, self-proclaimed histories, are fiction still, and even the best fictions, the Doctor notes, "teach young Minds to expect strange Adventures." Arabella has had adventures, and she has found a devoted hero in Glanville. She may have failed to be the heroine of a 17th-century romance, but her desire to be someone whose story is worth telling is satisfied as she becomes the heroine of an 18th-century novel.

—Jane Spencer

FINNEGANS WAKE.
Novel by James Joyce, 1939.

Begun soon after James Joyce finished writing *Ulysses* (1922) and continuing many topics from the earlier works, *Finnegans Wake* acts as a culmination of them and provides Joyce's "last word" on many topics.

Obscurity has been the *Wake*'s chief difficulty. In a text predominantly English, 50 or so languages have been enumerated, many in combination with other languages; Joyce accepted the term "portmanteau" from Lewis Carroll's *Through the Looking-Glass* to describe the combination words he devised. But the difficulty resides not so much in language as in the highly allusive—and frequently elusive—system of references. Joyce advised his public to study languages and Vico (1668–1744), who arranged history in recurring cycles of three declining phases followed by a regenerative "*ricorso*." Joyce arranged the novel in four books, with eight chapters in the first, four in each of the second and third books, and only one chapter in the fourth book or ricorso. Joyce intended the *Wake* to be a "universal history."

Therefore he identified the basic five temporal characters with eternal features of the Irish landscape: the father Humphrey Chimpden Earwicker with the "sleeping giant" mountain on the Dublin landscape, the wife Anna Livia with the River Liffey, the twin sons Shem and Shaun with tree and stone, and the daughter Issy with the cloud which will fall in rain on the river.

The *Wake* has two narrators, one to tell and one to question, exclaim, and comment; both occupy a position in the afterlife from which they can look down on the earth—in keeping with "after death" communications of the time—and see it clairvoyantly through its various phases of development. Thus the *Wake* begins and ends with the above-earth view of the river, at first circling the globe and at the end flowing out to sea. This unique point of view, which Joyce called "planes of narrative," provides for the basic characters to appear in various phases of time, so that Mutt and Jute are Neanderthal predecessors of Shem and Shaun and meet in 1014 on the former battlefield of Clontarf, now a part of Dublin city. This point of view governs, also, the penetration of several layers of human consciousness, including that of the dream in Book 3. The narrative method explains the assumption that the *Wake* is the "dream" of dead man whose form outlines the landscape.

Joyce sought to represent different phases of consciousness similar to the AUM of eastern philosophy, with its stages of waking conscious, dreaming conscious, and dreamless sleep; and these merge with the Viconian cycles. He called the book a "nightpiece," and scholars, frustrated with its difficulties, have asserted in turn that the *Wake* is a "stolentelling," that it is comprised of "heterogeneous bits and pieces" borrowed from other sources, and comprised of "whole vast sections of nonsense." Nevertheless, Joyce placed at the end of the novel an intriguing statement—"The keys to. Given."

Earlier, in *The Portrait of the Artist as a Young Man*, Stephen Dedalus announced a weapon of silence for his art; and Stephen closes the *Portrait* with an invocation: "Old father, old artificer, stand me now and ever in good stead." Now, it seems that the "weapon of silence" is a journalist named William T. Stead (1849–1912), who also provides the "keys" to the otherwise obscure system of reference.

Whatever the place or time, the characters converse inevitably about the "fall" and possible guilt of the father, whose initials HCE are repeated in innumerable variations—here comes everybody, haveth childers everywhere. Earwicker has committed a mysterious "sin in the park," based upon William T. Stead's investigation of child vice and white slavery in London in 1885, for which Stead prowled the parks. Knowing that he would have to enter the white slave traffic to "get the facts," he arranged for the abduction of Eliza Armstrong, a girl of 13 years. He published the series of articles exposing child vice and white slavery in the *Pall Mall*

Gazette, which he edited. The outraged populace accused him of deluging the city with a quantity of filth and with committing the crime he investigated. Although he accomplished his purpose—passage of the Criminal Law Amendment bill raising the consent age from 13 to 16—he served two months in Holloway prison for abduction and indecent assault. His trial provides for the 12 jurors of the *Wake*.

No two people have identical views of the Stead facts, and Joyce applies a concept from the *Arabian Nights* and renders "a thousand and one" variations of Earwicker's sin. Joyce divides the Stead history into Earwicker, who experiences it; Shem, who writes about it; and Shaun, who opposes it.

The *Wake*'s major characters and motifs may be sketched briefly in the facts of Stead's history, largely set forth in the four articles called "The Maiden Tribute of Modern Babylon." Stead accused "born gentlemen" of a conspiracy of silence like the stone covering putrefying corpses in Naples, and Joyce made Shaun the public-minded stone. Stead sought to bring light into the labyrinth (his word for London brotheldom), and Joyce connects Earwicker with the light-Osiris myth. After the first two articles had scandalized the public, Stead predicted he would succeed in rousing the conscience of the British people and shouted: "We knew we had forged a thunderbolt." Joyce makes a hundred-letter thunder word a tenfold motif. A Mansion House committee of three clergymen and one parliamentarian, formed to investigate the truth of Stead's findings, provide the basis for the *Wake*'s Four Old Men, who hover over the family's affairs.

Stead published Eliza Armstrong's letter "garlanded with kisses," and the *Wake*'s letter found in a midden is similarly composed and crisscrossed. Two women who assisted Stead with Eliza Armstrong had once been washerwomen. The day after the "filth" of his last article, Stead published a feature on laundresses; Joyce gave the first seven chapters to Stead's fate, and the eighth to a dialogue between washerwomen, the two "Maggies" of the *Wake*. With the dominant "cloacal" metaphor for Stead's exposé, Shem scandalously makes ink of his own excrement. The daughter Issy has all the facts that Stead published and uses them to sound naughty. These included clergy frequenting brothels, and a shady cleric haunts the romantic reflections of Anna Livia and Issy. Stead found that charwomen made excellent procuresses and that some policemen took bribes; Kate the cleaning woman completes the Earwicker household, and Constable Sackerson makes his rounds. Like the *Wake*'s "Ballad of Persse O'Reilly," Stead's reports became the subject of music hall lubricity.

Stead's historical novel *Here Am I; Send Me!* sets forth the ideal publican of Earwicker's occupation. In 1890 Stead began editing the monthly journal the *Review of Reviews*, to keep track of events all around the globe. His international travels and many languages treated in the *Review* account for Earwicker's international dimensions, developed in Books 2 and 3. The Earwicker children speak of a "Noblett's surprise" their father failed to attain; Stead was nominated for the Nobel Prize for Peace in 1901. The famous "Butt and Taff" dialogue of chapter 11 develops Stead's visit to Savastopol, bringing the "filth" of the Maiden Tribute with him, and Joyce linked this with his father's anecdote about the Irish soldier shooting the defecating Russian general. Stead died on the *Titanic* in 1912, and at the close of chapter 11 Earwicker slumps into his last doze as his ship sails out to sea. The *Titanic*'s maiden voyage and penetration by an iceberg provides the Tristan and Iseult analogy that opens chapter 12.

Stead became a spiritualist in the 1890's, and Book 3, the "dream" book, is largely devoted to a seance with Shaun acting as medium. Earwicker as ghost speaks through Shaun and announces his presence, "Bill of Old Bailey," where William T. Stead was tried. Stead, himself a medium talented with automatic writing, spoke through several mediums after his death, and frequently returned to the Maiden Tribute—the most decisive event of his life—in these messages, just as Earwicker does, and declares himself innocent.

Largely because of the Maiden Tribute, Stead said "The past has been like a nightmare, with a sudden awakening." Joyce adapted this for the most frequently quoted passage in *Ulysses*; with it Joyce opens Book 4, with the "awakening" over the sea, and honors Stead's posthumous request that the message of afterlife—Finnegan awake—be sent broadcast over the world.

With Stead the biographical original of Humphrey Chimpden Earwicker, and the missing spaces filled in with information from Stead's voluminous publications, of which the *Review* alone comprises 45 volumes, the *Wake* is revealed an historical novel, set primarily in the years 1885–1922 and looking toward the future in which archetypes recur.

—Grace Eckley

FOR THE TERM OF HIS NATURAL LIFE.
(His Natural Life.)
Novel by Marcus Clarke, 1874.

Marcus Clarke displayed his talent for research and for accurate recapitulation of interesting events from Australian history when his book *Old Tales of a Young Country* was published in 1871. One episode, "The Seizure of the *Cypress*," taken from James Bonwick's *The Bushrangers*, became one of the key episodes in *For the Term of His Natural Life*. Clarke read many other sources—histories, novels, government documents, and early journals—when he took a trip to Tasmania for his health in 1870 and lists them in the appendix to his novel.

Clarke maintains in the preface that Charles Reade (*It Is Never Too Late to Mend*) and Victor Hugo (*Les Misérables*) displayed the cruel treatment of felons, but that he purports to show the inexpediency of the transportation system which herds together offenders "in places remote from the wholesome influence of public opinion," totally at the mercy and whims of the gaolers; and while he recognizes that the British have ceased deportation to Australia, Port Blair still exists for Indians and New Caledonia for French prisoners. *His Natural Life* deals primarily with the maximum security prisons for repeat offenders and incorrigibles and not the penal system as a whole, which had, through the policy of chain gangs, assignment, and tickets-of-leave, provided the labor for the early development of roads, buildings, farms, and stations, paving the way for free emigration and the ultimate growth of a new nation. Brain Elliott, in his biography of Clarke, gives many other probable sources for the novel, as well as related works, stating that it was at first planned as a historical work, "but it emerged finally as a psychological romance."

The work was initially much longer when printed serially in the *Australian Journal*; but on the advice of Sir Charles Gavan Duffy, the plot was considerably tightened and the hero better motivated. Though the theme of revealing the brutality and bestiality that result when men are given absolute power over other men without public accountability is a powerful one, the story suffers from the disparity between absolute realism on the one hand, and deliberate contrivance and melodrama on the other.

An innocent man, Richard Devine, alias Rufus Dawes, is thrust into the meshes of the transportation system and into the clutches of a cruel, unfeeling gaoler, Lieutenant Maurice Frere, whose character and methods of discipline were based on those of John Price, superintendent on Norfolk Island for several years and later killed by convicts at Williamston. Through a series of incredible circumstances, Dawes, though actually saving people aboard the convict ship from mutiny and later saving the lives of the commandant's daughter and Frere, is wrongfully convicted in each instance and sent to all the maximum security prisons in succession—Macquarie Harbour, Port Arthur, and Norfolk Island—and becomes progressively more debased and hopeless, and increasingly persecuted by Frere. Ironically, the man who killed Lord Bellasis, whom Dawes was transported for robbing, is another convict, John Rex, the actual plotter of the mutiny, who later escapes from Macquarie Harbour by seizing the brig *Osprey* (based on the actual *Cypress* incident) and setting Frere, Mrs. Vickers, and Sylvia ashore. He later escapes from Port Arthur and returns to England to assume the identity of Richard Devine (Dawes) and inherit his fortune. Both were natural sons of Lord Bellasis. As a further irony, Reverend North, the prison chaplain at Port Arthur and later at Norfolk, is the person who really robbed Lord Bellasis. Furthermore, Frere, who is immoral and keeps Rex's concubine as a mistress for a time, is rewarded by getting Sylvia to marry him because, as a result of amnesia, she thinks Frere, not Dawes, saved her life.

Over a span of 18 years, Dawes is confined in maximum security, and Clarke describes, the real prisons (all inoperative at the time of writing) and the isolation, the punishment, the hard labor, the torture, the cruelty of the warders, and the hardening and debasement of the convicts whose sole thought was of freedom. Gabbett, who absconds from Macquarie Harbour in a party of four and from Port Arthur in a party of nine, each time returns alone. His character is based upon that of Pierce, an actual convict hanged for cannibalism. Dawes, who once attempts to escape by himself, is placed on Sarah Island as punishment and attempts suicide. Years later, on Norfolk Island, Dawes is the leader of the Ring, the secret rulers within the convict society who regulate internal affairs; and Frere, now Captain, more calculatedly callous, cruel, and malignant, tortures him with relentless fury using instruments specially devised for that purpose. To escape, Dawes and his cell-mates draw straws to determine who will kill one of their own. Thus, three escape the hell—the one killed, and the killer and the witness, who are hanged. Dawes is the witness and is condemned to die.

Given the subject and the circumstances, the rhetorical ending is appropriate. Reverend North, dipsomaniac and thief, the real cause of Dawes's imprisonment in the first place, develops an unholy passion for Sylvia, Frere's wife, who has finally concluded that her marriage to a coarse, cruel, and sensual man is no longer tenable. She is leaving on the *Lady Franklin* for Van Diemen's Land, and North is leaving on the same ship. He visits Dawes in his cell, prior to departure, to confess his duplicity with regard to the robbery and leaves the cell emotionally distraught, forgetting his cloak and hat. Dawes takes them and escapes, the boatmen thinking he is North. At sea, the ship is hit by a hurricane; Sylvia calls for help, and Dawes comes to her aid, at which time her memory of his former rescue returns full force. They are found locked in each other's arms, two corpses tangled in the rigging of the mainmast. Thus, love, pure and self-sacrificing, washes clean the horror and degradation of their lives. Their souls are finally freed, "recognizing each the loveliness of the other".

—Wesley D. Sweetser

THE FORCE THAT THROUGH THE GREEN FUSE DRIVES THE FLOWER.
Poem by Dylan Thomas, 1934.

Written when Dylan Thomas was about 18 and published in 1934 when he was 20, "The force that through the green fuse drives the flower" suffers from a number of youthful indiscretions: too rich and complex an imagery; a faulty parallelism in structure; an erratic accentual pattern; enjambments anticipating double readings that lead to obscurity instead of ambiguity. Nevertheless, it is a quintessential Thomas poem, crucial in tracing his development and in charting the juxtaposition of themes that preoccupied him in nearly everything he wrote: sex and death as each other's reflections both as mirror images and as antitheses. Further, this powerful poem transcends all of its flaws through an undeniable eloquence.

In two parallel stanzas, "the force that" nourishes us—which may be read as "whatever" nourishes us or "God who" nourishes us, without the slightest contradiction—is the same force that destroys us. The "I" who speaks is both poet and reader, therefore "we." Whatever urges flowers from their stems, and water from within the earth, pushes our lives forward by causing our blood to course through us. We cannot explain to the natural world, represented by the rock, nor can we explain to our veins, that all life draws its sustenance from the same source: "force," "God," "whatever."

In the third stanza, parallel in form but not in content, Thomas personifies that force as a "hand." In water, the hand can create with eddies and it can destroy with quicksand; the hand can control the wind with sails on ships and, just as sails must be hauled in, so must the human sail—the shroud—wrap us in death. In this instance, our inability to speak to the "crooked rose" of the first stanza or our "veins" of the second is paralleled in our inability to explain to "the hanging man" —the man who is hanged and simultaneously the man who does the hanging—that we are ourselves composed of the earth to which the body returns, assisted in transformation by the lime the hangman scatters to aid the corpse's decomposing.

Paraphrase at best is a clumsy necessity in threading through the intricacies of Thomas's overripe images, but it may be the only avenue along which the reader dares travel for fear of short-cut paths keeping him from the clear vision toward which the poem aspires in its difficult fourth stanza. It seems to be a more general comment on the specific instances that have preceded it. Here, time which we have invented by "ticking a heaven round the stars"—that is, time employed to measure the mortal limits of our lives and therefore of our conceptions of immortality—is lightly personified, drawing its own sustenance from our source, a word that perhaps not entirely by accident rhymes with "force." At the "fountainhead," paralleling the "mountain spring" and the "veins" in the earlier stanzas, time drinks or, rather, "leech[es]" since we both live and die because our "red blood" is driven by the "force." Here, that force becomes synonymous with time, our fabrication to justify our lives. Inevitably, the same force that "dries the mouthing streams" and thickens blood, turns it "to wax," although Thomas's familiar exchanging parts of speech insists that "wax" be read as both noun and verb. In the "lips of time"'s "leech[ing]," we draw sustenance from each other through "Love" that "drips and gathers," the "sores" of which will be "calm[ed]" by blood. The image is, then, both life-giving and life-taking; sex and death. Here, however, Thomas unnecessarily complicates the image: it is "fallen blood" rather than blood that has been spent or dried or spilled or turned "to wax," although in "the fallen blood" he may have intended to imply something of sacrifice in our proceeding through life toward death, menstrual as well as seminal. In the second half of the fourth stanza, Thomas returns to the wind. In a sense, the wind measures natural time through the weather's vicissitudes; but we cannot explain to it how time, that we have invented to measure our lives, has conceived of immortality through what we can see but cannot understand: "a heaven round the stars."

The couplet concluding the poem makes a staggering analogy. The "rose" of the first stanza is recalled through the couplet's "worm"; both are "crooked," separated by "Love" in the fourth stanza. We cannot explain to "the crooked rose" that what is life-giving and what is life-taking are interchangeable, manifested through love and death, beauty and ugliness, sex and decay, flower and phallus. Even the seasons marking time blur into each other, since "rose" and "worm" are both "bent by the same wintry fever."

As if to reinforce these approximations rather than to insist on actualities, Thomas locked his lines together through a series of half-rhymes rather than pure ones, both internally and terminally. Further, each stanza breaks between its five-beat observation and five-beat "dumb" response with a triple catalexis, the remaining two beats stopping unanswered in the silence of space on the page. Thomas's variations in form serve to clarify the density of his images, consciously or not; the result is a good poem, despite its difficulties.

—Bruce Kellner

THE FORSYTE SAGA.
Fiction by John Galsworthy, 1906–21.

Critics have been unkind to John Galsworthy; his reputation has not recovered from Lawrence's harsh criticism, and Woolf's facile dismissal of him as "a materialist." All who write about Galsworthy, however, agree that *The Man of Property* is his best work, and most are unanimous that it is an accomplished novel. Most also agree that *In Chancery* and *To Let* are less distinguished works. These three novels, connected by poetic interludes entitled "Indian Summer of a Forsyte" and *Awakening*, make up *The Forsyte Saga*.

The Forsyte Saga chronicles the life of an upper-middle-class family through three generations. The Forsytes belong to the city. Soames Forsyte comments at the end of the *Saga*: "Collectors, solicitors, barristers, merchants, publishers, accountants, directors, land agents, even soldiers—there they had been!" Galsworthy diagnoses and criticises their values and way of life through the tragic situation of Soames, and in the satirical portraits of his various aunts and uncles who, with little or no real affection for each other, maintain nevertheless an impregnable family solidarity. They meet together on such occasions as engagements and funerals, and exchange family news and gossip. The central action, however, focuses on the second generation of Soames and his cousin Young Jolyon. Soames is the "man of property" and epitomises the Forsytes. Young Jolyon explains the Forsytes to Bosinney: "My people . . . possess in a remarkable degree those two qualities which are the real tests of a Forsyte—the power of never being able to give yourself up to anything soul and body, and the sense of property." He describes himself as only half a Forsyte. This is because he leaves his family to follow his feelings and places a higher value on art and beauty than on property. (He eventually becomes a successful painter.)

Soames marries the beautiful but penniless Irene. In the course of *The Man of Property* Irene falls in love with Bosinney, the young architect Soames has engaged to build Robin Hill. (It is his acquisition of a country house that makes Soames a "man of property.") Irene, who stands for beauty and art (a strong theme in all Galsworthy's fiction) is to be enshrined in the house. Soames finally asserts his rights of possession over his estranged wife by raping her. Bosinney is so appalled when he learns of this he rushes out into the streets and is killed in a street accident. Irene leaves Soames.

In *In Chancery*, Soames's cousin, Young Jolyon, falls in love with Irene. Irene and Soames eventually divorce, and she marries Jolyon when she is free. They have a son called Jon. Soames makes a loveless marriage in order to secure an heir. He in time has a daughter Fleur to whom he is devoted. In this novel Galsworthy traces the Forsyte family history through the turn of the century and continues, in doing so, his analysis of property and possession. *In Chancery* begins with the statement: "The possessive instinct never stands still." The theme widens to include war and imperialism which stem from the urge to possess and control. Young Jolyon views the human condition within that framework: "A precious war! Domination of people or of woman! Attempts to master and possess those who did not want you!" (There is a gap in time between the second and third novels.)

In the third novel, *To Let*, Fleur falls in love with Jon. They meet secretly and try to discover why their respective parents do not wish them to see each other. Jolyon eventually tells his son about Soames's treatment of Irene, and Jon, out of loyalty to his mother, gives up Fleur and leaves the country. When Jolyon dies Irene joins her son in British Columbia. Fleur makes a loveless marriage. Robin Hill is on the market. *To Let* is a darker, more pessimistic work than the others. The new generation, embodied in Jon and Fleur, criticises the old. They want something different from the property-centred values of the Forsytes. Jon, who like his father before him associates war with acquisitiveness, says to Fleur: "The last generation thought of nothing but property, and that's why there was the war." Fleur adds that it is also the reason why their families quarrelled.

At the end of the *Saga* Soames thinks of the symbolic significance of Robin Hill. It is "the shell of the feud; and with the woman gone, it was an empty shell." In a melancholy mood of introspection he looks back on his life—centred in all its hopes and desires on Robin Hill—and concludes that, in addition to the house's no longer holding any meaning for him, the Forsyte way of life is over. Shifting then from the personal to the social scene and to the process of history he expresses a belief that the change he sees in evidence all around him is no more than "the interval of death between two forms of life, destruction necessary to make room for fresher property." He keeps faith with his beliefs but acknowledges at the same time that they can never satisfy "the melancholy craving in his heart."

—Stella McNichol

THE FORTUNES OF RICHARD MAHONY.
Novel by Henry Handel Richardson, 1917–29.

The Fortunes of Richard Mahony, like Henry Handel Richardson's first two novels, was based on personal history. In *Maurice Guest*, a novel about an English music student in Leipzig who fails in both art and love, she draws chiefly on her own experiences and observations as a piano student in that city (1889–92). In *The Getting of Wisdom* the story of the heroine, Laura, largely matches the history of the author's career as a boarder at the Presbyterian Ladies' College, Melbourne (1883–86). And the basic plot of her third novel—Richard Mahony's story—closely resembles in outline the history of her father, Dr. Walter Lindesay Richardson, from shortly after his arrival on the Ballarat goldfields in 1852 till his death in 1879. After making little money as a digger or storekeeper, he did better as a doctor, and very well indeed as a speculator in goldmining shares. He then went "home" to England for a couple of years, where he spent some time as a gentleman of leisure and some in medical practice, before returning to Australia to live in Melbourne. There, in opulent retirement, he devoted himself to study, chiefly of spiritualism, to which he became a convert. There too his wife Mary bore children, after they had shared many years of sadness at their failure to have any. He then took his family back to the old world, but during his grand tour he received news of a sudden reverse in his fortunes, and was obliged to hurry back to Melbourne and resume medical practice. He was a failure in a series of practices in different parts of Victoria, his physical and mental health deteriorated alarmingly, and in time Mary had to work as a postmistress while he was committed to a lunatic asylum. He eventually came "home" to die in the post office of a remote bush township.

So in writing her three major novels, Richardson had undertaken a journey back into the past, reshaping and coming to terms with her own experience and the experience of those nearest to her. She had driven progressively deeper within herself, first to memories of her young womanhood, then of adolescence, and at last to the terrible bedrock memories of childhood. Her father's vagrant, declining years had been her formative years of insecurity, embarrassment, and terror.

And those years, between her birth and her father's death (1870–79), are the historical basis of nearly half *The Fortunes of Richard Mahony*—the second half. But it is not in any way or at any point a mere novelisation. It is truly a work of fiction, an imaginative shaping of history and personal experience, in which many events and figures are given special importance, others given little or none, and others again are modified or conflated or chronologically transposed. Some of the most powerfully written episodes are inventions (for example, Mahony's brief visit to his mother and unmarried sisters in Dublin, and the death of his twin daughter). And some of the characters differ radically from the historical figures on whom they are based, most importantly in the case of Mahony himself. He, unlike the outgoing public performer Walter Richardson, is withdrawn, thin-skinned—a character chronically disposed to feel there is "a fly in the ointment," temperamentally closer to his chronically unsettled, reclusive author than to the man on whom he was nominally modelled.

Indeed the whole novel takes its tone principally from the character of its hero. Although from its beginning on the Ballarat goldfields until the onset of Mahony's decline it bears the outward marks of a family saga, with a large gallery of characters painted on a broad canvas (which has led some readers to complain of prolixity and tedium in the first two books), it always contains the elements of quite a different kind of fiction. It is pervaded by a spirit of uneasiness and chronic dissatisfaction, which slowly but relentlessly intensifies as the canvas narrows, the gallery of characters melts away, and the narrative focuses unsparingly on Mahony's disintegration and its effect on his family. At the same time the narrative point of view becomes less impersonal and omniscient; we are made to see things more partially, through the eyes of Mahony, Mary, and their son Cuffy (fictional counterpart to the child Ethel Richardson). Consequently we are given a direct, sympathetic experience of the working of their minds. Most importantly, we are able to comprehend from within the nature of Mahony's descent into psychological chaos. And in fact the later parts of the novel have been called a case-study. But if it alters in scope and mode as it proceeds, it has its own integrity, first because from the start it drives on with ever-increasing force to its inevitable, terrible ending; and second because it has a strong thematic unity. It begins with a young digger being buried alive, concludes with the burial of Mahony himself, and its dark tone is sustained by recurrent images and metaphors of burial, suffocation, and asphyxiation. As the story of a marriage, and a novel about migration, it presents Mahony's old world gentility and spiritual yearnings in continuing, increasing conflict with philistine materialism, which he sees both in Mary and in the raw colonial society on the barbaric continent of Australia. And by a bitter irony, it also shows that life in England irks and oppresses him as much as colonial experience ever has; and that, unlike his practical, warm-hearted wife, he is condemned never to feel at home anywhere.

Mahony is not simply a victim, a sensitive spirit crushed by a hostile world. He is also destroyed by his own pride and folly—by his rationalisations, self-deceptions, and impulsive decisions; his wilful, unthinking opposition to Mary; and his misguided quest for a material fortune while his deepest spiritual needs remain unsatisfied. There are elements of tragedy in the story of the very fallible Richard Mahony, who bears as much responsibility for his fate as those external forces over which he has no control. To read this story is a truly purgative experience, as writing it undoubtedly was for the author.

—Axel Clark

FOUR QUARTETS.
Poems by T.S. Eliot, 1943.

Twenty years separate *The Waste Land* from *Little Gidding*, the last of T.S. Eliot's *Four Quartets*. In spite of the interval, important signs of continuity unite the two works: most obviously the division of the poems into "movements" which reflect a "musical" conception of structure and the alternation of lyrical and discursive passages. Even the direct recourse to religious concepts in the *Quartets* is less innovative than might appear. The poems do not require the previous acceptance of any doctrinal formulation, but invite us rather to share in the exploration of a fully contemporary experience in which doubt, the difficulty of affirmative commitment, has a necessary part to play.

The first quartet, *Burnt Norton*, is concerned to establish a conceptual basis on which the later development may rest. After the initial tentative proposal of a possible convergence between time lived and time remembered—"What might have been and what has been / Point to one end, which is always present"—the first "movement" addresses itself to a past moment of personal illumination which might seem to confirm it. "Round the corner," "through the first gate" which seems, on reflection, to have opened into a "first world" of pure simplicity, the poem strives to recapture an experience which may indeed have been a "deception," but which might also offer the fleeting glimpse of a timeless reality. The fragments of past experience are held in precarious unity until the pressure of present reality returns them to their separate elements: "Go, go, go, said the bird: human kind / Cannot bear very much reality." Vision or illusion? In our incapacity, as time-conditioned beings, to hold fast to these moments of illumination only reflection, speculation on what has irretrievably vanished, can hope to tell.

To speculation, accordingly, we turn in the remainder of the first quartet. The experience in the garden seemed to suggest, while it lasted, that "To be conscious is not to be in time"; but, since only in time can it be remembered, the temporal element is inseparable from any continuing significance it may have. "Involved with past and future, / Only through time, time is conquered." To accept time as an ultimate reality is to risk turning our moments of timeless insight into illusions; but to deny the reality of the temporal is to render our experience, within its human limits, impossible.

The dilemma has particular application to the poet's creative endeavour. Language, the material of his art, shares in the necessary fragility of the temporal: "Words move, music moves / Only in time; but that which is only living / Can only die." Words "strain," "crack," continually "break" in the effort to express the timeless core of experience; and yet it is towards such expression, through a search for the "stillness," the achievement of the subsistent "pattern," that the deepest intuitions of art tend. To approach the timeless through the temporal, obtaining through the elements given by temporal experience the form that is the limited expression of a timeless reality, is at once the task of the artist and the obligation imposed upon him by his intermediate condition—poised "between being and un-being"—as a man.

Upon these conceptual foundations the following quartets build an expanding succession of meanings. The point of departure for *East Coker* is the disillusionment inspired, at a time of personal stress and collapsing certainties, by the approach of old age. "The long hoped for calm, the autumnal serenity" which we have been taught to expect as the reward of a lifetime's effort seems to have turned into a comfortless delusion. The disappointment, however, can be seen to contain a salutary warning against the temptation, inseparable from old age, to seek finality in an illusory "wisdom" based exclusively on past experience. "Home" may indeed be "where one starts from," and the end of the human journey in time may be sought, as the illuminating moment in the garden seemed to suggest, through a return; but between "beginning" and "end," the birth and death of each individual life, the degree of insight achieved necessarily changes and acceptance of this necessity is a condition of continuing life in the present. "Old men ought to be explorers": and again, "We must be still, and still moving." *Still*: ready, that is, to refrain from premature self-assertion in relation to a reality that is at each moment new, unpredictable, uniquely challenging; but equally *still moving*, ready to move with the current, rejecting the temptation to evade the dangerous challenge of the present by falling back upon judgments relevant only in the past.

The third quartet—*The Dry Salvages*—relates this doctrine of necessary renewal to a wider human context. Comparing the course of life—both that of the individual and that of the race to which he belongs—to the progress of a great river as it runs into the sea, the poem has recourse, more directly than at any previous point, to concepts which reflect the distilled experience of the poet's own Christian tradition. The only conceivable answer to "the bone's prayer to Death its God" is to be found in "the hardly, barely prayable / Prayer of the one Annunciation." What is "announced," presented as a redeeming possibility, is the related concept of "Incarnation": the spirit revealed through flesh, "The point of intersection of the timeless / With time": the possibility of a fresh approach to the "meaning," one which "restores the experience / In a different form, beyond any meaning / We can assign to happiness." This leads to a re-statement of the traditional notion of the "good death." Since, as we have already seen, the "pattern" of each human life is at any given point in time incomplete, its final sense can emerge only at the moment of death, when time ceases to be relevant and when the destiny of the individual is incorporated into that of the generations which have shaped the tradition to which his own efforts have now added their contribution. The moment of death becomes not an isolated point but one which covers the entire course of human existence. The end of the journey is present in its beginning, and experience becomes an invitation to confidence: "Not farewell, but fare forward, voyagers."

The last poem in the series, *Little Gidding*, is, theologically speaking, the most explicit. The acceptance of Incarnation leads naturally to an anticipation of the descent of the Spirit in tongues of fire. Once again, the poem proposes no short cut to spiritual peace. Its second "movement" offers, through a deeply personal meditation on "the gifts reserved for age," a conclusion as dismissive of easy consolation as anything in the sequence. Once again, the sense of guilt and personal inadequacy which shadows so much of Eliot's poetry makes its presence felt in "the rending pain of re-enactment / Of all that you have done, and been." The prevailing image of fire has a double significance, penitential and purgatorial, before it becomes the illuminating flame of Pentecost.

As the sequence moves to its conclusion, however, the doctrine of detachment developed in the earlier quartets becomes an "expanding" one of love beyond the intolerable importunities of "desire": a reconciling condition in which even those who were divided during their life-times by sincerely held convictions—such as those which separated committed men during the religious conflicts of 17th-century England—can be seen from the perspective of history as "United in the strife which divided them," gathered in the unity of "a single party." In a related way the poet's own struggle, sustained through a life-time, to find a medium adequate to express his meanings bears fruit in an instrument which has been perfected through succeeding generations and to which he is now making his personal contribution: that of a language

where every word is at home,
Taking its place to support the others,
The word neither diffident nor ostentatious,
An easy commerce of the old and the new,

The common word exact without vulgarity,
The formal word precise but not pedantic,
The complete consort dancing together.

The end of the poem, and of the series, returns to its beginning, but in a form clarified by the intervening development. It is true that "we die with the dying," accepting the necessary death implied in our temporal condition; but it is true also that "we are born with the dead" and may aspire to a state in which seeming opposites are brought together, reconciled in the lover's knot, the "rose" woven from the element of purifying and transfiguring "fire."

—Derek A. Traversi

FRA LIPPO LIPPI.
Poem by Robert Browning, 1855.

"Fra Lippo Lippi," a dramatic monologue in blank verse, is one of the poems which display Robert Browning's immersion in the civilization of the Renaissance. Browning establishes the atmosphere of his poem by placing his speaker, the Florentine painter and monk, Filippo Lippi, on the pavement outside the Medici-Riccardi palace, and having him refer to the altarpiece he is painting for Cosimo de'Medici, to the churches of the Carmine and San Lorenzo, and to numerous intimate features of the life of the time. Browning drew most of his material for his poem from the account of Fra Lippo in Giorgio Vasari's *Lives of the Painters*, but his persona is quite different both from Vasari's portrait and from the historical figure. As Browning's Fra Lippo speaks to the watchmen who have intercepted him on his return from a night of revelry in disreputable company, he exhibits a character largely invented by the poet himself and his philosophy of art echoes Browning's views. Browning places Fra Lippo as a realist who diverged from the religious idealism of the earlier painters, very much as Browning's poetry diverged from Romantic and Victorian conventions.

In explaining himself to the watch, Fra Lippo shows that he is an earthy, honest fellow, whose attraction to the pleasures of the flesh is part of a general delight with the world that leads him to depict it realistically in his painting. His joy is so irrepressible that he occasionally interrupts himself to sing folksongs. His account of the orphaned childhood which led him to become a keen observer, and of his first paintings, which portrayed the scenes and people of the neighborhood, is full of remarkable particulars that convey vivid glimpses of life in Renaissance Florence. The monk begins by admitting that his escapades are due to weakness of will, but this gradually changes to a mood of self-justification as he expresses his real views. The church authorities have criticized his paintings because they do not express religious feeling, saying that they represent a decline from the work of Fra Angelico and Lorenzo Monaco. But Fra Lippo defends his realism by declaring that taking pleasure in the visible world is a way of worshipping the God who made it. He says his escapades are a form of protest against hypocritical prohibitions against taking life as it is, and that it is the painter's mission to call attention to sights that others overlook. "Art was given for that; / God uses us to help each other so. . . . "

Nevertheless, Fra Lippo is reluctant to flout authority, feels that he has said too much, promises to "make amends" for his faults by painting a picture for the nuns of a nearby church, and closes his monologue by imagining that if he should appear in the company of virtuous people, he will be defended by the pretty girl who has modeled the figure of Saint Lucy in his painting. The picture he plans to paint is Lippi's "Coronation of the Virgin," which is described in some detail, not all of it accurate. Browning saw it in Florence, but it is also emphasized in an account of Lippi's life in Filippo Baldinucci's *Notizie de'Professori del Disegno*, one of Browning's sources of information about painters.

In this poem Browning has presented a remarkably vivid portrait of a vigorous, independent personality whose convictions about life's values compel him to challenge the discipline of the church. On one level, the conflict is an opposition of principle between individual liberty and institutional conformity, but on another, it is simply a case in which a man has been forced into an unsuitable role in life. As Fra Lippo says, "You should not take a fellow eight year old / And make him swear to never kiss the girls."

—Jacob Korg

FRANKENSTEIN.
Novel by Mary Shelley, 1818; revised edition, 1831.

Published anonymously before its author was 21, *Frankenstein* shocked some reviewers but was well received by readers. The book remains popular but is now less familiar than numerous film adaptations, many of which reduce and distort the original story of a young student who creates and then rejects a living being and is in turn destroyed by it. *Frankenstein* is a cautionary tale on at least two levels: like other gothic works, it speaks in veiled terms to a culture that persists in glorifying sentiment, reason, and material gain while refusing to acknowledge its own contradictions and the potency of other human motives; like later science fiction, it warns a technological age to examine and repair its relationships to its "creatures," material and human.

The novel's irony is achieved by contrasting points of view in embedded narratives, the first of which is contained in letters from an explorer, Robert Walton, to his sister. Walton, his ship locked in Arctic ice, rescues and befriends Victor Frankenstein, who is pursuing his Creature across the frozen sea. Victor's narrative is framed, amplified, and mediated by Walton's. Both men are romantic idealists; neither is aware of a divisive conflict between his adherence to sentimental domestic virtues and his obsession with attaining glory through scientific progress.

Victor recounts in glowing terms an idealized childhood. He does not admit, though critics have inferred, hostility toward a manipulative mother and stern but ineffectual father, ambivalent feelings for the adopted sister, Elizabeth, who is also his fiancée, and frustration at the irreconcilable qualities—domestic gentility and aggressive masculine ambition—his society demands of him. He tells, without explanation, of his estrangement from his family after his mother's death, and his spurning of the guidance of his university professors at Ingolstadt while he worked secretly on his bizarre project.

Neither does Victor explain why he rejected his Creature at its completion, but this too may be inferred: in creating it he has essentially created *himself*, projecting from his own character those traits his society has taught him to despise. He may not acknowledge these qualities as his own, but neither can he be rid of them. Unloved and uncontrolled, his nameless double attempts to do good but is soon driven to violence. The death of Victor's small brother in Geneva is more accident than murder, and Victor himself allows his family's ward to be executed when he refuses to support her innocence, of which he is convinced. Then, through the Creature's successive murders of Victor's friend Clerval and Elizabeth, Victor seems doggedly to abet his antagonist. His reluctant creation and then destruction of a female companion for the Creature, his doomed compliance in marrying Elizabeth despite the Creature's veiled threat to her life, his failure to prevent his bride's murder, all suggest a weakness as implacable as the Creature's strength. Seeing Walton's enterprise as similar to his, Victor presents his story as an attempt to save the explorer from his own mistakes, but remains sadly unaware of why he has suffered. Though he has failed, he says, "another may succeed"; he cannot at last renounce his course in spite of its disastrous consequences.

Only the Creature, whose narrative is central to the other two, recognizes the tragic dividedness implicit in Victor's life and his own. Rejected by his creator, he can find no other friend. His education, gained by listening secretly to a French family displaced by the Revolution (a family both like and unlike Victor's in certain significant respects), has shown him contrasts between society's ideals and practices. He has read Plutarch, Milton, Goethe; he has heard of the De Laceys' flight from political oppression. And he has found Victor's notes toward his own creation, from which he learns bitterly that all his qualities, including his hideousness to humankind, were deliberately given. His own needs have been thwarted at every turn. Given the nature with which Victor endowed him, he has literally no choice but to act, nor any choice of action but violence and revenge.

Victor has ignored the Creature's pleas for reconciliation, and Walton ignores—apparently—his eloquent *apologia* delivered after Victor's death; the explorer turns back toward England, but the book ends before he arrives there. At the end, too, the Creature still lives, though he has promised to immolate himself. He retreats into "darkness and distance," a continuing warning to those who undertake ambitious projects without self-knowledge.

Like other gothic fiction, *Frankenstein* has gained in reputation in the late 20th century. Its critics, especially since the late 1960's, have essayed biographical, psychological, sociopolitical, philosophical, and feminist readings. That the novel supports close, thoughtful, and varied speculation, while remaining a popular entertainment and a rich source of allusion for other artists, attests to its depth and strength.

—Mary K. Patterson Thornburg

THE FRENCH REVOLUTION.
Prose by Thomas Carlyle, 1837.

Thomas Carlyle became famous in 1837 for his *The French Revolution*, though a more discriminating readership might have already detected his greatness in his German translations, his influential essays, and above all in his startlingly innovative *Sartor Resartus*, written in a style more familiar in this century than in the first third of the 19th.

The French Revolution was also a revolution in its treatment of the recent past. For Carlyle stood in a curious relation to his subject matter. He had been born in 1795, and his student days in Edinburgh had been in wartime, his college left half-built as a result, his early newspaper reading of battles and the struggle with Napoleon. While he had visited Paris for a week in 1824 he was very much a Scot, product of a strongly pious background, an autodidact despite his university education, brilliantly verbal and fiercely omnivorous when it came to reading in history and literature. He had acquired enough German to introduce many of his contemporaries to Goethe and Schiller; he read Italian and French comfortably.

When he moved to Chelsea with his wife in 1834, it was to have access to major resources—major libraries, and the company of major thinkers such as John Stuart Mill who, as is well known, borrowed the manuscript of the first volume of Carlyle's history and accidentally allowed it to be burnt. Carlyle's recovery and heroic completion of the work is common knowledge. The work itself is less so. Hailed by the reviewers (not least by a penitent Mill) *The French Revolution* was extremely influential in its time, but until recent republication by the Oxford University Press had been overtaken by more recent historical treatment.

Carlyle's is an intensely selective analysis. Not for him the long exploration of the causes of the Revolution through a history of French society and the forces behind the breakdown of the agricultural system. Carlyle's analysis, shaped by his strong consciousness of the spiritual collapse of pre-Revolutionary France, begins with the dying Louis XV, the intrigue of palace and court, the shaky basis of Louis XVI's reign. Combining this selective but brilliantly focused recreation of vignettes from history with a profound understanding that the collapse of the monarchy, once started, was beyond human control and in the hands of an increasingly unpredictable and appalling mob, *The French Revolution* gathers speed as it conducts the reader through re-creations of great and justly famous set-pieces: the tennis court at Versailles, the fall of the Bastille, the flight of the royal family, the executions, the Feast of Pikes, the trials, the death of Danton and Robespierre, the collapse of the ideals of the Revolution, and the formation of new modes of society with grim forebodings of the Napoleonic period ahead.

Carlyle was content to stop there. As it did not seek to probe the prehistory of the Revolution, so the work stops short of the living memory of many readers of the first edition of 1837—the Napoleonic Wars, and their aftermath. The attention is focused on the Revolution from the crowning of Louis XVI to the rise of Napoleon, typically for Carlyle the forces of history encapsulated in a real, verifiable personality. The forces behind these personalities amply explain, for Carlyle, the Revolution: the intellectual and moral bankruptcy of the ruling classes and their dereliction of duty to the workers (whose savagery and barbarism are vividly portrayed after the fall of the Bastille). A writer who thought that heroes should govern and the governed should obey could only be horrified by a nation where the royal family lived in a fantasy world protected by self-interested courtiers, where the church had all but given up its spiritual duties, and where the fabric of a society had withered to the point where anarchy was the only response. All his life Carlyle feared that anarchy, and never more so than in the brilliantly evoked passages in *The French Revolution* where the streets of Paris run with blood, and the clang of the guillotine is heard over Europe.

Carlyle's vivid style, the hectic intensity of his narration, his gift of recreating historical personages and making the experience of history real and immediate made this book a telling one for his contemporaries, seeking to come to terms with their recent past. Without real analysis in the modern historical sense, *The French Revolution* transmitted a view towards the past, one in which moral and religious values had an important role, and where divine forces were seen acting out an inevitable tragedy in a country whose ruling classes had lost the right to rule. The relevance of this work to the troubled society of Carlyle's Britain in the 1830's and 1840's was not lost, and Carlyle went on in *On Heroes, Hero-Worship, and the Heroic in History, Past and Present*, and *Latter-Day Pamphlets* to hammer home to Victorian Britain the need to avoid a similar catastrophe.

—Ian Campbell

FRIAR BACON AND FRIAR BUNGAY.
Play by Robert Greene, 1589(?).

Written about 1589 and first published in 1594, Robert Greene's *The Honorable History of Friar Bacon and Friar Bungay*, which critics once considered as little more than a pleasant romantic comedy, is now interpreted as a nationalistic glorification of Tudor England and Queen Elizabeth. Greene creates an historical diptych in which the moral journeys that the 13th-century characters, Margaret, Bacon, and Prince Edward, undergo presage and parallel the rise of the Tudors and the ascendancy of Elizabeth. The discord which Margaret and Bacon encounter from love and magic, respectively, gives way to the harmony of the marital and political unions at Windsor Court, which represent the inevitable triumph of the Tudor line. As Peter Mortenson has stated: ". . . Eleanor-Europe is united with Edward-England in Albion. . . . The historical 'facts' symbolically achieve their prophetic epitome in Elizabeth; within the analogizing action of the play, the destruction and renewal pattern in the historical progress . . . to Elizabethan England is repeated in the festive structure of the plots of magic and love. . . . "

The play's 16 scenes take place in three settings: the country, including the East Anglian towns of Framlingham, Fressingfield, and Harleston; Oxford University, specifically Brasenose College, and Regent House; and the court as represented by Hampton Court and Windsor Castle. These settings constitute the major areas of English social, economic, intellectual, and political power. By having the representatives of the three settings interact easily, Greene creates an idealistic image of English society as both hierarchical in its insistence on the importance of aristocracy and egalitarian in its praise of ascendancy through personal merit. After a series of misadventures, the nobleman Lacy marries country maid Margaret in recognition of her noble character, and England is applauded as a felicitous combination of court and country, of monarchy and meritocracy, of class separation and social integration. This sense of integration among all classes and all parts of England, and between England and Europe invests the play with a spirit of beneficial circulation which is opposed by Bacon's necromantic plans to wall England off from Europe.

The journey motif is central to the play's social interactions, dramatic structure, and the themes of moral growth and national progress. The first scene depicts the dislocation arising from Prince Edward's lust for Margaret of Fressingfield, the daughter of the royal keeper. It is as if the court represented by the disguised Prince of Wales is intent on despoiling the pristine countryside as embodied by the virginal Margaret. Appropriately, Edward finally renounces his lust in the setting where it began, and the countryside returns to its former purity. Edward's return to Oxford marks his resumption of his identity as dutiful royal son and future husband of Elinor of Castile. The erstwhile wayward heir has matured and marries his proper bride, uniting their countries and ensuring a well-governed England.

Bacon's journey to moral regeneration is more complicated than that of Edward because he uses his magical powers for benign and evil nationalistic purposes. Bacon's construction of the brazen head represents the power and the danger implicit in the cultivation of the intellect fostered by Oxford University. By means of demonic magic, he attempts to construct a wall around England, a pursuit which is morally and politically opposed to the beneficial circulation created by the unions of Lacy and Margaret and Edward and Elinor. The brazen wall will "circle England round with brass" and rival "The work that Ninus reared at Babylon, / The brazen walls framed by Semiramis."

In late 16th century Protestant apologetics, Babylon is equated with Spain under Philip II, whose Armada was defeated by England in 1588. In Bacon's perverted dream of nationalistic and isolationist power, England will become a type of Babylon, but Greene has written *Friar Bacon and Friar Bungay* as a post-Armada dream play which unites England with Spain and the world in an image of circularity and communication. The narrow restrictionist circle of Bacon's abortive wall is replaced at the conclusion by the perfect circle of paradise: "That makes fair England like that wealthy isle / Circled with Gihon and swift Euphrates."

The play's scenes have alternated among country, university, and court settings. East Anglia as a place of innocence has been violated by lust, deception, necromancy, rivalry, and murder. But in the end Margaret is vindicated and raised to courtly status by her marriage. Oxford University has been the scene of hypocrisy, deception, rioting, necromancy, murder, and, finally, reconciliation and the reassertion of a proper national intelligence. Windsor Court is the summit to which the characters ascend: it is the crown of English society, the heart of its stature as nation. The chief residence of English rulers since William the Conqueror, the site of St. George's Chapel and the Order of the Garter, Windsor Castle epitomizes the English nationalism which Greene praises throughout *Friar Bacon and Friar Bungay*. In the final scene, England stands *primus inter pares*, surrounded by the world's leaders in an image of a united and circular world. Hierarchy and degree, virtue and service, interaction and egalitarianism, and beneficial imperialism and world unity are all celebrated in this fairytale ending.

—Frank Ardolino

THE FUNCTION OF CRITICISM AT THE PRESENT TIME.
Prose by Matthew Arnold, 1865.

Despite the absence of a detailed critical practice in "The Function of Criticism at the Present Time" and other essays in criticism, Matthew Arnold is generally acknowledged, by both proponents and detractors, to be the founder of "modern" English literary criticism's stress on literature's social function. Though few literary critics now unreservedly uphold Arnold's definition of literary critical practice as the attempt to "know the best that is known and thought in the world," Arnold's influence can nonetheless be traced in the works of literary critics as disparate as T.S. Eliot, Lionel Trilling, F.R. Leavis, Raymond Williams, and Elaine Showalter.

Arnold's emphasis on the social function of literature, and so on the important social task of the critic, must be placed in historical context. Arnold was writing at a time of democratisation in English culture. Though modern readers can find conservative his concepts of "disinterestedness" and the "touchstone," and his emphasis on "the best that is known and thought," he considered himself and his work (as school inspector, poet, and critic) to be a part of the democratising process. For Arnold, this democratisation necessarily meant that "religion" could no longer perform its traditional function; it was now, at a time when "exuberant self-satisfaction" and smugness characterised English politics in particular and society in general, that literature must provide that guide to conduct and feeling that religion once furnished.

At the same time, for Arnold, the "current of ideas" in which contemporary writers worked no longer provided the "fresh thought" that, for example, the society of Greece provided for Pindar and Sophocles, or that of Elizabethan England for Shakespeare. As a result, it is the function of the disinterested critic, who is the structuring principle in "The Function of Criticism," to see "the object as in itself it really is" and so ensure that the best ideas prevail, rather than those that are politically expedient. In other words, Arnold sees the need for a "disinterested" critic to prepare the ground for the "best ideas," that "fresh thought," which is so necessary for the "best" writing. Arnold outlines a three-stage process which he deems imperative "in the present time." In the first "epoch" as he calls these stages, the philosophers of the age generate the necessary "ideas." In the second, these ideas are culled or sorted through by critics in order to provide the creative writers, who are the third epoch in the process, with the "best" ideas to disseminate.

As argument for the necessity of this three-stage process, Arnold points to the romantic writers, and the source of their ideas, the French Revolution. Arnold first notes that "it seems strange that out of the immense stir of the French Revolution and its age should not have come a crop of works of genius." But, as he maintains, the romantics "had their source in a great movement of feeling, not in a great movement of mind." Their literature is consequently premature and, most importantly, too political. For Arnold, the ideas generated by the French Revolution too soon "quit[] the intellectual sphere and rushing furiously into the political sphere, ran, indeed, a prodigious and memorable course, but produced no such intellectual fruit as the movement of ideas of the Renascence."

In place of the immediate transportation of ideas into the political arena, Arnold advocates a time of contemplation, of sorting out the best materials, to be presided over by the disinterested critic: "Criticism first; a time of true creative activity, perhaps . . . hereafter, when criticism has done its work." Chris Baldick, in *The Social Mission of English Criticism*, has termed this critical practice Arnold's "doctrine of postponement." In many ways, it is Arnold's advocacy of a "time of critical contemplation" before action, his definition of "criticism" as an apolitical act, which problematises his modern critical reception.

For modern readers, Arnold's rhetoric in "The Function of Criticism" is particularly important. Structuring Arnold's argument throughout this work is a metaphor of procreation and cultivation which has an important impact on the presentation of ideas in the essay. Arnold distinguishes between the "fresh," "nourishing," and "quickening and sustaining" atmosphere of Shakespearian England, for example, with the paucity of "a crop," which "reap[s]" the "one fruit" that characterises the "atmosphere" of the French Revolution. Throughout "The Function of Criticism," this metaphor of successful and unsuccessful cultivation is utilised to describe the effect of critical practice. The critically-divisive passage on the child-murderer Wragg is a case in point. Arnold quotes the newspaper report of a young woman's murder of her child, juxtaposing this report with the "absolute eulogies" of contemporary politicians who jingoistically claim the "unrivalled happiness" of the "best race in the world." Arnold's point is that only by criticism "will these songs of triumph be induced gradually to moderate themselves . . . and to fall into a softer and truer key." But what is interesting to the modern reader is Arnold's choice of the "Wragg" incident. In contrast to the plenitude, the freshness, that distinguishes the products of a creative period that follows a critical one, "Wragg" characterises the sterility, here literally the infanticide, that marks the products of a creative age that has not benefited from a disinterested critical practice.

At the same time, the metaphor of cultivation / procreation structuring "The Function of Criticism" is complicated and contradictory. The "Wragg" episode, again, exemplifies this complexity. If sterility is associated with the absence of disinterested critical practice, it is also oddly associated throughout the essay with "the multitude," the "many," those "other people" who insist on "rushing furiously into the political sphere." It is the disinterested critic who cultivates—both generates and selects—or renders most cultivated, the best that is known, thought, and importantly, to be acted upon in the world. For the modern literary critic, it is this palimpsestic construction of cultivation which requires the most critical attention. Structuring that palimpsest is an Arnoldian anxiety about the "democratised" society in which literature and the critic must "function" that must be carefully assessed.

—Susan Hamilton

G

GAMMER GURTON'S NEEDLE.
Play by "Mr. S." (possibly William Stevenson), c. 1550–60.

Editions

Three Sixteenth-Century Comedies, edited by Charles W. Whitworth. 1984.
Four Tudor Comedies, edited by William M. Tydeman. 1984.

Critical Studies: *Shakspere's Five-Act Structure* by T.W. Baldwin, 1947; *The Staging of Plays Before Shakespeare* by Richard Southern, 1973.

Uncertainties surrounding the date and authorship of this short, lively mid-16th century comedy may perplex the scholar but need not trouble the reader, spectator, or amateur actor who encounters it. It is a university play, performed at Christ's College, Cambridge, the title page of the 1575 quarto informs us, "not long ago." That vague but tantalizing bit of information probably refers to the 1550's when the generally accepted candidate for authorship of the play, William Stevenson, was a fellow of the college and was involved in the production of plays there, according to surviving records. Although the quarto is the earliest known edition, a play called *Dyccon of Bedlam* was entered in the Stationers' Register for publication as early as 1562–63: Diccon is the leading character in *Gammer Gurton's Needle*. Despite its university origin, the play became known well outside Cambridge circles and remained so for some time after its composition and earliest performances. Imitated and referred to in other plays as late as 1599, it also figures in a polemical pamphlet in the late 1580's by the Puritan "Martin Marprelate," who pretends to accuse the Dean of Salisbury, John Bridges, of being its author. Admittedly, he does so only to discount it, but the fact that he mentions the play at all in such a context testifies to its reputation. Most curious of all, perhaps, is the fact that it was reprinted in 1661, a century or more after it was written.

The play's critical fortunes have fluctuated. Admiration for its "wit and invention," qualities already acknowledged by "Marprelate," has in recent years largely supplanted the 19th- and earlier 20th-century embarrassment at "the very rudimentary kind of humour which turns on physically disgusting suggestions no longer amusing to educated people" (Henry Bradley, 1903). Even Bradley could discern "real comedy, not quite of the lowest order" in some of the scenes. The humour that Victorians found objectionable is scatalogical humour of a naughty schoolboy kind, deliberately, gleefully indulged in this anarchic holiday romp by and for university men. Backsides and excrement as well as wallops, pratfalls, curses, and crude practical jokes are the essence of the play's exaggerated childishness. Probably it was part of a college festival of Misrule at Christmas, a medieval custom which lingered on in universities and Inns of Court long after the Reformation had suppressed it in churches.

The plot is tight and superbly structured, belying the madhouse atmosphere and frenetic action; that very incongruity is part of the fun. The prologue gives the plot in outline and the audience is invited to sit back, hold on to their seats, and enjoy the high jinks. Diccon the Bedlam appears and describes the scene in Gammer Gurton's household, where there is "howling and scowling . . . sighing and sobbing." We soon learn the cause of all the uproar: Gammer has lost the needle with which she was mending a pair of trousers for Hodge, her field hand—much ado about very little. Diccon's label "Bedlam" is misleading: it identifies him as an erstwhile inmate of the famous lunatic asylum in London, St. Mary of Bethlehem (as Edgar in *King Lear* pretends to be). But Diccon is far from mad; indeed, he has far more wits than anyone else. He is a vagrant, who steals a side of bacon while Gammer's household is preoccupied, but he is also and principally a prankster, a mischief-maker with a cruel sense of humour, and a master of ceremonies, moving easily and familiarly between play world and audience, promising "sport" and delivering it in abundance. He is in fact the motive force in the play, walking into a scene of confusion and exploiting it and its dimwitted actors for his own amusement and the audience's. Like the Vice of the English morality play, still a thriving genre at the time of *Gammer Gurton's Needle*, he insinuates himself into our confidence, promising us uproarious entertainment if we will let him manage events. The credulity and thick-headedness of the other characters make it absurdly easy for him to keep his word.

The old dame of the title, Gammer Gurton, her slow-witted labourer Hodge, her servant Tib (and Gib the cat), her irascible neighbour Dame Chat the alewife, the bibulous village curate Doctor Rat, the bailiff Master Bailey, and his silent catchpole Spendthrift—these are the rustic populace of the play's world. The dual plot, the loss of Gammer's needle (left in a pair of Hodge's trousers that he finds it necessary to change into, having soiled his other pair in terror at the imaginary devil that Diccon pretends to conjure), and Diccon's deliberate mischief-making—setting up a titanic battle between the two old women by feeding each of them lies allegedly coined by the other, persuading Dame Chat to set a trap for a supposed chicken thief, then leading the credulous, myopic Doctor Rat into it—is cleverly constructed by a dramatist well-versed in classical forms. This may be the first English play to be divided into five acts in imitation of Roman comedy. The audacious combination of classical structure and earthy, rambunctious subject matter is unique in English Renaissance drama. This remarkable little comedy continues to prove itself on both college and professional stages today, as it surely did on that of Christ's College, Cambridge, four centuries ago.

—Charles W. Whitworth

THE GARDEN.
Poem by Andrew Marvell, 1681 (written c. 1650–52).

Like the majority of Marvell's poetry, "The Garden" was not published until the posthumous *Miscellaneous Poems* of 1681. It is generally thought that it was written during the time he was living as tutor to Mary, the daughter of Sir Thomas Fairfax, at Fairfax's Nun Appleton estate in Yorkshire (1650–52). Fairfax, the commander-in-chief of the parliamentary forces in the Civil War, had resigned his commission when asked to lead an army to invade Scotland, retiring temporarily from public life. Two of Marvell's major poems, "Upon Appleton House" and "Upon the Hill and Grove at Bill-borow," are addressed to Fairfax, and focus on the issue of retirement by contrasting the natural world with the general's military past with its "Groves of Pikes" and mountains of "dying Men" ("Upon the Hill and Grove at Bill-borow)."

"The Garden" concentrates on the poet's own imaginative experiences within nature, but manifests a related concern with the causes and effects of retreat from the outside world. The first of the poem's nine stanzas sets the vain activity of men whose "uncessant Labours" are rewarded by the symbolic prize of a single tree ("the Palm, the Oke, or Bayes") against the richer real rewards of retirement where "all Flow'rs and all Trees do close / To weave the Garlands of repose." The second stanza presents the poet's own affirmation of these priorities, his discovery of quiet and innocence in the garden being the fruit of his escape from "busie Companies of Men." The poem thus seems to be firmly within the tradition of 17th-century retirement verse, in which the country's moral superiority is asserted over the city's corruption and ugliness.

The particular quality of this example, however, is to unite exceptionally intense versions of religious and sensual achievements of the solitary life. Quiet and innocence are "sacred plants" which, on earth, can only be found among the literal plants of the garden; but the solitude in which they can be enjoyed is "delicious." The poem's movement is thus towards all-inclusiveness, enclosing the essentials of all levels of human experience just as the flowers and trees merge into one whole. "The Garden" is often regarded as the culmination of Marvell's lyric poetry, his most complete expression of the concentration of soul and body into an ecstatic state which has been variously defined as Christian, Platonic, neo-Platonic, Plotinian, or Hermetic. For example, the idea of the garden as a re-creation of a prelapsarian, even pre-Eve, world can be read in terms of the Hermetic notion of an androgynous Adam. That Fairfax wrote a commentary on a translation of Hermetic writings may lend support to such an interpretation. On the other hand, it may simply be that Marvell is taking to its extreme conclusion a separation of natural goodness from human corruption: eroticism is purified by being transferred from human sexuality to an amorous nature. This is the point of stanza four, where Ovidian metamorphoses of Daphne and Syrinx into a laurel and a reed translate the god's sexual passions into devotion to nature.

However this much-discussed and variously interpreted poem is taken, its heart lies in the fifth and sixth stanzas, both structurally and thematically. The fifth represents the climax of sensuality, as the poet becomes the passive recipient of a luscious natural harvest of apples, grapes, nectarines, peaches, and melons. Ascertaining the tone of this stanza is particularly difficult: is it a serious presentation of total immersion in a natural paradise, the poet's identity being dissolved into nature; a re-run of the fall, with the poet stumbling on melons (the Greek word for apples); or a rather comic depiction of poet as victim of aggressive fruit? Uncertainty as to the precise nature of the experience is also a feature of the sixth stanza's simultaneous ("Mean while") withdrawal into intense mental activity. The mind is both supremely creative ("Yet it creates, transcending these, / Far other Worlds, and other Seas") and violently reductive ("Annihilating all that's made / To a green Thought in a green Shade"). Sensible objects are transformed onto a higher, purely intellectual plane, preparing for the soul to cast its "Bodies Vest aside"; yet the repeated "green" defines the achievement of mental pleasure through total identification with the "lovely green" which is the object of the poet's physical desire.

The puzzles of the poem rest on such paradoxes, rendering it both idealistically ecstatic and wittily earth-bound. Marvell's Fairfax poems confirm the sorry state of the public world as much as they describe a retreat from it: reality keeps breaking in to form a dialectical argument. So the final stanza of "The Garden" confronts the poet with nature's confirmation of the categories of human temporal existence. The garden contains a floral dial (not, as is sometimes claimed, a floral horologe: 17th-century floral dials were ornamental, with a gnomon to indicate the time). Time and labour ("th'industrious Bee") are as much a part of the garden as they are of the time-scarred world of "uncessant Labours" beyond it.

—W.B. Hutchings

GITANJALI.
Poems by Rabindranath Tagore, 1912.

Rabindranath Tagore, the author of *Gitanjali*, was born in 1861 in Calcutta, a member of a wealthy high-caste Bengali family. He was originally intended for the law and spent some time as a young man studying in University College, London. On his return to Calcutta he published his first volume of poetry, written in his native Bengali, rendered into English many years later as "Songs of Sunrise and Sunset."

On his marriage in 1884 he was put in charge of the family estate at Shileida on the banks of the Ganges and lived for close on 20 years a quiet country life devoted to writing, soon becoming recognised as the leading writer in Bengali. At the age of 40, after a short and unsatisfying involvement in Indian politics, he established a school for boys to which he devoted the great part of his capital. The emphasis was on creativity and contact with nature. During this period Tagore composed the 103 short lyrics that make up the contents of *Gitanjali*.

Tagore decided to make his own English translations of the Bengali lyrics in *Gitanjali* and these appeared in 1912 in a limited edition published by the Indian Society. The following year a trade edition appeared and its success was sensational. The London edition rapidly went into 20 reprints and Tagore followed up by publishing translations from his dramas and fiction. Tagore, writing in Bengali—a language few Europeans could understand—became famous almost overnight as a writer in English. In 1913 he was awarded the Nobel Prize for Literature, the first Asian writer to be so recognised.

It was *Gitanjali* that brought him to the notice of the world beyond India. It is a slight book of under a hundred pages, the lyrics all short; the nearest equivalent in English poetry a sonnet sequence. The poems are devotional and the English chosen for his translation is that of the King James version of the Bible. To English readers the lotuses and the Indian landscape might be alien, but the language was familiar—"Thou hast made me known to friends whom I know not. Thou hast given me seats in homes not my own. Thou has brought the distant near and made a brother of the stranger." The poet is seeking his Master, his God. But to the English reader (and possibly also the Bengali) the imagery is frequently ambivalent. The language of devotion is also the language of love and many of the lyrics in *Gitanjali* could be read as straight love-poems—"In the moonless gloom of midnight I asked her, "Maiden, what is your quest holding the lamp near your heart? My house is all dark and lonesome,—lend me your light.'" The echoes of ancient vedic Sanskrit hymns, a loving observation of nature and a sense of worship expressed in the exotic and ambiguous language of the Song of Solomon—it was a heady mixture, and the readers of 1912 made Tagore a cult figure. It is worth noting that the year 1912 also saw the publication of the great Grierson edition of John Donne. English metaphysical poetry too could blur the distinction between religious poetry and love poetry. The audience was ready.

What clinched the matter and established *Gitanjali* as a worldwide success was the introduction to the London edition, written by W.B. Yeats. The reputation of Yeats was by 1912 already considerable. He was a rising star—and in 1923 he too would become a Nobel laureate; his recommendation counted. The introduction is ecstatic: "I have carried the manuscript of these translations about with me for days, reading it in railway trains, or on the tops of omnibuses and in restaurants . . . these lyrics display in their thought a world I have dreamed of all my life long."

Yeats was well aware too of the ambivalence of these poems of worship: "Lovers, while they await one another, shall find, in murmuring them, this love of God a magic gulf wherein their own more bitter passion may bathe and renew its youth."

In today's more critical climate the poetry of *Gitanjali* in its English version pays the price for being both exotic and romantic. But one must remember that in Tagore's part of India his poetry (and the music he composed for it) is known to everyone from the highest caste to the lowest.

—Ian A. Gordon

THE GO-BETWEEN.
Novel by L.P. Hartley, 1953.

"The past is a foreign country: they do things differently there." The opening sentence of L.P. Hartley's *The Go-Between*, with its wistful cadences and sense of alienation from an earlier self, expresses the view of the timorous, repressed narrator, Leo Colston. The novel is concerned with his exploration of that foreign country; his quest is for the processes which turned the resilient child whom he resurrects for us into the adult who tells the story.

That adult is obliquely presented in the paragraph that follows, which exemplifies the narrative method that has made *The Go-Between* Hartley's most highly-praised novel. Examining "a battered red collar-box"—the evocation of period by means of realistic detail is beginning—Leo finds a cache of schoolboy treasures, untouched since his 13th birthday in July 1900. These are listed, apparently to provide authenticity at the opening of the novel; retrospectively we can see them as a commentary on Leo himself. The sea-urchins, "dry, empty"; the rusty magnets which have almost lost their power; negatives, tightly rolled; stumps of sealing-wax; a combination lock whose number he has forgotten: all these speak of deadness and enclosure, a life without energy or fecundity, lacking the power to attract or be attracted, devoted to suppression and denial. With the aid of the diary also in the box Leo revives memories, buried for more than half a century, of the traumatic experience which destroyed his emotional development at the very start of puberty, thus affecting his whole life. *The Go-Between* is a small-scale *Recherche du temps perdu*.

The use of symbolism, ever more tightly woven, continues throughout the novel. The amount might have seemed excessive had it been presented as authorial only, but this difficulty has been circumvented by making much of it, such as the omnipresent Zodiac, the product of Leo's fertile imagination. At school Leo apparently succeeds in vanquishing his bullies by "magical" spells, thus acquiring a half-belief in his own mysterious powers in a world of superhuman characters where external events reflect, and are intimately related to, his own personal affairs. This state of mind, which in an adult would indicate psychosis, is credible in an imaginative child—indeed the convincing portrayal of small boys, their behaviour, attitudes, and relationships, has always been considered one of the strengths of the book. Writing in 1953, Hartley was not to know how much children would grow in sophistication during the next half-century; his children remain convincing but now appear more like nine- or 10-year-olds than incipient teenagers—an unfortunate discrepancy which makes it harder to identify the child whose invented language impresses his peers as the height of wit with the adolescent responding with a "tumult of emotions" to the inviting but dangerous belladonna plant, a symbol of the sexually exciting Marian.

Leo, carrying messages between his hostess's daughter and Ted, her socially unsuitable lover, sees himself as Mercury, the messenger of the gods; soaring to new heights of experience, he identifies also with the mercury rising and rising in the thermometer as the summer heatwave continues. There are obvious parallels with *Lady Chatterley's Lover*, and also with Hardy's use of summer heat to symbolise sexual passion in *Tess of the d'Urbervilles*; here, however, not only the adult lovers, but also the pubescent Leo are "caught" in the sun's "fierce embrace." Sexually ignorant, but attracted and disturbed by Marian, Leo is vulnerable to her exploitation; it is one of the novel's many ironies that Ted, who attempts to suppress his own qualms at manipulating Leo by promising to tell him the facts of life, teaches him in the end by a demonstration which in different ways destroys them both.

Here for once *The Go-Between* seems forced. Ted has become a father-figure for Leo, as Marian, with her gift of the green suit, has taken on the role of a mother. The extent of Leo's disturbance depends on his Oedipal guilt, and for this it is necessary that he should feel that he has killed Ted (a destruction already prefigured on two occasions which Leo specifically links with the assumption of an adult role: the cricket match and the singing at the supper). Ted's suicide seems occasioned by this need, rather than by the demands of the character, who has already considered the army as an escape from his situation. Also unexplained, but less implausible, is the role played by Mrs. Maudsley. In the screen version scripted by Harold Pinter she was represented as sexually frustrated, trapped in a sterile marriage and bitterly jealous of a daughter who has gained the man she desires herself: this interpretation clarifies an area undeveloped by Hartley.

Controversy has been caused by the epilogue, seen as an anticlimax by several critics; for Hartley, who has expressed the view (in "My Own Work") that the lovers behaved "very badly," its purpose was to show "how [Marian's] sins found her out." The vitality of his creation has, however, for many readers obscured Hartley's moral purpose, and Leo himself is finally moved by her, for all his insistence on her self-deception: "the south-west prospect" of the Hall, which he sees again at the end, symbolises the life-enhancing aspects of the affair which neither he nor his creator can totally deny.

The Go-Between can be read in many ways—as a portrait of an epoch, a study of adolescence (it was an early example of this postwar genre), or a presentation of sexual forces in terms of timeless myth—but it is the tightly-woven symbolism holding the whole novel together in an intricate mesh, its Jamesian sense of form, that in spite of a certain self-conscious literariness provides it with a degree of depth and satisfying coherence.

—Margaret Forey

GOBLIN MARKET.
Poem by Christina Rossetti, 1862.

With few exceptions, Christina Rossetti's work has been treated with extraordinary indifference throughout most of the 20th century. The main exception has been *Goblin Market*, which achieved immediate recognition when it first appeared and has remained Rossetti's best-known and most-discussed work. Like most of the other great Victorian fantasies, *Goblin Market* has been variously interpreted; critics have dwelt especially on its erotic and its Christian elements. However, like her other works *Goblin Market* combines a very deliberately simple surface with complex suggestions. The genre (a combination of fairy tale, moral tale, and pastoral), the metre, (a rapid irregular line), the unpretentious diction, and the use of proverbs and sayings may all encourage a quick and easy interpretation that is seriously misleading. Rossetti's art frequently conceals as much as it reveals.

The first lines establish the poem's subjects, the young virgins, the goblin men, their commercial cry, "come buy," and the luscious fruit, listed in a catalogue like the flower catalogues of traditional pastoral. The first words of Laura and Lizzie voice the prohibition against the goblins' fruits on which the narrative is based; the analogy with the prohibition against specific fruit in Genesis is obvious. But not only must the sisters not eat, they should not allow themselves to be tempted: "we must not look at goblin men." The blushes and the tingling cheeks of the sisters perhaps suggest the sexual nature of the temptation. When Lizzie runs from danger, Laura is tempted to stay by her curiosity; the goblins seem like charming furry animals, clearly if perversely attractive. Laura buys the forbidden fruit with her own body—a golden curl, a precious tear. She sucks avidly—this is the verb consistently connected with eating the fruit—and goes home to Lizzie.

Lizzie greets her sister with "wise upbraiding," reminding her of Jeanie, who ate the goblin fruits and pined away, becoming a thing of such sterility that nothing will grow on her grave. Yet when they lie down together, what is stressed is not the difference between the sister who has yielded to temptation and the one who has resisted, but their similarity in beauty, purity, and love. The next morning, too, they share in the domestic tasks which in this poem seem idyllic. The difference between them is merely that one is content, "one longing for the night."

If Laura's actions have not corrupted her they have endangered her. She begins to suffer when she realises that Lizzie can hear the goblins while she cannot; that they now offer her only "baulked desire." In her frustration, she begins to pine and grow old. Lizzie, longing to help but afraid, returns to the story of Jeanie. At this point the connection between the fruits and sexual temptation is explicit: Jeanie died early "for joys brides hope to have." Nevertheless, realising that Laura is dying, Lizzie goes out to face the goblins: "And for the first time in her life / Began to listen and look." Unlike Laura, though, she is listening and looking with an altruistic purpose. When the goblins try to make her feast with them, they in turn are frustrated and turn to force. At this point Lizzie's strength is emphasized; like Laura she is described in listed similes, but while the similes applied to Laura suggest first her beauty and then her irresistible surrender—"Like a vessel at the launch / When its last restraint is gone"—the similes applied to Lizzie suggest her beauty and her strength against a mighty force. Laura in her temptation was like a "lily in a beck," whereas Lizzie is like "a lily in a flood," as well as a rock in the sea, a beacon in a stormy sea, a beleaguered city. She is strong in her purpose and in her delight in achieving that purpose; she has not tasted the fruit but is covered by the goblins with enough juice to save Laura. Her joyful energy is stressed when she runs home, running like one in fear but really urged on by "the kind heart."

Lizzie's jubilant cry to Laura has received considerable attention. Lizzie commands her sister: "Eat me, drink me, love me"; critics have commented both on the sacramental and (with some discomfort) on the erotic suggestions of her words. Laura's deliverance, however, seems to come not just from the juices on her sister's skin but from the fact that the kisses through which she ingests these juices are kisses of concern, a concern that makes her weep, refreshing "her shrunken eyes." The violence of her reaction to the juices is stressed in the last of the three simile lists as she falls

> Like the watch-tower of a town
> Which an earthquake shatters down,
> Like a lightening-stricken mast,
> Like a wind-uprooted tree
> Spun about,
> Like a foam topped waterspout
> Cast down headlong in the sea.

But after the violence of her fall she awakens entirely restored.

The poem ends in a future in which both Lizzie and Laura are wives and mothers. Laura tells her story to her children and points a moral generally understood as inadequate to the complexities of the poem: "For there is no friend like a sister / In calm or stormy weather."

The preceding paraphrase and commentary suggest the basis of some of the various interpretations, Christian, Freudian, feminist, and so on. (A particularly intelligent reading is Jerome McGann's in "Christina Rossetti's Poems: A New Edition and a Revaluation," *Victorian Studies*, 23, 1980.) Clearly the poem, the work of a committed Anglo-Catholic, is concerned with temptation, fall, and regeneration; clearly it has a sexual element; and clearly it deals with a woman's world and women's strength and weakness. It also combines a disturbing beauty with extraordinary energy and inventiveness.

—June Sturrock

THE GOLDEN BOWL.
Novel by Henry James, 1904.

The Wings of the Dove, *The Ambassadors*, and *The Golden Bowl* are the three major works that constitute the late phase of Henry James's career. Of the three, *The Golden Bowl* is the most complex and difficult. The surface action is deceptively simple with few events of apparent import. The novel falls into two parts, "The Prince" and "The Princess." The first part of the novel sets up the relationships and social conventions within which the game of the search for truth and meaning will be played.

Adam Verver, a rich American, has come to Europe with his daughter Maggie, to buy works of art for his collection. Along with various *objets d'art*, Verver also acquires a husband, the Prince, for his daughter and a wife, Charlotte Stant, for himself. Adam and Maggie are unaware that their spouses had had an affair that they were forced to abandon because they were not well-off enough to marry. Instead, the Prince and Charlotte separated, and Charlotte, a friend and contemporary of Maggie's, returned to America. It is on the eve of the Prince and Maggie's wedding that Charlotte appears in London, "extraordinarily alone," to witness the marriage of her dear friend. Charlotte's desire to find a perfect wedding gift, of the Prince's choosing, for Maggie, leads the ex-lovers on a search through London to a small antique shop in Bloomsbury where Charlotte discovers a golden bowl. The bowl is actually gilded crystal; it seems perfect but in fact is flawed. "Does one make a present," Charlotte asks, "of an object that contains, to one's knowledge, a flaw?" The golden bowl symbolises the fundamental flaws in the square of relationships that appear, superficially, to be so perfectly arranged and played out.

Maggie's feeling that she and the Prince "have made vacant, by their marriage, [Adam Verver's] immediate foreground" convinces her that the right course is for her father to remarry. Charlotte seems to be the ideal person to fill the empty space that Maggie perceives. Adam Verver's decision to marry Charlotte, is, however, founded on paternal concern and affection rather than on any passionate desire for either the state of matrimony or the person of Charlotte. Adam Verver makes this clear to Charlotte who, like Verver, seems satisfied to marry for the sake of Maggie's happiness. Ironically their union results in Adam Verver and Maggie spending more and more time together. The arrival of a grandson, the Principino, draws father and daughter still closer. The Prince and Charlotte, who by virtue of their domestic arrangements find themselves increasingly in each other's company, become lovers once again. This situation is sustainable because, on the surface, nobody "in the combination seemed estranged from anybody." The surface of their existence is, therefore, of paramount importance. The ability of the protagonists to maintain appearances is central to the working out of the game, but the cross-purposes that result lead to its eventual dissolution. By the end of the first part Maggie senses that all is not as it should be.

The complexity of the novel rests in James's subtle and searching exploration of the human consciousness, in particular that of Maggie, who, in the second part, comes across the golden bowl and confronts her husband with it, thus revealing her knowledge of his deception. Maggie manages to manoeuvre the Prince and Charlotte out of their lover-roles and into their respective spouse-roles by creating a gulf between them. She achieves this simply by not confronting Charlotte. Maggie knows the Prince will not tell Charlotte that they have been discovered. At the end of the novel Adam Verver and his wife leave for America; Maggie and her husband remain in England.

The movement throughout *The Golden Bowl* is one of perfect symmetry. In the elaborate game that is played out between the four protagonists each in turn takes control. Ostensibly the controller in the first part is the Prince, Maggie being essentially a passive figure. In the second part Maggie becomes the active mover of events as she takes on responsibility not only for her own life but also for her father's happiness; and as she does so, the Prince becomes an increasingly passive figure. At another level, it is Adam Verver who sustains the two marriages both through his money and, on a deeper level, his devotion to his daughter. Charlotte increasingly takes over events in her social role and it is in acknowledging her importance in this and in respect of her position as the wife of her father, that Maggie agrees to Charlotte's decision to take him to America.

The game which ends so neatly is, however, deceptive in its seemingly satisfactory conclusion: Maggie succeeds in saving her marriage but the price she has to pay is separation from the father she loves; Adam Verver promises Charlotte a new life but she has to relinquish the Prince. The surface resolution masks the novel's deeper ambiguity.

—Stella McNichol

THE GOLDEN NOTEBOOK.
Novel by Doris Lessing, 1962.

The Golden Notebook remains a staple coin in the currency of contemporary culture, registering since its publication 30 years ago the real gold value of novels that appeal to a general readership and engage, at the same time, scholars of the literary period. The most famous (and most famously difficult) work of Doris Lessing, *The Golden Notebook* has sold so far more than one million copies alone. Further, it has, like a forceful magnet, pulled to itself the fibers of many contemporary concerns: feminist, modernist and postmodernist, Marxist, psychoanalytical, philosophical, social, economic. For the novel is encyclopedic.

And it was prescient in its diagnoses of gender, class, and race as well as those political engagements and necessary disengagements in the morally exhausting years of the 1950's. "I suffer torments of dissatisfaction and incompletion because of my inability to enter those areas of life my way of living, education, sex, politics, class bar me from," the novel's female protagonist is made to observe, giving voice very early on in the novel to what has since been described as the woman writer's "anxiety of authorship." Present seemed what Simone de Beauvoir in France was then defining as "Other," the marginalized status of women's subjecthood and culture.

Nevertheless, *The Golden Notebook* took on a wide social sweep, embracing such matters as the Korean war, the colour bar in South Africa, the then current debates concerning politically correct roles for intellectuals and writers in the Communist Party of Great Britain, the McCarthy witch hunts in the U.S., the Czechoslovakian sabotage trials, the execution of Jewish writers in the U.S.S.R., the Hungarian uprising, the breakup of the left in the period following the revelation of Stalin's atrocities, then too Nikita Khrushchev's explosive speech before the 20th Congress of the Communist Party of the Soviet Union the morning of 25 February 1956.

And yet the story is ordinary enough. "The two women were alone in the London flat," announces the novel's limpidly simple opening sentence, the author forbidding from the outset any narrative courtship of a conventional marriage plot for her female heroine. Very soon the reader learns that the emblematically named protagonist, Anna Freeman Wulf, is a now unmarried and single parent engaged in hurt love affairs, ones which remain divorced from love, family, work, even political hope. A Marxist, a novelist, a writer, what then does she do through the course of the 666-page novel her author sends her through?

She thinks. She writes. And writes, and writes: diaries, journal entries, book reviews, news items, letters, parodies of commercial fiction, synopses of sessions with her psychiatrist Mrs. Marx, short story abstracts, film scenarios. All in separate notebooks, since Anna the novelist is suffering a writer's block and cannot create the novel the times demand: a "book powered with an intellectual or moral passion strong enough to create order, to create a new way of looking at life."

Then too, Anna's apparently free life is (as the novel's second line announces) "cracking up": sexually, politically, professionally, psychologically. So Anna keeps a journal. Anna explains: "I keep four notebooks, a black notebook, which is to do with Anna Wulf the writer; a red notebook, concerned with politics; a yellow notebook, in which I make stories out of my experience; and a blue notebook which tries to be a diary."

A persistent theme in *The Golden Notebook* is just this distrust of the whole writing enterprise. Obsessed by personal, social, and political fragmentation, the self-reflexive author-heroine interrogates narrative mimesis, veracity, and the duplicitous nature of storytelling itself. "I decided to use the blue notebook . . . as nothing but a record of facts. Every evening I sat . . . and wrote down my day, and it was as if I, Anna, were nailing Anna to the page. Every day I shaped Anna," an almost vertiginous narrator observes, dissecting the displacement of "I" into "Anna," fact into fictive artifact. Paradoxically in a novel about formlessness that questions the limitations of formal pattern, *The Golden Notebook* is shaped by a prodigiously patterned formal structure.

Lessing described the shape of the novel 10 years after its publication as consisting of a "skeleton or frame called *Free Women* . . . which could stand by itself. But it is divided into five sections and separated by stages of the four Notebooks, Black, Red, Yellow, and Blue. [Anna] keeps four and not one, because, as she recognizes, she has to separate things off from each other, out of fear of chaos, of formlessness—of breakdown." As they have already begun to dissolve one into the other, Anna eventually ends each Notebook to then start an important and new "Golden Notebook." Recording the mutual descent into madness of Anna and her American lover Saul Green, the inner Golden Notebook shows—as Lessing put the process in her preface—how characters "'break down' into each other, into other people, who form wholes." False binary divisions so summarily dismissed by Anna early on as "Men. Women. Bound. Free. Good. Bad. Yes. No. Capitalism. Socialism. Sex. Love . . ." dissolve. *The Golden Notebook*'s thematics become accessible. Counterpointed to the first theme of breakdown and replacing it is "the triumph of the second theme, that of unity." "[T]here is formlessness," Lessing was later to instruct, "with the end of fragmentation."

The tale itself resists the teller's claims about the end of fragmentation, at least as realized in the text. Certainly, it continues to be difficult for readers to defy Lessing's account of her own creation and so remain skeptical about authorial intention and actual achievement. Lessing is now very much a public persona, an international figure, traveling, accepting prizes (and regularly mentioned as a Nobel candidate), speaking, giving radio and television interviews; her authorial authority appears all the more unassailable 30 years after *The Golden Notebook*'s appearance. A new thing in literary history—this participation of a living author in the public scrutiny, explication, and exegesis of his or her own work—the practice has done much towards hardening into cliché initial critical reception. Thus Lessing has been for the most part taken at her word that *The Golden Notebook* was not autobiographical, that *The Golden Notebook* was not radical in its assumption that a female lens upon experience bore as much weight as that of a male, that *The Golden Notebook* was not a feminist tract for its time. For, of course, 1962 was the year when a woman, Doris Lessing, wrote, in a novel called *The Golden Notebook*, directly about women's situation in ways that have continued to influence the way women writers (Margaret Drabble, one among so many who have gone to school to Lessing's fiction) write about their lives. And read their lives. As readers will too.

—Virginia Tiger

THE GOOD COMPANIONS.
Novel by J.B. Priestley, 1929.

In *Rain upon Godshill* J.B. Priestley describes the Elder Breughel as an artist "with a broad appeal of the popular, tragic-comic, democratic kind, showing the crowd a vision of their own life"; these terms also aptly describe Priestley himself, especially with regard to *The Good Companions*.

Priestley had already written three novels and was to write many more, the most important being *Angel Pavement*, a dark, urban pendant to *The Good Companions*, and later *Bright Day, Festival at Farbridge*, *Lost Empires*, and *The Image Men*. Highly enjoyable and well made, weighty works, yet none had the impact of *The Good Companions*, the book which made Priestley famous, within a few months all over Britain, within a year in most parts of the globe. The reception by literary critics of this long novel was mixed, but the verdict of the public carried the day. Careful analysis shows the stunning success and lasting fame (further heightened by many stage and screen adaptations) are amply deserved.

Ultimately related to Chaucer's *Canterbury Tales*, this novel stands particularly in the tradition of Smollett's *Humphry Clinker* (1771) and Dickens's *Pickwick Papers* (1837) by showing the journeying through England of a group of people differing in temperament, age, sex, and social background. With such works it shares a warm-hearted and often farcical humour. This sets the English examples off from much continental picaresque fiction (though not from Cervantes's *Don Quixote*) and derives directly from Fielding, who dubbed the genre he helped to emerge with *Joseph Andrews* a "comic epic poem in prose"; the omniscient, eminently companionable and humane narrator of *The Good Companions* calls his story a "homely epic," but it is no less comic for that.

Like its analogues, the novel is a typical crisis story. One September, three widely separated characters: Jess Oakroyd from "Bruddersford," Inigo Jollifant in Fenland, and Miss Elizabeth Trant in the Cotswolds, turn a corner in their lives and take to the open road. Their meanderings fill Book One and convey multifarious impressions of central England and its inhabitants. Then the three paths, by a succession of wild and amusing accidents, converge on "Rawsley" (Barnsley?—a pity that Priestley adopted disguises for most places), where they meet the bankrupt remnants of a concert party called the "Dinky Doos." With Miss Trant's money, Inigo's music, the considerable talent among the professionals, and much enthusiasm the "Good Companions" are founded, get their act together, and perform (aided by Oakroyd's handyman skills) in the Midlands and Yorkshire. It is an uphill struggle in the autumn, during which more places and people come into view and some centrifugal forces already make themselves felt. The break after Christmas separates Books Two and Three. In March, at the height of their success, thugs hired by a worried local cinema operator smash up everything in the theatre at "Gatford." The party is over, and the "Good Companions" go their several ways, some of them in small groups, though all will stay in touch. For the three outsiders to the world of show business it was a sideshow anyway, though they would not have missed it for the world.

Closely looked at, the plotting impresses by its sheer ingeniousness. And Priestley gives the tale a strong structure as well as great pace, both artfully overgrown by the wealth of observation, incident, and character. Among the "Good Companions" themselves, Oakroyd, the quintessential Yorkshireman, the talented but too impressionable graduate Inigo, the charming, unpredictable Susie Dean, Jerry Jerningham ("Ai laike your playing. Jest what Ai warnted"), and Morton Mitcham with his banjo and boasting stand out; but all 10 are lovingly and convincingly drawn individuals. Also among the minor characters many are memorable, e.g., Miss Thong, the diminutive, indomitable seamstress (and most Dickensian character) and Mr. Timpany, the curly-haired "Second Resurrectionist." Indeed, the concreteness and liveliness of the novel stem from the fact that hardly anything or anyone is merely functional. And altogether there emerges an unforgettable, kaleidoscopic image of England and the English in the 1920's.

It has some of the realism in Priestley's grim account of the country in *English Journey*. However, the novel's realism resembles Breughel's—"a realism merging into the magical," with a "fairy-tale country" somewhere "just round the corner." There is also a "fairy tale" aspect to *The Good Companions* (see *Margin Released*).

It is due to the generally happy atmosphere and the ending, which fulfils nearly everybody's wishes; it is also due to Priestley's pervasive use of images tending to loosen the firm contours of man and world, to dynamise objects and situations and, especially through drastic disproportionateness of scale, to create an air of unreality. That mirrors the impressions of the three central characters, particularly after they have joined the world of the show—which, as the closing sentence of the book adumbrates, is itself representative of "a dream of life."

—Holger Klein

THE GOOD SOLDIER.
Novel by Ford Madox Ford, 1915.

Of Ford's 32 novels, *The Good Soldier* and the Tietjens tetralogy alone have continued to attract readers. The former has excited a good deal of admiration, but also perplexity—perplexity such that critics often seem not to be reading the same book. Much of this difficulty stems from the author's canny manipulation of point of view. *The Good Soldier*, which probes divisions within the self by playing on the psychological variations that unfold among a quartet of "good people," opens with one of those slight rhetorical shocks that sinew Ford's prose. "This is the saddest story I have ever heard," declares the narrator, John Dowell. It quickly becomes evident that he has been present while most of the action he recounts was happening. Why then does he speak of having *heard* about it? Precisely because he is the eyewitness who has seen almost nothing, who has to be told by Edward and Leonora Ashburnham about events in which he himself figures and which even now, as he composes his "memoir," remain largely incomprehensible to him.

The unreliability of Ford's narrator obliges the reader to engage in what amounts to collaboration, mentally revising and completing the story. Dowell mentions, for instance, that he and his wife Florence spent summers in Nauheim, a Hessian spa for cardiac patients, and then continues: "You will gather from this statement that one of us had, as the saying is, a 'heart,' and, from the statement that my wife is dead, that she was the sufferer." The inference would, however, be mistaken, and the reader discovers many pages later that Dowell knew it to be false when he sat down to write his chronicle. This coyness serves perhaps to compensate the narrator for the deception practiced upon him by his wife and friends. For nine years Florence carried on a liaison with Edward, of which Leonora, though not exactly complaisant, was fully aware; now the cuckold has their affairs at the mercy of his pen.

Dowell's conception of himself as a "fainter" Captain Ashburnham does not become explicit until the closing chapters. From the outset it is clear, however, that the narrator respects Edward's attainments as magistrate, landlord, and military officer, his loyalty to the essentially feudal traditions of his family. Of all the virtues Ashburnham lacks only one, constancy in his affections, and even that defect appears less a vice than a failure of self-understanding. Dowell himself possesses the emotional maturity of an early adolescent, and the love he bears for Edward is that of a pubescent boy for a slightly older contemporary, with all the narcissism and latent inversion one expects in such a relationship. Throughout the novel the narrator demands protection in the manner of a vulnerable child. Indeed his view of love appears to derive almost entirely from an early stage of the mother-son relation. When a man loves a woman, according to Dowell, what he desires most is "to lose his identity, to be enveloped, to be supported. . . . We are all so afraid, we are all so alone, we all so need from the outside the assurance of our own worthiness to exist." For all its poignancy, this expression of yearning reduces the male role to a passive acceptance of tenderness; in no way does it suggest what the man might bring to a love relationship, apart from his craving for solicitude.

Unlike Dowell, Ashburnham has a great deal to give others, and he is generous to a fault—toward his tenants, his troops, his mistresses, toward everyone except his wife, whom he "admires" but cannot love. Edward's appetites are robust and he needs a woman who can respond to them, a woman who must indeed be capable of providing the moral support Dowell regards as the mainspring of love, but who is, at the same time, prepared to receive his half-chivalrous, half-fatherly ministrations. Leonora, on the other hand, is undemonstrative, fiercely proud, and utterly without comprehension of her husband's romanticism or the traditions that, as lord of Branshaw manor, he wishes to uphold. His ward Nancy Rufford approaches the "ultimately satisfying woman" he seeks only in that her innocent grace and beauty actually do coincide with the idealized feminine image he has, hitherto, merely projected onto his lovers. That resemblance is sufficient, however, to engender a formidable passion, the more intense in that there exists no licit means of release. The fact that Nancy has been living under his roof, virtually as a daughter, casts an incestuous shadow over his love for her and renders the thought of its consummation intolerable. Reduced to its essentials, Ashburnham's agony proceeds from the contention between an overwhelming passion and unyielding moral constraints, precisely the dilemma that underlies so many classical tragedies. Yet the alembication of his story through Ford's irony, his remaining rhetorically a pawn of the spiritually arid, patronizing Dowell, makes it difficult for us to construe Edward's pathos as authentically tragic; that does not mean, however, that we should not take his doom seriously, for it prefigures a disaster of much larger scope. The forces that thwart love and lead to despair, insanity, and death for the major characters in the novel are just those that have set the time out of joint. Nearly all the decisive events in *The Good Soldier* occur, by seeming coincidence, on the 4th of August—the date, in 1914, that England was caught up in the final throes of that order whose paladin Ashburnham had been. Of the period prior to this calamity—*la belle époque*—Ford's friend and colleague Henry James remarked that "what the treacherous years were all the while really making for . . . is too tragic for any words."

—Richard K. Cross

GORBODUC.
Play by Thomas Sackville and Thomas Norton, 1562.

An address from the Publisher to the Reader, prefixed to the (authorised) 1570 printing of *The Tragedie of Gorboduc* (1565) records that the play was performed before Queen Elizabeth on 18 January 1561 [1562] "by the Gentlemen of the Inner-Temple" in London. The custom of presenting dramatic entertainments during the Christmas festivities at the four Inns of Court was an old-established one which resulted in the composition of many plays of serious import; in a sense they prepared the way for the more sophisticated masterpieces performed professionally on the Elizabethan and Jacobean stage. In terms of literary achievement, *Gorboduc* is considerably more subtle than some of the productions written for the Children of the Chapel Royal and other private acting companies. From the structural point of view it is more convincing than, say, *The Misfortunes of Arthur*, put on at Gray's Inn during 1588. This, too, draws on material from ancient British history, and likewise employs such devices as the chorus and dumb show. But the gripping dramatic "rhythm" of the earlier play—usually regarded as the first English tragedy written in blank verse—suggests that the authors, Thomas Sackville and Thomas Norton, had a keener sense of theatrical effect than Thomas Hughes, the author of *The Misfortunes of Arthur*.

What *Gorboduc* and *The Misfortunes of Arthur* have most in common is their use of conventions borrowed from the Latin dramatist Seneca (c. 4 B.C. to 65 A.D.), whose tragedies were enormously influential during the Renaissance period. In Seneca's plays, the *dramatis personae* include both human and supernatural beings, the ghosts of the departed urging those who survive to look upon acts of revenge as a moral imperative. Deeds of violence are commonly the outcome of internecine feuds, the various episodes giving scope for sententious utterances by both characters and chorus. Admittedly, *Gorboduc* does not follow Seneca quite as slavishly as do some other mid-century dramas; but the gloomy foreboding that human affairs are controlled by the will of the gods is never lost sight of. Another Senecan characteristic is the presence of allusions to classical literature, as when Gorboduc compares himself unfavourably to "happy Priam with his noble sons" in the opening of Act III. Sir Philip Sidney, in his *An Apologie for Poetrie* (1595) claimed that *Gorboduc* was "full of stately speeches and well-sounding phrases, climbing to the height of Seneca his style." And, undoubtedly, some of the rhetorical patterns favoured by the Roman dramatist are imitated; but the dramatic speech which Sackville and Norton regarded as appropriate, though hardly capable of conveying the nuances of meaning found in the mature work of Marlowe, Shakespeare, and their contemporaries, is at some considerable remove from the unimaginative dialogue found in some translations of the Senecan plays themselves.

The action of *Gorboduc*, like that of *King Lear*, originates in a heart-rending dilemma: namely, what is the wisest course for an ageing monarch to take when confronted with the problem of succession? The King, Gorboduc, has two sons, Ferrex and Porrex. Normally, his crown would be handed on to the elder, Ferrex. But Gorboduc thinks it fairer—in spite of advice to the contrary—to divide his kingdom "in two sundry parts," allocating the southern half of Britain to Ferrex and the area north of the Humber to Porrex. Somewhat naively, the well-meaning father takes it for granted that his sons will resist any temptation to quarrel over their inheritance, and relies on them to concentrate on the art of good government which they will learn from himself and his appointed counsellors. But Gorboduc reckons without the knowledge that his Queen, Videna, harbours an irrational hatred towards Porrex, while doting on his brother Ferrex. She therefore urges the latter to realise that his father's apparent even-handedness is likely to encourage the "growing pride" of Porrex, whose good faith cannot be trusted. Reluctant though he is to think evil of his younger brother, Ferrex yet allows himself to be persuaded by his mentor Cloyton (Duke of Cornwall) that his position is indeed in jeopardy—a fact later confirmed in a letter to the King from Dordan, one of Ferrex's counsellors. Ferrex therefore makes secret preparations so as to counter any attack by Porrex. For his part Porrex, interpreting Ferrex's menacing gestures as evidence of hostile intent, uses them as a pretext for an assault on his brother, whose realm he vows to invade "and seek the traitor-prince within his court . . ." affirming that "His wretched head shall pay the worthy price / Of this his treason and his hate to me. . . ." In the ensuing conflict, Ferrex is slain. After which Porrex makes his way to Gorboduc's court and with a clear conscience justifies his action to the horrified father who, however, is reminded that in part the tragedy has been caused by his wilful refusal to observe the principle of primogeniture. Meanwhile, Videna's obsessive desire for revenge—voiced in her colloquy with Ferrex in Act I—manifests itself when she most unnaturally murders her younger child. As Porrex's slaughter becomes public knowledge, the common people rise up in arms and destroy both Gorboduc and Videna. In true Senecan manner the Chorus declares that "Blood asketh blood, and death must death requite. . . ."

So far as the narrative is concerned, the play could easily end with Act IV. There being no power which can legitimately claim the right to govern Gorboduc's kingdom, the chances are that a foreign usurper (in the person of Fergus Duke of Albany) will attempt a *coup d'état*. A rightful heir to the throne is not forthcoming, so only chaos is likely to result. For political stability to prevail, national unity, deference to monarchical authority, and a measure of personal restraint are alone capable of saving the country from anarchy. Such moral teaching as this was highly relevant to the condition of England in the 1560's; fear of infiltration by unfriendly elements was common enough, and Elizabeth's own title to the crown did not go uncontested. With this in mind, it is possible to see *Gorboduc* as constituting a plea for national solidarity; the evil effects of usurpation are heavily underlined and veiled hints dropped that it behoves a ruler to choose his advisers wisely. But *Gorboduc* is something more than a propagandist tract. Taken as a whole, it has the vitality of authentic drama, and in spite of minor metrical and linguistic shortcomings offers a sustained consideration of an urgent human problem.

—E.D. Mackerness

GREAT EXPECTATIONS.
Novel by Charles Dickens, 1861.

Published in book form in 1861, *Great Expectations* is Charles Dickens's second-to-last completed novel. Being a novel narrated in the first person by its main character, it has affinities with other first person narrated novels of the period, such as Charlotte Brontë's *Jane Eyre*. Such novels trace the development of the narrator and main character from a sense of estrangement or alienation towards the recovery from that condition. They explore the nature of the narrator's alienation, reveal various false or inadequate attempts to overcome it, which usually lead to a spiritual or mental crisis, and, having confronted and overcome that crisis, the narrator finally achieves identity at the end of the novel, most often through fulfilment in love or marriage. First person narration is integral to a narrative structure which embodies the process of the protagonist's psychological reconstruction.

Though *Great Expectations* is clearly a novel in this tradition it diverges from it in important respects. Like *Jane Eyre* it opens by describing painful childhood experiences, but whereas in *Jane Eyre* we are encouraged to identify with how Jane felt at the time, in *Great Expectations* the narrator adopts an amused and ironical tone that indicates from the start that he has transcended the painful sense of estrangement from which he previously suffered. Thus a conventional happy ending is rendered unnecessary and gratuitous since the narrator's overcoming of his former condition is clear from his ability to look back on his earlier life with wry amusement. Dickens's original intention was not to provide such an ending but he was persuaded to alter the original ending and unite Pip and Estella, though there is still a note of ambiguity.

Though both endings can be defended, the original ending in which Pip and Estella are not united is arguably superior since one of the most interesting features of the novel is that it suggests, unlike *Jane Eyre* and numerous other novels, that romantic love is not the means of overcoming alienation but rather a product of it since Pip's recovery from that condition was not to be achieved through Estella returning his love, but by his attaining a mental emancipation which frees him from his former need of her.

Pip's mistake in his earlier life had been to confuse two different forms of alienation: the alienation of living in an apparently indifferent universe in which he has been left alive for no reason, his brothers and parents all being dead, and the social alienation of the criminal Magwitch. In the first scene of the novel Pip, confronted by the graves of his brothers and parents and exposed to a threatening nature, encounters the social alien Magwitch, a man rejected and condemned by society, and through helping him an identification takes place. Magwitch becomes the objective correlative of Pip's sense of estrangement and his fear of where it might lead. Other factors exacerbate this confusion. His sister, Mrs. Joe, has always treated him as if his existence is unnecessary yet when the upper-class Miss Havisham invites him to her house Mrs. Joe regards him as someone special and favoured by fortune, and when he meets Estella at Satis House her treatment of him as a person of no significance or importance seems to derive from his being merely "a common labouring boy!"

His escape from his working-class environment and the prospect of being a blacksmith for the rest of his life is so like a miracle that he sees his life as controlled by destiny. But when Magwitch, the very image of the alienation Pip believed he had overcome by being destined to become a gentleman, turns out to be the source of his social elevation this fairy tale is shattered. He can therefore no longer delude himself as to the reality of his own desire to escape from his working-class situation and life as a blacksmith and must recognise his guilt in rejecting the only figure of value in his early life, Joe Gargery.

The fact that the ex-criminal Magwitch was responsible for turning him into a gentleman shows that finding a socially acceptable form of identity is no solution to his original sense of alienation. Nor is there any suggestion in the novel that there is an ultimate solution to such alienation. Pip experiences no religious affirmation and love also cannot guarantee identity. His love for Estella was compromised by the fact that she was inseparable from his desire to find identity through becoming a gentleman. The fact that she turns out to be the daughter of Magwitch and a murderess reinforces the delusion he was under about it being his destiny to be a gentleman and to marry the fairy princess.

But the wry tone of the mature Pip as narrator and the irony with which he is able to look back on his earlier self indicates that he has achieved a psychological adjustment to his situation. He is able to live with guilt as an unavoidable part of life, both the guilt of being undeservedly alive while others are dead and the guilt created by his ambition, his rejection of Joe, and the fact that he was inadvertently responsible for Orlick's attack on his sister, supplying Orlick with both the motive and the weapon. The narrator's ironical tone indicates that he has achieved a mental transcendence that enables him to live with such guilt, though the conclusion of the novel suggests that there may be a price to pay for such transcendence since the mature Pip, even if one accepts the published ending, seems to be reconciled to experiencing little joy in life.

—K.M. Newton

GREEN MANSIONS.
Novel by W.H. Hudson, 1904.

Green Mansions, published in 1904, is W.H. Hudson's elegy for innocent Nature. Abel, from Europeanised Venezuela, a youthful, confident, civilised man, flees political persecution to the Guyanan forests, where he encounters the mysterious Rima. Among humans she is drab and diffident; in the forest she is transformed to something more than human, like Orpheus calming wild creatures, talking a strange bird-song language, communing openly with her dead mother, serenely alive in an undivided world. Abel and Rima share a brief love, a dream of union between the fallen and those in grace. But his intervention has thrown doubt into her life, and unwittingly set off the chain of events leading to her destruction. He inadvertently reveals her supposed grandfather Nuflo's deceitfulness about the proximity of her birthplace, whereupon she rushes in bewilderment on a fruitless quest for her kin. Savages who have avoided her forest, thinking her an evil spirit, take advantage of her absence to move in, murdering her when she returns alone. On discovering this Abel enters "a period of moral insanity," causing the entire tribe to be massacred by neighbouring enemies, before wandering alone in the forest through a bizarre penitential regression to find his way back to civilisation and Venezuela.

The book has some common ground with other "Lost World" or jungle romances, in which the late 19th-century imagination was projected onto a world shrunk by exploration and colonial development. The desire that uncharted places should still exist, harbouring creatures different from those we know, often consorted uneasily with the urge to track down and explain them, and *Green Mansions* shares some of this unresolved tension. It recalls Conrad in its pushing Western man to the far edges of his existence, and in its roundabout narrative technique stressing the secrecy and the burden of private, barely-communicable experiences. The book is distinguished by the fastidious evenness of its prose, always tending to subdue what in other hands would be high dramatic points, and the almost innocent reverberation of ripe symbolism through a text seemingly unconcerned to press it. Hence a snake lies between Abel and Rima at their first meeting. It coils harmlessly around her ankle, but bites him as he reaches towards her. He had found paradise, and been granted a moment's eye-contact with his Eve, before this entry into knowledge, of that in her which cannot be possessed, of her connections with others, of the fragility of her Dryad-state. And as exclusiveness dwindles, so the characters search restlessly for what is now lost or can only disappoint them: Rima for her land, her people, for the image of a redeemer she felt she had discerned in Abel; Abel for the elusiveness that will not stay his call, for "all the mystic, unimaginable grace and loveliness and joy that had vanished." The encounter with Eden also releases darker passions. While the tribesmen are presented throughout as innately vicious, Abel finds in himself an equally murderous will to extirpate whatever threatens or falls short of his ideal order, as if the glimpsed image of perfection were necessarily accompanied by the shadow of failure and betrayal. But after the disaster and his madness Abel seems to retrace in miniature the rude beginnings of civilisation: the discovery of shelter and fire; the awakening, via the enduring influence of Rima's memory, of a moral conscience and a tenderness born of guilt, rising to a visionary communion, reminiscent of the 95th canto of *In Memoriam*, of "our souls . . . like two raindrops side by side, drawing irresistibly nearer . . . crystallised beyond change," as if Rima and all she represented had suffered an ordained sacrifice for the sake of man's regeneration.

Raindrops had first occurred in connection with bird-song, the original source of Abel's fascination—"drops of melodious sound, which fell into my heart like raindrops falling into a pool to mix their fresh heavenly water with the water of earth." Hudson did as much as any writer to promote the study of wildlife in its own habitat, and one sign of Abel's incipient spiritual recovery after the catastrophe is his enthralled observation of the movements of a spider—counterpointing the passage immediately before his first sight of Rima, when he had detached himself from all other concerns to become absorbed in the minute details of animal behaviour. At such times the writing gathers an authority which can render trivial any routine objections to its far-fetched material. Raymond Williams mentioned the unembarrassed way Hudson could address subjects such as animism or mystic intimation, patiently attending to them as phenomena among others. There are dull stretches in *Green Mansions*, where the narrative interest peters out, but elsewhere the flow of the writing, smoothing over the ripples of detail, enacting in its form the imperceptible slow merging it takes as its subject, carries just that quality of attention—an exact care for natural things which is simply a way of being among them, without anxiety to squeeze a "truth" from them, or to flourish some idea which they supposedly illustrate.

—N.H. Reeve

GUESTS OF THE NATION.
Story by Frank O'Connor, 1931.

Frank O'Connor characterized the short story as a narrative expressing "an intense awareness of human loneliness," presenting "outlawed figures wandering about the fringes of society," figures such as "tramps, artists, lonely idealists, dreamers, and spoiled priests," whose "whole lifetime [is] crowded into a few minutes," showing "present, past, and future as though they were all contemporaneous" (*The Lonely Voice*, 1963). The opening and closing paragraphs of "Guests of the Nation" illustrate how skillfully O'Connor himself constructs this lonely voice and its distilled life.

O'Connor's participating narrator, Bonaparte, begins his account by reference to "the big Englishman Belcher," then in a casual parenthesis reveals that he and his fellows are not English ("we had picked up some of their curious expressions"). Such indirect exposition continues, in three economical paragraphs establishing without openly stating that the narrator and his companions, Noble and Jeremiah Donovan, are IRA soldiers guarding two British prisoners during the Anglo-Irish War (1919–21), and dramatizing that these official enemies actually behave as personal friends, playing cards together every evening, attending country dances, liking and trusting each other enough to argue even about religion and politics.

If such comradeship exists in this story, where is the marginal person, whose is the lonely voice? As is the case with many of O'Connor's stories, the narrator is alienated not only from other people but even from his younger self. His narration occurs far in the future, distanced by many years from the event he recounts; the vividness and immediacy of his story indicates the extent to which he has been marked forever by his early experience. Thus the older Bonaparte presents himself as a young soldier comfortable with his prisoners, only gradually coming to realize that these friends may have to be killed. The older Bonaparte quotes his younger self referring to the two captives by name as Belcher and 'Awkins (even playfully adopting Hawkins's cockney accent); but he regularly puts more general phrases such as "the enemy," "the prisoners," or "the hostages" in Donovan's mouth. The older narrator now understands what his younger self was then in the process of learning: that a man with a name, a man whose personal identity is acknowledged, is not so easily murdered as a man reduced to a category.

This learning process continues as the young Bonaparte spends a sleepless night struggling with the tormenting conflict between loyalty to his group (which includes some people, like Donovan, whom he does not like or even respect) and loyalty to his own developing sense of right and wrong (an experience something like O'Connor's own on the Republican side during the Anglo-Irish War and the subsequent Irish Civil War). The older narrator hints at the eventual outcome of that struggle when he states "in those days disunion between [IRA] brothers seemed to me an awful crime. I knew better after." As the moment of execution nears, the older narrator further indicates his changing values by condemning Donovan's explanations as "the usual rigmarole" and by contrasting Donovan's "cold and excited voice" with Belcher's "peaceable way." Donovan's easy cliché "It's our duty" is effectively discredited by the humanity of Belcher's last words: "I never could make out what duty was myself, . . . but I think you're all good lads, if that's what you mean. I'm not complaining." By remembering and selecting these remarks to report years later, the narrator indicates the distance he has travelled from the cause he once supported.

The last gunshot destroys not only a British soldier, but an IRA adherent as well: now Bonaparte feels "mad lonely." The bog where he helps bury Belcher and Hawkins may be part of the Ireland for which he had thought he was fighting, but now it seems "desolate" and "treacherous." In the final sentences of this quiet but fiercely critical story, O'Connor's narrator reports feeling alienated from the goals and values he previously held, alienated from his own people, even from his sympathetic comrade Noble and the old woman in whose house they were all staying; alienated from both earth and heaven, even "the birds and the bloody stars were all far away." The cosy dusk that opens the story gives way to darkness. The pleasant community of banter and card playing is replaced by isolation. The young soldier who felt like an adult at the beginning of the narrative feels "very small and very lonely" at its end, like a bereft child. The last sentence, "And anything that ever happened to me after I never felt the same about again," indicates the permanent fissure which exists between the narrator's morally comfortable youth and his present pain.

A brilliant reader himself, O'Connor felt that a short story should ring "with the tone of a man's voice, speaking." In virtually all his stories the real subject is the relation between the narrator and the event he recounts, the meaning carried by the tone of that voice. The wry humor which the title "Guests of the Nation" initially suggests by its gentle contrast of "guest" with "prisoner" finally sounds bitterly critical as the reader realizes how lonely and disillusioned is the voice that speaks, how isolated this ex-soldier feels from that nation in whose cause he murdered both an enemy-friend and his own youthful patriotic self.

—Kristin Morrison

GULLIVER'S TRAVELS.
(*Travels into Several Remote Nations of the World, by Captain Lemuel Gulliver.*)
Fiction by Jonathan Swift, 1726.

Gulliver's Travels marks the culmination of Jonathan Swift's career as a satirist. Though ostensibly written as an attack on the fantastic tales of travel writers, the book unfolds in two directions: one, concrete, historical, and political; the other, abstract and philosophical. Yet, the two prongs of Swift's satiric attack ultimately complement one another. After enumerating the abuses of Whig politics, economics, and science in the first three books of *Gulliver's Travels*, Swift reserves the fourth book for exploring the sources in human nature of those abuses. In that fourth book, Swift questions the commonplace Renaissance definition of Man as *animal rationale*, and after close, corrosive observation suggests an alternative: "*animal superbum*," the vain, or proud, animal.

Swift explains the premises on which he builds his travels in letters written in 1725, to his fellow Scriblerian, Alexander Pope. He hopes to prove the "falsity of that Definition *animal rationale*; and to show it should be only *rationis capax* [i.e., *capable* of reason]." Swift hopes to make his point with wit as well as indignation. He concedes his "Misanthropy" to Pope but insists that it differs from the Timonian—or Gulliverian—variety because Swift is capable of loving individuals although he, too, hates the species.

Herein lies a problem which has haunted Swift's critics from his day to ours. Where does Swift stand in relation to Gulliver? And especially to Gulliver's misanthropy at the conclusion to Book IV? Is Swift Thackeray's incipient madman, "filthy in word, filthy in thought, furious, raging, obscene"; Huxley's raging hater of "bowels"; or Arbuthnot's "happy man" who at 60 can still "write such a merry work?" Just as the book is composed of a mixture of overlapping genres—travel book, utopia, science fantasy, allegory, and beast fable, among others—so the voices of Swift and Gulliver frequently overlap, addressing us simultaneously, in a brilliant, uneasy combination of wit, humor and rage designed to keep us uncomfortable and off balance.

Gulliver's first two voyages, to the lands of Lilliput and Brobdingnag, closely examine the history of England and western Europe from the time of the Thirty Years' War and English Civil War to the mid-1720's. Book I allegorizes the political situation in England during the last years of Queen Anne and the first of George I—especially the growing Whig fear of Jacobite intrigues. Gulliver's size in Lilliput, 10 times that of the native inhabitants, symbolizes physically the magnanimity—largeness of spirit—that Swift saw as the preeminent moral quality of his two leading political friends, Oxford and Bolingbroke, who succeeded in negotiating the Peace of Utrecht, only to be swept from office upon the death of Queen Anne and accused—with some truth—of trying to restore the Pretender. Gulliver's bewilderment over the Junto's harsh treatment of him is designed to underscore what Swift saw as the decency and honesty of his friends attacked by paranoid, petty, and mean-spirited opponents. That initial intrepidity of the Lilliputians who conquer the "Man-Mountain" and demand that he serve them gradually reveals itself as the strutting pomposity of little men.

Swift's toying with perspectival relativity sets us up for a fall in interpreting Book II, the voyage to Brobdingnag. Drawn to identify with Gulliver's superior moral position in Book I, the reader is surprised to find Gulliver reduced physically and morally to a Lilliputian in the land of the giants. Gone are the generosity and tolerance which distinguished the protagonist earlier. Gulliver's braggadocio, his protective arrogance, increases in inverse proportion to the lessening of his dignity. Bespattered by a frog, teethed on by a baby, humiliated by a dwarf, mistaken by a monkey for its offspring, and used as a sexual plaything by court ladies, Gulliver compensates by defending his honor, and that of his nation and continent, in a series of conversations with the King of Brobdingnag. The monarch is both amused and appalled by Gulliver's conduct, on one occasion laughing at Gulliver's nice distinction between Whigs and Tories, and on another castigating "the Bulk" of Gulliver's countrymen as "the most pernicious Race of little odious Vermin that Nature ever suffered to crawl upon the Surface of the Earth."

Book III of *Gulliver's Travels* shifts the satiric focus to abuses in modern, and hence Whiggish, learning. Although Swift continues to make political points—for example, in the allegorical dispute between the floating island of Laputa and the city of Lindalino, which recalls Irish resistance in the mid-1720's to the introduction of William Wood's debased half pence into Ireland—most of the satire deals with corruptions in science and learning. Swift, a humanist who believed in the primacy of Socratic self-knowledge and felt that the study of scientific problems divorced from practical application was irrelevant and immoral, uses the silly and perverse experiments of the Lagadan academicians to mock the vanity and pride of "natural philosophers." Swift finds the misuse of historiography equally distressing. Living in the days of the Whig Ascendancy, Swift was acutely aware that history is generally written by the victors to justify their success. As a Tory historiographer, he attacks Whig historians, calling them "prostitute writers" who "ascribe the greatest Exploits in War to Cowards, the wisest Counsel to Fools, Sincerity to Flatterers, *Roman* Virtue to Betrayers of their Country, Piety to Atheists, Chastity to Sodomites, Truth to Informers."

Book IV of *Gulliver's Travels* allows Swift to explore the moral origins of the abuses outlined in the first three books. To the Christian Swift, Man is a flawed animal deeply afflicted by the cardinal sin of pride. Proud to be distinguished from beasts by the faculty of reason, Man forgets that abuse of this faculty lowers him beneath the beasts. Blinded by pride, Man must be reminded first, that he is not inherently reasonable, only capable of reason, and second, that he must distinguish between reason and rationalization—between the *proper* use of the faculty and its seemingly natural misuse for self-justification.

Through the visit to Houyhnhnmland, Gulliver learns with horror of the corruption of human reason and the enormity of human pride, and the reader sees Gulliver's discovery reinforced by the dramatic irony of the character's own behavior. Set between the equine, naturally reasonable Houyhnhnms and the humanoid but utterly bestial Yahoos, Gulliver uses pride and rationalization—not reason—to deny his moral resemblance to the Yahoos; however, Gulliver's violent hatred of the Yahoos ironically serves to link him more closely with those creatures in the reader's mind, especially after Master Houyhnhnm informs Gulliver that "the *Yahoos* were known to hate one another more than they did any different Species of Animals; and the Reason usually assigned was, the Odiousness of their own Shapes, which all could see in the rest, but not in themselves."

But where is Swift in this attack? Most recent rhetorical criticism carefully distinguishes between the voices of Gulliver and his creator. According to such criticism, it is the misanthropic Gulliver who will not hesitate to flay Yahoos, and not Swift. But in fact, Swift participates in both voices: just as in *A Modest Proposal* Swift attacks the cannibal heartlessness of 18th-century social planners while also admitting in a candid moment of dropped mask that he wishes some of his less patriotic countrymen could be "crucifyed," butchered and sold as "prime Daint[ies]." Swift remains elusively present, using Gulliver as his agent to castigate in the strongest language the vices and follies of mankind while simultaneously mocking the character as a dramatization of those very vices. Swift can thus laugh and rage at once, both engaged in, and divorced from, Gulliver's performance.

—David F. Venturo

H

HAMLET.
Play by William Shakespeare, 1601(?).

Hamlet is one of the central works of modern European culture, probably thought and written about more than any other play. In a comprehensive sense it is by now William Shakespeare's text plus its world-wide reverberations through centuries of theatrical interpretation, critical analysis, and reshaping by other creative authors—a vast body of "commentary" ranging from pious exegesis to malicious mockery. *Hamlet*'s intensity and complexity evoke seemingly infinite responses which say as much about their authors and periods as about the play.

The story derives from a 12th-century Danish history by Saxo Grammaticus. There are prototypes of Claudius, Gertrude, Polonius, Ophelia, Rosencrantz and Guildenstern, and of course of Hamlet himself, called Amlethus, son of Horwendillus; but there is no Laertes, no Fortinbras, and no ghost. The murder of Amlethus's father by his brother Fengo is public knowledge; Amleth is cunning (like Hamlet "mad in craft") and resolute (unlike Hamlet); it takes him long, but he achieves his revenge and becomes king. Saxo's Latin *Historiae-Danicae* was printed in 1514. In 1570 François de Belleforest published a French version of it in *Histoires Tragiques*, adding adultery to incest and garnishing the tale with strong misogynistic and moralistic animadversions. Belleforest's tale appeared in English as *The Hystorie of Hamblet* in 1608—and several phrasings suggest that the translator had seen Shakespeare's play.

Some English playwright—probably Thomas Kyd—used the Belleforest story for a play which is now lost. Critics call it the *Ur-Hamlet* and assume that this was Shakespeare's immediate source. References to it begin in 1589, and the promptbook may have belonged to Shakespeare's company. All we know for certain is that it introduced the ghost. However, Kyd's very successful *The Spanish Tragedy* (1589?), another early revenge play, is extant. It has a revenger, Hieronimo, who doubts and delays, and a woman who goes mad and commits suicide; furthermore it has some comic elements, a mixture of prose and verse, and a play-within-the-play. Presumably the lost *Ur-Hamlet* shared such popular features.

The very text of *Hamlet* presents grave problems. There exist three early, fault-riddled prints differing in hundreds of details apart from major divergences: the First, "bad" Quarto (Q1) of 1603, a pirated version based on memorial reconstruction; the Second or "good" Quarto (Q2) of 1604 / 05, based on Shakespeare's rough copy ("foul papers"); and the collected First Folio's (F) edition's *Hamlet* text of 1623, based on something like a promptbook transcript. The three texts are not quite discreet, Q1 was to some extent consulted for Q2 and Q2 for F. Q1, mutilated and garbled, contains about half the lines of Q2; Q2 is the longest text, containing about 230 lines not present in F (among them Hamlet's soliloquy in IV.4, "How all occasions do inform against me"), but lacking about 70 lines found in F. Neither Q2 nor F are viable without extensive editorial work—hence hardly two *Hamlet* editions are identical. For long, editors used F as copy text, variously emended from Q2; John Dover Wilson's edition of 1934 inaugurated an inversion of this procedure; the mid-1980's saw an Oxford-led return to privileging F as (possibly) embodying Shakespeare's revisions. But even the F version is far too long for normal Elizabethan (or modern) performance; Shakespeare may have envisaged variable, but substantial cuts in the theatre.

From its beginnings in the earlier 18th century, criticism has concentrated on the hero, Hamlet. This is not surprising, since he speaks nearly half the lines and the story is shown mainly from his point of view (which Horatio will perpetuate after the play). Moreover, we can share Hamlet's innermost thoughts—in the first four acts through his soliloquies, in act V through the intimate talks with Horatio which replace them. No-one else has a confidant; and Claudius is given only two asides (III.1 and V.2) and one soliloquy (III.3), Gertrude a single aside (IV.5), Ophelia one soliloquy (III.1), Polonius some baffled asides (II.2). Hamlet is thus not only central to the play, it is also difficult not to empathise and identify with him (some, including Tolstoy and Charles Marowitz, have managed it) even though many recoil, like Samuel Johnson, from his "soul-murdering" resolution in III.3 and his callous treatment of Ophelia in III.2—but only momentarily; later impressions efface these shadows.

The question dominating discussions since the later 18th century is: why does Hamlet not "sweep" to his revenge as envisaged early in I.5? He himself is puzzled by this, and is fascinating because, like most of us, he cannot account for all his thoughts, feelings, and actions. Explanations of the delay include his being too tender for such a rough task (Goethe), being a reflective, not an active man (Schlegel, Coleridge), his melancholy (Arthur Bradley), his activated Oedipus complex (Ernest Jones after Freud), his doubts in the Ghost up to III.2. (especially Wilson). What needs stressing is that, far from being a weakness of the play, this delay is one of its prime strengths. Just as Shakespeare humanises the villian by giving Claudius a ruler's poise and affability and by endowing him with a conscience, however feeble, Hamlet is interesting and attractive because he is *not* the simple revenger figure of Saxo's story or the Homeric tradition but, faced, like Orestes in the Greek *Electra* plays, with a real dilemma, is fully alive to its implications. Three figures—Pyrrhus in the Player's recitation of II.2 (though he hesitates for a moment), Fortinbras, and especially Laertes, who has no scruples at all—serve as foils to set him off.

Linked to the delay is the issue of revenge itself. Amlethus's story is set in pre-Christian times when blood revenge was an unquestioned duty; and Belleforest stresses the gulf between those barbaric times and his own period. Shakespeare has created a markedly Christian (not in all respects pre-Reformation) background. This as well as the presumed expectations of his target audience and the example of other revenge tragedies has led to hypotheses that the Ghost is indeed the Devil (as Hamlet surmises in the "cellarage" episode I.5 and the soliloquy II.2) and Hamlet his deluded or fully willing tool, inviting distant commiseration, reproof, and rejection. It is true that belief in purgatory and hence the possibility of ghosts coming from there had been denied by the Reformers, and that the Ghost's command infringes Christian ethic of all denominations: "Vengeance *is* mine; I will repay, saith the Lord" (Romans XII.19). Turning the play upon its head such critics overlook, however, that Elizabethan reactions to "ghosts" were less clear-cut than the new doctrine (cf. Roland M. Frye) and that their attitude to revenge did not always conform to their faith, as is borne out notably by the Bond of Association (1584), in which thousands of god-fearing gentlemen undertook to avenge a feared assassination of their queen.

Hamlet's delay, however variably motivated, leads to the revenge not being taken until there exists written proof of Claudius's guilt in other crimes (the "commission" Hamlet hands to Horatio in V.2) and the King has been denounced by Gertrude and Laertes, when Hamlet has more on his side than the word of a ghost, when killing Claudius is no longer the passionate deed of a grieved individual but appears as a necessary and public act of self-defence and retribution, and Shakespeare can accord his revenger figure an end opposed to others of the period: a death ennobled by royal praise and the promise of eternal rest. It is in the service of this strategy that Shakespeare makes Hamlet, who thinks and talks about so many issues, keep silent on the morality of revenge (as Anne Barton was among the first to stress) until V.2, when he can confidently ask "Is't not perfect conscience . . . ?"

There remains a string of minor problems and inconsistencies—Horatio knowing and not knowing the Court, Hamlet being called "young" in Act I but called 30 in V.1, and so forth (but that applies to other plays by Shakespeare and his contemporaries as well). There also remains a general numbness and bleakness; so much more than the royal house of Denmark has perished, while Fortinbras offers much less promise of renewal than Lucius in *Titus Andronicus*, Richmond in *Richard III*, and Malcolm in *Macbeth*.

Contrary to much critical comment, the play is tightly constructed and balanced. A case for a five-act scheme (absent in Q1 and Q2, partial in F) can be made; however, there are really three large phases of near-continuous action separated by weeks of time passing: I, II.1 to IV.4, IV.5 to the end. Each phase contains one full court scene mirroring emblematically, as it were, the state of play; in I.2 Claudius is at the height of his power, surrounded by his court, with Hamlet appearing as a wilful spoilsport and outsider; in III.2 the weights are not yet balanced, but Hamlet gains the initiative —compare the Court's exit in both scenes. In V.2, finally, the Court is decimated, Claudius has expended nearly all his proxies in the deadly struggle. Hamlet is at the centre, and when Claudius cries out "O yet defend me, friends, I am but hurt!" no one stirs. He has no friends; and his evident guilt now makes *him* the outsider.

The more closely one looks, the more one discovers the art of the mature dramatist at work. The play's flexible and forceful use of language has been noted early on, as has its richness in theatrical potential, which was appreciated even by so basically hostile an observer as Voltaire. From the first nervous challenge in the dark to the dead march at the end, we witness a succession of scenes apt to spark the imagination and remain in the mind—be it the tense play-within-the-play episode, or mad Ophelia dealing out flowers in IV.5, or Hamlet being undone by the gravedigger's equivocation and then musing over Yorick's skull in V.1. In a bout of modish iconoclasm Gary Taylor suggested that Shakespeare has been made and kept great by the cult grown up around him. Reading *Hamlet* alongside the large body of Elizabethan and Jacobean revenge tragedies suggests a different conclusion: by any criterion, the play stands out among its peers. And it retains its power to move most of us.

—Holger Klein

A HANDFUL OF DUST.
Novel by Evelyn Waugh, 1934.

A Handful of Dust was Evelyn Waugh's fourth novel and, like its predecessors, *Vile Bodies* and *Black Mischief*, is a satirical enquiry into the spiritual values of so-called civilisation. The hero, Tony Last, is the last of his line at Hetton Hall, a crumbling Victorian mansion of surpassing ugliness, built when the fashion for Arthurian romance was at its height, in a country village where the parson is so out of touch that he regularly preaches the sermons he used to preach in India, orating about ravening tigers and exotic camels and our dear ones far away at home. Tony likes going to church in dark suit and stiff collar, but is not sure whether or not he believes in God. Tony believes in tradition and spends nearly all his income in maintaining the house, with its staff of 14. His wife, Lady Brenda, is a social butterfly, trapped in country boredom. Tony and Brenda have separate bedrooms: hers is called Guinevere, after Arthur's faithless Queen. Brenda's lover is no Sir Lancelot, but a penurious and unprincipled social climber, John Beaver, whose mother is an interior decorator. She threatens to do up Hetton in white chromium. The Lasts have an only son, John Andrew, whose naive sayings endear him to us before Waugh, taking a hint from Thackeray's *Barry Lyndon*, kills him in a riding accident. Brenda has taken a flat in London to pursue her affair with John Beaver and is appalled to hear that "John" is dead. On hearing it is not John her lover, but John Andrew, her son, she bursts out, "Thank God." Brenda is self-condemned: she and her decadent friends speak a kind of "thieves' slang," transposing syllables.

They are all charlatans, and among them is a woman who fraudulently tells fortunes by reading not palms, but soles of the feet. John Andrew's death precipitates Brenda's decision: her letter declares, "I am in love with John Beaver and I want to have a divorce and marry him . . . " Tony is manoeuvred into "providing her with evidence," but the nightclub professional who accompanies him to Brighton brings with her one of Waugh's awful, whingeing children, who demands icecream for breakfast, and the "evidence" is not forthcoming. Tony has offered Brenda £500 a year, but Brenda's brother demands £2,000 for her and coolly suggests that Tony should sell Hetton. Tony recognizes this would be in order to "buy Beaver for Brenda" and he refuses. Brenda's supporters think Tony has behaved very badly.

Civilisation in Europe may be decaying and in the hands of social predators, but Tony faces a worse trial in the South American jungle, having impulsively joined an expedition to find a vanished city (which is illusory). His companion is eventually drowned, the natives are uncooperative, he suffers from terrible fevers, and is attacked by vampire bats, jiggers, and stinging insects.

Back in London, Brenda says to an old friend, Jock, that Tony is "off on some expedition with a crook doctor." Jock asks whether this is safe. Brenda replies blandly, ". . . The whole world is civilised now, isn't it—charabancs and Cook's offices everywhere . . . I'm very fond of Tony, you know, in spite of the monstrous way he behaved." Jock is Member of Parliament for a rural constituency and answers Parliamentary questions on pigs in such a way as to shelve all problems: a separate committee "have not yet made their report." Brenda is financially distressed, living on sandwiches, and without her money becomes unappealing to Beaver, who deserts her. Meanwhile, in the jungle, Tony's companion has set out to woo the Indians with trashy "trade goods," but his *pièce de résistance*, spotted green clockwork mice, sends them running in terror. Tony, ill and alone, is taken in by Mr Todd. He too is a child of corruption: his father was a missionary, who "was married to a white woman, but left her in Guiana to look for gold. Then he took my mother . . ." Tony is trapped in a living hell, compelled at gunpoint to read the works of Dickens over and over again to an illiterate semi-savage, while at home he is mourned as dead. Cousins inherit the estate, prune the servants, and turn it into a farm for silver foxes. Silver foxes, unlike the wild foxes John Andrew was learning to hunt for sport, are a commercial product. The heir hopes "by means of them . . . to restore Hetton to the glory that it had enjoyed in the days of his Cousin Tony."

As we have seen, the "glory" of Hetton is qualified: but Tony, despite his lack of imagination, in his blind loyalty to the limited values of English country civilisation, where Christianity has become moribund, had a basic decency missing from everybody else in the tale. Brenda comfortably marries Jock.

In an alternative ending, for serialisation in America, Brenda goes back to Tony, safely returned, after Beaver's desertion. Tony slyly takes over the London flat for his own purposes.

Admirers of Waugh are divided as to which is the worse fate, Tony's, or that of Guy Crouchback, in the *Sword of Honour* trilogy, a gentleman of old Catholic family, who remarries his faithless wife after her second husband dies, leaving her pregnant with an "heir" from another man's loins. Waugh, throughout his work, shows the world of high society as corrupt and corrupting. Decent traditionalists and middle-class professionals should leave it alone. But if British civilisation is decaying, savagery is a frightening alternative. Waugh was already a Catholic when he wrote *A Handful of Dust*, but not until *Brideshead Revisited* does he articulate his growing *contemptus mundi*.

—Valerie Grosvenor Myer

HANDLEY CROSS.
Novel by R.S. Surtees, 1843.

R.S. Surtees has had many admirers, ranging from Thackeray to Virginia Woolf. It cannot be said, however, that his novel *Handley Cross*, which first appeared in serial form in 1838, has always enjoyed unqualified praise. It did not bring its author the popular success which was to follow the publication of *Mr. Sponge's Sporting Tour* ten years later. Nor is it today generally considered to be in quite the same class as, say, *Mr. Facey Romford's Hounds* (1865). Joyce Cary, in an introduction to *Sponge*, goes so far as to describe *Handley Cross* as "a boring work," characterised by "a vein of mid-Victorian humour completely dead." Surtees's tale of hunting, drinking, cheating, and social manoeuvring in the fictional spa of Handley Cross is almost certainly too long—720 pages even in the "pocket" edition of 1854—to sustain an uncertain plot over which the author exercises only limited control. Yet, as Cary suggests, there is a special quality about Surtees's writing, and *Handley Cross*, perhaps because it is so undisciplined, provides a marvellous sense of a real world directly observed.

The action of the novel is centred on the town of the title, which we may surmise to be somewhere south of London. Surtees himself hunted with the Old Surrey, whose country was around Croydon and which features in the story as the hunting nursery of its hero, John Jorrocks, a cockney grocer of ample dimensions with a proclivity for strong drink and an overwhelming passion for pursuing foxes.

After some scene-setting, the first year of Mr Jorrocks's glory as Master of Fox Hounds at Handley Cross encompasses the time-span of the novel. The basis of the story is simple. Invited to take over the hunt by Captain Doleful, the self-appointed "Master of Ceremonies" at the up-and-coming spa, who sees an opportunity for advancement in the matter, Mr. Jorrocks needs no second bidding once the matter of "tin" has been resolved. Revelling in "the magic letters M.F.H.," he takes the field with a drunken huntsman called Pigg and a footboy as whipper-in, determined to make the foxes of the Vale of Sheepwash and Pinch-me-near Forest cry "Capevi!"

Here lies the first delight of *Handley Cross*—descriptions of hunting of astonishing vividness. Mr. Jorrocks's anticipation as hounds speak in covert, his joy as they go away on the line of a fox, the sight of him "pounding along, in a state of desperate perspiring excitement, all eyes, ears and fears" as he gets left behind, are almost as vital as the real thing—and explain why the novel has been so prized by generations of hunting folk.

There is, however, more to *Handley Cross* than a celebration of hunting. Surtees and Mr. Jorrocks, as it were together, lurch through domestic crises, the factional strife of Handley Cross, a fancy ball, a literally riotous hunt dinner, several ghastly private parties, and all manner of dubious deals over horses and hounds. Besides the brandy-soaked huntsman, snivelling whip and "MC" on the make, the novel is peopled with idle servants, insolvent soldiers, lunatic gentry, scheming mothers with daughters of marriageable age, an egomaniac hunting correspondent, and a whole gallery of rogues, snobs, crooks, shysters, and social climbers of every kind.

This anarchic mob of characters and the rather loosely connected events in which they take part are unified not just by Surtees's descriptive powers, but also by his humour. Cary's view notwithstanding, *Handley Cross* is consistently amusing, often hilarious. The inebriated Pigg's report on the weather after mistaking a cupboard for the front door ("Hellish dark, and smells of cheese") does perhaps smack of mid-Victorian farce. But numerous asides, a great deal of Surtees's inimitable dialogue, and several extended passages remain funny to modern sensibilities.

Certainly the denouement, if the novel can be said to have one, depends on the humour of mutual incomprehension which appeals quite as much today as it evidently did to Surtees. Mr. Jorrocks's conduct in stacking up "the dead bodies of fifty-three horses that had died of disease in the precincts of the town of Handley Cross" is no doubt prudent in a Master anxious to secure a supply of food for his hounds. Yet the operation is interrupted by "churchwardens, overseers, constables, &c." A fracas takes place, and Mr.

Jorrocks is brought before commissioners in lunacy who judge him insane, a consequence from which he escapes only after appeal to the Lord Chancellor.

What, beyond the humour, Surtees made of the world he observed so clearly, even ruthlessly, is difficult to say. The world brought to life in the pages of *Handley Cross*, and in his other novels including *Jorrocks' Jaunts and Jollities*, *Hawbuck Grange*, *Ask Mamma*, and *Plain or Ringlets?*, was boisterous, tough, and largely unselfconscious. The text of any of these works is about as far from an expression of modern angst as it is possible to get. Perhaps Pigg's motto says it all: "Brandy and baccy ill gar a man live for iver!"

—Lance St. John Butler

THE HANDMAID'S TALE.
Novel by Margaret Atwood, 1985.

Margaret Atwood's *The Handmaid's Tale* worries over the plight of women in a society governed by religious fundamentalists committed to bolstering a seriously low birthrate. In this "Republic of Gilead" fertile women serve as handmaids to infertile ones; each month, upon ovulation, the handmaid copulates with her mistress's husband. If conception occurs, the handmaid receives assistance in her labor from other handmaids, and then surrenders the child to her mistress. Having given birth successfully, the handmaid can rest assured that she won't be sent to the Colonies, where "unwomen" clean up toxic dumps and radiation spills.

Most readings of *The Handmaid's Tale* approach the text, quite rightly, as a dystopic novel; reactions focus on its horrific presentation of "theocratic ambitions of the religious right," on its understanding of the sinister implications of an exaggerated cultural feminism, and on its critique of our own gender arrangements. Many of these reactions then posit love as a force subverting Gilead's power. While such reactions make sense, readers also must attend to the novel's statements about love's tendency to follow decidedly conservative narrative forms. Drawing parallels between the handmaid Offred's relationships with the three men in her life—Luke, the Commander, and Nick—the novel subverts love's subversive force.

Not surprisingly, Offred takes pains to differentiate among the three men: Luke as her "real love," husband, and father to her child; the Commander as Gileadean "sugar-daddy"—powerful, distant, in control of her future; Nick as her illicit love, companion in crime. But the text makes a very different argument. All three men merge, and this merging requires us to reassess supposed distinctions among husbands, lovers, and commanders. In looking at Luke and the Commander, we see first that the two share a familiarity with various languages; like so many men of privilege throughout history, Luke and the Commander know the language of the classical curriculum and use this knowledge in a subtle reaffirmation of classical gender roles and inequalities. In addition to an interest in old languages, both Luke and the Commander share a penchant for the ways of the past. Luke spouts "old ideas" about women being incapable of abstract thought and men needing more meat, while the Commander provides Offred with outdated women's magazines, and escorts her to a brothel from the Hefner era.

These characteristics of Luke and the Commander contribute to an overall pattern of relational dynamics between these two men and women in the text. Because of their power, the men may serve as "passports" for women in their lives. After women lose their jobs and bank accounts, Offred turns to Luke as a passport provider. But just as the Commander will fail her in this respect (when he calls her into his study, she hopes to trade on his desire: it "could be a passport"), so too Luke: "He said the passports were foolproof. . . . Maybe he had a plan, a map of some kind in his head." The passports aren't foolproof, and Offred's language suggests that Luke's "plan" may be self-serving. At least in part, the novel is a story of his betrayal of her, of "love's" betrayal of her.

The Handmaid's Tale provides us with two male characters who mirror one another in personal characteristics and relational dynamics. Offred doesn't draw attention to parallels between the two men, and might protest against such connections but the text insists upon them. Atwood's novel encourages us to read the future in light of the past, and the past in light of the future; doing so, we cannot exclude male figures from our consideration—no matter how disquieting the results of such consideration. Here, recognition of similarity between Luke and the Commander *is* disquieting; it casts doubt not only upon the narrator's story of Luke's love, but also upon love stories generally.

"But wait," the romantic reader may object, "there's a third male in this story, and he does credit to the love plot." Various critics argue that Offred "breaks through to her courageous self" in relationship with Nick, and certainly we may acknowledge that Nick's intervention allows Offred to escape, tape her account, and thereby provide us with the story of her past. But despite these positive features, despite certain differences between Nick and Luke / Fred, the novel continues to represent the love plot as something potentially dangerous to women who entangle themselves therein. *The Handmaid's Tale* conveys these dangers in its representations of the effect on Offred of "being in love" and of the grammar according to which she articulates being in love. When in love with Luke, for example, Offred gives in to him, accepts his direction of her toward passivity; she does precisely the same with Nick, losing interest in Mayday and in the possibility of escape. She comments, "The fact is that I no longer want to leave, escape the border to freedom. I want to be here, with Nick, where I can get at him." She barely listens to Ofglen, and all political commitment she might be capable of making vanishes in light of her commitment to romance.

Equally worrisome is Offred's reliance upon traditional grammars with which to structure her relationship with this man. For example, Offred first employs the language of Harlequin romances to describe her visit to Luke's room; and when she revises this account, she falls into the language of old movies. Sadly, both "reconstructions" limit the range of activities and options available to male and female characters. Operating within these traditional grammars, Offred can individuate neither herself nor Nick; both fall into roles assigned to them by fairy tales and romances.

Every representation of romance in *The Handmaid's Tale*, including that most positive representation, Nick with Offred, is highly qualified, highly ambivalent. The novel wants to believe in "love" at the same time it expresses powerful reservations about how we typically realize this emotion. Finally, *The Handmaid's Tale* is a story of love's limitations, rather than its latitudes.

—Madonne M. Miner

HARD TIMES.
Novel by Charles Dickens, 1854.

Charles Dickens began *Hard Times* in January 1854 at the request of the publishers of *Household Words*, who looked to its editor to halt the decline in sales. He succeeded in doing so although he complained about the difficulties of planning and writing short weekly instalments which did not permit him to indulge his exuberant comic genius. The result was that the characters are strictly subordinated to the purposes of the plot, which is stark in outline, quite unlike the vast and labyrinthine plot of *Bleak House*, so that *Hard Times* is Dickens's shortest and most tightly structured novel. When it was published in volume form book and chapter titles were added that further clarify the representative significance of the main events. Factual education, for example, is examined in a chapter called "Murdering the Innocents." This concentrated parable-like plot which enacts its meaning economically and dramatically makes *Hard Times* unique in Dickens's oeuvre and, with the grim subject matter, perhaps accounts for the novel's low reputation for almost a century until F.R. Leavis revalued it in 1947, acclaiming some of the very aspects that had attracted adverse comment.

In terms of chronology, the novel belongs to the second, and more serious, phase of Dickens's career, and its sub-title *For These Times* and dedication to Thomas Carlyle underline the preoccupation with what the latter had called the "Condition-of-England question" in 1839. So eager was Dickens to present a convincing account of an industrial town that in January 1854 he visited Preston, where the cotton workers were in dispute with the owners. The immediate result was an article in *Household Words*, "On Strike" (11 February).

As in *Bleak House*, Dickens's account of English society is wide-ranging and deeply critical. However, in *Hard Times* he focuses on the alliance between Utilitarianism and industrialism that conditions and exploits the inhabitants of Coketown. Gradgrind, the misguided Utilitarian M.P., subjects children to a sterile education that inculcates only factual knowledge and the principles of self-interest. In the case of his daughter Louisa who marries Bounderby, a wealthy and powerful businessman and banker, that which has been repressed in her by her education and upbringing, namely wonder and spontaneity, leaves her vulnerable to the advances of the cynical and charming Harthouse. When Gradgrind is confronted with the ruin of his system, his affection for Louisa triumphs over his regard for his principles, and he abandons them.

Gradgrind at least has integrity, good intentions, and is capable of change; Bounderby is not. Exposed as a blustering and insensitive hypocrite, he responds, after a slight faltering, by continuing on the same course as inexorably as the relentless industrial processes that enslave the Hands and pollute the environment. The marvellously vivid and open-minded description of Coketown enforces the condemnation of industrialisation and conveys a strong sense of the constricted and routine lives of the Hands. This sense of being hemmed in is emphasised by the tiresome attentions of philanthropic and religious organisations who deplore what they regard as the Hands' idleness and immorality, and exhort them to reform and live by the principles of reason and self-interest. In presenting these features of urban industrial life, Dickens refers to Parliament as the "national cinder-heap" and mocks the method of statistical enquiry although the former often acted on the latter to effect genuine reforms. The simplified yet powerful presentation of the alliance between those who held political power and those who controlled the means of production evokes equally alarming responses as his depiction of Chancery in *Bleak House* and the Circumlocution Office in *Little Dorrit*: the system furthers the interests of the people who operate it more than those of the people it was designed to serve.

It was diagnoses such as these that alienated readers who had cherished the "inimitable" Dickens of *The Pickwick Papers*. On this occasion, Macaulay described the diagnosis as "sullen socialism." However, many readers have felt that although the social novelist clearly portrayed the injustice, exploitation and inhumanity of mid-19th-century England, the popular novelist stopped short of the logical conclusions. Slackbridge, the trade union orator, is swiftly dismissed and although an exchange between Bitzer and Mrs. Sparsit indicates the effectiveness of union solidarity, the authorial voice informs the reader that the Hands' belief that their sole hope lies in combining with one another is a delusion. Moreover, Stephen Blackpool, apparently a representative worker, refuses to subscribe to the union because of a mysterious promise to Rachael. Dickens's report on the Preston dispute in *Household Words* had praised the conduct of the striking cotton workers but then had concluded that the affair was "a deplorable calamity" that would cause much ill-feeling; in *Hard Times*, a strike is never considered and union membership is seen as an understandable mistake. Instead it is suggested by the words of Stephen Blackpool in a chapter entitled "Men and Masters" that the two sides will only draw closer together if individuals make the effort to understand and sympathise with one another. Similarly, while Dickens deplores the grimness of a typical English Sunday and the ineffective but respectable activities of the 18 religious persuasions in Coketown, he seems to endorse Rachael and Stephen's religious convictions which help them to endure their miserable lot, but also constrain them. While approving individual benevolence and religious belief, he seems sceptical about the possibility of organisations retaining integrity and fostering humane values.

Dickens locates these values in Sleary's circus, which, significantly, exists outside the social order and is not altogether respectable or prudent. In presenting the circus, Dickens does not lose his sense of what is comic, gaudy, and pretentious, yet he deftly establishes that its fundamental values are life-enhancing. The main embodiment of these qualities is Sissy Jupe, who is first offered as a force of natural goodness when she is symbolically contrasted with Bitzer in the schoolroom. Indeed, it is a potent indication of her life-affirming characteristics that she proves incapable of learning facts and drawing the correct conclusions from statistics. Later she succeeds in bringing the Gradgrind family to the realisation "that there is something—not an Ology at all—that" their "father has missed, or forgotten." Sissy is associated with the deep, natural and ultimately religious forces of life, but she remains a slightly insubstantial figure because the reader is often told of the effect she has on others, rather than being shown it. As an embodiment of goodness, she has links with Esther Summerson in *Bleak House* and Amy Dorrit in *Little Dorrit*: all three are young girls whose family circles have been depleted and yet they assume considerable responsibility for other people; and they find their reward and fulfilment in marriage. However, Sissy carries out her function almost unwittingly and thus avoids the taint of determined and self-conscious virtue that distances many readers from the other two heroines. Indeed, it is the dark-haired daughter of a stroller, drawing from Blake's conception of innocence and pointing forward to some of Lawrence's heroines, whose vitality and unforced selflessness make her the most resonant presence in Coketown.

—J.S. Shrimpton

HAVELOK.
Poem, late 13th century.

Edition

Havelok, edited by G.V. Smithers. 1987.

Havelok belongs with a small group of romances, including such works as *King Horn*, *Athelston*, and *Guy of Warwick*, which together make up "the matter of England." Their distinguishing characteristic is that they incorporate elements of the non-Arthurian legendary history of Britain in a story elaborated on the pattern of romantic folktale. The historical component in *Havelok* is slight. That the hero ultimately accedes to the thrones of England and Denmark is a circumstance recalling the period 1018–35 when Cnut ruled both kingdoms. The name Birkabeyn given Havelok's father is recorded as the nickname of a Scandinavian king who reigned from 1184 to 1202, but in Norway, not Denmark. The story's final point of contact with Scandinavian history involves a long-standing association of its hero with Olaf Sictricson. In conformity with the heroes of companion Middle English romances, Havelok first appears in Anglo-Norman chronicle and romance, in a passage in Geoffrey Gaimar's *Estoire des Engles* (1134–40), and later in the *Lai d'Haveloc* (1190–1220), an independent work superficially patterned on the *lais* of Marie de France. Both French sources attribute to Havelok the name Cuaran, familiar as the nickname of the Viking hero who became king of York in 941. This coincidence of names is a curiosity, but probably no more than that, the assumption once made that *Havelok* (*Abloc*) and *Anlaf* were etymologically related forms having been discredited. Other historical reminiscences are very localized. The provenance of both the main manuscript (Laud Misc. 108) and some minor fragments is Norfolk, but the story's associations are with Lincolnshire, the town of Lincoln itself and the seaport of Grimsby, for which the character Grim provides an eponymous founder.

Havelok recounts, in 3000 lines of octosyllabic couplets, a young man's struggle to reach maturity and to reclaim the patrimony treacherously stolen from him in his infancy. The hero survives an early attempt on his life, exile and poverty as the adopted son of a poor fisherman, and hard labour in the humble role of cook's assistant, before enforced marriage to a similarly abused princess initiates an amelioration of his fortunes. Havelok's imposing stature induces the wicked English regent Godrich to imagine that he can sophistically satisfy his promise to Goldeburgh's father Athelwold to marry her to the "highest" man in the kingdom, while making her ineligible to rule through her union with a peasant; by unwittingly marrying her to the as-yet-unrecognized heir to the Danish throne, he sows the seeds of his own eventual overthrow and execution. The story of Havelok's betrayal, humiliation, and ultimate restoration to privileged status conforms to what folklorists know as the male-Cinderella tale-type. The narrative progresses so methodically that routinely recurrent features, such as references to eating and to physical conflict, acquire significance as symbols which chart the hero's advancement as the plot develops. Variety is provided by the interweaving of the similar but subtly differentiated experiences of Havelok and Goldeburgh, and fusion of the process of maturing with a preparation for kingship individualizes Havelok's biography.

Articulating the qualities of a good king is a major thematic concern throughout the romance. It opens with an 82 line eulogy of Athelwold:

> He louede God with al his micth,
> And Holi Kirke, and soth ant ricth.
> Ricthwise men he louede alle,
> And oueral made hem for to calle.
> Wreieres and wrobberes made he falle,
> And hated hem so man doth galle;
> Vtlawes and theues made he bynde,
> Alle þat he micthe fynde,
> And heye hengen on galwe-tre:
> For hem ne yede gold ne fe!

It ends with the ousting of the usurpers, and initiation under Havelok and Goldeburgh of a regime destined to emulate that of the idealized English monarch. Although for extensive periods Havelok is without power or influence, and entirely subject to the authority of others, the account of his fortunes serves as a suitable vehicle for the advocacy of good government because the author assumes that the common man may embody the virtues necessary for a good king.

Havelok reflects singularly little influence of courtly doctrine. The absence of any sentiments associated with *amor courtois* is particularly noticeable, and well illustrated by Havelok's reaction to the suggestion that he should wed Goldeburgh:

> Hwat sholde Ich with wif do?
> J ne may hire fede ne cloþe ne sho.
> Wider sholde Ich wimman bringe?
> J ne haue none kines þinge—
> J ne haue hws, Y ne haue cote,
> Ne I ne haue stikke, Y ne haue sprote,
> J ne haue neyþer bred ne sowel,
> Ne cloth but of an hold with couel.

This preoccupation with the economics of marriage is stylistically closer to a fabliau such as *Le Vallet qui d'Aise a Malaise se met* than to a typical courtly romance. In conjunction with such "minstrel" features as appeals for attention, previews of forthcoming action, and a request for refreshment, this tone has been thought to indicate that the work was intended to appeal to a lower-class audience. But there is no reason to assume an audience different from that envisaged for Chaucer's *The Man of Law's Tale*, with which *Havelok* shares such phenomena as the duplication of episodes, and a dependence on instances of divine intervention to advance the plot.

The text of the romance in the Laud manuscript is bound together with a collection of saints' lives, and preceded with the rubric *Vita Hauelok*. It might therefore be compared with *The Man of Law's Tale* as an example of pseudo-historical romantic fiction with hagiographical colouration. Such is the unknown author's skill in integrating strikingly observed, albeit stock characters with a well-constructed plot, that *Havelok* would sustain the comparison well.

—Roy J. Pearcy

THE HAYSTACK IN THE FLOODS.
Poem by William Morris, 1858.

William Morris was only 24 when he published his first volume of poetry, *The Defence of Guenevere and Other Poems*. Since it was seen as the first book of Pre-Raphaelite poetry to appear before the public—neither Dante Gabriel nor Christina Rossetti, nor Swinburne, had yet published one—it met with a good deal of puzzlement and hostility. One reviewer saw it as evidence of "how far affectation may mislead an earnest man towards the fog-land of Art." But some of the poems did receive a more positive response, and "The Haystack in the Floods" was pre-eminent among these. Its subsequent critical acclaim has remained consistently high, owing to the interest of the story and the dramatic power with which it is rendered.

It is one of a group of poems in the volume which derived from Morris's enthusiastic reading of the *Chronicles* of Jean Froissart, probably in Lord Berners's English translation of 1523–25. Froissart was the French chronicler of the 14th-century wars between the English and the French in France. His *Chronicles* are notable for their vivid accounts of the often brutal and violent events of that disturbed time, and the young Morris—with his early devotion to medieval history, and his taste for action and commitment (and perhaps for what seemed a simpler world than that of the 19th century)—found among the stories several that appealed to his imagination. These include the dramatic fragment "Sir Peter Harpdon's End" and the memorable "Concerning Geoffray Teste Noire," but "The Haystack in the Floods" stands out even from these in its vigour and control.

It is written in octosyllabic couplets, which impart a certain briskness of manner. As is characteristic of these early poems, Morris sweeps the reader into a dramatic situation with no introduction of the characters:

> Had she come all this way for this,
> To part at last without a kiss?

It is only as we read on that we discover that "she" is Jehane, and that her long journey with her lover Robert has brought them only into an ambush, engineered by the enemy Godmar. The atmosphere is bleak and uncompromising: "The tears and rain ran down her face." Jehane is full of foreboding that she will be taken back to Paris, imprisoned, and thrown into the Seine to sink or swim, or else will have to marry Godmar. When they approach the enemy, Robert cries "'St. George for Marny' cheerily," but this is no heroic romance. His own men fail to follow him, and he is taken prisoner. Godmar baldly tells Jehane that he will kill Robert unless she gives herself to him. She refuses, and when he threatens further she continues to defy him—even though he speaks of giving her to the Paris people "to burn or drown" as a witch. Godmar's threat is made particularly distasteful by his sadistic dwelling on Jehane's physical beauty at this point:

> This were indeed a piteous end
> For those long fingers, and long feet,
> And long neck and smooth fingers sweet.

It is as if he finds sexual excitement in the thought of causing her death.

Jehane is given an hour to reconsider her decision. In this period the exhausted woman falls to the ground and sleeps with her "head on a wet heap of hay." On being awakened, she comes "strangely childlike" to Godmar, and says "I will not." The suggestion of a child lost in this violent adult world is poignant. Her decision prompts Godmar to immediate action, as Robert, his eyes dry, his lips firm, tries for the last time to touch Jehane's lips. On noticing this, Godmar thrusts them apart and turns on Robert. The powerful description of the murder gains force from being seen from Jehane's powerless point of view, and is driven forward in a long dramatic sentence, culminating in the blow struck by the "thin steel" as Robert's head is bent back by the hair.

The behaviour of Godmar and his men here is the opposite of the code of chivalry:

> So then
> Godmar turned grinning to his men,
> Who ran, some five or six, and beat
> His head to pieces at their feet.

Godmar then turns back to Jehane with a further command: she must return with him to the Chatelet. The three lines giving her response are effective in their controlled brevity:

> She shook her head and gazed awhile
> At her cold hands with a rueful smile,
> As though this thing had made her mad.

It might well have done; but Morris's technique is to withhold explanatory commentary. He concludes simply with a statement that takes us back to the title and the beginning of the poem:

> This was the parting that they had
> Beside the haystack in the floods.

The Victorians, including Morris, were greatly attracted to the Middle Ages, but they often tended to glamorize or moralize them. In this poem Morris creates an unforgettable drama of passion and violence, and leaves the reader to draw his or her own conclusions.

—Peter Faulkner

HEART OF DARKNESS.
Story by Joseph Conrad, 1902.

"Heart of Darkness," first published in *Blackwood's Magazine* between February and April 1899 and revised for inclusion in a separate volume in 1902, has become for many readers the quintessential modernist narrative. Its very title a suggestive metaphor, this novella has attracted a range of interpretations covering the full spectrum of analytical criticism. Although Joseph Conrad based his story on his earlier experiences in the Congo, he makes strategic use of the metaphysical potential of his subject, making the narrative neither simple nor straightforward. Deliberately minimal action and absence of a clear resolution compound the problems of meaning. In addition, Conrad's elaborate but often murky style creates a result so layered with different ironic possibilities that definite conclusions seem impossible. These narrative complexities heighten thematic orientation to give the work its distinguishing feature: an indelible forcefulness of moral concern. In this fashion the story creates a medium for surveying—and exposing—some major tenets shaping Western civilization and its colonialist adventures.

The literal actions of the story are structured sequentially as a journey, and it is the richly designed texture behind the unfolding of these events that gives the narrative its most important thematic significance. Its discourse embedded with classical and biblical allusions, the journey takes on the semblance of a mythic initiation, a ritual of descent and return. Charlie Marlow, the primary narrator, recounts his earlier adventure as a young man on an assignment as river steamboat skipper, an episode he now sees as the "culminating point" of his experience. Few specific names or locales are mentioned, but he crosses the Channel for an interview obtained through the influence of his aunt, secures the position, descends to Africa, and undertakes a mission upriver to the inner station to find and rescue Kurtz, his company's most productive trader. Although he must overcome great difficulties in his quest for Kurtz and discovers that the unrestrained Kurtz has become absolutely corrupt, Marlow effects the rescue. Kurtz dies on the return downriver, and Marlow, who very nearly dies of fever himself, returns to Europe where he lies—paradoxically—to Kurtz's fiancée, allowing her to continue to believe in Kurtz's grandeur. The ordering principle behind these events is not so much causal as spatial, and their eventual pattern can be seen, in fact, as circular.

The chronology itself moves by fits and starts and appears to break down entirely at times, as, for instance, when Marlow finds he must refloat his sunken riverboat and spends weeks waiting for rivets to repair it. The disjointed surface actions nudge the reader into seeking other unifying patterns, ones that appear laden with thematic import: the pervasive, unifying motif of the river; the juxtaposed light and dark color imagery; the Edenic qualities of the setting; the conflicts implicit in metaphorical forces pitted against one another; the epiphanic cycle of symbolic immersion and rebirth.

The other components of the narrative support and extend these thematic implications. The point of view, for example, is famous as an example of framed narratives. The largest part of the tale is told by Marlow, but his story is about a younger and very different Marlow from the older, alienated, Buddha-like figure who recounts the tale. Although Marlow appears in other narratives by Conrad, the layered perspectives surrounding his point of view in this story especially complicate his discourse. Marlow's story itself is contained within the first-person account of an unidentified narrator who listens to it with a group of businessmen aboard the *Nellie*, a cruising yawl in the Thames estuary. Even the audience to whom Marlow speaks needs to be taken into account to help interpret his story.

Countering the disjointed perspectives and the lack of a clearly established plot is Conrad's image-laden style, which helps create visual impressions and works to establish an allegorical or fablistic framework with primordial and natural dimensions of order such as the cycles of history and the turnings of the tide. The mysterious clues to Kurtz's character, the dead bodies, skulls, crypt-like residences, and oppressive natural surroundings build in increasing intensity until all these details appear to culminate into symbolic meaning. Conrad's fondness for abstractions such as "inscrutable," "inexplicable," and "unfathomable enigma" also compounds thematic meaning. Because of the economy of the novella format, many of the characters have a metaphorical rather than a mimetic cast: the knitting women who are "uncanny and fateful," "guarding the door of Darkness"; the elusive Russian trader; Kurtz's "wild-eyed and magnificent" African consort; or his ethereal fiancée. The symbolism is nowhere more apparent, though, than in Kurtz himself. Even though Marlow reveals Kurtz as the embodiment of the emptiness of contemporary civilization, he discovers himself bound to Kurtz, fated to be loyal to him as the "nightmare" of his choice. Marlow thereby displays another subtle paradox in his search for truth: there are no absolute answers, only a multiplicity of interpretations. His narrative serves to dramatize moral precepts, but at the same time it challenges assumptions about the nature of knowledge, the ways of perceiving, even about the act of reading itself.

—Thomas Loe

THE HEART OF MID-LOTHIAN.
Novel by Sir Walter Scott, 1818.

The Heart of Mid-Lothian is, by general consent, the finest of Sir Walter Scott's Waverley novels. After Shakespeare, Scott probably created a richer, more vivid, and more extensive cast of characters than any other British author, with the possible exception of Dickens (many of whose characters, however, sometimes seem to wear about their credibility the trappings of caricature).

Even in *The Heart of Mid-Lothian*, where for most of the story Scott's creative imagination is operating at white heat, there is a long preamble in which we learn that the whole story has been passed to us by Jedediah Cleishbotham, schoolmaster of Gandercleugh from the manuscript of his usher, Peter Pattieson. To make matters worse, at least in the eyes of his more impatient readers, in 1830 Scott added a further preamble, in which he explained how he heard the story of Jeanie Deans from Helen Walker, her real-life prototype. Those who are not Scott devotees may have sympathy with A.N. Wilson when he suggests that if the novel "were to arrive unsolicited on the desk of a London publisher for the first time today, there can be no doubt that he would want it to be heavily cut." Perhaps so; but the modern reader of Scott can get the most out of the Waverley novels only by surrendering himself or herself to the pace of the storytelling. The leisurely introduction to the tale, and its relaxed unwinding, serve to counterpoint the tensions of the main body of the novel.

Almost before he is aware of what has happened to him, the reader suddenly finds himself grippingly involved in the Porteous riots. Andrew Wilson, a criminal who commanded some public sympathy for setting on his guards the previous Sunday to allow his accomplice George Robertson to escape, has been hanged at the Tolbooth jail (from the nickname for which the novel takes its title). Captain Porteous, in charge of the execution, behaves with callous brutality toward the condemned man, and, when the crowd protests, orders his men to fire, killing six people. For this he is in due course tried and condemned for murder, but receives a reprieve from Queen Caroline, known to be anti-Scots in her outlook. Before Porteous can be freed, a mob collects in Edinburgh, advances on the prison, forcing a young clergyman, Reuben Butler, to accompany it and, after due religious observance, hangs Porteous. All this is described in magnificently paced prose.

In the jail also is Effie Deans, condemned under a cruel Scots law which assumed that when a secretly pregnant woman told no one of her condition and could not produce the child, she must be presumed guilty of child murder. The minister forced to officiate at the hanging of Porteous turns out, in fact, to have been the fiancé of Effie's sister, Jeanie. Both sisters are the children of old Davie Deans, a stern Calvinist and "left-over" from the days of the Covenanters; a man answerable to no one but his conscience and his God. Jeanie, the plainer of the two sisters, accepts his stern code of discipline. Effie, as so often happens in such constricting circumstances, rebels, attends dances illicitly, and takes as her lover the aforementioned George Robertson, in his youth something of a madcap. Robertson, leading the determinedly orderly mob attacking the prison, attempts to get Effie to flee from the Tolbooth during the confusion; but she is so bemused by his urging that she can only look on him with "mingled fear, affection, and upbraiding." As her own execution draws near, however, she begs her sister to save her.

Jeanie's conscience does not allow her to tell a lie. Both she and her father are wracked by the moral dilemma which imprisons their consciences. Effie's crime is not sexual indulgence, but concealment. Jeanie or her father have only to say that Effie told one or the other of them about her condition for her to be saved. George Robertson has only to come forward to marry her and, again, she will be saved. For their differing reasons, none can take the necessary saving action, though Robertson meets Jeanie at Muschat's Cairn and unsuccessfully tries to persuade her to lie to the court. Called to the box to give evidence, in response to Effie's cry "O Jeanie, Jeanie, save me, save me!" Jeanie can only testify "Alack! alack! she never breathed a word to me."

It was Jeanie's belief that if she trusted in Heaven, "she would experience its protection." She did. Revelation "came . . . on her mind, like a sun-blink on a stormy sea." If Porteous could be reprieved by the Queen, then so could Effie. Jeanie's journey to London and interview with Queen Caroline, whom she persuades to grant Effie a reprieve, keeps up Scott's inspired pace of storytelling. The touch is sure throughout, the writing taut, the character-drawing firm, even down to such details as the echo of the violent deaths on the gallows at the beginning of the book in the distant glimpse of Madge Wildfire's mother on the gallows which Jeanie catches as she passes through Carlisle on her way back from London.

The last quarter of the book has been judged by some critics to be weaker than the rest of it, if not actually superfluous. But this is assuredly not so, although admittedly the writing is slacker. While Jeanie's future life as a minister's wife is recounted at a more leisurely pace, the account of Effie's is "so condensed as to seem thinly melodramatic," as Scott's greatest biographer, Edgar Johnson so aptly puts it. Jeanie marries Reuben Butler, and is truthfully happy. Effie elopes with George Robertson, who turns out to be the son of an Espiscopalian clergyman but, unexpectedly, really Sir George Staunton, the heir to a baronetcy. As the dazzling Lady Staunton, Effie carries her restlessness into Regency London society, and achieves only superficiality. It has to be admitted that Scott's handling of the transformation of Robertson to Staunton savours a little of stagey contrivance, not to say implausibility.

Nevertheless, the novel transcendingly presents the virtues of truth as upheld by the sometimes rigid limitations of Scottish Presbyterianism. The portrait of a whole society—nothing less than the fabric of late 18th-century Scotland in fact—is there, forever focusing sharply onto a rich variety of detail with unswerving clarity, and revealing the human heart in all its priggishness, pathos, tenderness, and, sometimes, dogged energy. As Johnson again so succinctly puts it: "Even among Scott's other triumphs, the novel is unsurpassed," quoting the *London Magazine*: "Wert thou to live a thousand years, and write a thousand romances, thou woulds't never, old True-penny, beat thy own *Heart of Mid-Lothian*!"

—Maurice Lindsay

THE HEART OF THE MATTER.
Novel by Graham Greene, 1948.

The central figure of Graham Greene's *The Heart of the Matter* is Henry Scobie, deputy commissioner of police in an obscure West African colony during World War II. Amid a sea of corruption Scobie has managed to maintain an honesty born of a genuine love for the filthy, sweltering region he inhabits and for its people. His wife Louise, however, does not share this love, and is further disillusioned by Scobie's inability to get further promotion; Scobie, moved perhaps more by pity than by a love which is in some respects already dead, tries to arrange for her to leave for the comparative tranquillity of South Africa.

Not having the necessary money, he accepts a loan from Yusef, a Syrian businessman—much of the business of the colony is in the hands of the Syrians, as is the even more lucrative diamond-smuggling trade—which lays him open to blackmail; and Louise leaves. We next see him helping with the repatriation to this improbably British territory of a group of survivors from the sinking of a British ship; among them is a woman called Helen Rolt, whose husband of a few months has been drowned. Scobie enters into a relationship with Helen, which further worsens his position.

All of this is further complicated by the presence in the colony of a London-based spy called Wilson, who has fallen in love with Louise and tries various machinations to ruin Scobie; and also by Scobie's own Catholicism, which tortures him with his unfaithfulness. When Scobie hears that Louise is returning to patch up their marriage, he finds himself in an impossible position; he can only maintain his relationship to Louise by going to Mass with her which, in his eyes, completes his damnation. Sick at heart and losing hope of any kind of redemption, he confides in Yusef; one tragic upshot of this is that Yusef arranges for the murder of Ali, Scobie's trusted servant of many years.

The web is closing around Scobie, and his sudden elevation to the rank of commissioner only completes his sense of having sold himself to the devil. Aware that he is sealing his eternal damnation, he commits suicide, hoping that in that way he can at least prevent any further hurt to those whom he loves, but afterwards neither Helen nor Louise show any understanding of the reasons for his death, and it is left to the Catholic priest, Father Rank, to assert finally that "it may seem an odd thing to say—when a man's as wrong as he was—but I think, from what I saw of him, that he really loved God."

The crucial image in the book is the heart. Scobie is doomed to a perpetual questioning of his own motives and feelings, a ceaseless attempt to discover whether the various loves which he feels are genuine or are simply functions of an overwhelming sense of pity for the world and its inhabitants.

His method of suicide is to simulate angina, a heart-pain, and thus acquire the tablets which, taken in sufficient quantity, effect his death.

We are left in little doubt of Scobie's essential honesty and goodness; but circumstances are too much for him, and he is impaled on the dilemma of whether to put the love of God or the love of fellow-humans first. His entanglement with Yusef, which precipitates the death of Ali, begins only because of his wish to save Louise from further pain: "I am the responsible man," he says several times, calling attention to the sense of responsibility which effectively prevents him from acting to save himself while there are others to be saved.

The setting of the novel is richly and economically drawn: there is no heroism in this colonial situation, but neither is there blame. The major characters have inherited an impossible situation from their forebears, and their job is to make the best of it amid the appalling weather, the ceaseless greed, the lack of trust and understanding which prevails between the races, the snobbery and pettiness of the expatriate community. Scobie's house sits in the middle of a swamp, a powerful image for the forces of degradation and decay which are everywhere at work.

In such a world faith is difficult; Father Rank has been in the colony for 12 years, and doubts whether he has saved a single soul during that time. The goodness of God seems everywhere obscured by human malice: the figure of Wilson, the spy, is a masterly sketch of shallowness of feeling and embodies a destructive force which is not lessened by Wilson's callow ineffectuality as a human being.

Louise is herself a complex character, just as prone to snobberies and rivalries as the rest of the expatriates, trying to maintain a front of culture and intellectuality in the face of the difficulties of colonialism and war. Part of Scobie's tragedy is that he cannot separate his feelings of responsibility and pity for her plight, which he sees himself as having created, from love, which means that he finds himself most involved with her when she is suffering—and, indeed, this problem is repeated in his affair with Helen, whom he sees as in many ways a child in need of his protection.

But God moves in mysterious ways, and Scobie is able to cry out his love for Him even on his deathbed, leaving us with a characteristically ambiguous ending. Is Scobie saved or not? We are drawn to believe that he is; that the pity he has felt for his suffering fellow-mortals is in some way reciprocated by God's final pity for him, even though he dies in a state of damnation. Like all of Greene's work, *The Heart of the Matter* is in the last analysis a religious book, but in a special sense in that Greene uses the problems of faith to shed a brilliant light on our everyday worldly actions.

Greene's style is always terse, and here this terseness is at its best, with each small scene contributing to our sense of fearful claustrophobia as the web of corruption and half-truth closes around Scobie. There is a sense of inevitability which moves us through the novel: once the wheels have been set in motion there is no stopping them, which turns the novel into a genuine tragedy in which our own pity and terror in the face of suffering and pain is fully awakened and we are brought to see in Scobie's dilemmas a symbolic representation of our own.

—David Punter

HEARTBREAK HOUSE.
Play by Bernard Shaw, 1919.

The early 1920's saw the publication and production of the three plays which are possibly the finest and certainly the most ambitious of Bernard Shaw's long, prolific, and extraordinary career. The plays were *Heartbreak House*, first produced by the Theatre Guild in New York on 10 November 1920; *Back to Methuselah*, the immense five-play cycle that was intended to embody his fullest parable of Creative Evolution, and which was produced by the Theatre Guild in February and March 1922; and *Saint Joan*, which was produced by the Theatre Guild in late December 1923. During these years, Shaw was in his middle to late sixties, at a time of life when the creative evolution of most dramatists had long since ceased, but when he was at the very top of his powers.

Like most of Shaw's plays, even such classics as *Man and Superman* and *Major Barbara*, these culminating dramas received a plethora of imperceptive, denigratory, and even dismissive comments; and, with his experimental late plays, they remain among his least performed. There are probably two chief reasons for this neglect, one practical and one thematic. The practical is that the plays, like Ibsen's *Brand* and Strindberg's *To Damascus*, are startlingly long, dauntingly difficult, and much too expensive for any but a soundly subsidised theatre to stage. The thematic is that they make more complicated points and contain more pessimistic attitudes than the conventional theatre has usually embodied or, indeed, even attempted.

Shaw rather misleadingly called *Heartbreak House* "A Fantasia in the Russian Manner of English Themes," and so viewers were inevitably led to a comparison with Chekhov, in which a number of engagingly feckless people sit around in a country house and do nothing but talk for three or four acts. The misunderstanding, however, was a superficial one and unfair, in different ways, to both Chekhov and Shaw.

Chekhov's great comedies are far from static; indeed, they have a complicated plenitude of plot that would leave a Jonson or a Feydeau gasping. Shaw's play, on the other hand, has a welter of engrossing confrontations but hardly a developed plot at all. In fact, the only thing that remotely could be termed a plot is Ellie Dunn's conversion from romance, when she discovers in the very first act that Hector Hushabye has told her a series of comic-opera lies. Then she swiftly and stoically embraces the disillusionment of failed ideals. The other characters have even less of a revelation; they merely illustrate their characters, casually accept their social inutility and cheerfully welcome their deserved annihilation.

This sounds like, and indeed is, the most lugubrious of themes, but *Heartbreak House* could not be a Shaw play if its overt manner were at all dreary. His characters have such bumptious vitality, telling insight, and witty playfulness with language that they become not only enormously attractive but also provide a terrifically vigorous counterpoint to the theme. On the page, such an ebullient Shavian vigour may seem to reduce them to automatons, galvanized into a caricature of life by their creator's own liveliness. On the stage, in a production as sympathetic as that of the early 1980's which featured Rex Harrison as Captain Shotover, an unexpected dimension appears. There is intrinsic to the play a poignant sadness about the defeat of value, and these droll Shavian cartoons become the most touchingly emotional evocations of social man that Shaw ever wrote.

It is unusual to be moved by something as intellectual and yet as simplistic as allegory, and *Heartbreak House* is above all an allegory. The very set, "the after part of an old-fashioned high-pooped ship," emphasizes that this is the ship of state commanded by "cultured, leisured Europe before the war." Among the crew are Ellie, the youthful idealist in a world with no niche for idealism; Hector, the hero without employment; Hesione, whose beauty and charm are not enough and not even real; Mazzini Dunn, the inventor without power; Mangan, the exploiter whose capital is illusory; and, above all, Captain Shotover, the sage whose wisdom has been reduced to rum.

From such vivid cartoons, Shaw is able to draw not only telling emotion but profound meaning, and the Captain's last speeches are as pregnantly mordant as any of Captain Gulliver's. For instance: "The captain is in his bunk, drinking bottled ditch-water; and the crew is gambling in the forecastle. She will strike and sink and split. Do you think the laws of God will be suspended in favor of England because you were born in it?" Also, Hesione's final excitement and Ellie's radiance at the prospect of them, these charming and delightful failures, being shortly bombed into annihilation are as pessimistic and yet as triumphant a conclusion as a modern play has probably ever had.

—Robert Hogan

HENRY IV, part 1.
Play by William Shakespeare, 1596–97(?).

The First Part of King Henry the Fourth is the second play in William Shakespeare's so-called "second tetralogy" of works dealing with English history. Both in date of composition and chronology of historical material, it follows *Richard II* and precedes *The Second Part of Henry IV* and *Henry V*. Like these other plays its principal source is Raphael Holinshed's *Chronicles of England*. Its contemporary success, which seems to have been largely the result of the popularity of the Falstaff scenes, led to the publication of five editions within Shakespeare's lifetime, a number not exceeded by any of his other plays.

The main plot is economically set in motion in the first act. Henry IV deals brusquely with Hotspur (Harry Percy), son to the Earl of Northumberland, who is quickly persuaded to enter into complicity with the Scots (under Archibald, Earl of Douglas), the Welsh (under Owen Glendower), and Scroop, Archbishop of York, in a revolt against the king—whose legitimacy is in question owing to his own revolt against his predecessor, Richard II. Hotspur is contrasted with Hal, Henry IV's elder son and Prince of Wales, who idles away his time in the company of Sir John Falstaff, a notorious rogue; Hal himself claims, however (I.ii), to be deliberately blackening his own character in preparation for a triumphant "reformation." The end of the play sees the failure of Hotspur's revolt at the Battle of Shrewsbury, when the loyalists, strongly supported by the now soldierly and valiant Hal, carry the day.

The play is sometimes seen as a moralistic treatment of monarchy and the state, displaying the horrors of rebellion and the divine sanctions underpinning the monarch's rule. It is better understood, however, in terms of Shakespeare's creative freedom with an overall framework of political thought and political history; and in this sense the play transcends what was attempted in *Richard II*. Falstaff is much more than a symbol of the temptations which royalty rejects: he is the major force in a set of ironic and parodic parallels running throughout the play by which the grave and the comic, the noble and the disreputable aspects of warfare, valour, kingship, and even virtue itself are played off against one another. His wit is comically and subversively destructive not merely of the aristocratic and martial codes, but of human pretensions in general, and this not only in the scenes in which he explicitly mocks, for example, the King (II.iv) and the concept of Honour (V.i). The balance between sympathy and condemnation, delight and repulsion in our attitude to Falstaff is shifting and delicate, and the same is true of our response to the sets of values upon which he is made (implicitly and explicitly) to comment.

Further parallels which create a dramatic ambivalence towards these values are in evidence in other parts of the play. The Gadshill robbery (II.ii) is a comic counterpart to Henry IV's wish to deprive Hotspur of his spoils, the prisoners taken at Holdmedon (I.i). Hotspur himself mocks Glendower's fanaticism (III.i). And the ostensible hero of the piece, Prince Hal himself, is presented ambivalently; his attitudes are so enigmatic that his character has been interpreted in widely varying ways. Hal has been criticised as a cold-blooded prig (the speaker of the lines in I.ii in which he disdains his companions, seeing them only as a means to a selfish end) and, at the other extreme, celebrated as Shakespeare's ideal monarch. The truth seems to be that Hal, like the author of this play, is subject to conflicting pressures: he is both drawn to Falstaff and Eastcheap and yet repelled by them when the opportunity to revel in glory presents itself. Again, although there is nothing to suggest any insincerity when he gives the king his undertaking to "be more myself" (II.ii), he returns in the next scene to the tavern, where his participation in the life of idleness and roguery is no less unreserved. In Hal, as Samuel Johnson expresses it, "the trifler is roused into a hero, and the hero again reposes in the trifler." By the end of the play, however, he has come to appear genuinely heroic. He has changed places with Hotspur, the impressive but not unflawed incarnation of ardent valour: after killing Hotspur, Hal makes his rival's quest of honour seem superficial and vain when, having done his soldierly duty, he takes no interest in acquiring the credit for his exploit and offers to allow Falstaff to claim it (V.v).

What the play as a whole offers is not confusion or contradiction in the characters and their acts, but a special kind of complexity—a complexity that mirrors that of experience itself. Human values are sometimes viewed reductively, sometimes cherished as inspiring and ennobling; Shakespeare does justice to what is genuinely ambivalent in experience. And above all, the play evinces the most vivid delight in the world it both reflects and creates, with all its incongruities—centrally in Falstaff. "A plague of sighing and grief!" he exclaims: in the teeth of old age and death, Falstaff embodies the exuberant energies and appetites of life itself.

—Stuart Gillespie

HENRY IV, part 2.
Play by William Shakespeare, 1597–98(?).

Though in narrative terms a continuation of *The First Part of Henry IV*, *The Second Part* strikes the reader as a different play almost at once. Its action is less bouyant and energetic, its tone sometimes wistful and sometimes bitter. Shakespeare had to move from the irresponsible high spirits of part 1 towards a representation of Hal as a model monarch and the corresponding rejection of Falstaff, and the play's tone is set accordingly. Falstaff appears from his first entry (I.ii) as suffering the effects of old age and approaching death, and is immediately worsted by the Lord Chief Justice—who will eventually pronounce sentence on him. Hal is graver; his single scene with Falstaff before his coronation concludes with his abrupt departure as he blames himself for idleness (II.iv).

The outlines of Shakespeare's more general subjects in the second tetralogy are as clear in *Henry IV*, part 2 as in the other plays. The responsibilities of "the head that wears a crown"; the combination of qualities requisite for a prince; the current state and the future destiny of England; the ills attendant on rebellion: these matters are pursued in the conduct of the drama as a whole and directly addressed at certain points by the protagonists. Shakespeare's presentation of them extends in different directions from those of part 1, however. On his death-bed the care-worn Henry IV now admits the "crook'd ways" by which he acquired his crown; Hal, it is established, will enjoy an appearance of legitimacy to which his father was never entitled. The loyalists in this play are, indeed, in some ways scarcely better than the rebels: John of Lancaster's victory in IV.ii is achieved through a disgraceful deception which cannot be made palatable by critical arguments about Elizabethan attitudes towards rebellion. Shakespeare's exploration of national life now extends well beyond London: the Gloucestershire scenes render rural England in an comical-elegiac mood, full of inconsequential remarks, memories, futility, and the sweetness of ripe apples. This too is part of the kingdom which Hal must make his own. The Gloucestershire scenes have been called a glorious irrelevance, but the reader is more likely to agree on reflection that the public situation in the play is being "defined and judged in terms of a richly human context in which Falstaff's ragged regiment and the Cotswold conscripts are an indispensable part" (L.C. Knights).

By the end of the play Hal's greater qualities are to stand revealed, and near the close there will be a reconciliation between the prince and his father. The reconciliation (IV.v) is well-managed and moving. But Warwickshire's prediction must also come true: "The Prince will, in the perfectness of time, / Cast off his followers." The newly crowned King's dismissal of Falstaff has attracted much comment. Shakespeare attempts to prepare us for it in a variety of ways: by increasing the sordidness of Falstaff's way of life, decreasing his wittiness, and even, in a scene which our previous knowledge of the characters concerned renders less than fully plausible, making his friends Pistol, Doll Tearsheet, and Mistress Quickly responsible for a murder (V.iv). In trying to remove our sympathies from Falstaff, however, Shakespeare is evidently working against some of his own instincts, and has to labour to wrench the shape of the play to the purpose. The presentation of both Hal and Falstaff increasingly has the effect of a simplification of rich and complex material into something approaching a black-and-white morality drama. Shakespeare's problem was not entirely soluble, and in the end we are likely to "feel a good deal of pain and some resentment" (A.C. Bradley) at the new King's final speech to Falstaff, beginning:

> I know thee not, old man. Fall to thy prayers.
> How ill white hairs become a fool and a jester!

It is not only Falstaff's rejection but the manner of it that is hard to swallow. This speech, with its self-righteous air (reinforced by an echo of Matthew 25:12), asks us to accept a version of the past in which Hal was corrupted by his "misleaders" and is thus entitled to punish them. Hal has become the exponent of a mode of virtue which is embarrassing: the unattractiveness of his attitude here is uncomfortable because it is so closely involved with his brand of virtue. The play closes with a king who is a tower of stern moral strength, but who in banishing Falstaff has "banish[ed] all the world." In *Henry V* Hal will be more alone than any of Shakespeare's other kings.

—Stuart Gillespie

HENRY V.
Play by William Shakespeare, 1599.

> I will lay odds that, ere this year expire
> We bear our civil swords and native fire
> As far as France.
> (*Henry IV*, part 2, V.v. 105)

The promise held out by Lord John of Lancaster is fulfilled in *Henry V*. The play depicts the English conquest of France and the recognition of Henry as heir to the French crown. The action begins in April 1414 and ends with the betrothal of Henry to Princess Katherine, daughter of Charles VI, in May 1420. The main sources are Raphael Holinshed's *Chronicles* (1587 edition) and the anonymous play *The Famous Victories of Henry V* (1598).

Henry V was England's hero-king *par excellence*. The Chorus alerts us in his Act I prologue to the greatness of the theme and the proverty of its theatrical realisation:

> O for a Muse of fire, that would ascend
> The brightest heaven of invention,
> A kingdom for a stage, princes to act,
> And monarchs to behold the swelling scene!

To bring "the warlike Harry" before us "like himself" would require the richest rhetorical *inventio* and a whole kingdom instead of a wooden O. The Chorus urges the audience to compensate for theatrical limitations by using the power of thought. Shakespeare uses his Chorus, who delivers five prologues and an epilogue, to serve several purposes. He reminds the audience that it is witnessing not "true things" but imitations. He prepares the audience for developments such as the treachery of Richard of Cambridge (Act II prologue). He abridges historical time, eliding the five-year gap (Act V prologue) between the Battle of Agincourt and the peace conference at Troyes. Finally, the Chorus is used to "cancel the distance between performers and spectators . . . and . . . convey . . . the exhilarated involvement of Henry's people and Henry's land—and so of Elizabeth's" (A.R.Humphreys).

The play is varied in its ingredients and its tone. The opening of the Act II prologue stirs expectation: "Now all the youth of England are on fire, / And silken dalliance in the wardrobe lies." The Act IV prologue evokes the dread of the hours before the Battle of Agincourt: "Now entertain conjecture of a time / When creeping murmur and the poring dark / Fills the wide vessel of the universe." An aspect of the greatness of the play is inclusiveness: the encompassing of hope and despair, valour and "cold fear," high endeavour and farcical incident. As the fortunes of England advance, domestic and familiar ties are broken. The links with Henry's old life give way one by one. Falstaff's heart is "fracted and corroborate"; his death is narrated by the Hostess in II.iii. Bardolph and Nym are hanged. Mistress Quickly herself dies of venereal disease. The humiliation of Pistol by Fluellen (V.i) marks the extinction of Falstaff's band of irregulars. Pistol pronounces a valediction in his "Old I do wax, And from my weary limbs / Honour is cudgelled." This is one kind of darkening. Other contributions to the play's dark quality are the revelations of treachery within the English court and the self-doubt experienced by King Henry. Cambridge, Scroop, and Grey have been plotting to murder the King in return for French gold. Their unmasking, on the eve of the King's departure for France (II.ii), hints that gold was not the only motive force; Cambridge's plan to advance Edmund Mortimer to the throne is (indirectly) suggested (155–57). Nor does Henry forget the dubious legacy left to him by his father Henry IV. His soliloquy on the morning of Agincourt contains a coda (IV.i.295–311) lamenting the deposition and death of Richard II and acknowledging that

> . . . all that I can do is nothing worth,
> Since that my penitence comes after all,
> Imploring pardon.

Kingship is a burden; the circumstances in which Bolingbroke gained the crown cannot be willed away; but Henry must meet the demands of "the day."

A description of the play's spirit is incomplete without reference to Burgundy's oration in V.ii. In the last scene of this martial work Burgundy, fulfilling a choric role, speaks of the devastation of war and the blessings of peace. France, the best garden of the world, is choked by weeds; the coulter rusts; and nothing grows "but hateful docks, rough thistles, kecksies, burs, / Losing both beauty and utility." The speech is a noble drawing-together of Shakespearian concerns for the land, the garden, and the kingdom. The setting is all the more potent for being neither French nor English. Shakespeare's poetry of earth opens up a reality beyond the realm, the political entity, of France: here is the land itself.

The hero of the play has provoked immense critical disagreement. "The one commonplace man in the eight [history] plays" (John Masefield) is among the politer descriptions evolved by the anti-Henricians. But Henry's defenders have been eloquent. Perhaps the most ardent and persuasive is Charles Williams, whose classic essay on the play is included in Anne Ridler's *Shakespeare Criticism 1919–1935* (1936). Williams writes admirably on the legerity of spirit informing the St. Crispin's Day speech (IV.iii.18–67) and then continues, evoking the night-description that opens Act IV:

> The Muse, *entertaining conjecture* of a new and dreadful world, conjectured also a touch in the night, the thawing of fear, a royal captain of a ruined band, and conjectured the nature of the power of love and consequent lightness that thrills through the already poring dusk.

—Charles Calder

HENRY VI, parts 1–3.
Plays by William Shakespeare, 1591–92(?).

[*The First Part of the Contention betwixt the Two Famous Houses of Yorke and Lancaster* (1594) and *The True Tragedie of Richard Duke of Yorke* (1595) are defective reported versions of the plays subsequently published as *2* and *3 Henry VI* respectively.]

Though pockets of resistance remain, it is generally assumed that *Henry VI* is the unaided work of William Shakespeare and that the plays were written in natural sequence. The Arden edition of Andrew S. Cairncross (1957–64) directed attention to the "plays as plays" and showed that the energy hitherto expended on questions of authorship, collaboration, and revision could have been more profitably applied to examination of structure and rhetoric. The trilogy presents the life, reign, and death of Henry VI, who succeeded his father, Henry V, in 1422, and was killed in the Tower of London in May 1471 by order of Edward IV. *1–3 Henry VI* can now be seen as a large achievement in its own right and as a major component of Shakespeare's English history sequence.

The plan is ambitious, involving the conversion of a mass of chronicle material into a grand design. Shakespeare uses mainly *The Union of the Two Noble and Illustre Famelies of Lancastre & Yorke* (1548) by Edward Hall and Raphael Holinshed's *Chronicles* (1587 edition). (Holinshed is himself indebted to Hall for substantial portions of his narrative.) The chronicle material is compressed and reordered with great freedom but to strong purpose. The 177 lines of 1:I.i, for instance, telescope events which occurred between 1422 and 1450. Such boldness is justified, for the words and stage pictures convey the fragmentation and loss of purpose that afflict England after the death of Henry V. "Civil dissension is a viperous worm" warns the young Henry VI (1:III.i.72); it is dissension and private ambition which cause the loss of France and undo the work of Henry V. Part 2 shows the beginning of civil war in England; part 3 the triumph of the House of York and the murder of Henry VI. The trilogy ends with the delusive hope of Edward IV: "Sound drums and trumpets! Farewell, sour annoy! / For here, I hope, begins our lasting joy." All is prepared for the career of Richard III.

To cope with the shifting demands of his matter, Shakespeare deploys varying and responsive styles in accordance with the classical requirement of decorum. A high proportion of the text comprises politic and deceptive speech. Shakespeare shows great interest in the verbal methods of schemers and "machiavels." Cardinal Beaufort is a particularly gifted exponent of the language of dissimulation: supple, persuasive, polished. Richard of Gloucester also demonstrates early virtuosity (3:I.ii.18–31). While many characters use speech for concealment, King Henry uses it for revelation. His language has greater force, variety, and pithiness than has customarily been recognised. The affective and ethical properties of Henry's verse ensure that he stands out as a substantial and on occasion commanding exponent of Christian virtue, embodying the "pure integritie" ascribed by Hall to the historical King Henry. The banishing of Suffolk (2:III.ii) and the admonitions to the dying Beaufort in 2:III.iii show the King as no *roi fainéant* but an urgent spokesman for kingly and Christian qualities, "a keper of all goodnes."

Shakespeare the rhetorician is not in practice separable from Shakespeare the poet, for the very good reason that rhetoric is the art of persuasive speech. The orator in antiquity spoke to an audience in the lawcourt or the *Ekklesia* and used the most effective modes of appeal in order to persuade his hearers to vote or act in the way he desired. The dramatist uses his rhetorical skill to serve the varying requirements of his drama—lamentation, denunciation, vituperation, deception. The sustained monologues that are a feature of *Henry VI* exemplify Shakespeare's command of *artificiosa eloquentia* (eloquence based on the rules of art). There are the great moments when the Yorkist clan unloose their real thoughts in direct and impassioned address to the audience. York's solo in 2:I.i.215–60 reveals his burning desire for the crown and foreshadows the malevolent soliloquy of his son Richard in 3:III.ii. These speeches show us early Shakespearian style at its most vivid and energetic; for cold ferocity Queen Margaret's malediction in 3:I.iv.66–108 is unrivalled. In a different mode, there is the King's meditation on the field of Towton (3:II.v.1–54): a moving lament or *threnos* for the ordered life that has been broken by the civil war.

In *Henry VI* the action reaches to many corners of the realm and takes in many classes and occupations. The texture does not have the richness of *Henry IV*; there is not the same degree of circumstantiality or detail or counterpointing. But the trilogy does show us large events taking place—events which involve not only the magnates but also the people of England: citizens, clerks, conjurers, priests, prentices, pirates, beadles, butchers, and soldiers. The scenes depicting the rebellion of Jack Cade (2:IV) are marked by vigour and brutality; the swift violence of the gang is at work, "mindless" as far as Cade's followers are concerned, but ultimately inspired by York. And these events are set in time, being conditioned by competing ambitions and the pressure of past crimes and injustices. By part 3 the hatreds have descended to the next generation ("Thy father slew my father; therefore die"). So is fulfilled the prophecy of Warwick in 1:II.iv.:

> . . . this brawl to-day,
> Grown to this faction in the Temple Garden,
> Shall send between the Red Rose and the White
> A thousand souls to death and deadly night.

—Charles Calder

HENRY VIII.
Play by William Shakespeare and John Fletcher, 1613.

Published in the First Folio of 1623, *King Henry VIII* is considered to be the last play certainly written by Shakespeare, though some scholars still question this. They follow the Victorian critic James Spedding, who argued (from the poet Tennyson's impressions of the versification) that the play must be partly written by John Fletcher, Shakespeare's successor as playwright to the King's Men. Nevertheless, the play has a long history of spectacular performances including its first run, during which the wadding of a blank cannon-shot used in the staging set fire to the thatched roof of the first Globe Theatre, which burnt to the ground without loss of life as Sir Henry Wotton describes. After, if not before the burning of the Globe, the play would have been performed at the King's Men's indoor theatre at Blackfriars which occupied the same space where Queen Katherine's divorce trial was held. This would be quite appropriate because, unlike most Shakespearean plays, this one has consistently been performed with authentic historical costumes and settings based on Holbein's portraits of King Henry and his court, thus justifying Wotton's alternative title: *All is True*. In characterization and language the script closely follows Holinshed's chronicle recording the falls of the Duke of Buckingham, Cardinal Wolsey, and Katherine.

As often with Shakespeare's plays, *Henry VIII* was not the first to deal with its subject, which had been anticipated in part by Samuel Rowley's *When You See Me, You Know Me*. This uneven play scarcely approaches the sober intensity of Shakespeare's which has always impressed critics as it did Samuel Johnson, who found the treatment of Katherine's fall deeply moving. Johnson inspired the great actress Sarah Siddons to perform as Katherine in one of her best interpretations, admired because of its controlled realism. This matched the play's restrained and naturalistic style, which continues to reinforce the authenticity sought in the recent BBC television version, filmed at Tudor sites such as Leeds Castle and Penshurst. Despite notable touches of humour in minor court characters such as the Old Lady, the play largely avoids comedy. It follows the pattern of many of Shakespeare's earlier ones in showing the costly development of an effective political understanding in Henry VIII as he progresses from blunt hostility to the doomed Buckingham—while flirting adulterously with Anne Boleyn. The king's overdependence on Wolsey lasts until the rueful divorce from his loyal queen after a spectacular trial scene. Thereafter Henry achieves a more autonomous role by repudiating Wolsey's domination. After crowning Anne as his new queen with elaborate pageantry, he further demonstrates his own authority by frustrating a conspiracy to destroy Archbishop Cranmer. The diffident Cranmer matches Katherine, the play's female model of humility and rectitude. Cranmer survives with the king's protection to foretell (by Shakespeare's hindsight) the glories of the reign of the Princess Elizabeth, whose christening ends the play at a happy moment not wholly characteristic of Henry's later years.

The play's elaborate staging of this scene and the earlier coronation of Queen Anne has often been felt to make its performance an appropriate celebration for similar historical events, such as the coronations of George II and Elizabeth II. Indeed, the play may originally have been written to celebrate the marriage of the daughter of James I, another Princess Elizabeth, to the Elector Palatine in 1613. In performance *Henry VIII* has always been popular whatever critics may say, because of its spectacular effects. These are often favoured at the expense of the script, which is usually heavily cut, particularly the last act dealing with the conspiracy against Cranmer. Because of its pageantry, ritual, and settings, the play provided an important precedent for cinematic exploitation of spectacular history in 1911 when Beerbohm Tree filmed his elaborate stage production of the previous year. The play also provides a model for many other modern plays and films dealing with Henry VIII such as *Anne of a Thousand Days*, and *A Man for All Seasons*, not to mention Charles Laughton's virtuoso performance in *The Private Life of Henry VIII*.

Modern critical opinion has been mixed in its views, often finding the play to be a weak reversion to Shakespeare's earlier methods in chronicle plays such as *Henry VI* and *Richard III*, to which it provides a kind of sequel. The negative views result from an idea that its discontinuities reflect a divided authorship. For this there is no historical evidence, only conjectures of stylistic or internal inconsistencies resembling those in other plays once also therefore reassigned, but which are now held to be authentically Shakespearean. Recently there has been a steady shift to a more favorable interpretation of the play's unity and authorial integrity. Its structural and thematic unity lies in the recurrent rhythm including all the major characters from the aggressive Buckingham and the cynically manipulative Wolsey to the loyal and virtuous Katherine—who all progress from unjustified self-confidence in their roles to a truer understanding of their own limitations and their precarious state. Yet if they live in an uncertain world, the play shows it to be one governed ultimately by a providence which will secure the English Reformation through the triumph of Elizabeth I. This more positive mood matches that of the romances which Shakespeare also wrote in the last phase of his career, for which *Henry VIII* provides a kind of historical corollary or validation. The Tudor age is thus seen through a golden haze of nostalgia that softens the historical vision of the aging Shakespeare, whose final mood here is more serene and reconciled to human vicissitudes than it was in the earlier history plays. Perhaps in his last completed project Shakespeare wished to validate the mystical qualities of his late romances in more historical terms.

—Hugh M. Richmond

HENRY ESMOND.
(*The History of Henry Esmond, Esq.*)
Novel by William Makepeace Thackeray, 1852.

In *The History of Henry Esmond, Esq. A Colonel in the Service of Her Majesty Q. Anne: Written by Himself* William Makepeace Thackeray felt that he had "a better subject for a novel than any I've had yet." Unlike *Vanity Fair* or *Pendennis*, *Henry Esmond* focuses on Augustan England, a period that Thackeray had earlier (in their magazine publication) examined in the novels Catherine and Barry Lyndon. Having just completed a lecture series on English humorists of the 18th century, he felt well prepared to undertake a historical romance set in that time, though there were some who felt it unwise for him to turn his creative efforts to an earlier period. Most reviewers, however, felt that the novel was a success not only in style and story, but also in the many historical sources Thackeray utilized for the background of his narrative.

As John Sutherland has aptly pointed out, *Henry Esmond* "is a psychological drama crossed with a romantic plot in a historical setting." The narrator, looking back from old age in America, recounts the story of his maturation from the age of 12 to his early manhood and marriage. An orphan thought to be the illegitimate son of the late Thomas Esmond, Lord Castlewood, Esmond spends his early years at the Castlewood estate. During that period he becomes enchanted with Rachel, the wife of the new Lord Castlewood. Hers is an unhappy marriage that ends when Lord Castlewood is killed in a duel. In a dying confession he reveals that Esmond is the lawful Viscount of Castlewood. To save the estate for Rachel and her children, Esmond burns the confession and goes to prison for his part in the duel.

In a visit to Esmond in prison, Rachel accuses him of allowing her husband to be murdered. Bitter at this rejection from a woman he sought only to help, Esmond upon his release joins the army. After a successful military experience, he visits Rachel. At this point her love for Esmond surfaces, and she begs his forgiveness. During this visit to Castlewood, Esmond sees again Rachel's daughter Beatrix and falls in love with her, spending the ensuing years trying to win her affections. Her interests, however, lie in other directions. Following his involvement in a plot to place James Edward, an exiled Stuart, on the throne—a plot that fails—Esmond realizes that his real love is Rachel. Marrying her, he builds a new Castlewood in Virginia, where he lives contentedly and writes his memoirs. This last twist of the plot caused George Eliot to remark that *Henry Esmond* was "the most uncomfortable book you can imagine. . . . The hero is in love with the daughter all through the book and marries the mother at the end."

A basic theme of the novel is of course the seeking of a true identity on Esmond's part—a theme that is interwoven with English history of the time. From the isolation of illegitimacy Esmond moves to a position of legitimate nobility, at the same time becoming involved in his country's military and political conflicts. The work thus moves beyond being just a *Bildungsroman* to being a history as well. Esmond, as he writes his memoirs, hopes to bring a true sense of reality to history. "Why shall history go on kneeling to the end of time?" he asks. "I am for having her rise up off her knees, and take a natural posture." To make his own history more reliable, Thackeray appended some 400 notes to his novel. In a real sense, then, as Esmond seeks his true identity, he is also seeking a true history—one that is not distorted but accurate and one that addresses the cogent question of the relationship between interpretation and authority.

Some of Thackeray's contemporaries, Charlotte Brontë for example, felt that he had put too much history into the book. It is the love story between Esmond and Rachel, however, that provides the story with its basic mooring point. That story brings the characters to life, who in turn bring the book to life. Thackeray, according to George Brimley in the *Spectator* (6 November 1852), chose "for his hero a very noble type of the Cavalier softening into the man of the eighteenth century, and for his heroine one of the sweetest women that ever breathed from canvas or from book since Raffaelle painted Maries and Shakespere created a new and higher consciousness of woman in the mind of Germanic Europe."

One can make a strong argument that *Henry Esmond* represents the best of Thackeray's works, even though the novelist himself may have felt that he did not achieve his intentions. The irony here is perhaps best phrased by Charles Whibley when he praised the novel as "nearest to being the complete good book' which, he [Thackeray] said it was a shame the author didn't write."

—Wilton Eckley

HERO AND LEANDER.
Poem by Christopher Marlowe, 1598.

Hero and Leander was Christopher Marlowe's last poem and perhaps his last work. It is one of a number of English poems of a kind then fashionable, the classical erotic narrative, of which the first known example is Thomas Lodge's

Scilla's Metamorphosis (1589). Marlowe may have been led to write it by his earlier experience as a translator of Ovid's *Elegies* (also called *Amores*, since they all purport to express a lover's emotions and to relate his experiences); these undated poems probably belong to Marlowe's undergraduate days (1581–83). They anticipate *Hero and Leander* in using iambic pentameter rhymed couplets and also in making general observations, sometimes rather cynical ones, in an epigrammatic form.

The story of how Hero and Leander met and loved, and how Leander swam the Hellespont which separated their homes at Sestos and Abydos until at last he was drowned, was told in Greek by the poet Musaeus (5th century A.D.). Ovid himself had included two imaginary letters, one from each lover to the other, in his *Heroides*, a collection of such poetic letters. Marlowe's poem, though it anticipates the tragic outcome, narrates only the lovers' first meeting, Leander's first visit to Hero's tower and their exchange of vows, and his first swim across the Hellespont which ends with their night of love; whether Marlowe intended to finish the story is not known. It was licensed for publication a few months after his death (1593) but not published till 1598. In 1598 too another edition was published, in which Marlowe's fragment is divided into two books or "Sestiads" (derived from Sestos as Iliads is from Ilium) and followed by four further books completing the story. These additional books, and the verse summaries prefixed to all six books, are by George Chapman, whose contribution to the poem is in his own manner and not at all in Marlowe's. Another poet, Henry Petowe, published another completion of *Hero and Leander*, also in 1598.

Marlowe's *Hero and Leander* is an exuberant poem, full of high spirits and rich in invention. The mood is set by the opening description of the lovers, "Hero the fair, / Whom young Apollo courted for her hair, / And offered as a dower his burning throne," and Leander, whose locks, "Had they been cut, and unto Colchos borne, / Would have allured the venturous youth of Greece / To hazard more than for the golden fleece." When Hero, a priestess of Venus, goes to celebrate the feast of Adonis, the crowds that run to gaze upon her are compared to centaurs, "Wretched Ixion's shaggy-footed race," who, "Incensed with savage heat, gallop amain / From steep pine-bearing mountains to the plain" to see Diana's nymphs hunting. The temple where she officiates has a crystal pavement celebrating the loves of the gods ("There might you see the gods in sundry shapes / Committing heady riots, incest, rapes"), where words such as "bellowing" and "tumbling" convey boundless energy, and mention of crystal, sea-agate, and jasper creates an impression of richness that pervades the poem. When Leander swims the Hellespont his beauty attracts the courtship of Neptune, who at first mistakes him for Jove's minion Ganymede: Marlowe, who devotes more than 70 lines to this episode, exploits the erotic suggestion of the waves caressing Leander's body as he swims through them.

Mythology and imagery continually enrich the narrative. When Hero weeps after being struck by Cupid's arrow, Cupid turns her tears to pearls and winds them round his arm for a bracelet; he then goes to the Fates and solicits them to favour the lovers, but in vain, Marlowe explaining by a long mythological story of his own invention why the Fates are hostile to Mercury as well as to Cupid, and therefore why "to this day is every scholar poor," Mercury being the patron of wits.

Marlowe's ingenuity appears also in his witty handling of argument. Hero's vow of chastity, when the goddess she serves is Venus, allows Leander to point out the inconsistency of her moral position, amounting to sacrilege, as well as to argue against virginity in more general terms. Of course, his persuasion merely reinforces the effect of his beauty: "These arguments he used, and many more, / Wherewith she yielded, that was won before." From Ovid's *Elegies* and *Art of Love* Marlowe had learned the effectiveness of epigrammatic generalization, as in "Who ever loved, that loved not at first sight?" and "Seeming not won, yet won she was at length; / In such wars women use but half their strength."

Marlowe holds the balance remarkably steady between the rapturous and the ridiculous in this poem. His wit distances the reader from the lovers' passion; his sensuousness invites the reader not merely to observe but to participate in it.

—T.W. Craik

HINDLE WAKES.
Play by Stanley Houghton, 1912.

Hindle Wakes was first staged for two performances at London's Coronet Theatre, where it formed part of an ambitious repertory season by the Manchester Gaiety company. The year was 1912, and the "woman question" was the subject of heated debates inside and outside the theatre. Stanley Houghton's carefully crafted play was rightly seen as a challenging contribution to the debate, and its transfer from the Coronet in Notting Hill to the West End brought success through notoriety.

Fanny Hawthorn, a weaver at the mill owned by Nathaniel Jeffcote, spends the last two days of the holiday "wakes" week in Llandudno in the company of Jeffcote's son, Alan. When the truth comes out, her shocked parents conclude that Fanny must marry Alan. Leaving his rented house, Christopher Hawthorn goes with trepidation to the 14-bedroom pile of his boyhood friend, Nathaniel Jeffcote, where the rest of the play is set. Jeffcote, an indulgent but hard-headed father, accepts the logic that Alan must now marry Fanny. The reasoning is simple, though time has disrupted the language that expresses it. If Alan had gone to Llandudno with a "gay" woman (one who takes pay for pleasure) rather than a "straight" one, there would be no problem. Alan's tentative resistance is finally overcome in the play's only unconvincing scene, a dialogue with his fiancée, Beatrice Farrar, daughter of the owner of Hindle's second biggest mill (Jeffcote's is the biggest). The only dissentient voice is that of Mrs. Jeffcote, the only one, that is, until Fanny speaks her mind. She has no intention of marrying Alan because he's not good enough for her: "You're a man, and I was your little fancy. Well, I'm a woman, and *you* were *my* little fancy." If Fanny had suffered for her frank sexuality, critical objections would have been less vehement and the Vice-Chancellor of Oxford University would not have banned undergraduates from attending the play. But Fanny strides off to independence: "I'm a Lancashire lass, and so long as there's weaving sheds in Lancashire I shall earn enough brass to keep me going. I wouldn't live at home again after this, not anyhow!"

If *Hindle Wakes* were dependent on its content for its claims to attention, changing attitudes would have rendered it fatally innocuous. It is the fine tuning of its making, its accurate succession of confrontations that distinguish it. Concentration on Fanny's rejection of Alan has distracted attention from a much more remarkable interchange at the end of the play—the half-spoken female pact between Fanny and Alan's mother.

—Peter Thomson

THE HISTORY OF ENGLAND.
Prose by Thomas Babington Macaulay, 1848–61.

Thomas Babington Macaulay intended his *History of England* to supersede the fashionable novel on ladies' tables in Victorian England. He succeeded; and his aim suggests criteria by which the *History* must be judged.

As history it is a major achievement. Macaulay is usually decried for exaggerating the vices and virtues of his characters (notoriously the vices of Marlborough and James, the virtues of William), for practically fabricating evidence, for the uncritical use of sources, and for Whiggish partisanship. These accusations have some truth, but must be seen against the primitive state of English historical research during Macaulay's time. Without standing upon his achievements, his detractors would not have been able to see far enough to discern where the master fell short. Macaulay had the ability to organise an unprecedentedly vast range of source materials, mostly hitherto uncharted, into cogent (if arguable) patterns. None of the now-standard tools were available: Calendars of State Papers, the *Dictionary of National Biography*, the Public Records Office, comprehensive catalogues, and bibliographies of manuscript materials. By modern standards, he is not critical enough in his use of sources, but he was not naive, and pitted source critically against source; some of his distortions and errors may be attributed to the unorganized state of source collection and criticism rather than partisanship or malice.

Macaulay was the first English historian to portray the world beyond politics and war, beyond the upper, educated and politically active classes:

> It will be my endeavour to relate the history of the people as well as the history of the government, to trace the progress of useful and ornamental arts, to describe the rise of religious sects and the changes of literary taste, to portray the manners of successive generations, and not to pass by with neglect even the revolutions which have taken place in dress, furniture, repasts, and public amusements.

In this attempt, Macaulay became one of the first systematically to utilise non-political sources: broadsides, ballads, drama, poetry, folklore. In the range and organisation of sources, in charting some uncharted tracts (especially in the reign of William), and in broadening the scope of what counted as history and source, Macaulay achieved gains to which subsequent historians are all indebted. Finally, the scope of Macaulay's work is one which hardly any modern historian, with all his advantages, would contemplate, let alone execute with magnificence.

The historical achievement is important, but the *History* is also a work of literature: its triumph arises from Macaulay's attempt to reach a wide audience. Its literary qualities are not wholly separate from its historiographical qualities. It is a good story well told. Once begun, Macaulay is hard to put down. Each sentence leads carefully forward, each paragraph throws interest towards the next, and, as in a novel, each section or chapter concludes with a sense of more interest over the next page. Partly architectonic, this forward movement is also a result of style. Macaulay's sentences are clear and trenchant; structured around an endless variety of techniques, they please the intellect seeking information, the interest following a narrative and the aesthetic sense. Macaulay's style is not so magisterial and weighty as Gibbon's, and we miss his diverting cynicism, but it is more flexible, delicate, and various: it never palls. He has a strong sense for the dramatic. This can be seen in episodes such as the death of Charles II, or more subtly in the Massacre of Glencoe, or more powerfully in the conflicts between Parliament and King slowly brewing during the reigns of Charles II and James II, running over in the 1688 revolution, and maturing in the grand style in which Macaulay describes the celebrated conflict between James and William. Macaulay carefully structures the opening acts of an even larger-scale conflict, that between France and Europe, which culminated in Blenheim; but the work is unfinished. Literary attention to these conflicts probably led to some of the distortions of which Macaulay stands accused; but it also created the undying interest of the book as literature.

The personal, political, and military drama is varied by the inclusion of vignettes of character, manners, domestic and common life illuminating the main theme. In constant attendance, too, are descriptions of places and buildings: Macaulay travelled widely to see for himself, and his descriptions have the liveliness of those written with the eye on the object. They are not mere decoration, and Macaulay's use of topographical evidence is another pioneering feature of his history. Monmouth's rebellion is made not only more dramatic, but more comprehensible by the topographical descriptions.

The History of England speaks for Victorian England. It is humane, it moralises, and arrogantly assumes 19th-century Britain to be the pinnacle of civilisation. Because Parliament stubbornly defended its ancient liberties against the encroachments of the monarchy, England in the 17th-century still possessed a mediaeval-style limited monarchy. Thus, unlike the unfortunate countries of Europe who had allowed absolute monarchy to prevail, the 1688 revolution was peaceful and, to Macaulay, legal, when it came: "It is because we had a preserving revolution in the seventeenth century that we have not had a destroying revolution in the nineteenth." Macaulay values the revolution so highly that he avows it to be the last one: for, "the means of effecting every improvement which the constitution requires may be found within the constitution itself." Such (partisan) beliefs suggest boundless confidence in Britain's imperial mission. Some of these presuppositions and conclusions bother modern historians. But Macaulay wrote in an ancient tradition which held that history should instruct, both by precept and through interpretation; and if we distilled out the moral objective, we should lose much of the literary power.

—J.B. Lethbridge

THE HISTORY OF THE WORLD.
Prose by Sir Walter Ralegh, 1614.

The History of the World is a statement of the consonance of divine and natural law, and of the ultimate justice of all that transpires in human history. Accused of religious skepticism, Sir Walter Ralegh uses the tools of social and political analysis of the realist historiographical tradition of Machiavelli and Guicciardini and applies critical analysis to ancient beliefs and documents. Yet his ultimate purpose, like that of medieval historians, is to teach piety through historical example. This combination of *de casibus* portrayals and realist analysis persists in history-writing well into the 17th century in England, but Ralegh's successors—Bacon, Heylin, and Clarendon, for example—narrow the focus of their narratives—to a single reign, the reformation, a revolution—and while these historians assert the moral and religious lessons of history, they are primarily interested in the "secrets" of second causes in human affairs. In his preface to the *History of the World* Ralegh concedes that although, as a man of affairs, he might have been expected to write the "story of my own times, having been permitted to draw water as near the well-head as another," he intends to trace history from creation to the "unjointed and scattered frame of our English affairs." However, he completed only part of his narrative, ending in the 2nd century B.C. Realistic histories of such a scope were not successfully undertaken until Hume and Gibbon, neither of whom felt obligated to outline God's plan in the sweep of history.

Ralegh's purpose is explicit: to demonstrate to the present age that actions carried out for worldly ends have been relentlessly punished, and that Providence has doomed the edifices of human greed and ambition. Book One describes Creation, the Flood, and the subsequent proliferation of nations, and Book Two narrates the flight from Egypt, surveys the parallel histories of the kings of Israel, the Syrians, Troy, and Italy, and ends with the destruction of Jerusalem. With the Hebrew scriptures as primary source, the fulfillment of God's prophecy is immediately evident in these early books, although even there Ralegh explores the mechanism of Providence in human affairs. For example, Moses was placed in a position to save his people by the Pharaoh's fear of the Hebrews, "the next natural cause of the sorrows and loss which befell him and the Egyptian nation." Books Three and Four trace history through the ascendency of the Persians, the Peloponnesian War, and the actions of Alexander the Great, and Book Five the Roman victories over the Carthaginians and the Persians: throughout this narrative, civil and military leaders fail in the long run because they pursue their own ends, their appetites or interests. The dissension which followed the death of Alexander was a result of his cruelty, for example. Near the end of the history, Ralegh reinforces the didactic value of these portraits, asserting that the fate of empires depends upon the personal frailties of leaders: "But unto all dominions God hath set their periods; who, though he hath given unto man the knowledge of those ways by which kingdoms rise and fall; yet hath left him subject unto the affections, which draw on these fatal changes in their times appointed."

In addition to the sins of the flesh, most of these rulers have violated their responsibilities as governors. Ralegh traces the evolution of government, asserting that magistracy has a basis in nature, but also that "God himself kindled this light [of kingship] in the minds of men." Ralegh recognizes models of rule by one, few, and many, although it is clear that he perceives the greatest dangers in popular rule. Whatever the model, magistrates are the ministers of God, and history is replete with examples of those who were punished by God for resisting authority. The critical distinction between monarchy and tyranny is law—a monarch rules through the use of just laws and conscience (a recognition of divine law); tyranny (whether tryanny by an individual or tyranny by a city or nation) respects "only the pleasure of the commander." Asserting that the desire to rule is either the most noble or the most evil human predilection, Ralegh accepts Aristotle's definition of heroic virtue as a preference for "the weal public above all respects," but he goes on to say that the Christian king also adheres to divine law, is "religious and zealous in God's cause." The generals and tyrants responsible for the rise and fall of empires in this history offer an imitation of magistracy, like Alexander's generals-turned-kings, whom Ralegh describes as "these old tragedians . . . who begin to play their parts, with bigger looks and more boisterous actions, not with greater grace and judgment."

Old Testament narrative, particularly the Mosaic, is the keystone to Ralegh's history; his fundamental assumption is that these narratives are accurate, and he demonstrates that Egyptian history, the stories of Homer, and classical history and myth are chronologically consistent with them. However, the Scriptures aside, all other historical evidence and historical scholarship are subject to rational analysis. Especially in books One and Two, where the historical material is most remote, he critically evaluates the scholarship of biblical commentators, church fathers, and historians. He uses geography and etymology to locate Eden; he debunks the Egyptians' claim to 13,000 years of history; and after due consideration, he breaks rank with the majority of scholars in establishing the date of Moses' birth. He applies a similar rational scrutiny to mythical marvels—the golden fleece was wool that had been washed in a stream containing gold dust—although, in an interesting reversal, he shows that there is no natural explanation for the parting of the Red Sea. In this work Ralegh shows mastery of a vast body of scholarship, and draws, in numerous engaging passages, on knowledge gained in his travels, as in his affirmation of the existence of the Amazons.

There emerges from these analyses a recognition of the laws governing the realm of second causes. When addressing the claim that the Phoenicians invented writing, Ralegh counters that "letters were invented by those excellent spirits of the first age, and before the general flood," but observes that people all over the world have separately invented writing because "natural laws are common and general." Providence notwithstanding, the Machiavellian explanation of the vulnerability of the Persians to conquest—they did not have an independent nobility—is consistent with this theme in *The History of the World*. Near the end of the work, Ralegh observes "the great similitude found in worldly events," which he attributes to the fact that there is no great variety in those things "by which the wills of sundry men are overruled in managing the affairs of our daily life." In this, and in the numerous instances where he points out the trivial and personal causes of historical events, he approaches a natural, even psychological explanation of history. However, in the completed portion of this history, his focus on ancient civilizations and fallen empires enables him to hold natural causes and the hand of Providence in equilibrium. Human nature is the arena of Providence; in the long run, God punishes tyrants by allowing them to have their will.

—Sara B. Varhus

HOBSON'S CHOICE.
Play by Harold Brighouse, 1915.

Hobson's Choice is the best remembered of the plays of Harold Brighouse, one of the leading members of the

Manchester school of dramatists based at Annie Horniman's Gaiety Theatre in the early years of the 20th century. First produced in the U.S. and then in London in 1916, it remains a standard part of the current repertoire for professional and amateur actors. There was a notable production by John Dexter at the National Theatre in the mid-1960's, with Michael Redgrave, Joan Plowright, and Frank Finlay. A film version directed by David Lean in 1953, starring Charles Laughton and John Mills, caught the period feel adequately but was marred by the scriptwriters' insistence on "improving" much of Brighouse's more than adequate dialogue.

A piece which has survived so vigorously must obviously have much to say to succeeding generations, in terms both of dramatic values and of ideas. The period of the play is set back to the 1880's, the height of Victorian values. The setting is a boot and shoe shop in suburban Salford. Henry Horatio Hobson, the proprietor, regards himself as a paragon of Victorian imperial virtues: "I'm British middle-class," he asserts pompously, "and proud of it." He is not, though, above treating sycophantically such members of the gentry as occasionally patronise his shop. However, since the death of his wife and the rise of his shop's prosperity to the point where he feels safe in neglecting it and spending more and more of his time with his cronies in the Moonrakers Inn, the business is not quite as flourishing as formerly. It is only the industry and managerial skills of his 30-year-old daughter Maggie which enable trade to proceed on an even keel, together with the quality of the goods produced in the basement workshop. Foremost in skill among the boot-hands is the unassuming and semi-literate William Mossop, unambitious and contented in his exploitation. Maggie, though, less content to remain exploited, bullies and manoeuvres Mossop into marriage and the setting up of a rival establishment, gaining the support of her two younger sisters by arranging a situation in which Hobson is tricked into providing them with the financial wherewithal to marry the young men they have been surreptitiously meeting.

The inevitable result is the overtaking, and eventual taking over, of Hobson's business by the Mossops: the punning Hobson's choice of the play's title. In a final twist, Mossop, who has developed under Maggie's tutelage into a respected and successful businessman ("You'd be surprised the number of people that call me Mister Mossop now"), but has remained under her thumb, confronts and defeats her over the question of the name for the new shop, a sort of benign Frankenstein's monster whose creator welcomes his defection: "You're the man I've made you, and I'm proud," she says.

Particularly successful is the way that Brighouse retains sympathy and respect for the managing and overbearing Maggie ("I don't see why you should always get your way," one of her long-suffering sisters exclaims. "It's just a habit," she replies blandly). The declining Hobson and rising Mossop too are treated with subtle empathy and never guyed. The social milieu is both of its period and recognisable in its universality. There is an atmosphere of extreme Victorian gentility and respectability, a society in which Hobson, manoeuvred by Maggie into an out-of-court settlement for supposed trespass, sourly observes, "Good-class customers are not going to buy their boots from a man who's stood up in open court and had to acknowledge he was overcome [euphemism, of course, for drunk] at twelve o'clock in the morning." But family life, one feels, has not changed all that much. The dispute between Hobson and his two younger daughters on the morality of the then fashionable bustle must be repeated, *mutatis mutandis*, in every family in the land wherever there are teenage children and whenever the fashion changes.

—Michael Grosvenor Myer

HOLY WILLIE'S PRAYER.
Poem by Robert Burns, 1799 (written 1785).

This superb satire, too dangerous for Robert Burns to publish during his lifetime, was written early in 1785 soon after the church court judgment that gave rise to it. Its subject was a real person, William Fisher, an elder in Burns's parish of Mauchline, Ayrshire. He was a middle-aged bachelor given to drink and fornication on the sly. Despite these failings, however, Willie was wholly convinced that he was one of God's elect, and was the most pious, unctuous hypocrite among the evangelical or "Auld Licht" Calvinists in Mauchline. He was also active in the committee of the kirk session charged with sniffing out "backsliders" (most often sexual offenders) among the congregation. In this role as informer in matters of private morality Willie was both feared and despised; his own position was, of course, nearly impregnable—he never reported himself to the session. Late in 1784, however, he charged Gavin Hamilton, Burns's friend and landlord, with some rather trivial offenses for which the session issued a formal reprimand. Hamilton appealed the case to the Presbytery of Ayr, and in a public hearing held in January 1785, he was triumphantly acquitted. Burns imagines his accuser Holy Willie, who was made to look very foolish in the trial, going home after this defeat and praying to his Calvinist God of vengeance.

The prayer is an incredibly skillful burlesque, not only of the repulsive personality of Holy Willie, but of the whole system of belief for which he stands. It opens on a note of slow, pious deliberation, as Willie characterizes his God to one who

> Sends ane to heaven and ten to hell,
>   A' for thy glory!
> And no for ony gude or ill
>   They've done before thee.

In these quiet lines, almost before the reader is aware, Burns pulls the rug out from under the whole doctrine of election by placing it in the most absurd and appalling light possible. Especially effective is the subtle irony of "A' for thy glory." In the next stanzas Burns has Willie smugly congratulate himself for being one of God's chosen people, "A burning and a shining light / To a' this place." The sheer presumption of this is overwhelming—horrible, and yet, at the same time, grotesquely comic—to say nothing of the further irony of Willie's setting himself up as a shining "example" in the light of the squalid confessions that follow.

The confession passage (stanzas 6–9) deepens the picture of Willie's depravity, not only because he reveals himself as sinner ("fash'd wi' fleshly lust") and hypocrite, but more especially because of the way his twisted mind uses church doctrine to extenuate and even excuse his own weakness. The whining intonation comes through clearly as Willie abases himself in a humility that can only be seen as spurious after the sublime egoism of the preceding passage. He reminds the

Lord that we are all "defil'd wi' sin," that is, we are all infected by the original sin of Adam and therefore cannot help our wickedness. He makes clear that in his illicit affair with "Meg" he is not disturbed by any moral question; he worries only about his godly reputation. With "Leezie's lass" it wasn't his fault anyway because he was drunk at the time. The confession comes to a climax as Willie, still speaking in sniveling, whining style, attempts to give himself total justification:

Maybe Thou lets this fleshly thorn
Buffet Thy servant e'en and morn,
Lest he owre proud and high shou'd turn,
  That he's sae gifted:
If sae, thy han' maun e'en be borne,
  Until Thou lift it.

In other words, the whole thing is God's fault for having given him this cross of lust to bear, a cross that he, Holy Willie, will patiently carry until the Lord chooses to relieve him. The irony of the cant phrase "thy servant" here (and elsewhere) is withering.

Now that his confession is over and he has put himself right with God, Willie comes to the real point of his prayer as he turns viciously on his enemies and, kneeling before his God, spits out his bitter hatred of those who have made him look like a fool, and screams for revenge. Burns manages this sudden shift in style with breathtaking skill, as the abject meanness of Willie's soul comes out in a series of spiteful denunciations—of Gavin Hamilton, of the Presbytery of Ayr who acquitted him, and of Robert Aiken, the lawyer who defended him. Willie's hysterical raving culminates in stanza 15 when he asks for God's severest vengeance—"But for thy people's sake destroy them, / And dinna spare!" Having exhausted himself with this outpouring of rage and frustration, Willie closes his prayer with an oily supplication for blessings on his precious self. Here, once again, Burns effects the abrupt change in style from screaming anger to simpering, holier-than-thou complacency with matchless artistry; the final stanza fairly oozes with Willie's driveling piety:

But Lord, remember me and mine,
Wi' mercies temporal and divine!
That I for grace and gear may shine,
  Excell'd by nane!
And a' the glory shall be thine!
  Amen! Amen!

At least three sources of the extraordinary power of "Holy Willie's Prayer" may be discerned. For one thing, there is the utter convincingness of style, of the marvelously shifting styles in which Willie is made to speak. He was the kind of man whose ordinary talk was salted with biblical echoes and quotations and framed in the distinctive rhetorical pattern of evangelical preaching. Burns has caught this "ministerial" tone perfectly, so that we feel we are getting the living rhythms of Willie's speech—all slightly exaggerated, of course. At the same time, the pious style is turned against itself and becomes a mockery in the light of what Willie is actually saying. And this is done with such unerring skill that the reader finds it completely natural—Willie could not possibly have said it in any other way.

Second, the poem extends its meaning far beyond its immediate subject and becomes a universal satire on hypocrisy and fanaticism in every form. It is not just a personal exposé of a local reprobate, but a withering attack upon the system of belief that made Willie what he was. Burns's point is that the concepts of original sin and election as interpreted by the Auld Licht Calvinists made abominations like Holy Willie inevitable. In that sense, Willie may be seen as a victim of his own narrow, fanatical beliefs; and in an even wider sense he becomes a symbol of unwholesome bigotry everywhere and in all ages. Burns is not attacking religion here; he is attacking rigid thinking, what seems to him to be a false and irrational and unchristian kind of religion. By implication he is seeking a benevolent, rational, loving God in place of the monstrous deity of Willie's imagination. Seen in this perspective, the poem is a religious and philosophical document of universal interest and smashing power.

Finally, "Holy Willie's Prayer" is uproariously funny. Though the poem gives us a terrifying insight into the sewer of Willie's mind, at the same time Burns shapes his material to bring out the sheer ludicrousness, the absurdity of the elder's ideas of himself, of God, and of his fellow humans. The result is laughter—a mocking, cleansing laughter that convulsed Burns's Ayrshire and still echoes round the world.

—Allan H. MacLaine

THE HOMECOMING.
Play by Harold Pinter, 1965.

The Homecoming, written in 1964, is one of Harold Pinter's most enigmatic plays. Since the action on the surface seems so bizarre, the play has provoked various types of symbolic or allegorical readings, few of which are convincing. The characters and situations of the play are so powerful that attempts to translate them into symbols or archetypes lack credibility. But straightforward realistic readings seem equally inadequate. Can the play be understood or is it a work that departs so radically from probability that it can be regarded only as a work deliberately constructed to frustrate comprehension in the manner of certain postmodernist texts?

Though the latter possibility should not be dismissed, it should perhaps be adopted only as a last resort. The play is, I think, open to interpretation if one focuses on three interacting elements of it: language, psychology, stylisation. Pinter's radical innovation in his drama was to create a dramatic language that did not seek to exclude the banalities, repetitions, falterings, fractured sentences which are common enough in ordinary speech but which previous dramatists had avoided. Another innovation of his plays is that they show that even the most trivial linguistic exchanges are part of a struggle for dominance between the speakers and that language is as often used to conceal a person's motives and aims as to reveal them. Such plays as *The Caretaker* and *The Homecoming* are also not realistic in any simple sense. There is a strong comic element, largely the result of a subtle form of stylisation created through the use of inappropriate linguistic registers. Language, psychology, and stylisation interact perhaps more powerfully in *The Homecoming* than in any other Pinter play.

The play is made up of almost perpetual power struggles among the characters. Max, the father of the household, immediately challenges his son Lenny with the first words of the play: "What have you done with the scissors?" and each scene that follows consists of confrontation and struggle for dominance. Max is at the center of most of these confrontations. Though traditionally the father is head of the family,

Max is not regarded with respect by Lenny. It becomes clear that Max's late wife Jessie was the dominant figure in the family but with her death there is no agreed hierarchy. Lenny is contemptuous of both his father and his uncle Sam but Max continues to assert his right to dominant status. Max is, however, a contradictory character: though he identifies with the aggressive masculinity of his late friend MacGregor he plays a traditional female role in the household and resents the fact that Sam invades his kitchen.

It is into such a household that Max's eldest son Teddy, a professor of philosophy in America, comes with his wife Ruth. Though she does not express outward dissent it is clear that she resents Teddy bringing her here. Teddy is forced to go to bed without her but when she encounters Lenny she easily dominates him by an assertion of sexuality, the first time he has been dominated in the play. The most puzzling aspect of the plot is why Ruth decides to leave Teddy and agrees to act as a prostitute for the family, especially in the light of how Max treats her when she and Teddy come down for breakfast.

The family seems to be exploiting Ruth in the crudest way possible but the denouement of the play suggests that she is going to exploit and dominate them, re-enacting Jessie's role. Teddy has brought her to his parents' home to show the father he had previously deserted that now he is also a family man with three sons, thus healing the breach between them. But things go badly wrong. Instead he gives Ruth an opportunity to reject a way of life in America which does not seem to suit her. Whereas a sophisticated man like Teddy can dominate her, she is clearly more comfortable with outwardly aggressive men like Lenny and his boxer brother Joey, over whom she can easily exert power. When Teddy realises that Ruth is seeking to break free from his control he tries to leave with her immediately but an alliance between Ruth and Lenny frustrates this, and Max, resentful that Teddy has again been planning to reject his family, punishes Teddy by allowing Ruth to stay with them and agrees with Lenny's proposal to set her up as a prostitute.

When Teddy recognises that he is powerless to do anything about this, he refuses to give the family the satisfaction of seeing him defeated by outwardly appearing to be unconcerned. But the family's triumph over Teddy is hollow when they realise that they have taken in a woman who can dominate all of them. This is clear from the way in which she negotiates the terms on which she will act as a prostitute. Her legalistic discourse, which shows her mastery of the situation, and its dislocating register exemplify how the play brings together the struggle for power and a stylised control of language that is comic in its effect: "I would naturally want to draw up an inventory of everything I would need, which would require your signatures in the presence of witnesses." The family crumbles before her. Sam, who has desperately opposed Ruth becoming part of the family, collapses, perhaps because he is afraid that his lack of conventional male sexuality will be exposed by this woman. Joey is in thrall to her, and Lenny stands silent at the periphery of the scene. Max is afraid of what will happen: "She'll use us, make use of us, I can tell you! I can smell it." The play ends with Ruth triumphant, having liberated herself from a husband who had provided her with an uncongenial life style and found a way of life more suitable for a woman who enjoys dominating men by the force of her sexuality.

—K.M. Newton

THE HONEST WHORE.

Play by Thomas Dekker and Thomas Middleton, 1604 (part 2, by Dekker only, 1605?).

The Honest Whore part 1 was first performed by Prince Henry's Men in 1604, and first printed in the same year; part 2 was probably acted in 1605, but not printed until 1630. Although Thomas Dekker's name alone is on the title-page of part 1, Henslowe's *Diary* for 1604 notes payments for the play to Dekker and Thomas Middleton. Critics are divided as to the extent, if any, of Middleton's collaboration.

The setting is Milan, and conventional assumptions about Renaissance Italy govern much of the play: an all-powerful Duke oversees the action; the star-crossed lovers are aided by Friar Anselmo; there is a doctor principally skilled in poisoning; the major characters have tailor-made Italian names—Infelice, Bellafront, Candido. But the ambiance is recognisably mercantile London, with its shops, its apprentices (always rallying at the cry, "Clubs!"), and its riotous, gambling-mad young gentlemen. Part 1 ends with the English and the Italian milieux neatly fused—at Bethlehem Monastery, which combines Bethlehem House (the "Bedlam" Asylum) and the Italian friar's retreat. However, part 2 ends with an extended scene at the Bridewell Prison (described on the title-page as the "Comicall Passages of an Italian Bridewell") which, in its numerous details of administration, inmates and punishments, is quite specific to the facts of Dekker's London.

Hippolito loves the Duke's daughter, Infelice; to frustrate their love the Duke pretends that his daughter is dead. Friar Anselmo, a competent version of Friar Lawrence in *Romeo and Juliet*, brings the lovers together and mollifies the Duke. In a second plot, Candido is a merchant renowned for his patient and mild behaviour. His wife and the roaring boys of the town concoct some farcical schemes to make him lose his temper; they regularly fail. In a third plot, the courtisan Bellafront, intensely moved by Hippolito's disapproval of her life, amends, and tricks Matheo, her first lover, into marriage, thus becoming the "Honest Whore." In part 2, supposed to take place shortly after the events of part 1, Hippolito, now the Duke's son-in-law, has become a powerful courtier, while Matheo's recklessness and gambling have impoverished him and Bellafront. She petitions Hippolito for help, but he attempts to seduce her, reversing the arguments by which he had persuaded her to honesty in part 1. Meanwhile, Bellafront's father, disguised as a servant, protects her and finally convinces Matheo to reform. The merchant Candido has married again, and by an uncharacteristic show of wrath (heartily approved of by his friends and, presumably, the audience) he exacts submission and dutiful humility from his new wife.

The various plots, which intersect through some bridge characters and come together in the locations of Bethlehem Monastery and Bridewell in the two parts, are simple enough. The effectiveness of the play comes from Dekker's mingling of formal poetry and the crude speech of low-life realism, to create, respectively, the worlds of the Renaissance court and the London citizenry. Hippolito's ethical debate with Bellafront in part 1 follows a passage of her lively slangy chatter with some of her followers, joking with bawdy wit about the gallows and "cony-catching." Moments before, the audience has seen her at toilet, planning her modish appearance in collaboration with her genially corrupt servant Roger. Hippolito's solemn comments, delivered in formal verse, exactly focus on those topics which have been introduced in a more light-hearted, colloquial way—the reliance of a courtesan on the physical arts of make-up; the consequent void in her life after her beauty has gone; the way that a courtesan exists only for the social pleasure of other people, and consequently has no real personal identity. Hippolito's vision of a courtesan's nightmare—alone, faded, and subject to the violence of the law—is a sombre reflection of exactly those careless, lively moments we have earlier witnessed.

Similarly, though less darkly, the tomfoolery aimed at Candido's amiability is set into a large moral context when he explains himself before the Duke. He identified patience with godliness: "Why, 'tis the soul of peace: / Of all the virtues, 'tis nearest to Heaven." Christ, being the model of patience, was "the first true gentleman that ever breathed."

The ending of part 2 has some savagely comic passages in which the constable, the Masters of Bridewell, and the beadles haul some wretched "Harlots"—Dorothea Target, Penelope Whorehound, and Catharina Bountinall—to the punishments of whips, cartings, and hemp-beating. But the whole is presented before the Duke as a moral show or "fair." The prison's accoutrements are "emblems," designed to accomplish the Duke's high purpose "To purge our city, Milan" and, by example, to assure "that Hippolito . . . If he love truly, shall [Bellafront's] bed forbear."

Dekker's concern to identify significant moral issues in comic or knockabout moments is seen in his remarkable portrait of Bellafront's father, Orlando Friscobaldo—referred to in passing in part 1 but a major figure in part 2. Hazlitt describes the character in a famous phrase as able to "raise, revive, and give a new zest to our being." To a degree he is a conventional *pantalone*, hot-tempered, eccentric, ridiculously determined to stay young ("age hath not command of your blood, for all Time's sickle has gone over you, you are Orlando still"); but he is also shown as warm-hearted, sensible, and sensitive. To Hippolito's question—"Is your wife then departed?"—he touchingly responds, "She's an old dweller in those high countries, yet not from me. Here, she's here." His gruff sympathy for his daughter attracts Hippolito's comment, "I'm glad you're wax, not marble; you are made of man's best temper."

In his mixture of the farcical and the humane, Friscobaldo epitomizes Hazlitt's judgment of *The Honest Whore*: "simplicity and extravagance of style, homeliness and quaintness, tragedy and comedy, interchangeably set their hands and seals to this admirable production."

—Richard Morton

AN HORATIAN ODE UPON CROMWELL'S RETURN FROM IRELAND.
Poem by Andrew Marvell, 1681 (written 1650).

Andrew Marvell's "Horatian Ode" is arguably the most subtle political poem of the Interregnum. It is not only "Horatian" in that it is a neo-Roman public poem, but also in its imitation of the oblique method of argument used by Horace in his *Odes*: Marvell is using a clear classical precedent to create a poem which places much of the onus upon the reader, leaving the poet almost detached from his work, free to poise deliberately open readings.

Despite these ambiguities, the poem was still obviously considered sufficiently politically disturbing for it to be cancelled from all but two copies of the folio edition of Marvell's *Miscellaneous Poems* in 1681.

The immediate occasion of the poem is the return of Oliver Cromwell from his ferocious military campaign in Ireland in May 1650, and the anticipation of his subsequent campaign against the Scots. Marvell reviews the events which led to Cromwell's emergence as the dominant force in the parliamentary party: his military victories in the Civil War, the execution of Charles I in 1649, his increasing primacy in the uneasy Republic.

A first reading of the poem might suggest that it is a straightforward panegyric, albeit one which at least gives the executed king credit for dying bravely. The most obvious precedent for this would lie in Horace's "Regulus" Ode (III.v.) with its celebration of a Republican hero. Closer examination shows affinities with Ode IV. iv. which, while it celebrates military victories, begins, like Marvell's poem, with a reluctant young man being drawn from retired study to military action.

Marvell's praise of Charles I, as well as his reservations and ambiguities, have led some critics to conclude that the poem is "crypto-royalist," a covert attack on Cromwell. Others persist in seeing the poem as unambiguously parliamentarian. As far as can be discovered, at the time when the poem was written Marvell was still a constitutional monarchist, although he was coming to feel that only a strong leader could save Britain from chaos. In this poem, as throughout his works, Marvell remains intellectually independent: he poises ambiguities of imagery and frequently of syntax to make an inclusive statement about the nature of recent events. The poem is enriched by the variety of possible readings, as well as by its inclusion of detached meditations on the nature of power and governance, the perspectives of a historian applied to contemporary events.

The concluding stanzas may be taken as an index of the way in which this works: it is possible to read them as a confident anticipation of further military victories in Scotland and elsewhere. It is also possible to discern strange dislocations: the deer hunt goes wrong; the raised sword, like the sword of Aeneas, is warding off the gathering spirits of those whom Cromwell has killed; the concluding couplet could be triumphal, but it could also be a grim statement that there is no escape from the consequences of action.

—Peter Davidson

THE HORSE'S MOUTH.
Novel by Joyce Cary, 1944.

The Horse's Mouth is the last and, arguably, most entertaining volume of Joyce Cary's first trilogy. For anyone who has worked through Sarah Monday's tale as told by her in *Herself Surprised* and her employer, Mr. Hickson's, tale in *To Be a Pilgrim*, Gulley Jimson's Blakean picaresque narrative will come as the ultimate revelation. This impishly pathetic portrait of the artist as a dirty old man colors retrospectively the self-portrait of a frivolous and whimsically warm earth mother and that of the generous, vulnerable, and rich old man. If, however, as most readers do, we come upon Gulley in the flesh and without warning on the opening pages of his book, we must remain in the dark concerning the true nature of the other two, whose cases can be made only partially and between the lines of Gulley's wonderfully self-serving account of his waning years.

With some justice, Cary called this book a tragedy. Indeed, Jimson, who devotes all his energies and wit to the ends of painting, could be seen as a martyr to his art (and a hyperbolic version of the writer himself). A lovable rogue, he is the true goal-oriented man, but his goals coincide with no social norms and his methods are positively anti-social. By giving him his voice and his head, Cary lets us follow his actions, his motivations, and above all his wit at something approaching the speed of sound. The other protagonists may be unconsciously funny, Gulley is by turns consciously and unconsciously so, by turns the victim and the victimizer, the philosopher and the clown.

We are introduced to Gulley as he is released from prison, after he has served a term for harassing his benefactor, Mr. Hickson. Nothing daunted, he will try, and partially succeed in getting back at Hickson throughout this novel. But that is only one of half a dozen comic plot lines enlivened by Gulley's comic musings and one-sided descriptions of his actions. In the service of his art, Gulley is selfless, heartless, ruthless, and above all manipulative. But he is also a true descendant of William Blake, whose verses he repeatedly cites. Like Blake, this half-mad but thoroughly inspired painter (a muralist rather than a miniaturist) is a poet, but a poet given to describing landscapes in terms of a painter's colors, decking out his tawdry environment in absurd metaphorical finery: "Sun in mist. Like an orange in a fried fish shop. All bright below. Low tide, dusty water and a crooked bar of straw, chickenboxes, dirt and oil from mud to mud." Such is the opening passage which, after running through some lines from Blake, meanders into an oblique description of Gulley's unpromising situation before discovering that "the sun had crackled into flames at the top; the mist was getting thin in places, you could see crooked lines of grey, like old cracks under spring ice. Tide on the turn. . . . Emeralds and sapphires. Water like varnish with bits of gold leaf floating thick and heavy." The monologue continues rich and heavy with keenly perceived details, poetry constantly colliding with and greeting cold truth and wry wit.

If his goal is to beg, borrow, or steal enough money to buy paints and cover an enormous canvas or a wall, his days are filled leavened by contacts with a curious array of misfits and illuminés. There is the tough but soft-hearted lady barkeeper, Coker, "five foot high and three foot broad," a reluctant supporter whom he repeatedly cons. There is the Spinozan shoemaker, Plant; the ill-favored schoolboy admirer, Nosy, imbued with the teachings of Marx and Ruskin and thirsty for more; there is Gulley's aging bumptious ex-mate and model Sarah ("I've known some liars and crooks, but Sarah was the queen. Why, she couldn't ask you to have some more cream without putting the comether in her voice and shooting off her eyes and jerking up her front"); there is even Mr. Moseley ("A smart young man of fifty with a face like a raspberry, and suits and shoes so beautiful they make you look again. . . . Mr. Moseley is a prophet. He sells racing tips and takes bets"); and there is the effete art "cricket" Mr. Alabaster, etc. The result is a gallery as fetching and grotesque as anything Gulley or Hogarth might paint.

Gulley's adventures follow in swift succession: a catastrophic and larcenous visit to his benefactor's home; a philosophical evening of the Workers' Education Association at Plant's where he bumps erotically into Sarah; a visit to Sarah's house in quest of a cache of his paintings; the painting of the fall of Adam and Eve on the sly in a leaking studio; the desecration of Lord and Lady Beeders' apartment where Gulley devotes a wall to a huge painting of feet; the creation of the whale wall from which Gulley is mortally bulldozed. All of this and more, a trail of tribulations and outrage which would be terrible indeed were it not for Gulley's incredibly sharp and light-footed self-irony.

Ultimately, it is Gulley's voice that conquers all, his gift for the quip, his meticulously skewed vision of the world, a vision colored with erudition seemingly unbecoming in so seedy an individual. Gulley is a fascinating combination of character tropes drawn from a variety of literary conventions: the picaresque rogue, the suffering artist, the social satirist, the unreliable narrator. All of these and more, he finally inspires a considerable amount of affection and even credulity. Cary has managed something very difficult; he has turned stereotypes into something resembling flesh, convincing us that his wacky artist is actually a gifted as well as a suffering human being.

—David Hayman

THE HOSTAGE.
Play by Brendan Behan, 1958 (in Irish, as *An Giall*, 1958).

Originally written and performed in Irish as *An Giall*, Brendan Behan's *The Hostage* eventually developed through various stages into a different play, leaving behind its original naturalistic-tragic emphasis and achieving instead a satirical, highly comic flavor—opposite in tone to its original version. A good deal of the impetus for change came from Joan Littlewood of the Theatre Workshop, who, to an incalculable degree, rewrote parts of the play with Behan's acquiescence. In this new form, *The Hostage* became a huge success, especially on the London stage.

The hostage of the title is Leslie Williams, a young British soldier who is taken by the I.R.A. and is to be shot in reprisal for the death of a young I.R.A. prisoner being held in Belfast. What surrounds him may be the most exquisite manifestation of confusion ever presented on the Irish stage, as a rich variety of characters demonstrates that the only quality that is consistently valued is money: all else is devalued or undercut in some way. Intentional confusion on virtually all conceivable levels is in fact the play's unifying device, as through the many characters we lose sight of who is "right" or "wrong," who is living in the past or the present or is living for the future, who is on who's side—and who is for England, for Ireland, for neither, or for both. Thus are values and standards blurred.

The center of the political confusion is the aging, highly eccentric Monsewer, an English Protestant who is pro-I.R.A., has learned Irish, and patriotically continues to live in the time of the troubles, "making plans for battles fought long ago against enemies long since dead." The most important point, of course, is that the play's only selfless idealist is a madman who consistently mistakes dream and nostalgia for reality. Not surprisingly, the political turmoil caused by the fact that many Irish and English had indeed fought alongside one another in Europe is an issue Behan uses to some advantage.

That Monsewer has learned Irish is also a central element of the cultural confusion inextricably related to the political havoc. When for many years Monsewer persisted in speaking only Irish, no one was able to understand him and whenever he boarded a tram or bus "he had to have an interpreter with him so the conductor would know where he wanted to get off." Later, when Leslie asks, "what actually is a race?," this version of Behan's central theme culminates: Monsewer can provide no adequate response and the scene dissolves into pure humor—as when Leslie mistakes "Garlic" for "Gaelic."

Clearly, however, the dominant type of confusion is not political or cultural, but moral in nature. The most dazzling example is the case of Rio Rita—an effeminate construction worker who is also a homosexual. Rio de Janeiro, after which he is named, has long been associated with lax morality, so the nickname is appropriate, especially after we discover that Rio Rita and her black lover, Princess Grace, are carrying on a lesbian relationship; that is, both men play the female role in their homosexual union. Late in the play, therefore, when the heterosexual Mr. Mulleady joins the homosexuals in their hip-twitching dance, we are hardly surprised—nor when he ultimately dons then removes a mask and declares himself a secret policeman. His order that the two nuns be arrested for being I.R.A. men in disguise points to an allied theme: religious confusion. Both the old and new testaments are targets of Behan's satire as when we are told of Moses' belonging to the fire brigade, an obvious reference to the burning bush, and of Christ's having said that "every cripple has his own way of walking, so long as they don't cause strikes, rob, steal, or run down General Franco." Also worth mentioning here is the frequent linking of religion and sex, as when Miss Gilchrist prays fervently—*after* every illicit sexual encounter with Mr. Mulleady, both of whose names clearly echo those of the new testament's two primary figures.

To reinforce the central theme, Behan's stage directions insure that the verbal confusion is visually supported on the stage: "What happens next is not very clear. There are arguments all going on at once. Free-Staters against Republicans, Irish against English, homosexuals against heterosexuals, and in the confusion all the quarrels get mixed up and it looks as though everyone is fighting everyone else." Near the end of the play a melee breaks out and the key words in Behan's stage directions are "pandemonium," "confusion," and "chaos." An added layer of confusion is created through the author's self-conscious intrusion into the "reality" of his play: the characters refer directly to Behan by name, one of whom declares that Behan would "sell his country for a pint"; a few pages later occurs a thinly veiled reference to Behan's play, *Richard's Cork Leg*, which must have been in its earliest stages of composition.

However, the most striking type of confusion lies in the mood of the play, which consistently runs counter to the audience's "normal" expectations. For instance, at the very end of the second act, Williams learns he is likely to be killed and sees his supporters desert him, leaving him totally alone—emotionally very vulnerable, or so we would think. Instead of a heart-wrenching climax to the act, Behan gives us a hostage who requests music and then breaks into joyous song. Even more surprising, though, is the play's ending, where life and death themselves are confused. After having been shot dead Williams is resurrected by the author; rising from the dead, Williams joins the rest of the cast in song and dance. Those familiar with the history of drama will immediately recognize this play as a throwback to John Gay's *The Beggar's Opera* (1728), a biting satire that ultimately is highly celebratory rather than depressing, even though it deals with serious issues and culminates in the death of a charismatic character—who is promptly brought back to life among much happy singing and dancing. The clash between serious content and lighthearted tone points to the essential meaning of Behan's play.

What, in fact, *is* the purpose of the play's many interrelated manifestations of confusion? As in *The Quare Fellow* we have a community of outcasts that ultimately reflects the modern human condition, especially as it is uniquely displayed in Ireland. Both plays have at bottom a humanistic message that urges tolerance and acceptance of all humanity. It is pointed out, for example, that Williams, supposedly the enemy, is "a decent boy"; that "many a good heart beats under a khaki tunic"; that "there's good and bad on all sides"; and that "God gives us the brains, it's no credit to ourselves." The dance near the play's ending is "for all the outcasts of this world," who cannot be faulted for their essential state of being: for being who they are. None of us *chooses* to be an outcast in any particular way, though some of us, such as Behan himself, may certainly revel in our nonconformity.

Echoes of Frank O'Connor's *Guest of the Nation* (1931) are many, and the central point of each work is the same. But through its joy, humor, and sheer exuberance, Behan reaches more broadly and challenges us to accept one another as human beings not only in a wartime setting but in any situation where we reject others automatically because of vague "moral" or "patriotic" preconceived ideas. As Dunlavin put it so well in *The Quare Fellow*: we can hardly assign blame in life because, "when all is said and done, [each of us] is someone's rearing after all." We are who we are; we have not chosen to be who we are.

—Alexander G. Gonzalez

THE HOUND OF HEAVEN.
Poem by Francis Thompson, 1893.

Francis Thompson was a Roman Catholic who, destitute in London, eventually found a literary talent that he put to the service of his faith. He forms part of that group of late 19th-century Catholics, among them his friends the Meynells and the poet Coventry Patmore, who looked back through history to the high points of Catholic faith for their models and inspiration. This process was already evident in the work of Cardinal Newman (who joined the Roman church in 1845), in the Catholic element in the Gothic Revival in architecture, and in the medievalism of the Pre-Raphaelites, both phenomena of the 1850's. Thompson was born in 1859.

Unlike his great Jesuit contemporary, Hopkins, who forged a new poetic method, Thompson was more typical in his reversion to the middle ages and the 17th century. Thus his poems of 1893, and especially "The Hound of Heaven," were greeted by one reviewer as "the return of the 19th century to Thomas-à-Kempis." Similarly the debt of the poem to the 17th-century mystic poet Richard Crashaw (also a Catholic) is evident. In poetic terms Thompson may be seen as a late adherent of the metaphysical style—the violence of the image of God as a large dog pursuing, burning, and generally chastising the poet is familiar to us from Donne and others ("Batter my heart, three-personed God . . . ").

But the poem is of the 19th century for all that. In the first place, whereas the anxiety in Donne and Herbert is generated by the fear that God will be angry with sin, by Thompson's time the anxiety hints that it might be about unbelief. At the end of the poem, for instance, the poet wonders "Is my gloom, after all, / Shade of His hand, outstretched caressingly?" The typical gloom of the Victorian doubter may, by a metaphysical paradox, demonstrate the existence of the divine.

The tone of the verse, and its rhythms, associate it with the pagan songs of Swinburne or the hedonistic melancholy of Thompson's close contemporaries, Dowson, Housman, Johnson, Wilde. Certainly it is the rhythm of "The Hound of Heaven" that carries the poem forward and with it the reader. Thompson achieves a match between subject and rhythm that makes a considerable impact especially in the refrain, four times repeated in different variations, of which the first version runs:

> But with unhurrying chase,
> And unperturbèd pace,
> Deliberate speed, majestic instancy,
> They beat—and a voice beat
> More instant than the Feet—
> "All things betray thee, who betrayest Me."

The sense is well conveyed of the irresistible force of the divine; such an ineluctable pursuit can have only one ending although the poem has started:

> I fled Him, down the nights and down the days;
> I fled Him, down the arches of the years;
> I fled Him, down the labyrinthine ways
> Of my own mind; and in the mist of tears
> I hid from Him . . .

These two examples show the way Thompson manages to control our reading through the printing of his verse: line-length and indentation together with heavy punctuation produce the cadences he wants and force us to take the pursuit seriously. It is not immediately obvious that we would be able to take God seriously as a sort of divine Hound of the Baskervilles were this not so well done.

The rhythm is reinforced by an overall design, not of a regular stanza length or rhyme, but of a development in the different sections that shows a progression of thought: the opening section ("I fled Him") is followed by the first version of the refrain; we then hear of the poet's pleadings to escape from God, a longer section marked twice by the line "Fear wist not to evade as Love wist to pursue" which is followed by the second version of the refrain. This is followed by one of the two longest sections of the poem which describes the attempt to find meaning in Nature and is again followed by the refrain (now "Nigh and nigh draws the pace"). The second of the long sections sees the poet overwhelmed by God ("Naked I wait Thy love's uplifted stroke") which is followed, without the refrain intervening, by the section where God's voice speaks at length: "'Lo, all things fly thee, for thou fliest Me! / Strange, piteous, futile thing, / Wherefore should any set thee love apart?' " This is followed by the final section, the six-line refrain again, starting this time "Halts by me that footfall" and ending "I am He Whom thou seekest! / Thou dravest love from thee, who dravest Me."

The language and the imagery of the poem are a fascinating mixture of the 17th century with the 19th. From the 17th we get the paradox direct: the poet finds his own "betrayal" in the "constancy" of God's "servitors" to Him, describing their actions as "Their traitorous trueness, and their loyal deceit." Equally we feel the presence of Donne in the questions to God: "Ah! must Thou char the wood ere Thou canst limn with it?" and "must Thy harvest fields / Be dunged with rotten death?" Behind this lies the Authorised Version: "My days have crackled and gone up in smoke." From the 19th century come the typical images involved in these lines: "Across the margent of the world I fled, / And troubled the golden gateway of the stars, / Smiting for shelter on their clangèd bars." or these: "Yea, faileth now even dream / The dreamer, and the lute the lutanist; / Even the linked fantasies, in whose blossomy twist / I swung the earth a trinket at my wrist."

Even to an age of less faith than Thompson's there is a power in "The Hound of Heaven" to move, as well as an excellent example of how poems are made from other poems, for it is a work that is transparently intertextual.

—Lance St. John Butler

THE HOUND OF THE BASKERVILLES.
Novel by Arthur Conan Doyle, 1902.

Despite the commercial success of Arthur Conan Doyle's series of stories based on the fictional detective Sherlock Holmes, the pressure of repeated contracts requiring Doyle to produce the stories month after month caused him to put at least a temporary end to the illustrious detective in 1893. In "The Final Problem," published in the *Strand Magazine*, Holmes, after successfully solving cases through two novels and two dozen short stories, apparently tumbled into Reichenbach Falls, grasping his evil nemesis Moriarty in a death-lock. For nearly eight years, while Doyle devoted himself to his other writings and served in the Boer War, no new Holmes stories appeared to satisfy an eager public.

When Doyle decided to bring Holmes back in the *Strand* in August 1901, he carefully established that the case was one that took place previous to Holmes's disastrous encounter with Moriarty; he was not truly resurrecting his famous detective, at least not at that time. *The Hound of the Baskervilles*, serialized in nine monthly installments, was instantly successful, and remains among the most popular and memorable of the 56 stories and four novels Doyle based upon Holmes and his friend and biographer Dr. Watson. Although Doyle claimed that he originally intended to create the story (based on a folk legend related to him by his friend Fletcher Robinson) using a different set of characters entirely, he returned to the protagonist and general formula that had made him successful—and famous. The result was a sharp increase in sales in the *Strand*, and Doyle once again became the most popular author in England. A year after the last episode of *The Hound of the Baskervilles* appeared, Doyle, flattered by the renewed demand for his hero, began a new series of Holmes stories, revealing that Holmes did not, after all, die in the falls at Reichenbach.

Whereas the other three Holmes novels become somewhat tediously bogged down in lengthy flashbacks, due to Doyle's skillful plotting, *The Hound of the Baskervilles* presents a structured sustained narrative that is difficult to achieve in detective fiction. In this novel we see Holmes and Watson locked into a brooding, even hostile Darwinian universe, an indifferent cosmos whose presence overshadows their lives and throws the world of Baker Street into its proper perspective. Doyle implies this cosmological perspective by establishing an historical framework with the story. The Baskervilles, we are told, are a very old family; the manuscript detailing their legend dates back to 1742. Still, the Baskervilles are recent interlopers on Devonshire moor, despite their house which has stood there for a century and a half. Long before them the moor was inhabited by "neolithic man," humans who disappeared centuries before, leaving behind only their barrows, bones, and primitive stone huts. Older than either the Baskervilles or these prehistoric humans is of course the moor itself, which, like Hardy's Egdon Heath, is a place where primal forces dominate. Grimpen Mire destroys the evil Stapleton, but it also drags under the harmless heath ponies and presumably is the final resting place of countless neolithic humans as well as the dinosaurs that preceded them. It is against this eternal landscape that the drama of the hound is played out, and it is through the juxtaposition of the present with this larger timeless universe that Doyle establishes the sense of a Darwinian universe.

By plucking his characters from their snug Baker Street flat and placing them in the middle of such a desolate and primitive atmosphere, miles from civilization, Doyle increases their vulnerability. On the moors they are alone in a way that they can never be in London, alone in time and space and far from the achievements of a civilized world, facing the fundamental forces of the universe. This confrontation with cosmic powers increases the terror of the novel. In such a place as Dartmoor forces may exist that civilized man has forgotten and long ceased to believe in. Here, Watson's trusty revolver, which is always so reassuring in most adventures, may be absolutely worthless and of no more real advantage than the neolithic man's stone axes. Of course, even three revolvers are not enough to conquer a truly supernatural force, but as it turns out, the detective and his friend are heavily overarmed. A lot of ammunition is spent, but the mysterious apparition turns out to be only a dog after all. Although Holmes is able to dismiss the Baskerville legend as "fairy-tales," Watson, and Doyle's readers, are successfully misled into believing that the legends and superstitions might just be true after all. What Holmes establishes clearly is that these fairy-tales are simply that. There is nothing truly supernatural in a Darwinian universe. What is most frightening about it, in fact, is that it has had all its magic removed; the world evolves for natural, not supernatural, reasons.

After Holmes is able to dispatch the hound and the evil Stapleton sinks to his death in Grimpen Mire, Doyle immediately returns the novel to the detective's snug retreat in London. It is a "raw and foggy" November night and Holmes and his chronicler are sitting "on either side of a blazing fire in our sitting-room in Baker Street." Security fairly exudes from the pages as Holmes, pipe in hand, sits back to explain the mystery to Watson and the reader in Doyle's formulaic conclusion. Here in Baker Street, Holmes and Watson can temporarily block out the indifferent universe they found at Dartmoor. Restaurants are nearby, tickets for the opera are in hand, Darwin and his threatening theories can be momentarily banished as easily as Watson shuts out the rain and darkness. Clearly Doyle has immediately juxtaposed this cozy scene with the disturbing vision of Grimpen Mire so that a Victorian sense of order can be restored to the novel. Holmes always projects a powerful image of security in Doyle's stories; he stands beside Watson, a virtually omnipotent figure, with the strength and the insight to sweep away fear and confusion and cast light into even the most obscure dark corners. This final scene is necessary to restore the equilibrium of the novel, a novel in which Doyle modified his traditional detective formula slightly to allow his hero to peer beyond the physical facts into the mystery of life itself.

—Don Richard Cox

THE HOUSE OF FAME.
Poem by Geoffrey Chaucer, written c. 1379.

In the first 58 lines of *The House of Fame*, its narrator emphatically denies that he understands dreams, although in making this disclaimer he surveys medieval theories of their causes, categories, and significance. This opening gambit leads to an unequivocal assertion that his own dream on the 10th of December was the most wonderful ever dreamt and to the promise that he will tell it completely—that is, as he can remember it. These oscillations between uncertainty and precision prepare for the wittiest and most disconcerting of Geoffrey Chaucer's dream visions. For 2158 lines of octosyllabic verse he swings between elevation and bathos, confidence and scepticism, before breaking off in mid-sentence when a man of great authority is about to make an announcement.

Who this authoritative figure might be, and what he might say, invite speculation. It is difficult, however, to imagine any serious tidings, given the swirling confusion of true and false rumours in which he appears. Furthermore, if *The House of Fame* is an occasional poem leading toward a specific piece of news, it is a long preamble to a tale. Formal invocations, promiscuously addressed to Morpheus, Christ, Venus, the Muses, and Apollo, divide the poem into three books. In Book I, the dreamer visits a glass temple of Venus, decorated with a version of the *Aeneid* curiously abridged so that the emphasis is on lovers' falsehood. From the desert outside this temple he is rescued by a golden eagle, who in Book II addresses him familiarly as "Geffrey" and tells him that Jove has granted him a trip in the house of Fame, "So that thou wolt be of good chere." A single house of Fame seems to be promised, but Book III provides two. In the first, an ornate palace, the goddess appears in her role as renown; in the second, a whirling wicker house full of tidings, Chaucer portrays the growth and spread of rumour, the second variety of fame.

Although the poem is often criticized as oddly proportioned or carelessly constructed, the four settings of the dream provide a clear pattern, as oppressive scenes alternate with scenes of high comedy. The glass temple of Venus, emphasizing love's brittleness, is linked with the beryl palace of renown, built on a foundation of ice. Both are grand, artful, delusive, and finally sterile. Often the palace is identified with the "house of Fame," but it is the house of rumour which corresponds to the eagle's description of how all speech moves to Fame's dwelling, where the dreamer will hear varied and wonderful news. The dreamer complains after visiting the palace that he has heard "no such tydyngs" as the eagle promised, and the relentless demonstration of Fame's caprice in the palace would be a strange gift from Jove, whose announced intent is to grant the dreamer "som disport and game" after his long and unrewarded service of Venus. The lively house of rumour shares the comic gaiety of Geffrey's flight with the eagle, though not the philosophical consolation given in the eagle's Aristotelian and Boethian lecture on the movement of all things to their proper place.

Recurrent invocations are one sign of literary ambition in the work, notwithstanding Chaucer's claim in the invocation to Apollo that he is concerned more with matter or "sentence" than with craft. The poem is packed with references to books and authors, classical and medieval—Virgil, Ovid, Claudian, Dante, Macrobius, Anticlaudianus, and a host of others. In renown's palace poets and historians support pillars representing various cities, their own names preserved along with that of their subjects. Their standing is, however, far from secure. However closely authors and authorities are identified, these figures are placed suspiciously close to the minstrels, tellers of tales, magicians, and charlatans found in architectural niches of the palace. In the hall of Fame the goddess arbitrarily distributes glory, ill-repute, or oblivion. One of the six writers upholding the renown of Troy accuses Homer of favoritism to the Greeks. As the abbreviated *Aeneid* found earlier in the dream vision shows, literary works are subject to distortion in reading and retelling.

The abruptness with which the poem breaks off frustrates desire for a simple resolution, and uneasy scribes of two 15th-century manuscripts left blank space for copying an ending, if one should turn up. Given Chaucer's theme—the uncertain relationship of truth to dreams, authors, and authority—the break is a paradoxically satisfying conclusion. While nothing is concluded, the final impression is not the vanity of human wishes in the realms of Venus and Renown but the cheerful, chaotic bustle of life in the house of rumour, the carnival spirit there as figures tumble over themselves, full of curiosity for tidings more apt to be amusing than enlightening.

—Kay Gilliland Stevenson

THE HOUSE OF LIFE.
Poems by Dante Gabriel Rossetti, 1870 and 1881.

Dante Gabriel Rossetti's *The House of Life* made its first appearance as "Fifty Sonnets," among the "Sonnets and Songs towards the Work to be entitled 'The House of Life'" in *Poems* (1870). The sonnets were increased in number to 101 (to which was added an "Introductory Sonnet") and rearranged, with the Songs detached from the sequence, when *The House of Life* was republished in *Ballads and Sonnets* (1881). Though the 1881 sequence is divided into two parts, "Youth and Change" (sonnets i-lix) and "Change and Fate" (1x-ci), the work provides little sense of chronological arrangement or narrative; nor is it likely that it should, in view of the fact that it draws together sonnets written as early as 1847 and as late as 1881.

The introductory sonnet, "A sonnet is a moment's monument," declares that the poet's purpose is to reveal the soul in its awareness of life, love, and death. Love is the constant theme: many of the sonnets represent a not altogether successful attempt to spiritualize love, using the imagery and notions of Dante, but without Dante's Christian theology and his clear distinction between Platonized courtly love and Christian truth. So Rossetti sometimes rises no higher than religiosity or pious sensuality, as in "Heart's Hope" (sonnet v in the 1881 sequence):

Lady I fain would tell how evermore
Thy soul I know not from thy body, nor
Thee from myself, neither our love from God.

In "The Soul's Beauty" and "The Body's Beauty" (1xxvii, 1xxviii, originally written to accompany Rossetti's paintings of, respectively, *Sibylla Palmifera* and *Lilith*) the lover cannot catch the "flying hair and fluttering hem" of the soul's beauty though he pursues her "passionately and irretrievably, / In what fond flight, how many ways and days"; but the body's beauty

Draws men to watch the bright web she can weave,
Till heart and body and life are in its hold,

and the two are never reconciled. Sometimes Rossetti's pious sensuality is only a gesture, as in "Secret Parting" (xlv), where "as we kissed, her mouth became her soul." Elsewhere, something more elaborate is intended, as in "Love's Redemption" (in its 1870 version before being revised as "Love's Testament" [iii] in 1881):

O Thou who at Love's hour ecstatically
Unto my lips dost evermore present
The body and blood of Love in sacrament;
Whom I have neared and felt thy breath to be
The inmost incense of his sanctuary.

The image, though, is vague, and the idea vaguer. As often, the incense fumes around Love's altar cloud Rossetti's meaning.

This is not always the case. "Silent Noon" (xix) has qualities of fresh, crisp, static particularity such as we find in the Pre-Raphaelite paintings of Holman Hunt and Millais. The painter's sharp perception and grasp of detail crystallize and communicate honestly an intense experience. So too in "Sudden Light":

I have been here before,
But when or how I cannot tell:
I know the grass beyond the door,
The sweet keen smell,
The sighing sound, the lights around the shore,

and in that fine rendering of exhausted sorrow, "The Woodspurge." Both those poems appeared among the Songs appended to the incomplete version of *The House of Life* in *Poems*, 1870.

Rossetti's most memorable poetry, like Wordsworth's, explores the landscape of memory; but all too often for Rossetti memory is a nightmare of remorse. He recognizes his failure to sustain his idealism in life, and is haunted by guilt over lost opportunities in life and art. Remorse deepens into self-disgust and disintegration of personality:

Look, in my face; my name is Might-have-been;
I am also called No-more, Too-late, Farewell;
("A Superscription," xcvii);

God knows I know the faces I shall see,
Each one a murdered self, with low last breath.
"I am thyself,—what hast thou done to me?"
"And I—and I—thyself," (lo! each one saith,)
"And thou thyself to all eternity!"
("Lost Days", lxxxvi).

Four sonnets, written in 1868 and called, collectively, "Willowwood" (xlix-lii), most poignantly speak for a man divided against himself. Here the past invades the present, dumb, lonely figures—representing the lost days—stand beneath the trees, and the corpse of the wife rises to the surface of the hidden river. The images, at once personal and archetypal, convey a powerful sense of remorse brooding over the dead days. This "thicket" image in "Willowwood," "the rustling covert of my soul," is almost obsessive in Rossetti's work. It is this sinister, demonic region where love meets death, rather than the angelic sphere of "The Blessed Damozel," that Rossetti recreates most convincingly.

—A.J. Sambrook

HOWARDS END.
Novel by E.M. Forster, 1910.

Howards End is "a condition-of-England" novel, asking directly, who shall inherit England? Geographically, the action is centred in London, with scenes in Swanage, Shropshire, and Hertfordshire, where the modest house of the title is situated. The old house in the country, with a vine growing on it, beside an ancient wych-elm and delightful meadow, resists change and modernization. Germany (as civilized and humane, anything but a potential enemy) and Italy also have a small part in the novel, and the Empire too is touched on.

The central conflict is between the Schlegels and the Wilcoxes. The Schlegel household, two sisters in their twenties, Margaret and Helen, and teenage brother, is affluent. They are half-German and stand for the values of culture: they hear Beethoven's Fifth Symphony almost every time it is performed in London. Yet they know that culture is a means and not an end: the end is the Bloomsbury cultivation of personal relations. The Wilcox family consists of Henry Wilcox and his three crass children. He is a successful businessman, head of the Imperial and West African Rubber Company, sending his younger son to work in Nigeria. Henry's motto is "Concentrate"; he can see life steadily but not whole.

Mrs. Wilcox, however, who inherited Howards End, is quite different, representing the traditional values of the country: "she worshipped the past" and "the instinctive wisdom the past can alone bestow had descended upon her." Transplanted to London, she dies suddenly. Her spirit is continued by Miss Avery, a wise, mysterious old farm woman.

A fourth element is a lower-middle-class couple, the Basts. He is a humble insurance clerk who aspires to culture despite his poverty. Forster admits that he is leaving out "the very poor," who "are unthinkable, and only to be approached by the statistician or the poet."

The epigraph of the novel is "only connect," and thus Margaret Schlegel becomes Henry Wilcox's second wife. She has come to respect businesslike virtues, asserting: "More and more do I refuse to draw my income and sneer at those who guarantee it." She also starts to question her own beliefs, asking her sister: "Do personal relations lead to sloppiness in the end?" The Schlegels attempt connection with Bast, but he is timid and suspicious. Helen eventually becomes pregnant by him, an act, like the marriage of Margaret and Henry, that some have found implausible.

At the end Margaret and Henry are settled at Howards End, and Helen's baby (uniting culture and the lower middle class) plays happily in the sun with the ploughman's son. The magical hay-field has a "sacred centre," producing "such a crop of hay as never!" Wilcoxes, however, suffer from hay fever, and this happy ending is qualified: Henry Wilcox is broken, his elder son in prison, while Margaret says that she cannot love a child and Helen that she cannot love a man. Though the "red rust" of London suburbs is spreading towards the house, Margaret claims: "Very early in the morning I feel that our house is the future as well as the past."

Business values are found wanting. Culture as understood by most humans is faulted too, but Beethoven towers above them. "One can trust" him because he shows both the defeat of "goblins" and the possibility of their return.

The beauty of the English countryside—tamed in Hertfordshire, spectacular in Shropshire, all-embracing looking from the Purbeck Hills, where "the imagination swells, spreads and deepens, until it becomes geographic and encircles England"—remains very valuable, as support, consolation, and inspiration. Indeed, "England's hope" lies in yeomen, rooted in the country (unlike the mobile middle class), keeping "to the life of daylight," carrying "forward the torch of the sun." This is a Wordsworthian cult of nature, diluted a hundred years later.

Stylistically, Forster is modest and disarming. He starts casually with "One may as well begin with Helen's letters." He indulges in a flight of fancy about King's Cross station suggesting "infinity," then undercuts it prosaically with "If you think this ridiculous, remember that it is not Margaret who is telling you about it." Most striking, he builds patterns of images around, for instance, glass and rabbits, to be noted at second reading, and repeats numbers of phrases, such as the "panic and emptiness" understood by Beethoven and the outer life of "telegrams and anger" of the Wilcoxes.

"Only connect" applies not only to Schlegels and Wilcoxes, but to the inner and outer life ("of course the inner life is superior, but it's medieval to brood on it") and "the prose and the passion." "Only connect, and the beast and the monk, robbed of the isolation that is life to either, will die." While some have re-phrased this tag as "if we only could connect," Forster, though usually tentative, nevertheless is giving clear advice on the means to the good life.

—Malcolm Page

HUDIBRAS. See the Writers entry on **BUTLER, Samuel** (born 1613).

HUMPHRY CLINKER.
(*The Expedition of Humphry Clinker.*)
Novel by Tobias Smollett, 1771.

Humphry Clinker, Tobias Smollett's last novel and one published just three months before his death in 1771, is his best loved and most admired work. Smollett's best earlier novels, his first two, *Roderick Random* and *Peregrine Pickle*, are picaresque in genre, and so present the adventures of tough and unscrupulous young loners: brutal contests of wits, rapidly shifting exotic settings, and excoriating social satire provide the excitement. *Humphry Clinker* transforms picaresque into something rich and strange, a fascinating blend of travelogue, psychological novel, and comic romance.

Perhaps because he wrote the novel away from the broils of London, in an Italian villa overlooking the Mediterranean, perhaps because he was in failing health and knew death was near, perhaps in response to the new vogue during the 1760's for fine feeling and sympathetic communion (epitomized in the fiction of Sterne), *Humphry Clinker* contemplates life with acceptance, even celebration, rather than protest, and has, as the earlier novels did not, the subtlety and serenity of fully achieved art. Its title, *The Expedition of Humphry*

Clinker, indicates this change: whereas Smollett's earlier novels had been entitled, according to picaresque formula, *The Adventures of* . . . , this title is much more oblique. The novel's central figure is actually Matthew Bramble, a touchy, hypochondriac Welsh landowner, who has embarked with his family in a tour of Great Britain on the advice of his doctor. The novel's expedition is in quest of Matthew's health, and that quest is achieved by the novel's end—because Humphry Clinker, a young outcast who is so simple-minded and humble as to be helpless in society, joins the party and becomes Matthew's servant and eventual saviour. Humphry, who in outer form resembles the picaresque antihero but in spiritual terms is his opposite, only joins the "expedition" one-quarter of the way through the novel, and then as simply another one of many servants.

The fictional situation is, in fact, oblique in many ways. It is apparent from the outset that Matt Bramble's ailments are psychosomatic: his physical diseases (his attacks of gout, for instance) are caused by mental and emotional dis-ease. Embittered, aggrieved, and preoccupied with himself, Matt, like Lear, needs an ounce of civet to sweeten his imagination, and only when his outlook upon life is free from its poison will his body be well. Furthermore, as the head of his travelling household, Matt provides a humble domestic image of the diseased king of traditional story: because he is unwell, all the members of his travelling household are also infected. His sister, the old maid Tabitha, has become a shrew, able to show her genuine affection for her brother only by browbeating him and by hoarding money diverted from his estate. Jery Melford, Matt's nephew who has just graduated from Oxford, is dominated by prickly snobbishness and sophomoric disdain for his own family; Lydia, Jery's naively romantic younger sister, nurses a broken heart because she has fallen in love with an itinerant actor (who has been angrily rejected as unsuitable by Jery). The family as a unit is also diseased: cut off from each other, resentful, suspicious, lacking in sympathy. By the novel's end, all the individuals are well, and the family itself has become "a family of love," in the words of Tabby's maid, Win Jenkins, whose semi-literate and wildly funny aspirations to gentility amplify the theme of discontent.

The novel's narrative method introduces further complexity. Unlike Smollett's earlier novels, *Humphry Clinker* is told in letters. Each of the main figures in the Bramble household writes to a correspondent, and in each case the epistolary relationship provides an image of the character's situation. Matt writes to his doctor, Dr. Lewis, recounting his symptoms and gauging the effects upon him of his new surroundings; Tabby Bramble writes to the housekeeper back at Brambleton Hall in Wales, issuing orders and complaints; Jery writes to a titled friend in Oxford, somewhat strenuously maintaining a sophisticated, disengaged, worldly air; Lydia writes breathlessly to a confidante who was with her at a school for girls in Gloucester and knows all about Mr. Wilson, the actor; Win Jenkins, who is agog at the new world before her, writes to a fellow maid at Brambleton Hall. The two men, Matt and Jery, write about two-thirds of the novel's letters, with Jery, whose reports are the closest to being objective, recounting about half the novel; the three women (Tabby, Win, and Lydia) punctuate this rather phlegmatic flow of narration with their own surprising and distinctive accounts of events. Humphry alone among the major characters writes no letters,

The novel's method is thus full of psychological interest (and here Smollett no doubt registers the impact of Richardson): the Bath or London seen by Matt Bramble is set against the very different perceptions of Jery, Lydia, Tabby, and Win. Hazlitt considered *Humphy Clinker* "the most pleasant gossipping novel that ever was written" for just this reason. The epistolary method is also a vivid embodiment of the state of the family, each member cut off from the others by personal preoccupations: by the end of the novel, letters are no longer needed, not only because the family's travels are about to end, but also because the family members can now communicate directly and openly with each other.

The novel puts its satisfactions as a travelogue to even further use. The British settings, if not exotic, provide symbolism as well as psychological interest: out of variety an image of life as an integrated whole slowly emerges. The circular tour of the Bramble family through the whole of Great Britain, beginning and ending in Wales, and in between swinging through southern England, northern England, Scotland, and back into the centre of England again, embodies the wholeness eventually achieved by each person and by the family unit. They have seen on their way rural and urban life, rich and poor, frauds and solid citizens, the leisured and the hardworking—and even, in the long central section of the novel which takes place in Scotland, discover the primitive feudal past existing side by side with the progressive urban present.

These leisurely travels are punctuated by two accidents in which the family carriage is overturned. Each provides a "revolution" in the novel's plot. As a result of the first accident, at Marlborough Downs in southern England, Matt's footman is dismissed for disrespect to Tabby, and Humphry Clinker, who seems nothing but a feeble-minded, bungling tatterdemalion, is hired on. Humphry's advent, however, is the turning point of the novel. He not only brings to the group love and loyalty (he refuses to be fired when Tabby objects to his ragged breeches); he not only exposes the group to genuine disease, misery, and destitution; he not only professes Christianity openly and embodies the Christian ethic of humility and love; he not only represents the nature from which all the family members are estranged; perhaps as important as anything, he provokes Matt to laugh for the first time in the book, and to laugh out of delighted sympathy with Humphry's child-like humanity. Humphry is immediately proved to be a miracle-worker. Tabby, outraged at the prospect of his joining the group, tells Matt that either Humphry must go or she will; Matt, renovated by Humphry's example, retorts with new authority that either Chowder, the ugly cur Tabby dotes on and uses as a means of terrorizing the family, must go or she will. Tabby, strangely moved by her brother's new sense of responsibility for and to her, immediately accedes, and Humphry's appearance causes the disappearance of the noxious Chowder. Saving powers have joined the group, and once Humphry is seen in these terms, it is clear why Smollett includes no letters from him: he is what the others must comprehend and attain.

The second overturning of the family carriage, which occurs near the novel's end, is equally pivotal. This time the family is spilled into flood waters, and Humphry rescues his master, who almost drowns. Matt is brought back to life, reborn, an event that had been foreshadowed in a comic episode at Scarborough, when Humphry, seeing Matt bathing and fearing that he would drown, dragged the naked Matt ashore by the ear. This rebirth symbolism is underlined when the sodden Brambles take refuge at a nearby gentleman's estate, and there the plot is suddenly resolved. The nearby gentleman turns out to be Mr. Dennison, Matt's old friend and thus highly respectable, and Lydia's Mr. Wilson is discovered to be George Dennison, his son. Amid these revelations, Humphry is discovered to be the illegitimate son of Matt himself, and so this "love-child" becomes Matt's legal as well as natural heir. Humphry and his love Win Jenkins are now free to marry; Lydia is free to marry George Dennison; Tabby, now much gentler, agrees to marry the eccentric, penniless, and touchy Scotsman, Captain Lismahago (ironically, the one unattached male of her age that she has not pursued wildly). The book ends, in comic fashion, with these three marriages—and Wales, England, and Scotland are once again united.

Though Win Jenkins has virtually no role in the plot and writes relatively few letters, she is the novel's keynote figure. Her great characteristic is her unintentional profanity. Determined to write genteelly, and yet lacking the education that would allow her to write accurately, her aspirations to become a Prioress end up making her sound like a Wife of Bath. A typical sentence of Win's is: "Last Sunday in the parish-crutch, if my own ars may be trusted, the clerk called the banes of marriage betwixt Opaniah Lashmeheygo, and Tapitha Brample, spinster." Win's letters are thus not only full of delightful wordplay; they also symbolize the wholesomeness of unadulterated nature, overspilling and dwarfing conventional niceties. This is why Win's nakedness, much to her embarrassment, is exposed again and again during the action; why she is a suitable bride for Humphry himself; and why she is given the final letter in the novel. It should be no surprise that James Joyce considered her the great achievement of 18th-century fiction.

—Bruce Stovel

HYDE PARK.
Play by James Shirley, 1632.

Partly set in Hyde Park, recently opened to the public, James Shirley's play is specific in the details of its location and in its nicely discriminated perceptions of social class. It presents, in the polite world of Caroline London, the loves and intrigues of a group of idle young men and women, ranging from young sparks with no shortage of money but some diffidence and uncertainty about their manners, to Lord Bonvile, a grand nobleman who is nonetheless happy to court the commoner Julietta. The play reflects a coterie society, with which the sophisticated audience at the Phoenix Theatre in Drury Lane could identify. Unlike older comedies of love, there is no authoritative royal or ducal figure to sort everything out; the servants are pert rather than vulgar or manipulative; the characters come together not at the court but at the horse races.

These leisured classes are in transition; for example, Bonavent, missing at sea for seven years, cannot recognise a social event—"Pray, is this a dancing school?" he asks, when ushered into a wedding party. "I know not how to foot your chamber jigs," he observes, and the ladies think that he dances "something like . . . a hobby-horse." But social insecurity does not affect only a newcomer. The modish Jack Venture has written a "very ballad . . . and a coarse tune" about the horses, but is too embarrassed to sing it ("You shall pardon me") until Lord Bonvile—totally self-assured—persuades him that some healthy vulgarity is not amiss:

> Why, does any tune become
> A gentleman so well as a ballad?
> . . . Leave these crotchets
> To men that get their living with a song.

The lively song heralds the shift of scene from fashionable London houses to Hyde Park; the characters wander in groups through its walks, meeting, crossing, and avoiding each other in subtly managed staging. The high points are the servants' footraces and the horse races, where both gentlemen amateurs and jockeys take part—Pepys reports that in a Restoration performance horses were brought on the stage. The park setting, where the action is resolved, is a true-to-life equivalent to the magic places of earlier romantic dramas, for at the end all the characters act with probity and elegance.

While the naturalistic aspects of the play reflect the everyday life of London society, its three distinct plots are romantic and conventional. Bonavent, captured by pirates and presumed dead, returns just as his wife's seven-year vow of celibate widowhood has expired and she is to marry again. Trier tests the constancy of his beloved Julietta by attempting to prostitute her to Lord Bonvile. Mistress Carol, who scorns men and marriage, is tricked by her suitor, Fairfield, into an agreement that leads her finally to accept him. The plots are only connected because their participants belong to the same smart set, and constantly exchange confidences and remark on each other's adventures.

Each plot investigates the roles of men and women in this culture; the most interesting is that of Mistress Carol, the vivacious man-hater. She is self-consciously aware that her freedom comes from her rejection of the conventions normally governing woman's behaviour. But her commitment to a free, active and decisive life is shown as undesirably masculine. She muses, "Were I a man," and wonders how her cousin Mistress Bonavent can bear to marry again when she is rich and self-reliant. Carol believes that plentiful material possessions are all that one needs to be totally happy. Like a male bravo, she readily and ridiculously takes offence, polarising differences of opinion and exaggerating trivial matters. When Fairfield comments mildly that she is "ingrateful," she ironically concludes the line for him: "Abominably peevish, and a wench / That would be beaten, beaten black and blue." When he approaches too closely she responds, "Prethee let my body alone."

The trick played on her to restore her to womanly dependence is one which removes her power to act and to decide. Fairfield asks, "You must swear to perform truly what I shall desire." As he allows Carol the opportunity to make any exceptions, she agrees, stating the obvious provisos: she must not be forced to love and obey him, she must be free to do thus and so. But Fairfield's binding oath is puzzling and negative: "by that oath / I bind you never to desire my company / Hereafter." A man may select a lover and change his mind; this crucial male advantage Carol has bargained away for what is a silly (and typically male) wager. Of course, she cannot now stop thinking of Fairfield and desiring his company. But *Hyde Park*'s sexism is not doctrinaire; unlike Shakespeare's Kate, Carol is not humbled. After her witty duels with Fairfield, he notes, "Each other's now by conquest." Similarly, the other plots end with graceful agreements.

The young men and women in *Hyde Park* bet extravagantly and cheerfully on the horses; the lovers offer diamonds and pearls; their language is filled with elaborate courtly metaphor, boasting of their honour and joking about maidenheads, high fashion, and nakedness; kissing and compliment follow each encounter. Sober-minded critics condemn the play as decadent; contemporary theatre-goers seemed attracted to its glittering frivolity. The play epitomises Caroline ideals of generosity, polish, and wit, no doubt presenting to its first audiences a flattering mirror-image of how they would wish to be seen.

—Richard Morton

I

I, CLAUDIUS and CLAUDIUS THE GOD.
Novels by Robert Graves, 1934.

Although published separately, these novels form a single work: an "autobiography" of the fourth Emperor of ancient Rome. In *I, Claudius* he recounts his first 50 years, as a minor member of the Imperial family; the book can be read independently. *Claudius the God* covers his reign, and makes best sense when read in sequence.

Until this century, historical novels depended chiefly on verisimilitude, on a head-on depiction of the past reminiscent of panoramic paintings. Whether the mode was melodrama (as in *Ivanhoe*, say, or *The Three Musketeers*) or was psychologically more complex (as in *Salammbô*, say, or *The Scarlet Letter*), a main source of reader interest was meticulous description of the detail of past lives—artefacts, especially, giving a sense of place and time. In the 20th century, historical novelists began to dig deeper into character and motivation, taking their cue both from the case-histories of psychoanalysis (often published as first-person accounts) and from films, in which the presence of well-known actors (Laughton or Garbo, say) produced its own sense of detachment, of counterpoint between action and background, which could be used to make critical and ironical points.

This is precisely Robert Graves's method in the Claudius books. His intentions are revisionist, and his method is paradox, Suetonius, Tacitus, and other ancient historians dismissed Claudius as a drooling halfwit, whose survival to the age of 50 was inexplicable, and whose career as Emperor alternated between eccentricity and tyranny. Graves's research took account of the undeclared bias of such sources (Suetonius's prurience, for example, or Tacitus's republicanism), and his starting points were the questions "If Claudius was such a fool, how did he survive, why was he made Emperor, and how did he reign so successfully and for so long (13 years)?" His answer was to depict Claudius as the wiliest politician in Rome, using physical disability to mask his shrewdness from his murderous family, and only allowing it open expression once he was hoisted (willy-nilly, after a palace coup) on to the Imperial throne.

This interpretation works brilliantly in *I, Claudius*. It allows Graves to savour every scurrilous rumour in his sources, every hint of political deviousness or scandal—and at the same time to pour doubts on any he chooses by framing them in Claudius's sceptical, quizzical comments. He depicts the Imperial family as a gang of prototype *mafiosi*, murdering and power-broking under the baleful eye of the Empress Livia, their Godmother. Claudius is presented as an intelligent human being, with modern sensibilities, trapped in an epic soap opera whose other characters are as dangerous, and as far above question, as the gods and heroes of ancient myth. (In a later novel, *The Golden Fleece / Hercules, My Shipmate*, Graves works the same trick in reverse: he takes myth-characters, Jason and the Argonauts, gives them human sensibility, and so creates a counterpoint between sympathetic human character and fantastic event which animates the book.)

Graves builds Claudius's character on two known facts: that he was an amateur historian (dry as dust, ancient writers sneer), and that he stammered. From these hints Graves creates a man who approaches every situation—from deciphering Samnite inscriptions to choosing wine for dinner—by means of painstaking research, sifting evidence, pondering, and taking time before he speaks. Claudius is a fool who knows his folly (and trades on it), a bore who presses his point home to the last word (usually devastatingly insightful), a man fascinated by the past who is unexpectedly given the chance (when the palace guard make him Emperor) to reinflect today in terms of yesterday, literally to make history come alive. The book's measured, digressive manner is Claudius's own style; its vision of events seems to be Claudius's own—until we remember that it is actually just as invented as he is, that apart from the coincidence of names and places, none of what Graves tells us may have any similarity at all with Roman history, as it was actually lived.

In *Claudius the God*, the method is the same but the effect is different. In this book Claudius moves centre stage, and recounts his reign. He tells us of verbal skirmishes in the Senate, of real wars in the Middle East and Britain, of enlightened social legislation, and about his private life (in which he is cuckolded by a beloved, younger wife). He ceases to be commentator and becomes protagonist—and the risk is tedium, a catalogue as dull as the man who makes it. Ancient historians claim that Claudius was as bloodthirsty an emperor, as arbitrary, as any of his predecessors. In *Claudius the God*, he is given the chance to justify every action, to present one side of every story. The stories, individually, are as lively and as far-fetched as any in *I, Claudius*, but lack of contrast makes them seem less true. Given the subject-matter of the two books—the implausible mayhem of *I, Claudius* and the enlightened rationality of *Claudius the God*—this is remarkable, perhaps the final irony in a work whose energy depends, from first page to last, on paradox.

—Kenneth McLeish

I HID MY LOVE.
Poem by John Clare, written late 1840's.

John Clare's unique work is still being brought to light, edited, newly valued, and to find a single representative poem, one that contains all the particular aspects of his poetry, seems scarcely possible. A small group of poems might suggest his range and quality: these could include "It Is the Evening Hour," with its delicate easy metre, perhaps the most perfect of all the "Mary" poems; the autumnal and haunting "Now Is Past," which pursues the *now* in time; the awesome "An Invite to Eternity," a brief poem of echoing greatness; "Clock-a-Clay" for its summer lightness and detail. The moving prose account of Clare's foot journey from the Essex asylum to his Northampton home must be read too. And one other poem should join the list—"I Hid My Love," which, for a number of reasons, seems as fair a choice for a single piece as any.

The early rural nature writings are essential Clare, but they do not tell of Clare's whole life story, his special journey of the mind. Certain recurring themes belong to his extraordinary later work, and something of each, and all, can be found in "I Hid My Love." Nature remains an intrinsic part of fact and vision, seen, as always, not in terms of landscape and distance but in the details of leaves and grasses, insects, stones, the dew on a flower. Increasingly, though, these things reflect or become intensified with his joy or grief. There is his obsessional love for the dream-girl Mary (long dead, whether or not he knew it), always near, always far, never quite attained, even in poetry. There is his perception of time, stilled or racing and urgent. And almost always too, however strange or "mad" the poem, we find him knowing his own predicament, never ceasing to search for his own identity.

In the opening verse of "I Hid My Love," with its whispered rush straight into the secret that he must tell but cannot share, the familiar is not yet menacing, though it is seen and felt with the heightened sensibility, the disturbing intensity of focus that—quite brilliantly—marks the poem. Memory is still the link with and separation from a reality that must not meet his inward gaze—for is it true reality? Nature is still his ally and consoler—but an image too of the dream-girl herself. "Where e'er I saw a wild flower lye / I kissed and bade my love goodbye."

In the central verse the tempo changes. Clare enters a charmed dream-memory (a woodland scene) and a calm replaces the uneasy air of verse one. The bee (always looked on fondly) is a thing of kindness ("The bee kissed, and went singing by"); the dream-love, no longer lost, is part of nature itself, magically held in time. (See the mysterious line "She lay there all the summer long": an image of sleep or death?) While nature seems to share his secret, he is free.

But in the third and final verse, the "greenwood dells" give way to the rough human world of "field and town." The sereneness and ecstasy are no more. The light breeze can "knock him down"; the fly's buzz seems "A lion's roar." Disturbingly, the bee sings ballads (songs of sadness, violence, lost love, death?)—loudness is everywhere. Silence itself "Has found a tongue / To haunt me all the summer long." Now even nature cannot free him from the bond, the riddle to which he alone knows the answer.

"I Hid My Love" was one of the many poems written in the Northampton Asylum, where Clare lived from 1841 to his death (at 70) in 1864. It was a civilised place, giving him plenty of freedom. By great good fortune, the house steward, W.F. Knight, who came in 1845, took an interest in his unusual charge, provided him with paper, and collected each day's writing. These poems, Knight explained, he "faithfully transcribed from pencil originals which were so obliterated that without referring to the Author I could not decipher. Some pieces will be found unfinished, for Clare will seldom turn his attention to pieces he has been interrupted in while writing—and in no instance has he ever rewritten an single line."

Among Knight's transcripts is the poem "I Hid My Love." Though it is not dated, its quality and the fact that it is complete suggest that it belongs to the earlier years at Northampton, the middle or later 1840's, a time for Clare of high inspiration. His verses were to grow more and more fragmentary with time. A curious echo of the poem in our own century might be worth noting; it almost certainly inspired the familiar anthology piece "Lost Love" by Robert Graves. "Lost Love" runs to the same metre, describes the same intensified perception. The lover's eyes "are quickened so with grief / That he can watch a grass or leaf / Every instant grow." He hears "the clashing jaws of moth / Chumble holes in cloth"; "the maggot's weak / Clamour rings in his sad ear," as, without relief, he seeks lost love. Graves's poem is without Clare's Blakelike depth ("I Hid My Love" offers more on each re-reading); it is a tribute none the less. Graves did indeed read Clare. "I find myself repeating whole poems of Clare's," he wrote in 1955, "without having made an effort to memorize them. And though it was taken as a symptom of madness, that one day he [Clare] confided in a visitor, I know Gray—I know him well,' I shall risk saying here with equal affection, I know Clare—I know him well. We have often wept together."

—Naomi Lewis

THE IDLER. See **THE RAMBLER.**

IDYLLS OF THE KING.
Poems by Alfred, Lord Tennyson, from 1859.

Alfred, Lord Tennyson's fascination with the Arthurian cycle of Malory was life-long. The first draft of "Morte d'Arthur," eventually published in 1842, dates from the end of 1833 when he heard the news of Arthur Hallam's death; and the poet was still revising some of the later idylls shortly before his own death in 1892.

Malory is a diffuse and repetitive writer, and it was natural for Tennyson to select and simplify. But one alteration to Malory's narrative was particularly significant. In Malory, Mordred, the traitor and destroyer of the fellowship of the Round Table was Arthur's son, born of incest with his sister. Tennyson, influenced possibly by the accident that the king's name was the same as his beloved friend's makes Arthur wholly pure, surrounded with a complex symbolism of light, and at some points, almost a Christ-figure. Some critics, of whom Swinburne was the most vehement, have complained that this change spoils the balance of the story. Certainly, in "Guinevere" (1859), there is a disturbing double vision; on the one hand, Arthur, in terms of the actual story is the deceived husband forgiving the now repentant wife. But the source, and the emotional feeling of the scene, seems to be derived from the scene in John's gospel, where Christ forgives the woman taken in adultery. Obviously, the two views are not compatible.

The single theme which links all the stories together is the fragility of civilization. The barbarism and confusion which follow the collapse of Rome, "the slowly fading mistress of the world," gradually give way to the brief period of Arthur's rule and the loyalties of the Round Table. But these are soon under threat, and in the last idylls, "The Last Tournament" and "The Passing of Arthur" (which incorporates material from the early "Morte d'Arthur"), the city is destroyed, replaced by a bleak and terrible desert landscape, Lyonesse is about "to sink into the abyss again," and Mordred is killed by Arthur, having accomplished the destruction he sought. The very last line: "And the new sun arose bringing the new year" suggests a cyclical movement of time and the possible restoration of civilization in another form.

Order is always under threat, not only from treacherous enemies, but from the inner weakness both of men and women as persons and of their institutions. The knightly code itself, which is the metaphor for all loyalty, honour, patriotism, and responsible citizenship is productive of anger and violence, as is well shown in the mortal combat of the two brothers Balin and Balan. Whether we think of them as rivals or as symbolic representatives of the warfare of the inner self with itself, the scene in which they lie together dead, reconciled only when mortally wounded, is a visible emblem of the failure of peace and order.

Love is a wayward and destructive passion. The adultery of Lancelot and Guinevere is the original flaw in the system, which causes honour and dishonour to be inextricably intertwined, leading to lies, deceptions, and disillusionment. Elaine's love for Lancelot is chaste, but hopeless and destructive. The two are brought together in a remarkable scene ("Lancelot and Elaine" 1225 ff), when Guinevere petulantly hurls the precious jewels presented by Lancelot into the river, where they fall beside the barge which is carrying the dead Elaine to her burial. The adultery of Tristram and Isolt is ended by the treacherous blow from behind, struck by Isolt's royal husband, Mark, whose cry "Mark's Way" forms the only two words spoken by him in the entire cycle. Pelleas begins as the extreme idealist of love, believing both in the purity of Guinevere and in that of his own love, Ettarre. His disillusionment is correspondingly extreme ("Why then let men couple at once with wolves"). He becomes the Red Knight, the leader of a group at once hostile to the Round Table and a deliberate parody of it, where the men welcome dishonour and the women boast of being harlots.

A threat of an entirely different kind to the Round Table is presented by the Holy Grail. It is not suggested that the vision of it is illusory, only that the quest is beyond the strength of most who attempt it; and the search for the spiritual life on the part of those who are too weak-willed for it disrupts the social order, and corrupts those who mistakenly attempted it.

The poem's visionary landscapes both show forth the brittle unreliability of things, and enable Tennyson to compensate for his comparative weakness of dramatic representation. For a landscape may become a subtle equivalent of the mood and feeling of persons. So the long temptation of Merlin by Vivien is imaged in the breathless heat and its climax of success in the ensuing violent storm. The threatening, constantly changing and magical landscape of "The Holy Grail" represents the solitary inward suffering of the bewildered quester.

Some contemporary readers, such as Ruskin and Hopkins, were sceptical of Tennyson's apparent escape from his own time into the Middle Ages. But Tennyson's genius was not well-suited to dealing with the topical. He preferred to approach the problems of the 19th century, and his own pessimism about the prospects for the 20th by indirection. The nature of the threats to Camelot is so general, and so deeply embedded in the nature of the world and of the race that he cannot be fairly charged with evading the troubles and dangers of his own time. The blank verse in which all but a few short lyric passages are written is a finely modulated instrument, which can move easily from the comparatively pedestrian to a high eloquence or memorable aphoristic wisdom.

—A.O.J. Cockshut

IMAGINARY CONVERSATIONS.
Prose by Walter Savage Landor, 1824–29 and 1853.

The personality and style, the inaccessibility but rewarding uniqueness of Walter Savage Landor are all evidenced in this much-quoted extract from a letter to his early biographer John Foster: "I shall have as many readers as I desire to have in other times than ours. I shall dine late; but the dining-room will be well-lighted, guests few and select. I neither am, nor ever shall be, popular. Such never was my ambition."

The prediction was accurate. This larger-than-life, energetically obstinate egoist, as quick to kindness as to anger, was and is more admired than read. He is often obscure, blinkered, and irritating; but there are wisdom and beauty, and what can only be described as a presence, in both the poetry and the prose that cannot be ignored. *Imaginary Conversations* is the bulk of the prose.

Some of the unpopularity of *Imaginary Conversations* can be attributed to their continual onslaught on complacency. The essayist William Hazlitt, a younger contemporary, pointed out that the English are certainly "the most uncomfortable of all people in themselves and glance askant at the disturber of their peace." Landor had a moral purpose that would not be deflected by conventional standards, rarely even by reality, a purpose most lucidly expressed in the conversation "Florentine, English visitor and Landor":

> If men were to be represented as they show themselves, encrusted with all the dirtiness they contract in public life, in all the debility of ignorance, in all the distortion of prejudice, in all the reptile trickery of partisanship, who would care about the greater part of what are called the greatest? Principles and ideals are my objects: they must be reflected from high and low, but they must also be exhibited where people can see them best, and are most inclined to look at them.

Such stringent, and at the same time egocentric, measures make Landor unsympathetic, not to say prejudiced in his attitudes to, for example, Plato, Dante (comparing him unfavourably with classical writers), Byron, and the Roman Catholic church. Against this must be weighed the noble phrases he gives Cicero to espouse his philosophy:

> Everything has its use: life to teach us the contempt of death and death the contempt of life. Glory, which among all things between stands eminently the principal, although it has been considered by some philosophers as mere vanity and deception, moves those great intellects which nothing else could have stirred, and places them where they can and most advantageously serve the Commonwealth. Glory can safely be despised by those only who have fairly won it: a low, ignorant, or vicious man should dispute on other topics.

The above excerpts can only serve as hints; *Imaginary Conversations* needs to be appreciated in detail, since it is its resistance to classification that has dampened the enthusiasm of eminent critics, from Hazlitt and Leslie Stephen at the time, to F.R. Leavis and others of the 20th century, and daunted prospective readers.

The conversations were built on Landor's profound knowledge of the classics, and the reader is assumed to have a considerable familiarity with Greek and Roman literature, art, philosophy, and mythology. They are a mixture of personal essays, satires on contemporary ideas and customs, and dramatisations of ideologies through historical characters. Although Landor's voice is unmistakable throughout, some of the conversations are more dramatic, in the sense that Landor reconstructs his characters' minds first before embracing them with his own; in other pieces his characters are puppets; and in some he switches from drama to discursive essay and back again.

The characters are from classical times to the 19th century, and among those usually identified as the most successful are the following (volume indicated): Aesop and Rhodope (I); Louis XIV and Père La Chaise (II); Fra Filippo Lippi and Pope Eugenius IV (II); Romilly and Wilberforce (III); Melanchthon and Calvin (IV); La Fontaine and La Rochefoucauld (IV); Leofric and Lady Godiva (V). Several commentators have considered the classical ones as being the best; frequently singled out are Marcus Tullius and Quintus Cicero (II), Alfieri and Saloman the Florentine Jew (IV), and Diogenes and Plato (I).

Landor is effective as a literary critic, although too inconsistent and unsympathetic for modern tastes. It is necessary to have in mind Professor Proudfoot's dictum—Landor "does not merely read books, he lives them." The insights are worth patient harvesting; the most memorable being those where he makes functional use of imagery. Here is Boccaccio, with Landor's voice, describing the critic's job, in *The Pentameron*. "He walks in a garden which is not his own; and he must neither gather the blossoms to embellish his discourse, nor break the branches to display his strength . . . "

A key tenet in Landor's conversations between literary men is that to be lapidary is not necessarily to be devoid of feeling. Enough has been quoted to indicate Landor in this mode, most notably in the ceremonious epigrams of Cicero's little speech. Characteristically, Landor is marmoreal even when (in the shape of Boccaccio) he is advising Petrarch to be plain: "In the loftiest rooms and richest entablatures are suspended the most spider-webs; and the quarry out of which palaces are erected is the nursery of the nettle and the bramble." When he is at his best, Landor's striking epigrams are the product of strong feeling; he has been claimed as an inspiration by several great writers of recent times, including Yeats, Pound, and Eliot.

—Brendan Hennessy

THE IMPORTANCE OF BEING EARNEST.
Play by Oscar Wilde, 1895.

The Importance of Being Earnest, Oscar Wilde's last and finest comedy, opened at the St. James Theatre, London, on 14 February 1895. Avoiding the melodrama and sentiment of Wilde's three earlier fashionable dramas, it is even more artificial than any Restoration comedy of manners among those that staked out the genre. The subtitle of the published version, *A Trivial Comedy for Serious People*, points in several directions. "Serious" and "Earnest" carry different levels of punning ambiguity for different segments of the audience. After enjoying, for three acts, paradoxes of the sort that the Savoy operas of Gilbert and Sullivan had made popular, readers might find ungrateful Wilde's stage direction to "whistle some dreadful popular air from a British Opera." Cigarettes are so prominent in the text that in 1956 the New York Public Library could draw upon its Arents Tobacco Collection to publish manuscripts and typescripts of a four-act version shortened in 1895 for performance.

The opening scene establishes an epigrammatic manner and the aesthetic reversal of Victorian values. The servant Lane, who did not think it polite to listen when his master played the piano, answers the charge that he consumed his employer's champagne: though he was married only once and then in consequence of a misunderstanding, he knows that a bachelor's champagne is better than that in a household demoralised by marriage. The employer remarks that the lower classes are of no use unless they set a good moral example. The servant's name refers, typically, to Wilde's publisher, John Lane.

The play's two sparring couples are by definition young, attractive, well-off, and idle. John Worthing, who is in London to propose to the Honourable Gwendolen Fairfax, is known to his friend Algernon Moncrieff as Ernest. Algernon's recovery of a cigarette case inscribed by "Cecily" to "Jack" forces John to admit that the name Ernest is one he assumes in town; in the country, where his ward Cecily Cardew lives with a governess, Miss Prism, he is Jack. He prevaricates to shield Cecily from acquaintance with the gluttonous Algernon. Throughout the play, Algernon emblematically consumes sandwiches and muffins laid out for other guests. Algernon's name for duplicity is Bunburying: to avoid dreary appointments, for example with Lady Bracknell (his aunt and Gwendolen's mother), he has invented Bunbury as an invalid in the country whom he must attend in emergencies.

Edith Evans made the high point of Act I her own in several stage productions, a film of 1952, and a recording. Simultaneously heartless and convincing as a concerned mother, Lady Bracknell catechizes Jack to determine his fitness for marriage to Gwendolen. Her comments on his responses are a stream of Wildean epigrams. She is glad he smokes, for a man should have an occupation of some kind. She is glad that nothing has tampered with his natural ignorance. She is sorry to hear that his house in town, essential for an unspoiled girl like Gwendolen, is on the unfashionable side of Belgrave Square. When she learns that he is an orphan found in a handbag at Victoria Station by the late Mr. Cardew, who named him Worthing for a trivial reason typical of the play, Lady Bracknell rejects him explosively: to lose both parents looks like carelessness.

Act II opens with Cecily telling Miss Prism how she wishes that her very serious guardian would allow his wicked brother Ernest to visit so that Miss Prism might have a good influence over him. After an interlude wherein Prism, author of a three-volume novel, reveals her designs on the dull-witted Canon Chasuble, Algernon arrives, claiming to be Ernest Worthing. With Algernon off-stage, Jack enters dressed in black, which he explains as mourning for his late brother Ernest. As Cecily repeats unyieldingly what Gwendolen had declared in Act I, an unwillingness to marry any man not named Ernest, the two young men separately seek to be christened Ernest by Dr. Chasuble. Through several reversals of situation, dialogue that dramatically distinguishes the over-protected Cecily from the urbane Gwendolen also reveals their kinship in the skills of avoiding personal discomfiture.

In a scene in manuscript, later dropped, Algernon is arrested for debt. The remaining Act III fits neatly into place every character, every detail only seemingly incidental, and every paradox of the plot. Cecily has a sufficient income to marry Algernon, and admiration for his sacrificial willingness to be christened. Bunbury, "found out" as fatally ill, has gone the way of Jack's "brother." Jack is discovered to be in fact Algernon's older brother, christened as Ernest and (instead of her novel) thrust absent-mindedly into the handbag by Miss Prism. Jack is at once elated and humiliated to discover that he has spoken truth all along: he was named Ernest and had a brother. The delicate amalgam of artificial comedy, parody of melodramatic Victorian drama, glancing social satire, and farce has shown the unimportance of being earnest —except for the few insiders who knew homosexuality as "love in earnest"—and has demonstrated the corollary success of triviality. When played as pure aesthetic form, the piece is highly theatrical and full of characters believably motivated.

H.G. Wells called it "good nonsense, excellent fooling"; Harold Child praised the triumph of a "fantastic, irresponsible world." George Alexander, manager of the St. James Theatre, removed the playwright's name from the hoardings when Wilde was arrested for acts of gross indecency with other male persons, and he suppressed Wilde's name again in 1901, but after a lucrative production in 1909 (the second of Alexander's four revivals) he continued to flourish in the role of Jack and issued a souvenir edition of "dear *E*" in the format of Wilde's collected works.

—Carl Woodring

IN MEMORIAM.
Poem by Alfred, Lord Tennyson, 1850.

When Alfred, Lord Tennyson was ennobled for his poetry it was because he had become the poet of his times. His representative position, and his peerage, both seem to have derived from *In Memoriam*, his great elegy for his friend and fellow-student Arthur Henry Hallam who died in 1833. In the 1830's Tennyson's position was that of a lyric poet much under the influence of the work of Keats, but in the 17 years that elapsed between Hallam's death and the publication of his extended lament Tennyson matured into his own style. In the lyrics that make up *In Memoriam* he found his own poetic voice properly for the first time.

Typically for the High Victorian era that was to follow it, the themes of the poem are death and doubt. The first of these was always popular with the Victorians who invented a complexity of mourning and a style of funerary art that can seem exaggerated to a later generation. The second theme, doubt, is profoundly connected in the poem to the new evolutionary explanation of the universe that was emerging in the 1840's and 1850's; this did not find its full expression until the publication of Darwin's *On the Origin of Species* in 1859 but it was "in the air" around Tennyson at Cambridge and elsewhere much earlier than that.

Tennyson had a difficult engagement to his future wife, Emily Sellwood, during the years of composition of the poem and it appears that he needed, finally, to convince her that his Christian faith was sound before she would agree to marry him. With this in view he sent her a privately-printed version of *In Memoriam*, to which he had recently added the prologue, some months before its official publication. Astonishingly, it convinced her that her fiancé was indeed a Christian.

Perhaps the prologue goes some way towards explaining this. With its addition the poem at least opens with a direct invocation of Christ: "Strong Son of God, Immortal Love." But a careful reading of the rest of the poem reveals more of doubt than of faith while much of the prologue itself shows anxiety about religious faith. Having invoked Christ it continues: "Whom we, that have not seen thy face, / By faith and faith alone embrace. / Believing where we cannot prove, . . ." The emphasis is on the reasons to doubt rather than on the reasons to believe, and this tone remains dominant:

> Thine are these orbs of light and shade;
>   Thou madest Life in man and brute;
>   Thou madest Death and lo, Thy foot
> Is on the skull which thou hast made.
>
> Thou wilt not leave us in the dust:
>   Thou madest man, he knows not why,
>   He thinks he was not made to die;
> And Thou hast made him: Thou art just.

This is not merely elegiac gloom (the mourning was long since over by the time Tennyson wrote the prologue) it is a species of pessimism about metaphysical matters that gives us the clue to much of the rest of the poem. For although God officially exists in these quatrains, there is a despairing tendency to question his relationship to man that amounts to serious doubt. God made light, yes, but also shade; life but also death, his foot is on man's *skull*, significantly. Man comes to dust and yet we trust that somehow God will bring him back to life. Those words "trust" and "somehow" are repeated in the poem on several occasions, always stressing the uncertain nature of good ("Oh yet we trust that somehow good / Will be the final goal of ill," "Yet if some voice that man could trust / Should murmur from the narrow house" and so on); along with words such as "Yet" and "But" they offer a key to the poem.

The doubt comes from the fact of death. Tennyson said that he would despair if he ever came truly to doubt God or Immortality, yet Hallam's death and the anguished question as to where Hallam now was and whether they would meet again put an immense strain on these beliefs. Death in *In Memoriam* "keeps the keys of all the creeds" for only after death will the truth be revealed, though it may be the truth that all religion is untrue.

The poem's lyrics are separate from one another and most of them can be read as units more or less successfully; a lyric such as "I envy not in any moods" (no.27) could be anthologised separately without huge loss. But undoubtedly the poem works best as a whole. It has a vague structure, passing through three years of mourning, showing us three Christmases and moving towards some sort of (very tentative) resolution. Above all, its emotional register pervades all its constituent parts which would therefore lose something if cut off from it. When evolution is the topic (in lyrics 54–56 for instance) we are still aware that it is personal grief that has provoked these thoughts and that it is not only the answer to life's mysteries that is "Behind the veil, behind the veil" but the whereabouts of Tennyson's friend too. A good comparison in this respect would be Shakespeare's sonnets which can be read separately but which are nonetheless a sequence.

Lyric 48, in which Tennyson describes his own method in the poem, asks us not to take his "short swallow-flights of song" too seriously as intellectual arguments; the "slender shade of doubt," he protests, has become "vassal unto love." But this is nonetheless the great poem of Victorian doubt as the poet himself recognises when he proclaims, in an astute move, that "There lives more faith in honest doubt, Believe me, than in half the creeds." *In Memoriam* is a great elegy, a great poem of doubt, and an excellent picture of the early Victorian frame of mind. It is also characterised by an extraordinary euphony and a masterly use of the rhythms of English.

—Lance St. John Butler

INTIMATIONS OF IMMORTALITY FROM RECOLLECTIONS OF EARLY CHILDHOOD.
Poem by William Wordsworth, 1807.

William Wordsworth's "Intimations of Immortality from Recollections of Early Childhood," begun in 1802, first published in 1807, is his greatest and most talked-about lyric, and one of the high points of English literature. It has propagated for millions a reverence for childhood. For good or ill, it remains a major romantic assertion of imagination as creative awareness vital to individual growth.

Its honorific title, "Ode," lays claim to complexity in lyric utterance, exalted exclamation, and rapid transitions of tone; it points to variation in metrics, line-length, and length of stanzas, characteristics descended from Pindar by way of the irregularity of Abraham Cowley and justified by the romantic claim that thought and feeling organically determine form. The control of sound is masterly throughout. Its title summarises an argument deducible from the poem that a child's sense of unlimited, indestructible glory can return in flickering moments to the adult.

The ode begins on a May morning when the joyous singing of birds and bounding of lambs reminds the speaker of the poem of his childhood. Present joy pales in memory of the glory felt in childhood, when there were no objects because no objectivity, no distinction between I and it, nothing between I and there. Whether a bird actually sings from joy is irrelevant; early stanzas of the ode treat consciousness as sovereign. Successive stanzas increase the uncertainties of relationship among self-awareness, consciousness of other, reports of the senses, and intimations of the infinite.

The first four stanzas ask where the child's sense of glory has gone. In the continuations between June 1802 and 1807, stanzas V–VIII offer a dark view of growing up; the final stanzas, IX–XI, peer less somberly into the dimmed light of maturity. Poetically rather than theologically, stanza V proposes that a child remembers its heavenly pre-existence.

Ways of seeing are explored, not by logic, but by associations and transitions of feeling, expressed in metaphors of astonishing power. The cascade of metaphors continues to fascinate after long familiarity. Clouds of glory trailing from the infant are shaded and eclipsed as the prison-house of objectivity restricts the joy of existence. Like sacred moonlight to a priest, the child sees its vision "fade into the light of common day." In stanza VI, drawing upon pastoral romances of the Renaissance that invert the adoption of Moses by Pharaoh's daughter, the infant is a prince of God found and raised as a foster-child by Mother Earth, a homely nurse who claims him as her own. The ode gives a further turn to the proverbial blind leading the blind: adults, blinded by objective separation of self from other, lead the visionary child into blindness. Thus custom like unceasing winter buries the life of the child under an irremovable frost.

In the stanzas celebrating partial recovery, adults are embers in which the fire of divinity occasionally flickers. Eternal Silence sometimes penetrates the noise of mundane life. The being that has drifted far inland from its oceanic origin has intimations of oceanic oneness—as if the ocean-born in inland exile carried a conch-shell and listened to its intimations of the beckoning sea. Engaged in adult games, we can return through imagination to the real life of children sporting on the shore. With such consolation, the speaker of the poem can hear the birds of May sing and can watch the lambs bound, not without exclamatory envy, but without destructive regret for what is lost. Despite irreversible, objectifying maturity, the "philosophic mind" (calm though aware of loss) can, through love of brooks, clouds, meadows, and the meanest flower, endure.

Critics who have lamented Wordsworth's prolonged "decline" from the exalted faith of this ode, and other critics as well, have regretted among the rapid transitions of tone the humor of the stanza on the imperial prince raised by the ignorant shepherdess Earth, proud of her larder. They have rejected yet more insistently the satire of the stanza that follows, which treats worldly parents of a later age as descendants of the complacent nurse. Husband and wife fondly regard the child trailing glory as their pygmy-sized creation playing store. He learns the adult games of business, getting and burying with artful ceremony, competition, and war as he rehearses for the stages of life defined by Shakespeare's Jaques. He is an ordinary version of the extraordinary Master Betty, who was enacting Romeo and Hamlet in 1803–04, when not yet 15, on the stages of major theatres from Belfast to London.

If it was captious of Coleridge to ask how an ignorant child could be "best Philosopher," the ode is full of phrases inviting conjecture: the "timely utterance" that brought relief; the Virgilian-sounding winds that "come to me from the fields of sleep"; the "Tree, of many, one"; the Immortality that broods like day over the child, a master over a slave; and the concluding "Thoughts that do often lie too deep for tears." Other memorable and widely remembered phrases give lyric embodiment to the essences that unify the vaulting stanzas: light, silence, fresh flowers, rolling and flowing waters, the creative potential of creatures.

—Carl Woodring

IOLANTHE.
Opera by W.S. Gilbert, music by Arthur Sullivan, 1882.

The seventh light opera on which W.S. Gilbert and Arthur Sullivan collaborated, *Iolanthe*, or *The Peer and the Peri*, was the first to have its premiere (25 November 1882) in the Savoy Theatre, recently built by Richard D'Oyly Carte, their impresario, to house their works. Having satirized and / or parodied a court of law, the army, navy, melodrama, and the Aesthetic Movement, Gilbert now turned his wit upon the British political system and combined it with a parody of Victorian fairy plays.

Some quarter of a century before the opera begins, Iolanthe, a fairy, has broken fairy law by marrying a mortal. She has been banished and has had a half-mortal son, Strephon, now an Arcadian shepherd. Her human husband believes her dead; he himself has risen from barrister to Lord

Chancellor and is attracted by one of the wards in Chancery, Phyllis, a shepherdess, who is engaged to Strephon. They are to be married on the day when the action opens, although they do not have the Lord Chancellor's permission.

At the beginning of act one, the Queen of the Fairies pardons Iolanthe and promises to help Strephon whenever he is "in doubt or danger, / Peril or perplexitee. . . ." The House of Lords enters in procession and full coronation regalia to beg Phyllis to marry one of them. They are led by Lord Mountararat and Lord Tolloller, who try to convince her that peers are as virtuous as the lower classes.

Phyllis rejects their offers, but the Lord Chancellor refuses to let her marry Strephon. When Iolanthe appears to comfort her son, the eavesdropping peers convince Phyllis that Iolanthe is Strephon's inamorata—an easy mistake since fairies never look older than 17, a situation Gilbert had exploited in "The Fairy Curate" (*Fun*, 1870). Angrily, Phyllis engages herself to Lord Tolloller and Lord Mountararat simultaneously. Strephon calls the fairies to his aid, and they enter "Tripping hither, tripping thither" in a parody of pantomime fairies. The Lords refuse the Queen's explanation, and the Lord Chancellor infuriates her by taking her for the proprietor of a ladies' seminary.

To punish these presumptuous mortals, the Queen announces that Strephon will enter Parliament from one of her "pocket boroughs" and that both Lords and Commons will be forced to pass all his bills and measures. Among other reforms Lords will be chosen by competitive examination. Triumphant peris and horrified peers defy each other in the first act finale, the longest Sullivan ever composed.

Act two takes place by moonlight in Palace Yard, Westminster, with the Houses of Parliament in the background, a set praised by reviewers for its "rare fidelity." Here a lonely sentry, Private Willis of the Grenadier Guards, muses over government. He thinks it comical that every child at birth "Is / either a little Liberal, / Or else a little Conservative!" He also observes that if members of Parliament have brains, "They've got to leave that brain outside, / And vote just as their leaders tell 'em to."

The fairies arrive, only to be chidden by Lords Mountararat and Tolloller for magically influencing votes to support Strephon's parliamentary reform measures. The fairies are attracted to the peers, and their Queen herself admits that if it were not forbidden by fairy law, she would worship Private Willis. Mountararat and Tolloller now press Phyllis to choose between them, but she refuses, saying that they are both equally rich and both equally plain. This almost provokes a duel, but the lords decide that love is not worth being killed for and resume their friendship, leaving Phyllis free to return to Strephon. He explains that his mother is a fairy, and they decide to get married immediately and change their minds afterward in "the usual way." The Lord Chancellor, however, has finally convinced himself to give his own consent to his own marriage with Phyllis—a leading example of Gilbert's use of a plurality character, i.e., one character with multiple, mutually exclusive functions which contradict, support, or contrast with each other.

The young lovers beg Iolanthe to go to the Lord Chancellor on their behalf. Veiled, she pleads unavailing, disclosing her identity only as a last resort. The *Era* called this scene "really exquisite" in melody. In one of Gilbert's few poignant moments, the Chancellor recognises his wife, and she prepares for death, having broken the fairy law a second time. But as the Queen raises her spear, all the fairies and peers rush in to say they have all married each other. The Queen hesitates, and the Lord Chancellor suggests a "legal" solution: add a negative so that the law becomes its opposite and every fairy must die who does *not* marry a mortal. To save her own life the Queen proposes to Private Willis. Wings spring from the mortals' shoulders, and they all fly away to fairyland "up in the air, sky-high, sky-high. . . . "

In thus integrating the political and the supernatural, Gilbert used as a basis the 19th century "fairy love" plot exemplified in such works as Andersen's "The Little Mermaid", La Motte Fouqué's *Undine*, and Bellini's *Norma* (where the fairy is a Druidess). In 1869, Gilbert had written a burlesque of the last work, called *The Pretty Druidess*, but in it and *Iolanthe* he changed the usual tragic ending by a solution satirizing both law and logic—a favourite kind of Gilbertian resolution. He also treated Strephon's dual nature with strict but impossible logic. As this half-fairy/half-mortal says, "My body can creep through a keyhole, but what's the good of that when my legs are left kicking behind? I can make myself invisible down to the waist, but that's of no use when my legs remain exposed to view!" Other clichés of fairy-lore are caricatured in the tall, robust Queen of the Fairies, who says Iolanthe taught her "to curl myself inside a buttercup . . . to swing upon a cobweb . . . to dive into a dewdrop. . . ." This Queen was originally costumed as Brünnhilde, and Sullivan underscored Gilbert's visual parody by introducing delicately Wagnerian echoes, including the Rhine Maidens' song.

Gilbert's political satire evident in the above synopsis is still comic after more than a hundred years, but it was much sharper on the opening night of *Iolanthe* when the performance included two songs soon deleted to shorten act two. In one, Mountararat describes a universal genius De Belville, unrewarded until his uncle dies and leaves him a seat in Parliament and a fortune. Then his merit is acknowledged by taking him from the Commons, where his abilities would be useful, and putting him in the Lords, where his talents will have no scope. The other song, "Fold your flapping wings," is sung by Strephon, who attacks Parliament's lack of social concern and repeats one of Gilbert's favourite serious themes, that is, that environment makes the drunkard and thief. William Beatty-Kingston, the *Theatre*'s reviewer, objected strongly to this number as being out of place in a comic opera and to Gilbert's politics as "bitterly aggressive." Other critics were not so offended.

Although it has never attained the great popularity of the more ebullient *H.M.S. Pinafore* and the more tightly plotted and happier *Mikado*, *Iolanthe* is probably Gilbert's best libretto, its satire still applicable. Gilbert's metrical dexterity and ingenious rhymes, moreover, are at their height here, in such numbers as the Lord Chancellor's Nightmare Song ("When you're lying awake with a dismal headache"), in the linguistic competition of the Lords and fairies in the first act finale, and in such lines as "I wouldn't say a word that could be reckoned as injurious, / But to find a mother younger than her son is very curious, / And that's the kind of mother that is usually spurious. . . ." The onomatopoeia of the peers' entering chorus, "Loudly let the trumpet bray," emphasized by Sullivan's orchestration, contrasts with the pastoral lyrics of Strephon and Phyllis to whom Gilbert also gave a duet filled with literary "conceits": "Thou the tree and I the flower— / Thou the idol, I the throng— / Thou the day and I the hour— / Thou the singer, I the song!"

The librettist was also his own stage director and controlled the visual aspects of the opera from the costumes to the exact shade of moonlight in act two. An enchanting innovation was the use of the electric stars worn in the fairies' hair in this act. *Iolanthe* ran for 398 performances, and has been revived regularly.

—Jane W. Stedman

J

JANE EYRE.
Novel by Charlotte Brontë, 1847.

Similarities between *Jane Eyre* and fairy-tale have often been noted, and on a very simple plot level the influence is obvious. We should thus not be too worried by the magical coincidences which allow the heroine to gain her ends so spectacularly. An element of wish-fulfilment in the story appealed to Victorian readers and still appeals, helping this to become one of the most universally popular novels in English. The fairy-tale elements do not end with the plot, however, and are exploited throughout the novel. Jane, whose surname is *Eyre*, is compared by Rochester to an elf. It is clear that in Charlotte Brontë's terms the feminine "spiritual" element is civilising the unprepossessing masculine one, guarding and taming him until he is fit for union with her. Jane, however, is no conventionally pretty young woman. Her creator linked Jane with herself and according to Elizabeth Gaskell told her sisters, "I will show you a heroine as plain and small as myself, who shall be as interesting as any of yours."

A psychoanalytic view of the book might see the masculine psyche split between the immoral but good-hearted Rochester and the rule-bound pair Mr. Brocklehurst and St. John Rivers. The latter presents himself to Jane's sense of duty, and she is seriously inclined to marry him, until an incorporeal voice (that of Rochester communicating through telepathy) challenges her choice and recalls her to her deeper emotional commitment. The fiery aspects of the feminine are locked by Rochester in the attic at Thornfield in the shape of his mad wife Bertha, who makes several efforts to reveal herself and is finally disclosed on the occasion of Jane's would-be marriage to her legal husband. It is not only duty which demands that Jane should leave the house. The author clearly intends us to notice that Rochester has failed to trust Jane as a fellow human; her refusal to stay should not be seen purely as an acceptance of Victorian convention.

The obvious gothic elements in *Jane Eyre* are used symbolically. Symbolism has also been detected in the names of the localities through which the heroine passes: Gateshead, Thornfield, etc. In connection with this, we may recall the Brontës' early attachment to *The Pilgrim's Progress*. Jane also shows some complex pictures to Rochester, which she has drawn herself and which evoke insoluble problems of her being. These deeply revealing sketches seem to echo actual pictures drawn by Charlotte Brontë her brother and sisters.

The search for originals in *Jane Eyre* became an industry soon after its publication. Thus Lowood was quickly discovered to represent Cowan Bridge school, where the author's two younger sisters had caught diseases from which they subsequently died. But Rochester has no original, though he may take some traits from M. Constantin Heger, the Belgian schoolmaster she met in 1842. His descent from the Byronic hero of the Brontës' childhood imaginations is clear. Though the Rivers sisters mirror to some extent in an idealised fashion the home personas of the Brontë sisters, they are not to be confused with the real Emily and Anne. Yet the improvement in Charlotte Brontë's writing when she sets her novels in England or Belgium, abandoning the imaginary worlds of her childhood, is obvious to anyone who has read through the juvenilia.

There are many elements of visual description in *Jane Eyre*, some showing acute observation, like the landscape of the road to Hay on the January day when Jane first meets Rochester. Bewick's woodcuts are not far from this scene. Bewick is also present in the very first scene where Jane is hiding from her cruel cousins. The author's short-sightedness meant that she studied landscape partly through Bewick and other engravers. The coldness of the winter scenes in Bewick emphasises the loneliness of some humans, and this chimes with the Brontës' interest in orphans and the tyranny of the adult world over the world of childhood. The scenes involving Mr. Brocklehurst, including those at Lowood, explore the nature of childhood resentment.

Brontë was able to use *Jane Eyre* as a critique of evangelical religion, which exerted some attraction for her own personality, but which she rejects here as heartless and mechanical, though the sense of duty exhibited by St. John Rivers is not disparaged. He is approved as a conscientious parson, but his inconclusive relationship with Rosamond is presented critically. The empty ritual of Bible reading at Lowood while Miss Scatcherd torments her victim provides a bleak image.

Jane Eyre was on the whole well received by the early critics, who noted its passion and warmth. The first-person narrative enabled them to come close to the life experience of the underprivileged heroine and sympathy was quickly established. It is possible to see the book as a feminist text, both in the sense that the female first person is the emotional centre of the story, and also since Rochester and the other male characters are shown as inadequate. He learns through suffering, but it is not clear whether St. John Rivers is capable of learning, and Brocklehurst is a stereotype. Subsidiary female characters, "good" or "bad," are generally more credible than the male, though Bertha Mason is seen externally: deviant, outraged, and menacing. *Jane Eyre* successfully raises the "woman question" high on the agenda, but it was perhaps more important still to the author to portray Jane as a champion of the human race, irrespective of gender. She clearly stands for the individual against a deforming society, a child rather than a girl only against harsh education, a servant rather than merely a governess against the bland superiority of the gentry, represented by Blanche Ingram, and sincerity against the blandishments of wealth which considers it can buy anything.

However, the traditional plot, in which an oppressed orphan magically but deservedly overcomes loneliness and finds a strong partner who is finally fit to be her equal is clearly a major reason for the success of the book. It stands, among other things, as the archetypal romance, by which many subsequent novels have been influenced. The character of Jane is imbued with so much life that generations of readers have believed in her as the real author of the book.

The genuinely popular nature of the novel at one time led critics to underestimate its artistry, but in recent years its importance has been readily acknowledged.

—Edward Chitham

JOSEPH ANDREWS.
(The History of the Adventures of Joseph Andrews and of His Friend Mr. Abraham Adams.)
Novel by Henry Fielding, 1742.

Joseph Andrews, Henry Fielding's first novel and the first great comic novel in English, came into being as the result of external "accidents," just as do most of the scenes in the novel. The first accident was that Fielding, the most influential playwright of the day, had been deprived of his profession when Walpole's government, stung by Fielding's fierce stage satires, passed the Licensing Act in 1737. Though Fielding proceeded to qualify as a lawyer and half-heartedly took up law practice in 1740, and though he edited the *Champion*, an opposition journal, from 1739 to 1740, he was at this point in his life at loose ends: a man with literary ability (not to mention an ailing wife and young children) who had yet to find his métier.

Then the second "accident" occurred. In November 1740, Samuel Richardson published *Pamela; or, Virtue Rewarded*, a novel in letters depicting the growing love and eventual marriage between a 16-year-old servant girl, Pamela Andrews, and her lustful master, Mr. B. *Pamela* was immensely successful. Fielding must have been outraged by the universal acclaim: within four months he wrote and published *Shamela*, a travesty applying the technique of *reductio ab absurdum* to *Pamela*'s smug morality and naive epistolary narration, and a year after that, in February 1742, he published *Joseph Andrews*, a second fictional response to *Pamela*. But whereas *Shamela* had been a brief demolition-job, *Joseph Andrews* is a full-length, carefully considered creation of another kind of novel from Richardson's. If Richardson's novel probed the inner experience of one or two characters, Fielding would survey the whole of his society; if Richardson made character primary, Fielding's imaginative centre is the comic concatenation of events (as arranged by Fortune/Providence/Art); if Richardson entrusted the narration to his characters and appeared himself only as the editor of their letters, Fielding steps forward as a shrewd, genial narrator, highlighting his own artifice. Fielding's first novel formulates a debate, and a dialectic, that would ever after define the possibilities of the novel form.

The novel's full title is revealing: *The History of the Adventures of Joseph Andrews and of His Friend Mr. Abraham Adams, Written in Imitation of the Manner of Cervantes, Author of Don Quixote*. The allusion to Cervantes suggests that what follows will be a comedy of the open road, told with selfconscious art. Even more significantly, the title points to a double focus. The novel will present the story of Joseph Andrews, Pamela's chaste young footman-brother, who will withstand the lascivious advances of his employer, Lady Booby, the aunt of Pamela's Mr. B. ("Booby" being, in Fielding's view, the full name concealed by Richardson's discreet initial), and win through to marriage with his true love, the milkmaid Fanny. But, the title suggests, this main plot is only half the story: the other half consists of one of the great comic figures of English literature, Parson Abraham Adams, the curate within Lady Booby's household and companion to Joseph and Fanny in their travels.

Of little importance in the plot, Adams is negligible to the superficial eye, and to most of the novel's characters. Impoverished, dependent on his social betters, bedraggled and unseemly in deportment, Homerically absentminded and guileless, he is ignorant of the actual world and knowledgeable only about the ideal world propounded in books. Yet, like Falstaff or the Wife of Bath, or indeed like Don Quixote, Adams is less a person than a force of nature, gifted with unfailing, superabundant energy, childlike directness and wholeness of feeling, and a moral heroism that becomes all the more dignified as his cassock grows all the more ragged. Capering about the room with joy, groaning with sorrow, quick to strike evildoers with his crabstick, unable to learn, or to pause, or to see his own wild inconsistencies, Adams, as his name suggests, is mythical in stature.

Adams was clearly a favourite of Fielding's: the last paragraph of Fielding's carefully argued preface to *Joseph Andrews* is devoted to Adams, whose character is called "the most glaring" in the novel and one "not to be found in any Book now extant." (Joseph, by contrast, goes unmentioned.) And in the last chapter of *Tom Jones*, Fielding's masterpiece, we learn Adams has been made tutor to the children of Tom Jones and Sophia Western. Adams has also been a favourite with the novel's readers. The poet William Shenstone, reading *Tom Jones* in 1749, said, "I see no Character that is near so striking as Mr. Abraham Adams. *That* was an *original*, I think; unattempted before, and yet so natural that most people seem'd to know the Man." And James Beattie, the Scottish poet and critic, described Adams in 1783 as "next to Don Quixote, the most ludicrous personage that ever appeared in romance."

Adams's ludicrousness has both satiric and comic dimensions. He is an ideal vehicle for satire, since, like Don Quixote, he expects the world he encounters to conform to the ideals he has imagined—only to find that landowners, judges, lawyers, doctors, innkeepers, even clergymen, even his own wife, all consider Christianity something that should be confined to Sunday church services.

And just as Cervantes's work begins as a satire upon farfetched romances and opens out into glorious comedy, Adams is even more important as a comic than as a satiric figure. Fielding's preface to *Joseph Andrews* outlines a conception of comic writing as corrective and so satiric: as Fielding analyses it, we laugh at what is ridiculous, and that boils down to Affectation, which in turn results from either Vanity or Hypocrisy. However, Fielding's practice controverts his theory. Our laughter at (or, more precisely, with) Adams is deeply affectionate: the more ludicrously he is entangled with the intractable world, the more dignified and moving he becomes. Parson Adams is a sign of, and contributes to, a great shift in comic sensibility; it was in mid-18th-century England that both Don Quixote and Falstaff were for the first time taken to be comic heroes and not simply ridiculous buffoons.

All the same, the Joseph–Lady Booby–Fanny plot is handled very artfully. The first 10 chapters of the novel are carefully limited to parody of *Pamela*: Joseph responds to physical advances by the newly-widowed Lady Booby in much the same manner as Pamela does to Mr. B., even writing two letters to his sister in her characteristic tone of shocked virtue. But Fielding conceals until the start of Chapter 11 the crucial fact that Joseph maintains his chastity because he is in love with Fanny: the parody has been unimpaired, but now the comic quest-romance can begin. And begin it does in Chapter 12: Joseph, dismissed by Lady Booby, sets out from London to Lady Booby's country estate, where Fanny lives, and is immediately robbed, beaten, stripped naked, and left for dead; his helpless need for charity meets with a great range of typically human responses from his fellow-travellers, not one of whom turns out to be the Good Samaritan. Fielding's road show is under way, and it will continue just as it began.

Furthermore, the four books of the novel are elegantly structured: the first half of Book One and Book Four are largely stationary and bracket the adventures through rural England of Joseph, Adams, and Fanny. (Fanny, having heard of Joseph's dismissal, has set out to find him, and the two lovers meet on the road.) The first 10 chapters of Book One are set in Lady Booby's house in London; Book Four takes place at Booby Hall, her country estate. Lady Booby and her city entourage reappear in Book Four, and so does the stagey kind of comedy established in the first chapters of the novel.

Adams is unable to learn, but Joseph is. He matures through his travels, unobtrusively but artfully, a progress that is all the more evident because it exists beside Adams's inability to change. It is significant that, when Fielding returns to parody of *Pamela* in Book Four, he no longer presents Joseph as a ludicrous male version of Richardson's heroine; rather, the parody is sustained by introducing into his own fiction the leading figures of Richardson's novel—Mr. B., newly and strenuously genteel, and Pamela herself, socially gracious but a cold-hearted snob.

Joseph, in short, is needed if the novel is to have a plot, and Fielding, drawing upon stage conventions, gives the novel an ingenious one. Joseph turns out to be the son of Mr. Wilson, a country gentleman encountered by Adams, Joseph, and Fanny on their travels. Joseph can now marry Fanny, who had just been discovered to be Pamela's sister (though in the end *not* Joseph's brother), and Adams is given a handsome living. Mr. Wilson not only resolves the plot, but he is central to the novel in at least three other ways. In narrative terms, his long account of his misadventures in London broadens Fielding's depiction of English society. In moral terms, he embodies the solution to which the novel is moving: he has been saved by love, marriage, family life, and retirement from the vain world. In philosophical terms, Wilson's country life is an image of the goodness of human life—though right after Adams likens the Wilsons' life to the golden age, Fielding shades his idyll by showing the Wilson children's pet spaniel shot by the local squire's son out of pure malice. If evil will not prevail, it is still present.

Fielding created in *Joseph Andrews* a kind of novel—which he terms in his preface the "comic Epic-poem in Prose"—that he would develop even further in *Tom Jones*. Already in this early work we find Fielding's most distinctive feature as a novelist: the ever-present omniscient narrator, knowledgeable, genial, allusive, often ironic and always wise. As in *Tom Jones* (and in complete contrast to Richardson's novels), the action is disposed neatly into books and chapters; there are essays on general topics before each book and witty chapter titles; events are recounted with selfconscious artifice (battles, for instance, are described in mock-epic diction). Cervantes had found an English successor.

—Bruce Stovel

A JOURNAL OF THE PLAGUE YEAR.
Fiction by Daniel Defoe, 1722.

The remarkably prolific and versatile Daniel Defoe published his *A Journal of the Plague Year* in 1722; and while composition of the work seems to have been stimulated by a sudden outbreak of plague in Marseilles in 1720, Defoe is concerned to chronicle the Great Plague that came over from Holland and swept England, particularly the densely urban areas like London, in 1665. Often referred to as the "Poor Man's Plague," its rampant spread is historically attributed to overcrowding and lack of hygiene and proper sanitation. Though there were three previous outbreaks in the 17th century, the 1665 bout was most severe, claiming the lives of at least 70,000 out of a population of a half million. In its journalistic and accurate account of the plague, this work is sometimes seen as more of an historical document than imaginative literature: it is full of facts, figures, tables, mortality bills, detailed anecdotes, and remedial laws and procedures to combat the spread of the disease. But it is much more than a journal. It not only presents visions of 18th-century social and psychological experience common to much of Defoe's fiction, but it depicts and explores the experience of human beings under tremendous stress, and under the hideous and terrifying conditions which many of Defoe's contemporary readers would have reluctantly remembered with only too much clarity, conditions which (along with the devastating London fire of 1666) were seen by many as divine retribution or judgement upon a sinful and wayward people.

Early in the book it becomes clear that while the journalistic facts are important, they are really only the backdrop to the main focus which is on the human emotions and behavior *generated by* the plague and by the sense of entrapment in an urban doom. Through numerous anecdotes the book reveals the incomprehensible and irrational behaviour that can result from extreme stress: at one point a group of drunken louts in a tavern ridicule a miserable man who has just lost his entire family to ghastly deaths (a portrayal of "denial" perhaps); at another point a man forcibly kisses a woman in the street and then gleefully informs her he is infected with the plague ("misery loves company" or the perverse feeling of having "life and death power" over others); at another point a terrified man throws himself into a pit where the dead are being daily dumped and buried (the human desire for the painfully inevitable to be "over with"). The book also investigates human susceptibility to superstition and desperation in the face of extreme adversity, as it reveals a plethora of quack cures and preventative measures from bizarre rituals to soothsaying to astrology to magic charms that "possessed the heads of the people very much." Most poignantly Defoe explores the fundamental dichotomy of the human being's duty to self versus his duty to others around him—especially to those very close such as family and dear friends (or, in the case of doctors and clergy, their patients and congregations): does one choose to do the "sensible thing" and flee to protect one's own life? Or does one reaffirm one's allegiance to those to whom one is responsible and risk death?

Indeed, this is the dilemma confronting the narrator (known only by the initials H.F.) at the beginning of the book. H.F., "not knowing what to do" in the face of so many people fleeing (and so many others dying), eventually decides (upon reading the 91st Psalm which promises that "no evil shall befall thee, neither shall any plague come nigh thy dwelling") to do his Christian "duty" to stay, warn, pray for, and help those in need. He chronicles events with great precision, saying that he is writing a history, not preaching a sermon; and he focuses as much on human interest stories and vignettes as he does on facts and figures. In so doing he becomes a representative consciousness of that extraordinary time in history: through H.F. Defoe manages to bring the past alive in human terms, to conflate the day-to-day observations into a large recollected event—a nightmare which, paradoxically, exists through time yet seems timeless in the increased irrelevance of chronology as the situation becomes almost apocalyptically chaotic. The book seems timeless also because in recording such a period in history it touches on some strikingly modern themes such as the human sense of interpersonal alienation, spiritual isolation, the anxiety and paranoia of congested urban life, and the absurdity and meaninglessness of life in the face of human attempts to construct or impose higher meaning and direction onto it. But the important difference is in the outcome. The plague ends, England is delivered from evil, and human belief and trust in God and His infinite wisdom are gratefully reaffirmed: "'Blessed be God . . . and let us give thanks to Him, for 'tis all His own doing, human help and human skill was at an end."'

Not only was there a substantial amount of literature at this time which was concerned with apocalyptic forebodings, there was a virtual flood of "plague literature" between 1665 and 1722. But Defoe's *Journal* can be seen as the most outstanding exponent of this genre for a number of reasons. First, its moralizing is not as heavy-handed as that of others: while people presumably are to learn from this scare to fear God and behave accordingly, Defoe recognizes that people are people, and after the plague is over "they sang His praise, but they soon forgot His works." Second, the protagonist is much more recognizably human than the more authoritative—almost semi-divine—voices of other plague narrators. H.F. constantly admits his fallibility and alludes to the fact that he is reporting only what he has seen or heard: he differentiates between fact, observation, hearsay, apocrypha, and the unknowable, thus making his presence at once more immediately felt *and* more amiably reliable. Third, Defoe's narrator has a clearer sense of social consciousness than other narrators who refer to *man* in categorical terms: Defoe recognizes that the plague was much worse for the poorer classes who were trapped and could simply not afford to flee—and H.F. continually claims that "the poor people were to be pitied" on so many occasions because of their disproportionately hopeless conditions. Finally, Defoe's prose style conveys a sense of gripping immediacy; he frequently works with loose sentences that tend to accumulate in the manner of breathless street gossip and unpremeditated outcome, thus making his *Journal* a very compelling work of art which possesses, as Anthony Burgess noted in his edition, "the truth of the conscientious and scrupulous historian, but its deeper truth belongs to the creative imagination."

—Richard Arnold

JOURNEY'S END.
Play by R.C. Sherriff, 1928.

Immensely successful in the decade between its production and the outbreak of World War II, R.C. Sherriff's *Journey's End* might have been expected to have dwindled by now into a dated and sentimental relic from the era of the well-made play. While "He was skipper of rugger at Barford . . . a jolly good bat, too" or "How topping—to have played for England!" may express, in their faded slang, attitudes which a handful of present-day Barfords foster even today, Raleigh's open hero-worship, like Stanhope's brand of clean-limbed decency ("so keen on the fellows in the house keeping fit . . . frightfully down on smoking—and that sort of thing") now seem as out-moded as his naive excitement about the glories of war. But, as recent productions on stage and television have shown, the merits of the piece remain remarkably undimmed. Its portrait of men under pressure, the tensions and camaraderie of the claustrophobic life of the trenches, is still excellent theatre and, at the close, deeply moving.

Sherriff's knowledge of his subject was first-hand, and the authenticity of his presentation of war is one of the reasons why the play remains alive: there are no glamorised heroics, but damp, rats, broken beds, unappetising food, cramped living conditions, irksome inefficiency, the sheer tedium of long periods of inactivity, and, above all, the ever-present danger. The humour with which the piece is shot through is not decoration tacked on with an eye to the box office, but a necessary strategy for survival in conditions of extreme stress: its omission in the 1988 BBC version made for a grimmer, yet in some ways less poignant, play.

Against this background the tensions that arise between the well-contrasted main characters, the five occupants of "a dugout in the British trenches before St. Quentin," stand out sharply. The dugout itself operates as another source of pressure: a dreary haven from the horrors "up there" which yet could—and for Raleigh does—become a tomb, it forces the officers to live on top of each in a world where only whisky provides a real, if temporary, escape.

The restricted setting presents a problem for the producer. Monotony and confinement are of the essence of the play: a handful of men sit around a table and talk, or eat; one or two leave, others come in. They are "all just waiting for something" which, when it happens, takes place off stage. Some variation is achieved by lighting: the moonlight of the first scene changes to morning sunlight which brightens and fades in succeeding scenes; the celebratory meal in Act III is lit "quite festively" by "an unusual number of candles," providing a striking contrast to the final pre-dawn scene, which starts and ends in darkness. By emphasising that the action is virtually sequential (the play almost observes the dramatic unities) these changes also mark, silently, the relentless approach of the "big attack" which has been expected from the start.

But the demands of drama for action, movement, change are met less by visual variation than by rises and falls in the emotional temperature. These are skilfully plotted: Hibbert's breakdown, the suicidal raid, the death of Raleigh are interspersed with moments of wry comedy, nostalgia, or the grim call of duty that takes Stanhope away even from Raleigh's corpse. There are occasional longeurs, particularly the static expository scene between Osborne and Raleigh early in the play; although Raleigh's enthusiasm is tellingly contrasted with the cynical *sauve qui peut* attitude just seen in the departing Hardy, and though Osborne's cautious warning that war "tells on a man," hints at difficulties ahead, the pace here is slow. In Act III, another lengthy *tête-à-tête* is easier to handle, for this time dramatic tension springs from the huge gap between the reality known to Osborne, and Raleigh's illusions, and the slow build-up to the raid adds to the suspense. The raid itself is the first major climax of the play. It is something of a theatrical *tour de force* to have created a moment of such dramatic intensity by means of an empty stage; it is typical also of Sherriff's stagecraft that he maintains the suspense by withholding news of Osborne's death until the interrogation of the terrified prisoner is complete, and the jubilant Colonel, unmindful of the cost, is brought up short by Stanhope's bitter sarcasm.

Before and after the raid, the fluctuating relationship between Stanhope and Raleigh provides the centre of interest. Here the insufficiency of Stanhope's motivation must be called a weakness, though in performance this is masked if his edgy hostility is seen to be covering the near-hysteria of a man close to breaking point. The revelation that Stanhope copes by drinking heavily would seem in itself insufficient to damage his unofficial engagement, and his desire to go away "for months" and live "in the open air" before he can return to his fiancée appears unwarranted. A more plausible explanation of this sense of pollution and the dangers of exposure might be thought to be hinted at in his drunken anecdote in Act III, "She said, 'Not in these trousers—in French'," but although the pressures under which Stanhope lives have been vividly portrayed, Sherriff was evidently reluctant to risk alienating the audience's sympathies by developing this theme.

Political aspects of the war are not explored; in spite of Raleigh's moment of illumination—"It all seems rather—*silly*, doesn't it"—Stanhope's question to the coward Hibbert as to what would happen if "we *all* say we can't," is a rhetorical one. Instead, we are presented with men enduring the well-nigh unendurable, and somehow retaining their humanity in spite of it. For all its pathos, the ending is not without a sense of "what may quiet us in a death so noble."

—Margaret Forey

JUDE THE OBSCURE.
Novel by Thomas Hardy, 1895.

Thomas Hardy's last novel, *Jude the Obscure*, is also his bitterest and most schematic. Undeflectably pessimistic, it is partly a protest against social oppression, partly a metaphysical arraignment of the wrongness of the world. His preface puts emphasis on the universality of his theme: "a deadly war waged between flesh and spirit." It is true that the book's hero tries hopelessly to harmonise the dual demands of his nature; true, too, that he is trapped between two contrasting women, spiritual Sue and fleshly Arabella. But behind this theme lies something even larger—what Hardy called "the tragedy of unfulfilled aims." *Jude the Obscure* is about the pain of disappointment—frustration, disillusion, loss.

The book is constructed quite deliberately to exemplify these qualities. Hardy told Edmund Gosse that he desired to show "the contrast between the ideal life a man wished to lead, and the squalid real life he was fated to lead . . . The idea was meant to run all through the novel. It is, in fact, to be discovered in *everybody's* life." This master-thesis is reinforced by the novel's main structural principle: ironic juxtaposition. Again the device was deliberately deployed. Hardy stated: "Of course the book is all contrasts, or was meant to be in its original conception . . . e.g., Sue and her heathen gods set against Jude's reading the Greek testament; Christminster academical, Christminster in the slums; Jude the saint, Jude the sinner; Sue the Pagan, Sue the saint; marriage, no marriage, &c. &c."

Persistently, this use of juxtaposition suggests the ideal destroyed by the actual: worthy hopes and aspirations collapse into squalor and failure. This is the pattern that imposes itself on the life of the eponymous hero. Aspiring to the spirit, Jude gets the flesh: as he strolls along rehearsing his litany of uplifting classical authors, sensuality rudely assails him in the form of a greasy pig's pizzle hurled by a leering farm girl. Later, when he really does want "the flesh"—sexual communion with his beloved Sue—he is tortured by a merely spiritual affection that shrinks from physical contact. Numerous other contrasts confirm Jude's fate. As a child he dotes on "the dear little birdies": his kindness is curtailed by the blows of an angry farmer. On his first night in Christminster he speaks out loud to the past alumni of the university city: the only reply, both banal and hostile, is the voice of a suspicious policeman. Enraptured by a hymn, he seeks its composer, convinced that such a high-souled artist would readily understand his earthly temptations: the man he finds is a grasping snob about to go into the wine trade.

The narrative pattern is doggedly consistent: rapture, hope, idealisation, followed by disillusion. The two main areas to which it applies are sexual relations and education, but in these a sharp, specific note of social protest begins to make itself heard. Though Hardy later feigned innocence of any subversive motivation, the book's social criticism provoked much outrage ("Jude the Obscene," "dirt, drivel, and damnation") and remains a potent part of its appeal. Christminster, which shimmers alluringly at a distance, proves a deathly and rejecting fortress. Descriptions of the college architecture dwell on rottenness, gloom, and decay. But it is also made clear that Jude's exclusion is directly due to poverty. As Sue says bitterly to him later, "you were elbowed off the pavement by the millionaires' sons."

Despite Hardy's subsequent disclaimers, the book also mounts an onslaught on marriage. In this it has affinities with the contemporary New Woman novels, which questioned marriage and urged "free union." In *Jude the Obscure* the crescendo of criticism becomes at times almost comic (Father Time tells Sue she does *look* like Jude's wife, "'cept he seems fond of you, and you of him"), but underlying such gleefully grim ridicule is a serious critique of monogamous morality—the belief that all sexual relations outside marriage must automatically be condemned, all inside sanctioned and approved. This belief, or the pressure it exerts, is responsible for virtually every disaster: Jude's initial marriage to Arabella; Sue's expulsion from training college; Phillotson's loss of his livelihood; Jude's lost job as a church restorer; Sue's notice to quit from lodgings in Christminster (which leads directly to the deaths of the children); Sue's return to Phillotson and his acquiescence; and of course, throughout the book, the Church's bland blessing on grotesquely unwise marriages—Jude's to Arabella (twice) and Sue's to Phillotson (twice).

Hardy's criticism of marriage is linked with his criticism of the university. Illustrating the book's epigraph, "The letter killeth," both are rigid institutions dependent on forms and ceremonies. Surveying the colleges, Father Time enquires: "Are the great old houses gaols?" They are: but gaols which lock people out. The university excludes people eminently suitable for study because of its insistence on traditional forms of entry. Marriage, conversely, incarcerates people eminently unsuited to live together because of its insistence on traditional forms of relationship.

It is not possible, however, to read *Jude the Obscure* entirely in social terms. As elsewhere in his treatment of tragedy, Hardy stirs in metaphysical ingredients: the fatal curse on the Fawley family; talk of destiny and "malignant stars"; and the lugubrious child Little Father Time, never a breathing, believable boy but a walking, croaking, philosophic symbol ("He was their nodal point, their focus, their expression in a single term"), whose grisly actions are presented as proof "of the coming universal wish not to live"—a Schopenhauerian doctrine. Characteristically of Hardy, the novel vacillates between a social and a cosmic perspective. What remains fixed, indeed diagrammatic, is the pessimistic thesis about human disappointment. At the end of his novel-writing career, Hardy appears to have become impatient with everything but the points he wishes to prove. *Jude the Obscure* is not so much a great novel as the unadorned blueprint for one.

—David Grylls

JULIUS CAESAR.
Play by William Shakespeare, 1599.

It seems that William Shakespeare wrote *Julius Caesar* in 1599, immediately after *Henry V*, the last in his series of English history plays. His main source, Plutarch's *Lives of the Noble Grecians and Romans*, evidently inspired him to talk more frankly about politics and political motivation. His attitude to rulers (and God's endorsement of them) is more sceptical, even disrespectful, than had been possible in plays which needed to justify kingship in general and the Tudor dynasty in particular.

The critical questions raised by the play start with the title: is this play about Julius Caesar? All the actions for which Caesar is famous are ignored by Shakespeare; even the war which had left him effectively in supreme power in Rome is mentioned only casually; instead, we are shown just the last phase of his life when his attempt to have his position made official precipitates the successful revolution by Cassius and Brutus which is the central subject of the play. As well as drastically abbreviating the dictator's career, Shakespeare kills him off during Act II and allows him very few moments at the centre of the stage before that, arguably reducing him to the status of a minor character in his "own" play.

Though he may have nothing to do, and not very much to say, he is universally talked about. All the actions of the play are undertaken in relation to him and he is an obsession with those who distrust or hate him even more than with those who hang on to his coat-tails. Cassius, his inveterate enemy, sees him as a "Colossus" round whom "we petty men" crowd; and some critics seem to agree, regarding the other participants as essentially minor. Yet there is no play of Shakespeare so full of personalities realized completely yet economically, and at least three of them—Brutus, Cassius, and Antony—bring out the dramatist's full powers and are, especially in their interreactions, of absorbing interest.

If there is a dominant figure in the play it is Brutus: "Et tu Brute?—Then fall Caesar!" Brutus is not a politician; he is a stoic, a moral philosopher who is, if anything, anti-political. Although clearly disturbed by what Caesar is up to, he does not act until goaded by Cassius, ignoring appeals to ambition but responding energetically when individual freedom is threatened by Caesar's imperial designs. His soliloquy in Act II when he concludes that he must kill Caesar has been dubbed unsatisfactory, one critic claiming that it denies Brutus any credible motive for the assassination. But Shakespeare's Brutus, scrupulously setting aside Cassius' accusations, puts the case most favourable to Caesar, and still can see no alternative to killing his friend. Brutus is not stimulated by jealousy like Cassius or excited at the prospect of blood-letting like Antony. His speech at Caesar's funeral is universally rated as much inferior to Antony's. It is certainly less successful with the crowd, but if personal integrity, respect for one's audience, and a powerful appeal to the idea of freedom based on the dignity of the individual are any measure of worth, then Brutus' speech is impressive.

This is not to say that Shakespeare shares Brutus' vision of his fellow men. The play opens with the fickle plebeians, forgetful of their former enthusiasm for Pompey, turning out to celebrate Caesar's triumph. The sycophancy of Caesar's court discourages confidence in human dignity. The senators are cowards, Cassius a schemer, and Antony a crook. And even Brutus is not untouched by Shakespeare's irony; for he continues to think people are uninfluenced by the pressure of others when he himself has just been manoeuvred towards action by Cassius.

The interplay of these two friends clarifies the strengths and weaknesses of each. Cassius thinks self-interest is everything, and considers Brutus a fool for not realizing this: "Caesar doth bear me hard; but he loves Brutus. / If I were Brutus now, and he were Cassius, / He should not humour me." Nevertheless his envy of Caesar is transformed by his passion into a powerful indictment of Roman degeneracy under a dictator. Each man feels affection for, and patronizes, the other: each is essential to the conspiracy, and not just for the obvious reason that Cassius is its organizer and Brutus its moral guarantor. Cassius needs Brutus' conviction to sustain his own belief in the assassination and consequently (and fatally) accepts subordination to Brutus' leadership.

Antony is the most volatile character, the joker in the pack. Initially no-one takes him seriously. It is Caesar's death which transforms Antony. He has no principles and no belief in liberty or individual rights, but he is roused to anger by the mutilated body of his hero. Grasping intuitively the power of blood, he pledges himself to crown the dead Caesar and discovering his capacity as demagogue he turns the crowd into a mob, the weapon of his revenge and means of his own rise to power. We see the moral character of the new Antony in the mean little scene in which he and Octavius casually swap death sentences on each other's relatives.

In contrast there follows a surprisingly emotional scene between Brutus and Cassius. Brutus has just received news of his wife's suicide; outcast from Rome, he suspects his closest ally is not backing him up (is perhaps even prepared to leave him to fight Antony alone) and his self-control and impartiality give way. His unfairness to Cassius has the curious effect of drawing the audience closer to him, and prepares for the moving farewell of the friends. The two men have traced parallel but opposite courses: Brutus stepping out of his role as idealist, and stooping to the imperfection of living, destroys himself, but becomes more human: Cassius, the self-proclaimed egoist dies for love of Brutus and liberty.

The last act of the play brings out the alternative interpretations of the assassination, Brutus' view and Antony's. Brutus' friends are "the last of all the Romans" fighting to maintain their liberty: they are also, as Caesar's ghost has warned Brutus, the conspirators over whom retribution hangs. Nevertheless, in defeat the behaviour of the republicans is marked by fidelity, generosity, and grace—no recriminations when failure is snatched out of the jaws of success. Their suicides are death in the "high Roman fashion." Caesar's revenge is accomplished and acknowledged, but Cassius and Brutus die unrepentant, paying the price without regret. Remembering the reproach of the dying Caesar, Brutus half-humorously responds as he kills himself: "Caesar, now be still; / I kill'd not thee with half so good a will."

In writing the first of the major Roman plays Shakespeare offers both a more tragic and a more ironic vision than does any of his previous history plays. *Julius Caesar* effectively contradicts the possibility of uniting king and country or hero and politician so reassuringly affirmed in the person of Henry V, but soon to be even more radically questioned in *Hamlet*.

—Moira Megaw

THE JUNGLE BOOKS.
Stories by Rudyard Kipling, 1894–95.

The idea of a human child pursued by a tiger who stumbles into a wolf den and proceeds to dislodge a cub from the mother's side so that he might feed is an electrically-charged beginning for the series of stories interlaced with verse that comprise Rudyard Kipling's *Jungle Books*. Although Kipling did not invent the talking beast tale, his collection set standards for its use, so that subsequent works in the genre are measured against his intriguing moral ambivalence of characterization and his thematic use of the absolutes of the Law of the Jungle. It is in the play between these two elements that the dramatic tension of the stories is found.

Many critics have noted that what chiefly distinguishes Kipling's animal characters is that they are true wild animals, even when we recognize and respond to their individual patterns of behaviour. The sinuous grace of Bagheera, the panther, is an extension of Bagheera's personality; while Baloo the Bear is comforting and stable, Bagheera exudes danger and unpredictability. Mother and Father Wolf and their children are shadowy, benign figures, but Akela the Pack Leader has stature and nobility which is played to good effect against the fickle self-centeredness of many of the young wolves of the Seeonee pack. The Bandar-log, or Monkey people, are lawless, customless dilettantes, unable to match man in ability to infer and predict, and unwilling to imitate the rest of the Jungle in adherence to the Law. Finally, Kaa, the ancient Rock Python, even when he aids Mowgli, is truly reptilian, capable of arousing admiring horror in the other characters and in the reader.

It is in the story "Kaa's Hunting" that we see Kipling at his unsentimental best. When Mowgli is kidnapped by the Bandar-log, Baloo and Bagheera solicit Kaa's help, citing as a hopeful sign the fact that Kaa is always hungry and loves to feast on careless monkeys. When Mowgli is rescued, Kaa settles down to mesmerize the monkeys, a process that is a prelude to their serial demise. Mowgli finds this educational, as he is unaffected by Kaa's chant, but Baloo and Bagheera nearly succumb, and all three know that no consideration of the loyalty due to erstwhile allies would have interfered with Kaa's feeding had Mowgli not wrested them from his spell.

Besides the intervention of Kaa, Mowgli owes his survival in this episode to his mastery of the Law of the Jungle, a mixture of mythic strictures, culture and tradition, and ordinary common sense. In creating Jungle society, Kipling envisioned a balanced hierarchy. Hathi the Elephant is the most wise and so rules, but all the Jungle fears the Little People of the Rocks (bees) and avoids confrontation with Tabaqui (the hyena) whose bite when mad can cause hydrophobia; thus the little and the great, the hunters and the scavengers coexist in an ordered universe that gives structure and limits to what seems at first glimpse like childhood's vision of freedom for Mowgli. In fact, although he is raised in the Jungle and so spared school, Mowgli is taught, rewarded, and punished by Baloo and Bagheera to make him a law-abiding member of his society, much like any village child.

But Mowgli is not a village child, nor is he, despite his own best efforts, a wolf. Twice within the tales Mowgli goes forth from the Jungle to sample the ways of men; the first time he is expelled by the Pack and will be expelled by its human counterpart in the village, but the second time, in fulfillment of Akela's dying prophecy, he is driven by his own nature which in the end cannot be satisfied save by the love of his own kind. The sadness of his parting from all whom he has loved in the Jungle creates an elegiac strain; although deeply satisfying in the way of the truly inevitable, the end of the stories is also melancholy and haunting.

Scattered through the first and second *Jungle Books* are stories featuring animal protagonists who are not a part of Mowgli's world. Still, when set beside the rhythms created and sustained in the latter, the former do not seem out of place, more an extension of themes and motifs found in the Mowgli stories—thus Rikki Tikki Tavi celebrates resourcefulness and loyalty, while the White Seal sounds again the theme of leaving what is known in pursuit of a higher good.

Besides these elements, what connects all the stories is Kipling's ability to awaken in children an eager and rapt response to his characters and settings. The rabbits of *Watership Down* and the farm animals of *Charlotte's Web* are only two literary descendants of those Jungle dwellers, and they, like Kipling's creations, inhabit worlds where terror, danger, and sudden death threaten the weak, the gentle, and the lovable. After Kipling, even animals who talk must be, in the most durable way, real.

—Judith N. Mitchell

JUNO AND THE PAYCOCK.
Play by Sean O'Casey, 1924.

Sean O'Casey's most famous literary achievement, *Juno and the Paycock* was the first play to run two weeks at the Abbey Theatre and marked an important shift in the Abbey toward urban drama and away from the peasant drama of Synge. This play, in fact, in its realism achieves for urban Ireland what Synge did for rural Ireland; its tone is seriocomic, as in most of Synge's drama—humor mixed with violence, heroism, and disillusionment. It is also a brilliant mix of realism with farce and melodrama.

The characters are all superb creations. Boyle, the peacock of the title, relies on ostentatious yet insubstantial displays that serve only to prop up his burgeoning ego. He is lazy, resisting all effort to find work, and self-centered, concerned, for instance, about his daughter's pregnancy out of wedlock only as it socially reflects on him. Anti-heroic in the extreme, he relentlessly undercuts any heroic qualities the other characters may possess. Joxer Daly, his chameleon-like crony who adapts his personality to whatever demands he finds in any particular situation, is an ingratiating toady with a wide streak of treachery in him. The banter between Boyle and Joxer is considered by many to be O'Casey's finest literary creation.

Boyle's son, Johnny, honorably wounded in the Easter 1916 rising and later in the Irish Civil War, has become lately a disillusioned and frightened coward who by betraying a comrade insures his own retaliatory death. Mary, his sister, is sincere, intelligent, and hardworking, but is frustrated in her ideals and in love. The play's highly melodramatic ending is heightened by the coincidence of the discovery of her pregnancy coupled with the execution of Johnny.

Juno, Boyle's wife, is the soul of the play. She is honest and, even if uneducated, intelligent. She realistically sees religion as socially ineffective but is among the first to resort to sincere prayer in time of crisis. Hers is the burden of reality, counter to her husband's delusions and her children's idealism. And, as her name suggests, she is of heroic stature—a goddess figure from Roman myth, a universal symbol of the suffering of womankind, motherhood personified.

An unavoidable key question is whether or not the play is naturalistic. At first glance, it would appear so: the initial stage directions repeat the code words and phrases of the naturalistic philosophy—"circumstances," "forces," and "degraded by [the] environment." Johnny's "choice" to participate in the rising is no real choice: being merely a young, idealistic boy at the time, how informed could his "decision" have been? Was he not really just swept away by the fervor of the times? As for Mary, it makes no sense for her to love such a cold, unlovable man such as Bentham, but she is slave to what the naturalists would call a "chemism"—a sexual attraction that defies intellectual control. Juno, however, makes the free choice that undermines such a reading: she elects to leave her husband, that naturalistic dead weight that has for a lifetime been dragging her down with him. If such a choice is possible, then the play cannot be purely naturalistic.

Yet despite all this negativity, the play *is* comic at times, frequently descending to the level of farce. Boyle's struggling to remove his trousers then searching for his braces, which are draped around his neck the whole time, is a hilarious scene, as is Mrs. Madigan and her drinking. Boyle's assertions early in the play that a man who doesn't drink cannot possibly be a true Christian also play very well.

The play's conclusion deserves separate discussion. Despite its melodrama—or perhaps because of it—the end is emotionally crushing: Johnny has been shot, Mary is pregnant and abandoned, the Boyles' financial delusions have evaporated and been replaced by the reality of huge debts, and the family has completely disintegrated as a unit. The apartment has been stripped virtually bare—clearly symbolizing the stripping away of all fantasies and pretensions, because all that remains is stark reality. It is therefore even more appropriate that the play does not end with Juno but with the drunken Boyle and Joxer instead. With their incoherence and incomprehension the anti-heroic emphasis dominates. The humor at this point is both horrifying and grotesque. Boyle has given his love to the false Joxer (fantasy) instead of to his family (reality). In his delusions, spirit, and exaggerations, Boyle richly deserves the title of Falstaff's modern Irish counterpart.

—Alexander G. Gonzalez

K

KIM.
Novel by Rudyard Kipling, 1901.

Although long dismissed as little more than a healthy boy's book, *Kim* is now more generally regarded as Rudyard Kipling's most successful novel, one in which content, style, form and theme are successfully interwoven with memories of the author's childhood in India to create a story that appeals on several levels. The author speaks of *Kim* in his autobiography, *Something of Myself*, almost as if he is unsure whether to regard it with pride or disparagement, calling it "nakedly picaresque and plotless." This, actually, is not a very satisfactory description. True, it does share some of the characteristics of a picaresque novel. Its two main characters, a Tibetan Bhuddist lama and a young orphan boy of mixed race, called Kimball O'Hara, bear a distinct resemblance to Cervantes's Don Quixote and his squire, Sancho Panza. The two also engage in a series of adventures—some exciting and some amusing—as they make what appears to be a rather casual journey around India. Yet, unlike the heroes of a genuinely picaresque novel, both the lama and Kim do develop as characters, and their journey has a clearly defined purpose. The lama is seeking a river that will wash away sins, while Kim is searching for "a Red Bull on a green field," which is the regimental crest of the Mavericks, with whom his father had served as colour sergeant. Their dual quest provides the thread around which Kipling artfully weaves his narrative.

The lama and his young companion travel widely by train and along the Grand Trunk Road and eventually Kim falls in with the Mavericks. He is taken over by the regiment's chaplains and packed off to military school, where he his bullied and treated as a "nigger." Meanwhile, the lama goes off to join the temple of the Tirthinkers at Benares. Eventually Kim is released from military school through the good offices of a Colonel Creighton and with the financial assistance of the lama he is sent to St. Xavier's School. There his formal schooling properly begins, and this is followed by a less orthodox education under the tutelage of Lurgan Sahib, who initiates Kim into the complexities of the "Great Game," after which he is inducted into the British secret police.

While Kim appears to have come to an important stage in his life's journey, which ironically parallels the "triple trial of strength" performed by the Buddha as described by the lama early in the book, the lama himself still seems far away from a successful conclusion to his quest, despite his saintly character. What is wrong, Kipling suggests, is that the lama mistakenly believes that one attains "merit" by freeing oneself from the "Wheel of Things," in contrast to Kim, who flings "himself wholeheartedly on the next turn of the wheel." At last, when Kim and the lama reach the hills the lama realizes the futility of trying to live above life rather than in it. There they become involved in a pitched battle with a Frenchman and a Russian, precipitated by the Russian's attempt to seize the lama's sacred chart, which angers the lama and provokes in him the very human desire for revenge. As the lama realizes at last that it is virtually impossible to subdue the spirit entirely, and one is in any event dependent on others, he becomes a candidate for grace. At that moment the sacred river gushes forth at his feet and his soul ascends, "wheeling like an eagle" to heaven.

Although *Kim*'s major theme is the superiority of the active life over the contemplative, there is a secondary one which is political. Throughout the novel the British army is made to seem brutal and insensitive, while the mass of Indians are depicted as dishonest and venal. Neither seems fit to rule. Only the secret police, which enrolls the best elements of each and whose hero is Kim, "friend of all the world," the offspring of an Irish father and an Indian (possibly Eurasian) mother, acquits itself with honour and intelligence. What Kipling appears to be saying is that effective rule in India can be achieved only if the best of both races unite in the interests of India as a whole.

But *Kim* is far from being simply a novel with a message. Its form and content are seamlessly fused in a way that Kim himself would recognize. After his ordeal in the hills, the hero is nursed back to health by the motherly Maharanee of Saharanpore. He gradually regains his strength and simultaneously an awareness of his true identity. Previously he had felt that "his soul was out of gear with its surroundings—a cog wheel unconnected with any machinery, just like the idle cog wheel of a cheap Beheea sugar-crusher laid by in a corner." He recites his name several times and asks: "What is Kim?" Then, "with an almost audible click he felt the wheels of his being lock anew on the world outside. Things that rode meaningless on the eyeball an instant before slid into proper proportion." Everything in the world Kim finally realizes, is "real and true—solidly planted upon the feet—perfectly comprehensible—clay of his clay, neither more nor less."

This recognition that everything in the world has its place and all are united in one vast design, is mirrored in the form of the novel itself. As such, *Kim* demonstrates that Kipling, often viewed as an unrepentant imperialist, was not only a writer of superior talent but was also a man whose view of life may have been more liberal and humane than is often supposed.

—John M. Munro

KING JOHN.
Play by William Shakespeare, 1594–96(?).

King John differs from the remaining eight English chronicle histories William Shakespeare wrote before 1600 in not being part of a cycle where one reign leads into another, with prophecy and recall of events from play to play. John's reign, from 1199 to 1216, is dramatized in isolation, with only a reminder of Richard the Lionhearted. Although Shakespeare has created causal links between events that seem to cover far less time than their actual 17-year span, he has not developed the obvious cohesiveness that we might expect from a play standing alone. There is no climactic battle that all events point toward, despite a great deal of military action. Nor does John provide a center, for in mid-play he changes from a commanding ruler to a mean, weak shell, and Philip Faulconbridge must hold play and kingdom together. When strong, John lacks the charisma of Henry V; when weak, he lacks the poeticism of Richard II; when mean, he lacks the energy of Richard III. His title is shaky, and his efforts to retain the crown against a more valid claim by Prince Arthur increase the political manoeuvres and opportunism that characterize much of the play.

Shakespeare turned to Holinshed's *Chronicles* and other histories for some details, but much of his material had already been dramatized in his immediate source, the two-part *The Troublesome Reign of John King of England* (c. 1591). There have been attempts to demonstrate that *The Troublesome Reign* is an earlier draft or a bad quarto of *King John*, but it is generally regarded as a separate, anonymous work. Shakespeare treated it like any other source, eliminating several factual scenes and the coarse anti-Catholic humour, and changing the emphasis on some events. By compressing the two short parts into one play, he created a sense of speed and urgency. Most important, he developed some characters quite differently. Prince Arthur seems younger, and instead of debating rationally, makes a bid for pity. Semi-fictitious Philip Faulconbridge retains his humour, but is made the center of much of the action in a bold move combining fiction and history.

Today John's rule is remembered chiefly for Magna Carta. Many of Shakespeare's contemporaries, however, saw Queen Elizabeth's reign as the successful culmination of a movement John had begun. John's defiance of Rome in Act III makes him very like a spokesman for Protestant England and presages the break under Henry VIII, which Elizabeth reaffirmed after the Marian interlude. Pandulph's excommunication of John was a forerunner of the Pope's excommunicating Elizabeth and absolving Englishmen of allegiance to her. The fear of outside intervention was still very much in English minds, and Arthur's dependence on Austria and France would have made him seem to the audience too weak to rule. The abortive French invasion in Act V reminded Elizabethans that they had just escaped the Spanish Armada and might face another incursion. Faulconbridge's closing lines, ". . . Naught shall make us rue / If England to itself do rest but true," were both summation and reassurance.

The development of Faulconbridge is Shakespeare's great achievement in *King John*. Philip's honesty and patriotism, and his ability to address the audience, often saying what needs to be said, give the play strength. In a world where most seek personal gain, Philip is willing to admit bastardy, forgo his inheritance, and follow John and Queen Elinor to France. His comments on his new knighthood as Richard I's son, his observation on "commodity" (self-interest), his joking defiance of the Duke of Austria, his refusal to jump to conclusions about Arthur's death, and his steadfast patriotism make him the most attractive character. He steps into the vacuum left as John collapses, after trying to remind John to "Let not the world see fear and sad distrust / Govern the motion of a kingly eye." John only retreats further, giving Philip "the ordering of this present time." The development of the character and movement of the play are such, in fact, that we are surprised when Shakespeare, bound by fact, suddenly introduces Prince Henry to take over his dying father's throne, rather than letting it revert to Faulconbridge, who seems so qualified.

Many modern critics have noted that the contrast between Faulconbridge's honour and the political machinations of many of the other characters provides an organizing principle for the play. There are only a few innocent victims. Blanche, John's niece, hastily engaged to the French Dauphin to settle the siege of Angiers, is left helpless and deserted when Pandulph, the Papal Legate, splits France and England. Although Arthur and his mother, Constance, are also victims, they seem less innocent, for they will gain a throne if their cause succeeds. Their supporters, however, waver, and Arthur, whom Shakespeare keeps a child, arouses pity as he pleads successfully for his eyes, and dies trying to escape. John and Philip of France have power, but they use it badly. John defies, then submits to Rome. He debases the military triumph of Arthur's capture by plotting the Prince's murder. France plans to destroy the English lords once England is conquered. Even the English lords are opportunists, using Arthur's death as an excuse for their already planned defection.

While Faulconbridge and the tension between honour and opportunism help unify the play, there are also rhetorical devices that add coherence. Personification is important: commodity becomes a "smooth-faced gentleman." Many images embrace war, blood, violence, and fire. Fire-related words are singularly important, adding urgency, emphasizing feelings, or heightening pain. Constance has "kindled France," heated irons threaten Arthur's eyes, the lords "burn in indignation," and Prince Henry's hot tears do not sooth the dying King's "burned bosom."

A study of details helps emphasize Shakespeare's achievement in a play that at first glance seems diffuse and weak.

—Frances A. Shirley

KING LEAR.
Play by William Shakespeare, 1605.

King Lear is clearly one of the world's greatest plays. It is also one of the most complex and ambiguous.

The text itself offers problems. Behind the play are two editions: a quarto volume printed in 1608 and the folio printed in 1623. Not only are there variations in words and phrasing, but the quarto has about 283 lines not in the folio and the folio has about 100 lines not in the quarto. Editors have traditionally included all the lines from both texts. Recent scholarship argues, however, that the two texts represent two versions of the play, the folio possibly a revision by Shakespeare of the quarto. The play is subtly different depending on which version we read.

But even if we focus on one or the other version, the play is immensely untidy. It conforms to none of the unities of place, time, or action. It has an involved secondary plot and an exceedingly antiformalistic structure. Some critics have pointed to Lear's unclothing himself in the storm (III.iv) as the turning point, but, from there, even if we stay with Lear, the plotline hardly follows a straight path. A crisis begins the play; the hero's ill fortunes unfold through several acts; the action rises in Act IV with the reunion of Lear and Cordelia, only to be followed by the tragic end. Some readers have described the play's structure as that of a tragicomedy with tragedy tacked on at the end.

Different eras have approached the play in radically different ways. The 18th century could not bear its ending: Nahum Tate's 1681 redaction which eliminated the Fool and ended the play with the marriage of Edgar and Cordelia held the stage for more than a century. Today that is considered a sentimental reduction of the play; but the 20th century has been far from uniform in its response. The characters are so multi-faceted, the play's movement and thematic development so complex that it sustains very different readings and productions.

The abruptness of Lear's action in the first scene to many readers seems problematic. Why does Lear behave so rashly —giving up his power, insisting that his daughters be rewarded in response to how much they say they love him, disowning Cordelia when she refuses to flatter, banishing loyal Kent when he interferes? "Why" is probably unanswerable: the 20th century is more interested in causes, the Renaissance more interested in effects, results. But what Lear's action and words reveal about him is the complex stuff of an actor's interpretation. The rigid, autocratic, almost monolithic Lear in Peter Brook's 1971 film rendition contrasts with the slight, childlike Lear, playing with his Fool as his proclamation is read, in Grigori Kozintsev's 1971 film.

Cordelia, in this first scene, is also far from simple. Is she guilty like her father of measuring love quantitatively? (Half of her love goes to her father, she tells him, half will go to her husband.) Many see her love transcending such metaphors, but, still, why does she so refuse to bend? Her father wants / needs to be persuaded that she loves him. Can't she reassure him? In Akira Kurosawa's remarkable 1985 film *Ran* based on the Lear story, Saburo, the Cordelia character, is outright rude, intolerant of his father's show of weakness. For many, Cordelia in her love cannot cater to Lear's weakness or blindness. She cannot participate in the belittlement of her father perpetuated by her sisters' dishonesty. She is both strong and innocent. Although in a sense she is sacrificed, she is not a martyr.

Lear is hardly a positive figure at the beginning of the play. When do we begin to sympathize with him? Goneril and Regan's manipulative insincerity is evident in their preposterous overstatement of their love in the first scene and their readiness to find fault with Lear is clear in their exchange that ends the scene, but do they have good reason? Are, for example, Lear's followers, "disordered" and "deboshed," as Goneril claims? Many readers feel such claims are concocted. Albany, Goneril's husband, shows no knowledge of the knights' unruliness and when Goneril justifies her treatment of Lear to him, she does not mention that argument. Regan and Cornwall identify the good Edgar as one of Lear's "riotous knights," which encourages us to mistrust any such description of the knights. But there is no definitive textual evidence either way. In Brook's *King Lear* the knights are rowdy; in Kozintsev's they are not.

Lear clearly changes in the play. The king in court in the first scene, no matter how interpreted, is very different from the old man, companioned by his fool and a mad beggar, howling at the wild storm, stripping off his garments, or the man at Dover adorned with wild flowers "mad as the vexed sea." And that Lear is different from the Lear who awakes, his wits restored, and kneels before Cordelia. His journey leads him to understand he has wronged Cordelia ("I did her wrong"), to have empathy for the poor and dispossessed ("I have ta'en / Too little care of this"), to discern the world's corruption, to know he has been "flattered . . . like a dog," to understand himself: "I am a very foolish fond old man." But different critics and directors / actors have plotted his change differently, some even denying that in the end Lear learns anything at all.

The subplot in *Lear*, the story of Gloucester and his two sons, one who destroys him and one who preserves him, intersects on several occasions with the Lear plot. But its most important function is as an analogue that supports and extends the meaning, the texture, the implications of Lear's story. And like Lear, Gloucester's change is obvious in some ways and in others not easy to plot. He begins as a gullible man and a follower. He grows in courage and initiative, aiding Lear, confronting openly Lear's children, until blinded and thrust out of the gates, a desolate old man, he understands his previous blindness: "I stumbled when I saw." But, ironically, his understanding / vision is still partial. If I could but "see" Edgar "in my touch," Gloucester says as Edgar stands before him unrecognized, "I'ld say I had eyes again!" Edgar nurses him, leading him to Dover and the carefully constructed fantasy of his suicide and miraculous rescue, teaching him to "bear / Affliction" with patience. The text provides some suggestion, however, that he is a recalcitrant learner. Twice later in the play he looks hopefully to death only to be again snatched out of its clutches by Edgar.

His son Edgar also changes. Edgar is stripped of his name and, like Lear and Gloucester, thrust into a cruel world. Disguised as a Bedlam beggar, he is reduced to the lowest form of humanity—naked, "unaccommodated man." Later as guide to his father he becomes a peasant, and finally an armed knight. He learns the value of indirection, the inadequacy of optimism, the harshness of life. He is capable of fighting aggressively for himself and others against his brother. The extent of his strength and his position among the survivors, however, depend on numerous decisions of interpretation, as well as what text is used. In the quarto Edgar emerges as rather callous and self-indulgent, and it is Albany who delivers the last lines of the play. In the folio Edgar has more dignity and maturity, and, as the future ruler, speaks the last lines.

Goneril, Regan, Edmund, have all been the unfavored children of their fathers. Modern readers have often been sympathetic in particular to Edmund's anger at being treated as unnatural because he is a "bastard," though any such sympathy is quickly blotted out by his cold cruelty to his brother and father. In the end, however, he is not a simple force of evil. He acknowledges the noble bearing of the unnamed knight before him. He is moved by Edgar's description of their father's death and tries to countermand his earlier order that Lear and Cordelia be killed. Finally, there is a pathos in his response to the deaths of Goneril and Regan, the two women who fought over him: "Yet Edmund was beloved," he says simply. Some directors have seen this side of Edmund as expendable. In Laurence Olivier's 1983 television film, most of Edmund's positive lines are cut; in Brook's version, Edmund's effort to save Lear and Cordelia is completely eliminated.

The play ends with the destruction of evil: Cornwall, Goneril, Regan, Edmund all lie dead. But it also ends with the destruction of good: Gloucester, Lear, Cordelia are also dead and Kent is dying. The play is a harsh one, pervaded by animal images, images of lechery, perjury, "undivulged crimes," of poverty and madness, of the "sulphurous pit" and the "fiend," of a raging, pitiless storm and even more pitiless human cruelty. Brook, influenced by Jan Kott's comparison of *King Lear* and Samuel Beckett's *Endgame*, conceived of the play as nihilistic, and existential image of corruption and emptiness. But there are other interpretations. Gloucester's famous speech, "As flies to wanton boys are we to th' gods; /

They kill us for their sport," comes before he understands the faithful, nurturing love of Edgar; and Lear's final tirades against human corruption come before he too learns of the love of Cordelia, the one "daughter / Who redeems Nature." For many readers and directors (Kozintsev, for example) the power of the Cordelia and Lear's recognition scene and the beauty of Lear's words to Cordelia as they are taken off to prison survive the pain of the play's ending. Near the end of the play Edgar describes Gloucester's death: finally knowing his guide to be his son, Gloucester's heart "Twixt two extremes of passion, joy and grief, / Burst smilingly." Lear dies in agony at Cordelia's death; yet there is ambiguity even in that death. Lear's last words are, "Do you see this? Look on her! Look her lips, / Look there, look there—". Does he die thinking she breathes? Does he, like Gloucester, die smilingly?

King Lear defies definitive interpretation. Its potential and life are greater than any one reading, any one production. Indeed, that very capacity is at the heart of its greatness.

—Susan T. Viguers

KING SOLOMON'S MINES.
Novel by H. Rider Haggard, 1885.

King Solomon's Mines is, arguably, one of the greatest adventure stories ever written. Published in 1885, it became an overnight sensation, a bestseller which made H. Rider Haggard a household name. It has been in print almost continuously ever since, and has been filmed several times. It is a seminal work, spawning countless imitations, and creating a new genre: the "lost world" exploration adventure. The elements combined in *King Solomon's Mines* for the first time are now items in a well established formula: a fast moving plot, a "lost" or "forgotten" civilisation which preserves primitive cults and superstitions, violent action, fabulous treasure, awesome ancient temples, and a small group of clearly delineated (if not caricatured) heroes.

The book prefigures much of the popular fantasy writing of the 20th century by drawing extensively on ancient societies—those of Egypt, the Vikings, and the Old Testament—to create a new fictional world. The hero, Allan Quatermain, a white hunter, is approached by Sir Henry Curtis to act as a guide in the search for his brother. With them go Captain Good, and the native warrior Umbopa. With the aid of an ancient map, the four journey through a desert, across the mountains named Sheba's Breasts, to Kukuanaland. Once there, they become involved in the struggle to overthrow the despotic King Twala, in favour of Umbopa, who is revealed to be the true heir to the Kukuana throne.

Some of the armies of Kukuanaland join them against Kwala's forces, and a great battle ensues, which is won by Umbopa. The heroes then explore King Solomon's diamond mines, led by the old hag Gagool. She entombs them in a rock cavern, but they escape. The heroes return to civilisation, and on their return journey meet Curtis's brother.

In Allan Quatermain Haggard finds his ideal narrator, as is testified by Quatermain's reappearance as the narrator of many of the author's subsequent African adventures. Quatermain is tough, bluff, and self-deprecating in the English manner. On the first page he tells us "I am a timid man and dislike violence," though he has killed "many men" and 66 lions. In a tongue-in-cheek introduction Quatermain apologises for the plain language of his tale, but adds "'a sharp spear,' runs the Kukuana saying, 'needs no polish.'" In fact, Quatermain's spare style and vivid descriptions are ideal for his material, which is composed almost entirely of spectacle and incident. The worst elements in his style can be traced to a juvenile humour (the book is dedicated to "all the big and little boys who read it"). Hence the embarrassing schoolboy jokes surrounding Captain Good are mercilessly overworked. Good's white legs, false teeth, glass eye, and whiskers are all taken as signs of semi-divine status by impressionable natives. Yet the juvenile ethos is also responsible for much of the book's attraction as an adventure story. One aspect of this is an absorbing interest in military tactics and weapons. Quatermain lists precisely all the guns taken by the heroes: "the reader will observe that . . . the cartridges were interchangeable, a very important point." Another is the fascination with bloodshed and with death. In the course of the tale we meet corpses preserved by an astonishing variety of means. Jose da Silvestra, a Portuguese nobleman, is deep frozen "fresh as New Zealand Mutton" for three centuries, while the kings of Kukuanaland are preserved by being turned into human stalagmites. Watching over these bodies is an enormous effigy of Death himself.

Quatermain comes into his own in his descriptions of the great set pieces of the book, such as the heroes' pretence of darkening the moon during the eclipse, and the great battle against Twala's forces. In the latter, Haggard is drawing directly on first-hand accounts of battles in the Zulu wars, which he recorded during his years in the Transvaal.

Throughout Haggard's writing, death is one of the themes which inspires him most, and is the subject of the most memorable, and poetic, lines of *King Solomon's Mines*. These come in the stark solemnity of Umbopa's speech in chapter 5, which begins "What is life?"

While Quatermain claims that "there is not a *petticoat* in the whole history" woman is by no means absent. Banished from conscious view, the sexual element returns to the tale in distorted form. The travellers penetrate a forbidden country whose landscape represents a woman's body magnified to a geographical scale. Crossing Sheba's Breasts (which have nipples thousands of feet high), they find themselves in a fecund valley where a brook flows, "bordered with dense masses of a gigantic species of maidenhair fern."

Once in this territory, threatening female images abound: the wrinkled and Methuselan Gagool (who prefigures Ayesha in *She*), the witch-finders, dressed only in snakeskins and girdles of bones, whose touch sends men to instant death, and the grim monolithic statue of Astarte, "of great though severe beauty."

This last figure draws attention to the one scene which cuts across the ethos of a romance with a darker and more serious note: the appearance of "the silent ones." These are the first of a long line of colossal statues in Haggard's fiction. They play no part in the plot, but punctuate the landscape with symbolic forms of fearful or mystical significance. The "Silent Ones" (one representing a devil, one a remote but cruel god, one a severe Goddess) provide early evidence of the mystical and religious concern which became more and more important in Haggard's writing as his career continued. It is one of the strengths of the "lost world" novel that it can easily accommodate such content. In Haggard's fiction, the unexplored interior of Africa becomes, like Stoker's Transylvania, the country of the imagination. All things are possible within it. *King Solomon's Mines* begins Haggard's "exploration" of this Africa, projecting dreams and fantasies into the heart of a dark continent.

—Edmund Cusick

KINSHIP.
Poem by Seamus Heaney, 1975.

Interpretation of "Kinship" requires knowledge of historical evidence made available to Seamus Heaney by P.V. Glob's *The Bog People* (1969), which gives a full account of the sacred spring wedding, first described by Tacitus, once celebrated by Germanic tribes in a "holy grove" on "an island of the ocean." The chosen bridegroom, with attendants of the sacred chariot of the bride Nerthus, the fertility goddess, was killed and "straightway swallowed" by the lake where the sacrificial rites were carried out, causing "a mysterious terror" in the populace. Bodies of these victims and "cloven oak" representations of Nerthus are among the items which Glob records as having been preserved by and recovered from the Danish bogs.

This myth allowed Heaney to combine his growing fascination with the peat bog as emblematic of Ireland and his feelings about the political situation in a number of poems which have received much critical attention. "Kinship," centrally placed in *North* and the longest piece in the book, is the conclusion and culmination of these poems, which first began to appear in *Wintering Out*. Previous pieces concentrated on specific finds, but the subject of "Kinship" is the poet himself, as the poem investigates alternately the nature of the actual land and the poet's identification—the "Kinship" of the title —with the sacrificial victims. As he explores his national history and his own deepest feelings Heaney discovers that he possesses primitive impulses and reactions, like the dog that flattens itself a place in the undergrowth—another "nest in the bracken"—on the kitchen floor. Eventually he is forced to abandon his attempt to find adequate expression for the sufferings of his native land, unable to achieve the necessary detachment.

Even in the opening section, where the terrain is objectively described, the identification of the poet as Nerthus's lover and bridegroom begins: "I love this turf-face." Sections II and IV explore the nature of the bog as life-giver, preserver and destroyer, connecting fertility and death as in the ancient ritual. Sections III and V are narrative, concerned directly with the poet and his desire to identify with the peat-diggers. Digging in the bog has always been for Heaney symbolic of the poetic process, in which he contemplates Ireland's past and uncovers the depths of his own mind: a sense of continuity with his peat-digging forebears is attained through this image.

The second section reveals the poet's uncertain and ambiguous response to his divided land. It preserves treasures, yet is a "midden"; it is a source of life, yet "slime kingdoms ..of.. dirtied eggs" evokes sexuality with apparent revulsion. Heaney explores Celtic roots ("bog / meaning soft"), while the heavily-stressed short lines and the kennings ("Earth-pantry," "bone-vault") suggest the influence of Anglo-Saxon verse. Acknowledging the bog's "dark side," the poet finds this also in himself. Section IV proclaims the land's power: it is the antithesis of Yeats's enfeebled civilisation, the centre which could not hold. Womb and grave, the bog devours its offspring in an endless process, and the poet feels drawn to it, though "weeping" and "gravity" suggest his unease.

In sections III and V Heaney uncovers buried artefacts connected with peat-digging. First the lifting of a turf-spade covered by spring growth is sensuously described; but action and language have erotic overtones, and the incident is ominously linked with the unearthing of a representation of Nerthus. A note of awe and fear is introduced as the goddess rises to confront him: "catkin and bog-cotton tremble." The attempt to dig brings only a beloved who seeks a victim. Suggestions of the erotic continue in V with "cupid's bow" and the reappearance of "lips," but this confident scene is set, significantly, in Heaney's youth, when he rejoiced in his association with the driver of the turf-cart, seen as godlike in his masculinity and power. The epithets applied to the driver may suggest a combination of Apollo and Prometheus, hinting at the benefits that Heaney once supposed the poet could confer on mankind. He appears here to inhabit an exclusively male world, but the adorned cart and his status as "privileged / attendant" are reminders of the fate of those who ministered to the sacred chariot, and it is Nerthus who dominates in the final section.

Here, Heaney abandons his attempt to interpret Ireland's tragedy. Aware of the incredulous gaze of the outside world, he merely records the blood-bath, shown by verbal links, to an earlier section ("sour" and the homophonous "mother") as pertaining to the very nature of the land; but he denies Wallace Stevens's dictum that the mind can create through poetry "something that will suffice." "Sacred heart" introduces the Catholic aspect of the problem, giving new overtones to the preceding "faithful"; while media reactions are hinted at in the plea to Tacitus to return as a fair reporter. The poet meanwhile achieves only "a desolate peace." Slaughter appears accepted; but the poem ends with Heaney as victim, torn to the last between conflicting reactions.

"Kinship" is perhaps Heaney's most disturbed formulation of his difficulties in responding to Ireland today. For some, the myth to which he resorts appears to distort the actual situation too one-sidedly and comfortably (despite the gruesome "gargling"); yet the final section is powerfully moving. The poem also weaves together themes and language from the first half of the book, while connecting this, through an auditory link between "island of the ocean" and the ensuing title, to the more confrontational pieces that follow. In addition to displaying the preoccupations and characteristics of Heaney's mature work, "Kinship" shows a structural ability which he has not yet matched elsewhere.

—Margaret Forey

THE KNIGHT OF THE BURNING PESTLE.
Play by Francis Beaumont, c.1607.

Francis Beaumont's *The Knight of the Burning Pestle* is one of the most accessible of Jacobean dramas. It is a remarkably funny (and obvious) farce, but it is also a pointed (and not so obvious) play on the theme of illusion and reality, the relation of audience world to fictive world—a theme as modern as it is Jacobean.

The play begins with an actor delivering a prologue, but he is almost immediately interrupted by a man from the audience who climbs onto the stage and insists on seeing a play that will honor the "commons of the city." The Citizen is soon joined by his Wife, who is similarly vocal about her desires. What ensues is the concurrent performance of two plays, one directed by the Citizen and the Wife and the other the company's intended play, scenes from one alternating with scenes from the other.

The Citizen and the Wife's play stars their apprentice Ralph. It is an outstanding example in English literature of a burlesque of the chivalric tale, with numerous similarities to *Don Quixote*. In his first scene Ralph enters reading one of the same books that influenced Don Quixote. Like Don Quixote, Ralph becomes a knight errant—actually, a "grocer-errant," naming himself the Knight of the Burning Pestle—and sets out to rescue distressed damsels and accomplish "feats of arms." In the tradition of the knight from La Mancha, he causes trouble when he thinks he is helping, assumes knights are exempt from such conventions as payment for room and board, pulls others into his chivalric fictions, fights a so-called "giant," holds in his heart a local wench ("black thumbed Susan") and graciously declines the favors of an exotic princess. Ralph's story does not, however, have the philosophical and emotional richness of Cervantes's novel: it is simply ridiculous exaggeration. And unlike Don Quixote, who returns home defeated and ill, Ralph's final episodes at home show him very much in command. He leads his men as Lord of the May and later as city-captain at Mile-End, and his triumphant death (with its glorification of his trade) is one of the funniest in literature. "I die, fly, fly my soul to Grocers' Hall. Oh, oh, oh, etc.," he cries.

The company's play is also about an apprentice, but one the opposite of Ralph, one who distresses his master. Jasper, apprentice to the merchant Venturewell, is dismissed from service because he dares love his master's daughter Luce, for whom Venturewell has other plans. Although a fuller and more coherent story than Ralph's, this one is also farcical. The merchant's antipathy is unreasonable; Luce is unwaveringly faithful; Jasper's sudden decision to test his beloved is preposterous; the rival suitor, Humphrey, is preeminently silly; the merchant's sudden, total change of heart is absurd. The characters are caricatures; the plot elements formulaic.

Humor, however, is not only present to point up the ludicrousness of popular artistic taste. In the figure of Merry thought—Jasper's father and the center of a secondary plot in the company's play—mirth (surely the audience's experience of the two plays) is aligned to health. Merrythought—destitute, old, faced with the supposed death of his son Jasper, but still merry—ends in the position of power, the power to create the play's happy ending. He obtains the forgiveness of the merchant for Jasper. He takes back his responsible, but unkindly wife, who left him in distaste for his profligate merrymaking. And he imposes mirth on the whole group. "'Tis nought but mirth," they all sing in the final song of the play, "That keeps the body from the earth!"

Humor, both satire and mirth, also defines the Citizen and the Wife. Beaumont satirizes their artistic naivety, their merchant-class values, their self-absorption. Their inability to distinguish between illusion and reality is as striking as Don Quixote's own. When Jasper draws his sword on Luce, the Wife cries to her husband, "Away, George, away! rise the watch at Ludgate." And at one point she herself is about to speak to Venturewell on behalf of Humphrey. The Citizen and the Wife's values are made clear by their responses to the company's play. The Wife is drawn to the wrong characters: the merchant, Humphrey, and Jasper's priggish brother Michael. Jasper, in contrast, arouses her aversion. She and her husband are materialistic and pro-authority. As the play progresses, eventually ending very differently from how the Wife would have devised, she simply loses interest in it. They see what they want—the glorification of their own Ralph, bringing honor, of course, to themselves. They are not, however, reduced to caricature. The warmth of their relationship, their enthusiasms, their generosity make them positive. The Wife is initially drawn to Merrythought (until he denies his wife reentry into his house), and behind that attraction seems a genuine good-naturedness, the capacity for which is the concluding blessing of the play.

Their limitations yet their liveliness and warmth are part of what makes them two of the most rounded, realistic characters in all Elizabethan and Jacobean comedy. Their realism is the key to the sophistication of Beaumont's handling of illusion and reality. The Citizen and the Wife never act like characters in a play; they seem as much a part of the audience as the gentlemen in the audience to whom the Wife speaks. In contrast, the farcical nature of the inner plays calls attention to their being artifice. Play world and audience world, illusion and reality, seem clearly separated. Only, what seems real is as much a part of the play as what seems fiction. The play is a spoof on audience tastes and values, but it is also a more complex vision of how difficult it is to differentiate between illusion (or wish-fulfilling fantasy) and reality. We, the *real* audience, are set up to be as taken in by the Citizen and the Wife as they are by the plays they are watching. Do we, like they, see only what we want to see, see nothing that would challenge our sense of ourselves?

—Susan T. Viguers

KRAPP'S LAST TAPE.
Play by Samuel Beckett, 1958.

Samuel Beckett's short play is a dramatised reflection on time and memory, and confirms the early influence on him of Proust. In many ways the best introduction to the play is Beckett's witty and sardonic essay on the French novelist, although it dates from 1931, more than 25 years before the play, which was staged in 1958. *Krapp's Last Tape* was Beckett's third piece for the theatre, his reputation having been established only four years previously by the success of *Waiting for Godot*.

The play presents us with an old man (Krapp is apparently barely short of the biblical three score years and ten—perhaps a hint of the exemplary nature of his case) who prepares to record a tape reviewing the past year in his life (just as he has habitually done each year on the eve of his birthday). His preparation involves listening to a previous year from his series of birthday retrospectives, recorded when he was about 39—"at the crest of the wave," as he puts it. In its turn that tape was not only a reflection upon the year just past but a commentary on yet another earlier tape made when he was about 27. At 27 Krapp had already established these habits of retrospection, so that by the time the 69-year-old Krapp adds his "last" tape (perhaps only with the sense of latest) the effect of the series is like that of mirror images inside mirror images, presenting us with a long temporal perspective, within which successive Krapps look backwards in scorn or mystification upon their predecessors. When the kinship is acknowledged it is with bitter sarcasms at the younger self's pretensions and illusions; at times earlier selves are encountered as deluded strangers and viewed with hostility or incomprehension. The question of identity amid this habitual process of reiterated denial, flux, re-definition, and contraction is rendered problematical. Krapp is of course always the same (and conspicuously the prisoner of his habits—witness the weakness for bananas, and for drink, his sexual relations, the whole apparatus of ledger and tape-recorder, etc., and yet forever changing as the perspective from which he views himself shifts.

Although action is conspicuously absent, thanks to the innovatory use of the tape recorder, these conflicts between successive Krapps are nevertheless highly dramatic. What the younger Krapp thought of (ironically) as "memorable" and "unforgettable" either does not interest the older man or drives him to exasperation. The climactic ironic conflict comes in the play's final moments when a still defiant but embittered Krapp listens to the falsely confident and assertive voice of Krapp at 39 summing up: "Perhaps my best years are gone. When there was a chance of happiness. But I wouldn't want them back. Not with the fire in me now. No, I wouldn't want them back." The tape runs on into silence. How much he wants back the very things he set his face against all those years ago is of course demonstrated by his repeated playing of the passage on the tape that is annotated in the ledger by the phrase "goodbye to Love." What is dramatised for us is the process of ageing, of loss, of living in time, which constitutes the "exfoliation" of identity Beckett had described in *Proust*. And Krapp's election for rational control, for the light, his refusal of the "hopeless business" of love, the chaos of emotion, his balking at the limits of self and order (signified repeatedly by his concern with the "eyes" of the various women of whom he speaks) have conspired to leave him isolated and alone. Proust taught us that love and friendship are self-deceptions, Beckett had said in 1931, "Wisdom consists not in the satisfaction, but in the ablation of desire." On these sterile but rational premisses Krapp has conducted the orderly progress of his life. To no avail, for now the final darkness gathers about him.

The repetitions constitute the formal mode of the inner quest for the ideal core of the onion, the excavatory, centripetal process by which one searches for one's own identity. It is a process which in *Proust* he had described as for him the one valid form of artistic endeavour. The essential condition of mankind's loneliness is in one sense what stands revealed by the play. Krapp fully justifies the assertion that man is a creature that cannot come forth from himself.

Repetition moreover involves the meta-dramatic elements within the play (the notion of a text endlessly replayed to a detached but engaged audience, the white boots, clown's nose, banana skins). We go on repeating ourselves—and would like to go on doing so *ad infinitum*: "once wasn't enough for you." The recording ensures the possibility of repetition, which hindsight denies. What the repetitive pattern infers is the essentially inescapable nature of the central obsessive concern. The same holds true for the linguistic and symbolic repetitions in the play—the interplay between black and white, light and dark, etc., which are pervasive.

The dramatic structuring of the play also depends upon a series of reiterations and repetitions, for as Krapp plays the tape which makes up most of the text of *Krapp's Last Tape* several times over, never does he play precisely the same section of the tape twice; he always begins or ends in different places. Plainly this device provokes curiosity and defers its satisfaction so that we do not hear the very end of Krapp's tape until Beckett has gathered into those moments their fullest implication.

Krapp has striven to keep control, to keep emotion at bay, to bring everything into the light of rational control. His is the very opposite in this sense of Proust's emotional indulgence. The apparently random allusions to previous tapes (of Krapp at 27 and 39) in fact direct us to moments in his life when first his father and then his mother died. (Death is the ultimate promise of life-in-time.) His reference to these events is characteristically unemotional, and consistent with his approach to his own imminent death. Emotion is held in check. Unfortunately for Krapp, the undirected, involuntary aspect of the tape-memory confronts him with episodes from his own past which are truly forgotten and are now therefore truly re-experienced (Proust's madeleine episode). This encounter with his own emotional life—in particular his involuntary memory of the girl in the punt—renders him vulnerable at the very moment when he is trying to gird himself for death, defended by irony, cynicism, comic stoicism. The false confidence of the middle-aged Krapp sounds intensely ironic to the confused, angry, embittered (yet stoical) figure who sits and listens, and who in spite of himself desperately wants to "be again." In Beckett's world, rationality provides no adequate defence (though it may seem the only available one) against the absurdity of human existence. Life is a condition that, according to Beckett, "admits of no palliative."

—Brian W.M. Scobie

KUBLA KHAN.
Poem by Samuel Taylor Coleridge, 1816 (written 1797).

Traditionally regarded as an unfinished, somewhat chaotic account of an opium-induced dream, Samuel Taylor Coleridge's "Kubla Khan" has teased the imagination of critics almost from the moment it was written. The poet, himself, however, has left a description of its genesis which would appear to preclude all speculation. He wrote in a preface to the poem that he had composed it in his sleep, after taking an "anodyne." He had been reading an account of Xanadu by the Elizabethan travel writer, Samuel Purchas, and had fallen asleep over it, awakening three hours later after having experienced a dream. It was especially vivid, and in Coleridge's own words, he took "pen, ink and paper and eagerly wrote down the lines that are here preserved." Indeed, the poet continues, the poem might have been even longer had he not been "called out by a person on business from Porlock, and detained by him above an hour." On his return, to Coleridge's "no small surprise and mortification," with the exception of "some eight or ten scattered lines and images, all the rest had passed away."

Many have found difficulty in believing that Coleridge was able to write down "Kubla Khan" at one go in the spontaneous manner he describes. Still others doubt that the poem is as Coleridge describes it, a "fragment." On the contrary, it is now generally believed that the poem has a quite logical structure and far from being merely a phantasmagoria of colourful images, it makes a statement about the nature of the artistic imagination. However, such is the fluid nature of the poem that it is difficult to ascribe a precise meaning to it, or, in particular, to determine whether Coleridge has written a general celebration of the poetic imagination or whether one is justified in seeing it as a figuring forth of the theory of the imagination expounded in his prose treatise, the *Biographia Literaria*.

The opening description of the pleasure dome reveals a combination of pleasure and sacredness, which were for both Coleridge and his friend Wordsworth essential features of true poetry. However, its well-ordered precision, reinforced by the heavy alliterative binding of key words, suggests also that it might be intended to reflect the operation of what Coleridge specifically referred to as the "fancy," in which the poetic spirit is set in motion by the "conscious will." In the second stanza, which explores the kinds of passionate and miraculous experiences with which romantic poetry deals, Coleridge also suggests the way the creative imagination operates, concluding that it is often under threat. This, more specifically, could be a description of how Coleridge's "primary imagination" operates, reconciling opposing ideas and images in one indivisible whole, the "miracle of rare device / A sunny dome with caves of ice."

In the final stanza, where the poet appears to recollect and describe a moment of extreme rapture, he goes on to express the wish that he might revive and prolong that moment through an act of artistic creation, so as to experience again his previous ecstasy. This, certainly, has strong suggestions of Coleridge's theory of the "secondary imagination," which "dissolves, diffuses, dissipates in order to recreate." The poem ends with a suggestion of the ambiguity of the poet's status, blessed with vision yet, like all prophets, separate from the crowd and potentially dangerous.

While "Kubla Khan" may be read as a general statement about the workings of the poetic imagination or, more particularly, as a demonstration of the operation of Coleridge's "fancy" and "primary and secondary imagination," as defined in his *Biographia Literaria*, it is also possible to find in the poem's densely woven texture meanings which radiate out from the central theme of poetic creation. For example, as many critics have noted, this blessed activity creates a state of being akin to that enjoyed by our first parents in the Garden of Eden; there are several echoes of Milton's description of Eden in *Paradise Lost*. Moreover, there is also a suggestion of the important role played by woman in guiding the poet's spirit, analogous to Beatrice's conducting Dante or Goethe's *ewige weibliche* who leads the poet on high in the second part of *Faust*, a role which Coleridge looked to Sarah Hutchinson to play in his own life.

Such resonances deepen the poem's meaning rather than suggest alternative readings, which is no doubt why "Kubla Khan" has endured so well. Surrealistic, symbolic, evocative, "Kubla Khan" stands quite apart from other English Romantic poetry of the time; it belongs to a tradition more spiritedly followed in Europe than in England, where Wordsworth's more homely poetic influence evoked a more sympathetic response.

—John M. Munro

L

LADY AUDLEY'S SECRET.
Novel by Mary Elizabeth Braddon, 1862.

Lady Audley's Secret is a well-written thriller which established a literary reputation, helped define a fictional form, and introduced an important literary type. The form was the sensation novel, the controversial sub-genre that dominated the popular fiction of the 1860's; and the immense success of *Lady Audley's Secret*, one of the bestselling novels of the 19th century, ensured that Mary Elizabeth Braddon was recognized, along with Wilkie Collins, as the leader of this school. The literary type was Lady Audley herself, the first of those beautiful fiends abhorred by many contemporary reviewers and the subject of renewed critical interest today.

Lady Audley's Secret contains all the major features of what was to become the sensation novel formula, with its obsessive emphasis on disguised identities and social alienation. To Audley Court, a tranquil little world removed in space and, architecturally, in time from the hubbub of mid-Victorian life, comes Helen Talboys, who has assumed a false identity and bigamously married Sir Michael Audley. As the action of the novel unfolds with the efforts of Robert Audley, Sir Michael's nephew, to penetrate the mysteries which surround Lady Audley and her own increasingly violent efforts to defend her false position, Braddon concentrates insistently on the alienating consequences of Lady Audley's imposture. Sir Michael is estranged from his daughter; Robert is exiled from Audley Court and estranged from his friends in London; George Talboys, Lady Audley's first husband whom she attempts to kill, feels compelled to leave England secretly and must "endure the loneliness of an existence which separated him from every friend he had ever known"; and finally Sir Michael too must become "an exile from his own house" to escape his wife's polluting presence. Appropriately, when Lady Audley's mask is stripped away, she is in turn deprived of her social identity, immured in a Belgian *maison de santé* under a false name, and the novel concludes with Talboys's return and the establishment by Robert Audley of a new domestic haven.

Despite this conventional closing vision, in which virtue triumphs and mid-Victorian anxieties about social identity and the threat of alienation are comfortingly allayed, there were features of this and other sensation novels which dismayed contemporary reviewers. Sensation novels emphasized plot rather than character analysis. They obscured the traditional boundaries between realism and romance, setting the passions and crimes associated with gothic fiction and transpontine drama in the contemporary world of telegraphs and railways, Pre-Raphaelite painters and dreary suburban developments. They suggested that mystery and crime were a frequently hidden but omnipresent feature of modern middle-class life, and often encouraged sympathy for morally ambiguous characters. Their popularity was deemed a frightening sign of the decay of taste and morality, and their depiction of women one of their chief offences.

Blonde and beautiful, a talented painter and musician beloved in the neighborhood of Audley Court, Lady Audley is also a bigamist, arsonist, and attempted murderess. In her and her successors, the angel in the house becomes a demon, an image of woman's capacity for passion and wickedness. Reviewers recognized in her the intrusion into fiction of a New Woman, whose existence outside the overheated world of the sensation novel they wished to deny. It is precisely Lady Audley's subversion of fictional conventions and cultural norms that has attracted critical attention in recent years. In *A Literature of Their Own*, Elaine Showalter contends that, in characters like Lady Audley, Braddon and others

> made a powerful appeal to the female audience by subverting the traditions of feminine fiction to suit their own imaginative impulses, by expressing a wide range of suppressed female emotions, and by tapping and satisfying fantasies of protest and escape. . . . As every woman reader must have sensed, Lady Audley's real secret is that she is *sane* and, moreover, representative.

However, subversion in *Lady Audley's Secret* is not confined to the title character and the novel's female readers. Robert Audley, though less frequently discussed, no less clearly attacks the foundations of Victorian life. A briefless barrister, contentedly idling away his existence in bachelor quarters in the Temple, Robert is a "young philosopher of the modern school" who denies that life is serious and refuses to be earnest. As he tells Lady Audley, "I have enrolled myself in the ranks of a profession, the members of which hold solemn responsibilities, and have sacred duties to perform; and I have shrunk from those responsibilities and duties, as I have from all the fatigues of this troublesome life." When the disappearance of his friend, George Talboys, forces him grudgingly to accept the role of amateur detective, Robert denies the sanctity of womanhood too in misogynistic outbursts like the following:

> "It's all woman's work from one end to the other. . . . They are Semiramides, and Cleopatras, and Joan of Arcs, Queen Elizabeths, and Catharine the Seconds, and they riot in battle, and murder, and clamour and desperation. . . . To call them the weaker sex is to utter a hideous mockery. They are the stronger sex, the noisier, the more persevering, the most self-assertive sex. . . . I hate women," he thought savagely.

Lady Audley and Robert Audley challenge conventional assumptions about woman in similar ways; but when the former is declared mad and the latter converted by love for Clara Talboys to a life of purposiveness and domestic bliss, orthodoxy prevails, for the sensation novel is not ultimately a literature of protest but melodrama renovated for a middle-class audience. The special appeal of *Lady Audley's Secret* and the sensation novel generally is in part the pleasure of an exciting tale well told, but also the ability of this form to express the anxieties and hostilities of mid-Victorian readers within a familiar and cathartic framework.

—Randolph Ivy

LADY CHATTERLEY'S LOVER.
Novel by D.H. Lawrence, 1928 (and later versions).

D.H. Lawrence began work on what was to become *Lady Chatterley's Lover* in Italy in October 1926; he first published the novel there in 1928. Lawrence's practice of repeated rewriting produced three versions of the Chatterley story—*The First Lady Chatterley*, *John Thomas and Lady Jane*, and *Lady Chatterley's Lover*, the last being the version with which we have been most familiar since its publication by Penguin in 1960, and the accompanying obscenity trial.

Lady Chatterley's Lover was D.H. Lawrence's last extended effort to persuade or antagonize readers, particularly English readers, into a recognition that what they took to be commonsense, the *via media*, level-headedness, reasonableness was, in fact, dull and deadening mediocrity. *Lady Chatterley's Lover* is not a temperate book, but the work of a man *in extremis*; and extremity has its absurdity as well as its brilliance. The novel is perhaps now paying the price which the passage of time exacts from any form of extremity, originality, or idiosyncrasy of thought—a degree of absurdity and silliness. The novel marks the extreme point of what Lawrence called his "thought-adventure," and while it may not represent his finest thinking, it lays bare, in stark and exciting ways, his fundamental premises, and their potential contradictions and tensions. Lawrentians have always regretted that *Lady Chatterley's Lover* is the work for which Lawrence is best known. Consequently they have ignored it, dismissed it, domesticated it, or have rescued from it a few set-pieces which we may safely admire. The wider reading public has appropriated *Lady Chatterley's Lover* in a variety of ways—as pornography, as a contribution to the campaigns against censorship and for civil and sexual liberties, as a counter-case which has energized the feminist cause. But *Lady Chatterley's Lover* bears, at most, a tangential relation to these appropriations. It is an idiosyncratic novel; it is a more humorous novel than has been recognized; above all, it is a shocking novel. But the shock of *Lady Chatterley's Lover* lies less in its subject matter than in its modernity of styles. It is marked, like so much of Lawrence's writing, by an extraordinary and disturbing fluidity of voices, tones, and registers—a fluidity which "throws" the reader, challenging any distinctions we may have between the serious and the trivial, between what does and does not matter, between what requires reverence and what invites mockery.

To the modern world which he so thoroughly rejects, Lawrence opposes the sexually explicit and adulterous relationship of Lady Constance Chatterley and her gamekeeper, Oliver Mellors. Feminist critics have objected to what they see here as Lawrence's bullying veneration of male sexuality and the phallic imagination. There is some truth in the attack, but Lawrence's treatment of sexuality is too idiosyncratic to be representative of a general male chauvinism. Moreover, men and male sexuality are the objects of a great deal of mockery and comedy in *Lady Chatterley's Lover*, comedy which both the novel's admirers and its critics, equally sombre, have hitherto failed to note. In fact, Connie's and Mellors's sexual explorations lead to a moving and largely persuasive affirmation, not of male power, but of the value of touch and tenderness. Thus, at the novel's close, Mellors learns a new creed: "I stand for the touch of bodily awareness between human beings . . . and the touch of tenderness." During the writing of the novel, Lawrence toyed with the possibility of *Tenderness* as a title for his work, a title which reflects the novel's true emphasis.

But *Lady Chatterley's Lover* seems insufficiently aware of what Mellors himself calls "All the complications" of a world which "allows no hermit." Thus the question of a sustaining social context for Connie's and Mellors's relationship hovers anxiously at the periphery of *Lady Chatterley's Lover*, but is never adequately answered. Intermittently, Mellors wonders vaguely about a future life in the Colonies. But the novel ends, leaving the couple waiting, apart, for the various entanglements of their previous marriages to be sorted out. And this is just as well, since the most plausible indication of their future together which *Lady Chatterley's Lover* gives us is of Mellors set up as a farmer with the help of Connie's capital. Lawrence is careful *not* to inquire too closely into where the money comes from. But to present the couple living on this is to present a relationship subsidized by the society which the novel so vehemently reviles: Lawrence terminates his narrative before this contradiction emerges too blatantly. It is a problem which Lawrence never satisfactorily addresses nor resolves. And *Lady Chatterley's Lover* is not alone in this respect: in their endings, *Sons and Lovers*, *The Rainbow*, and *Women in Love* all equivocate over, or evade the problem of defining a sustaining social context for their central characters' happiness. Moreover, the evidence of the unsatisfactory and nomadic nature of Lawrence's own life suggests that the problem of finding of a "new world" was one that, in his life as in his art, he never solved.

—John M. Lyon

THE LADY OF SHALOTT.
Poem by Alfred, Lord Tennyson, 1832.

Published in the volume of 1832 and revised for the 1842 *Poems*, "The Lady of Shalott" is Alfred, Lord Tennyson's first treatment of Arthurian legend and is based on an Italian romance, *Donna di Scalotta*, Shalott being Astolat and the Lady resembling Elaine, the maid of Astolat, whose story Tennyson was to recount in *Idylls of the King*. The poem belongs to the romantic tradition, and its richly sensuous imagery recalls Keats, while the air of mystery and abrupt shifts of scene and image create a vivid, dream-like quality comparable to that of "The Rime of the Ancient Mariner." Like Keats and Coleridge too, Tennyson uses narrative to suggest, indirectly and paradoxically, ideas about human life. The central themes concern isolation, apprehension of reality, and the proper province of art.

Initially the Lady resembles other of Tennyson's isolated maidens—Mariana, Oenone, the Soul in "The Palace of Art." Dwelling in the island tower, she is barred from the outside world by the four grey walls, the river, and the threatened curse; and her alienation is increased, not alleviated, by the window, through which she is forbidden to look, and the mirror, which provides her only view of the world. At first her solitude seems to ensure peace and to possess its own attractiveness, depicted by the wolds, the long fields, and the slowly winding river. But the serenity of the landscape belongs only to the Lady's perspective, and the reference to the "reaper weary" (line 33) hints that, viewed from another perspective, the scene would be very different. Moreover, the reaper's whisper, "'Tis the fairy / Lady of Shalott" (lines 35–6), indicates directly the Lady's essential foreignness.

Part two takes up these suggestions to develop a sense of imprisonment and stagnation. The river is now a whirling eddy, and the road a busy highway, down which passes a spectrum of medieval society—market girls and damsels, abbots and shepherds, knights and ladies. From this activity the Lady is separated, and the curse, the mirror, the unending weaving suggest that she is in fact buried alive, excluded from the sorrows and joys of human life. It is the reflection of two lovers that first prompts her to rebellion as she declares, "I am half sick of shadows" (line 71). Her subsequent rejection of the conditions of her magical, protected environment precipitates the dramatic climax and the thematic development of the poem.

The sudden intrusion of Lancelot brings into sharp focus the conflict between the Lady's world of shadows and the real world of human concerns and passion. Riding in the sunlight, he represents the brightness and dynamism of Camelot, and the details of his appearance—the glistening armour, bejewelled bridle and saddle, silver bugle, and burnished helmet—coalesce to produce an image of dazzling radiance. That Lancelot's world contains its own dangers is obliquely suggested by his warrior status: although he comes in peace, singing the Tirra lirra song which is an expression of his vital energy, he appears "a bow shot" from the tower; he is dressed in full armour, riding his war horse; and he is on his way to Camelot, seat of military prowess. Nevertheless, the pull of human ties induces the Lady to defy the curse, and as she looks out of the window, she sees the blooming lily, the helmet, and the plume, symbols of nature, heroic glory, and love. In leaving the tower, then, she enters the mortal world of time, movement, change, and death.

The consequences are immediate. A storm arises, and the straining wind and complaining stream contrast sharply with the earlier enchanted landscape of little breezes and clear river. Embarking on the river, suggestive of the progress of human life, the Lady asserts her human identity by writing her name upon the boat, and then, like all human beings, begins her journey to death, chanting the song of her life as she does so. She has chosen contact with Camelot, even at the price of her own destruction, and achieves her goal as she gains the marvelling, if fearful, recognition of the citizens and the awed reverence of Lancelot, ironically unaware that he is the cause of her death. She has exchanged shadows for reality and has escaped from a sterile death-in-life, moved into the world of experience, and finally suffered death, a natural part of the human condition.

But the Lady's story has a further, more ambiguous significance in that it deals with the role of the artist. As a weaver, the Lady is a dedicated artist, working night and day, but her seclusion, while it enables her to create a magical and beautiful web, prohibits her from active involvement with humanity. Thus the poem presents a conflict between the artist's need for withdrawal and the demands of human contact and social responsibility. When she leaves the tower, the Lady forsakes her art as she has hitherto practised it, and the web is torn from the loom. This is not to say, however, that she abandons art entirely. Instead, the art of the tapestry is replaced by the art of the song, which reflects the complexities and contradictions of human life, since it is both loud and low, both mournful and holy, the result of her entrance into life and the accompaniment of her voyage to death. Thus the poem perhaps suggests that, despite the appeal of solitary detachment, the artist cannot achieve full self-realization without participation in the tumult of human life.

"The Lady of Shalott" defies rigid interpretation. The Lady's choice has been seen both as a triumphal move to engagement with life and as a violation of the detachment necessary to her art, and analysis of the poem ranges from explanation of the Platonic symbolism of light and shadow to deconstructionist readings of the Lady as an allegory of the poetic text or "signatory act." Certainly the poem is problematic and reflects Tennyson's own inner conflicts. Ultimately, however, the central paradoxes—that freedom and love may involve destruction and that acceptance of life is also acceptance of death—are also the paradoxes of the human condition itself.

—Muriel Mellown

THE LADY'S NOT FOR BURNING.
Play by Christopher Fry, 1948.

The Lady's Not for Burning delighted its initial audiences with its poetic exuberance. Playgoers whose experience with modern verse drama had been limited to Eliot's tightly controlled style welcomed the metaphors, images, and puns in Christopher Fry's first full-length comedy. Although this facility with words would be called a weakness a decade later as dramas portraying an inarticulate working class took the stage, it is the hallmark of Fry's style, and cannot be ignored when we examine other aspects of the play.

When Thomas Mendip speaks of "The sky's pale belly glowing and growing big, / Soon to deliver the moon," or Alizon Eliot calls Humphrey "a winter in my head," audience responses to these people are mediated by the metaphors. The coldness Alizon evokes goes beyond a mere expression of dislike. Unfortunately, long decorated speeches do sometimes seem to substitute for a deeper probing that would help to explain motivations and reactions. On the other hand, there is more to the play than flowing words.

Fry wanted to write dramas corresponding to different seasons, and *The Lady's Not for Burning* represents spring. The outpouring of sensuous imagery is part of a larger representation of awakening or rebirth. Thomas moves from his early death-wish to a resolve to follow Jennet Jourdemayne; Jennet, condemned for witchcraft, escapes burning and grows fond of Thomas; Alizon, who has left a nunnery, avoids an arranged marriage; the orphaned clerk, Richard, leaves his dutiful life to elope with Alizon; the old rag man Jennet has supposedly killed has a real awakening from a drunken sleep. All participate in a metaphoric rebirth, and all but old Skipps leave the market town of Cool Clary with its dull officials and populace.

The play is distanced from 20th-century reality by its medieval setting, and by fantasy that makes the happy ending seem quite believable and sufficiently motivated. Thomas, disgusted by his wartime experiences, arrives demanding to be hanged, never explaining why suicide would not have sufficed. Instead Fry shifts the focus onto the reaction of protocol-bound officialdom. Thomas, though, must carry the play, with long speeches that range from poetically descriptive to sardonically observant. He develops from his existential "I breathe, / I spit, I am" to a wondering admiration of a Creation that could include laughter. Fond of language, he criticizes Jennet at characteristic length: "Madam, if I were Herod in the middle / Of the massacre of the innocents, I'd pause / Just to consider the confusion of your imagery." Mayor Tyson tries unsuccessfully to deflate him by calling him "an unappetizing young man / With a tongue too big for (his) brains." Fortunately, Fry had excellent verse speakers to play Thomas in the early productions that established the play. Alec Clunes, who had sponsored the work, premiered it, and John Gielgud took it to the West End and Broadway.

The other actors must also handle individual verse idioms easily, for no one reveals feelings by brooding silences or inarticulate one-word replies. Jennet talks eloquently of her desire to live and of the eccentric behaviour that has made her a target; Hebble Tyson is often clichéd as he tries to cope with the unexpected with authoritative statements; Margaret Devise domineers as she addresses Tyson and her sons; Justice Tappercoom runs to strings of short phrases with earthy imagery; and Skipps, ill-educated, mangles words in the only prose segment. Physical action is kept off stage. Hot-tempered Nicholas on stage assaults his brother, Humphrey, alliteratively as a "crapulous, puddering pipsqueak."

A more socially oriented author might have used the story as an obvious statement against incompetent officialdom everywhere, but Fry lets his audience make what allegorical connections they will. Thomas knows that to be executed he must have killed a man, but he can produce no body, so he is doomed to live. His quest for execution runs counter to Jennet's desire to escape burning. Ironically, she is doomed on equally slim evidence, for there is no proof that she turned Skipps into a dog. Thomas is a bothersome stranger. Jennet is locally well-known—a woman who dabbles with the scientific materials she inherited from her father, speaks French to her poodle, and has property that will come to the town if she is burned. Fry structures the play so that the two are imprisoned together where they discuss life and develop affection.

The same predictable kindling of love occurs between dutiful Richard and spunky Alizon. On the day of her engagement party, she rejects the apparently respectable Humphrey, a lecherous self-seeker. Fry adds a twist as Nicholas declares his intention of saving her from his brother. There is tension as these plots develop, with the poetry sometimes heightening, sometimes dissipating it. Imagery can add intensity; conversely, a decorated speech may obscure the urgency a brief utterance would underscore.

The two love stories, never isolated, are most closely linked at the end, when Alizon and Richard interrupt their elopement to bring back Skipps, then quietly slip off again during the excitement at his return. With the rag man alive, the only charge against Jennet is eccentricity, which does not warrant burning. She and Thomas are free to leave together, though Fry never explains why she may not simply go home. Leaving house and possessions, she fits into the April mood of renewal as she starts on a fresh path with Thomas.

The final movement is dispersal, rather than the togetherness that often characterizes comedies. The all-inclusive party had come earlier. Now the unseen mob outside must go home without a hanging or a burning. In immediate postwar Europe, Thomas's weariness and disgust were understandable. The suspicion of the eccentric may also have seemed familiar. People welcomed *The Lady's Not for Burning* not only for its poetry and romanticised notion of a medieval town, but also for its portrayal of an escape from the humdrum and from despair.

—Frances A. Shirley

THE LAKE ISLE OF INNISFREE.
Poem by William Butler Yeats, 1890.

"The Lake Isle of Innisfree," first published on 13 December 1890, in W.E. Henley's *National Observer* and later included in *The Rose* section of William Butler Yeats's *Collected Poems*, was written when the poet was living in Bedford Park, a suburb of London. This was the time when Yeats was still striving to find his authentic poetic voice, being attracted both by the dreamy romanticism of such poets as Keats and the Pre-Raphaelites (notably William Morris) and the more particularised world of Ireland and Irish myth. In the first section of his *Collected Poems*, aptly named *Crossways*, these two influences seem finely balanced, eight poems on Indian and Arcadian themes being included in the first part, followed by another eight on Irish themes in the second. It was, of course, the Irish influence which was to endure and, in Yeats's own estimation, "The Lake Isle of Innisfree" was the first properly Irish poem that he wrote.

Its genesis Yeats described in his autobiographical novel, *John Sherman*, and more briefly in a letter of 30 November 1922, replying to some schoolgirls who had asked him if Innisfree was a real island. The idea for the poem came to him, he said, while walking along Fleet Street in London, feeling "very homesick" for the Sligo countryside where he had spent much of his childhood and youth. He heard "a little tinkle of water and saw a fountain in a shop window which balanced a little ball on its jet and began to remember lake water." From this "sudden remembrance came my poem Innisfree, my first lyric with anything in its rhythm of my own music."

This was also the time, Yeats continued, when "I had begun to loosen rhythm as an escape from rhetoric and from the emotion of the crowd that rhetoric brings, but I only understood vaguely and occasionally that I must for my special purpose use nothing but the common syntax. A couple of years later I would not have written that first line with its conventional archaism—'Arise and go'—nor the inversion in the last stanza."

Thus, stylistically, "The Lake Isle of Innisfree" is a poem in which we can sense Yeats edging towards the more fluid, colloquial rhythms that characterize most of his mature work. However, it still remains a rather mannered exercise, and in Yeats's later years he admitted that he had often thought to exclude it from his *Collected Works* but found it difficult to do so because it had become so popular.

Yet, the dream-laden world which Yeats evokes is precisely described. More important, while the main concern of the poem appears to be the sights and sounds of the Sligo countryside, Yeats is also aware that the region he describes is heavy with mythic associations. In fact, although Yeats does not make these explicit, already we can detect faint traces in this early poem of his later determination to universalize his personal experience by linking it with Irish folklore and myth.

As he points out in a headnote to his poem, "The Danaan Quicken Tree," there was on the island of Innisfree an enchanted tree, whose berries were "the food of the *Tuatha de Danaan*, or faeries." Moreover, as he makes clear elsewhere in the *Autobiography*, this tree has other characteristics which link it with the biblical tree of knowledge of good and evil and the fate of Adam and Eve. In the same passage he states that the idea "to live some day in a cottage on a little island called Innisfree" came to him after he had heard his father reading from Thoreau's *Walden* and thereupon he thought "that having conquered bodily desire and the inclination of my mind toward women and love, I should live as Thoreau lived, seeking wisdom."

This idea came to him shortly after he had met the unpredictable beauty Maud Gonne, to whom he had been introduced by the Fenian leader John O'Leary in 1889; Yeats fell in love with her immediately and was to be tormented by her wayward passionate nature until his death. Therefore, while "The Lake Isle of Innisfree" on one level expresses simply the poet's desire to leave behind the grey pavements of London in favour of the verdant tranquillity of Sligo, on another it reflects his wish to escape into a world free from the frustration and emotional complexities which Maud Gonne's presence aroused.

Read independently from Yeats's other work, "The Lake Isle of Innisfree" appears to be a fairly conventional, escapist piece, not significantly different in tone from other *fin-de-siècle* poems of the time. However, when viewed within the context of *The Rose* section of his *Collected Works* it takes on added significance. Together with "A Faery Song" and "A Cradle Song," it celebrates that blessed state of the pure in heart who are enwrapped in the illusions described in another poem of the same section, "The Rose of Peace." This, Yeats suggests in the same poem, is not necessarily an unalloyed ideal; it can only exist within a framework which also includes reality. As such, the dream-like state envisioned in "The Lake Isle of Innisfree" must be seen as reality's antithesis, an essential correlative in Yeats's vision of the duality of the universe, symbolized by his interlocking "gyres" and the "Great Wheel" of his later poetry and prose.

—John M. Munro

LALLA ROOKH.
Poetry and prose by Thomas Moore, 1817.

After a gestation of some five years and a year's delay because of depressed trade, Thomas Moore's *Lalla Rookh: An Oriental Romance* was finally published on 27 May 1817. Longman, Moore's publisher, gave him the biggest advance yet offered for a long verse narrative; the first edition sold out in a fortnight; six more followed in less than a year, and *Blackwood's* proclaimed Moore "the most ingenious, brilliant and fanciful Poet of the present age. . . . " Edgar Allan Poe called him the world's most popular poet.

Moore originally conceived of *Lalla Rookh* as an oriental (i.e., Middle-Eastern) version of the rhymed tale popularized by Sir Walter Scott. Before he finished it, however, Lord Byron published his own romantic oriental poems. This disheartened Moore, who wrote that now "when I make my appearance, instead of being a leader as I looked to be, I must dwindle into an humble follower. . . . " And, indeed, there are Byronic strains in Moore. Nevertheless, in 1814, Byron dedicated his *Corsair* to Moore with an allusion to his forthcoming poem. When it did come, *Lalla Rookh* proved to be what Howard Mumford Jones called "the culminating point in political Orientalism."

The book consists of four verse tales within a prose framework. Like Scott, Moore combined historical and imaginary characters and events. His prose heroine, the beautiful Lalla Rookh, is Aurungzebe's daughter, for whom a marriage has been arranged, sight unseen, with the young King of Bucharia. Superbly accompanied, she sets out from Delhi for her wedding in the Vale of Cashmere. Among her train are Fadladeen, the self-important Chamberlain of the Haram, and Feramorz, an elegant young poet, sent by the bridegroom to beguile the tedium of the journey. This he does by reciting to Lalla Rookh, her ladies, and Fadladeen, who criticises his verses severely. Moore uses this captious character for comic relief, to satirize critics, and to disarm possible objections to his own work by putting them into a comic mouth.

As they near Cashmere, Lalla Rookh realizes that she loves Feramorz, but dutifully moves forward through splendid scenes to meet the King of Bucharia, who, to her delight, is—Feramorz himself! They live happily ever after, and Fadladeen is struck with admiration for the royal verse style.

The first of the interior stories, "The Veiled Prophet of Khorassan," was the most popular, allusions to it continuing into the 20th century. Here Moore combined gothic motifs with more modern concepts of the psychology of grief and of fanaticism. The Prophet is Mokanna, who conceals his monstrous visage behind a silver veil and his monstrous hatred of mankind behind a crusade for freedom. Thus, he exults, he will "sweep my darkening, desolating way, / Weak man my instrument, curst man my prey!" Young idealists who believe that Mokanna is heaven-sent supply his fanatic army, and beautiful women his haram.

Fairest of these, Zelica, has a mind "turned astray" by the supposed death of her beloved Azim. The Prophet subjugates her sexually and morally by making her believe that submission to him will win her a blissful afterlife with Azim. Mokanna "marries" Zelica in a charnel-house where she is forced to drink blood and swear a fearful oath before the watching corpses. Azim, however, is alive and the newest recruit to the "holy war." Despite her degradation, he urges Zelica to escape with him. She cannot. Azim then joins the Caliph's army besieging Mokanna. In a hopeless last stand, the Prophet poisons his few surviving followers, shows them his hideous face as they die, and leaps into a flaming well which will consume him utterly. Thus future votaries will believe he has returned to heaven and will continue his lethal work. "Kings yet unborn shall rue Mokanna's name. . . ." Disguised in Mokanna's discarded veil, Zelica rushes on Azim's spear and dies. For years he prays for her until, forgiven, she appears in a dream. Then "He and his Zelica sleep side by side."

Moore followed this turbulent poem with the simpler, shorter "Paradise and the Peri" in which a Peri attempts to enter Heaven by bringing it the "most dear" gift. Flying over exotic geography, she returns unsuccessfully, first with a hero's last drop of blood, shed against tyranny, then with the sigh "of pure, self-sacrificing love." Finally she brings the tear of a repentant sinner, which opens the Eternal Gate.

The theme of freedom in the first two narratives furnished the plot of the third, "The Fire-Worshippers." These are Ghebers, or Persians, who cling to Mithra and resist Muslim oppression. Their dauntless leader, Hafed, and the remaining Sons of Fire harass the Arabs from a ruined shrine on a mountaintop. One night Hafed seeks the Emir to kill him, but instead, finds his daughter Hinda, "all truth and tenderness and grace. . . . " She loves the unidentified stranger, the Persian Romeo to her Arabian Juliet.

A traitor betrays the Ghebers to the cruel Emir, who sends his daughter away by sea and prepares to attack. Hinda's ship, however, is seized by Hafed's men; she finds who her beloved is and warns him. Once again she is sent away for safety. Glowing with martyrdom, the Fire-Worshippers prepare a pyre of "every wood of odorous breath," but first they surprise the Arabs and fight fiercely to the last man—Hafed. Dying, he fires the funeral pile; Hinda sees its light and drowns herself. Their requiem is sung by a Peri beneath the sea. Long, long will the brave and the fair "weep for the Chieftain who died on that mountain, / They'll weep for the Maiden who sleeps in this wave."

In a footnote Moore suggested that "The Fire-Worshippers" may have a "doubleness of application," and it is obvious that the embattled Ghebers, faithful to their old religion, are also the Roman Catholic Irish, struggling for religious toleration. Moore himself had been a college friend and admirer of Robert Emmet, the Irish revolutionary executed in 1803. Hafed and Hinda recall Emmet and his sweetheart, Sarah Curran, whose memories Moore also preserved in two of his *Irish Melodies*: "Oh! breathe not his name" and "She is far from the land."

Feramorz's last poem is a rhapsody on "The Light of the Haram." In fragrant floral imagery he tells how Jehanguire and his adored sultana, Nourmahal, are reconciled after a lovers' quarrel. The Sultana's appearance as a masked Arabian singing girl at a Feast of Roses foreshadows the revelation that the King of Bucharia has masked as a poet. The rhapsody is prolonged by descriptions of luscious fruits and by legends of flowers.

In fact, a prolixity of imagery and authenticating allusion is characteristic of *Lalla Rookh* as a whole. Moore's preparatory reading included works by Dow, Gibbon, Sir William Jones, Morier, Taverner, D'Herbelot, and many others who appear in the first edition's more than 50 pages of end-notes. The prose framework is written in the ornate, epithetical style which the West regarded as Oriental, and both prose and verse are filled with local colour and "unnatural" natural history. For instance, the ladies eat violet sherberts, while in Heaven the Peri will feast of "the Tooba Tree, / Whose scent is the breath of Eternity!" Hafed wears a Gheber "cushee"; the Huma bird never touches the ground, and amber is "a concretion of the tears of birds." The *British Lady's Magazine* accused Moore of concealing "immorality, impiety and voluptuous vice" under gorgeous draperies. On the other hand, the *Edinburgh Review* thought that if "the beauteous forms, the dazzling splendours, the breathing odours of the East" were too lavish, the noble feeling of the poem compensated for their superfluity. In their day, moreover, the depictions of these sights and sounds served as a travelogue.

The metres of *Lalla Rookh* are irregular, anapaests and trochees frequently substituting for basic iambs (and vice versa) to give a sense of swift movement. Likewise, Moore used rapid open couplets with occasional quatrains or more complex rhyme schemes. There are also inserted songs, the most familiar of which is the nostalgic "Bendemeer's Stream."

Musicians have often been attracted to *Lalla Rookh*, especially as it was rapidly and widely translated. Both Félicien David and Anton Rubenstein wrote operas based on the framing narrative, and Villiers Stanford one on "The Veiled Prophet of Khorassan." Robert Schumann composed a choral work from "Paradise and the Peri" and Sir Granville Bantock a dramatic cantata "The Fire-Worshippers." Other composers setting Moore's work include Sterndale Bennett, Clay, Barnett, and Jongen.

—Jane W. Stedman

L'ALLEGRO and IL PENSEROSO.
Poems by John Milton, 1645 (written c. 1631).

In spite of the apparent limpidity of John Milton's verse in "L'Allegro" and "Il Penseroso," much critical discussion has focused on the question of what these two matching yet contrasted poems are actually about. Interpretations have been affected by their assumed date: connection with the Horton period, which led to attempts to identify the scenery with specific localities in that area, is now generally dropped in favour of the summer of 1631, when Milton was still at Cambridge; this has drawn attention to traditions of academic argument, so that the pair have been regarded as asserting the rival merits of different temperaments, or as a development of the debate about Day and Night in Milton's first "Prolusion." Growing understanding of 17th-century theories of melancholy have also helped interpretation, showing that Il Penseroso is to be taken as the Contemplative Man, possessed of the Aristotelian melancholy felt to be indispensable to various forms of genius, including the poetic.

That the poems are to be seen as a pair has never been in doubt. Each opens with the dismissal of an undesired opposite—"loathed Melancholy" or "vain deluding Joys"—in a ten-line introduction which is Italianate in its rhyme-scheme and variation of long and short lines, but succeeded by irregular octosyllabics which frequently gain or lose a syllable, or adopt trochaic rhythms, producing an overall effect of lightness and grace. Each celebrates the chosen quality, personified and attended by appropriate companions. In so doing it shows the influence of the *encomium* which, as Milton would have learnt at school, required that the subject be praised for his ancestry, qualities, features, friends, and actions (Milton's subjects, in fact, are both represented as divine females). Each shows interest in effects of light and dark, in particular of half-light; and each makes use of an approximate 24-hour structure, though "L'Allegro" begins this at dawn and ends before cockcrow the next morning, while "Il Penseroso" starts at night and ends before the following day has reached evening. Some critics have described the poems as showing the Cheerful Man's or Contemplative Man's day, but this is to make their structure too rigid: it is a strange day which includes both summer and autumn ("L'Allegro," 88–90), and the day/night format is in each case followed by a more generalised passage in which the rural pleasures are succeeded by urban ones: towered cities, tourneys, masques, marriages, and theatres, or the academic cloister and college chapel of "Il Penseroso." Both follow this with a section on the effect of vocal music, which for the Cheerful Man provides the final delight, though the Contemplative looks forward to an old age spent acquiring "something like prophetic strain" in a hermit's cell. The final couplet in each case pledges allegiance, though the "if thou canst give" of "L'Allegro" may be felt the more tentative.

These obvious links have led readers, unnecessarily, to think of the poems as presenting opposed, rather than merely different, qualities. But there is no true opposition here: that would require speakers whose calibre of mind differed, as well as their occupations, which has been recognised by those who see the poems as presenting two moods in the same man, or even as showing Milton pulled between the development of different aspects of himself. So viewed, the question must be regarded as already decided in favour of "Il Penseroso," for Melancholy has not only the last word, the fuller description, and the more positive ending; it also has religious connotations which Mirth does not attain.

Much of the charm of these poems derives from their mingling of the general and the particular, and from two strands in their descriptions of the rural scene, one deriving from Milton's first-hand experience and one from his reading. The detailed realism of the "minute drops" falling from the eaves, the unexpected colours of the grey and russet fields, the observation that the moon appears to stoop when clouds drift across its face, have not come from literature; at the same time, both poems are deeply imbued with pastoral imagery. This is most evident in the country figures scattered through the landscape of "L'Allegro" (itself "trim" and anthropomorphised, with bosoming trees and hens parading as dames). The happy ploughman, milkmaid, and shepherd are succeeded by equally idealised Arcadian rustics. Like *A Midsummer Night's Dream*, whose influence in these poems has been noted, "L'Allegro" happily mingles the classical with the English folklore tradition. The "stories" told here are of Faëry Mab and Robin Goodfellow; they are told in company and convivially accompanied by "nut-brown ale." In "Il Penseroso," on the other hand, the tellers are Chaucer and Spenser through the medium of the printed page, and even drama is here not seen but read. The real world, for Milton, cannot be kept separate from the world of the imagination.

The comprehensiveness of these poems may indeed be seen as the key to their meaning. Once frivolity and morbid retreat from life's joys have been rejected, all pleasures that the exterior and interior worlds can offer are joyfully seized upon. This universality is most clearly demonstrated in the improbable landscape of "L'Allegro," which unites extremes: rocky-topped mountains are found in apparent proximity to daisied meadows; wide rivers and shallow brooks appear; the only visible habitations are a castle and a cottage; and the lowland pastures that produce the "tanned haycock" are twinned with "upland" hamlets.

Yet from this compendium the pleasures of love or even close companionship are conspicuously absent. The Cheerful Man participates as an observer, while the Contemplative chooses to "walk unseen" and withdraws for his deeper studies to "some high lonely tower." (In "L'Allegro," on the other hand, where nature has been preferred as Mirth's progenitor, not only to wine, but also to love, the tower appears as the subject of romantic but uninvolved speculation.) It is not fortuitous that dreaming is mentioned in both poems: they are, as Johnson called them, "noble efforts of the imagination," but the imagination of a youthful poet, still upon the threshold of adult experience. Hence their delighted sense of infinite possibilities.

—Margaret Forey

LAMENT FOR THE MAKARIS.
Poem by William Dunbar, 1505–08.

William Dunbar's *Lament for the Makaris* displays a major poet, at the height of his powers, treating some of the great literary commonplaces, the transiency of the world, the death of friends, and the fearful recognition of one's own mortality. Its affinities with François Villon's *ballades* "Des dames des temps jadis" and "Des seigneurs du temps jadis" help account for the frequently drawn comparison between the Scots poet and his French contemporary. Despite the familiarity of the theme, and the conventional nature of the several devices by which it is elaborated in Dunbar's handling, the ultimate expression is uniquely individual and profoundly moving.

The *Lament* comprises 25 quatrains of iambic tetrameter rhyming aabb. The liturgical refrain, *Timor mortis conturbat me*, from the Office for the Dead, appears in several other Middle English poems, including Lydgate's "So as I lay this othir nyght." Dunbar may be indebted to this work, and to the same poet's "Testament," for some sporadic verbal echoes, and Lydgate's *Daunce Machabree* perhaps influenced the development of stanzas 5 through 11, but the stock nature of the materials makes specific attribution difficult. Use of the Dance of Death motif is supplemented by a brief evocation (stanza 5) of another motif, that of *vado mori*, and this section also includes a reference (stanza 2) to the traditional triad of the World, the Flesh, and the Devil. In conjunction with the refrain, these stereotype variations on the theme of death's universality conspire to produce an effect of relentless progression towards an inevitable conclusion.

This effect is reinforced at every turn by the end-stopped lines, the balanced phrases, alliteration, and both internal and terminal rhyme. The device of ringing changes on an obscured but immutable pattern is used to bind stanzas 13 through 22, where the constant is a syntactic unit featuring the auxiliary verb *hes* ("He *hes* tane Roull of Aberdene"). "He" (death) has only one variant, "That scorpion fell," throughout this section; for "tane" are substituted "done devour," "done infek," "berevit," "endit," "slaine," "reft," and "done roune"; and variants for the objects of death's visitations sound the roll call of the dead poets of Scotland. Addition of particularizing adjectives and adverbs, and recourse to inversions ("Clerk of Tranent eik he hes tane") and transpositions ("Schir Johne the Ros enbrast hes he") help orchestrate the virtuoso performance, but within it the grammatical marker sounds the monochord of irrecoverable loss.

The poem as a whole is saved from monotony by a pervasive ambiguity which influences the narrator's voice and controls the overall structure. This ambiguity first appears in the opening stanza:

> I that in heill wes and gladnes
> Am trublit now with gret seiknes
> And feblit with infermite:
> *Timor mortis conturbat me.*

Since the poet survived the occasion of this poem by several years, the genuineness (real or imagined) of any potentially fatal physical disability has been questioned, and the idea advanced that at issue rather is the poet's guilty sense of himself as a man "who has taken pleasure in temporalia." In fact the poem's subsequent development embraces both possibilities. In the next stanza the narrator identifies himself as a member of the Christian community, subject to the temptations of deadly sin, and confronted with the omnipresence of death in a mutable world. This leads into a vision of death's expanding dominion over the living of whatever age, sex, or profession, and to a reasoned acknowledgment that no one can escape his tyrannical power. The argument to this point precisely prepares the way for the conclusion of the last stanza, where the pronominal forms reassert the communal values of the second stanza:

Sen for the deid remeid is none,
Best is that we for dede dispone
Eftir our deid that lif may we:
Timor mortis conturbat me.

This perfectly logical progression is interrupted, however, at the juncture where the survey of the occupations subject to death's authority gives rise to the thought that the poet's own metier is not exempt:

I se that makaris amang the laif
Playis heir ther pageant, syne gois to graif;
Sparit is nocht ther faculte:
Timor mortis conturbat me.

The narrational "I" makes its first appearance here since stanza 1, and it introduces the idea of *ubi sunt* which dictated the choice of title made by an early editor, David Laing. Rather than an expanding vision of death's dominion, this *topos* articulates the poet's sense of the gradual annihilation of the group with which he is most intimately affiliated. Since the speaker, sick though he is, must expect to outlive the last poet mentioned, Walter Kennedy, who "In poynt of dede lyis veraly," it is the lament of a last survivor, and it captures something of the heroic pathos of its Anglo-Saxon antecedents in this genre. As the listing of the makers progresses, the epithets with which they are addressed, "gude," "maister," "gentill," begin to agglomerate, "gud gentill," "gud maister," as though the poet's respect and affection for those designated his "fallowis" intensifies with his sense of their diminishing numbers.

Emotionally the movement of this section climaxes with the alternate conclusion of the penultimate stanza, which again uses the first-person pronouns of stanzas 1 and 12, and reprises the syntax of stanzas 13 through 22:

Sen he hes all my brother tane
He will nocht lat me life alane;
On forse I man his nyxt pray be:
Timor mortis conturbat me.

The two conclusions stand in a diptychal relationship to one another, and between them define the range of meaning for *timor mortis*. In the last stanza the phrase signifies that salutary fear of death which serves to keep in focus spiritual preparation for the end of the pilgrimage of life. It generates a conclusion as orthodox as that found at the end of *The Wanderer*. But, as in that poem, this religious resolution transcends, without entirely denying or assimilating, the fear which stems from a stupefying consciousness that a sentient being will cease to be.

—Roy J. Pearcy

LAMIA.
Poem by John Keats, 1820.

John Keats's "Lamia" could be said to set a trap for its critics. Like Coleridge's "Christabel" the poem has a peculiarly atmospheric power, generated by the evocation of illusion and uncertainty, glamour and magic. When this mystery is subjected to cold reason, Lamia and Lycius are killed, and the poem itself is ended. How does one analyse a poem which condemns analysis?

The poem employs several devices to remove it from the encroachments of conscious reasoning. Lamia's first act—the transforming of Hermes's sight by magic to reveal the object of his desire—prepares us for the opening of a chimeric world of fantastic beauty. Lamia's power is the power to fulfill fantasies. In its opening words, "upon a time," Keats announces the poem's location in Faerie, which we should understand according to Coleridge's definition as "the country of mental space." The invocation of Mount Olympus and English Fairies are designed to tease us out of rational thought into the realms of the marvellous.

"Lamia" is a fantasy; it is also a dream. We enter the poem through the God Hermes, whose life is born out of dream: "It was no dream; or say a dream it was, / Real are the dreams of Gods, and smoothly pass / Their pleasures in a long immortal dream." Like a dream, the poem is concentrated around a number of arresting visual images and transformations. Within the poem, a dream-like sense of the unfamiliar is generated by a series of encounters with that which is "other," sacred or occult. A nymph is taken by a God, a man meets a Goddess, mortal men of Corinth enter a paradisal mansion, a sage confronts a demon. Each character is drawn across a threshold of awe, wonder, or dread. Our own world is itself thrown into new and strange perspective by the evocation of other realms. Lamia explores the blessed domains of Elysium, the underworld of Hades, the mermaid-guarded Queendom of the Sea Goddess Thetis, and the Temple of Vulcan, before she finds Lycius in this world.

Lamia's identity is itself mysterious: something between a monster and a Goddess. She is able to command elemental spirits, yet is herself held in thrall to an enchantment. Keats's descriptions of her are no more than the assertions of conflicting possibilities: "Striped like a zebra, freckled like a pard, / Eyed like a peacock, and all crimson barred"; "She seemed, at once, some penanced lady elf, / Some demon's mistress, or the demon's self." We are left with little in the way of definite form: only a confused swirl of light, colour, and magic. At the heart of this confusion is a paradox: that of the seductive serpent. In Christian symbolism the snake is the embodiment of evil; but Keats draws attention to other symbolic overtones of the snake. Hermes bears the Caduceus, a staff formed by a wand and two intertwining serpents, a symbol of his authority, and also of healing.

Lycius's first meeting with Lamia highlights the fluidity of her identity. As he approaches her the verse moves subtly from his physical journey to his wandering thought:

Over the solitary hills he fared,
Thoughtless at first, but ere eve's star appeared
His fantasy was lost, where reason fades,
In the calmed twilight of Platonic shades.

The "Platonic shades" wherein his imagination moves mirror the actual twilight through which he walks. Lamia appears to him in both the inner, psychical, and the outer, physical landscape. As the preceding lines have warned us, Lamia is the incarnation of Lycius's wish: "Jove heard his vows, and bettered his desire." The hero's greeting of Lamia displays what his "desires" are. Lycius throws out a range of fantasies for Lamia to fulfil, ranging from nymph to Star-Goddess. Lamia, after flaunting the power of a Goddess, "throws it off" to select the form most calculated to captivate him. Lycius is duly transported from trance to trance.

The scene as he first beholds her is one which epitomises Keatsian yearning. The adoration of love is expressed through a physical image, drawn from the most intimate sense, taste. Lamia is an inexhaustible cup to match Lycius's unquenchable desire. Arousal and gratification of the senses are both the principle which governs poetic creation and the impulse which drives fictional characters. Lamia's account of her first sight of Lycius is heavy with the lushness of Keatsian overstimulation. Lycius, himself an object of desire to her, appears standing at the doors of the temple of Venus, amid baskets of aphrodisiac herbs. Revealingly, Lamia's account of Heaven is of a state differing from ours only in the intensity and availability of physical pleasure. Again, we see Hermes fall like a star from Heaven, but his decent is neither Luciferic nor Promethean, merely Priapic. His goal is a naked waternymph.

Lamia's palace represents the consummation of this principle, created to gratify all the senses with joyous enthusiasm. Keats's genius with the persuasive power of sound is comparable to Tennyson's. It is, however, pressed to more immediate use than the creation of effects for landscape: "When in an antechamber every guest / Had felt the cold full sponge to pleasure pressed. . . ." Into this world enters Apollonius, whose art would commit the ultimate sin of "unweaving the rainbow." Lamia is, of course, "rainbow-sided."

Lycius's bliss is destroyed not merely by cold reason, however, but by his own hubris. Lycius seeks not only to enjoy the delights of magic, but to expose them to the world of temporal reality. He displays his treasure to "the herd," seeking their praise. His overweening pride outsteps the boundaries of what is possible, and he is punished.

In conclusion, it is interesting to assess Lamia in the light of the author's own comments on it. In a letter to George Keats of 18 September 1819 he wrote: "I am certain there is that sort of fire in it which must take hold of people in some way—give them either pleasant or unpleasant sensation. What they want is a sensation of some sort." "Lamia" does have fire—the fire of erotic and imaginative excitement. It is Keats's fascination with sensation (and in particular his affinity with the physical) which transforms what is sensational into what is sensuous. In Keats's hands a classical tale of the supernatural becomes a journey into fantasy and physical pleasure, exploring the boundaries of each.

—Edmund Cusick

LAVENGRO.
Fiction by George Borrow, 1851.

The tutelary deity of *Lavengro*, George Borrow's best-known work, is Daniel Defoe. Its novelistic forebears are *Robinson Crusoe* and *Moll Flanders*. Borrow's decision to make much of this fact in the narrative would seem to locate this autobiographical fiction in the mainstream of the English novelistic tradition. However, *Lavengro* complicates the procedures of Defoe. Instead of treating fiction as fact, Borrow treats fact as fiction treated as fact. If a radical rearrangement of facts can be classified as a fiction, *Lavengro* is a polyvalent instance of the genre replete with intertextual effects and self-reflexive in the extreme. A lively but baggy affair, it is filled with encyclopedic detail, embedded narratives, satirical portraits and larger-than-life minor characters. Beyond that, it partakes of the conventions of the *Bildungsroman*, the *Kunstlerroman*, the picaresque novel and the spiritual quest.

In a narrative filled with names, many of which are caricatural, most of the towns are nameless and the narrator himself takes on the pseudonym Lavengro, which is Gypsy for word-master. Far more than a mere observer, Lavengro is a complex and unpredictable individual with a startling range of moods, a powerful voice, a vigorous wit, and an array of masks. His own voice is supplemented in the frequent dialogues by others as distinctive and strange, and he can shift at will from low comedy to high, from tenderness to pathos, from the elegiac to the grotesque.

Borrow's subtitle, *The Scholar, The Gypsy, The Priest*, takes us beyond characterization and social/moral roles and points up some of the mystery with which this book is instinct. The narrative can be divided into three segments, each corresponding to a stage in the protagonist's development, each written in a major novelistic mode. We begin with the "scholar," whose *Bildung* is conditioned in part by the fact that his father, an impecunious officer, takes his family from base to base in Ireland, Scotland, and England. This seemingly undisciplined and ill-endowed second son becomes, as a result, a splendid example of the resourceful autodidact. He picks up his learning on the wing, so to speak, not only from the very streets, woods, and fields that surround him, but from the very air he breathes. A wild child and youth, he associates with the Gaelic-speaking Irishmen despised by his father and learns their language before falling in with Gypsies, who give him his honorific title. It is during the book's first third that he discovers and develops his remarkable gifts as a linguist, picking up Welsh, Old Norse, German, and Armenian, to say nothing of Latin, Greek, and Hebrew with very little outside help, eventually using the Bible as an all-purpose key.

Unlikely as it seems, this account of the making of a philologist is anything but dry. Borrow is closer to a Tom Jones than to a Blifil. Though rigorously "moral," he is seldom priggish and he repeatedly gets into scrapes, dealing with all manner of individuals from all walks of life as might a picaro. It is to the picaro's existence that the term "gypsy" applies on one level, for the Gypsy people into whose ranks the hero is inducted seem best to define his relationship with the English society and culture to which he most emphatically belongs. That is, he lives apart and largely by his wits but maintains his strong, if troubled, English identity intact.

The first or *Bildung* segment of *Lavengro* follows the narrator over the often rocky terrain of childhood and adolescence giving us splendid accounts of the landscape, history, and customs of the places inhabited by the peripatetic military family. The second or *Kunstler* segment finds the hero in a hostile London where he tries to make his way as a writer. At this point, his Gypsy alter ego, a version of the "noble savage," makes his presence felt. This Gypsy prince or "Pharaoh," Mr. Petulengro, is a resourceful "master of the horseshoe" or blacksmith, as thoroughly at home in his marginalized role as the spiritually unsettled narrator is miserable, guilt-ridden, and displaced in his various habitats. (Perhaps it is to this radical displacement that we owe the thread of anti-semitic disparagement that mars and marks this and other works by Borrow.) It appears that Lavengro is most marginalized in the midst of the most English of cities, hence he is most the Gypsy in relation to the social norm. Destitute and depressed, he battles the odds, serving uncompromising taskmasters while trying unsuccessfully to market the literary production of his youth, his translations from the Welsh and the Norse classics. In his efforts to survive, this serious scholar produces a compendium of criminal lives and trials while associating with a variety of colorful characters: ranging from a charmingly dissolute Irish nobleman, to an apple woman who doubles as a thieves' fence, to an enigmatic Armenian merchant. His last urban act is to write and sell under the pressure of extreme need an adventure novel for the pulp trade.

The apple woman and the Armenian introduce into the London sequence the sort of embedded narratives that will dominate the conventional "road" narrative (*The Priest*). In it the narrator leaves the city afoot to clear his head and raise his spirits. What follows is a group of three studies in extreme neurosis: the tale of an obsessed gentleman writer, the tale of a sin-ridden Welsh lay preacher, foreshadowing the harrowing account of the narrator's own anxiety attack.

During this period, to aid a distressed family, Lavengro purchases the equipment of a tinker. While training himself in that trade, he re-encounters and encounters four powerful characters: Petulengro; the Gypsy witch Mrs. Hearne, who sees him as a threat to her people and poisons him; the redoubtable Flaming Tinman with whom he fights an epic battle; and the resourceful Belle, a tall handsome girl raised in a workhouse, with whom he joins forces. A fifth figure, the priest of the subtitle, is literally a Jesuit missionary cast in the role of the devil and haunting the last segment of the novel. We might also say that Lavengro's emotional and spiritual crisis, melded with those of the gentleman author and the Welsh preacher, is consolidated by his encounters with the red-headed priest. The novel ends on an enigmatic note with the embedded narrative of a coachman, who has crossed metaphorical swords with that same priest in Italy.

Viktor Shklovsky has called Sterne's *Tristram Shandy* the very type of the novel. In much the same (perverse) way, we could say that this thoroughly eccentric book is a serious 19th-century equivalent of Sterne's comic masterpiece.

—David Hayman

LAYS OF ANCIENT ROME.
Poems by Thomas Babington Macaulay, 1842.

It was, appropriately, Thomas Babington Macaulay who coined the much (and often ironically) quoted formulation, "Every schoolboy knows . . .", appropriately because, for many generations, every British schoolboy (and girl) did know Macaulay's poem "Horatius," first of the four ballads which constitute his *Lays of Ancient Rome*. The story, taken from Livy and other historians, tells of how the eponymous "captain of the gate," with two companions, patricians like himself, saved Rome from the Tuscan armies levied by "Lars Porsena of Clusium" to restore the Tarquins, by defending the only bridge across the flooded Tiber until the citizens had hewed it down, thus denying the attackers access to the city.

Concepts of patriotism have been eroded in Britain since about the 1950's. Up till then, the poem, often under some such stirring title as "How Horatius Held the Bridge," was much anthologised for schools, as an exemplar of virtues like love of country, heroism, and honour even to brave enemies, as when Horatius, the bridge being down, swims for his life across the flooded river, and "Even the ranks of Tuscany / Could scarce forebear to cheer."

The other three poems have never been so generally familiar or popular. In "The Battle of the Lake Regillus," some of the same characters appear as in "Horatius." Herminius, one of Horatius's co-defenders of the bridge, meets his end in single combat with the Latian champion Mamilius. We learn that the villainous Tarquin, "False Sextus who wrought the deed of shame," at whose appearance in the earlier poem, "On the house tops was no woman but spat towards him and hissed, / No child but screamed out curses and shook its little fist," is deservedly haunted by the ghost of the wronged Lucretia.

At the climax of the poem, the gods Castor and Pollux appear at the head of the Roman armies and assist in putting the foe to flight. There is, Macaulay points out, an analogy to such a superstition as late as the supposed appearance of St. James to Cortes's troops in Mexico, "in an age of printing presses, libraries, universities, scholars, logicians, jurists, and statesmen."

"Virginia" tells of the desire of a tyrannical patrician for the daughter of the honourable plebeian Virginius. He plots to obtain her by making a deceitful dependant claim her as a stolen slave, and a corrupt patrician court gives judgement in his favour. But the plot is thwarted when the girl's father, to save her from the "taunts and blows, the portion of the slave," and even more from the "nameless evil that passeth taunt and blow, / Foul outrage which thou knowest not, which thou shalt never know," publicly stabs her to death; whereupon the downtrodden mob is inspired to rebellion and the long-suspended Tribunes are restored. In the final poem, much the least dramatic or interesting, the seer Capys prophesies to Romulus and Remus the future glories of Rome. Each of the Lays is given a precise date, place, and occasion when it may be supposed to have been appropriately composed and declaimed to honour the memory of the event recorded.

Although there were, as this brief summary will suggest, strong elements of Victorian patriotism and morality in Macaulay's inspiration, it is clear, from his characteristically learned and lucid preface to the collection and headnotes to the individual poems, that his main motive was an attempt at scholarly reconstruction. Convinced that the early period of Rome's history, as related by Livy, Dionysius, and others, was based on traditional oral, rather than reliable written, sources, Macaulay aimed to imagine the ballads on which the four stories, variously treated by different historians, might have been founded. He cites as analogies variant versions of the same event in British history in ballads from Percy's *Reliques*, and Hume's having relied, in his *History of England*, on William of Malmesbury's 12th-century chronicle, without having cited William's acknowledged use of what he admitted to be historically unreliable traditional balladry.

Moreover, Macaulay admits to certain ironic elements in his reconstructions. The supposed author of "Horatius," with his yearning for "the brave days of old," when "none was for a party . . . all were for the state . . . the great man helped the poor and the poor man loved the great," is characterised by the author as "much given to pining after good old times which never existed." On the question of which Roman virtues should be emulated, he admits in the preface several which should not, notably "the illiberal sneers at the Greeks, contempt for the arts of peace, ungenerous exultation over the vanquished. The old Romans," Macaulay admits, "had some great virtues . . . but Christian charity and chivalrous generosity were alike unknown to them."

The *Lays of Ancient Rome*, taken and read as a whole, are more subtle and less tendentious than they have traditionally been given credit for. On the other hand, prefaces and headnotes and scholarly exegesis had no place in the sort of school books which, for so many years, excited and inspired the young with the deeds of Horatius. And indeed the Lays are undeniably stirring and (especially in "Virginia") poignant; and, despite occasional clumsiness and occasional over-sophistication, the ballad manner is effectively caught. It is a pity that, although they remain constantly in print in the Everyman collection of Macaulay's *Essays*, they should have dropped so completely out of "every schoolboy's" formative experience.

—Michael Grosvenor Myer

LEVIATHAN.
Prose by Thomas Hobbes, 1651.

Motivated by the political crisis that resulted from the English Civil War of the 1640's, Thomas Hobbes attempted in *Leviathan* to present a theory of civil government. Unlike his *De Cive*, written in Latin for scholars, this new work was to be written in English and directed to the popular English reading audience. Published in 1651, the book is a comprehensive and powerful examination of absolute government as it derives from a covenant between the ruler and the ruled to protect the citizenry and to secure peace. The frontispiece of the book, dominated by a crowned giant made up of tiny human beings and bearing a sword and crozier, served as a graphic depiction of absolute government—frightening, in a sense, to contemplate, yet necessary for the good of the human race.

Man in Hobbes's lexicon is a creature of both passion and reason, who lives through the use of his senses, which are inherent, and his faculties, which are learned and cultivated by study and industry. For the latter, speech he believed was the key. He would have agreed with the Greeks in their use of the word *logos* for both speech and reason. The meaning of words was crucial to Hobbes. Indeed he would have agreed also with Confucius's advice that to set government in order, one must first set his family in order; to set his family in order, one must first set himself in order; to set himself in order, one must first call things by their right names. Without clarity of speech, man's faculties are as straws in the wind.

The challenge, of course, throughout the history of man has been to bring reason to bear on passion and thus to move man above the law of nature which, to Hobbes, leads to the condition of war, where every man is pitted against every other man and where justice and injustice have no relevance. For the law of nature gives man the right to anything and everything as well as the right to use any means to preserve himself—"there being no obligation on any man, which ariseth not from some Act of his own." Life under the law of nature is precarious indeed and marked by fear and anxiety—a life where man's passions lead him in many directions in a constant seeking for power that ends only with death, because, says Hobbes, "he cannot assure the power and means to live well, which he hath present, without the acquisition of more." Power, morever, is the basic gauge by which men judge other men. To control power and to allay fear and anxiety, man has sought mutual cooperation with his fellows by forming societies—from primitive tribes to highly organized states. For Hobbes in *Leviathan* the most effective form of government is that headed by the absolute sovereign, who provides the common power to which all men must defer. For without this common power, there can be no law, no security, no peace.

By virtue of the covenant made between the sovereign and his subjects, the former is the ultimate legislator, executor, and interpreter of laws. He may, moreover, deprive individuals of rights and property. In this sense, the covenant is not a mere contract. If it were, each individual would have to effect his own contract with the sovereign. Put another way, life and peace must be preserved, not rights and property; and to this end individual men must be subject to "a Common Power, to keep them in awe, and to direct their actions to the Common Benefit."

While Hobbes did not deny God, but rather saw Him as the prime cause, he distrusted organized religion as a possible source of civil discord. Hobbes's God, like Milton's, was beyond human powers of description and argumentation. The papacy, on the other hand, was "no other than the ghost of the deceased Roman empire, sitting crowned upon the grave thereof." While much of *Leviathan* deals with religion, Hobbes obviously was more interested in outlining a secular vehicle for the curbing of man's passions to enable the world to go forward, reasonably and peacefully—that vehicle being the absolute sovereign.

Leviathan is a book that befits its title and that will be read and discussed as long as humans endeavor to solve their own riddle of existence. As for Hobbes, his hope was that his work would eventually "fall into the hands of a Soveraigne, who will consider it himself . . . without the help of any interessed, or envious Interpreter; and by the exercise of entire Soveraignty, in protecting the Publique teaching of it, convert this Truth of Speculation, into the Utility of Practice."

—Wilton Eckley

THE LIFE OF SAMUEL JOHNSON.
Prose by James Boswell, 1791.

James Boswell's *The Life of Samuel Johnson* is best understood not in the context of biography in the 20th century, but rather as an instance of 18th-century life writing: a large category—inclusive of autobiography, biography, literary biography, travel literature, memoirs, journals, and criminal biographies—which demonstrates the universal preoccupation during this period with the data of individual lives and experiences. Unlike the panegyrics and *de casibus* portraits of the previous century, which portrayed men and women within the framework of religious doctrine or the ethics of a rigid social hierarchy, the more realistic narratives of the 18th century sought the meaning of lives in behavior—in actions, letters, speeches, and the fundamental habits of mind. Boswell advertised that his *Life of Johnson* offered more information than earlier narratives. (He was referring in particular to those by two other Johnsonian friends, Hester Lynch Piozzi and Sir John Hawkins.) Although the biography proceeds chronologically from Johnson's birth to his death, its great length and complex structure are due to the variety of biographical information included in it. Because the basis of the *Life* is information which Boswell gathered through his "acquaintance of Dr. Johnson," which began in 1763, the bulk of the biography addresses the last 21 years of Johnson's life. Even during this period of friendship, Boswell and Johnson were frequently separated, so Boswell relies on secondhand reports of Johnson's activities and conversation, prints his own and others' correspondence with Johnson, and, in one instance, includes Johnson's journal of a trip to France. The *Life of Johnson* also functions as a literary biography; Boswell offers in his narrative extended analyses of Johnson's works.

Boswell's intense interest in the minute particulars of life is evident in the journals which he maintained throughout his life. Since the discovery of the Boswell papers earlier in this century, scholars have recognized that the *Life of Johnson* emerged from this larger body of life materials, and just as Boswell's journals present not a static and complete picture of himself, but a self-portrait in progress, discontinuous and contradictory, so the *Life of Johnson* reveals Boswell's struggle to delineate the character of Johnson in the recorded conversations, letters, and diaries available to him.

When, in various places in the *Life*, Boswell discusses the process by which he "recollected and recorded" Johnson's conversations, he offers not transcripts, but recreations: "when my mind was, as it were, *strongly impregnated with the Johnsonian aether*, I could, with much more facility and exactness, carry in my memory and commit to paper the exuberant variety of his wisdom and wit." (Late in the biography, he slyly reports that when Johnson put his shorthand to the test, it was proven to be quite inaccurate.) That Boswell as biographer is not simply an objective observer and recorder is also seen in the numerous instances in which Boswell raises topics with Johnson for the purpose of hearing his reaction, as he admits that he did in introducing the topic of ghosts on a number of occasions, and in staging confrontations—the dinner with the radical Wilkes, for example. Although it seems that Boswell assembles for posterity an anatomy of the great author's thoughts on a variety of recurring topics like religious belief and custom, government and subordination, moral law and behavior, and literature, the *Life of Johnson* is more fundamentally an exploration of the extent to which a coherent character emerges in these verbal dramas. Critics have observed that Boswell presents not one, but many portraits of Johnson: the heroic, the mock-heroic, the man of principle, the man who "argues for victory." He dwells on the contradictions in Johnson's nature, for example, in the continuing discussion of Johnson's religious faith and his profound fear of death, and, while at times he speaks in awe of Johnson, he also dwells on his ungainly physical appearance, walk ("moving along"), and mannerisms.

When Johnson himself observes in *Rambler* 60 that "no species of writing seems more worthy of cultivation than biography, since . . . none can more certainly enchain the heart by irresistible interest, or more widely diffuse instruction to every diversity of condition," he affirms the didactic function of biography, although significantly the "instruction" occurs through the empathy felt by the observer for the biographical subject. Similarly, the most persistent images of Johnson in Boswell's *Life* are found in his relationship with his young biographer; Boswell's perceptions of his subject of more than 20 years—his reverence, irritation, and ultimately his identification with Johnson are a central focus of the narrative. Although Boswell describes his first meeting with Johnson as a mock-heroic encounter in which he is almost driven from the field, he asserts early in the biography that he can "scarcely believe that [he] had the honour of enjoying the intimacy of such a man." He is once so dazzled that he cannot remember Johnson's conversation, yet he later preens himself when a legal opinion which he has penned is praised at the expense of one which Johnson wrote for him. Just before he tells of Johnson's death, Boswell assures the reader that he will make no more mention of himself, but that the references to himself are due to "the peculiar plan of his biographical undertaking."

The process of portraying Johnson, of affirming his sincerity in the welter of recorded talk, is of supreme personal importance for Boswell; when in the middle of his narrative Boswell regrets that he no longer felt "that aweful reverence with which I used to contemplate Mr. Samuel Johnson," he remarks that what he had taken to be a great mystery "is owing to the cloudy darkness of my own mind. I should be glad that I am more advanced in my progress of being, so that I can view Dr. Johnson with a steadier and clearer eye." In the conventional character with which he concludes the biography, Boswell asserts that Johnson was consistent in his basic principles, and that his contradictory nature was evident only "in his manners, and in the display of argument and fancy in his talk." This faith in Johnson's sincerity above all other virtues, in an essential and intelligible character, stands in ironic contrast to the verbal data of this biography—the arguments, the eloquent but inconsistent opinions recorded over time, and the conversations and anecdotes forged by Boswell himself.

—Sara B. Varhus

LITTLE DORRIT.
Novel by Charles Dickens, 1857.

Little Dorrit was serialised over 19 months, each shilling number having two etched illustrations by Charles Dickens's regular collaborator Hablot K. Browne ("Phiz"), who worked to his instructions. Although many of the relationships within the large cast and elaborate mystery plot are not explained until near the end, the needs of overall unity and of each monthly number involve a delicate balance of parts and the "weaving" of many "threads."

While set in the 1820's, it is a very topical work of the 1850's, written against a background of financial crashes and frauds, unstable governments, a corrupt Civil Service, and military disaster in the Crimea. Dickens's later fiction shows little faith in British ability to assign responsibility or initiate change within the general social malaise. Institutionally, this is represented in the blight which the Circumlocution Office and the Barnacles cast on the few positive characters. In his comprehensive analysis Dickens ranges from London slums to Hampton Court Palace, from Marseilles prison to Venetian palazzo, illustrating a social and economic flux, where the traditional governing class is decayed and the rising middle class ruthless and acquisitive. In the decade of Britain's Great Exhibition he portrays a nation based on competitive materialism, near moral collapse.

The narrative method enacts this sense of unease and disorder as we confront seemingly separate stories and widely diverse groups of unrelated characters, with many questions of motive and identity. By the end, the complex structure produced by revelations going back 40 years and by coincidental meetings of characters (devices inherited from earlier fiction and popular theatre) results in a tightly-woven unity underpinning a coherent social vision. A series of repetitions, parallels or contrasts of characters or situations prevent a simple linear reading. The rather ineffectual hero Clennam, for instance, becomes partner to the eminently practical engineer Doyce, in turn contrasted with the condescending Meagles and the Barnacle determination "not to do"; the quietly selfless heroine, Little Dorrit, is contrasted with her shallow sister Fanny, with the tortured anger of Miss Wade and Tattycoram, and with the cold worldliness of Mrs. Gowan and Mrs. Merdle: there are patterns centred on marriage, money, family, personal morality. Similarly, episodes parallel or comment on others: Old Dorrit's self-deception about his "duty" to preside over his fellow prisoners ironically comments on the toadies' inviting Merdle's political patronage as a "duty to Society," and prepares us for Merdle's exposure as a criminal. Flora Finching's amorous nonsense about her "secret understanding" with the bewildered Clennam parodies the serious mystery he half senses at the heart of the plot. Dickens analyses a complex modern society where people are acted on by unseen forces beyond individual comprehension: Miss Wade's comments in chapter 2 point to the certain accomplishment of destined relationships, even as Clennam finally realises that his life-long toil and return from China have been a journey towards a "vanishing-point" in Little Dorrit.

The complex plot-structure is reinforced by a density of metaphor and recurrent symbolic imagery characteristic of Dickens's late works. The opening chapter establishes patterns of sunlight and shadow which run to the last sentence of the novel, sometimes literal, sometimes indicating the unhealthy forces in society (the criminal Rigaud, Merdle, the Circumlocution Office, Mrs. Clennam's repressive house); numerous images of travel and Clennam's sense of his life on "the flowing road of time" present characters' lives as a journey or more specifically a quest. The dominant image in illustration and word, however, is of imprisonment, from the tainted Marseilles jail, through the quarantine house, a "bolted and barred" Sunday London, Mrs. Clennam's dark and sterile moral bondage, to the central example of the Marshalsea, which the Dorrit family seem to carry with them and impose on Venice and Rome: to Little Dorrit, "this same society in which they lived, greatly resembled a superior sort of Marshalsea." The prison imagery touches many: Merdle seems perpetually handcuffing himself; the Circumlocution Office is like a "place of torture for convicts." This both unifies the vision of society and extends from the literal to the metaphoric, representing a state of mind which conceals or denies reality: if Merdle (who dies a naked suicide) or Casby (exposed by shearing of his locks) are conscious frauds, Fanny Dorrit or Mrs. General can exist only through eye-averting fictions, and Old Dorrit and Mrs. Clennam are locked in self-deception about the past. Plain truth, associated with Doyce and Little Dorrit, is what finally saves Clennam in the recognition of his destiny, as the dramatic revelations sweep away the past and his mother is challenged by the "overwhelming rush of reality." This generalising power of the connecting imagery moves the novel beyond the merely topical to present the human condition in "the prison of this lower world."

In the huge cast, many individuals or groups are distinguished by symbolic names, characteristic speech, or vivid description: the Barnacles, for instance, have a gentlemanly use of many words to obstruct action: "such formalities as are required to be observed in so doing, may be known on application"; Pancks blows "like a little labouring steam-engine." Old Dorrit's halting speech reflects not only his literal imprisonment but the contaminated relationship between language and reality. (The range and vitality of Dickens's language in narration and dialogue would require an essay in themselves.) Clennam and Little Dorrit are created more intimately, through access to their point of view, and in contrast to many of the stereotyped and externalised characters common in Dickens. They are not as immediately vivid as the comic immortals, such as Flora Finching with her muddled romantic fantasies, or the melodramatic villain, Rigaud, but their worth is established through the contrasts and through the interior moral exploration. Little Dorrit remains a strange heroine, child-protector of both father and future husband; but in her symbolic role within the novel's patterns of image and morality she holds the quiet centre of a vast and turbulent stage.

—Ian McGowan

THE LIVES OF THE ENGLISH POETS.
(Prefaces, Biographical and Critical, to the Works of the English Poets.)
Prose by Samuel Johnson, 1779–81.

Samuel Johnson's 52 contributions to *Prefaces, Biographical and Critical, to the Works of the English Poets*—to give the work its original title—constitute a key document for understanding significant 18th-century theories of poetry. It would be no exaggeration to say that from its pages we can obtain, either directly or by inference, a perspective on English literary culture which is astonishingly comprehensive. The plenitude of observations, interpretations, anecdotes and evaluative assessments is presented in a style exactly suited to Johnson's authoritative manner; the humorous asides and unexpected insights ("He [Swift] had a kind of muddy complexion, which, though he washed himself with Oriental scrupulosity, did not look clear") add a touch of immediacy much needed if biography is to rise above the level of casual reportage. Yet Johnson never descends to gratuitous banter. In the *Life* of William Shenstone, for instance, after treating playfully that poet's strange obsession with landscape gardening, he discloses that this harmless pursuit caused Shenstone the embarrassment of having to endure unfavourable comparison with his more opulent neighbour, Lord Lyttelton, whose much larger estate lay close to Shenstone's "little domain." And Johnson concludes: "Where there is emulation there will be vanity; and where there is vanity there will be folly."

That particular *Life* tells us much about Johnson's approach to the biographical aspect of his task. He invariably aims to establish the exact particulars of his subjects' careers and to correct inherited misconceptions; and he also elicits relevant traits of character which underlie mental and spiritual inclinations. He thus comes down heavily on Edmund Waller for being a kind of intellectual Vicar of Bray; writes with amused tolerance of William Collins's habits of procrastination; and commends the tender philanthropy of Isaac Watts ("To the poor . . . he allowed the third part of his annual revenue . . ."). In considering human motivation,

Johnson shows uncommon psychological acumen, along with a compassionate awareness that misfortunes or weakness of resolution may well explain the culpable misuse of talent to which some men of letters have been subject.

The poets of whom Johnson writes range from the "metaphysical" Abraham Cowley (born 1618) to Thomas Gray (died 1771)—covering the whole, that is to say, of the so-called "Augustan" era of our literature. To the modern reader, some of the names represented in the *Lives of the Poets*—Blackmore, Fenton, Pitt, and Tickell—are hardly important enough to warrant serious attention; but even when memorialising such minor figures as Edmund Smith, John Hughes, and William Broome, Johnson brings to our notice features of contemporary authorial practice which would probably have escaped the attention of less vigilant individuals. But it is in his discussions of the major poets that Johnson really comes into his own (the *Life* of Richard Savage, incidentally, stands somewhat apart from the rest because of Johnson's preoccupation with the recriminations and intrigues which undermined Savage's equanimity). For Johnson, literature is a serious pursuit which has direct relevance to the ordering of human existence in its moral and intellectual aspects. The author's function is to make essential discriminations acceptable to his reader with the aid of figurative language deployed in the service of agreeable enlightenment. The end of literature, he says elsewhere, is to instruct: the end of poetry is to instruct by pleasing. The poet will therefore deal in "truths" which have the widest application to the affairs of all rational beings. This is not to say that only didactic poetry has merit; but Johnson does imply that a serious author must use circumspection in choosing the literary conventions he thinks most appropriate to his purpose.

The legitimacy of fiction is one subject on which Johnson is anxious to clear his mind. He frowns on any recourse to unorthodox imaginative activity if this merely leads to the indulgence of levity; but the exquisite fable unfolded in Pope's *The Rape of the Lock* is completely justified since it gives rise to "elegance of description and justness of precept. . . ." Johnson's tendency to rate literal expression above allegory causes him to respond uneasily when confronted by devices which result in fanciful elaboration; and when dealing with poetic idioms of which he does not appreciate the rationale, Johnson can be surprisingly obtuse. His dismissal of the metaphysical poets is a good example of this, and his characterisation of Milton's *Lycidas* as "easy, vulgar and therefore disgusting" because it is in the pastoral mode uncovers another blind spot. Not that Johnson's castigation of other pastoralists in the *Lives* was without justification; for, as T.S. Eliot observed, the literature of Johnson's day was cursed with the pastoral convention, which explains why the rational mind of the critic refused to countenance such an apparent affectation. What Johnson overlooked, of course, is that despite Milton's reference to himself and Edward King as shepherds driving their flocks afield and the intermingling of Christian and pagan elements in *Lycidas*, this pastoral elegy succeeds in transcending the convention which Milton adopted.

Johnson's suspicion of departures from decorum in literary composition is apparent in his deliberations on the language of poetry. On all occasions, he contends, the writer should maintain "good sense" and consistency, eschewing phrases and images which arouse mnemonic irrelevances or violate propriety. One reason for his mildly contemptuous observations on English poetry earlier than the 17th century lies in his conviction that the "barbarity" of earlier ages was hostile to metrical regularity and appropriateness of diction. Before the time of Dryden, he says, there was "no system of words at once refined from the grossness of domestic use, and free from the harshness of terms appropriated to particular arts. Words too familiar, or too remote, defeat the purpose of the poet. . . ." From one point of view this apologia for the "poetic diction" of much 18th-century verse is reasonable enough, since a poem overloaded with demotic expressions runs the risk of being ridiculed. On the other hand, few would deny that the occasional admission of those elements of vocabulary which Johnson found obnoxious can have the effect of achieving qualities of raciness and immediacy which would otherwise be lacking. Another topic on which Johnson adopts a dogmatic posture is that of religious poetry. This he regards as unlikely to please because "Contemplative piety, or the intercourse between God and the human soul cannot be poetical . . . ," and in any case the "topics of devotion are few." To admirers of George Herbert, this proposition will not hold water; but Johnson insists that pious verse can merely "help the memory and delight the ear . . . but it supplies nothing to the mind. . . ." The implication that religious poetry belongs to an inferior order of invention comes strangely from a man who raised no objection to the utterance of carefully premeditated prayer.

But for all its author's prejudices, *The Lives of the English Poets* remains a masterpiece of provocative thought delivered in prose of unfailing liveliness. Dogmatic and assertive Johnson may be; but his crotchets are outnumbered by the innumerable passages in which reasonable argument prevails over obstructive partiality. Johnson is both an able theorist and a fine practical critic (see, for instance, his analysis of Pope's *Essay on Criticism*) whose massive intellect is brought to bear on questions of perennial importance to lovers of literature. In the romantic period Johnsonian prose was thought to be too stereotyped to be of much further use by practitioners in the art of criticism. But few would now dissent from James Boswell's view that *The Lives of the English Poets* is "the richest, most beautiful, and indeed most perfect, production of Johnson's pen."

—E.D. Mackerness

THE LONDON MERCHANT.
Play by George Lillo, 1731.

The London Merchant; or, The History of George Barnwell tells the story of an innocent but impressionable young man, George Barnwell, who is much loved by his master, the merchant Thorowgood, his fellow-apprentice Trueman, and his master's daughter Maria. George Barnwell is seduced by an adventuress, Millwood, and in his infatuation he steals money from his master. The theft is discovered by Trueman, who tries to cover it up for a time, and then the money is replaced by Maria, who also hopes that her father may not discover his beloved apprentice's fall from grace. Millwood has, meanwhile, sensed the possibility of larger gains and she urges George to murder his rich uncle, Barnwell, in order to inherit his estate. George hesitates, but in the end infatuation proves stronger than conscience and he goes to do the deed. However when he meets his uncle he hesitates, drops his pistol, and, in a moment of panic, stabs Barnwell to death. The scene ends, however, in a sentimental reconciliation of the dying man with his killer, the prelude to a succession of further scenes of forgiveness and reconciliation in the remainder of the play. Millwood's wickedness is revealed by her servants, who are appalled by her guiltiness and desert her, and in due course both she and George go to the gallows, he sustained by the blessings of his sympathising friends, she impenitent to the last.

George Lillo's play belongs to the period which saw the beginnings of the realistic and the domestic fictional development which includes the work of his admirer and fast friend Henry Fielding. By comparison with heroic tragedy and dramas in verse, Lillo's play, for all its shortcomings, must be seen as representing a major step towards naturalism. At the time, and for years afterwards, it was prized for treating mercantile life seriously, portraying natural familial emotions, and preaching valuable moral lessons to the young. Written in prose and clearly, if simplistically characterised, it does indeed use its characters to act as choric presences, commenting on the main action (in which George Barnwell's soliloquies often serve as commentary on his own dilemma as he struggles between the impulses of appetite and grace): the characters often invite the audience to share their sense of the terribleness or the pathos of events by the strength of their pained emotions. The play may, in this respect, be seen as an early example of the literature of sensibility or feeling which was to develop in Fielding's novels and to attain its greatest development in the work of Goldsmith, Henry Mackenzie, and Sterne. The final scenes show this particularly clearly. Thorowgood, the master, feels lively compassion for his erring apprentice. Trueman, his fellow, also rushes to the condemned cell to voice undying friendship and share in a sentimental scene of forgiveness. Maria appears as George is about to be taken to the gallows, avows her feelings and faints away. Forgiveness greets George wherever he looks, echoing the forgiveness which his uncle bestowed upon him as he died. Throughout, the play counterbalances scenes showing the wickedness of Millwood and the hapless George's infatuation with others which appeal to the audience for sympathy as characters on stage show the extent to which affection for a once-admired youth can survive disappointment and compassion blot out their recognition of crime.

Essentially, George Barnwell is represented as a victim. Charles Lamb has some scathing sentences in his essay "On the Tragedies of Shakespeare, Considered with Reference to Their Fitness for Stage Representation" (1812) ridiculing lazy spectators who sighed over Othello's death and George Barnwell's last moments in the condemned cell and found them both "so moving." But it is certainly Lillo's hope that we will be moved. For the character of George Barnwell is a study in weakness: in how conscience can be stilled till wicked deeds are done, though thereafter conscience is sure to revive. Against this Lillo sets the character of the ruthless adventuress Millwood, a figure who in Defoe's hands would have been a natural survivor, like Roxana, but here must come to a bad end, having driven a hapless and infatuated youth to crime. The energy of Millwood's character, however, can still be felt: she perhaps represents the 18th century's most remarkable short study in aberrant female psychology.

Lillo wished his play to be morally useful and he felt that the recognisable nature of its setting and its characters, taken from the ranks of the London mercantile class would increase its immediacy and force as a moral corrective. Eventually the play came to be performed at certain times as an Awful Warning to youth concerning the dangers of illicit passion and disobedience to one's superiors: a custom which Charles Lamb decried. It seems possible, too, that Fielding's admiration for the play proved less than durable. In *Joseph Andrews* elements of Millwood's character are absorbed into that of the sexual predator Lady Booby, while her attempted seduction of Joseph incorporates parodied features from Millwood's seduction of the hapless George Barnwell and recognisable passages of their conversation.

—William Ruddick

LOOK BACK IN ANGER.
Play by John Osborne, 1956.

8 May 1956 remains a very important date in the theatrical history of Great Britain and the rest of the English-speaking world, for it marks the first performance of John Osborne's *Look Back in Anger*, a play that revolutionized mid-20th-century British theatre. England suddenly had a new and vital international voice, a playwright who wrote passionately, honestly, and with an intensity that characterized him as the leader of a new group of writers later called the "angry young men." Arnold Wesker and John Arden were among the playwrights who would be so categorized, and Tom Stoppard would later say that the excitement generated by Osborne led him to think of himself as a dramatist. Though Osborne's style remained *sui generis*, the playwrights who followed could take their craft more seriously because of the respect that Osborne's work commanded.

But is *Look Back in Anger* more than theatrical history? Does the play continue to have theatrical qualities in addition to its historical importance? As Robert Egan declares, 30 years of successful revivals suggests that "it has not lost its special energies as a theatre event" (*Modern Drama*, September 1989). A domestic drama focusing on the tumultuous marriage of Jimmy and Alison Porter, the main source of this play's power lies in the striking portrait of its main character, the irascible, passionate, and even petulantly cruel Jimmy. A 25-year-old operator of a sweet stall in a large midland town, Jimmy is overeducated for his employment, artistic, bitter, hypersensitive—and angry about nearly everything. From the opening moments of the play Jimmy's verbal abuse toward his wife Alison and their friend and neighbor Cliff Lewis is difficult to categorize. Does Jimmy rail affectionately to express unusually expansive energy or does he cut to the quick in order to maim and scar? When her friend Helena Charles supplants Alison and becomes Jimmy's mistress, the ambivalence remains, just as it does when Alison returns and the Porters reconcile, ending the play by embracing one another and indulging in their familiar and affectionate baby-talk game of "squirrels and bears."

In Jimmy Porter, Osborne created a character who could not be taken lightly. A kinsman to Molière's Alceste, Jimmy cannot be reduced to a simple quotient; his rich complexity forces from the audience and ambivalent response of love and hatred, respect and scorn, acceptance and rejection. His cruelty raises the heat of the audience's response to such an intense level that one must seek an explanation for his uncivilized behavior, the way an audience feels compelled to try to explain Iago's "motiveless malignity."

Osborne provides the audience with explanations for Jimmy's behavior, but he offers them with such skill that the audience's ambivalence toward Jimmy is not resolved. The most famous speech from the play suggests that Jimmy's anger expresses his generation's disillusionment over England's failure to deliver on the promises of its post-World War II welfare state:

> I suppose people of our generation aren't able to die for good causes any longer. We had all that done for us, in the thirties and the forties, when we were still kids. There aren't any good, brave causes left. If the big bang does come, and we all get killed off, it won't be in aid of the old-fashioned, grand design. It'll just be for the Brave New-nothing-very-much-thank you. About as pointless and inglorious as stepping in front of a bus.

Another and perhaps more compelling explanation for Jimmy's behavior lies in his response to his fractured love life. As Helena leaves him, Jimmy complains that he cannot find a woman of similar intensity and commitment to face with him the life's suffering:

> They all want to escape from the pain of being alive. And most of all, from love. . . . It's no good trying to fool yourself about love. You can't fall into it like a soft job, without dirtying up your hands. It takes muscle and guts. . . . Was I really wrong to believe that there's a—a kind of—burning virility of mind and spirit that looks for something as powerful as itself? The heaviest, strongest creatures in this world seem to be the loneliest. Like the old bear, following his own breath in the dark forest. There's no warm pack, no herd to comfort him. That voice that cries out doesn't *have* to be a weakling's, does it?

When Alison returns, she has suffered her "first loss." The baby she had conceived with Jimmy has died and she has lost her fertility. Yet her pain seems to bring her closer to Jimmy, and the play ends with them in some kind of renewed relationship. Have they found a stronger bond through suffering or have they just retreated to a smaller world where "we'll be together in our bear's cave, and our squirrel's drey, and we'll live on honey, and nuts"? The rich ambivalence in *Look Back in Anger* leaves us wondering, brings us back to experience the play again, and gives Osborne's landmark drama its enduring power.

—Terry Nienhuis

LORD JIM.
Novel by Joseph Conrad, 1900.

Joseph Conrad began writing *Lord Jim* in 1898 as a novelette, but after its first parts had been serialized in *Blackwood's Magazine* beginning in October 1899, he extended his story into a full-length novel whose installments ran until November 1900. In it, Conrad's favorite narrator, the veteran seaman Marlow, examines the case of a young merchant ship officer who commits the crime of abandoning his vessel and its passengers during a storm, and then seeks to vindicate himself by undertaking the leadership of a beleaguered tribe of people in Borneo. The tale is based on two separate chapters of British colonialism in southeast Asia. In August 1880, a ship carrying Muslim pilgrims to Mecca was deserted by its British crew who thought it was sinking, but the ship was towed into port the next day. The affair created a great scandal, there was a court of inquiry, and the offending officers were penalized. Conrad also had in mind as a model for his protagonist the figure of Sir James Brooke, an English soldier who helped a Bornean tribe to fight off their enemies and became their leader as the Rajah of Saráwak.

The career of Conrad's hero includes experiences from both of these episodes. Jim claims that when he abandoned the pilgrim ship which is later brought into port safely, together with its deserted passengers, he jumped from its deck involuntarily. Yet he has displayed cowardice before, and when he reviews the events, he is led to the conclusion that he is guilty, even if he did not intend to jump, because men are responsible for their actions even if they lack free will. He is indirectly condemned when a brilliant young officer who witnesses the court of inquiry commits suicide, presumably because he fears he may disgrace himself as Jim has. After the inquiry Jim becomes a drifter, roaming from port to port to avoid those who know about his past. When Marlow consults the philosophic German trader, Stein, about him, Stein diagnoses Jim's case as that of a romantic egoist, and recommends that he undertake to live up to the proud image of himself that has been endangered by his act of cowardice.

Accordingly, Jim goes to a village in Borneo where Stein has a trading post, and helps its people defeat the neighbors who are oppressing them. He becomes their hero and their magistrate, falls in love with one of their girls, and Marlow, when he comes to visit him, finds that he has regained his confidence, and has forgotten the weakness he once displayed. His uncertainty reappears with fatal results, however, when an English desperado and his gang attack the village. Jim conquers them, but when the outlaw suggests that there must be something in Jim's past that deprives him of the right to pass judgment on him, Jim, conscious of his old guilt, agrees to let him go. As a result, the son of the village headman is killed, and Jim gives himself up to be executed as the one responsible for it.

These events are attended by irresolvable moral ambiguities. They are acted out against the backdrop of Conrad's intuition that the universe is a chaos whose evil constantly threatens to invade human motives, and that the prime virtue men can display is "fidelity" to each other. Jim's fault is characterized as "a breach of faith with the community of mankind." But the question of his ultimate morality is never really settled because the novel offers glimpses of some larger purpose that transcends superficial altruism. Because he believes that events cannot be judged from "the language of facts that are so often more enigmatic than the craftiest arrangement of words," Conrad employs some remarkable narrative innovations to split open the facts and expose their moral complexities.

The two sections of Jim's career are presented consecutively, but the episodes of the story are told in an order very different from that of their occurrence. In this way, the significance of each situation changes as other parts of the story become known. The novel begins in mid-point, after Jim's disgrace, when he is working on shore as a clerk, and before the reader can know the reason for his furtive behavior. Only after the inquiry has begun do we learn how the cowardice of the deserted ship's crew was exposed by a brave French lieutenant who brought it into port. In addition, Conrad tells his story through several narrators (most of whom, however, report to Marlow), who bring different perspectives to bear on Jim's situation, so that the novel has the form of a circle of moral evaluations which seem to exhaust the possibilities of judgment. Finally, the narrative is marked by numerous symbols and images that convey messages differing from those of action and character, and give the text a powerful poetic dimension that augments the traditional fictional resources. Through these methods, the disruption of chronology, the dispersion of the narrative point of view, and the use of symbols as significant elements of the story, *Lord Jim* expanded the possibilities of fiction and anticipated developments in the 20th-century novel.

—Jacob Korg

LORD OF THE FLIES.
Novel by William Golding, 1954.

William Golding's *Lord of the Flies*, the *Robinson Crusoe* of our time, enjoys—like the earlier island story of shipwreck and survival—a pre-eminent place in cultural lore. Both cultural document and modern classic, the novel has provoked enormous critical attention at the same time as it has prompted great general interest—and has sold millions of copies. An obdurate and uncompromising fable about how boys—very British boys—will be beasts if the constraints of authority are withdrawn from their closed world, *Lord of the Flies* has proved to be a literary and popular success, known and discussed beyond the confines of the academy: two feature film versions of the book have been produced and the book may well be the most internationally taught of contemporary novels. It has also, like its author, been "endlessly discussed, analysed, dissected, over praised and over faulted, victim of that characteristic 20th-century mania for treating living artists as is they were dead," as the novelist John Fowles once observed. In fact, Golding's first novel is not nearly so long as the critical commentary it has spawned.

The story itself is by now familiar. A group of schoolboys, educated by British public schools in a system designed to control an empire, are dropped on an edenic island in the Pacific Ocean. There they confront the task of survival. First the boys proceed to set up a pragmatic system based on a "grown-up" model: government, laws, shelters, plumbing facilities, and food supplies. Quickly, however, the society disintegrates under the dual pressures of aggression and superstition. Signal fire becomes defensive hearth, then ritualistic spit; nighttime darkness becomes monstrous "beast" to be propitiated by totemic pig heads. Hunting becomes killing as Jack's hunters break loose from Ralph's fire-keepers to form a tribal society with gods, rituals, and territory at the island's end. When two boys from the original group invade this territory they are killed, Simon ritually as a totemic beast and Piggy politically as an enemy. Finally a scapegoat, Ralph, is hunted down so as to offer his head to the Lord of the Flies, when the adult world intervenes in the person of a naval officer. The fable concludes with the pathetic image of the survivor, Ralph, crying for the "end of innocence, the darkness of man's heart, and the fall through the air of the true, wise friend called Piggy."

And yet "[h]ow romantically it starts!," wrote E.M. Forster, his 1962 introduction to *Lord of the Flies* being influential in establishing Golding the unfashionable allegorist, writing from deep religious convictions about mankind's essential depravity. He "believes in the Fall of Man. . . . his attitude approach[ing] the Christian; we are all born in sin, or will all lapse into it." But the text itself bears no such single or stable meaning, a matter made evident by its susceptibility to a range of critical interpretations: religious, philosophical, sociological, psychological. As moral fable, it examines individual disintegration; as political fable it explores social regression, while as mythic fable it offers an account of prelapsarian loss. Other readings seem equally pertinent. Using the lens of Freud's *Three Essays on Human Sexuality* or *Totem and Taboo* opens *Lord of the Flies* to a reading where the boys become representative of various instincts or amoral forces. In anthropological terms, the boys' society could be seen to mirror the societies of prehistoric man; theirs seems a genuine primitive culture with its own gods, demons, myths, rituals, taboos. Then again, viewed from the position developed by Hannah Arendt's *The Banality of Evil*, *Lord of the Flies* can come into focus as a dystopia, showing how "intelligence (Piggy) and common sense (Ralph) will always be overthrown in society by sadism (Roger) and the lure of totalitarianism (Jack)."

"[I]sn't it cracking an opusculum with a critical sledgehammer?" the author was later to remark in response to these abstract accounts, ones that so often obscured the book's primary strength. For *Lord of the Flies* is first and foremost a gripping adventure story about English schoolboys, related ironically—indeed, subversively—to another boys' story, R.M. Ballantyne's *The Coral Island* (1857). *Lord of the Flies'* main characters are, like *Coral Island*'s, named Ralph and Jack—though Ballantyne's third character, Peterkin, is split into two boys: Peter and Simon. Shipwrecked on an uninhabited island, Ballantyne's boys lead prosperous lives whereas Golding's boys progressively deteriorate. When at the end a naval officer, surveying the hideous children before him, remarks: "I should have thought that a pack of British boys—you're all British aren't you—would have able to put up a better show than that—I mean . . . Like the *Coral Island*"), the intertextual allusion is more than ironic. For *Coral Island* functions throughout as an embedded narrative; by recasting the 19th-century tale from a post-World War II perspective, *Lord of the Flies* refutes conceptions of the civilized child and—by extension—the civility of men.

Such a revisionary strategy informs other narrative features, ones characteristic of Golding's subsequent fictional practice: the distinctive use of visual symbol where significance is saturated in and sutured to naturalistic detail, the coda reversal with its point of view on events contradicting initially established expectations; the habit of delayed disclosure; the method of interlocked design where chapter, episode, character, description, internal allusion, motif, and image pattern are integrated so meticulously that they reflect back thematically upon one another.

Present as well in the figure of Simon is a feature of Golding's work that has remained—despite charges of allegorical reductiveness—a stubborn conception in the Golding mythopoeia: the holy fool. Forerunner to *Pincher Martin*'s Nat, *Darkness Visible*'s Matty, or *Rites of Passage*'s Parson Colley, *Lord of the Flies'* unsimple Simon comes to be wise. Sitting before the Lord of the Flies, a stinking, fly-ridden pig's head on a stick, Simon recognizes in human nature the real beast. Simon is then ritually murdered, meeting the fate of those who remind society of its own complicity. The ritual enacts the confinement and destruction of the boys' own terrors; they kill Simon as a beast, his death momentarily exorcising their fears. Piggy's death marks the inadequacy of the rational, logical world: the symbolic conch is smashed as the blind Piggy falls into the sea. Ralph alone remains, to be hunted down as fire sweeps through the island, thus signalling the naval ship and bringing about the schoolboys' rescue.

Rescue is always ironic, so the contemporary sensibility records, and *Lord of the Flies* has complied. As a text interrogative of its time, *Lord of the Flies* has meant many things to many people. Golding himself insisted upon one theme—one so transformed by the resonance of the fiction that it resists any allegorical abstraction. *Lord of the Flies* declared its author is "about grief. Grief, grief, sheer grief."

—Virginia Tiger

THE LORD OF THE RINGS
(includes *The Fellowship of the Ring*, *The Two Towers*, *The Return of the King*).
Novels by J.R.R. Tolkien, 1954–55.

J.R.R. Tolkien's massive chronicle of events in Middle-Earth is a great masterpiece of modern fantasy, the work with which other fantasies are repeatedly compared and contrasted. It has been estimated that by 1968, shortly after its paperback publication, *The Lord of the Rings* had been read by 50 million people. Although Tolkien saw the work as a single novel, divided into six books, the publishers found it advisable to subdivide it into three separate volumes, *The Fellowship of the Ring*, *The Two Towers*, and *The Return of the King*. Hence it has become popularly referred to as a trilogy, but it is actually one continuous narrative.

Tolkien spent 13 years in the writing of this complex work. He saw the fantasy writer as a "subcreator" who invented a "secondary world" differing from our primary world but enhancing its meaning for us. For his own secondary world of Middle-Earth, he provided a complete history, mythology, geography, several races of rational beings, and several disparate languages. The central plot of the novel deals with the Third Age of this invented world, during which a great battle between the forces of good and evil takes place. The focus of the struggle is a ring of power in the possession of the Dark Lord, Sauron. Only the destruction of this ring will save Middle-Earth from his tyranny. A fellowship of seven individuals representing five of the free peoples (men, elves, dwarves, wizards, and hobbits) undertakes the quest to destroy the ring.

Tolkien's ingenuity in creating original races and vivid characters is responsible in part for the book's wide appeal. His concept of the elves is highly original, for they are not at all like the diminutive creatures of folklore. They are impressively tall, and some live in trees in a lovely timeless country where grow silver trees with golden leaves. Skilled with arrows and talented artisans, they are also immortal, a feature which endows them with a sense of sadness in a mortal world. The hobbits in contrast are quite little, about three feet tall and with furry toes. A happy race, which delights in food and festivities, they nonetheless provide the heroes who will take on the dangerous mission of destroying the ring. The ents are an entirely original creation. Tree spirits, they move about and speak in their own distinctive language, but they look like trees with feet.

Tolkien's outstanding individual characters include the wizard Gandalf, the oldest ent Treebeard, the jolly nature spirit Tom Bombadil, and gracious elven queen Galadriel, and the stubborn, persistent hobbits, Frodo and Sam, who overcome extraordinary dangers and problems in their seemingly hopeless quest. The evil figures are also memorable, ranging from the Dark Lord to the voracious spider, Shelob.

As in most effective novels, the characters in this work are strongly individualized, with growth and development throughout and with dramatic inner conflict. The hero Frodo, for example, does not find it simple to carry out the burdensome quest, and even after the deed is achieved (in a very ironic way) he feels loss and regret. Tolkien also uses the devices of splitting and doubling as modes of characterization. The pitiable Gollum, whose only concern in life is the ring, which he calls his "precious," represents an aspect of Frodo. Several other characters are paired as doubles.

Tolkien's professional background provided him with inspiration for many of his ideas. As a linguist, he enjoyed creating new languages, as a result of which the novel contains not only words but even songs in such languages as elvish. As a medievalist, he was also familiar with the literature and mythology of the Anglo-Saxons and the Middle Ages. A few of the episodes are modeled on similar events in *Beowulf* and in Norse myths, and some of his names are drawn from mythic sources. His languages are designed to suit the nature of their speakers. The elvish words are melodious and mellifluent, while the crude orcs speak a harsh, guttural tongue.

Part of the appeal of Tolkien's fantasy saga is the satisfaction of experiencing a world which is coherent and meaningful. Events here are never random, and nature is never indifferent. Elements of nature, such as trees, sunlight, and mountains, are endowed with an awareness of what goes on in Middle-Earth. A malicious willow tree, an unwilling dawn, and an angry mountain cause serious problems for the fellowship.

One of the purposes of fantasy, according to Tolkien, is to help the reader rediscover his own world from a fresh perspective. His novel succeeds in this aim. For those who have looked at trees so much that they no longer really see a tree, the appearance of the ent transforms that awareness. Reading about Middle-Earth invites the reader to see places and events in nature with a renewed sense of wonder. The result is a joy which transcends catastrophe, which elevates the reader's consciousness beyond any expectation of a merely happy ending.

At the end of the novel, the Third Age is about to end. The Fourth Age will be that of humans, and the elves, dwarves, wizards, ents, and hobbits will no longer be around. The vision is sad, but the reader's experience of having known them is a satisfying one.

—Charlotte Spivack

LORNA DOONE.
Novel by R.D. Blackmore, 1869.

R.D. Blackmore defined his third novel, *Lorna Doone*, in a rather circular fashion, as a "romance" because, he said, "the incidents, characters, time, and scenery, are alike romantic," and although his work was not the only one of the 1860's to challenge the prevailing realistic style, it was nonetheless an anomaly and at first little appreciated. After a couple of years, however, it did gain a readership, due in part, Blackmore suspected, to the interest in the marriage of Princess Louise and the Marquis of Lorne, and it has remained the most enduringly popular of Blackmore's novels. Its ultimate success can be attributed partly to the romantic qualities of which Blackmore speaks—the idealized, almost mythic characters, elemental conflicts, and awe-inspiring landscape—but also to the complex historical consciousness informing the novel, to the affectionate authenticity with which Blackmore recreated west country agricultural life, and to the engaging, self-deprecating, yet shrewdly perceptive tone assumed by the protagonist, John Ridd, in narrating the novel.

Set principally on Exmoor in Devon and Somerset, Blackmore's tale embellishes local legends of the Doone gang, a decadent family of 17th-century noblemen living by plunder and extortion after losing their land in the north through legal chicanery. The romantic plot concerns the developing relationship between the narrator Ridd, a yeoman farmer whose father is murdered by the Doone gang at the beginning of the novel, and Lorna Doone, a beautiful girl whom Ridd originally believes to be a child of one of the Doones. Later, however, he discovers her to be the daughter and heiress of an English nobleman, abducted as a young child by the Doones and intended as a wife for Carver Doone, the most ruthless of the brigands. An equally romantic subplot involves Ridd's highwayman cousin Tom Faggus, a former blacksmith ruined by a lawsuit, who, like the Doones, turns to a life of crime. Admired for his daring exploits and his generosity with stolen money, he eventually settles into the generally sober life of an honest citizen after marriage to Annie, Ridd's sweet-tempered sister.

The characters are defined by superlatives—Lorna the most beautiful, Ridd the largest and strongest, Carver the most brutal, even the snowfall is the deepest in generations—and scenery and plot are alike handled with an almost operatic disregard for probabilities. In the melodramatic climax of the novel, for example, as Ridd and Lorna exchange wedding vows in the parish church, Lorna is suddenly shot by Carver Doone, an event which leads to the final battle between Ridd and Carver at the eerie Wizard's Slough.

Because it is set in the latter half of the 17th century during the political turmoil of the 1680's, *Lorna Doone* invites consideration as historical fiction. Charles II and Chief Justice Jeffreys appear briefly, and Ridd is nearly swept up into Monmouth's abortive rebellion of 1685 and is threatened with execution as a rebel after the battle of Sedgemoor. There is, however, another dimension to Blackmore's historical imagination, more important to the novel than these peripheral figures and events. Conceiving of the instability of the time as a transition from a violent but romantic past to a calmer, more prosaic present, he imposes upon the form of his novel an analogous process of historical change. The extermination of the Doone gang creates a safer though less exciting countryside. Carver's affectionate young son Ensie becomes a model English schoolboy, Tom Faggus a respectable bourgeois, and Annie an avid consumer of the latest gadgets. By the end of the novel even Mother Melldrum, the local Exmoor prophetess, has died, and the Mother Melldrum Inn has appropriated her name. As a figure of ancient mystery now exploited by modern advertising, she foreshadows the boost to west country tourism that Blackmore's novel would itself provide.

In contrast to the consciousness of historical change in the novel is its timeless pastoralism. The novel has been much praised for its detailed descriptions of agricultural life, by, for example, Thomas Hardy, who noted its keen perceptions of "little phases of nature." In addition, *Lorna Doone* is informed throughout by the values of pastoralism—the independence, the physical wholesomeness, and the moral soundness of rural life. These values foster a staunch conservatism illustrated by Ridd's frequently reaffirmed loyalty to the royalist cause and even by his respect for the Doones' social position, yet at the same time they nourish an iconoclastic individualism which repeatedly questions the nature of true nobility and ridicules pomposity.

Judged by the criteria of realistic fiction, *Lorna Doone* no doubt lacks such virtues as an acute psychological insight, a tightly knit structure, and a profound analysis of the nature of society. Judged in its own terms, however, it remains a work of singular power and charm, written in an idiosyncratic, often rhythmic and poetic style. Still today it draws hundreds of literary pilgrims to the west country to climb the waterslide into the "real" Doone Valley and to pay homage to the creator of one of the most memorable myths in Victorian fiction.

—James E. Byer

THE LOVE SONG OF J. ALFRED PRUFROCK.
Poem by T.S. Eliot, 1917.

T.S. Eliot's early poem "The Love Song of J. Alfred Prufrock" is a portrait of impotence and futility remarkable for its modernity of idiom and form, and the modulation it achieves between images of contemporary urban, middle-class tedium, and a rhetoric of prophetic revelation.

The impotence is Prufrock's, the protagonist who cannot find it in himself to articulate the question with which he is (by his own account) consumed. His determination wavers, his visions give way (bathetically) to revisions. His hesitations, inhibitions, and anticipations combine to ensure the endless deferral of his question. Prufrock capitulates and we are never quite sure to what—to something in himself, or to something in a social milieu filled for him with imagined tyrannies? The reader is left to little more than hints and guesses.

For the reader then, the poem is a frustrating experience, the more so because it had begun so promisingly, with the proferred complicity and intimacy that conventionally lies behind so many poet/reader relationships here made explicit —"Let us go then, you and I." It is an offer that takes us nowhere. The narrative line founders and is immediately bemused by the repetitions of "Do I dare?" and "Do I dare?" The cat-like fog, the unfamiliar image of the etherised patient, offer already discomfitting because discordant signals —the leap that turns to sleep—stasis, rest, comfort, enclosure, an entrapment, a threatening silence, isolation. Explanations are deferred (in the way of texts with their readers), but the promise is never quite redeemed. Indeed the language anticipates the process of reading in a way that is quite specific—the language of *lead* and *follow* and *intent*—but denies the question about the question—or defers it until (we are as readers to suppose) more facts are revealed by "our visit."

The rhythm and pattern of the verse are certainly insistent and urgent, perhaps neurotically repetitive. Eliot's use of rhyme has something to do with it, taken with his variable line lengths, and his deployment of alliterations. (The poet himself acknowledged the influence of the French poet Laforgue on the rhyme and *vers libre* rhythms of his verse.) The disquieting of the reader is achieved above all by the repetitive, incantatory manner of his language, not only the repeated phrases and sentences—"there will be time" or "do I dare?"—but the insistent weaving of word repetitions through passages like the following:

> And I have known the eyes already, known them all—
> The eyes that fix you in a formulated phrase,
> And when I am formulated, sprawling on a pin,
> When I am pinned and wriggling on the wall,
> Then how should I begin
> To spit out all the butt-ends of my days and ways?
> And how should I presume?

And then, of course, at the level of sounds, there are the alliterations and assonances operating here as they do throughout the poem, and the internal and end-rhymes. The degree of formal patterning in Eliot's verse is considerable and sophisticated. The syntax of his verse paragraphs, the control of rhythm and pace, the characteristic contraction in those lines that mark the end of his paragraphs— "Before the taking of a toast and tea"—these constitute formal aspects of the poem that induce even as they imitate the reader's frustration. The poem provides an alternation between passages of quickening pace and expansive gesture that yet cannot discover the resounding closure that they seem to promise, and lines which instead contract and offer a bathetic alternative.

> And indeed there will be time
> For the yellow smoke that slides along the street
> Rubbing its back upon the window-panes;
> There will be time, there will be time
> To prepare a face to meet the faces that you meet;
> There will be time to murder and create,
> And time for all the works and days of hands
> That lift and drop a question on your plate;
> Time for you and time for me,
> And time yet for a hundred indecisions,
> And for a hundred visions and revisions,
> Before the taking of a toast and tea.

Closure is here expected to be dis-closure, revelation; and that unfulfilled expectation constitutes the characteristic rhetorical strategy of the text. One need only look at the closing lines of each of the verse paragraphs to confirm that this is so.

If we return from a formal level of discussion to what we might call the level of character, what appears to intimidate and disarm Prufrock's need to speak is his profound sense of the pointlessness, the futility, of any attempt to communicate his "message." It is futile to try because he does not believe that anything he might have to say would be understood:

> If one, settling a pillow by her head,
> Should say: "That is not what I meant at all.
> That is not it, at all."
>
> If one, settling a pillow or throwing off a shawl
> And turning toward the window, should say:
> "That is not it at all,
> That is not what I meant at all."

The world that would not understand is dominated by women of his own cultured and leisured middle class, those women who "come and go / Talking of Michelangelo." There seems little doubt that the inhibition is created in part by the fact of their being women, that is to say, it is a sexual inhibition. The poem registers throughout a neurotic sexual consciousness; Prufrock is morbidly fascinated by and fearful of female sexuality. "Arms that are bracleted and white and bare / (But in the lamplight downed with light brown hair!)" is a passage in which the oppositions of bare/hair, white/brown, and bracleted/downed define terms (positive/negative) to register that revulsion and recoil.

The title indeed seems to point us towards a sexual interpretation of the poem as a whole—in which Prufrock's question is either a proposal or a proposition. The intimacy of the scenes between Prufrock and the unnamed female encourages us to believe that the question concerns their personal relationship. It has often been noted that there are very powerful echoes of Marvell's poem "To His Coy Mistress," that archetypal poem in the *carpe diem* tradition—a tradition whose whole point is the urgency of immediate action, and a poem which presses this point with magnificent confidence. Eliot has Prufrock muse:

> Would it have been worth while,
> To have bitten off the matter with a smile,
> To have squeezed the universe into a ball
> To roll it towards some overwhelming question

And speaks earlier of "having the strength to force the moment to its crisis."

Marvell's lover proposed:

> Let us roll all our strength, and all
> Our sweetness, up into one ball:
> And tear our pleasures with rough strife,
> Thorough the iron gates of life.

The reminder of Marvell is instructive, for Marvell's lover has the advantage of (admittedly ironic) self-belief. For him the persuasions are powered by dominance and delight (sexual and linguistic), are paradoxically at once destructive and creative. His argument is levelled against Time and Death, in sexual defiance; also against their Silence. Eliot's Prufrock, on the other hand, is enfeebled and defeated. Sexual defiance avails him nothing; his song is muted. This ironic function of the allusion connects also with the other allusions in the poem, particularly the one to *Hamlet*—"No! I am not Prince Hamlet, nor was meant to be"—for Hamlet's situation within the convention of revenge tragedy is itself likewise ironic. Hamlet questions the ethics of action in ways that subvert the convention at its very foundations—hence the sporadic action and the uneven pacing of *Hamlet*, the hero's oft-remarked procrastination. Hamlet shares other characteristics with Prufrock, of course, the sexual revulsion noted above, for one. But it is his distinctive aversion from a belief in the efficacy of action, and from the ethics of action, that marks him out among Elizabethan and Jacobean avengers, and peripheralises him within that complex of assumptions that constitute the world of revenge plays. Heroism is only ambiguously related to action in Hamlet's case. He is the appropriate progenitor for Eliot's yet further marginalised "hero." He is related therefore through a problematisation of the very notion of "hero." "An attendant lord, one that will do / To swell a progress, start a scene or two" now occupies the centre of the stage. It is a process that is confirmed and extended by Stoppard's *Rosencrantz and Guildenstern Are Dead*. The tradition provides the means to re-define the stature of our representative protagonists. The notion of the marginalised and diminished figure as a 20th-century archetype is founded in Prufrock. Powerless and intimidated, without either the insistent assurance of Marvell's lover, or the hesitant and impetuous responses of which Hamlet yet remains capable, "I have measured out my life in coffee spoons."

Yet there remains the question of the question. If the world of social intercourse not only inhibits the posing of the question, and does so by being incapable of understanding it, between the questioner and his world there seems to be a problem of language or communication. Prufrock considers oblique ways of bringing the question to the surface, into words: "Shall I say, I have gone at dusk through narrow streets. . . ." Another suggestion—"To say: 'I am Lazarus, come from the dead, / Come back to tell you all, I shall tell you all'"—would seem to take the question out of the realm of sexual exchanges merely, and into the realm of silence. And Lazarus is joined by others in the poem whose presence implies a question that certainly turns on the issue of death and whatever we might mean by the meaning of life. Hamlet is of course just one such character whose preoccupations are greatly taken up with that bourne from which few travellers return (after all his father is one such, Lazarus another). The epigram from Dante points us in precisely the same direction, to the question of life beyond death, and to the expectation that it cannot be spoken of: "If what I hear is true, no one ever returns alive from this place," Montefeltro tells the visitors in *Inferno*, "so I will tell you without fear of dishonour." John the Baptist is another such mediator between this world, the world of experience, and whatever Reality may lie beyond it. (John the Baptist is also of course the victim of female sexuality, of Salome, the *femme fatale*.) Even Marvell's poem was written, as has been suggested, within a perspective that laid emphasis upon death and the "fine and private place" that awaits us all, and in the shadow of its silence.

In the light of Eliot's later poems, it is tempting to see this network of allusion and reference as indicative of a straining against the limits of the temporal, a quest for the spiritual or eternal dimension beyond our knowledge. The denial—"I am no prophet"—does not deny the need for prophecy, rather the appropriateness of prophecy in these times. There is no longer any place for what was once thought of as prophecy; nor is there any language proper to that function. We are presented instead with a world of social triviality and banality, a world of illusion behind which reality lies masked; and our language is employed in the service of that illusion. It is surely this pressure upon language and upon vision that makes sense of his assertion that he is "almost, at times, the Fool." (We assume, presumably, Lear's fool.) The question becomes a *prophetic* questioning.

Pound defended the ending of the poem as necessarily unresolved and open. Closure for such a poem he thought inappropriate. In fact, the final section is of great significance in bringing the reader to an understanding of the poem. The distinction between the full and enriched life in "the chambers of the sea" and the banal world to which we are called to return by "human voices" is the distinction between life and death, paradoxically expressed. The sea held strong positive associations for Eliot which are evident throughout his work. It is an image symbolic of that fuller, eternal reality, the timeless dimension to which death or creative imagination gives us access. In life itself one drowns, cut off from the imaginative world of mermaids singing each to each. Whether Eliot already has in mind religious/spiritual salvation, or salvation through art, or both is perhaps not unambiguous.

—Brian W.M. Scobie

LOVERS OF THE LAKE.
Story by Sean O'Faolain, 1957.

First collected in *The Finest Stories of Sean O'Faolain*, "Lovers of the Lake" is one of the best examples of how O'Faolain rewrote the agenda of the Irish short story. A good deal of his early work was devoted to analyses of Irish political and cultural conditions, and O'Faolain's reputation rests not only on his accomplishments in the short story but, perhaps to an equal degree, on the commitment of his nonfictional prose, particularly that produced in the 1930's and 1940's. The periodical which he founded in 1940, the *Bell*, is commonly regarded as a landmark in the development of Irish intellectual life in the years following the establishment of an independent Ireland, when such a life was most needed and greatly lacking.

O'Faolain's early stories tend to be anatomies of the various intellectual and institutional insufficiencies of the new Ireland which the author's generation brought into being. These works often have disillusionment for their theme, are critical in tone, and are neither metropolitan nor bourgeois in their orientation. It would be misleading to suggest that O'Faolain stopped producing stories of this kind once he resigned the editorship of the *Bell* in 1946. Nevertheless, from about this time his work becomes more ironic in tone, focused more on individuals than on their contexts, more inclined to feature elements and aspects of European taste and culture, and typically presenting characters whose state of material comfort is accompanied by unwonted experiences of moral complexity. In a word, these stories tend to portray the Irish as though they believe themselves to be grown-ups rather than the aimless ragamuffins of history or the embittered victims of their own political independence. Much as his early stories have been admired, it is the work produced after 1946 which have given O'Faolain a lasting place in the modern annals of the form.

The couple in "Lovers of the Lake," Jenny and Bobby, are representative of O'Faolain's revised cast of characters. Rather than husband and wife, much less the isolated individuals typical of his earlier stories, they are mistress and lover. Bobby is no less than Doctor Robert Flannery, the eminent Dublin surgeon and conventional atheist, while Jenny is the estranged wife of a successful businessman. Class lines are identified as promptly as blood lines would be in Irish fiction of an earlier time, and these lines are emphasised with details of the couple's dress, taste, and general material ease.

Representative O'Faolain characters the pair may be, but they are not, however, typical of Irish society, as Jenny's opening observation about the dress of the suburban tennis-players on whom she is "looking down." The Irish are generally not known for either their atheism or their amorousness. In addition, Bobby and Jenny are presented as being detached from the tribal intimacies of Irish life, such as inconveniently large families, spiteful neighbours, and the whole array of political, cultural, and sectarian affiliations which function as impersonal social sources of identity. It is from the interplay between contrasts in status, levels of freedom, and degrees of responsibility (not to mention responsiveness) that the story elicits its broader themes.

Jenny's decision to travel to St. Patrick's Purgatory at Lough Derg, off the inhospitable coast of Donegal, Ireland's north-westernmost country, both links her to and differentiates her from commonplace Irishness, embodiments of which are skillfully deployed throughout the detailed, but not overbearing, account of the pilgrimage. Bobby, as orthodox an atheist as he is a sensualist, considers her decision to be illogical at best, yet finds himself unable to relinquish her to the enactment of it. The personal difficulties which arise between Jenny and Bobby in the course of their penitential sojourn are not simply, or necessarily, emblematic of larger cultural themes. Rather, their ability to find in this unequally shared experience a deeper, more tolerant, and arguably more catholic basis for their relationship is expertly projected in the story.

At the same time, however, the lovers come to a renewal of their love in the context of the lake, one of the age-old holy places of Ireland, rich in tradition, flagship of the purgative and puritanical strains of Irish Catholicism. That the adulterous couple emerge with their humanity enhanced rather than intimidated emphasises the story's individualist rather than communal orientation. But such individual development would not have taken place without the formal presence of a communal rite. Jenny and Bobby reappraise their relationship on the basis of differences between them revealed by the pilgrimage. The openness of the story's playful contradictions expresses the freedom which is individuality's talisman.

—George O'Brien

LOVE'S LABOUR'S LOST.
Play by William Shakespeare, 1594 (?).

Love's Labour's Lost is generally thought to have been among William Shakespeare's earlier plays, probably first performed by 1595, but the quarto edition, published in 1598, speaks of the text: "As it was presented before her Highness [Elizabeth I] this last Christmas. Newly corrected and augmented." The script is unusual for Shakespeare in that there is no known source or precedent for it, though many of the characters derive from contemporary French history and also appear in Marlowe's *The Massacre at Paris* and Chapman's *The Conspiracy and Tragedy of Charles, Duke of Biron*. The contemporary King of Navarre (who became Henri IV of France in 1589) was a popular Huguenot leader for Elizabethans, and seemed likely to end the French civil wars of religion by a military victory which would create a French Protestant monarchy allied to the Tudor one. A play about the romantic Gascon origins of Henri de Boubon thus had great appeal. The youthful escapades of this hero (at the Nérac conference, 1578) establish a pattern Shakespeare repeated in Prince Hal's excesses in *Henry IV*. To avoid political offence when both plays were printed in 1598, Shakespeare renamed the comic Oldcastle (a Lollard martyr) Falstaff, and Henri, King of Navarre, became Ferdinand.

In parodying the academic affectations of the court of the youthful King, Shakespeare exploits and ridicules many of the verbal characteristics of the university wits such as Marlowe and Lyly who were his rivals in the theatre, with occult allusions to Sir Walter Ralegh's mysterious School of Night. The play is a pastiche of Renaissance literary styles, an exercise in verbal pyrotechnics through which Shakespeare displays the full range of his verbal skills, from endless puns to virtuoso debates on outrageous topics such as the virtues of fickleness or of loving an ugly woman. Shakespeare both exploits and ridicules the extravagant euphuism of the Spanish Don Armado, the Latin pedantry of the schoolmaster Holofernes, as well as the naive idealism of the academically ambitious young men of the court of Navarre. All these male pretensions are overthrown by the witty realism of the Princess and her ladies whose arrival for diplomatic negotiations signals the collapse of the puritanical academy established by the King. These lively ladies anticipate the assertive behaviour of many later Shakespearean heroines when they treat the young men's intellectual ambitions with humorous scepticism, reaching a point of wholesale ridicule of their Russian Masque and Pageant of the Worthies, in which first the courtiers and then their associates are totally humiliated, and abandon all their pretensions. The news of the death of the father of the Princess confirms the replacing of intellectual frivolity with harsh realism when the ladies impose a renewed discipline on their admirers to test the sincerity of their erratic affections. The play thus ends provocatively without the conventional resolution of marriage and the subordination of the women. Its concluding choric songs match the women's realism by mocking the picturesque promiscuity of youthful Spring while noting harsh Winter's sober virtues. Here, as throughout the play, literary sophistication is thus subordinated to the practical demands of society in ways that undercut the academic and literary credentials of Shakespeare's theatrical rivals.

Many of Shakespeare's classic effects are mapped out in this play, with its theme of the tempering of a naive hero which is to be repeated in later comedies by Orlando, Claudio, and Angelo. Berowne's contribution to this evolution matches the jaded scepticism of a Faulconbridge, a Falstaff, a Benedick, or a Lucio. These sceptics' impact is reinforced by the kind of assertively witty heroines in many later Shakespearean comedies such as Portia and Beatrice, of whom the Princess of France and her ladies are successful prefigurations. This princess and her ladies match the feminism and sophistication of the Valois courts as perfected by the *escadron volant* of the Queen Mother Catherine de' Medici: Shakespeare derives many of his dominant women from France: Marguerite d'Anjou in *Henry VI*, Rosalind in *As You Like It*, and Helena in *All's Well*. However, the assertive Princess's brunette attendant, the sharp-tongued Rosaline, matches Shakespeare's own Dark Lady and her analogue, Cleopatra. The play reverses the gender roles of another early Shakespeare play, *The Taming of the Shrew*, showing women tempering the vagaries of male egotism rather than a husband dominating a wife.

For a long time the elaborate language of the play was regarded as too esoteric and rhetorical to attract popular audiences, but its suitability for elegant productions in the opulent style of Fragonard and Watteau has ensured many successful productions in recent years, such as those by Peter Brook at Stratford in 1946 and by the Oregon Shakespeare Festival in 1987. The low-life critique which its clown Costard makes of aristocratic pretensions also shows a lively humour which has considerable modern appeal. As with its first productions, the play can still successfully both exploit and ridicule upper-class elegance and sophistication. It shows a youthful playwright scoring brilliantly off the pretensions of his theatrical rivals with their university backgrounds, which he clearly does not share or envy. In doing so he maps out his own distinctive creations for the future in which he deftly adapts history to suit contemporary tastes and concerns.

—Hugh M. Richmond

LUCKY JIM.
Novel by Kingsley Amis, 1954.

Kingsley Amis's first novel, *Lucky Jim*, has often been placed alongside John Wain's *Hurry On Down* and John Osborne's *Look Back in Anger* and treated as part of an "Angry Young Man" movement that swept through British society during the relatively comfortable Macmillan era. A common enemy of this new breed of writers, apparently, was the Establishment and the various institutions such as the public schools and the civil service that supported it.

Even though it is commonly agreed that Amis was a vocal and prominent member of a vibrant literary movement in the 1950's, the labels "angry" and "anti-Establishment" may seem ironic when applied to *Lucky Jim*. The striking quality about "lucky" Jim Dixon, after all, is that he is able, for the most part of the novel, to repress and keep at bay in delightfully comical ways his frustration and anger about living in a class-ridden society that seems set against the lower-middle classes and in favor of the privileged few. Dixon does indeed spend much of the novel doing battle against attitudes and characters that he calls phoney, pretentious, or overly sophisticated: from the "arty get-ups" of his girlfriend, Margaret Peel, to the Brahms and Delius soirees arranged by his senior colleague, Welch, to the continental airs of Welch's two artsy sons, Bertrand and Michel. However, although his conscience tells him to do physical damage against these types, much of the deliberate and, at times, farcical humor of the novel lies in Dixon's ways of channeling and diverting his obvious anger: by either resorting to violent interior monologues or by breaking out into one of several appropriately fashioned facial postures, such as the "Martian-invader face" or the "Evelyn Waugh face." In general, Dixon spends most of the novel trying hard to seem honest and decent on the outside when on the inside a different voice urges: "What wouldn't he give for a fierce purging draught of fury or contempt, a really efficient worming from the sense of responsibility?"

Not until the end of the novel does Dixon finally express his anger and contempt, ironically as he is delivering a lecture on "Merrie England" to the Antiquarian and Historical Society. Fuelled by drink, he starts to imitate the voices and accents of those whom he reviles before proceeding to articulate in his own clear voice what it is that makes him loathe the "Merrie England" crowd, as well as "the homemade pottery crowd, the organic husbandry crowd, the recorder-playing crowd," and so on. Even though the performance loses Dixon his job, luck finally comes his way and at the end of the novel he is seen embarking on a train for London to work as private secretary for a wealthy patron of the arts.

Not only does Dixon exchange his unchallenging teaching job at a drab provincial university for a more prestigious job in the capital, he also trades in his girlfriend for a ritzy upper-middle-class woman, Christine Callaghan, whom he had originally loathed as a representative of the very class that stood for privilege and phoney pretentiousness. The turnaround seems curious and suggests that, despite Dixon's earlier posturing against upper-class elitism, he seems content eventually to buy into the same system.

In a prophetic way, perhaps, the novel predicts and accounts for Amis's own subsequent rise to literary fame and prosperity, Comparing *Lucky Jim* with the later novel *One Fat Englishman* reveals interesting differences: both are campus novels, but wheras Dixon is mainly involved in humorous encounters with class rivals, Roger Micheldene, a fat and celebrated English writer visiting America, spends the entire novel unleashing a hostile animus against American types and institutions. As critics were quick to point out, "lucky" Jim had turned sour and Amis himself, it seemed, had become an entrenched and sardonic member of the very literary and social establishment that *Lucky Jim* railed against with such great comic effect.

—Robert S. Burton

LYCIDAS.
Poem by John Milton, 1638.

Lycidas (written November 1637), an elegy commemorating the death by shipwreck in the preceding August of John Milton's fellow collegian at Christ's College, Cambridge, Edward King, was commissioned by a group of King's friends for inclusion in a memorial volume of poems, *Justa Eduardo King Naufrago* (1638). Its second appearance was in Milton's collected early poems (1645). The poem's subtitle, *In this Monody the Author bewails a learned Friend, unfortunately drowned in his passage from Chester on the Irish Seas, 1637. And by occasion foretells the ruin of our corrupted Clergy then in their height*, immediately directs attention to Milton's political concerns: *Lycidas* combines a private utterance of grief with a statement about England's rebirth out of the destruction of an Anglican church that had, as Milton saw it, become too Catholic-oriented and worldly.

Lycidas announces itself as a monody; that is, a funeral ode uttered by a solitary voice. But it is a monody that is consciously indebted to the formal characteristics of pastoral elegy as practised by the 3rd century B.C. Greek poets Theocritus, Bion, and Moschus and then as imitated by Virgil. The reader who comes to *Lycidas* from Theocritus's *Idyl* 1, Bion's *Lament for Adonis*, Moschus's *Idyl* 3 (the *Lament for Bion*), and Virgil's 5th and 10th eclogues, will see that Milton's elegy is a complex web of allusions to, and echoes of, these poems, just as it is also an intertextual celebration of the work of more contemporary neo-Latin writers (Castiglione, Sannazaro) and English pioneers of the pastoral elegy in the vernacular such as Sidney and Spenser. The name "Lycidas" appears in, among others, Theocritus, Bion, Virgil, and Sannazaro; the question "where were ye nymphs?" (line 50) translates Theocritus, *Idyl* lines 66–9 via Virgil's translation of the same lines in *Eclogues*, 10. 9–12; Orpheus and Arethusa come from Moschus; and even the oaks of line 186 are the property of Theocritus, Bion, and Virgil as well as of the English countryside.

Such intimate echoing of poetic predecessors has particular point in an elegy, for by recalling their words the writer is, in effect, re-calling them, making them live again, thereby offering the power of memory as a definitive gesture against time and death. Furthermore, recalling the words of poets is a way of pointing to a major theme of the poem: *Lycidas* is about King's death and the envisioned liberation of England; it is also about Milton's thoughts about his own poetic vocation and its vulnerability to the fact of death. More precisely still, it is about Milton's dialogue with his Greek pagan forebears concerning the problem of death and the erasure of self that death entails. Although it is a poem in which Milton triumphantly affirms his Christianity, we must recognise that *Lycidas* records a struggle: King's premature death causes a deep crisis of faith which the text expresses and attempts to resolve.

Lycidas is divided into 11 paragraphs (or stanzas) with the following line totals: 14/10/12/13/14/ /21/18/29/33/21//8. This is no random array as the symmetrical spacing of the repeated totals reveals: 14 . . . 14/ /21 . . . 21.

Lycidas has 11 stanzas because, following the Roman festival of the dead, the *parentalia*, the number had taken on the meaning of elegiac lament (Ovid, *Fasti*, 2. 567–8): hence the 11 stanzas of Milton's other elegy "On the Death of a Fair Infant." But *Lycidas* is actually divided 10 + 1 stanzas, because the elegy itself is completed by the end of the 10th stanza with the recognition that Lycidas is immortal, and the final stanza is a retrospect directing attention for the first time to the monodist himself. Ten, the number of circularity and completion, "of return to God" (Heinrich Cornelius Agrippa, *Three Books of Occult Philosophy*, 1651) symbolises Lycidas's redemption, therefore; and the symmetrical subdivision into units of five stanzas directs us further into poem's arguments. Stanza 1 (14 lines) is answered by stanza 5 (also 14 lines), thus implying an equation on the symbolic level between Lycidas, prematurely dead, his body tossed by the sea, and in stanza 5 Orpheus, archetypal Greek poet who, like the dead Lycidas at line 158, visited the underworld and who, also like Lycidas, died suddenly and violently and, dead, floated on the waters. But to the Renaissance mythographers Orpheus, because of his descent into the underworld and his return, and because he was a supreme musician and poet, was a symbol (or type) of Christ; and when his head was thrown into the river Hebrus and floated downstream (lines 61–3) it sang triumphantly (Ovid, *Metamorphoses*, 11). Thus, the parallel between Lycidas and Orpheus works symbolically. If we add to this the fact that Druids (line 53) were, in Milton's political vocabulary, emblems of British liberty as well as proponents of poetry and prophecy and believers in the immortality of the soul, we begin to see how the redemption of Lycidas through the poem's structure is also an image of the redemption of Britain (Lycidas's body "becomes" a Druidic body because King was drowned off Mona [Anglesey] near that point which had seen the massacre of the Druids by Caesar's Romans).

Similarly, stanza 6 (21 lines) is answered by stanza 10 (also 21 lines). In the former the poet is tempted to abandon the rigours of his trade for sexual pleasure but is reproved by Phoebus Apollo, god of poetry; in the latter Lycidas enters heaven, redeemed from the sea by the Christological sun, and hears the "nuptial song" that celebrates the union of Christ and his church (Revelation 19:7 and 21:2).

This song cancels out the delights offered by Amaryllis and Næera (stanza 6) just as the resurrected sun displaces pagan Apollo. When, moreover, we notice that line 181 ("wipe the tears for ever from his eyes") echoes Revelation 7:17 and especially 21:4, we see, too, how Milton has turned elegy into visionary political statement; for these verses in Revelation 21 announce the "new heaven and . . . new earth" that many thought the Civil War was heralding. The wiping away of tears, together with the last half of Revelation 21:1 ("and there was no more sea") erases grief (the "melodious tear" of line 14) and the destructiveness of the ocean, leaving only the memory of the poem's fresh waters (Dee, Hebrus, Camb, Arethusa), symbols of regeneration generally.

Lycidas also exploits the symbolic implications of the actual cause of King's death, shipwreck: the sinking of the "perfidious bark" recalls the traditional ark of the church (derived from Noah's ark)—"faithless" under royalist Anglo-Catholic dominion—as well as allegorisations of the human body (sinful and frail at best) as a ship battered by the seas and winds of temptation. The poem is, in fact, Milton's most densely structured and complex work.

—Douglas Brooks-Davies

M

MACBETH.
Play by William Shakespeare, 1606.

No literary work is more wreathed in superstition than *Macbeth*. Notoriously, actors avoid naming it, employing instead cautious circumlocutions such as "the Scottish Play." Within the text itself Macbeth acquires a similar status: "This Tyrant, whose sole name blisters our tongues." The reasons for this are obvious. *Macbeth* includes invocations of evil spirits, apparitions from the underworld, and the working of black magic on stage. In *As You Like It* Hymen appears to consecrate marriage, and Zeus appears in *The Tempest*. Both figures reflect the spirit of the plays which they enter. *Macbeth* is entered by Hecate, goddess of witchcraft. The protagonist is so evil that he must not merely be killed, but destroyed: in the final scene his head is brought on stage. In literary, rather than theatrical terms, the play is a study in evil, fate, and the supernatural.

The central paradox (in a play which communicates truths through paradox) is that while Macbeth becomes a murderer and tyrant, he remains the hero. His heroic status has two causes. First, the narrative of *Macbeth* takes its tragic hero far past the point (if such a point exists) where he has triumphed through his sin. Macbeth's triumph is a hollow one, troubled by constant insecurity. He does not enjoy the fruits of kingship. His crime leads him only into a perpetual struggle with the forces of chaos and with the shapes of his own disturbed mind. Yet when all is lost Macbeth fights on, his courage adding a pathos to his confrontation with death and damnation.

Second, Macbeth is involved in a superhuman battle against forces that are more or less than mortal. In this conflict he must engage some at least of the audience's sympathy, for his opponent is the common enemy of man. All mankind is represented in Macbeth: his story marks out a Faustian path which is timeless—the destruction which falls on those who are beguiled by satanic promises. In our recognition of this, Macbeth, of all tragic heroes, arouses (according to Aristotle's dictum) not only pity, but fear. At stake is our belief in the beneficence of the universe. The plot of *Macbeth* is true to the world of Greek tragedy in its presentation of the world as a dangerous place governed by a malign fate.

To sustain the central paradox—the heroic murderer—is difficult. The play accomplishes it by a number of means. First, the action distances Macbeth from his atrocities. We see Macbeth kill only one man, and that is in battle at the end of the play. Second, Macbeth is introduced to us as the hero of his generation, whose bloody ruthlessness marks the epitome of honour. Through it he has saved the Kingdom for a King who is himself too old to take to the field. His heroic slaughter in battle is, significantly, compared to the crucifixion: "Another Golgotha." In launching on his new path as traitor and despot he exercises the same bloody determination which distinguishes him in the warrior society depicted in the play. Third, Shakespeare seems deliberately to undermine the moral or dramatic stature of all who oppose Macbeth. Dramatically, Macduff should be the hero, but dramatically he is weakened by his incautious neglect of his family. He is further reduced in our eyes at the moment when Macbeth, believing himself to be invulnerable, offers Macduff mercy. Malcolm is the other potential hero. Yet the crucial scene (IV.iii) in which Malcolm reveals his character to the audience is confusing. The bulk of Malcolm's lines are spent in lengthy condemnation of his own monstrous vices, culminating in the declaration that he is worse than Macbeth himself. Then, in a brief 12 lines he reverses his original speech by announcing himself to be of pure and virginal virtue. In a world of deception and obscurity he has hardly proved a touchstone of integrity. Furthermore, in what is a short text, none of the other characters are allowed enough room to develop into satisfying heroes. Banquo is an obvious choice for hero, as he may have the strength to resist the temptations to which Macbeth has yielded (though his dreams are troubled). However Banquo is an early victim and speaks no more after the third act. Fourth, in literary terms Macbeth is pre-eminent. The sensitivity of his imagination is matched by a poetic eloquence which maintains our fascination with him. The vividness of his soliloquies is compelling. His speech of V.v., "Tomorrow and tomorrow and tomorrow," is an anthem of bitter despair which strikes a chord with all our feelings of the futility of life.

Macbeth is one of the most explicit of Shakespeare's works in dealing with the spiritual realms. The play presents both the power of Christianity and the forces raised by black witchcraft. These forces assume a particularly British identity. The witches themselves are emanations of the earth. Evil is made manifest through elements of the natural world: the bat, the wolf, the rook. *Macbeth* depicts a conflict fought both above and below. It brings the occult dimensions uncomfortably close. The cosmology referred to by Lady Macbeth assumes the continual presence of listening spirits of evil, waiting to be invoked. The invisible world presses in close around the corporeal:

> Come, you spirits
> That tend on mortal thoughts . . .
>
> Come to my woman's breasts
> And take my milk for gall, you murdering ministers
> Wherever, in your sightless, substances,
> You wait on nature's mischief.

At the heart of the spiritual battle is the murder of Duncan. This is conceived not in criminal terms, but in religious ones, as an act of sacrilege: "Most sacrilegious murder hath broke ope / The Lord's anointed temple and stole thence / The Life o'the building." Once again, there are echoes of the crucifixion (the Lord's anointed). Duncan's body, like that of Christ, is the temple of God. After his murder, as after the crucifixion, the sun is eclipsed. This supernatural violation has a devastating effect on the natural order. Macbeth's description: "And his gashed stabs looked like a breach in nature / For ruins wasteful entrance" proves prophetic. The breaches of Duncan's wounds are rents in the natural order through which darkness and confusion pour, covering the land. Scotland is overwhelmed by the darkness that the Queen invoked. She herself is left spiritually injured, as the Doctor informs us, needing "light by her continually." Waves of darkness and terror flood the land till Scotland itself "bleeds." Banquo, Macduff's family, and countless others are engulfed. Yet at their furthest reach these waves ebb back, and close in contracting circles around Macbeth. Nature pushes in to heal the breach, marching visibly across the stage against him. Finally Macbeth is left alone, encircled, and awaiting death.

The spiritual dimension to this countermovement is acknowledged by Macbeth's opponents: "Macbeth / Is ripe for shaking, and the powers above / Put on their instruments." It is most powerfully demonstrated in the person of Edward, who appears at the point where the dramatic tide turns. The structure as well as the themes of the play balance him against Macbeth. Edward is no warrior King, however, but an angelic figure blessed with the charismatic gifts of the holy spirit. Above and below there is polarisation. The king of Scotland is in league with dark powers, while the English king is a saintlike servant of God.

More than any other of Shakespeare's tragedies *Macbeth* can be read as an extended poem. The text of the play is characterised by an extraordinary density of image, meaning, and symbol. Threads of imagery run through the play, first appearing in words, then brought to life on stage. There is an almost musical exploration and reworking of images and motifs: darkness, Hell, daggers, blood, feasting, drinking, dress, sleep, medicine, and motherhood. The effect of this symphonic orchestration of images is peculiarly atmospheric. The text of the play creates a fertile imaginative space in which words and thoughts gather energy to themselves and become real. Many of these images are drawn from nature.

Birds, traditional symbols of the soul and of the spiritual realm, appear frequently. Banquo's identification of the martin with sanctity proves fatally ironic. Lady Macbeth's preparation for her guests is signalled by a dark ornithomancy of her own: "The raven himself is hoarse / That croaks the fatal entrance of Duncan / Under my battlements." Rooks, crows, and ravens, all associated with magic, appear as symbols of grim portent. Macbeth himself is a "hell-kite." The most significant of these images is the owl, sacred to Hecate. The owl first utters its cry as Duncan is murdered. After the murder, the disorder in nature is symbolised by the slaying of a falcon, a royal bird, by an owl. Lady Macduff presages her own murder in her image of the owl falling on the wren.

What we could call the "magical" quality of language—its apparent capacity to bring to pass what has existence in words—is most evident in the words of Macbeth and Lady Macbeth. Lady Macbeth's rebuke "Was the hope drunk / Wherein you dressed yourself? Hath it slept since?" for example, connects with a web of details surrounding the murder. She will make the grooms drunk to commit the murder, while she herself will need wine to fortify her spirits. Macbeth will dress himself in his nightgown—the garb of sleep—to pretend innocence.

Two of Macbeth's own most powerful speeches come as he prepares for the murders of Duncan and Banquo (II.i. 49–60 and III.ii. 40–55). As the idea of the murders grow he unleashes a stream of incantatory imagery. It is in these speeches that he draws closest to the supernatural evil aroused by the witches (only at these times does he speak the name of Hecate). Part of what gives these speeches their uncanny power is that he does not seem to be in control of them. His imagination opens to a sequence of images—the pale moon, the wolf, the rooky wood—which appear almost to be speaking *through* him.

The relationship of the witches to language is of particular interest. When Macbeth asks, of the witches' ritual, "what is't you do?" their answer, "A deed without a name," is significant. The deed they are working belongs to the other, "sightless" world: mortal language cannot grasp it. No name exists in this domain for the acts of the world beyond. Macbeth has strayed not only beyond the writ of law, but beyond the scope of the lexicon to where language itself fails.

When that world manifests itself in this one, the language it adopts is baffling. It proffers rich promises, but holds in them the seeds of their own negation. (Banquo is indeed "happier" than King Macbeth, but that is saying little.) As the witches themselves cross the border of the visible and the natural, even of the possible, so their words bridge the gap between the present and the future. The prophecies of the witches reach into the occluded realms beyond the horizon of human comprehension. From these realms come the twists of fate that reverse the meaning of the symbols Macbeth believes he understands. Truth from the underworld is always ambiguous. The witches speak to Macbeth in paradoxes and riddles. The supernatural expresses itself in mortal language by the assertion of opposites, "Fair is foul and foul is fair." The use of this antithetical language is one of the signs of emergent evil. As Macbeth contemplates Duncan's murder he is drawn into the imaginative shadow-land where he thinks the unthinkable, "Nothing is but what is not." Even Macduff, troubled by Malcolm's deception, speaks in oxymoron: "Such welcome and unwelcome things at once / 'Tis hard to reconcile." The riddling of the witches, while fatal to those who trust in it, is not conventionally malign. In his final confrontation with the witches it is Macbeth who pronounces five curses, the last one falling on himself, "And damned all those that trust them." His curse is fulfilled.

Macbeth fits into wider patterns of tragedy. The essential tragic concept of *hamartia*—the mistake with far reaching consequences—is magnified by recourse to the supernatural. So, too, is the theme of the ruinous effects of the corruption of women—the theme which runs through all Shakespeare's tragedies.

—Edmund Cusick

MAC FLECKNOE.
Poem by John Dryden, 1682.

Mac Flecknoe's principal target is Thomas Shadwell, a minor playwright who for over a decade before the poem's composition had been publishing his views on literary and dramatic matters as well as second-rate plays. Shadwell had boasted that he was the true heir of Ben Jonson in dramatic comedy, a claim which drew forth John Dryden's scorn and ridicule. The resulting poem pillories Shadwell in a narrative fantasy depicting him as the subject of a grotesque coronation ceremony. Shadwell had written of himself in the grandiose terms appropriate to a monarch—as the master of the "Province of Comedy"; Dryden portrays him as the legitimate ruler of the empires of folly and boredom. He is chosen as the future monarch of literary dunces by Richard Flecknoe, a notoriously bad Irish poet and current emperor of "all the realms of *Non-sense*," who eulogises, elects, blesses, and prophesies a reign of unsurpassed dullness for his chosen successor. Instead of being the rightful heir of Jonson, Shadwell is the true "son of Flecknoe"—which is the meaning of "Mac Flecknoe."

The poem is a mock-heroic. The trivial subject is treated in a ludicrously high-flown style, replete with allusions to classical epic. Virgil's Aeneas sails up the Tiber to be crowned in Rome; Shadwell progresses up the Thames: "About thy boat the little Fishes throng, / As at the Morning Toast, that Floats along."—where the fishes' "Morning Toast" is the disgusting accumulation of rubbish and sewage in the river. Similarly, Shadwell is crowned with poppies, symbolising his dullness (and the sleep induced by reading his dull works), where the Roman emperors were garlanded with laurels. Dryden also draws on Milton and on the Bible to expose Shadwell's huge pretensions. When Flecknoe is shown "High on a Throne of his own Labours rear'd," for example, the phrase recalls Satan in *Paradise Lost*, who sits "High on a Throne of Royal State." Many allusions are made to Shadwell's own plays too; indeed the poem ends with two of Shadwell's own characters playing a stock comic trick on Flecknoe.

Dryden's mock-heroic style and allusions help the poem, at its best, to rise above the personal abuse which formed part of his motivation. *Mac Flecknoe* is more than a mere lampoon: Dryden can be seen as addressing, intermittently, the threat of dullness and cultural anarchy represented by poetasters and the insidious power of intellectual pretentiousness in general. Intermittently rather than comprehensively, however: Dryden's poem is a triumph of witty (and often vulgar) deflation with moments of more wide-ranging satire, rather than a comprehensive analysis of the cultural world. It was left to Alexander Pope, some 50 years afterwards, to develop the latter subject in *The Dunciad*—a poem Pope acknowledged to be based on *Mac Flecknoe*.

Nevertheless, Dryden's poem contains much that is delightful. The comic magnificence of the figures of Flecknoe and Shadwell is especially striking, and suggests that Dryden had opened himself to a range of feelings wider than the term "satire" might normally suggest. The vivacity of Dryden's verse on these figures seems to proceed not from the self-gratification of pillorying them but from a genial delight in their absurdity:

> Some Beams of Wit on other souls may fall,
> Strike through and make a lucid intervall;
> But *Sh*—'s genuine night admits no ray,
> His rising Fogs prevail upon the Day:
> Besides his goodly Fabrick fills the eye,
> And seems design'd for thoughtless Majesty
> Thoughtless as Monarch Oakes, that shade the plain,
> And, spread in solemn state, supinely reign.

Only monarchs, trees, and Shadwell are able to enjoy the supreme bliss of wholly unshakable self-confidence; and while the satirical point is clear, there is also a glow of wonder at the comprehensiveness of Shadwell's self-deception. He may be a monarch only of folly; but most men are not monarchs at all.

—Stuart Gillespie

THE MADRAS HOUSE.
Play by Harley Granville Barker, 1910.

Recent revivals of Harley Granville Barker's *The Madras House*, *Waste*, and *The Voysey Inheritance* have startled audiences by the author's wit, complexity, and immense theatricality. This is a healthy reaction, for, of the handful of important modern English dramatists, Barker has been until lately one of the most ridiculously ignored. The reasons may be partly that his plays, particularly *The Madras House*, are difficult in themselves as well as very expensive to stage. *The Madras House* requires a cast of 25, four elaborate sets and about 40 costumes, six of which at least would be very costly.

Nevertheless, Barker's theatricality should not have been surprising, for he was a leading actor of his day as well as probably the most innovative and exciting play director. Indeed, until his regrettable early retirement from active stage work, his mentor and intimate colleague had been the brilliant dramatic Proteus Bernard Shaw. In other words, Barker's consummate play-writing experiments were grounded in a thorough understanding of every aspect of the practical theatre.

The Madras House was first produced in London in 1910 by the American entrepreneur Charles Frohman. Together with Galsworthy's strong but conventional *Justice* and Shaw's hilarious but subtle *Misalliance*, it was to have been the vanguard of an attempt to form an intellectual repertory company for the commercial stage. The attempt was courageous but hopelessly unsuccessful, and it is possibly no exaggeration to say that its failure retarded the development of the English drama for years.

A prime difficulty of *The Madras House*, other than its costliness, was that it quite dispensed with the traditional foundation of the overwhelming majority of western plays, both ancient and modern. That is, plot. Or at least the kind of plot that, in an Aristotelian fashion, embodies a story with a beginning that leads through causally connected and increasingly tense incidents, up to a climactic confrontation that is quickly resolved by a satisfying denouement. *The Madras House* does contain two nominal plots: the broader is the sale of the Madras House, a firm which designs women's fashions; and the more specific is the nominal continuation of the marriage of Philip Madras and his wife Jessica. The Philip and Jessica story does have an importance for the true plot, but the sale of the firm is only a device to bring a number of disparate people together.

The true plot is not determined by the dramatizations of actions but by the explications of attitudes; and the attitudes which Barker explores are the principal social ones, whether expressed or tacit, taken to the role of women in the modern world.

Act 1 dramatizes the social milieu of the middle-class, in which Mrs. Huxtable has taken on the rigid and narrow opinions of the bourgeois wife, and her six daughters wastefully await a respectable proposal of marriage that will allow them, then, to assume their mother's attitudes. This act also brilliantly contains the author's most delightful satire of vacuous conversation, and concludes with a parting at the door involving no fewer than 15 "good-byes." Act 2 dramatizes two attitudes: that of Jessica who is expensively turned out in the trappings of a successful marriage but is childless and ignored by her bored husband; and that of Miss Yates, a working girl who has become pregnant but is determined to remain an independent, unwed mother.

Act 3 treats the subject of woman as depersonalized feminine object, and the strength of the act is that the mannequins who model the expensive gowns are regarded completely impersonally—as is the idea of woman-as-consumer who will automatically purchase the product. Act 4 is quite the most complicated and compares the totally submissive woman of a polygamous society with the difficult and emerging role of woman as the equal partner in a monogamous marriage. The view of polygamy is brilliantly embodied in Philip's urbane and wayward father Constantine who has become a Muslim and settled down in Arabia; and the possibilities of an ideal monogamy are explored in the final dialogue of Philip and Jessica.

This bare account of the thematically structured plot does much injustice to the absorbing intricacy of the argument and none whatsoever to the consummate dramaturgy. To note but two qualities, however, Barker provides a marvellously etched and often quite subtle characterization, with a wealth of telling small details; and he also writes a deceptively simple dialogue which nevertheless contrives to carry an unusual weight of intellectual content for a play. Despite his nominal realism, Barker is not simply an experimental writer, but such a master of his original dramatic form that it is taking the modern stage as long to assimilate his work as it did that of Chekhov.

—Robert Hogan

THE MAID'S TRAGEDY.
Play by Francis Beaumont and John Fletcher, before 1611.

The Maid's Tragedy is a blend of ingredients from two literary forms of its day, the revenge play (such as *Hamlet*) and the prose romance (such as Sidney's *Arcadia*). From the first comes the dramatic conflict and its violent resolution, from the second the idealized characterization of the classically-named participants. The action is set in the royal court of Rhodes at some indefinite time, but this court is recognizably contemporary—like the costume, as the woodcut illustration on the first edition's title page (1619) makes clear.

The plot turns upon the marriage between Amintor, a young gentleman, and Evadne, the sister of Amintor's friend, the soldier Melantius. Their marriage has been arranged, and a sumptuous masque commissioned, by the King; in obeying the royal command Amintor has deserted Aspatia, to whom he was engaged to be married. After the celebration Evadne refuses to go to bed with her husband, announcing to him that she is the King's secret mistress and that their marriage is a mere screen. So great is Amintor's reverence for kingship that his natural urge to revenge his injury is paralysed: all he can do is ask Evadne to be discreet in her sin and keep up the pretence that they are a happy couple. Next morning they play their parts so well that the King privately reproaches Evadne with having let Amintor lie with her; she denies it and compels the wretched Amintor to confirm her statement. In the following scene Melantius, suspicious of Amintor's outward gaiety, forces him in the name of friendship to reveal the truth, and resolves to kill the King for whoring his sister and so dishonouring him and his family. To secure himself after taking revenge he needs the island's fort, which is in the keeping of Aspatia's father Calianax, a cowardly dotard whose long-standing hostility towards Melantius has been intensified by Evadne's supplanting of his daughter; when asked for the fort because "I would kill the King / That wronged you and your daughter," Calianax suspects a trap and, asking for time to reflect, goes and tells the King. Meanwhile Melantius goes to Evadne and so strongly denounces her guilt that he persuades her to kill the King with her own hand; she meets Amintor and tells him of her penitence but not of her intention. At a banquet for the bridal couple the King privately taxes Melantius with Calianax's accusation, which he easily rebuts while continuing in an undertone to ask the old man for the fort, and Calianax, beside himself at the King's incredulity, finally yields. Melantius's revenge is next endangered in another way: the King has sent word to Amintor that Evadne must come to his bedroom, and the enraged Amintor is eager to kill the King in order to safeguard Evadne's new penitence. Melantius overcomes him by insisting that a king's life is sacred. Evadne has now arrived at the King's bedroom, where she finds him asleep, ties his arms to the bed, reproaches him with corrupting her, and stabs him to death. Melantius, from the fort, proclaims the justice of the deed, and the King's brother and successor pardons him for instigating it. In the last scene Aspatia reappears, disguised as her own soldier-brother, and compels Amintor to fight a duel in which she is fatally wounded. As she lies dying Evadne bursts in, her hands bloody, and appeals to Amintor to take her as his true wife because she has expiated her sin, but her murder of the King horrifies him, and at his rejection she stabs herself. Aspatia recovers sufficient consciousness to reveal her identity to Amintor and forgive him her sufferings. Upon her death he too kills himself, surviving just long enough to take leave of Melantius, who resolves not to outlive his friend despite the new King's care to preserve his life.

Three incidents are derived from different sources: Melantius's behaviour in the accusation scene, from a collection of historical anecdotes by Valerius Maximus; Evadne's binding and stabbing of the King, from a gruesome story by Bandello; and Aspatia's self-contrived death, from Sidney's *Arcadia*. Their combination, and the rest of the plot, is the dramatists' own. Fletcher's hand is agreed, on stylistic grounds, to be conspicuous in four scenes, Melantius's interview with Evadne, Evadne's killing of the King, the scene at the fort, and an early scene in which Aspatia is shown lamenting her desertion. Dryden praised the plot for its mingling of expectation and surprise: nothing, for example, prepares the audience for Melantius's interview with Evadne or for Aspatia's disguise, but the King's death is inevitable once Evadne has vowed to effect it. Some of the developments have been considered artificially theatrical, in particular the so-called "quarrel scene" in which first Melantius challenges Amintor for calling Evadne a whore and then Amintor challenges Melantius for resolving on an act of revenge that would dishonour Amintor for his passiveness, but in its whole design the play is strongly unified, particularly by the frequent presence of dramatic irony and by the emphasis on sexual passion and on honour. Though it is Amintor and Evadne who are at the heart of the plot, the title is not inappropriate in view of Aspatia's crucial importance in the final scene and her contribution to the pathetic tone of the ending. The device of the young woman disguised as a young man is frequent in romantic comedy and tragicomedy (as in *Twelfth Night* and *Philaster*, in both of which the situation is sustained throughout) but it is here exceptionally used in a tragedy. Calianax is a mainly comic figure, with his testiness and cowardice, yet at the end his discovery of his dead daughter is a poignant moment.

Though much is said about the divine nature of kingship, the play does not bear out Coleridge's charge that the authors were servile royalists. The King's royalty does not excuse his wickedness nor defend him against punishment, and Amintor's principles are placed in contrast with those of Melantius. *The Maid's Tragedy* is, however, by no means a political problem play, but a tragedy of situation and emotion.

—T.W. Craik

MAJOR BARBARA.
Play by Bernard Shaw, 1905.

Bernard Shaw was less impressed by Ibsen's symbolism and characterization than by the instances when characters sat down for a discussion of some important problem that was being dramatized. His own works often carried the discussion technique he adapted from Ibsen to a far greater length than any debates he found in *Ghosts* or *A Doll's House*. Shaw believed that plays should be vehicles for social change, stimulating thought about a whole range of subjects he and his Fabian Socialist friends found compelling. *Major Barbara* is a typical example of Shavian dramaturgy in its mix of mildly comic situations, witty dialogue, and those static moments when several characters argue over their philosophies of life or social views.

To make these discussions work on stage, Shaw often creates strong, lively, somewhat unusual figures. Andrew Undershaft, foundling inheritor of an armaments empire, is unashamed of his work and an advocate of making money and providing his employees with a utopian mill town. He is given a worthy opponent in his daughter, one of Shaw's strong women, who is a thoroughly committed major in the Salvation Army, offering the poor bread and diluted milk in return for their conversions, and distressed that the Army could take tainted money from her father and a distiller to continue its mission. Although Shaw does not write romantic scenes, he does include a fiancé for Barbara, Adolphus Cusins, who seems at first destined always to teach Greek, but develops into a worthy successor to Undershaft.

Around this trio are grouped figures that verge on caricature, including Lady Britomart Undershaft, tradition-bound, who has refused to live with her husband since he insisted on passing the armaments works to another foundling rather than to their son. The son comes close to being a straw man in the discussion scenes, for he insists he knows the difference between right and wrong, while Barbara comes to realize that the distinction is not simple. "Cholly" Lomax, Sarah Undershaft's fiancé, is the chief butt of audience laughter as the rather dim university graduate given to meaningless slang. In the second act, at the West Ham shelter, another group of rather flat characters surrounds the trio: the tough-talking Cockney bully whom Barbara soon deflates, the unemployed "poser" who testifies to his conversion in return for handouts, two older victims of poverty, and two Army women. Undershaft has agreed to visit the shelter and see Barbara's world, if she in return will come to his factory. Shaw is not a strict realist, but in this act he makes his audiences aware of the hard lot of people who must rely on charity. He shows the Army itself pinched for money and in danger of closing the shelter until capitalist benefactors make huge contributions. Barbara suffers a crisis of faith when Mrs. Bains, the Salvation Army Commissioner, accepts this tainted money as an answer to her prayers, and the problem of right and wrong grows more complex.

Shaw once declared that the world is composed of idealists, realists, and philistines. Undershaft is obviously a realist from the start. Barbara, with too much of the Shavian Life Force in her to collapse completely, moves from idealism to a measure of realism in the last act. Cusins, with a streak of idealism, is technically a foundling and possesses the vigor that Undershaft is looking for in an inheritor. He insists that if he takes over the factory, he will select the proper customers for his munitions. We assume Undershaft is right, however, and that Cusins will soon be driven by the business, and be selling to everyone.

If it were simply a matter of settling the inheritance, Shaw would still have created an effective satiric comedy that called attention to poverty and unequal distribution of wealth, and opened the question of the way men amassed fortunes that enabled them to make spectacular gifts to worthy causes, and gave them knighthoods and lordships in return. In many of his plays, Shaw pointed to a problem but offered no real solution. In *Major Barbara*, however, he complicated the issue further by showing an ideal community where the Salvation Army is not needed. People are well-fed and housed, have exemplary social services, are educated, have churches that they attend on full stomachs, and have a social hierarchy where they live in harmony. The irony is that these peaceful people produce the means of destruction and death, and benefit from suffering. With characteristic iconoclasm, Shaw has a munitions maker rather than a pottery or furniture manufacturer as his beneficent employer. Undershaft is modelled on Alfred Nobel, although he creates a sparkling town rather than a number of prizes. Barbara is not convinced that her father's business is right, but at the end of the play she has decided that she will live in the town, where the workers with explosives are genuinely religious, believing "There must be some truth or other behind all this frightful irony." Where the power of money has eradicated "the crime of poverty," she will try to save souls and create spiritual power.

In addition to the major targets, Shaw has barbs for a number of attitudes. He notes that Undershaft's Jewish partner, Lazarus, is blamed for the Undershaft rapacity. He contrasts Lady Britomart's idea of poverty on £1600 to Barbara's ability to live on a pound a week. He even specifically attacks Barnardo homes that snap up the bright foundlings and make them fit only to teach conventional wisdom.

Current productions often cut some of the long discussion in the third act. But the reader can have even more of Shaw's philosophy than the theatre-goer, for Shaw also wrote a preface almost half the length of the play. It deals with work, punishment, the Salvation Army, his lack of indebtedness to foreign writers, minimum wage, and a number of other issues. The preface serves as a background to a challenging play.

—Frances A. Shirley

THE MALCONTENT.
Play by John Marston, 1602–03(?).

John Marston's most famous play, *The Malcontent*, was first staged at the Blackfriars Theatre. The staging is clearly intended for the small, indoor stage of the Blackfriars and for performance by the boy actors of the Children of the Queen's Revels. The play was later adopted for performance by the adult actors at the Globe, however, as is clear from the Induction written for that occasion, presumably by John Webster. In this Induction, peopled by actors in the adult company, we learn about the custom of sitting on stage in the indoor theatres, and we are also told that since the boy actors stole the play about "Jeronimo" from them, they are retaliating by stealing this play, about "Malevole." The episode reveals a glimpse into the intense theatrical rivalry of this time.

The setting of the play is a corrupt court in Genoa. The corruption is communicated theatrically in the opening scene, when a supernumerary actor comes on stage spraying perfume into the air. The presence of courtiers like Bilioso and court hangers-on like the bawd, Maquerelle, also typifies the Elizabethan convention of the depraved Italian court. The rightful Duke, Altofronto, has had his position usurped by Pietro, who now reigns. Unknown to the new Duke, the old has returned in disguise as the malcontent Malevole, who now plays the unofficial role of court fool.

The central role in the play is thus polarized: the rightful Duke Altofronto, scarcely able to speak in his own voice except to his one remaining friend at court, and the malcontent Malevole, an outspoken satirist. Altofronto's legitimate claim to the throne of Genoa is the central motivating factor in the plot, but it is Malevole's strident moral voice which in fact dominates the play. Much of Malevole's language echoes the medieval theme of *contemptus mundi*, or contempt for the world, a Christian view which despised this world in contrast to the heavenly world of the afterlife.

> World! 'tis the only region of death, the greatest shop of the devil, the cruelest prison of men, out of the which none pass without paying their dearest breath for a fee; there's nothing perfect in it but extreme, extreme calamity.

The language which reviles worldliness coalesces with that of the satirist, so that Malevole's speeches are rich in animal imagery, in physical disgust, in sensory indulgence. At frequent points in the play, Altofronto's serious blank verse shifts suddenly to Malevole's outrageous hyperbole, as when he berates the foolish Bilioso: "old ox, egregious wittol, broken-bellied coward, rotten mummy."

The protagonist is a divided figure throughout most of the play. Although the Duke is restored to the throne at the end, the audience senses that the malcontent role he has been playing so forcefully has actually become an integral part of his nature.

The remaining characters are largely conventional or parodic. Aurelia is the lustful Duchess, Maria the faithful wife, Celso the true, loyal friend, and Pietro the somewhat inept overreacher as usurper. The most fully realized characters outside of the central role are two parodic ones, Maquerelle and Mendoza, the self-styled villain. Maquerelle's speech pours out in Rabelaisian detail, whether she is reciting a recipe for posset to restore youthful beauty, or spreading court gossip. Mendoza parodies the Machiavellian villain, violating every precept of successful villainy in the process. Swearing to trust no one, he trusts everyone and is betrayed; he hires the disguised Duke to kill himself and in general makes mistakes in every evil act he attempts.

One of the most intriguing aspects of the play is its sheer theatricality. When it was performed in London in the 1960's, the reviewers remarked on the modernity of its metatheatrical precepts. Throughout the play, beginning with the Induction which features actors talking about the parts in the play, and ending with a spectacular masque, the entire drama evinces a sophisticated sense of the theatre. In this play which threatens from the start to be a revenge tragedy, the subject of death is handled with theatrical finesse. At one point the body of the courtier Ferneze is lying on the stage, supposedly stabbed to death, during a soliloquy and an extended dialogue, when it suddenly comes to life and calls for assistance. During the final masque, several characters who have been presumed dead, reappear in full life. Death in this play is clearly an actor's gesture, not the real thing.

The tradition of the fatal revels at the end of a play had been established since Thomas Kyd's *The Spanish Tragedy*. Here the concluding revels scene is introduced in the same vein. The courtiers are all masked, and the assumption is that someone will be killed. The masquers surround Mendoza, the conniving villain, but in actuality no one is killed. Instead the masque fulfills its purpose in revealing the identity of the ruler. It is here that Malevole unmasks to identify himself as the Duke and resume his position. It is here that the couples are reunited, and here that the villains are expelled from court. At the end Malevole/Altofront refers to the "actors idly departing" reminding us that we are seeing a play.

—Charlotte Spivack

MAN AND SUPERMAN.
Play by Bernard Shaw, 1903.

Man and Superman was the last play Bernard Shaw had to issue in book form to reach a public, while theatrical managements ignored his work. As a result, the text has a chameleon identity. Presented, with long descriptions of characters, as literature for readers, it is part of a complex of approaches to a core of ideas related in the author's thought: an essay (the prefatory "Epistle Dedicatory") and a Blakeian collection of aphorisms ("The Revolutionist's Handbook") being included with what may be regarded as two plays, one an Edwardian comedy, the other a philosophical debate between characters from a historical-legendary costume drama. Taken together, these different elements amounted to the most ambitious claim Shaw had yet made on contemporary attention and the nearest to a summing-up of his world view at that time. He made no attempt to conceal indebtedness to Schopenhauer and Nietzsche for the terms of his arguments, though the cultural groundbed of the work is wider and deeper than that. The world view includes self-analysis, using the mythic figure of Don Juan which he had already adopted as a key to his own personality, and focusing on matters which reflected his own situation as a militant socialist orator, an artist and master of words, lately married to a "green-eyed millionairess" and now and forever a figure of bourgeois respectability. Though he connived with Granville Barker's making-up to look like the author in the first performances of the comedy, Shaw's pose is consistently objective, directing interest away from self outward to the universe. He claimed to have modelled Tanner on H.M. Hyndman.

He did not expect the comedy and the debate to be presented together on the same occasion; Edwardian audiences were unprepared for such a marathon. Even Granville

Barker's company performed them on different days, though encouraging audiences to see both. Since then, there have been a number of productions incorporating the Don Juan play as the Act III dream of Jack Tanner, and there is general critical agreement that this is the most satisfying and interesting form of presentation, giving depth to the already scintillating frame-play, setting up a multitude of perspectives and a mutually critical relationship between the Edwardian plot and the philosophical interpretation cunningly presented as fantasy. When performed separately, as *Don Juan in Hell*, static discussion is enriched by the mythic dimension, the allusive relation to a 17th-century story and visual interest (Shaw engaged Charles Ricketts to design the costumes after Velasquez in a black velvet setting for the first production); and his paradoxical interpretations of the story and characters are crowned by a pyrotechnic verbal display. The introduction of snatches of music from Mozart's *Don Giovanni* underlines the operatic nature of the work. No-one alive today can report first-hand on the early playing, though Granville Barker is known to have cultivated a style of rapid and flexible delivery; but many can still remember Alec Clunes's virtuoso interpretations (attended by the elderly Shaw), in which Juan won the debate hands down and his long speeches were applauded like operatic arias, while others testify to the powerful cunning of the Devil in Charles Laughton's platform performances. In relation to the frame-play, this dream interlude presents a passionate intoxication with words and ideas that anchors it to the personality of Tanner. The doctrine of Creative Evolution here propounded was henceforth identified as Shaw's principal creed. The Edwardian comedy does not call it into question, but may raise doubts about its immediate applicability.

The comedy of Ann Whitefield's pursuit of Jack Tanner for a husband follows on logically from the earlier play, *Candida*. That exposed the weakness of a Christian socialist and this, the vulnerability of a socialist millionaire, while also catching the factional squabbles of the left in a net of Gilbertian satire through a conference of brigands in the Sierra. Perfectly acceptable as a useful, self-critical in-joke at a Fabian Society conference, transferred to the stage of a public theatre the play opens socialism in general to the happy mockery of middle-class audiences. It fulfils the hopeful expectations of such audiences as well as any of the conventional plays Shaw as critic had attacked: the girl gets the boy in the end, fortune is added to fortune, the will of Ann's father is fulfilled and a tranquil, secure, comfortable future is promised for the privileged group, with the only threat soothingly contained within marriage.

Contemporary attention was drawn to the shocking(?) revelation of courtship as a strenuous covert pursuit of the male by the supposedly passive female, condemned by the manners of the day to conceal her initiatives in order to remain respectable. Though Shaw's skill keeps the play amusing today, it seems very remote from modern social experience of conflict and anxiety. It may do some work in our world negatively, by triggering a reaction against its anodyne blandness. One critical solution is to overleap the present time of the comedy with the authority of the end of the Don Juan dream, and look to the future for the more highly developed breed of humanity female instinct seeks. There are less despairing possibilities. Shaw's dramatic form was more effectively revolutionary than Tanner's, or Juan's, arguments. Even the comedy in isolation outrages the tenets of the well-made play, the contemporary form of classical structure, with such pranks as the chase from England to Spain, the on-stage motor car, and an action based on the pratfalls of a clown-hero; it equally outrages careful Ibsenite naturalism with its blatant rhetoric and near-farcical plot, being more closely related to popular dramatic forms based on variety—from Shakespearian comedy to 19th-century pantomime: "Harlequin Don Juan" if the dream transformation is included.

Within the covers of the book, "The Revolutionist's Handbook" can explode the Whitefield world. On stage, Shaw's silences may work ironically: he has contrived an insulated milieu for his conventional happy ending with no glimpse of the sources and cost of the Whitefield–Tanner wealth; the women in the play are untouched by any impulse towards social liberation, indeed thinking he sees a sign of this in Violet is one of Tanner's most ludicrous mistakes. Accepting marriage and motherhood as their only conceivable adult function to be achieved by lying and concealment, they confirm hypocrisy and willed ignorance as effective bulwarks against social change. Tanner's dream discovery of Creative Evolution may be self-justificatory or consolatory. A fear of women and of the attractiveness of maternal protection are certainly projected through *Man and Superman*, but unresolved contradictions, the clash of unreconciled styles, the association of pleasant emotions with mental restlessness all defy closure and invite frequent reinterpretation.

—Margery Morgan

THE MAN OF FEELING.
Novel by Henry Mackenzie, 1771.

The Man of Feeling rates a passing mention in histories of the novel as an exercise in the hyper-sentimental; so pure a specimen of the cult of sensibility might even be said to be indispensable. Most of the episodes serve to illustrate Harley's delicacy of feeling, and tears fall abundantly over distressed orphans and veterans, ruined women, unexpected kindnesses, a trusty old dog, the "romantic melancholy" of a shepherd's horn, etc. Yet if the book's tone and many of the incidents appear dated or trite, the provisionality of its construction seems surprisingly modern, or postmodern. Henry Mackenzie is invisible (publication was anonymous): an unnamed Editor acquires from a country curate a fragmented manuscript (parts have been used for gun wadding) in which an unnamed Narrator ("a grave, oddish kind of man" known as "The Ghost") recounts passages in the life of Harley. This degree of distancing, in a novel of sympathy, is remarkable. What might be considered problems in point of view (the Narrator's unexplained omniscience) and unity (a large number of interpolated stories) seem less significant than the obliquity of the narrative. Mackenzie's text is, moreover, an essay in "the art of the fragment": we begin with chapter 11, many chapter numbers are wanting, and three chapters are *called* "fragments."

In its emotionalism and its diffuseness, *The Man of Feeling* reminds most readers of Sterne—Mackenzie's denial of any influence is scarcely credible—especially when it assumes a theology of Sensibility, with an elect and a damned. The Narrator declines to describe Harley's joy at helping Emily Atkins because "one half of the world would not understand it" and the other half needs no description. The trouble with this outlook is the ease with which it becomes the self-appointed superiority of the persona of Harley's pastoral, who salutes other "souls of more delicate kind" who eschew pleasure but have sensibilities "To the sons of the world still unknown" (one of many hits at "the world"). Even those he calls his "friends" do not understand him, nor would he wish to possess their temperaments. His virtue is invulnerable in its smugness.

Sterne aside, Mackenzie touches many familiar chords of the Georgian novel of feeling. Here are both graveyard melancholy and the joy of finding that duty and happiness sometimes coincide; the pleasures of charity (Harley's, his father's, Miss Walton's, old Edwards's); and a warning that reason is a mere machine. The love of Harley and Miss Walton is delicately Platonic, while their sympathies derive from Terence's *homo sum*. There is even an attack on the barbarities of Bedlam Hospital. *The Man of Feeling* is a sweet concentrate of the sentimental literature of the time.

But it has a harder, less self-indulgent side, more obviously related to the nascent romanticism of the period, that ranges itself against "the world" in various ways. First comes Harley's unworldliness: he lacks self-interest, and the sophistication to see through London's sharpers, causing him to forsake the city for the more innocent countryside halfway through. The Narrator soon associates himself with this outlook: "we take our ideas from sounds which folly has invented" in this "world of semblance." The indictment is broadened to Europe in "The Pupil: a Fragment," where Sedley exclaims of the villain Respino, "If this is the world's honour. . . ." "The world" is also what (ostensibly) keeps Harley from Miss Walton and thus causes their tragedy, "for, according to the conceptions of the world, the love of a man of Harley's fortune for the heiress of £4000 a year is indeed desperate." We feel, however, that their excessive delicacy and reticence also play a role.

The meaning of "the world" is not everywhere the same, but some of the social views expressed help clarify it. The story of Miss Atkins shows how the plays and novels of circulating libraries can undermine a young reader's morality. The Narrator suggests that aristocrats should be held to a high moral standard, that sometimes "opportunities for nobler accomplishments have only served to rear a fabric of folly." Harley has a long speech attacking the moral basis of the British Empire. The force of the attack on the establishment and mainstream culture sometimes requires satire, as in the Swiftian railings of "The Misanthropist" (chapter 21) and the Fieldingesque stagecoach ride during which several different temperaments and social orders display their foibles and are lectured by Harley.

Roughly the obverse of this theme shows up in the second half of the novel, as the action returns to the country and we are shown how vulnerable its traditions are to the encroachments of "the world." Edwards's troubles began when the family farm became a victim of the new agro-economics, delivered by a London attorney turned country steward. Harley sees his old schoolhouse "silent, unroofed, and desolate," pulled down by the squire "because it stood in the way of his prospects," and the green where he played despoiled by "the sacrilege of [the] plough." Mackenzie's preferences in landscape and scenery support this nostalgic idealization of "the deserted village." Harley first sees Edwards as a character in a scene painted by Salvator; the cottage where Harley installs the old man and his grandchildren is a bucolic idyll, a genre painting by Gainsborough. Harley significantly couches his one moment of poetic self-expression, "Lavinia," in pastoral terms.

But Mackenzie's sentimentality did not extend to concluding the book on a note of rural mellowness; the last pages are dominated by a mood approaching *contemptus mundi*. In their final interview Harley tells the Narrator that he cannot, and does not want to, live in a world that is "in general selfish, interested, and unthinking. . . ." The Narrator himself ends the book by warning us that the sight of Harley's peaceful grave "will make you hate the world." "Feeling" is at last shown to be incompatible with this world; its true home is elsewhere.

—Richard Bevis

THE MAN OF MODE.
Play by Sir George Etherege, 1676.

Sir George Etherege's *The Man of Mode; or, Sir Fopling Flutter* was first produced and published in 1676, and, if not quite the greatest of Restoration comedies, certainly embodies the pattern at its most typical. For that very reason, the play was admired in its own day for its witty realism, but, depending on the spirit of the age, alternately condemned and defended ever since. It embodied to many the amorality and licentiousness that Jeremy Collier so vigorously attacked in his influential *A Short View of the Immorality and Profaneness of the English Stage* of 1698. Richard Steele in 1711, preparing the way for his own practice of sentimental comedy, called it a portrayal of "nature in its utmost corruption and degeneracy." In the 19th century Macaulay in attacking Restoration comedy in general referred to Etherege's contemporary Wycherley as like the skunk "too filthy to handle, and too noisome even to approach." In the 20th century, L.C. Knights went beyond invective to find Restoration comedy not so much immoral as "trivial, gross, and dull."

Etherege and his colleagues have, however, always had their defenders, although Lamb in 1822 attempted to disarm criticism by asserting that Restoration comedy existed entirely outside of reality, in a never-never land of its own, in "the regions of pure comedy, where no cold moral reigns." In its own day, however, the charm of the play was that, with its hero Dorimant so closely modelled on Rochester, it accurately reflected a small, privileged and sophisticated segment of society. That was also the view of John Dennis, the play's first effective defender, in 1722, as it was of modern critics such as Thomas H. Fujimura, Bonamy Dobrée, James Sutherland, and Jocelyn Powell, go beyond the matter of morality to a consideration of artistic value.

To the reader of the 1990's, the play's artistry is undeniable. Its well-defined characters, headed by that enchantingly theatrical bundle of affectation Sir Fopling, have lost little of their power to please. Dorimant remains as fluent and perceptive a wit as Shaw's Jack Tanner, while Harriet is a cleverer foil than Ann Whitefield was in *Man and Superman*. Medley is as droll a man about town as any of Oscar Wilde's, and even the shoemaker and the orange woman are vignettes worthy of Ben Jonson. The play's language may lack the strength that Congreve finds in balance and antithesis; it may not rise to the bitter power of Wycherley, or possess the fancy and fluency of Vanbrugh. However, its use of irony, of simile and metaphor not only imparts a richness to the action, but actually reinforces the spirit of play which underlies and impels the action.

The play dramatizes the game between the sexes, and the weapons are intrigue and suavity of language. The stakes are the domination of one partner and the defeat of the other. The symptoms of winning are the retention of independence and of unruffled social aplomb. The symtoms of losing are dependence and an uncontrollable outburst of frustrated emotion. In terms of Etherege's intrigue, the possibilities of win, lose, or draw are seen in what happens to the main women characters in their conflicts with Dorimant.

Each of these three little plots has its development. Mrs. Loveit rises from her initial rage to a momentary triumph when she arouses Dorimant's jealousy about Sir Fopling. He, however, erases his discomfiture, turns the tables, and reduces her to spluttering fury. Bellinda weakly resists but then weakly succumbs to Dorimant's seduction. She, however, is let off without public exposure because her resultant emotion is not rage or revenge but shame and acquiescence in losing. Harriet refuses to let either her rhetorical or her emotional defences down, and thereby ensures that Dorimant will pursue her to the country and, indeed, to the altar. For all of its presumed immorality, then, this Restoration play ends with the prospect of as conventional a marriage as the most hidebound moralist could wish.

The immorality of *The Man of Mode*, like that of much Restoration comedy, is really more superficial than basic. It is true that the chief characters are often rakes and licentious ladies who attempt to snare the weak and credulous by witty word warfare and cunning plots. But although the characters ruthlessly play at the game of love, the stakes are real enough, and so Etherege's drama does not really exist in Lamb's never-never land. Etherege's terms may be more urbane and his counters more suave than usually exist in actuality, but the values at stake are the perennial issues of courtship. This fact makes *The Man of Mode*, as well as the best work of Etherege's contemporaries, as germane today as it was in the late 17th century.

—Robert Hogan

THE MAN WHO DIED.
(*The Escaped Cock.*)
Novella by D.H. Lawrence, 1929.

Mark Schorer, in his *D.H. Lawrence* (1968), expressed the belief that in *The Man Who Died*—written just before Lawrence's death—Lawrence had said "what he had almost all his life wanted to say." Blending eastern and western myths, balancing the familiar oppositions of submission and domination, Lawrence in this novella focuses his theme of physical regeneration in the most spiritual of beings, the risen Christ. Although Lawrence refrains from using the names Christ or Jesus and calls Mary Magdalene Madeleine, he adheres to the gospel of St. John, with the man who died emerging from the sepulchre, meeting Mary Magdalene and the disciples, and ending not ascended into heaven but living to do "many other things" on earth.

At first titled *The Escaped Cock*, the story opens with a very virile and splendid cock—a Christian symbol of the resurrection—owned by a peasant and tied by the leg, just as the man who died awakens painfully, also tied with bandages and linen, and bereft of the former ideals; they have died with him. The cock's crowing to the spring dawn animates him, and he takes recuperative shelter with the peasant. The cock, banishing the ghostly night of death, helped the god of medicine Aesculapius to cure the sick; and the man who died, watching it, begins a repudiation of his former teaching while he takes inspiration from the cock's virility.

Having known the spiritual half of life, the man who died must come to know the physical half. His awakening to the male physical life occurs with his observation of the virulent cock, tugging against restraints and treading the hens. His illumination with the female occurs when the cock of Judea gives way to the sun-loving lotus of Lebanon. These symbols blend the religion of Christ with that of Osiris.

Developing a reverence for the earth and physical life, the man who died comes to understand the selfishness of his former interference with the souls of men. Meeting Madeleine he invokes the *noli me tangere* of Christ to say "Don't touch me," and he uses this phrase to hold himself aloof from others until it gradually becomes redefined. He tells Madeleine that he has outlived his mission, has brought betrayal on himself and wronged "poor Judas." Giving now appears to be a form of domination, and he who gives too much satisfies his own vanity at the expense of the receiver. Virginity itself is a form of greed. His compelling others to his will caused his death. The holy Word seems only an annoyance, another interference, like the midge that bites at evening. Meeting two of his disciples, he explains nothing.

Identifying the egotistical compulsion to impose one's will on others, he knows that this was his fault. The thought sickens him now. He decides to wander the earth, a healer, and dresses the part of a physician, taking the cock with him until he leaves it to its fertile hens and its freedom. Like it, he has escaped from the domination of his former existence. He begins a solitary journey of exploration that takes him by winter to Lebanon.

A young priestess of Isis celebrates the goddess in search of the slain Osiris, to be reunited with him and bring forth Horus. Like the lotus quickened by the rays of the sun and symbol of the womb of the world, she waits for the re-born man. In calm equilibrium, she holds herself aloof from the common sexual life of slaves—the male dominating, the female submitting. In meeting the man who died, however, quickened by the "blood consciousness" that Lawrence found wiser than the intellect, she admits him to her temple and believes him to be the risen Osiris.

The man who died has turned from healing the soul to healing the body; he knows that he had no healing power like "the flame of this tender girl." For her, his body with its wounds resembles the severed body of Osiris. With her anointing his wounds, he reaches the climax of his understanding; he had asked his people to serve him with "the corpse of love." If he had kissed Judas with live love, "perhaps he would never have kissed me with death." He now interprets the words "Upon this rock" to mean "On this rock I built my life," and it is the penetrable rock of the living woman. "I am risen" means the phallic rise. Atonement has three meanings. The new physical atonement that the Father had hidden from him is fatherhood itself. His wounds are suns bringing the priestess her atonement with the sun of Osiris. The great atonement is being in touch with the sea and the rain and woman and the invisible Isis; all these and the unseen sun are "all in touch, and at one."

Possessions, likewise being redefined, should be kept to the self. While the peace of the priestess is threatened by the possessiveness of her mother, his peace is threatened by the Roman soldiers, who would possess him, and the slaves who would sell him to them. He leaves the priestess with child, and promises to return like Osiris in the spring. Escaping by boat, he knows that he has sowed the seed of his life and his resurrection and he has put his touch on this woman.

Lawrence closes this mystical drama with another mixed symbol—that of the "gold and flowing serpent" that the man who died feels "coiling up again, to sleep at the root of my tree." Western meanings suggest that, being physical, he awaits physical death. Eastern meanings suggest the chakras that, based in the groin of regeneration, rise to coil round the spinal tree. Subtly, then, Lawrence represents in this symbol the words of immortality: "I am the resurrection and the life."

—Grace Eckley

THE MAN WHO LOVED CHILDREN.
Novel by Christina Stead, 1940.

Among Christina Stead's 15 substantial books, *The Man Who Loved Children* is the only one to have enjoyed the admiration of readers as well as critics over a long period of time. It failed with both on first publication in 1940. After 25 years, during which its underground reputation developed, it was reprinted to introduce to a subsequent generation its ruthless examination of an American family, probed below its own quick with relentless and even maddening deliberation. Some readers will object to its garrulity, its diversions, its insistence on including virtually everything. (Weighing in at 527 pages, it is sufficiently ample, but perhaps it was originally longer and then cut just before publication since the dust jacket indicates over 800 pages.) Other readers will grow impatient with the private language in some of the dialogue that from time to time obliges Stead to spell out in parentheses what wordplays, puns, and whole phrases are supposed to mean. No reader, however, will abandon the novel untouched by it, and no reader who stays the course will ever entirely awaken from the nightmare of its conclusion, at once terrifying and gratifying. Until recently, *The Man Who Loved Children* was the only one of Stead's books to have been reprinted, both in hardcover and, more significantly, in a paperback edition suitable for college courses where it surely belongs in any consideration of the American novel. That Christina Stead happened to be an Australian whose four earlier novels were set in Australia and on the continent without any indication of an American sensibility in no way alters that observation about one of the most "American" American novels of the 20th century.

This sprawling, exasperating novel about the decline and fall of a family is so staggering that it cancels out Stead's familiar flaws—a ripe and sometimes overwhelming prose, an indiscriminate inclusion of extraneous detail, a pitiless scalpel honing too heavily peopled plots—and allows her great gifts for characterization and a lethally clear view of human relationships to reinforce her narrative. The Pollits are a catastrophically mismatched couple living in ramshackle Tahoga House, which serves as a battleground for the cold war of their marriage until both the house and the husband and wife descend to their own shadows in the matching shambles of a slum's Spa House and open aggression. Surrounded by too many children and too many expenses, interfering but well-meaning relatives, and memories of an elegant world in which she was gently bred, Henrietta (called Henny, Moth, Mothering, since everybody has several cloying nicknames) has long been estranged from her husband. She rages against him through their children in vicious and frightening harangues. Sam Pollit's retaliation against his wife, simultaneously irritating and falsely charming, is to suffocate their children with malicious jealousy of them masquerading as love. Stead filters her vision, however, through the sensibilities of Louisa (Louie, LooLoo, Loozy), Sam's daughter by his dead first wife. As the perceptions of this oversized, clumsy, altogether remarkable girl develop, so do those of Stead's readers. They have no alternative but to admit with palpable horror the accuracy of hate and to cringe before familiarity. Louisa has learned to survive Henny's ugly beratings and Sam's interminably childish effusions, by centering on a private self neither of her monstrous parents is capable of recognizing, diseased as they are by the bile of their own self-deceit. In the end Louisa is the only child strong enough to survive this domestic holocaust, but she will bear its permanent scars for the rest of her life. So, of course, will the other children who survive, but less well, lacking her age and self-possession: Tommy; Evie; Ernie, turned humorless miser; the twins, Saul and Little-Sam, cowed into grief—all already warped in various ways. Henny's attempted murder and suicide that draw *The Man Who Loved Children* to its conclusion are as justified as they are inevitable, and disclosing this epiphany spoils no surprise. Louisa escapes to "take a walk around the world," never to return. Sam who loves children ends in possessing them alone, but when they are old enough to escape the smothering thrall in which he holds them, Sam himself will be a lonely child.

The Man Who Loved Children, for all its sprawl, has a narrative drive linking several marvelous set pieces: Henny's confrontations with her lover; Sam's government assignment in Malaya (during which the family functions oddly well and oddly ill without him); Louisa's dispassionate killing a cat; visits to the homes of relatives; Louisa's schoolgirl crush on her teacher; Louisa's one-act tragedy for the children to perform that serves as a mirror of the novel's central conflicts; a penultimate horror when Sam commandeers the children into boiling down a giant marlin to grease and tallow, leaving a stench which permeates their bodies as well as their souls; and of course Henny's vengeful suicide. Set pieces or not, they are sequentially inextricable from each other—few novels seem so resistant to excerpting—and Stead's triumph is in part having made of them so indestructible a single work. If it suffers because Stead lacks a strong sense of proportion—too often concentrated at too great a length on this scene, that circumstance, distant relatives, Henny's numbing invective, Sam's windy locutions—patient readers are unlikely to want to sacrifice much from this finally satisfying novel.

—Bruce Kellner

MANSFIELD PARK.
Novel by Jane Austen, 1814.

Mansfield Park was written at a pivotal point in Jane Austen's career and marks a dramatic change of direction. The first three novels she composed (*Sense and Sensibility*, *Pride and Prejudice*, and *Northanger Abbey*) were drafted between 1795 and 1799, while the author was in her early twenties and living happily in her parents' home at Steventon

Rectory in Hampshire; they are gay and witty works that follow naturally upon Austen's juvenilia, the high-spirited parody-novels such as *Love and Freindship* written to entertain her family.

Austen's fourth novel, *Mansfield Park*, was written after a gap in her novel-writing career of more than 10 years (a fragment of a novel, *The Watsons*, was begun and abandoned in about 1804). During this blank period the Austen family had broken up, following the death of Austen's father in 1801, and Austen, her ailing mother, and her elder sister Cassandra found themselves without a permanent home, moving from one lodging-house to another in Bath and Southampton. In 1809, however, Austen recovered her spirits and resumed novel-writing: her older brother had inherited a large estate at Chawton in Hampshire and settled the three women in Chawton Cottage on the estate. Austen immediately revised *Sense and Sensibility* and had it published in 1811. She then turned to revising *Pride and Prejudice*, which was eventually published in 1813. At the very same time, Austen, now in her late thirties, began writing a counter-statement to *Pride and Prejudice*—*Mansfield Park*, the first of her three later novels (to be followed by *Emma* and *Persuasion*).

This biographical context helps explain why *Mansfield Park* is unique among Austen's novels. Dark and sombre in tone, morally intransigent and even embattled in vision, the novel has the quietest and least outgoing of Austen's heroines and very little of her characteristic verbal irony. The author's own estimate of the novel is apparent in a letter written in 1815: she remarks of *Emma*, then in press, that "I am very strongly haunted with the idea that to those readers who have preferred *Pride and Prejudice* it will seem inferior in wit, and to those who have preferred *Mansfield Park*, very inferior in good sense."

Mansfield Park is called after an estate, unlike Austen's other novels, and the estate is arguably the most important entity in the novel. Sir Thomas Bertram, its owner, a pompous and distant, if well-meaning, man, is surrounded by equally ineffectual people: his remarkably indolent wife, Lady Bertram; his two sons, the scapegrace Tom and the earnest Edmund, destined to be a clergyman; his two flighty and spoiled daughters, Maria and Julia; and Lady Bertram's widowed, sister, the vain and domineering Mrs. Norris, who actually runs the household.

Mansfield Park, however, is a moral and social bulwark much greater than the flawed people who inhabit it. This becomes apparent when, out of charity, Sir Thomas agrees to raise Fanny Price, the novel's heroine, the eldest daughter among the nine children of Lady Bertram's other sister, Mrs. Price, and Lieutenant Price, a naval officer without much in the way of income, ambition, or ability. Fanny comes to Mansfield Park at the age of 10. The quiet, humble, and sensitive girl is terrified; in several brief but effective vignettes (the only childhood scenes in Austen's novels), Edmund alone befriends and protects her. Out of her gratitude to him is born the love on which the novel turns. Paradoxically, the Bertrams' mistreatment and neglect of their poor relation joins with Edmund's consideration for her to develop in Fanny a hidden, lonely strength of character. She becomes an embodiment of the moral code that gives Mansfield Park its real value.

As she would do in *Emma*, Austen divides the action of the novel into two parallel sequences: a symbolic prelude is presented in volume 1 of the standard three volumes, and the main plot line is developed over volumes 2 and 3. Just as Emma's arrogant delusions over Harriet Smith and Mr. Elton provide a self-contained action anticipating her follies over Jane Fairfax and Frank Churchill, Fanny Price's integrity is twice tested by appeals to her gratitude. The first time, in volume 1, the whole Bertram family, even Edmund, expect her to take part in the play they are staging; in volumes 2 and 3, all the Bertrams again, and again even Edmund, expect her to accept a marriage proposal from the wealthy, handsome, and charming Henry Crawford. In both cases, Fanny refuses, and thereby hangs the tale.

Both of Fanny's crises are precipitated by the presence at Mansfield Park of Henry Crawford and his sister Mary, who have come to visit their uncle, Dr. Grant, the Rector of Mansfield. A little older and much more sophisticated than their Bertram counterparts, Henry and Mary have been raised in London by their dissolute uncle: they come to Mansfield, in fact, because their uncle has just settled his mistress in his house. Full of energy, drama, and poise, Henry and Mary embody the restlessness and self-absorption of modern life: if Fanny points back to Richardson's heroines Pamela and Clarissa, the Crawfords look ahead to the world of *The Great Gatsby*. The younger Bertrams are fascinated by the Crawfords; Henry and Mary, finding life in the country dull, each decide to turn fascination into conquest. Mary, seeing Edmund's involuntary infatuation with her and genuinely believing that to be a clergyman is to opt out of life, sets out to make his devotion to her overcome his devotion to religion; both Bertram girls are clearly available, but Henry decides Maria is more of a challenge, since she is engaged to marry, for dynastic reasons, the wealthy but slow-witted Mr. Rushworth.

Fanny's first crisis, over the family theatricals, shows that she alone understands and resists the moral disarray at Mansfield Park. Sir Thomas has gone to the West Indies, and in the holiday world created by his absence the family decides to put on a play. The real appeal of the project lies in the actual play chosen, the German melodrama *Lovers' Vows*, and in the casting: the production allows Henry Crawford to play-act lovers' vows to Maria, and also allows Edmund, who was at first unwilling to participate, to be wooed by Mary Crawford. Fanny alone sees the delusions, the blurring of reality and fantasy, into which all have fallen; she alone remains aware of the impropriety of the project—an impropriety symbolized by the transformation of Sir Thomas's library into the green-room and evident in everyone's feelings of guilty consternation when Sir Thomas unexpectedly returns on the final page of volume 1.

Fanny's moral independence is even more severely tested by the novel's major crisis, which immediately develops. Once Maria has married Mr. Rushworth, Henry Crawford begins to notice Fanny, and rapidly moves from the thought of "making a small hole in Fanny Price's heart" to falling deeply in love and proposing marriage. There are many ironies here: that Crawford should be the first to appreciate Fanny's value; that Fanny should succeed where Maria and others have failed; that Mansfield should conquer the Crawfords as well as vice-versa; that Henry has little chance of success because of Fanny's hidden love for Edmund. The greatest irony, however, occurs when Sir Thomas and Edmund champion Crawford's suit and expect Fanny, as their dependent, to bow to their wishes out of gratitude; Fanny, however, just as she had in the theatricals episode, resists those in power at Mansfield Park and adheres to its moral code (which stipulates that marriage should be based upon love and not social eligibility).

An episode unique among Austen's novels resolves this plot. Sir Thomas, exasperated by Fanny's independence, determines to send her back to her family in Portsmouth for an extended stay: "A residence of eight or nine years in the abode of wealth and plenty had a little disordered her powers of comparing and judging. Her father's house would, in all probability, teach her the value of a good income." Again, ironies abound. Sir Thomas is partly right: Fanny's own home proves to be the most squalid, cramped, disordered, even sordid, setting in Austen's fiction. But what Portsmouth underlines for Fanny is the moral, not social, value of Mansfield Park: the consideration and dignity that underlie daily life there. Fanny's exile only strengthens her integrity—but the separation undoes Crawford's new dedication to virtuous love. After some months, he meets Maria Rushworth, reasserts his power over her, and the two elope. Further disasters follow. Julia takes advantage of the ensuing turmoil to elope with a foolish suitor. Even Edmund is shattered: he finally sees that Mary Crawford is the female equivalent of Henry when she treats Maria's and Henry's conduct lightheartedly, as folly and no more. To make matters worse, Tom Bertram, the dissipated heir, becomes seriously ill. Mansfield Park is in collapse, and Fanny is recalled to comfort the shattered family. Edmund, now disillusioned, turns to Fanny; they marry, and the novel ends with them settled in Mansfield Parsonage, the spiritual heirs and upholders of Mansfield Park.

In the end, the two most striking things about *Mansfield Park* are its heroine and its insistent moralism. Fanny Price is completely unlike Austen's other heroines. Lacking in the vivacity, poise, and sophistication that are their primary characteristics, she is also socially dependent, lacking in privilege, as none of the others are. Furthermore, the main plot of the novel presents, not the heroine's delusions, but a clear-sighted heroine waiting for the man she loves to awaken from self-deception; in this it is unlike the other Austen novels except for *Persuasion*. But, of course, Fanny's absence of other strengths highlights her strength of character—what she makes out of what she has been given.

The novel is also the most obtrusively moral, and the least ironic, in the Austen canon. Several moral themes are inescapable: responsibility, self-knowledge, humility, education, to name only a few. Austen's decision to emphasize "good sense" has also made *Mansfield Park* the most controversial of her novels. Many of the most respected of her critics—Lionel Trilling and David Lodge, for example—have championed it for its profound moral insights; the response of many other readers can be summed up in the title of Kingsley Amis's well-known essay on the novel, "What Became of Jane Austen?" Whatever the verdict, most readers will find that it tests and extends their powers of judgment.

—Bruce Stovel

MARIUS THE EPICUREAN.
Novel by Walter Pater, 1885.

Marius the Epicurean: His Sensations and Ideas is Walter Pater's only novel, and one of the few pieces of work published in his lifetime not to appear first in periodical form. Although possessing certain characteristics of imaginative fiction, such as a central character, attention to relations among characters, and detailed presentation of setting, the plot and narrative dimensions are frequently obscured (and even lost) by the incidence of other discourses and genres, notably those of philosophy, history, and criticism. It is unsurprising that John Morley, editor of the *Fortnightly Review* judged *Marius the Epicurean* unsuitable for monthly serial publication, a form which exploits suspense.

Written in the wake of the reiterated objections to the Epicurean philosophy of *The Renaissance*, the novel was Pater's attempt to take up the subject matter of the controversial Conclusion to the earlier volume, and deal "more fully" with it in order to satisfy his critics. It is evident, however, from the course of the novel as a whole, that Pater's position had changed in the dozen years since he had written *The Renaissance*, and while parts of the novel pertain to the Conclusion, its overall shape expresses a different sensibility. To a reader of *The Renaissance* with its disavowal of Christianity and absolutes of any character, Pater's claim in the later work that "the highest Platonic dream is lower than any Christian vision" signals the nature of that new sensibility while affording Pater infinite scope for the depiction of the pre-Christian sensibility at its best. Another distinct change is the nature of the novel's prose, which is more in command of the nuances of structure, diction, and tone, so that sentences which resemble the following sample are the very building blocks of the novel:

> And the inside was something not less dainty and fine, full of the archaisms and curious felicities in which that generation delighted, quaint terms and images picked from the early dramatists, the lifelike phrases of some lost poet, preserved by an old grammarian, racy morsels of the vernacular, and studied prettinesses:—all alike, more playthings for the genuine power and natural eloquence of the erudite artist, unsuppressed by his erudition, which however make some people angry, chiefly less well "got up" people, and especially those who were untidy from indolence.

Between 1872 and 1885 Pater continued to write for the periodicals, and planned similar volumes from themes in other essays which, however, he subsequently decided not to publish: one on Greek studies and another on Shakespeare. It might be said that in his choice of 2nd-century Rome, a period of transition between pagan and Christian, he avoided the danger posed by the subject of Greek culture, now commonly associated with homosexual discourse, and complicated by the violent and grotesque elements in his essays of the 1870's on the decadent afterlife of ancient Greece.

Marius the Epicurean offered Pater many opportunities: it remained within his professional academic sphere of the classics where his knowledge and imagination were most tenaciously lodged, it could avail itself of the commonplace comparison between Victorian Britain and the Roman Empire (thus facilitating Pater's attempt to explain the code of conduct recommended to the young in *The Renaissance*, for example), it cunningly found a vehicle for autobiography in the fictional genre of *Bildungsroman*, and allowed Pater to introduce a glimpse of historical Christianity and its intellectual and spiritual potential. As the narrator of the novel is visible, and palpably situated in the 19th century, the comparison of the two periods constitutes an important element of the novel, one which is eased by the availability of the parallel between the two empires at the time.

The novel tells the story of Marius, a follower of the Cyrenaic philosophy of pleasure, whose intellectual cast of mind is shaped by his successive and intense friendships (preeminently first with Flavian and then with Cornelius, a young soldier of the Empire who harbours Christian knowledge and belief) in the Rome of Marcus Aurelius, the Stoic. It is a pagan world whose brutality and dearth of medical knowledge permit Pater to pursue his preoccupation with death, and to dramatise the argument that the failure of the pagan religions to cope with death convincingly and to provide a satisfactory framework for life leaves the way open to Christianity to dispel the melancholy and sadness with faith, charity, and peace. Moreover, the evident interest of the novel in friendships between young men registers the transition between the initial relationship between Marius and Flavian which is terminated by the death of the latter from the plague, and the second friendship, informed by Christianity. It ends with Marius's sacrifice of his own life for that of his friend whose stake in the (Christian) future and in the optimism Christianity offers is dramatised by his projected marriage with Celia, an idealised Christian woman. Celia is the only female main character in this novel peopled by men. The death of Marius the Epicurean is also cleverly gathered into the new wisdom by the device of the error of the strangers among whom he dies who take him for a believer and administer communion to the grateful but passive dying man. The conclusion of the novel draws attention to the attraction of the early Church for those who took the path to Rome in the 19th century, and the interest within the novel not only in the best case for the pagan but for the Roman Catholic church as well.

In one of the many memorable phrases in the novel Pater recommends to his youthful contemporaries "truant reading," and many elements of the novel could be termed "truant" to the same degree as *The Renaissance*. Many of its passages contain references and combine discourses in such a way that readers alive to aesthetic vocabulary and texts may produce readings not available to general readers. Although ostensibly in the most popular genre of its day, the novel, there remains an inescapable difficulty in the prose and an abstract and philosophical level of argument which the fictional narrative only negligibly leavens; the readership of *Marius the Epicurean* seems certain to have been smaller and more select than that for *The Renaissance* despite the appetite of the Victorian public for novels of religious doubt and faith as diverse as Newman's *Loss and Gain* and Mrs. Humphry Ward's *Robert Elsmere*. *Marius the Epicurean* repays its readers with subtly imagined detail of decadent Rome and incorporates skilfully many classical texts of the period. Its halting, exquisite progress toward the end of the sway of the pagan and the advent of the Christian manages to be a muted celebration of both.

—Laurel Brake

THE MARRIAGE OF HEAVEN AND HELL.
Prose and poetry by William Blake, 1793(?).

"Exuberance is Beauty." *The Marriage of Heaven and Hell* both states and exemplifies this. It is the most humorous and immediately enjoyable of William Blake's Prophetic Books. The wit can be enjoyed and the essential points understood without any special knowledge. Then one may go on to investigate the context. It was written probably between 1790 and 1793, the early years of the French Revolution. In the opening "Argument" the angry prophet threatens the old order in France, and in the concluding "Song of Liberty" the falling king is on one level Louis XVI. But, as always in Blake, history is caught up into a larger vision. The Prophet comes in clouds and fire, heralding Apocalypse; with the king fall the restrictive codes which have prevented man from being fully human. During 1789–93 Blake was writing his *Songs of Experience*, which with the earlier *Songs of Innocence* show "the Two Contrary States of the Human Soul"; and in *Thel* and *Visions of the Daughters of Albion* was asking why Innocence should descend into Experience. *The Marriage* continues the exploration of the meaning and relationship of these and other states. Relating it to Blake's life one remembers that he was 33 in 1790, that he had been—to some extent still was—an admirer of Swedenborg, and that he was an engraver. Swedenborg, the Swedish philosopher, had dated the beginning of a new dispensation 33 years earlier. But his presentation of heaven and hell as permanent states to which the good and the wicked would be confined now seemed to Blake to be "predestination after this Life . . . more Abominable than Calvin's . . . Cursed Folly."

The renewal Blake hoped for in 1790 would be not the entry of the "good" into an exclusive "heaven," but an explosion of revolutionary energy which would seem "hellish" to the conventional and would lead to recognition of the holiness of all life. He saw himself as the prophet of this change, and Swedenborg's writings as being discarded like the linen clothes of Jesus at the Resurrection (Plate 3). He was engraving his prophecies on copper plates, etching away the surface with acids to let the words and designs stand out, "displaying the infinite that was hid" (Plate 14).

"To generalise is to be an Idiot." So it is best to concentrate on a few themes and passages. The central theme is announced in Plate 3: "Without Contraries is no progression." Full humanity is not to be attained by suppression, but by bringing all man's potentialities to fruition. Good and Evil, Heaven and Hell, Reason and Energy, Angel and Devil—the words being used in deliberately perverse ways—are to be "married." One can recognize profound truth here, and enjoy the exuberance of the writing, and still doubt whether Blake shows what he purports to do. To show a marriage some positive content would need to be given to "Heaven" and "Angel" as well as to their contraries. But Blake is of the Devil's party, and gives him all the best tunes. In the climax of the action the Angel becomes the narrator's "particular friend," but only after he has "become a Devil" (Plate 24). *The Marriage* is a celebration of energy rather than of a union of contraries. Before dealing convincingly with this theme Blake needed to develop his later recognition that there are negations as well as contraries. However "good" and "evil" may be used in special senses to mock the pious, the real good (not passive) and the real evil (not active, but negative and destructive) shown in *The Marriage* and in the *Songs* are simply opposites. The "starry king" must be brought down; the Angel must renounce his self-righteousness. "The Negation must be destroyed to redeem the Contraries," as Blake will later put it (*Milton*, 40:33).

The central, prose part of *The Marriage* parodies Swedenborg, who often alternates philosophical discourses with "Memorable Relations" of his being carried up to heaven and of his dialogues with angels, etc. Blake pokes fun at Swedenborg's claim to familiarity with heavenly spirits, and obliquely puts forward his own ideas. One must recognise the strong dramatic element—not say "Blake says" but "Blake makes so-and-so say," and then try to see the total vision by putting together the various perspectives. Thus in the first "Memorable Fancy" the narrator descends, unlike Swedenborg, into hell and gathers "Proverbs of Hell." The Proverbs' "Infernal Wisdom" is expressed with great force and concision—"Eternity is in love with the productions of time," "One thought fills immensity"; but one must remember that they are "Proverbs of Hell" and need questioning and interpreting. "He who desires and acts not breeds pestilence." Must one act out *all* desires? "The cut worm forgives the plough." How is one to understand this? In the second "Memorable Fancy" the narrator has Isaiah and Ezekiel to dine with him. When they speak of discovering "the infinite in everything" and of the "Poetic Genius," these are Blakean insights; but when Ezekiel goes on to say that "we so loved our God, that we cursed in his name all the deities of surrounding nations" so that all nations have come to "believe the Jews' code and worship the Jews' god," one supposes that the prophets and even the narrator who is convinced by them are being treated ironically. Even a religion starting from true vision degenerates into an exclusive code. In the fourth and wittiest "Memorable Fancy" an Angel and the narrator in turn try to impose his own way of seeing on the other. The narrator's vision is preferred, but the implication is that there are many perspectives, none of which is final and all-inclusive.

Questionings and subtleties are cast aside in the concluding "Song of Liberty." However equivocally the scene of fiery boy (later named Orc), born of Eternal Female (Enitharmon) rebelling against jealous king (Urizen) may later be treated, now it is presented with delight. At this stage the young revolutionary is dominant over the master of multiple perspectives.

—P.H. Butter

MARTIN CHUZZLEWIT.
(The Life and Adventures of Martin Chuzzlewit.)
Novel by Charles Dickens, 1844.

Martin Chuzzlewit was published in monthly parts from 1843 to 1844. Like most works by Charles Dickens it was written while the printing was already under way. Today it is usually accorded a transitional position between the early narratives and the major novels of his maturity.

Dickens claimed that he had composed the novel with a "general purpose and design" in view, endeavouring to depict the most common of human failings, selfishness. While it has been conceded that the book does indeed exhibit egoism in a variety of forms, the author's avowed intention to write a unified narrative has not always been accepted. Yet we should fail to appreciate the complexity of the composition if we overlooked a thematic coherence which is in fact furthered by its structural diversity.

Martin Chuzzlewit, whose "life and adventures" the novel purports to record, may seem vastly superior to his brutal cousin Jonas Chuzzlewit, but there can be little doubt that he is similarly motivated. Self-love is indeed a trait which all members of the widespread Chuzzlewit clan and many of their associates share, though it may manifest itself differently. In Martin, as in his grandfather, the other and, it would seem, omnipotent Martin Chuzzlewit, it appears in the shape of excessive pride. Pecksniff's self-regard, conversely, is masked by hypocrisy, possibly the least forgivable weakness on Dickens's moral scale, whereas scheming and defrauding become an end in themselves for the tricky Montague Tigg. Ironically, even Augustus Moddle's dramatic desertion of his bride Cherry Pecksniff, which is presented as a just retribution for the latter's heartlessness, arises from a modicum of self-interest.

Martin Chuzzlewit, which anticipates the panoramic novels of the later Dickens, is best approached as a combination of several plots arising from different situations. Martin, the title-figure, has chosen to fend for himself rather than submit to his authoritarian grandfather. Abused by Pecksniff, he seeks his fortune in the New World, from where he returns chastened and matured. The American chapters, which caused some annoyance in the United States, can only be read as a concentrated satire; they should not be dismissed as an obvious digression. Exposed to the crass materialism and conceit of a young civilization, Martin loses his inflated self-esteem and may now be trusted to advance to a responsible position in society.

While this educational process is taking its happy course, Jonas Chuzzlewit progresses along different lines. Spoilt by an indulgent father, the crude go-getter deteriorates into a murderous monster that finally destroys itself. Dickens's keen interest in the criminal mind and in human behaviour in extreme situations made him devote considerable attention to Jonas's decline. Besides, the stark contrast between these grim scenes and the less turbulent, comic, or even pastoral parts forms an important element in the novel's structure.

Pecksniff certainly pursues his aspirations in a smoother mode. It is noteworthy to what extent social or even professional pretensions serve a wish for self-aggrandizement in *Martin Chuzzlewit*. Pecksniff has set up as an architect without qualifications, yet his role-playing and posturing make up for the deficiency. Acting the master-builder, a man of professed rectitude who has modestly withdrawn to a rural retreat, he pursues his deviant practices until he is brought to book by Old Martin Chuzzlewit, whom he had planned to wheedle out of his property. It is fit and natural that Pecksniff should eventually be put down. Yet the image of the sanctimonious hypocrite will linger on unharmed, as a Dickensian character is wont to do. And then there is Sarah Gamp, midwife and nurse, another of Dickens's indestructible figures. Like Pecksniff, she is a coarse materialist whose moral and professional claims are entirely unfounded. At the same time, she impresses us as a magnificent comic creation, embedded in a world of make-believe which she herself seems to have fashioned. Mrs. Gamp, always armed with her cumbrous umbrella, ever ready to pronounce wisdom through oracular sayings, has attained a prominence well beyond the Chuzzlewit saga, in which she fills a minor function only. But it would be wrong to depreciate her relevance to the novel. Driven by a sentimentalised ruthlessness and imperturbable vigour, she might be seen as a grotesque excrescence of the life-force that so richly sustains the narrative flow.

Yet the novel would still lack fullness if it comprised selfish personages only. Greed, jealousy, envy, all the human failings connected with egoism, do not appear in Tom Pinch. Were it not for his credulous naivety and ungainly shape, dear Tom would come too close to the stock-figure of the good-natured man to carry conviction. Cunningly dismissed by Pecksniff, whose true nature he has at length perceived, Tom is secretly supported by Old Chuzzlewit, although he does not realize this. As would seem typical of the early novels of Dickens, money is often transferred but never earned in *Martin Chuzzlewit*, whose hero advances to a comfortable subsistence after having singularly failed to provide for himself. But is Martin really the hero of the book? There can be no doubt that his vagaries reflect the traditional progress of the epic protagonist whose prolonged struggles are finally rewarded by a happy match. Conversely, there is little about him that might appear exemplary. True virtue, courage, a selfless regard for the needs of others are rather found in Tom Pinch, whose profound decency passes beyond Martin's comprehension. And yet it is Martin who gains the hand of the much-tried beauty, whereas Tom's true devotion remains unfulfilled. The text shows that Dickens must have been quite aware of this seeming anomaly. After all, Tom expressly submits to the contingencies of real life, which seldom correspond to the pattern of romance: "There is a much higher justice than poetical justice my dear, and it does not order events upon the same principle." Despite the fairy-tale atmosphere that clings to *Martin Chuzzlewit*, Dickens is evidently moving towards a more comprehensive, a more realistic view of the human condition.

—Herbert Foltinek

MARTIN MARPRELATE PAMPHLETS
(*The Epistle*, *The Epitome*, *Mineral and Metaphysical Schoolpoints*, *Hay Any Work for Cooper?*, *Martin Junior*, *Martin Senior*, *The Protestation*).
7 prose tracts 1588–89.

Edition

The Marprelate Tracts 1588–1589, edited by William Pierce. 1911.

Critical Studies: *An Historical Introduction to the Marprelate Tracts*, 1908, and *John Penry*: *His Life*, *Times*, *and Writings*, 1923, both by William Pierce; *Thomas Cartwright and Elizabethan Puritanism* by A.F. Scott Pearson, 1925; *John Penry and the Martin Marprelate Controversy* by D.J. McGinn, 1966; introduction by A.G. Dickens to *The Marprelate Tracts 1588–89* (facsimile), 1967; "Rhetoric and the Dramatic Satire of Martin Marprelate" by R.A. Anselment, in *Studies in English Literature*, 10, 1970; *Martin Marprelate, Gentleman*: *Master Job Throkmorton Laid Open in His Colors* by Leland H. Carlson, 1981; "Robert Waldegrave: The Printer as Agent and Link Between Sixteenth-Century England and Scotland" by Katherine S. Van Eerde, in *Renaissance Quarterly*, Spring 1981.

These pamphlets, written by an anonymous 16th-century author writing under the name of "Martin Marprelate," were part of a Puritan protest movement challenging the prevailing doctrines—and hence the hierarchy—of the Anglican Church during the latter part of the reign of Elizabeth I. In 1586 the Archbishop of Canterbury, Whitgift, in an effort to stifle the protesters, procured a decree giving him (and the Bishop of London) the power of suppressing seditious or slanderous books and also giving him full control over the operation of all printing presses in England. (He had no jurisdiction in Scotland, then a separate kingdom.)

The Marprelate series was a direct result. The pamphlets were set and run off on a printing-press that was secretly moved around various parts of England, until Waldegrave, the printer-owner, ultimately took fright and fled; other secret presses then took over but by the end of 1589 the authorities had closed them down and punished such offenders as they could discover. By 1593 the government stepped into the affair and set up harsh penalties for any attack on the church. The controversy went underground. "Martin" was never discovered and Waldegrave the original printer found a haven in Scotland where he became royal printer to King James VI.

Seven of the Marprelate pamphlets have survived, among them the lively *Epistle*, *Protestation*, and *Hay any worke for Cooper?*, the latter title being a wordplay on the street cry of London barrel-makers and on the name of Thomas Cooper, Bishop of Winchester. All the Marprelate pamphlets are in the form of attacks on the Anglican bishops, highly personal abuse ("You grosse beastes . . . pestilent dunces") being mingled with more sober passages expounding Puritan doctrine.

Were they solely protest pamphlets they would now be merely part of the troubled history of the church of the period and not part of the literary history of England. What gives them literary importance is their prose style. They were written in the first person in colloquial and conversational idiom, using the vigorous slangy vocabulary in which Elizabethan spoken English is so rich.

The bishops felt they had to answer the Martin attack—and in the same popular idiom. They turned to a group of young writers, all university men, all up until then writers of the currently fashionable "literary" written prose: John Lyly, Robert Greene, and Thomas Nashe. For John Lyly (author of the elaborately written prose of *Euphues*, 1578) the writing of his anti-Martin *Pappe with a Hatchet* (1589) was simply an exercise in a different kind of rhetoric. But for Robert Greene and Thomas Nashe the invitation to write colloquial religious pamphlets was a turning-point. Both had been educated at St. John's College, Cambridge, the college of Cheke and Ascham, who had been strong advocates of the principle "to speake as the common people do, to think as wise men do."

The flurry of counter-invective against Martin lasted little more than a year. When it was over Greene and Nashe had found their prose style and their *métier*, journalistic commentary on Elizabethan life presented in a richly colloquial style that has seldom been equalled. It was in due course to provide a major foundation for the English novel. In the history of English literature the Marprelate pamphlets are consequently something of a curiosity. Their impact was to be more important than the works themselves, and in an area unintended by the original author. Their intended influence on the religious thought of the day was slight. Their unintended influence on the development of English prose was incalculable.

—Ian A. Gordon

MARY BARTON.
Novel by Elizabeth Gaskell, 1848.

Manchester, the "shock city of the 1840's," as Asa Briggs has called it, was where Elizabeth Gaskell had lived for nearly a decade and a half, when her husband William encouraged her to think of writing a novel as a means of coping with her grief after the death of her infant son in 1845. She first thought of a historical tale set in Yorkshire, but the here-and-now quickly bore in upon her.

Mary Barton is a tale of Manchester life about the cotton workers who, in the words of the preface, were "doomed to struggle through their lives in strange alternations of work and want." There were two phenomena underlying the human suffering, the one environmental in the actual conditions of life and work, the other socio-political-economic, in the constraints that imposed such conditions. Some novelists like Frances Trollope and Charlotte Elizabeth (Tonna) metaphorically entered the factories and described the circumstances of industry; others like Disraeli and, less directly, Dickens, dealt in the broader background causes. Gaskell, who knew Manchester better than any of them, did neither, but none excelled her in telling how people actually lived.

The novel begins in a time of temporary prosperity, but that soon passes; and from the happy holiday atmosphere of Greenheys Fields we move to the impoverished dwellings of the workers and, most notably, to the squalid hovel of the Davenports, itself to be quickly contrasted with the wealth and luxury of the Carsons' manufacturers' household. There was a long history of class division in Manchester, only most explosively demonstrated in the Peterloo massacre of 1819. Gaskell sets her novel in the 1839–42 period which included the great Chartist demonstration on Kersal Moor.

Despite its title, the central character is John Barton, the intelligent and well-intentioned workman whose better impulses are destroyed by his inability to understand the suffering brought upon him and, for him more importantly, upon his fellow-workmen who are less able to cope. This is the result not least of his fundamental Christian beliefs. References to the story of Dives and Lazarus run like a refrain throughout the novel. Barton's trusting nature contributes to the pathos of his belief that the delegation to Parliament will enlighten the ignorance of those in authority and lead to legal reform. After the failure of the delegation there is despair, and the industrial atmosphere darkens with the meeting between masters and workmen and in its wake, as a result of Harry Carson's cruel cartoon, the Union's imposition of murderous revenge, a task which falls by lot upon Barton, ironically so because he had not been present at the fateful meeting.

Counterpointing the social disintegration, at the centre of which is John Barton, has been the personal history of his attractive daughter Mary, who is beloved by the steady and equable workman, Jem Wilson, but also pursued by Harry Carson. The original sub-title of the novel was to have been *A Manchester Love-Story*, but, though this aspect remains prominent and indeed is dominant in the latter stages of the novel, Gaskell's interest seems to have become centred principally upon the social facets of the tale. Indeed, she suggests in a letter that she could have wished to call the novel "John Barton."

In tracing Mary's history, the novelist is concerned to show how her development enables her, after initial mistakes, to discriminate between infatuation and love and to distinguish in her respective suitors the difference between outward wealth and inner worth. In the background as example and warning stands Mary's aunt, Esther, who by a like attraction to a wealthy suitor had been betrayed into prostitution. It is she who warns Jem Wilson about Harry Carson's designs upon Mary and thus sets up the train of events which lead to Jem being accused (wrongly) of Carson's murder. These events—the trial and the urgent pursuit of Jem's cousin, who is about to sail from Liverpool but can produce an alibi—give a fine narrative urgency to the latter stages of the novel, to be followed by the account of John Barton's last days and final reconciliation with Carson, Harry's father, who had come seeking his own revenge for his son's death.

Some have considered this stage too artificial; and indeed it is contrived, but in the best sense of that word, to convey Gaskell's overriding moral concern about our common humanity. Dives and Lazarus had indeed met together. But she has no solution for the immediate social problems. Jem Wilson and Mary Barton marry, but they cannot stay on in Manchester. They emigrate to Canada and a new start in a new world. Overall, *Mary Barton* is a powerful, if at times uneven book, justly praised on its appearance and retaining a strong appeal ever since.

—Arthur Pollard

MAUD.
Poem by Alfred, Lord Tennyson, 1855.

Alfred, Lord Tennyson's *Maud: A Monodrama* is perhaps best understood in the light of its original title *Maud; or, The Madness*. The work is an intimate portrayal of the morbid and disturbed state of mind of its narrator. Both the peculiarity and the appropriateness of its form are indicated by the later subtitle. A monodrama is a drama which could be performed by one person. It is also, in modern terminology, a dramatic monologue: a poem supposedly delivered by a single character at a particular (often momentous) point in time. *Maud* is not one dramatic monologue, but a long series of such lyrics. It therefore allows us to witness the changing mental state of its narrator, as the mood and thoughts behind the monologues undergo violent changes. The bleak desperation of the opening verse, for example, "I hate the dreadful hollow behind the little wood" is in sharp contrast to the famous romantic lyric "Come into the garden, Maud" (I, XXII). Tennyson employs considerable variation in both the verse-form and the metre of the lyrics. This helps to maintain our interest in a poem which has neccessarily a narrow, obsessional focus.

The story that a reader pieces together through these monologues is one of a young man whose father was ruined by the Lord of the neighbouring Hall and committed suicide. The Lord's daughter, Maud, returns to the Hall, and the hero, who worships and courts her, eventually wins her favour. They are opposed by Maud's brother, and the hero kills him in a duel. He then flees abroad, and goes mad, before finding new life in the hope of serving in war. The convention that a dramatic monologue can only contain an indirect exposition adds to the puzzle of trying to piece together the objective story and the suspense of the love story.

The history of the work's composition testifies to its interest in probing deeper and deeper into the origin and psyche of its hero. The first part to be written was the lyric "Oh that 'twere possible" (II, IV). To render this poem intelligible, Tennyson wrote a preceding one, and that too required a predecessor, and so on. "The whole poem," according to Aubrey De Vere's account in Hallam Tennyson's *Alfred Lord Tennyson: A Memoir*, "was written, as it were, *backwards*." It is a poem of peculiarly intense concentration. The course of the narrative is tortuous but relentless. In Part I it spirals inward around Maud, the "milkwhite fawn" at its centre, circling also through the cycle of hope, infatuation, and despair of the narrator. This is graphically demonstrated by the changing physical viewpoint of the narrator as he traces circuits of the landscape. We meet Maud in the village street, glimpse her riding across the moor (I, VIII), see her in church (I, XI), hear her singing in the garden (I, V), and look down on her from the hill top (I, IV, II). This movement is reversed after the climax. In Part II the hero is spun outwards—literally through his sudden exile to France and psychologically through his madness. Part I is intensely rooted in the English countryside. The Hall, the village, the Church, the shore, and the moor serve almost as icons of an idealised rural England. Yet it is at the same time an inner landscape. As in *Wuthering Heights*, the visible landscape is resonant with meaning. The narrator's grim first line signals an impassioned identification with his surroundings. The world which we enter in *Maud* is the world within the narrator's head. Each outer landmark charts some inner crisis or memory.

Tennyson violates the conventions of landscape symbolism to produce some startling effects. Emotionally potent touch stones of England, or of Englishness, are subverted: "Walked in a wintry wind by a ghastly glimmer, and found / The shining daffodil dead, and Orion low in his grave." (I, III). Spring's most familiar constellation is symbolically overthrown, the world is askew, and the Wordsworthian beauties of nature have perished. The disturbance of the narrator's psyche is portrayed by disruption of elements familiar to the reader's own inner landscape.

Elsewhere, the symbolism of flowers and stars is used extensively. "Sad Astrology" is ironically invoked to express the hero's existential loss of faith in the order of the universe. "Cold fires yet with power to brand / His nothingness into man." (I, XVIII) Traces of astrology also appear in a way that seems validated by the narrator, however. At the climax of the love story, his tryst with Maud, Venus "the planet of love is on high." In the penultimate lyric (III, VI) the narrator is returned to the earlier scene of desolation and sees above Orion's grave the "glorious crowns" of Auriga and Gemini (I, III, I). The spirit of Maud, who herself is "star-sweet" (I, III) and his "leading star" (I, IV, II) points to Mars shining in Leo, as a portent of war. The mention of Auriga (the Charioteer) reinforces the warlike omen, but the presence of Gemini high in the mid-heaven may suggest a duality, if not a continuing instability, in the hero's mental state.

Flowers occur again and again in the narrative, always invested with symbolic value. Maud's garden "of roses and lilies" echoes the tension between passion and purity in the narrator's mind. The garden itself gives hints of the violent denoument: "A lion ramps at the top / He is claspt by a passion flower" (I, XIV). Elsewhere animal symbolism is used to represent the narrator's contemptuous feelings: Maud's brother is an "Assyrian Bull" (I, VI). Her father a wolf (I, XIII, III). Maud's other suitors are a rabbit and a titmouse. In contrast, angelic imagery accompanies Maud (see I, VIII). Maud receives the full force not only of the narrator's love but of his thwarted idealism and longing for redemption. Her beauty is: ". . . the one bright thing to save / My yet young life in the wilds of Time" (I, XVI, V). She is transformed in his fantasy into something celestial. From an imagined glimpse of her hand he sees her: ". . . like a glorious ghost, to glide / Like a beam of the Seventh Heaven." (I, XIV, II). "Some peculiar mystic grace" (I, XIII, III) he believes, enabled her to be conceived without sin or taint from her father.

The narrator is also concerned with religion, politics, and philosophy, but his movements into these areas have less to do with reasoned speculation than with expressions of horror against the world. At times, however, the bitter force behind these passages results in biting polemic:

> Grimy nakedness dragging his trucks
> And laying his trams in a poisoned gloom
> Wrought, till he crept from a gutted mine
> Master of half a servile shire
> And left his coal all turned to gold (I, X, I)

The narrator longs for a populist leader who can redeem the nation (I, X, V): he longs also for war. It is significant that he first begins to fall in love with Maud when he hears her singing a martial song.

The final passages of Part III, in which he eagerly embraces the cause of war, are ambiguous. We have more than enough evidence to doubt the narrator's sanity. Earlier dismissive references to pacifism invite us to question the principles he is proclaiming, and his claims for war as a force which will regenerate the moral life of the nation seem wildly far-fetched. It does seem though, that in the last stanza, he has found a greater trauma in which to sink his own: "I embrace the purpose of God, and the doom assigned."

—Edmund Cusick

THE MAYOR OF CASTERBRIDGE.
Novel by Thomas Hardy, 1886.

Most readers have felt that the *Mayor of Casterbridge* was in some ways untypical of its author's work, though they have differed widely about its merits. Thomas Hardy himself "fancied he had damaged it more recklessly as an artistic whole . . . than perhaps any other of his novels." He attributed this to the requirements of serial publication. Others have admired it for a classic simplicity, an inner logic of events, which most of Hardy's other novels lack. As Hardy's preface of 1895 recalled, it was rooted in the oral traditions of his childhood, which recalled as real events the sale of a wife, the hunger of the 1840's, and a royal visit to Dorset.

On first appearance, the book received more critical acclaim, without achieving more popularity, than Hardy's previous novels. It was perhaps the turning-point in his reputation; henceforth he was recognized as one of the leading novelists of an age adorned also by Meredith and Henry James, after the deaths of George Eliot and Trollope. It is more urban than his other major novels (except perhaps *Jude the Obscure*)—selling the produce of the land is more prominent than growing it—and the narrative is unusually dominated by the single personality of the hero. Hardy's early memories of Dorchester are formative, and there is a constant insistence on the town's Roman origin. The opportunity to make more use of the ancient mound of Maiden Castle, so much anterior to the Roman invasion, and so full of material for prolonged Hardyesque meditation is unexpectedly scanted.

Chance plays a lesser part in the plot than in most Hardy novels. Henchard's original error in selling his wife, the drunkenness from which he escapes for a time (but not permanently), and his mistake in allowing Farfrae to remain in the town and become his rival and eventual conqueror, determine much of the book's course. The thought of *King Lear* seems to have been pervasive in the author's mind throughout the writing, and becomes explicit for the reader at the end when Whittle plays the part of Shakespeare's Fool, and is addressed by Henchard thus: "What, Whittle, and can you really be such a poor fond fool as to care for such a wretch as I!" Even more uncharacteristic perhaps, is the portrayal of Henchard's foil, the hard-headed, sentimental Scotsman, Farfrae, who likes singing songs about home, because it costs nothing, and says at a crisis involving life and death "that will make a hole *in a sovereign*." Farfrae's triumph is the inevitable one, of calculation over wayward passion, of new machines over old customs, of genteel manners over rough, unpredictable, anti-social ways. The story is so told that Henchard is always wrong, Farfrae always right, yet it is always Henchard who possesses the reader's sympathy. Perverse and absurd, yet touching, is the twisted sense of fairness which induces him to tie one hand behind his back before engaging in a fight to the death. The workers prefer Farfrae as employer, because they are freed from Henchard's unpredictable rages, but the reader notes sourly the meanness of Farfrae in reducing the wages.

Mrs. Henchard's naivety in believing that the sale could give the sailor a legal and moral right to be her husband strains credulity; but in Elizabeth-Jane Hardy has presented a telling contrast between the old country ways and the new. Henchard's determination that she should be a "lady" and eschew country dialect words is pathetic, yet thoroughly credible; and her thoughts on things in general reflect some of the author's own meditations, softened by common-sense femininity, and the absence of that extreme wildness of imagination which was inseparable from the author's genius.

The background of uneducated characters, tied to a primitive culture that is passing, is painted here in harsher colours than in *Far from the Madding Crowd*. Superstition and irrationality are less graceful and more cruel. The skimmington-ride represents the popular consciousness, and the fortune-teller is hard and cunning. Symbolism is less obtrusive than in most Hardy novels. But two symbolic images stand out, remembered perhaps by readers for whom many other things have worn faint: the picture of Henchard, contemplating suicide, gazing at his own simulacrum in the water; and the caged bird which he fruitlessly brings as his offering for Elizabeth-Jane's wedding.

Henchard's will contains some of the most eloquent and memorable words Hardy ever wrote. It is characteristic of Hardy that these words should be read from a crumpled scrap of paper, placed at the head of the bed of the dying man. In the grandeur of their content, and the rough simplicity of their form, they reveal Hardy's genius, defective in form, lacking the polish of art, yet possessed of high imaginative powers:

> & that I be not buryed in consecrated ground.
> & that no sexton be asked to toll the bell.
> & that nobody be wished to see my dead body.
> & that no murners walk behind me at my funeral.
> & that no flours be planted on my grave,
> & that no man remember me.

Perhaps these words are all the more impressive because they sound so alien to the busy, progressive age in which they were written, and so unlike the other great moments of its literature.

—A.O.J. Cockshut

MEASURE FOR MEASURE.
Play by William Shakespeare, 1604(?).

Like other of William Shakespeare's "problem plays," *Measure for Measure* has a complex plot. Vincentio, Duke of Vienna, hands over rule to Angelo, counting on him for strict enforcement of the law, and partly to test his austere character. The Duke adopts disguise to observe events. Claudio has made Juliet, his wife-to-be, pregnant: Angelo sentences him to death for fornication. Isabella, Claudio's sister, a novice nun, is brought to plead on his behalf. Her virtuous demeanour excites Angelo's lust, and he offers to release Claudio in return for sex. Isabella tells her brother, refusing to save him. The Duke intervenes, and through his plotting, Mariana, once betroathed to Angelo, acts as substitute bed-partner. Angelo does not thereafter pardon Claudio. The Duke now finds a substitute severed head, but tells Isabella her brother has been executed. The Duke's return to Vienna is announced. In the complex denouement, the Duke's disguise is finally removed by Lucio, a dissolute gentleman who has slandered him. Angelo surrenders to judgement: the Duke manoeuvres Isabella into pleading, with Mariana, for Angelo's life. Finally, the Duke reveals that Claudio is still alive, and in sequence marries Angelo to the formerly jilted Mariana, punishes the slanderer Lucio by obliging him to marry a woman he has acknowledged fathering a child upon, and rewards himself by proposing to Isabella. Sub-actions involve a lively group of dissolutes, and the lowest instrument of the state, Abhorson, the hangman.

Measure for Measure is a variant on the unjust judge narrative, in which a judge sexually coerces a maiden through his power to pass sentence on her brother. In most analogues the girl agrees to the Judge's coercion. Shakespeare precipitates crisis by having Isabella refuse:

> Then, Isabel, live chaste, and brother, die:
> More than our brother is our chastity.

These lines, pointed as they were by Shakespeare with rhyme to get Isabella's decision totally clear to his audience, have never really been forgiven the character. Explanations based on Isabella's vocation cannot make the problematic quality of her decision disappear.

The play settles its action upon the concepts of remedy and redemption. The words "remedy," "redeem," and "redemption" appear more often than in any other play. Redemption is the absolute act:

> Why, all the souls that were, were forfeit once,
> And He that might the vantage best have took
> Found out the remedy

but can only be imitated on earth amid the difficult moral density of society by approximations in which compromise appears. Isabella asserts "foul redemption" in what Angelo would have her do, "nothing kin" to lawful mercy. Yet she herself must refuse mercy to her brother:

> Is there no remedy?
> None, but such a remedy as, to save a head,
> To cleave a heart in twain.

Isabella cannot redeem her brother: "O, were it but my life, / I'd throw it down . . . As frankly as a pin"—her generosity is too large for the situation, irrelevant. Instead, a remedy must be concocted for Angelo's fall and her intransigence: the device of a substitute bed-partner.

The Duke's intervention into the traumatic interview between Isabella and Claudio ("to the love I have in doing good; a remedy presents itself") can been seen as the imposition onto the drama of contrived and unpersuasive compromise. To an extent the Duke has controlled the action from the start. The opening dialogue suggests how far the Duke counts on Angelo proving a severe magistrate. Our resistance to his controlling power is gratified when the pardon he complacently announces turns out to be a confirmation of sentence from Angelo, and by the ungovernable Lucio. By the fifth act, every character except Lucio has been manipulated by the Duke into words, actions, and the timing of both at his direction alone. His tendency to experiment with people, which breaks Angelo, finally claims Isabella, when she kneels to beg forgiveness for the man she believes responsible for her brother's death, on the grounds that "a due sincerity" governed Angelo's deeds "Till he did look on me." Unlike Angelo, the Duke can make Isabella compromise, wins her from her cloister as his partner.

This play contains three of Shakespeare's finest scenes of confrontational dialogue: Isabella and Angelo's two meetings, and Isabella giving her decision to the anguished Claudio. Act V is brilliantly contrived: attention switches from character to character, each actor gets a turn at centrality, to surprise and be surprised. The poetry in which Shakespeare's drama is written (until supplanted by the prose of the scenes contrived by his proxy the Duke) is of disturbing power. As testimony to this: Samuel Johnson, in old age, compounded his neurotic habit of making noises with a continued mumbling. Eventually friends realised that he was locked into a sub-vocalisation of Claudio's speech to Isabella on the horror of death:

> Ay, but to die, and go we know not where;
> To lie in cold obstruction, and to rot . . .

—Roy Booth

MELMOTH THE WANDERER.
Novel by Charles Robert Maturin, 1820.

The vogue for gothic fiction which spanned the last decades of the 18th century and the first of the 19th produced many strange works, but Charles Robert Maturin's *Melmoth the Wanderer* has a good claim to be called the strangest. Certainly it is one of the largest and, in narrative terms, the most confusing and the most difficult to summarise.

The story begins with Young Melmoth attending at the death of a relative in Ireland and inheriting a manuscript; he finds that it tells the story of one Stanton and his encounters with a mysterious figure, who first promises Stanton that he will encounter much misfortune, culminating in a spell in a madhouse, and then, when this prophecy is fulfilled, appears to him in his adversity offering to give him his freedom in exchange for his soul. This is reminiscent, as is the whole book, of the Faust legend. The mysterious figure is identified as a relation of Young Melmoth who should have been dead long ago. While he is pondering on the manuscript, a shipwreck brings to his door a Spaniard called Moncada who tells him a further story which is even more horrific and involves the same mysterious figure of Melmoth's un-dead ancestor, who thereupon becomes the key character in the book.

More stories come thick and fast, and all of them involve the ancestor Melmoth attempting to find an individual in such depths of despair that he would be willing to trade his soul for escape; they are set across 150 years, and range through Europe to the Indian Ocean. Most of them are highly coloured, and grim with death and horror, for it is in conditions of torment that Melmoth is, of course, most likely to find somebody who will accept his deadly bargain.

But in his quest, Melmoth is unsuccessful: he finds nobody, however desperate their plight, who is willing to surrender their soul, and in the end he appears in person to his young relative, announcing that he has had no success and that he has come home to await his end, the end consisting in his being dragged away by demons, initially into the sea, but we presume thence into the flames of hell which he has failed to avoid by visiting them upon another.

The central idea of Maturin's book—the search by a doomed soul for another to take its place—is not original, neither is it unusual among romantic and gothic writers. What is unusual is the author's skill in bringing to life the various scenes of terminal deprivation which he depicts. He also manages to do this with considerable wit, which he partly owes to one of his avowed masters, Cervantes. This wit is appropriate because Melmoth is portrayed as a man of extreme intellect and rhetoric; like Faust again, it is his real gifts which have been his undoing.

Maturin, a Protestant Irishman, was violently anti-Catholic, and this provides the clue to one of the linking themes behind the book, which is the horror of the notion of divine vengeance. Maturin himself clearly thought that he was depicting the evil behind the Catholic notion of God; for readers at the time and since, this anti-Catholicism seems more anti-religion in general, and Maturin provides some sustenance for this idea in the words of a dying and very evil monk:

> All saints, from Mahomet down to Francis Zavier, were only a compound of insanity, pride, and self-imposition;—the latter would have been of less consequence, but that men always revenge their impositions on themselves, by imposing to the utmost on others.

But the real skill of the novel, and what makes it still worth reading, is the subtlety of Maturin's portrayal of extreme emotional states. There is room for only one example. Moncada is tortured by monks who, in order to break his resistance to taking the vows, enter into a communal pretence which involves affecting to be frightened of him:

> The terror that I inspired I at last began to feel. I began to believe myself—I know not what, whatever they thought me. This is a dreadful state of mind, but one impossible to avoid. In some circumstances, where the whole world is against us, we begin to take its part against ourselves, to avoid the withering sensation of being alone on our own side.

This is part of an extremely sensitive account of some of the consequences of persecution. Moncada attempts to escape, and is thwarted at the moment when his light expires: "we lay", he says,

> . . . not daring to speak to each other, for who could speak but of despair, and which of us dared to aggravate the despair of the other. This kind of fear which we

> know already felt by others, and which we dread to aggravate by uttering, *even to those who know it*, is perhaps the most horrible sensation ever experienced. The very thirst of my body seemed to vanish in this fiery thirst of the soul for communication, where all communication was unutterable, impossible, hopeless.

It is in this kind of passage that the real strengths of *Melmoth the Wanderer* lie: in the depiction of the psychological contortions of which people are capable under conditions of duress. Maturin had a formidable understanding of the mind and its more remote recesses; although a very significant question remains, which is whether he was genuinely describing reactions of minds under the pressure of persecution, or whether he was in fact writing about paranoia and out of a state of paranoiac consciousness in himself. No doubt the two things cannot really be separated; but certainly the novel itself is interesting, at least in part, because it does not enable us to draw that distinction, and we feel that the outer world and the inner world cannot be clearly separated.

—David Punter

MEMOIRS OF A WOMAN OF PLEASURE.
See **FANNY HILL.**

THE MERCHANT OF VENICE.
Play by William Shakespeare, 1596(?).

The Merchant of Venice is the darkest of William Shakespeare's romantic comedies. No other comedy threatens its title character with imminent death or portrays its villain as an outsider with a thirst for blood. No other comedy engages such serious issues as the contrast between law and grace or between mercy and justice. And no other comedy is so lacking in comic characters and comic scenes. More important than all these, no other comedy is so dominated by a single character, nor is any other character in Shakespeare so fully developed in five short scenes. In the text, Shylock has a much smaller role than Portia or Bassanio. But in the theater, for the 250 years during which the history of this play can be documented, Shylock is the role which has attracted great actors from Charles Macklin to Henry Irving to Laurence Olivier. In fact, some productions (e.g., Irving's in 1879) ended the play with Shylock's final exit, turning Shakespeare's comedy into the tragedy of Shylock.

On what grounds is *The Merchant* regarded as a romantic comedy? Primarily because the line of action involving Portia makes her a captive princess who can be released only by Prince Charming (Bassanio). She is imprisoned by the will of her dead father, condemned to marry any man who has the kind of insight that distinguishes between a deceptive appearance of worth (the gold and silver caskets) and true worth (the lead casket). That Bassanio should succeed is dictated by the romantic nature of the plot, not by any qualities apparent in his character. Fortunately it is clear that Portia is in love with Bassanio, and in Shakespeare's romantic comedies lovers always have their way, as do Gratiano and Nerissa and especially Lorenzo and Jessica (whose elopement is quintessentially romantic).

But the title character, Antonio, belongs in a quite different kind of play. His mysterious sadness and his apparent willingness to die to prove his love for Bassanio suggest the world of tragedy. The bond he signs with Shylock is unromantically explicit about the three-month term and the consequences of forfeiture. His contempt for Shylock finds no comic expression, and at the end of the play he is the odd man out among the pairs of happy lovers.

As for Shylock, he is sui generis. He is too powerful for a romantic comedy and too grotesque for a tragedy. He has been hindered and insulted by Antonio, for which he wants to kill the merchant. Is he a man of great soul or a greedy miser? His thirst for revenge suggests an anger that a petty spirit could not feel. But his unwillingness to pay the price for that revenge, his bargaining instead for as much money as he can get, reduces his stature. And his confused lament over his daughter and his ducats suggests a grotesque inability to distinguish between them. Above all, he is a Jew. In his most famous speech he asserts the fundamental humanity of his nation, but the Christians persist in calling him "the Jew" and the laws of Venice make him an alien. Gratiano may be the most rabid Jew-baiter in all literature. Certainly no character in any other Shakespearean comedy undergoes a defeat as crushing as Shylock's.

Portia is the instrument of that defeat. This fairy tale princess becomes an avenging angel. In IV.i she delivers the famous mercy speech, memorized by generations of school children. But when she springs the trap, catching Shylock in a legal quibble, she shows him no mercy. In making the scene so tense and riveting that it can hardly fail in the theater, Shakespeare created an adversary whose spirit was as hard and whose tactics were as devious as Shylock's. Portia can be witty and gamesome; she is submissive to her father's will and quite thoroughly in love with Bassanio. But the trick she plays on Bassanio and the accusations she levels against him in the final scene are part of a test which is not entirely playful: she makes it clear that she intends to keep the upper hand. There is a vein of steel in Portia that has made the role a challenge second only to that of Shylock.

The Merchant has been a popular play for 250 years, but the deaths of millions of Jews under Hitler's regime cast a shadow over this comedy. Modern critics and scholars find in it such serious issues as racial prejudice, economic injustice, and the struggle of women to escape male domination. But audiences are still moved by its emphasis on love's power to overcome great odds and to achieve a musical harmony made all the more attractive by its contrast to the dissonance of a flawed world.

—Thomas Wheeler

THE MERRY WIVES OF WINDSOR.
Play by William Shakespeare, 1597.

The Merry Wives of Windsor is unusual among William Shakespeare's plays in being evidently composed for a particular occasion. In its final scene a character impersonating the Fairy Queen has a speech full of complimentary allusions to Windsor Castle, Elizabeth I, and the Order of the Garter. This speech, together with allusions to a German duke who is coming to Windsor, connect the play with the Garter Feast of 23 April 1597, at which one of the newly elected Knights was Baron Hunsdon, the new Lord Chamberlain and the patron of the theatrical company to which Shakespeare belonged, and another was the Duke of Württemberg, who was elected *in absentia*. The probability that Lord Hunsdon commissioned the play for this occasion need not rule out the tradition (first recorded in the early 18th century) that Elizabeth I desired to see Falstaff in love.

In courting, at the same time, the wives of two Windsor citizens, Falstaff's ulterior motive is to get his hands on some of their husbands' money. Mistress Ford and Mistress Page, who learn Falstaff's game by comparing the identical love-letters that he has sent them, decide to teach him a lesson. Ford, who is a jealous husband, is also taught a lesson. Learning from Falstaff's disaffected hanger-on Pistol that the fat knight covets his wife, he disguises himself under the name of Brook and becomes Falstaff's confidant; and learning from Falstaff of the assignations that he has made, he twice searches his house for him, without success, and is forced to apologize. After the second search he is let into the secret by the wives, and a final plot against Falstaff is contrived, he having already been thrown into the Thames when hidden in a basket of washing and beaten out of the house when disguised as an old woman. This time he is persuaded to disguise himself as the ghost of Herne the Hunter, wearing a pair of antlers, and to come to a rendezvous in Windsor Park at midnight. There he is terrified and tormented by a troop of pretended fairies, denounced for his schemes, and at last forgiven and invited to a general supper at Page's house. Also invited is Fenton, a young gentleman who has used the fairy revel as an opportunity to marry the Pages' daughter Anne, thereby forestalling her two unwelcome suitors who are the respective choices of her father and mother.

The play is a by-product of the English history plays that Shakespeare was writing at the same time. Besides Falstaff and Pistol it contains Bardolph, Nym, Mistress Quickly, and Justice Shallow. Shallow's kinsman, a foolish young man called Slender, is one of Anne's unwelcome suitors, and the other is Doctor Caius, a choleric Frenchman by whom Mistress Quickly is employed as his housekeeper. They provide much of the play's incidental humour, and so does Sir Hugh Evans, the Welsh parson of Windsor, whose verbal mannerisms correspond to Fluellen's in *Henry V*.

Though often disparaged as though it were a pot-boiler and a second-rate farce which degraded Falstaff, *The Merry Wives of Windsor* is a well-constructed comedy, making the most of the scenes at Ford's house and of the disguised Ford's interviews with Falstaff at the Garter Inn. Shakespeare's source for this part of the plot is a story in a collection by Ser Giovanni Fiorentino (another of which supplied the main plot of the slightly earlier *Merchant of Venice*), but he has substituted his own wholesome morality for the amoral sexual opportunism of the original, without falling into the fault of writing moralistically: as Mistress Page says, "Wives may be merry, and yet honest too." The second of Ford's searches, where he throws out all the contents of the washing basket and later cudgels the would-be seducer in utter ignorance of his real identity, so that he is a victim of dramatic irony at the very moment when he is a dispenser of justice, is particularly rich in this moral humour. The final scene, with the midnight wood, Falstaff's antlered disguise, the pretended fairies, and the topical compliments, brings to the play a new element of fantasy, but it is an element that is easily accommodated, and it must have contributed greatly to the original audience's enjoyment, though the topical compliments are nowadays usually omitted in the theatre. The tormenting of the antlered Falstaff may have connections with folk-rituals celebrating the defeat of winter or of death, as some 20th-century criticism has maintained. In the main, however, it is as a lively "citizen comedy"—Shakespeare's one attempt in this form, and his play with the highest proportion of prose to verse—that *The Merry Wives of Windsor* makes its mark.

—T.W. Craik

MIDDLEMARCH.
Novel by George Eliot, 1872.

Not many Victorian novels have the name of a town for the title. Here, the imaginary name is rich in meanings. "Middle" suggests ordinariness, and "march" both a borderland and the long haul of years that make a lifetime. The name perfectly fits the book's main theme, the clash between the workaday world and exceptional talents, aims, and ideas. The book's great merit is to hold the balance equal, neither disparaging nor idealizing those who aim above the common mark. Dorothea Brooke, Ladislaw, Casaubon, and Lydgate are all, in different ways, aiming at great achievement. All are flawed, so that their failure, or imperfect success, is due as much to an enemy within as to external forces and provincial stupidity. Dorothea is naively idealistic, intellectually precocious, and childishly retarded as a woman. Ladislaw is a romantic dreamer; Lydgate's "spots of commonness" cause him to exclude the feminine from the serious concerns of life, and to allow a tradition of gentlemanly superiority to mar his high intellectual aims; while Casaubon dreams of being a pioneering genius when he is only a dry-as-dust professor with no imagination.

Against these exceptional people are ranged the ordinary stuff of provincial society: Dorothea's sister, Celia, whose common sense is shown in the early chapters as neatly puncturing her sister's inflated bladder of dreams; Mrs. Cadwallader, one of the author's best humorous characters, whose witty worm's-eye view is felt as a relief to readers fatigued with high-mindedness; Mr. Brooke, who may hold strong views, but will never allow them to harm his comfortable position as a stingy landlord, and Rosamund Vincy whose remorseless will easily triumphs over her husband, Lydgate's superior intelligence. The ordinary people have clearer aims, fewer inhibitions, fewer doubts, and grasp their limited goods unerringly. Fred Vincy is the ordinary person of weak will, who needs and finds in Mary Garth a stronger will to direct his own. The sinister element in life is present in Featherstone and Raffles, who try to drag others down to their own level. Caleb Garth and Mr. Farebrother are contrasted with the idealists in a different way; they find their ideal in the humdrum; they have no illusions either about themselves or the world, they reflect the author's strong conservative sense of limits. They are exceptional in knowing they are not exceptional, and in making full allowance for the weakness of others. Thus Garth is able to forgive Fred Vincy's careless extravagance with his money, and Farebrother to understand that powerful forces, which Lydgate does not understand, will cause him to vote against his friend in the chaplaincy election in favour of a man he does not know.

Following the tradition of comedy, the classic English novel deals more minutely with courtship than with marriage. *Middlemarch* is unusual in that two of the three most important marriages in the book occur early enough in the story to be fully assessed by the reader. The first two, Casaubon–Dorothea and Lydgate–Rosamund, are handled with masterly insight. Each of the four is self-deceived as well as disappointed. Casaubon imagines that he can move easily from a life of solitary industry to the delights of love, at the same acquiring an ardent, uncritical admirer, to soothe his self-doubts and the sting of hostile scholarship, and an unpaid secretary. Dorothea imagines that an intellect (which, in any case, she much overrates) can compensate for the masculine heart and body which her feminine nature will later crave. Rosamund thinks that Lydgate's good birth will neutralize his workaday profession and comparative poverty. Lydgate supposes that a pretty, delicate girl will be easily moulded to his wishes, forgetting how effortlessly she has coaxed him out of his bachelor state, showing already her greater shrewdness, will, and egoism. By making the woman more sympathetic in one marriage and the man in the other, Eliot comes nearer to what is essentially human in her characters' needs, aspirations, and illusions. And she does not forget or let us forget that the unsympathetic Casaubon and Rosamund also have the ability to suffer.

The third marriage, Ladislaw–Dorothea, is more problematic, and not only because it comes too near the end to be seen developing. Early readers of the book (published in serial form) were sometimes struck by a sense of spiritual affinity between Lydgate and Dorothea, and some even fantasized about an eventual marriage of the two. Does this suggest that Ladislaw is a second-best for Dorothea? One of the book's few flaws, perhaps, is that the author does not squarely face this question. Did she know, unconsciously, as we do, that Ladislaw is too much of a restless dreamer to settle down to the realities of domestic life? A certain uncharacteristic feverishness in the writing in the description of their final coming together suggests that perhaps she did. The unconvincing attempt in two passages at the book's beginning and end to identify the blundering and often comic Dorothea with St. Teresa seems to show an emotional rebellion on the author's part against her own clear-sightedness, as if one part of her nature regretted that she was so intelligent.

Bulstrode is one of the book's most notable achievements. The way he dresses his ambitions in the "severe robes" of Evangelicalism is a fine corrective to the unsympathetic, and often unfair, treatment of similar figures by Eliot's predecessors, Thackeray, Dickens, and Trollope. The subtle insincerities that help to bring about the death of the hated blackmailer, Raffles, and the devotion of Bulstrode's wife when the hiss of the world is against them, are finely handled. In the world of the book as a whole, self-deception is ubiquitous, but never the same in one case as in another. The resonance of contrast between them is one of the reader's chief pleasures.

—A.O.J. Cockshut

A MIDSUMMER NIGHT'S DREAM.
Play by William Shakespeare, 1595(?).

One of William Shakespeare's finest early plays is the comedy *A Midsummer Night's Dream*. Scholars cannot now date the year of its writing or first performance with absolute certainty. But given internal evidence (verse style, allusions to specific historical events, etc.) most authorities think it first was staged about 1594 or 1595, possibly as part of an actual wedding celebration attended by the queen. Whatever its date of composition, *A Midsummer Night's Dream* represents the artistry of a skilled poet and dramatist.

Shakespeare sets his play in Theseus' Athenian palace, in a purposely vague antique period. His aim is not to write realistic social comedy but a fantasy suitable for the magic of a summer night in a never-never place and time. (Ironically, the play's events seem to occur on the eve of May Day rather than on that of Midsummer's Night.) Unlike *The Comedy of Errors* or *The Taming of the Shrew* composed earlier, *A Midsummer Night's Dream* exhibits reduced reliance on classical antecedents as Shakespeare worked toward developing his own more romantic style of comedy. In the world of this play, audiences certainly laugh *with*, not *at*, the objects of the jokes.

Blank verse is the author's main staple in *A Midsummer Night's Dream*. Still, there are passages of rhymed verse, too, at moments of high passion in the love plot and during the several songs and invocations that dot the play. Distinct social classes are delineated by different dialogue patterns as often is true in Shakespeare's dramas. Courtiers and royalty of both human and fairy realms speak in blank verse with some rhymed couplets ending scenes. The aristocratic lovers in the play likewise use blank verse though with frequent splurges of rhymes, given the intense nature of young love. At times, the verse spoken in the fairy realm—especially during songs and Puck's casting of spells—shifts into a brisker meter, usually octosyllabics. Prose dialogue, on the other hand, dominates the speech of the workmen who prepare a play for the nuptial revels of Theseus and his bride Hippolyta. The poetry permeating this comedy needs to be well-rendered, because it is poetry which creates the shifting moods and the prevailing fantastic tonality.

In design as well as in language, *A Midsummer Night's Dream* displays an adroit playwright at work. Four discrete but intersecting story lines mesh in smooth conjunction. Serving as an outer frame for the play is the pending wedding of Duke Theseus of Athens and his captive bride Hippolyta, Queen of the Amazons. No conflict as such characterizes their plot function. As monarchs of a peaceful land, they are to establish a festive tonic key for the play and to establish a four-day time frame for the other plots. First of the active stories to unfold concerns four young lovers caught up in dispute. Hermia and Lysander love one another and want to marry; Helena loves Demetrius who in turn, however, does not love her but rather Hermia. Egeus, Hermia's father, wants Demetrius for his daughter, not Lysander. The four end up wandering the woods near Athens. Their bizarre adventures furnish one main source of laughter, because with the help of a magical love potion, the affections of the lovers are shifted several times. Eventually, as in most comedies, the *right* pairs will match up to join Theseus and Hippolyta in a grand marriage festival at play's end.

The woods in question are abode for Oberon, king of the fairies, and his queen Titania. Whereas Theseus rules over civilised Athens, Oberon is monarch of the dark, unknown wild woods. Oberon and Titania currently are at odds, their love having gone awry. Only another dose of magic resolves their disagreement, allowing them to reunite in happiness at the end. A group of Athenian craftsmen—called "mechanicals"—also happen into the same forest to rehearse a court entertainment in privacy. They intend to stage a play about Pyramus and Thisbe, a pair of ill-fated lovers, at

Theseus's celebration. Oberon's servant Puck magically transforms Bottom, the most exuberant of the workmen, by replacing his own head with that of an ass. And Titania, under Oberon's spell, will fall madly in love with the man-animal Bottom has become. Shakespeare elicits wild farce from the strange interactions of the mortal and fairy kingdoms.

A theme found in many of Shakespeare's subsequent plays is first examined here. The court, or city, represents stability, common sense, and sophistication. But formalized structures and attributes rarely help in matters of love which typically are irrational. So, often the scene in a comedy alternates between court and forest. The natural setting seemingly provides the innocence and healing ethos which allow the solving of personal problems, particularly those concerning love. In such plays as *The Winter's Tale*, *As You Like It*, *The Tempest*, and even to some extent *The Merry Wives of Windsor* and *The Merchant of Venice*, it is the salving essence of the woods that permits humans a fresh perspective.

For most audiences, *A Midsummer Night's Dream* emerges a light comedy built on magic and fantasy. The notion of "dream" is prominent in the play, and Puck, also known as Robin Goodfellow, proves adept at turning one's dream—or nightmare—into reality. Through Oberon's magic love potion, the fickleness already inherent in young love is reinforced. Some observers wonder if the youths would have behaved any differently in the forest without the potion. In contemporary times, some productions emphasize the underside of both fairy and mortal worlds in the play. Puck's cultural lineage leads back to a half-demon "pook" figure, with strong devilish associations. Recent stagings parlay that fact into a psychosexual premise, concentrating on the loss of inhibitions that can occur in the asocial context of the woods. Titania's love for a beast is seen as further evidence of a no-holds-barred axis running through *A Midsummer Night's Dream*. Yet, for most audiences everywhere, the play will remain pretty much what it has been since its first performance: a delightful fantasia on ingredients derived from the classics, medieval fable, and popular culture. When melded, as Shakespeare miraculously succeeds in doing, the separate elements effect a prime example of Elizabethan romantic comedy.

—C.J. Gianakaris

THE MILL ON THE FLOSS.
Novel by George Eliot, 1860.

The most autobiographical of George Eliot's fictions, *The Mill on the Floss* draws on her childhood in the Warwickshire countryside, recalled some 30 years later, her struggles to assert herself against a background of stifling conventionality, and her painful love for her brother Isaac. There are important differences: Eliot, unlike Maggie Tulliver, suffered frustration but always had enough money to pay for lessons in the subjects that interested her. She was never reduced, as poor Maggie is, to relying on church services for the only music available after the sale of the family piano. The rebellious girl-child had been invented in fiction by Charlotte Brontë in *Jane Eyre*, but the turbulence of Mr, Tulliver's "little wench" owes much to the young Mary Ann Evans, who also tried with all her might to be good.

The first chapter paints a scene of rural beauty, but the life within it is not idyllic: the second chapter opens with Mr. Tulliver's ruminations, in dialect, about giving his son an "eddication" which will fit him for "one o' them smartish businesses as are all profits and no outlay, only for a big watch-chain and a high stool." We do not get much impression of the man's wisdom. The conversation between him and his wife is inconsequential. We learn that their daughter is more intelligent than their son, and that Maggie is "too 'cute for a woman . . . an over 'cute woman's no better nor a long-tailed sheep: she'll fetch none the bigger price for that."

Mrs. Tulliver is unconvinced that Maggie's intelligence is not damaging while she is still small: "it all runs to naughtiness." She complains the child is "half an idiot" in practical matters, and her hair refuses to curl. Clearly Maggie's prospects of intellectual encouragement are not good. Mrs. Tulliver is concerned with cleanliness and respectability. The interaction of her and her sisters, formerly the Misses Dodson, is the comic highlight of the book. With them, Eliot creates a picture of provincial life in the early years of the 19th century which shows both their admirable self-respect and their absurdly narrow views.

Maggie objects to doing patchwork, "tearing things to pieces to sew 'em together again." And she does not want to please her Aunt Glegg by doing it, because she doesn't like Aunt Glegg. Like other children, Maggie cuts her own hair. She jealously pushes her pretty blonde cousin Lucy into the cow-manure, and runs away to join the Gypsies, planning to become their instructress and queen. Four-year-old Mary Ann Evans, unable to play a note of music, sat down at the piano in order to impress the servant with her prowess, and the mature Eliot ruthlessly satirises this aspect of her younger self. Even more painful is her treatment of that lordly bully, brother Tom, secure in his conviction of superiority to any mere female, and in his right to rule. Maggie slavishly worships Tom and lives for his approval. All this childish emotion was revisited by the writer after her own brother had rejected her for living with George Henry Lewes, yet being unable to marry him.

But after Mr. Tulliver becomes a bankrupt, our perception of Tom changes: he is no intellectual, but he is a young man of integrity, and at 16 sets to work in his Uncle Deane's wharf, saving money and paying off his father's debts. Tulliver is reduced to working for his old enemy, lawyer Wakem. Maggie "gets religion" and decides to renounce the world and its pleasures. But one secret pleasure remains to her: she meets Wakem's hunchback son, Philip, in the disused quarry, the Red Deeps. Philip is the intellectual companion Maggie needs after the family books are sold. Philip wisely tells her she is merely trying to "stupefy" herself.

Maggie has not yet grasped that "renunciation remains sorrow, though a sorrow borne willingly" (Book 4, chapter 3). The real theme of the novel is Maggie's attempt to come to terms with the loss of her brother's love. The story betrays unease: it says the love between the children was mutual, yet we never see Tom's affection, apart from family pride, in action—we have to take it on trust. The portrait is resentful, its respect grudging. The story slackens when Maggie and Lucy's young man fall in love and go boating, which causes Maggie, who has improbably renounced him anyway to avoid hurting Lucy and Philip, to lose her reputation. Because the love-object is neither handsome Stephen nor handicapped Philip, the conflict is insoluble. There is nothing to do with the brother and sister but reunite them in death by drowning. Eliot could not invent credible lovers for Maggie or convincing reasons for her brother's sternness, because the real reasons for the breach between the author and her brother were too personal and too painful. So she has to say goodbye symbolically to the children she and her brother used to be.

Eliot sets Maggie's provincial struggles in contrast to "good society," which

> is of very expensive production, requiring nothing less than a wide and arduous national life condensed in unfragrant deafening factories, cramping itself in mines, sweating at furnaces, grinding, hammering, weaving under more or less oppression of carbonic acid . . . based entirely on . . . the emphasis of want, which urges it into all the activities necessary for the maintenance of good society and light irony . . .

It is for such generalised wisdom that the reader turns to Eliot (although some complain of "prosiness" and "preaching").

—Valerie Grosvenor Myer

MILTON.
Poem by William Blake, 1804–08(?).

Milton is the most attractive, partly because the shortest, of William Blake's long prophetic poems. There are two main strands of narrative—the Bard's Song and the story of Milton's journey to self-renewal. The former is difficult, contains little of Blake's best writing, and may well be passed over at a first reading. All one needs to grasp is that it is the Bard's story of Satan's usurpation of the prophetic role that leads to Milton's recognition of his own errors. Milton descends to earth, enters into Blake, his successor, into whom Los, the eternal Prophet, also enters. He unites with his female counterpart Ololon. The scattered elements of full humanity come together, leading to the appearance of Jesus, the divine humanity, and bringing us to the brink of Apocalypse.

This bald summary does no justice to the richness and complexity, nor the irritations, of the poem. It is comforting to have a thin thread of narrative to follow; but this is not mainly a narrative—rather a series of related visions. At first one enjoys some marvellous passages, between which one stumbles over much that seems obscure, repetitive, tiresomely didactic, difficult to connect. As one re-reads, other parts come to life and one sees more relationships between them. Perhaps some day one will see the whole consort dancing together, as some commentators claim to do; but most readers will remain in alternate excitement and perplexity.

Milton is, among other things, Blake's *Prelude*, showing in the narrator and in Milton the poet's "call," his fall into inner division and his recovery of wholeness through imagination. The large statements are at the best given substance by being embodied in visions we can all see if not fully understand, and dramatised in encounters between characters who are more than symbols for abstract qualities. Los is not just a symbol for imagination. He is the Eternal Prophet, sometimes a moving character in himself, more often so when he is seen as acting in his "Sons," especially in Blake. In the accounts in Plates 21 and 22 (using Keynes's numeration in *Complete Writings*) of Milton and Los descending to him, we see Blake in his house in Lambeth stooping to do on his sandal, a shaft of sunlight falling from behind on his foot. Seeing "the infinite in all things" he experiences the sun as Los, Apollo the sun-god; feels the greatness and terror of his calling to be a poet-prophet. A way has opened into eternity along which he, now shod, must walk. Later the hitherto shadowy Ololon and Milton become real and touching when they descend, a virgin of 12 years and a severe and silent figure in black, into Blake's cottage garden at Felpham (Plates 37 and 38). At the end, as trumpets sound for Apocalypse, Blake falls terror-struck on his path, and wakes "to Resurrection and Judgement in the Vegetable Body" with his wife trembling at his side. In the combination of the vast and homely visions of eternity are directly experienced. A similar effect is produced in Plate 31, where the lark, leading the other birds, rises to sing a joyous song of morning, and the wild thyme and other flowers give up their scent, filling "the air with an innumerable Dance." The statement that in the centre of every flower "Eternity expands Its ever during doors" is given substance by rhythm and image. Lark and thyme have symbolic meanings, and retain their identities as bird and flower. Such effects are too rare. Too often the doctrine is insistently and repetitively stated; vision is not seen, as Blake knew it must be (*Jerusalem* 91:20–21), "in its Minute Particulars." Milton's solemn speeches are at odds with the self-annihilation they preach. The Los in Blake battles, not always successfully, with the Urizen in him.

A difficulty for most readers is the proliferation of symbolic characters, introduced abruptly without explanation, and of wide-ranging allusions. In the best passages the action shows and the images convey the essential meanings, which are then reinforced and extended by the allusions. One such is the encounter between Milton and Urizen in Plates 18:51–19:14. Urizen is associated with rocks, snows, freezing; he solidifies clay into marble; he pours icy fluid onto Milton's brain from his cold palm, trying to baptize him into his faith, into the acceptance of rigid, inhuman systems. Milton is encountering an aspect of himself, his own school-divine God. He resists by taking red clay and trying to make a human body for Urizen. His action is reminiscent of Christ's use of clay and spittle to restore sight to the blind man in John 9:6–7, as well as of the creation of Adam in Genesis 2:7. Other biblical allusions are to Mahanaim, where Jacob had a vision of angels (Genesis 32:1) before wrestling with God and seeing Him face to face; to Succoth, where Jacob built a house (Genesis 33:17); and to Beth Peor, where the Israelites rested before entering the Promised Land (Deuteronomy 3:29). The meaning grows as we meditate on these allusions, but is not totally dependent on them. But what are we to make of it when we are told that "Hand, Hyle and Coban surround" Milton "as / A girdle, Gwendolen and Conwenna as a garment woven / Of War and Religion"? These are mere names, not given any substance until *Jerusalem*, and then not much. Blake's belief in his inspiration—"the authors are in eternity"—makes him inconsiderate of his readers.

The confrontation of Milton and Urizen may be compared with that between narrator and Angel in *The Marriage of Heaven and Hell*. The earlier work has the greater exuberance and humour, the later more wisdom. The doctrine of contraries is now given substance. Urizen is to be redeemed, humanised. The wish to tumble down the sneaking villains is still present; but the new emphasis on forgiveness of sins and annihilation of the Selfhood offers a more hopeful path to salvation. Blake's vision never solidified into a system; his mythology is always changing. This is a source of difficulty (for instance, in *Milton* Satan is sometimes the old Satan who can be redeemed, sometimes the new Satan, a mere Negation) and of strength. Few will find "a perfect whole" in

Milton, but many may find the puzzling succession of visions more honest and exciting.

—P.H. Butter

THE MIRROR FOR MAGISTRATES.
Poetry, 1559 (and later revisions).

Editions

The Mirror for Magistrates, edited by Lily B. Campbell. 1938.
Parts Added to The Mirror for Magistrates, edited by Lily B. Campbell. 1946.

Critical Studies: *Tudor Conceptions of History and Tragedy in A Mirror for Magistrates* by Lily B. Campbell, 1936; "Recent Studies in *A Mirror for Magistrates*" by Jerry Leath Mills, in *English Literary Renaissance*, 9, 1979; "Modes of Perception in the *Mirror for Magistrates*" by Lawrence D. Green, in *Huntington Library Quarterly*, Spring 1981; "*The Mirror for Magistrates* and the Shape of the *De Casibus* Tragedy" by Paul Budra, in *English Studies*, August 1988.

Although singularly influential in the history of early modern English literature, the *Mirror for Magistrates* remains a relatively unexplored text. Granted, in most historical accounts it is duly noted as a major source for many of the historical tragedies of late 16th- and early 17th-century theater, and its complex progress as a printed book has received scrutiny from bibliographers. Formally, the work has been examined as a consequential step in the development of various literary genres (narrative poetry, dramatic monologue, historical mirror, and epyllion); a sprinkling of studies has marked its experimentation in both meter and diction, situating its poetics in a larger scheme of stylistic evolution. Criticism of the last 50 years has been reasonably consistent in perceiving the *Mirror* as a sturdy bridge between medieval *de casibus* tragedy and the more dazzling matter of late Elizabethan and Jacobean drama. But few modern commentators have found it a compelling piece of literature in view of dominant critical interests, and still fewer would support Sir Philip Sidney's aesthetic assessment as recorded in his *Defence of Poesy*: "I account the *Mirrour of Magistrates* meetely furnished of beautiful parts." Moralizing metrical monologues on the falls of great figures, except as these appear in the most admired examples of early modern drama, have tended not to arouse much critical admiration in the 20th century.

There are signs, however, of a new curiosity about this work, particularly as notions of history become more complicated and readings of historical texts more sophisticated. Its role in civic propaganda, as a tool for disseminating an authorized Tudor interpretation of prior political history, has begun to be noted. One of the most popular books of the 16th century, the *Mirror* offered a contemporary audience lessons in appropriate political behavior through its didactic and sometimes grisly narratives of retribution; recently, critics have begun to think about the possible intentions, contradictions, and effects of these narratives, their functions in a discourse of public responsibility. As Gary Waller reminds us in his *English Poetry of the Sixteenth Century*, the *Mirror* is in many ways representative of a ubiquitous literature that has until now been relegated to the margins of critical concern: "the bulk of the poetry extant from at least the first three-quarters of the sixteenth century is unremitting in the way it subordinated itself to the public needs of the regime." New critical questions have generated new critical foci, and the *Mirror* may prove to be a particularly useful point of investigation.

If attention to this work has been slow in coming, the problem may be attributable in part to the difficulty of grappling with the text *qua* text. The collection of narratives signalled by the title *Mirror for Magistrates* is not coherent, unified, and stable but unusually polymorphic and polygenetic, made up of various quantities and combinations of selectively revised stories by multiple authors in variant editions. Studies of provenance have relied heavily on the accounts given by author William Baldwin in his prefatory letters in the first edition (1559). In the epistle to the reader he explains that the book was originally conceived as an English continuation of Lydgate's *The Fall of Princes* (a 15th-century adaptation of Boccaccio's *De casibus virorum illustrium*). Approached about writing the narrative sequels, Baldwin in turn persuaded seven other writers to join him in composing the stories, whereupon it was determined that the best point of departure would be the reign of Richard II and that the tales would be derived from those of various English chroniclers. (These are identified later in the text as Fabyan, Hall, and Sir Thomas More.) The dedicatory epistle, "To the nobilitye," indicates that the work was begun and partially printed four years before its present publication, this prior production having been "hyndred by the lord Chauncellour that then was." Lily Campbell's critical edition of the *Mirror* cites bibliographical data which point to John Wayland as the printer who originally secured Baldwin's services and commenced the ill-fated printing; Campbell's hypothesis is that his edition was suppressed because of the book's clear reliance on Hall's chronicle, specifically banned in 1555. Thomas Marshe was to print the authorized first edition of 19 tragedies (without *The Fall of Princes*) and many of the expanded versions that came after.

In his dedicatory epistle Baldwin complains of having had many promises of help but little actual cooperation in the project, such that he has had to end the work abruptly "till the rest be ready: which with Gods grace (if I may have anye helpe) shall be shortly." All those who did contribute to the first anthology have yet to be definitively identified. Baldwin and George Ferrers are the only commissioned writers explicitly named within the edition. On the one extant leaf of text from the suppressed 1555 edition, a "master Chaloner," thought to have been Thomas Chaloner, is identified as the author of the monologue by Richard II, and a later edition attributes the tragedy of Owen Glendower to Thomas Phaer. The tale of Edward IV, an older poem serving as the conclusion of this group, is introduced as Skelton's. In 1563, this collection was reprinted with eight new tragedies: Ferrers's life of Somerset, Thomas Churchyard's story of Jane Shore, [John?] Dolman's "Hastings," Thomas Sackville's "Buckingham" with its impressive induction, Francis Seager's "Richard Plantagenet," [Humphrey?] Cavyl's "Blacksmith," and the tragedies of Lord Rivers and the poet Collingbourne. Why some of these tales, containing evidence that they were written before the reign of Elizabeth, were delayed until this point is not clear.

The edition of 1571 shows a reordering of the tragedies but no new ones, and in 1574 another edition with only minor variations was published as *The Last Parte of the Mirour for Magistrates*. In the same year, Thomas Marshe published a companion volume, entitled *The First Parte of the Mirour for Magistrates*, containing 16 tales of ancient Britons from Albanact to Nennius, all by the poet John Higgins. This volume, with one additional tale, was published in a subsequent edition in 1575, which we find occasionally bound with a reissue of the *Last Parte*. In 1578 a newly revised *Last Part* appeared with two additional tragedies, of Eleanor Cobham, Duchess of Gloucester, and Humphrey, Duke of Gloucester.

Also in 1578 appeared *The Seconde part of the Mirrour for Magistrates*, which consisted of 12 new tragedies composed by Thomas Blenerhasset, covering the period "From the conquest of Caesar, unto the commyng of Duke William the Conquerour." This effort to fill remaining historical gaps was not included, however, in a 1587 edition of the *Mirror* which connected Higgins's work, now expanded to a total of 40 tales, to the main corpus in a continuous format. In this volume four new tragedies were added to the 29 of the *Last Part*: the tragedy of Sir Nicholas Burdet, Churchyard's tale of Wolsey, and two old Scots narratives on James IV of Scotland and the Battle of Flodden Field. Thus, by 1587, the text of the *Mirror* had grown from 19 stories to 70, excluding the efforts of Blenerhasset.

Even then, however, the book was not to stabilize. In what critics uniformly agree to have been a disastrously muddled redaction, Richard Niccols combined the three sets of stories —drastically adding, cutting, and rewriting—and included work of his own—in a tome that appeared in print in 1610, 1619, 1620, and 1621.

When we talk of *The Mirror for Magistrates*, then, precisely what text do we mean? Critics taking a "purist" stance have attempted to define the *Mirror* as just those English tragedies which can be shown to have been part of Baldwin's original plan. In their view, the later additions tend to obscure and dilute the political aims of the earlier collection—especially the critique of specific contemporary political conduct through historical parallels. Others, pointing to early modern literary adaptations of work by Higgins and Blenerhasset, argue for a more inclusive view; some have observed that the earlier tales show a political ambivalence, a concern not only with the display of clear retributive justice but also with the exploration of fortune as accident or contingency. As suggested above, recent attention to the *Mirror* focuses less on editorial and authorial intention and more on the play of political ideologies through the various editions (including that of Niccols). The concern is to examine the role of this book in the development of Tudor state identity and increasing centralization.

The flux and diversity of *The Mirror for Magistrates*, its contradictions and complications, make it a rich field for further investigation. As literary and historical studies are increasingly integrated, and as new sets of critical questions are generated, we will no doubt see increasing scrutiny of its characterizations of people and power. And if increased attention may be said to benefit the literary artifacts of previous times, we may confidently predict that the fortunes of this text will rise.

—Janis Butler Holm

MR. PERRIN AND MR. TRAILL.
Novel by Hugh Walpole, 1911.

Subtitled *A Tragi-Comedy*, Hugh Walpole's third novel was written while he was still in his twenties. It probably owes less to his boyhood experiences at King's School, Canterbury, for which he retained a lifelong affection, than to the year he spent as a master at Epsom College shortly after leaving Cambridge. As for its literary origins, it may owe something to the school scenes in *David Copperfield* and other novels by Dickens; in its turn it set a fashion for novels and plays about school life of which later examples are James Hilton's *Goodbye Mr. Chips* and Terence Rattigan's *The Browning Version*.

The book was written in two months and completed on 4 September 1910. Publication followed on 25 January 1911. Walpole said that he "never knew an impulse to do something so strong," and according to his own account the idea for the story occurred to him one day as he was crossing the King's Road, Chelsea, on his way to the Court Theatre: "I was in the very middle of the King's Road when I suddenly saw Mr. Perrin staring at me. By the time that I had reached the Court Theatre, a brief five minutes, the whole of the story was outlined in my mind." The same account makes two other observations of interest. One is that "the Umbrella incident" was the germ of the narrative and was based on an actual incident (in the novel Traill's carelessness in taking Perrin's umbrella by mistake has far-reaching consequences and forms the pivot of its construction). The other is that Traill is "what I would have liked to be" and Perrin "what I thought I was." In response to Walpole's comment (in the preface to a 1935 reprint) that "As a matter of fact . . . I was neither" his biographer, Rupert Hart-Davis, retorts "As a matter of fact he was both."

As if to reinforce the first of these points, the original title was *The Umbrella*, successively rejected in favour of *The Brown Hill*, *Green-Apple Orchard*, and the final title. The American edition appeared as *The Gods and Mr. Perrin*.

The novel was a popular success and was admired by, among others, H.G. Wells and Arnold Bennett, the latter writing in an article on Walpole in 1914 that it showed "the hand of the born and consecrated novelist." Two of Walpole's friends, however, were less indulgent in their private comments. Robert Ross told him that he had made an "absurd" error of judgment in not allowing Traill to die at the end: "You were writing an 'unpleasant' story. Why didn't you stick to your art and ignore popularity?" Henry James, in a long letter of 15 April 1911, first praised the book's "life and beauty and reality," describing it as "represent[ing] a very marked advance on its predecessors," then proceeded to criticize it severely, finding one of the main characters a failure ("you . . . take such pains to demonstrate that Mr. Traill was, as a vessel of experience, absolutely *nil*"). In a subsequent letter James damned Walpole's heroine even more thoroughly ("I don't think your *girl* was really an experience of anybody's"). It cannot be said that these strictures are unfair, and Walpole was perhaps recalling them when he wrote in his journal long afterwards (1924) that in writing the book he had been "filled with" his subject, "Schoolmastering," "but the characters . . . were puppets to me." Another journal entry declares that it is the "truest" novel he ever wrote.

It was in the year after the publication of *Mr. Perrin and Mr. Traill* that James wrote to Walpole his famous letter insisting on the central importance of form and stigmatizing the kind of 19th-century novel that resembles a "tasteless tepid pudding." While it is true that Walpole's fluency often lapses into carelessness, he made a considerable effort in this novel to achieve dramatic concentration. The number of characters is relatively small, the setting is confined to one place, and the time-scheme restricted to a single school term, from September to Christmas. He successfully conveys the suffocating atmosphere of boarding school life, where tempers become more frayed and relationships deteriorate as the weeks go by, and the bitterness and malice of many of the schoolmasters (including the tyrannical and sadistic headmaster) is at times powerfully rendered. The main action concerns the feud that develops between two contrasting characters: Mr. Perrin, a lonely and unattractive bachelor who has spent 20 years at the school, and Mr. Traill, fresh from the university, enthusiastic and athletic, who falls in love and becomes engaged to the girl on whom Perrin has unrealistically had his eye.

The climax of the story, when Perrin first intends to murder his rival and then rescues him from drowning at the sacrifice of his own life, degenerates into melodrama and sentimentality, and the real strength of the story is in its presentation of mounting tension as trivial incidents fuel the resentment and antagonism bred in the claustrophobic atmosphere of an institution that seems to have excluded almost completely the rest of the world. Its most serious weakness is the psychological shallowness of the protagonists, though it is only fair to add that the conventions of Edwardian middle-class fiction imposed restrictions on, for example, a fuller exploration of the sexual origins of Perrin's unhappiness and his jealousy of the younger man.

Moffatt's, the third-rate public school that is the scene of the action, is located in Cornwall—partly to increase the sense of isolation, but also to discourage too ready identification with Epsom College. As a public school boy himself, Walpole makes it clear that his attack is not upon the system itself (as a character says in chapter 4, "the first-class public school . . . [is] a different kind of thing altogether") but on inferior institutions that unsuccessfully imitate their betters. Walpole's convictions, however, seem to be dictated less by a concern for educational reform than by snobbery (a characteristic also evident in his depiction of the "little science master" of working-class origins in chapter 8).

—Norman Page

MRS. DALLOWAY.
Novel by Virginia Woolf, 1925.

Mrs. Dalloway is perhaps Virginia Woolf's most widely read novel, sharing several traits with those other works of high modernism, Joyce's *Ulysses* and Eliot's *The Waste Land*. Set in one day in June 1923, and located in a small part of central London, it nevertheless brings in many characters, places, and other times and extradiegetic events through memory and association. It is in many ways a painful, emotionally searing novel which Woolf controls through adroit transitions in free indirect discourse, spatial and temporal jumps, interwoven stories, and complex ordering.

Clarissa Dalloway seems at first to be a unexceptionable character involved with trivial concerns: ordering flowers for her party that evening, fixing a dress, shopping. But she has reached certain boundaries of her life. The well-to-do wife of an M.P., she is 51 and has just recovered from an illness which left her with a lasting heart condition. She realizes that she cannot be at the center of her husband's concerns, as he rushes about London attending meetings and luncheons, and she has a poor relationship with her daughter Elizabeth, feeling she has lost her to the outcast tutor Miss Kilman. She is envious of the courageous Lady Bexborough and the politically involved Lady Bruton. She is worried about the success of the party that evening and from time to time she thinks of her old friend, Peter Walsh, who has returned temporarily to England after five years in India.

These different and minor concerns are given far greater depth than a summary can indicate by Woolf's technique (which is interior monologue or free indirect discourse rather than stream-of-consciousness). As we follow Clarissa in the course of her day, we see her perceptions and memories continually call to her mind the other characters at earlier key points in their lives: Sally Seton when she was an intellectual free spirit some 30 years earlier, or the moment when Clarissa chose to marry Richard Dalloway instead of Peter Walsh. Clarissa's personal sense of time is in constant tension with objective chronology (exemplified by the ringing of Big Ben breaking into Clarissa's thoughts, ordering her day, moving her onward to her party). Memories mix in fragments of other times; Clarissa's day is a synchronic passage.

Clarissa's story and thoughts are interwoven with the activities and thoughts of Septimus Warren Smith, a shell-shocked veteran of the war who sees his dead comrade, gets messages from trees, and hears the birds speak in Greek (a symptom of one of Woolf's own periods of breakdown). The preoccupations of the Dalloway circle are constantly juxtaposed with the mad thoughts of war-damaged Septimus and his fretful, torn Italian wife Lucrezia. An autodidact, he went to the war for England, for Shakespeare, for an ideal construction of English womanhood. After the death of his friend Evans, after he had congratulated himself for seeing so many die in the war, during the peace Septimus lost his mind.

His story and appearances undercut the satisfied and superior characters of the Dalloway circle for whom the war is an increasingly distant memory, something definitely over. Clarissa Dalloway's fragile mental state has been helped by her wealth and social position, by the little private room in which she reads and naps and cries, by the predictable sight of the old woman in an upstairs window across from her own house each evening, by her husband and doctor paternally protecting her. Septimus's doctors, on the other hand, tell him to buck himself up, that it doesn't look right for English manhood to tell his wife he wants to die; he is told to take up sports or a hobby, to rest, not to read poetry. Sir William Bradshaw, the expensive doctor Lucrezia consults, prepares to send him to a rest home in the countryside, and when Bradshaw comes to see Septimus he jumps from a window, impaling himself on the area railings.

Bradshaw is used as the point of connection between Clarissa and Septimus. Bradshaw is presented almost as a caricature of the British establishment: smug, decisive, judging normality by himself and his wife, condemning anyone who deviates from that norm. He attends Clarissa's party that evening and momentarily shocks everyone by speaking of Septimus's suicide, almost ruins everything, Clarissa thinks, because he brought death to her party. Clarissa must retire to gather strength from her props, and then she returns to stand at the top of the stairs in the triumphal moment which ends the book.

It has only been recently that Woolf criticism has begun to emphasize the social and historical dimensions of *Mrs. Dalloway*, treating the previously neglected areas of its satire and irony, the consciousness of class and gender, the foregrounding of various types of intolerance for differences, especially in the female characters (Sally Seton, Miss Kilman) and the men who are considered failures (such as Peter Walsh and Septimus), or considered the background of the war and its victims (both the immediate victims and those in the years after the war). *Mrs. Dalloway* has come to be seen less as a typical work by one of the few women writers studied in the modern British canon, and more as something continuous with the other major works of modernism.

—Leonard Orr

MRS. WARREN'S PROFESSION.
Play by Bernard Shaw, 1898.

In the 1902 preface to *Mrs. Warren's Profession* Bernard Shaw declares: "*Mrs. Warren's Profession* was written in 1894 to draw attention to the truth that prostitution is caused, not by female depravity and male licentiousness, but simply by underpaying, undervaluing, and overworking women so shamefully that the poorest of them are forced to resort to prostitution to keep body and soul together" (*Plays Unpleasant*). Elaborating further on his authorial intentions, Shaw directs attention to two of the play's social subplots: in letters he explains the importance and integrity of "incest episodes"; and in the 1902 preface he introduces an analogy between the censorship *of* his play and the censorship *within* his play.

Although most critics do not accept "Shaw on Shaw" wholeheartedly, they generally take their cue from him. Thus, critical analyses of *Mrs. Warren's Profession* almost always foreground discussion of the play's indictment of society as responsible for prostitution, often make reference to its suggestion that prostitution may lead to incest and occasionally comment on its exposure of society's self-censorship. Highlighting both causes and effects of the profession/occupation of prostitution, these readings pay scant attention to other possible meanings of the word "profession." While aware of the thematic importance of "profession" *as* "occupation," I want to focus on the play's manipulation of two other meanings of the word "profession": 1) "to declare openly, announce, affirm; to avow, acknowledge, confess"; 2) "to lay claim to, often implying insincerity; to make protestation of; to pretend to" (*Oxford English Dictionary*, vol. 7, 1888). Curiously, the two definitions undermine each other. The first suggests a full disclosure; the second denies such disclosure, insisting that declarations, affirmations, and avowals involve pretense and withholding. Throughout Shaw's play, characters simultaneously reveal/conceal themselves, making pretense of profession. This repeated dynamic necessitates a re-assessment of the play's final, seemingly positive act of profession: Vivie's declaration that she will pursue her work.

The play's first important example of a profession undermined is Mrs. Warren's revelation to Vivie of how and why she chose to support herself through prostitution and brothel-keeping. Rather than work herself to death in a lead factory for the economic benefit of its owner, Mrs. Warren works for herself; she sells her looks, and puts in a claim for openness with regard to how she has managed: "Whats the use in such hypocrisy? If people arrange the world that way for women, theres no good pretending it's arranged the other way." Impressed with such forthrightness, Vivie embraces this "unmentionable woman" as her mother—until Crofts, in Act III, reveals the partial nature of Mrs. Warren's profession: she spoke in past tense when she should have been using present. Thus, in Act IV, Vivie dismisses her mother, pointing to what has been concealed in her revelation: "You explained how it came about. You did not tell me that it is still going on."

Similarly partial is Crofts's profession with regard to this business. Wooing Vivie, he discusses the business in which he and Mrs. Warren are partners: "Of course you know by your mother's being in it that it's perfectly straight and honest. . . . I dont know whether youve found in travelling how hard it is to find a really comfortable private hotel. . . . Well, thats all it is." But that's not "all it is" and when Vivie comments that she knows the nature of this business because her mother told her, Crofts curses, "The old——." He smothers the damning epithet, just as he has attempted to smother the more unsavory aspects of his interaction with Mrs. Warren—while supposedly telling Vivie "all about it." Crofts makes one other profession of importance. Before leaving the stage to Vivie and Frank, he introduces Frank to Vivie as his "half-sister, the eldest daughter of the Reverend Samuel Gardner." We have no way of testing the truth of this profession, but given Crofts's motivation to lie, it makes sense to read this as yet another example of profession as pretense.

We might expect honest declaration from the Reverend Gardner, but he too disappoints. With regard to the paternity of Vivie, he provides Frank with a statement "tantamount to a denial"—a statement to be distinguished from real denial.

In different ways, both Frank and Praed also enact duplicitous professions, one espousing "love's young dream" (while unwilling to live on money made from the underside of this dream), the other espousing the "Gospel of Art" (without any awareness of how this Art supports itself).

More unsettling than any of these professions-turned-pretense, however, is Vivie's announcement in Act IV that she does not "want to be worthless." She says to her mother, "I am like you: I must have work. . . . But my work is not your work, and my way is not your way." We may be inclined to read Vivie's profession here as the positive assertion of a morally responsible woman; she will put in her hours at the office, support herself, earn more than she spends. But just as the professions of all other characters contain an element of pretense, so too Vivie's declaration: her work and her way are very much akin to her mother's. As an actuary, computing insurance risks and premiums, Vivie provides the icing on capitalism's cake; ironically, she is as deeply enmeshed in buying and selling of lives and in speculating upon bodies as is her mother. According to Shaw's final stage direction, Vivie "goes at her work with a plunge, and soon becomes absorbed in its figures." The nature of these figures should disturb us, as should Vivie's "absorption." Her profession about the "worthiness of work" includes no mandate for assessing the nature of one's work, evaluating ways in which it sustains or challenges social and economic structures. Finally, Vivie's profession, like all others in the play, represses as much as it reveals.

—Madonne M. Miner

MODERN LOVE.
Poem by George Meredith, 1862.

This sequence of 50 16-line stanzas exhibits the skills of a poet who was also a novelist. It tells the coherent, well-motivated story of a failed marriage, and has the novelistic elements of psychological analysis, a setting in contemporary social life, a conflict-driven plot, and well-defined scenes of action and conversation. The husband who is the narrator through most of the poem is a romantic who suffers disillusionment when his wife is unfaithful, and resorts to brutality and cynicism. The poem's exposure of the couple's jealousy, hypocrisy, and hostility to each other might be regarded as a response to the Victorian idealization of love in such works as the Brontës' novels and the ordinary love lyrics of the period. Its observation that "Passions spin the plot" is not a romantic assertion that feelings are primary, but a condemnation of irresponsible emotion, for the next line reads, "We are betrayed by what is false within."

The autobiographical element of *Modern Love* is unmistakable. Nine years after George Meredith married Mary Nicholls, the widowed daughter of Thomas Love Peacock, she was unfaithful to him, like the wife in the poem, and, like her, died unhappily, though not as a suicide, the year before the poem appeared. It seems certain that Meredith himself experienced many of the feelings his narrator expresses, though the actual events of the marital disaster were not the same.

Modern Love is not a continuous story, but rather a series of scenes and moods that outlines a sequence of events clearly enough. There are no transitions between the stanzas, which shift abruptly in mood and setting, achieving effects of startling directness. The poem opens with a stanza describing the couple lying side by side in bed and suffering from the consciousness of their alienation from each other. As it continues, the husband displays conflicting feelings, saying that he knows of his wife's infidelity, and is tempted to denounce her or even to punish her, but cannot act in this way because he still loves her. One dramatic, tightly-woven stanza describes a scene in which the husband wakes his wife to confront her with letters she has written to her lover. Intricate ironies arise as the two pretend to be on their usual terms, both when they are alone and when they are in company. The meditations on morality, human nature, and self-respect that punctuate the narrative achieve considerable originality because they reflect the conflict between the husband's cynicism and his effort to adhere to conventional idealism. His state of mind is rendered complex as he thinks of a love affair of his own, and wonders if he has the right to feel aggrieved.

In an effort to find consolation, the husband turns to another woman, who is described as beautiful and witty, but she does not satisfy his romantic ideals, and their relationship is a superficial one: "I am approved / It is not half so nice as being loved . . ." The social comedy that characterizes Meredith's novels appears as the wife and mistress meet, and praise each other's weakest points. But the unspoken hostilities of the occasion make the scene an act in the husband's tragedy. He believes he is in love with his mistress, but nevertheless feels jealousy when he sees his wife with another man, and recalls the intensity of his first love. There is a movement toward reconciliation, which no doubt reflects the effort of Meredith's wife to come back to him, but a night spent together seems only to put the seal on their alienation from each other. Nevertheless, a frank talk in a natural setting as they walk along the shore restores confidence between the two, and even love—"The hour became her husband and my bride." But, in a swift denouement, the wife takes poison and is found dead on the seashore, and the husband believes she has killed herself in order to free him to go to the other woman.

Modern Love develops its psychological insights with a sophistication, realism, and irony that are seen elsewhere in Victorian poetry only in the work of Robert Browning and Arthur Hugh Clough. The stanzas vary in tone as the husband's feelings fluctuate among grief, resentment, remorse, and contempt. He has a good sense of his wife's feelings, and realizes that she is undergoing a conflict much like his own; in spite of their animosities, the two are seen to feel pity for each other.

The language of the poem is direct and economical, much of it imitative of actual speech. The complex psychological states of the people are conveyed through remarkable images, many of them employing birds and animals. The stanza beginning "Love ere he bleeds, an eagle in high skies," depicts the husband's change of feeling through a little allegory in which the eagle of love is struck by an arrow, and can only drag along the ground, shedding drops of blood, thus becoming transformed into a serpent. The husband applies the allegory in this way: "I had the eagle in my bosom erst: / Henceforward with the serpent I am cursed."

The poem's narrative point of view shifts in a puzzling way. The opening and closing stanzas are spoken in the third person, as though by an objective narrator, while most of the other stanzas are the husband's speech, though some of these slip into a third-person mode, and some of the stanzas of general observation or reflection might be assigned either to the husband or the narrator. Some critics think these represent two figures, but there is also the view that the husband shifts his perspective from time to time in telling his story. In spite of this instability, there are no sharp discrepancies among the attitudes expressed by the different voices. All find the mysteries of love unfathomable, and would agree with the lament of the impersonal narrator in the last stanza,

> Ah, what a dusty answer gets the soul
> When hot for certainties in this our life!

—Jacob Korg

MODERN PAINTERS.
Prose by John Ruskin, 1843–60.

John Ruskin is above all a teacher; *Modern Painters* his pedagogical *magnum opus*. Beginning as a brief defence of Turner's art, it grew to five lengthy volumes, where, in order to offer his defensive interpretation of Turner's painting Ruskin interprets painting and the arts in general, nature, man, and society. A moral task begun in the fervour (and language) of evangelical faith, it continues after the loss of that faith, in the fervour of faith in the value and potential of human life.

Ruskin begins by setting down the principles of his criticism—what defines the greatest art: ideas of power, imitation, beauty, relation, and most importantly, truth to nature. Turner had been criticised for lacking this last, yet Ruskin believed him to possess it above all modern painters. Thus he argued that neither Turner's art nor nature had been accurately seen. *Modern Painters* is an attempt to teach readers to see the art properly. But before he can teach us to see truth to nature, Ruskin must teach us to see nature. Accordingly, as great Renaissance artists studied every detail of anatomy, Ruskin begins with a study of nature in its finest, even scientific, detail, under the headings beauty in clouds and truth in clouds, and so on. Lack of knowledge is a handicap in seeing; of clouds for instance we do not know what makes them float, how they are coloured, nor how they are outlined. These discussions, of skies, mountains, trees, leaves, the stamen of plants, always referring to nature and to Turner, are often technical, but the exposition is always clear. Ruskin not only teaches us to see nature, but, in order that we might see, to draw and paint. Thus prepared, we can be taught to see Turner's work—which has throughout been our constant reference.

The conclusion of the whole matter lies in the last chapters of the fifth and final volume. These contain detailed exegeses of Turner's *The Garden of the Hesperides* and *Apollo Slaying the Python*. Ruskin not only interprets the paintings to the external sight, but also iconographically and mythologically to the inward, applying the themes thereby discovered to the state of contemporary England in the style of an Old Testament prophet exhorting a people to repentance and change in prose of considerable poetic power. *Modern Painters* has taught us to see with our eyes, but also to see the inwardness of art, to understand, and to see its significance for ourselves and our culture. The connections between the interpretation of art and society are many, but we may summarise thus: if we cannot see the truth of nature and art we fail also to see accurately the nature, and hence the political and economic organisation, of ourselves and our fellows. This theme is brought to a head in the final chapter. It is often expressed in terms of seeing and interpreting: "the things to be desired for man in a healthy state, are that he should not see dreams but realities; that he should not destroy life, but save it; and that he should not be rich, but content." Again, in terms of understanding art: "in order to teach men how to be satisfied, it is necessary fully to understand the art and joy of humble life." Education is a form of interpretation itself, "developing or 'drawing out' the human soul." As often in English criticism the critical and aesthetic point becomes a moral one. Not power and mastery—the laws of the Devil—but understanding (seeing) and love—the laws of "God walking in the garden at cool of day." An economical system built on the assumption that men are self-seeking will make men brutish in its service; economists who believe only that law have failed to see nature (in this case man) accurately. To these blind leaders Ruskin writes: "you shall have death's crown, with the worm coiled in it; and death's wages with the worm feeding on them; kindred of the earth shall you yourself become; saying to the grave, 'Thou art my father'; and to the worm, "Thou art my mother and my sister.'"

Ruskin conducts the book as a logically sound treatise: every point is to be established conclusively from first principles. This veneer lends a diffuse book a superb controlling organisation, but is deceptive. Ruskin's technique is to make a series of assertions, and then to argue from them. Why we should accept these assertions is not apparent to a critical or unsympathetic reader. And quite why in strict logic we should accept other dubious points such as some of Ruskin's definitions, etymologies, mythological interpretations, and just plain pronouncements, is also unclear. But Ruskin teaches that there are other techniques of persuasion than logic, and other ways of arriving at truth. He is a teacher in the highest sense of the word: a sage. There is a suggestion of prophecy and poetry about his prose. Ruskin's rhetorical tropes are those of the preacher; one who aims not to convince by logic, but to speak truths and to convict. The making of the following minor point is typical: "It is red to which the colour-blind are blind, as if to show us that it was not necessary merely for the service or comfort of man, but that there was a special gift or teaching in this colour." The logic cannot establish the point; nor does the point need to be thus established. Ruskin is illustrating and explicating, not proving; teaching, not deducing; convicting, not convincing. The "as if" is here sufficient.

This illustrates the most important characteristic of the book. It is not primarily a logical treatise, it is a work of criticism, and, as all good criticism, its techniques of argument are servants to its insight. It is full of the insight and wisdom of learning and experience, whether it be in the seeing of nature or art, the technique of representing truth to nature, the history and moral relevance of art, the reading of a particular painting, or above all in the seeing of human nature, life, and institutions. We may fail to trace a purely logical thread, but we do not miss prophetic insight, exhortation, and abundant wealth of fertile ideas. We learn, too, a great deal about painting, about seeing, and about nature. We are wise to come now to *Modern Painters* with reservations, but it teaches despite them.

—J.B. Lethbridge

A MODEST PROPOSAL.
Prose by Jonathan Swift, 1729.

The "modest" proposal is that the children of the Irish poor should be fattened until they are one year old, and then butchered and eaten. The 10 pages of dispassionate economic argument in which Jonathan Swift advances this proposal are among the most shocking pages in English literature and perhaps its foremost example of irony.

Swift's pamphlet is built upon the adage that desperate diseases require desperate remedies: if this is the only remedy, the patient is sick indeed. The Dean of St. Patrick's Cathedral in Dublin since 1713, Swift was an indignant observer of the Irish nation's exploitation: in his eyes, the Irish were being eaten alive by their English rulers. His pamphlet simply takes this somewhat trite metaphor and advocates it with deadpan literalness. English landlords, "as they have already devoured most of the parents, seem to have the best Title to the Children." England is referred to late in the pamphlet as "a Country which would be glad to eat up our whole Nation without [Salt]."

This cannibalistic conceit is presented ironically, through an imaginary speaker, a persona capable of conceiving and arguing for such a plan. Swift wrote about two dozen pamphlets on the state of Ireland between 1728 and 1733, but whereas the others, now forgotten, present straightforward arguments in propria persona, *A Modest Proposal* is ostensibly the work of a "projector"—a private citizen who proposes sweeping schemes for public benefit. Like Swift's most famous persona, Dr. Lemuel Gulliver of *Gulliver's Travels*, the projector is a materialist, a man of modern science. He is, however, unlike Gulliver, a theorist and a social scientist. He is a utilitarian, always pointing to the larger public good, and as a social scientist he brings scientific methods of reasoning to bear upon human ills. He thus relies upon precise statistics, deadening and neutral scientific language ("It is true a Child, just dropt from its Dam, may be supported by her Milk, for a

Solar Year"), and the passive voice (only children should be slaughtered, he explains, since the Irish adults are dying "as fast as can reasonably be expected").

In short, the disease that Swift diagnoses is not so much addressed by the speaker as embodied in him: it is his ghastly and naive inhumanity that is at the root of the problem. His complacent inability to see what he is advocating is a measure of the general failure to see, and it is Swift's purpose to shock us into seeing in his blindness an image of our own.

This blindness is especially evident in the full title and in the opening and closing paragraphs of the pamphlet. Its full title is *A Modest Proposal for Preventing the Children of Poor People in Ireland, from being a Burden to their Parents or Country; and for making them beneficial to the Publick* (similarly, later in the tract the modest proposer says that mothers will be "sure of a Settlement for Life, to the poor Babes"). The enormous ironies in these bland terms are underlined in the pamphlet's opening sentences: there the speaker feelingly describes the misery evident on the streets of Dublin and concludes, "whoever could find out a fair, cheap, and easy Method of making these Children sound and useful Members of the Commonwealth, would deserve so well of the Publick, as to have his Statue set up for a Preserver of the Nation." With preservers like this, who needs destroyers?

A deeper irony also emerges here: the proposer is just as immodest as his proposal. His vision is of himself as a hero as much as it is of the commonwealth preserved. He is, of course, entirely unaware of this egotism; in fact, it is his monstrously inadequate conception of selfishness that makes his final sentence so beautifully ironic: "I profess, in the Sincerity of my Heart, that I have not the least personal Interest, in endeavouring to promote this necessary Work; having no other Motive than the Publick Good of my Country, by advancing our Trade, providing for Infants, relieving the Poor, and giving some Pleasure to the Rich. I have no Children, by which I can propose to get a single penny; the youngest being nine years old, and my Wife past Child-bearing."

In its form, Swift's pamphlet is lucidly logical. Step by step, the speaker outlines the problem, defines his solution, shows its benefits (both direct and indirect), considers and dismantles the obvious objections, shows his proposal's superiority to other measures, and concludes with a modest disclaimer. Of course, the surface logic only accentuates the irrationality and barbarity beneath this bland surface. In the same way, in the pivotal sentence of the essay, the one in which the modest proposal is actually stated for the first time, devious syntax and studied wording almost succeed in concealing the meaning: "I have been assured by a very knowing American of my Acquaintance in London, that a young healthy Child, well nursed, is at a year old, a most delicious, nourishing, and wholesome Food; whether Stewed, Roasted, Baked, or Boiled; and, I make no doubt, that it will equally serve in a Fricasie, or Ragoust."

Furthermore, the many benefits adduced with wonderful ingenuity by the projector allow Swift to anatomize the diseased body politic. Once again, the cures highlight the disease: "Thus the Squire will learn to be a good Landlord, and grow popular among his Tenants. . . . The poorer Tenants would have something valuable of their own, which, by Law, may be made liable to Distress, and help to pay their Landlord's Rent. . . . Men would become as fond of their Wives during their Pregnancy, as they are now of their Mares in Foal."

Swift quite deliberately lets the ironic mask slip near the end of the essay. His projector has just made what he considers a climactic point: if it is undeniable that his scheme will lessen the population of Ireland, that is in fact its designed and primary advantage. The projector then says, "Therefore, let no man talk to me of other Expedients: . . ." and proceeds to list about a dozen very practical measures, such as a tax upon absentee landlords. These measures were printed in italics in the original editions, and they were the very proposals that Swift was making at this time in his non-ironic pamphlets. This list of positive expedients completes the undermining of the projector, climaxes the argument-by-inversion, and forces us to realize that the ironist's mask of black humour is used in the service of committed and humane values. We have not been simply sporting with horrors. Human action can and should change human ills—and once that is grasped this ostensibly reasonable man and his apparently logical proposal are all the more horrifying.

—Bruce Stovel

MOLL FLANDERS.
(*The Fortunes and Misfortunes of the Famous Moll Flanders.*)
Fiction by Daniel Defoe, 1722.

Moll Flanders was first published in 1722, and may be counted among the earliest of novels in English. The term "novel," however, should be applied to this work with some caution; much of the interest of *Moll Flanders* lies in Daniel Defoe's blurring of the distinctions between autobiography and novel, and between fact and fiction.

To see how circumspect with the term "novel" Defoe himself is, we need look no further than the opening lines: "The World is so taken up of late with Novels and Romances that it will be hard for a private History to be taken for Genuine. . . ." But Defoe's protestations that the story can be taken as a true record, only leave the reader wondering in what sense this narrative can be taken as true or real. The narrator asks us to accept the story as Moll's own, as told by her, but freely admits to having made some alterations in the text—the location and extent of which he does not disclose.

Even if we accept Moll as the novel's narrator, it is difficult accurately to identify the narrative voice. The Moll who does the narrating often seems to be inconsistent with her younger self who enacts the adventures. The young Moll's financial fortunes fluctuate wildly and she spends much of the novel living by her wits in the London criminal underworld. The older Moll lives a life of financial security in Virginia. The older Moll frequently, and emphatically, regrets her former immoral activities, but just as often she ignores or excuses them.

Defoe uses this double narrative time scheme in order to impede any easy moral judgment on the reader's part. A good example of this is the episode in which Moll steals a child's necklace. The older Moll, looking back and reflecting on the event, introduces it as a matter of grave moral significance: "the Devil put a Snare in my way of a dreadful Nature indeed." But in the story that follows, the narrating Moll is absorbed into the very detailed and immediate account of the adventure, which we experience with the *younger* Moll who is enacting it. By the time Moll has described in detail her route through London, considered the value of the necklace, and speculated on the culpability of the child's parents for letting "the poor little Lamb" out alone, the original observations of the older Moll, about the devilish nature of the deed, seem to have been forgotten and she comments "However, I did the Child no harm."

The way in which Moll recounts her adventures is highly plausible. She tells us episodes as they occur to her, in a roughly chronological sequence. The novel is not intricately plotted; Moll's manner of narration is anecdotal, complete with incidental circumstances, interjections, and outbursts. Moll's method of storytelling is persuasive; she seems to be very close to the reader. But this familiarity is deceptive.

In many ways we do not have a clear picture of the heroine of *Moll Flanders*. What is her real name? What are the names of her children? We are not told what she looks like—she can appear older or younger than her actual years. She is attractive as a woman, but can pass as a man. We find out more about the value of the goods Moll steals than about the woman herself. In fact, we know very little about the facts which normally give an individual their social identity.

Moll is as interested in money as she is in love or sex. At the older brother's attempt to seduce her she remarks "My Colour came and went, at the Sight of the Purse, and with the fire of his Proposal together." She is genuinely fond of her banker husband, but his function as a banker is of as great importance to her as his affection. Money is the gauge by which Moll judges all her activities.

In this way, the novel interacts with the early 18th-century society in which it was written. Defoe reveals, through Moll, not only the kind of necessity that drives the urban poor to a life of crime, but also the kind of society which allows Moll to prosper. The success of a mercantile class had made social distinctions, previously based on hereditary rank, open to the influence of money. Social identities became fluid; money could bring power and prestige.

Moll's social identity is unfixed because she uses it in a system of trade, selling sex, affection, or the goods she steals. She moves through social degrees—a prostitute, the wife of a banker, a successful plantation owner—not primarily in order to gain respect, but to accrue capital and finally to attain her professed goal of financial security.

—Penelope Fielding

MOLLOY, MALONE DIES, and **THE UNNAMABLE.**
Novels by Samuel Beckett, 1955–58 (in French, as *Molloy*, *Malone meurt*, and *L'Innommable*, 1951–53).

The trilogy *Molloy* (1955), *Malone Dies* (1956), and *The Unnamable* (1958) is the culmination of Samuel Beckett's experimentation in prose fiction. The aforementioned dates are those of Beckett's own translations of the works into English, though they were originally written in French and published in Paris, the first two in 1951 and the last in 1953. Beckett himself has said that he began writing in French because the language had a softening or weakening effect upon the edge of his prose style, and even further "*en française c'est plus facile d'écrire sans style*." Whatever the case, the trilogy is certainly a concerted attack upon the conventions of fiction, upon style, narration, character, and closure. To some, it represents the exhaustion of language, since, as the novels evolve, and page piles upon page, language becomes stripped of its properties of both denotation and connotation.

In *Molloy*, the reader is immediately plunged into uncertainty by a first-person narrator who is not at all sure of his own identity and a narrative that consistently curls about itself and refuses to move forward in any definite direction. It would seem that the speaker is indeed Molloy, sitting in his mother's room and writing, controlled by a sinister man who appears each week to pick up completed pages and leave a designated amount of money, but with none of this can Molloy be completely at ease. The story he tells has to do with a proposed visit to his mother, whom he calls Mag while she calls him Dan, though this is not his name, a mother with whom he communicates by rapping with his fist upon her skull. Though he is never to arrive at his mother's house, Molloy becomes embroiled in a series of adventures on his journey, wheeling himself along with crutches on a chainless bicycle. Soon enough, he runs over and kills a little dog belonging to a woman known only as Lousse, who imprisons him for an indeterminate length of time. The reader clings to details such as these in the hope that the narrative mists will lift, only to find that Molloy will somehow escape to continue on his way, sucking pebbles from the beach, staggering and crawling toward oblivion. "All I know is what the words know, and the dead things, and that makes a handsome little sum, with a beginning, a middle and an end."

The second section of *Molloy* makes it clear that Beckett is intent upon the destruction of logic, of undermining the relationship of cause and effect. If Descartes could assert that "*Cogito ergo sum*," Beckett might reply that "*Cogito ergo cogito*." Now a man named Jacques Moran, with a son also named Jacques, receives a message from an envoy named Gaber, sent by someone named Youdi, to embark upon a quest for Molloy. What Moran is to do when he finds Molloy, what he is to say or how he is to proceed, is left unspecified. Moran will never reach Molloy, but during Moran's travels he more and more begins to resemble the quarry he has been dispatched to snare. The second section of *Molloy* becomes a dark mirror of the first. Moran's legs will stiffen, he will procure a bicycle and become lost in a dark forest, and finally Gaber will send him home to where he began. There he will sit down to write, as the narrative comes full circle, but with a difference. The section's opening: "It is midnight. The rain is beating on the windows," is repeated and counterstated by its conclusion: "It is midnight. The rain is beating on the windows. It was not midnight. It was not raining." The overt contradiction of the sentences leaves both the speaker and the reader in a quandary that cannot be satisfied in a conventionally logical or fictional way. If we cannot look outward to character delineation and plot resolution for a solution, then we must remain at the mercy of a voice that continues to tell stories simply for the sake of their telling.

We are left in all three novels with a Beckettian voice whose characteristics constantly reinforce the need and the impossibility of communication. Slowly but surely shorn of all physical capabilities as the fictions roll on (the narrator of *The Unnamable* is an indecipherable creature sitting in a jar), Beckett's speaking entity who seems to be searching for silence is paradoxically notable for his garrulousness. The words pour forth from him in waves, and single paragraphs that go on for several pages indicate an urgency that simply will not allow a pause. This voice is self involved and self reflexive, grotesquely comic, yet it has no direction. It is prone to asides and qualifications, assertions and their opposites, contradictions and complaints. It can begin stories, but it cannot seem to end them, if it had any intention of doing so in the first place. It is aware of its fictional contemporaries like Murphy, Watt, Mercier, and Camier, and will call them by name, but it does not remember their histories. Gradually, it becomes apparent that all the voices in the trilogy are but aspects of a single consciousness, whether it be titled Molloy, Moran, Malone, Mahood, or Worm, all alter egos of the aptly named Unnamable.

Malone of *Malone Dies* is a case in point. Confined to a bed in what appears to be an insane asylum, Malone controls his environment with a long, hooked stick that enables him to manipulate objects in his room, while he writes in a notebook with a tiny stub of pencil. With nothing to look forward to but death, he has decided to while away the time by constructing fictions. "I think I shall be able to tell myself four stories, each one on a different theme. One about a man, another about a woman, a third about a thing and finally one about an animal, a bird probably." Yet he is incapable of living up to his plan. Beginning with a tale about a serious young man named Saposcat or Sapo, Malone is diverted to a description of oafish farmers named Lambert, but even this is not to be completed. The writer cannot carry on with the narrative thread. "In his country the problem—no, I can't do it. The peasants. His visits to. I can't." Soon Sapo has metamorphosed into Macmann, a creature who bears an eerie resemblance both to Malone himself and to Molloy. Awakening in an Irish asylum called the House of Saint John of God, Macmann will end up on a bizarre boating excursion, sponsored by the institution's wealthy patron Lady Pedal, that is interrupted by a murderous attack on the party by the brutal attendant Lemuel, wielding a hatchet.

This brief synopsis makes the narrative seem somewhat coherent, which it is not, but the twisted absurdity of the events serves to emphasize the nihilistic cosmos in which Beckett's characters exist. Malone's last words, uttered in a prose that has lapsed into incoherence, reflect the chaos that has overwhelmed his thought processes. "Or light light I mean never there he will never anything there any more." The circularity of the journeys of the characters necessitates an endless repetition to which each of the speakers is doomed. They are launched upon expeditions to nowhere, trapped in a language that has lost its meaning, enslaved by a world that has passed into sterility. Perhaps the most obvious question to ask is why they do not cease the struggle and give up, accepting silence as a refuge, if not an acceptance of what is. Malone provides at least a partial answer. "Live and invent. I have tried. I must have tried. Invent. It is not the word. Neither is live. No matter. I have tried."

What allows Beckett's characters a good measure of nobility, despite their squalid surroundings, is that they decline the option of becoming mute, even in a world where they assume that no one is listening. No matter how much their physical surroundings may deny them the luxury of freedom of movement, still Molloy, Malone, the Unnamable, and their fellows retain their freedom of choice. There is no outside force or evil entity that forces them to write, to express themselves, and their manuscripts are testaments to their refusal to bow down before a nonsensical world. The Unnamable will retire from the struggle only in his own time and on his own terms, as he declares "The search for the means to put an end to things, an end to speech, is what enables the discourse to continue." It would seem that only death can put an end to the discourse, and even then the trilogy indicates that the place of one defunct Beckett speaker will immediately be taken by yet another. The Unnamable reminds himself: "you must go on, I can't go on, you must go on, I'll go on, you must say words, as long as there are any." In its own bleak way, the trilogy is a tribute to the resilience of the human spirit in a universe gone mad.

—Michael H. Begnal

THE MONK.
Novel by Matthew Gregory Lewis, 1796.

Written in 10 weeks by a 19-year-old embassy attaché, *The Monk* was an instant and sensational success. The author (whose identity was revealed in the second edition as M.G. Lewis, M.P.—now just 21) became known and lionized as "Monk" Lewis, despite complaints from several quarters about the unsuitability of the work as the product of an M.P., and threats (never realized) of prosecution for obscenity and blasphemy. Lewis's story certainly contained plenty of material to offend the British clergy, despite its setting in Madrid under the Inquisition; lust and ambition run riot among the supposedly holy Capuchins and the Sisters of St. Clare. The eponymous monk, Ambrosio, brought up by the Capuchins on whose doorstep he was left as an infant, has risen to become Abbot through his singular holiness, profound knowledge, and outstanding oratory; but, like Shakespeare's Angelo in *Measure for Measure* (to whom Lewis refers in an epigraph), his apparently impregnable virtue is not proof against the attractions of a beautiful young woman. Ambrosio's fall, which involves him in sorcery, rape, incest, and murder, is the result both of his monastic upbringing, which allowed "every vice which had fallen to his share, to arrive at full perfection," and of demonic intervention.

The novel provides the double thrill of transvestism and sacrilege, when the novice Rosario, whose company Ambrosio so enjoys, seems at first to be a besotted young woman, Matilda, the spitting image of the beautiful Madona whose portrait Ambrosio worships (not without carnal stirrings). Ambrosio surrenders to temptation, but soon tires of Matilda, despite her lasciviously described sexual skill, and falls obsessively in love with the innocent Antonia, who is drawn to him (emotionally rather than sexually) without understanding why. Enlisting Matilda's aid he attempts to seduce Antonia through black magic, killing her mother, Elvira, when she foils the attempt. He then drugs, kidnaps, and finally rapes Antonia in a vault among the decomposing corpses of nuns, killing her to prevent her rescue by, and marriage to, Lorenzo. After suffering the extremest tortures of the Inquisition, he sells his soul to the devil to escape execution, incidentally discovering that Matilda is in fact a demon in human shape, sent to lead him to destruction. The devil gloatingly informs him that Antonia was his sister and Elvira his mother; Ambrosio attempts, too late, to repent, and dies a protracted and horrible death.

Ambrosio's lack of compassion for Lorenzo's sister, the unfortunate Agnes, however, has already placed him as a villain before he succumbs to attraction for Matilda; indeed, what happens to him is partly a consequence of the pregnant Agnes's curse when he betrays her attempt to escape from the strict convent of St. Clare. The sadistic Prioress, furious with Agnes for disgracing the convent in the opinion of the austere Ambrosio, derives obvious satisfaction from faking Agnes's death and imprisoning her in a vault below the convent, with only lizards, toads, and the putrefying corpse of her illegitimate child for company. (The narrator derives apparently equal satisfaction from recounting the death of the Prioress, torn limb from limb and trampled underfoot by the angry mob raised by Lorenzo, who storms the convent to rescue his sister, by now nearly starved to death.) Agnes nevertheless recovers to marry her lover, Raymond, whom only family treachery and supernatural intervention had separated from her in the first place.

As the summary suggests, *The Monk* is a lurid tale, abounding with prophetic dreams, exotic drugs, enchantments, magic mirrors, and ridiculed superstitions coming horribly true; when Raymond and Agnes attempt to turn the local legend of the Bleeding Nun to their own advantage, the real Bleeding Nun puts in an appearance and proceeds to dog Raymond wherever he goes until he finds out how to exorcise her. There is an element of adolescent nastiness in the narrative, dwelling lovingly on grotesque details of putrefaction and torture. But despite the obviousness of Lewis's desire to shock, *The Monk* is genuinely shocking. Where Ann Radcliffe's novels raised the spectre of incest only to veer away from it at the last minute, Lewis makes incest and matricide central to his protagonist's fate. The supernatural has far more than a merely atmospheric role to play in Lewis's novel, and he is not afraid to make Lucifer appear in the dungeons of the Inquisition to bargain for Ambrosio's soul (though with characteristic irony he makes Lucifer renege on his side of the deal, since Ambrosio fails to read the small print before signing in blood). Unlike Radcliffe, Lewis does not bend the supernatural to the laws of rationality, but allows them to coexist as equally important systems. Ambrosio's fate is overdetermined: original sin, education, environment, the corrupting influence of power, ordinary human lust, or diabolical intervention? Lewis never provides a comfortable answer.

—Caroline Gonda

THE MONKEY'S PAW.
Story by W.W. Jacobs, 1902.

"The Monkey's Paw" was first published in 1902 in a varied collection of short stories called *The Lady of the Barge* by the admirable popular short story writer W.W. Jacobs. His normal vein at its best is comic tales about sailor men on leave or humble villagers. In "The Monkey's Paw" he surpassed himself with a story in the usual lower-middle-class setting but of a grim mythic quality and moral depth.

A soldier returns from India to tell a family of old friends his adventures and gives them the sinister magical Monkey's Paw with due warning. It will grant three wishes. Elderly father, mother and only son take it lightly. They wish for £200 to pay off the mortgage. The money comes, but as compensation for the son's death at work. The mother's anguished passion for her last child leads her to persuade her husband to wish for the return of their son, though the father believes the wish to be "false and wicked." The son had been mutilated beyond recognition and was 10 days in his grave. The second wish is made and a violent knocking is heard at the front door. The mother tries desperately to open it. In bitter despair the father uses the third and last wish, the knocking ceases, the mother at last opens the door, but the street is deserted.

The setting is economically but clearly evoked. A cold wet winter's night encloses the cosy little house, though the house itself grows cold at night and is lit only by candles. The deep desires and hidden sorrows of the humdrum decent life of quiet people are touched by the visitor from the mysterious East.

Though the plot is fantastic with its folkloric "rule of three" it has a significant relation to the domestic realism. The plot shows that if in ordinary life you violate "destiny" and try to manipulate ordinary reality by unnatural processes, you will pay a severe penalty. The ancient yearning for the return of the beloved dead and the horror of death are simultaneously evoked. Mistakes once made cannot be repaired. Death cannot be overcome by a false material resurrection. There are no short cuts, no easy ways out. The moral applies to more than magic. Fantasy gives us a general moral truth told in a moving fiction.

—Derek Brewer

MORTE ARTHURE (Alliterative).
Poem, late 14th century.

Editions and Translations

King Arthur's Death: The Middle English Stanzaic Morte Arthur and the Alliterative Morte Arthure, edited by Larry D. Benson. 1974.
The Alliterative Morte Arthure, edited by Valerie Krishna. 1976.
The Alliterative Morte Arthure: *A New Verse Translation*, translated by Valerie Krishna. 1983.
Morte Arthure: *A Critical Edition*, edited by Mary Hamel. 1984.

Critical Studies: *The Tragedy of Arthur* by William Matthews, 1960; *The Alliterative Revival*, 1977, and *Alliterative Poetry of the Later Middle Ages*, 1989, both by Thorlac Turville-Petre; *The Alliterative Tradition in the Fourteenth Century* edited by Bernard S. Levy and Paul E. Szarmach, 1981; *The Alliterative Morte Arthure: A Reassessment of the Poem* edited by Karl Heinz Göller, 1981; "The Alliterative *Morte Arthure*: The Story of Britain's David" by R.A. Shoaf, in *Journal of English and Germanic Philology*, April 1982; "Heroic Kingship and Unjust War in the Alliterative *Morte Arthure*" by Michael W. Twomey, in *Acta*, 11, 1986.

Now generally recognized as one of the major achievements of the alliterative revival, *Morte Arthure* survives in a single manuscript, Lincoln Cathedral 91, written by the scribe Robert Thornton and dating from around 1430–40. How much earlier than this the work was composed is a matter of dispute, dates as early as 1365 and as late as 1402 having been suggested. As preserved in this manuscript, the poem consists of 4346 alliterative long lines, regularly divisible into half-line units. The second half lines particularly reflect the poem's heavily formulaic character. Additional evidence about the manuscript tradition can be gleaned from the Winchester manuscript of Malory's *Tale of King Arthur and the Emperor Lucius*, for which the Middle English poem furnished the principal source.

The *Morte Arthure* itself derives ultimately from the pertinent section of Geoffrey of Monmouth's *Historia Regum Britanniae*, probably by way of *Le Roman de Brut*, an Anglo-Norman verse redaction by Wace. Episodes akin to Arthur's premonitory second dream appear in both Laȝamon's *Brut*, a Middle English verse reworking of Wace, and in the 13th-century French prose romance *Mort Artu*. Since neither provides a satisfactory source for the alliterative poem, this common feature may imply that all three works are indebted to some augmented, and no longer extant, version of Wace. Also incorporated in *Morte Arthure* are materials from two Old French Alexander-romances, the *Voeux du Paon* and the *Fuerres de Gadres*, and a *chanson de geste*, *Fierabras*, the latter perhaps by way of the Middle English *Sir Ferumbras*. In its descriptions of Arthur's campaigns, the poem has also been assumed to reflect incidents associated with Edward III's struggle to assert his claim to the French throne during the early stages of the Hundred Years War. The perceived parallels with historical events support an early date for the poem, but they may be fortuitous, or, if genuine, derived from later written records.

Arthur in Geoffrey of Monmouth has many attributes of the archetypal mythic hero, and as they deal successively with Geoffrey's account both Wace and Laȝamon augment this aspect of their source. But very little of it survives in *Morte Arthure*. Arthur first appears as ruler of a magnificent imperial court whose prominence has been won by force of arms. When he dies from wounds suffered at the last battle in Cornwall, he undergoes an ordinary mortal's fate and is buried at Glastonbury. Between these poles, the narrative contours trace the theme of armed combat, treated according to the conventions and in a spirit akin to that of the *chansons de geste*. The vigorous, richly descriptive style generally associated with alliterative verse imparts to the battle scenes a horrifyingly vivid realism:

By that swyftely one swarthe þe swett es byleuede,
Swerdez swangen in two sweltand knyghtez,
Lyes wyde opyn, welterande on walopande stedez;
Wondes of wale men, werkande sydys,
Facez fetteled vnfaire in filterede lakes,
All craysed, fortrodyn with trappede stedez.

The scale of martial encounters in the *chanson de geste* ranges from events as grand as defending Christendom to events as narrow as enforcing feudal vassalage. The *Morte Arthure* begins on the grand scale (Lucius), then narrows (Duke of Lorraine), and concludes with an episode (Modred) combining elements of both. Such a variety problematizes the morality of Arthur's role, and this situation is aggravated by the author's eclectic use of his other source materials.

Digressions preserved unchanged from an otherwise transformed source, or imported into an alien literary environment, create a disjunctive effect which the poet seems deliberately to have cultivated, since the most important examples of this procedure are emphatically demarcated by passages of rhetorical *descriptio loci*. The first instance of generically discordant intrusion occurs with the episode of the giant of Mont St. Michel, carried over from the *Historia Regum Britanniae*. It presents Arthur as a monster-killing culture hero, a role similar to that assigned him when he hunts the boar Twrch Trwyth in *Culhwch and Olwen*. Geoffrey's legendary history accommodates such a figure comfortably, but in the middle of a realistically described campaign the episode is incongruous, and depicts Arthur in a way not easily reconciled with his portrait elsewhere in the work. During the siege of Metz, Gawain, in the course of a typical romance adventure, defeats in single combat a knight, Priamus, who converts to Christianity and switches allegiance from the Duke of Lorraine to Arthur. The moral issues raised by the episode are at odds with those operative in the immediate narrative context, and the scene helps isolate Gawain from the moral framework applicable to the activities of Arthur and Modred, both of whom eulogize him after his death.

The most significant of these interpolated passages, however, is that describing Arthur's dream of Fortune's Wheel and the Nine Worthies. Its location in the narrative identifies Arthur as the victim of a typical *casus*, discovering the betrayal by Modred which will precipitate his bad fortune at the very moment when he is about to be crowned emperor by the pope. Counsellors asked to interpret the dream speak with the moral authority of hermits guiding knights-errant on the grail quest, and speak of Arthur's sin in spilling innocent blood. Those looking for a unifying principle in *Morte Arthure*, and wishing to associate it with the conflict between heroic values and penitential doctrine frequently explored in the alliterative revival, have been led by these circumstances to categorize the poem as a medieval tragedy of Fortune, and to see Arthur as guilty of *hubris* in moving from resisting tyranny to practicing it. Unfortunately, while nothing in the text absolutely defies assimilation to such a scheme, nothing confirms it either. Nor can the consistency of the emotionally charged style nullify the effects of generic promiscuity to support a view of the poem as a condemnation of warfare and its attendant horrors. Such an interpretation might readily be drawn from passages of the kind quoted earlier, but its validity is undermined by the fact that the wounds inflicted on a giant in a *märchen*, and the wounds suffered by the hero (but cured with a magic salve!) in a *roman*, are described with the same gusto for gory detail.

Morte Arthure is without doubt a great work of literature, but its greatness is not to be found in any architectonic statement of moral truth. If any single criterion can be extrapolated from the work, it might be that moral judgments on the behaviour of fictional characters are either orthodoxly Christian or generically determined.

—Roy J. Pearcy

LE MORTE DARTHUR.
See the Writers entry on **MALORY, Sir Thomas.**

MOUNTAIN LION.
Poem by D.H. Lawrence, 1923.

D.H. Lawrence's poem "Mountain Lion" was written in January 1923 at the Del Monte Ranch, Questa, New Mexico, where he lived for a short time. The ranch was situated "in the higher, forested foothills of the Rockies, seventeen miles from Taos" (F.B. Pinion, *A Lawrence Companion*), and the scenery, the altitude, and the time of year are all evoked in the poem. The name "Lobo" at the end of the poem is that of a nearby mountain.

It was one of the last poems to be written for Lawrence's collection of verse, *Birds, Beasts, and Flowers*, completed in February 1923 and published later the same year. (The title of the volume, taken from the Victorian hymn "Now the day is over" by Sabine Baring-Gould, recalls the importance of hymns among Lawrence's earliest literary influences: see, for example, his poem "Piano" and his essay "Hymns in a Man's Life.") It appears in the section of the volume titled "Animals," as does the well-known "Kangaroo."

A mountain lion is not strictly speaking a lion but a large feline mammal, *felis concolor*, with a greyish-brown coat and a long tail; a native of North America, it is also known as a puma or cougar. The simple incident described in the poem is, as so often with Lawrence, presumably autobiographical: on a mountain walk, he meets two Mexicans carrying the dead animal and, continuing his walk, finds the empty lair and regrets the death of the beautiful and irreplaceable creature. Sixty years after Lawrence's death, the emotion and the conviction expressed have a highly contemporary ring: he feels sadness and anger at the wanton slaying of the animal—an action symptomatic of man's indifference to the non-human world. There is perhaps a false note near the end of the poem, in the strident rhetoric of "how easily we might spare a million or two of humans / And never miss them," a curiously insensitive way of making his point at a time when World War I and its mass slaughter of Lawrence's own generation were a very recent memory. But the real strength of the poem lies in the delicate portrayal of the wild creature's beauty and uniqueness: paradoxically, his re-creation of its vitality is prompted by the sight of its carcase, so that from death itself comes a sense of urgent and unique life.

Lawrence's sympathy is not felt across the distance that separates human from animal but involves a momentary identification with its existence, as when he thinks of it watching "out of the shadow of the cave in the blood-orange rock. . . ."

Like many of Lawrence's poems, "Mountain Lion" is written in free verse, mingling long and short lines and dispensing with rhyme. The absence of these formal elements of traditional verse is to some extent compensated for by the use of two devices: repetition and parallelism. The former is well illustrated by the description of the dead animal:

> Lift up her face,
> Her round, bright face, bright as frost.
> Her round, fine-fashioned head, with two dead ears;
> And stripes in the brilliant frost of her face, sharp,
>   fine dark rays,
> Dark, keen, fine rays in the brilliant frost of her face,
> Beautiful dead eyes.

Here the words "round," "bright," "dead," "brilliant," "fine," "dark" and "frost" are interwoven into a complex pattern of emphases; the effect is closer to that of spontaneous speech under the pressure of feeling than to traditional verse.

Parallelism is in evidence at the moment when the Mexican hunters are encountered:

> They hesitate
> We hesitate.
> They have a gun
> We have no gun.

and again when the two parties go their separate ways:

> They go out towards the open;
> We go on into the gloom of Lobo.

Here the contrast is pointed and, especially in the first quotation, the short lines communicate a sense of drama.

Some lines in the poem, however, make use of metrical patterns that come close to the regular rhythms of conventional verse: in "And out to the dim of the desert, like a dream, never real . . ." the free verse moves close to a regular anapaestic line.

In many respects the poem is highly characteristic of its author. Like so much of Lawrence's work, it springs directly, and to all appearances immediately and spontaneously, from personal experience. Its evocation of an alien atmosphere—the distinctive scenery of a vast mountain range, and even the thinness and sharpness of the air at a high altitude in winter—is vivid. The sensibility, particularly the concern for the uniqueness of the individual life and the otherness of a wild animal, is that which informs many of his writings in prose and verse. And the style and verse-form exemplify his search for new modes of expression, though the influence of Whitman is probably significant.

—Norman Page

MUCEDORUS.
Play, 1598.

Editions

In *Shakespeare Apocrypha*, edited by C.F. Tucker Brooke. 1908.
In *Three Elizabethan Plays*, edited by James Winny. 1959.
In *Elizabethan Plays*, edited by Arthur H. Nethercot, Charles R. Baskervill, and Virgil B. Hetzel. Revised edition, 1971.
A Contextual Study and Modern-Spelling Edition of Mucedorus, edited by Arvin H. Jupin. 1987.

Critical Studies: "*Mucedorus*: Most Popular Elizabethan Play?" by George F. Reynolds, in *Studies in English Renaissance Drama* edited by Josephine W. Bennett, Oscar Cargill, and Vernon Hall, 1959; *The Predecessors of Shakespeare* by Terence P. Logan and Denzell S. Smith, 1973; *Elizabethan Popular Theatre: Plays in Performance* by Michael Hattaway, 1982.

Mucedorus has been called the most popular Elizabethan play. Although the number of editions is no sure measure of popularity—theatre companies had reason to keep popular plays out of readers' hands—*Mucedorus* went through 17 editions between 1598 and 1668, so the play is undoubtedly a good measure of popular taste. Authorship and date are both uncertain. In 1619 it was still in the repertory of the King's Men and was performed before King James "with new additions."

The plot centers on the usual features of the romantic comedies of the 1590's: a love triangle in which Princess Amadine rejects a morally unworthy courtier for a man of seemingly humble station, a flight of the lovers from an unfriendly court to the woods, separation there, the final discovery of Mucedorus's true princely rank, and general reconciliation. The style is invigorated with the devices of Senecan tragedy, namely debates between Comedy and Envy as Induction and Epilogue, and passages of stychomythia. A typically Senecan plot against Mucedorus's life, in which he kills his courtier rival's agent, leads the Princess to declare her love and flee with Mucedorus. The play is further enlivened by a bear, a Wild Man, and a rustic comic, who becomes the courtier's servant. At the start of the play, after he has wandered away from his father's court in Valencia disguised as a shepherd, Mucedorus rescues Amadine from the pursuing bear. Later she is abducted by the Wild Man. Though a cannibal, he is in thrall to her beauty and saves not only her life but Mucedorus's, who, rather ungratefully, slays him. The interest of the action is not in the portrayal of the characters, who have been aptly described as functions of their situations, but in the interweaving of the actions. There is a touch of the folktale in the reduplication of the bear in the Wild Man.

The vigour of the action sweeps along in simple, serviceable verse that pauses for occasional set-pieces. Here, for example, is the Wild Man wooing Amadine:

> Thou shalt be fed with quails and partridges,
> With blackbirds, larks, thrushes and nightingales;
> Thy drink shall be goat's milk and crystal water;
> And all the dainties that the woods afford
> I'll freely give thee to obtain thy love . . .
>
> The satyrs and the wood nymphs shall attend on thee
> And lull thee asleep with music's sound,
> And in the morning when thou dost awake,
> The lark shall sing good morn to my queen,
> And whilst he sings, I'll kiss my Amadine.

This trope is more familiar to us in the words of Titania or Volpone, but the pleadings of this gentle monster are closer to real nature than their more fanciful versions.

It has been suggested that the pleasure of *Mucedorus* lies in our recognition of forms and conventions. Yet there are many Elizabethan plays where those forms and conventions lie inert. What brings *Mucedorus* alive is the blithe insouciance with which those conventions are handled and the mix, as in the quoted passage, of the workmanlike and the extravagant.

—Anthony Graham-White

MUCH ADO ABOUT NOTHING.
Play by William Shakespeare, 1598(?).

"Benedik and Betrice," Charles I wrote on the title page of *Much Ado about Nothing* in his copy of the Second Folio edition of William Shakespeare's *Works* (1632)—one of many indications that the self-deceiving recalcitrant lovers of what began as the subplot have always dominated the play. Yet, this mature comedy (written late 1598 / early 1599) is a tightly woven piece in which all elements are needed and cohere.

Much Ado offers few textual problems. It has been shown that the first print, a Quarto (1600), must have been set from Shakespeare's autograph (so-called "foul papers"), with typical carelessness especially in speech headings and stage directions; the text is full of minor slips, but good on the whole. For the First Folio (1623) setting from a copy of the Quarto bearing corrections and various changes compatible with playhouse practice can be inferred; the result is largely the same text, with some interesting variants, old and new slips, but no independent authority. Modern editions are based on the Quarto.

The Hero-Claudio plot is traditional; the closest model, among the many stories of falsely accused young women, is Matteo Bandello's No. 22 of Timbreo di Cardona and Fenicia, daughter of Lionato de' Lionati at Messina under King Piero of Aragon. A free translation appeared in volume 3 of François de Belleforest's *Histoires Tragiques* (1569), but Shakespeare seems to have relied on the original, published in *Novelle* (1554). In Bandello's and similar stories as found in Ariosto's *Orlando Furioso* and Spenser's *The Faerie Queene* the slander stems from a disappointed rival lover, thus furnishing a specific motive rather than the general, rabid malignity of Shakespeare's Don John.

Hints of a Beatrice figure have been found here and there by scholars, and young men refusing obedience to love have usually been punished by the little God, as, for instance, Valentine in *The Two Gentlemen of Verona*; nevertheless, Beatrice and Benedick are not only Shakespeare's creation—that applies to each and every element, whether developed from a specific source or not—but also his invention. So are the benign but (saving Francis Seacoal, the Town Clerk of IV. ii) hilariously incompetent townspeople: Dogberry, Verges, and their crew.

Much Ado has the highest proportion of prose among Shakespeare's comedies, and its flexibility as well as its sparkle are remarkable. With Beatrice's conversion scene (III. i) as the main exception, verse is reserved for the emotional peaks of the melodramatic Hero-Claudio plot. Overall, there is nothing "Illyrian" about Messina, which remains the place of action throughout—no change here to a pastoral environment as in *A Midsummer Night's Dream*, *The Merchant of Venice*, and *As You Like It*. The atmosphere and tone remind rather of Windsor in *The Merry Wives* (which also has a very high proportion of prose); and remind of Padua in *The Taming of the Shrew*, with which *Much Ado* shares the plot element of an unconventional pair of lovers proving more sympathetic as well as successful than others. Indeed, in *Much Ado* we are even surer of that, despite Benedick's final repetition, at the very end, of the play's *leitmotif*—the assumption of female "lightness," or rather the males' obsessive fear of cuckoldom.

With few exceptions the principal men in Shakespeare's comedies are inferior to the women in one or several respects. Rarely, however, do most fall so far below them as in *Much Ado*. Benedick stands out; his weaknesses are comical, not least his vanity; and in his battles of wit with Beatrice he is worsted; but he is pleasant, generous, and courageous—witness his frankness and warmth in his conversion scene (II. iii) and the undertaking to challenge and if necessary to "kill Claudio," as Beatrice demands for the sake of her wronged cousin Hero (IV. i). The rest are a sorry lot—Leonato begging his daughter to have at least the decency to die, Claudio proving even shallower than Bertram in *All's Well*, and much meaner, the Prince gullible enough to believe his brother John and callous enough to concur with Claudio's spiteful gesture.

And yet we easily acquiesce in the happy ending where all is cleared up and forgiven—as we knew it would be. Several factors contribute to this assurance, a prerequisite for comedy. The sequence of episodes shows us the discovery of the vile trick by the watchmen (III. iii) and thus indicates the eventual redress before we see the disastrous effects (IV. i).

Don John is such a cardboard villain, one simply cannot take him and his henchmen seriously. The weight of the Beatrice-Benedick plot with its psychological truth and its verbal sprightliness (finer than the scraps of Rosaline and Berowne in *Love's Labour's Lost* and less sober than the duels of the gay couple in Restoration comedy) is a counter-indication to an unhappy outcome, as is the mere existence of Dogberry and Verges with their sunny innocence as well as their fumbling logic and language. Shakespeare is the opposite of an absurdist playwright; with such people around, we can be certain that all will indeed be "suffigance" (Dogberry, III.v), and that the "much ado" is really "about nothing."

—Holger Klein

MURDER IN THE CATHEDRAL.
Play by T.S. Eliot, 1935.

"The great vice of English drama from Kyd to Galsworthy has been that its aim of realism was unlimited." So T.S. Eliot had written in an essay of 1924. When, some 10 years later, he composed his first play he was still of the same mind. He knew that at all costs he must avoid imitating Shakespeare, which would not be easy because perhaps none of our poets has had a more thorough knowledge of and admiration for him. He would go further back for inspiration, though not exactly for models to imitate, to the mediaeval *Everyman*, and to Aeschylus. For a recent pathfinder, he had the example of Yeats; though his admiration here will have been combined with a wariness of a pagan example. Milton's *Samson* had been militantly Hebraic rather than Christian. Only *Everyman* possessed a Christian spirit upon which Eliot could build.

The invitation to produce a play for the Canterbury Festival meant that the choice of Becket's martyrdom had an obvious local appropriateness, though, as we shall see, an Anglican setting for a Catholic event was to involve the author in inconsistencies.

As in Aeschylus, the Chorus would be central to the drama, though unable to act in it. The link between the experience of Thomas and that of the women of Canterbury is close, while the Priests, the Tempters and the Knights exist at a comparatively superficial level of mere action, mere opinion, mere topicality. Thomas and the women exist, feel, and suffer at the heart of the drama in a pattern of timeless moments. The foreboding of the women before the murder and their horror afterwards are the central experiences which the audience shares. They are more eloquent than Thomas. The simplicity of the dramatic structure, and the paucity of event, and especially the close parallels between each tempter and the knight with the corresponding number ensure a formal elegance. The drama of murder and martyrdom is performed twice: once in Thomas's mind, then in his actual suffering. After his death, when the knights speak directly to the audience, the 12th century and the 20th are brought together. There is a kind of comic relief which is distinctly sinister. But in ironically celebrating the subordination of the Anglican church to the state, Eliot ignores (it is hard to imagine that he really forgets) the fact that in real history the king had to bow to papal authority and purge himself of complicity with the deed.

The dramatic method requires a wide range of tones in verse and prose, from the first tempter, who speaks in homely aphorisms, to the abstract philosophizing of the fourth. The chorus moves from the plain accounts of the hardship of ordinary life in early choruses (though with suggestions of terror in allusions to parallels like the betrayal of Christ by Peter) to the eloquent polysyllabic horror of the late choruses. A world in which everything is always the same ("the labourer bends to his piece of earth, earthcolour, his own colour, / Preferring to pass unobserved") is the background for a single memorable event. For the audience to come to feel that they are at the same time witnessing events in the 12th century, and celebrating them liturgically, the prose sermon and the recital at the beginning of the second part of parts of the liturgy for the days between Christmas and 29 December, the day of martyrdom, have both a special importance. This sense of a timeless celebration then receives a neat ironic contrast with the anachronistic 20th-century chat of the guilty knights to the public represented by the audience. Here it is specially important that a possible 20th-century secular misunderstanding, that Thomas sought martyrdom for his own glory, has been anticipated in the dialogue between Thomas and the fourth tempter, which is in some ways the dramatic climax of the play. It is very characteristic of Eliot that before this moment of dramatic intensity he should make use of material from the stories of Sherlock Holmes ("Who shall have it? He who will come. What shall be the month? The last from the first?") When the fourth tempter says, in answer to Thomas's question: "Supreme, in this land?" "Supreme, but for one," he is tempting him to worship the devil under the guise of worship of self. The rejection of this is the spiritual climax, which reduces the murder, important though it must be, to a secondary position. This, perhaps, though the murder is nearer to the stage action than it would be in Aeschylus, is Eliot's equivalent for the Greek convention of having violence off-stage. The murder is distanced by thus being anticipated in an inward dialogue with the tempter, as it is also by the singing of Dies Irae and the prolonged meditation of the chorus which follows.

The deliberate bathos of the following scene with the prosaic knights allows the audience an opportunity for thought and questioning to follow intense emotion. Here, as throughout, contrasts are carefully modulated and remarkably effective.

—A.O.J. Cockshut

MY FIRST ACQUAINTANCE WITH POETS.
Prose by William Hazlitt, 1823.

"My First Acquaintance with Poets" is one of the finest of all brief autobiographies and a key record of the first great phase of English romanticism. In it William Hazlitt recalls how after hearing Samuel Taylor Coleridge preach at Shrewsbury in the early part of 1798 he then met the poet and experienced the magnetism of his conversation and his personality. Later in the year Hazlitt was to visit Coleridge in Somerset, and the impact of the joint company of Coleridge and Wordsworth—at Nether Stowey, Alfoxden, and on a brief walking tour to the Valley of Rocks at Lynton in Devon—on the would-be writer (then just 21 years of age) is vividly re-created.

"My First Acquaintance with Poets" expands material first published in Leigh Hunt's periodical the *Examiner* six years earlier, on 12 January 1817. There, in the form of a letter to the Editor, Hazlitt recreated the tremendous impression which hearing Coleridge preach had made on him and he contrasted the radicalism of that 1798 sermon with the Toryism of Coleridge's "The Statesman's Manual" (then recently published), complaining that Coleridge had now comprehensively betrayed his early promise. The intention of Hazlitt's piece was directly political, but when, six years later, he cut out the original accusatory conclusion and expanded the material beyond his account of Coleridge's preaching to record the whole history of his relations with the authors of *Lyrical Ballads* up to the point of the book's publication and their departure for Germany in the autumn of 1798, he turned a political attack into a celebration of the power of Coleridge and (to a lesser extent) Wordsworth to awaken a young man's imagination and energize his mind towards the development of its innate potential.

In traditional autobiographical form, "My First Acquaintance with Poets" offers a double portayal—of Wordsworth and Coleridge at the height of their innovative powers on the one hand, and of Hazlitt himself on the other. The essay has five main sections. The account of Hazlitt's walk to Shrewsbury and the impact made on him by the sermon he heard Coleridge preach there, which first made him feel the awakening power which Coleridge could exercise upon the faculties of a young man's mind, reproduces the material originally published in 1817 almost without change. But this is now followed, and balanced, by a sketch of Hazlitt's father, an elderly Unitarian minister, who found in biblical criticism food for his imagination as well as for his faith. The meeting of the veteran minister with Coleridge the tyro preacher now ensues, while his father's reaction ("to think that Truth had found a new ally in Fancy!") maintains Hazlitt's concern with Coleridge as an exponent of the romantic imagination. The essay also maintains a political content, less obviously present than when it began life in 1817, but nonetheless there throughout: at this point it may be noted that Hazlitt's record of the conversation after dinner is chiefly concerned with Godwin, Mary Wollstonecraft, Holcroft, and other Radical figures of the 1790's. Hazlitt's own recollections of his conversations with Coleridge then and the following morning, when he accompanied Coleridge for part of his walk home, move us forward towards the story of his visit to Coleridge at Nether Stowey and his characterisation of Wordsworth and Coleridge together at the time immediately before the publication of *Lyrical Ballads*, which then opens into the narrative of their visit to the Valley of Rocks and Coleridge's conversation during the trip.

Although mostly written 25 years after the events which it chronicles, "My First Acquaintance with Poets" recreates a springtime of poetical and (for Hazlitt) political ardour which can only be matched by Dorothy Wordsworth's *Alfoxden Journal* (very different in focus as it is) and the poems of *Lyrical Ballads* which Hazlitt heard read by their creators from the original manuscripts, seated under the trees of Alfoxden Park. "The sense of a new style and a new spirit in poetry came over me," says Hazlitt, and a sense of the originality and freshness of the poems which Wordsworth and Coleridge were writing at this time is strongly projected through his prose. The essay also offers vivid sketches of the physical appearance of the two poets at this period. As a young man Hazlitt trained as a portrait painter before turning to the writing of biography, criticism, and essays, so he catches the vivifying details. From these we learn of Wordsworth's "convulsive inclination to laughter about the mouth" and Coleridge's nose "the rudder of the face, the index of the will" which was "small, feeble, nothing." These and other physical characteristics are worked up into psychological portrayals showing considerable insight; while the fragments of conversation which Hazlitt recalls are equally valuable for what they retrieve of the opinions concerning politics and literature (often otherwise unrecorded) of the two poets at the period of their closest intellectual companionship.

The undertow of disappointed Radicalism in Hazlitt's account is easily overlooked unless the frequency with which references to the political figures of the 1790's occur in the recorded conversations, and their full resonance, is recognised. Hazlitt's own self-portrayal as a young man is, by contrast, memorably and sensitively projected throughout. His excitement at Coleridge's sermon, his gratitude for Coleridge's praise of his first faltering remark in the after-dinner conversation, his excited anticipation of the visit to Nether Stowey, and his vivid memory of the events of that stay will be felt by every reader. His portrayal of Wordsworth in 1798 is also invaluable, but above all it is the enduring fascination of Coleridge that is recreated in the essay with obvious gratitude. For all their later disagreements, Hazlitt does not hesitate to assert his belief "That my understanding also did not remain dumb and brutish, or at length found a language to express itself, I owe to Coleridge."

—William Ruddick

MY LAST DUCHESS.
Poem by Robert Browning, 1842.

The subtitle "Ferrara," which names an Italian city famous during the Renaissance, gives us the setting for this dramatic monologue, one of Robert Browning's best-known poems in the mode. No exact date is given but clearly the Duke who speaks the poem is one of those Machiavellian reprobates, inevitably Italian, who peopled the imagination of English writers from the 16th century to the time of the gothic novel (in decline by the 1830's). A context of corruption, poison, arrogance, and elegant evil is thus created, all of which form an essential background for the understanding of the poem. It is barely relevant, though true, that Browning based "My Last Duchess" on an incident in the life of a real Duke of Ferrara in 1561.

In addition to cultural context, the reader has to supply a large part of the drama that makes this monologue "dramatic." It is, thus, an exercise in half-revelation that requires the reader to take an active role, a requirement enhanced by the rather tortuous syntax. We explore the Duke's mind, and the events that are hinted at, through a dense medium. But the revelations are sufficient for us to be certain of the truth by the end.

Thus, when we read the list of things that the late Duchess appeared to value equally highly ("My favour at her breast / The dropping of the daylight in the west, / The bough of cherries . . .") we are being told that the Duke expects his wife to value a present he has given her (which is, of course, a *favour*) more highly than a beautiful sunset and, generally, as the highest of things. Similarly, the Duke harps on his "nine-hundred-years-old name" as if that were something that a bride should consider the greatest of "gifts." Clearly, if a little obliquely, we come to realise the arrogance of the man who stands condemned out of his own mouth. He chooses "never to stoop," expects his wife to smile a special smile for him and no one else, and, it dawns on us, murders her ("I gave commands; / Then all smiles stopped together") for what is almost a whim. Her offence is no one specific crime but a friendly if bland personality that has irritated her husband by not pandering to his notion of his own importance.

Once we have the events of the poem sorted out we can begin to see that Browning offers us further revelations. The Duke, for instance, may have murdered his wife on more than a whim, perhaps being obsessed by sexual jealousy. There is a hint of this in the delight with which he shows his interlocutor the painting, hidden by a curtain that is pulled back by none but the Duke himself, and imagines that Fra Pandolf may have complimented the Duchess about the inimitability of the "faint/Half-flush that dies along her throat." Connected with this is her tendency to blush and the (repeated) "spot of joy" that many things, too many in the Duke's view, could call into her cheek. And "'Twas not / Her husband's presence only" that could produce this effect on her. An obsessive desire not to be cuckolded and a maddened sense that he cannot conquer his wife seem to lie behind these details.

But the Duke is a dilettante too. The poem opens and closes with an invitation to contemplate an art object (the painting of the Duchess, the Neptune cast for the Duke by "Claus of Innsbruck"). There is some sort of aesthetic game being played here alongside the darker motives. The ending, accordingly, is both sinister (he will serve his *next* Duchess the same way, presumably, or, alternatively, is only interested in her dowry) and rather comically inconsequential. Perhaps he is only interested in acquiring money, after all; when he refers to his "just pretence" to a good dowry the word "pretence," standing out at the end of a line, is intended as another revelation—technically it means "claim" but we cannot separate it from the notion that the Duke is acting a part. All this is made possible by Browning's full use of the dramatic possibilities of his genre—we become acutely aware of the interlocutor, presumably some sort of ambassador from "the Count" whose daughter he is seeking to marry, although this person never utters a word that we hear. Instead the Duke reveals more and more about himself.

Browning nearly defeats the reader entirely at several points where his delight in opaque grammar obscures meaning. The sentence beginning "Who'd stoop to blame," for instance, is quite impossible to make sense of on a first reading, but in general the handling of syntax and of the iambic couplets that the poem is made up of enhance its effect. Thus towards the end of the poem the Duke protests that his proposed new Duchess is, of course, an object in her own right apart from her dowry. He does it thus:

> . . . his fair daughter's self, as I avowed
> At starting, is my object.

The double break created by ending the line in the middle of the subordinate clause increases our sense of the somewhat vacuous and hesitant protest that is being made. The mind and moral quality of the man are revealed by what is, after all, a series of technical devices brilliantly handled but not necessarily felt. As ever Browning appears complicated and clever rather than complex and thoughtful.

—Lance St. John Butler

THE MYSTERIES OF UDOLPHO.
Novel by Ann Radcliffe, 1794.

The Mysteries of Udolpho has come to be seen as the archetypal tale of gothic terror. It is, famously, the book which leads Catherine Morland into folly in *Northanger Abbey*. Its most notorious elements are its most memorable —the gloomy, crumbling, and labyrinthine castle of Udolpho, and Montoni, the archetypal gothic villain: proud, wilful, revengeful, and vicious.

However the novel is much more than a thriller. It is a novel of sensibility and of taste. Ann Radcliffe is as at pains to provide moral edification as she is to arouse our terror, as the book's final paragraphs make plain. It is also a novel about landscape. A large proportion of its considerable length is given over to visual descriptions of scenery, particularly that of the mountains over which Emily journeys. The skill of these passages is the more impressive as Radcliffe never saw at first hand the scenes she describes.

The whole novel is, arguably, constructed according to the same principles of taste that govern Radcliffe's fictional landscapes—principally those of balance, contrast, and the element of the picturesque. The sublime contrast between the jagged peak or chasm and the soft woody slopes below is echoed by the violent contrast of the idyllic family home at La Vallée with the grim Udolpho. This contrast extends to character: St. Aubert, Emily's father, is a man of almost saintly virtue. Montoni, who comes to stand *in loco parentis*, is a fiend.

The pictorial element of the picturesque is likewise transferred to the novel. Hence the action is punctuated by descriptions of peasants dancing in costume, and by the pageant of Neptune in Venice.

We see this process operating in microcosm in Emily's own art (she is both painter and poet). The principles of taste serve to organise and mould the products of her own imagination, even of her own fantasy. Her poems replicate, with a higher degree of aesthetic concentration, the effects of the novel. Hence poems such as the "Storied Sonnet," "Stanzas," and "The Pilgrim" set lonely figures in sublime landscapes, and rehearse the themes of terror, pathos, virtue, and sudden death. Others deal with fanciful descriptions of nature. "The Sea Nymph" is a ballad of a mermaid and shipwrecked mariners in which Emily's fantasy projects her into the world suggested by the pageant of Neptune—the picturesque returning to pathos. Emily's painting is guided by the same principles, and has a moral purpose. While she is still facing the direst of fates herself, Emily draws a picture of imagined scenes, depicting sad stories, "as a tear fell over the pictured griefs, which her imagination drew, she would forget, for a moment, her real sufferings."

The terror aroused by *The Mysteries of Udolpho* is compounded of many elements: horrible sights, claustrophobic confinement, the fear of the supernatural, and, most tellingly, the suspense as to what cruelty may next befall the heroine. Radcliffe was at pains to distinguish her own art of terror from the cruder, more sensational art of horror. Terror is to be found in fearful expectation of the dreadful; horror is a face to face confrontation with it. Horror thrives on gruesome details, whereas terror avoids it.

The Mysteries of Udolpho bears out her ideals well. While there is violence in the book (battle, bloodshed, and murder) the bulk of it happens "off-stage," as it were, and reaches the reader only by report. The book is driven along by fearful anticipation rather than by bloody shocks. Occasionally however, the novel does throw up shocking images, for example, a corpse lying soaked in blood. These are all the more disturbing as we do not expect them. At the climax of her stay at Udolpho, Emily faces the continual fear of rape, which cuts through the romantic conventions of the novel with an uncomfortable immediacy.

Radcliffe periodically relieves the tension with the quasi-Shakespearian device of Emily's dialogues with her servant Annette. Annette is gullible and garrulous, feckless and affectionate. Her simplicity panders to the reader's superior discrimination, arousing both humour and pathos.

The suspense generated in the novel is of the intellect as well as of the emotions. Our fear and curiosity are aroused in equal proportions. Radcliffe mastered the art of the detective story long before it became an art form in itself. She gives the reader all the facts necessary to solve her mysteries, but does so in such a way that we jump to the wrong conclusions. A false trail is laid which suggests that Emily is the daughter of the Marchioness de Villeroi. St. Aubert is seen weeping over a portrait of the Marchioness, who is rumoured to have had a secret marriage, and to whom Emily bears a striking resemblance. The denouement is both surprising and satisfying: St. Aubert was the late Marchioness's brother, and Emily is her niece.

Similarly, Radcliffe sets up circumstances which powerfully suggest the presence of the supernatural. Ghostly figures are glimpsed, disembodied voices speak, and spirits are rumoured to walk abroad. But this too, is part of an elaborate puzzle, and only at the end of the novel are the natural explanations of these phenomena revealed. Radcliffe gains all the terror and mystery that the supernatural can arouse, while, finally, disavowing such ideas as irrational superstition.

Finally, *The Mysteries of Udolpho* is also a novel about how to be—the most virtuous and wholesome way of feeling. St. Aubert, on his death bed, warns Emily that: "We become the victims of our feelings, unless we can in some degree command them. . . . Always remember how much more valuable is the strength of fortitude, than the grace of sensibility." Montoni counsels her: "If you will not release yourself from the slavery of these fears . . . forbear to torment others by the mention of them. Conquer such whims, and endeavour to strengthen your mind."

Emily's sensibility is very much at issue. While, morally, Radcliffe condemns any self-indulgence on Emily's part, artistically she relies on it. It is Emily's hypersensitivity which serves on the one hand to add to the terror of her tale, and on the other, to increase our sympathy for her in her misfortunes.

—Edmund Cusick

THE MYSTERY OF EDWIN DROOD.
Novel by Charles Dickens, 1870.

After a five-year break from writing novels, Charles Dickens began work on his last book, *The Mystery of Edwin Drood*, in late 1869. In poor health, and weakened by decades of hard work and the strain of his very successful series of public readings, Dickens for the first time included in a book's contract a clause stipulating the arrangements in the event that he should die before the novel was completed. The stipulation proved to be prophetic, for on 9 June 1870, with exactly half of the book written, and only half of that published in serialized form, Dickens died, leaving behind no notes or plans that indicated what he intended to do with the unfinished novel. Although there was some public speculation that Dickens's associate Wilkie Collins might step in and conclude the uncompleted mystery, such a move was never seriously contemplated. Instead, Dickens's friend and executor John Forster oversaw the publication of the remaining material, restoring some of Dickens's deletions and dividing and retitling some chapters in order to fill the space remaining in the book's last three monthly numbers.

According to Forster, *The Mystery of Edwin Drood* was to describe "the murder of a nephew by his uncle," with the last chapters portraying the murderer, John Jasper, in his prison cell awaiting his execution. As a starting point Forster's remarks seem reasonable enough and apparently agree with the fragment of the novel we have, but dozens of books and hundreds of articles have focused on how Dickens might have concluded the novel in the space he had remaining. The debate, which has continued over the last century, has primarily focused upon Dickens's health as well as his overall concept of the book.

Basically there are two camps. Those who believe Dickens was stung by the success of his friend Wilkie Collins's mystery novels such as *The Moonstone* and *The Woman in White* see Dickens as challenging Collins on his own ground. These critics assume that Dickens applied all his genius to creating what would have been the ultimate mystery novel, a book full of tricks, twists, false clues, and unexpected revelations; such a book would of course have a surprise ending. For these readers, any fact that seems obvious can only be a false trail; on the other hand, any subtle nuance suggests a clue that will ultimately loom large and will undoubtedly be followed up later.

Other readers see Dickens as not being so clever. These critics argue that plots were never Dickens's strength, and that now, in the twilight of his career, he was not going to do anything radically different from what he had already done. Although some of these critics praise the novel for its traditional Dickensian strengths—characterization and atmosphere—others take a more harsh stance; George Bernard Shaw, for instance, dismissed the novel as "a gesture by a man three-quarters dead." Observing that Dickens underwrote several of his monthly numbers, some see him as exhausted and trapped by his plot, the stress of maintaining the mystery finally killing him; even more gloomily, others, noting that the book's final chapter seems to forecast Dickens's demise, have suggested the author virtually willed his own death to avoid working out the puzzle.

The controversy over the novel's ending focuses on three recurrent issues: 1) whether Edwin Drood is dead or alive; 2) John Jasper's role in the murder (if there was one); and 3) the identity of the apparently disguised detective Datchery who shows up in Cloisterham to look into the murder. According to sources closest to Dickens—John Forster, Charles Dickens, Jr., and Luke Fildes, the book's illustrator—the first two questions are easily resolved. Edwin Drood is dead and John Jasper strangled him. Despite this agreement among those who actually knew Dickens and discussed the novel with him, many subsequent readers have remained skeptical and added their personal touches to the novel; hundreds of theories abound. The "resurrectionists" argue that Drood was never killed, either because he simply leaves Cloisterham on his own or because he manages to survive an assault. Others contend that because Jasper obviously seems to be the murderer he cannot be so, for there is no mystery in this. Some have it both ways by arguing that although Jasper believes he kills Edwin, Drood somehow escapes death; Jasper is thus a murderer in spirit but not in fact. Even more ingenious, and, given the evidence, more likely, is that Jasper possesses a split personality. The "good" Jasper is dedicated to finding his nephew's killer, while the "evil" Jasper is in fact the very person the choirmaster seeks. The two halves were to be united in the condemned cell when Jasper discovered he himself committed the crime. Frequent references to mesmerism, post-hypnotic suggestion, and Jasper's drug-induced trances all support this explanation, and allusions to double selves can be found in earlier Dickens novels.

The identity of Datchery is a game with even more players and theories. Many readers see him as Drood himself, returning to solve his own murder. Every other eligible character in the book, male and female, has at one time been suspected of being Datchery, with particularly spirited debates focusing on the qualifications of Bazzard and Helena Landless. Dozens of actual conclusions to the novel have been written demonstrating these theories, some attempting to imitate Dickens's style, some purporting to have been written by Dickens or Wilkie Collins, one alleging to have been dictated by Dickens's ghost. Dramatizations of the novel have also been popular; a recent American musical version allowed audiences to vote for the ending they preferred, a most democratic way to resolve the puzzle.

Recently critics have tried to go beyond the unanswered questions and examine the book's statements on racism, imperialism, hypocrisy, and the church. Many have praised the novel's tone, symbolism, and somewhat subdued style. The final chapter in particular, with its lyrical descriptions of the cathedral, suggests to many that Dickens was writing a novel that, if finished, would have stood among his best.

—Don Richard Cox

N

NEW GRUB STREET.
Novel by George Gissing, 1891.

New Grub Street, George Gissing's one acknowledged masterpiece, is a sustained, bitter study of the writer's plight in contemporary, commercialised society. Set in late-Victorian fog-choked London, it depicts a degrading struggle for survival among those who seek to live by print. Its atmosphere is unrelievedly literary. All its major characters are word-producers—reviewers, editors, novelists *manqués*. It deals with the drudgery of research, the torments of fictional composition, the demands of magazine deadlines. Though Gissing sticks to what he knows, the book's themes clearly have a wider application. Literature, here, is a microcosm of the modern commercial world.

New Grub Street examines how social problems bite into individual lives. The deepest problem is poverty, a powerful corroder not merely of happiness but of decency and self-respect. That poverty degrades is persistently asserted; yet in this society the alternative to poverty is the lure of commercialisation. The novel suggests—with some exaggeration—that in the 1880's an unprecedented flood of commercialism overwhelmed the literary world. With the vast expansion of the reading public, literature has become just another commodity, exposed to the forces of the market. Hence the rise of popular journalism, such as Whelpdale's magazine for "the quarter-educated," *Chit-Chat*, the substitution of periodicals for books, the proliferation of literary "advisers," and all the venal practices of the metropolitan literary racket.

If poverty corrodes, commercialism corrupts: writers must choose between integrity and success. This dilemma (which Gissing felt to be his own) is nailed into the narrative by character contrasts. The most obvious is that between Edwin Reardon and Jasper Milvain. Both agree that the current standards of the literary world are corrupt; but whereas Reardon rejects them and fails, Milvain exploits them and succeeds. Reardon is a man of the old school who will not, or cannot, "make a trade of an art." Sensitive, conscientious, painfully slow, he strives for work of intrinsic merit rather than ephemeral popular appeal. Jasper is a new man and a tradesman: what he aims at is money and money's benefits—physical comfort, social esteem, travel, luxurious living. Literature for him is a means to this end. Under no illusion about the merit of what he writes, he realises that success as a writer is not wholly dependent on merit. Other things are needed too—sufficient capital, influential friends, or an advantageous marriage. Marriage is the means by which Gissing links his love stories to the novel's social thesis. With books converted to commodities, people are reduced to investments. Showing this, the book's character-contrasts are supplemented by parallel relationships.

The crucial pattern in the plot is the way that Jasper's relationship with Marian reduplicates that between Reardon and Amy. Initially it seems not a comparison but a contrast. The married couple are breaking apart, the lovers are apparently uniting. But Gissing exploits his three-volume format (much discussed in the text itself) both to build up and undermine the contrast. The first volume ends with marital hostility, the second with the lovers' engagement. Both endings, though, are fraught with foreboding, and in the final volume Jasper betrays Marian just as Amy had deserted Reardon. Even the emotional predicaments are repeated. One might compare the meeting between the married couple, where Amy is repelled by Reardon's shabbiness and then begins "to feel ashamed of her shame," with that between the lovers in Regent's Park, where Jasper observes "with more disgust than usual, the signs in Marian's attire of encroaching poverty," and yet "for such feelings he reproached himself, and the reproach made him angry." The third volume ends with Jasper and Amy, advocates of the commercial approach to literature, united in complacent bliss—winners, both financially and amorously.

Underpinning the novel's narrative is a Darwinian conception of the present and a nostalgic vision of the past. Competition in the modern market is a ruthless fight for scarce resources, including a suitable mate. For several characters, success and survival depend on extinction of a rival: Milvain and Reardon, Amy and Marian, Whelpdale and Biffen, Fadge and Yule. Behind this panorama of strife are two wistful historical vistas. One is the 18th-century Grub Street of Johnson, hard, sordid, but comparatively heroic: the *new* Grub Street, the book suggests, lacks its redeeming features. The other is the non-commercial grandeur of the classics: "Yes, yes," reflects Reardon, reading the *Odyssey*; "*that* was not written at so many pages a day." Yearning evocations of Johnson and Homer rebuke the ignominy of the present. But, as Reardon sadly discovers, they have no power to change it.

New Grub Street is sociologically informative, but also morally and psychologically subtle. Refusing to sentimentalize its failing protagonists, it offers no absolute moral standards to set against its chronicle of commercial encroachment, nor even the lesser satisfactions of simple condemnation. Subsequent developments in art and society have certainly not reduced its relevance. As George Orwell and many others have noted, it retains its capacity to disquiet.

—David Grylls

A NEW WAY TO PAY OLD DEBTS.
Play by Philip Massinger, 1625(?).

The action of Philip Massinger's *A New Way to Pay Old Debts* is conventional plot and counter-plot—the outmanoeuvring of a powerful man by playing on his greed and gullibility; Massinger borrows some characteristic features from Thomas Middleton's *A Trick to Catch the Old One*, successfully performed some 20 years earlier. But *A New Way to Pay Old Debts* is unconventional in its social realism, documenting the collision between two contemporary social philosophies—the profit-oriented business ethics of Sir Giles Overreach (whose name and character echo those of the infamous financier, Sir Giles Mompesson) and the benevolent aristocratic ideal represented by Lady Allworth. Key words, such as "honour," "grace," and "noble" are reiterated with meanings distinct to each speaker's point of view.

For Sir Giles, wealth is essentially a weapon—to crush his enemies, to manipulate the law, to attract useful hangers-on and to enforce a glamorous marriage for his daughter. For Lady Allworth, the wealth she possesses is not a necessary component of nobility; honorable lineage and natural generosity are more important. Even the disorderly and extravagant lifestyle of Frank Wellborn is not incompatible with innate gentility.

The "cruel extortioner" Sir Giles Overreach has two specific aims in the play—to destroy his wastrel nephew Wellborn, and to marry his daughter Margaret to Lord Lovell. Margaret and Tom Allworth, Lovell's page, are lovers. Wellborn persuades the rich widow Lady Allworth to join him in a plot against Sir Giles; by showing affection to Wellborn and seeming to grant him control of her property, she will stimulate Sir Giles's greed ("All that is hers is mine, as I will work him") and make him careless. Lovell, in fact Lady Allworth's suitor, also deceives Sir Giles, pretending to court Margaret while encouraging Tom Allworth's wooing. Finally Sir Giles's schemes are frustrated by his misconceptions and by the treachery of his own venal followers; the collapse of his hopes drives him insane.

The main action serves to accommodate a number of scenes and speeches illustrating the conflicts of Caroline society. For example, Wellborn, an old patron of the innkeeper Tapwell, is rejected when he runs out of funds. His question, "Is not thy house, and all thou hast, my gift?" receives the mercenary response: "I find it not in chalk; and Timothy Tapwell / Does keep no other register." Wellborn's arguments reflect a curious version of *noblesse oblige*: "Am I not he / Whose riots fed and clothed thee?" Similarly, Lady Allworth and her servants scorn Wellborn in his rags, until he reminds them of his noble blood, and his generosity to her late husband: "Are we not base rogues, / That could forget this?" asks the cook. Debts of money are all that matter in Sir Giles's world; for Lady Allworth, debts of gratitude are more important.

Throughout the play, Sir Giles equates his wealth with power over the aristocracy. He describes in detail how he can seize the estates of bankrupt gentlefolk, and he berates Margaret ("The blest child of my industry and wealth") when she is embarrassed to be served by Lady Downfall: "that was once attended / With persons not inferior to myself / In birth."

The contrast between industry and social status is not perceived only by Sir Giles. Lord Lovell chillingly explains to Tom Allworth why he cannot accept Sir Giles's bribes:

> I would not so adulterate my blood
> By marrying Margaret, and so leave my issue
> Made up of several pieces, one part scarlet
> And the other London blue.

(i.e. "scarlet" for nobility; "blue" for trade).

The relationships of servants and masters, patrons and clients, tradespeople and gentry, are assessed throughout the play, always with the conclusion that loyalty flows from the old ideals of aristocracy, and that capitalism breeds selfishness and betrayal. Sir Giles's agents, Justice Greedy, who thinks of nothing but his belly, and Marall, a corrupt attorney, desert him when it serves their purpose. Finally, Sir Giles's extortionate behaviour is seen as unchristian, and his discomfiture is a "precedent to teach wicked men . . . when they leave religion, and turn atheist."

The resolution at the end of the play centres on the lovers' marriages and two comic reversals: Sir Giles, throughout the spokesman for a flinty practicality, loses all control and runs mad; Wellborn, the careless and disorderly spendthrift, joins the troops of Lord Lovell and dedicates himself to a life of military discipline. Yet these reversals are not unprepared for. Sir Giles has from the beginning shown a hot temper and a violence of expression; Wellborn has managed his trickery with strategic skills. The play's final moments, then, are consistent and satisfying.

—Richard Morton

NEWS FROM NOWHERE.
Fiction by William Morris, 1890.

William Morris was a man of many interests and most of them are reflected in his futurist romance, *News from Nowhere*. He was an accomplished rather than a great poet, and his most ambitious work in verse, *The Earthly Paradise*, showed a great discontent with the Victorian world he lived in, combined with a nostalgic yearning for classical antiquity and especially for an idealized medieval world of happy warriors and happy craftsmen and free cities liberated from the yoke of feudalism—a preoccupation he shared with his friends, the Pre-Raphaelites on one hand and the genial anarchist, Prince Peter Kropotkin, on the other.

Morris's medievalism led him towards an exaltation of hand workmanship and a hatred of the tyranny of the machine, and hence of capitalism and the Industrial Revolution. He not only became a leader of the handcraft movements of the later Victorian era, having a considerable influence on new trends in design and architecture, he also gave his dislike of present society an expression in an extremely libertarian form of socialism. He was first a member of the Democratic Federation, but later led away a radical splinter group which became the Socialist League.

According to the framing story of *News from Nowhere*, it was after a meeting of the Socialist League, where the shape of a future society was discussed, that the narrator, William Guest, went home, fell asleep, and found himself in England two centuries in the future. What follows can hardly be described as a novel, for it is almost wholly didactic in nature. The only adventures the narrator really has are intellectual ones, as more and more aspects of this ideal society of the future are revealed to him by the various kindly citizens who guide him and inform him during his brief sojourn.

What Morris offers is a Utopia, but an unusual one. Writers of Utopias—and this applies equally to anti-Utopias like *Brave New World*—from Plato to Sir Thomas More onwards, have generally offered planned societies operated by elites of intellectuals. Utopia is, almost by definition, an authoritarian society where change has ended because all is for the best. Morris, with a refreshing difference, offers the picture of an attractive libertarian society, with no rules, no plans, but a general desire to live as freely and fully and happily as possible.

In accordance with such a desire, England has undergone profound changes which have removed the circumstances hostile to happiness. Assisted by a mysterious source of power that removed the need for drudgery as opposed to work, the people of Nowhere (Utopia translated into English) have dissolved the evil towns of the Industrial Revolution, have abolished Blake's "dark, Satanic mills," and have turned London into a kind of garden city.

The beauty of this renewed environment, and the good nature and physical beauty of the people who inhabit it, going about their cultivation and their craftsmanship, make *News from Nowhere* on one level a book of extraordinary charm, with its revived and clearly coloured medievalism giving it some of the vivid luminosity of the great Books of Hours. But there is a solid and sometimes dense didactic underlayer, as William Guest is passed on from citizen to citizen and learns about the England that has come into being after a violent revolution some time in the past (Morris places it in 1952).

Morris never called himself an anarchist, though he associated closely with anarchists in the Socialist League and was personally close to Kropotkin, and the reasons why he made his own distinction between anarchism and the kind of socialism he projects are hard to determine when one reads *News from Nowhere*, for it is in effect one of the few anarchist utopias, in which nothing is planned, nothing regulated, and growth and change continue.

Government and its apparatus have vanished, with the Houses of Parliament turned into a dung warehouse. There are no soldiers to be seen, and no policemen. Prisons and punishment have vanished, and the principal public buildings are combinations of markets and moot halls where the people of each locality can gather to make whatever common decisions they need. But the economics suggested by the markets is as devolved as the politics suggested by the moot hall. Money and property alike have come to an end and have been replaced by an ethic of sharing, so that the farmers and the craftsmen bring their products to the market where they are freely offered (not exchanged) to those who need and appreciate them. The craftsman expects nothing from his finest work but that it will be in the possession and use of someone who appreciates its beauty and the quality of its workmanship.

There is no directly portrayed dramatic action in *News from Nowhere*, and certainly none that involves William Guest before he awakens to a disillusioning tomorrow in his 19th-century home in Hammersmith. Yet he is aware that there are perturbations even in the happy world of Nowhere. For human beings remain less than angels. Violence and emotional cruelty sometimes flare up; there are homicides and broken marriages. But nothing is treated as a crime or aggravated by punitive laws, and in the end we are reassured with the thought that people have not been stamped into uniformity by any Utopian plan. But in spite of these concessions to emotional probability, Morris was too intent on teaching a lesson to have written a true novel, and so *News from Nowhere* remains the most charming of political tracts.

—George Woodcock

NIGHTMARE ABBEY.
Fiction by Thomas Love Peacock, 1818.

In the spring of 1818, Thomas Love Peacock found himself fighting against low spirits occasioned by the departure of his intimate friend, Shelley, for Italy. *Nightmare Abbey* is a loose amalgam of the thoughts aroused by three separate impulses, regret for Shelley, amused disgust at the mannered gloom and affected misery of some recent literature, and a wish to turn the now-antiquated tradition of the gothic novel to comic effect. To this are added, without much sense of artistic decorum, an attack on the German transcendent philosophy as introduced by Coleridge, and a parody of fanciful scientific speculation embodied in Mr. Asterias's mermaid. The parts do not fit into a satisfying whole, and those, like Marilyn Butler, who have ingeniously argued that they do, have failed to convince.

The comic tone derives its force from the Augustan spirit, steeped in Greek literature and "pagan" wisdom of a man who, despite his affection for Shelley, cannot see what all the fuss is about in the turbulent emotions of his literary contemporaries. This leads to a certain lack of discrimination; the reader may be tempted to suppose that Coleridge's subtlest thoughts were as affected and absurd as the egoistic exhibitionism of Byron when he drank claret out of a human skull. By calling Southey Sackbut (a reference to one of the perquisites of the Poet Laureate), and by an irritable footnote about Burke, whom he accuses of "prostituting his own soul, and betraying his country," he diminishes the force of his own satire. It is easy to say, but very difficult for the reader to believe, that everyone the author happens to disagree with is insincere and venal.

Some of the humour is repetitive and subject to the law of diminishing returns, as with Mr. Listless's endless questions to his servant. There are some sharp hits at Byron, as when Marionetta says: "surely no one who cordially and truly either hates or despises the world will publish a volume every three months to say so." But the comic Byron, admittedly more in evidence after 1818 than before, who is the source of the poet's lasting reputation, is conspicuous by his absence. Though some of Mr. Flosky's speeches are amusing, and some are clever, parodies of passages in Coleridge's prose works, the spirit of Coleridge is completely missed, because his obscurity is wrongly treated as deliberate obfuscation produced by a man more anxious to impress others with his profundity than to search for truth. For all his intelligence and deep learning, there is something of the common-sense Philistine in Peacock, as there is in many Augustans. Everything, they seem to imply, is really very simple and obvious, if only everyone wouldn't make such a song and dance about it.

Two features are characteristic of all Peacock's work. The first, of which we see an instance in the collision and fall of Scythrop and Toobad in chapter 3, is the farcical translation of abstract principles or wayward theorizings into fantastic events. The comic effect is heightened both by the contrast with the ultra-romantic scene just before when Scythrop pleads with Marionetta for a mingling of the blood from the veins of each to be drunk as a "sacrament of love," and by Scythrop's boyish impulse to turn the trivial misfortune of the fall downstairs into a cosmic event signalling the proof of Toobad's pessimistic philosophy.

The other staple feature of Peacock's books is the mingling of ordinary passions and selfish views with a high-flown intellectual theory. This is seen, for instance, when Toobad, in chapter 4 gives abstract arguments to support his wish for his own daughter to be preferred to Marionetta as a bride for Scythrop.

This contest of the two girls, Marionetta and Celinda, for the hand of Scythrop, culminating in the elopement of each, one with Listless and the other with Flosky, gives the book what plot it has. Some readers have thought they detected a tasteless reference to Shelley's two wives: Harriet, who had already killed herself when the book was written, and Mary. Others have seen the contest as an allegory of a literary one, Marionetta representing comedy, and Celinda tragedy, an interpretation which Peacock himself may seem to support by referring to Thalia, the Muse of Comedy, and Melpomene, Muse of Tragedy. Two points at any rate are clear: many readers must have been reminded of Shelley's two wives, whether the author intended this or not. And the closing words of the book "Bring some Madeira," with which Scythrop makes up his mind to forget both girls have the author's emphatic endorsement. Throughout Peacock's work, wine and food bring together in happy agreement characters who can find no ground of intellectual meeting, as in the scene in chapter 11, when Glowry, Cypress, Larynx, Flosky, Listless, Scythrop, Asterias, Toobad, and Hilary all fill their glasses.

Peacock's attitude to the real Shelley and to the Scythrop of the book shows an unusual combination of feelings in his nature. He is at the same time fascinated by ideas and emotionally detached from the excitement they arouse in more sensitive spirits. Most of his satire is aimed at monomania; and the critic takes his stand on a personal, slightly quirky, version of traditional Greek and Augustan views. Moderation, balance, common-sense, enjoyment without excess of the pleasures of the senses, these are his watchwords. A man who has these can take the higher pleasure of argument and philosophizing calmly and without injury.

—A.O.J. Cockshut

NIGHT-THOUGHTS.
(*The Complaint; or, Night-Thoughts on Life, Death, and Immortality*.)
Poem by Edward Young, 1742–46.

Edward Young was already an experienced writer in various genres when he composed the work by which he is best known. He had achieved theatrical success with *Busiris*, produced at Drury Lane in 1719, while his series of satirical poems, begun in 1725 and collected as *Love of Fame: The Universal Passion* in 1728, established the form of "characteristical satire" and influenced Pope's *Moral Essays*. Having taken holy orders in 1724 and become royal chaplain in 1727, Young's poetic output seemed—apart from an occasional patriotic piece—to have come to an end. But, approaching the age of 60, Young discovered a fresh form, one which combined the rhetorical excitements of "graveyard poetry" (the most extreme example of which is Robert Blair's *The Grave* of 1743) with the large scale of the reflective, philosophical poem. Rather than the abstract, *a priori* reasoning of Pope's *Essay on Man* or the deist tendencies of Thomson's *The Seasons*, *Night-Thoughts* operates mainly in the tradition of Christian apologetics, with the emphasis on the truth of revelation and the Christian assurance of immortality.

Like *The Seasons*, *Night-Thoughts* grew over a period of time. The first three Nights were published in 1742, Nights four and five in 1743, six and seven in 1744, the eighth in 1745 and the final Night in 1746. All nine were collected in 1750. There is no completely formal structure to the poem, for it consists mainly of a series of discursive, personal meditations on universal themes of life, death, immortality, and religious faith. Some narrative shape is given by recurring figures, notably Lorenzo, a young man whose susceptibility to the pleasures of the world and the errors of atheism is often the object of the poet's address. His "real" identity and those of other named figures (Philander, Narcissa) have proved the subject of some misguided investigation and guesswork.

The first five Nights are devoted to broad reflections on life and death, with central themes and concerns being repeated and emphatically re-affirmed. In Night 1 ("On Life, Death, and Immortality"), the poet is woken from "short (as usual) and disturb'd repose" to hear the tolling of a bell which prompts him to thoughts on the passing of time and the insubstantiality of worldly things. Only the eternal world can console us, asserts the poet, as, referring to the death of their mutual friend, Philander, he warns Lorenzo to be constantly prepared for death. The manner and tone of the poem, serious moralizing expressed in a series of pointed aphorisms, are established at this stage. The death of Philander is used in Night 2 ("On Time, Death, and Friendship") as a means of reworking the theme of time and introducing that of the value and happiness of true friendship, when "heart meets heart." The third Night ("Narcissa") narrates the death of the young and angelic Narcissa shortly after that of Philander, and expresses emotively the poet's intense sorrow at her loss. From this example, Young draws general observations on the need to focus the mind on the Christian virtues and on the next life in order that death can be properly viewed as the "crown of life." The longer Nights 4 and 5 ("The Christian Triumph" and "The Relapse") elaborate the assertion that only assurance of immortality can free human kind from its fear of death and set life's vicissitudes in true perspective. This assurance is granted by Christ's triumphant sacrifice: "Touch'd by the cross, we live; or, more than die."

The remaining nights concentrate more firmly on Christian apologetics. The sixth and seventh are two parts of a whole, "The Infidel Reclaimed: Containing the Nature, Proof, and Importance of Immortality." Although Young still employs fictional and real examples (the seventh Night opens by referring to the recent death of Pope), it is ideas which are now dominant, in particular the key theme of the whole poem, immortality as a necessity for our present existence. Arguments are adduced from the wonders of nature, the evident superiority of spirit to matter, and life's meaninglessness without a belief in immortality. A powerful passage in Night 7 expresses the despair created by lack of faith. In effect, then, these "arguments" are emotional at basis. Night 8 ("Virtue's Apology") continues on this tack through a series of rhetorical evocations of life's emptiness as a means of persuading Lorenzo to believe that "Bliss has no being, virtue has no strength, / But from the prospect of immortal life." The huge final Night, at 2434 lines by far the longest of the nine, sets out to be the "Consolation" to the preceding "Complaint." It begins by repeating earlier themes, but the substantial part consists of a "Moral Survey of the Nocturnal Heavens," an ecstatic exercise in the physico-theological mode, ranging over the wonders of the universe ("Orb above orb ascending without end!"). Young is, however, careful not to admit deism by also insisting on the parallel power of revelation. Combined, these assertions dispel night and herald eternal day.

Night-Thoughts was for a long time a widely read poem, both in England and abroad. New editions at home were an almost annual event until the mid-19th century, while translations into French, German, and Italian appeared by 1770. Its subject matter, didacticism, length, and exclamatory style have all contributed to its present neglect. Nevertheless, the poem can still make a powerful impact, combining as it does striking individual lines with cumulative impressiveness. Blank verse can be used in a paragraphic manner, but Young adds an epigrammatic force whose directness and antithetical structure forge memorable sayings: "A perpetuity of bliss is bliss"; "Time wasted is existence, used is life"; "A Christian is the highest style of man." The whole poem is held together by a distinct voice, urgent and emotive, committed to flights of the imaginative sublime. It has, as Johnson puts it in his *Life* of Young, "the magnificence of vast extent and endless diversity."

—W.B. Hutchings

NINETEEN EIGHTY-FOUR.
Novel by George Orwell, 1949.

Nineteen Eighty-Four has been regarded a futuristic novel prophesying the takeover of the world by a merciless totalitarian tyranny, and also as a tract against communism. In fact, it was neither. Its intent was admonitory; it was meant as a warning against negative tendencies in our society, and here George Orwell did not intend to single out communist Russia specifically, as he had done in his earlier fable-novel, *Animal Farm*. He wanted us to recognize that the perils were everywhere.

Completed in 1948, *Nineteen Eighty-Four* envisaged an England 36 years ahead, controlled by a totalitarian party upholding the doctrines of Ingsoc. It is part of Oceania, one of the three great empires, all similar in their structure, which rule the world, intermittently at war and tyrannising the marginal territories of what we now call the Third World.

This political structure, so unlike that of the democracies, is given an uncanny reality by the fact that in other respects Orwell's novel is non-futuristic, and the cityscapes are those of the London of the 1940's, even more shabby and battered by the sporadic warfare, while the standard of living is even more deprived than that of wartime London.

Complete as the tyranny is made to seem, with its all-pervading Thought Police and the vast machine for the concoction of propaganda and the rewriting of history known as the Ministry of Truth, its success is clearly not total, and two workers in the Ministry of Truth, Winston Smith and his lover Julia, set out on their private rebellion, which in his case is inspired by a recognition of how the facts of the past are being distorted to serve present policies and in her case by a hedonistic rebellion against the sexual puritanism which is an inevitable aspect of the totalitarian order.

Winston and Julia imagine they have found a perfect refuge to follow their "degenerate" private lives in a room in the prole districts of the city (for society is now divided into two sharply divided classes, the Party, and the proles who have no political life but some personal freedom), and they become involved through a high party official, O'Brien, in what they are led to imagine is a network of disaffection, centred on the great enemy of the state, a certain Goldstein, who is reminiscent of Trotsky, the great enemy in Stalinist Russia.

But their little nest of pleasure turns out to be a trap, and O'Brien is a betrayer, an agent of the Thought Police; Winston finds himself in the dreaded Room 101 in the Ministry of Love, the police headquarters. In a long process of torture and mental conditioning, Winston is broken down physically and subordinated mentally to the will of the regime, and thrown out of the machine like a rag to spend the days that remain to him in a café frequented by broken rebels like himself, all awaiting elimination at the will of the Party.

Nineteen Eighty-Four is both realistic and satirical. The verisimilitude of the background of London in 1948 transferred to London in 1984 is compelling, yet at the same time it is a satire as well as a representation of the world of 1948, with its built-in Utopian tendencies, and as such it is often extreme to the point of caricature; the Ministry of Truth on this level is a caricature representation of the great propaganda agencies of World War II and especially of the BBC where Orwell worked some unhappy years; Goldstein's account of Oceania is a caricature of Marxist historiography; Newspeak is a caricature of Basic English; and the beetlelike Party members are caricatures of the socialist doctrinaires whom Orwell had already flayed in *The Road to Wigan Pier*.

But at this point a basic dichotomy appears, for Orwell's intentions in writing *Nineteen Eighty-Four* were not entirely satirical; he also wanted to issue a warning about the future, and it is hard to be satirical about the future. One is tempted to be either optimistic or pessimistic; the first carries the danger of romanticism, the second of melodrama, and both are prominent in the novel. Winston's rebellion is largely supported by his romantic nostalgia for the past, and the nostalgic tone is enhanced by the frequency with which he experiences attractive yet ominous dreams that set the tone for his adventure, an adventure as fragile and vulnerable as the tiny bit of moral magnified within the glass paperweight which he treasures as a fragment of the past.

That fragment is broken as his dream is subsumed in the nightmare of Room 101, when the novel moves into melodrama, whose false light many critics believe distort the final chapters of *Nineteen Eighty-Four*. Yet even the quality of Grand Guignol and the echoes of Poe that hang over the doings in Room 101 cannot diminish the revelation Orwell makes at this point. He himself once said of Swift that he possessed "a terrible intensity of vision, capable of picking out a single hidden truth and then magnifying and distorting it." Orwell picked on the hidden truth that Bakunin once knew and which the Marxists obscured—that the love of power is stronger and more perverting than any material or economic motive. He magnified and distorted the insight into a vision more terrifying than anything in Swift.

Yet there is a further ironic aspect to the book. Intermittently Winston recognizes the insanity of his torturer O'Brien and of his prophecies of an unending world of slaves and masters. And though Winston surrenders, we know there will be others like him, which is the only reason why Room 101 exists, and that, as Orwell said elsewhere, even if the slave society is created it "will not endure, because slavery is no longer a stable basis of human society."

—George Woodcock

NORTH AND SOUTH.
Novel by Elizabeth Gaskell, 1855.

Elizabeth Gaskell's *North and South* was serialized in Dickens's weekly *Household Words* from 2 September 1854 to 27 January 1855, where it was preceded by Dickens's own novel set in the industrial north, *Hard Times*. (Dickens and Gaskell conferred, to avoid overlap.) He much admired her work (*Mary Barton* "most profoundly affected and impressed" him) and published much of it in his weeklies, though he found her unpractised and unskilled in serialization and insisted on some alterations. For the book edition she restored some of this material, and added chapter titles. Dickens had named the novel *North and South* (Gaskell had intended to name it after its heroine); opinions differ on how wisely Dickens thus directed readers' attention and how far the story is helpfully seen in relation to the spate of "industrial" or "social problem" novels. Gaskell's first novel had been *Mary Barton: A Tale of Manchester Life*. Here returning to that city she calls it Milton-Northern, in Darkshire, partly to avoid the controversies and recriminations which had followed her earlier work, and the narrative is now centred less on working-class characters than on employers.

The novel's opening is bumpy. It starts in London where 18-year-old Margaret Hale has for some years been living with an aunt and cousin in elegant circumstances but is now moving to the family home at Helstone in Hampshire, where her father is the parson. No sooner has she got there and rejected an offer of marriage (the suitor then almost disappears from the narrative) than she discovers that her father feels obliged on conscientious grounds to resign from the Church. Mr. Hale and his doubts do not prove, however, to be a centre of attention; rather, this is a device for moving the family (in chapter 6) to Milton-Northern where Hale can make a living as a tutor. The novel effectively gets going in chapter 7 with their arrival in Milton, which Margaret—it is her activities and consciousness that dominate the novel—finds physically, socially, and ideologically very alien and, at first, repulsive. Gaskell, a southerner by birth, who had spent much of her life in rural Cheshire, married a Manchester minister of religion, and had thus personally trodden the path which occurs so often in these socially exploratory novels, as the genteel and sensitive but ignorant outsider confronts the new social and economic circumstances of a factory town or other such environment. The novel also uses another popular fictional situation from the period—the tensions, misunderstandings, and possible fulfilment when sexual attraction takes place across a major cultural or class divide. Many novels begin, too, with a marriageable young person arriving in a new place.

The slow-ripening relationship between Margaret and the active and forceful manufacturer John Thornton—to some degree a matter of "Prejudice and Pride"—is complicated by local industrial unrest during a recession in the cotton trade, in which Thornton is prominent. Margaret, who has made some acquaintance with working men and their families, is more sympathetic to their cause. A strike and a riot ensue (as often in this kind of fiction); Margaret and Thornton get involved, and her trying to protect him from assault leads to his first—and premature—courtship attempt. But the industrial and North/South themes are intermittent: this is basically a domestic/courtship novel, though indeed the obstructions conventionally needed to delay the wedding bells to the finale here mostly take regional, cultural, social, and ideological forms. (Gaskell contemplated but rejected the idea of giving Margaret a rival, though the unsatisfactory episode of her brother Frederick makes Thornton think that he has one.) Margaret arrives in Milton sure that nobody in "trade" can be a gentleman, whereas her poverty-stricken ex-parson father is educated, professional, and therefore an ex officio one. But the stranger's eye she brings to Milton does help the reader to explore the ethos of the living and working conditions in the new industrial towns, and her discussions and disputes with Thornton and others involve important issues about master/man relationships, the ethics of capitalist enterprise (the narrator calls it "the deep selfishness of competition") and trade union activity. This is informed by Gaskell's 20-odd years' residence in Manchester (she alone of this type of novelist had such experience) as a goodwilled middle-class lady and "a true Christian—(only people call [me] socialist and communist)." The reactions of Margaret's parents to this new environment, and of Thornton's proud, redoubtable, and possessive mother to Margaret, further illustrate North/South—and *nouveau-riche*/traditionally genteel—differences, which include not only modes of employment but also manners and such matters of taste as interior decoration.

Much of the plot paraphernalia of current fiction appears: coincidence, a mystery man, a dying girl, plenty of other deaths ("I wish to Heaven her people would keep a little firmer on their legs!" said Dickens of an earlier *Household Words* story), a timely plot-solving legacy. Inevitably as in other cross-cultural courtships (e.g., Disraeli's *Sybil*) the eventual union involves a diminution of attitudinal differences. Thornton sees the necessity for a less impersonal, more sympathetic attitude to his employees, "cultivating some intercourse with the hands beyond the mere 'cash nexus'" (Carlyle's influence is apparent here), and he recognizes the possibility of error for "men groping in new circumstances . . . full of difficulties that must be encountered . . . not merely pushed aside for the time." Margaret, on her return to London, finds herself missing the sincerity and earnestness of Milton conversation. Little is seen of Helstone in the narrative—the South is mostly represented by the exiled Hale family's reactions to Milton—but Margaret, who earlier had idealized it, later becomes more conscious of its shortcomings (brutal and poorly-paid agricultural work, vicious superstition) and, on briefly revisiting it, while responding nostalgically to its prettiness, she realizes that she, and it, have changed and that she could not return there. She has enlarged her mind and sympathies—has grown up. Gaskell is adroit throughout in conveying shifts in outlook and emotional life of which the protagonists are imperfectly and belatedly aware.

—Philip Collins

NORTHANGER ABBEY.
Novel by Jane Austen, 1817.

Northanger Abbey was not published until after Jane Austen's death, an earlier attempt to publish having been unsuccessful. The primary impulse in its composition, like that of *Pride and Prejudice* and *Sense and Sensibility*, was a desire to parody those forms of fiction which were most popular at the time—the gothic novel and the sentimental novel centering on a young woman's exposure to the dangers of society.

Catherine Morland is Austen's youngest heroine. She is also her most undistinguished, having neither Elizabeth

Bennet's wit and fine eyes, nor Eleanor Dashwood's sense and balance. Youth and inexperience are her most distinguishing characteristics. Her only knowledge of the world outside her secure and happy home has been gained from novels which present a picture of beautiful, talented, and artistic young heiresses running a gamut of dangers from evil uncles/guardians who try to get control of their fortunes by forcing them into insupportable marriages, immuring them in lonely fortresses and convents, or even murdering them. The scene of these novels is, inevitably, a wild mountainous region with chasms, ravines, precipices, and old, decaying castles and abbeys which are themselves full of hidden rooms, secret passages, ominous portraits, and old chests with mysterious manuscripts detailing past horrors and atrocities. Alternatively, beautiful and virtuous heroines living in recognizable English landscapes, find that their path to true love is impeded by low relations or by wicked suitors determined to compromise them in the eyes of their high-minded lovers and the more respectable members of that society in which they should rightfully move.

Austen, always so careful to indicate the major theme and tone of the novel in the first few sentences, immediately establishes Catherine as utterly unheroic. "No one who had ever seen Catherine Morland in her infancy would have supposed her born to be a heroine. Her situation in life, the character of her father and mother, her own person and disposition, were all equally against her." She is plain, tomboyish, comfortably off, not an orphan or an heiress, her parents are kind and sensible, she has no innate though untaught aptitude for art or music; in short she is perfectly natural and ordinary and good-tempered. She does, however, undergo a series of adventures similar to those of the heroines of a Fanny Burney or an Ann Radcliffe novel. She is prevented from walking with Henry Tilney by the foolishness of John Thorpe; it appears that she has been impolite to Henry's sister and so must defend her behaviour. She is left relatively unguarded in her coming out in the society of Bath by the indolence of her guardians there and is, consequently, exposed to social embarrassment and boredom.

Since *Northanger Abbey* is a happy book, all of these incidents are no more than minor evils, ordinary, domestic, quickly remedied, and attended with no tragic consequences. The same is not entirely true of the "gothic" elements of the novel. When Catherine goes to visit Northanger Abbey it is, at first, her own overheated imagination which causes problems. Saturated in the excitement of books like *The Mysteries of Udolpho*, she expects to find adventure in the romantic abbey. She is overcome with the idea of reading hidden documents, only to find in them nothing more exciting than a laundry list. Then she imagines the rather gruff General Tilney to have made away with his wife, or to have her secretly hidden somewhere in the grounds of the Abbey. So taken up is she with these fantasies that she is careless of the consequences of her imaginings and has to be brought back to a sense of reality and proportion by Henry Tilney, playing the role, which is to become familiar in Austen's novels, of educator of the young heroine.

On the simple level of plot, Austen is debunking the excesses of other novels by grounding her heroine and story in a familiar domestic setting and pointing out that gothic-style adventures are unlikely to take place in the Home Counties. On another level, she is simultaneously asserting the importance of the novel form and reprimanding those who think it trivial "women's reading" and not fit for Sunday perusal. Henry Tilney, one of her ideal young men, whose views are firmly endorsed throughout, actually admits to enjoying novels. In this he is echoing an authorial intrusion which, stylistically clumsy though it may be, is important as an early statement of Austen's novelistic intentions. "'And what are you reading, Miss—?' 'Oh! it is only a novel!' replies the young lady; while she lays down her book with affected indifference, or momentary shame. 'It is only "Cecilia," or "Camilla," or "Belinda";' or, in short, only some work in which the greatest powers of the mind are displayed, in which the most thorough knowledge of human nature, the happiest delineation of its varieties, the liveliest effusions of wit and humour, are conveyed to the world in the best chosen language."

With this view of the potential of the novel, Austen moves in *Northanger Abbey* away from mockery of existing novels to a realistic account of believable wickedness in the Home Counties. Burlesque gives way to satire as she reveals that General Tilney's interest in Catherine is based solely on the erroneous idea that she is an heiress. When he learns that she is poor he cruelly exposes her to the undeserved hurt and humiliation of being turned out of Northanger Abbey and to the very real dangers of travelling unescorted by public conveyance over 70 miles to her home, separated from her friend and her lover, and ignorant of what she can have done to merit such treatment. In the process, a novel about the undue influence of gothic horrors on a receptive but undiscriminating mind becomes a moral tale of the evils of subordinating happiness and an estimation of the worth of others to monetary considerations; in short to a discussion of one of Austen's permanent themes and a revelation of her inevitable progress from the parodic to the moral.

—Anne Clune

NOSTROMO.
Novel by Joseph Conrad, 1904.

As an epic novel of adventure in an exotic setting, *Nostromo* is the most complex example of a popular Edwardian category. Like the novella "Heart of Darkness" it combines a critique of imperialist activity in an undeveloped country with an existential quest, and critics dispute, sometimes quite bitterly, over which aspect of the book, the political or the metaphysical, is predominant. In the Author's Note he wrote in 1917, Joseph Conrad speaks of writing *Nostromo* "in the heat and clash of my own conflicting emotions." The record of those conflicts in the book's deep structure is a principal source of its power to engage and fascinate through successive readings and to generate divergent interpretations. There is no novel which more requires re-reading for the sense of difficulty and perplexity to give way to admiration, not of the technical cleverness, but the achieved result.

Conrad gives fictional reality to an entire country, Costaguana, focusing mainly on its chief port, Sulaco, and the surrounding district. Its topography and history, the ethnic divisions in its population, political factions and social groupings, the process of its industrial development and its relations to the rest of the world are not inert background; they inhere in the trajectory of the novel, in the characterisation of the figures shown in close-up, and not least in the undifferentiated crowds of peasants and labourers, skilled industrial workers, armies, and refugees that move continually through Sulaco, its harbour and hinterland. This model of a sphere of imperialist influence (represented by the visit of Sir John from England and Mr. Holroyd from the U.S.), and Conrad's prescient location of it in Latin America, has proved easily identifiable with recent actualities—in Chile or Salvador, but also the Philippines or Vietnam—and has been widely influential on a whole category of novels and films, often through Graham Greene as intermediary. Zdzislaw Najder's belief that Conrad was "really" writing about Poland in this work may trigger a recognition that *Nostromo* is based on a radical analysis of historical process and of human beings acting "in history."

A cyclic view of history is implied in the accounts of Costaguana's successive revolutions, the references back from the conditions of modern exploitation to the Spanish conquest and occupation, and reminders of the Inquisition in the systematic torturing of Dr. Monygham and Hirsch. Tyranny and oppression reassert themselves after every violent upheaval. At the level of character, historical determinism is mirrored in Nostromo's fatalistic attitude. It is also implied in Conrad's spare but potent use of myth: the myth of original sin, the "paradise of snakes" and the fall into knowledge and self-consciousness; and the myth of the earth's treasure and its guardians, ambiguously placed in chapter 1 as a legend "within men's memory" which may look forward or back to the main action of the novel. Conrad tests the historical logic of capitalism in the working-out of a specific enterprise commanded by Charles Gould, a Costaguaneran of English stock, whose initial vision of the development of the silver mine as the source of general prosperity, order, justice, and stability, proves ultimately dehumanising to him, divisive and oppressive to the country. The novel has been interpreted as Marxist in tendency or by default, but it intimates a new revolution to come, whose proletarian conspirators meet, after Separation when l'Albergo d'Italia Una is no more, in the Café Lombroso (named for the now-discredited student of criminal types). Capitalism and communism are locked into the same system of historical materialism.

The first of the major difficulties facing the reader comes in the form of tangled chronology, as episode is related to episode by apparently digressive modes of association. (One of the least shadowed humorous touches in the novel is the simple Captain Mitchell's insistent call for his chronometer.) This is part of a general indirectness of approach: a kaleidoscopic method of frequently shifting temporal perspectives and centres of consciousness, yielding a sense of teeming life, simultaneities of action, a mesh of variously interrelated events and characters, a mass of detail, echoing phrases and images holding the essence of events or personalities. The presentation and interpretation of characters is often indirect, achieved analogically as when the Master of the Mine acknowledges the bandit self-styled Master of the Campo, or in the contrast between Decoud and Monygham, both of whom act out of devotion to a woman. Charles Gould is presented directly in his silences, the twisting of his moustaches and his spurs, through his wife's love and Monygham's compassion for her; but he is represented at the centre of the novel by Nostromo, the silver in human form, his nickname "our man" as Gould is the man Holroyd "runs" in Costaguana, and Nostromo's awakening from innocence to knowledge matches the moment of Gould's self-recognition before he is altogether engulfed by the mine.

Conrad's view of society admits no heroes, though it respects Giorgio Viola's reverence for Garibaldi. Nostromo performs before the crowd in the role of a stage hero—he would not be out of place in *Carmen*—and meets his death from old Giorgio's bullet, fired in defence of honour, in the mode of romantic melodrama. Sotillo "of many teeth," feigning sickness in his hammock, is a caricatured horror of *opéra bouffe*. Theatricality is Conrad's device to subdue realism to the general convention of moral fable and bridge the gap between the narrative of events and the extensive analytical commentary foisted within Captain Mitchell's obtuse presentation of Sulaco to an anonymous tourist.

The most crucial difficulty confronting the reader is of relating the account of Decoud's end to the rest of the book. Within the adventure-novel convention it is a long-drawn-out anti-climax, but no part of the book is more powerful and memorable than this version of the familiar fable of man isolated from society as a castaway on an island. The scepticism of the intellectually brilliant Decoud is intimately related to Conrad's own ironic and pessimistic cast of mind and had to be dealt with. Confronted by "a universe of incomprehensible images," a Nothingness which mirrors the void in himself, Decoud conceives "the first moral sentiment of his manhood," the sense of a wasted life. His suicide is a not ignoble surrender to the vast unknown. It was anticipated in Chapter 1's presentation of a theatre of action endowed with meaning: the Golfo Placido which fills with "blind darkness" is also a "sanctuary," an "unroofed temple." *Nostromo* as a whole balances on the verge of an absolute pessimism, as Conrad undercuts even the self-knowledge and sacrifice of Monygham and represents Mrs. Gould's compassion in the image of a fairy with a silver tea-service. But she, too, has a symbolic counterpart in Linda who, at the end of the book, cries out her love as her eyes strain towards the horizon, over which hovers ambiguously a silver cloud.

—Margery Morgan

O

ODE ON A DISTANT PROSPECT OF ETON COLLEGE. Poem by Thomas Gray, 1747.

Ode on a Distant Prospect of Eton College is the earliest of the small number of truly distinguished poems Thomas Gray produced during his lifetime. It was written in the summer of 1742, eight years before the great *Elegy Written in a Country Churchyard*, and is in some ways a preparation for it. Gray himself had gone to Eton College, the most famous of the English schools for boys, along with his close friends Richard West and Horace Walpole, and the poem is in part a nostalgic reminiscence of his experience there. The grim forebodings in the second half of the ode reflect Gray's depressed frame of mind immediately after the early death of West. In genre it is an "Horatian" ode, a quiet, contemplative kind of poem (like the *Elegy*), as distinguished from the more passionate "Pindaric" odes ("The Bard" and "The Progress of Poesy") that he composed many years later.

In its verse form the poem is extremely complex and difficult, containing exactly one hundred lines divided into 10 stanzas of 10 lines each. Metrically each stanza is basically iambic tetrameter, except that lines 2, 4, and 10 are trimeters, with a fixed rhyme scheme of A B A B CC D FF D. This very confining pattern is repeated consistently in all 10 stanzas, and it enhances the overall impression of formality and high seriousness that the poem conveys. The opening quatrains, with their alternating lines of four and three feet and their tight rhymes, are especially distinctive and have an impressive lapidary quality in most stanzas, while the final trimeter line has a very effective clinching or summarizing function. The fact that Gray, working within these incredibly rigid constraints, is able to achieve a smooth flow of words, a feeling of polished ease, is a technical triumph of a high order and an important part of the pleasure the poem gives us.

In its overall structure the ode is equally masterful. It divides neatly into two halves: the first five stanzas evoke the childish joys of the schoolboys, the last five depict the adult miseries that await them. Line 52—"The little victims play!"—is the turning point, at almost exactly the center point of the poem. In his opening stanza Gray pictures himself viewing Eton College and the Thames valley from a distance, from the heights of Windsor Castle. It is indeed a "distant prospect," both in space and in time, and this is a key factor in the poet's strategy. The emotions Gray gives vent to are, of course, deeply personal in origin, but he wishes to transform these feelings and ideas into universals, to give them general relevance; and to do so requires a certain distancing of himself as narrator from the schoolboys he contemplates. He says in stanza 2 that the faraway vista of the college is soothing to his "weary soul" as he recalls his own childhood. In the next stanza, addressed to "Father Thames," he wonders what the boys of today are doing, and he re-creates his own youth, not directly but obliquely, by imagining the lives of current Etonians (stanzas 3–5). He sees them as heroically, naively living in the present, full of joy with no serious concern for the future. In stanza 6, however, the poet shifts his focus to the pains and sorrows of adult life that await the innocent boys. The next three stanzas go on to portray these miseries in gloomy detail, resulting from the Passions ("The vultures of the mind"), from Ambition, from the physical decay of old age and death, and so forth. Finally, in stanza 10, the speaker concludes that the happy boys of Eton are better off not knowing about the harsh realities of mature human experience.

The style of Gray's ode has often been adversely criticized in this century as being too artificial, cluttered with "poetic diction" and rather labored personifications. The third stanza, where Gray describes sporting activities, is notorious: the poet asks Father Thames "Who foremost now delight to cleave / With pliant arm thy glassy wave?" This is, indeed, a strange and slightly absurd way to picture young lads swimming in the river, and it has caused problems not only for modern readers but even for 18th-century ones like Edward Gibbon, the historian, who made gentle fun of the whole passage. Some readers have complained that the language here is so roundabout that it is not entirely clear just what the boys are actually doing! Two points in Gray's defense, however, need to be made. First of all, the truly excessive diction is confined to stanza 3; the other nine stanzas are relatively free of it. Second, it was no part of Gray's purpose to render a specifically realistic picture of Etonian sports; in fact, such detail would have distracted the reader from the philosophic idea that is at the center of the ode. He needed only to *suggest* these activities in a general, impersonal fashion, and the artificial diction is a way of achieving that.

On the other hand, Gray's style in this ode is frequently eloquent, and the reader who can get beyond stanza 3 will find much to admire. The image of the boys escaping off-limits on forbidden rambles into the countryside (stanza 4), for example, concludes with the memorable lines, "They hear a voice in every wind, / And snatch a fearful joy." Even better is the opening quatrain of the sixth stanza, the turning point of the poem:

> Alas, regardless of their doom,
> The little victims play!
> No sense have they of ills to come,
> Nor care beyond today . . .

Here it will be noted that the diction, far from being artificial, is remarkably simple, direct, and powerful; and this is true also of the moving quatrain in the final stanza:

> To each his sufferings; all are men,
> Condemned alike to groan:
> The tender for another's pain,
> The unfeeling for his own.

These lines lead smoothly into the speaker's conclusion that the boys in their fool's paradise are better off not knowing of the universal misery that lies ahead; he says, in unforgettable words: "No more: where ignorance is bliss, / 'Tis folly to be wise."

The Eton College ode, on the whole and despite some inflated language, is a poignant and impressive piece of work. For it Gray provided an ancient Greek motto from

Menander, which translates as follows: "I am a man, a sufficient excuse for being unhappy," and these words sum up the point of view of the speaker, a suffering adult reflecting on the carefree joys of his youth. The poem gives us a dual vision: that of the naive boys seen in a distant garden of Eden, and that of the disillusioned grief-stricken man musing on their innocence and ignorance. Both visions reflect Gray's own personal experience in both phases of his life, but he employs various devices (stately diction, a far vista) to distance himself from the specific joys and agonies in order to make the contrast a universal one for all people in all times. By virtue of some touching and powerful phrasing that looks forward to his masterpiece, the great *Elegy* of a few years later, and by virtue of superb craftsmanship, he largely succeeds.

—Allan H. MacLaine

ODE ON A GRECIAN URN.
Poem by John Keats, 1820.

The stanzaic pattern of John Keats's odes varies from 10 to 18 lines and from three to eight stanzas. The prevailing pattern consists of 10 lines composed of a quatrain rhyming *abab* and a sestet rhyming in variations of *cde*, the same for both "Ode on a Grecian Urn" and "Ode to a Nightingale." Both odes also have similar movements, similar tensions between the eternal and the mortal, and similar speculations about immortality; but the former, because of a calculated or inadvertent ambiguity in the last two lines has probably aroused more controversy and commentary than any other poem in the English language. Harvey T. Lyon in *Keats' Well-Read Urn*: *An Introduction to Literary Method* (1958) has compiled over 80 such critiques by prominent scholars and authors, none of which agrees in every respect in interpretation and evaluation with any other.

The subject is ostensibly a Grecian urn, both a work of art and a receptacle for the ashes of the dead; but it is a composite urn, not a particular one, even "overwrought" with "marble men and maidens," more in keeping with the Elgin Marbles than terracotta; and the subject thus becomes the creative imagination in poetry as well as in the visual arts. The difference between *to* a nightingale and *on* an urn is significant and suggests a greater detachment from the subject in the latter.

Three distinct movements are apparent in these odes: first, the external description of the subject; second, the entering into and becoming one with the subject, creating through imagination an absolute empathy with the experiences suggested; and third, the emergence and separation from the subject, with a commentary about or evaluation of the experience. The process involved in the second movement is what Keats thought of as negative capability, the ability to lose consciousness of one's identity in the creative process so that the creation and the creator are one.

Stanza I is merely suggestive of the scenes on the imaginary urn of "leaf-fring'd legend"—men or gods pursuing reluctant maidens, musicians, and "wild ecstasy"; but the significance of the art form is that of a record of an earlier time and culture. Stanza II begins the apotheosis of "unheard melodies" of an eternal sort which "pipe to the spirit" across the chasm of centuries, of trees perpetually in leaf, and "bold lovers" who, though never achieving their bliss, will love forever and their loves "be fair." In stanza III, Keats, at least momentarily and with great intensity abandons himself to total sensuous rapport with the boughs for which it is perpetual Spring, with the never-tiring melodist, "For ever piping songs, for ever new," and with the lover who can look forward always to warm fruition, a "happy love" "For ever panting, and forever young." But then—so much for negative capability—we are plunged into the reality of Keats's living anguish—terrible desire, constant frustration, and the daily awareness of his impending mortality, "a burning forehead and a parching tongue," just as in the "Ode to a Nightingale" "Where youth grows pale, and spectre-thin, and dies," all symptoms of his tubercular affliction. The experience is at once felt and an indelible contrast etched between the transience of the human condition and the relative permanence of art. Stanza IV is an outward drifting, describing this time a religious procession with a garlanded sacrificial heifer led by a priest to an unknown altar for an unknown purpose. Stanza V brings us back to our own world to consider the implications of art and eternity, the words "Cold Pastoral!" breaking the spell. And it is from what the urn tells to man generation after generation that a seemingly eternal controversy has emerged.

Because Keats heavily punctuated his letters with dashes in place of periods and because he was terminally ill at the time of the final publication in book form and unable to edit the text, no authentic reading can be established beyond a reasonable doubt and the intent of the last two lines of the poem must remain ambiguous. "'Beauty is truth, truth beauty,'—that is all / Ye know on earth, and all ye need to know." Obviously, if both lines were enclosed in quotation marks and "Truth" and "Beauty" both capitalized, the urn would be suggesting, in effect, that beauty is the absolute truth for which man is seeking and that he need know no other. Newell F. Ford's *The Prefigurative Imagination of John Keats*: *A Study of the Beauty-Truth Identification and Its Implications* (1966) is based on a concordance and a study of Keats's use of the word "truth." His conclusion is that the preponderant use tended toward the relativistic. In other odes, Keats notes that "Beauty cannot keep her lustrous eyes" and "She dwells with Beauty—Beauty that must die," so it is obvious that Keats was aware that all beauty is not eternal or absolute. On the other hand, he does say in "Endymion" that "A THING of beauty is a joy for ever." Many critics believe that the portion of the last two lines of the "Ode on a Grecian Urn" following the dash are addressed by the poet to the reader. Others feel that they are addressed by the poet to the urn which, being secure and fixed in its beauty and having no knowledge of earthly pain and anguish, is ironically unaware of any other truth.

Keats unquestionably achieved the all-consuming ambition of his very brief life—to be ranked among the poets. His unique and memorable poetic diction, his intense and sensuous imagery, his effective use of tension and ambiguity, and the paradox that "dost tease us out of thought" have made "Ode on a Grecian Urn" a living monument to the creative imagination.

—Wesley D. Sweetser

ODE ON MELANCHOLY.
Poem by John Keats, 1820.

Before analysing the poem, a brief word is necessary on the concept of melancholy itself. To the Romantics, the word no longer signified a state of clinical gloominess, strangeness, and solitary wanderings. By now, it also implied a positive, heightened sensibility which could, of course, bring inspiration to the artist. A second important point is the paradoxical romantic belief that pain can be an essential part of pleasure. These two ideas are integral to an understanding of John Keats's "Ode on Melancholy."

The first stanza dwells very much on negatives at both lexical and syntactic levels. The first line contains four direct negatives (No, no, not, neither), one image of death (Lethe) and one of distortion (twist). The remainder of the stanza elaborates on the theme, and there is an abundance of nouns (many drawn from nature) suggesting death: wolf's bane, nightshade, rosary, yew-berries, beetle, death-moth, owl, sorrow, shade. There are also negative adjectives and adverbs: pale, poisonous, mournful, drowsily, and a verb: drown. Another classical allusion (Prosperine) likewise suggests death.

What is fascinating about the use of verbs in the first stanza is the interplay between the active and passive connotations. An initial active imperative (go) is followed by a passive (suffer); similarly, the imperative "make" is succeeded by the passive, "let." This typically Keatsian procedure (other examples can be found in the "Ode to a Nightingale") leads to a deconstruction of the position of the speaking subject, who is neither master nor victim. This confusion of control is finally resolved in the emphatic use of the future tense "will come . . . And drown" (lines 9–10). This establishes death as dominator. The final line of the first stanza could be seen as a transition between stanzas one and two. "Soul" encompasses both the death of the first stanza and the life of the second. "Wakeful" forms a direct contrast with "drowsily" of the previous line, and again anticipates the second stanza.

Stanza II reverses this posture and foregrounds melancholy in the positive aspects. There is no control over the advent of melancholy, but at least we are now being given suggestions as to how to implement it in an aesthetically positive sense when it does occur. In contrast to the death-laden connotations of the first stanza, we now move to an affirmation of life forces (e.g. melancholy comes from heaven, in the month of April, and, by syntactic ambiguity, can be seen as fostering droop-headed flowers). At this point, we therefore move to imperatives of positive action, in which hyperbolic verbs like "glut" subsume the negatives of sorrow and in which Keats exploits the positive connotations of "morning roses" and peonies (a flower of healing, named after the god Paeon). Even the anger of a mistress is turned to positive account, as the "imprisoning" and "feeding" gives the poet aesthetic sustenance. It is interesting that the typically Keatsian synaesthesia is exemplified in the last six lines of the stanza as scent (rose), sight (rainbow), sound (anger), touch (soft), and taste (feed) combine to form a sensuous unity in contrast to the dissociative processes of stanza I. Similarly, at the syntactic level, the triply-repeated "or" replaces the "nor" of stanza I.

Stanza III, while remaining affirmative, introduces a modal shift to abstractions such as Beauty, Joy, Pleasure, Delight, Melancholy. This stanza represents the resolution of the conflicts presented in stanzas I and II. Melancholy is oxymoronically linked with beauty (cf. "aching pleasure") and deconstructs her sovereignty with the realisation that, in the very moment of triumph, Beauty "must die" and Joy "bid adieu."

The final six lines of the poem can be seen as a kind of code, articulating the binary opposition that has been the underlying matrix of the entire text: at the heart of Delight (sanctified by the word "temple") dwells Melancholy, exercising her sovereignty. Keats develops this with highly explicit sexual imagery as he concludes that only he who is capable of appreciating this paradox can, with his "strenuous tongue" "burst Joy's grape." (This forms a structurally-integrated contrast to the "poisonous wine" of stanza I.) Such a privileged person (i.e., the poet) can alone "taste" (oxymoronically) the "sadness of her might," leaving himself, paradoxically, one of melancholy's conquests ("trophies"). Once again, Keats has reversed the passive and active modes, as in stanza I, and has expressed the aesthetic in terms of the sensuous.

—Anne Katherine Monaghan and A.W. Lyle

ODE TO A NIGHTINGALE.
Poem by John Keats, 1820.

At 23 John Keats came into his own as a great English poet with the odes written in May 1819. Perhaps the greatest, the "Ode to a Nightingale," dramatizes the profound emotion to which the bird's song moves him. Almost hypnotised by the song's beauty, the poet is drawn out of his ordinary awareness of the human world. The first effect is physiological and the poem's evocation of physical sensation (yet linked to cultural values) is extraordinary. The poet feels as if he has taken poison ("hemlock") and is sinking into the forgetfulness of death, hearing only the bird singing "of summer in full-throated ease." In emulation, to ease his own throat and alleviate the "fever" of human life he thirsts for wine, real wine though redolent of myth and tradition—"Hippocrene," "Dance, and Provençal song." He hopes—his nerve endings hope—to escape "The weariness, the fever, and the fret" of ordinary consciousness through man's ancient comfort, wine. The bubbles will wink at reality; he can "leave the world unseen, / And with [the nightingale] fade away into the forest dim."

But how can he be with the nightingale if he lets himself "dissolve"? Consciousness is necessary. Bacchus and his beasts are rejected in favor of the conscious and willed act of poetic imagining. The "viewless" (invisible) wings of Poesy transport the poet to the imagined world of the nightingale while shutting out the "view" of the world's fever and fret. There follows a remarkable passage in which the poet imagines himself imagining. From the "here" (line 24) of the daily world Poesy transports the poet to the "here" (line 38) of the nightingale's world. This is not, however, the daytime "melodious plot" of stanza 1 with its "beechen green and shadows numberless." It is suddenly "night," and although the moon may be shining far above, "here there is no light," and the poet "cannot see." It is as if Keats had closed his eyes the better to imagine. The poet's imaginative effort in identifying the flowers about him only by their scent helps us experience vicariously his imaginative effort of placing himself in the woods with the nightingale. The "forest dim" itself seems to be imagined, since the last stanza presents the real landscape as a rural but not a forest scene.

The wish to escape from the feverish daytime world into a nighttime world of absolute beauty is a death wish. To be released from time is to die. The deathlike sensations of drinking poison or wine and dissolving have their climax when the poet, having escaped to the nightingale, imagines himself in "embalmed darkness," corpselike, surrounded with flowers. The way to avoid life's fever and fret, which after all are caused by the death-threat of disease and age, is to die while one is conscious only of beauty, to pour forth one's soul in death while the nightingale pours forth his in ecstasy. Then the bird's song of summer would become a "high requiem" for the poet and for figures out of the past or from literary tradition, such as Ruth, or those who drowned in "perilous seas, in faery lands." The dead poet, deaf as well as blind, would have "become a sod." At the end of the poem the literary tradition, in stanza 2, so full of "Dance and Provençal song and sunburnt mirth," has become "forlorn." The flight from "The weariness, the fever, and the fret / Here, when men sit and hear each other groan" has ended by finding the threat of "perilous seas" and Ruth standing "in tears among the alien corn." Human tragedy is the theme of high requiems. And whether one is nursing one's brother while he dies of tuberculosis (as Keats had recently done) or sitting under a plum tree after breakfast writing the "Ode to a Nightingale" (as he is now doing), human life is necessary to the perception of love and beauty. With a switch of perspective, the nightingale's song becomes a mere "plaintive anthem" and itself dies, "buried deep." The intense claustrophobic atmosphere of the "embalmed darkness" where one "cannot see" gives way to a series of visual images of open landscape: "Past the near meadows, over the still stream, / Up the hill-side." Fancy is a "deceiving elf" to pretend that she can provide a make-believe world of absolute beauty into which we can escape from responsibility.

"Was it a vision, or a waking dream?" The attempt to escape which is dramatized in the poem is clearly a dream. But seeing the impossibility of escape, seeing the dependence of the timeless on time, of the ideal on the actual, of the self upon others, of the subjective on the objective, this seeing, which is the total poem, is certainly a "vision real" (Keats's draft). The ode does not wink reality like wine bubbles, or stand "Darkling" "where it cannot see" or throw open casements only on forlorn unpeopled sea-scapes. Keats has not left us with the bad choice between grim reality and an aesthetic cheat. The poem sees that above blind illusion "the Queen-Moon is on her throne, / Cluster'd around by all her starry Fays." Like Ben Jonson's Elizabethan "Queen and huntress, chaste and fair" this is a symbol of order and relationship. This strongest visual image in the poem is negated neither by the "embalmed darkness" of the poet's viewless fancying nor by the "leaden-eyed despairs" and the loss of Beauty's "lustrous eyes" in the weary daytime world. Through the "verdurous glooms" blows a little light to remind us that somewhere (and in this poem) the poetic vision reigns over both ideal and actual. "The Queen Moon is on her throne"—"haply."

—David R. Clark

ODE TO THE WEST WIND.
Poem by Percy Bysshe Shelley, 1820.

"Ode to the West Wind," written by Percy Bysshe Shelley near Florence in 1819, was published with *Prometheus Unbound* in 1820. As one of the most frequently anthologised poems in English, it is one of a dozen lyric poems normally called upon to define the English Romantic movement.

Its particular lyric mode is prayer, a poet's exclamatory petition to the strong west wind of October as a prodigious power known by its effects. To prominent critics of the 1930's the poem exemplified a rhetoric of uncontrolled emotion, but it is organised as if by a public accountant paradoxically certified to approve a work structurally unique. Dante's terza rima, in which the middle line of each tercet rhymes with the first and third line of the next, is modified in five numbered sections such that each consists of four triplets followed by a couplet. Each section, then, forms a stanza of 14 lines—a sonnet. In each sonnet, 12 lines of progressive, propulsive rhyming, *aba*, *bcb*, *cdc*, are abruptly resolved in *dd*.

Autumn leaves driven in the first sonnet, clouds driven in the second, and waves driven in the third are envied in the first triplet of the fourth sonnet by a poet who would be driven as they are because the proud force of his early youth has been beaten into failure. The three prolusory sonnets on driven leaves, clouds, and waves each end in the same rhyme-sound and the same plea to the wind, "O hear!" The final sonnet pleads with the wind to enter the poet and scatter his thoughts abroad. He is Milton's Samson ready to redeem a people. Stuart Curran has called the ode "a purgatorial song of secular Christian triumph."

Each sonnet contains a variation on the principle that the west wind is destroyer and preserver: the autumnal wind scatters seeds for burial through the winter so that the revivifying "azure sister" of the spring may evoke buds, hues, and odours. Each also interweaves the metaphors and motifs of the others. In the second, the wind-blown commotion of the sky is a stream on which, from the tangled boughs of ocean and upper air, clouds are driven like leaves. In the third, vegetation reflected in a bay of the Mediterranean has its complement in the foliage of live coral disturbed by autumnal storms.

The repletion of metaphor accounts for erroneous impressions of decorative excess. The wind, an enchanter chasing ghosts, drives the pale and livid leaves of autumn like plague-stricken multitudes. (G.M. Matthews has noted that Shelley's four colours for dead leaves were the four colours of contemporary anthropologists' four races of humanity.) Like a hearse, the wind transports the corpses to their winter graves. The howling wind is the dirge of the dying year, as lengthening night closes like a vaulted dome over the year's sepulchre. The sleeping Mediterranean (like sleeping Italy) has reflected, like dreams, the ruined villas along the shores of the Bay of Baiae; as the fierce wind intruding from the Atlantic disturbs those dreams, its cleavage into billows brings a sympathetic response in the "sapless foliage" undersea. The invention of a diving box with windows, making possible accounts by naturalists of soft coral, provided a factual basis for Shelley's evocation, at once scientific and idealistic, of a harmonious universe of love.

"Oh! lift me as a wave, a leaf, a cloud!"—the poet cries in lamentation like a prophet in travail over the deadness of his time to spiritual purpose. He offers his recently inert self as a conduit for the power to awaken earth: "Make me thy lyre, even as the forest is." Do it by restoring me to my true self.

The second section is a meteorologist's delight. Photographs have been offered in support of scientific description to confirm the accuracy of detail in the poem concerning autumnal storms, torn cirrus clouds (like hair uplifted "from some fierce Maenad"), water-spouts, and other phenomena of the Ligurian Sea which are utilised symbolically in the poem. The Contemporary scientific search for a single, unifying cosmic power in the force of electricity underlies Shelley's metaphoric use of the electric cycle of ocean, vapours, clouds, lightning, thunder, hail, and rain. The search for cosmic unity links the rain cycle with the swaying and blanching of undersea growth in sympathy with billows fleeing from a cold wind. Like electricity, the west wind is a cosmic power seen only in its effects on earth, sky, and sea.

The final line, "If Winter comes, can Spring be far behind?", encapsulates a prophetic view of history. Europe, like the poet, has been pummelled into lethargy. The revolution that began in France has failed; the long reach of the Holy Alliance suppresses freedom everywhere; Tuscany, birthplace of the poem, languishes under foreign rule. In England, homeland of the expected readers of the poem, reactionary laws and actions by a conservative government are understood by Shelley to be massacres of innocence. Such tyranny enslaves itself and ensures its own demise. The inevitability that "congregated might" will burst in black rain and hail appeals to the pacifist Shelley as a law of self-inflicted retribution, but history is replete with evidence that spring does not end a cycle that includes recurrent autumns and winters.

—Carl Woodring

OF DRAMATIC POESY.
Prose by John Dryden, 1668.

John Dryden was already established as a playwright when the London plague of 1665 closed the theatres. He retreated to the country and spent some leisure hours putting into shape his ideas (and some alternative ideas) on playwriting techniques. When the theatres reopened he returned to the London stage, publishing his essay, *Of Dramatic Poesie*, in 1668. As a practising dramatist in various genres he did not feel he had necessarily to follow some of the practices he had advocated in the essay (notably on the use of rhyme in drama) and in his later essays he sometimes shifted his critical stance. But he regarded *Of Dramatic Poesie* as an important work in its own right and when he issued a second edition (1684) he made only stylistic alterations and did not adjust any of the critical views of 1665.

The essay takes the form of a discussion among four participants, who are given the classical names of Eugenius, Crites, Lisideius, and Neander, the latter representing the views of Dryden himself. Each participant is allotted a section in which he expresses his views on an aspect of dramatic writing and is then answered by one of the others, who states the opposing point of view. There are occasional short interpolations from one or other of the four but the lay-out of the work is in effect a series of miniature critical essays.

Though the issues are controversial, the tone throughout is non-polemic. The interlocutors state their case or their reply in the courteous and easy conversational register characteristic of most late 17th-century prose. Dryden later came to regard the tone as perhaps over-familiar—the 1684 edition, for example, alters the original "the age he lived in" to "the age in which he lived" but the impact of both editions is essentially the same.

Two major topics are discussed in the first part. In the final section a minor topic, rhyme in drama, gets an airing but as Dryden's dedicatory epistle cancels out these views, the issue need not detain the modern reader. The virtue of the essay lies elsewhere.

The first major topic is Ancients versus Moderns. Crites defends the superiority of ancient classical drama, its use of the three Aristotelian unities, and the acceptance of these in French classical drama. Eugenius responds with a defence of the freer structures of English drama, which had absorbed but improved on what classical drama had to offer.

The second discussion is French versus English. Lisideius proclaims himself in favour of Richelieu's strictures on French drama which, conforming strictly to the three unities, is built around a central figure, does not permit (as even Jonson did in *Catiline* and *Sejanus*) any variation from a single serious tone, allows no subplot, and by narrating off-stage violent action is more effective than the English use of violence on stage—death scenes in English drama, Lisideius claims, are regarded by audiences as comic rather than tragic.

All of these points are taken up by Neander (the word means "the new man" and is intended to represent Dryden himself, socially a "new man" alongside the upper-class members of the group, and also a "new man" in his critical attitudes). He finds the long declamatory speeches of French classical drama dull, its concentration on a single central figure offering the beauties of a statue not that of a man. English drama has more variety of characters and the blend of serious and comic in English plays gives greater pleasure. These propositions are not made in a critical void. Dryden/Neander backs up his opinions with specific examples and offers to present an analysis of a Jonson play. Eugenius interupts by asking for a "character of the author." Neander's reply is a brilliant few pages on the characteristics of Shakespeare, Beaumont and Fletcher, and Jonson; and this is followed by a detailed "examen" or analysis of Jonson's *Epicoene; or, The Silent Woman*.

This whole central section is a landmark in English literary criticism. The short appreciations of the four great Elizabethan/Jacobean dramatists have never been equalled for compression and critical acuity and the long analysis of the Jonson play is the first empirical criticism in English. Setting aside the various literary theories the participants had enunciated, Dryden keeps his eye on the object and states where and why he finds the play excellent. It is the first example in English of the close reading of a dramatic text—by a writer who is not merely a critic but a practising and successful dramatist, examining with an expert eye the work of another practising and successful dramatist. It is not for nothing that Dryden has been called the father of English criticism.

—Ian A. Gordon

THE OLD CURIOSITY SHOP.
Novel by Charles Dickens, 1841.

Charles Dickens's fourth novel, *The Old Curiosity Shop*, has received less critical attention than some of his later masterpieces, but there is no doubt at all about its enormous success with Dickens's contemporaries. Before its serialization ended, the circulation of the magazine in which it originally appeared had reached 100,000, a record that was to be unsurpassed by any of his major novels. In particular the fate of the heroine, Little Nell, aroused widespread interest in England and America. Later in the century a reaction against what was seen as the novel's self-indulgent sentimentality set in, and Ruskin, Wilde, and others attacked it. In Dickens's own time, however, it did much to develop the close relationship between the novelist and his readers: as his biographer and friend John Forster observed, it was crucial in making the "bond" between them "one of personal attachment."

Little Nell has received so much attention, favourable or unfavourable, that it is easy to forget that there are substantial portions of the story in which she makes no appearance. There are in fact two sides to *The Old Curiosity Shop*, one sentimental and pathetic, with overtones of Shakespearean tragedy (especially *King Lear*), the other comic and grotesque, attractively blending realism (in its presentation of

London low life) and a vein of fantasy (notably in the figure of the hideous and malevolent dwarf, Daniel Quilp) that owes something to folktales and fairy stories.

Accompanied by her grandfather—a kind of Lear to her Cordelia—Nell flees the menace and corruption of the city in a quest for safety and peace. Her journey, part symbolic, part realistic, takes her through an inferno-like industrial landscape to a rural haven that seems to belong to an earlier age; and George Cattermole's illustrations for this part of the novel emphasize the picturesque as well as the funereal aspects of gothic architecture and church monuments. What Nell finally attains is the peace of death, and the description of her deathbed is a set-piece of highly wrought metrical prose—again, almost the equivalent of a passage of Shakespearean blank verse.

Modern critics have recognized, however, that there is another side to Nell, who is the object of predatory sexual desire, a kind of Red Riding Hood pursued by the wolf. Quilp in particular offers a study, remarkable for its period, in rampant sexuality and unbridled energy; it is significant that such a character could only be presented in the early Victorian period in terms of the grotesque, and there is point in James Joyce's reference to the novel as "the old cupiosity shape."

The other, contrasting aspect of the novel is represented by the whimsical and endearing figure of Dick Swiveller, an amiable anti-hero who befriends the servant girl known as the Marchioness. A victim of her employers' ill usage, she serves as parallel and counterpart to Nell. The scenes in which Dick and the Marchioness appear contain some of Dickens's finest comic effects, and the tenderness of her care for him when he is ill contrasts with the more insistent sentimentality of the scenes involving the heroine. Dickens wrote a passage indicating that the Marchioness was the illegitimate child of Quilp and the mannish Sally Brass, but later deleted it as (presumably) too *risqué*.

Nell's journey across a large part of England provides Dickens with the opportunity to introduce a variety of scenes and characters in the manner of his earlier versions of the picaresque such as *The Pickwick Papers* and *Nicholas Nickleby*. Among these is Mrs. Jarley's travelling waxwork show, one among many examples of Dickens's lifelong fascination with theatre, performance and display.

Dickens had a considerable personal involvement in the novel, and especially in that part of it dealing with the death of the child who is its central figure. In a letter written in January 1841, as serialization of the novel drew to a conclusion, he wrote that he had tried in the book to "do something which might be read by people about whom Death had been, with a softened feeling, and with consolation." This may suggest that he had had Nell's fate in mind from the outset, hence it is not surprising that he turned a deaf ear to the many pleas from friends and readers that he should spare her life. Dickens had had fairly recent first-hand experience of the death of someone close to him whose memory may have been idealized in the person of Nell: his sister-in-law Mary Hogarth, who lived with Dickens and his wife, had died in his arms on 7 May 1837 at the age of 17 after being suddenly taken ill. Her loss had a profound effect on Dickens, and his preoccupation with the death of a young girl in this novel may represent an attempt to come to terms with his own feelings.

Appropriately enough, in view of its two contrasting aspects, the novel had two illustrators, Hablot K. Browne ("Phiz") and George Cattermole. While the former was concerned with the comic and grotesque elements, the latter was more concerned with the picturesque and the pathetic, from the early portrayal of the shop itself to the depiction near the end of Nell's last days in the secluded village. The styles of the two illustrators form an effective contrast.

As G.K. Chesterton pointed out, the title is somewhat puzzling since the antique shop plays only a minor role in the novel. Its significance should probably be seen as symbolic rather than realistic, foreshadowing Nell's escape from a menacing present to the world of the antique, where, ultimately, safety lies only in death.

—Norman Page

OLD MAN'S STORY.
Story by Frank Sargeson, 1940.

In vision, method, and effect "Old Man's Story" typifies the short stories collected in *A Man and His Wife*, Frank Sargeson's most influential volume. The vision is that of the puritan anti-puritan who attacks and even attempts to reverse the ethical judgements of New Zealand puritanism, challenging the reader to reconsider its stereotypes and stock responses. The method by which that vision is communicated and that effect on the reader is gained is only seemingly casual, actually achieving great suggestion and compression beneath the simple, idiomatic prose of its first-person narration. As Sargeson has said (in *More Than Enough*), his method leaves "a good deal to become intelligible to the reader only upon the condition of a halfway meeting," the reader's imagination coming out to meet the writer's.

An analysis of that method shows a surprising complexity beneath the simple surface: the narrator is telling the story of an old man telling him a story of that old man's youthful experience with an older man (who told *him* stories). There are thus four distinct levels of awareness: the boy who had a "tremendous experience" that was "too big for him to be at all clear about until later on in life"; the old man that that boy became, attempting to communicate that experience; the narrator, a decent but limited man, who senses that "there was something in the story" that the old man "wanted to make [him] see," but who cannot quite get it; and the implied author, invisible, but felt in the arrangement of the story, inviting the reader to see more in the story than can the boy, old man, or narrator.

The opening frame, more than simply a natural way into the story, implicitly establishes the old man's purpose in telling his story. The narrator, sitting at the waterfront, watches the old man reading the paper and seems to misjudge his murmured "Terrible" in response to a reported court case involving an older man and a young girl, assuming that he is making the usual puritan punitive judgement. However, the old man soon indicates that his remark is more a response to the prison sentence meted out in the case, and thus his story is implicitly an explanation of how he arrived at such a position. As Sargeson himself said in an interview (quoting an earlier critic), the story is really about "the birth of charity."

The story the old man tells implies that he was raised a puritan. From his aunt and probably his mother he had as a boy received the ubiquitous "official" view of the female moral guardians that sex is a dirty, basically male business, made acceptable only by marriage and procreation. During the summer of which he tells the story, from Bandy, the "hard case" hired hand on his uncle's farm, he picks up the "unofficial" male view that sex is a male exploit like fighting. The two views are different sides of the same coin, as closely related in his puritan culture as the sermon and the smoking room story. However, what his culture does not prepare him for is Bandy's behaviour with Myrtle, the orphan girl who comes to work on the farm. To the aunt and uncle, Bandy's interest in her can mean only that he is a dirty old man who ought to know better, but when the boy sneaks up to spy on Bandy and the girl in the garden swing at night he discovers not the sexual adventure that he imagined but rather an expression of tenderness. The experience is too much for him, as he sees that "he had managed somehow to get life all wrong"; from thinking that "he'd got to know what was what" he comes to understand that "he had a lot to learn."

At that point, "the old man seemed to think his story was finished," and for him it was, for the scene on the swing was the beginning of his realization of the inadequacy of the puritan view of sexuality, in both its "official" and "unofficial" sides. The narrator does not seem to understand that significance, but in briefly drawing out the rest of the story from the old man—that Bandy and the girl were later caught together in Bandy's room, that the girl was sent back to the orphan's home, and that Bandy committed suicide soon after—he unwittingly underlines the human cost of the puritan code. It is left to the reader to put it all together, to wonder at "human life with its deep mystery of personal motive and behaviour" (as Sargeson puts it in *More Than Enough*), beyond the simple moral judgements of puritanism. Vision and method have united to implicate the reader in a profound experience.

—Lawrence Jones

OLD MORTALITY.
Novel by Sir Walter Scott, 1816.

It is a commonplace that *Old Mortality* is among the very greatest of Sir Walter Scott's Waverley novels. Seldom, however, is it regarded as supreme among them, despite its acknowledged virtues—its narrative pace; its formal strength; its adult concern with history, politics, and revolution; its confident symbolism; its grave tone. Enthusiasm for it is predominantly cool and judicious, thanks, perhaps, to the absence of a towering central character, or to its setting in one of the less colourful and more complicated moments of Scottish history, or to the comparative lack of grandeur in its landscapes. It is a novel designed to appeal to the head rather than to the heart.

Its *raison d'être* is the supplanting of myth by historical probability. A traditional sentimentalisation of those staunch, stern upholders of Presbyterian principle, the Covenanters, and a corresponding view of their royalist opponents as licentious oppressors, had become for many "a design in snow and ink" (to quote Stevenson). Scott's respect for folk-memory with its strong, tragic simplicities yields to his historian's sense of complexity and contradiction in human motivation and behaviour. It was not just his worldly fairness, however, which provoked the partisan criticism of Thomas M'Crie and others: in addition to Scott's clear balancing of justice and blame on both sides, the reader senses how Scott feels these plebeian Presbyterians as alien to him, alongside the aristocratic heartiness of the royalists, brutal as they are. The treatment of Claverhouse, above all, modulates from the cold and ruthless oppressor of tradition to the agreeable companion who preserves the life of the hero, Henry Morton. Claverhouse admits he is as much a fanatic as the Cameronian homicide, Balfour of Burley, but Scott's Claverhouse is the embodiment of courtesy who will end as he hopes, at Killiecrankie, in epic style, "pressing one day some well-fought and hard-won field of battle, and dying with the shout of victory in my ear." Scott's view of Balfour's essential nature, on the other hand, is depicted in the symbolism of the Covenanter's favourite hiding-place on the moor, a romantic but terrible retreat which embodies the isolation, danger, and terror of his personality: his end is that of a man of violence, merely, drowned while in a vindictive death-grapple with a trooper. Seldom did Scott make his hesitations about romantic individualism more clear.

Despite two battles and a siege, however, the conflicts of the novel are not merely military: they are about states of mind. For much of the novel, when swords are not clashing, Scott offers a conflict of discourse instead. The mannered, pseudo-biblical argot of the Covenanters is the distilled language of fanaticism—sublime, stupefying, and comic by turns. Their opponents, in the persons of Claverhouse and Sergeant Bothwell, are given speech which is more attractively conversational, but almost as vigorous in image and rhythm. Against these is set the gravely polished, poised, bloodless speech of Morton, of Edith Bellenden, and of Evandale, Morton's political and amatory opponent and friend. Their coolly rational utterance never deserts them, whether confronting the end of love, or of life itself:

> "Nothing short of my life, you would say?" replied Morton, in a calm, but melancholy tone; "I believe that will be entirely in the bosoms of my judges. My guards spoke of a possibility of exchanging the penalty for entry into foreign service. I thought I could have embraced the alternative; and yet, Miss Bellenden, since I have seen you once more, I feel that exile would be more galling than death."

Were Scott simply writing a love story, such stuff would be merely comically inadequate. For these lovers, however, love provides no alternative domain, no passionate withdrawal from the world: rather, it is interfused with cruel, historical actuality. In this context, the language of tender hearts is no expression of passionate individualism. It becomes, rather, the utterance of central, society-nurturing instincts as opposed to the destructive passions of ideological adversaries. But if love, here, becomes social sanity, it is nevertheless seen as a supreme value. These grave, sane, chivalrous lovers are passionately believed in by Scott and the sober Morton can be seen, by at least one critic, as a "fanatic of the centre." Consciously inverting romance, Scott sees sexual love here as a calming, sane impulse: this transformation of literary tradition is one of the book's surprises.

Another surprise is an ambiguity deeper than that conflict between emotional attachment to the past and rational welcoming of progress which marks other Waverley novels. Here, even his reason gives Scott cause for sorrow. The novel can be read, admittedly, as an optimistic work, for it depicts the flow of British history steadily banishing fanaticism and violence. It ends with the dawn of a better political age. Yet it is not just a history lesson, and is as much concerned with exploring abiding human impulses as it is with interpreting a historical moment. And what it contemplates is the limited influence of moderation and reason: these sane young people are blown about by the gales of fanaticism in others, and their story is a sad one. Scott relegates the tale of their future happiness to a satirical final chapter, underlining that happiness ever after is found only in books pandering to less than serious readers. The essential story of the trio of lovers ends in woe with the last breath of Evandale.

In other novels, Scott makes the experience of his central characters echo the larger movements of history: progress for British society brings happiness for the individual. Here, the personal story tells of frustration, and if the larger movement of passing time sweeps away fanatics like Burley, it is also the occasion of the deepest human woe: these lovers are united in death, even if not their own. Old Mortality himself is not just a link with the Covenanting past. He embodies a larger consciousness of mortality, of time, and of *lachrimae rerum*.

—David S. Robb

THE OLD WIVES TALE.
Play by George Peele, 1591–94(?).

Among the comic dramatists of the 1580's and early 1590's, when romantic comedy held the stage and the satirical and citizen comedy of Dekker, Jonson, Marston, and Middleton had not yet been born, George Peele, Robert Greene, John Lyly, and Shakespeare were prominent. Peele, one of the "University Wits" along with Marlowe, Greene, Lodge, Nashe, and others, wrote in a variety of genres, including mythological pastoral, biblical tragedy, and English historical drama. He also tried his hand at anti-Spanish propaganda with *The Battle of Alcazar* in the post-Armada fever, and wrote several pageants for court and civic shows. But the work by which he is best known is his shortest play and probably his last, *The Old Wives* [Wife's] *Tale*, published in 1595. (The singular possessive seems right: the tale in question is the one told in the play, which becomes the play itself, by Madge, the "old wife".)

The quarto text is very short, only 1170 lines. Its brevity and the curiously attenuated, sketchy, or simply incomplete nature of much of the plot has exercised editors and critics. Is the play as we have it complete, as Peele conceived and wrote it? Could it have been, as the title page claims, acted by the Queen's Men, one of the leading adult companies of the early 1590's, or was it a play for children? The number of characters, many of whom make only brief appearances, the inclusion of songs and dances, and the very light-hearted, fairy-tale-like quality of the action itself have led many readers to believe that it must have been composed for a children's company. Are the many inconsistencies and puzzles in the text accidental or deliberate, part of the intended effect of a rambling, dream-like nocturnal tale told by a sleepy, forgetful old woman? In any case it is quite without precedent in Elizabethan drama.

Unprecedented too is the astonishing mixture of genres in such a small scope. *The Old Wives Tale* is a sort of compendium of Elizabethan forms and conventions. Whatever Peele's intentions may have been—and we are unlikely ever to know—the effect of the little play, even in reading, must be both laughter and delight, as Sir Philip Sidney distinguished them in his *Defence of Poesy*. The ludicrous bumptiousness of the braggart knight and suitor Huanebango (a near cousin to Udall's Roister Doister) and the broad knockabout comedy of the churchyard scene in which the dead Jack's friends try to intimidate the Sexton and Churchwarden into giving him a proper Christian burial, provoke laughter, derisive or mirthful. Other elements—the romance of the hero Eumenides' and the two brothers' search for the spellbound maiden Delia, held captive by the wicked conjurer Sacrapant, the parallel but very sketchy subplot of the young man Erestus turned into an old man by the same conjurer while his beloved Venelia runs through the wood maddened and mute with grief, the benevolent ghost Jack coming to the hero's aid—these induce pleasure of a different kind.

Critics have usually emphasized either the play's fantasy, folktale quality, its dream-like delicacy and enchantment, or its parody, satire, and farce. More recently, it has been recognized that both or all of these readings can be accommodated, that the openness of the texture belies the slightness of the fabric. It is indeed made up of several genres, some of which are simultaneously parodied: folktale, romance, pastoral, masque, folk ritual, farce, classical comedy. Add songs and dances, spectacular effects, magic, elements of *commedia dell' arte* and wordplaying, logic-chopping clowns, in an unpredictable compound of verse and prose, and we begin to appreciate the extraordinary, unclassifiable quality of Peele's miniature masterpiece. It has, furthermore, a complex metadramatic dimension imposed by the setting of the play as a non-dramatic event, a tale told by an old woman to her guests as they sit by the fire in her cottage in the woods. This frame occupies the first hundred lines or so: Madge and the two lost pages who have come upon her husband Clunch in the woods and are taken home by him, settle down to listen to a story while their fellow and the smith go off to bed (these two actors were no doubt required for other parts). Madge begins her "Once upon a time, long ago" sort of tale, gets muddled, forgets where she was, and suddenly the characters of her story materialize and drama takes over from narrative. Madge and her auditors remain on stage as spectators and commentators; "morning" comes as the play-within-the-play ends. We are back in the cottage with Madge rubbing her eyes and offering breakfast. A play which calls itself an old wife's tale, in which her tale becomes even as she tells it a play in which various characters flit in and out, in plots apparently unrelated to each other, some of them telling tales of their wanderings—such is the fantastical structure of Peele's strange and wonderful play. At the very end, we are jolted into another time scale, when the old woman wakes up and speaks in the past tense of having seen or heard all this before, when she was the hearer or spectator, not the teller. This final disorientating wrench leaves us as uncertain of our bearings in space and time as the lost pages who begin Peele's play or the bewitched, wandering, ghostly characters who perform the old wife's magical tale.

—Charles W. Whitworth

THE OLD WIVES' TALE.
Novel by Arnold Bennett, 1908.

The Old Wives' Tale is the best of Arnold Bennett's Five Towns novels about life in the Potteries. It is a novel on a large scale chronicling the lives of two sisters brought up in Bursley; one sister remains in Bursley to live a conventional life as wife and mother, never moving from the house in which she was born, the other elopes with a handsome young man and then survives and eventually achieves success in France after he has abandoned her. This beautifully crafted novel explores the entire lives of the two sisters.

The first part, named after the mother, Mrs. Baines, covers the youth of the sisters Constance and Sophia, and ends after the marriage of Constance to Samuel Povey, the chief assistant in the family draper's shop, and the elopement of Sophia with the attractive commercial traveller Gerald Scales. In this part of the novel Bennett creates the feel of life in the small provincial town of Bursley with all its delights and its narrowness. He does this through his focus on the Baines house and shop in the corner of St. Luke's Square. It is in this house that the sisters are born and will in turn die. When Mrs. Baines leaves the house at the end of the first book she feels that her life is over. The house is so crucial to the family's maintaining its continuity into another generation that Bennett endows it with a mythical quality: "Old houses, in the course of their history, see sad sights, and never forget them!" The house also sees scenes of delight such as the spirited Sophia's extraction of Samuel Povey's tooth, or the children's party at which the four-and-a-half-year-old Cyril disgraces himself by snatching a piece of cake from the little girl beside him and cramming it into his own mouth. Bennett tells Constance's story in the second part and Sophia's in the third. In the final part, "What Life Is," the sisters are re-united in the house in St. Luke's Square.

Bennett, who was brought up in the Potteries, left the region as a young man, learned his craft from the French realists, and became a sophisticated cosmopolitan interested in the *avant-garde* movements in the arts. Yet he returns to his origins again and again to express his vision of the beauty and interest of life. He finds interest in what is most ordinary and unassuming, like the life of Samuel Povey; Constance comes to appreciate the human grandeur of the man who had been considered not good enough for her: "She saw him [in death] as an object pathetic and wistful, not majestic. And yet she genuinely thought that there could not exist another husband quite so honest, quite so just, quite so reliable, quite so good, as Samuel had been."

Bennett speaks of the "manifold interest" of the position of the two sisters on the opening page of the novel. What ultimately is "interesting" in the ordinariness of most people's lives is the profound layer of human significance underlying all the waste and pettiness and frivolity. This is expressed in Sophia's moment of shock when she looks on the corpse of the old man who had once been her handsome young husband: "What affected her was that he had once been young, and that he had grown old, and was now dead." As she reflects on their youth and on how he had ill-treated her she looks in a mirror and sees "a forlorn woman, who had once been young, and now was old." What she recognises is evidence of the same pattern of time working itself out in her own life. The pattern repeats itself in different forms throughout the novel, as youth and age are continually found to exist in relation to each other. This is indicated emblematically, for instance, in Bennett's description of Sophia and her mother: "They sat opposite to each other, on either side of the fire—the monumental matron whose black bodice heavily overhung the table, whose huge rounded face was creased and wrinkled by what seemed years of joy and disillusion; and the young, slim girl, so fresh, so original, so ignorant, with all the pathos of an unsuspecting victim about to be sacrificed to the Minotaur of Time." And as if to bear this out Bennett will write of Constance when she is old: "The naive ecstasies of her girlhood had long since departed . . . the price paid for experience and self-possession and a true vision of things." He adds that the "vast inherent melancholy of the universe" did not exempt her. It is ultimately the "riddle of life" that Sophia confronts in the presence of her dead husband that concerns Bennett in his fiction.

Although the world Bennett created in *The Old Wives' Tale* is that of small-town provincialism, his interest is in the universal nature of the individual and the particular. Bursley is a typical place, but it is also the microcosm through which Bennett can explore the universal situations of the human condition—youth and age, life and death. The Five Towns world is "England in little, lost in the midst of England, unsung by searchers after the extreme; perhaps occasionally somewhat sore at this neglect, but how proud in the instinctive cognizance of its representative features and traits!"

—Stella McNichol

OLIVER TWIST.
Novel by Charles Dickens, 1838.

Charles Dickens's second novel, serialized from February 1837 to March 1839 in the recently-launched magazine *Bentley's Miscellany*, of which Dickens was editor, and published in three volumes in November 1838, was an astonishing performance, not least because it was written and published alongside *The Pickwick Papers* until November 1837 and then alongside *Nicholas Nickleby* from April 1838. In his mid-twenties, Dickens displayed enormous energy and self-confidence in thus producing two serials simultaneously (he never did so again) and in so ostentatiously declining to repeat the hugely successful Pickwick comic formula with a "Son-of-Pickwick" sequel. Instead, his new novel was concerned with crime, evil, death, deprivation, social injustice, and urban squalor, and was mordantly satirical about the New Poor Law (1834), thus engaging many interests and talents not accommodated in *The Pickwick Papers*. It was original too as the first English novel centred on a child; and childhood became a Dickens speciality.

But as Robert A. Colby shows in his "*Oliver Twist*: The Fortunate Foundling" (in *Fiction with a Purpose*, 1968), the abandoned orphan, often illegitimate like Oliver, was familiar in fiction, as was the criminal setting, in the then-popular "Newgate novels." As Blake's poem "The Little Boy Lost" witnesses, childhood experience and suffering had emerged as a significant new topic in romantic poetry, and Dickens was personally impelled towards it by memories of his own preteenage years when, with the rest of the family in prison and himself alone and thrown into manual labour, "I might easily have been," he recalled, "for any care that was taken of me, a little robber or a little vagabond": no accident, indeed, that Oliver's first encounter in London is with a member of a criminal gang who "befriends" and seeks to recruit him.

Starting in a workhouse and culminating in Newgate, the novel announces two central concerns of Dickens's fiction: seeing characters in relation to institutions, and referring to important topicalities. How to deal with paupers, criminals, and children were urgent and controversial issues, in which Dickens took a prolonged and well-informed interest, outside as well as in his fiction. Similarly, the parenthetical episode of Oliver's nearly becoming an apprentice chimney-sweep alluded to a scandalously dangerous juvenile job which also engaged the attention of Blake and of philanthropists and reformers.

"Life in London, as revealed in the pages of Boz, opens a new world to thousands born and bred in the same city," wrote the *Quarterly Review* (June 1839). Dickens is explicitly exploratory when he imagines "a stranger" discovering with the "utmost astonishment" the Jacob's Island area where Bill Sikes meets his violent end. The young Queen Victoria was among such readers who found "excessively interesting" these accounts of "squalid vice" and "starvation in Workhouses." But Dickens was exploring individual as much as social evil in his depiction of Fagin and Sikes and their associates. Murder and its aftermath (powerfully enacted in Dickens's last and most spectacular public reading, *Sikes and Nancy*, 1869) provide the final sequence, and Dickens presents intensely Sikes's guilty mind and Fagin's terror as he faces trial and execution.

These emotional climaxes to the novel are impressive, but its plot denouement, like some other elements, belongs to fictional convention rather than engaging Dickens's imaginative conviction. Oliver's predictably felicitous outcome, while mildly gratifying, results from multiple coincidences, and few readers long remember exactly how he is related to the Maylies and Mr. Brownlow, to whom he is miraculously restored, while his impeccably middle-class attitudes and accent, despite his workhouse and gangland upbringing, no more aspire to realism than does the presentation of Nancy as a prostitute and gangster's moll. Thackeray at the time complained that Dickens "dares not tell the truth concerning such young ladies," though many readers were moved by this pitiable golden-hearted-whore figure. The "good" characters are poorly presented as is the obligatory but rather perfunctory love story, though Dickens was attempting something new by making Rose Maylie a (supposed) bastard, and her illness and near-death drew upon his memories of the recent sudden death of his beloved sister-in-law Mary Hogarth.

The novel is most alive in its presentation of physical, social and moral evils and in Dickens's new-found ironical narrative tone. Also, despite its murky subject matter, it retains Dickensian humour. As a bullying beadle, Mr. Bumble makes Oliver's life miserable, but Bumble is also a comic figure, and when he marries and falls to "the lowest depth of the most snubbed henpeckery" he adds gloriously to the ranks of that popular stereotype; and he exits splendidly, on learning that husbands are legally responsible for their wives' actions, with the memorable statement that "If the law supposes that, the law is a ass—a idiot. If that's the eye of the law, the law is a bachelor . . ." But the novel's most remarkable speech is Oliver's in chapter 2 (unforgettably depicted, as are other major moments, in George Cruikshank's illustration): "Please, sir, I want some more"—a wonderful instance of Dickens's mythopoeic capacity, even in his early career, to encapsulate in a few simple words a perennial element in the human condition.

—Philip Collins

ON LIBERTY.
Prose by John Stuart Mill, 1859.

John Stuart Mill's essay *On Liberty*, begun in 1855 and published in 1859, is the most trenchant work available on its subject and for readers of English the central and most influential. Concerned particularly to gain freedom for the individual from the tyranny of common opinion, Mill distinguished the needs of the individual from the concerns of society, freedom of belief from freedom to act, moral suasion from law, education from instruction, and self-regarding actions from acts that affect the interests of others. The essay has five chapters: 1. Introductory; 2. Of the Liberty of Thought and Discussion; 3. Of Individuality, as One of the Elements of Well-Being; 4. Of the Limits to the Authority of Society over the Individual; and 5. Applications.

The introductory chapter sets forth a few principles and reveals several assumptions. The author, like his Utilitarian father, James Mill, assumes that the normal human being is "progressive," rational, and the best judge of its own needs and desires. The only justification for interfering with an individual is "to prevent harm to others"—to prevent not merely physical hurt but harm to the interests of another. Mill has no fear that civilisation, which conquered barbarism, might suffer a reversal. He praises Alexis de Tocqueville for identifying the most intrusive despotism of contemporary transatlantic states as the natural intolerance of the mob, or mass. Democracy—or a homogeneous society—nourishes mediocrity. Society must respect liberty of conscience, liberty of tastes and pursuits, and freedom to unite in groups. The most nearly metaphysical of Mill's principles is reserved for the final chapter: the free have no right to be *not* free; one may not sell oneself into slavery.

Liberty requires that experience be interpreted by "free and equal discussion." We can be justified in assuming the truth of an opinion, for the purposes of action, only if there has been and is (as assumed in science) complete freedom of contradicting and disproving. Like a privileged Jesuit, one should become acquainted with all opposing views—as a good in itself and as a good for the future of society. The ultimate appeal must be to "utility in the largest sense, grounded on the permanent interests of man as a progressive being," for belief in abstract truth leads to the sentimental view that truth will always prevail. Throughout the essay, liberty means absence of restraint.

Chapters 2 and 3, acknowledging an intellectual debt to Wilhelm von Humboldt, reiterate that the individual must be free to achieve a harmonious development of personal powers. Liberty is necessary "to enable average human beings to attain the mental stature which they are capable of." For society to enjoy improvement rather than suffer the stagnation of custom, genius must have "freedom to point out the way." Mediocrity must be opposed by "great energies guided by vigorous reason and strong feelings strongly controlled by a conscientious will." Everybody, Mill asserts, believes in originality, in the discovery of new truths. Yet the average person is naturally intolerant because "moderate in inclinations."

If an errant individual does no hurt to the interests of others, society may remonstrate, reason, persuade, or entreat; it may punish by reprobation and avoidance; it may not compel. For evil consequences to others, however, society must punish. Here Mill asks not for restraint or reform, but for punishment. He preserves his distinction between (primarily) self-regarding and (primarily) other-regarding actions by asserting that society may punish an individual for neglecting family or creditors, but not for drunkenness as a cause of such neglect.

The principle of freedom from interference does not apply to children, nor to backward states where the race is in its nonage (and therefore in need of fostering by a civilised nation). The exemption of persons declared insane apparently goes without saying, for Mill specifically exempts the "delirious." Government and society must cease, however, to treat the labouring classes as children. Mill's generic use of "man" for human is a linguistic issue only; he notes the greater need of women for emancipation from inequity and custom. Free trade, though a good, is irrelevant to individual liberty. The suggestions of possible applications given in the final chapter mitigate the rigour of the principles. The "probability of damage" may under some circumstances justify prior restraint. Drunkenness is a crime in one who has earlier proved violent when drunk. The sale of poison may be regulated though not prevented; a government may discourage stimulants by taxation because government's responsibility to protect requires taxation and it is better to tax stimulants than necessities. Restrictions and guarantees are permissible with regard to public gambling houses and pimping for fornication, but Mill declares himself undecided concerning more stringent measures. Offences against decency may be punished from "objection to publicity." Government should require education, but should not, lest it hinder diversity, provide education directly. Almost as a recovery of first principles, Mill commends modes and laws of divorce that consider the adults equally with the children.

This defence of unpopular conduct, critics have noted, came from one who had lived with another man's wife. To the argument itself, four distinct kinds of objection have been raised: that the essay offers inadequate guidance; that it contains confusing contradictions; that excessive claims for the individual ignore collective needs that protect and foster individuals; and, especially in the later decades of the 20th century, that Mill grants too much power to the state, or ignores the ordinary individual for the greatest good of the greatest number, or seeks to replace Christianity with rational, secular development, or erects his own intellectual elite into an ideal. John C. Rees, Mill's most careful reader, has confirmed minor ambiguities and contradictions, but defended the text in detail from its chief critics.

—Carl Woodring

ON THE MOVE.
Poem by Thom Gunn, 1957.

In a world still largely innocent of the homoerotic significance of motorbike and leather jacket (later common currency in the California of its setting), and unaware of Thom Gunn's own homosexuality (which came out only after the 1967 volume *Touch*), "the Boys" of "On the Move" broke in 1957 as figures of the existential restlessness made popular by a youthful Marlon Brando's performance in the film *The Wild One* (1954) and by Jack Kerouac's novel *On the Road*, also published in 1957. Though the rebellion of the Beat generation informs this poem, signalled in the very slogan which provides its epigraph, "Man, you gotta Go," it is counterposed by other, highly literary and philosophical influences. The poem's posture owes as much to the existentialism of Sartre and Camus which Gunn had imbibed as a Cambridge undergraduate as to the laid-back lifestyle he found in California, where he had gone to study with the scholar-poet Yvor Winters, dedicatee of a poem in the same volume, and the model for the tight rhyme scheme, traditional syntax and stanza, and measured attitudes of the verse.

In keeping with its easy riding between low life and high culture, the poem provided not only an image for the young bikers of a generation in revolt, but also a manifesto and title for that most academic of literary movements, "The Movement" itself, which in the 1950's proclaimed its hostility to a previous generation's rhapsody and rant represented by Yeats and Dylan Thomas, and opted instead for a deadpan metric, strict rhyme, and a plain, unmetaphoric language of statement and argument rather than exclamation and effusion. Though its language is richer and more varied than the typical "Movement" poem, "On the Move" is certainly a textbook example of the kind of writing to which this diffuse movement aspired, as popularised by A. Alvarez's introduction to the Penguin anthology *The New Poetry* in 1962.

The opening if not quite the title poem of Gunn's first volume, *The Sense of Movement*, "On the Move" contains in its penultimate stanza the crucial shift which translates a simple fact of existence into an existential philosophy of becoming. A "movement" one is passively born to becomes "*the* movement" joined in an act of selfconscious choosing:

> One is not necessarily discord
> On earth; or damned because, half animal,
> One lacks direct instinct, because one wakes
> Afloat on movement that divides and breaks.
> One joins the movement in a valueless world,
> Choosing it, till, both hurler and the hurled,
> One moves as well, always toward, toward.

The poem is indeed full of movement, from its opening verbs of glad animal motion, the blue jay "scuffling in the bushes," the gust of birds that "spurts across the field," "the wheeling swallows" through to the final stanza's image of the bikers:

> A minute holds them, who have come to go:
> The self-defined, astride the created will
> They burst away. . . .

Yet if that last verb suggests violent activity, it also contrasts the self-questioning fatuity of human life with the "direct instinct" of animals. The motorbike may here update Plato's parable of the charioteer, but it also emphasises Gunn's belief in the arbitrariness of human motive and the "absurdity," in an existentialist sense, of all such activity in "a valueless world" where direction is simply "where the tyres press." The Boys have come simply to go: they are always just passing through, the only point of their travelling the journey itself, its "motive" in the end simply flight from the irritation of staying in one place. This indeed is the conclusion of the poem:

> At worst, one is in motion; and at best,
> Reaching no absolute, in which to rest,
> One is always nearer by not keeping still.

The absolute is desired yet felt at the same time to be nugatory, in contrast with the self-sufficient "hidden purpose" of the blue jay in the opening lines. The impulse of the epigraph, hovering between command and vacuous self-justification, is not founded on any basic conviction, for, lacking the "instinct" and "poise" of the animal, "one moves with an uncertain violence." The repeated "one" depersonalises the human subject at the very moment that it separates it off from the rest of creation as a selfconscious creature with a species-being, able to make those generalising statements which, in the very universality to which they lay claim, deprive their utterers of "direct instinct."

The paradoxical nature of this highly intellectual search for an instinctual poise is self-evident and indeed part of the poem's ironic complexity of celebration. The human mind is admired in its perverse quest for the impossible at the very moment that its absurdity is displayed and apologised for. Existence precedes essence: before the Boys can burst away, "self-defined" on their "created will," they are creatures of a distance that "throws them forth." In that distance they are at first "Small, black, as flies hanging in heat," and the echo here of *King Lear* ("As flies to wanton boys so we are to the gods: / They kill us for their sport") is in keeping with the rich Shakespearian allusiveness of this volume and its sequel, *My Sad Captains*.

The most sophisticated system of belief by which we rationalise our existence is, in the end, no more adequate than the incoherent self-justification of the biker's slogan, both alike "the dust thrown by a baffled sense / Or the dull thunder of approximate words." Sense (meaning here both the bodily senses and the idea of meaning, fused in "the sense of movement") is "baffled" like the bike's engine, to protect us from the roar of an amoral indifferent power which we have to master while never fully understanding. The obscuring dust, the merely approximate words, are necessary if we are to stay in control of a power that could easily overwhelm us if we tried to subject it to rational analysis. By strapping in doubt, the Boys assume a pose of robustness which substitutes for any authentic identity, becoming that which they pretend to be. (This is a version of Sartre's existentialist proposition that a waiter is a man acting the part of a waiter.) In refusing to think about the meaning of their existence they almost invent a kind of meaning out of the meaningless noise of creation, fabricate a "shape" which offers an imaginary "Exact conclusion [to] their hardiness." In the "donned impersonality" of goggles and leather jackets they contain from moment to moment that hum of energy which "Bulges to thunder," perpetually threatening to break out of human control. But if this thunder is "held by calf and thigh" they are in turn held in their passage through space and time by the forces they negotiate, both hurler and hurled. ("A minute holds them, who have come to go" recalls perhaps Shakespeare's sonnet 15: "everything that grows / Holds in perfection but a little moment.") In this act of will, a difficult balancing act in which only continuous unquestioning forward motion keeps them stable, "Men manufacture both machine and soul, / And use what they imperfectly control / To dare a future from the taken routes."

So with the poem, which also dares its original future from verse routes taken by a variety of illustrious predecessors. Itself maintaining the balance and poise it admires in the Boys, the poem stays firmly in the saddle of an energy that drives it relentlessly forward towards unknown destinations. What strikes one in retrospect is the remarkable authority and assurance with which this second volume by a young writer proclaims its doctrine of human uncertainty, facticity, and factitiousness. The cool confidence of the poem is, in contemporary parlance, "really cool," combining existential chic with a rhetorical cheek worthy of Yeats the artful dodger, one of the "known whereabouts" from which it bursts away. For if the Movement eschewed Yeats's domineering high blarney, it is clearly a potent influence here, evident in the masterly control of an eight-line stanza which delays closure for its second rhyme for a further six lines, and in the facility with which the poem moves from concrete image to generalised assertion, juxtaposing philosophical abstraction with verbs of intense physical action. For all its insistence on part solutions, the poem comes to rest with considerable finality on the idea of human restlessness, the last word "still" providing purpose and completion to the poem even as it denies ordinary mortals that completed purpose reserved for birds and saints.

—Stan Smith

ON THE WOUNDS OF OUR CRUCIFIED LORD.
Poem by Richard Crashaw, 1646.

O these wakefull wounds of thine!
  Are they Mouthes? or are they eyes?
Be they Mouthes, or be they eyne,
  Each bleeding part some one supplies.

Lo! a mouth, whose full-bloom'd lips
  At too deare a rate are roses.
Lo! a blood-shot eye! that weepes
  And many a cruell teare discloses.

O thou that on this foot hast laid
  Many a kisse, and many a Teare,
Now thou shal't have all repaid,
  Whatsoe're thy charges were.

This foot hath got a Mouth and lippes,
  To pay the sweet summe of thy kisses:
To pay thy Teares, an Eye that weeps
  In stead of Teares such gems as this is.

The difference onely this appeares,
  (Nor can the change offend)
The dept is paid in *Ruby*-Teares,
  Which thou in Pearles did'st lend.

Any reading of Richard Crashaw's "On the Wounds of Our Crucified Lord" should deal, perhaps sooner than later, with the intent of the questions posed in the opening stanza. Here, though his initial rhetorical strategy is to be indecisive (1–2), Crashaw immediately responds to that stance by implying that his own questions are insignificant (3–4), merely a matter of imaginative classification: the significance of Christ's wounds, whether mouths or eyes, remains that we are saved by the fact of their existence. Why then raise the questions? Surely to cause us to dwell upon the appearance of the wounds, to have us see them in such detail that we, like the poet who has already done so, might determine for ourselves that they *are* like mouths or eyes. Stanza 2 reveals as much, for here the poet makes more specific his already grotesque metaphors and casts them into the realm of paradox—they are both "blood-shot eyes" and "full-bloom'd lips."

Throughout the first two stanzas, then, Crashaw forces us into a sense of Christ's awful physical pain at the crucifixion by causing us to see clearly and by prodding us to resolve his paradox by analyzing its workings. If we do not rush to symbolic meanings the paradox thrusts upon us the physical facts of a human crucifixion. In clinical terms, nailing a human hand or foot to an unraised cross-tree will cause circular punctures, and the weight of a human body pinioned by nails to a standing cross-tree will cause punctures to become gashes. With such a wound an initial puncture might still remain evident, while a tearing will cause the flesh to "blossom" out along its length, developing "lips." That Crashaw's intent is to have us realize these gruesome details is well borne out by the way in which the wound images appear in the penultimate line of the poem. Here, in the single image "*Ruby*-Teares" the wound metaphors, which have been structurally parallel throughout the poem, converge in a pun on "tear-drop" and "tear gash."

At the third stanza we face an abrupt shift in visual perspective from the particular wounds of the dead but elevated Christ on the cross to the general form of the prostrate but live Magdalene weeping at his feet. Certainly, Magdalene symbolizes all repentant humanity, but more significant is the extent to which Crashaw develops the Christ-Magdalene relationship throughout the remainder of the poem.

Within the third stanza we easily recognize the appearance of a conceit drawn from the world of commerce in the play on "repaid" and "charges," particularly appropriate in the light of Magdalene's former trade. But the ground for this conceit has been established already in stanza 1 in the ingenious use of "supplies" to mean "to fulfill a lack" and "to stand as a substitute for." Christ's blood makes up for humanity's inherent failure and his death-wounds are a substitute for our spiritual deaths. But "supplies" is also an image of the marketplace, and in stanza 2 Christ's wounds have been purchased "at too deare a rate." In stanza 3 Magdalene's current tears and kisses already have been "repaid" by Christ, no matter how many sins might be charged against her or how much she charged for her kisses in the past. Stanza 4 extends the conceit of a commercial transaction along with the conceit of wounds as mouths and eyes; but in line 3 ("To pay thy Teares, an Eye that weeps") they coalesce in a contrastive allusion to Old Testament justice—an eye for an eye. Justice under Christ also demands an eye for an eye, but in return for the blood from his eye-like wound only the tearful eye of repentance and sympathy is required of the sinner, clearly a bargain in terms of the marketplace. Though Magdalene may have been a shrewd tradeswoman in the past, taking money payment for the "summe of . . . [her] kisses," no longer need she drive a bargain. Her spontaneous, hence freely given, tears and kisses make her the receiver of instant justice (mercy) under Christ.

The commercial transaction is given more point in the final stanza where the poet stresses at once the inequality of the transaction *and* the significance of that fact. When one exchanges a pearl for a ruby in the marketplace, some additional compensation would accrue to the holder of the more precious stone, but the difference between pearl and ruby is only apparent ("The difference onely this appeares")—a mere classification honored by those whose values are based in the material world, the Platonic world of appearances. After all, there is little difference between Magdalene's tears and Christ's blood. Both are emblems of love, and no "offense" can be taken over the seeming inequity of the exchange. However, in another sense the greater price of Christ's payment is insisted upon in the last two lines, wherein the distinction between paying and lending is emphasized. Christ pays with his life; Magdalene merely loans tears. True, her tears are a love commitment, but her life will go on and humans will err. Although saved for all time through her belief in Christ, she cannot cry forever and may sin again. Moreover, the distinction alludes at the same time to Magdalene's earlier career, to the difference between giving love freely and forever and lending "love" momentarily for payment.

Perhaps a more interesting dimension of Crashaw's double conceit is the way in which it evokes the poem's anagogical meaning. In the first two stanzas the images of mouth and eye are first metaphoric and then symbolic: initially they cause us to see wounds clearly; later they are emblems of spiritual sustenance. But in stanzas 3 and 4, where the speaker addresses Magdalene directly, we are led to recollect the sexual nature of Magdalene's sins by the continued development of the commercial conceit. With this awareness the phrases, "Thy charges," and, "To pay the . . . summe," become more resonant, and the idea of Christ as Magdalene's *physical* suitor arises as we formulate from the poem's details the following overly simple abstraction: "Christ pays for Magdalene's love." The effect is propitious. Our need to suppress the absurd and sacrilegious idea of Christ and Magdalene as lovers in the profane sense impels us toward the poem's ultimate meaning: at her death Christ will be Magdalene's Heavenly Bridegroom; meanwhile, even in death he is her spiritual suitor. But the antecedent awareness of Christ as a lover who gives all for his lady's love or who, as a customer of Magdalene, gives much more than he gets are important, if uneasy, intrusions upon our consciousness. For through these evocative analogues Crashaw enables his reader to measure the spiritual magnitude of Christ's sacrifice and to evaluate its significance, in short, to apprehend mystery by the intellect. In his first stanzas Crashaw avoided the cliché, "He died for our sins"; in his address to Magdalene he expresses the poem's anagogical meaning while avoiding the most common of religious metaphors, providing us instead with the kind of allusion whose ingenuity epitomizes the concept of wit in religious poems during the post-Renaissance era.

This dense poem shows us a Crashaw unlike the celebrative poet of the Theresa pieces, where lyrical exuberance sweeps us along; or unlike the eccentric poet of certain epigrams and some stanzas in "The Weeper," where extravagant and bizarre conceits evoke the patronizing smile, despite our awareness of their post-Reformation context. Here, where metaphor is carefully controlled, tone deftly handled, and meaning obliquely revealed, is evidence of a true metaphysical poet functioning in the service of his faith.

—Frank Fabry

ORCHESTRA.
Poem by Sir John Davies, 1596.

Published in 1596, *Orchestra* is generally regarded as reflecting Sir John Davies's thoroughgoing commitment to the cult of Elizabeth I as exemplified in the visual arts of the period, pageant, entertainment, and the poetry of Spenser and Ralegh. Although not dedicated to her (as was Davies's longest poem, *Nosce Teipsum*, 1599), or addressed directly to her (as were the *Hymns of Astraea*, also 1599), it is nevertheless a celebration of harmonious order which ends with a vision of Elizabeth in her characteristic cultic role as moon queen and restorer of the Golden Age.

The poem exists in three distinct forms: a manuscript version from 1595; the printed version of 1596 which is 18 stanzas longer and dedicated to a companion of Davies's in the Middle Temple, Richard Martin; and the version revised by Davies for republication in 1622 which was dedicated to Prince Charles and announces itself on the title page as being "not finished." This is, however, a pretence. Davies had quarrelled with Martin, wished to re-use the poem, and decided that the simplest way to do this was to erase all references to Martin, add a few stanzas, suggest that some (on Queen Elizabeth) were missing, then let the work limp to a halt with a couple of etceteras.

The poem's new dedicatee, within three years to be Charles I, was an excellent dancer who, like Elizabeth before him, espoused dancing as an image of cosmic harmony brought to earth to exemplify the well-governed state. Hence the poem's title (which also glances at Lucian's *Peri orcheseos*), the etymological significance of which tends to be lost on most of us today: the *orchestra* was the space in the Greek theatre where the chorus danced and sang. The 1596 title underlined this (*Orchestra: Or a Poeme of Dauncing. Judicially prooving the true observation of time and measure, in the authenticall and laudable use of Dauncing*) as did the pithier title of 1622: *Orchestra. Or a Poeme expressing the Antiquitie and Excellencie of Dauncing. In a Dialogue betweene Penelope, and one of her Wooers.*

Although originally written for lawyers, maybe as a disputation in favour of dancing at a time when it was under Puritan attack as frivolous and licentious (for example, by Philip Stubbes in his *Anatomy of Abuses*, 1583), the poem's topic asserts political commitment: dancing was no mere pastime or social grace but a symbol of stability to a court and society that were nervously aware how necessary such images were.

From this point of view it is interesting that the poem's plot shows a queen being persuaded from scepticism into belief: Davies has invented an episode from the concluding books of Homer's *Odyssey* where Penelope, in her husband's continuing absence, is assailed by suitors. He selects one of the main suitors, Antinous, and imagines him winning the queen with arguments about the role of dance (as love, as co-operation, as mutuality) in the universe. The end of the poem shows Penelope persuaded: Love, on Antinous's side, gives him a "crystal mirror" which Antinous then hands to Penelope. As she gazes into it she sees Elizabeth as the virgin moon queen surrounded by "a thousand sparkling starres": in other words, Elizabeth as the apotheosis of all that Penelope, as Odysseus's "chaste . . . Queen", signifies. (Contemporary readers would have noticed the parallel with Spenser's epic poem in praise of the queen, *The Faerie Queene*, III. ii. 18-2, where there is a magic mirror which, like Penelope's, can reveal future events.)

The mirror is a Platonic emblem of Truth, and Elizabeth herself was often described as the mirror of heavenly virtue (for example, *Faerie Queene*, I proem, stanza 4), so that the symbol supplies a fitting conclusion to a poem which has, through Antinous, proposed the commonplaces of the universal structure as originally described by Plato in his creation dialogue, the *Timaeus*. For Plato, the universe was sustained through numerically expressed proportions: it is harmony, audible manifestation of friendship or affinity, that defines the relationship of creator to created, the balance of the four elements, and the relationship of the planets to each other. Davies's Antinous, accepting this world view, argues that it is not so much harmony *per se* that sustains the cosmos but dancing, and that dancing was established not by friendship (Plato's *philos*) but by the more ancient and powerful Love (the *eros* of the *Symposium*). This proposal is consonant with the image of Elizabeth as Queen of Love (in Davies's own *Hymns of Astraea*, for example) and also marks the conflation of Platonism with biblical myth; for the vision of a universe engaged in the constant celebratory play of dance which Antinous expounds throughout the poem is inspired by Proverbs 8 in which rejoicing and play are present in the cosmos "from the beginning."

From consideration of dancing's antiquity Antinous proceeds to describe the motions of the heavens in terms of dance, moving on to the elemental dance, the dance of all earthly things (flowers dance in response to the sun, for example, in stanza 55), the development of social dancing, and music itself as dance ("So Musick to her owne sweet tunes doth trip"). To Antinous (who is, we remember, making a case) everything that moves dances through "Loves maze." Even the metamorphoses of the mortals and gods recorded by Ovid are versions of dance.

Orchestra has canonical status today because E.M.W. Tillyard resurrected it, in an edition of 1945, as the prototypical exemplification of what he had called, in his book of the same name, *The Elizabethan World Picture* (1943). Davies would have appreciated the way Tillyard found in his poem an emblem of order amid the stresses of World War II, for he published it himself as an exercise in propaganda at a time when internal and external political pressures, together with the queen's increasing age, were fragmenting the whole idea of a cult of Elizabeth. *Orchestra* is thus knowingly exploring a fiction. Its triumphant conclusion is that the myth of Love's relationship with Dance has created the image of Elizabeth and her court—has, in other words, constructed the Elizabethan icon. But the poem's textual revisions show that it knows that its conclusion is subject to revision and modification, that myths outlive their time: in 1622 the queen, 19 years dead, can only be registered as an absence ("Here are wanting some Stanzaes describing Queene Elizabeth"), and her cult recognised for the temporary phenomenon that it was.

—Douglas Brooks-Davies

THE ORDEAL OF RICHARD FEVEREL.
Novel by George Meredith, 1859.

The Ordeal of Richard Feverel, George Meredith's first realistic novel, either puzzled or offended most of its initial readers and met, at best, a tepid critical reception. Quickly removed from the shelves of Mudie's Circulating Library after some patrons found it "dangerous and wicked and damnable," it failed to produce the financial success for which Meredith hoped. Substantially revised in 1878 and then again in 1896, it remains, however, a work of striking originality still difficult to evaluate by traditional standards: as Virginia Woolf exclaimed, "What an odd conglomeration it is!"

But it is a rich and complex conglomeration as well, one in which Meredith extends the stylistic possibilities and challenges the conventional categories of fiction. Ranging from the cleverly epigrammatic and aphoristic to the casually conversational to the florid and poetic, the style is carefully adjusted to the situation and characters. Critics have particularly noted the poetic qualities of chapters 23 and 46, the former an idyllic portrait of Richard and Lucy's love, the latter a demonstration of the healing powers of nature.

More disorienting to readers than the varied style of the novel is its tragicomic nature. In many ways Meredith arouses the expectation of a conventional comic resolution in which the young lovers triumph over a hostile parent. The minor characters, for example, constitute a rich gallery of comic types, often referred to by comic or ironic epithets (the Wise Youth, the Eighteenth Century, the Saurian); the chapter titles sometimes suggest a comic structure ("In Which the Last Act of a Comedy Takes the Place of the First") as do numerous allusions to New Comedy and to such works as *The Tempest*. It is not surprising, then, that many readers have found the tragic conclusion, with the death of the only wholly admirable character, arbitrary and forced.

Yet Meredith himself saw the situation of Richard and his father as inherently tragic, and, as recent critics have recognized, the comic expectations arise from a partial reading of the novel. The young lovers, like those in *Vanity Fair*, overcome the obstacles to their marriage and are united comparatively early in the novel, yet the conflicts produced by vanity and egoism persist and lead unswervingly to misfortune. In blending the conventions of comedy and tragedy, Meredith invites his readers to perceive the action from different perspectives; the purely comic perspective, embodied as it is in the novel by the worldly, disengaged cynic, Adrian Harley, is shown to be ultimately inadequate.

The initial impulse behind *The Ordeal of Richard Feverel* was painfully immediate and personal to Meredith, a fact which partially explains its complexity and ambivalence. In 1857 Meredith's wife Mary Ellen ran away with a minor Pre-Raphaelite painter, Henry Wallis, leaving Meredith with a young son. Similarly, at the beginning of the novel the wife of Sir Austin Feverel has fled with a dreadful poet named Diaper Sandoe, leaving Sir Austin to raise his son Richard alone. Meredith's bitterness is apparent both in his ridicule of Sandoe and in his unwillingness to grant Lady Feverel more than a vague and shadowy existence. Remarkably, however, Meredith treats Sir Austin in an objective, even ironic manner, allowing the reader to perceive the contribution he probably made to his wife's behavior.

Sir Austin's responsibility for his son's upbringing enables Meredith to explore several themes in which both he and his readers of 1859 were interested—the concept of evolution, the nature of education and the value of educational systems, and the role of egoism in even the most benign relationships. Believing, on the one hand, that human beings are perfectible if their development is properly controlled and, on the other, that all Feverels are singled out for a special ordeal, Sir Austin devises a system and a schedule by which to regulate his son's intellectual and moral growth and, particularly, to restrain his sexual inclinations, seen by Sir Austin as the chief threat to perfectibility. In short, as Adrian Harley, Richard's cousin and tutor observes, "Sir Austin wished to be Providence to his son."

Sir Austin's attempt to usurp the role of Providence produces an effective variation on the form of the providential novel, familiar to Victorian readers through such works as *Jane Eyre*. Meredith creates a world in which nature and instinct, like Providence, if unhindered, will arrange human lives properly: he emphasizes repeatedly, for example, that nature, without the aid of Sir Austin's exhaustive searches, has provided the ideal mate for Richard. But blinded by egoism and class prejudice, Sir Austin forces the rigors of his system into conflict with the promptings of nature, with tragic consequences.

Sir Austin's system does not, however, compel the prolonged separation of the lovers, once united, and in that separation, with Richard's consequent infidelity, lies the principal weakness of Meredith's plot. Though not a serious flaw, the circumstances under which Richard alone petitions his father in London do appear contrived in order to allow Richard opportunity for infatuation with the seductive Mrs. Mount. Worse, these circumstances arouse in Richard an air of patronizing superiority toward his wife, whom he thinks of as a "poor little thing," causing him to resemble George Osborne of *Vanity Fair*.

Fortunately, in recent years the reputations of Meredith and of *The Ordeal of Richard Feverel* have begun to recover from what F.R. Leavis called the "necessary demolition-work" of such critics as E.M. Forster. Perhaps their attacks were an inevitable response to the excessive praise of Meredith's admirers at the turn of the century. Now, however, we can see that while his novel may not be as great as his most ardent supporters claimed, it is far better than his detractors admitted, a novel which addresses issues of enduring importance and produces fertile innovations in the form and style of fiction.

—James E. Byer

THE ORIGIN OF SPECIES.
(*On the Origin of Species by Means of Natural Selection; or, The Preservation of Favoured Races in the Struggle for Life.*)
Prose by Charles Darwin (1809–82), 1859 (6 revisions, 1860–76).

Edition

The Origin of Species: A Variorum Text, edited by Morse Peckham. 1959.

Bibliography: *The Works of Darwin: An Annotated Bibliographical Handlist* by R.B. Freeman, 1965; revised edition, 1978.

Critical Studies: *Life and Habit: An Essay after a Completer View of Evolution*, 1877, *Evolution Old and New*, 1879, revised edition, 1882, 1911, and *Luck or Cunning as the Main Means of Organic Modifications?*, 1886, all by Samuel Butler; *Darwin among the Poets* by Lionel Stevenson, 1932; *Darwinism and the English Novel* by Leo J. Henkin, 1940; *Darwinism: Competition and Cooperation* by M.F. Ashley-Montagu, 1952; *Darwin's Century: Evolution and the Men Who Discovered It* by L.C. Eiseley, 1958; *A Century of Darwin* edited by S.A. Barnett, 1958; *A Book That Shook the World: Anniversary Essays on Darwin's Origin of Species* by J.S. Huxley and others, 1958; *Darwin and Butler: Two Versions of Evolution* by Basil Willey, 1960; *Darwin: Evolution by Natural Selection* by Gavin de Beer, 1963, as *Darwin: A Scientific Biography*, 1964; *Darwin and His World* by J.S. Huxley and H.B.D. Kettlewell, 1965; *Darwin: The Years of Controversy* by Peter J. Vorzimmer, 1970; *Darwin and His Critics* by David L. Hull, 1973; *To Be an Invalid: The Illness of Darwin* by Ralph Colp, 1977; *Darwin: A Companion* by R.B. Freeman, 1978; *Darwin* by L. Robert Stevens. 1978; *Darwin* by Peter Brent, 1981; *The Impact of Darwinism* edited by D.F. Bratchell, 1981; *Evolution Without Evidence: Darwin and the Origin of Species* by Barry G. Gale, 1982; *Darwin* by Jonathan Howard, 1982; *Darwin's Plots: Evolutionary Narrative in Darwin, George Eliot, and Nineteenth-Century Fiction*, 1983, and "'The Face of Nature': Anthropomorphic Elements in the Language of *The Origin of Species*," in *Languages of Nature* edited by L.J. Jordanova, 1986, both by Gillian Beer; *The Survival of Darwin: A Biography of a Man and an Idea* by Ronald W. Clark, 1984; *The Vital Science: Biology and the Literary Imagination 1860–1900* by Peter Morton, 1984; *Darwin's Metaphor: Nature's Place in Victorian Culture* by Robert M. Young, 1985; *The Darwinian Heritage* edited by David Kohn, 1985; *Darwin for Beginners* by Jonathan Miller, 1986; *Darwin and the Novelists: Patterns of Science in Victorian Fiction* by George Levine, 1988; "Darwin Issue" of *Proteus*, Fall 1989.

This book may have taken the longest to write and may be the most influential work since the Bible. Further, since Charles Darwin himself is such an exemplary product of the programs for the gradual accumulation of knowledge stemming from the British Royal Society, the European Enlightenment, and the Protestant ethic of working hard with the raw material of this world (what Bacon called "The Book of Nature") one can hardly say that only *he* wrote it in the usual sense of authorship. Nevertheless, Darwin was the author—there at the right time and the right place. It was his vision of non-speciation and his data, from years of gathering and evaluating observations from the *Beagle* voyage, from his memberships in domestic breeding clubs, and from his studies of barnacles, earthworms, and small birds, that dramatically brought into focus the final attack on the ancient Aristotelian notions of genre and fixed speciation. From the scientific revolution onwards, thinkers had been uneasy with ancient ideas about "classes," or permanent and ordained types, that somehow governed nature without changing. No observations seemed to support this traditional human hope for fixity. When Darwin's massive and yet humble book appeared, the evidence and the articulation were persuasive enough to give the "non-class" view of things its modern champion. Heraclitus, Epicurus, and Lucretius may have been "Darwinian" in the ancient world; but it was only after the publication of this book that the world dared to believe again in such open-ended possibilities for material growth, development, and death.

The Origin of Species nearly did not get written. Darwin had delayed the final writing both because he loved accumulating his data and because he wanted to be sure he had collected enough. But when, on 18 June 1858 he received the famous letter from Alfred Russel Wallace describing Wallace's own recent independent arrival at the same conclusions Darwin had been working on for 25 years, the book had to be put in final form. Darwin finished the work in March 1859, and it was published on 24 November. He was co-discoverer with Wallace of the principle of natural selection, but *The Origin of Species* was the masterwork that carried the argument.

A typically fine and slow sentence written as Darwin moved inexorably toward the lyric conclusion of the book suggests how much data he hoped, at least, to offer as evidence for his vision of "descent with modification."

> When we no longer look at an organic being as a savage looks at a ship, as something wholly beyond his comprehension: when we regard every production of nature as one which has had a long history; when we contemplate every complex structure and instinct as the summing up of many contrivances, each useful to the possessor, in the same way as any great mechanical invention is the summing up of the labour, the experience, the reason, and even the blunders of numerous workmen; when we thus view each organic being, how far more interesting—I speak from experience—does the study of natural history become!

The actual analysis of the mechanism of natural selection as Darwin derives it from the "artificial selection" practices of breeders sounds just as careful, slow, and Whiggish as the sentence above. This is the clock-mechanism argument from design of the 18th-century Deists spread across the time and space of a marvelously inter-locked and dynamic nature. Darwin's fourth chapter and the summary of that chapter are the keys to this mechanism. He emphasizes "divergence of character" under the Malthusian pressures of population, that is, increasing specialization. He praises the role of "extinctions"—a lot of them, also, under the pressures for survival that he had learned about from Malthus. And like the complex ship image above, Darwin's image for (and illustration of) the tree-like shape of development as well as residual modifications that remain in disuse show the interrelation of all life—extinct, living, and yet to be.

Far from being brutal and "red-toothed" as Tennyson feared, Darwin's vision in *The Origin of Species* is a beautiful and lyric image of unity and community. Not only his final picture of the "tangled bank" that is often quoted but also the weight of all his detail envisions one large life force on this planet which, as W.B. Yeats wrote later, is "past, or passing, or to come." Beyond fine writing, the scientific revolution in all this is Darwin's stubborn insistence that divisions of speciation are arbitrary and essentially flow into one another. Small differences of biological varieties tend to increase until they equal the greater differences we call species, but there are no clear species. Modern biologists and geneticists are not now so sure, but this wonderful theory turned the world of human certainty upside-down—although in this work he does not speak directly of human evolution at all. A standard college text on evolution sums up the importance of *The Origin of Species* as "the most influential book ever written on any biological subject."

—Donald M. Hassler

OROONOKO.
Novel by Aphra Behn, 1688.

Oroonoko; or, The Royal Slave is the most significant of Aphra Behn's novels. Although in her own time Behn enjoyed recognition as a dramatist, her reputation today rests to a much greater extent upon her contributions to a then newly-emerging art form—the novel—and to *Oroonoko* in particular. V. Sackville-West called this novel Behn's "most original contribution" to English literature. *Oroonoko* has been analyzed in terms of the role of the tragic hero in romance, the effects of the personal narrative, the early development of the emancipation novel, and the novel as roman à clef—here, a thinly-disguised political intrigue.

Initially, *Oroonoko* captivated its audience as a tragic romance. Prince Oroonoko, who leads a slave revolt, is tall, handsome, brilliant, and beloved, "the first glorification of the Natural Man." He is a "noble savage," "capable of governing wisely, had as great a Soul, as politic maxims, and was as sensible of power as any Prince civiliz'd in the most refined Schools of Humanity and Learning."

Sadly, Oroonoko's brilliant and happy career is short-lived as he confronts a series of tragic events that reshape his life. Behn offers an ironic view of the naive faith in justice of Oroonoko and his beloved, Imoinda. We see Oroonoko's gradual transformation into a tragic figure fully conscious of the power of evil and capable of confronting its destructive force. Combining romance and intrigue, Behn portrays Oroonoko and Imoinda as innocent, virtuous, star-crossed lovers, whose peace and happiness in both the Old World and the New are sacrificed to evil forces. Even Thomas Southerne's weak adaptation of *Oroonoko*, roundly panned by the critics for its poor verse, failed to diminish the audience's enthusiasm for the hero.

Behn's claim that her tale was based on first-hand experience has attracted attention and stirred controversy among later critics. Southerne writes in his "Epistle Dedicatory," published shortly after Behn's death, that "Behn told his [Oroonoko's] tale" in her salon many times before she actually wrote the novel. Behn herself claims "I was myself an Eye-witness, to a great part, of what you will find here set down." Other novelists such as Defoe and Richardson also used female narrators and claimed their fictions were true, but their works provoked no negative criticism because of these claims. Behn's statement incited a series of attacks that reflected upon her novel as a work of art. Principal among these attackers was Ernest Bernbaum who accused Behn of deliberately lying about having been in Surinam, and consequently sought to discredit the value of her novel.

In the 20th century, Maureen Duffy and Angeline Goreau seemingly settle the matter. Both biographers corroborate the likelihood of Behn's sojourn to Surinam by carefully retracing her journey through documents and records. Behn shaped her sense of excitement into a dramatic first-person narrative with evocative descriptions of the sweet citrus groves of Coramantien, the flora and fauna of Surinam, and circumstantial references to the names and ranks of various government officials. From Oroonoko, she gathered information about his near-death encounter with an electric eel that she fashioned into a scientifically accurate episode. The electric eel's danger, unknown outside of Surinam, is but one example of Behn's scrupulous attention to detail that became a model for many future novelists using a first-person narrative.

Oroonoko, often considered the first emancipation novel, drew attention to the glaring disparity between the desire of traders to gain economic influence and power through slavery, thus enhancing the British Empire's growth, and their Christian principles that forbad human enslavement. The book, popular in 17th-century England, was translated and reissued in France and Germany, where readers saw it as an important social document. Between the appearance of *Oroonoko* and Harriet Beecher Stowe's *Uncle Tom's Cabin* (1852), no work in English literature makes so plain the argument against slavery.

Behn's emancipation theme, however, does not follow simple abolitionist lines. The growth of Oroonoko into a tragic figure undergoing ritual destruction deepens the pathos of the slavery theme. In Oroonoko Behn presents a traditional military hero who himself made slaves of conquered enemies. After his own betrayal to slavery, he learns of its horrors first-hand and is transformed. He must reconcile what he has learned to understand about European religion and history from within a system that demeans and humiliates not only himself, but Imoinda. The dilemmas Oroonoko faces embody the problems, and the death and destruction, the New World would come to face with slavery.

—Adelaide P. Amore

OSSIAN.
Poems by James Macpherson, 1760–63.

These are "poems" that are clearly more important for their potential, reputation, and influence than for their actuality as poems. James Macpherson claimed they were translations from ancient texts in Gaelic or Erse, but he could never produce the original poems. Following his death in 1796, a committee of experts on Scottish history and literature studied the matter extensively and finally issued a report in 1805 concluding that Macpherson's texts were in part original work and in part freely adapted versions of Celtic ballads. Hence scholars and critics who are committed to a clear, Lockean analysis of literature have been offended from the start by Macpherson's work. Samuel Johnson demanded firmly in print that he produce his originals. On the other hand, Macpherson's achievement in these "forgeries" is remarkable. He has embodied one of the great themes of "modern" literature—the longing for roots and for the Ancients. Johnson himself, who would secretly read chivalric romances about knights in armor (and the contemporary illustrations of *Ossian* show the warriors, wholly anachronistically, in armor) made the difficult journey to the Western Scottish Highlands with Boswell, in part, because he hoped to discover authentic sources for the imaginative "romance" of a native Homer. In other words, Johnson's indignation at being duped was to some extent *self*-indignation at how susceptible he himself was to what he called "diseases of imagination."

Furthermore, since the theme of discovering "roots" is also a major program of modern science (biological evolution, archeology, even the first seconds of creation in physics), Macpherson's blatant creativity challenges some of our dearest methodologies. Like James Joyce, he seems to be telling us that the best we can do is "to forge" out of the mists of the past the great heritage of our paternity and nationality. Certainly following Macpherson's lead (and long before Joyce made it the highest art in *A Portrait of the Artist*), writers of national epics in the 19th century such as the Finnish *Kalevala* and the American *Hiawatha* built long "poems" of the heroic past on the most meager of textual evidence.

When Macpherson began to publish his creative adaptations from the misty past, there had already been a century of collecting and theorizing about native ballads. This urge goes back, at least, to the extensive antiquarian library of Samuel Pepys that became a key source for Bishop Percy's immensely popular *Reliques of Ancient English Poetry*. Joseph Addison had argued, also, in a *Spectator* series that the ballad of "Chevy Chase" conformed *nearly* to the rules for classical epic. Conversely, centuries of church-driven and fully "civilized" scholarship on the Roman Empire in the West (material that Gibbon used in his massive history) provided the data on the barbarian tribes just out of focus, lurking on the edges, so that primitivism was waiting to be called forth like a bastard son as an alternative to the rational "civility" of traditional classical literature. In historical essays that he published with his translations, Macpherson makes extensive use of Roman history to date the lives of his hero Fingal and his poet son Ossian just before Christianity came with the Romans to the north of Briton.

Following a rather Augustan literary apprenticeship in which he wrote heroic couplets, Macpherson published *Fragments of Ancient Poetry Collected in the Highlands of Scotland* in 1760. He was encouraged by the eagerness of the reading public for some alternative to Augustan poetry and for some native epic heroics and so, in the following year, announced that he had discovered during trips into the Highlands an "epic" about the 3rd-century hero Fingal as written by his son Ossian. In 1761, six books of the epic poem *Fingal* appeared and in 1763 eight books of a related epic titled *Temora*. Macpherson's English for all this work is in the form of a flowing, and yet strangely generalized, prose; and this is the same verbal form that he used a decade later in his miserable translation of the *Iliad*. Ossian's style, however, seems even now to be appropriate to an 18th-century Scottish nostalgia for a misty, lost past.

The poet Ossian himself spends more time lamenting a sense of lost paternity—loss of the Ancients, loss of the fatherland, a presaged loss of Fingal—that seems clearly Macpherson's own obsession. He wrote Jacobite history later. Johnson had commented to Hugh Blair, who championed the work, that anyone could write such material "if he would *abandon* his mind to it." Macpherson wonderfully abandons himself in rhapsody after rhapsody, lament after lament; and there is very little narrative structure to the set. Here is a typical exchange from the section titled "Oithóna: A Poem," which Blake used as the basis for his *Visions of the Daughters of Albion*: "Sadness shall come, like night on thy native streams; for thou art fallen in thy youth—My fathers, replied the stranger, were of the race of the mighty; but they shall not be sad; for my fame is departed like morning mist." Such writing was a great influence on the rising mists of Romanticism.

—Donald M. Hassler

OTHELLO.
Play by William Shakespeare, 1604(?).

Othello has perhaps produced more divergent critical responses than any other of William Shakespeare's tragedies. For 19th-century critics Othello was a noble figure and Iago was the ultimate in evil. This critical tradition culminated in A.C. Bradley's reading of the play in his book *Shakespearean Tragedy*. T.S. Eliot was the first major critic to depart from this view when he claimed that Othello in his final speech before killing himself was "*cheering himself up*. He is endeavouring to escape reality, he has ceased to think about Desdemona, and is thinking about himself." F.R. Leavis went further and claimed that Iago exercises such power over Othello because "he represents something that is in Othello—in Othello the husband of Desdemona: the essential traitor within the gates." The focus of the tragedy shifted to Othello himself and for Leavis Iago was reduced to "not much more than a necessary piece of dramatic mechanism." For another influential 20th-century critic of the play, John Bayley, Iago is "deadeningly trivial." Iago had thus been reduced from being a fascinating study in evil to being merely a catalyst who brings forth forces which exist within Othello himself.

Yet Iago's role in the play is so large that the play must be weakened if he is seen as a mere dramatic device. On the other hand, Bradley's over-concentration on Iago tends to take the dramatic focus away from Othello. It is likely that readings of the play will always be distorted if either Othello or Iago is elevated at the expense of the other. Both should be seen as central to the tragedy.

The play is perhaps most persuasively interpreted, therefore, as a study in contrast, Othello representing the noble or master and Iago the servant or slave. There are numerous references in the text which illustrate such a contrast. For example: "Is this the noble Moor whom our full Senate / Call all in all sufficient?" (IV.i.261–2); "O thou Othello that was once so good, / Fall'n in the practice of a damned slave" (V.ii.294–5). Iago rejects his inferior role: "I follow him to serve my turn upon him: / We cannot all be masters, nor all masters / Cannot be truly follow'd" (I.i.42–4), and his motivation in seeking to destroy Othello is thus best understood as the slave's resentment of the master's superiority. He is determined to reveal that Othello's noble qualities are a sham, by reducing him to being a man "eaten up with passion." If Othello's nobility can be shown to have no substance Iago will emerge as superior because of his greater cleverness.

Iago's strategy is based on persuading Othello to accept that appearances can be deceptive: "Men should be that they seem; / Or those that be not, would they might seem none!" But he counts on Othello failing to draw the logical conclusion that this applies also to "honest Iago." The self-conscious reflectiveness necessary to create such sublety of mind is not reconcilable with the noble mentality, which is characterised by straightforwardness, trust, and a lack of self-consciousness. In contrast Iago possesses such self-conscious cleverness and subtlety in abundance and combines it with a scepticism that regards all spiritual concepts and values with contempt. He succeeds in gaining power over Othello by persuading him to accept that his intuitive beliefs are untrustworthy, that appearances are deceptive, and that testing and proof are necessary before one can be certain of anything. When Othello asserts "prove my love a whore" he is in Iago's power. Thus the man of "noble" qualities who was "all in all sufficient" and "Whom passion could not shake" loses his intuitive faith in Desdemona's faithfulness, resorts to the ignoble practice of eavesdropping, and becomes a victim of uncontrolled passion, desiring to tear Desdemona to pieces.

Yet Iago's triumph over Othello and noble values is not total. Bradley is right up to a point when he claims that Othello in the fifth act regains his self-control and is the master of his emotions. The noble man reasserts himself. Killing Desdemona is an impersonal act, undertaken for honourable reasons, "else she'll betray more men." Most recent critics have, however, rejected this reading and, following Eliot and Leavis, have viewed Othello as guilty of gross self-deception. But this produces over-concentration on Othello's psychology. A more persuasive reading is that the play reveals the tragic defeat of the man of noble qualities. Even if his motives are honourable in his own eyes, this does not alter the terrible fact that he is going to kill an innocent woman.

The tragedy of the situation is that Othello's noble qualities are insufficient to cope with the world. A man whose qualities are adequate in the sphere of war against the Turks proves vulnerable in the realm of domestic intrigue. In order to see through Iago's deception, Othello would have needed to possess the intellectual sublety and self-reflective cleverness that he signally lacks. Yet one cannot criticise him for lacking these attributes since they are irreconcilable with the kind of qualities one associates with nobleness. But, as the play clearly shows, in certain situations such calculating cleverness and self-conscious sublety of mind may be necessary if one is to master the world. Critics who have attacked Othello for being too eager to believe Iago and for failing to see through his lies can be accused of implicit sentimentality in that they assume that the noble man's qualities and the calculating, self-conscious cleverness of the "slave" can be reconciled, and that Desdemona can be saved. The play is a tragedy because such a reconciliation is shown as not possible.

Iago should also be seen as part of the tragedy since his self-conscious cleverness and corrosive resentment prove no more adequate to the world than Othello's noble qualities. He obtains no pleasure or benefit from destroying Othello and in the end he too is destroyed. His life is one of joylessness and total isolation from others, typified by his retreat into silence at the end of the play. But Iago can no more change his slave-like qualities by incorporating the qualities associated with the noble man than Othello can incorporate the qualities associated with Iago. The play's tragic message is that human beings can never attain sufficient completeness to be masters of their world.

The centrality of both Othello and Iago to the tragedy is emphasised by the fact that there are various parallels between them; both, for example, suspect their wives of being unfaithful and Iago, like Othello, finally kills his wife. But perhaps the most interesting parallel is that both love Desdemona. As Iago says: "Now I do love her too." But again we have a study in contrast. Iago's love for Desdemona is purely on a physical level, as the sexual language he uses in relation to her throughout the play graphically demonstrates. Othello's love for Desdemona is in contrast spiritual. He requests that Desdemona join him in Cyprus but asserts that he does not do so "To please the palate of my appetite . . . But to be free and bounteous to her mind." On meeting again in Cyprus, before the marriage has been consummated, he states: "If it were now to die, / 'Twere now to be most happy." When Iago convinces Othello of Desdemona's sexual appetite, his spiritual conception of her cannot accommodate it and he believes she must be killed. Iago's sexual love for her also leads to the desire for her death. Unable to achieve the spiritual apprehension of such a woman which would allow him to view her without resentment even though denied access to her sexuality, he wishes to destroy her as he cannot possess her. It is he who suggests to Othello that she be killed in the very centre of sexuality, the marriage bed: "strangle her in her bed, even the bed she hath contaminated."

It is another of Iago's successes that he reveals that underlying the idealism of Othello's spiritual love there is an unacknowledged sexuality. And though in the fifth act Othello seems to have transcended his earlier sexual jealousy that led him to abuse Desdemona as a strumpet and strike her, when he believes that her response on being told that Cassio is dead is a confession of guilt he again emphasises her sexuality as he kills her: "Out, strumpet!," "Down, strumpet!" The one-sidedness of both Othello's and Iago's love for Desdemona makes them jointly responsible for her death. The play is thus also a tragedy of love in that it suggests that a complete form of love in which the spiritual and the sexual are equally balanced and reconciled is humanly unattainable.

Desdemona might seem to contradict this view since her love for Othello is both spiritual and sexual. But this unification is achieved at the expense of an adult relation to his otherness as her love for him is essentially childlike. Even the total change that takes place in Othello does not affect her feeling for him. Her willow song is about a woman who died for love despite the fact that "he she lov'd prov'd mad, / And did forsake her." She seems prepared for death at Othello's hands though she pleads for her life. It would be wrong, however, to criticise her form of love. No form of love in the play, Othello's, Iago's, or Desdemona's, is entirely adequate in the world of the play and this is why love is seen in tragic terms.

—K.M. Newton

OUR MUTUAL FRIEND.
Novel by Charles Dickens, 1865.

Charles Dickens's last complete novel appeared some five years after its predecessor, *Great Expectations*, and it shows signs of new and deep meditations on old themes, especially class and money. Twemlow, one of the few born gentlemen in the book, is now subordinate to the flashy new rich, like Podsnap and Veneering, and glad, in his poverty, to be asked to their tables. The new wealth is both vulgar (see, for instance the amusing description of the Veneering's monstrous table decorations) and transient. Bankruptcy may soon succeed opulent display. Money seems less and less a reward for work or a family inheritance, and more a matter of speculation. When it is inherited, as by Boffin, it is held by someone whose class position and lack of education makes him feel ill at ease and ineffective, despite generous intentions. A great change has come over Dickens's view of the charitable use of riches, since the time when the Cheeryble brothers (in *Nicholas Nickelby*) had spread happiness and gratitude in their path. Now, Boffin feels thwarted by his inability to give with good effect, hemmed in by parasites, adventurers, and dubious philanthropists. Moreover, it has ceased to be certain who really has wealth and who has not. The Lammles marry in their delusion that the other partner is rich, and find themselves poor. Fledgeby, the miserly money-lender, conceals his identity behind the Jew, Riah, whom no one will believe when he truly protests that he is a mere agent. Dickens was influenced here by a letter from a Jewish correspondent, who complained that the villainy of the Jew, Fagin, in *Oliver Twist*, might excite prejudice. So he set himself to paint a Jew of immaculate moral purity, who would nevertheless be engaged in the traditional Jewish pursuit of money-lending. The moral contrast between him and the detestable Fledgeby, often ironically called "christian" is an extreme one.

At the same time as they have been pushed more to the margin of the social world, the gentlemen by birth have become more sympathetic. Twemlow, Wrayburn, and Lightwood are not very much use in the working world, but they are far more attractive than their gentlemanly predecessors in Dickens's work. Their idleness is treated with wry amusement rather than satire. Wrayburn's moral struggles over his affection for Lizzie Hexam, his rivalry with Headstone, and his eventual decision to marry Lizzie are portrayed with a sympathy which may well have suprised the book's first readers.

Headstone is perhaps the most original and convincing of all Dickens's numerous murderers. Like most murderers, in fact, but unlike many of his Dickensian predecessors, he is a respectable citizen, with a definite place in the social system. Dickens has combined in him a tale of wild passion and violence with one of his most thoughtful studies of educational change. He is a new type of trained teacher; and, for him, as for his protégé, Charlie Hexam, respectability—belonging to the middle class through professional qualification—has all the romance that their humble and disreputable origins can give it. His obsession with Lizzie is wholly convincing, as is his impotent rage when taunted by Wrayburn.

Dickens had always been the poet of London, but here we find a new, stranger London, dominated by the river, and its "birds of prey," Hexam and Riderhood, who make their living by robbing the corpses the river washes up. But, though the river of the first chapter is repellent and associated with crime, its function in the book's structure gradually changes. It becomes a purifying force. People who fall into it are changed. Riderhood believes that his narrow escape from drowning makes him invulnerable to the fate of actual drowning which eventually overtakes him. Wrayburn is changed from a man uneasily contemplating the seduction of Lizzie to a man determined to brave the laughter of the world by marrying her. It is the special virtue of Dickens's symbolism that it is rooted in a closely observed reality. This applies both to the river and to the dust-heaps, which constitute much of Boffin's wealth, and which were, in fact, as Mayhew testifies, enormously valuable properties. The old Dickensian theme of the parent (or in *The Old Curiosity Shop*, the grandparent) guided and controlled by a young girl here undergoes a bizarre transformation in the relation of the dolls' dressmaker to her drunken father, whom she terrorizes with a ferocity at once cruel and pathetic. The author's ruthlessness is seen in the heartless account of his death in a street accident. And the old satire on public institutions is revived in the savage description of Betty Higden, preferring death in the street to being the inmate of a workhouse.

All these threads are interwoven with what is, ostensibly, the main plot, the story of Rokesmith's disguised return from supposed drowning and his romantic love for the mercenary but redeemable Bella Wilfer. The over-sweet sentiment here is sharpened, though, by the acid portrait of the selfish posturings of Bella's mother and sister, and by the very convincing pretence of miserdom which Boffin makes as a warning to Bella in her mercenary tendencies.

—A.O.J. Cockshut

THE OWL AND THE NIGHTINGALE.
Poem, late 12th-early 13th century.

Edition

The Owl and the Nightingale, edited by E.G. Stanley. 1960; revised edition, 1972.

Critical Studies: *The Owl and the Nightingale: Sources, Date, Author* by Kathryn Huganir, 1931; introduction by N.R. Ker to *The Owl and the Nightingale* (facsimile), 1962; "Henry II and *The Owl and the Nightingale*" by Anne W. Baldwin, in *Journal of English and Germanic Philology*, 1967; *Early Middle English Literature* by R.M. Wilson, 3rd edition, 1968; "The Patrons of *The Owl and the Nightingale*" by J.C. Russell, in *Philological Quarterly*, 48, 1969; *The Owl and the Nightingale: The Poem and Its Critics* by Kathryn Hume, 1975; "*The Owl and the Nightingale* and English Law Court Procedures of the Twelfth and Thirteenth Centuries" by Michael A. Witt, in *Chaucer Review*, Winter 1982; "*The Owl and the Nightingale* and the Bishops" by Nicolas Jacobs, in *Medieval Literature and Antiquities* edited by Myra Stokes and T.L. Burton, 1987; "Flying in the Face of Tradition: A New View of *The Owl and the Nightingale*" by Alexandra Barratt, in *University of Toronto Quarterly*, 56, 1987; *Middle English Debate Poetry and the Aesthetics of Irresolution* by Thomas L. Reed, Jr., 1990.

After the Norman conquest, some alliterative verse modeled on the conventions of Old English poetry continued to be written. However, under the influence of French poetry, *The Owl and the Nightingale* inaugurates a fresh spirit and new style in early Middle English. The poem's wit, urbanity, *courtois* vocabulary, and octosyllabic couplets have often been cited as evidence of the 12th-century Renaissance spirit in the English vernacular.

Originally composed in a southeastern dialect, perhaps that of Surrey, the poem survives in a southwestern dialect in two manuscripts, British Library MS Cotton Caligula A.ix, and Bodleian Library MS Jesus College 29. The medieval catalogue (c. 1400) of the Library at Titchfield Abbey in Hampshire also lists "De conflictu inter philomenam et bubonem in anglicis," most likely a copy of the poem, now lost. Although some editors date the Cotton manuscript before 1250 on paleographical grounds, Ker believes it impossible to date either manuscript more precisely than to the second half of the 13th century. Internal evidence indicates the poem was composed after the death of Henry II in 1189 and before the accession of Henry III in 1216.

The extant manuscripts offer no hint of the poem's author. A 17th-century owner, almost certainly Thomas Wilkins, records a verse from a leaf no longer extant that mentions one John of Guildford, but nothing connects him definitely with *The Owl and the Nightingale* rather than with other French and English poems in the manuscript. The only person mentioned in the poem is Master Nicholas of Guildford, a learned cleric apparently dwelling in Portesham, Dorset, in the diocese of Salisbury, before whom the argumentative birds agree (their only point of unanimity!) to submit their case for judgment. One purpose of the poem seems to have been to bring Nicholas, whose wisdom, prudence, righteousness, and mature discrimination both birds praise (lines 191–214), to the attention of his superiors and so win for him promotion, although even on this point commentators are divided, particularly as the English vernacular was in this period a poor cousin to Latin and Anglo-Norman. Master Nicholas may have been a canon lawyer and Oxford professor, Master Nicholas of Aquila, whose family seat was near Guildford, or Nicholas de Guildford, Nicholas *filius Thoraldi*, or Nicholas, Archdeacon of London, but attribution of the poem to Nicholas (no matter who he was) remains controverted. A recent suggestion ascribes the poem to women in the Benedictine monastery at Shaftesbury.

The poem observes the conventions of the *debat* (also known as *altercatio* or *estrif*), a popular genre in the 12th and 13th centuries. Essentially poetic disputations in which two or more opponents debate competing views, medieval Latin *debats* encompass a wide variety of antitheses: summer and winter, gold and lead, wine and water, soul and body. Unlike the Latin *debats* (particularly *Winter and Summer*) which are its closest analogues, however, *The Owl and the Nightingale* contains no neatly organized argument of balanced speeches, and the classical allusions of the Latin models are replaced here with proverbs ascribed to Alfred and exemplary tales drawn from the *lais* and fables of Marie de France ("Laustic," the fables of cat and fox, hawk and owl) and Aesop. The influence of Alexander Neckam's *De natura rerum* has also been recognized. Although the author uses legal terminology sporadically, the extent to which English law court procedure (common-law or canon law) or rhetorical training at university shapes the poem remains a matter of contention.

Like the Latin debates, *The Owl and the Nightingale* generates its dialectic from the character of the contestants—the solemn Owl on her ivy-clad stump and the merry Nightingale on her bough of blossoms. The argument proceeds in a series of charges and counter-charges, many secondary allegations later recurring as major indictments. The nightingale, as plaintiff, states the initial complaint: the owl is ugly, her habits foul, her origins base. The owl threatens physical violence, but the birds agree to let Nicholas judge the case. The nightingale restates the indictment, adding that the owl is also blind by day, an accusation the owl unequivocally denies. She claims her song signals the hours of night prayer and that, in contrast to the nightingale, she sings in moderation. The nightingale responds that she sings only in the spring, linking the owl's song with winter and adversity. The owl turns that censure into a virtue, linking her song to Christmas, and in her turn accuses the nightingale of licentiousness. The nightingale attempts to respond, but the owl claims it is her turn to attack.

She accuses the nightingale of possessing a single skill, at the same time delivering three minor counter-charges that parallel the nightingale's earlier attack—the nightingale is ugly, lives by the privy, and eats dirty food. The nightingale defends her single skill by linking it to the joyousness of Christian worship. The owl returns to the attack by bringing up an earlier, incidental charge that the nightingale sings of secular, licentious love, as evidenced by her failure to sing in northern Europe where missionaries are needed. The owl furthers this rebuke by connecting the nightingale with courtly love, particularly with adultery. The debate ends with a discussion of love, marriage, and adultery, leading to another threat of physical combat, which the Wren, king of birds, is called upon to prevent.

Nearly everyone agrees that the dispute is allegorical, but interpretations of the contest vary widely. Among the antitheses that have been suggested are pleasure vs. asceticism, or the active and secular life vs. the contemplative, monastic life, the minstrel vs. the clerk, joy vs. sorrow, art vs. philosophy, or the newer lyric poetry opposed to the older didactic poetry. Some commentators have seen the poem as political commentary *a clef*: Geoffrey, Archbishop of York, for instance, as the owl, his opponent Richard I, or Thomas à Becket as the owl, Henry II as the nightingale. The lack of a coherent subject in the avian squabble has led some critics (notably Kathryn Hume) to construe the poem as a burlesque-satire.

The Owl and the Nightingale is one of the earliest English poems to use the octosyllabic couplet based on continental French models, although the considerable freedom with which the poet employs anacrusis, trochaic substitutions, alliteration, and occasional clashing stress has led some commentators to connect the line more closely to the native English fourstress line. The style is conversational, the effect colloquial. In its verse form, its *debat* genre, and its *courtois* vocabulary, *The Owl and the Nightingale* marks a clear break with the Anglo-Saxon poetic past.

—Richard H. Osberg

THE OWL AND THE PUSSY-CAT.
Poem by Edward Lear, 1870.

"The Owl and the Pussy-Cat" translates into nonsense Edward Lear's own journeys as a landscape painter and writer. The most famous nonsense song, it was written later than the first *Book of Nonsense* (1846), which contained cheerful and subversive limericks with clear-lined woodcuts. Visual and verbal nonsense came easily to Lear: in its apparently reasonable and mildly crazy world he could relax, forget shyness, relate to children whom he loved. He could also forget his worries about money, and the problems of the artist who had constantly to woo his upper-class friends and visitors into buying his pictures. Sadness, aggression, loneliness, and guilt could all be explored in the nonsense worlds, leaving Edward Lear, artist and writer, with an acceptable public face.

"The Owl and the Pussy-Cat," like most of the nonsense, was written for children. It began as a gift for Janet, a sick child, daughter of Lear's friend John Addington Symonds, who was wintering, like the artist, in Cannes in 1867. The poem was first published in *Nonsense Songs, Stories, Botany, and Alphabets* (1870). It was a story of travel, and a neat subversion of a serious Victorian romantic ballad. The illustrations underline the text's suggestion of a prudently organised voyage: domestic care and good sense decree honey and money as obvious necessities. We are not asked to think of the traveller's actual eating and spending habits.

Lear loved drawing birds; his first commissioned work had been ornithological. He was also devoted to cats, and when finally settled in San Remo in 1871, he soon acquired a lifelong companion: the striped, but tail-less Foss. Owl and cat are total opposites, yet, in the everyday world, they have a strange facial likeness, and in this nonsense song they become ideal partners. The pea-green boat, the Cat holding the rudder, the Owl serenading his love to the music of his guitar: every detail seems perfectly appropriate once the reader has accepted the initial nonsense proposition: "The Owl and the Pussy-Cat went to sea . . . " In this topsy-turvy world owls do not have to fly and cats do not dislike large quantities of water. The narrator never questions the calm of the journey and "a year and a day" pass by without a hint of surprise. The "land where the Bong-tree grows" holds no threats because it is immediately taken for granted. The reader is not concerned with the strangeness of a Bong-tree, but with the familiar Pig who, so luckily, happens to have a ring "at the end of his nose." The ring once purchased, the marriage goes forward, presided over by a convenient and helpful Turkey.

By the light of the moon, on the edge of the sand, the union of the Owl and the Pussy-Cat is celebrated with feast and dance. This peaceful journey to a happy land is unusual in Lear's nonsense songs which contain, for instance, the melancholy Dong waiting vainly for his Jumbly girl, and the Jumblies themselves who ignore all warnings of danger and go to sea in a sieve.

The dialogue throughout this song is simple, with a childlike air of taking everything for granted. No questions arise, the marriage is celebrated, the only "nonsense" words are "Bong-tree" and "runcible." The first is easy to accept, as vaguely exotic, the second, a favourite word of Lear's, can mean almost anything, but has pleasant connotations. The needs of metre and syntax sometimes condense the dialogue:

". . . are you willing to sell for one shilling
  Your ring?" Said the Piggy, "I will."
So they took it away, and were married next day
  By the Turkey who lives on the hill.

but this is quickly understood as a sense within nonsense.

Lear's nonsense, more than his paintings or journals, brought him some kind of fame. He set "The Owl and the Pussy-Cat" to music and sang it, after dinner, in countless appreciative Victorian drawing-rooms. On his last journey, to India, in 1874, he was drawing an owl for one little girl when another begged "O please draw a Pussy-Cat too!—because you know they went to sea in a boat." Lear was gratified to discover that the child had learned "this remarkable poem" at school. The pea-green boat had sailed to the lands of the British Raj.

The 1894 introduction to *Nonsense Songs, Stories, Botany, and Alphabets* points out that "Nonsense has proved not a mere putting forward of incongruities and absurdities, but the bringing out of a new and deeper harmony of life in and through its contradictions." "The Owl and the Pussy-Cat" combines "contradiction" with "harmony," in a nonsense world of voyaging and romance, with marriage and a necessary domesticity. The poem celebrates a partnership that Lear, in his long life, sadly never achieved. But the pea-green boat sails on as it has done ever since it was launched on its journey, for Janet Symonds, in 1867.

—Ruth Pitman

OWLS DO CRY.
Novel by Janet Frame, 1957.

Janet Frame's first novel, *Owls Do Cry*, offers a representation of family relationships and of the construction of "madness" that prefigures many of the central preoccupations of the liberation movements of the 1960's. Critiques produced then by R.D. Laing, David Cooper, and the women's liberation movement show striking similarities to those offered in Frame's fiction. Yet her work moves far beyond any element of "case study"—though her next novel, *Faces in the Water*, was to be made required reading for the staff of some New Zealand mental hospitals. Her dazzling, often ironic, sometimes humorous playing with words allies the novel also with those post-modernist texts that rupture language to show the gaps and dissonances of conventional accounts of patriarchal society and ideology.

The text tells the story of the Withers family—Amy and Bob, and their four children, Francie, Daphne, Toby, and Teresa or Chicks. Francie is burnt to death while a teenager, Toby is epileptic and a dealer in second-hand goods, Daphne is incarcerated in a mental hospital for many years. Only Chicks leads a "normal" life, but her diary narration of her day-to-day life (the dominant discourse of which is the women's magazine) is satirically exposed as resembling Laing's "appalling state of alienation called normality" ("We were both silent then, and depressed. I agreed—If only something could be done about the State of the World"). The narrative operates through mobilising, kaleidoscopically, a series of binary oppositions: sanity/madness; rational/intuitive; conscious/unconscious; growing up/childhood; rubbish/treasure. *Tales of Treasure* was Frame's original title. The children search for treasure, which includes books like fairy tales by the Grimm Brothers, at the dump; their father grumbles, "they can't tell what's rubbish from what isn't rubbish."

The text is of and about working-class family life. This is perhaps why Frame's representations of a state of alienation from contemporary capitalist and consumerist society avoid the often patrician detachment of those of, say, Patrick White. Her habitual writing strategy is the transfiguration of cliché—but from inside popular usage, not from outside.

In an essay entitled "Beginnings," Frame writes of abandoning early a career as a teacher: "I walked from the room and the school, from 'this' world to 'that' world, where I have stayed and where I live now." Inhabiting "that world" is posed as a mode of resistance to the "normal," the world of repressive institutions like the family and the asylum; retaining a critical perceptive imagination makes it possible to combat, on an individual level at least, pervasive pressures to live out the dominant ideology. Such refusal of incorporation, however, also leads inevitably to the punishment or destruction of those who resist. Frame herself writes in the second volume of her autobiography of having narrowly escaped a leucotomy. Daphne is forced to have one: "We're going to change you so that you'll be able to live in the world and be just like other people, and you'll like that, won't you?"

The novel's title, drawing on a line of Ariel's song from *The Tempest*, is revealing both in its principles of selection and its context. The time when "owls do cry" is the threatening night in which birds of prey hunt. But there are two other dimensions to Shakespeare's text:

> Where the bee sucks, there suck I
> In a cowslip's bell I lie;
> There I couch when owls do cry.
> On the bat's back I do fly
> After summer merrily: . . .

Lying in a cowslip's bell evokes a supposed security and confidence of a childhood in the orbit of the mother—recalled both with nostalgic longing as the source of nourishment: "I used to climb on her knee and pull open her blouse, and take her tittie in my mouth, for there was no one who came after me to say—It's mine," and negatively as a model of women's oppression ("an old worn letter-box," "Amy Withers always made pikelets for peace"). The freedom of flying "on the bat's back" through the darkness is not attained by any protagonist in the novel. Daphne rejects the illusion of her mother's protection: "*Come in you naughty bird / the rain is pouring down / what would your mother say / if you stay there and drown? / You are a very naughty bird / you do not think of me / I'm sure I do not care / said the sparrow on the tree.*" When her father (who has bemusedly authorised her leucotomy) comes to visit her before the operation, we are told that Daphne "felt safe under the hat. The rain could not fall and her mother would not have to be standing at the door and crying out—Come in you naughty bird, out of the rain. Daphne smiled then, remembering she was a don't-care sparrow, and threw the hat into the corner."

Institutionalised "caring" is represented as destructively violent in its effects—the family is *not* a cowslip's bell (the breast metonymised into nourishment of real needs), a "haven in a heartless world"; the asylum offers no refuge from the owls for the sparrow but rather functions, through its instruments of sexualised repression ("Turn on, my love, he will say, and reach for the switch, and caress the red luminous eye with his gentle hand"), to return "deviants" to "normal" life. By the end of the novel, the family has withered away. If the Epilogue is read as a summarised sequel, Toby has been arrested for indigence and Bob is in a home for old men, vaguely remembering only his wife—and primarily in her symbolic function of making pikelets. Daphne has escaped the asylum but at the price of having become someone suitable to be forewoman at a Blakean dark satanic mill—not a road to independence through paid work, but a "taking hold like the mill girls of the wrong magic and the wrong fairytale."

—Carole Ferrier

P

THE PAINTER OF SIGNS.
Novel by R.K. Narayan, 1976.

The Painter of Signs is firmly set in Malgudi and in the timeless modern India of R.K. Narayan's imagination, and the motor of its plot is something peculiarly Indian: the Gandhi government's campaign to persuade peasant villagers of the importance of birth control. Nevertheless, it rivals *The Man-Eater of Malgudi* (about Vasu the ambitious taxidermist) as the most European of all Narayan's books. Specifically, it is structured not in his usual linear, streamlike way but like Euripidean tragedy. At the start, two incompatibles are brought together; as the story proceeds, they seem to be moving towards accommodation, though neither in fact changes or develops; about three-quarters of the way through there is a moment of irreversible crisis; self-understanding is achieved—and at the end, in the most Euripidean stroke of all, the story explodes expectation, scampering in a direction which makes us think again, with new irony, about all that has gone before.

In Euripides's plays, the central conflicts are often between the (psychologically compelling) humanness of the characters and the unbending, unavoidable necessities of fate. What happens is in the end surprising and shocking because our sympathy for the characters' personalities has led us to expect, to hope for, a different resolution of their dilemmas. Narayan is superficially gentler, but no less philosophically relentless. In *The Painter of Signs*, as so often in his work, the central conflict is between Old India, embodied by the hero's devout Hindu aunt, and New India, symbolised by the heroine's unwavering and uncritical devotion to the birth-control campaign. The central character Raman, the painter of signs himself, is tugged in both directions, and his plight is both ridiculous (as he blunders without understanding between one relationship and the other) and tragic (because he can discover no way out of his dilemma, because the resolution he thinks he thinks he has found turns to ashes in his hands). Narayan subverts the Euripidean structure even as he uses it, but it nonetheless underlies the story, supplying formal tension and beautifully controlled.

For the rest, *The Painter of Signs* once again exhibits Narayan's characteristic minimalism. As in all his books, he reduces teeming India to one small town, three or four characters, a couple of relationships. He spends time on tiny details, each of them a vital clue to character—the smoothness of the wood Raman uses to make his signs, the spareness of Daisy's office at the Family Planning Centre, the coarse grey hair of Raman's aunt (once, in her days of youthful hope, a beauty), the uncomprehending, eager eyes of the villagers, high in the Mempi Hills, to whom Daisy unavailingly explains the need for smaller families, the missing of a bus. Raman's house, like his soul, has no furniture at all, and his only luxuries are the materials of his craft (each sign is a work of art, though no customer ever realises it) and his pile of tattered books, World's Classics which carry him into realms of the imagination which he understands even less than his day-to-day Malgudian reality.

Narayan selects the events of his plot in a similarly thrifty way, making each moment stand for a thousand incidents. The flowering of love between Raman and Daisy—the triumph of Raman's hopes—is signalled by a single hand-touch beside a river at evening. The impossibility that Daisy's peasant campaign will succeed is apparent (except to her) as soon as Raman finds that the only surface suitable for his slogans is the wall of the village fertility shrine. (The shrine's peppery, 100-year-old priest is one of Narayan's funniest minor characters.) The collapse of Raman's happiness begins when his aunt casually announces that she is buying a one-way ticket to Benares. This kind of focusing is familiar, once again, in European drama—Beckett, especially, comes to mind—but its frugal richness is rare in western novels. Even the shorter works of Hesse or Gide, Narayan's nearest fictional analogues, seem by contrast both prolix and unenlightening.

It is, I think, a tribute to Narayan that all this critical rummaging for comparisons and contrasts seems to take us further away from the novels, to obscure more than it illuminates. *The Painter of Signs*, like all his mature work, has for its main quality a limpidity of meaning, matched absolutely by form and utterance, which makes explication otiose. Narayan never seems to be saying very much; your main emotion as you read is delight in a simple tale told without fuss or fret; but the story lingers long in both mind and heart. This is not due to literary sleight of hand—which is why it evades analysis. Nor is it because Narayan is artless. The book's simplicity is unforced, natural, and resonant: prose-poetry.

—Kenneth McLeish

PALLISER SERIES.
6 novels by Anthony Trollope, 1864–80.

Anthony Trollope's Palliser novels trace the political career of Plantagenet Palliser, nephew and heir of the Duke of Omnium, who eventually becomes Prime Minister of England. The series consists of six works: *Can You Forgive Her?*, *Phineas Finn*, *The Eustace Diamonds*, *Phineas Redux*, *The Prime Minister*, and *The Duke's Children*. Where Trollope's Barchester series loosely concentrates on church life, his Palliser series concentrates on parliamentary life. The Palliser novels are often called Trollope's political novels, and this is, perhaps, a more apt title for the series, since, while the texts follow the career of Palliser and his wife, Glencora, who appear in each work, four of the six focus on other characters. Phineas Finn, for instance, an Irishman who longs for a political career, dominates both *Phineas Finn* and *Phineas*

Redux, where Lizzie Eustace is the primary subject of *The Eustace Diamonds*, and Alice Vavasor of *Can You Forgive Her?*

The series revolves around politics, and, indeed, its own political nature is apparent in its conscious project. Although these novels often condemn some of the machinations of Parliament, they generally work to support and justify a certain standard of life. They attempt to affirm the values and the norms of a conservative, bourgeois Victorian lifestyle. It is in this that the novels have grown in appeal, for the ways in which they subvert their conscious project is of particular interest to contemporary critics. The novels become intriguing exemplars of a conservative, bourgeois Victorian ideology, and as they seek to justify that ideology, they also, inadvertently, expose its flaws. This process is perhaps most evident in the textual portrayal of women.

Trollope was a self-admitted opponent of women's rights, and his texts attempt to legitimize his belief that women are inferior to men, should be guided by men, and should accept their "proper" place in society as wives and mothers. Yet, in the novels' efforts to vindicate their ideological view, they in fact depict the oppressive and unjust nature of the system they seek to support. Each text depicts the unhappy fate of Victorian women, and its attempt to resolve the conflict it has dramatized is ineffectual and foregrounds the necessity of social change.

The first novel of the series, *Can You Forgive Her?*, draws attention to the plight of women in Victorian society. Its protagonist, Alice Vavasor, wishes to be useful, but discovers that she can only be of use as a wife. As a woman, she is barred from any other activity. Alice initially jilts the "worthy" John Grey, but, ultimately, learns to appreciate his qualities. The text asserts that Alice has matured and left her foolish ways behind, but the language used to describe Alice's acceptance of Grey's proposal is disturbing:

> She was pressed by him as in some countries the prisoner is pressed by the judge,—so pressed that she acknowledged to herself silently that any further antagonism to him was impossible . . . She shrank from him, back against the stonework of the embrasure, but she could not shrink away from his grasp. She put up her hand to impede his, but his hand, like his character and his words, was full of power. "Alice," he said, as he pressed her close with his arm, "the battle is over now, and I have won it."

The language, here, suggests that Alice does not happily accept her role as wife, but that it is forced upon her, and if she must be forced to comply with it, then it cannot be "natural" for her to assume it. Therefore, despite its effort to normalize its ideological view of woman as wife and mother, the text implicitly asserts that that view is constructed, and is not natural at all.

Glencora Palliser provides a further example of a woman who has been compelled to perform according to society's rules. Glencora is the victim of an arranged marriage, and tries to find fulfillment in life as a social leader. Her efforts are unsuccessful, however, and her dissatisfaction with her marital status is evident in one of her final appearances in the series, when she reflects that

> [s]he had toiled and struggled, she had battled and occasionally submitted; and yet there was present to her a feeling that she had stood higher in public estimation as Lady Glencora Palliser,—whose position had been all her own and had not depended on her husband,—than now she had done as Duchess of Omnium, and wife of the Prime Minister of England.

Glencora's desire for an independent existence is impossible. A Victorian woman cannot function successfully in an unmarried state, and her only hope lies in marrying a man who will make her happy. Glencora tries to save her daughter, Mary, from the hardships of an arranged marriage, and encourages her to marry the man she loves. Palliser is opposed to the match, and tries, in *The Duke's Children*, to force Mary to align herself with the mate he has chosen for her. He does eventually accede to her wishes, but what is made clear is that a woman's fate depends upon a benevolent male decision. While the texts imply that all decent men have the best interests of their women at heart, they also demonstrate that this is not always the case.

In *The Eustace Diamonds*, the long suffering Lucy Morris must work as a governess while she waits for her future husband, Frank Greystock, to "claim" her; until that time she is at the mercy of her employers. As she endures hardship, her solicitor fiancé flirts with his client, Lizzie Eustace. Nonetheless, despite his treatment of Lucy, the text presents Greystock as an "honourable" man, and implies that, in him, Lucy has found a fine husband. And, indeed, in light of the fate of other women in the series, most readers will agree that Lucy is fortunate in her choice.

In *Phineas Finn*, Lady Laura Standish has depleted her fortune in coming to the aid of her brother's gambling debts, and must marry to replenish the familial coffers. Although she loves Phineas Finn, she chooses to marry Mr. Kennedy, a taciturn Scot. The marriage is an unhappy one, but Laura is unable to disentangle herself from it legally, and must exile herself to Dresden to escape her husband's abuse. Although the texts work to support the British justice system, they have difficulty supporting a system which accords women so few legal rights. And Laura is not the only example of a woman trapped in a disastrous marriage. Emily Wharton, in *The Prime Minister*, suffers the same fate when she falls in love with and marries Ferdinand Lopez, an unscrupulous fortune-hunter. Emily learns of her husband's shady business dealings, yet is unable to extricate herself from the marriage. When Lopez decides to emigrate to Guatemala, Emily has little choice but to follow him. Fortunately (and conveniently) Lopez commits suicide and frees Emily; however, he frees her only to enter another marriage. While this marriage promises to be better, the novel has made it clear that if a woman has the misfortune to marry poorly, she is at the mercy of her husband.

There are female characters in the series who refuse to conform to the Victorian ideal of woman. Lizzie Eustace decides to trust only to herself, and rejects her male counsellors' advice. Lizzie had married a wealthy old man, who has died, and she becomes involved in various legal battles when she insists on keeping her deceased husband's family jewels. The text condemns Lizzie's behaviour and portrays her as manipulative, unscrupulous, and deceitful. To dramatize its "moral" that women who break society's rules meet with unfortunate ends, the novel pairs Lizzie with Mr. Emilius, a preacher with a dubious past. In *Phineas Redux*, Mr. Emilius murders Finn's political enemy, and is convicted of bigamy. The irony of this moral lesson lies in the fact that Lizzie fares no worse than Laura Standish, who has done nothing to deserve her fate.

The one female character who flouts conventions and prospers is Madame Max Goesler. Madame Max is a widow who falls in love with Phineas Finn, and actually proposes to him, thus violating the rules of female decorum. Finn initially refuses her, but when he is accused of murder, in *Phineas Redux*, and Madame Max secures the evidence that acquits him, he accepts her proposal—along with the money she brings to the match. However, while this provides a neat solution to Finn's financial and marital plight, many 20th-century readers will find the marriage disappointing. The weak, if likeable, Finn is hardly a suitable match for the intrepid Madame Max.

Although the novels overtly assert that woman should trust to man to guide her throughout life, they also foreground the problems within their ideologically constructed view of woman. Far from justifying the system they ostensibly support, the texts demonstrate its untenability, and, if they justify anything, it is the need for social reform. In this, the Palliser series assumes new significance for contemporary critics, since it becomes an exemplar of the ways in which an ideological treatise will hold, within itself, a critique of its own conscious project.

—Priscilla L. Walton

PAMELA.
Novel by Samuel Richardson, 1740–41.

Samuel Richardson's *Pamela; or, Virtue Rewarded* was first published anonymously in two duodecimo volumes on 6 November 1740, though it bore the date 1741. It was subtitled "In a SERIES of FAMILIAR LETTERS FROM A Beautiful Young Damsel, To her PARENTS. Now first Published In order to cultivate the Principles of VIRTUE and RELIGION in the Minds of the YOUTH of BOTH SEXES." The first novel by Richardson, a London master printer, *Pamela* may well, depending upon definition, have been the first novel in English. Richardson's great rival for the title of first English novelist is Daniel Defoe, a generation earlier. Both men wrote books which fit our general definition of the novel—a long fictitious prose narrative whose events grow out of each other or out of the nature of its protagonist. If we demand, however, that the creator of a new genre be consciously aware that he is creating a new form, not merely ringing lively changes upon an older one, the title belongs to Richardson, for Defoe still seems to view and present his novels as episodic extensions of the journalistic pseudo-autobiographical account. Richardson, in contrast, lets his characters see and state plainly that their lives are the stuff from which a novel could be made.

Yet the impetus for Richardson's first novel, like that of Defoe's, was essentially non-belletristic. Richardson was so, a printer (publisher). Two of his bookseller friends asked him to put together a collection of *Familiar Letters* which the lower classes could use as models. (The writing of socially acceptable letters is one of the most difficult skills for the upwardly mobile to master.) Richardson showed an unusual ability to project himself into the characters writing these model letters and was particularly taken with that of a young serving maid whose chastity was being threatened by her young master. As a 13-year-old Richardson had written love letters for three young women of his acquaintance (a sort of androgynous Cyrano); now he set aside the letter book for a while and in two months wrote instead the first draft of *Pamela*. The book appeared anonymously as letters from a real serving girl, with Richardson assuming the persona of editor.

The plot of *Pamela* is simple. Pamela's parents, decent and literate persons, have been reduced by a financial catastrophe to her father's digging clay ditches. They have had to put their daughter out at 12 as a serving girl to a good lady, who has educated and cultivated her but who has just died, leaving Pamela, at 15, in a house now run by the young master, Mr. B. He is attracted to Pamela, shows her marks of his favor, makes it increasing plain that he hopes to seduce her. She is drawn to him but afraid of him, particularly after he kidnaps her to his Lincolnshire estate. By her wit and her virtue, she wins him over to an honorable marriage; they are married before the novel is two-thirds over, but she still must cope with problems involving high-born neighbors, a haughty sister-in-law, her husband's illegitimate six-year-old daughter, and a spoiled and willful husband himself.

There had been other epistolary narratives before Richardson, but none had aroused the immediate and widespread attention (applause and attack) that his did. Among its admirers was Alexander Pope, who stayed up much of the night to finish it and asked Dr. George Cheyne to make his warm compliments to Richardson, telling him he had read his book "with great Approbation and Pleasure." Likewise, Samuel Johnson would later praise Richardson as an author who had enlarged our knowledge of human nature and of the human heart, although he admitted to Erskine that if one were to read Richardson for the story, his impatience would be so much fretted that he would hang himself. Read him instead for the sentiment, he advised, with the story only giving its occasion. But if *Pamela* completely won over two of the major figures of 18th-century literature, it hopelessly antagonized a third—Henry Fielding—who saw Pamela as a conniving upstart who did not know her place and simply used her physical charms to win what she wanted: a marriage for above her station. The adulation heaped upon the novel by many of its readers infuriated Fielding, who took his revenge in two imitations of *Pamela: An Apology for the Life of Mrs. Shamela Andrews* (first published 2 April 1741), a bawdy parody in which Pamela has become a loose-talking and loose behaving illegitimate city child of an Irish bawd, a girl profligate and scheming, carrying on with Parson Williams and bearing his child. Less than a year later (22 February 1742), Fielding brought out a second response to Richardson's *Pamela* in *Joseph Andrews*, which grew into much more than simply a second parody of Richardson. Its first and last parts burlesque Richardson, but its center is an original novel in itself.

Fielding's *Shamela* and other attacks upon *Pamela*, but more especially admiring attempts to provide sequels to Richardson's immensely popular novel, drove Richardson to providing a sequel himself. On 7 December 1741, he brought out his own sequel. Always overshadowed by its predecessor, *Pamela II* centers its interest upon Pamela's first child, Billy, and her reaction when Mr. B. comes ever closer to an affair with a Countess. This flirtation is the major conflict of *Pamela II*, although there are also interesting debates on whether Billy should be breast-fed (Pamela wants him to be, Mr. B. does not) and on what parts of Locke's theory of education will work and what will not—and the proud and indulged Lady Davers is still a formidable sister-in-law.

Although not the first of the epistolary narratives, *Pamela* was the most influential and famous of them, but it is not told solely in terms of letters. For much of the novel, Pamela is being held incommunicado on the Lincolnshire estate and cannot write letters at all. Instead, she keeps a journal. At a few other points Richardson intervenes in the persona of editor and simply summarizes the plot events. Most of the letters are from Pamela herself, directed to her parents; the pattern has not yet become the infinitely rich and complex one of the letters in *Clarissa*. (Even in *Pamela II* the epistolary technique is becoming more complicated, though Richardson also loses some of his ability to write "to the moment" in his sequel—a technique in part 1 which is much more exciting but less plausible.)

Ultimately *Pamela* (like *Clarissa*) is a novel about sexual empowerment. The woman is engaged in sexual combat with a man both attractive and frightening to her, one who is her superior in social rank and in physical strength. Her only weapons are words—her oral wit and her pen, the new instrument of defense and attack which has replaced the needle as a woman's best implement. The woman is engaged in a race as to whether she can, in Carolyn Heilbrun's terms, teach the man to be androgynous (to have some of the gentler and less aggressive traits generally thought of as feminine) before he asserts his physical masculinity and rapes her. She must endeavor to do so chiefly though her speech and her writings; each man (Mr. B. and Lovelace) intercepts and reads the letters or journals written by the woman. In Clarissa's case Heilbrun sees the failure of androgyny; though Lovelace reads and is moved by Clarissa's letters, he is himself so unstable, undisciplined, aggressive that he rapes her anyway. But Pamela, seemingly gentler and less intellectual than Clarissa, achieves the triumph of androgyny, outmaneuvering and winning over Mr. B. to respect and honor her.

Two incidents in *Pamela* show the struggle for empowerment at work—and Pamela's means of handling that struggle. The first is the psychological climax of the novel, when Pamela almost kills herself. In her most serious escape attempt, after she has been held prisoner on the Lincolnshire estate for a month, Pamela squeezes through a window one midnight, drops down to the ground, and throws her upper-coat, her neck handkerchief, and her round-eared cap into the pond, so that her pursuers will waste their time there rather than looking for her outside the estate. But when she reaches the gate, she finds that Mrs. Jewkes has changed the lock; she tries to climb over the door, only to have the bricks give way and throw her back to the ground, stunned and injured. She cannot escape; she cannot get back into the house without her escape attempt being detected. Suddenly the sham suicide in the pond seems a real possibility. She drags herself back to the pond edge and contemplates with pleasure their remorse at finding her dead, but sound theology intervenes, and she realizes that she must not arrogate to herself the divine power of saying when her life may end. Perhaps all these trials have been God's plan to make her totally dependent on His grace. She accepts her fate, waits till morning in an outbuilding for wood and coal, accepts Mrs. Jewkes's abuse for her escape attempt, and records the whole incident in her journal. The episode is recounted with strong psychological power; when Mr. B. reads the account, he is moved and softened by it. It becomes one of Pamela's most powerful devices in moderating him before he can attack her.

The other incident is one in which Mr. B. appears to have entire verbal control but does not. The Restoration and 18th century was fond of presenting balanced sets of marriage conditions, in which each lover stated what he or she desired in the behavior of the other. The most famous instance of such an exchange is that between Mirabell and Millamant in Congreve's *The Way of the World*. In *Pamela*, after Mr. B. has married her, he gives her 48 rules for proper wifely behavior; she gives him none. It appears to be a very one-sided exchange. But Pamela, reporting the 48 conditions to her parents, frequently comments upon them in italics—and the comments are often what characters earlier in the novel have described in her as "pert," muttered objections, sharp responses which she makes, indicating that Mr. B. is behaving in an unjust or unreasonable or indecorous manner. She has won the main victory with the marriage; she is quietly refusing to concede some lesser points as well. Once again, Mr. B's apparent victory is not as simple as it first appears.

Pamela then is a very optimistic novel. In treating the theme of sexual empowerment, it suggests that by using the instruments available to her—the spoken and written word—quickly and deftly and wisely, the female can soften and sensitize the courting male sufficiently that he will ultimately cease to be physically and sexually dangerous to her, and will accept her partially on her own terms. In turn, she must learn to trust him and to rely upon him. Only then, as Pamela says in response to item 32 on Mr. B.'s list of marriage terms, can husbands and wives be, as they ought to be, also friends.

—Frances Mayhew Rippy

PARADISE LOST.
Poem by John Milton, 1667.

John Milton wrote in the invocation to Book 9 of *Paradise Lost* that he was "long choosing and beginning late" (26) his epic subject on the Fall of Man. Indeed, he took some years to decide on this subject, his early writing showing his concern with epic. Later he speculated on whether he should write an epic or a drama, with stress on a religious subject and on the religious function of the poet. He considered several biblical topics for dramas in classical forms, and wrote drafts of a play on the Fall. The opening lines of this drama became part of Book 4 of *Paradise Lost*. By 1657 or 1658, or perhaps just after the Restoration, Milton began *Paradise Lost*. He finished it in 10 books by 1663 or 1665, publishing it in 1667, and reissued it in 12 books in 1674, the year of his death.

The sources of *Paradise Lost* include the Bible, the epics of Homer, Virgil, Ovid, Dante, Ariosto, Camoëns, Tasso, and Spenser, and medieval and Renaissance drama. Milton's treatise, *De Doctrina Christiana* (*Christian Doctrine*), shows many religious values that underlie the poem. He used his vast knowledge of the Bible and the great literature of the past to expand the brief account of the Fall in Genesis 2 into a poem of more than 10,000 lines. He wanted his poem to be comprehensive and universal.

As an epic *Paradise Lost* adopts many of the conventions of epics—a statement of the subject in the opening lines, invocations, scenes on earth, in heaven, and the underworld, dramatic dialogues, extended descriptive passages, elaborate similes, divine messengers, prophecies, and dreams. Like other epics *Paradise Lost* begins in the middle of the story (the aftermath of the war in heaven). Milton, however, transforms the epic conventions he adopts.

In a note Milton cites the precedents in verse: "The Measure is *English* Heroic Verse without Rime, as that of *Homer* in *Greek* and *Virgil* in *Latin*" ("The Verse"). His version of the meter used in classical epics is blank verse, a new medium for the English epic. One of its features is that the "sense" is "variously drawn out from one Verse into another" ("The Verse"). The effect is a strong onward movement necessary in a long poem. Milton's style is "grand" as befits a religious epic, but there is wide variation in it. The poem has many voices, moods, and descriptive interests varied within themselves.

Paradise Lost concerns "Things unattempted yet in Prose or Rhyme" (1.16). Its theme is "Man's First Disobedience" (1.1), the first causes of man's sinful nature, and so reveals something about sin in all times. Its characters are God, the Son, Satan, Adam and Eve, and the good and bad angels. It explores Heaven, Hell, Earth, Eden, infinite space, Chaos, and time's beginning and its end. Its action involves the cosmic struggle between good and evil for the fate of humanity. Since it deals with truth and the highest virtues, *Paradise Lost*'s concerns are greater than those of past epics. Therefore, as Milton asserts the superiority of a Christian reality to pagan myth, he indicates that he will try to surpass past epic poets, mainly Homer and Virgil, if he gets the inspiration he seeks.

Milton does not present *Paradise Lost*, his first publication after the Restoration, to readers on his own authority, but on the authority of God's Spirit. After defending the Regicide and after giving 20 years of his life as well as his sight to the failed cause of republican rule, he was a marked man. The invocations in Books 1, 3, 7, and 9 of *Paradise Lost* show the blind and discredited Milton asking for God's aid in a worthy task. He depreciates his own powers and owes all that he achieves to power outside of himself. If he is to "justify the ways of God" (1.26), God's Spirit will have to speak through him. He believed that his poem was an inspired creation.

The first two books of *Paradise Lost* concern the causes of the Fall and how humanity got to its present condition. Satan is part of the cause, and so the first two books are devoted to him and his followers. Satan gives several great orations; this alone makes some readers admire him as the "true hero," but they must see what he says and judge it apart from his great eloquence. Indeed, Milton never lets readers be deceived by Satan's poses. He provides key statements, like "Vaunting aloud, but rackt with deep despair" (1.126), which show that there is a public and a private side to Satan. Furthermore, in Satan's encounter with Sin and Death, Milton presents loathsome portraits, lest readers be seduced by Satan's person and eloquence and forget what evil really is. Satan begot Death on his own daughter, Sin; this foul and sordid story shows up evil vividly and makes it repulsive. Satan attributes to God his own motives and ideas. He sees no justice in his fall, except that might makes right—which Satan can understand, but which has nothing to do with God's justice. In Book 4 truth comes out in solitude: Satan admits his debt to God and His easy yoke, but he cannot submit; his pride is too great and he fears shame. Satan, no more inclined to evil than the angels who remained faithful, spoke otherwise as a public figure. Like other fallen angels, he cannot understand that servitude to God is the greatest freedom. His mental torture is worse than his torture in hell and he can never escape it. Milton, however, has a grand view of Satan's character: Satan is full of complex feelings, but he gradually loses his luster throughout the epic.

As Satan tries his evil, God frustrates him the more and turns his evil to good. This is apparent in Book 3 when God explains how He works to offset Satan's evil. Some readers find God difficult to accept because he defends His justice in light of Adam and Eve's sin. He explains, for example, that their sin means death for humanity, that He made them free to choose Him or Satan in order to give their allegiance meaning (merit only exists in freedom), and that humanity will be able to utilize grace (given sufficiently to all) for salvation. Milton, however, has reason to present God as he does, for Scripture itself does. Besides, God must speak truly for He *is* Truth. Moreover, divine dialogue is a sacred fiction that shows two of God's qualities, justice and mercy, which are never separated. God the Father is the voice of justice; the Son, a part of Him, is the voice of mercy. When the Son, the working agent of the Father, comes to pronounce sentence on Adam and Eve in Book 10 he is God, both judge and intercessor. Dialogue between the Father and the Son is really a dialogue of one. Milton describes divine things in human terms, which is a rationale for the method of *Paradise Lost*.

Unlike most epics, *Paradise Lost* has two heroes, Adam and Eve. Milton depicts them as the best examples of the race, made with adult consciousness, but there is a fine naive quality in their narration of the dawn of their lives. They first learn about themselves and their abilities and then their thoughts turn to God. They have the dignity to be curious *before* their sin; curiosity is no offense against God, if kept within limits. Not "immutable," they are "perfect" for as long as they obey (5.524).

Adam is formed for "contemplation" and "valor" (4.297), Eve for "softness" and "sweet attractive Grace" (4.289); man's qualities are assumed to be higher than woman's. In Milton's view there is a natural hierarchy in the order of things, but a person is no less free for acknowledging it and deference is a virtue. Eve freely submits to Adam; love is not absent from Paradise. For Milton wedded love is the only true love; based on mutual esteem, it recognizes the natural superiority of the male. Although man is superior to woman in the natural order, Eve becomes Adam's moral superior in Book 10 when she accepts her responsibility for her sin and brings Adam to accept his responsibility for his failing. In addition, Eve has the last words: "By mee the Promis'd Seed shall all restore" (12.623); her words round out the pattern of glory, ruin, and restoration with which the poem began.

Before the Fall Adam and Eve know all that it behooves them to know, that is, all that is relevant to their relation to God. They are "Sufficient to have stood" (3.99), despite the subtlety of their foe. In Books 4 and 5 their morning and evening prayers show their knowledge of the "goodness infinite" (4.734) that made them and the universe. In fact, Book 7, an account of creation, is a hymn celebrating God's plenitude and variety. Adam and Eve see God's grandeur in His creation and that all creation should worship Him. They know why they should feel gratitude toward God and obey Him. As creatures they owe Him a debt not payable.

When Adam and Eve need to know more than they can learn by themselves, God sends the angel Raphael to warn them of Satan's presence and his methods. In Book 6 Raphael narrates the war in heaven, which shows that the rebel angels were free and had the strength not to sin. This is an explicit warning to Adam and Eve to obey God. God gives them every chance. Adam, however, knows that there is a weak link in his armor; he is susceptible to Eve's beauty. Raphael tells him to love Eve, but to love God first by obedience. Nevertheless, in Book 9 Adam falls into sin by passion, Eve by vanity and curiosity for new experience. Adam chooses a lesser love over a greater: Eve rather than God. Eve trusted her reason above the divine command not to eat of the tree. Milton called their sin "mortal Sin / Original" (9.1003–1004).

Adam learns in a dramatic way in Books 11 and 12 that the "Fruit" of sin is "Death" and "all our woe" (1.1–3). Death begins for all creation and the children of Adam and Eve share in their corruption by heredity. The historical perspective Adam gets includes few good moments, with the exception of heroes of faith like Abraham and Moses who point the way to the "great deliverer" (12.149) to come. The prophecies lead to Christ the Savior who will destroy Satan within the hearts of believers and, at the end of time, destroy Satan and Hell altogether. Then Earth will be transformed to a field of glory.

As they learn of God's plan for salvation, Adam and Eve learn that by imitation of the Savior they can achieve an inner paradise "happier far" (12.587) than the paradise they lost and that it can be achieved without institutions of any kind. For all it shows of human weakness and defeat, *Paradise Lost* ends in hope: "Some natural tears they dropp'd, but wip'd them soon; / The World was all before them" (12.645–46). Adam and Eve keep heart as exiles and take their "solitary way" (12.649) out of Eden to start human history. The poem ends quietly with a beginning.

Soon after its publication John Dryden (as reported by the early commentator Jonathan Richardson) recognized *Paradise Lost* as a monumental poem: "This Man Cuts us All Out, and the Ancients too," and, in his lines "On Milton," he put him in the company of Homer and Virgil. Perhaps Dryden felt that Milton's epic had the dignity of Homer and Virgil's epics—England now had its epic poet—but that his surpassed theirs in the scope of the subject he treated. Indeed, no other epic poet had ever attempted to treat a subject as vast as Milton's treatment of the Fall of Man, dealing, in a Christian framework, with primary questions of beginnings and endings, of good and evil, and of human destiny in the universe. *Paradise Lost*, having immeasurable influence on literature, is generally regarded as the greatest non-dramatic poem in English.

—Timothy C. Miller

PARADISE REGAINED.
Poem by John Milton, 1671.

Published with *Samson Agonistes* in a 1671 volume, *Paradise Regained* probably was composed, in a relatively short span of time, after the completion of *Paradise Lost*. We need not take too literally Thomas Ellwood's claim to have inspired the poem ("Thou hast said much here of paradise lost, but what hast thou to say of paradise found?"); but his anecdote does provide evidence for the period of composition that is corroborated by John Milton's nephew Edward Phillips, who also inaugurated the tradition of defensive comparisons to the larger poem: "Possibly the subject may not afford such variety of invention, but it is thought by the most judicious to be little or nothing inferior to the other for style and taste."

In this narration of Christ's trials in the wilderness, Milton chose to follow the order of temptations in Luke 4:1–13 (turning stone to bread, the kingdoms of the world, the pinnacle of the temple), providing a dramatic sequence superior to that in Matthew (stone, pinnacle, kingdoms). He augments the gospel temptations with incidents shaped from other biblical material (Jesus' dream) or invented (the banquet scene). Theology and traditions of biblical commentary are invaluable resources for comprehending just what is at issue in the encounters and the particular nuances with which Milton endows them. The three desert temptations were identified with the primal temptations in the Fall—the world, flesh, and the devil—the second Adam succeeding in tests the first Adam failed. Milton follows Protestant tradition in, for instance, presenting the stone-to-bread offer as a temptation to distrust in Providence, rather than the appeal of appetite. The encounters further involve the definition of Christ's threefold office as mediator, his roles as prophet, priest, and king (see Milton's *De Doctrina Christiana* I.xv).

Although the pairing with *Samson* has provoked some efforts to read the poem as drama, Milton deliberately presents it as an epic: a narrative divided into books and displaying such epic signatures as invocation, catalogue, epic simile, council scene, panorama, heroic encounter, but all oddly attenuated, reduced to an essence. Eighteenth-century editors responded to Milton's own distinction in *The Reason of Church Government* between two kinds of epic "whereof the two poems of Virgil and Tasso are a diffuse, and the book of Job a brief model," recognizing the parallels to *Lost* and *Regained* as "diffuse" and "brief" epics. Twentieth-century scholars have restored a tradition of commentary on the Book of Job as an epic and confirmed its status as model for a line of brief biblical epics. These insights enhance the significance of the six overt references to Job, making the reader more responsive to other Jobean allusions and actions within the poem.

The entire poem has a puzzle quality to it, nowhere more evident than in the structure. The division into four books remotely may own something to Virgil's *Georgics*, more immediately to Giles Fletcher the Younger's *Christs Victorie and Triumph* (1610), and certainly to the four evangelists. But the formal structure corresponds neither to the chronological (books to days) nor to the episodic (books to major temptations) in a predictable way. Equally difficult is the overlapping and reduplicative character of the trials and the elusive quality of their thematic imprints. Are Adam's trials of distrust, ambition, and vainglory to be seen in the three major temptations or in the subset of banquet, wealth, and glory? Are the latter to be understood as preparatory to the kingdoms of the world, demonstrating Christ's kingship over himself, or as something distinct? If the stone temptation devolves into an argument about Christ's prophetic office and the kingdoms test the definition of his kingly office, is the priestly role to be seen in the temptation of the pinnacle or the banquet in the wilderness or both? Boundaries dissolve and distinctions constantly blur in the poem; the reader's balance is more precarious than that of Jesus standing on the pinnacle of his father's temple.

Throughout, the aggressor Satan sets the terms of the encounters and debates, "as a swarm of flies in vintage time, / About the wine-press where sweet must is pour'd, / Beat off, returns as oft with humming sound" (4.15–17), while with Jobean patience Christ endures the assaults. Thus, many of the confusions are deliberate, attempts by Satan to goad Christ to premature action, to remain under the order of law, to accept an inferior type of himself, or to falsify his mission. Others reflect Satan's own imperfect comprehension of Christ or his own anxieties; the kingdoms of the world is the most extensive temptation because there Satan feels most threatened. The biblical echoes in their dialogue offer a seminar in hermeneutics, Jesus countering Satan's preoccupation with kingship by his own with priesthood. The style has direct affinities with that employed in the final two books of *Paradise Lost*; rather than the grand epic style, it identifies with an Augustinian tradition of an expanded and chastened low style, appropriate to the humility of the Gospels and of the Incarnation itself, achieving subtlety and resonance through imitation of biblical rhetoric and metrics.

Paradise Regained operates on a number of levels at once: it glances at contemporary controversies such as those over a learned ministry and over millenarian expectations; it resonates with many of the theological complexities concerning the Son of God that occupied Milton in the *De Doctrina*; it provides a dense introduction to biblical typology. For most readers, however, its accessibility will be in the presentation of Jesus as a private man withstanding the incessant and bewildering assaults of evil. For Milton, as for Jeremy Taylor, Christ is "the Great Exemplar" to mankind; and the emphasis on his humanity is nowhere more evident than in the concluding lines: "hee unobserv'd / Home to his Mother's house private return'd" (4.638–39). The poem earned Coleridge's discriminating praise: "Readers would not have been disappointed in this latter poem, if they had proceeded to it with a proper preconception of *the kind* of interest intended to be excited in that admirable work. In its kind, it is the most *perfect* poem extant. . . . "

—Raymond B. Waddington

THE PARLIAMENT OF FOWLS.
Poem by Geoffrey Chaucer, c.1380.

Geoffrey Chaucer's *The Parliament of Fowls*, a dream vision of 699 lines in rhyme-royal, was written in the late 1370's or early 1380's; more precise datings, particularly those claiming to link the poem to the specific occasion for which it was composed, have not won general acceptance. In fact, the only real consensus to have emerged about *The Parliament* is that the poem is a remarkable artistic achievement capable of supporting a myriad of diverse interpretations.

The poem's first section (1–28) is devoted to a discussion of Love, which Chaucer as first-person narrator claims to know only from his reading. Having revealed that to learn "a certain thing" he had taken up Macrobius' commentary on Cicero's *Somnium Scipionis* (*The Dream of Scipio*), the narrator summarizes the *Somnium*, observes that he has what he doesn't want but lacks what he desires, and falls asleep (29–94).

The narrator then describes a dream in which Africanus (a character in the *Somnium*) states that he has come to repay Chaucer for his diligent reading, and conducts him to a gate leading into a walled garden. The gate, suggesting the gate of Hell in Dante's *Inferno*, bears two inscriptions—one praising and the other cautioning against love. Unable to choose between entering and leaving, the narrator is finally shoved into the garden by Africanus.

In the garden, Chaucer encounters a series of personified abstractions from the tradition of courtly love, including Cupid, Beauty, Jealousy, and Venus herself. Finally, Chaucer comes upon the Goddess of Nature, presiding over a St. Valentine's Day assembly at which the birds choose their mates. Nature outlines the rules to be followed and orders the royal male eagle (the tercel) to begin. The royal eagle claims the female (the formel) perched on Nature's hand, but is challenged by two other male eagles of lower rank who present their own claims.

After some lower birds protest the delay, Nature orders each class to choose one bird to present its view. Finally, Nature assigns the choice to the female, who asks for an additional year in which to make her choice. Nature agrees, the other fowls choose their mates and sing a roundel in her honor; their noise wakes the narrator who turns to other books, hoping to encounter something which will improve his lot.

Although scholarship has revealed a great deal about the various sections of the poem, key questions about *The Parliament* remain unanswered. *The Parliament* can with confidence be placed within a 10-year period, but the narrator's seemingly definitive statement in line 117 that at the time of his dream he saw the planet Venus in the north-north-west has been interpreted as meaning everything from "saw it in the year 1380 [or 1374 or 1377 or 1382]" to "did not see it at all" or "saw it in an unpropitious position," depending on the point a particular interpreter wants to make.

The equally attractive hypothesis that the poem is an allegorical celebration of a particular royal engagement or marriage has enjoyed a similarly checkered history. The suggestion made a century ago that the formel eagle represents Anne of Bohemia while the three tercel eagles stand for Richard II of England, Charles of France, and Friedrich of Meissen dates the poem to 1380. More than 50 years ago this view was rejected on the grounds that the reference to Venus in line 117 rules out 1380 and was replaced by ones proposing a wide range of different dates and different royal personages and ones arguing that Valentine's Day alone was sufficient justification for the poem; but the theory reappeared during the 1980's, buttressed by new interpretations of Chaucer's astronomical reference.

While every feature of *The Parliament* is familiar to readers of medieval literature, it seems almost impossible to establish one overall meaning for the poem. The inexperienced narrator whose reading provides the frame for the dream-vision is a variation on similar figures in two of Chaucer's other early poems, *The Book of the Duchess* and *The House of Fame*; and Chaucer refers to Macrobius' commentary on the *Somnium* in both these poems as well as in the translation of the *Roman de la Rose* attributed to him. But because the narrator does not specify what he hopes to find in his reading of the *Somnium*, critical opinion has interpreted Chaucer's summary in a variety of ways: as political advice to King Richard, as a condemnation of earthly love, and as a justification of the kind of earthly love which serves the general welfare, to name a few.

The Garden of Love and its inhabitants are conventional in their details, but the gate's inscriptions have proven a puzzle; interpretations have ranged from seeing them as descriptions of two different types of love (earthly and heavenly) to regarding them as a reminder of the dualism inevitably present in earthly love. Much the same is true of Venus and Nature, the two principal symbolic figures within the garden, who figure as opponents in some interpretations, as allies in others.

The parliament of the birds and the speeches of the eagles have proven particularly challenging. While each eagle may be pleading the case for a historical suitor, critics have also viewed this section as a satire on the pretensions of the noble birds and/or the lack of understanding of the lesser fowl; as a debate about courtly love, or about faithfulness in love, or at any rate about something having to do with love; and as the final stage of the process, begun in the *Somnium* section, of reconciling earthly love with the Christian life, or of illustrating the dichotomy between the two.

In its optimistic open-endedness, the conclusion of the poem—the formel's decision not to decide, the harmonious song of all the birds, and the narrator's decision to continue his search—justify and reinforce the many readings *The Parliament* invites and supports. One may never determine just what the poem is about, but the search is worth the effort and, more importantly, a great deal of fun.

—William D. Reynolds

A PASSAGE TO INDIA.
Novel by E.M. Forster, 1924.

A Passage to India, E.M. Forster's last novel, was published in 1924. Recalling his two visits to India and simultaneously interweaving with them fragments of his three-and-a-half-year stay in Egypt, it is the culmination of his fictional work.

Forster may be seen principally as a novelist of ideas; the epigraph of *Howards End*, "Only connect," is the theme of all his novels, but in *A Passage to India* it has overtones of the impossible. The yearning exploration of personal relationships in the novel is set against the vast divisive backcloth of the sub-continent of India with its teeming population, its racial tensions, its linguistic confusions, and the political anguish of a subjugated race, riven with dissension, yet longing for freedom and nationhood.

While Forster's earlier novels are fairly traditional in plot and in form—births, marriages, and deaths giving them shape and an apparently omniscient narrator controlling the point of view—this last novel is both more adventurous and more subtle. Despite Virginia Woolf's assertion that Forster was putting "new wine into old bottles," *A Passage to India* owes much to the dialogue of narration which was occupying the novelists of the early decades of the 20th century. The plot itself breaks the mould: though Mrs. Moore dies and Fielding gets married offstage, these events are relatively unimportant; it is her life, not her death, that places Mrs. Moore at the centre of the story; her desire to "connect," to harmonise diversity, is based on her belief in the inalienable selfhood of the individual, which transcends the discords that divide mankind. Ronny and Adela express a faith in "the sanctity of personal relationships" but their understanding of individuals is tinged with innate, in Adela almost unrecognised, attitudes to race, colour, and creed that confine them; Adela thinks that Aziz "might attract women of his own race and rank," but appears unable to think of him purely and simply as a human being. Mrs. Moore, on the other hand, meets him on equal terms and, describing him to Ronny, it does not occur to her to mention that he is an Indian.

The plot is strongly reinforced by the method of its narration. The three sections of the novel, "Mosque," "Caves," and "Temple," have symbolic significance in Forster's tripartite scheme. They represent the three Indian seasons, Cold Weather, Hot Weather, and Rains; they are dominated by three religions, Islam, Christianity, and Hinduism; they contain respectively the Exposition, the Catastrophe, and the Resolution. The first two sections begin with a chapter of authorial comment which not only sets the geographical and political scene but also adds cosmic significance to the story: the sense of mystery and muddle which pervades the novel, the implication of realms beyond the human and physical are established in these chapters and in other passages of authorial comment throughout the novel. Yet, though the narrative method appears to imply the omniscience of a generally non-intrusive third-person narrator, the author as God, such an implication is subverted by subtle authorial interventions and even subtler use of the occasional interior monologue. Though much of the narration is achieved through straightforward and traditional storytelling methods, the reader's understanding of characters and events is at times enlarged by direct entry into a character's stream of consciousness; thus we learn of Aziz's secret dream of building a mosque and of Mrs. Moore's disillusion with Christianity.

More significantly, the use of symbol and motif to control the progress of the plot is fully developed. The dominant symbol of the novel is the echo; it is present in many forms, from the echoing "ou-boum" of the Marabar Caves, to the series of layers of kites . . . vultures . . . sky and the spaces beyond, to the echoing replacement of colonial administrators. Once established, the echo motif becomes a vital narrative device as every recurring image echoes its previous appearance and is in turn echoed on its next occurrence. Closely associated with the echo are the many images of circularity—the immense vault of the night sky, the round hollow caves, the snake with its tail in its mouth. The interconnection of these and many other images and motifs achieves a richness of texture in the novel and establishes layers of meaning which, lying beneath the surface, evoke haunting recollections that influence our reactions to events; Mrs. Moore's wasp becomes a symbol of universal tolerance which the two missionaries, Mr. Sorley and Mr. Graysford, are unable to embrace and with which, later, Professor Godbole attempts to come to terms, while the kites which hover over the failure of the Bridge Party are ominously recalled by the Brahmany kite which flaps over the scene at the Marabar Caves.

When the novel moves to Mau in the final part, romantic tradition would perhaps suggest that a harmonious resolution of personal relationships is being prepared; though the geographical location has changed, Aziz and Fielding meet again and over them hovers the memory of Mrs. Moore, strongly recalled to Aziz's consciousness by the presence of her son Ralph. Yet Forster defies his readers' hopes and expectations and takes the modern, realistic approach; as representative of a subjugated race, Aziz can never make terms with his conqueror. In the end personal relationships prove to be insufficient to overcome the racial barriers and the sky and the earth cry out against such a possibility. But the novel ends with a slender hope; the words "not *yet*" and "not *there*" seem to indicate that in some other time and place friendship between east and west will be possible.

—Hilda D. Spear

PATIENCE.
Poem by the Gawain Poet, late 14th century.

Patience is extant in a single manuscript, MS Cotton Nero A.x., which was produced in the late 14th century. The poem is written in the alliterative verse characteristic of the north and west of England at this period, and its dialect is that of the northwest midlands. Accompanying it in the manuscript are three other alliterative poems in the same dialect: *Sir Gawain and the Green Knight*, *Pearl*, and *Cleanness*. When they were first studied it was assumed almost without question that the poems had a common author, and although it is now recognised that many of the resemblances between the poems are properties of the literary conventions to which they belong, many, perhaps most, of those who have worked on the poems still believe that they are the products of one hand.

Patience illustrates the value of that virtue by means of a single exemplum, the story of Jonah, who is presented as a type of impatience. It opens with an assertion of the value of patience in soothing the pain of the heart which has been wounded by scorn, or in some other way. At this point the narrator seems to leave open the possibility that patience may be able to influence external as well as internal causes of unhappiness, but soon focuses exclusively on the psychological benefits of the virtue. Paraphrasing the Beatitudes he keeps close to the sense of his original until he substitutes "Blessed are those who can govern their hearts" for "Blessed are those who suffer persecution for the sake of justice." He then pictures, with a touch of irony, the Beatitudes as courtly ladies who ought to be wooed. Turning to his own condition he remarks wryly that since Lady Poverty is so importunate in her advances to him he will entertain himself with Lady Patience as well. Punning on "need" and "suffering" he satisfyingly establishes a necessary connection between the two qualities: the poor man must suffer need / must necessarily suffer (be patient), therefore patience and poverty are necessarily companions. Patience is thus established as a willing acceptance of the inevitable.

Within this context Jonah acts as an example of *im*patience, not only in his refusal to go to Nineveh, but in his anger against God's pardoning of the Ninevites, and the destruction of the ivy. In keeping with the idea of patience the poet has established, the stress is on Jonah's folly in thinking himself able to avoid the edicts of his creator; he is blind, a witless wretch, in his attempts to avoid the inevitable.

The poet alters the biblical account quite markedly, expanding the narrative by the inclusion of extra dialogue and by the addition of concrete, realistic details. There is a vivid description of the sailors preparing to set out, and the belly of the whale is described at length. The beast is so huge that Jonah glides through his mouth like a speck of dust blown through the door of a cathedral, and the corner of the gut where he comes to rest is as huge as the hall of a castle. Jonah's movements irritate the beast and cause it to vomit, and when he is cast onto dry land his clothes are filthy. Such vividness serves a symbolic as well as a realistic function, for the evil smell associates the whale's belly with Hell and the devil, and Jonah's filthy clothes signify his sinful state.

As well as steering our responses by direct comment on Jonah's folly, the poet also exposes the nature of Jonah's shortcomings through the very structure of the poem, counterpointing his rebellions and hestitations with the immediate obedience to God's word of other characters and natural phenomena which are endowed with consciousness and will. Thus God calls on the winds to raise a storm and they are so eager to obey that there is no time between His command and their execution of it, and on a human level the sailors pause only long enough to be sure that they have understood. The readiness of the sailors to obey is paralleled by the speed with which the people of Nineveh repent, just as the worm that devours the root of Jonah's woodbine (the poet's translation of *hedera*) and the west wind that brings hot weather recall in their obedience the earlier winds and the whale.

Although Jonah's rebellion is treated with some comedy the poem invites a complex response, for if his attempts at evasion are rendered ludicrous by virtue of God's omnipotence, his very helplessness in the face of a seemingly arbitrary power provokes the sympathy of the reader.

Ironically it is through Jonah's *im*patience, through his angry assertion that the destruction of his woodbine is no trivial matter, that God is led to justify himself, to proclaim an order based on His mercy and a patience greater than that of his human creation.

The poem ends with the narrator's application of the story to his present circumstances and audience, and the last line of the poem echoes, and intensifies by the addition of the word "noble," the opening assertion that "patience is a virtue although it may often displease."

—Anne Samson

PEARL.
Poem by the Gawain Poet, late 14th century.

One of four poems (the others are *Sir Gawain and the Green Knight*, *Cleanness*, and *Patience*) preserved uniquely in British Library MS Cotton Nero A.x., *Pearl* is universally acclaimed a masterpiece of English literature for its technical virtuosity and ambitious doctrinal theme. Dated to the last quarter of the 14th century and written by a single scribe in a difficult northwest midlands dialect, the manuscript contains four illuminations that, although poorly executed, direct attention to the poem's critical episodes: the first depicts the jeweler-dreamer in the earthly "erber," asleep on the blossomy mound where he has lost his pearl; the second shows him exploring the gem-lighted river landscape of his dream vision; the third illustrates his meeting with the pearl-maiden, resplendent in white linen and crowned with pearls; and the fourth represents him catching a glimpse of the New Jerusalem where the Pearl-maiden now dwells in the company of the 144,000 virgin brides of Christ.

Although a number of ingenious arguments have linked *Pearl* (as well as *Saint Erkenwald*) with various possible authors—Ralph Strode, David Rate, John Prat, John of Erghome, and most recently several men named John Massey —the *Pearl*-poet has eluded certain identification; even common authorship of *Pearl* and *Sir Gawain* remains controverted. It seems likely that the author was a clerk, perhaps attached to a noble household; collectively, the poems suggest a poet keenly attuned to the complex theological issues of the late 14th century and widely read in the popular literature, including the *Roman de la Rose*, Dante's *Commedia*, *The Aeneid*, Boethius' *Consolatio de Philosophia*, and perhaps even Boccaccio's *Olympia*, which earlier in this century had been urged as the immediate source for *Pearl*. The poem echoes many passages from the Vulgate Bible, particularly Revelations (54 verses), Psalms (12 verses), and Canticles (8 verses) and also demonstrates importantly the influence of medieval lapidaries (the opening line, for instances, replicates a lapidary formula).

In the central debate, the Pearl-maiden fuses *courtois* language and theology. "Cortasye," as the jeweler-dreamer comprehends it, is an order grounded in rank and station. The Pearl-maiden's definition ("Of courtaysye, as saytȝ Saynt Poule, / Al arn we membreȝ of Jesu Kryst") offends his sense of justice, for how could a two-year-old, who knows neither creed nor Pater, become a Queen of Heaven? In response, the Pearl-maiden recounts the parable of the vineyard (Matthew 20), an exposition of essential and accidental grace: "For þe grace of God is gret innoȝe," the refrain line of stanza group XI and the doctrinal center of the poem. His response, that such grace is too generous, provides the occasion for her account of Christ's earthly and heavenly role as *sponsus*.

When first published in 1864, *Pearl* was universally deemed a father's elegy for his two-year-old daughter ("þou lyfed not two ȝer in oure þede"). In 1904 however, Schofield argued that the poem was an allegory, the Pearl-maiden representing pure maidenhood. In this century the balance of critical opinion has shifted frequently between elegiac and allegorical interpretation. As an elegy either for a lost daughter (from *margarita*, Latin for pearl; Margaret, daughter of the Earl of Pembroke, and Margaret, daughter of Edward III have been suggested), or for a woman with whom the poet had a romantic relationship, elegiac interpretations see as central to *Pearl* the jeweler-dreamer's initial anguish at the loss of his Pearl and the ultimate reconciliation of his will with God's. Awakening from his dream, the jeweler commends his pearl "In Krysteȝ dere blessyng and myn," a formula often ending letters from parents to children.

On the other hand, allegorical interpretations based on scriptural and exegetical traditions variously identify the pearl as the eucharist, as the pearl of price (the *pretiosa margarita* of Matthew 13) symbolizing Christ, as holy innocence, as the loss and recovery of eternal life, as virginity, as a symbol of Paradise, as the Church, or as the reward for purification of the soul. The *Pearl*-maiden herself has been read as a literary device expressing the lesson of divine grace, as a female guide and instructor (like Dante's Beatrice), or as the jeweler-dreamer's own soul.

Much of *Pearl*'s brilliance resides in its formidable technical virtuosity. The poem astonishes with its numerological and prosodic complexities: 1212 lines in 101 stanzas rhymed ababababbcbc. Groups of five stanzas (and one of six) are linked by a refrain and the repetition of key words or phrases from the last line of the stanza in the first line of the next (*concatenatio*). Concatenation also occurs between groups of stanzas, except between lines 720 and 721, perhaps a deliberate omission. The link words in each stanza group seem to underscore the poem's thematic structure ("Prynces paye," for instance, the linking phrase of the last stanza group, suggests that every soul is a pearl pleasing to Christ). There is as well much wordplay and a reliance on the conventions and vocabulary of *courtois* love poetry. The meter is accentual-syllabic. Generally there are four stressed syllables in a line; these are frequently alliterated. The numbers 5, 6, 8, 12, 60 and 101 have numerological significance and dominate the poem's structure. Like *Sir Gawain*, *Pearl*'s opening line is echoed in its last lines. This circularity, and other structural and prosodic features, seem to have thematic significance, especially the three landscapes of earthly garden, terrestrial paradise, and heavenly city, which have been linked with emotional, didactic, and sacramental stages of religious growth as well as with a spiritual itinerary of sense, intellect, and inspiration.

For its passionate artistry and complex emotion, *Pearl* has no parallel in Middle English poetry.

—Richard H. Osberg

THE PEARL.
Poem by George Herbert, 1633.

The 1633 title page of *The Temple* describes George Herbert's poems as "Sacred Poems and Private Ejaculations." There can be no doubt to which category "The Pearl" belongs. Like "Affliction" and "The Cross," it springs directly from recognisable circumstances of his personal history. "The Pearl" is unmistakably a review of the experiences as scholar, courtier, man of the world, that have made Herbert what he is. This review is set within the framework of a colloquy with God.

The allusive title subtly colours the whole discourse. There is no mention of a Pearl within the poem, but the biblical reference directs the reader to the parable in St. Matthew's gospel which likens the Kingdom of Heaven to "a merchant-man seeking goodly pearls, who when he had found one pearl of great price went and sold all that he had and bought it." The poet presents learning, honour, and pleasure not as mere distractions but as goodly pearls, the rejection of which entails a genuine sacrifice.

Though Herbert consecrated his poetic gifts to God at an early age, it was not until he was 32 that he was ordained deacon, and he then postponed for another five years the decision to become a priest. "The Pearl" appears in a manuscript written prior to the Bemerton poems, and it may well belong to the period when, discontented alike with academic and courtly-political life, he was still hesitating to commit himself to the sacred office of priest.

The language of the poem is notably energetic and concentrated. In the first three stanzas the speaker is self-assertive, piling clause on clause in rapid succession, emphatically amplifying his points. Only in the last stanza does the pace slacken, for here the whole passage is a direct address to God, hitherto invoked only in the brief refrain that has concluded each verse—"Yet I love thee."

Though the poem's argument is perfectly clear, and the notion of a transaction is sustained until midway through the final stanza, the imagery and phraseology are sometimes difficult—more so for modern readers than for Herbert's contemporaries, who would have been more responsive to biblical allusions.

The first stanza conveys the excitement of a Renaissance scholar as he surveys the range of knowledge available to the enquiring mind. (Herbert was a friend of Bacon, whose *Advancement of Learning* had appeared in 1605.) Traditional learning, distilled and conveyed through learned institutions, is supplemented by natural philosophy. Astrology and alchemy are still the province of scholars, and the voyages of explorers literally open up fresh territories for the mind to ponder.

A sardonic tone pervades the second stanza. Herbert knew well enough (and not merely through family connections) that the life of courtiers, diplomats, and politicians, though accorded honour, is not necessarily honourable. He is known to have done his best to exchange the restricted opportunities of Cambridge for a career in the service of the state. The poem reveals distrust of the ways of the world, but there is also a high-spirited appreciation of the cleverness needed to take advantage of chances for advancement. Ambition may entail a willingness to pledge oneself to burdensome responsibilities and to form reckless alliances. Thus there may be a note of penitence in the concluding words "Yet I love thee."

The third stanza is not at all penitential. It proclaims the enchantments of pleasure and the liveliness of the senses, and its mood is passionate, almost defiant. Music, one of Herbert's abiding joys, is immediately associated with Pleasure; strains, lullings, relishes, and propositions would have been understood as precise musical terms by his musical contemporaries. The ruefully comic notion of Conscience outnumbered by the five senses is juxtaposed with the refrain "Yet I love thee" in a way that few devotional poets would think of attempting. More inward-looking and self-revealing than the first two stanzas, this one marks a transition from what can be discussed in public—alternative careers—and what can only be referred to God.

In the final stanza, the latent parable of the merchant surfaces in the commercial imagery of a bargain with God. Legal and financial terms are frequent in biblical and theological references to God's dealings with his people. But the poem ends on a note of tender gratitude. Herbert introduces the idea of the labyrinthine difficulties of reaching a wise decision, acknowledging that he could not have found his way out of the maze without divine guidance. There are implicit references to Greek mythology, but Ariadne's rescuing cord becomes a kind of rope-ladder, by which the soul makes its ascent. God's mercy, not human ingenuity, provides the solution.

Herbert distilled some of his best poetry from what he described as "spiritual conflicts." "The Pearl" is a fine example. Strikingly personal, psychologically revealing, it is more easily accessible to the non-Christian reader than many of Herbert's devotional poems.

—Margaret Bottrall

PERICLES.
Play by William Shakespeare and George Wilkins, 1608(?).

Of the 38 plays now generally acknowledged as comprising the Shakespeare canon, only two, *Pericles* and *The Two Noble Kinsmen*, were not included in the First Folio of 1623. *Pericles* gained belated entry into the canon in the Third Folio in 1664. But Alexander Pope excluded it from his edition of 1725 and it was not restored until 1780, by Edmund Malone. Since that time, while it has figured regularly in editions of Shakespeare's works, it has enjoyed comparatively little popularity on the stage, and its text has been the subject of considerable controversy and speculation. Only a few decades ago, it was rarely included in discussions of Shakespeare's "late plays," though it shares many features with the dramatic romances of the last few years of Shakespeare's full-time activity as a playwright.

Heminges and Condell may have omitted *Pericles* from the First Folio because they knew it was not entirely by Shakespeare (though that consideration did not deter them from including *All is True* [*Henry VIII*], which they surely knew to be a Shakespeare-John Fletcher collaboration). Or they may have had available no text except the obviously corrupt quarto of 1609, apparently based on a reconstruction from memory by some of the actors who had performed the play. That Shakespeare is not responsible for the first nine scenes (Acts I and II in the Third Folio's unreliable division) has been recognized intuitively by many readers of the play and demonstrated by a number of modern editors and textual scholars. Just who was responsible has been much debated. The most likely candidate is George Wilkins, a minor playwright and novelist who had previously provided at least one successful play for the King's Men, and who may well have begun *Pericles* then handed it over to the company's chief dramatist for completion. In any case, Wilkins capitalized on the play's popularity in the theatre by publishing a prose version closely based on it: as author of a good part of the play, he would have been in a very good position to rewrite it in narrative form and thus make a bit more profit from it. For the parts he had not written and hence knew less well or not at all, he relied more heavily on another, earlier prose version by Lawrence Twine (c.1575), republished in 1607. That reprint, another source for the play itself, must have given Wilkins—if the initiative was his—the idea for a play on the well-known story. His novella announces itself as "being the true history of the play of Pericles, as it was lately presented by the worthy and ancient poet John Gower." Gower appears as presenter and chorus in the play, introducing the action, commenting on it, and filling in parts of the rambling, romance narrative that the dramatists chose not to show. The reason for the resurrection of the 14th-century poet in a 17th-century stage play is that the real Gower had written a lengthy version in verse, of the classical legend of Apollonius of Tyre in his *Confessio Amantis* (Book VIII); it was a principal source for the play, as it had been for Shakespeare's *The Comedy of Errors* 14 or 15 years earlier. The intertextual relationships of all these versions are complex; what is missing is the original, full version of the play, or anything like it. Both Wilkins's prose tale and the play quarto of 1608 must be seen as reported versions of that missing original that was performed by the King's Men.

The playgoer is less aware of textual difficulties than the reader. The reassuring figure of Gower guides us through the improbable tale of chivalry, shipwreck, separation of families, endless journeying, incest, treachery, virtue, courage, miraculous resurrection, and moving reunion. If some of the verse in the first few scenes is rough, it only sounds deliberately archaic, like an old oft-told tale. Gower turns the quintessentially romance narrative into stage drama before our eyes. As in all his later, romance-based plays, but more so here than elsewhere, Shakespeare seems content to leave the improbabilities and wonders of romance as they are, not to try to account for them or naturalize them, but rather to submit—and submit his audience—to them in all their outrageous unlikelihood. Gower is there to refer us to the book where the story is recorded, his authority, teasing us by *showing* us that which cannot ultimately be shown, but only heard and taken on faith, or a more than willing suspension of disbelief.

The play is surprisingly moving in performance, as more and more modern revivals are proving. The gamut of human emotions are portrayed and evoked. We are invited to share with Pericles his horror when he discovers, in the first scene, that the princess he woos is the incestuous mate of her father King Antiochus, his grief and impotent fury when his newlywed wife Thaisa dies in childbirth at sea, his shock at the treachery of Cleon and Dionyza whose country he has saved from famine and who plot the murder of his daughter whom they have raised with their own child. We are further horrified at the degradation to which Marina, now a young woman, is subjected in the brothel to which she is sold by the pirates who capture her from Dionyza's hired murderer and whose proprietors threaten her with dire punishments if she will not consent to become a whore. These responses are counterbalanced by the humorous, homely wisdom of the fishermen who rescue Pericles from shipwreck, the happiness of his idyllic marriage to Thaisa, daughter of the jovial king Simonides, relief at Marina's escape from the brothel, amazement at the revival as from the dead of Thaisa by the physican Cerimon, and speechless wonder at Pericles's own revival from the comatose state to which he had sunk in his misery, a revival brought about by the uncanny musical skill of the maiden brought to him on shipboard by the governor of Mytilene: of course, it is his long-lost daughter Marina. The scene of recognition between father and daughter is superbly moving. Shakespeare is unrelenting and in the very next scene, father and daughter are reunited with wife and mother at the temple of Diana in Ephesus where Thaisa has been a priestess. The complete family is found at last, with a new member, son-in-law and husband, drawn into it, the governor who has protected Marina after being converted to virtue by her purity when he met her in the brothel. The play has moved through a series of imperfect or broken or incomplete or blighted families to this image of a whole one at the end. Characters and audience alike are overwhelmed by the "sea of joys" rushing in upon them. Indeed, the sea, in both its benign and destructive aspects, is central. This and the other conventions and motifs of romance of which Shakespeare was especially fond and which he employed in so many plays, from *The Comedy of Errors* to *Twelfth Night* to *The Winter's Tale* and *The Tempest*, are present in concentrated, unadulterated form in *Pericles*. The virtues of romance, its mythical aspect, its engagement with universal human experience, the age-old essentials of existence—birth and death, love and hate, time and place, courage and fear, power and vulnerability, grief and joy—are nowhere in his works more strikingly affirmed.

—Charles W. Whitworth

PERSUASION.
Novel by Jane Austen, 1817.

Jane Austen's last novel in anything like finished form appeared the year after her death, showing not exhaustion but interesting developments of theme and technique. The opening in summer 1814 is historically precise, as 20 years of European warfare draw to a close and, newly enriched by their prizes, the naval captains who had defended Britain return to land. Captain Wentworth comes from the world of action, success, unpredictability, and urgent emotion to the decayed moral and social world of the landed gentry represented by the Elliot family, which in 1806 had thought him a "degrading" match for Anne in terms of property and rank: by these social standards she had been persuaded to reject him, partly as she thought for his own sake. Against this background of change and decay, Austen focuses on Anne's search for fulfilment through a quiet assertion of her individuality and recognition of her possibly irreversible error; we witness the crucial stages in a longer personal and social process.

Anne is not one of Austen's high-spirited young heroines: past her prime, she is seen in terms of "prudence, self-denial, sacrifice," an acceptance of social duty and principle which conflicts with her love for Wentworth and the need to maintain the self's integrity. Austen gradually moves her focus from family to individual to show with sympathy the impossibility of Anne's now making a spontaneous declaration of her undying affection. Access to her point of view reveals the sad irony of her attempts to persuade herself that her love is a thing of the past, as Austen juxtaposes her quiet strengths and the more positive or romantic attitudes of her contemporaries. William Walter Elliot has a regency glamour, while the vigorous Wentworth is naturally attracted by the assertive determination and spirit of Louisa Musgrove which lead, however, to her fall on the Cobb at Lyme Regis. This famous episode shows Austen's confidence in a complex direction of readers' responses, as the melodramatic tableau of Wentworth's initial response gives way to scenes of comic hysteria as characters collapse, scream, and jostle; the warrior is enfeebled, while the retiring Anne instinctively takes on the decisive quality formerly associated with Louisa; as she moves off stage, Anne grows in strength as her constancy to her living emotion for Wentworth contrasts with her family's fixation with dead social values. A capacity for real growth and change is one of this novel's tests of moral worth.

Austen's technical skill repeatedly appears in her manipulation of point of view to mingle comedy and pathos: in Chapter 8, Mrs. Musgrove's sentimental recollection of her dead son who had served with Wentworth provokes in him both amusement at her self-deception and consideration for a mother's feelings; the emotional crisis for Anne—"actually on the same sofa" as Wentworth—is seen with interior sympathy, but complicated by her awareness of the substantial female barrier between them, who effectively parodies Anne's feelings about constancy, and by the narrator's tart comments on Mrs. Musgrove's "large fat sighings." Anne welcomes the encounter with Wentworth at the concert, then suffers through the impossibility of speaking out directly to deny any interest in his assumed rival, Mr. Elliot; repeatedly, moments of potential intimacy are disturbed by a third party, highlighting the problems of establishing relationships between individuals subject to the codes and pressures of society. Giving access to the thought of the heroine and then moving back to the narrator's more detached and ironic view of a situation, Austen subtly prevents a fixed response: for readers as for characters, much in the novel is characterised by hesitation and doubt. A rare opportunity for comparative analysis of Austen's art is provided by the surviving manuscript cancelled chapter of *Persuasion*, for which she substituted Chapters 22 and 23. The superiority of the reworking is seen in her use of a semi-public situation, in which Wentworth can overhear Anne's commitment in her conversation with Captain Harville; his declaration of love through a letter rather than speech; Anne's "absolute necessity of seeming like herself" to conceal her emotion from her family; and the comically unnecessary attentions of Mrs. Musgrove. The rewriting both heightens our sense of the personal crisis in the social context and throws greater responsibility on Anne to claim for her sex the privilege of "loving longest, when existence or when hope is gone."

The normal Austen pattern is for a young heroine to marry her social superior and settle to a landed existence. In *Persuasion*, the fading heroine marries an outsider, a self-made man with a dangerous profession, recognising that from the feudal world of the Elliots she can bring little to the naval community. If the novel ends on the stability of marriage—"she gloried in being a sailor's wife"—the "tax of quick alarm" at future war signals her entry into an uncertain world unknown to her sister heroines. Austen's ability to dramatise through the personal and family histories the wider national change in relationships between social classes and the problems of individual identity in a time of challenge to communal values is a remarkable testimony to her still growing artistic powers in the year of her death.

—Ian McGowan

PETER PAN.
Play by J.M. Barrie, 1904.

It is not always realised that—a few private oddities apart—J.M. Barrie produced only one work for the young. But that one, a major myth of the new century, was written in many forms over many years, before and after the actual stage production. Indeed, it is fair to say that few works discussed in the present volume can have a more curious history than *Peter Pan*, "that terrible masterpiece," as Peter Davies (see below) once called it. Where for a start is its authentic form to be found? Though that first stage production was in 1904, the play had to wait several years for a definitive printed version. The "story," the full-length definitive narrative (the longest, best, most satisfying of all the versions) did not appear until 1911. Yet clues can be found in Barrie's quite early adult writings.

Certain facts in Barrie's life have so fundamental a part in the making of *Peter Pan* that they should be set out here. He was a small-town Lowlands Scot, one of a weaver's large family. When David, the mother's favourite child, was killed in a skating accident on the eve of his 14th birthday, James, then aged 6 and hitherto of little account, set himself to compensate for the loss. The obsessive relationship that grew between mother and son was to mark the whole of his life, as writer and as man. Another intense relationship began towards the end of the century, when the once penniless young journalist had, quite rapidly, become the rich and celebrated novelist and playwright. This was with Sylvia and Arthur Llewellyn Davies (she was the daughter of George du Maurier) and their several—eventually five—small sons. These boys, devoted childish listeners, were in an immediate sense the kindlers of *Peter Pan*—Jack, Peter, and Michael (as their names confirm) especially.

In print, the magic boy first appeared by name in Barrie's adult novel *The Little White Bird* (1902), a strange first-person narrative about a wealthy bachelor clubman's attachment to a little boy, David. Taking this boy for walks in Kensington Gardens, the narrator tells him of the elusive Peter Pan, who can be found in the Gardens at night, when the gates are closed. A little girl (not motherly Wendy but a sturdy likeable child called Maimie Mannering) bravely stays behind at dusk, though her brother runs away, and she becomes Peter's friend. Four years later these chapters were taken out and reprinted as a separate book called *Peter Pan in Kensington Gardens*, with pictures by Arthur Rackham: its verve and magical atmosphere make it well worth reading today. Told verbally this was the form first known to the Davies boys.

But the roots of the tale go very much further back. In *Margaret Ogilvy* (1896) Barrie recalled how his mother's childhood had ended at 8, when she had to become the family's housekeeper. "The horror of my boyhood was," he noted, "that I knew a time would come when I must also give up games, and how it was to be done, I saw not." More revealing still are his novels *Sentimental Tommy* and *Tommy and Grizel*. Tommy, a clever, feckless dreamer who—disastrously—can't face adult responsibilities, plans a work of fiction:

> a reverie about a little boy who was lost. His parents find him in a wood singing joyfully to himself because he thinks he can now be a boy for ever; and he fears that if they catch him they will compel him to grow into a man, so he runs further from them into the wood and is running still, singing to himself because he is always to be a boy.

But Barrie, unlike Tommy, had a shrewd and positive streak, and the gift of turning fancy into fact. Only a writer of great assurance could have hoped for a theatrical production of *Peter Pan* with its extraordinary cast and sets and flying devices. Beerbohm Tree, who had first offer, thought it hopelessly unworkable, original to excess. But Charles Frohman was more adventurous, and the vastly successful opening productions, on both sides of the Atlantic, were his.

Like most of Barrie's work, *Peter Pan* has been adored and reviled for much the same qualities: what some perhaps call charm, others call the sentimental and whimsical. Possibly neither group has taken into account Barrie's outstanding craftsmanship as a playwright, or of his easy gift for gripping a reader's interest on the printed page. The sentimental and whimsical were certainly part of his stock-in-trade, but they were not accidentally used; by the time he wrote *Peter Pan*, the hard glint in the sentimentalist's pale blue eyes becomes increasingly evident. (It is, indeed, a wonderfully *heartless* book—as Barrie was well aware: see the final line of the novel.) A touch of self-satire can possibly be observed even in the obsessional mother-theme. Wendy is given many good lines, in the novel particularly; note her watching the mermaids "combing out their hair in a lazy way that quite irritated her"; note her scornful feelings when Hook has her tied to the mast.

> No words of mine can tell you how Wendy despised those pirates. To the boys there was at least some glamour in the pirate calling, but all that she saw was that the ship had not been scrubbed for years. There was not a port-hole on the grimy glass of which you might not have written with your finger "Dirty pig"; and she had already written it several times.

Yet her role holds the seeds of its own defeat. "You need not be sorry for Wendy," writes Barrie. "She was one of the kind that like to grow up. In the end she grew up of her own free will a day quicker than other girls." By ceasing to be a child, she rapidly loses Peter, Ariel of the child-world. She loses in every sense the power to fly. The Wendy portrait, begun with such simple charm (the name was the pet-name of William Ernest Henley's short-lived daughter) has clearly got out of hand, reflecting an unadmitted conflict in Barrie himself.

Peter Pan: landmark or signpost? The first far more than the second; it seems to have stunned imitation at any notable level. Pan-followers ran to coyness rather than wit; and this affects the work's reputation still. True, it did give an impetus to theatre for children; it can also be said that it brought into the open the growing cult of childhood and fairies in writings meant for adults. From Grahame's *The Golden Age* in the 1890's to Milne's *When We Were Very Young* in the 1920's, this cult took in work of de la Mare, Eleanor Farjeon (*Martin Pippin*), Rose Fyleman, Saki, James Stephens (*The Crock of Gold*)—and other prose and verse, now classed as children's reading, which were certainly published for adults in their day. With *Peter Pan* the process works in reverse. Both play and novel were (like *Alice*) specifically meant for the young, but are now (like *Alice*) of increasing interest to adults. *Peter Pan* mirrors its time; it mirrors, though more obliquely, its author's mind. As an instance: Barrie first made his name (and almost wrecked it in his home town) by using his local Scottish background for copy. In *Peter Pan* the Scot is hard to trace. But in fact it is the northern stranger's eye that finds such appeal in the Edwardian middle-class nursery; in the social mystique of Kensington Gardens; in the *mores* of prep school and public school. Is not Hook himself, most enigmatic of pirates, abjuring "bad form" even in death, an old

Etonian? James Hook . . . odd that the author should give him his own name. But nothing is really simple in this work. How to explain the dog-kennel father, say, so many years pre-Thurber?

The position of *Peter Pan* today is a curious one. It is at once known and not known. Like other invented myths (Crusoe, Gulliver) its persons and ideas have currency among many who have neither read nor seen what Barrie wrote. Those who *do* read (or listen) often meet it only through feeble brief retellings (there are, alas, a number of these in print). They are missing much; the full text abounds in richness. *Peter Pan* is the secure child's dream of danger, of wild distances, of freedom from adult rules—but always (as in Sendak's *Where the Wild Things Are*) from a safe home base. It incorporates the traditional boys' adventure yarn which had so much delighted Barrie himself when young; indeed, much of the pirate/redskin material can be seen as a brilliant take-off of the genre. Peter himself is the absolute leader and hero-figure, the animator of action. But the children are not only onlookers; they are *in* the event, as themselves. It incorporates magic; the children actually fly. All these elements are combined on an island which accommodates redskins, pirates, mermaids, wolves with the greatest ease. For the young, the whole thing is a feast which lasts the longer by the skill—the continual sleight-of-hand—with which it is served. A "terrible masterpiece," yes, but a work of genius, the most complex and original of all its author's works, and a mine for Barrie-explorers.

—Naomi Lewis

THE PICKWICK PAPERS.
(The Posthumous Papers of the Pickwick Club.)
Novel by Charles Dickens, 1837.

The Pickwick Papers, Charles Dickens's first novel, is an astonishing achievement for a man of 24. It lacks some of the complexity of his later fiction but it is a substantial work, as long as the greater novels which earned Dickens his fame. It maintains a consistency of tone and shows a certain strength of characterisation even if the tone is somewhat facetious and the characters rather stereotyped.

Dickens had clearly digested a good deal of the picaresque tradition before embarking on *Pickwick* and it is his reading rather than his observation of "life" that fills up most of the volume. The picaresque conventions are adhered to rigidly: the plot consists of a series of somewhat random journeys undertaken for the purpose of providing incidents and adventures for the novelist to recount; those incidents and adventures are primarily physical in nature and farcical in effect; a cheerfully ironic attitude is taken towards everything and everyone encountered, even towards the hero himself; digressions are permitted and, finally, there is a great deal of eating and drinking.

All this comes from *Don Quixote* (Mr. Pickwick and Sam Weller are versions of the Don and his faithful Sancho Panza), as well as from the French picaresque *Gil Blas*, both of which were translated into English by Smollett in the mid-18th century, from Smollett's own *Roderick Random*, from *Tom Jones*, and from their imitators. This is not the tradition of psychological or sociological analysis nor of romance or serious adventure. It is the tradition of the comic and the farcical with possible moral applications. It continued after this work (see for example Thackeray's picaresque *Barry Lyndon*) but by then Dickens himself was writing his more serious and more obviously "Victorian" novels.

Pickwick takes us from London into Kent, up to Ipswich, across to Bath and so on, always coming back to London as the centre of operations. But this is not yet the London of *Our Mutual Friend* or *Oliver Twist*. In keeping with its 18th-century origins, the novel stresses the standard picaresque ingredients—the inn, the coaching-office, the journey, the dinner, the ball, and, always, the quantity of alcohol consumed. Most of the characters are venal or horrible in one way or another. Even the members of the Pickwick Club are not spared; Mr. Pickwick calls his friend and follower Mr. Winkle a humbug and an impostor when he discovers that, in spite of boasts of sporting prowess he can neither shoot a gun nor skate. But the Pickwickians have a certain innocent folly rather than evil natures.

Pickwick himself is a sort of grown-up child, as are many others whom we meet; only Pickwick's servant Sam Weller is nearly a grown-up and he helps the author to laugh at the pretentions of the others. The women are mostly vain and obsessed with male attention, the men are mostly vain, foolish or bullies. They are stock characters—the jealous little man, the cowardly boaster, the idiotic constable. Even the less reprehensible personnel are made from a recognisable mould—Mr. Wardle is the bluff, hospitable English squire, Mr. Snodgrass the romantic poet and so on.

Equally recognisable are their adventures: between their large meals they are overturned in coaches, hit by cricket balls, accidentally shot, caught in the gardens of girls' schools at night, and chased about in their nightgowns, victims of mistaken identity. Resourceful servants help their masters not to make complete fools of themselves but in general they *are* fools and will remain so, for there is no moral development in the picaresque.

One can see some of Dickens's later concerns and qualities in *Pickwick* but these are not the picaresque elements of the novel. They appear when he introduces the law, for instance, or when he lights on a truly original character, which he does in the case of Mr. Jingle. The law is satirised with a touch of the bitterness of *Bleak House*—Messrs. Dodson and Fogg, the venal solicitors, foreshadow that novel in their names, their clerks, and the extreme degree of their unscrupulousness. Attached to the Inns of Court are a number of macabre and gruesome stories which Dickens delights in telling us and the "Tale of the Queer Client" in particular makes us think of the horrors of Chancery which the later novel will expound so forcefully. When Pickwick is consigned to the debtors' prison, the Fleet, the descriptions rise to something of the surrealist horror that we will find again in *Little Dorrit*. The "Chancery prisoner," for instance, who has been in the Fleet for 20 years describes his friendlessness thus:

> Friends! . . . If I lay dead at the bottom of the deepest mine in the world; tight screwed down and soldered in my coffin; rotting in the dark and filthy ditch that drags its slime along beneath the foundations of this prison; I could not be more forgotten or unheeded than I am here.

Equally, we find in *Pickwick* some of the germs of what will become Dickens's remarkable narrative powers and his extraordinary prose style. Only rarely in this novel does he actually rise to the heights of his greatest work but Mr. Jingle's telegraphic mode of speech and, in particular, his description of playing cricket in the West Indies in chapter 7, show the brilliant extravagances to which Dickens will rise so often later in his career. Sometimes too, Sam Weller's cockney wisdom is delivered with something of the flavour of the speech of later villains and heroes.

One inevitably, then, looks before and after as one reads this work. It is moulded almost entirely from the 18th-century picaresque (this is not merely a structural matter—Pickwick is actually carried about at one point in a sedan chair) and depends intertextually upon it, while for all other non-picaresque elements in the novel (such as they are) we are irresistibly drawn into comparisons with the Dickens's major fiction of the 1850's and 1860's.

—Lance St. John Butler

THE PICTURE OF DORIAN GRAY.
Novel by Oscar Wilde, 1891.

Oscar Wilde's *The Picture of Dorian Gray* was first published in the July issue of *Lippincott's* magazine on 20 June 1890 and in book form in July 1891. The novel was immediately controversial because of the ethics of the aesthetic doctrines it seemed to embrace. Critics have since approached the book from a variety of positions: as an autobiography of Wilde's life, as gothic melodrama, and as an aesthetic novel. Of these approaches the last is the most consistent in clarifying the novel's themes.

Wilde was an outspoken proponent of the Aesthetic Movement which Walter Pater, influenced by the Pre-Raphaelites, helped define in his book *The Renaissance* (1873). In the "Conclusion" Pater stated "to burn with this hard gem-like flame to maintain this ecstasy, is success in life." As a student of Pater's at Oxford, Wilde had embraced Pater's ideas, and in London Wilde had adopted the pose of an aesthete. Pater removed his "Conclusion" from the 1877 version because Wilde and others had made the Aesthetic Movement too embarrassing for him, and he did not adopt their extreme views.

However, the French symbolists' ideas were more sympathetic to the Aesthetic Movement. And Wilde borrowed the phrases "art for art's sake" from Gautier's Preface to *Mademoiselle de Maupin*. The 11th chapter of *The Picture of Dorian Gray* is also strongly influenced, though not as much as earlier critics thought, by Huysmans's novel *A Rebours*. Consequently, Wilde's only novel is strongly grounded in the Aesthetic Movement.

In *The Picture of Dorian Gray* the aesthetic is built on the tension of opposites. Richard Ellmann in an article "The Critic as Artist as Wilde" first saw the opposites in Wilde's critical essays, "The Critic as Artist" and "The Decay of Lying," and in this novel. Ellmann's biography of Wilde also extends this theory, and the rest of this essay is based on Ellmann's ideas. The primary opposite in the novel is that art, while detached from real life is also very much involved with it. Wilde illustrates this in *The Picture of Dorian Gray*: when Lord Henry Wotton, a friend of the artist Basil Hallward, tempts Dorian by talking about youth and beauty and becoming a spectator to life, he makes a prayer or wish, that his portrait grow old while he remains young. Dorian moves from the human (real life) sphere and becomes living art while the picture assumes Dorian's human traits, taking on his sins and his age and recording them as distortions in Hallward's full-length painting of him.

The aesthetic experiment, however, is a failure. Dorian, at first unaware of the change that has taken place, falls under the influence of Lord Wotton's aesthetic creed. Watching a play in a second-rate theater, he falls in love with Sybil Vane, a beautiful actress. However, he has not fallen in love with the woman; he has fallen in love with her art. When Sybil falls in love with him, she loses her ability to act well. Unlike Dorian, she prefers the real to the artificial. As Dorian is now himself art, he cannot understand Sybil's inability to perform well, and loses his interest in her. Thus when Dorian takes Wotton and Hallward to the theater to see her act and her acting ability is gone, he tells her that he can no longer marry her, and she commits suicide. Dorian has sinned against love, and the picture records this in an alteration to a facial feature.

Once Dorian realizes the implications of never growing old, he buries himself both in art and in experiences of all kinds, especially experiences of a darker nature. He corrupts both men and women, eventually murders Basil Hallward, and finally kills himself by stabbing the picture with a palette knife, which returns both he and it to their natural spheres of existence. Dorian is a failure at living a perfectly aesthetic life. No one can. Ellmann believes that Wilde wrote the "tragedy of aestheticism," becoming a martyr to the aesthetic creed.

However, one must not jump to the conclusion that Wilde rejected the aesthetic doctrines himself. He added a preface to the 1891 book which stated the aesthetic principles in epigrammatic form. These principles were opposite to what the novel itself demonstrated. Again Wilde balances opposites by extremes. Extreme aestheticism cannot be lived, but neither can one live solely in reality. Consequently, truth must lie somewhere on the plane between pure aestheticism and pure reality.

The Picture of Dorian Gray has been a perennial favorite of readers. It retains a freshness that many other gothic novels do not, and its mysteries are still as fascinating as when they were first penned. The idea of living life without fear of death or its consequences is as old as the Faust legends and the Irish Celtic myths, but in *Dorian Gray* Wilde breathed new life into the legends by infusing them with the doctrines of the Aesthetic Movement and allowing Dorian "to burn with a hard gem-like flame."

—David A. Upchurch

PIERS PLOWMAN.
See the Writers entry on **LANGLAND, William.**

PIG ISLAND LETTERS.
Poems by James K. Baxter, 1966.

On the dust jacket of *Pig Island Letters* James K. Baxter's words are repeated from that of his preceding book, *Howrah*

Bridge and Other Poems: ". . . the first part was written some time ago by a man who thought he was a New Zealander; the second part lately, in the past two or three years, by a man who had become, almost unawares, a member of a bigger, rougher family." Titles of both these books are 'anti-poetic.' Howrah Bridge is the hideous railway bridge in Calcutta; "Pig Island," Baxter notes, "is used to refer to the whole country [of New Zealand]." All Baxter's earlier titles are romantic, rhetorical: *Blow, Wind of Fruitfulness*, *The Fallen House*, *In Fires of No Return* are representative. In *Howrah Bridge* C.K. Stead noted "a new voice . . . that of the mature Baxter," and, "With *Pig Island Letters* the informal tone predominates. The voice becomes rougher, more natural, though the poems are quite as well made." Baxter himself (interviewed by John Weir) said of the title sequence: "There is a certain breakdown of form that occurs, but there is an advantage in spontaneity, I think, and in authenticity. I wanted that: just someone speaking authentically. . . . I thought 'That book will break the critics' teeth.' I felt happy about it." *Pig Island Letters* still embodies Baxter's continuing themes and scenarios, but, to reverse the proverb, a too often sleazy synthetic silk purse of "poetry" can be seen changing into the bristling pig's ear of "language charged with meaning." The twin thematic frames are, in Weir's words: "No other New Zealand writer has expressed as keenly as he the conviction that man inhabits a fallen state," and, from Baxter himself: ". . . our island is . . . an unjust, unhappy one." *Pig Island Letters* is a volume of *stasis*, terminus of one "poetic" career, springboard to ". . . something / Nobody counted on," to (adapting Weir) "the necessary purgation which robbed his life of gentility and his tongue of rhetoric," that is, to Jerusalem, to the "sonnet" sequences *Jerusalem Sonnets*, *Jerusalem Daybook*, *Autumn Testament*. *Howrah Bridge* (a response to six months in India in 1958 and 1959) is the turning-point, but the only substantial work between *Pig Island Letters* and the Jerusalem titles is *The Rock Woman* (1969), 53 selected poems of which only nine are new.

The poems of *Pig Island Letters* were written from 1961 to 1965; Baxter gave the three next years to literary employment and fellowships in Dunedin; in 1968 a "vision" called him to the tiny Wanganui Maori settlement of Jerusalem, and in early 1969 he went there. This was his ultimate choice of a life that transcends, though it no way repudiates, art.

Pig Island Letters appears in three sections. The title sequence is of 13 poems dedicated to Baxter's friend, the novelist Maurice Shadbolt, with whom Baxter had shared a "gap" of creative sterility, "The menopause of the mind," the topic of the opening poem; the *stasis* he has reached. The second section has 14 poems, for the most part notably more austere and pared of rhetoric than section one, three using the rhymeless Durrell-derived pentameter couplets first seen in *Howrah Bridge* ("Elephanta") which became his medium for the Jerusalem sequences. One poem represents, unevenly, Baxter's very personal genre of vernacular colonial ballad. There are three Lowellesque, melodramatic vignettes of chaotic middle-class familial and sexual life. There are 39 lines—irregular syllabics?—of brilliantly comic self-mockery, "The Cold Hub": satori—here "Nada"!—from freezing awake all night on a park bench. Section three has nine poems, all in syllabic stanzas except for the final uneven obituary tribute to the Auckland printer Bob Lowry, "Ballad of One Tree Hill" (neither ballad in form nor using Baxterian vernacular; Lowry, in the old bad Baxter rhetoric announces, "I am a dark river").

The second poem of the opening series begins memorably:

From an old house shaded with macrocarpas
Rises my malady.
Love is not valued much in Pig Island
Though we admire its walking parody, . . .

These poems are general meditations, with much autobiography, on (says W.H. Oliver) "art, poetry, politics (rather dubiously), memory, miracle and prayer, and also anger, cunning, mockery and humour." A memorable picture in the ninth poem, "The poet as family man / Head between thumbs at mass" contrasts with ". . . the other / Convict self . . . ," and ends ". . . The poem is / A plank laid over the lion's den." The 13th poem is a lean and brilliant dialogue between Our Lady and a soul (Baxter's) at Heaven's gate; its end offers a diver encountering an underwater spring: "As that wild nymph of water rises / So does the God in man."

Section two's excellent couplet poems—"East Coast Journey," "Waipatiki Journey," "At Taieri Mouth"—all use a radical Baxter scenario, "man alone" at the land's edge, autumnal or wintry, dourly eschatological. "East Coast Journey" concludes in an old man's desire for ". . . the arms of the eater of life, Hine-nui-te-po" (Polynesian Great Lady of Darkness) "With teeth of obsidian and hair like kelp / Flashing and glimmering at the edge of the horizon." "The Watch" (marine) unites, off New Zealand's coast, Baxter and Elpenor.

The final syllabic poems include two on ancestors but, after a harshly gentle "To a Print of Queen Victoria"—"I advise rest, Madam"—they are dominated by the superb "Tomcat." The postman returning—"I thump up the steps through bush / at 4 p.m."—is, of course the real-life Baxter—but the cat?

. . . the old fool;
stood, body hard as a board,
heart thudding, hair on end, at
the house corner, terrible,
yelling at something. They said,
"Get him doctored." I think not.

Small masterpiece of cadence and timing this poem is, yet, he has "the snaffle and the bit all right / But where's the bloody horse?" At the end of the line, *stasis*; three years of literary Dunedin's acceptance confirmed, paradoxically, that the "Convict self" will not be "doctored"—it will become the pilgrim to Jerusalem.

—Peter Alcock

PILGRIMAGE.
Novel by Dorothy Richardson, 1915–38.

Pilgrimage was the final title given to a long novel by Dorothy Richardson, published in four volumes in 1938, which had been slowly appearing in instalments over a period of 20 years. The first section, entitled *Pointed Roofs*, had been published in 1915. *Pointed Roofs* was on its first appearance read as a self-contained novel and hailed by a percipient reviewer in the *Saturday Review* as "an original book." Its 11 successors were similarly read and reviewed as "novels" (though Katherine Mansfield, who reviewed two of them, considered them rather as a "nest of short stories").

Richardson herself preferred to regard each of these successive volumes as a "chapter" of a longer work in progress and it was not until the entire work was published that her plan for a *roman fleuve* was fully apparent.

Richardson was—as her first reviewer noted—original. A contemporary of Joyce, Mansfield, and Woolf, she pioneered with them the technique of narration that has come to be known (though she was not herself satisfied with either description) as the stream of consciousness or the interior monologue. But while the reputation of the other three pioneers has grown steadily over the years, *Pilgrimage*—and Dorothy Richardson—has lurked in the critical shadows. Yet *Pointed Roofs* come out before *Ulysses* and *Mrs. Dalloway* and "At the Bay," and its technical skill owes nothing to any other writer.

Pilgrimage is unashamedly autobiographical. Richardson's heroine Miriam through each successive section mirrors the experiences of the author. Many authors have used their own life-history as the basis of a novel. Richardson differs from them in holding steadfastly through nearly 2000 pages to a single point of view. Everything is seen through Miriam's eyes and expressed through her conscious observation and the verbalised expression of her unconscious. The technique is the stream of consciousness pushed to its limits.

She broke new ground in one other important direction. It is commonplace now to assert that female writers differ from male writers in their entire use of language. The English language is aggressively masculine. Richardson was in 1915 a pioneer: "Feminine prose," she wrote in her preface to the completed novel, "should properly be unpunctuated, moving from point to point without formal obstruction." Her use of a new syntax was quickly noted by Woolf, no stranger to the problem: "She has invented . . . a sentence . . . of a more elastic fibre than the old, capable of stretching to the extreme, of suspending the frailest particle, of enveloping the vaguest shapes . . . It is a woman's sentence."

Why then the neglect, for a writer so highly praised in her time? For she is a neglected writer—one of the best studies of her is frankly entitled *Dorothy Richardson*: *The Genius They Forgot*. Her contemporaries (and, to isolate the issue, only women contemporaries are cited) Woolf and Mansfield have prospered in edition after edition and have attracted a whole library of commentary and criticism. *Pilgrimage* had to wait nearly 30 years for a second edition in 1967 and a further 12 years for a new edition in 1979. The critical books on her, though enthusiastic, are few. One of the most appreciative of them has a preface which opens with the kiss of death: "It is with the *dulness* of Dorothy Richardson that we must begin." How can any writer survive such criticism—and from her admirers?

Basically, the problem with *Pilgrimage* is the drabness of the life of the heroine. Miriam, the central figure, is intelligent, sensitive, but locked in a lower-middle-class milieu that echoes the life of the author—governess, translator, hack journalist, fighting a grim battle all her life for mere survival. That she survives is a triumph. But the battle, in spite of the subtleties and skill deployed in its narration, is too dispersed and attenuated for the result to be considered major artistry. Mansfield in stories like "Pictures" and "Miss Brill" can capture it all in a few pages of concentrated prose. During her lifetime, Richardson noted sadly that people bought her first volumes and then her readership fell away.

For the persistent reader, who is prepared to take *Pilgrimage* at its own pace, there are many rewards, a new sensitivity, a new and dazzling use of prose, new insights. But it is difficult to see Richardson, in spite of her originality of approach, ever being regarded as one of the major writers of the century. Her work lacks the taut discipline and overall control of form of which Woolf is such a master.

—Ian A. Gordon

THE PILGRIM'S PROGRESS.
Fiction by John Bunyan, 1678 and 1684.

The Pilgrim's Progress was the first bestseller in English literary history. Part I written almost certainly during the second half of John Bunyan's first imprisonment, 1660–72, and published in 1678, had gone through 13 editions by the time of Bunyan's death in 1688. In the verse preface to Part II (1684), Bunyan calls attention to its unprecedented popularity, and to the number of translations and of "counterfeit" versions of his work. This success was not a matter of passing fashion. *The Pilgrim's Progress* has never since been out of print: no other 17th-century text (save the King James Bible), no other committedly Puritan work, and nothing from a writer of Bunyan's social class has enjoyed such an extensive readership or exerted such a lasting influence.

In *The Pilgrim's Progress* the definitive modern genre—the novel—is nascent, for it is distinguished from the body of 17th-century fictions by its realism. The circumstantial details of the journey are mundanely familiar; the incidents on the road are commonplace; the conversations between travellers are colloquially idiomatic. Unlike the exotic realms of romance, the world of *The Pilgrim's Progress* is not socially, temporally, or geographically remote. Bunyan's characters are equally readily recognisable. Each is a moral type, but, individualized through the deft use of telling detail, rarely only a type. The characterization usually passes from the allegorically representational to the realistically exemplary: "Not Honesty in the *Abstract*, but *Honest* is my Name" says one of the pilgrims. Bunyan's pastoral awareness that failings coexist with faith in human beings precludes the categorical presentation of persons as either entirely vicious or entirely virtuous. The protagonist, Christian, is conspicuously a prey to doubts and misgivings, and is prone to making mistakes. Socially insignificant, an unemployed vagrant in rags it seems, he is no romance hero: fiction had never before treated such a figure with anything but contempt. (Bunyan's radicalism in this respect is more than merely literary; there is a good deal of biting social comment and satire in *The Pilgrim's Progress* in which persons of gentle birth or prestigious status are invariably hypocrites or villains.) To Christian's ordinariness is due not only much of the appeal of the fiction but also its persuasiveness: if Christian can succeed on the quest, so can the reader. Whether Christian *will* succeed remains, however, a question throughout Part I. The outcome may be doctrinally certain, but it is not given to Christian, any more than to most believers, to be unassailably confident of his salvation. Since it is his fallible and often apprehensive point of view which shapes much of the narrative, experiential anxiety outweighs dogmatic precepts. The reader's awareness of Christian's own vulnerability and uncertainty is far stronger than the sense of predetermined election. Tension and suspense are the consequence. When Christian asks "*How far is it thither?*", the Shepherds gnomically reply, "Too far for any but those that *shall* get thither indeed"; the discovery of their identity must await the end of the story.

Novelistic *The Pilgrim's Progress* may be; it is not, however, a novel. The verse "Apology" to Part I shows Bunyan uncomfortably aware that his work will not satisfy the generic expectations of readers accustomed to Puritan sermons and practical divinity. He tells that, having planned a tract upon "the way / And race of Saints," he fell "suddenly into an Allegory" which so rapidly expanded that he was forced to abandon his intended work and allow his imagination free rein. Nevertheless, his imagination worked through the modes and techniques with which he was familiar. *The Pilgrim's Progress* shares with all Bunyan's other writings that didactic and edifying purpose which was the only justification for literary creativity recognised by the Puritan tradition. Its innovative originality consists less in rejecting the techniques of Puritan prose than in realising their imaginative potential.

Thus, the episodic structure of *The Pilgrim's Progress* is related to homiletic technique. Each episode functions as a discrete exemplum, closing with an expository conversation between the pilgrims which draws out its significance. This is most clearly so in Part II, where Great-heart repeatedly explains to Christiana and her companions the import of what has just occurred. Such use of exemplary anecdotes and incidents, drawn commonly from experience, was a standard device of Puritan preachers. Often, they would develop such anecdotes into short narratives, which might be attributed to speakers other than the preacher. An entire work might be cast in dialogic form, as was one of the most popular guides to godliness, Arthur Dent's *Plain Man's Path-way to Heaven* (1601), a book known to Bunyan. It was Bunyan's innovation to set the interlocutors in motion within a plot, but the ruminative discussions in *The Pilgrim's Progress* continue to occupy stationary moments separate from the scenes of action and are often indistinguishable in manner from passages of homiletic exposition. Realism was equally characteristic of Puritan divinity, with its insistent practical bias: only by addressing the actual everyday circumstances of persons could its advice carry conviction. And for more than a century Puritan homiletics had insisted upon the need for a plain style in order to be able to reach ordinary people. In several of his works Bunyan explicitly endorses this rejection of erudite allusiveness and elaborate syntax. Among more radical Puritans (citing I Corinthians 2), this emphasis could lead to rejection of the need for an educated ministry, and in several of his works Bunyan himself defiantly asserted his ignorance as a strength: "I never went to school to *Aristotle* or *Plato*, but was brought up . . . among a company of poor Countrey-men"; "I have not . . . borrowed my Doctrine from Libraries. I depend upon the sayings of no man: I found it in the Scriptures of Truth."

To the "Scriptures of Truth" Bunyan owed the controlling metaphor of his fiction. The way "as straight as a Rule can make it" recalls the distinction drawn in the Old Testament wisdom literature and prophets between the straight way of the righteous and the crooked way of the wicked; the image was given a specifically Christian significance in the dominical saying "I am the way" (John 14:6). The interpretation of such Old Testament texts in Hebrews (especially chapters 3 and 11), which see the patriarchs as "strangers and pilgrims in the earth," journeying to a "heavenly country," a "continuing city," provides the essential structure for Bunyan's pilgrimage from the City of Destruction (Isaiah 19:18) to the Celestial City. As Bunyan's marginal references indicate, each particular incident in *The Pilgrim's Progress* has similar biblical warrant, but Bunyan's genius had also another inspiration. A poor countryman might be excluded from the dominant literate and international courtly culture of the time, but he had access to an oral tradition, which, in a period antedating general literacy, might be no less vital. Clearly, the giants and hobgoblins of Bunyan's story are of folkloristic origin, and its delight in riddling, the often odd perspectives and proportions of its scenes, and the way locations appear or dissolve before us, suggest the motifs and movement of folktale.

The air of unreality, of dream, which, for all its verisimilitude, is found in *The Pilgrim's Progress*, owes something to this folkloristic heritage, but it is more immediately the result of Bunyan's Puritanism. He was habituated to treating the visible world as a revelation of invisible truth. Persuaded that divine and infernal powers were active in creation, he sought to understand God's will and nature from what he perceived in the world about him. Reality was itself an allegory. This is most readily appreciable from Bunyan's emblem book for children, *A Book for Boys and Girls*, in which he draws from everyday things a series of monitory and hortatory morals. Precisely the same technique is used for the scenes in the Interpreter's House. In *The Pilgrim's Progress*, realism is never an end in itself; Bunyan is, in contemporary terminology, "spiritualizing the creatures," treating the real world as a revelation of divine truth. The numinous is no less a feature of *The Pilgrim's Progress* than the realistic. It may anticipate the novel, but it is also our last allegory, a bridge between the medieval and modern worlds.

—N.H. Keeble

THE PLAIN-DEALER.
Play by William Wycherley, 1676.

The Plain-Dealer is, of William Wycherley's four comedies, the one which displays the most variety of content and style. Its subplot, in which Freeman overreaches the litigious Widow Blackacre, to whom he has been paying mercenary court, and succeeds in securing an income and the discharge of his debts without even having to marry her, is a simple comedy of humours, peppered with law terms and diversified with her independence-seeking son Jerry and her other suitor the superannuated wit Major Oldfox. Its main plot, whose connections with the subplot are of the slightest, is a comedy of intrigue, with a strong moral and satirical flavour, employing occasional blank verse as well as the customary prose.

This main plot revolves around four chief characters: Manly, the plain dealer of the title; Olivia, his false-hearted mistress; Vernish, his false-hearted friend; and Fidelia, his true-hearted unknown admirer, who has assumed the disguise of a young man in order to be near him. The play opens topically with Manly returned to London after sinking his ship rather than allow it to be captured by the Dutch, then at war with the English. He was intending to emigrate to the Indies in his aversion to the general insincerity at home, and had left half his fortune, mostly in jewels, in the hands of Olivia, expecting her to follow him later under the protection of Vernish. Olivia has no intention of joining him, associates with foolish wits and flatterers, and quarrels with him when he appears, finally informing him that she is married (but not to whom) and that therefore he cannot expect her to return his jewels, and that if he has anything more to say to her he can employ his young companion (Fidelia) as his messenger. Manly, still ensnared by his passion for her, orders the disguised Fidelia to be his go-between, for he must lie with her, and when Fidelia reminds him of Olivia's ingratitude he declares that he will lie with her out of revenge. Fidelia (like Viola in Shakespeare's *Twelfth Night*) goes about her task reluctantly. When she returns, she reports (unlike Viola) that Olivia loves the messenger and not the suitor. Manly at first furiously concludes that the young man has lain with her; this being denied, he urges him to do it and thus cuckold her secret husband; and still meeting resistance he determines to accompany him himself and "act love, whilst you shall talk it only." Olivia, waiting in the dark for the young man, is surprised by the return of her husband (who is Vernish) from the country, gets rid of him temporarily, and then welcomes the expected lover, but when she goes to the bedroom it is Manly who follows her; having achieved his aim and returned to Fidelia he requires her to stay and make another appointment so that he can bring witnesses and publish Olivia's shame. Vernish returns, intercepting Fidelia, who by confessing her sex escapes a duel only to face a rape, and presently, having escaped that too, tells Manly her adventure without disclosing that she is a woman. He is naturally puzzled at the husband's supposed gullibility, and when he tells the story to Vernish (whom he still supposes his friend) Vernish is more puzzled still, as well as secretly enraged at Manly's success. In a final melodramatic encounter at Olivia's house Vernish is fought and worsted, he and Olivia are denounced, and Manly recovers his jewel-casket and, discovering Fidelia's identity, gives it to her ("Then take for ever my heart, and this with it").

In so far as the plot turns upon Fidelia's dilemma and is resolved by her identification and Manly's proposal of marriage, *The Plain-Dealer* is a romantic comedy of intrigue; but in so far as its title highlights Manly's uncompromising nonconformity to social pretence and scene after scene dwells on the moral shortcomings of society in general, it is a moral satire. Besides all the usual satirical topics—including the abuses of the legal system in the subplot—great stress is laid on insincerity. In this respect *The Plain-Dealer* goes beyond Molière's *Le Misanthrope*, from which Wycherley has taken the notion of the social rebel: Alceste is presented as extreme, though estimable, and is dismissed to misery and voluntary isolation; Manly is presented as estimable, though extreme, and is dismissed to happiness, union with Fidelia, and wealth (for she has £2000 a year). Though some critics maintain that Manly is as much the object of Wycherley's satire as its mouthpiece, they do so only by measuring him against their own moral values. Wycherley's own moral criticism is explicit and copious, and from it Manly is exempt. Olivia's first scene (II.i) for instance, is a lengthy demonstration of her hypocrisy and malice, with her cousin Eliza underlining all the evidence for the audience's benefit; into it Wycherley has worked a defence of his own *The Country-Wife*, modelled on Molière's defence of *L'École des femmes*. The play's prologue, spoken by the actor of Manly, puts the author's intention beyond doubt: "And where else, but on stages, do we see / Truth pleasing, or rewarded honesty? / Which our bold poet does this day in me."

—T.W. Craik

THE PLAYBOY OF THE WESTERN WORLD.
Play by J.M. Synge, 1907.

J.M. Synge's most famous play, *The Playboy of the Western World*, extended the horizons of Irish theatre so far that a conservative "patriotic" backlash became inevitable. The play's realistic yet humorous portrayal of the rural Irish set off the notorious "*Playboy* riots" of 1907: complaining among other things of profanity about the use of the word "shifts," the Dublin audience disrupted several performances with tin horns and other noisemaking ploys, and eventually scuffling broke out; the reaction in New York reached new lows: Lady Gregory tells us that a variety of rotting vegetables were thrown at the stage, as well as capsules filled with "asafoetida," and that more scuffling occurred resulting in 10 arrests. In addition to the wild language, the protesters objected to a plot in which an Irish lad claims to have murdered his father with a spade and is then regaled as hero in a rural community. Yet the play is based on a real murder case, where a man indeed killed his father with a loy, was hidden from police by villagers, and finally was safely shipped off to America.

The 1907 preface is a manifesto of sorts and gives some idea of the play's more revolutionary aspects. In it Synge acknowledges his debt to the "folk imagination" of the Irish people and declares that his characters speak only plain language or language that he has actually heard in Ireland. His purpose is to render not only "reality, which is the root of all poetry, in a comprehensive and natural form," but also the joy of life—which Synge felt was lacking in the intellectual drama of his time. Part of his method, therefore, is to focus upon character much more than on event.

The play's characters are, in fact, well delineated and quite memorable. Shawn Keogh vividly represents all that is most contemptible about mindless conservatives: hiding cowardly behind the standards set by his religion, Shawn is afraid of anything that threatens the status quo. That includes Pegeen Mike, his intended, a beautiful woman with a fiery disposition who could not possibly be more his opposite in nature. Where Shawn grovels, Pegeen is defiantly proud, independent, and free-spirited. Another strong female character is the lusty Widow Quin, a 30-year-old woman of keen intellect and loose morals who proves an able competitor for Pegeen when it comes to the affairs of love. But of all the characters the one on whom most scholars necessarily base their interpretation of the play is Christy Mahon, the man who arrives in the village claiming to have killed his own father.

Synge's protagonist is a young man who, several critics have noted, takes his self-image from cues offered by the people around him—which accounts for the play's several mirrors: their role is to symbolize Christy's search for his self-image, for clearly he is a man who really does not know himself or his potential to succeed in life. For instance, when he lived with his father he reflected his father's poor expectations of him—lazy, ugly, stupid, clumsy, and afraid of girls. But when he arrives in Mayo he finds people in need of a messiah who can lift them spiritually, who can save them from their mundane and boring existences—and that is what he becomes: a romantic hero who is energetic, handsome, intelligent, noble, and of tremendous sexual appeal to the women he encounters. Christy's transformation is confirmed when the Widow Quin is able to convince Christy's father that the triumphant young athlete on the beach is *not* his own son. That Christy is after all a Christ figure is virtually a universally accepted interpretation now. It has been pointed out that his name is a lesser form of Christ's, as befits the seriocomic nature of the play; that he is the son of Mahon (man), as Christ was; that Christy's father is said to be "like holy Joseph"; that at the height of his popularity Christy is paraded along the beach on the back of an ass, as Christ was when he entered Jerusalem; that the people of the community exalt him in order ultimately to betray him and pull him down, as happened to Christ; that Pegeen's three denials of having anything to do with Christy are equivalent to Peter's three denials of knowing Christ; that Christy's binding and wounding echo Christ's; that reference to "the sins of the whole world" followed by "In the name of Almighty God" points again to Christ; and that both are, finally, saved by their fathers.

Political parallels have also been drawn. Christy can be seen as a reflection of Parnell, who also was raised by his people only to be torn down and disgraced. And like several Irish rebellions that were backed a great deal in theory but received far less support once revolt was actual, here Christy's first supposed murder of his father fires the peasant romantic imagination; however, his second attempt, when witnessed in actuality, merely horrifies and repels the villagers, who desert his cause. In each case the average Irishman has rejected the salvation offered him.

Christy's second attempt at murder is, in fact, a pathetic attempt to regain his miraculous lustre, lost when his "dead" father reappears and makes a liar out of the newborn romantic hero. Christy's first attempt, however, provides an opportunity for discussing the play's tremendous capacity for humor. It seems his father has ordered the usually docile lad to marry the Widow Casey—an intolerable command because the woman is twice his age, weighs over two hundred pounds, walks with a limp, is blind in one eye, and is noted for "misbehavior with the old and young"! Such a marriage would benefit his father financially but ruin Christy's whole life, hence his act of rebellion. Much of the laughter for the modern reader derives from quirks of the peasant lifestyle and psyche, some manifestations of which defy analysis—as when Susan accuses Sara of once visiting "the man bit the yellow lady's nostril on the northern shore"; or when Jimmy tells us of a man "kicked in the head by a red mare, and he went killing horses a great while, till he eat the insides of a clock and died after."

Finally, some discussion of the rejection theme is necessary, for negative choices abound on a variety of levels: Christy twice rejects his father, and later the Widow Quin; Pegeen first spurns Shawn and then Christy; the villagers repudiate authority (the police), subsequently Christy, and ultimately the Catholic social establishment, which is indirectly a target of mockery throughout the play. All of these actions serve to illuminate the dominant theme of the play: Christy, who has spiritually uplifted his people, is expelled by them, even as Christ was lauded then rejected by his. Synge's pessimistic message, finally, seems to be that, as a species, we long for some sort of spiritual salvation—but are thoroughly incapable of embracing it when it is offered.

—Alexander G. Gonzalez

THE PLEASURES OF IMAGINATION.
Poem by Mark Akenside, 1744; revised edition, 1772.

The Pleasures of Imagination, Mark Akenside's major poetic work, was, in its first version, a youthful production (he was 22 when it was published in 1744). Its command of an individual blank verse is remarkable, achieving a distance from that of Milton or Thomson. Indeed, in his "Design" Akenside acknowledges classical rather than modern influences, the "simple" style of the Greek poets as refined by Virgil and the "familiar epistolary way of Horace," while also paying tribute to Pope's example in the writing of philosophical poetry. But Akenside's subject, "tending almost constantly to admiration and enthusiasm," demands its own style, which he describes as "more open, pathetic and figured."

In thematic terms, his subject, the power of imagination and the principles underlying its operation, leads him initially to derivative elements. The first book sets out the main categories of the imagination and connects them with the Shaftesburian doctrine of an identification of Beauty and Truth. These categories are a triad of the sublime, the wonderful and the fair, clearly derived from Joseph Addison's definition of the pleasures of the imagination as proceeding "from the sight of what is great, uncommon, or beautiful" (*Spectator* 412, 23 June 1712). But Akenside goes beyond Addison in the depth of his investigation of the sources of aesthetic pleasure, and he also seeks to demonstrate the principles poetically as well as simply defining them. Hence the sublime is rendered in the mind's "resistless ardour to embrace / Majestic forms, impatient to be free, / Spurning the gross controul of wilful might," and the fair (or beautiful) through an evocation of the classical vale of Tempe. Significantly in view of the tendency of later aesthetic thought to pay particular attention to the power of the sublime, it is actually the beautiful which receives most extensive treatment, for it is this principle which allows the Platonic / Shaftesburian connection with moral categories. Beauty is the "lovely ministress of Truth and Good," and forms with them an indissoluble trinity. The elevation of Akenside's vision is marked by a rising scale of nature which measures physical forms as, ultimately, inferior to those of the mind: "Mind, mind alone . . . / The living fountain in itself contains / Of beauteous and sublime." The imagination is thus most strongly stimulated by ideals, such as virtuous friendship or devotion to liberty of the kind manifested in Brutus. Since God is the highest truth, that scientific knowledge which teaches us of the wonders of creation is the most important imaginative power in our observation of such beautiful objects as a rainbow.

Book 2 takes the passions as its chief topic, emphasizing their force and their truth ("Nature speaks / Her genuine language") even when the feelings are of sorrow, as Akenside attempts to illustrate in an extensive allegory. But it is the third book, with its lengthy analysis of the processes of poetic creation, which provides the most significant and influential of Akenside's ideas. The poet, as Akenside himself demonstrates in the course of the poem, synthesizes the beauty of nature and the power of the mind, a synthesis of physical and mental directly related to that at the centre of Akenside's definition of imagination. The creative processes include associationism and memory, and the act of creation itself is a "Promethean art" by which the poet "Into its proper vehicle . . . breathes / The fair conception." Thus, in this high estimation of creative activity, the poet is related to the divine principle.

These ideas, which have come to be (often all too lazily) associated with "romanticism," undergo some re-definition in the later version of the poem which Akenside left unfinished at his death in 1770. The Addisonian triad is reduced, no doubt under the influence of Edmund Burke's *A Philosophical Enquiry into the Origin of Our Ideas of the Sublime and Beautiful* (1757–59), to two. The sublime and the fair are now given their source directly in God, rather than in the mind. Thus Akenside is moving in the direction of a dialectic between human and divine vision rather than, as in 1744, between internal and external pleasures. Similarly, the subject matter of Book 2 is located more clearly within human and divine frames of reference, with God's will as the "perfect virtue" to which all human creation aspires. A fragment (130 lines) of a new Book 4 contains the most intriguing development of Akenside's ideas. Here a renewed, eloquent paean to the powers of the poet (or bard, as Akenside now says) to shape and control place and time is both connected to divine creativity ("His prevailing hand / Gives to corporeal essence life and sense") and made to emerge from Akenside's account of his own early experiences of the beauties of nature in his native Northumberland. An act of memory brings the poet close to those moral lessons which "fix'd the colour of my mind / For ev'ry future year," lessons granted when "all alone, for many a summer's day, / I wander'd thro' your calm recesses, led / In silence by some pow'rful hand unseen." Rather than casting Akenside in the simplifying mould of a "romantic precursor," we should recognize the two versions of *The Pleasures of Imagination* as valuable 18th-century aesthetic documents and poems of achievement which question conventional categories of literary history.

—W.B. Hutchings

THE PLOUGH AND THE STARS.
Play by Sean O'Casey, 1926.

The Plough and the Stars was first performed at the Abbey Theatre to angry audiences, outraged by Sean O'Casey's irreverent treatment of the Easter Rising of 1916. The title refers to the flag of the Irish Citizen Army, a paramilitary group formed to defend Irish workers during the great lock-out of 1913. Under the leadership of James Connolly (who was shot by the British for his role in the Rising), the Irish Citizen Army joined forces with other paramilitary organizations to launch the Rising.

Set in the slums of Dublin before and during the Easter Rising, *The Plough and the Stars* dramatizes a world receding into chaos. What has not been achieved by poverty is accomplished by the insurrection: the immediate dangers of street fighting accelerate the physical and spiritual decay inherent in tenement life. By shooting at the people who, for the most part, appear indifferent to their patriotic appeals, and by provoking the shelling and occupation of Dublin by the British, the Irish Nationalists in the play make an already difficult life intolerable for the tenement dwellers.

As O'Casey presents them, the Nationalists have a negative but energizing sense of history. The Voice in Act II, whose words are borrowed snippets from Patrick Pearse, one of the executed leaders of the rebellion, consistently presents a death-involved version of the past as the basis for action in the present. The Voice views Irish history as a seesawing between English outrage and abortive Irish risings: "they [the British] have left us our Fenian dead, and while Ireland holds these graves, Ireland, unfree, shall never be at peace." This is a view that not only tolerates, but courts death as a means of renewing the wounds and pain of foreign occupation. The Voice believes that the Nationalists' ultimate purpose, the independence of Ireland, need not be realized for them to be successful. From the Voice's evocation of the Fenian dead and his reliance on the imagery of blood sacrifice, it is clear that the shedding of blood constitutes an immediate and desirable goal. *The Plough* presents the Rising as the logical consequence of this view of Irish history.

The dramatic center of the play is not, however, the Rising, but the disastrous intersection of this moment of historical crisis with the lives of the economically deprived and politically naive characters. Although the majority of characters in *The Plough* implicitly oppose the Rising, preferring to loot rather than to fight, they are unable to resist the force of events, and they are unable to alter the unnecessarily destructive effects of those events on themselves. The resulting casualties, mainly from war, but also from poverty, are Jacobean in scope: Mollser, dead of tuberculosis; Jack and Nora's baby, stillborn; Jack, Bessie, and Langon, dead in the fighting; Nora, mad; Fluther, Brennan, Uncle Peter, and the Covey, taken prisoner; the house, occupied. When the curtain comes down, victorious British soldiers are sipping tea and singing, with unconscious irony, "Keep the Home Fires Burning" in Bessie's otherwise deserted room, while Dublin, revealed in the window at the rear of the stage, burns.

It is not surprising that, despite great comic moments, high points like the fight in the pub, or Bessie and Mrs. Gogan's shoving match for possession of the looted pram, a sense of depletion, of wasted talent, and unfulfilled potential, permeates the play. While many of the characters in *The Plough* embrace life, their actions remain isolated gestures of affirmation that lack positive consequences. O'Casey, in fact, suggests that these characters are handicapped not only by external conditions of poverty and war, but by their own attitudes. Their most debilitating attitudes involve the related concepts of time and change. Most of the characters have only the most superficial sense of living in history. For example, Jack Clitheroe, who goes out on Easter Monday with the Citizen Army, is the character most likely to interpret history in the same way as the Speaker. But Jack is motivated by personal vanity, not by public concerns. The Covey's professed socialism is the closest any of the characters comes to seeing his or her life as part of a larger historical sequence distinct from the Nationalist vision. Yet the Covey's socialism is less an expression of ideological commitment than it is an infantile game of intellectual one-upmanship.

The characters not only lack a sustaining view of history, but, like the Voice in Act II, they are obsessed by a consciousness of imminent death. Perhaps the most transparent and self-defeating strategy for camouflaging the fear of death is Mrs. Gogan's perverse habit of celebrating it. Violent death sanctioned by an angry God features prominently in the comments of Bessie and Peter. This obsession with death diverts the characters not only from protesting their intolerable economic conditions, but from developing even a minimal opposition to the patriotic frenzy that, at the very least, might have stopped Jack from fighting and kept Nora from going mad. In concentrating on the ubiquitous presence of both natural and violent death without seriously addressing the possibility of social amelioration as a partial solution, these characters increasingly paralyze themselves.

Having been pushed by their intellectual and economic limitations, and by the force of events, to the periphery of history, there the characters make their strongest commitment to decency, compassion, and fellow-feeling. Nora braves the bullets looking for Jack; and Fluther, alarmed that Nora has gone off into the fighting, ignores the danger in the streets in an effort to find her. As the fighting intensifies and Nora goes into premature labour, Bessie volunteers to go outside to find a doctor. Unfortunately, these gestures of human-heartedness have little effect in conditions of such radical disintegration. They do, however, suggest a reservoir of goodness in the characters, reserves that they ought to have been able to use for their own collective benefit instead of squandering them in futile gestures.

—Bernice Schrank

POEMS OF 1912–13.
Poems by Thomas Hardy, 1914.

In these lyrics, written in the months immediately following his first wife's death, Thomas Hardy, the most private of major poets, drops the pose of philosophical detachment that he maintains in his earlier lyric poems and deals directly and powerfully with the complex emotions that his loss has occasioned. Although his headnote for the poems is "Veteris vestigia flammae," which he translates as "relics of the old fire," the surprise for Hardy is that the love he once felt for this woman has now burst once again into intense flame. After years of emotional estrangement from her, he now remembers the beautiful and free-spirited young woman whom he had fallen in love with, and he bitterly regrets the blindness and carelessness that led to their forgetting that love.

Hardy was later to say that he had never written so many poems in so short a space of time and that he felt in those days that he was "in flower" though "his flowers were sad colored." He added, "A loss like that makes one's brain vocal." Certainly the variety of verse forms, some experimental for Hardy, the intriguing shifts in point of view, and the simplicity and directness of the language and imagery suggest that these poems are a more immediate expression of emotion than the philosophically abstract lyrics he had earlier produced. Indeed, Hardy went through much soul-searching before including these poems in the 1914 collection *Satires of Circumstance*, and his decision to publish them marked a new stage in his career as lyric poet.

Although Hardy does not attempt to impose a dramatic or philosophical structure on the collection, the poems are best considered as a whole, not as separate works. Indeed much of their power and comprehensibility depends on their cumulative effect. His use of shifting points of view, for example, allows a complexity of emotional and psychological development that a consistent point of view would not. Of the 21 poems, six are apostrophes addressed by the husband to the dead wife; more curiously, three are spoken by the spirit of the dead woman; nine are first-person accounts of the man's experience without the woman he has lost, many of them stimulated by a visit to the places in Cornwall where he had first known her; and three are written in the third person, providing a somewhat more objective view of the experience and the people involved. Each of these points of view has its own purposes and advantages: in the apostrophes to the dead wife, we see both the power of the speaker's passion and the intensity of his regret and loneliness as in this concluding section from "The Going":

> Well, well! All's past amend, Unchangeable. It
> must go.
> I seem but a dead man held on end
> To sink down soon.

The poems we hear in the voice of the wife's spirit are more distant, more chilling in their finality, as in the conclusion of "His Visitor" when she returns to find her house so changed that she must "rejoin the roomy silence, and the mute and manifold / Souls of old." In the other first-person poems, we find the man struggling with the irony of a world that goes on despite his loss, as in "A Circular" that comes to announce the season's fashion to a woman "in a shroud." Finally, the third-person poems provide an outside view of matters, as in "The Phantom Horsewoman" in which Hardy has a speaker describe him as a man of queer ways whose inner visions grow stronger as his body withers. These poems introduce a strongly personal lyric voice in Hardy's work, but their greater significance lies in the fact that, as F.B. Pinion has observed, they "comprise the most genuine love-elegy in the English language."

—Wade Jennings

THE PORTRAIT OF A LADY.
Novel by Henry James, 1881.

The Portrait of a Lady is the culminating work of Henry James's early period, a quintessential Victorian novel that yet adumbrates those particular qualities, architectonic and narrative, that James contributed to the development of the 20th-century novel.

The reader can perceive the older and newer impulses at work by comparing chapters 6 and 42. In chapter 6 a confidential narrator offers an analytic verbal portrait of Isabel Archer, enjoining the reader's indulgence and sympathy for a young heroine in whom theories may take the place of knowledge of the world, whose self-esteem may cause her to believe too much in her own opinion, and whose idealism and innocence may lead her into complexities she little anticipates. In short, "her errors and delusions were frequently such as a biographer interested in preserving the dignity of his subject must shrink from specifying." Not only the narrative manner in such a passage, but also James's theme is Victorian, the marriage market and the relationship of money to marital options. Will money bring Isabel freedom of choice or make her an object of social predators? What effect has money upon her own imagination? In chapter 42, which James notes in his retrospective preface as "obviously the best thing in the book," Isabel sits by the fire pondering what her husband has asked of her this evening, examining her marriage: "It was very well to undertake to give him a proof of loyalty; the real fact was that the knowledge of his expecting a thing raised a presumption against it. It was as if he had had the evil eye; as if his presence were a blight and his favour a misfortune. Was the fault in himself or only in the deep mistrust she had conceived for him? This mistrust was now the clearest result of their short married life; a gulf had opened between them over which they looked at each other with eyes that were on either side a declaration of the deception suffered." Here the action has moved inward, the point of view focused in the heroine's own consciousness, and the range of vision narrowed to what she herself can see and interpret. Question replaces answer, metaphor supersedes explicit statement, as Isabel searches for the similitude that will convey her intuitions and feelings. Such a passage is nearer to the late James in point of view and figurative language, and anticipates the 20th-century psychological novel which his own subtler experimentation fostered at the turn of the century.

The carefully crafted structure also looks to the later James. In his celebrated Preface to *The Portrait of a Lady*, written for the definitive New York Edition of his works, James has much to say about the architectonics of his novel, how he laid it brick by brick, building it outward from the initial perception of the character of Isabel Archer by devising those relations with other characters and those settings which would best reveal his heroine. "Such is the aspect that to-day *The Portrait* wears for me: a structure reared with an '*architectural*' competence . . . that makes it, to the author's own sense, the most proportioned of all my productions after *The Ambassadors*."

The Portrait of a Lady is also the crowning work, from his early period, in James's development of his theme of international contrast. Its plot is very simple and has been recognized as that of a fairy tale, in which the heroine must choose among three suitors; her fortunes must depend thereafter upon the wisdom of her choice. The first two suitors, Caspar Goodwood, an American businessman, and Lord Warburton, an English aristocrat, manifest national as well as personal characteristics, the dangers of ruthless self-assertiveness and of hereditary forms and obligations. Isabel's chosen suitor, Gilbert Osmond, is an American living abroad, who has absorbed effete and corrupt aspects of European civilization together with European aestheticism and sophistication. He becomes the principal foil for Isabel's new-world virtues of enthusiasm, innocence, and aspiration. Secondary characters, Mme. Merle, who betrays Isabel into this marriage, and Henrietta Stackpole, who remains her friend despite it, define similar polarities. Isabel's fate is left in the balance at the end. Having chosen wrongly, will she desert her husband or slavishly perpetuate the form of an empty marriage? Will she live by the memory of her deceased cousin Ralph Touchett, whom she now perceives as beloved? Or for the sake of her stepdaughter Pansy Osmond, to preclude a similar fate for her?

"The obvious criticism," James wrote in his *Notebooks*, "will be that it is not finished—that I have not seen the heroine to the end of her situation. . . . That is both true and false. The *whole* is never told; you can only take what groups together." Here again James analyzes his own salient qualities, his concern with form and the characteristic open-endedness of his fictions.

—Jean Frantz Blackall

A PORTRAIT OF THE ARTIST AS A YOUNG MAN.
Novel by James Joyce, 1916.

A Portrait of the Artist as a Young Man is a *Bildungsroman* depicting the development of James Joyce's semi-autobiographical persona, Stephen Dedalus. In subject the work is a typical novel of education. Stephen's problems are those of any adolescent rebelling against authority. His aim is to achieve some personal authenticity. But Stephen's typical problems take on a firmly particular cast from their setting, late Victorian Dublin. The struggle for Home Rule, the death of Parnell (leader of the Irish parliamentary caucus), and the church's disputed involvement in his fall, are key issues of Stephen's childhood. So is the nationalist Gaelic League of his young manhood. Stephen will not join, taking the view that programmatic allegiances limit individual freedom, and that in any case Ireland betrays those who fight for her. Irish history and politics is one net Stephen must evade to achieve his freedom. Another is rigorist Catholicism. Stephen's Jesuit education shapes his adolescence. Intellectually it gives him a framework of thought from Aristotle and Aquinas which is helpful in its rigour, though its particular conceptions are later inadequate to his needs. For Stephen's developing sexual feeling the Catholic ambience is more problematic. The traditional Catholic view of eternal punishment for sin is articulated in a fearsome sermon on the torments of Hell (which Joyce drew from a 17th-century Italian sermon actually translated in Dublin in 1868). This sermon causes Stephen to feel total self-revulsion and a sense of guilt which issues for some time in complete sexual abstinence. The context of traditional Catholicism gives a particular and highly intensified shape to what is fundamentally a typical adolescent problem.

Though Stephen is in part any adolescent boy in a particular setting the novel is also "a portrait of the artist." Writing, too, therefore, is central. From the beginning Stephen has a special fascination with language—the sounds and suggestions of individual words, and the music of verbal patterns. Later the novel depicts the experience behind a piece of Stephen's writing, the process of composition, and the finished poem—which is probably in Joyce's terms a failure, musically beautiful but formulaic: it excludes all that is ordinary in the originating experience, as Joyce's own art does not. Stephen is also shown as the inevitably selfconscious modern artist working out his own aesthetic ideals. For Stephen art is static, not kinetic—it does not cause either desire or loathing. Art has therefore no didactic moral function, as it had for most English 19th-century novelists. This apparent doctrine of art for art's sake is qualified by Stephen's own literary responses. He is helped in being anti-Victorian and internationalist by his favourite writers: Byron and Shelley—rebels, outcasts and heretics; Ibsen and Flaubert—morally scandalous and formally experimental. It is clear, too, from Joyce's letters that Joyce thought of his own work as having at least an oblique moral function through what it revealed. The nicely polished looking-glass of *Dubliners* is a first step towards the spiritual liberation of Ireland; Joyce is attempting to create "a conscience in the soul of this wretched race." The same thought is Stephen's final flourish. But true art is in no sense propagandist. For Stephen, "the artist, like the God of creation remains . . . invisible, refined out of existence, indifferent." It is a doctrine of impersonality which Joyce derived from Flaubert, and which arguably *A Portrait*'s complex play of sympathy and irony around Stephen does not wholly carry out. The aspect of aesthetics which Stephen does not discuss in *A Portrait*, though it is central to its earlier form, *Stephen Hero*, is the theory of the epiphany—by which Joyce meant a sudden revelation of something in the objective world, or moment of subjective realisation, which the artist transcribes. Whether Stephen does not discuss this because by the time of *A Portrait* Joyce thought the theory less important, or whether he thought it so important that it was too good for the young Stephen, is a matter of dispute. The religious terminology (Joyce also referred to the epiphany as "eucharistic") indicates how much Stephen's sense of himself as artist is related to the vocation he experiences for the priesthood. It is to a considerable degree the aesthetic aspects of the church that attract Stephen. He rejects the church for art because the artist is a superior priest, not the interpreter of a particular theology but "a priest of the eternal imagination."

Though traditional in its subject, *A Portrait* is experimental in mode, style, and structure. The experimental mode is particularly evident if the novel is compared with *Stephen Hero*. *Stephen Hero* follows Joyce's actual biography with less shaping than *A Portrait*, and Joyce is present in it as a narrative voice directing the reader's responses. In *A Portrait* there is no commentating voice. Authorial commentary is oblique, through implications of structure, tone, and imagery. *A Portrait* is also experimental in style. Joyce registers a child's point of view in diction and syntax, by seeing at times from within the young Stephen's partial comprehension, and by not differentiating the actual world of the fiction from Stephen's fantasies. At times the reader is presented with indicative tableaux and left to extrapolate a relevance to the whole. The work ends with a fragmentary diary which is particularly open in its implications. Though it has no plot *A Portrait* is carefully shaped. Each chapter rises to a climax of some success for Stephen which the next reflects back on from a different perspective (though not, as is sometimes argued, one necessarily ironic of Stephen). A similar potential shift of perspective attends the novel's symbolism. Stephen sees his extraordinary name as a prophecy: he is Daedalus, the imaginative builder. He can be seen, too, as the overweening son, Icarus, who flies too high and is destroyed. As with many modernist open texts the reader is involved in constructing meaning. Clearly Stephen is in some degree Joyce himself. The title tells us this, and scholarship can tell us more: Stephen's views on aesthetics, for example, are derived from Joyce's Paris and Pola notebooks (now published in his *Critical Writings*). Clearly too the author is not entirely to be identified with his fictional persona. But just how each reader judges the final degree of sympathy and irony is one of the work's most vexed interpretative questions.

—David Fuller

PREFACE TO LYRICAL BALLADS.
Prose by William Wordsworth, 1800.

William Wordsworth's Preface to *Lyrical Ballads*, a collection of poems produced by Coleridge and himself in 1798, was first published with the 1800 Second Edition as a considerable expansion of the First Edition's short preliminary "Advertisement." Further and final additions appeared in 1802.

This prose piece is in part defensive, aiming to deflect received and anticipated criticism of the seemingly unrhetorical language with which the Ballads, and Wordsworth's contributions in particular, render "incidents and situations from common life" by depicting uniquely humble characters in their natural rural environment.

It also forms, however, a calculated manifesto which spurns the affected phrase-making and elevated jargon of 18th-century poetic diction, seeking to liberate as the poet's medium "the real language of men in a state of vivid sensation."

In the opening lines, the Preface recognises that the poems will seem to many "materially different" from what might be expected in "the present state of the public taste" and, after admitting that he and Coleridge will be breaking the formal contract of poetic expectation, Wordsworth begins to outline their object of reclaiming poetry as the appropriate affective means of exploring primary experience unconstrained by social pretension and, thereby, of reaching more towards a comprehension of the nature and growth of the human spirit in organic sympathy with the natural world which sustains it.

The Preface is thus a primary text of the English Romantic endeavour and self-consciously seeks to attain a purifying of the affections and an ennobling of that nexus of sensibility where feeling and thought are made immanent of each other —a dismissal of Augustan binary assumptions which surprisingly permits an almost atavistic continuity with the early 17th century metaphysicals.

Wordsworth also newly celebrates the poet as the rightful "upholder and preserver" of this theory of intense recognition, thus aligning his apologia with Shelley's later "Defence" of poets as "the unacknowledged legislators of the world." And here also, in its less philosophical stretches, the Preface asserts the primacy of poetry, or more accurately metre, over prose, articulates new challenges for a reinvigorated poetic diction, and distinguishes this authentic enterprise from the increasingly stultified verse of the 18th century.

The essay may be seen, in retrospect, as holding a distinctive place in the lineage of English critical theory. Despite its ostensible reaction against the poetry of immediately previous generations, some of its most pertinent claims on behalf of the poet closely echo Pope's praise, some 90 years before, of the writer of that which "oft was thought but ne'er so well express'd" in the *Essay on Criticism* and middle passages of the Preface seem to reach back, in their authentication of the sensibility of pleasure, to Sidney's 16th-century *Defence of Poesy*.

There again, in its own short passages involving "practical criticism" of stanzas by Gray, Johnson, and Cowper and in its psychological probing of the way in which "language and the human mind act and react," the theories, some one hundred years on, of I.A. Richards seem to be as present as the more obvious contemporary indebtedness to the claims of the associationist school of psychology pioneered by David Hartley and particularly influential on Coleridge's *Biographia Literaria*, which should stand with Wordsworth's Preface as the twin gates of expositional access to English Romanticism.

Though the Preface is in no way overtly political, it resonates with the reactions of the times. The enfranchising of, to use Wordsworth's own phrase, a new "class of Poetry" and poetic subject might be seen as an appropriate and an inevitable outcome of a decade which had seen the young Lakeside intellectuals intense with the implications of continental revolution.

But the Preface registers an evolutionary, rather than a revolutionary, movement and Wordsworth's celebration of metrical form, which dominates the concluding sections of the Preface and which, he argues, creates the only qualitative distinction between poetry and prose, derives from metre's provision of regulation and security amidst the contingencies of a wilful vocabulary and subjective impressions. Metre thus may measure and portend the "sense sublime" that "rolls through all things," as articulated in Wordsworth's most profound Lyrical Ballad, "Lines Composed a Few Miles above Tintern Abbey . . .," and thus does the technical analysis within the Preface determine upon a "similitude in dissimilitude" or a "tempering and restraining" of its otherwise revolutionary subject.

Wordsworth's manifesto may be distinguished in heralding a new poetic sensibility and method but it thus retains the consolation of formal regularity as well as of a, literally, informing historicism or conservative regress. The poet's work necessarily emanates from an evolving process of retrospection and reflection; the "overflow of powerful feelings" may be "spontaneous" but the contributory emotions must be "recollected" and the poet must be affected "more than other men by absent things as of present." Even the most vivid thoughts are primarily "representatives of all our past feelings" and there is an intuitively conserving impulse to secure the present by the past.

It is this process of recollection, with the metrical distancing of the apprehension from the original experience, which ultimately identifies Wordsworth's literary liberation more as that of the poet's own mind than of any truly authentic or naturalistic depiction of the minds of "real men" which is the Preface's perhaps patronising intent. The "gaudiness and inane phraseology" may have been stripped from the verse as a corrective to the recent degradation of poetic diction which is closely narrated in the final passages of the Preface. However the poet's "principle of selection" will also eliminate all that is "painful or disgusting in the passion" and thus, some might suppose, render the experience of such characters as Michael hostage to the stylising impulses of Wordsworth's ennobling sentiments.

There is little here of that probing towards the naturalistic, gradually encouraged by the 19th century's other great literary evolution, that of the novel, which, to the Preface, is a "frantic" form. Nor, even, will such a theory of "emotion recollected in tranquillity" lend itself to the singular voice of the dramatic monologue which awaited the liberating rhythms of Browning.

The tendency to solipsism is, instead, latent in the ordination of the new poet here described and the perhaps inevitable move during the next decades was from the poet Wordsworth as "a man speaking to men" to the poet speaking in *The Prelude; or, Growth of a Poet's Mind* to and of himself but with such a resonant and empathetic self-rendering as would lay claim to any sensitive mind's accord.

—Paul J. Smith

THE PRELUDE.
Poem by William Wordsworth, 1850 (written from 1798).

For generations of readers (and for writers as various as Virginia Woolf and Matthew Arnold) William Wordsworth's *The Prelude* has had the power to make clever literary artifice seem trivial. At one point in the poem, Wordsworth dismisses scornfully what he calls the "quick turns / Of self-applauding intellect"—and it is, instead, with the flux of feelings that this great, slow, serious masterpiece is mainly preoccupied. Accordingly, retrospection is its mode, for Wordsworth attached crucial importance to "past feelings," as he declared in the preface to *Lyrical Ballads*.

The Prelude virtually invented autobiography as we know it. That very word "autobiography" is unrecorded in English before the period when Wordsworth was writing. New words appear when new phenomena need to be labelled; and autobiography, as Wordsworth practised it, seemed startlingly innovative. "It was," Wordsworth commented later, "a thing unprecedented in literary history that a man should write so much about himself." That phrase "so much" applies to more than just its eventual bulk; the process of composition extended over half a century. After beginning work on it in the year when the *Lyrical Ballads* volume was published (1798), Wordsworth kept revising it for much of the rest of his life and left it unpublished when he died in 1850. Thus the significance of this poem is inseparable from its textual history. It first took shape in a version of less than a thousand lines, and this (reconstructed from manuscripts and published only in recent years), gives us the core of what was later amplified to 14 books comprising about 8000 lines.

One might say that the dominant theme in this "core" poem of 1798–99 is the awakening of the imagination through experiences of childhood and adolescence. The proto-*Prelude* records a number of intensely emotional encounters between the poet (as child or youth) and various aspects of his natural environment, moments of heightened awareness that he calls "spots of time," through which his imaginative capacities seemed somehow to be nourished. This is not simply "nature poetry." The external physical world is significant only in relation to the poet's inquiry into his own nature as one who sees himself both as representative of other people and also as set apart from them by a special literary vocation. To uncover and explain the life of his own mind, the lines of development that led to the person who writes about them: the poet's desire to do this is apparently a basic impulse of his initial composition. However, with the subsequent process of textual elaboration, *The Prelude* reaches for images that might sustain a grander structure. In the opening passage of the enlarged Book 1, the poet-narrator seeks to orient himself both within the world of nature and within a literary tradition. These lines transform, through several specific allusions, the closing sentence of Milton's *Paradise Lost*, and at the same time situate their speaker in a landscape where directions are unclear. What kind of figure is this "I," and what will be his trajectory through the poem?

The structure of *The Prelude* (in its final 1850 version) has been described by some critics as a quest, and there is something of that in it—a search for poetic enlightenment. Framed thus, the poem might be read as having two main stages, each climaxing in a "peak" revelatory experience: the crossing of the Simplon Pass (Book 6), which produced a sense of intense apocalyptic bafflement, and the climbing of Snowden (Book 14), which produced a final visionary illumination. But "quester" can hardly encompass the figural permutations of the protagonist's manifold selfhood. Even within the first hundred lines or so of Book 1, he has already represented himself as a kind of priest, truant, fugitive, pilgrim, labourer, and hermit. These shifts in self-characterisation are part of a more general fluctuation between two different language registers. One of them draws on the local speech of a rustic environment, using simple and regionally particular locutions that approach "the language of conversation in the middle and lower classes of society" (the formula that Wordsworth proposed in his preface to *Lyrical Ballads*). Alternating with that, the other register draws on an elevated cultural heritage represented stylistically by the sonorous blank verse patterns, elaborate syntax, and rich diction of Miltonic and Shakespearian poetry. The narrator is placing himself and his implied readership partly within that formal, prestigious tradition in the very act of declaring a certain measure of independence from it. This ambiguous cultural situation, intricately linked to several social changes in late 18th- and early 19th-century England, underlies the motile relations between *The Prelude* and a number of established literary genres and rhetorical practices: philosophical verse essay, effusive ode, elevated epistle, distended lyric, Miltonic epic, pastoral idyll, rustic rumination, topographical sketch—elements of these forms all mingle in ways that to Augustan taste would have seemed indecorous if not downright incongruous, along with newer forms, notably the intimate "conversation poem" recently invented by Coleridge (to whom *The Prelude* is addressed). Against that varied background the irresolute wanderer of Wordsworth's poem repeatedly allegorises his historical situation as writer and as self-marginalised countryman.

—Ian Reid

PRIDE AND PREJUDICE.
Novel by Jane Austen, 1813.

Despite the spate of scholarship that has demonstrated otherwise, *Pride and Prejudice* for the general reader remains and is likely to continue to remain a romantic love story with a Cinderella conclusion in which the provincial heroine marries one of the most eligible bachelors of the realm. Jane Austen's own depreciation of her art as carved on "two inches of ivory" has permitted readers to look upon her fictional world as well-constructed conventional romance. The cult of "Janeites" has contributed over the years to an image of a kindly maiden aunt amateurishly working away in the quietude of familial domesticity. Forever imprinted on the minds of movie-goers who have relished the acting of Laurence Olivier and Greer Garson is a *Pride and Prejudice* expressing a charming love story. The novel itself belies the absurdities of such notions.

Pride and Prejudice is a realistic portrayal of a particular segment of late 18th-century society, its conventions, and its values. Austen begins by focusing on the injustices of an entail system that denies inheritance to female heirs. She exposes the desperation of women whose sole assurance of security resides in the marriage contract. When a woman of Charlotte Lucas's intelligence must be grateful for the opportunity to ally herself to an unmitigated fool like Mr. Collins, the cruel values of a social system are given a human face. For all Mrs. Bennet's gaucherie, she may be forgiven the urgency that she feels about marrying off five daughters whose doweries would not satisfy a travelling salesman. However attractive Mr. Bennet's wit, his callousness concerning the young women's plight, as his daughter Elizabeth comes to recognize, is less than admirable. The coming to town of a contingent of soldiers and the holding of a festive ball by which unmarried young ladies may be able to make matches may not be earthshaking events like the Industrial and French Revolutions of the time, but in the society that Austen depicts, they are no less realistic. Austen's realism may be different from the truths expressed in the panoramic novels of such predecessors as Fielding and Smollett, but it is equally honest and faithful to the world with which she was concerned.

Unlike the titles of those works of earlier writers that bore the names of their heroes, Austen's title conveys its theme, which is the exploration of the values being challenged by the actual merging of social classes taking place in the period. Elizabeth Bennet's relations with Darcy and, to a lesser extent, Jane Bennet's with Bingley allow Austen to examine the psychological struggle that accompanies the union of the bourgeoisie with the aristocracy. Both sides are bound by familial connections and loyalties; pride and prejudice are not the exclusive province of either side. To accept Darcy as a suitor requires Elizabeth to forgive him for his opinions of her family, particularly, but not exclusively, Mrs. Bennet. She is too intelligent not to recognize her mother's vulgarity, but there is no way that she is willing to deny the connection for to do so would be to deny part of herself. Darcy, conscious of his own worth and proud of his heritage, desires Elizabeth, recognizes her qualities, admires her independence, but cannot tolerate her family; still, he, too, must deny the truth about his connections.

Austen's skillful handling of her narrative provides a resolution that ultimately allows her main characters to place individual worth above family connections. If Elizabeth is burdened by her mother, Darcy cannot escape the vulgarity of his aunt, Lady Catherine de Bourgh. When Elizabeth's sister Lydia falls prey to the wily Wickham and brings disgrace to the Bennets, it is no more than Darcy has experienced through his sister's betrayal by the same villain. If Darcy's side is over-matched by a comparison of the gross conduct of Bingley's sisters with the generosity and honesty of Elizabeth's aunt and uncle, let alone the goodness of Jane, Elizabeth herself cannot escape the connection with Collins and the foolishness of her younger sisters. In the end the two lovers must come to realize that their relationship is more important than their connections and must reconcile themselves to the truth if they are to find happiness with each other. Austen does not offer them an easy solution.

Austen's artistry is most evident in her use of point of view to create the realism of her characterization while offering her strong social statement. An omniscient author, from the opening sentence, allows for ironic comment. Still, the focus is on Elizabeth. In the beginning this develops slowly, providing both suspense and credibility. Caught up in her own pride and prejudice, Elizabeth early in the novel cannot be trusted as a judge, particularly of Darcy's feelings. Ultimately, she moves away from the cynicism that engulfs her father; she acknowledges the falsity of her judgment of Wickham; she understands herself and Darcy as she moves to maturity.

Unquestionably a delightful story, filled with unforgettable characters, and gratifying in its conclusion, *Pride and Prejudice* is much more than that. It combines romance with a sensitive portrait of a young woman's development and offers an honest and realistic depiction of a change in English society as it affected people in their everyday lives.

—Robert D. Spector

A PRIEST TO THE TEMPLE.
See **THE COUNTRY PARSON.**

THE PRIME OF MISS JEAN BRODIE.
Novel by Muriel Spark, 1961.

It was an index of the reputation that Muriel Spark's first six novels published in just three years had gained her that the *New Yorker* printed her seventh complete in one issue in 1961. The fact also points to its brevity: 128 paperback pages. Nevertheless, the narrative's chronological time span (1930 to at least 1959) and the complexity of the social, political, ethical, and theological issues which it raises make it a major work. Furthermore, a stage adaptation, a film, and a television series helped within a few years to make its principal character a byword. It is interesting to speculate as to why a vain, self-deceiving woman with confused religious views and extremely silly political opinions should appeal so much to such a wide public.

The Prime of Miss Jean Brodie deals with an Edinburgh schoolteacher in her forties who has decided that she is in her "prime." (It would be hard not to associate this with menopause.) She is at loggerheads with Marcia Blaine's School for Girls, where she teaches, over her approach to her work. She despises science and maths, values poetry and fine art above them, and devotes educational time to telling her charges about her holidays in Italy (she greatly admires the dictator Mussolini) and of her, perhaps wholly imaginary, fiancé, slain in World War I. A group of six 10-year-old girls, around 1930, become her "set" of favourites, and keep in touch with her.

The "story" (which jumps backward and forward) takes us down to the eve of World War II, when one of her group, Sandy Stranger, "betrays" her, informing her headmistress of the improper influence which Brodie had exercised on a fellow pupil whom she encouraged to go to work for Fascism in Spain, where she was killed. Brodie is dismissed. There are flashes forward to much later events, post-war, from which we learn that none of the "Brodie girls" achieved the elevated roles in life, involving aesthetic dedication or missionary self-sacrifice, that she had urged on them.

A great deal of the novel is concerned with "sex"—a subject which Sandy and her friend Jenny Gray at one stage study with absorbed prepubescent fascination. Miss Brodie "loves" Teddy Lloyd, the school's one-armed art teacher, but since he is married she rebounds upon the feckless but rich music master, Lowther, whose mistress she becomes. She wills her pretty pupil, Rose Stanley, whom she imagines as a future artist's model, to sleep with Lloyd as a surrogate for herself. Instead, it is Sandy, the clever one with piggy little eyes who goes to bed with him, before betraying Miss Brodie and then entering a convent.

This complex tale has betrayal as its main theme. Sandy's motivations are not fully clarified—and are perhaps impossible to clarify. (Sandy's point of view is privileged during much of the narrative, yet it is made clear that her memory and her vision of events may both be unreliable.) Though Miss Brodie's pro-Hitler politics are distasteful to her, a developing religious commitment is surely more weighty in Sandy's betrayal. She believes that Brodie herself has betrayed her "set." She has elevated herself as a false prophet, antinomian, above the moral law: her authoritarian political views are related to the Calvinist belief, still entrenched in the Scottish psyche, that some people are "elect," others unsaved. However, Brodie does not even have the merit of possessing coherent theological views.

This is Spark's only novel set in her native city, Edinburgh, to which, in exile, she claims to remain deeply attached. (Indeed, it is her only novel set in Scotland, though *The Ballad of Peckham Rye* has a Scottish protagonist derived from Scottish notions of diabolism.) Brodie stands clearly within the Scottish tradition. The protagonist claims descent from a famous Edinburgh criminal of the late 18th century, a Deacon of his Guild and Town Councillor who was respectable tradesman by day, robber by night. Deacon Brodie, though a historic figure, relates to famous antinomian and "double" characters in Scottish literature: to Burns's hypocritical "Holy Willie," Hogg's extraordinary *Justified Sinner* and to Stevenson's *Dr. Jekyll and Mr. Hyde*.

Edinburgh is sharply and richly evoked. Miss Jean is seen in part as a typical Edinburgh spinster of her generation. The city of the 1930's is not spared criticism, with its hideous central slums and the genteel humbug of its middle class. Poverty, unemployment, fascism, war, religion are all handled with serious effect.

But nothing set down so far explains this novel's great popularity. Like all Spark's best work, it has room for wit, comedy, and beauty. Brodie herself is beautiful. Her affectations in manner and speech are rendered—endearingly—hilarious. Equally funny are the imaginary encounters of young Sandy with such literary personages as Alan Breck, the Lady of Shallot, and Mr. Rochester, and the written attempts by her and Jenny to fictionalise Miss Brodie's life. This very "literary" work "sends up" literature—or a Brodiesque notion of it—"something rotten."

Spark has written: "I don't claim that my novels are truth—I claim that they are fictions out of which a kind of truth emerges. And I keep in my mind that what I am writing is fiction because I am interested in truth—absolute truth." Such "truth," for Spark, must be Roman Catholic truth. But for readers of Brodie who are not Catholic, the effect may be one of "poetic truth," found in passages of acute wit and sudden lyrical intensity. Spark's earliest ambition as a writer was to be a poet. Her intricate, teasing narrative in *The Prime of Miss Jean Brodie*, and her refusal to clarify, omnisciently, what exactly it signifies, suggest that she still considers poetry to be a superior form to fiction.

—Angus Calder

THE PRISONER OF ZENDA.
Novel by Anthony Hope, 1894.

For many people *The Prisoner of Zenda*'s entitlement to recognition rests on little more than the fact that it introduced the word "Ruritania" into the English language, the name given by Anthony Hope to an imaginary Central European country in which this, his most popular novel, is set. In a sense, this is appropriate for the word "Ruritania" does evoke swashbuckling adventure and amorous intrigue, which reminds us that we should not take Hope's far-fetched plot too seriously. Essentially a fast-moving entertainment, *The Prisoner of Zenda* is unlikely to be regarded as an important milestone in the history of the English novel, yet, while its characters are wooden, its plot is well constructed, and for the social historian it may have some significance as an expression of early 20th-century attitudes.

The idea for *The Prisoner of Zenda* came to Hope, as he tells us in his autobiographical *Memories and Notes*, when the author-barrister was walking back from the Westminster County Court, where he had just won a case. Suddenly, the word "Ruritania" came into his mind as being suitable for a legendary country in which a tale of romantic adventure might be set. Then, seeing two men who bore a remarkable resemblance to one another, the idea of a plot began to grow. Returning to his chambers he mulled over the outlines of a narrative and within a month had completed a first draft.

Hope never took himself seriously as a writer and appears to have viewed his literary career with ironic detachment. Consequently, there is some ambivalence in much of his writing, an unwillingness to commit himself wholeheartedly to the creation of an action-packed story. In *The Prisoner of Zenda*, however, he appears to be sufficiently emotionally involved with his plot and characters to prevent the novel from becoming a virtual parody of the kind of yarn most suited to his literary talents. Rather different is *Rupert of Hentzau*, *The Prisoner of Zenda*'s sequel, where at times Hope seems to be mocking the romantic idealism which the earlier novel upheld.

The Prisoner of Zenda records the adventures of Rupert Rassendyll, a red-haired Englishman of independent means, related to Rudolph of Elphenburg, heir to the throne of Ruritania, whose coronation he decides to attend. The day before the two men are celebrating and Rudolph is drugged by his brother, Black Michael, who also wishes to be king. As a result, Rudolph is unable to attend his own coronation, and the king's faithful friends, Sapt and Fritz, urge Rassendyll to take his place, the two men having a remarkable resemblance to one another. The plan is successful and at first no one suspects the impersonation but eventually Black Michael finds the real king and locks him up in his castle at Zenda. This forces Rassendyll to continue with his masquerade and devise a plan to free him. Meanwhile, he has fallen in love with the Princess Flavia, who is supposed to marry the real king. She is loved by the people and to satisfy them Rassendyll must declare his intention of marrying her. For a moment he is tempted to marry her in earnest and betray the king; however, he resists and devises a plan to free Rudolph instead.

The first attempt to free the king fails but the second achieves its aim, though not according to plan. Rupert of Hentzau, one of Black Michael's bodyguards, is in love with a handsome widow called Antoinette de Mauban, who does not reciprocate his affections, preferring Black Michael instead. This provokes Rupert of Hentzau's jealousy and he kills Black Michael, fleeing into the forest hotly pursued by Rassendyll where they fight and Rassendyll barely escapes with his life. By now the true king is free, which means that the way is open for him to marry Flavia. Rassendyll is still in love with her and for a moment they consider running away together, but Flavia recognizes that her first duty is to her people. Rassendyll returns to England; the royal marriage takes place; peace and security in Ruritania are assured. Even so, the love between Rassendyll and Flavia continues, and every year they exchange single red roses, symbol of their undying love.

Although *The Prisoner of Zenda* is an entertaining story, Rassendyll's self-righteousness; his indifference to other people's suffering; his unquestioning acceptance of the authority of the monarchy, irrespective of the integrity of the man in whom royal power has been invested; his evident unwillingness to respond to Flavia's womanly charms; all these the modern reader will find faintly disquieting. Even so, such jarring features are unlikely to obtrude. What matters are the twists and turns of the plot, the narrow escapes and exciting encounters between good and evil. These are the qualities which have ensured the novel's continuing popularity, and while we may fear momentarily for the well-being of the good characters, the reader has no doubt that in the end virtue will triumph and vice be vanquished.

Thus Hope belongs in that company of early 20th-century writers such as H. Rider Haggard, A.E.W. Mason, and Stanley Weyman, who made names for themselves simply by writing good stories. True, *The Prisoner of Zenda* does have a moral of sorts—that private feeling should be always subordinate to the public good—but this is little more than a reflection of prevailing attitudes and may hardly qualify as an important theme.

—John M. Munro

PRIVATE LIVES.
Play by Noël Coward, 1930.

On its initial reception, *Private Lives* was described by critics as "tenuous," "thin," "brittle," "gossamer," "iridescent," and "delightfully daring." It is enduringly popular.

As Noël Coward said himself, it is a reasonably well-constructed duologue for two experienced performers, with a couple of extra puppets thrown in to assist the plot and to provide contrast. The leads were originally played by Coward himself and by Gertrude Lawrence, with the young Laurence Olivier in the supporting role of Victor.

Elyot and Amanda have, it seems, no jobs and no money worries: they flit about the world at whim, wear good clothes, smoke cigarettes, and indulge in witty badinage. Coward the hard-working dramatist was at pains to make his writing and performing seem effortlessly sophisticated, in an atmosphere of wealth and leisure. The play dramatises the durability and irrationality of sexual desire, and the tendency of lovers to quarrel. Once the artificiality of the initial situation is accepted, the rest follows naturally. Elyot and Amanda were married for three years and were divorced five years before the play opens. They find themselves in adjoining suites in an hotel in France on their second honeymoons. The balcony setting is an ironic echo of *Romeo and Juliet*. Elyot and Amanda, initially embarrassed, recognize they are still in love and elope: memorably, Elyot says to Amanda:

> You're looking very lovely, you know, in this damned moonlight. Your skin is clear and cool and your eyes are shining, and you're growing lovelier and lovelier every second as I look at you. You don't hold any mystery for me, darling, do you mind? There isn't a particle of you that I don't know, remember, and want.

Amanda replies softly, "I'm glad, my sweet."

This sexual suggestiveness, within the limits of decorum, still has the power to stir and move. As Coward himself admitted, there is little further plot and no further action after Act I, with the exception of the rough and tumble fight between the reunited Elyot and Amanda at the end of Act II. Before it comes a full 40 minutes of dialogue between Amanda and Elyot, which demands alert and sophisticated comedy acting.

Another reason *Private Lives* is loved is that it has such funny lines. Elyot tells Amanda he has met his second wife at a house-party in Norfolk. Amanda replies drily, "Very flat, Norfolk." It is funny because underneath the trite observation lie both Amanda's jealousy and her wish to diminish the events which led to Elyot's second marriage: Norfolk is physically "flat," and Amanda suggests that social events taking place there must of necessity be boring. Yet she is making polite chit-chat, as convention demands. In creating a brittle social world, Coward draws on traditional celebrations of romance, and of society fictions, and tests them. He is the heir of Congreve and Wilde. The bitching between Amanda and Sybil recalls the sparring between Wilde's Gwendolen and Cecily.

The subject of the play is the sex war: Elyot says reprovingly, "It doesn't suit women to be promiscuous." Amanda replies tartly, "It doesn't suit men for women to be promiscuous." Elyot and Amanda are modern and secular: they do not believe in heaven or hell. Amanda's creed is "being kind to everyone, and giving money to old beggar women, and being as gay as possible." Elyot rejects the "quest for ultimate truth" and suggests laughter and flippancy are the best answer to "the futile moralists who try to make life unbearable": yet later he admits to Victor that "flippancy may cover a very real embarrassment." He covers it at one stage by chattering on about a fountain that goes "plopploppploplop." Elyot admits that he and Amanda, too, are laughable, "figures of fun." He echoes Marvell's appeal to his coy mistress and Shakespeare's "youth's a stuff will not endure" when he begs Amanda, "Come and kiss me, darling, before your body rots and worms pop in and out of your eye sockets."

Elyot teases Amanda for her vagueness, when she is trying to justify her reluctance to go to bed with him too soon after dinner: "Chemical what d'you call 'ems: please try to be more explicit." Here a man deals with a rebuff to his virility by taking issue with the language in which the woman's emotion is expressed: mutual misunderstanding delicately dramatised. There is a certain brutality beneath Elyot's polished exterior: "Some women ought to be struck regularly, like gongs." He is astute enough to recognize the brute facts of human nature under the social surface and shrewdly grasps that Amanda and Sybil want their men to fight over them. Elyot is the only character in the play with a sense of irony. He himself is too civilised and rational to fight. He and Amanda epitomise the generation of Bright Young Things (Coward's own term), afraid of sentimentality but still in the grip of their passions.

—Valerie Grosvenor Myer

THE PRIVATE MEMOIRS AND CONFESSIONS OF A JUSTIFIED SINNER.
Novel by James Hogg, 1824.

In *The Private Memoirs and Confessions of a Justified Sinner*, James Hogg, heir to the Border tradition of oral narrative, created a fiction from the stuff of ballads: a tragic tale of murder, of the destruction of a family, of the supernatural. That it is *not* a ballad is a major part of its meaning.

Two half-brothers grow up separately, split by that great division of religion, politics, and culture which dominated the 17th century. Meeting as young men in the party-torn Edinburgh of 1704, the puritanical Robert Wringhim persecutes the sociable, loose-living George Colwan who is eventually found slain. The mystery surrounding his death, on investigation, is found to involve a mysterious friend who does not seem normally human. When the law finally attempts to bring Wringhim to book, he has disappeared. These events are recounted in a lengthy "Editor's Narrative" which introduces the novel proper. The work then goes over the same ground from Wringhim's point of view, and reveals him as a wretched heir of the worst traditions of Protestant extremism: he is brought up to despise other men as damned sinners, yet to fear them for the persecutions his pride and antagonism provoke. Assurance of his salvation coincides with his finding, in the mysterious Gil-Martin, a companion who induces him to murder in the name of his beliefs. As his career of mayhem progresses, and as he increasingly loses his sense of the integrity of his own personality, Wringhim tries to flee Gil-Martin whose haunting becomes increasingly diabolical. Wringhim commits suicide in an isolated corner of the Borders, and over a century later, a mummified corpse is found, buried with the text of *The Private Memoirs and Confessions of a Justified Sinner*. The tale of its finding is recounted in an appendix.

A ballad tells a tale, however extraordinary, with unflinching and unequivocal matter-of-factness: its narrative can be carried by the merest flash of information ("And their hats were o' the birk"). Meaning and emotional power are entirely coincident with a narrative the status of which is never in doubt. In Hogg's novel, the fact, nature, and meaning of every event is in doubt; and all enmeshed in this fiction—characters, "editor" and reader alike—suffer unrelieved (indeed, ever-deepening) uncertainty. At one point as he flees from justice, Wringhim becomes accidentally enmeshed in the threads of a loom: the bizarre image is a key one expressing a baffling and terrifying entrapment. Tormented by the ultimate Christian uncertainty, the destination of his soul, and baffled by the complexities of the moral life, he joyfully commits himself to the extraordinarily destructive certainties of the antinomian. Infinitely worse complexities are thereby unleashed. Hogg's identification of one of Christianity's theological extremes with the Devil himself is but the boldest of many bold ironies in the book.

Essentially, however, this work is not about religion. It is an exploration of the limitations of human certainty, and of the dangers inherent in the romantic cult of morbid individualism. As David Groves argues, Wringhim is to be ranked with the Ancient Mariner, with Prometheus, and with other romantic figures as an explorer of his own individuality. Like them, he increasingly finds that his isolation brings the disintegration of his personality, but for him there is no Mariner-like rapprochement with the world of men. In Wringhim, the instinct for exalted individualism is hardened by the carapace of religious belief and, like Scott in his treatment of so many of his Byronic villains, Hogg combines a treatment of the Scottish past with a criticism of the romantic present.

The certainties of the heirs of the Edinburgh Enlightenment, however, are undermined in this novel as completely as the pretensions of the romantic avant-garde. The Editor's inability to create a coherent and conclusive account of the events surrounding George Colwan's death is matched by his incomprehension of Wringhim's document: his rationalist mind cannot admit its most obvious implication of a supernatural reality.

The Editor, however, is clearly fascinated and so is the reader: both are entrapped by doubt as to the reality which this text inhabits. We find in the opening narrative a fiction which seems firmly realistic in mode—it is a historical whodunit—but which contains a strong trace of the supernatural. When we turn to Wringhim's actual confession to resolve the dilemma we find it does no such thing. For one thing, the constant possibility of a psychological explanation for these apparently supernatural events is always there to tease us: we cannot rest easy in either reading. In addition, the pull towards an allegorical interpretation is as strong for us as it is for the Editor on the last page of the novel.

Nor are things made any easier by the introduction into the last section of actual historical personalities: Lockhart and Laidlaw from the Scott/*Blackwood's* circle—and Hogg himself.

Wringhim and the Editor abhor mystery and uncertainty. So, at one level, does any reader, and Hogg has designed his narrative puzzle to engage his reader's deepest instincts towards comprehending fictional data. We strive for a ballad-like certainty from which, as heirs of the Enlightenment, we are debarred. At another level, the novel satisfies with its extraordinary poise and confidence. Hogg's web is made up not only of a large-scale structural originality, but also of a more labyrinthine narrative progress: extraordinary invention is coupled with immense grace in the conduct of the narrative sequence. Most striking of all, Hogg is a master of style and builds on his ability to imitate a range of modes of speech and thought a series of ironic self-revelations to equal those in the novels of Galt. And at such moments as when he is recounting the circumstances of Wringhim's birth—and, even more, those of his death—he reveals a poet's sureness with language to fuse a surface certainty in the telling with a reality of complete uncertainty. His vision permeates his writing at all its levels. No wonder that one commentator longs to apply the word "perfection" to this book.

—David S. Robb

THE PRIVATE PAPERS OF HENRY RYECROFT.
Fiction by George Gissing, 1903.

The volume of short meditations titled *The Private Papers of Henry Ryecroft* came as something of a surprise from an author who had made his reputation, over a period of more than 20 years, as a novelist. George Gissing had planned to write a book of this kind since 1887 by developing and augmenting material from his personal notebooks, and he completed it in 1900 and 1901 while he was living in France. First published serially in four instalments in the *Fortnightly Review* between May 1902 and February 1903 under the title, "An Author at Grass," it became his best-known book and is regarded as a minor classic.

In his preface Gissing sketches his character, Ryecroft, as a widower of 53, in poor health, who has been freed from the toil of a writer's life by an unexpected inheritance, and lives quietly in a cottage in Devon, communing with books, nature, and memories. The essays are said to be selections from Ryecroft's diary, but they clearly reflect Gissing's tastes and temperament, and contain so many of his own ideas and experiences that they have a strong autobiographical flavor. However, as the volume's epigraph, "*Hoc erat in votis*" suggests, the peaceful conditions of Ryecroft's life represent an ideal that Gissing himself never realized.

Ryecroft's thoughts are expressed within the context of a well-defined character. He is a man who feels that his life's work is over, and is placidly resigned to the failures of the past and the isolation of the present. He is deeply grateful for the tranquillity that has at last been granted to him, impatient with many features of the modern world, and passionately devoted to the natural scenery that surrounds him. After his years in London, he derives intense pleasure from observing flowers, the sunrise, birds, the changes of season, and trivial episodes of his solitary life.

Ryecroft's comments on questions of social justice and morality undoubtedly represent Gissing's own views, and provide a kind of key to the social criticism of his novels. "I am no friend of the people," he declares, explaining his anti-democratic feelings by saying that he values the individual but fears the masses. Ryecroft, like Gissing, was once a radical, but because he has lived among the poor, he harbors no illusions about them, and when he says that they do not share his values, we understand, by referring to Gissing's novels, that he means their indifference to art and culture. His pleasure in the security of his home now makes him realize that he values property and individualism. He claims that his new prosperity has made him especially sensitive to the evils of poverty, but he modestly declines to become a reformer, and is content to keep his ideals to himself, believing that, "the world is better, not worse, for having one more inhabitant who lives as becomes a civilized being." He echoes the theme of Gissing's novel *New Grub Street* by writing of struggling professional authors with a mixture of compassion and contempt, and condemns war and militarism, recalling that he rebelled against the military training imposed at school.

But there are also signs that some of Gissing's views were shifting. Ryecroft says that he has come to value the wisdom of the heart over that of the brain, and asks whether leaders who depend on intellect possess the more important virtues of sympathy and honesty. Analyzing his life-long antagonism to science, he concludes that he feared it because, as he now sees, it threatens human sympathy and intelligence. Not a religious man, he is nevertheless glad to respond to childhood memories at Christmas time, and he reconsiders Puritanism, giving it credit for bringing vigor and discipline to English intellectual life. Ryecroft's definition of Art as "an expression, satisfying and abiding, of the zest of life," seems, if anything, to be a retrospective criticism on Gissing's part of the pessimism of his novels.

Viewing his native country from the perspective of his residence in France, Gissing gives Ryecroft many thoughts about England, its climate, its food, and the character of its people. He approves of its form of government as a practical one, reflecting both the common sense and the idealism of the English, and warns against the encroachments of democratic feeling. It is wrong, he says, to consider the English hypocritical. Their fault is rather a sincere conviction of their moral superiority, which enables them to deceive without feeling dishonest.

Ryecroft's leisure gives him time to ponder the great mystery of the meaning of life. Gissing's agnosticism, his youthful enthusiasm for Positivism, and thoughts from the Stoic philosophy of Marcus Aurelius contribute to meditations which question the existence of a deity and the justice of the universe, and speculate on the possibility of an age of reason free of supernatural ideas. These musings end, inconclusively, in a "calm of achieved indifference," a peaceful mood of resignation and acceptance.

Gissing said that *The Private Papers of Henry Ryecroft* was written "with gusto," that "it contains the best literary work I can hope to turn out," and that none of his other books could be compared with it "in point of English." While there are occasional moments of passion and enthusiasm, the prevailing style is quietly suggestive and meditative, verging on the conversational. Readers were captivated by its charm, nostalgia, candor, and intimacy. Some were critical of Ryecroft's passivity and indifference, but many more found something encouraging in his spirit of calm, resigned contentment, and in the balance between his stoical acceptance of the world's evils and his love of tranquillity and the beauties of nature.

—Jacob Korg

PROMETHEUS UNBOUND.
Play by Percy Bysshe Shelley, 1820.

Called (by C.S. Lewis) the best long poem written in English in the 19th century, *Prometheus Unbound* was Percy Bysshe Shelley's attempt to fulfil an ambition general to the Romantic poets: to write a great long poem. Written in 1818–19, *Prometheus Unbound* was in part designed as an implicit comment on counter-revolutionary politics in Britain. Its greatness lies in the fact that it portrays an eternal rather than a merely temporal struggle between the forces of tyranny and liberty in the persons of Jupiter and Prometheus. Based loosely on the legend of the Titan, friend of man and punished for his friendship by a jealous Jupiter, Shelley's Prometheus bears a close relationship to Milton's Satan, here presented in a form purged of ambition, envy, and revenge. The plot is that of an inverted *Paradise Lost* rather than that of Aeschylus's Prometheus trilogy, which ends in reconciliation. In Shelley's poem, Jupiter is overthrown and humanity (dramatically personified in the heroic Prometheus) is triumphant.

But Shelley does not simply invert Milton's themes in the service of revolutionary politics. Had he done so, critics would not have found the poem difficult or obscure, or have been as dismissive of it as has sometimes been the case. *Prometheus Unbound* is no simple allegory of radical struggle. It is also an account of the cyclical nature of history, an analysis of the limits of human knowledge, a Platonic fable of our attempt to find absolute truth on earth, and a poem which seeks to define eternity as being, in Blake's phrase, in love with the productions of time. Overlaying all these is a language of quite remarkable sensuousness and simultaneous remoteness, the outpourings of a poet who ". . . feeds on the aerial kisses / Of shapes that haunt thought's wildernesses. . . ."

We are directed several times in the poem towards what such "shapes" may be, perhaps most notably in the famous speech of the Earth in Act I, with its assurance that there are "two worlds of life and death," this and a shadow-world. It is in the shadow-world that "all that faith creates or love desires" is to be found: that is, the action of *Prometheus Unbound*, which is concerned with faith in liberty and the desire of sexual union, a subject which dominates the last part of the poem. Thus Shelley is displaying to us a shadow-world, a world where our secret desires for liberty and love can fulfil themselves. The immediacy of his language and its simultaneous curious remoteness is a facet of the fact that he is displaying a world like and yet unlike our own: a world eternally present, and yet, like our own desires, mortal. Here the action of liberation takes place.

The remoteness of this struggle for liberty from real politics is further emphasized by the fact that it is not Prometheus whose agency overthrows Jupiter, but Demogorgon, a strange figure who dwells in darkness and cannot be easily identified with any traditional human or mythic force. The name derives from a mediaeval philosopher, Theodontius, who used it to identify the father of the gods. For Shelley, Demogorgon is a more complex figure. On one level he is, literally, "people-monster," the principle of united democratic action. On another, he is the operation of Time within Eternity, a contradiction in terms borne out in the statement "the deep truth is imageless." Both a creator and dispeller of shadows, Demogorgon is an ambivalent agent who distorts the simple anti-Miltonic images of the plot still further. He is both terror and redemption; perhaps on some level he represents Shelley's feelings about the fruitlessness (and yet perhaps the need) of political violence to gain revolutionary ends.

The deposition of Jupiter is a provisional victory. In the final hymn of triumph, Demogorgon speaks of the possibility that "The serpent" of tyranny will once again gain power. History is viewed as cyclical. Shelley draws here on the ancient image of the ouroboros-worm, its tail in its mouth, wrapped round the earth. He can only be kept at bay by Love, the bird who from the ". . . narrow verge of crag-like agony, springs / And folds over the world its healing wings." Christian images of dove and snake are here adapted by Shelley for the purposes of his own myth-making.

Prometheus Unbound is a stupendous vision of human potential, with a plot which at first sight seems to have unlimited faith in that potential. On closer examination, qualifications emerge. Human beings are limited by the very desires they so long to fulfil: "Nor yet exempt, though ruling them like slaves, / From chance, and death, and mutability. . . ." Only contingent knowledge of the world is available. No one has full knowledge (Plato's noesis): all are limited, and to the central question who (or where) is God? Demogorgon merely answers (three times) "He reigns." Shelley's triumph is to give a climactic utterance to desires for freedom which he knows are finally provisional: to give us ". . . hope, till Hope creates / From its own wreck the thing it contemplates." The cycle goes on.

—Murray G.H. Pittock

THE PROVOKED WIFE.
Play by Sir John Vanbrugh, 1697.

Sir John Vanbrugh's third play, *The Provoked Wife*, produced at Lincoln's Inn Fields in the spring of 1697, was immediately popular and, with some alteration, remained so for more than a century. The author made the first revision in 1725, when he wrote two new scenes for Act IV, converting Sir John Brute's disguise as a parson into that of a "woman of quality." Later productions softened the language and at least one aspect of the plot: David Garrick made Lady Brute's flirtation with Constant an elaborate practical joke leading to a complete reconciliation with her husband.

The Provoked Wife is a comedy in the true spirit of the Restoration, and the influence of earlier writers is evident. The character groupings echo those of Otway's *The Soldier's Fortune*, while the same kinds of couples are seen in Etherege's *She Would If She Could*. Like his predecessors, Vanbrugh claimed he wrote for gentlemen, "to divert (if possible) some part of their spleen in spite of their wives and their taxes." Yet his voice is his own, and if he utilizes the love chase, the wit combat, and the sharp edge of satire, his central focus is on the marriage of Sir John and Lady Brute.

As in *The Relapse* and *The Provoked Husband*, Vanbrugh takes the question of marital incompatibility as his theme, but in this play neither side is given unconditional sympathy. Sir John married for lust ("because I had a mind to lie with her, and she would not let me") and Lady Brute for money. Now they find themselves trapped in an unhappy union with divorce out of the question, since it requires proven adultery and an act of Parliament. Sir John's mistreatment of his wife leads her to consider the possibility of taking a lover and, although she does not actually succumb during the play, the conclusion is ambiguous enough to cause speculation about the future.

Contrasted with the false values that created this situation is the love chase of Heartfree and Bellinda, in which honesty, true affection, and enlightened self-interest combine to make a good, if not ideal, match. When Bellinda frankly admits, "I can't say I wou'd live with him in a cell upon love and bread and butter," adding at once, "I would rather have the man I love, and a middle state of life, than . . . twice your Ladiship's splendour," she underscores the moral view that commonsense and decency are to be prized above the false values of fashion.

Vanbrugh himself said that the work had "no mighty plot," and, in truth, the story line of *The Provoked Wife* is little more than the typical Restoration love chase with a bitter-sweet ending. It is, however, neatly balanced with enough complications to keep the interest from flagging. The action is divided between two triangles: Sir John, Lady Brute, and Constant in the first, and Heartfree, Bellinda, and Lady Fancyfull in the second. These triangles continuously meet, mingle, and overlap, altering the plans of the characters and the progress of the plot by unexpected turns. To the modern audience, the frequent use of asides, letters, overheard conversations, and devious servants may appear contrived, but they were standard theatrical conventions of the time, and Vanbrugh employs them with skill. Interspersed among the main points are specialty moments, and the disguise scenes give the drunken Sir John a bravura moment of comedy, while gratuitously introduced songs display the talents of performers who have no part in the story but give color and richness to the atmosphere.

If the plot is not outstandingly original, the characters and dialogue provide ample compensation. Sir John, an unreconstructed rake, may be a dismal husband, but his outrageous behavior is thoroughly comic, whether he is trying to hoodwink a constable or bemoaning his married state in a manner that foreshadows Sir Peter Teazle in Sheridan's *The School for Scandal*. The neglected wife, Lady Brute, has the spirit of the Restoration woman. Later in the century, she was made into a sentimental heroine who soliloquizes, "A good part of what I suffer from my husband may be a judgment upon me for my cruelty to my lover," but in Vanbrugh's original version she is more candid, "Virtue's an ass, and a gallant's worth forty on't." Heartfree and Bellinda, the model lovers, owe much to Benedick and Beatrice as they wittily joust their way to the altar.

The outsiders who form the odd corners of the two triangles, Constant and Lady Fancyfull, are also out of Restoration comedy. Constant too is a rake, and, although his courtesy and decency (by rakish standards) make him more sympathetic than Sir John, his quest for Lady Brute's favors reveals the same desire for sensual satisfaction. The malicious coquette-prude, Lady Fancyfull, is the female version of the traditional fop whose concentration on superficial elegance has so distorted her moral values that she is beyond the point of redemption.

The tone is consistently satiric, and none of the characters is exempt. In the last act, everyone is subject to Vanbrugh's scrutiny of contemporary fashions. Lord Brute discovers Constant's passion for his wife, Lady Brute's virtuous resolve begins to weaken, and a spurious letter casting doubt on Bellinda's chastity breaks Heartfree's pose as a cool-headed lover. Order is restored and true values established in the last scene when Lord Brute is forced to come to terms with his marriage, Lady Fancyfull is exposed in all her ridiculous triviality, and the true lovers are united.

Vanbrugh, coming at the end of a tradition, did not have a strong influence on the playwrights who followed, and moralists have criticized his work. In 1698, Jeremy Collier charged it tried to justify adultery, while others condemned its "profane" language. Today the consensus regards the moral structure as firm: brutish husbands get what they deserve (cuckoldry), honest men get good wives, false values and actions are bound to be exposed. As an example of the elegant, witty comedy of manners, *The Provoked Wife* holds a respectable place in the canon.

—Helene Wickham Koon

THE PROVOST.
Novel by John Galt, 1822.

By the time the Scottish novelist John Galt came to write what many consider to be his finest novel, he had already published a book on his Mediterranean travels, a life of Cardinal Wolsey and four novels, by far the most important of which was *Annals of the Parish*, in which the elderly Reverend Mica Balwhidder paints a human picture of a Scottish village, Dalmailing, during the reign of George III. This novel achieved and retained popularity in English, much as *Lawrie Todd* has kept Galt's name alive in Canada, the country he served as an administrator.

In *Annals of the Parish*, Galt again used the form of presenting old papers supposedly come upon. This was followed by the three-decker *Sir Andrew Wylie*. For all its excellencies of character-drawing and the expression of human frailty, Galt was unhappy in this fashionable extended form, and returned to the rambling formula of *Annals of the Parish* for his next novel, *The Provost*, which is contained in a single volume.

Modelled on Baillie Fullarton of Irvine, who had run the burgh council when Galt was a boy, and whom he believed, erroneously, to be dead (Fullarton, by then a very old man, survived to present Galt with the Freedom of the Burgh of Irvine in 1825) Provost Pawkie records the events of Gudetown (Irvine). Being a Royal Burgh, Provost Pawkie has more momentous events to describe than had the minister of Dalmailing, but Pawkie's observations are as carefully detailed and couched in as rich and picturesque a Scots idiom as Balwhidder's. Pawkie, a worldly cloth-merchant by trade, is, of course, a much more ambitious character, freer in his speech and much concerned with the degree of string-pulling in office which was permissible by the standards of public service at the time without descending to "jookery-cookery." While self-interest is never allowed to come before public duty, it is not to be despised if it can be made to follow properly behind.

The range of matters he describes take in balls, council functions, the erection of street lamps and the funding of a newspaper, as well as a duel, the arrival of a naval press gang, and even the quite unsentimental treatment of the hanging of a beautiful young woman for murdering her child. So wide is the range of small-town activity, indeed, and so wittily philosophical many of Pawkie's social observations, that what we see unfolding before us is the change in relationship between the newly-married men of trade and the old gentry in the wake of the French Revolution and the Industrial Revolution. Chronicling the hard times on which some of the gentry had fallen, Pawkie observes: "We thought less and less of them, until, poor bodies, the bit prideful lairdies were just looked down upon by our gawsie big-bellied burgesses, not a few of whom had heritable bonds on their estate." This was an issue further developed by Galt in two later novels, *The Entail* and *The Last of the Lairds*.

For the most part Galt's great novels of manners, though no doubt initially inspired by Scott, deal mainly with contemporary, or near-contemporary situations—the notable exception being *Ringan Gilhaize*, which was written favouring the Covenanters, in response to Scott's *Old Mortality*. Like Scott, too (except in "Wandering Willie's Tale"), Galt employs Scots solely for dialogue. Doubts have been expressed (by David Daiches and others) as to whether Galt is portraying his characters wholly sympathetically, or is not perhaps occasionally holding them up ever so slightly to the ridicule of his English readers, with their carefully-chosen quaint words and obviously old-fashioned ways. This may be so. It is certainly a suspicion likely to arise, at least in the minds of his 20th-century Scottish readers, used to the critical acerbities of Hugh MacDiarmid on this prevailing national literary tendency. Galt's use of Scots can be eclectic, as Jennie W. Aberdein—the critic who, in her *John Galt* (1936) did more than most to restore Scottish interest in Galt—put it, he "frequently violates the forms and functions of words, ruthlessly twisting them to his will, coining new words and making hybrids or monstrous compounds" to suit his fancy and enable him to say what he wanted to say.

Yet true or not, Galt's characters and their dialogue, especially when unencumbered by the "galling harness" of a plot, as he put it, record with style, good-humour, linguistic vitality, and the compelling ring of social accuracy, the men, the women, and the manners of an age already losing the physical isolation that had enabled many native features of their Scottishness to survive. In none of his novels is the balance of this stylistic perfection so obviously well-sustained as in *The Provost*.

—Maurice Lindsay

PURGATORY.
Play by William Butler Yeats, 1938.

This brief intense play belongs to the general category of symbolist drama associated with intimate or studio theatres. It has connections with Maeterlinck's *Little Plays for Marionettes* and was a taking-off point for Samuel Beckett's short theatre pieces. William Butler Yeats's *Purgatory* shows specific resemblances to some of Strindberg's late chamber plays (named on analogy with chamber music), particularly the first scene of *Ghost Sonata*, in which an old man and a young one observe a Stockholm mansion which proves to be the house of life, and *The Burned Site*. The separation between an illuminated area of visual focus and foreground figures that comment, question, and narrate is a version of the classical dramatic distinction between central actors and chorus also found in Maeterlinck's *Interior*. It is the relocation of the climax and dramatic gravity of the play in the chief choric figure which sets *Purgatory* apart.

Written in the year before his death, *Purgatory* draws upon Yeats's long practical experience of working in and with Dublin's Abbey Theatre, as well as his careful and purposeful studies in world drama, especially Shakespearian and Greek tragedy and the Japanese Noh plays. He had been one of the founders of the Abbey as a privately financed national, even nationalist, theatre, intended to concentrate on Irish myth, legend, and history, and the life of the peasantry in its repertoire. His involvement in the production of plays had introduced him to Edward Gordon Craig's visionary ideas of stage design and lighting. De-materialising the stage to free spiritual expressiveness combined with the symbolist aim of creating a synthesis of all the arts to engage the soul of an audience. In *Purgatory* Yeats shed some of the obvious exotic features of the plays he had written from 1917 onwards: there are no musicians, no folding and unfolding of ceremonial cloths, no stylised dance at the climax, not even the beautiful costumes of aesthetic theatre. Certainly this play achieves the miraculous moment which so many of Yeats's mature poems and plays celebrate and evoke; but the supernatural here rises out of forms of common life and contemporary consciousness. T.S. Eliot remarked that Yeats had now solved his problem of writing modern drama in verse. His metre accommodates a laconic and sometimes abusive vernacular, a distancing, percussive brusqueness, allusive snatches from *King Lear* and nursery rhyme, learned wit, and meditative emotion without breaking the form or the unity of the dominant character. The directness of utterance, like the simplicity of structure and action, is a sign of mastery and concentration learnt as much through the writing of poems as of plays; for Yeats's plays complete the spectrum of his poetry and do not represent a secondary activity.

Early criticism from Catholics of the unorthodox doctrine of purgatory outlined in the play was a distraction. There is no direct acknowledgement in the dialogue that the play is a meditation on Irish history, but the figurative nature of its story is clearly indicated ("Study that house . . . And that's symbolical; study that tree . . ."). The house is identified with the generations of Ascendancy culture since Aughrim and the Boyne; the tree is a symbol of dynasty and of the soul, especially the soul of a motherland, now "riven" by a past thunderbolt. Insistence on the span of 16 years (the Old Man's age when he killed his father, the Boy's age in the present when he is stabbed) points the way back from 1938 to the Treaty of Partition and the subsequent chaos, as it is also likely to recall the rebellion of 16 years from the start of the century; but the play sets up a general stylistic resistance to crude decoding as historical allegory: the likely consciousness of an Irish audience is enough. The intersecting double action, which stresses racial degeneration and social decline over three generations, recedes into greater depths of time through a framework of fatalism, the eternally recurrent dream corresponding to the cyclic view of historical process. The Old Man is a highly sophisticated creation, summing up in his person the heroic figures of Oedipus, who killed his father and loved his mother too well, and Cuchulain, who killed his son, but expressing a modern intellectual consciousness of his situation and actions despite his pedlar's garb. It is he who interprets national decline in terms of class—the treachery of the aristocratic young woman (like Strindberg's Miss Julie) in mating with a groom from the stables—though the opening words of the play, "Half-door, hall door," point towards the misalliance. Yet the nature of the dramatic medium limits his functioning as a privileged interpreter. Although the Boy eventually sees the ghost of his grandfather at the illuminated window of the ruined house, the hoofbeats are heard by the Old Man only (though the sound is highly effective theatrically if heard by the audience); and Yeats directs that he hears them return as he stoops to pick up the scattered coins—a conventional sign of barren materialism, in Irish drama, since J.M. Synge's *In the Shadow of the Glen*. The tragic figure of the double murderer, whose attempt at a ritual purification through blood sacrifice has failed, ushers in a final, universal perspective on human suffering, guilt, and helplessness.

—Margery Morgan

PURITY.
See **CLEANNESS.**

PYGMALION.
Play by Bernard Shaw, 1914.

Pygmalion, premiered in Vienna (October 1913) was Bernard Shaw's first play to enjoy real financial success in England and has remained his most popular work. The London premiere (1914) was sensational, the reviews like love letters, and the play has enjoyed success ever since. The filmed version (1938) and the musical *My Fair Lady* (1956, filmed in 1964) were equally successful and only added to the stature of the original.

Despite its seemingly plastic adaptability, *Pygmalion* is actually a carefully crafted play, a well-made play with a classically structured plot. It is an actor's delight, and does not demand complicated staging, though it does offer lush scenic possibilities, as both the film and the musical demonstrated. Shaw's satire seems muted, and for many the play creates its own rather warm world and evokes an era poignantly, almost lovingly. Shaw appears to be honestly fond of all his characters, even Henry, whose introduction in the stage directions sets Shaw's tone: "he is so entirely frank and void of malice that he remains likeable even in his least reasonable moments."

For a curmudgeon to be somehow lovable is unusual, but that curious conjuction of possibilities explains a great deal about Shaw's characterization and why actors are challenged by it. Eliza's transformation from flower girl to someone capable of moving in the highest social circles offers marvelous theatrical possibilities. Even Mr. Doolittle, Eliza's father, with just two relatively short appearances on stage, often steals the show. He claims to be one of the "undeserving poor," but his honesty and worldly common sense demand recognition. When he is finally "rewarded" with money, middle-class status, and the necessity of respectability, his fate clearly parallels that of his daughter, but his new status (unlike Eliza's) has been achieved so effortlessly, so undeservingly that it cautions us not to take too seriously Eliza's own hard-won victory.

Although not a celebration of the work ethic, Eliza's transformation is central to the plot, which Shaw keeps sharply focused. Mr. Doolittle's story is as close as we come to a subplot. Technically, the plot hinges on a bet which Henry makes with Colonel Pickering that he like Pygmalion can transform Eliza from a "draggletailed guttersnipe" into someone who could pass as a duchess. Henry relies upon his knowledge of phonetics, and from the outset the effort is clearly a form of scientific experiment. Henry will play the comic Dr. Frankenstein—a presumptuous and meddling scientist. Mrs. Pearce, the housekeeper, and Henry's mother are both concerned about what will happen to Eliza should Henry succeed, but nobody really wants him to fail. At first Eliza's problem is in learning to pronounce words acceptably, but she is very quick, and soon it becomes clear that her real problem will be in mastering the class system with all its complex markers. That becomes apparent during Eliza's introduction to society (Act III), which she survives in spite of her use of "bloody" and her ignorance of what subjects of conversation are socially acceptable. Henry helps to save her by dismissing all her mistakes as "the new small talk," but his own boorishness makes clear that he alone cannot effect the desired transformation. Nonetheless, Eliza's success in that climactic scene suggests that Henry can eventually win his bet.

The drama takes on larger dimensions after Eliza has passed her final test and been mistaken for a princess. Since Henry and Pickering fail to give her any of the credit, she is hurt and angry, and decides to end the game by refusing to play the docile Galatea to her "creator" any further. In this stalemate the play ends, but not before Shaw indulges his own views concerning the battle of the sexes. In Shaw's view (here put in Henry's mouth), what men desire is "a consort battleship" of equal intellectual power, a partnership of equals. Henry does not, however, offer her love or marriage—both of which are apparently beyond his emotional capabilities, so the story ends without resolving the question of what will become of Eliza. Her rise from rags to riches has been Cinderella-like; Shaw just denies Eliza her prince.

Like many superior works of art, *Pygmalion* lends itself to many interpretations and resists being easily categorized. It is a comedy of manners with all the wit and sophistication that implies, yet none of the characters seems flat or stereotypical. Even Mrs. Pearce is a refreshing mixture of sensitivity and stuffiness. The play is realistic, as Shaw himself took pains to explain in his discussion of the ending: "I cannot conceive a less happy ending . . . than a love affair between the middle-aged, middle-class professor, a confirmed old bachelor with a mother-fixation, and a flower girl of 18." Yet Shaw himself labelled the play a "Romance" and much of its charm derives from its use (admittedly ironic at times) of romantic myth and fairy tale. Indeed, the very ambiguity of Shaw's ending leaves a romantic "reading" of the play quite possible. One need not assume that Henry has seen the last of Eliza, nor even that life with Freddy would be as bad for Eliza as Henry insists.

Shaw's dialogue is often brilliant, and if his language once seemed unusually bold, it now seems almost genteel. Shaw was, in fact, not even the first to use "bloody" on stage. Like

Henry himself, Shaw believed that speech itself was the key to social distinctions. A final irony is that the play itself demonstrates that phonetics, even language, is just part of a much more complex structure. What Eliza needed to know was not just how to speak, but also how to act. Colonel Pickering, a true gentleman, helped her more, she claims, to achieve the self-respect that was the basis of her success. Thus, Henry, as Pygmalion, is a flop, and Shaw proves himself a better artist than linguist.

—Harold Farwell

R

R. ALCONA TO J. BRENZAIDA.
("Remembrance.")
Poem by Emily Brontë, 1846.

Early in 1844 Emily Brontë began to transcribe her poems—those she wished to keep—into two notebooks. One of these she called "Gondal Poems"; it is now in the British Library. The other—now in private hands in the U.S.—was for her personal (that is, non-Gondal) writings. The poem beginning "Cold in the earth" is in the Gondal book with the title R. ALCONA TO J. BRENZAIDA and the date 3 March 1845—a high creative period in Brontë's life. But a few months later, in the autumn of that year, the writing both of poetry and of the Gondal saga would come to a stop. Charlotte Brontë's "discovery" of the notebooks brought all private writings into the undesired daylight of "the world without," where they could not thrive. Ironically, this closing of one gate seems to have led to another—the writing of *Wuthering Heights*.

Gondal is both known and unknown; echoes, fragments, and references survive, but all the prose narratives were destroyed, almost certainly by Emily Brontë herself. The imaginary-kingdom game begun by the four child Brontës had lasted, for her, almost to the end of her life. But the Gondal kingdom did not remain a childhood world. It advanced with her as she grew, a wild terrain in which the special aspects of life which absorbed her could be endlessly played out: endurance, stoicism, valour, self-sufficiency, landscape and weather, solitude, memory, exile, the reach of imagination, visionary experience (nothing though of orthodox relgion), death. It was a place of orphans and foundlings, princes and warriors, dungeons and palaces, passionate emotions, violence, heroic action, Byronic recklessness. Something of these is in all of her Gondal poems—recognisably in "Cold in the earth." No need to interpret this poem as evidence of a lost love in Brontë's life, in the wilful manner of yesterday's fictional biographers, and of cinema fantasists to this day. As an observer she was well aware of human behaviour. For herself, however, she stood apart from all close human relationships, except with her sister Anne.

"Cold in the earth" is among the best known of Brontë's poems, if not the best understood. It was in the 1846 selection, the sisters' first venture into print, though given there the uninspiring (and non-Gondal) title of "Remembrance." It is of course an apt anthology piece with its striking opening line, its riveting phrase of "fifteen wild Decembers" (which covers so much more than time in its three words), and its suggestion—to those ignorant of Brontë history—of some dark personal drama. But its power comes from Brontë's "inner world," and it does not lose its strangeness with rereading. It is elegiac in kind, but it is also something other than that. In most of the great elegies the sharpness of loss is tempered by distance, beautified by imagery. Brontë almost never ornamented her work with similes. In this poem passions are not diminished but held down, and crossed by paradox. What are the "sterner desires," the "darker hopes" that beset the mourner? Memory itself is both "rapturous pain" and "divinest anguish." With the mountains, heath, and fern leaves, the brown hills that yearly melt into spring, indeed, with the wild Decembers, we are in Brontë's own country as much as in Gondal; here, as often, they merge; there is no division. Most of all the poem is a statement of stoicism, Brontë's deepest personal quality. For

> when the days of golden dream had perished
> And even Despair was powerless to destroy,
> Then did I learn how existence could be cherished
> Strengthened and fed without the aid of joy.

It is not only the theme, the detail, the atmosphere that make the poem so unmistakeably a work from Brontë's hand. The *manner* is the other essential element. As with most of her poems the form seems simple enough—here, a five-iambic quatrain with *abab* rhyming. Looked at again, it is not simple at all. Every alternate line starts with an arresting clang or beat: "*Cold* in the earth . . .," "*No* other Sun . . .," "*Then* did I learn. . . ." Before you have lost the impact it occurs again. By contrast, at the end of each of these lines is an additional light syllable which has the haunting effect of an echo. At the same time the metre carries with it all of her typical suppressed (or not suppressed) urgency, her "condensed energy" in Charlotte Brontë's lucky phrase. You are left with a sense of hurrying motion, a rushing sound, even, underlying the actual words.

Who were R. Alcona and J. Brenzaida? Gondal sleuths have attempted to reconstruct what they can from the poems, the diary letters, and other chance clues, but there can be no absolute answer. R. is probably Rosina, J. Julius, but the Gondal characters seem to change their names continually. Far more to the point is what the poem foretells of a work certainly in the author's mind at the given date, possibly already mapped out, her final masterpiece *Wuthering Heights*.

—Naomi Lewis

RAIN.
Story by W. Somerset Maugham, 1921.

Though Somerset Maugham wrote 19 novels and 24 plays, his reputation in English literature may ultimately rest on his hundred or so short stories. Among these, "Rain" (or "Miss Thompson," the title under which it was first published) is one of the finest and certainly the best known.

One of the most widely-travelled authors of the 20th century, Maugham made made lengthy journeys through the South Pacific and Far East between the world wars, and from these experiences he fashioned a fictional world uniquely associated with him. This is the milieu of the colonial administrator attempting to rule empires by an appearance of superior laws, discipline, and moral conduct. But where Kipling celebrated imperialism, Maugham reveals the cracks in its facade and, in the words of one critic, shows that the White Man's Burden was often his wife's adultery, his own alcoholism, or their uncontrollable appetites. Frequently, Maugham places his European officials in alien environments which, though with less dramatic results than the degeneration of Kurtz in Conrad's "Heart of Darkness," destroy their balance and drive them to acts of violence and despair.

"Rain" is a product of Maugham's first great South Seas journey in 1916, and its origins can be found in three entries in his *A Writer's Notebook*. Following numerous rejections—no doubt because of its subject matter—it was published first in H.L. Mencken's the *Smart Set* and then with five other South Pacific stories in *The Trembling of a Leaf* in 1921. This collection and *The Casuarina Tree* appealed to cynical war-weary readers longing for the escape of exoticism, though they were studies of colonial mentality rather than romantic sojourns on idyllic islands.

Despite arising from Maugham's first-hand observations, "Rain" is an almost archetypal tale of an encounter between a harlot and a priest, of conflict between the spiritual and the sensual. Having origins in the Middle East in the 7th century, it was powerfully rendered in a novel with which Maugham would certainly have been familiar, Anatole France's *Thais*, the story of an austere and humourless monk who sets out to convert a famous Alexandrian courtesan and ends by going mad with desire for her.

The antagonists in "Rain" are Sadie Thompson, a prostitute who has been expelled from Hawaii, and the Rev. Alfred Davidson, an intense and stern missionary who has worked to convert the natives for years. Though Graham Greene commented that Maugham "has done more than anyone to stamp the idea of the repressed prudish man of God on the popular imagination," much of the force of "Rain" comes from the restraint and objectivity of the portrayals of the missionary and the prostitute. Davidson is frightening in his fanatical priggishness and religious zeal, but there are courage and sincerity in his efforts. Sadie, though sympathetic in her seeming powerlessness, is coarse, vulgar, and far from beautiful.

In Maugham's early play *Lady Frederick*, a woman says "I've often noticed that the religious temperament is very susceptible to the charms of my sex," and the theme of "Rain" is that religious fanaticism is an expression of thwarted sexual passion. This is never stated but masterfully conveyed through the conversation of Davidson and his equally prudish wife, who complains of not being able to find a single "good" girl in any of the native villages and proudly announces that "no one has danced in our district for eight years." The story gains power, moreover, by the absence of any conversation between Davidson and Sadie as he tries to convert her or any description of his attempt to seduce her and his consequent suicide.

Instead, Maugham filters the events through one of his favorite devices: the detached *raissonneur*. In the Pacific with his wife to recover from a war wound, Dr. MacPhail is a balance to Davidson in his objectivity, tolerance, rationality, and disinterestedness. Typical of many such characters in Maugham's work, however, MacPhail is merely an observer and unable to influence the action. In this, he is less effective and forceful than Davidson.

MacPhail does not judge the behaviour of the antagonists but he is a shrewd witness and subtle filter of events. At the end, for example, when Davidson has killed himself from guilt about his desire for Sadie, Maugham brilliantly reveals that Mrs. Davidson understands and has shared her husband's sexual repression. "To the doctor," Maugham writes, "she seemed unnaturally composed . . . Her voice was hard and steady. Dr. MacPhail could not understand the look in her eyes. Her pale face was very stern." Similarly, when Maugham ends his story with the *coup de canon* he learned from Maupassant, it is MacPhail to whom Sadie reveals Davidson's fall: "You men! You filthy, dirty pigs! You're all the same, all of you. Pigs! Pigs!"

The action of "Rain" takes place over several claustrophobic days while the characters are quarantined at Pago Pago, and the sense of repressed passion and explosive religiosity is heightened by brief but effective descriptions of incessant, maddening rain. Maugham ascribes to it a kind of malignity and primitive power that seems to have a fury of its own that makes the characters powerless before it, just as the missionary is ultimately powerless against sexual desire.

Richard A. Cordell has suggested that the implications of unhealthy ascetism and sexual repression made "Rain" a pioneer in Freudian fiction, and certainly Maugham employs a device with unmistakable Freudian elements. After several days of attempting to convert Sadie, Davidson dreams of the mountains of Nebraska, "huge mole-hills, rounded and smooth," which MacPhail remembers had once reminded him of a woman's breasts.

Greene is probably right that the image of Davidson haunts the public attitude to missionaries, but this is due as much to stage and film as to the printed word. A dramatized version by John Colton and Clemence Randolph was a sensation in New York and London, and "Rain" has been made into three feature films and many television and radio adaptations.

—Robert L. Calder

THE RAINBOW.
Novel by D.H. Lawrence, 1915.

D.H. Lawrence's quest within *The Rainbow* for values and for the appropriate form is as important to the experience of reading the novel as his polemic. Lawrence wanted to write about the passions of men and women in a new way. He also wanted to re-create himself and to urge his readers to re-create themselves. Lawrence felt that the novel form is particularly suited in its spaciousness for proposing, testing, and discarding formulations as its author seeks truth. *The Rainbow*'s unfolding process presents a history of his struggle for fulfillment. *The Rainbow* dramatizes Lawrence's quest for the kind of fiction that is appropriate both for passionate sexual relationships between men and women and for the struggle within each man between, to use his terms, mind-consciousness and blood-consciousness.

The Rainbow is Lawrence's quest to rediscover mankind's instinctive, libidinous, biological potential which he believed lay underneath the trappings of the social self that civilization has both produced and required to play acceptable roles. Lawrence argues that passionate sexual relationships are not only beyond man's understanding, but beyond man's conscious control. That in *The Rainbow* Lawrence meant to propose a strikingly different kind of novel is clear from his frequently quoted letter about characterization: "I don't so much care about what the woman *feels*—in the ordinary usage of the word. That presumes an *ego* to feel with. I only care about what the woman *is*—what she IS—inhumanely, physiologically, materially . . ." (5 June 1914).

The Rainbow is both a prophetic novel and a family chronicle. In the very first pages, the anonymous pre-verbal Brangwens represent the reaffirmation of the primitive instinctive origins of man. They dominate the space they inhabit as if they were 20 times or 50 times the size of normal men. They are giants of the earth bestriding their land like Colossi. For Lawrence this generation represents mythic forbears whose example still has meaning for modern man. Even as the opening renders the energy within nature and the men who are inseparable from nature, it announces the hyperbole, myth, and process that are central to the novel's aesthetic. After the canal and the railroad are introduced, the familial, agrarian life is no longer possible. Thus within Lawrence's myth of the giants of the earth, the Nephelim version of the creation myth, he also proposes a fortunate fall. The women are not content to live in "the drowse of blood intimacy." They feel that their world is anachronistic once industrialism touches it. They begin a quest for a richer life, for a life that contains an awareness of oneself and the world beyond the farm.

Tom and Lydia provide the first principle of Lawrence's grammar of passion. Lawrence uses the relationship between Tom and Lydia to show that *passionate* attraction takes place beneath the conscious level and disarms the intellect and the will. Lydia is roused to life despite her intention to withdraw from passionate attachments after the death of her husband. Lydia articulates Lawrence's basic premise in the novel: "Between two people, the love itself is the important thing, and that is neither you nor him. It is a third thing you must create."

The Anna and Will section corresponds to the passionate struggle that raged between Lawrence and Frieda while he wrote the novel. In the Will-Anna relationship, Lawrence explores the second principle of the grammar of passions: each person must bring an independent existence to marriage.

The chapter entitled "Anna Victrix" defines the problem of man and woman after they have awakened to self-consciousness and are no longer in rhythm with nature in a pastoral world. "Anna Victrix" is an ironic title. By winning —by overwhelming will with her sexuality—Anna loses. Anna is indifferent to the outside world, but like Lawrence she needs to find a balance between mind-consciousness and blood-consciousness.

Lawrence proposes as the third principle of his grammar of passions that certain elect souls can struggle by themselves to fulfillment, and can reconcile blood-consciousness and mind-consciousness, if they are true to their own impulses and if they avoid submitting to lesser beings and social conventions. Choosing a female as his surrogate enabled Lawrence to achieve distance and objectivity. Like Lawrence, Ursula is torn, on the one hand, between the female "secret riches" of the body and, on the other, the "man's world" of work, duty, and community. When Lawrence's chronicle reaches the contemporary world of the turn of the century, the Brangwen quest for symbols becomes more urgent because it mimes his own central concerns.

Ursula's oscillation between the demands of the conscious self and the passional self continues in an upward spiral to the novel's final pages as she moves toward the unreachable goal of what Lawrence calls "full achievement" of herself. At the close Lawrence and Ursula are inseparable. When she agrees to marry Skrebensky, her capitulation to conventions mimes Lawrence's own fear that he lacked the strength to break free.

The final vision is not only Ursula's but Lawrence's. It is the moment to which the narrative and the narrator have moved. The novel has redefined God to be something remote, whose presence pervades nature but is indifferent to man's individual quest. (Ursula thinks: "What ever God was, He was, and there was no need to trouble about him.") Yet God also becomes the name of each individual's fullest potential, the aspect of life that is immune to Dr. Frankstone's mechanism. ("I don't see why we should attribute some special mystery to life.") Thus Ursula is recognizing the God within her when she understands that "Self was a oneness with the infinite. To be oneself was a supreme, gleaming triumph of infinity." Such an insight is an essential prelude to the ending. Although Genesis is her favorite book, and her grandfather's death in a flood established him as a Noah figure, she mocks God's command to Noah: "be ye fruitful and multiply." Ursula must discover what Lawrence sees as the meaning of that myth—as a figuration of death followed by rebirth, despair by hope—if she is to carry out the Brangwen promise. Her vision of the rainbow is the fulfillment of God's Covenant that he will never destroy the things of the earth.

—Daniel R. Schwarz

RALPH ROISTER DOISTER.
Play by Nicholas Udall, 1553(?).

The missing title page of the unique surviving copy of *Ralph Roister Doister*, now at Eton College, has left us with mysteries of authorship and date not unlike those posed by the contemporary *Gammer Gurton's Needle*. Fortunately, in this case there is solid external evidence which leaves no doubt as to who the author was and very little as to the year in which it was written. Thomas Wilson quotes in full in the third edition of his book on logic, *The Rule of Reason*, published in January 1553, a love letter written by Ralph Roister Doister, the titular comic hero of Nicholas Udall's play, to the widow Dame Custance and deliberately misread by the mischievous Matthew Merrygreek in Act III; the misreading produces a comically absurd declaration of affection by the witless would-be lover. Wilson, who also quotes the correct version of the letter, names Udall, his friend and former teacher, as author of the "interlude" from which his example is taken. The reference appears in neither of the earlier editions of Wilson's book, first published in 1551. The play must therefore have become known to him shortly before his third edition appeared, that is, in the latter part of 1552. Udall, appointed canon at Windsor Chapel in the summer of that year, probably wrote his play especially for a royal visit to Windsor by the young, ailing King Edward VI in September. A license to print "a play intituled *Rauf Ruyster Duster*" was issued to Thomas Hackett in 1566–67, and the surviving copy, now without its title page, was probably printed about that time.

This play is lighthearted, impeccably clean school drama, designed to entertain a young, unwell, and terribly serious Protestant king. It was no doubt performed by the choristers of the Chapel Royal at Windsor. Its five-act structure is that of the Roman comedy it imitates; it vies with *Gammer Gurton's Needle* for the title of the first English "regular" comedy, that is, one constructed according to the "rules" supposedly laid down by Donatus, a late Roman grammarian and commentator of the works of the dramatist Terence. Udall, an Oxford graduate, scholar, schoolmaster, translator, and humanist, knew the Roman drama and its scholarship well: he had published a collection of extracts from Terence, *Flowers for Latin Speaking*, a sort of handbook of eloquence for students, in 1533, the year before he became headmaster at Eton. His sanitized English comedy draws mainly upon Plautus's *Miles Gloriosus* and Terence's *Eunuchus*. Udall added songs and a mock requiem to exploit the talents of his young players. Servants and musicians swell the cast, providing parts for any number of extras; all the boys in the school might participate in the royal event.

Matthew Merrygreek, the mischievous flatterer and parasite who is Roister Doister's go-between in his hapless, hopeless wooing of the virtuous widow Christian Custance, derives from the English Vice as well as from the Roman type of the cheeky, clever servant. Like his counterpart, Diccon of Bedlam in *Gammer Gurton's Needle*, he boasts of his parasitic way of life in the opening scene. In practice though, this aspect of the character is virtually forgotten as he throws his energy and wit into the game of pretending to further his idiotic patron's love suit, while busily sabotaging it and mocking and insulting him for the audience's amusement. The prologue promises "mirth with modesty" in its invective "against the vainglorious." The mock-hero's vanity is certainly deflated, but then he never poses a serious threat to Dame Custance's virtue anyway. She replaces the witty courtesan of Roman comedy: a sober, upright English Christian widow fending off the absurd suitor's advances, honour intact, while awaiting the return of her fiancé, the merchant Gawin Goodluck. Once Merrygreek has taken her and her friend Tristram Trusty into his confidence and enlisted their aid in his plot to gull the braggart, the audience is in no doubt about the outcome.

The mock requiem, organized by Merrygreek when Roister Doister threatens to expire from unrequited passion (III.iii), the deliberately misread letter (III.iv), with the correct reading supplied in the next scene by the Scrivener who copied it out, the mock battle in which the would-be chivalric lover is routed (IV.viii), songs and marches for servants and retainers—Udall added these ingredients to the typical Roman comedy recipe and recast the whole in romping rhymed couplets. Stirred by the ubiquitous Merrygreek, who is both master of ceremonies and *agent provocateur*, it becomes a unique creation. The English humanists from Thomas More onward recognized the value of drama as a training and propaganda vehicle. Here Udall puts it to the service of Reformation education: a vernacular, domesticated English comedy in imitation of the Roman drama the pupils knew so well, which aimed to inculcate the Protestant virtues of piety, sobriety, and perseverance. His play provides "mirth with modesty" and furthers the training in elocution and public bearing so esteemed of the humanists. From the prologue to the song at the end, Udall systematically converts the often cynical, racy, amoral comedy of his Roman models into forthright, jolly, English, unequivocally moral Protestant entertainment. In his deft and lively adaptation, Roman comedy is fully absorbed into English dramaturgy. More than any other play of the period, *Ralph Roister Doister* both epitomizes the early Tudor achievement and anticipates that of the major Elizabethan comic dramatists, including Shakespeare.

—Charles W. Whitworth

THE RAMBLER.
Periodical edited by Samuel Johnson, 1750–52.

THE IDLER.
Series of essays by Samuel Johnson, 1758–60.

Samuel Johnson's best-known periodical essays, the *Rambler* (208 essays published between 20 March 1750 and 14 March 1752) and the *Idler* (104 essays published between 25 April 1758 and 5 April 1760) include moral essays, short fictions, oriental tales, allegories, and letters from fictional correspondents. They reflect many of his preoccupations: the scholarship of the *Dictionary*, the criticism and life-writing of the edition of Shakespeare and the *Lives of the English Poets*, his lifelong concern for the poor, and his work as political journalist and commentator; they are, however, along with *The Vanity of Human Wishes* and *Rasselas*, primarily important as expositions of Johnson's moral philosophy. In both series, Johnson makes specific reference to the audience, the didactic spirit, and the timely topics of the *Tatler* and the *Spectator*, but the lessons which he draws are, when compared to these great predecessors, usually more general in their application and timeless in their reference.

The *Rambler* touches upon an array of topics: critics and criticism, the pastoral, biography, antiquarianism, poverty, the miserable plight of prostitutes, and Milton's versification, to name a few. The moral essays on such topics as Hope, Friendship, Stoicism, Fame, the Private Life, and Penance and Repentance usually dwell on folly rather than villainy, and the Rambler offers a morality of lived experience rather than systematic moral philosophy; for example, while in 64 he characterizes friendship as a "constant and warm reciprocation of benevolence," in 160 he also observes that friendship is difficult because we are divided by education and habits of life "almost into different species."

A persistent theme, which he establishes in numbers 24 and 28 on the dictum to "know thyself" and touches on in numerous succeeding essays, is the tension between the essential moral self and the false selves and dissipating activities of human beings—lovers, writers, aspiring youth, young girls, and even the Rambler himself. Like the Tatler and Spectator before him, the Rambler comments on customs and social behavior, but his unique insight is that in expressing our identities—pursuing our goals—we usually betray ourselves, and that human relationships are subverted by the customs and fashions which we embrace. He frequently dwells on the follies and delusions specific to females, who, he suggests in 39, are limited by their education and the "custom of the world." While essays in the Spectatorial tradition often address a female audience and female education, in the Rambler's essays and in particular in his fictional tales, the female experience exemplifies the fabric of vain poses and false appearances in which all human beings participate. It is significant that the persona of the Rambler—the sombre, solitary man of learning—is in many instances defined by his distance from (and, at times, his attraction to) female society.

Numerous letters and stories—in particular, the letters addressed to the Rambler by the fictional Hymenaeus and Tranquilla—also focus on the subject of marriage and the extent to which personality (that aggregate of passions and customs) makes satisfactory human relationships impossible. The Rambler frequently explores the hopes and frustrations of being an author—an occupation fraught with the potential for the deception of others and the self; in 77 he suspends his usual gentle resignation to assert that nothing is more wicked than an author who sets out to deceive his readers. Writing, like costume and disguising throughout the *Rambler*, demonstrates that human discourse is often a masquerade.

Although the *Idler* also addresses poverty, friendship, marriage, and the vanity of most human aspirations, it differs from Johnson's earlier series in its greater topicality, considering such newsworthy issues as the Insolvent Debtor's Bill, the custom of announcing marriages in the newspapers, advertisements, and the general lack of real news in the newspapers. Several essays expose the futility of war and the military life, as in 5, where the Idler suggests that women are particularly suited to serve in the army because of their triviality and narcissism. The Idler's fictional characters are for the most part urban shopkeepers whose fortunes are tied for better or for worse to their work; few of the aspiring gentlewomen and men of the Rambler's tales are represented, and while the loss of fortune or the collapse of expectations often places the Rambler's characters in desperate straits, in the *Idler* inheritance received usually provides the means for such characters as Dick Minim, Tim Ranger, or Tom Tranquil to pursue foolish ends.

However, the pervading theme of the *Idler*—a theme that Johnson elaborated most fully in *Rasselas*, which was written while he was publishing the *Idler*—is that human activity and business afford merely the illusion of accomplishment, and that the mind only disguises its vacuity with curiosity and exploration. The persona of the Idler himself is characterized by the state of being busy about nothing, of seeking a kind of oblivion in a crowded mind. In the first essay, he asserts that "the diligence of an Idler is rapid and impetuous," and in the third he observes that new images and ideas relieve the "languor and lassitude," the "miseries in idleness." This is the dilemma of the Lockean mind occupied with an unpredictable and perhaps meaningless succession of images: as the Idler suggests in 17, natural scientists are fundamentally Idlers, and in 101, even the studious pass a great part of their lives attending to trivial matters. The passage of time seems never to afford the opportunity for decisive and meaningful action: fictional characters in the series pass unsatisfactory lives in a "bustle of pernicious activity," or like Rasselas, paralyzed in inactivity and anticipation.

In both the *Rambler* and the *Idler*, Johnson works within and at the same directs irony at the conventional role of the periodical essayist as observer and adjudicator of the passing scene. In *Adventurer* 95, he observes that while all human behavior can be attributed to a few passions, these, in combination with "prevailing opinions and accidental caprices, make such frequent alterations on the surface of life, that the show while we are busied in delineating it, vanishes from the view, and a new set of objects succeeds. . . ." The immediate subject of the moralist is by definition illusory; as the Idler observes in 32, "in solitude we have our dreams to ourselves, and in company we agree to dream in concert." There is in the end only one lesson to be drawn: as the Rambler asserts in 17, the only certain corrective for human folly is a recognition of "the uncertainty of our duration."

—Sara B. Varhus

THE RAPE OF LUCRECE.
Poem by William Shakespeare, 1594.

William Shakespeare's two substantial narrative poems, *Venus and Adonis* and *The Rape of Lucrece*, were written around 1592, when, with the closure of London theatres due to the severity of the plague, his usual creative medium was not easily available to him.

The Rape of Lucrece in particular bears implicit and sometimes ironic indications that this solely literary medium dissatisfied the playwright and that the formal rhetorical structures, unmediated by the accidental nature of stage performance, imposed an authorial burden of authority and a tendency to absolute meaning which Shakespeare seems unwilling to support. As a result the poem contains a remarkable range of self-critical tropes and anti-poetic referents and takes as its subject a story whose every aspect negates creativity, destroys worth, and spuriously generates meaning or interpretation primarily as a solace for its pain.

These two examples of the epyllion, or short epic in verse, were extraordinarily popular and ran to some ten editions in Shakespeare's own lifetime. They contrast strongly in mood and *The Rape of Lucrece*'s heartless story is rendered with a desperate and unleavened fatalism. Using Ovid and Livy as narrative mentors, Shakespeare describes how Tarquin, "inflamed" with lust for Lucrece whose virtues and beauty had been passionately described and whose fidelity proven by her husband Collatinus, steals away from the Roman camp to seek lodging with Lucrece at Collatium. During the night he forces her chamber door, rapes her, and flees. Lucrece, in desperate plight, sends for her father and husband and kills herself after relating her dreadful story and determining their avowal to revenge.

The poem contains many fine examples of contemporary rhetorical practice and also metaphor and narrative method of a quality peculiar to Shakespeare. The remarkable 120-line formal tirade against Opportunity is masterly, as is the inclusion of Lucrece's *contemplatio* upon pictures of the Trojan war. This latter diversion, however, bears in upon the poem's own potential cynicism and its determination to fashion a hermeneutic such that the meaningless horror of what it describes might be glossed with the consolation of significance.

The painting is "lifeless life" made of "conceit deceitful" and Lucrece plunders it in an attempt to find a sympathy between art and experience. As with Hecuba, in whom "the painter had anatomis'd Time's ruin, beauty's rack and grim care's reign," Lucrece feels herself transmuting into myth, destined like Hamlet, Macbeth, and other later Shakespearean protagonists to become the deed's creature and a victim of story's symbolism.

Thus, as in the tragic dramas, every aspect of this poem takes its significance from its relation to the structuring entity of a violent action whose effects are obvious but whose "meaning" becomes the anxiety of the work. *The Rape of Lucrece* turns on that single act of rape, the intellectual "premeditation" of it and later reaction to it, and it shows how character becomes an inexorable part of the meaning given to the action and how it is determined by the response to that action. For both Tarquin and Lucrece need to redescribe and reidentify themselves in the context of this event to which they are now mythically bound. They both become objects of interpretation rather than protectors of their private feelings.

Premeditation and review, that is the future and the past, formalise the event in narrative verse; the present is the peculiar domain of drama created of witness and an audience's respect, its looking back. Decorum might be one reason why Shakespeare provides no explicit relating of the rape but, in the polluting sexual innuendo of Tarquin's approach to Lucrece's chamber, it is clear that we are intended to imagine the event figuratively before occurrence:

> The locks between her chamber and his will
> Each one by him enforc'd, retires his ward . . .
> . . . his guilty hand pluck'd up the latch
> And with his knee the door he opens wide.

At the moment of rape itself, the poem recedes into an authorial dirge with an element of artistic abdication. Feeling the impossibility of engagement with the event, it instructs us to create our own impressions: "Imagine her as one in dead of night / From forth dull sleep by dreadful fancy waking." But the dreadful fancy is denied the aspect of realisation and language merely pursues more language in the quest for meaning. Language, after the act, becomes the dialectic subversion of event, its rhetorical control amounting to contemporary alleviation of "opportunity's" untransmutably tainting presence. Thus the acts of speaking and writing are fraught with difficulty in this poem and the manner of intellection is seen to be antithetical to the weight of feeling.

> . . . she prepares to write
> First hovering o'er her paper with her quill,
> Conceit and grief an eager combat fight,
> What wit sets down is blotted straight with will.
> This is too curious good, this blunt and ill.
> Much like a press of people at a door,
> Throng her inventions, which shall go before.

Conceit and grief also combat in Collatinus who, in attempting to articulate, so speaks "that no one could distinguish what he said" and Tarquin abuses rhetoric, even in "disputation" with himself, such that words are instruments not of meaning but of self-persuasion "urging the worser sense for vantage still." Lucrece, fighting for dignity through language, grasps frantically at any rhetorical solace till she subsides into a glut of hackneyed metaphors—six standard issue comparisons within as many lines. Her disorganised rabble of platitudes is the mindless repetition of a studied gnomic exercise and she quickly turns on it, "Out idle words, servants to shallow fools / Unprofitable sounds, weak arbitrators."

At the conclusion, Lucrece's father, like the poem's readers, searches the event for significance and is troubled as surfaces shift and action evades language's interpretation: "If in the child the father's image lies, / Where shall I live Lucrece is unlived?" The event and its narration have "unlived" her; an anti-dramatic annihilation. As an actual reflection of himself, she sustained his own self-awareness. This, then, is the story of how Lucrece lost life to become, herself, a story, but her death, by extension, also negates her paternal creator. "O from thy cheeks my image thou has torn, / And shiver'd all the beauty of my glass, / The I can no more see what once I was."

Language presses in upon those truths within us that shun the tongue but it lacks presence to redeem them. *The Rape of Lucrece* reminds of what we are not and Shakespeare returns willingly to theatre for the release of drama where the eyes of audience and performers might meet in a proper respect.

—Paul J. Smith

THE RAPE OF THE LOCK.
Poem by Alexander Pope, 1714.

Alexander Pope's *The Rape of the Lock* is the most famous (and most frequently anthologized or reprinted) poem of the Restoration and 18th century, the foremost example in English poetry of the mock-epic, and one of the most outstanding examples in English of satire and of the heroic couplet. Pope was 23 when he sold in 1712 the two-canto version of the poem to Lintot; especially in its expanded version two years later, it assured his reputation as a major English poet.

The Rape of the Lock was by inception an occasional poem, though it grew far beyond its occasion. Robert, Lord Petre, had cut off a lock of Arabella Fermor's hair. The two prominent Catholic families became estranged over the incident; John Caryll, from a third important Catholic family, asked the young Pope to write a poem which would laugh the two families back into a reconciliation.

This two-canto version, a mock-heroic burlesque in heroic couplets, retells the incident of the stolen lock. Arabella Fermor (now Belinda) rises late and journeys on the Thames to Hampton Court Palace, where she joins Lord Petre (now the Adventrous Baron) and the rest of their party of belles and beaux. The Baron has already resolved to secure the lock and has made appropriate sacrifices and prayers to receive this boon. Their world of high fashion takes refreshments (coffee and tea) and disports themselves. Clarissa hands the Baron the scissors; he cuts off Belinda's lock of hair. Upset and enraged, she and the other belles attack the beaux (chiefly verbally) and win the battle when she throws snuff in the Baron's face and threatens him with her bodkin (no longer an Elizabethan dagger, now simply an ornamental hairpin). But in the altercation the lock has been lost and cannot be restored. Pope consoles Belinda with the relative permanence of art: through this poem, the lost lock has in the best Ovidian fashion been stellified, has become a shooting star which will outlast even the life of Belinda.

Within the next year Pope resolved (against the advice of Addison, who found the poem *merum sal* as it stood) to add "machinery" to *The Rape of the Lock*. From the Rosicruceans he borrowed the sylphs and the gnomes (in their previous existences, coquettes and prudes), making Ariel and the other sylphs serve the mock-epic function of benevolent protective deities, sending Umbriel, the chief gnome, down into the Cave of Spleen, that haven of female neuroses, to fetch back a bag of sighs and a vial of tears to precipitate the altercation between the belles and the beaux. To this earlier mock-epic battle he adds a second, that of the game of ombre. Pope modified this 1714 version of *The Rape of the Lock* (immediately and immensely popular) once again in

1717 by adding Clarissa's summation speech to Belinda and the others, in which Clarissa advises Belinda (unsuccessfully) to abjure the conflict with the beaux, instead preserving good sense, good humor, and merit, because these are qualities which outlast physical beauty (and which, by implication, help even aging belles to continue to attract beaux). It is Clarissa's moral—and it is as much of a moral as Belinda is likely to understand—but it does not necessarily define the limits of Pope's satiric message. As total theme it is suspect because it is spoken by Clarissa, who earlier in the poem precipitated the crisis by handing the Baron the scissors.

The Rape of the Lock has often been interpreted as if its theme were nothing beyond Clarissa's statement, as if it were solely a laughing look at the foibles of female high society in the early 18th century. Hazlitt, for example, spoke of it as "the most exquisite specimen of *fillagree* work ever invented. It is admirable in proportion as it is made of nothing." But a good deal more than fillagreed nothing seems to be going on in this satire. If it is the goal of any satire to hold up (at least implicitly) an ideal by which present performance is critically measured and found inferior—if all satire writes on Belshazzar's wall that the thing it describes has been weighed in the balances and found wanting and suggests what weighs more heavily on the other scale of that balance—then *The Rape of the Lock* is measuring not only coquettes but all of fashionable society in the 18th century and finding it dwarfed. It is not yet so much a society with inverted values as one in which trivialities and important things have all assumed the same value. In a society and among a social class with much money and much leisure, no painful choice need be made; there is wealth and time enough for everything, trivial and important. The society which Pope describes largely has that luxury of non-choosing. The danger is that when they must make hard decisions, they will choose the trivial.

If this is the underlying theme of *The Rape of the Lock*—that this is a society which falls short by refusing to choose between what matters and what does not—then Pope has adopted three devices peculiarly suited to convey this theme: the heroic couplet, the mock-epic, and zeugma.

The heroic couplet balances two rhyming, end-stopped lines of iambic pentameter, with one line played off against the other and even the smaller segments of a single line (before and after the caesura) played off against each other—or against those parts of the succeeding line. This arrangement is particularly effective if the played-off parts are of decidedly unequal value, as the readers note but the participants do not, e.g., "Forget her Pray'rs," or miss a Masquerade. . . .

Likewise, the entire force of the mock-epic is particularly suited to satirizing a loss of sense of values. By its nature, the mock-epic looks at things modern and finds them less heroic than things in the classical or Miltonic worlds. The epic battles have here become card games and snuff-throwing; the descent into Hades goes instead into a cave of female hysteria; benevolent Greek deities have become sylphs and malicious ones gnomes; Achilles's seven-fold shield has become a layered and behooped and whalebone beribbed petticoat; the genealogy of weapons has become the history of Belinda's ornamental hairpin; at the Baron's sacrificial altar he burns 12 gilt French romances, three garters, a glove, and billets-doux and lights the fire with three amorous sighs. Thus Pope finds the mock-epic structure especially useful for making his thematic point: upper-class Augustan society, unlike classical or Miltonic heroic society, has no clear sense of values.

Finally, Pope advances his themes by utilizing in *The Rape of the Lock*, more effectively than it has probably been utilized in any other English poem, the rhetorical device of zeugma, in which a word is placed in the same grammatical relationship to two other words of very different absolute value. (More precisely, Pope is generally utilizing the device of syllepsis, in which the yoking is grammatically correct but ideologically wrong—but zeugma is a more general term for all such linkings.) *The Rape of the Lock* is rich in zeugma; the device always reinforces Pope's theme of the absence of discriminating values in contemporary English high society. Ariel (and sylphs are former belles) fears that Belinda may "stain her Honour, or her new Brocade . . ." "Or lose her Heart, or Necklace, at a Ball." When Belinda's lock is cut off, she shrieks as other women of her society scream "When Husbands or when Lap-dogs breathe their last. . . ." On Belinda's dressing-table are found "Puffs, Powders, Patches, Bibles, Billet-doux." Hampton Court Palace is the place where Queen Anne "Dost sometimes Counsel take—and sometimes *Tea*." So far, leisure and money have left these people free to take all things seriously, the trivial along with the serious. If cutting off the lock is called a rape, an assault, Belinda would presumably be at least equally upset by a real rape. But the poem gives dark hints that this society, if forced to choose between trivialities and significances, will choose the trivial. Already Belinda would rather that the Baron had robbed her of any hairs except this socially visible lock on her head; already judges sign death sentences and jurymen reach death verdicts hastily in order to get home to dinner; already virtue is sacrificed in the name of honor (reputation).

Certain literary works flourish because their content seems ideally suited to a particular literary device in which the poet couches that content. So Poe's "Bells" seems almost created to exemplify onomatopoeia and related musical devices; Keats's odes, to display synesthesia. In the same way, Pope's *Rape of the Lock* is one of the enduring successes of English poetry because its theme of the indiscriminate confusion in his contemporary high society—that which matters being muddled with that which does not—finds its perfect vehicles in the heroic couplet, the mock-epic, and the rhetorical device of zeugma.

—Frances Mayhew Rippy

RASSELAS.
(*The History of Rasselas, Prince of Abyssinia.*)
Fiction by Samuel Johnson, 1759.

Written in the evenings of one week under the pall of Samuel Johnson's mother's fatal illness and death, *The History of Rasselas* stands as a brilliant example of Johnson's style and distillation of his moral thought. The book is a Menippean satire in which, by definition, the characters serve as vehicles for philosophical debate. Throughout the tale, Johnson explores the inevitable unhappiness of the human condition in a mundane, mutable world. But he never falls into cynicism or despair, even when he ironically contrasts the subtle differences between hope and delusion in the lives of his characters. In the end, Johnson strikes a balance by offering his readers the religious consolation of "the choice of eternity" while never losing sight of the problems attendant on the choices of everyday life.

The story centers on the predicament of Rasselas, the fourth son of the Emperor of Abyssinia. Like all of his siblings, Rasselas finds himself confined to an Edenic "happy valley" until his time should come to succeed to the throne. Eden, however, turns out to be a prison; the eldest son may leave only upon the death of the Emperor; the daughters and the younger sons have little prospect of release. In order to make the captivity "blissful," once a year the Emperor opens the iron gates of the valley, and all the nation's "artificers of pleasure" are called to an eight-day feast so that "every desire" of the royal offspring might be "immediately granted." The most successful entertainers win a prize which proves no bargain at all: permanent confinement to the valley.

Johnson unequivocally illustrates the limits of human satisfaction by demonstrating how even this surfeit of pleasure fails to please for long. In his 26th year, Rasselas grows dissatisfied with his lot. By observing animal creation, Rasselas has discovered a basic difference between man and beast: "I am hungry and thirsty like [them], but when thirst and hunger cease I am not at rest; I am, like [them], pained with want, but not, like [them], satisfied with fulness." This metaphorical hunger of the human imagination—its perpetual dissatisfaction with what it has and its desire for something beyond what it possesses—lies at the moral and theological center of the book.

Rasselas is shaped by a profoundly ironic and fortuitous conception of life. Circumstances rarely work out according to plan and much happens merely by accident; hence, the rather loose plotting of the story. For example, a once-esteemed sage tries to persuade Rasselas of his good fortune by contrasting the pleasures of valley life with the miseries of the outside world, only ironically to pique the prince's interest in escaping in order to see those miseries.

Rasselas naively resolves to search beyond the valley for the "choice of life"—for that mode of existence which will make him permanently happy. Accompanied by his mentor, the poet and sage Imlac, his sister, Nekayah, and her maid, Pekuah, Rasselas escapes through a tunnel to the outside world. Even before the band leaves the valley, however, it becomes clear that the search is doomed to failure. In an inscribed tale, Imlac tells Rasselas the story of his life. Years before, he too, had hoped to make the perfect choice, only to discover at last that no such thing exists; that whatever happiness one achieves merely comes as a by-product of pursuing one's everyday affairs. Rasselas, however, learns nothing from Imlac's story; Johnson implies that human wisdom must be earned through one's personal experience; that the examples of others rarely prove instructive.

Johnson always felt a strong taboo about directly addressing religious subjects in a secular work. Nevertheless, in a secularized version of Solomon's "all is vanity" survey from Ecclesiastes, the prince and his friends search for happiness through a series of binary oppositions: in palaces and huts, in the teeming city and the hermit's cave, in married and single life; but neither alternative in any pair of choices offers satisfaction; everyone insists on his or her own unhappiness, yet all persist in envying someone else's bliss.

Imlac uses the "anti-sublime" to teach the fundamental emptiness of human endeavor in chapters 30 to 32. He takes his young friends to see the Great Pyramid of Egypt in order to illustrate "that hunger of imagination which preys incessantly upon life." Even the pharaoh could not find an object large enough to fill his mind for long: "He who has built for use, till use is supplied, must begin to build for vanity, and extend his plan to the utmost power of human performance, [merely] that he may not be soon reduced to form another wish." For Johnson, in contrast to Edmund Burke, the pyramid evokes divinity through its *lack* of substantial grandeur; only the divine "stability of truth" is capable of truly filling the mind, and that only exists in heaven.

Rasselas has sometimes been unfavorably compared with Voltaire's *Candide* for its lack of narrative bustle, but in fact, the long intervals of quiet are punctuated by moments of intense activity—but activity which is forced on, rather than initiated by, the characters. In contrast to Voltaire, Johnson focuses on the countless ways in which human beings waste time pursuing the "choice of life" when the "choice of eternity" looms before them. Perhaps the chief problem, Johnson suggests, lies in spending too much time resolving, and not enough in attempting to live. It is rarely noted that "young" Rasselas passes about a dozen years on the road and is nearly 40 by the end of the story.

The much misunderstood last chapter of *Rasselas* explores the conflicting uses of human resolve as a preparation for, or a postponement of, action. The little band of travellers does *not* return to Abyssinia in the "Conclusion in which Nothing is Concluded." They have only "*resolved* . . . to return"; Johnson leaves them in stasis, *thinking* about their next move. Yet, Johnson does not mean wholly to discredit resolution: if life indeed offers "much . . . to be endured, and little to be enjoyed," hopeful resolve, when not harmfully delusive, offers comfort beyond an unsatisfying present by hinting at a future which points toward the fulfillment of "eternity."

—David F. Venturo

REBECCA.
Novel by Daphne du Maurier, 1938.

Daphne du Maurier's *Rebecca* is that rarest of species, a bestseller in which the reader never discovers the heroine's name, and in which the Byronic hero quite literally gets away with murder. A successful cross between two genres (gothic romance and murder mystery) the novel exploits the norms of the one to reinvigorate the conventions of the other, breathing fresh life into a formula apparently on the verge of extinction. Readers recognised the book's borrowings from illustrious predecessors—*Great Expectations* in the case of the young beauty shaped by an older woman to wreak havoc on the male sex (Rebecca-as-Estella) and *Jane Eyre* (a plain second wife whose eponymous predecessor represents everything which she is not, a mysterious set of apparently inhabited apartments, fire which destroys the Great House and reduces its patriarch to helplessness). Echoes of *Bluebeard*, *Cinderella*, and *Sleeping Beauty* increase the archetypal suggestions. In contemporary terms the revival of interest in popular fiction and in female gothic makes *Rebecca* significant in terms of both class and gender politics. For the Marxist reader, it appears to respect Marx's dictum, that the British bourgeoisie rule through a surrogate aristocracy. The hero, Maxim de Winter, representing the landed gentry, fails to find happiness with a wife who apparently possesses "beauty, brains and breeding," and subsequently marries a young girl from an inferior social milieu. The adaptation of the heroine to the world of the landed estate culminates in her appearance at a fancy dress ball in the guise of an aristocratic ancestor, producing a disastrous reincarnation of Rebecca's previous costume. The reappearance of Rebecca's body at this point, and the revelation of aristocratic appearances as mere charade, sets in motion the detective plot, the destruction of Manderley, the ascendancy of the heroine over a chastened hero, and a quiet valorisation of middle-class paradigms.

As Roger Bromley notes (in *Literature and History*, Autumn 1981), however, *Rebecca*, as a bestseller, is difficult to align with any simple pattern of readership along class lines, even in 1938 with depression behind and war ahead. The Oedipal attractions of the plot are a crucial factor. Besotted by her father, Gerald, a matinee idol, du Maurier viewed her mother (and various actresses) as rivals for his affection. The discovery of love-letters written to her husband by a preceding fiancée (*Observer*, 23 April 1989) appears to have reanimated older jealousies and prompted the novel. The second Mrs. de Winter marries a man twice her age who infantilises her and openly declares that there is "a certain type of knowledge I prefer you not to have." All obstacles to their affections are removed, however, by the discovery that he never loved Rebecca. Having gained the love of the father-figure and disposed of the quasi-mother (Rebecca announces her pregnancy and is promptly shot) the heroine vanquishes Rebecca's surrogate (the witchlike Mrs. Danvers) and reduces her husband in his turn to doggy, childlike dependence. Rarely has a novel offered such a rich harvest for wish fulfilment. The discovery of the murder substitutes as secret knowledge for the sexual knowledge of the Oedipal format. Significantly the triangular configuration is maintained, with Maxim, the heroine, and Frank Crawley in the know, but with asexual Frank as the childish figure whose awareness cannot be acknowledged.

The empowering of the heroine, who finds her identity and emerges from her repressions by part-identification with her "double," occurs nevertheless within a conservative sexual framework. Artistic, cultivated Rebecca, a free spirit who laughed at men and loved whom and where she chose, remains voiceless, presented only through the self-serving accounts of others. By striking a pact with her husband to present a perfect marital facade in exchange for erotic freedom, Rebecca does no more than many aristocratic males. (The de Winters' is almost an arranged marriage, though Rebecca does the arranging.) Yet both Rebecca and Mrs. Danvers are criminalized, in Maxim's place. Role-reversal and subversion of male ideology are ruthlessly punished. Even worse, the subsequent revelation that Rebecca had cancer converts murder into mercy-killing. (The Hays office was less forgiving; in the film version Rebecca's death is attributed to accident.) Ambiguities remain, however. In the novel dreams come true only to be spoiled, and to that extent du Maurier writes against the usual romance convention. At the beginning she deflates the glamour of courtship with a series of deft touches. (Eno's fruit salts are mentioned in the proposal of marriage.) At the end, as Manderley burns and Mrs. Danvers gets off scot-free, the heroine dreams of Rebecca's face appearing in place of her own in the looking-glass. The de Winters' is clearly a Pyrrhic victory, and the possibility of Rebecca lingers on, a ghostly presence to haunt the reader. In the next reworking of the story (Jean Rhys's *Wide Sargasso Sea*) the suppressed first wife was to form the centre of a feminist parable and revindication of women's erotic freedom.

—Judie Newman

THE RECRUITING OFFICER.
Play by George Farquhar, 1706.

George Farquhar's *The Recruiting Officer* presented a refreshingly new kind of humor when it opened on 8 April 1706, for it maintained the spirit and gaiety of Restoration comedy without the sophisticated Court wit that was beginning to lose favor with London audiences. A good part of the attraction came from the characterizations: the dashing Captain Plume, written for his friend Robert Wilks, and the spirited Silvia, a breeches role for the beautiful Anne Oldfield. *The Recruiting Officer* made its debut late in the season, but it was performed more than 10 times that spring, garnering three benefits for its author, and went immediately into the repertory where it remained a staple for almost two hundred years.

The theme is the traditional love chase involving two young couples, but with a difference: the purpose is marriage. The way to the altar has sufficient stumbling blocks to keep the plot moving, but the scenes between lovers are neither the lecherous battles of the previous era nor the emotional tempests of sentimental drama. Farquhar neither satirizes nor preaches lessons. He is, however, quite capable of satire, and much of the action involves a mocking view of the recruiting practices resulting from the Mutiny and Impressment Act of 1702, designed to swell the ranks of the army. Yet in both areas, his touch is light, and the wit, though sharp, leaves no bitter aftertaste.

The structure forms an architectural whole: characters who seem peripheral at first (Brazen, Balance, Bullock) are, in the end, discovered to be integral parts of the action, the satiric theme of recruitment is the foundation for the love theme (it is the need for soldiers that brings Plume into the town), the two pairs of lovers are inextricably linked by Melinda's maid, Lucy. There are no scenes of gratuitous entertainment—even the songs define characters or establish the emotional temperature.

Setting the play in Shrewsbury, far from the customary London haunts, is also unusual, and the change of locale not only offers an unconventional background but a wide range of characters aside from standard courtiers and their ladies. Farquhar exploited the opportunity by creating a variety of ordinary people from farmers to country magistrates. He has fun with all of them, but he is careful to make it clear in the preface that his purpose is "a comedy, not a libel," and that he had no intention of making "the town merry at the expense of country gentlemen."

He has a superb sense of theater, and, although his ear for dialogue (particularly the provincial accents) is fine, he does not indulge in repartee for its own sake. Situation takes precedence over clever language, as in the scene in which two rustics accept the "Queen's picture" on a coin only to find it means they have enlisted in the army. He uses all the resources of the stage—lost, found, and forged letters, overheard conversations, and misunderstandings at every level. He makes a masterful use of disguise when Silvia, dressed in her brother's suit, passes herself off as a young man. The device is less forced than appears, for 18th-century men's costumes, with their stiff, brocaded coats, multitudinous ruffles and, above all, elaborate wigs, can still make a woman seem a credible boy.

The characterizations reveal both charm and skill. The lovers are sincere, likable and, above all, honorable. Silvia's sudden increase in fortune almost places her out of the impoverished Plume's reach, Melinda's inheritance has reversed her relationship with Worthy, moving her from dependent to despot. In each case, honor is the deciding factor: Plume's willingness to give up the army and Worthy's honest love for Melinda leads to a happy conclusion. Plume and Silvia are perfectly matched in humor and spriteliness. He may have been the typical gallant in the past, but, once genuinely in love, is content to settle into monogamy, while she makes no secret of her feelings and actively pursues the same goal. Worthy and Melinda make an interesting contrast: the sober young man and the coquette do not seem to suit each other, yet their characters are complementary, partly because she is not a true coquette. When the reason for her behavior is known, her flirtation with Brazen merely becomes a test which Worthy passes when his love proves genuine.

The provincials are treated with comparative gentleness for an age which regarded non-Londoners only as fit targets of ridicule. The illiterate, simple-minded Bullock, his naive sister, Rose, and their counterparts, descendants of Shakespeare's rustics, are amusing but not contemptible. Only the men who manifestly want to join the army end up in the ranks, while Rose is actually rewarded with the post of Silvia's maid.

Farquhar's sharpest satire is directed less toward people than process, and the courtroom scene clearly indicts the abuses of an act that allows military expedience to ignore human welfare. In terms of characters, he is less kind to the army. The guileful Sergeant Kite cajoles, outwits, and when all else fails, unfairly deceives men into joining the army. Captain Brazen is even less appealing with his snobbery, his overt search for a rich wife, and his constant, if inaccurate, name-dropping. Even here, however, good humor prevails: Kite retains his office, Brazen loses Melinda but gets all the volunteers when Plume resigns his commission.

Farquhar wrote only one more play, his last (and best) *The Beaux' Stratagem*, but *The Recruiting Officer* has remained almost as great a favorite. Although the references to the Mutiny and Impressment Act held topical meaning to the audiences of his own day, they are not essential to the comedy. The characters and situations, familiar to all ages, continued to delight audiences throughout the 18th and 19th centuries. It is still occasionally revived, still seems fresh, and still brings roars of laughter in the theatre, fulfilling every requirement of that most difficult of all genres, pure comedy.

—Helene Wickham Koon

REDGAUNTLET.
Novel by Sir Walter Scott, 1824.

Redgauntlet is one of the most important works of Sir Walter Scott's later career. In it, he returns to a subject raised in *Waverley*, his first novel: the Jacobite uprisings of the 18th century. Unlike the 1745 rebellion in *Waverley*, one of the central events in *Redgauntlet*—a plot to reinstate Charles Edward Stuart ("the Young Pretender") to the throne in 1765—has no basis in historical fact. Nevertheless, like many of Scott's works, *Redgauntlet* is about history and the shaping force that history has upon the lives of individuals.

The novel examines the factors that make up the identity of the individual, and asks if it is possible for the self to escape the identifying forces of history and society. The principal Jacobite conspirator, Hugh Redgauntlet, believes in the absolute power of historical determinism. He tells his nephew, Darsie Latimer, that "The privilege of free action belongs to no mortal." He sees a pattern in his family history which drives Redgauntlets to dangerous, and often fatal, adventure.

Darsie is almost convinced by this idea as he catches a fleeting glimpse of a horseshoe mark—emblem of the hereditary family curse—in his own forehead. But ultimately Darsie is a man of the Scottish Enlightenment. He is less interested in reviving a heroic past, than in debating the philosophical nature of freedom.

Scott is well known for his ambivalent feelings about Scotland's heroic past and the romantic appeal of Jacobitism. This novel is no exception. On the one hand, seen against the romantic scenery of his glen, or riding along the Solway Firth, Redgauntlet is a figure of enormous energy and power. Yet much of his heroism seems anachronistic, belonging to a past which is not directly presented in the novel. We learn of his past exploits in the after-dinner conversation of ageing, ineffectual Jacobites. In the light of the modern world of the novel, Redgauntlet seems a rather shabbier figure, indulging in underhand practices. But the past cannot be overlooked. It reveals the secret of Darsie's birth and family; past mistakes return to haunt Nanty Ewart, the freebooter who helps Alan; "Wandering Willie's Tale," set in a past world, has relevant information for Darsie about courage and action.

Redgauntlet sees history as an almost supernatural force preserving constant characteristics in people. He is scathing about the modern world, the commercial and legalistic Edinburgh where Darsie grew up with the Fairfords, and believes that his nephew can reject it. Once Darsie has shed the "grovelling habits" of this "poor-spirited class," his uncle is convinced that he will fulfil "the web of destiny" and answer the call "of honour and of patriotism." The novel, however, has alternative views about history. During the course of *Redgauntlet*, the characters function in an historical as well as a geographical no-man's-land around the Solway. Here they can abandon their social identities while friendships are made or tested. Alan dramatically deserts a court case in order to find Darsie, Joshua Geddes leaves his Quaker way of life for the same reason, and Nanty Ewart abandons his smuggling to protect Alan.

But despite this respite, the characters must return to the same society that they left. History is shown to be a progression of change, not a circular, interconnected web, as Redgauntlet had called it. Alan will become a lawyer in the town of "Clinkdollar," leaving the reader wondering if this is intended to indicate a decline into the sort of petty commercialism despised by Redgauntlet. Darsie is to become Sir Arthur Redgauntlet, but will belong to an aristocracy wanting the intensity and animation of his uncle. The novel's end, in which this information is supplied, is told by the fictitious narrator, "Dr. Dryasdust." Dryasdust's very name suggests that he is much further removed from the story than the reader has been, as he or she followed it through letters and journals. *Redgauntlet* offers no easy conclusions.

Although Scott often uses internal narrators to preface, or comment on the main narrative, *Redgauntlet* remains unusually diverse in its narrative techniques. Scott experiments with different ways of conveying the story: letters, a journal, tales told by characters, and third person narration. The early part of the novel, unusually in a work by Scott, is composed of letters between Darsie and Alan. The rest is divided between Darsie's journal, which he writes after he has been kidnapped and imprisoned by his uncle, and a third person narrative concerned mainly with the adventures of Alan. This section reveals differences not only between its two protagonists, but also between first and third person narration. The reader is close to Darsie's immediate thoughts and feelings but always one step behind Alan as he moves from one encounter to another. This allows Scott to maintain the framework of a picaresque adventure novel, while also experimenting with the more psychological characterization of the static, contemplative Darsie.

—Penelope Fielding

THE RELAPSE.
Play by Sir John Vanbrugh, 1696.

Prompted by a financial crisis at the Theatre Royal in Drury Lane, whose manager Sir Thomas Skipwith was his friend, Captain John Vanbrugh hastily wrote *The Relapse*, a sequel to a hit of the preceding season, Colley Cibber's *Love's Last Shift* (January 1696). His first performed comedy (21 November 1696), *The Relapse* triumphed, keeping the company from bankruptcy. Outdistancing Cibber's original, Vanbrugh's sequel held the stage during the first half of the 18th century, took new life from a revamped, bowdlerized version by R.B. Sheridan (*A Trip to Scarborough*, 1777), and, 300 years later, still enjoys revivals.

As a sequel, *The Relapse* stands in originality between *The Provoked Wife*, probably the first-written of Vanbrugh's plays and the only one that is fully his, and the other eight, later comedies he completed, all adaptations. It taps his considerable gifts for immediate effects—vivid characters, striking scenes, wit, language that rings true—and lets him exploit with some complexity the moral and emotional material he found in Cibber. Cibber had shown a rake reclaimed: Amanda spends a passionate night with her husband Loveless, who after seven years' absence abroad does not know who she is; when he learns that her true love by day is as compelling as her ardor by night, he gives up libertinism for her arms and heart. By way of worldly demurrer, Vanbrugh shows the rake relapsing, seduced by the love (or strong interest) and sexiness of Amanda's widowed cousin Berinthia. Worthy, who in *Love's Last Shift* had arranged Loveless and Amanda's reunion, now incites the affair between Loveless and Berinthia, hoping to provoke Amanda to cuckold her unfaithful husband with him. Despite her anger, however, she remains true, thereby reclaiming Worthy to virtue here as she had reclaimed her husband in Cibber's comedy. At the end of *The Relapse*, the "vice" of Loveless and Berinthia is unpunished, the "virtue" of Amanda unrewarded, and Worthy's new moral zeal likely to be short-lived, if one judges by Loveless's example.

Much of this plot, in Vanbrugh's hands, is very amusing, if acid, but still more amusing and acid is the second plot, which develops Cibber's Sir Novelty Fashion into the English stage's greatest fop, the drawling egoist Lord Foppington. (Cibber himself, Vanbrugh's close friend, first played the part and for almost 40 years made it his own.) Foppington's rakish brother Tom Fashion returns penniless to England, like the prodigal husband in *Love's Last Shift*. He, though, is spurned when he asks his kin, the lord, for help. Cibber's Loveless had been morally reclaimed by a wife through a disguise and seduction plot; Tom resolves to be financially reclaimed by those same means. Masquerading as Foppington, Tom weds and beds his brother's betrothed, a rich, spoiled, lustful, pubescent country girl named Hoyden Clumsey. She is as naively gross as Lord Foppington is affectedly exquisite, but her narcissism equals his. If the marriage of the loving Lovelesses suffered from a relapse, this marriage of Tom and Hoyden, mismatched pragmatists, surely will suffer—or enjoy—many lapses and relapses.

By broadening Cibber's cast to include country as well as city folk, a social scale from Lord Foppington down to Hoyden's old nurse, and a wide moral range from Amanda to the wholly callous Foppington and Hoyden, Vanbrugh complements *Love's Last Shift*. He does not cynically rebut it, but shows the fragility of its happy resolution. Characters in *The Relapse* who begin with illusions lose them. The firm structural arrangement that marks the end of *Love's Last Shift* also vanishes in the relative disarray of *The Relapse*, where the two narrative lines echo each other but otherwise remain separate, here and there perfunctorily joined and both, of course, open-ended. This formal looseness no doubt results from Vanbrugh's having to write *The Relapse* so quickly, and was acceptable to him because he saw his play largely as a comment on Cibber's. By contrasting with the neatness of *Love's Last Shift*, his disorder serves a purpose.

The Relapse was one of the plays that the moral censor Jeremy Collier singled out as offensive in his *A Short View of the Immorality and Profaneness of the English Stage*. To his attack on its "Blasphemy and Bawdy," Vanbrugh protested in return that comedy should "shew People what they shou'd do, by representing them on the Stage, doing what they shou'd not." In fact, he sets so many moral hares running in *The Relapse*, and pursues them along such mazy paths, that one would have a hard time making satire from his skeptical view of human antics. The effect of *The Relapse* is not to prevent relapses. Though Vanbrugh's rakes lack the glamour of those in comedy of the 1670's, he makes their treachery amusing and also makes Tom's fully excusable. By leaving moral distinctions up to the audience to discern, he guarantees that the last morally discerning people, those most in need of moral reform, will learn nothing while being well entertained. Modern audiences, like those of the 1690's, have not found this a drawback.

—Eric Rothstein

RELIGIO MEDICI.
Prose by Sir Thomas Browne, 1642.

In its own day *Religio Medici* was a contentious book. Reprinted frequently, it was translated during Sir Thomas Browne's lifetime into French, German, and Dutch. It was, however, not originally intended for publication. The first draft (1634) was composed in "leisurable hours" for the "private exercise and satisfaction" of its 30-year-old author. Dr. Thomas Browne, having studied medicine in Montpellier, Padua, and Leyden as well as Oxford, was embarking on the practice of the profession that was to bring him fame and prosperity. His extensive essay is an intellectual stock-taking. He might have had in mind the lines from Sir John Davies's

Nosce Teipsum (1599): "Myself am centre of my circling thought, / Only myself I study, learn and know."

Though he continued to describe it as "a memorial unto me," he revised the first draft in 1636, and let copies be made for a few close friends. These circulated more widely than he anticipated, and in 1642 a London bookseller printed *Religio Medici* without the author's permission and anonymously. In the following year Browne sanctioned an emended version, acknowledging authorship of the little book. This had already, in the pirated edition, attracted a remarkable amount of attention. It had even been reissued bound up with the *Observations* of Sir Kenelm Digby, a Roman Catholic virtuoso, who had devoured it in a single night and set down, for a friend, his immediate impressions.

Educated readers in the 1640's were apt to be passionately interested in religious topics, quick to seize on controversial points and to pounce on heresies. Digby's comments on Browne's unorthodoxies, though censorious, were far less hostile than those of Alexander Ross, whose *Medicus Medicatus* (1645) was a venomous attack, based on a total misapprehension of the nature and purpose of *Religio Medici*. Browne's speculative mind and tolerant temper exposed him to misunderstanding in an age of religious controversy. Today it is his unequivocal piety that impresses; not simply his loyalty to the Anglican church, but the spirituality which moved him to the prayer that concludes *Religio Medici*—"Thy will be done, though in my own undoing." In any case, the attraction of the book nowadays does not depend on the specifically religious themes. What makes it perennially fascinating is Browne's genius for self-observation and self-delineation. In language of singular flexibility, he conveys the characteristic qualities of his own mind and heart. And the personality that emerges is a most engaging one.

Yet Browne's intention was not primarily autobiographical. Rather, it was to register his achieved position as regards faith and morals. The first part of *Religio Medici* is concerned largely with doctrine. It exhibits the range and richness of Browne's learning, and is more carefully constructed than Part II, which deals with Christian behaviour. Essentially a Renaissance man, Browne could take all knowledge to be his province; and if his scepticism disturbed his contemporaries, it is his credulity that is likely to provoke some amusement today.

Wide-ranging as his interests were, love of the English language was evidently an abiding passion. Writing was an art that Browne continued to cultivate during his long life as a doctor and antiquary. Eventually his fondness for ornate diction and solemn cadences led to a prose style that is wilfully idiosyncratic; but *Religio Medici*, in accordance with its varied subject matter, is variegated in style, sometimes homely, sometimes sublime. Browne diverts us, as Montaigne does, with confidential asides, enabling us to get to know him. But when, as so often, he is moved by wonder, the poet in him takes charge. Scientifically knowledgeable, he nevertheless brings a poetic imagination to bear on metaphysical problems, and relies on metaphor to convey his deepest insights.

Written at the very end of a great cultural tradition by a man with a sure command of imaginative eloquence, *Religio Medici* perpetuates a moment of poise between the traditional Christian past and the expanding scientific future. Browne's omnivorous, amateurish kind of learning became old-fashioned during his long span of life, and post-Restoration standards of prose were diametrically opposed to fantasy and magniloquence. But his reputation revived when romantic critics rediscovered the riches of 17th-century literature. *Religio Medici* made a profound impression on Coleridge, who recognised in the "enlightened physician" a kindred spirit. It still exercises a powerful fascination for readers interested in the art of self-portraiture.

—Margaret Bottrall

THE RENAISSANCE.
(*Studies in the History of the Renaissance.*)
Prose by Walter Pater, 1873 (and later revisions).

Walter Pater's collection of essays appeared initially in 1873, under the title *Studies in the History of the Renaissance*. This was abandoned in all subsequent editions in favour of *The Renaissance: Studies in Art and Poetry*, after a sceptical reviewer in the *Westminster Review* denied its claim to "the historical element." Frances Strong Pattison's complaint proved easier to answer than others, from varied sources, which constituted the critical reaction to this book. While *The Renaissance* was largely a collection of controversial articles which had already appeared in periodicals between 1867 and 1872, the confirmation of Pater's apostasy in the broad daylight of book publication provoked rabid response in reviews and even in sermons. John Morley, editor of the *Fortnightly Review*, from which some of Pater's essays had been drawn, stands out as one of the few who welcomed this first book by the Fellow of Brasenose College, Oxford.

Pater's work commanded notice on several counts: its philosophical positions, its historical notion of the Renaissance, its prose, and its form. Late 20th-century readers will be more conscious than Pater's contemporaries of its eclecticism: its treatment of art, artists, art criticism, and literature over a 500-year period—subjects which span distinct discourses, languages, and cultures; we are also more able to acknowledge publicly the book's recommendation of Greek models of male bonding and gay love, an argument which its first Victorian reviewers only covertly noted.

In the Preface and the Conclusion to the volume, Pater presented his arguments in their starkest and clearest form. He recommended that the enjoyment of art rather than its teaching function was uppermost, and that this pleasure from art consisted in the discernment of moments of beauty, moments which are ever changing and passing, and beauty which is relative and inherent within artistic form, not content. Because receptivity was paramount, Pater recommended the shedding of commitment to fixed ideas of any kind, lest they inhibit this ideal openness to experience of art or, Pater adds provocatively, life. In these two short essays which frame the literary portraits which make up the bulk of *The Renaissance*, Pater provides his readers with a nomenclature (he is an "aesthetic critic") and an outline of a position which implicitly denies the social and moral purposes expected of art, and which substitutes relative aesthetic values (such as pleasure and form) for absolute Christian truths (with their cargo of teaching and content).

In Pater's Preface and Conclusion, both the accord of art with morality and the advocacy of pure medieval art championed by John Ruskin and the social and religious claims for art made by Matthew Arnold are addressed, and rejected. Arnold, the former Professor of Poetry at Oxford, and Ruskin, the current Slade Professor of Art, represent two alternatives which, although crucial to Pater in his formative years, are neither adopted here in the early work, nor in the later writings where Christianity has more sway. To Arnold's scientific, disinterested aim of the critic, "To see the object as it really is" Pater adeptly counters with "in aesthetic criticism the first step towards seeing one's object as it really is, is to know one's own impression as it really is." To Ruskin's interdict against the Renaissance, Pater insists "beauty exists in many forms. . . . all periods, types, schools of taste, are in themselves equal."

If Arnold and Ruskin signify those authors whose writings Pater reacted against, there is in *The Renaissance* an array of figures whose positions Pater either openly adopts or appropriates and a far greater number whose positions are surreptitiously purveyed, with Plato, Goethe, Hugo, and Rousseau exemplifying the former group and Swinburne, Baudelaire, and William Morris the latter. Pater is particularly artful in quoting others without acknowledgement of the source or, indeed, indicating quotation at all. Taking on the mask of the lives and views of his "historical" subjects, Pater makes contentious material, such as (Michelangelo's) vehement passions, (Leonardo's) taste for the grotesque, and (Winckelmann's) preference for Greek love, appear in these "portraits" as descriptive. All reappear as characteristic subjects in other contexts in Pater's later work.

If *The Renaissance* can be viewed as a pastiche of Pater's previous work including recycled book reviews and review articles, with the Conclusion a famous example of an unacknowledged fragment of a review of some poems by William Morris, so the volume can be said to contain the seeds of almost all of Pater's subsequent work. The biographical form adopted for the essays on Pico della Mirandola, Botticelli, Della Robbia, Michelangelo, Leonardo da Vinci, Du Bellay and Winckelmann is to reappear prominently in Pater's short stories, most of which adopt the form of the imaginary portrait as does his only novel, *Marius the Epicurean*. Pater's twin and pre-eminent interests in culture and theory / criticism are clearly signalled here, not least in the theoretical argument imposed on these disparate pieces by the critical framework of the Preface and Conclusion. The tendency in *The Renaissance* to discuss present preoccupations in terms of alternative models and authority from the past is characteristic of his period (see Carlyle's *Past and Present* and Tennyson's *The Princess*) and of Pater who was by profession a classicist. The legacy of classicism and its multiple forms continues to pervade Pater's work, with English literature (suppressed with William Morris's name in *The Renaissance*) coming more into view subsequently. So provocative to his enemies did Pater deem the Conclusion to be that in 1877 he deleted it entirely from the second edition, hoping to defuse the charge of corruption of the young. The additional factor in the formula of provocation to be found in the book is the seductive, suggestive tone of its sinuous and artful prose. Pater's care for style is notable here in a plethora of set pieces (such as the evocative and memorable paragraphs on La Gioconda and the tombs by Michelangelo in the sacristy of San Lorenzo), more than a decade before his famous essay on "Style," published in 1888.

Pater's criticism has continued to be of interest from his day to ours. The emphasis in *The Renaissance* on the reader/critic, aesthetic form, culture, the dissolving subject, quotation, and defamiliarisation, have been taken up by our own contemporaries, while the work is of historical moment for its impressive negotiation of aestheticism and Victorian science and philosophy.

This collection of essays which fits so uncertainly into our later, institutionalised separation of art, philosophy, and literature, proves absorbing to read: its combination of continuity and fragmentation is rich, and its succession of short biographical essays border on fiction in their narrative element and intricate figured language, while they include philosophy, science, and critical theory. Pater designated "imaginative prose" as the special art of the modern world, and that is what he wrote.

—Laurel Brake

THE RETURN OF THE NATIVE.
Novel by Thomas Hardy, 1878.

Thomas Hardy's sixth published novel, *The Return of the Native*, was his most ambitious to date and initiated a sequence of tragic novels that reached its culmination in his great works of the 1890's: *Tess of the d'Urbervilles* and *Jude the Obscure*. Its immediate predecessor, *The Hand of Ethelberta*, had attempted a vein of comedy and satire in a largely urban setting; it had not been commercially successful, and as Hardy notes in his autobiography its appearance had caused "general disappointment at the lack of sheep and shepherds." It is therefore not surprising that in *The Return of the Native* he once again favoured the kind of rural setting that had helped to make *Far from the Madding Crowd* a success. Egdon Heath, which is evoked in a set-piece at the very beginning of the novel and continues to brood over the entire story, is in fact very close to the cottage in Higher Bockhampton, near Dorchester, in which Hardy spent his childhood and early youth.

The new novel was offered initially to Leslie Stephen, the distinguished editor who had published *Far from the Madding Crowd* in the prestigious *Cornhill Magazine*. At this stage only the earlier portion of the story had been written, and Stephen, concerned for the reputation of the *Cornhill* as a family magazine, took fright at the way in which the sexual relationships in the novel seemed likely to develop, and declined it. This was thus an early and relatively minor instance of the problems Hardy was to encounter somewhat later in his career: the obstacles imposed by editorial caution, and a form of unofficial censorship, in the way of a novelist who wished to deal frankly with questions of love, marriage, and sex. Its reception among contemporary reviewers was mixed, but the fact that the presentation of rural life was widely discussed suggests that by this stage in his career Hardy was already becoming identified in the public mind as a regional novelist.

Like most of Hardy's novels, *The Return of the Native* is a love story and in particular a story of love disappointed or frustrated. Diggory Venn, the silent but faithful lover of Thomasin Yeobright, is hurt by her marriage to Damon Wildeve, whose classical forename contrasts with the homely "Diggory" and whose surname carries a hint of wildness (names are often symbolical in Hardy). But Wildeve has married Thomasin only as an act of revenge against Eustacia Vye, who has married Clym Yeobright, the "native" of the title, less from love than because she hopes he will carry her off from her rural backwater to a glittering life in Paris. When Clym undergoes a spiritual revulsion against the artificial life of the city, Eustacia resumes her relationship with Wildeve—a relationship now adulterous on both sides. As this outline suggests, there is something diagrammatic and almost geometrical about the network of interrelationships between the major characters, and this is a feature characteristic of Hardy's work as a whole. (In a letter dated 4 January 1896 to his friend Edmund Gosse, Hardy refers to "the rectangular lines of the story" in *Jude the Obscure*.)

Eustacia herself is a figure of unusual interest, and her kinship to Emma Bovary was recognized early, though Hardy insisted he had not read Flaubert's novel at the time. (*Madame Bovary* had appeared in 1857.) According to Hardy's description, Eustacia bears a strong physical resemblance to the type of tall, dark-haired, and languorous female depicted in the paintings of the Pre-Raphaelite Brotherhood; as so often in Hardy's fiction, the visual element is strongly and precisely realized. Temperamentally, she has a romantic longing for escape, but her emotion also possesses a social dimension, for the circumstances of her life afford no outlets for her passionate and independent spirit. She has something in common with such figures as Tennyson's Mariana and his Lady of Shalott, and her death has a certain inevitability. She represents one of the earliest of a series of studies in Hardy's fiction of the gifted woman whose life is intolerably cramped and confined by the social order.

Diggory Venn has a different kind of interest as a half-realistic, half-supernatural figure who illustrates Hardy's capacity for blending different modes of fiction. His occupation as a "reddle-man" (dealer in red dye used for marking sheep) places him firmly in a specific culture and setting, but his habit of appearing and disappearing without warning, his silent observation of the doings of others, and his part in such fantastic scenes as the game of dice with Wildeve conducted by the light of glow-worms, suggest a non-realistic, almost folk-tale dimension. His marriage to Thomasin at the end of the story was an afterthought and a concession to popular taste, Hardy's original intention having been to let him steal silently away at the conclusion.

Hardy seems to have seen the drama of these individual lives, played out in a confined and obscure setting, in relation to tragic conceptions that override the limitations of time and space. In particular he may have taken as a model the Shakespearian tragedies that he had studied so carefully, and it is significant that the climax of the action occurs at the end of the fifth "book," the structure of the work thus corresponding to the five acts of Shakespearian drama (the sixth book is a kind of epilogue). There is even, as at the end of *Hamlet*, a funeral procession. In the process Hardy was not only seeking to endow his own work with a high seriousness that raised it above the bourgeois fiction of the day, with its concern with social trivialities: he was also raising the stature and enlarging the scope of the Victorian novel itself.

—Norman Page

REVELATIONS OF DIVINE LOVE.
Prose by Julian (Juliana) of Norwich (c. 1343–after 1416), written c. 1373 and c. 1393.

Editions and Translations

A Shewing of God's Love: The Shorter Version of Sixteen Revelations of Divine Love, edited by A.M. Reynolds. 1958.
The Revelations of Divine Love, translated by James Walsh. 1961.
Revelations of Divine Love, translated by Clifton Wolters. 1966.
Revelations of Divine Love, edited by Marion Glasscoe. 1976.
Julian of Norwich's Revelations of Divine Love: The Shorter Version, edited by Frances Beer. 1978.
A Book of Showings to the Anchoress Julian of Norwich, edited by Edmund Colledge and James Walsh. 2 vols., 1978.

Critical Studies: *The English Mystics*, 1927, and *The English Mystical Tradition*, 1961, both by David Knowles; *English Mystics of the Fourteenth Century* by T.W. Coleman, 1938; *Juliana of Norwich* by P.F. Chambers, 1955; *The English Religious Heritage* by Conrad Pepler, 1958; *Julian of Norwich: The Teaching of a Fourteenth-Century Mystic* by Paolo Molinari, 1958; *English Spirituality* by M. Thornton, 1963; *English Prose Style: Margery Kempe and Julian of Norwich* by Robert K. Stone, 1970; *The Influence of Richard Rolle and Julian of Norwich on the Middle English Lyrics* by Mary Arthur Knowlton, 1973; *On Julian of Norwich, and In Defence of Margery Kempe* by E.I. Watkin, 1979; *The Middle English Mystics* by Wolfgang Riehle, 1981; *Love Was His Meaning: The Theology and Mysticism of Julian of Norwich* by Brant Pelphrey, 1982; *God Is Our Mother: Julian of Norwich and the Medieval Image of Feminine Divinity* by Jennifer P. Heimmel, 1982; *An Understanding of Love According to the Anchoress Julian of Norwich* by Patricia Mary Vinje, 1983; article by Ritamary Bradley, in *An Introduction to the Medieval Mystics of Europe* edited by Paul E. Szarmach, 1984; article by Christina von Nolcken, in *Middle English Prose* edited by A.S.G. Edwards, 1984; article by Catherine Jones, in *Medieval Women Writers* edited by Katharina M. Wilson, 1984; *Julian: Woman of Our Day* edited by Robert Llewelyn, 1985; articles by Ritamary Bradley, David A. Foss, and Debra Scott Panichelle, in *Downside Review*, July 1986; *Julian of Norwich* by Austin Cooper, 1987; *Julian of Norwich: Mystic and Theologian* by Grace M. Jantzen, 1987.

The Revelations of Divine Love: A Book of Showings is an autobiographical account of 16 visions received by Julian (Juliana) of Norwich on 13 May 1373, and subsequently recorded in two texts. The first is commonly called the Short Text and was written soon after the visionary experience; the second, the Long Text, is a greatly expanded version of the account, written 20 years or more after the initial visions.

Much of what we know of the background to Julian's work we have learned from personal comments in her texts. We know, for example, that Julian received the 16 showings, as she calls them, when she was 30-and-a-half years old and that they came to her during a serious illness. She recorded the experience in the Short Text, describing the visions as either bodily visions, ghostly visions, or visions given to her understanding. The Short Text focuses on the corporal or bodily visions, primarily of the tortured and bleeding body of Christ. We know also that an interval of 20 years or more passed during which time Julian probably became an anchoress, a situation which allowed her to pray and meditate on her experience. The result of this contemplation is the Long Text, over twice as long as the original which, while leaving intact the bodily visions, expands greatly on the spiritual and intellectual visions. Both texts give a chronological account of the visions as they appeared to Julian at intervals over a period of two days. Long popular with a limited audience for its spiritual teachings, the 1978 publication of the text with preface and appendix by Colledge and Walsh has opened it to the critical analysis of a much wider audience. Critics now consider Julian's revelation not only as an invaluable record of a mystical vision but also as a literary work in which she displays traditional medieval concepts and concerns. In assessing Julian and her work, we must look at her as a visionary but also as a writer—learned, observant, in the mainstream of 14th-century medieval thought. She writes both as a traditionalist and as one who looks ahead.

In considering Julian's work as a visionary experience similar to that of other 14th-century mystics, one immediate discovery is the correlation between Julian's categories of visions and the traditional categories of visions. She says that she saw the visions by bodily sight, by words formed in her understanding, and by ghostly sight. Thus her visions correspond with corporeal, imaginative, and intellectual visions of the medieval and classical scheme. It is also obvious from Julian's text that she shares with other medieval writers a mistrust of Imagination. Quick to acknowledge that visions could and were frequently denounced as mere products of the Imagination and therefore subject to misinterpretation, Julian continually stresses the visual quality of her showings, and that she most often refers to them as *showings* reinforces this point. She relies heavily on the act of physical sight, even in her ghostly revelations and those given to her understanding, or perhaps especially in these since they are the ones most subject to misinterpretation: "This vision was shewyd to my vnderstandyng"; "The eye of my vnderstanding." She is also explicit in distinguishing between visions and dreams as she makes clear when she refers to a dream that she had during an interval between revelations, once again reflecting a medieval concern. Julian's dream was of Satan, and she says, "This vgly shewyng was made slepyng, and so was none other." In addition, as Colledge and Walsh indicate, Julian has a thorough knowledge of medieval *colours*, those rhetorical figures used by medieval writers.

She also shows the influence of the medieval sermon and 14th-century church iconography as she acknowledges in the Short Text: "I leevyd sadlye alle the peynes of Cryste as halye kyrke schewys and techys, and also the payntyngys of crucyfexes." Julian, the homilist, and the artist share a similar concern with the bleeding body of Christ, with Christ as Plowman, with the divided heart of Christ, with Mary.

Thus in these and in other instances she writes much as a traditionalist, but she is also and ever a visionary, both in that she writes of her visions and in that she sees beyond her own world, her own time, and becomes one who writes of universals. And nowhere is this more evident than in her development of the parable of the Lord and the Servant and the Christ-Mother metaphor. These two most critical additions to the Long Text are found in Revelation 14 and show the great spiritual and intellectual growth of Julian between the writing of this text and her earlier one. She uses the parable and the metaphor in two ways: to explain two terms critical to the mystical experience, in-dwelling and "oonyng," and to illustrate her understanding of the visionary experience and its emphasis on love.

The parable with its imagery indicative of landscape illustrates clearly the two concepts by associating our life in Christ with that of a lord dwelling in his kingdom: "His [the lord of the parable, allegorically God the Father] syttyng on the erth, bareyn and desert, is thus to mene: he made mannes soule to be his owne cytte and his dwellyng place." A little later she writes, "And I sawe no dyfference between god and oure substance, but as it were all god." Thus the ultimate mystical desire, to become one with the creator or "oonyng," is affirmed.

Her development of the Christ-Mother metaphor accomplishes this same end but perhaps even more vividly. The image of the walled city is a particularly medieval concept, but the image of mother and child is universal, and even though Julian was working within a well-established theological tradition, she gives a richness and paradoxically a homeliness to the image not found before. For instance she adds the concept of nourishment: "Oure precyous moder Jhesu, he may fede vs wyth hym selfe." She also adds to the image the ideal of an eternal womb: "Oure savyoure is oure very moder, in whome we be endlesly borne and nevyr shall come out of hym." And finally, she uses the image explicitly to illustrate both in-dwelling and "oonyng": "He toke oure sensuall soule, in whych takyng he vs all havyng beclosyd in hym, he onyd it to oure substance."

Thus by appealing to universals, Julian effectively defines two mystical terms and at the same time shows her audience most clearly that she understands the meaning behind her visions: "Woldest thou wytt thy lordes menyng in this thyng? Wytt it wele, loue was his menyng."

In an age of war, plague, and famine, Julian of Norwich wrote of the redemptive value of love and established her place in the literary canon.

—Gayle H. Miller

THE REVENGER'S TRAGEDY.
Play by Thomas Middleton or Cyril Tourneur, c. 1606.

The Revenger's Tragedy fuses the allegorical traditions of the morality play and the ironic intrigue of Jonsonian comedy with revenge tragedy formulae to create a Jacobean masterpiece. The play, according to its title page "sundry times acted by the Kings Maiesties Seruants" and published in 1607, suffered critical neglect until the 20th-century re-evaluation led by T.S. Eliot. The play, published anonymously, was assigned to Cyril Tourneur by Edward Archer in 1656, an attribution uncontested until the 20th century when alternative names were proposed, particularly Thomas Middleton.

The unnamed Italianate court of the play condenses every vice attributed to Italy in Elizabethan imaginations—devious poisoning, judicial hypocrisy, and sexual sin. The vision of Italianate corruption and sin presents and excoriates the dreadful other, the dark Italy of English Renaissance imaginings, and at the same time makes an oblique commentary on the contemporary Jacobean court. The play occurs in a court characterized by lust, incest, rape, and murder, in which the central fountain of justice—the ducal throne—is contaminated by its occupant. The audience is guided to moral discrimination of ducal crimes by Vindice, who uncovers the sins beneath "costly three-pil'd flesh." Vindice's stance as the castigator of ducal sin has produced critical commentary which sees Vindice, a character indebted to Marston's Malevole in *The Malcontent*, as contaminated by the very sin he names. Modern psychologizing of character has blurred the morality roots of the play. The names—Castiza, Gratiana, Lussurioso, Ambitioso—signal the allegorical type rather than the realistic individual. The vigor of the play's presentation of sin should not mask its denunciation of aristocratic abuse of privilege.

Vindice's revenge has been set in motion by the murder—nine years earlier—of his mistress, poisoned by the Duke whom she refused as a lover. Vindice is given further impetus by the death of his father recently dead of neglect, the "nobleman's consumption." The murder of Gloriana, his dead mistress, is recapitulated in the death of Antonio's wife, a suicide after her rape by the Duke's stepson, the junior brother, a rape unpunished in court. The presentation of the body of Antonio's wife, a virtuous suicide like Lucrece, exposes the danger that the ducal family poses to chaste women. Tyranny unchecked is represented by the crimes of lust of the ducal family. The Duchess commits incest with the Duke's bastard son, Spurio. Lussurioso seduces with gold. Junior brother rapes. Justice is blocked when the criminal sits in the ducal chair. Vindice disguises himself as Piato, and is employed by the Duke's heir, Lussurioso, only to find himself hired as pander to his own sister. The criminal progression of sexual crime has in no way modified since Gloriana's death, though Castiza, Vindice's sister, proves valiant against the blandishments of the pander. Direct vengeance against the head of state is blocked, but Vindice uses ducal lust to trap the murderer.

The intrigue, as carefully constructed as a Jonsonian comedy, involves a series of ironic reversals. Vindice, disguised as Piato, finds himself hired to pander his own sister when to his dismay he catches an unexpected victim, his mother, Gratiana, eager to prostitute her daughter. Lussurioso, expecting to discover his stepmother incestuously in bed with her lover, Spurio, finds instead his father lawfully asleep with his wife. Ambitioso and Supervacuo, meaning to order the execution of Lussurioso, instead arrange the beheading of their younger brother. Vindice in his own clothes is hired to kill his disguised self, Piato. In the final ironic coup, Vindice's confession of his murder of the Duke is met with horror and he is sentenced to death. The intrigue has a macabre humor as if devised to amuse a detached and ironic god. Making emphatic the inexorable mechanisms of an ironic justice, this play could be called "The Theatre of God's Judgment."

The title, *The Revenger's Tragedy*, signals the centrality of vengeance in the play and may mark the writer's challenge to the type. *The Spanish Tragedy*, revised in 1602, Marston's *Antonio's Revenge*, and *Hamlet* all precede *The Revenger's Tragedy* which dispenses with various Kydian devices. The revenger's delay precedes the opening of the play. No ghost demands revenge. Instead, Gloriana's skull itself serves as *memento mori* and instrument of vengeance. Dressed in robe and headdress the skull becomes a participant in Vindice's deadly trap for the Duke. The play-within-the-play, as in Hamlet's "Mousetrap," is transmuted into a literal device for execution.

The play's deserved reputation is grounded not only in the spectacular scenes of vengeance and the skillful plotting but in the language. The opening soliloquy in which Vindice addresses "the shell of death," once the "bright face" of his lady, and his later question "Does the silkworm expend her yellow labors for thee?" are justly famous, as are the rich evocations of a lustful court. The play with its central spring of vengeance is propelled by a process that dramatizes metaphor, most vividly in the moment when Vindice constructs a device which forces the Duke to confront the bare bone of truth.

—Karen Robertson

RICHARD II.
Play by William Shakespeare, 1595–96(?).

In *Richard II* William Shakespeare explores the nature of monarchy as an institution, and the problems created by that institution for individuals—both monarchs and subjects. The political dynamics of the monarchy proved to be the central issue in the historical plays Shakespeare wrote about the troubled times from the reign of Richard II to that of Richard III. This grand project was begun as early in Shakespeare's career as 1590, with *Richard II* reaching production at the middle point between the earliest of the Henry plays (*2 Henry VI*, written 1590–1) and the last (*Henry V*, produced 1599). Not coincidentally, *Richard II* is thematically central to the entire project as well since it gives clearest voice to the questions, "What is the nature of kingship?" and "What obligations does kingship create for monarchs, and for subjects?"

Richard II tells the story of a king who is not, as a man, suited to the office, and furthermore lacks the self-awareness to understand that fact and compensate for it. As portrayed by Shakespeare, Richard is profligate and arbitrary; his whimsy and self-indulgence lead him to actions which are no less than tyrannical. But even tyranny can be endured, as Machiavelli pointed out, until it turns its attention to the economic well-being of a prince's subjects. Upon the death of the "time-honored Lancaster," old John of Gaunt, Richard seizes Gaunt's vast property and revenues to the exclusion of the rightful heir, the banished Henry Bolingbroke. Bolingbroke returns from exile, finds supporters anxious to take up his cause, and proceeds systematically to dismantle Richard's misrule, protesting all the while that he has come only for his own. Power shifts *de facto* from Richard to Bolingbroke, and Richard is eventually forced to abdicate the crown in favor of Bolingbroke. This linear progression of power from Richard to Henry is given a cyclical spin, which projects the action into the Henriad, when the murder of Richard is committed under indirect commission from Henry, replicating the murder of Thomas of Woodstock at the command of Richard—the act of tyranny which initiated the action of the play. The cryptic reference (V.iii) to Henry's son, Hal, another profligate young man (like Richard?) suggests that Henry's regime may suffer from its own brand of mis-rule. In short, Henry becomes the tyrant, Richard the victimized subject.

Of central interest in this play is the question of what a king can and cannot do. When Gaunt laments the banishment of Bolingbroke in Act I, Richard removes four years of the sentence in consideration of his uncle. "Such is the breath of kings," Gaunt notes, that they can, with a word, change another's life so profoundly—even to the taking of that life. And yet there are limits to the power of the monarch, since four years will matter little to Gaunt who will not live to see even six winters come and go. When Richard protests that Gaunt has many years to live, Gaunt replies "but not a minute which thou canst give." Richard's failure as a king is tied up in his inability to recognize the limits of monarchical power; he begins to gain our sympathy when he comes to terms with those limitations in his famous meditation on the "death of kings."

Richard's violation of Bolingbroke's customary rights as Gaunt's heir is anticipated when he curtails, in a symbolic disruption of ritual, the trial by combat between Bolingbroke and Mowbray. Richard's uncle, York, tries to tell the king that his own position depends as much upon custom as Bolingbroke's: "Take Hereford's rights away, and take from Time / His charters and his customary rights, / Let not tomorrow then ensue today; / Be not yourself. For how art thou king / But by fair sequence and succession?" By discarding customary right and ritual, Richard makes his kingdom vulnerable to the power politics which dominate the Henriad and find their supreme incarnation in Richard III. York's question, "But how art thou king?" echoes throughout the entire cycle of the Lancaster-York plays. Still, Shakespeare remains ambivalent on the issue of custom and rite; the trial by combat which Richard interrupts is itself shown to be a mockery of justice, as seen not only in the Bolingbroke-Mowbray episode, but also in the nearly-comic Aumerle episode (V.i) with its flurry of charges and counter-charges, all to be settled by combat in a world where the honor of one's word has lost all force of meaning.

While concerned with the broad issue of political theory in this play, Shakespeare does not neglect the ethical dilemmas faced by particular characters. When confronted with tyranny or rebellion (or when caught between the two, as in the case of York) how should one respond? Gaunt had watched his profligate nephew rule for years, silently lamenting the leasing out of England, but does nothing to curb Richard. Gaunt is rebuked for his inertia by Woodstock's widow: "Call it not patience, Gaunt, it is despair . . . That which in mean men we entitle patience / Is pale cold cowardice in noble breasts." Suffering with patience becomes Richard's theme, who earlier had initiated the suffering of others. From the time he lands in Wales, Richard begins to learn what it is to suffer, to have to choose between hopeless action and despair. For most audiences, this suffering has the effect of mitigating our contempt for his earlier behavior.

This sympathy arises, in part, because Richard's means of coping with suffering is one which Shakespeare himself would have a particular sympathy for: the telling of a tale. When first confronted with the hopelessness of his situation, Richard implores us to "sit upon the ground / And tell sad stories of the death of kings," and later tells his queen in her grief to: "Tell thou the lamentable tale of me / And send the hearers weeping to their beds." The telling of the tale lessens the burden of the hearer: "And in this thought they find a kind of ease, / Bearing their own misfortunes on the back / Of such as before have endured the like."

—David A. Summers

RICHARD III.
Play by William Shakespeare, 1592(?).

Richard III, the last in William Shakespeare's early series of plays dealing with the collapse of the traditional feudal order in 15th-century England, is the work of a young dramatist engaged in exploring the possibilities of his art, creating as he goes along the very idea of a "historical" drama. What began, perhaps two years earlier in the first *Henry VI* plays, as little more than a series of episodes presented in sequence, emerges in *Richard III* as an action deliberately shaped in accordance with a coherent reading of history and a dramatically viable idea.

This idea is given its focal point in the presentation of the main protagonist. Richard dominates the play at every point, both by his presence on the stage (the role is the longest, after Hamlet, that Shakespeare gave to an actor in any of his plays) and by the fascination which he exercises on those who become his dupes and his discarded victims. The entire conception, by which an actor playing his part before an audience in the theatre embodies a character engaged in creating a dramatically self-conscious image of himself for the benefit of those around him, emerges from the soliloquy which opens the play. Richard's repudiation of the "sportive tricks" and dishonest fictions which prevail in a society from which he feels himself excluded is balanced by his wry recognition of himself as a being physically misshapen and morally deformed: an outsider excluded from "love's majesty" (the phrase, which will be given its full significance at the end of the play, carries an unwilling admission that stands out despite the sneer that seeks to cover it), but who retains despite this recognition of moral deformity a powerful sense of human plausibility. The contrast between this plausibility and the horror of what he actually achieves is a primary factor in the creation of the play's distinctive irony.

The successive stages of Richard's career take the form of a deliberately patterned action, ascending to the moment in which he achieves the "golden round" which he has so intensely pursued only to fall away, once his goal has been attained, in a descent which leaves him finally alone, faced by the isolation which his pursuit of power as a self-sufficient goal has from the first implied. For so long as he is engaged in using and discarding the victims who provide the steps for his rise to power, the confidence expressed in his comments seems to reflect a perverse, upside-down creativity which anticipates the villains of later and greater plays—notably Iago and Edmund—who similarly seek to control the action of their respective plays by manipulating the fate of their victims.

In accordance with this conception, Richard's power to shape the course of events deserts him as soon as his goal has been attained. The pursuit of power has been sweet: but, once attained, the question remains: "Power, to what end? for what?" The crown as an object of desire has been obsessively attractive as a compensation for other, more human exclusions; but, like Macbeth after him, having achieved it Richard finds that the possession brings only a descent into unnatural and senseless brutality. The infant Princes are duly butchered in the Tower; but by now his pleasure in his contriving has been replaced by a sense of emptiness, a nervous grasping at improvisations which seem less products of his active, confident devising than useless and repetitive attempts to postpone the inevitable. The sense of doom which he seeks to remove from his thoughts weighs increasingly upon him as he contemplates his final isolation. The principal external mouthpiece of this sense, carried over from the preceding plays but now increasingly urgent in its expression, is the aged Margaret, widow of the murdered Henry VI, who has survived the ruin of ambitions savagely pursued through a life-time and who now joins the pitiful band of her fellow survivors as an implacable voice from the past giving choral utterance to the pattern of retribution which overshadows Richard's last days.

It is important, of course, to remember that Shakespeare in writing these plays was aware of the need to respond to an "official" interpretation of the events shown. The defeat and death of the tyrant on Bosworth Field was also the occasion of the first Tudor's assumption of power as Henry VII. Shakespeare, willing no doubt as most of his contemporaries were to give proper value to the peace which they believed they owed to these events, uses them for dramatic purposes of his own. Richard's final dream before the decisive battle confronts him with the shades of his victims in a nightmare obliteration of the distinction between "substance" and "shadow," reality and illusion which is the outcome of his perverse choices. "Richard loves Richard; that is, *I am I*!" To be excluded, in the words of the opening soliloquy, from "love's majesty" is to find oneself at the last faced by the impossibility of self-evasion, of escape from the limits of the isolated self.

Richard's nightmare is contrasted with the "fairest boding dreams" that accompany his rival Richmond's sleep and leave him "jocund" in the face of the trial before him. On the field of battle Richard's final speeches to his dwindling followers revive for a moment some sense of his qualities as a leader of men, one capable of enacting "more wonders than a man" and "daring an opposite to every danger." Yet this final burst of frenzied activity can by now only cover a last attempt at self-evasion. As we follow Richard to his death, we can hardly avoid establishing a parallel—one of several in the play—with Macbeth. Like Macbeth, he succumbs to the death which the nature of his choices has implied, and which his final defiant gesture in the face of fate cannot evade. Richmond is duly crowned, like Malcolm after him: like Malcolm he looks forward to the healing effects of "smooth-faced peace" and announces the end of bloody strife and the restoration of "smiling plenty" and "fair prosperous days." The play has been Richard's tragedy, to which the first Tudor contributes no more than this necessary, final resolution; but in this restoration of life after the final exhaustion of the destructive impulses of conscious, willed evil one of Shakespeare's most abiding concerns is given a logical and impressive expression.

—Derek A. Traversi

RIDERS TO THE SEA.
Play by J.M. Synge, 1904.

Literary mythology centres the flowering of J.M. Synge's genius on his discovery of the primitive life of the Aran Islands. Here, it is said, folk tale and local anecdote supplied his plots; the life of the islanders and their response to the natural world about them inspired his great themes; and their Irish speech—rendered into his own poeticized Hiberno-English dialect—made possible the distinctive linguistic style of the plays.

However, *Riders to the Sea* is the only one of Synge's plays to be set on Aran and unlike the other plays, even the nominally tragic *Deirdre of the Sorrows*, does not offer the tragicomic, joyous affirmation and transcendence through imagination that characterizes Synge's distinctive vision.

The play's one act takes the form of a classic tragedy, beginning on a note of foreboding and ending on one of wearied resignation, "No man at all can be living for ever, and we must be satisfied." The main character is Maurya, a woman who has lost her husband, her father-in-law, and four of her six sons to the sea. As the play opens she waits for news of the body of a fifth drowned son, Michael, with the boards to make his coffin propped up against the wall of the cottage in which the play is set. The action of the play consists mainly in trying to establish if the body found floating many miles to the north is that of Michael; in Maurya's unsuccessful attempts to keep her one remaining son, Bartley, at home; in the *caoine* (keen) over the body of dead Bartley; and in Maurya's final submission to the unchallengeable power of the sea.

Like all Synge's plays *Riders to the Sea* is based firmly on reality. In his journal, afterwards published as *The Aran Islands*, Synge noted those details of island life which most impressed him. He noted the absence of trees on the islands which necessitated the importation of wood for coffins; the tradition of knitting distinctive patterns in jerseys and stockings so that drowned men could be identified; the persistence of pre-Christian customs of *caoine* and wake, marks of wild protest at death; and the bright red petticoats of the women which seemed to Synge another form of defiance of the grey seas, the grey rock, and the grey skies over Aran. Here, in this "primitive" place, far removed from the "false joy" and illusory protection of civilization, Synge felt that it was possible to discern and to portray older, permanent patterns of human response to the fear of loneliness, old age, and death and to the omnipresent and malevolent power of the encircling sea.

However, these realities also had potential as dramatic symbols. The white boards presage the death of Bartley; the daughters counting the stitches in the stocking of the drowned man become embodiments of the fates spinning and snipping the thread of life; Maurya is prevented from handing the bread of life to Bartley since he is doomed and she ritually and symbolically empties the last of the holy water over the body of her last son. In the realm of the imagination, into which all Synge's plays leap from their realistic basis, black hags fly over the sea, ghosts reach out from the sea to gather the living to themselves, the reassurances of the priest about the mercy of God are dismissed as irrelevant, and the natural balance between youth and age is upset.

The governing power of this world is not God but the sea. "Is the sea bad by the white rocks?" asks Cathleen at the beginning and at the end Maurya can rejoice that, having taken everything from her "there's nothing more the sea can do to me." The sea is not passive and impersonal. It is active, greedy, and malevolent. Bartley is not drowned at sea but, riding his horse to the pier, is knocked off into the sea below by the grey horse ridden by the ghost of his brother.

The climax of the play is Maurya's great *caoine* for her husband and sons and the accompanying antiphonal chorus of the other islanders keening this death and their own dead men. In the everlasting battle with the sea humans will always lose. Maurya's battle is over. Poverty, loneliness, and death will be her lot but she has been made to exemplify the endless courage of man confronting rather than trying to escape that battle with hostile natural forces which Synge sees as the fundamental, inescapable human condition.

—Anne Clune

THE RIGHTS OF MAN.
Prose by Thomas Paine, 1791–92.

With an abiding interest in people's struggles for freedom around the world, Thomas Paine was a master rhetorician who, in a simple and direct style peppered with emotional outbursts, produced an array of works that have had a profound influence on readers for two centuries. Among these works, *The Rights of Man* has been widely viewed as a textbook for revolution.

Having spent 12 years in America, during which time he championed the cause of the American Revolution in such notable writings as *Common Sense* and *The Crisis*, Paine returned to his native England in 1787, planning to build an iron bridge across the Thames in London. His interest in the French Revolution, however, took him to France in 1789, from where he began to write enthusiastic letters regarding events in France to Edmund Burke. The latter did not share Paine's enthusiasm, fearing that it might spread to England. So concerned was Burke that he published in 1790 his *Reflections on the Revolution in France*, an attack on the leaders and principles of the revolution and on the violence and excesses that resulted. It was not that Burke decried the concepts of liberty and freedom; it was rather that he felt that these concepts would have a better chance of being realized in a nation with a settled system of law and justice than in one where the uncontrolled fury of the masses would lead to chaos and violence. Paine's response to Burke was *The Rights of Man*.

Like *Reflections*, *The Rights of Man* had an enormous circulation—so much so that the British government, uneasy about its effects, sought to suppress it. William Pitt saw much merit in Paine's views, but noted that "If I were to encourage Tom Paine's opinions, we should have a bloody revolution."

In the first part of *The Rights of Man*, appearing on 13 March 1791, Paine harshly criticizes Burke for what he, Paine, considered an unjust and unprovoked attack on the French Revolution. For himself, Paine says, "I am not contending for nor against any form of Government, here or elsewhere. That which a whole Nation chooses to do, it has a right to do." In his argument, Paine draws a clear distinction between men and principles, pointing out that the French were not revolting so much against Louis XVI as against "the despotic principles of the government." In short, the French Revolution was "generated in the rational contemplation of the rights of man" and was, therefore, positive in essence. Paine reminds the reader that, like customs and manners, governments can become obsolete and that change in governments is not only inevitable but welcome because the rights of the living are more important than laws made by men long dead. "Man is not the enemy of Man," he says, "but through the medium of a false system of government." Underlying all of these points is the idea that government is essentially the management of the affairs of a nation and, therefore, is rightly the property of the whole community. This truth, according to Paine, explains the republican system established by both America and France.

The second part of *The Rights of Man* continues with an attack not only on Burke, but also on the hereditary principles espoused by monarchists. "Conquest and tyranny, at some early time, dispossessed man of his rights, and he is now recovering them," Paine notes as he begins a review of society and civilization, along with old and new systems of government and of constitutions. His hope for better governments and better constitutions is based on what he sees as "a morning of reason rising upon man on the subject of Government that has not appeared before." Perhaps men did leave the state of nature because moral virtues were insufficient to allay their predatory instincts, but that does not, in Paine's view, diminish their natural rights. If indeed there are to be civil rights, they must find their source in these natural rights, and they must, above all, be under constant scrutiny to make sure that they do not impinge upon man's individuality nor upon his freedom of action.

Paine was indicted for treason in May 1792 but managed to escape to France before he could be arrested. There, in an ironic twist of events, he was elected to the French National Convention. His conduct, however, offended many, and after a prison sentence, he returned to America in 1802, where he lived until his death in 1809.

The Rights of Man, along with his other writings, shows Paine to have been a strong advocate of liberty. His spirited, argumentative style of writing made him an apt spokesman for the causes he espoused.

—Wilton Eckley

THE RIME OF THE ANCIENT MARINER.
Poem by Samuel Taylor Coleridge, 1798.

"The Rime of the Ancient Mariner" is generally regarded as one of Samuel Taylor Coleridge's very few achieved masterpieces. It is a narrative poem of some 600 lines, written in traditional ballad stanzas and divided into seven parts.

At the beginning a figure known only as the "wedding-guest" is accosted by the Mariner; and although he is in haste he is virtually hypnotised into hearing the old man's story. This story concerns a sea voyage, in the course of which the ship is becalmed amid the ice of the South Pole. However, there appears an albatross, whereupon a wind springs up; but the Mariner kills the bird. A worse becalming ensues:

Day after day, day after day,
We stuck, nor breath nor motion;
As idle as a painted ship
Upon a painted ocean.

Water, water, every where,
And all the boards did shrink;
Water, water, every where,
Nor any drop to drink.

The very deep did rot: O Christ!
That ever this should be!
Yea, slimy things did crawl with legs
Upon the slimy sea.

The other sailors blame the Mariner for their dreadful plight. He finds that the albatross is hung about his neck. Amid a welter of supernatural portents, another ship is sighted, but her crew turns out to consist of Death and "the Night-mare Life-in-Death," who are gambling for the sailors' souls. The other men die, leaving the Mariner "alone, alone, all, all alone, / Alone on a wide wide sea." He tries to pray and fails, but then sees a host of watersnakes. He finds them beautiful and blesses them, and the moment he does so the albatross drops from his neck.

The dead men come back to a kind of life and, under the guidance of "the Spirit from the south-pole," man the ship back to the equator; but a dialogue between two spirits reveals that the Mariner still has "penance" to do for his murderous act. The sailors are transported to Heaven, leaving the Mariner alone again but now in sight of his own homeland. He is rescued, although those who rescue him see him as the Devil; and from then on, as he now explains to the wedding-guest, he is constrained to a life of wandering in which he is forced to tell his tale over and over again. The poem ends with the wedding-guest, "a sadder and a wiser man," turning away from the wedding feast in dismay.

The major theme of the poem is guilt and punishment, and this reflects aspects of Coleridge's own pathology, as an opium-addict and a man of notoriously unreliable habits. The law the Mariner breaks is referred to as the law of hospitality, but really his crime is to break the web which should connect all living things together in love, and although he does this unwittingly punishment is inevitable. He is only freed from this doom—and that partially—when he sees the water-snakes:

Within the shadow of the ship
I watched their rich attire:
Blue, glossy green, and velvet black,
They coiled and swam; and every track
Was a flash of golden fire.

O happy living things! no tongue
Their beauty might declare:
A spring of love gushed from my heart,
And I blessed them unaware:
Sure my kind saint took pity on me,
And I blessed them unaware.

These watersnakes might well be the creatures the Mariner saw earlier and referred to then only as "slimy things"; what happens here is that he perceives them as living, individual, beautiful, and by perceiving them in that way he re-enters the web of life from which he had previously exiled himself by shooting the albatross. It is also very important that he blesses them "unaware"; no act of the human will can really compensate for evil, but there are moments of spontaneous love which save us. Here Coleridge is expressing a major romantic theme, for romanticism hinges on the notion that spontaneous, unconscious acts have more value than those which we produce through the exercise of will.

The figure of "Life-in-Death" represents becalming not only in the nautical sense but in the wider meaning of a loss of direction, something which Coleridge always feared as a poet and as a man. Coleridge regarded the poet's vocation as both a blessing and a curse—a blessing in that it put one directly in touch with the "divine" imagination, but a curse in that the gift of poetry isolated a man from his fellow-mortals, a theme also developed in "Kubla Khan."

There were many "wanderers" in romantic literature, including the Wandering Jew and Melmoth the Wanderer: these and the Ancient Mariner held the function of warning other people of the fate of those who go against divine law, even if that law is unjust or if one was ignorant of it at the time one transgressed. The Mariner himself is condemned to serve as a living warning, and it is highly significant that the person who is forced to hear his tale is described as a wedding-guest, for he is somebody who is on his way to celebrate all that is best about human communality, and it is precisely at this point that he encounters this grisly reminder of the ever-present possibility of isolation.

One of the peculiarities of the poem is that, although it can be read as a Christian allegory about divine retribution and repentance, much of the machinery Coleridge uses is pagan, and indeed the whole tone of the poem suggests an older, more violent world than the Christian one—the various spirits are clearly more animist than Christian, and the descriptions suggest a world in which natural phenomena have their own life irrespective of divine justice. We may connect this with Coleridge's superb use of the ballad form; both the pagan elements and the traditional, song-like metrics conjure up a sense of a realm which pre-dates humanity, and with which we have to make our peace. The sailors themselves are unsure what to make of the albatross, and in the immediate aftermath of the shooting are divided as to whether the bird was angelic or diabolic.

The realm Coleridge is describing is one of primitive superstition, beyond will or rational judgement; we might also refer to it as a realm of dream, and Coleridge signifies this particularly in his use of colour imagery. When the curse is upon the ship, we see a "bloody Sun," in a "hot and copper sky," while

About, about, in reel and rout
The death-fires danced at night;
The water, like a witch's oils,
Burnt green, and blue and white.

This is reminiscent of a wrongly developed photograph: the shapes are recognisable, as they might be in our dreams, but a colour-shift has occurred so that what might otherwise appear beautiful or sublime now appears as a nightmare.

The story of the voyage in itself might lead us to despair; but the framing narrative, involving the wedding-guest, at least suggests a possible hope, which is that if we could properly hear and attend to the meaning of the Mariner's story, then we might ourselves become, sadder indeed, but wiser; although this wisdom might itself be a terrible thing to bear, since it involves remaining constantly aware of the injustice and isolation at the root of human experience.

—David Punter

THE RING AND THE BOOK.
Poem by Robert Browning, 1868–69.

Robert Browning, browsing among the offerings of a bookstall in the square of San Lorenzo in Florence one year before the death of his wife, Elizabeth Barrett Browning, bought, for a pittance, a collection of documents and letters containing the legal arguments, pro and con, presented in the trial of Count Guido Franceschini and his four accomplices accused of triple murder in Rome in 1698. The date of Browning's purchase was June 1860, and the collection, now known as the *Old Yellow Book*, is housed in the library of Balliol College.

That Browning immediately recognized the potentiality of his purchase as a source for a poem of some magnitude is implied by the speaker's (clearly Browning) description in Book I of *The Ring and the Book* of his absorbed reading of the story while walking through the streets and on the terrace of Casa Guidi. Book I also contains his explanation of the metaphor comparing the process of crafting a gold ring from raw metal to the poet's creation of a poem from factual accounts, a process paralleled with the creative power of God, albeit with human imperfections. The imagination of the poet-artist transforms facts to a work of art as the artisan's alloy transforms the metal into an object of art. Hence the title, which, emblematically, joins his wife's Etruscan *ring* with his poem, the *book*.

Modern scholarship has concluded that *The Ring and the Book*, containing some 21,000 lines of blank verse, may be regarded as conceived at the time of the discovery of the "facts" in the *Old Yellow Book*, but that Browning probably did not commence work on it in any serious way until 1864 and that much of it was composed in the ensuing year. The completed work appeared at the close of 1868 and January 1869.

A summary of the narrative and identification of the principal characters must precede the inevitable questions of Browning's use of the dramatic monologue and his position on relativism. Count Guido Franceschini of Arezzo, an impoverished, middle-aged aristocrat desperately in need of money, arranged, in 1693, to marry Francesca Pompilia Comparini, age 13, daughter of Pietro and Violante Comparini, a couple with new wealth who were eager to marry their daughter into the aristocracy. Violante had kept the secret of Pompilia's birth—that she was a foundling of the lowest origin whom Violante had passed as her own—in order to fulfill the conditions of an inheritance. The parents, eager to be associated with the Count, also moved to Arezzo, but, after four months, left in disgust at the realization of Guido's poverty and instigated proceedings against him in order to regain Pompilia's dowry. After more than three years had passed, years in which, according to Pompilia, she endured every kind of cruelty and humiliation, and, according to Guido, years in which he constantly confronted an intractable and unfaithful wife, on 23 April 1697 (St. George's Day), Pompilia, in the early stages of pregnancy, fled in the company of a young canon, Giuseppi Caponsacchi, to whom she had appealed and whose intentions were to rescue her. Overtaken by Guido within sight of Rome at Castelnuovo, the couple were arrested. Pompilia, after a month at a convent, was sent to her parents to await the birth of her child, a son, born in December. Guido, desiring to keep the child as his in order to claim inheritance, gained entrance with his four accomplices to the Comparini household by identifying himself as Caponsacchi. They murdered the parents on the spot and left Pompilia with 22 stab wounds which were to prove fatal. The baby was not harmed. All five were caught, arrested, and after the trial (documents recorded in the *Old Yellow Book*), convicted and sentenced to die on 22 February 1698. Guido as a nobleman was beheaded, and his accomplices hanged before a huge crowd.

The first question which must be addressed concerns Browning's use of a series of dramatic monologues as the optimal method of transforming the crude legal accounts into the realm of art. The 10 monologues which more or less recapitulate the main narrative are framed by Books I and XII in which the 19th-century poet (Browning) addresses his British public, thus creating a kind of prologue prefiguring the events and an epilogue in which the speaker recounts four reports on the aftermath of the executions, a device which tidies up the loose ends of the narratives. This lurid tale presents the problem of incorporating a host of melodramatic elements: the child of prostitution, the old goat or wolf as husband of a child-bride, the villainous servant, the rescue in the night, the chase and capture, and the culmination in bloody murder by stabbing, topped by the equally bloody executions. By weaving the woof of the melodramatic episodes with the web of the introspective and evaluative voices of public opinion, Half-Rome, The Other Half-Rome and Tertium Quid; of the main characters in the story, Guido (earlier and later speeches), Caponsacchi, and Pompilia; of the two advocates, Archengelis for Guido and Bottinius for Pompilia; and of the final judge, the Pope, Browning seizes the opportunity to expose the thought processes, the self-awareness and the self-deception, the love and the hate in his characters as they respond to the ponderous pressures of guilt, forgiveness, betrayal, and loyalty in their confrontations with Heaven and Hell. Their speculations and recollections comprise the psychological stress which determines or influences their points of view and their choices. This marriage of external action in moments of crisis with internal meditative analysis and revelation is characteristic of Browning's monologues and of the genre in general, but in *The Ring and the Book* it is given full play.

Closely related to Browning's psychological interest in employing the dramatic monologue is, as he notes in Book I, the engagement of the reader's judgment in the conflicting testimonies. The conflicts and contradictions while sharpening interest and affording variety (". . . What mortal ever in entirety saw?") do not ultimately conceal or deny truth, "The variance now, the eventual unity, / Which make the miracle." Browning is digging for "the lingot truth," not sifting the sands of relativism. At the final hour, Guido, in the agony of his second speech as he faces death on the block, remains the hypocritical and greedy villain-sinner. The Pope, as he wrestles with the relativism of historical decrees in his debate with himself, does not break under the awesome responsibility of holding Guido to the sentence of death, though he may hope his soul can be saved by a flash of truth. His judgment of Caponsacchi, "the warrior-priest," excuses any doubts of him as flaws. His assessment of Pompilia elevates her to the status of martyr-saint.

Browning, in this attempt to extract the truth from the *Old Yellow Book* fashions all his characters with the freedom permitted to the artist. But it is in his expansion of the roles of Pompilia, Caponsacchi, and the Pope, that his imagination affords him the maximum freedom in his delineations and in his efforts to find and express the truth: "Because, it is the glory and good of Art, / That art remains the one way possible, / of speaking truth, to mouths like mine, at least."

The Ring and the Book represents Browning's brilliance as a poet in all its facets. His positive religious posture is clear, his skill in pushing moments to their crises is amply illustrated, and examples of his assimilation of Italian mores permeate the work. The scope of the poem permits Browning to exercise his special talent in altering the iambic line by interrupted thought and parenthetical additions. It permits him to utilize imagery and metaphor enriched by his fascination with science, particularly animal and insect life, and, finally, it provides space for pithy and lengthy comments as well as graceful allusions to biblical and literary sources, ancient as well as modern. *The Ring and the Book* can, indeed, be seen as a compendium of knowledge ranging from classical times to the Victorian age. It embraces much of western heritage, particularly the Judaic-Christian heritage on which its values rest. In addition, it points toward the emphasis our modern world places on the lonely choice.

—Meredith B. Raymond

THE RIVAL QUEENS.
Play by Nathaniel Lee, 1677.

Nathaniel Lee's fourth and most popular play was first performed at the Theatre Royal in Drury Lane on 17 March 1677. As it deals with the demise of an absolute monarch, it was appropriate that Charles II attended. By contemporary and modern consensus Lee's best tragedy, *The Rival Queens; or, The Death of Alexander the Great* dramatizes, with great license, the last days of Alexander the Great. Intoxicated with notions of his own divinity and consequently deaf to reason and responsive to flattery, Alexander enters captive Babylon ripe for tragic reversal. Suspicious of plots, he has executed some of his most trustworthy advisers; vainglorious, he has humiliated anyone sceptical of his divinity; and lustful, he has betrayed his wife Statira with an earlier spouse, Roxana. His irrational excesses end with his impaling of his most loyal soldier, Clytus; with the stabbing of the virtuous Statira by an insanely jealous Roxana; and with Alexander's own poisoning by the dissimulating Cassander.

In earlier plays Lee had proved his resourcefulness in ransacking history for theatrically exciting subjects; but nowhere is the action brisker nor the style more ambitious than in *The Rival Queens*. Generically the play is a hybrid: part rhymed heroic drama urging admiration for those most noble in renouncing the fleshly for the ethical; part affective tragedy written in blank verse and imploring empathy for the suffering of flawed but essentially worthy protagonists; and part unashamed melodrama. Critics concur that in *The Rival Queens* Lee exploits all the resources of the baroque Restoration stage to produce "tumultuous," "spectacular," and "rhetorically powerful" theater. Where they violently disagree is over the worth of his accomplishment. Those who defend Lee as a disciplined artist interpret the plot as "thoughtful and coherent," the characterizations as psychologically "profound," and the language as "poetically powerful." Those who denigrate mad Nat Lee as a neurotic pseudogenius interpret the plot as "incoherent" and "inept," the characterizations as "shallow," and the language as "blustering rant."

Appreciative critics stress Lee's compelling dramatization of Alexander's psychopathology, his powerful depiction of a charismatic leader unable to moderate his heroic excesses. J.M. Armistead ably orders Lee's creation by seeing the contending characters as projections of Alexander's fragmented psyche and the plot as the social chaos wrought by psychic disease. Hostile critics stress that such order as the play possesses derives from the inherited truisms of heroic drama with its balanced characterizations and couplets while Lee's definitive additions are bombast and unashamed sensationalism.

For good or ill Lee's hyperbolic language has to be heard to be believed. When Alexander fears his beloved Statira may be dead he cautions himself:

Keep down, ye rising sighs,
And murmur in the hollow of my breast,
Run to my heart, and gather more sad wind,
That when the voice of fate shall call you forth,
Ye may, at one rush, from the seat of life
Blow the blood out, and burst me like a blatter.

Statira's sister pleads that to implore Alexander to spare the life of her lover,

I'll follow thus forever on my knees,
And make your way so slippery with tears
You shall not pass.

When, a few lines later, Alexander revokes his unjust sentence, Statira embraces his knees exclaiming,

Why are you so divine to cause such fondness
That my heart leaps, and beats, and fain would out
To make a dance of joy about your feet?

From the day the play opened reaction to Lee's rhetoric was strongly polarized. John Dryden, whose *All for Love* owes much to *The Rival Queens*, lauds Lee's lines as the triumph of "nature . . . over wretched art," criticizing "those drones" who "accuse / The too much vigor of your youthful muse." In contrast, Alexander Pope drew from Lee's drama for examples of poetic descent in *Peri Bathous*; and Colley Cibber ridiculed the play line by line in a burlesque *Rival Queans*. Addison pursues the mean in *Spectator* 39, seeing "the impetuosity of his genius" but wishing "he had restrained it, and kept it within its proper bounds" and lamenting that his grand thoughts are "frequently lost in a cloud of words."

Lee's play was one of those most frequently performed and printed in the hundred years after its opening. Today, despite historical interest and recent interpretive ingenuity, *The Rival Queens* survives for its few readers because of its rhetorical excesses. It remains a rollicking roller coaster ride from pathos to bathos; and its sudden descents from the sublime to the ridiculous are as delicious to the learned palate as they are astonishing. When the passionate, abandoned Roxana cries that "My soul is pent, and has not elbow room," who cannot smile; and who can withhold sympathy when, just lines later, she refuses the sexual advances of Alexander's loathsome enemy:

Disgraced Roxana, whither wilt thou fall!
I ne'er was truly wretched till this moment. . . .
What, shall I leave the bosom of a deity
To clasp a clod, a moving piece of earth
Which a mole heaves?

—Harry M. Solomon

THE RIVALS.
Play by Richard Brinsley Sheridan, 1775.

Richard Brinsley Sheridan began his brief career as a playwright with a work that has become a classic of the English theater. The opening, however, was inauspicious, for the first performance on 15 January 1775, was a dismal failure, "too long" and tedious. It was withdrawn at once, Sheridan spent a month pruning and revising, and when it was offered in its present form on 27 February it was an immediate and permanent favorite.

As is fitting for a comedy of manners, the satire of *The Rivals* is in the gentle Horatian mode, aiming at folly rather than vice, but for all his mildness, the author has a sharp eye for the ridiculous: pretensions to elegance, exaggerated romantic notions, arranged marriages, sentimentalism gone mad. It is more akin to the comedy of Congreve than to the contemporary style which for a generation had been edging closer to the French *comédie larmoyante* and which Sheridan himself seemed to find absurd.

The setting in Bath, which he knew well, allowed not only a wide range of targets but an attractive background, for the fashionable watering spot drew all elements of society to its center. Earlier, Beau Nash had established certain traditions of propriety (gentlemen could not wear swords or use foul language), but for all its claims as a health spa, Bath maintained a holiday spirit where the relative informality permitted adventurers to rub shoulders with aristocrats, where it is not inconceivable that a penniless Irishman could hope to find a wealthy wife.

The rivalry of the title is for the hand of Lydia, and the most obvious is Absolute's pretended competition with his alter ego, Ensign Beverley, but other characters are also involved. Acres thinks he is contending with Beverley, O'Trigger with Absolute; in a broader sense, Lydia is the unwitting rival of Mrs. Malaprop for O'Trigger's affections, while Faulkland's instability makes him his own rival for Julia. The constant deceptions and intrigues provide insight on characters as they solve problems or plunge more deeply into difficulties with unexpected turns of the plot.

The action is complex but clearly presented. The central plot is anchored in Absolute's pursuit of Lydia and the other lines develop from it; Acres's part is connected through his hopeless passion for Lydia, the O'Trigger / Malaprop line through mistaken identity. The subplot is less closely tied and is, in fact, a parody of the sentimental. It is the reversal of the Absolute / Lydia situation, for in this case the steady one is Julia, and Faulkland is the hypersensitive hero who brings his troubles on himself. Without breaking the comic mood, their story comes close to ending unhappily, and the suggestion of serious consequences to unbridled emotion adds a sobering touch of commonsense to the laughter.

The characters are richly varied. Lydia Languish, whose head is so filled with romantic novels that her ambition is to marry a poor ensign and live on love, little Bob Acres, a favorite of comedians, is a study in bravado and cowardice, the hot-tempered Sir Lucius O'Trigger adds a touch of Irish humor, and Jack Absolute's cleverness and ingenuity not only allow him to outwit everyone but reward him with the prize. Sir Anthony and Mrs. Malaprop are examples of what the older generation should not be, and much of the comedy derives from frustrating their plans.

As in his other comedies, Sheridan uses the resources of the stage to full advantage. Visual humor is present throughout; Lydia hastily conceals her forbidden romances from her aunt ("put *The Innocent Adultery* into *The Whole Duty of Man*"), Mrs. Malaprop listens in on conversations, and Acres undergoes a last-minute lesson in gun etiquette. Misunderstandings abound, mostly centered on Absolute's masquerade as Beverley. Knowing this, the audience can appreciate the irony of Lydia's devotion to Beverley, the coinciding of Sir Anthony's and Absolute's choice of bride, Acres's request that Absolute be his second in a duel with Beverley, and Mrs. Malaprop's mistaken assumption of O'Trigger's affection. Letters further the plot but are also devices that often involve servants. The timid David is too frightened even to touch the challenge note, the crafty Fag reads everything and utilizes the information for his own ends, the greedy Lucy capitalizes on them by delivering to the highest bidder.

It is in his dialogue, perhaps, that Sheridan displays true brilliance, though he is less interested in wit for its own sake than in the comic lines that arise from character and situation. At one point or other, every character speaks at cross-purposes. Even Absolute is not exempt when he refuses to marry the girl he thinks his father has chosen for him. Acres, O'Trigger, and Mrs. Malaprop are in a constant state of misapprehension, sometimes deliberately created by Absolute, sometimes by their own egocentric views. A good part of the comedy lies in misleading words: Absolute simultaneously establishes his own identity with Mrs. Malaprop and deceives Lydia into thinking he is Beverley, O'Trigger swears undying love to "Delia," not knowing she is the aunt and not the niece. But Sheridan's ultimate achievement is in the character whose name has become a part of the language itself, Mrs. Malaprop. Her creative approach is evident in almost every speech. She complains that her niece is "as headstrong as an allegory on the banks of the Nile," she compliments Absolute as "the very pine-apple of politeness," and she is proud of her own "oratory" which includes "a nice derangement of epitaphs." Her speech on the education of a young lady who should have "a supercilious knowledge" without becoming "a progeny of learning" is a masterpiece of malapropisms.

Sheridan's career as a playwright lasted only five years and he wrote only five original works, but two, *The Rivals* and *The School for Scandal*, have been ranked with the comedies of Shakespeare and Congreve. Along with Goldsmith, he has been given the credit for returning "laughing comedy" to the stage. It is not surprising that he is regarded as a major dramatist, or that *The Rivals* is still a part of almost every theatrical season.

—Helene Wickham Koon

THE ROAD.
Play by Wole Soyinka, 1965.

As with most of the plays that Wole Soyinka wrote in the decade after returning to his native Nigeria in 1960 after university study in Britain, *The Road* combines features of the indigenous Yoruba performance tradition with techniques which he had learned while working as playreader at London's Royal Court Theatre. The play is thus a complex dramatic demonstration of the principles of cultural hybridisation which some theorists have argued is integral to post-colonialism.

The Yoruba element which Soyinka introduces into most of these plays is that of the Egungun festival, a tradition of masquerading which venerates the spirits of the ancestors. Since the spirits are believed to possess the masked dancers, the dance is highly sacramental, and the assumed religious dynamics of the performance are such that contact between the performers and the general populace must be prevented by the presence of youthful flagellants. In an earlier play, Soyinka used a flogger to break through the other characters and clear a space with his long whip, after which the space is ritualistically sprinkled with water; in this play, the flagellants carry a dog tied to a stake and brandish matchets. Whatever the religious orientation of the audience, the effect of the masquerade is both intimidatory and awesome, although there is sometimes a hint of a comic dimension also.

In *The Road*, Soyinka combines Egungun performance with another Yoruba element, that of Agemo, "a religious cult of flesh dissolution." This he defines as "a visual suspension of death," "an arrest of time," a phase which "includes the passage of transition from the human to the divine essence." Just as masquerading challenges the concrete nature of a dramatic role, allowing ancestral identity to dominate or merge with that of the character and possibly performer, similarly Agemo collapses the sense of time and chronological ordering. Together, the principles complicate and sometimes block the personal interactions which occur on the stage.

The European presence in the world of the play is announced in the introductory stage directions describing the play's single set: the corner of a church and a wagon full of salvaged motor parts. Most of the characters will also show evidence of the residual colonising presence: Salubi in a chauffeur's uniform, a cannabis-smoking, Americanised thug called Say Tokyo Kid, and a deranged Professor in Victorian tails and top-hat whose vatic rhetoric gives him a special authority. At the start, it is nearly dawn, and several of the menials are sleeping. An element of suspense comes through Murano, who moves among the sleeping figures and disappears; in fact, he is a recently-dead person in his Agemo phase, on a different plane of existence, and throughout the play his muteness means that there is constant uncertainty about the degree of sensory contact that exists between him and other characters. The first act is predominantly comic, with a satirical indulgence in issues of status and pretension, but the stature of the Professor remains ambiguous: he may be just an absurdly fossilised local hero, or his obsessive sermonising about death may have a connection with the real carnage on the highway which seems to be set up to help the car wreckage business. The act ends with the suggestion that the Professor does have a special level of contact with Murano.

The second act is more complex and sombre. It begins with a narrative—which develops into an enactment—of the horrific truck accident in which Murano was killed. The action is generated initially by the Professor's morbid curiosity and subsequently by the confused and emotionalised memory of the driver, but there is also a more substantial factor of collective imagination because Murano was actually leading a masquerade at the time of the accident, and his mask is concealed in the truck on stage. Time, place, and role crumble as narration merges with enactment, but the stage presents the two truck drivers frantically trying to get away from the flagellants who are searching for their leader; one driver picks up a whip and becomes involved in the flogging, while the other desperately puts on the mask and becomes frenzied, blinded by the dead man's blood. The Professor is questioning, documenting, and commenting on much of this, and the play ends with the Egungun peaking, the drivers fighting, and the Professor, fatally stabbed, delivering a sermon on the Road while the mask spins by itself.

That the Road itself has many available metaphorical dimensions is obvious, and some of these must be associated with ersatz colonial technology and the vulture-like consumerism that this breeds in societies. But the Road, with its predators and its interpreters, coexists as a dynamic and destructive totem with Ogun, the Yoruba deity who feeds on dogs, and the two factors produce the rich texture of hybridisation that is Soyinka's ironic statement of the dilemma of the post-colonial quest for identity.

—Howard McNaughton

ROBINSON CRUSOE.
(*The Life and Strange Surprising Adventures of Robinson Crusoe, of York, Mariner.*)
Fiction by Daniel Defoe, 1719.

Although some critics consider *Robinson Crusoe* the first English novel, a reader who picked it up in 1719 would have been struck less by its novelty than by its continuity with existing forms. Clearly it was trading on the popularity of travel literature, particularly William Dampier's *Voyages* (1697–1709), and narratives of the ordeal of Alexander Selkirk, the real-life Crusoe. Equally plain would have been the author's pitch to the large audience for religious literature. A generation after Bunyan and Milton, he promises to give "a religious application to events," and "to justify and honour the wisdom of Providence." Yet from these familiar materials Daniel Defoe made something transcendent: the one book that Rousseau used in the "natural education" of Emile; the patriarch of a great tribe of imitations, such as *The Swiss Family Robinson*; the children's classic and scholarly puzzle of our time.

Critics have wondered whether *Robinson Crusoe* is really a novel or a myth, with most of them preferring the latter. Virginia Woolf thought the book "resembles one of the anonymous productions of the race," and Ian Watt groups it "not with other novels, but with the great myths of Western civilization." The book's deficiencies as a novel—social and psychological realism, dialogue, style, etc.—are in any case patent. But the question then becomes: a myth about what?

Watt argues that Crusoe embodies the archetype of *homo economicus* and that Defoe's verisimilitude supports a materialist ethic. Certainly England in 1719 would have enjoyed the image of the small shopkeeper acquiring stock from the shipwreck and taking inventory in his island cave ("it was a great pleasure to me to see all my goods in such order"). But Crusoe is more than a shopkeeper: he is one of the merchant adventurers who were then helping to found the Empire. He leaves his crowded homeland to seek his fortune, gains a foothold on the coast of new territory, establishes agriculture and a fortified base, reconnoitres the hinterland but leaves it untamed, subdues or converts the heathen, and eventually departs, granting limited self-government without relinquishing title, and leaving the colonists to remit to the Motherland. If this involves slavery, that is how colonies work. (As a journalist, Defoe promoted colonial commerce, raising only economic, not moral, objections to slavery.) So we find Crusoe selling his fellow escapee Xury, and importing African slaves for his Brazilian plantation.

Compelling and timely though it was, this theme is only one aspect of the book, and recent scholarship has preferred to emphasize the spiritual or didactic side: *Robinson Crusoe* as confessional literature, recounting the salvation of an erring soul. After all, Defoe was a Dissenter, like many of his readers, and religious allegory was central to the Puritan experience. So Crusoe calls going to sea against his father's wishes his "original sin" and refers to himself after the first storm as a "true repenting prodigal." On the island Crusoe, fighting off despair, decides that Providence has "ordered everything for the best": his stranding becomes one of those Fortunate Falls beloved of Puritans. His religious life takes the forms popular at the time: an "Enthusiastick" vision that converts him to "born-again" status just nine months after his landing, opening the Bible at random for guidance, ecstatic testimony, and so on.

This level of the book is one that some modern readers find mechanical and unconvincing. There may even be a hint of mischief in the pages leading up to Crusoe's attempt to instruct Friday in Christianity; Defoe lets his hero stumble into one theological difficulty after another. But even critics who reject the religious reading often acknowledge a spiritual dimension, such as a quest motif or an allegory of Defoe's life (a view that he encouraged).

It is fitting that the book contains these disparate elements. Puritanism was a fusion of economic and religious impulses much like Max Weber's "Protestant ethic": the pious will prosper, and prosperity argues piety. Defoe's business was to mirror the world that he and his readers knew, not to simplify it, so he alternated physical adventure and spiritual introspection, success and failure, the manual and the sermon.

Underlying and uniting these elements is the bedrock theme of isolation. To be isolated is, literally, to be "islanded" (*isola*); the survivor, the capitalist, the colonist, the soul are all, ultimately, isolates. Defoe, wrote Virginia Woolf, "persuades us to see . . . the solitude of the human soul." At the beginning of his *Serious Reflections*, a sequel, Crusoe writes at length on the "Silence" and "universal act of solitude" that is life. And it is not just Crusoe: virtually all of Defoe's characters are outsiders, cut off from society, from which we infer his imaginative identification with them. Moll Flanders is "islanded" by her friendless womanhood, as is Roxana, and in *A Journal of the Plague Year* the survivors are confined to an island of health in a sea of plague.

But it was *Robinson Crusoe* that struck a nerve. It would take pages to list the hundreds of translations, revisions, adaptations and imitations, many preserving the name "Robinson." It is difficult for us to write or read a story of isolated survival—and we have many—without Crusoe making his presence felt. In J.M. Barrie's *The Admirable Crichton*, the lower-class butler, not the inept aristocrats, proves to be the true Robinson; William Golding subverts our Defovian responses in *Pincher Martin* to create an existential fable. In retrospect, Defoe can be seen to have moved away from Donne's "No man is an island" towards the modern outlook preserved in Arnold's "To Marguerite—Continued": "Yes! in the sea of life enisled, / . . . We mortal millions live *alone*."

—Richard Bevis

RODERICK RANDOM.
(*The Adventures of Roderick Random.*)
Novel by Tobias Smollett, 1748.

Although scholars disagree on the extent of the picaresque influence on Tobias Smollett's works, with few exceptions, they place *Roderick Random*, his first novel, well within that genre. Smollett himself acknowledged his indebtedness to LeSage's *Gil Blas*, his translation of which appeared in the same year as the publication of his novel. Kinship not only with *Gil Blas*, but with such ancestors as *Guzman de Alfarache* and *Lazarillo de Tormes*, marks all the fictional features of Smollett's novel: the structure of its plot, its characterization, and its literary purpose.

Like the traditional picaresque, Smollett's work employs a journey motif. Roderick and Hugh Strap, his picaresque pair, begin their adventures in a village in northern Scotland, their birthplace, and Smollett uses the setting to satirize education as well as familial and town relationships. After taking on the profession of schoolmaster and exposing the deceitfulness of apothecaries, his main characters go on the road. Their arduous trip to London becomes a vehicle for displaying the various hazards awaiting travellers on English highways. In London itself the perspective is that of the outsider, and the two naifs suffer the indignities inflicted by city tricksters who prey upon innocent dupes. Smollett's episodic structure allows him to include the sad history of the unfortunate Miss Williams, a prostitute whose downfall should warn Roderick, but his characteristic picaresque nature does not permit him to learn from experience.

The journey motif, intended to expose as many of the vices of contemporary society as possible, requires Smollett to go beyond the bounds of his native shores. Taking off from the funniest scenes in the novel in which Smollett savagely attacks naval examination boards and political corruption, the novel moves on to an exploration of the harshness of shipboard authority and warfare. His picaresque technique provides a realistic portrait of the unheroic and gruesome details of battles. Then, in rapid succession, he offers an outsider's view of colonial life in Jamaica; a satire on "bluestockings," women so caught up in intellectual matters that they lose sight of everyday reality; and the absurdities of French civil and military life.

Adventure piles on adventure, all with a single intention—as Smollett declares in his preface—to awaken his readers to "the sordid and vicious disposition of the world." Returned to London, Roderick applies his picaresque tricks to attempts to dupe high society. He goes on to con visitors to the resort of Bath and to uncover the impostures of doctors. Even when his fortunes send him to prison, the satiric character of the picaresque narrative continues as Smollett ridicules the pretenses of the literary and theatrical establishments of his time. Only in the long romantic coda that begins with Roderick's return to Jamaica, takes him on a triumphant return first to London and then Scotland does Smollett break from the traditional picaresque and lose the tone of his novel. It does not represent a turning away from the genre in his structure, but rather the weakness of a young novelist who does not know another way to bring things to an end.

As with any picaresque, the structure of *Roderick Random* poses problems for its characterization. Panoramic presentation does not allow for depth in the people of its fictional world. Beginning with its eponymous hero, the novel is replete with characters defined by tag names, whether such nautical figures as Lieutenant Bowling or Captain Oakum, or such single-trait figures as the homosexual Captain Whiffle and the intellectual "lady," Mrs. Sagely, or the mean-spirited Launcelot Crab, or the outrageous literary fools, Banter and Ranter. Smollett's strength is his ability to bring them to life and make them credible through that intensity in his writing which was so much admired by Dickens, who employed the same techniques to make caricature convincing. Even with the stereotypical Welshman Morgan and Irishman Mackshane, one Roderick's shipboard friend and the other his adversary, Smollett knew how to make them more than the stock figures current on his contemporary stage.

But most particularly it is the characterization of Roderick—one of the two fictional elements that provide the unity of the rambling structure of the novel—that marks Smollett's achievement. Two things motivate his character: pride and revenge; attack the first, and the second is certain to follow. Introduced in the very first episode, these character traits are repeated throughout the novel and become the very basis for holding the novel together even as they expand our understanding of the hero and develop our vision of the world he inhabits. The same rhythmic device—repetition and progression—marks the satiric intentions of the novel. The satire begins with individual targets, progresses to more and more objects of scorn, until we recognize that what Smollett offers is a thorough satiric assessment of his entire society in a narrative that describes "modest merit struggling with every difficulty to which a friendless orphan is exposed."

In *Roderick Random* Smollett takes an established genre, adds to it a generalization of his own personal experiences, and adapts it for an English audience attuned to a didactic message. The effect was to produce the first genuine migration of the continental picaro to English soil.

—Robert D. Spector

ROMEO AND JULIET.
Play by William Shakespeare, 1594–95(?).

Romeo and Juliet has provided our culture with its archetype of tragic young love, giving rise to creations as diverse as opera, orchestral music, ballet, musical, literary parody, and comic routine. But the myth of Romeo and Juliet bears a somewhat loose relation to the particulars of this early play, a play which, surprisingly perhaps, finds its most immediate affinities with William Shakespeare's comedies of love.

Romeo and Juliet is marred by what seems, on the dramatist's part, an excessive will to tragedy. There are too many, not too few, reasons why things go wrong in this play. We are offered a social setting in hot Verona which emphasizes the intimate relation of sexuality and violence. The lovers are from families long involved in a destructive and seemingly interminable feud. There is, in Romeo's and Juliet's love, an excessive haste, and *occasional* intimations that something inherent in their love itself makes for its self-destructiveness. Lest we be in any doubt, a Chorus appears at the beginning of the play and, in a manner atypical of Shakespeare, pre-empts dramatic suspense, affording a jumble of terms which declare emphatically the tragic outcome of the story we are about to witness:

From forth the *fatal* loins of these two foes
A pair of *star-cross'd* lovers take their life; . . .
The fearful passage of their *death-mark'd* love,
And the continuance of their parents' rage,
Which, but their children's end, nought could remove,
Is now the two hours' traffic of our stage . . .

Continuing throughout the play, there is a verbal insistence, accompanying every turn of the action, on the malevolence of Fortune or Fate or the stars. But, if we attend to plot and action rather than to the words of *Romeo and Juliet*, we find an accumulation of accidents and implausibilities, all too easily averted. Mercutio is mortally wounded in the confusion of Romeo's intervention in a brawl. Tybalt returns to the scene of the fight all too conveniently. Romeo could so easily have carried Juliet off with him to the safety of Mantua, in the way that Lysander elopes with Hermia in *A Midsummer Night's Dream*. Friar John, delayed by the plague, fails to tell Romeo of the *faked* death of Juliet. Romeo arrives at the tomb, just a few moments too soon. Juliet awakes a few moments too late. The Watch arrives at precisely the wrong moment, causing Friar Laurence to desert the suicidal Juliet for reasons which, like so much of this play, are none too clear.

Yet the play remains a masterpiece in its exploration of the experience and languages of love, an exploration it shares with such comedies as *As You Like It*. Like that comedy, *Romeo and Juliet* involves its audience in a process which effects, first, the demystification, and, subsequently, the revitalization of love's language: the hyberboles and tropes of the lover, exposed as too well-worn clichés at the play's opening, are again brought to grip and to express a particular and intense reality. We first encounter Romeo, "in love" with a Rosaline who never appears in the play, and comically trapped in self-perpetuating conventionalities of expression. He is mocked by Mercutio, and, initially, we feel that the truth entirely belongs with this bawdy and forthright materialist. But, after Romeo's first meeting with Juliet, a new urgency and energy enters his words, and we, the audience, come, with Romeo, to dismiss Mercutio as one who "jests at scars that never felt a wound." The mocking and realistic role transfers itself, more subtly, to Juliet, who tests Romeo much as Rosalind tests Orlando in *As You Like It*. The couple's language breaks beyond the confines of closed couplets into a more free-flowing blank verse and triumphs in a dramatic aubade (III.v) which is rightly valued as some of the finest love poetry in the language.

This is not to argue that the play is a comedy. *Romeo and Juliet*, despite the clumsiness of its plotting, affords, scenically and poetically, numerous instances of tragic intensity: but the play is a lyrical rather than a dramatic tragedy. This is nowhere more true than in the last act, an act encumbered by an excess of stage business and the Friar's bumbling and summary reiteration of a plot with which the audience is already fully familiar. Amid such ineptnesses, both Romeo and Juliet articulate an extraordinary lyricism of love and loss. The end of the play sees the lovers dead, and the feud over—but over only because none of the younger generation remains alive to continue it. The overt rivalry gives way to a more insidious form of competitiveness as the old fathers promise to outdo each other in the grandeur of the statues they will raise to Romeo and Juliet. We must wait until *The Winter's Tale* for the cold opulence of such statuary to be again transformed into warm human flesh.

—John M. Lyon

ROSALYNDE.
Fiction by Thomas Lodge, 1590.

Thomas Lodge was about 27 years old when to allay the tedium of a commercial voyage to the Canary Islands he wrote the pastoral romance *Rosalynde: Euphues' Golden Legacy*. Addressed specifically to "Gentlemen Readers," he notes that "every line was wet with a surge and every humorous passion counter-checked with a storm," adding, "If you like it, so." This flippant statement was clearly geared to an Inns-of-Court audience, but it was also clearly recalled by Shakespeare when in 1598/99 he adopted the plot and characters of Lodge's novel in *As You Like It*. There was good reason for Shakespeare to look to this publication since Lodge's romance demonstrated great popular appeal, going through 11 editions before 1640 (as against only two of the play).

Rosalynde derives in part from the pseudo-Chaucerian *The Tale of Gamelyn* (c. 1350); as it was still unpublished, Lodge must have had recourse to a manuscript from which he took the name of Sir John of Bordeaux, father of the two sons who win the love and the hands of the two heroines. But in the handling of the tale he adds a good deal, substituting for its Robin Hood outlawry a pastoral context in the forest of Arden and inventing the romantic plot involving three sets of lovers whose "passions" he treats with lightly mocking humour. In the interweaving of the various episodes the thematic emphases reflect 16th-century attitudes and thus give a degree of tonal weight to what is essentially a diverting tale.

The dying Sir John's unequal legacy to his sons initiates the action by arousing the jealousy of Saladyne toward his younger brother Rosader. As part of his legacy Sir John also includes a number of "wise saws and modern instances" (*As You Like It*, II.vii.156) for their edification; they should seek after honor, avoid ambition, serve the commonwealth, but, above all, they should avoid love, the reason being that "women are wantons and yet men cannot want one"; however, "chaste, obedient, and silent" a woman may be, she will still reveal sufficient vanities to offset her virtues. It is the countervention of this legacy that becomes the determining theme of the romance.

Nonetheless, this misogynist point of view receives some verbal support, first, from Rosalynde when she is disguised as Ganymede and is maintaining the decorum proper to a male. "You may see what mad cattle you women be. . . . They delight to be courted, and then they glory to seem coy; and when they are most desired, then they freeze with disdain." Later, it receives further support from the disdainful shepherdess, who readily acknowledges that an "ounce of give-me persuades a woman more than a pound of hear-me." Though she herself shuns her pastoral lover—for a time—the other characters, once they congregate in Arden, are quickly receptive to their natural promptings. Ultimately, despite exile, revenge, and outlaws, the complications of the plot are resolved by love and amity—an ironic inversion of the legacy.

A parallel to the situation of the two heroes is that of the girls. Alinda, daughter of the usurping King of France, is the dearly loved friend of Rosalynde, whose banished father is now dwelling in the forest of Arden. A wrestling tournament at the tyrant's court provides the means by which the wicked Saladyne believes he will rid himself of his brother as well as the occasion for the instant enamourment of Rosader and Rosalynde at the scene of the competition. The vagaries of the tyrant lead, first, to the banishing of Rosalynde, then of his daughter, and, finally, of Saladyne; their destination, as it turns out, is Arden, where Rosader, accompanied by his faithful retainer Adam, also arrives.

In this pastoral retreat Alinda becomes the shepherdess Aliena and Rosalynde her page Ganymede, the locale providing a sharp contrast to the courtly life of Rosalynde and Alinda with its political strife and to the country life of Saladyne and Rosader with its fraternal strife. To the exiles it appears idyllic—a *locus amoenus*, which, in accord with 16th-century attitudes, is presented as something artificial rather than natural:

> The ground where [two shepherds] sat was diapered with Flora's riches, as if she meant to wrap Tellus in the glory of her vestments. Round about in the form of an amphitheatre were most curiously planted pine trees interseamed with lemons and citrons, which with the thickness of their boughs so shadowed the place that Phoebus could not pry into the secret of that arbor; so united were the tops with so thick a closure that Venus might there in her jollity have dallied unseen with her dearest paramour. Fast by, to make the place more gorgeous, was there a fount so crystalline and clear that it seemed Diana with her Dryads and Hamadryads had that spring as the secret of all their bathings. In this glorious arbor sat these two shepherds, seeing their sheep feed, playing on their pipes many pleasant tunes, and from music and melody falling into much amorous chat.

Here the characters disport themselves, eating such country cates as the locale affords, enjoying sweet prattle—sweeter than all their courtly junkets—but most of all playing the part of lovers. Here Ganymede masquerades as Rosalynde in order to test Rosader's skill in wooing. When this device leaves him ill-satisfied, they agree on a jesting match which afterwards proves a match in earnest.

Among his interweaving themes, Lodge emphasizes the 16th-century concern with the relation between nature and nurture, Rosader, for example, possessing a prodigal wit but, thanks to his envious brother, lacking the art provided by education. Such natural capacity necessarily includes the ability to love with the disdainful shepherdess providing—but only for a time—a negative instance; as Aliena-Alinda notes, "Women must love or they must cease to live." Linked to this nature-nurture theme is the role of fortune—"variable with every object and constant in nothing but inconstancy." Response to its fluctuations is seen to measure an individual's nature.

Locale, situation, and plot provide Lodge with opportunity to exhibit his stylistic skills. The subtitle with its reference to John Lyly's popular novels—*Euphues: The Anatomy of Wit* and *Euphues and His England*—indicate that he is employing to some degree the euphuistic manner, this mostly by references to natural history—fortune is like the chameleon—or to mythology—Rosader compares himself with Ixion, thinking to possess a goddess but embracing only a cloud. The pastoral context allows Lodge to introduce many delightful songs and sonnets, e.g., "Love in my bosom like a bee" and one denigrating love that Shakespeare seems to echo in Sonnet 129. There are also blazons and soliloquies that function as debates as well as a great variety of Renaissance motifs included in both the poetry and the prose sections. This blending of the two modes, the deft plotting, and the witty style result in a work that still has considerable appeal.

—Elizabeth Story Donno

ROSENCRANTZ AND GUILDENSTERN ARE DEAD. Play by Tom Stoppard, 1966.

Rosencrantz and Guildenstern Are Dead was Tom Stoppard's first major theatrical success. It typifies the work of the first phase of his creativity, up to *Travesties*. Within the framework of absurdism he takes a "root" text, and juxtaposes it with his own material. In *Rosencrantz and Guildenstern Are Dead* the "root" text is, of course, Shakespeare's *Hamlet*.

He takes the two minor court sycophants, Rosencrantz and Guildenstern, and elevates them to be joint protagonists, while Claudius, Gertrude, Polonius, and Hamlet make occasional walk-on appearances in their own play. This enables Stoppard to make a statement about the theatre and theatrical expectation—a theme prevalent in much of his writing. He conducts several germane discussions on the nature of art. And, by inverting a classical work where critics constantly strive for "meaning," and by showing an inversion where life appears entirely without purpose, where dramatic characters cannot even recall their own names, and have no concept of why they have been "sent for," he is able to issue the absurdist challenge that we should make radical reassessments of all our comfortable innate assumptions about life.

Hamlet with its familiar words occasionally spills over into the metaphysical annex where Rosencrantz and Guildenstern are waiting to discover the meaning of their summons, and futilely attempting to plumb Hamlet's secret as they adjust their own lives to the predetermined but meaningless pattern within which they subsist.

Also, the players who, in the original *Hamlet* occupy a minor role in Act II, are elevated to the centre of things by Stoppard. Their leader, particularly, is a wily, pragmatic, and infinitely world-weary old ham, whose remarks on art, theatre, and life provide some of the play's richest and most pungent moments. His delightful *reductio ad absurdam* of the great Jacobean classics hits home the harder coming within the context of Stoppard's *Hamlet* inversion. Discussing stage realism the Player confides: "I had an actor once who was condemned for stealing a sheep—or a lamb, I forget which—so I got permission to have him hanged in the middle of a play—had to change the plot a bit but I thought it would be effective . . . and you wouldn't believe it, he just wasn't convincing. It was impossible to suspend one's disbelief . . . the whole thing was a disaster!—he did nothing but cry all the time—right out of character—just stood there and cried. . . . Never again."

Such a speech contains the essence of Stoppard's particular absurdism. It challenges us to reassess the relationship between imagination and reality, and the intermediary role played by art in wedding the two. It reduces an argument to the utterly preposterous, yet the tone is so superficially earnest and reasonable that, while the Player is speaking, it is almost possible to fall into the dreadful gulf he digs between common sense and surrealist insanity. No wonder Stoppard once spoke of his art as "ambushes for the audience."

Act I of *Rosencrantz and Guildenstern Are Dead* introduces the theme of chance, order, and reason. Rosencrantz and Guildenstern, in a typically absurdist limbo—"a place without any visible character"—are tossing coins. The coin has landed heads 85 consecutive times, and the ensuing debate sets the tone for much of the intellectual games playing which is to follow.

We learn that they have been "sent for," but they have no concept of why. The spectator who knows *Hamlet*, of course, is perfectly aware that they are destined, without any free will of their own, to play the already-written roles of court spies, and that their destiny is sealed. All their talk of probability, free will, and chance is a vain irony.

They encounter the Players, also walking out of limbo towards Elsinore where they are destined to perform. They offer a play/exhibition to Rosencrantz and his partner, but just at the moment it is to happen—and just as the first tails turns up on a coin—*Hamlet*, Act I, scenes i and ii supervenes, and they receive their commission to discover Hamlet's secret. This task simply confuses them further, and leads to a characteristic Stoppard word game—"Questions"—where every line of the dialogue must comprise a question. Apart from showing what hopeless inquisitors they are, this brilliant passage also demonstrates the subversive power of words themselves—another Stoppard preoccupation.

Act II gives us the play-within-a-play (*The Murder of Gonzago*) in a version which weirdly melts into *Hamlet* itself, so that Rosencrantz and Guildenstern actually watch the Players perform the moment when they—Rosencrantz and Guildenstern—arrive in England with the exchanged letters containing the mandate for their own deaths. Thus they get an appalling preview of their own literary and "real" destiny, but they watch totally uncomprehendingly—for after all, if they are in a play, and we haven't got this far yet in the script, how *can* they know that they have just previewed their own deaths? Again the Player's comments upon illusion and reality underpin the theatrical inversions and subversions and sustain the performance.

Act III steps beyond the strict confines of Shakespeare's script, and becomes Stoppard's fantasy reconstruction of the boat journey Hamlet describes in Act V scene i, when he substitutes the death warrants, jumps ship, and returns to Elsinore. These events are sketched out in Stoppard's Act III, but, deliciously, we find that the Players are aboard too, still surviving, despite being in jeopardy for their performance at Elsinore.

Rosencrantz and Guildenstern's attempts to imagine what it will be like when they arrive in England are poignantly and ironically interspersed with speculations about death, identity, free will, and destiny: "Who are we that so much should converge on our little deaths?"

An atmosphere of crepuscular fatalism closes in on the play's last moments. "There must have been a moment at the beginning, where we could have said—no. But somehow we missed it." They drift disconsolately from view. Then, with a convulsive light-change, we melt to a tableau of the last moments of *Hamlet*, the dead scattered over the stage, as the English Ambassador announces Shakespeare's words "Rosencrantz and Guildenstern Are Dead."

—T. Bareham

THE ROVER.
Play by Aphra Behn, 1677.

The source for Aphra Behn's play *The Rover* is Thomas Killigrew's lengthy closet drama *Thomaso; or, The Wanderer*, written in the 1650's and published in 1664. *Thomaso* needed extensive cutting and recasting to fit it for the stage, and though Behn used many of its incidents and some of its dialogue, the overall shape and controlling tone of the play are her own. She uses the conventions of Spanish intrigue comedy with great skill, producing a tightly patterned, fast-moving plot, with contrasting pairs of lovers, multiple tricks, disguises and mistakes, and conflicts between love and honour, often leading to duels. First played at the Duke's Theatre in Dorset Gardens in March 1677, *The Rover* soon became one of Behn's most popular works. It was very frequently performed up to the 1740's, and revived in the 1750's, but after that disappeared from the stage until very recently, when it has become one of the few Behn plays (others include *The Feigned Courtesans* and *The Lucky Chance*) to be given 20th-century performance.

It must have originally delighted royalist taste as a nostalgic glimpse of an idealised cavalier past. Set in Naples during the Interregnum, it follows the adventures of a group of "Banished Cavaliers" whose loyalty to their king has robbed them not only of estate and fortune but the responsibilities that go with them. For the moment it is by thoroughly enjoying themselves that they can best prove their allegiance to the future Charles II, now, like Behn's hero, "a rover of fortune," though still "a prince aboard his little wooden world." Its appeal is not just topical. It is Carnival time in Naples, and many of comedy's enduring carnivalesque delights are brought into play. Hellena's father is away, and with his authority temporarily withdrawn she and her companions only have to contend with a rather easily fooled brother in order to join the festivities and find lovers. Hierarchies are reversed and a fool gets his comeuppance when the "jilting wench" Lucetta entices the silly country gentleman Blunt into her chamber, drops him through a trapdoor into a sewer, and robs him. The old Spanish general is dead, and his mistress Angellica Bianca has the money and freedom to choose a lover for herself.

The 1670's saw the flourishing of the most licentious of Restoration comedies. Wycherley's *The Country-Wife* (1675) and Etherege's *The Man of Mode* (1676) both celebrate, if somewhat ambivalently, the rake-hero: successful seducer, wit, and controller of plots. Behn is partly using this pattern with her rover, Willmore, who first wins his way into Angellica's bed—she even gives him money instead of charging her usual exorbitant fee—then discards her in favour of Hellena, a rich and marriageable virgin. Willmore, however, is no clever schemer, being much more likely to ruin his friend Belvile's plots by mistake than to think up any of his own. The women play a more active role than he does, and many of the scenes focus on their point of view. Witty Hellena and her sober sister Florinda are both plotting to avoid unwanted destinies planned by men: in Florinda's case, forced marriage to Antonio, in Hellena's, imprisonment in a nunnery. Angellica is treated with a sympathy most unusual in Restoration comedy's handling of a rejected mistress: her choice of love and desire over financial gain is taken seriously, as is her disappointment. Women's vulnerability in love is shown differently in Florinda, whose attempts to find her true love, Belvile, nearly end in disaster. She is mistaken for a whore and is in danger of being raped by Blunt and even by the supposedly likeable Frederick and Willmore; briefly, the play shows a dark underside to its holiday humour.

The heroine Hellena, however, is determined not to share her sister's vulnerability. Hellena is Behn's creation: the character called Helena in Killigrew's play is an old blind prostitute humiliated by the other characters. Behn takes the name and creates a new character. Killigrew's hero marries a virginal heroine, a woman all virtue, helplessness and submission. In *The Rover* her role is split between Hellena and Florinda. Florinda gets all the victimization, Hellena gets the hero. She is active, and disguises herself as a gipsy and then as a boy to get what she wants. Her skill with words gives her the power to evade her brother's control and negotiate an acceptable relationship with her lover. She is an inventive interpreter of others' words: when Florinda dutifully tells Don Pedro "I shall strive to do as shall become your sister," Hellena glosses this as "that is, to be as resolved your way as he is his"—a radical re-reading of the brother-sister relationship, and an assertion of the importance of woman's will which is central to the play. Hellena is an attempt on Behn's part to create a female counterpart to the rake, equally careless and free. She names herself "Hellena the Inconstant," and Willmore, marrying her, promises not to bother about her honour; at one point she is even addressed by his epithet of "rover."

However, we are kept aware that Hellena's victory is at Angellica's expense, and Behn was perhaps dissatisfied with it for that reason. In her sequel *The Second Part of The Rover* (1681), she coolly dispatches Hellena to an early grave, and then re-runs the contest between a courtesan and a rich virgin for possession of Willmore. This time the courtesan, La Nuche, wins.

—Jane Spencer

RUBÁIYÁT OF OMAR KHAYYÁM.
Poems by Edward FitzGerald, 1859 (and later revisions).

After Tennyson's *In Memoriam*, the *Rubáiyát of Omar Khayyám* was perhaps the most popular poem of the later 19th century. Like the poems of Byron in an earlier period it was much favoured by romantically-inclined Victorians for reading on picnic parties, having an ideal combination of the sensual and the pleasingly melancholic, qualities which permitted it at once to be a poem of escape from Victorian convention (not to say industrialism) and a poem offering an alternative philosophy to the official Christianity of the time.

The original quatrains ("Rubáiyát" means "quatrains") were composed in Farsi (known to the 19th century as Persian) by the poet, astronomer, and mathematician Omar Khayyám who was born in the province of Khorassan in the later 11th century and died in 1123. Omar intended each quatrain to be read separately but Edward FitzGerald managed to create a certain continuity between them to form a loose pattern that moves from dawn to night and from life to death. It is apparent that FitzGerald drew on his extensive knowledge of Persian poetry to supplement what he found in the manuscripts—some of the lines and even one whole quatrain are absent from Omar's original collection. FitzGerald preserves the verse-form of the original but he does not adopt the mystical implications that later generations of Muslim commentators claimed to find in it; thus the famous "wine" we are exhorted to drink seemed to the Sufis to stand as a symbol for divine power while for FitzGerald, and probably for Omar himself, although clearly not simply fermented grape juice, it is very much more nearly a literal drink than an image of Islamic grace. FitzGerald prefers to stress the anti-Islamic and hedonistic side of Omar, both in his selection of quatrains to translate (the 1859 edition has 75, the 1868 edition 110, the 1872 and 1879 editions 102, while the various manuscripts of the Farsi original contain anything from 159 to 564 stanzas) and in the brief "Life of Omar Khayyám" appended to the second and subsequent editions of the *Rubáiyát*.

The appeal of the *Rubáiyát* to the Victorians (we can consider it as a Victorian English poem) may have lain in its subversion of religion but it replaces religion with a *carpe diem* sensual epicureanism that has had a wide appeal throughout western literature from Horace to Ernest Dowson whose "Vitae summa brevis" was obviously indebted to FitzGerald: "They are not long, the days of wine and roses: / Out of a misty dream / Our path emerges for a while, then closes / Within a dream." Here are the themes of Omar: the swift passage of time, the hurrying to oblivion, the moment of pleasure brought by wine and roses, by the intoxication of the senses and the fragile beauty of the earth.

Proper names lend an aura of Persian romance to these themes:

Iram indeed is gone with all his Rose,
And Jamshyd's Sev'n-ring'd cup where no one knows;
  But still a Ruby kindles in the Vine,
And many a Garden by the Water blows.

The exact references hardly matter, the significance is obvious—the famous, even famous flowers and drinks, depart, but there are still gardens and wine for us, though only for a time, for:

Whether at Naishapur or Babylon,
Whether the Cup with sweet or bitter run,
  The Wine of Life keeps oozing drop by drop,
The leaves of life keep falling one by one.

These are the only consolations: religious asceticism, much canvassed among Shi'ite Muslims, is a waste of time: "Come fill the Cup, and in the fire of Spring / The winter garment of Repentance fling." Worldly ambition is vain:

The Worldly Hope men set their Hearts upon
Turns Ashes—or it prospers; and anon,
  Like Snow upon the Desert's dusty Face,
Lighting a little hour or two—is gone.

Philosophy cannot stay the passage of time any more than religion:

Why, all the saints and sages who discuss'd
Of the Two Worlds so wisely—they are thrust
  Like foolish Prophets forth; their Words to Scorn
Are scatter'd, and their Mouths are stopt with Dust.

The true philosophy is a sort of agnostic nihilism: the poet proclaims "I came like Water, and like Wind I go" glossing this in the next quatrain:

Into this Universe and *Why* not knowing
Nor *Whence*, like Water willy-nilly flowing;
  And out of it, as Wind upon the Waste.
I know not *Whither*, willy-nilly blowing.

And yet this is only a sort of nihilism, for Omar, like the Victorians, while doubting and dismissing, felt the threat of an unseen determinism. For the 19th century this took the form of evolution (the *Rubáiyát* was published in the same year as Darwin's *The Origin of Species*) while for Omar it was very like a Muslim God, a fatal Allah, but still a determinism: men are pots, thrown by a Potter, or chess pieces:

'Tis all a Chequer-board of Nights and Days
Where Destiny with Men for Pieces plays:
  Hither and thither moves, and mates, and slays,
And one by one back in the Closet lays.

Under these circumstances, so reminiscent of the world views of Tennyson and Hardy, where "The Moving Finger writes; and, having writ, / Moves on," the best life is the one devoted to pleasure and love, but of a delicate and melancholy kind. The ideal is to be "Here with a Loaf of Bread beneath the Bough, A Flask of Wine, A Book of Verse—and Thou . . ."

There is a beautiful music in FitzGerald that is worthy of Tennyson or Swinburne at their best. Read in any of the four, widely varying, editions, the quatrains offer the quintessence of a pleasantly sad fatalism rendered in the elegiac tone of a true poet. They tell us as much about Victorian culture as they do about medieval Persia.

—Lance St.John Butler

RURAL RIDES.
Prose by William Cobbett, 1830.

William Cobbett's *Rural Rides* owes its lasting repute and readership to the peculiar combination it offers of well-recorded travel observations, polemical arguments regarding the changes wrought in the lives of English country people as a result of the early 19th century agrarian revolution, and eloquent nostalgia for a rural way of life Cobbett had known as a child and which the pattern of his life had forced him to abandon.

Cobbett himself was the son of a Surrey farm labourer, born in 1763 when the enclosure movements that would wreak such havoc in the English villages had hardly begun. One day in 1784 he set off to a village fair and on an impulse boarded a coach to London, where he took the King's Shilling and served the next seven years in the garrison of Fredericton in remote New Brunswick, where he rose to the rank of sergeant-major.

His time in the army gave him both leisure to acquire an education and a cause in which to use it, for he ferreted out the corruption at work in managing the finances of the Fredericton garrison. Buying himself out of the ranks, he returned to London and exposed the misdeeds of his officers, which led to his persecution and flight, first to France, then to the U.S. where he began his activities as a satirical writer ("Peter Porcupine") and was again in trouble, prosecuted for libel. Returning to England, he joined the Radical cause, and though he lived and worked most of the rest of his life in London, publishing the *Political Register* which earned him a term of imprisonment for writing against flogging in the army and another brief exile in the U.S., he never lost his love of the land and tried for years to run a farm even when he was deep in radical journalism and in trouble with the authorities.

In 1821 Cobbett settled in Kensington and, except for growing a few seeds for sale, abandoned farming. But more and more he became concerned with the life of the farmer and farm labourer, and the way the landowners and the government acted in concert against them, and it was to gather material he could publish in the *Political Register* that he started his journeys of inspection. These began in 1821 and continued until 1832, with Cobbett, in the later years, venturing into the midlands and the north country as far as the Scottish border. For the first and best edition of *Rural Rides* (1830) he chose the travels of a limited period, from 25 September 1822 to 26 October 1826.

This collection of journeys has an extraordinary unity of tone and structure, partly because they were undertaken in a limited area of southern England (15 counties), and partly because—unlike some of the earlier and later journeys on which Cobbett travelled by coach, these were literally rides. Going on horseback through lanes and paths, talking to people along the road and stopping at cottages and farms not only enabled Cobbett to understand more intimately what was going on in the countryside, but gave his narratives a close texture and a remarkable and sustained continuity of interest.

Time and territory helped to unify the Rides; they took place in the middle of the decade preceding the great Labourers' Revolt of 1830, at a period when, though no violence was yet visible, an explosion of some kind was becoming inevitable. This fact gives them a special documentary value like that of Arthur Young's *Travels in France* which described the agricultural condition of France in *1787* and illuminated the causes of the great revolution two years later. Cobbett's territory is that which burst into the flame of burning barns and cornricks during the Labourer's Revolt. The early Rides cover the counties between the Thames and the English Channel where the revolt began—the country of downland and weald and fertile valleys which was Cobbett's native soil. In the last and greatest of the Rides, which continued for three months, covered 568 miles and occupies about two-fifths of the 1830 *Rural Rides*, this original territory of Cobbett's formed the base for a long expedition that extended westward as far as Gloucester, Hereford, and Worcester on the Welsh border. The special character of this area goes far towards explaining Cobbett's attitudes during the 1820's. The country of *Rural Rides* was barely touched by the Industrial Revolution; in a few of the towns he visited there were dwindling remnants of an ancient weaving industry but nothing more. On the other hand, the Agricultural Revolution, with its enclosures and its proletarianization of the farm worker, was more advanced and certainly more drastic in its effects than in any other part of England. Finally, this was the region most subject to the sinister centralizing influence of the Wen—as Cobbett called it—of London. It was the area where the displacement of the old landowners by the "new men," made rich by the Napoleonic wars, was most obvious. *Rural Rides*, in other words, presents the social picture of a limited region, the countryside of south England, in a time of drastic transition, and this gives the book a great unifying theme.

But soon, in the eyes of the reader, the Rider becomes almost as important as his rides. For a man then in his late fifties, Cobbett showed an extraordiary physical strength. He could perform an arduous day's ride over difficult country, lasting from dawn until after dark, with neither food nor drink until evening and a drenching at the end of it all, and remark merely that he considered a good soaking an excellent cure for "the hooping cough." His physical strength was accompanied by an awesome robustness of temperament. He liked to find and overcome obstacles, to take "the stern way," and even to the point of folly he insisted on reaching the goals he set himself. His thought had the same headstrong quality as his actions. He was stubborn in argument, passionately irrational in defence or attack, and downright in his prejudices; he hated wholesale, by classes, creeds, and races: Anglican parsons and Unitarians, bankers and brokers, Jews and Scots, and above all Quakers. He detested canals and stage-coaches, tea and potatoes, and lived long enough to lay his curse on the railways. Yet he was the kindliest of men who would go without food on his rides to give the cost of his lunch to some poor family at nightfall, and all he asked, like his great successor George Orwell, was a politics based on decency, and a sufficient material life and enough freedom for all men. There is not a scrap of ideology in *Rural Rides*, though a vast amount of social criticism and condemnation.

—George Woodcock

S

SAILING TO BYZANTIUM.
Poem by William Butler Yeats, 1928.

In April 1928 William Butler Yeats wrote to Lady Gregory that he was looking again at the volume of his poetry he had published earlier that year: "Re-reading *The Tower*, I am astonished at its bitterness." Although he was now recognised and honoured as a great poet, and at last happily married, he felt embittered by the turmoil of the modern world (see, for example, "The Second Coming" from the previous volume of his poetry) and by his acute awareness of life's transience. All natural life must die, and he too is ageing, though his creative powers, he felt, had never been greater. These are the themes of *The Tower*, and in its opening poem, "Sailing to Byzantium," he rages at mortality and old age. He longs, like many people, particularly when growing old, for some sense of permanence and spiritual peace, a state free from change and decay. In Yeats's case he feels especially the world's lack of concern with spiritual and artistic wisdom and achievement.

The emphatic "That" at the beginning of the poem states dramatically the modern world is not for the old, but belongs to the young. The opening stanza is a celebration of the fecund natural world. Yet even in the midst of that rich vitality Yeats in the phrase "Those dying generations" reminds us of the indissoluble interconnection of creation, birth, and death. This "sensual music" of the natural world so seduces man that inevitably he neglects the wisdom of the past and its intellectual and artistic creations. The importance of these is affirmed in the stately rhythm and lapidary quality of lines such as "Monuments of unageing intellect."

The rich sensuality of diction in the first stanza intensifies the scorn, in the next, for the paltry tattered scarecrow of old age. All that the soul (the spiritual side of man which in spite of its own wishes is tied to the mortal flesh) can do is to try and learn delight and joy through artistic contemplation and creation, but the only way to this is by studying the great artistic and intellectual achievements of the past: the "Monuments of its own magnificence." And therefore Yeats (or rather the persona, the I, which he adopts in this poem) has come to Byzantium, where he feels he can escape from the flux and fret of the mortal world, and achieve some permanence and stability. The journey to Byzantium is a symbol of the search for spiritual life and intellectual joy.

Byzantium, the capital of the eastern half of the Roman Empire, which survived Rome's fall by a thousand years till its capture by the Turks in 1453, represented for Yeats a place where perfect unity of being—psychological and social, intellectual and artistic—was possible. In *A Vision*, he writes: "I think that in early Byzantium, maybe never before or since in recorded history, religious, aesthetic, and practical life were one." There, since no earthly "singing school" exists, he implores the sages or saints represented in a mosaic (a characteristic Byzantine artefact), to assist the usual historic and natural process by taking him out of nature into "eternity." By calling it an "artifice" Yeats emphasises its distinction from the natural and its connection with the artistic. The cry to be released from human mortality is passionate and anguished: "Consume my heart away: sick with desire / And fastened to a dying animal." (Like a "battered kettle," "tied to me / as to a dog's tail," he states in the next poem, "The Tower," where the same image is used.)

When he has escaped from this natural bodily shape, he will never take a form "from any natural thing," but that of an artificial golden bird: "I have read somewhere that in the Emperor's palace at Byzantium was a tree made of gold and silver, and artificial birds that sang." This bird is the symbol, or emblem, of the soul, of art, and of the artist's imagination (that is, both its creative product and the artist's own identity which the artefact embodies), and of the permanent free from the messy flux of life. It stands in sharp contrast to the "dying generations" of birds at their song and the instinctive joy of mortal human life celebrated in the first stanza. Ironically, as his friend Sturge Moore pointed out, "such a goldsmith's bird is as much nature as man's body," especially if it only sings to the court of Byzantium of "what is past, or passing, or to come": that is, of life and its transience which Yeats seeks to escape.

Yeats tried to correct this fault, as he felt it to be, by writing the more explicit rejection of "all complexities of mire and blood" in the poem "Byzantium" included in his next volume of verse, *The Winding Stair*. Nevertheless, he never removed "Sailing to Byzantium" from his work and wrote many more poems in which he vacillates between the rival claims of the soul and the body, of art and life, before emphatically declaring in one of his last poems, "The Circus Animals' Desertion," his clear recognition, as a writer, of the importance of, and his commitment to, the "foul rag-and-bone shop of the heart." This affirmation of life had already been implied, albeit unconsciously, in the rich and passionate ambiguities of "Sailing to Byzantium."

—David Astle

SAINT JOAN.
Play by Bernard Shaw, 1923.

It was the suggestion in 1920 of Sydney Cockerell of the Fitzwilliam Museum, Cambridge, that stimulated Bernard Shaw to explore the material that developed into the play *Saint Joan*. The Maid of Orleans had been canonized that year but Shaw's fascination with historical figures goes back to his treatment of the young Napoleon in *The Man of Destiny* and Julius Caesar in *Caesar and Cleopatra*. In Caesar, Shaw attempts to present an early model of his ideal figure of which Joan is a later version: the person who combines the vision to sense that he or she is part of the "Life Force" with the practical ability to turn this vision into reality. The "Life Force" is an integral part of Shaw's theory of "creative evolution," which he fully developed in the preface to *Man and Superman*. Shaw proposes that mankind is progressing toward higher and higher forms of intellectual development; it was his response to the "social Darwinism" of the period which attempted to justify the appalling social and economic conditions of industrial England in the late 19th century as the "survival of the fittest."

Another of the elements in the character of *Saint Joan* stems from Shaw's antipathy toward the "womanly woman," as he regarded the stereotypical female who had been advanced as Victorian England's ideal of feminity: passive, fragile, and dependent on a man in any crisis. Shaw's earliest theatrical portrait of a woman, Blanche Sartoris, in his first play, *Widowers' Houses*, is of a "strong-minded" young person who challenges the man who woos her. Such notable females as Vivie Warren, Candida, and Ann Whitefield, the "mother for the Superman" in *Man and Superman*, culminate in the figure of Major Barbara, Shaw's most complex portrait of a woman prior to Saint Joan.

There is much of Barbara that is later found in Joan. Both are inspired by religion; both are headstrong, independent women; both are determined to change the established order. But while *Major Barbara* is a comedy that ends with a promised marriage between Barbara and her poet-philosopher, Cusins, Joan is the solitary heroine of a tragedy that ends with her martyrdom.

Saint Joan, then, is the culmination of Shaw's growth as a dramatic artist; it contains the elements of classical tragedy that Shaw had scrupulously avoided in all his prior work, yet it has the Shavian wit and pointed "message" that marked most of his earlier efforts. Shaw was awarded the Nobel Prize for Literature in 1925, clearly in recognition of *Saint Joan* as his crowning artistic achievement.

The first three scenes of the play follow the conventional "birth of a hero" plot that is standard in historical melodramas. Joan wins over the skeptical noblemen and the Dauphin to her cause and then inspires Dunois to lift the siege of Orleans. Shaw, as if thumbing his nose at the conventions of melodrama, inserts a small "miracle" in each scene in order to lead the audience into assuming that he also regards Joan as a "Saint" in the conventional sense. In the first scene, the eggless hens begin to lay as soon as Joan arrives; in the second, she "miraculously" detects the disguised Dauphin in the midst of his courtiers; in the third, the wind needed to speed the boats across the Loire to lift the siege of Orleans conveniently begins to blow as she prays.

But it is apparent in the brilliant fourth scene between the English nobleman, Warwick, and Peter Cauchon, the Bishop of Beauvais, that Shaw is up to something more than historical melodrama. In this scene, Shaw shows how Joan, as a true rebel, has instilled anxiety into the hearts of these two powerful men. Her appeal to the French as a nation concerns Warwick who fears that his feudal rights will be taken away by "Nationalism"; her "protest of the individual soul against the interference of priest or peer between the private man and his God" is seen by Cauchon as a direct challenge to the authority of the church: "Protestantism."

Shaw, in his preface, declares Joan a "genius," "a person who, seeing farther and probing deeper than other people, has a different set of ethical valuations from theirs, and has energy enough to give effect to this extra vision and its valuations in whatever manner best suits his or her specific talents." This difference in "ethical valuations" is what leads Joan to her isolation from her allies, as is revealed in the fifth scene, and ultimately to her own destruction in the famous trial scene which marks the dramatic climax of the play.

In one of his earliest comments on the play he was yet to write, Shaw insisted that Joan had received, considering the nature of the accusations against her, a "merciful" trial in which she was not tortured. This insistence that her martyrdom was not a simple matter of deliberate cruelty on the part of the church is dramatized in the trial scene in which Joan condemns herself out of her own mouth. Shaw's point is that Joan's vision of her own world was too uncompromising to be accepted by even the most "tolerant" and humane theologians of her time.

It is in the epilogue, however, that he brings his point home, not merely for the period in which Joan lived and died, but even five centuries later in 20th-century England. As the newly sainted Joan asks all of her adoring admirers from the past and present whether they would wish that she "rise from the dead, and come back to [them] a living woman . . .," one by one they leave her until she is again as solitary as she was when she began her pilgrimage. Shaw's own plaint—that the monstrous irrationality of World War I had served as a repudiation of all his hopes for a rational future for mankind—can be heard echoing in Joan's plea at the conclusion of the play: "O God that madest this beautiful earth, when will it be ready to receive Thy saints? How long, O Lord, how long?"

—Joel Shatzky

SALOME.
Play by Oscar Wilde, 1894.

Oscar Wilde wrote *Salome*, his vivid, ornate, claustrophobic one-act play, in French. This seemed appropriate to many, because his Salome was immediately seen as a continuation of the Decadent or Symbolist tradition treated by French artists (Baudelaire, Gautier, Flaubert, Mallarmé, and the painter Moreau), and especially by Huysmans, author of that textbook of Decadence *A Rebours* (*Against Nature*). So Wilde's Salome has been widely seen as "*fin de siècle femme fatale*."

Sarah Bernhardt (over 50 at the time) agreed to play Salome in London, and only during rehearsals was the production censored, under an old law forbidding the representation of biblical characters on stage. The play was published in French in 1893, and in an English translation in 1894, after Wilde had extensively revised the unsatisfactory version produced by his friend Lord Alfred Douglas.

Wilde took significant liberties with the Bible story, conflating three different Herods, producing a fanatical Baptist in Jokanaan, and giving Salome's central motive for demanding Jokanaan's head not as her mother's prompting but as thwarted lust for the prophet who refuses even to look at her. But Wilde echoes the Bible throughout, especially in Jokanaan's words, and this increased general unease over the play.

William Archer, contemporary theatre critic and champion of Ibsen, saw Salome, intriguingly, as "an oriental Hedda Gabler," and Jane Marcus has expanded this, showing how the clear French sources obscure a suggestion of the New Woman of Ibsen, paralleling Salome's dance with that of Nora in *A Doll's House* and her character with Hedda

Gabler's. Marcus even declares: "Salome was probably the only English 'New Woman' who was directly derived from Ibsen." Hedda too was described as "a revolting, abominable, heartless woman" and "infinitely perverse." Ibsen's exposés of the repression of 19th-century women and his efforts to emancipate them from male expectations were admired by Wilde, and for *Dorian Gray* and *Ghosts* the same hysterical abuse was heaped on both writers.

As usual then, part of Wilde's achievement in *Salome* is a combination of major traditions, the Decadent one in which Salome is associated with witches, vampires, sirens, and cruel sphinxes, and the Ibsen one where the self-discovery and emancipation of women was being flaunted at panicky audiences. The result is a combination of extraordinary emotional power. Wilde's own additions include the dance of the seven veils, Jokanaan's prophecy of Salome's death, and Herod's final order for the soldiers to crush her under their shields.

Wilde's play has three central characters, Salome, Jokanaan, and Herod, although many critics have concentrated only on one or two of these. It has been suggested that Salome's demand for Jokanaan's head is at least in part revenge for the long imprisonment and death of her father, or for Jokanaan's attacks on her mother, but it is difficult to find this in the play. When Salome hears Jokanaan, she wants to see him, and when she sees him she wants his body. When he spurns her she determines to kiss him on the mouth—even if he must be decapitated first. Her obsession blots out anything else.

Her lust for Jokanaan is paralleled by Herod's for her. Herod is a more complicated character than Salome. He is not only obsessed by lust, he is moody: persistently determined to be happy, though ridden by fear, guilt, and evil omens, and he is comic in his evasiveness. He tries to transfer his guilt to Herodias, even accusing her of sterility as he gazes at her daughter. All this is underlined by Herodias, whose limited literal mind makes her the principal critic of the larger, "poetic" characters. Minor characters repeat that anything beyond the senses is ridiculous: disputing about angels, believing in a God one cannot see, the heightened language of Jokanaan, the suicides of Stoics are all ridiculed before Herodias ridicules the disputing Jews and at last Herod himself with his peacocks. Where other characters see the moon as a little princess, a dead, naked, mad or drunken woman, or as a little piece of money, Herodias sneers at the "poetry": "The moon is like the moon, that is all."

Jokanaan's language is often biblical, but overall he is harsh, even hateful, and as determined, as obsessive in his denunciations as Salome and Herod are in their lust.

Wilde himself noted that the play is built on "recurring phrases that bind it together like a piece of music with recurring motifs": no wonder Richard Strauss used it directly as libretto for his opera, cutting occasionally, but only for brevity. It also relies heavily on the tripartite structure common to traditional fairy-tales and to Wilde's own: Herod offers Salome the equivalent of three wishes, but her perverse and appalling request is immutable, so that his solemn promise to her is as crucial and inevitable as Dorian Gray's prayer about his portrait.

—Isobel Murray

SAMSON AGONISTES.
Play by John Milton, 1671.

John Milton's primary source in *Samson Agonistes* is Judges 13–14 but his treatment has little in common with the folkloristic manner of the Old Testament's tale of riddling, superhuman strength, and barbaric revenges. Biblical material is given classical form. In a prefatory prose note, Milton presents his text as an example of tragedy "as it was anciently composed," the "gravest, moralest and most profitable" of all poetic genres. This claim, and details of his poem's structure and metre, Milton justifies by instancing the Greek tragedians, Aristotle, Cicero, Plutarch and "The Apostle Paul himself" who quotes Euripides in 1 Corinthians 15:33. He is at pains to distinguish true tragedy from the "common interludes" of the 17th-century theatre which intermix "comic stuff with tragic sadness" and introduce "trivial and vulgar persons." A Puritan as well as a classical sensibility appears in his insistence that his blank verse poem "never was intended" for stage performance.

Following these precedents, Milton's drama is set in one location (the prison at Gaza) on a single day (the last of Samson's life) and is composed of dialogues between the blinded and imprisoned protagonist and a succession of visitors: his father Manoa, his wife Dalila, and a Philistine champion, Harapha. A Chorus of Hebrew friends comments upon what passes. After these exchanges, Samson agrees to go with a Philistine officer to perform feats of strength at "a solemn feast" held in honour of the Philistine god Dagon. There, it is reported by a fleeing Hebrew, Samson pulled down the pillars of the "spacious theatre" which contained "Lords, ladies, captains, counsellors, or priest, / Their choice nobility and flower," destroying both them and himself.

Two aspects of the drama have particularly engaged critics. First, since Samuel Johnson opined in his *Lives of the English Poets* that "the intermediate parts have neither cause nor consequence, neither hasten nor retard the catatrophe," the integrity of the structure and coherence of the plot have been debated; second, the so-called "Hebraic" spirit of this classical tragedy on a Christian theme has troubled many commentators, who find it distressingly vengeful, a "morally disgusting" (the words are John Carey's) celebration of the wanton and bloody destruction wrought by Jehovah through his barbarous champion.

The resolution of both issues is intimated by the title, which bestows upon a Hebrew name a Greek epithet signifying: a contestant at the games; a champion; and one engaged in spiritual struggle and development. The Samson of the opening soliloquy, oppressed by the knowledge that his preordained mission has failed through his own folly, is "past hope, abandoned," as he believes, by God. Spiritually blinded, emotionally exhausted, he is imprisoned in his own despair: "Myself, my sepulchre, a moving grave." The assured resolution evident in Samson at the end of the drama would be quite beyond this figure who, incapacitated by lassitude ("My hopes all flat, nature within me seems / In all her functions weary of herself"), desires only to be left untroubled by further demands ("the strife / With me hath end"). The ensuing exchanges are the means by which he rediscovers his commitment and his identity as "a person separate to God." In their attempts to exercise control over the defeated Samson and to determine his destiny, each of his visitors, in the ironic way characteristic of tragedy, achieves an effect opposite to their intentions: Samson refuses Manoa's scheme to secure his release by political negotiation; he rejects Dalila's attempt at reconciliation; he is not overawed by Harapha. Aroused by their proposals and compelled to confront his own guilt, he comes to a renewed belief in the possibility of divine forgiveness and in himself as an agent of the divine will. He is hence able to see in the officer's command a providential opportunity to serve. And though the outcome, determined by the biblical story, is bloody, this is neither planned nor premeditated by Samson. He goes not knowing what to expect: "I begin to feel / Some rousing motions in me which dispose / to something extraordinary my thoughts . . . / If there be aught of presage in the mind, / This day will be remarkable in my life / By some great act, or of my days the last." The ironic knowledge that it will be both is the privilege of the reader. This is to go not in vindictive self-assertion but in submissive self-denial.

This reassurance that God does not abandon his chosen ones would speak particularly both to Milton himself, a leader of the lost Puritan cause and, like Samson, blind, and to the Puritan's nonconformist heirs, whose plight, as "prisoners chained," is mirrored in Samson's. That their persecution after the Restoration, brought before "unjust tribunals, under change of times," is inescapably called to mind by the reflections of the Chorus (lines 667–704) upon God's incomprehensible, and apparently unjust, dealings with his elect, is one of the strongest arguments for the late dating of the poem's composition.

—N.H. Keeble

SARTOR RESARTUS.
Fiction by Thomas Carlyle, 1836.

Thomas Carlyle's *Sartor Resartus* ("The Tailor Re-Tailored") is a motley concoction roughly in the shape of a novel and divided into three books. In Book One an unnamed English Editor discovers a German book entitled *Die Kleider, ihr Werden und Wirken*, or *Clothes, Their Origin and Influence*, by an obscure German philosopher named Diogenes Teufelsdröckh. Excited, yet puzzled, by the German work, the English Editor seeks out more information about the author, working under the assumption that biographical facts will help him in understanding the Clothes Philosophy, as the Editor labels Teufelsdröckh's thought. Book Two consists of the Editor's biographical construction of Teufelsdröckh's life from multifarious records contained in six paper bags, along with the Editor's running commentary. And finally Book Three contains a potpourri of additional Teufelsdröckhian materials which the Editor organizes thematically.

The major reason for Carlyle's work is to explain his view that old forms of society and culture must be replaced by new ones. As a result, Carlyle must examine his contemporary, unworkable forms of society and show how they fail to function properly. This effort takes him to a treatment of symbols and appearances in an effort to recognize sham symbols and proper symbols. This is Carlyle's primary goal in almost everything he wrote thereafter. And even though *The French Revolution* made Carlyle famous, *Sartor Resartus* was his first genuinely original work, one which struck the best minds of Victorian England in profound ways. It became a cult piece for later Victorians.

The heart of Carlyle's work is romantic. And even though it owes more to German romanticism than to English, this skeptical view of shams is much like Shelley's attempt to see beyond the surface of Mont Blanc. Finally, Carlyle's view is pantheistic, for one of the major goals of *Sartor Resartus* is to renew mankind's wonder of the world.

These two goals, one destructive and the other constructive, are at odds with one another. The conflict is explained by German romantic irony. While one goal destroys the old, worn-out forms of society, the other may simultaneously create a new one. This is done with the knowledge that the new form will itself in time be outmoded. But society can't be remade successfully until the old form is exploded. *Sartor Resartus* is then as radical an expression of the central motive of the French Revolution as may be had in English letters. Everything is in a constant state of Heracleitian flux.

Carlyle's understanding of symbols reveals his contradictory goals. As he has Teufelsdröckh say, symbols both reveal and conceal. This view is Carlyle's reception of German idealistic philosophy, probably initiated by his study of Friedrich Schiller's discussion of dialectic in *The Aesthetic Education of Man*. There, the idea of *Aufhebung* constitutes the same balancing of destructive and constructive tendencies found in Carlyle's definition of the symbol. In the synthesis of dialectical oppositions, the moment of *Aufhebung* takes something from the old oppositions and makes this into something new; there is a simultaneous creation and destruction. Just so with Carlyle's symbol: something is revealed in a symbol, even a natural object reveals something of God. But something is concealed as well: one cannot finally get behind the symbol. Perhaps this is a romantic way of saying that the sign is not the same as its referent.

Since *Sartor Resartus* embodies such a complex and paradoxical view, there is little wonder that its genre is difficult to determine. In the fourth essay of the *Anatomy of Criticism*, Northrop Frye links *Sartor Resartus* both to anatomy and confession since it is both an encyclopedia of sundry knowledge and has autobiographical elements, especially in Book Two. This view places *Sartor Resartus* in a category of mixed novelistic forms along with *Tristram Shandy*, *Don Quixote*, *Moby-Dick*, and *Finnegans Wake*. Its hopes for a better society give it a utopian coloring while its skepticism about human nature allows it to be seen as a distopia as well. These contradictory tendencies can be seen in Teufelsdröckh's echo of Goethe's "Here or nowhere is America."

The closest associates to Teufelsdröckh and the Editor are Don Quixote, Uncle Toby, and other such oddballs who see metaphysical dimensions in everyday matters. Critics have recognized for a long time Carlyle's debt to Jean Paul Richter's *Humoristen*, late 18th-century humor characters whose idiosyncrasies render them ridiculous. But the satire is tender and often self-reflexive. Following hints from Friedrich Schlegel's aphorisms on romantic irony, Carlyle creates an eccentric who gently laughs at his own eccentricities.

—Lee C.R. Baker

A SATIRE AGAINST REASON AND MANKIND.
Poem by John Wilmot, Earl of Rochester, 1679.

In his poem "Tunbridge Wells" Rochester had surveyed the specimens of humanity visiting the spa town, and concluded: "Our selves with noise of Reason we do please / In vain, Humanity's our worst Disease," with the result that it was "with Remorse, / I us'd the Insolence to mount my Horse." This specific point was to be developed by Swift in Book IV of *Gulliver's Travels*, but the general point of animal superiority to humans forms the basis of Rochester's *A Satire Against Reason and Mankind*. He gives it an additional twist by making the basis of that superiority what is normally the source of their inferiority, lack of reason.

The structure he uses is based on Boileau's *Satire* VIII, from which he borrows many phrases and ideas; and he is also indebted to Hobbes, La Rochefoucauld, and Montaigne. Nevertheless, it is a personal statement of a philosophy of life. The statement is then qualified at the end. This is typical of Rochester: here in his greatest poem, as always, he is never simple. The verse form is the heroic couplet, heavily end-stopped, but otherwise handled with great flexibility and a very informal diction. The conversational tone is characteristic, but especially appropriate here since the poem is a kind of dialogue.

It begins with an extension of the idea from "Tunbridge Wells": Rochester would prefer to be any kind of creature rather than Man, precisely because men prefer Reason, that "*Ignis fatuus*, in the *Mind*," before "instinct" and "sense." Many a court wit could have started a poem like this, and played with the idea in a spirit of merry cynicism. In Rochester's poem we see at once that depth, and darkness, which makes him by far the most impressive of the court poets. For him Reason is useless because it cannot keep man afloat in "doubts boundless Sea"; that is it cannot deal with the only problem that matters—Death:

> Hudled in dirt, the reas'ning *Engine* lyes,
> Who was so proud, so witty, and so wise.

All philosophies, and here in particular that of Hobbes, are vain pretensions. Therefore since we cannot "know" the world, it makes sense to "enjoy" it. This is a definitive statement of 17th-century libertinism; but one made against the starkest of backgrounds.

Rochester proceeds to introduce a clergyman who attempts to defend Reason; but he is quickly put down, first by reiteration of the vanity involved in the assertion that man's mind "can pierce / The limits of the boundless Universe," and second by a new idea, of two kinds of Reason. Rochester asserts "I own right *Reason*," that is a Reason that obeys and serves the senses. This may seem inconsistent with what has gone before, but in fact this section is a bridge to the moral centre of the poem. Lines 127–158 embody a comparison between the animal and human worlds which evolves into a statement on the nature of man. It is a vision that underlies and explains, not only Rochester's poetry, but in a sense the whole world of Restoration literature. It is this period's equivalent to the Jacobean vision of Lear's "poor, bare, forked animal"; and no less terrifying. Rochester sees the essential nature of man in terms of violence and treachery:

> *Birds*, feed on *Birds*, *Beasts*, on each other prey,
> But savage *Man* alone, does *Man*, betray:
> Prest by necessity, they kill for Food,
> *Man*, undoes *Man*, to do himself no good,

and explains this by the Hobbist concept of the search for Security:

> For hunger, or for Love, they bite or tear,
> Whilst wretched *Man*, is still in arms for fear;
> For fear he armes, and is of Armes afraid,
> By fear, to fear, successively betray'd.

This is a specific reference to distrust of standing armies, one of the great constitutional issues of the day; but its message to a world of nuclear weapons is obvious.

This brilliant passage, concluding with its logical, mordant paradox, that "all Men, wou'd be *Cowards* if they durst," stands then as Rochester's commitment to a deeply pessimistic view of mankind. Or it would, if the poem ended here. It does not. Rochester goes on to say that if he can find just one good man, at Court or in the Church, "I'le here recant my *Paradox* to them." This may of course just be a typical shifting of ground; but it also shows an awareness of an alternative. Rochester is prepared to consider the possibility of virtue, and presumably God, existing; but he wants some kind of proof. This may throw some light on his controversial "conversion." It certainly confirms that, as he wrote to his wife: "I myself have a sense of what the methods of my life seem so utterly to contradict." In poetry, in life, and in death, Rochester is always ambiguous.

—P.E. Hewison

SAVED.
Play by Edward Bond, 1965.

Saved was central to the drive that finally ended the Lord Chamberlain's power to censor English theatre. The controversy over Edward Bond's second produced play stemmed from profane language and from two scenes, one overtly sexual, one shockingly violent. Bond refused to modify the language or cut the scenes, the censor refused to license the play for performance, and the Royal Court Theatre ran it as a club production. Critics tended to side with the censor at first, and the media paid special attention to the sixth scene, where a gang of young toughs attack a baby left alone in its pram, first smearing it with its fouled diaper, then stoning it to death.

By the 1969 revival, the censor was gone, the furor had died, and people re-evaluated the work. Critics now saw the violence as part of a larger social pattern revealed in the play. They admitted that *Saved* had a cohesiveness of language and structure that many had at first refused to recognize. In fact, people began to feel that an earlier scene, where the baby's cries were ignored by its family, was more horrifying than the behavior of the men in the park.

Public outrage came in part because Bond did not include social or moral pronouncements in his text. Although in the introduction he does comment on the lack of moral sense among the young, and questions how the killing of one infant compares with the fire bombing of whole cities during World War II, in the play itself he presents situations on stage without taking a stance. He allows the audience to see people in their normal surroundings—a slum living room, a cafe, a park—generally going about their normal business, and the audience is shocked into asking questions about the effects of society on those people.

The working-class men and women in *Saved* have jobs and homes, although comments about the jobs suggest that they are deadening. These people would probably never be able to analyze the frustrations we see revealed in their brief remarks, but as they meet and talk in short, often monosyllabic phrases, we see their callousness and self-centeredness and hints of viciousness that lead to the baby's death.

The opening of the play suggests moral casualness when Pam brings Len home and, after conventionally comic delays as her father passes through on his way to work and Len asks questions, procedes to seduce him. Months pass and Len stays on as paying boarder, although Pam has tired of him and is now pregnant by Fred, the confident young man who rents boats in the park. Len gradually emerges as the most caring, least self-centered young person. He worries about the child and declares to Pam, "I ain't leavin' that kid." "Why?" she asks. "With you." "It ain't your kid."

The abrupt dialogue is characteristic. Bond has very few speeches that are over a line long. The curt phrases convey facts or responses to a situation. Replies are almost never softened, and there are very few instances where anything approaching a probing explanation is given. There is, however, a rhythm to the exchanges, which are frequently laced with expletives or couched in Cockney slang.

Beyond this spareness of speech, there are even more important patterns of non-communication. They range from the drugged infant's inability to cry out in response to the pain inflicted on it to Pam's parents' refusal to speak to each other. Often there is a self-centeredness that leaves people talking into the air as others carry on their own conversations. The distressing fourth scene, when the baby cries in the bedroom, desperate for attention, while Pam turns up the telly to mask the sound and Len and her parents refuse to take responsibility, drives home to the audience the lack of what we like to think of as normal caring instincts.

Later, Pam ignores the baby when Len brings it to her bed, and it is no surprise that she stupifies it with aspirin to quiet it. When she finally pushes the infant, who is never referred to by name, to the park, she is more intent on finding Fred, than on taking care of a child who has already had "newmoanier." Fred's "Yer wan' a stop thinkin' about yerself," and Len's horror that she has left the brake off the pram are part of a pattern of details that Bond creates which comes to a climax in the stoning.

While a series of scenes has built up Pam's irresponsibility and Len's ineffectiveness, another episode highlights the viciousness of the gang of youths. In the third scene, they joke about a recent fatal accident. Peter, the ring-leader, had deliberately not avoided hitting a boy who then caromed off his car into a passing truck. There is no remorse, and only a vulgarly dismissive "accidents is legal." These are obviously people who lack the conventional decencies.

Although the stoning is meant to shock, and certainly succeeds, it is very clearly part of the fabric of life of these people. Youthful rough-housing can easily turn nasty. As horrifying as the death of the infant is Pam's casual return to push the pram off, mouthing conventional words without checking her child's condition. Only Fred is imprisoned, and returns a hero.

There are a few positive moments in *Saved*. Harry, Pam's father, does come to Len's room to say goodnight. Mary feeds Len, perhaps seeing in him a replacement for her son, who was killed in the same park, equally impersonally, by a bomb. And in the last scene, Len mends a chair. But in that last scene, no one in the living room speaks, and Bond offers no solution to the social malaise he has shown in grimly realistic details.

—Frances A. Shirley

SCENES OF CLERICAL LIFE.
Stories by George Eliot, 1858.

Serialized in *Blackwood's Magazine*, January–October 1857, when she was 37, these three stories were George Eliot's first attempts at fiction, though "It had always been a vague dream of mine that some time or other I might write a novel" ("How I Came to Write Fiction," manuscript dated 6 December 1857, published in her *Letters*). She was encouraged in this by George Henry Lewes, with whom she lived from 1854, himself a novelist and leading reviewer of fiction, and she may retrospectively be seen preparing herself for her new literary role in review articles in the year or so before she began on *Scenes of Clerical Life* (available in her *Essays*, edited by Thomas Pinney, 1963), where she enunciates principles for fiction akin to her practice and authorial statements in these stories. She is scathing about "Silly Novels by Lady Novelists," in a review completed days before she began writing *Scenes of Clerical Life*, and praises artistic "realism" (a critical term recently imported from France and popularized by Lewes). Her penny-plain male pseudonym was partly a protection against her being mistaken for a silly lady novelist. Another emphasis of these essays is that art should extend readers' sympathies.

Eliot had "a strong disinclination" against writing prefaces, but here and in her next fictional work *Adam Bede* (1859) the narrator offers (over?-) ample instructions about how and why to read these stories. The hero of her first story "The Sad Fortunes of the Rev. Amos Barton" is

> in no respect an ideal or exceptional character . . . but was palpably and unmistakably commonplace . . . 'An utterly uninteresting character!' I think I hear a lady reader exclaim . . . who prefers the ideal in fiction . . . Yet these commonplace people—many of them—bear a conscience; . . . they have their unspoken sorrows, and their sacred joys . . .

Her publisher Blackwood wanted "a pleasanter picture" of provincial life and urged her to "*soften* your picture as much as you can. Your sketches this time are all written in the harsher Thackerayan view of human nature," but she responded that her artistic bent was to "the presentation of mixed human beings in such a way as to call forth tolerant judgment, pity, and sympathy." Thackeray regarded her as a disciple; she did not, though she thought him "the most powerful of living novelists." The influence of Scott and Austen is more evident, in her presentations of community and character, and in the astringently ironic and witty element in her style.

The unglamorous curate Amos Barton wins his parishioners' sympathy after his errors and tribulations, culminating in the premature death of his wife Milly (a much-admired episode). The heroine of "Janet's Repentance" occasions "the first intelligent treatment of alcoholism in English fiction" (John Sutherland): she is driven to drink by a brutally unhappy marriage but repents and devotes herself to good works under the influence of the Evangelical clergyman Mr. Tryan. Here again Eliot shows great originality—Evangelicals generally appeared in novels as sanctimonious killjoys—and the more creditably because, although in her youth she had been earnestly pious, she was now an unbeliever, if still respectful towards Christian ethics and sympathetically aware of the sustenance that faith and worship could provide. Some readers indeed, curious about the identity of this impressive new author, surmised that George Eliot was a Cambridge-educated clergyman, and surprisingly few realized that "he" must be a woman (Dickens being an emphatic exception, and he rightly acknowledged too the stories' "extraordinary merit").

"Mr. Gilfil's Love-Story" is the least original of these stories, and the least "clerical." Maynard Gilfil, a predecessor of Amos Barton at Shepperton Church, seemed a dull old stick but in earlier years his life had briefly been disturbed and irradiated by "passion and poetry" during his courtship of and brief marriage to Caterina Sarti, conventionally beautiful and, with her Italian background, conventionally passionate. She had preferred the attentions of Captain Wybrow (the first of Eliot's series of upper-class sexual bounders) and when frustrated had nearly murdered him, but Wybrow died anyhow, and Caterina accepted Gilfil's adoring consolations—a love-triangle to which his clerical avocation and duties are irrelevant. Like Amos Barton and Janet Dempster, however, Gilfil manifestly experiences "sad fortunes." Eliot initiates her "bourgeois tragedy" theme, and her most characteristic adjective is frequently present—"we poor mortals . . . poor little Caterina's nature . . . The poor bird was beginning to . . . vainly dash its soft breast against the hard iron bars of the inevitable." So is Eliot's characteristic involvement of the reader in her characters' dilemmas and imperfections: "Caterina, *like the rest of us*, turned away from sympathy which she suspected to be mingled with criticism" (italics added).

The narrator presents himself as having inhabited the Midlands locations of these stories and as remembering the places and some of the characters, or accounts of them. As Warwickshire readers quickly recognized, this was true: Eliot was using memories of her birthplace Chilvers Coton ("Shepperton") and its adjoining mansion, Arbury Hall ("Cheverel Manor"), and of nearby Nuneaton ("Milby") where she attended school, and of people who had lived there in, or just before, her youth. *A Study of Provincial Life* was the subtitle of her later masterpiece *Middlemarch*: that "study" begins in *Scenes of Clerical Life* which also exhibits her constant determination to depict fully the community within which the major characters operate. She displays a fine command of dialect and of the humours, pettinesses, and solidities of both male (tap-room) and female (tea-party) groups and a strong sense of how their opinions and inclinations bear upon the protagonists' fates. These are fully and vividly populated small-scale social worlds.

Eliot's blend of humour and pathos was highly praised by most reviewers: she, like Lewes, would have accepted Anthony Trollope's definition of the novel as "a picture of common life enlivened by humour and sweetened by pathos," a definition which did not, for serious artistic purposes, outlive the century. "The exquisite truth and delicacy, both of the humour and the pathos of those stories I have never seen the like of," Dickens generously wrote to her (18 January 1858), detecting "such womanly touches" that, as he specified them to her publisher (27 January 1858), if he was wrong in his surmise about the gender of "that admirable and charming writer, . . . a woman's mind has got into some man's body by a mistake that ought immediately to be corrected." But Eliot, while certainly displaying the feminine insights that Dickens noticed, was also already exhibiting that intellectual toughness and wide acquaintance with life that were then often considered the prerogative of what she later described as "A man's mind—what there is of it . . . " (*Middlemarch*, Book 1, chapter 2).

—Philip Collins

THE SCHOOL FOR SCANDAL.
Play by Richard Brinsley Sheridan, 1777.

Like his earlier masterpiece *The Rivals*, Richard Brinsley Sheridan's *The School for Scandal* offers a plethora of well-etched comic characters and a brilliant succession of superb comic situations, including one of the most effective in all English comic drama, the famous screen scene. It is probably, however, the corruscatingly witty language that has made *The School* Sheridan's most admired play and that has kept it constantly on the boards ever since it was first produced at Drury Lane on 8 May 1777.

The scandal scenes in particular have been considered a triumph of wit, and they will only work, indeed, because they are witty. The danger of these scenes, especially in a poor production, is that they are static. Nothing happens in them. The plot does not advance, and one viewer at the play's première was even heard to grumble that he wondered when the author was going to get on with the story.

But, of course, the story itself is not well structured. Despite its careful preparation, practically nothing is made of Lady Sneerwell's infatuation for Charles. The important plot business of Snake's forgery is briefly lugged in at the end of the play and as briefly disposed of. The heroine, Maria, has such a small part that she is offstage through most of the crucial acts and, amazingly, is not even confronted with the hero until the very denouement in Act V. Nor are the elements of the story all that fresh. The rich relative just returned from the West Indies is lifted directly from the well-known novel by Sheridan's mother, *Memoirs of Miss Sidney Bidulph*; and the quarrels of Sir Peter and Lady Teazle probably owe more than a little to the quarrels of Sir Harry and Lady Flutter in his mother's successful play *The Discovery*.

Yet despite every charge of hoary devices and maladroit plotting, the play triumphantly succeeds. As with *The Rivals*, one could pile up a dozen instances of what Sheridan had to do with his plot, yet did not. But, also as with *The Rivals*, one must admit that what he did do instead is so delightful, so lively and so absorbing that his audience is thoroughly satisfied. The arguments between the Teazles, the baiting of Sir Peter by the School, Charles's auction of the family pictures and the double deception of the screen scene offer such a droll succession of comic situations that they easily compensate for the lack of a well-ordered plot.

Sheridan was no dramatic innovator, and his characterization in the play makes much use of familiar stock types. But although Mrs. Candour and Sir Benjamin Backbite offer no fuller characterization than their names imply, Sheridan invests the parts with such fresh and felicitous detail that the old types sparkle anew. However, the Teazles, who are the familiar figures of the crusty old husband and the flighty young wife, are drawn with such affection for their foibles that they become rather more individualized and memorable than their types. Joseph is basically the character of the hypocrite, but Sheridan's sisters found him most reminiscent of their older brother Charles; and in Joseph the playwright does seem to cut beneath the surface and to find contradictions and even something approaching complexity. Thus, Joseph is not only a meaty acting part but also probably closer to reality than the great comic monsters of a Volpone or a Tartuffe. Charles Surface grows out of the type of the rake from Restoration comedy, but the character has none of the hardness of Etherege's Dorimant or Wycherley's Horner. Indeed, it is hardly stretching the point to see in Charles some of Richard Sheridan's own carelessness and casual mismanagement. But, like everyone, Sheridan had a good deal of tolerance for his own foibles, and so does the audience have a good deal of tolerance for the erring but basically good-hearted Charles. From this crucial attitude, much of the sunniness of the play can be traced.

That sunniness is a much-needed antidote to the delightful but cruel malice of the scandalous scenes which take up much of the first two acts. This is particularly the case because the scandalmongers are mainly opposed by Maria and Sir Peter, the unmalicious characters who are able to counter the witty malice with no more than ineffective direct statement or stuffy honest dignity. Yet, while neither Maria nor Sir Peter is a match for witty malice, that does not mean that a match could not have been found. A well-equipped Shavian wit, such as Sidney Trefuses or Don Juan, could have more than upheld the side of sense and worth with equal rhetorical cleverness and by substituting gaiety for malice.

Nevertheless, despite all of Sheridan's borrowings and botches, the play is so eminently stageworthy that one would have to say of Sheridan, as Shaw said of himself, "that he touches nothing that he does not dust and polish and put back in its place much more carefully than the last man who handled it."

—Robert Hogan

THE SEA, THE SEA.
Novel by Iris Murdoch, 1978.

There are two main clues to the meanings of *The Sea, The Sea*, Iris Murdoch's 19th—and still arguably her best—novel. The first is the title; the second, Murdoch's commitment to Platonism and its fusion, in her fiction of the 1970's with her interest in Buddhism.

The title invokes the first stanza of Valéry's "Le Cimetière marin" (a poem quoted in *The Unicorn*, 1963), in which the narrator confronts his own change through death as he gazes at *La mer, la mer, toujours recommencée* (The sea, the sea, perpetually renewed) and meditates, in a way relevant to Murdoch's Platonism, that "the Dream is knowledge." Valéry's juxtaposition of water and earth, flux and reflux, with images of enclosed deadness, is picked up at the novel's beginning as the former actor and theatre director Charles Arrowby arrives at his retirement home by the sea to write his autobiography and describes the village's *cimetière marin* (seaside graveyard), concentrating in particular on a tombstone engraved with a " 'foul anchor' and the simple inscription: *Dummy* 1879–1918." The sea in Murdoch's fiction invariably signifies the unconscious mind and, as in *The Black Prince*, metamorphic power. Lizzie, one of Charles's former lovers, once played Ariel to his Prospero in a performance of Shakespeare's *The Tempest* (another text allusively omnipresent in the novel): Charles remembers this and then, later, Lizzie turns up and actually sings "Full fathom five" as Charles nearly drowns ("Nothing of him that doth fade, / But doth suffer a sea-change . . . ").

The sea thus suggests the depths of Charles's buried self and his unacknowledged memories that, now he has retired to brood and write and—that most difficult of tasks in Murdochian thinking—"learn to be good . . . and repent of egoism," thrust themselves forward, demanding to be heard. (Eventually, practically every character who has featured large in his life arrives at Whitsun, the feast of the Pentecostal speaking in tongues and mutual comprehension that also originally, and significantly for the novel's water symbolism, celebrated the newly baptised and their transition from the dead corporeal self to the reborn spiritual self.) A key supporting image in this respect is Charles's recurring vision of the sea snake, uncanny reminder of the unknown, that is later "explained" when, as often in Murdoch's fiction, the main character confronts an art work which, on this occasion, is Titian's *Perseus and Andromeda*. The sea dragon from which Perseus rescues the girl is, in a sense, Charles's monster; but it is the monster metamorphosed into the subject of art, the stuff of the unconscious caught, examined, transformed and thereby, to some extent at least, understood.

In the same year that she published *The Sea, The Sea*, Murdoch gave an interview in which she explained that "ideas in art must suffer a sea-change," thereby identifying the central metaphor of "Full fathom five" and the transmuting power of art with her favourite notion that the quest for the good is achieved by rejecting egoism and morally reductive fantasies. The sea thus also represents that process of transformation which is, at bottom, the subject of the novel: the escape from egoism to goodness (compare Murdoch's remark in *The Sovereignty of Good* that "goodness is connected with the attempt to see the unself") is, in Charles's case, measured in terms of his break with the world of theatrical illusion and specious magical control and his confrontation of his self's darker unconscious images through the initially egotistical, but actually humbling, attempt at autobiography. The novel records the process by which Charles's fantasies are confronted for what they are—distortions of particular reality, self-deluding, self-consolatory, self-pitying (for Murdoch "good art reveals what we are usually too selfish . . . to recognise, the minute and absolutely random detail of the world").

Our initial two clues are therefore in effect aspects of each other: "Dummy" is the repressed self—analogous to the sea monster—of buried fears and resentments; he is also the body left behind by the soul which the novel inspects, interrogates, and lays to rest again. He has various forms, the most obvious of which is Hartley, Charles's childhood sweetheart whom he finds, totally by chance (except that chance is a tricky concept in any Murdoch novel) in his chosen retirement village. She is married and has a son. Her husband, Ben—*le mari* as Charles punningly calls him—is (perhaps) a tyrant; their adopted son Titus ran away two years previously. Charles sees his mission as that of Perseus to Hartley's Andromeda, rescuing her from monster Ben in the name of his own love for her. Charles tricks and imprisons her, refusing to listen to her protests that his perception of their relationship is a false and perniciously destructive obsession.

Another form of Dummy is Titus himself, whom Ben becomes convinced is actually Charles's son and whom, upon his arrival, Charles tries to possess. Titus eventually drowns—another image from the unconscious to be interrogated then quietly relinquished, but only after he has been connected with another art work, this time Rembrandt's portrait of his son Titus. Charles sees it and the Titian during the same gallery visit then has a loss of consciousness which is, simultaneously a heightening of awareness out of which emerges his cousin James.

James is Charles's symbolic twin, a wiser Cato to his Henry (to use the polarities of Murdoch's immediately preceding novel), admired and envied for his intelligence and wealth, whose reappearance announces another return of the repressed, the exhumation of yet another Dummy. He, too, dies, and at the end of the novel Charles inherits his London flat, which is filled with Buddhas and other signs of his commitment to the east including a "casket . . . like the ones in which lamas are accustomed to keep demons prisoner."

At the end the casket is empty, its demon, like the novel's various dummies, departed. It is James who voices the novel's central dilemma and gives us a particular image through which to understand it. As a convert to Tibetan Buddhism he transposes the Murdochian Platonic metaphor of striving for the good by purging bad fantasies into a slightly different key by explaining to Charles the concept of *bardo*, the limbo in which "the souls of the dead, while waiting to be reborn, wander . . . meet[ing] all kinds of demons there [which] the learned ones regard . . . as subjective visions." He also discloses that "the gods themselves are dreams" and that at the moment of death you are given a chance "to become free . . . of attachment, cravings, desires." This suggests that Charles's solitude at the end, his occupation of James's flat, and the empty casket, mark, just possibly, his chance to be free, and raises in turn the possibility that the whole novel, with its thronging images, has either been an extended exploration of the "moment" of Charles's actual (or symbolic) death or the record of his wanderings in *bardo*.

—Douglas Brooks-Davies

THE SEAFARER.
Poem, in 10th-century manuscript.

Edition

The Seafarer, edited by I.L. Gordon. 1960.

Critical Studies: "The Interpretation of *The Seafarer*" by Dorothy Whitelock, in *Essential Articles for the Study of Old English Poetry* edited by J.B. Bessinger and S.J. Kahrl, 1968; "Setting and Mode in *The Seafarer* and *The Wanderer*" by D.G. Calder, in *Neuphilologische Mitteilungen*, 72, 1971; "The Modern Reader and the Old English *Seafarer*" by W.A. Davenport, in *Papers on Language and Literature*, 10, 1974; "The Meaning and Structure of *The Seafarer*" by Roy F. Leslie, in *The Old English Elegies* edited by Martin Green, 1983; "Genre(s) in the Making: Diction, Audience, and Text in the Old English *Seafarer*" by J.M. Foley, in *Poetics Today*, vol. 4, no. 4, 1983.

The Seafarer, preserved in the late 10th-century manuscript known as the Exeter Book, is regularly grouped with such other Old English poems as *The Wanderer*, *The Ruin*, *The Wife's Lament*, and *The Husband's Message* as elegies or elegiac lyrics. Because of the strength and beauty of its descriptions of the sea, modern readers generally find *The Seafarer* more accessible than the other elegies, and Ezra Pound's translation of the poem's first half demonstrates the work's continuing attraction for 20th-century translators. Nonetheless, the poem poses a series of puzzles for its readers. Estimates of the most likely date for the composition of *The Seafarer* range from the late eighth to the early 10th century; interpretations of the poem's meaning as well as definitions of its genre are equally varied.

So deliberately ambiguous are the poem's vocabulary and syntax that readers disagree about such basic issues as whether it should be read—as I shall read it—as the interior monologue of one speaker or as a dialogue (the break coming in line 33) between an experienced sailor and an inexperienced tyro. Moreover, many early critics maintained that the poem originally ended at line 64a, or at line 102 which concludes a folio, and that a Christian interpolator later added 60, or 22, lines of sermonizing whose connection to the rest of the poem is not immediately apparent and whose text and metrics are frequently corrupt. More recent commentators accept *The Seafarer*'s integrity but disagree about the way and the degree to which it is to be read allegorically and about the connections between the poem's first and second halves.

The poem's first section (lines 1–64a) contains two subdivisions. In the first (1–33a) the poem's persona provides an apparently autobiographical account of the sufferings he has endured while on ocean voyages, contrasting his own direct experience of the wintry sea with the landsman's ignorance of it.

With line 33b the narrator shifts to the present time, telling his audience that his spirit is now prodding him to visit the faraway home of aliens / exiles. Following a gnomic passage to the effect that every man is so concerned about the outcome of his own sea journey as to think of nothing but the "rolling of the waves," the seafarer makes the paradoxical statement that the very beauties of Spring urge on the prospective traveller. The section concludes with the speaker reaffirming his intention to set sail despite the landsman's inability to understand his motivation.

The second half of the poem, decidedly homiletic and formulaic in tone, makes no mention of either the sea or sea voyaging. After acknowledging that old age and death will destroy the transitory pleasures of earth, the poet reworks the traditional heroic formula which calls for individuals to act in ways that will keep their names alive in the future into a call for virtuous actions which will deserve praise from both men and angels. The poet then catalogues material things which have passed away and, finally, exhorts his readers to fear God, live humbly, and keep in mind that heaven is their ultimate home.

Those who read *The Seafarer* allegorically contend that even if its persona had been intended as an actual pilgrim (*peregrinus*), the poem's original audience would automatically have moved beyond the concrete referent and responded in terms of the abstract idea(s) which explain the pilgrim's actions. According to many interpretations of this type, the persona becomes a representative of all Christians; the ever-changing sea a symbol for the transitory material world; the distant land a figure for heaven; and the sea voyages emblems for life (or if one distinguishes between the seafarer's previous journey and the one he is about to embark on, for life and death respectively). Particular allegorical readings vary one or more of these components, postulating, for example, that the first voyage is intended to recall the disorder which entered the world following the sin of Adam and Eve.

Those who do not read *The Seafarer* as an allegory are nearly unanimous in rejecting the view that the poem is simply an account of the irresistible attraction the sea exerts on certain people. Instead, they maintain that while nowhere in the poem is there a direct call for an allegorical interpretation, the religious language and references necessitate a more complex interpretation. Like Dorothy Whitelock, such readers take the sea voyage literally as a "pilgrimage for the love of God" (*peregrinatio pro amore Dei*) and view the persona as an actual pilgrim who leaves his homeland and for a time, which may be the remainder of his life, dwells as a stranger in a strange land, preparing his soul for heaven.

Some critics maintain that there is no need to choose between a literal and an allegorical reading, arguing that the presence of an allegorical level (or levels) in the poem does not mean that the seafarer and his experiences must be taken as nothing more than symbols.

—William D. Reynolds

THE SEASONS.
Poem by James Thomson, 1726–30.

Urged on by the success of his descriptive, blank verse poem *Winter* (1726), James Thomson wrote *Summer* (1727), *Spring* (1728), and then completed *The Seasons* in 1730 with *Autumn* and "A Hymn on the Seasons." For this version of 1730, he also revised and expanded the previously published poems, a practice he was to keep following with reissues of *The Seasons* till his death in 1748. He won great popularity. *The Seasons* was reprinted by itself or in Thomson's *Works*, in English or translation, some 170 times during the remainder of the 18th century alone. Above all were admired his eloquent evocations of the year's cycle, which touched readers increasingly taught, during the 18th century, to love the natural world. *The Seasons* was also the first long blank verse poem of high quality after Milton. Through its stylistic blending of Milton's epic mode, Roman descriptive verse, and tragic stage dialogue, it offered a rich model for later long poems in blank verse.

Thomson carried the principles of the first version of *Winter* into *The Seasons* as a whole. Set in the countryside, where unblunted nature dominates, the *Winter* of 1726 depicts the rhythms of that nature as it is experienced. It combines description and reflection or moral meditation, in an order that imitates the movement of a representative speaker's mind as he surveys the actions of winter, creating and destroying. Thomson's focus upon a single season and a single moral and aesthetic sense of life gives *Winter* a compound unity, while variety comes from the many forms the season takes and from the range of tones taken by the speaker's voice, urgent, musing, nostalgic, awestruck, or pious. Through the speaker's urgency, his imperative verbs and his now minute, now expansive descriptions, the wintry world itself is made doubly present: as God's darkly understood domain and as an overwhelming environment. These features all appear in *The Seasons*, adapted to the differing impressions that each time of year creates. The flocks wandering in *Winter*'s snow yield to the thwarted lover who pines in *Spring*, suffocating winds and tornadoes that rage in *Summer*, hunters who carouse in *Autumn*, and so forth, with full scenic and moral variety.

Thomson also augmented the features of the first *Winter*, written by him as a young Scot recently transplanted to England. By 1730 and surely thereafter, he wrote as a Briton, on behalf of a country rapidly assuming cultural dominance. More and more, *The Seasons* became a poem in which nature passed under a kind of cultural dominance too. *Winter* had portrayed human beings among other creatures within nature and, simultaneously, as subjects of moral and sensory experience. To these perspectives, Thomson added a third, humans as readers who had to reflect upon nature and its creatures, including humans themselves. In *The Seasons* nature's moral laws and its laws of structure and generation emerge for the reflective mind. Narrative vignettes express what is most typical of it, most elegantly illustrative. The "feel" of *The Seasons* is that of various orders to various degrees infusing rich, undisciplined particulars.

As a result of this process, the ever-lengthening, ever-exfoliating poem lost the simplicity that *Winter* had first presented. Multiple ways of understanding and a density of assorted particulars—sensory, narrative, scientific, and moral—diverted the reading process, altering Thomson's original balance between unity and heterogeneity. This led him to still more elaboration, sometimes toward overt moral statements. Such passages have perturbed some modern critics. They neither call on Thomson's strength as a descriptive poet nor show originality, for they are meant to anchor the poem in common, shared wisdom, which is by nature conventional. But it is hard to see how *The Seasons* could fulfill its epic design without the shifts in perspective and large views of pattern that they provide.

Ultimately, God's moral and cognitive truth underlies *The Seasons*, and for Thomson, witnesses to that cognitive truth are the facts of science. Using scientific laws, Thomson could bring regularity into an apparent thicket of immediate facts and perceptions. Mysteries of the solar system, fogs, insects, and water flow, deciphered by "natural philosophy," all show nature both complex and legible. He could also dignify his readers by giving them a penetrating eye as well as a widely observing one. Furthermore, the scientific theme is progressivist and patriotic as well as timeless and oriented towards God. Within their own lifetimes, many of Thomson's audience had experienced a great burst of British scientific progress, through Newton, Halley, Boyle, and others in the Royal Society.

As a patriot, Thomson takes the torch from the specifically philosophical poets of an emulable antiquity, Lucretius and the Virgil of the imperial *Georgics*. He reminds one stylistically of Milton, a British modern who recaptured the splendors of antiquity, and his style too suggests the terminology of modern British science. His Latinate words often have scientific as well as Miltonic force or flavor ("umbrageous," "incult," "hard agglomerating salts"), and his compound words ("mazy-running," "full-descending") evoke similar Latin usages ("celeripes"). Such a lexicon also stresses a reality so profuse that the common words of English must be stretched to contain it. As the moralizing and science anchors *The Seasons* in common truth, for Thomson, so its allusive texture anchors it in its heritage, not only literary but also broadly cultural. Through making his distinctive yet echoing language match his inherited, personal subject, Thomson pays tribute to the past, emulates it, makes it his own, and goes beyond it as a British poet very much of a new time with a new momentum.

—Eric Rothstein

THE SECOND COMING.
Poem by William Butler Yeats, 1920.

"The Second Coming," written in January 1919, grew, according to William Butler Yeats's widow, from his "apprehensions about the socialist revolutions in Russia, Germany and Italy during and after World War I" (Donald Torchiana, *Yeats and Georgian Ireland*, 1965). In the first drafts, the opening lines are succeeded by the raw statement: "The Germany of Marx has led to Russian Com[munism] / There every day some innocent has died" (see Jon Stallworthy, *Between the Lines: Yeats's Poetry in the Making*, 1963). Faced by this information, the critic usually argues that Yeats universalises each little local catastrophe, transforming it into a larger image of apocalypse which transcends history, to offer a timeless tragic vision of the human condition. Certainly the movement from particular to general is a regular procedure in Yeats's finished work, even when his poems bear the date of their inception in their title, as with "September 1913," "Easter 1916," "Nineteen Hundred and Nineteen," and the Coole Park poems. Nevertheless, such a strategy too frequently enables the critic to dispose of Yeats's embarrassing philosophical and political ideas as irrelevant to literary discussion, exculpating his poetry from responsibility for the various unpleasant extremisms he espoused in his long life (including support for fascism), and allowing the reader to flirt with attitudes which would be loathsome in the "real world." In the end, it is an argument which diminishes Yeats's stature as a great poet of moral utterance.

In reality, poems such as this become much more polemic *because* they don't name their actual target. Yeats's revulsion at the murder of the Tsar's family, which the drafts reveal to be the occasion of the poem, is reasonable enough. But by suppressing its occasion, the finished poem then goes on to make sweeping statements about the nature of historical change in general as a process which is *always* for the worse, always a matter of "blood-dimmed tides," in which *everywhere* the "ceremony of innocence" is drowned. By presenting its ferociously partisan sentiments in the guise of disinterested cosmic vision, a poem such as "The Second Coming" seeks endorsement for its reactionary sentiments, and encourages readers to find confirmation for their local prejudices in the commanding universal statements of art, when those statements are in fact as local, particularised, and prejudiced as the readers'. This is complicated when, as here, the moral posture of the poem is deeply ambivalent. For it is clear that, while Yeats laments the destruction the poem envisages, he also exults in that destruction as a necessary prelude to renewal, part of that "widening gyre" of history which, in *A Vision*, he presented as the inevitable movement of the modern era.

According to a note Yeats wrote for this poem, history is composed of two vast interlocking gyres, one inside the other, rotating in opposite directions, one expanding as the other contracts, around a common centre. Historical events are shaped by the turbulence created by their conflicting pulls:

> the end of an age, which always receives the revelation of the character of the next age, is represented by the coming of one gyre to its place of greatest expansion and of the other to that of its greatest contraction. At the present the life gyre is sweeping outward, unlike that before the birth of Christ when it was narrowing, and has almost reached its greatest expansion. The revelation which approaches will however take its character from the contrary movement of the interior gyre. All our scientific, democratic, fact-accumulating, heterogeneous civilisation belongs to the outward gyre and prepares not the continuance of itself but the revelation as in a lightning flash, though in a flash that will not strike only in one place, and will for a time be constantly repeated, of the civilisation that must slowly take its place.

The two thousand years of the Christian era are now reaching their end, to be succeeded, antithetically repeated and reversed, by the coming of the Antichrist predicted in the Revelation of St. John, a monstrous parody of the child born in Bethlehem, who will inaugurate a new and brutal dispensation.

The poem embodies this idea of history as a pattern of repetitions at the level both of language and event. The repetition with which it opens, "Turning and turning," sets up a linguistic routine which continues through the poem. It is reproduced in the play between "falcon" and "falconer," and in the parallelism both within and between lines in the rest of the first paragraph. The two pithy clauses, "Things fall apart; the centre cannot hold," describe the same event from different points of view (points which correspond to and repeat those of the falcon and the falconer respectively) and attribute a kind of simultaneous causality to the process: things fall apart *because* the centre cannot hold. But this line is then paralleled and repeated by the next line of what seems to be a (loosely) rhyming couplet, where the active "cannot hold" is translated into the passive "is loosed upon." The abstraction of "Mere anarchy" (a word which hovers between cosmology and politics) is narrowed down to the more concrete and emotive "blood-dimmed tide," and the two processes revealed as one by the repetition of "is loosed," which converts a metaphor of political control (linking back to the feudal and aristocratic grasp of the falconer) into the impersonal one of loosened flood waters, culminating in that powerful "drowned." The passive voice, here and throughout, gives the impression of a process in which human agency is no more than a hapless instrument and victim of vast impersonal forces—centripetal forces which in the first four lines seem to equate political disintegration (the falcon's disobedience to its master) with the break-up of gravity itself. By the time the second paragraph opens, the syntactic parallelism has reached such a pitch that the two lines beginning "Surely" differ only in their interchangeable synonyms, where "*the* Second Coming" gives precision to the vaguer "*some* revelation" (compare "somewhere"). Repeated, this phrase then becomes a powerful incantation, calling up as if inadvertently the "vast image" that succeeds it (though the poem carefully avoids imputing causality to sequence: "Hardly are those words out / When . . . ").

There is a certain rhetorical insistence to the poem, which only half conceals the deep uncertainty in which it is founded. The repeated "Surely" lays claim to more conviction than it warrants. The repeated phrase "the Second Coming" itself magically calls up the "vast image" which appears to resolve the status of an utterance poised between question and assertion; but there is nothing in the poem which actually gives this image objective status. There is an effective contrast between the blank and pitiless *gaze* of the beast, objective, unseeing, and the subjectively troubled *sight* of the poet. Revelation is a process of visual revealing. This image which "Troubles my sight" emerges from *Spiritus Mundi*, the collective unconscious, in Yeats's words "a general storehouse of images which have ceased to be a property of any personality or spirit." Though Yeats wishes us to see this "vast image" as an objective thing, the poem acknowledges that it is something subjectively *imagined* before it can be objectively externalised, a revelation before it is a coming.

In the same way, we cannot pin the event down to a real place and time. Its location is vague ("*somewhere* in sands of the desert") and all the specificity with which the poet describes the rough beast depends on rhetorical sleight of hand. The assertiveness of that emphatic present indicative initiated by "Is moving its slow thighs" seems to be confirmed by the powerfully concrete and particular verb "slouches"—a word which like "rough beast" calls up the suppressed class feelings in which the poem originated: proletarians slouch. Despite the apparent confidence of the assertion "but now I know," we see that the whole supernatural vision is sustained by a mere rhetorical question which *presumes* that which it merely in fact *posits*: the actual existence of the "rough beast." (Compare a similar strategy with regard to the supernatural in, for example, "The Statues," "What stalked through the Post Office?", and in "To Dorothy Wellesley," "What climbs the stair?")

The reeling of the desert birds (presumably low-class collectivist vultures) sets up an antithetical motion to the turning and turning of the (aristocratic and solitary) falcon. Carrion not hunting birds, they converge with ungrateful plebeian indignation upon the beast that will supply their dinners. Though Yeats clearly loathes both birds and beast, we can feel too the sinister attraction their brutish vitality holds for him, concentrated in those powerful verbs, "reel," "vexed," "slouches." The somewhat abstract vocabulary of the first section, highly latinate and conceptual, "centre," "anarchy," "ceremony," "innocence," "conviction," "passionate," "intensity," palls beside the immediacy and visual concreteness of the second, focussed by its apocalyptic image. If the beast represents the "filthy modern tide" of a proletarian century, it has also the archaic inhuman majesty of those fabulous animals Yeats would have passed regularly in the Assyrian Room of the British Museum. The flood which merely drowns in the first section is more of a desert than that sea of sand teeming with new and monstrous life in the second. The phrase with which the poem ends emphasises that this is a new beginning as well as a (possibly deserved) end, and Christ's rocking cradle, vexing stony sleep to nightmare, is hardly a positive image of the order now to be overthrown. Yeats's antithetical imagination here makes him the match for a century which both fascinated and repelled him. "The Second Coming," like so much of Yeats's best work, reveals what Patrick J. Keane in *Yeats's Interactions with Tradition* (1987) calls "the notoriously conflicted tone of the speaker, his mingled anguish, terror, and exultation." This ambivalence is a deep energy and resource of the poem.

—Stan Smith

THE SECOND MRS. TANQUERAY.
Play by Arthur Wing Pinero, 1893.

Female suicide drama had almost become a European vogue in the decade before Arthur Wing Pinero wrote his most famous play, *The Second Mrs. Tanqueray*, and the topic had been made considerably more problematic by the plays of Ibsen and Strindberg. The depth of Pinero's familiarity with their work is debatable, and the continental yardstick has not always treated his achievement favourably; however, the play's impact on its first London audience was momentous and its critical resonance continued for a decade, so that its significance in terms of cultural history remains unquestionable.

When Paula Tanqueray goes upstairs and kills herself at the end of the play, it seems as if harmony will be restored in the patriarchal world of the drama. Whatever her intentions, she has been the complicator of the central action, and her death—which some have seen as obliging—is certainly a simplifying gesture for Aubrey Tanqueray. However, the cause of her psychological turmoil and suicide is complex, with the result that audience manipulation is by no means as straightforward as had become traditional in the "well-made play," and a variety of perspectives may attract a degree of sympathy. Paula is by no means merely the stereotypical "woman with a past," to be condemned on sight, and she articulates her dilemma with a vigorous allusiveness that engrosses any audience. But Pinero's dramatic strategy seems also designed to ensure that we see at least some aspects of the problem through the eyes of Aubrey.

The first act—unlike the other three—is set in Aubrey's bachelor apartment in London, and includes several characters who will not appear again. The main subject of conversation is Aubrey's proposed second marriage, and the effect of these considerable demands on production resources is to establish an emphatically male perspective, with two bachelors and two married men providing the context for Paula's first entrance. Coming to a bachelor's quarters late at night, she offends the sense of propriety of both characters and audience. She describes a dream she has had about marriage to Aubrey and presents a letter which chronicles her earlier life; Aubrey's response is to burn the letter without reading it and say "Yes, yes. Eat some more fruit." The male rejection of Paula's attempt at the exposure of her private self seems complete, and she is reduced to a one-dimensional commodity in a male market.

Since Paula is presented as bargaining up from her position as a "fallen" (or at least experienced) woman in a world of male dominance in the first act, and even mentions suicide as a resort if her marriage to Aubrey does not come about, the male categorisation of women's expectations seems explicit. However, the act ends with Aubrey receiving a letter from Ellean, the daughter of his first marriage who has hitherto lived in a convent, announcing that she will come to live with him in his "loneliness." So Aubrey finds himself in the exclusively male dilemma at the first act curtain, caught between Paula, an apparently reformed woman with a past and Ellean, who, because of her cushioned existence to date in a hermetically sealed-off environment, is essentially a—highly abnormal—woman without a past.

Aubrey's position is virtually static, and the play's conclusion seems to vindicate this pose. Pinero makes no attempt to dramatise—as a later playwright might have done—the inner anguish from these conflicting demands of two women. The women, similarly, are relatively static as characters, but the play gives them each one grand entrance and one major piece of character development. For Ellean, this consists in moving out into the real world on the other side of the "Black Moor" to have her first amorous engagement; this is unsuccessful, but she is left ready for other relationships. Paula, by contrast, tries to efface her past (as Aubrey has symbolically done by burning the letter) and present herself as a socially acceptable, good, married woman, but her past targets her in the form of Ardale (her former lover who is now attracted to Ellean), and she commits suicide precisely as she said she would in the first act.

Paula's character at the time of the première was clearly informed by the fact that she was created by Mrs. Patrick Campbell, who had been celebrated as a female heavy earlier in her stage career. But Paula's behaviour is dominated by a quest for acceptability: she does not have to tell Aubrey about Ardale, and the second act shows—at some length, in both comic and poignant terms—that she has outgrown the proclivities of her former social circle. If Paula is the victim of her past, Aubrey may, conversely, be seen as an oppressor, in that he has imposed an absence of identity on Ellean for which he has to answer in the course of the play. Until now, Aubrey has played God with Ellean: keeping her in a convent, preventing her from seeing "what the world is like on the other side of the Black Moor," and having the "one great desire" to keep her "ignorant of evil." If the play's resolution is seen by some as a denial of Paula's right to exist, it may equally be seen as a denial of Aubrey's right to play God on these terms.

—Howard McNaughton

THE SECOND SHEPHERDS' PLAY.
Play by the Wakefield Master, 15th century.

The Second Shepherds' Play is undoubtedly the best known of the English mystery plays, yet ironically it is the least typical of the genre. Whereas the majority are usually closely tied to their biblical and apocryphal sources, this one takes for its main plot a folktale about a stolen sheep; and whereas characterisation, dialogue, and stage movement are so often rudimentary in the other plays, in this one they are so skilfully managed that the play has become a popular perennial for study and for theatrical production.

This is the better of two shepherds' plays by the Wakefield Master, and probably they were treated as alternatives. The *First Shepherds' Play* also makes extensive use of folktale, but the burlesque treatment of the squabbling and mock-feasting by the shepherds seems not to come together to make such a unified play. The two have close links with a third, that of the Chester cycle of mystery plays, which also concentrates on the worldly and often foolish behaviour of the shepherds before the announcement of the birth of Jesus. Thematically this behaviour has been said to represent the state of fallen humankind before the Redemption, but it is equally likely that the shepherds had become associated with knockabout comedy and that their play was regarded as a point of comic relief within the cycle.

At the beginning of *The Second Shepherds' Play* the shepherds enter individually, each complaining about one thing or another—upstarts and landlords, shrewish wives, hunger, the weather—and agree to cheer themselves with a song. With the arrival of Mak, a notorious petty criminal, they are on their guard, but agree to let him stay so long as he sleeps between them. Mak, however, contrives to steal a sheep and conveys it to his cottage, where his wife swaddles it in a cradle. The shepherds' frantic searches bring them to the cottage, but the sheep remains undiscovered, disguised as a newly born child. Only after they have left does one think of returning to make a gift to the baby—a kindness which leads to the discovery of the sheep and to the punishment of Mak by tossing him in a canvas sheet. An angel appears singing the *Gloria* and announces the birth of Christ. The shepherds, admiring the singing, attempt to emulate it, then rehearse some of the Old Testament prophecies of a Saviour's birth, before travelling to Bethlehem to present their gifts.

The non-biblical part of the play gives the Wakefield Master opportunity to explore some of his favourite themes. The audience is involved by the fact that the shepherds are characterised as Yorkshire farm workers, and search for their lost sheep in Horbury Shrogs, a place just south of Wakefield. They complain of contemporary abuses such as "purveyance" and "maintenance," and speak directly to the men of the audience warning them of the misfortunes of marriage. Their style of speech is colloquial and involves traditional sayings such as "Ill-spun woof always comes out badly," probably a popular proverb around Wakefield, which was a centre for wool spinning and weaving. When asked who are his "child's" godparents Mak names them as Parkin, Gib Waller, and John Horn, possibly local characters, two of whom appear also in *The First Shepherds' Play*.

The inventive use of the Mak story makes for excellent theatre. The action would not have been confined to the pageant wagon (the moveable stage on which some of the mystery plays were performed), but requires two distinct locations, representing moorland outside a town and Mak's cottage, with an open acting space between. Through this space the actors move in well-managed changes of scene, as when the shepherds, approaching the cottage, comment in advance on the discordant lullaby sung by Mak and his wife. Singing is, in fact, a recurrent preoccupation, and set pieces by the angel and the shepherds probably enhanced the production. Humour, dramatic irony, and tension come together in the cottage scene, as the suspicious shepherds question Mak and he protests his honesty, "otherwise let this be the first meal I shall eat today" (pointing to the cradle). The discovery of the sheep is brilliantly managed:

> What the devil is this? He has a long snout!
> He is deformed. It's wrong for us to wait about.
> He is rather like our sheep . . .

And all this naturalness is achieved despite the Wakefield Master's use of his characteristic nine-line stanza with its varying length of line and its complicated internal rhymes.

The sheep-stealing story is also a clever parody of the story of the Nativity, a link which might have been enhanced in production by making the cottage serve also as the stable in Bethlehem. Mak's wife is a grotesque contrast to the Virgin Mary, and the swaddled sheep (at one point called a "horned lad") is the devilish antithesis of Jesus himself. It is extraordinary that the Wakefield Master was able to get away with such boldness, but we have every reason to be thankful that he did.

—G.A. Lester

THE SECRET AGENT.
Novel by Joseph Conrad, 1907.

The Secret Agent is the middle volume of Joseph Conrad's three pessimistic, sardonic novels centered on political strife and intrigue, bracketed by *Nostromo* (1904) and *Under Western Eyes* (1911). Of these, *The Secret Agent* is the most heavily ironic and melodramatic, lacking the numerous intermediating narrators and embedded texts which provide distance and complication of transmission in the other works. When Conrad subtitled the book a "simple tale," he perhaps meant in terms of these narrative structures, since he certainly couldn't have meant the work was clear and unambiguous. The story has a comparatively small group of characters in a restricted area of London during a brief period.

The novel centers on the shabby family grouping of Verloc, his wife Winnie, and her retarded brother Stevie. Verloc is portrayed as lazy and brutal, yet somehow active enough to be a police informer, an agent provocateur, leader of a group of anarchists, and a spy for a foreign embassy (these activities are so disreputable that Verloc's front is that of a pornography dealer). Winnie Verloc, who emotionlessly minds the counter and takes care of the stock, does not love her husband but married him in order to provide for her brother and crippled mother. She cherishes the illusion of Verloc and the childlike Stevie as father and son and feels it was worth giving up all of her desires for anything better in order to have gained some security for her family.

In the claustrophobic atmosphere of the *sub rosa* world portrayed by Conrad, everything is motivated by distrust, authority, suspicion, betrayal, and tense mutual surveillance and coercion. Verloc is the most active figure in this bleak London, meeting secretly with Chief Inspector Heat of Scotland Yard and the Russian agent Vladimir, speaking with the fanatical anarchists and nihilists who form his terrorist band (Michaelis, Yundt, Ossipon, and an American called "the Professor"; none of the terrorists are British), and planning the symbolic bombing of the Greenwich Observatory (based on a real incident of 1894, this attack on the first meridian would be an attack on science, the current fetish of the British middle class, explains the Embassy official who assigns this "outrage" to Verloc). All of the anarchists, who always disagree with one another, are grotesques: indolent, overweight, supported by the intelligence apparatus of the different countries and the "International Red Committee," in love with their own vivid representations of what damages they might one day cause, what destruction there might be around them. The most dangerous member of the group, the Professor, works on perfecting detonators and claims to be a living bomb, with explosives wrapped around his body and the rubber bulb which would set it off always in his hand. The forces of law and order are little better, with the stupid and very nearsighted Home Secretary (whose pet project is a bill to nationalize fisheries) and the interfering and credit-grabbing Assistant Commissioner (even Inspector Heat, the most positively presented official, identifies with common criminals and feels that they support him in his work against the terrorists).

When Verloc uses the trusting Stevie to carry the bomb to the Observatory, and Stevie is accidentally blown into tiny bits that must be shovelled up by the police, the secure world constructed by the stolid Winnie collapses. The last words of Verloc are described in this way: " 'Come here,' he said in a peculiar tone, which might have been the tone of brutality, but was intimately known to Mrs. Verloc as the note of wooing." Winnie kills Verloc by stabbing him with a carving knife (in a scene reminiscent of Tess's stabbing of Alec d'Urberville in Hardy's novel, rendered more squalid in Conrad by the surrounding and the circumstances). She seems to awaken with the shock of her brother's death, and rebels against the dehumanized life she has led with Verloc, the cloistering, the secrecy, and his sexual demands. Ossipon happens by and Winnie immediately gives her trust to him, just as she had earlier trusted Verloc, and again this trust is betrayed. She will flee the country with Ossipon and Ossipon agrees, although stricken with fear; he steals her money and she quietly throws herself into the English Channel. At the end of the book Ossipon is reading the newspaper account of the "Suicide of a Lady Passenger." "Comrade Ossipon was familiar with the beauties of its journalistic style. '*An impenetrable mystery seems destined to hang forever. . . .*' "

An important element of the book is the relationship of the narrator to the various characters, and the different tones and levels of sympathy shown by the narrator, who sometimes speaks in the first person (see Jakob Lothe's *Conrad's Narrative Method*, 1989). *The Secret Agent* is a rich and complex novel, fully an equal to *Nostromo* and *Under Western Eyes*.

—Leonard Orr

THE SECRET SHARER.
Story by Joseph Conrad, 1912.

The captain-narrator of Joseph Conrad's "The Secret Sharer," separated by a "distance of years" from the meeting with Leggatt, recounts a tale of initiation in which he successfully overcame debilitating emotional insecurity to command his ship. The significance of the events for the sensitive and intelligent captain is that he discovered within himself the *ability to act* decisively that he had lacked. As a younger man, the captain doubted himself, felt a "stranger" to the community to which he belonged, and wondered if he should "turn out faithful to that ideal conception of one's personality every man sets up for himself secretly." His concern *now* is to present the issues in terms of what Leggatt meant to him. Although he certainly knows that harboring an escaped murderer represents a threat to a maritime civilization and a violation of his own legal and moral commitment, his retelling ignores this.

The captain's interpretation of his experience dramatizes the process of his coming to terms with what Leggatt symbolizes. In reductive terms, Leggatt is a man of unrestrained id and underdeveloped superego. The captain, an example of hyperconscious modern man who fastidiously thinks of the consequence of every action to the point where he cannot *do* anything, is his opposite. Self-doubt and anxiety create an illogical identification with Leggatt as his "double." He risks his future to hide the man he regards as his "other self." To avoid discovery, he begins to act desperately and instinctively without conscious examination of the consequences of each action. Leggatt's presence creates situations where the luxury of introspection is no longer possible. Symbolically, the captain completes himself. He finds within himself the potential to act instinctively and boldly that his "double" exemplifies. It can be said that his adult ego is created by appeasing the contradictory demands of the id and superego. Despite the evidence that Leggatt murdered another man in a fit of passion, the captain holds to a belief in Leggatt's control and sanity and insists that the killing was an act of duty. But the reader does not forget that Leggatt commits a horribly immoral act which *he does not regret*.

The effect of Leggatt's presence is to disrupt the ship's community and to raise further doubts in the minds of the captain's officers about his own self-control and sanity. The captain becomes more neurotic because he has to consider whether his every sentence and every word might reveal his secret. He now has twin loyalties, mutually exclusive, to the man whom he is harboring and with whom he identifies, and to his ship. Paradoxically, the desperation of his paranoia, of his belief that he is constantly being scrutinized by his subordinates, leads him to give his "first particular order." When threatened, he "felt the need of asserting myself." The pressure of circumstances makes it increasingly difficult for him to distinguish between himself and Leggatt. Like Eliot's Prufrock and Joyce's Gabriel Conroy, the integrity of the captain's personality is threatened by a disbelief in the authenticity of self.

Before Leggatt's appearance, the captain is immobilized by self-consciousness and self-doubt. The character of Leggatt is a function of the captain's need for someone to share the burdens of loneliness and anxiety. When he hears of Leggatt's alternatives (to keep swimming until he drowns or is welcomed on board the captain's ship) he responds, "I felt this was no mere formula of desperate speech, but a real alternative in the view of a strong soul." The captain recalls that "the voice was calm and resolute. A *good* voice. The *self-possession* of that man had somehow induced a corresponding state in myself" (emphasis added). But this contrasts with his original response of seconds before: "He seemed to struggle with himself, for I heard something like the low, bitter murmur of doubt. 'What's the good?' His next words come out with a hesitating effort." Jumping from one assertion to another without empirical data, the captain continues to convince himself of Leggatt's resemblance to him on such flimsy grounds as that they are both "young." Although he tells us that they looked identical, he later admits that Leggatt "was not a bit like me, really." His original, flattering description of Leggatt is continually modified until it is almost contradicted. Before Leggatt even begins to explain how he killed a man, the captain has excused him: " 'Fit of temper,' I suggested, confidently." Insisting upon the value of his second self enables the captain to discover himself morally and psychologically. But the process of idealizing his "double," his "other self," into a model of self-control, self-confidence, and sanity is arbitrary and non-cognitive.

Leggatt is flippantly conscious of the possible analogy between Cain and himself: "The 'brand of Cain' business, don't you see. That's all right. I was ready enough to go off wandering on the face of the earth—and that was price enough to pay for an Abel of that sort." It disturbs the conventional morality of the captain to be on the side of Cain; but for a time he becomes an Abel figure in protecting his double: "The very trust in Providence was, I suppose, denied to his guilt. Shall I confess that this thought cast me down very much?" Yet it is soon clear that both men contain Cain and Abel elements. Leggatt plays the role of Abel when he willingly leaves the ship and thus helps the captain through the crisis. The captain's Cain identity derives from our realization that, to fulfill his own aspirations, he must abandon Leggatt. The persistent allusions to the Cain-Abel myth suggest that each man must continually confront an unresolvable conflict between self-fulfillment and commitment to others.

The captain is as much Leggatt's secret sharer as Leggatt is the captain's. Indeed, each of the two men has a partial understanding of the other, but each *believes* the other's partial understanding to be complete. In this sense, too, Leggatt is the captain's double. Paradoxically, Leggatt disrupts the captain's psychic health, and hence the order of the ship, at the same time as he is a catalyst for a more efficient integration of both the captain's personality and his fitness to command. The only way for the captain to satisfy his conscience, now that he has cast him from his boat, is to create the myth of a triumphant departure, for even retrospectively he cannot admit that he might have sacrificed Leggatt in order to preserve his own position. Yet, for the reader, Leggatt is a tragic, lonesome figure, branded not only by the standards of civilization, but by the captain himself as an outsider destined to wander the earth. It is the teller who has fulfilled the implied prophecy of a new destiny. He had lived up to an ideal conception of himself by proving his ability to command and by establishing his hierarchical position as captain.

—Daniel R. Schwarz

SENSE AND SENSIBILITY.
Novel by Jane Austen, 1811.

Jane Austen's first novel to be published, *Sense and Sensibility* was developed from a sketch in letters ("Elinor and Marianne") begun some 15 years earlier. Its title seems to locate it firmly in a neoclassical, dualistic moral world where the values of reason and restraint, embodied in Elinor's good sense, will finally triumph over the impulsive, romantic sensibility of her sister Marianne. Yet even by its second chapter, any readerly security in such terms as "justice" and "good sense" is immediately put at risk as John Dashwood and his wife Fanny use rational calculation and prudent self-interest to hide their greed from themselves as they "sensibly" persuade one another that the intent behind the father's deathbed legacy of £3000 to his daughters, John's stepsisters, can be satisfied by an occasional gift of fish and game. Just as the novel's first scene shows how Sense can become a screen for coldness and cruelty, so too the novel as a whole dramatizes the gaps that occur between language and behavior, feeling and action: gaps that the unscrupulous exploit, the naive are trapped by, and the wise must use every resource of imagination to repair, or at least understand.

In this deceptively expressible world the two elder Dashwood sisters (Margaret, the youngest, is largely forgotten by the reader, and the author) try to work out their destinies, discover and narrate their own stories, by very different models. Like all of Austen's young women, both implicitly acknowledge that financial security and social stability, let alone enhancement, depend on marriage. Yet Marianne assumes that that relation should found itself on the unmediated openness of one freely expressive heart to another; her sister, that marriage is first a social contract, mediated by a language that, in turn, preserves a rational and decorous civilisation as a stay against humankind's baser instincts. Both sisters choose, and apparently are chosen by, men of appropriate character: Elinor's Edward Ferrars (brother of her stepbrother's wife) is a man all of whose works "centered in domestic comfort and the quiet of private life" and who is "too diffident to do justice to himself"; Marianne's Willoughby, conversely, with his "lively spirits," "open affectionate manner," and "natural ardour" is "exactly formed to engage Marianne's heart."

Each sister, however, is deceived: following Willoughby to London after his sudden and unexplained removal from Devonshire, Marianne is cruelly cut by him, in the novel's most powerfully dramatic scene (" 'Good God! Willoughby, what is the meaning of this?' ") at a party they attend with their cousin Lady Middleton; Elinor, ministering to her distraught sister (who has been rejected in favor of an heiress), supresses her own recent and painful discovery that Edward has been secretly engaged for four years to Lucy Steele, a vulgar, scheming climber. Both sisters also soon learn that Willoughby had previously seduced and abandoned, pregnant, the 16-year-old ward of their taciturn friend Colonel Brandon. Much confusion is brought about by (among other events) Edward's being disinherited for his unsuitable engagement to Lucy, his initial refusal to break off the engagement (out of a strict sense of honor) even after Lucy wants her freedom when she realizes he will be an impoverished clergyman, and comic confusions involving Edward's foppish brother Robert, who takes his brother's place in Lucy's affections and ambitions. Marianne, never fully recovered from the illness brought about by unrequited love, collapses again with fever en route home to Devon. Willoughby, rushing to what he assumes will be her deathbed, makes a confession and apology to Elinor, who is passionately moved by his distress, and by her sympathy for his economic impotence. After recovering, Marianne comes to see virtue in Brandon, who offers a living to Edward, and the sisters marry prudently at last: Elinor and Edward, in the Parsonage at Delaford, "had in fact nothing to wish for, but the marriage of Colonel Brandon and Marianne, and rather better pasturage for their cows," while Marianne, "born to an extraordinary fate . . . to discover the falsehood of her own opinions, and to counteract, by her conduct, her most favourite maxims . . . found herself at nineteen, submitting to new attachments, entering on new duties, placed in a new home, a wife, the mistress of a family, and the patroness of a village."

Though the novel's final paragraphs seem to celebrate happiness and power ("patroness of a village") gained through submission and accommodation to society and the taming of impulsive vitality, the narrator's sly ironies ("better pasturage," "extraordinary fate") point toward a level of awareness no character in the novel is allowed, and the author herself partly suppresses. Together, Elinor and Marianne represent the sort of disciplined imagination later found in such complex characters as Elizabeth Bennet (*Pride and Prejudice*) or Anne Elliot (*Persuasion*), but much of *Sense and Sensibility*'s depth exists in implication: in the erotic energy of Willoughby and its devastating effect on Marianne (nearly fatal) and Elinor (who decides not to tell her sister the full truth of Willoughby's confession); and in the complex representation of power relations, whereby men ruthlessly dominate and manipulate women, women have only their sexual marketability as defense, and both sexes are imprisoned in a structure that denies most people (except perhaps for clergymen and gentleman farmers) useful work as a source either of wealth or personal worth.

—William W. Heath

A SENTIMENTAL JOURNEY THROUGH FRANCE AND ITALY.
Novel by Laurence Sterne, 1768.

The original title page of *A Sentimental Journey* had no need to name Laurence Sterne. The narrator, Parson Yorick, had first appeared in his serial novel *Tristram Shandy* for part of which he is as dead as his ancestor, the jester in *Hamlet*. (At Versailles he identifies himself to the Count by pointing to the printed play: "Me, Voici!") Sterne had identified himself with the conflated priest-jester, and had even published his own sermons under Yorick's name. He had travelled in France 1762–64 and to Italy in 1765, using the earlier experience for Tristram's travels in Volume VII. In his final book, of which the part dealing with Italy remained unwritten, there is thus an elaborate play with the common identity of author and the masks through which he had won enormous fame.

In the preface, characteristically at some distance from the abrupt opening, Yorick distinguishes his motives and methods from those of conventional travellers. "Sentimental" was a new, non-pejorative concept, popularised by Sterne, suggesting refined or elevated emotion; Yorick is not interested in routine tourist sites but in occasions for the liberation and cultivation of his own responses. Structurally, the novel therefore seems to consist of a rather disjointed series of scenes and episodes; however its unity depends not on plot but on the controlling consciousness of Yorick, who both exposes and analyses his own emotion. Towards the end, he glories in "Dear Sensibility! source inexhausted of all that's precious in our joys, or costly in our sorrows!. . . . that I feel some generous joys and generous cares beyond myself—all comes from thee, great, great SENSORIUM of the world!" The arrangement of the text into short sections beneath headings—"The Snuff Box: Calais"—both mimics guide books and focuses our attention on the novel's lack of factual information and its concentration on the superficially trivial episode, often of someone in distress, which is best appreciated by the true sentimentalist; it also draws attention to the immense self-awareness of the narrative, whose spontaneity is precisely calculated to highlight this series of set pieces. Thus we remember the dead ass, the Parisian grisset, the starling, or Maria (whose story also appears in *Tristram Shandy* IX, 24).

This cultivation of feeling, especially pathos, is in part a heightening of a widespread movement of the time, but Sterne characteristically complicates our response by an ironic awareness of its artifice and vulnerability: as Yorick solemnly tries to reflect in the coach on the mourner's love for his dead ass, the postillion unfeelingly lashes his horses into a gallop inappropriate to this mood: "he'll go on tearing my nerves to pieces till he has worked me into a foolish passion, and then he'll go slow, that I may enjoy the sweets of it." The frustration is part of the whole response to a world which cannot live up to his hopes.

A sentimentalist naturally has a particular and feeling interest in women, and here, despite Yorick's protestations, Sterne excels in a delicate ambivalence which shades into innuendo and *double entendre* in a way never caught by his many imitators (for instance Henry Mackenzie in his *The Man of Feeling*). The episode of the grisset shows him seeking "a face not likely to be disordered" by his request for instructions, his rapid move to feeling her pulse, the "combined looks of simple subtlety—where whim, and sense, and seriousness, and nonsense, are so blended, that all the languages of Babel set loose together could not express them—they are communicated and caught so instantaneously." Finally, the sentimentalist allows himself to be overcharged for gloves by slightly less than he wishes. The immediately following section makes innuendo of his trying to enter through a door as the Marquesina is coming out, and his going home with her: "the connection. . . . gave me more pleasure than any one I had the pleasure to make in Italy." The episodes with the *fille de chambre* show Yorick's consciousness of flirting with danger as his protestation of virtue ambiguously cuts across his story of unbalancing her in his bedroom: whenever providence tries virtue, "let me feel the movements which rise out of it, and which belong to me as a man, and if I govern them as a good one, I will trust the issues to thy justice." If women occasion characteristic episodes of this sort, Yorick is impelled by the pathetic story of Maria, which he read in the pages of his "friend, Mr. Shandy," to seek her out as one of his "melancholy adventures": "I know not how it is, but I am never so perfectly conscious of the existence of a soul within me, as when I am entangled in them." Women can remind Yorick of his fleshly humanity, but in his sympathetic weeping with Maria he is raised to a more spiritual level of response: "I felt such undescribable emotions within me, as I am sure could not be accounted for from any combinations of matter and motion."

But the novel's final scene returns, via the elaborate negotiations as to his overnight sharing a room at an inn with a lady and her maid, to innuendo as the reader is invited to speculate how they undressed. It ends tantalisingly in mid-episode as, "nature and patience both wearing out," Yorick breaks his treaty of silence and, apparently accidentally, catches hold of the maid in the dark. The open-endedness is appropriate to a work which from its abrupt opening in dialogue defies many conventions of both travel book and well-made story, blurring the distinctions between literature and "life" (is Yorick a character in Shakespeare, in *Tristram Shandy*, a "real" traveller, or Sterne himself?). Sterne's method focuses through dramatisation and reflection on the difficulties of consistency and self-knowledge, even in the seeming clearest-cut situations: the economy, awareness of flux, and combination of comedy and pathos are his legacies from this brief masterpiece.

—Ian McGowan

SERJEANT MUSGRAVE'S DANCE.
Play by John Arden, 1959.

A discussion of *Serjeant Musgrave's Dance* might well start where John Arden started: "In the ballads the colors are primary. Black is for death, and for the coalmines. Red is for murder, and for the soldier's coat the collier puts on to escape from his black. Blue is for the sky and for the sea that parts true love." And the white snow isolates the town and the figures seen against it. Against this background he envisaged the action in the sudden shifts from stillness to furious action he had seen in Japanese films and in westerns. Visually, the play can offer strikingly clear images, as in the memorable spareness of the original Royal Court production of 1959.

The play's import is a lot less clear. This is primarily because Arden uses a gambit rare in the theatre: he asks the audience to shift its sympathies during the performance. He has said, "I resent plays in which the audience is brought in by the author to take one side of the argument." He also dislikes the audience's habit of deciding what an author's social standpoint is and then expecting to follow that assumption to the play's conclusion. In his 1957 play, *The Waters of Babylon*, the holocaust victim Krank turns out to be the internment camp guard Krankiewicz. In *Live Like Pigs* we first sympathize with the Gypsies who are being forced to settle on a council estate, then see how destructive they are to their neighbours' lives, so that the title we had assumed was ironic turns out to be literally true. To *Serjeant Musgrave's Dance* we bring the habit of identifying with the central character, and that identification is reinforced as we learn that he and the three soldiers he leads are not recruiting, as they have proclaimed, but are deserters on a mission to protest against war. It may be as late in the play as the climactic scene in which Musgrave runs up the skeleton of a dead soldier instead of a flag in the town square and orders his men to shoot down the townspeople that the audience realizes that he is "wild-wood mad." The scholar, interpreting the play, can find viewpoints stated or implied that seem to offer alternative philosophies to Serjeant Musgrave's dance, a circular dance of death, an unending cycle of violence. But an audience cannot turn back to reinterpret the play.

Warning Annie, the barmaid, to stay away from his men, Musgrave says:

> Our work isn't easy, no, and it's not soft: it's got a strong name—duty. And it's drawn out straight and black for us, a clear plan. But if you come to us with what you call your life or love,—*I'd* call it your indulgence—and you scribble all over that plan, you make it crooked, dirty, idle, untidy, *bad*—there's anarchy.

Here Arden masks his own inclination—in 1966 he described himself as having been attracted to anarchist ideas for some time—in Musgrave's disapproval. Similarly, in *Left-Handed Liberty* it is into the mouth of the "bad" King John that he puts the wish to keep the clauses of the Magna Carta loose "because by this very laxness they go some way to admit the existence of dandelions, of disobedient women and ribbons of cloth-of-gold." The poles of the world of *Serjeant Musgrave's Dance* are those in Krank's key speech in *The Waters of Babylon*:

> all the rest of you,
> With your pistols and your orations,
> And your bombs in my private house,
> And your fury, and your national pride and honour.
> This is the lunacy.
> This was the cause, the carrying through
> Of all the insensate war
> This is the rage and purposed madness of your lives,
> That *I*, Krank, do not know. I *will* not know it,
> Because, if I know it, from that tight day forward,
> I am a man of time, place, society and accident:
> Which is what I must not be.

In *Serjeant Musgrave's Dance* Annie ignores Musgrave's order and goes to the men where they sleep in the stables. The youngest soldier, Sparky, tells her "we don't need his duty, we don't need his Word. . . . Your life and my life—make our *own* road, we don't follow nobody." Sparky is killed in a muddled fight over his trousers and his attempted desertion. This, Attercliffe tells Musgrave, "wipes the whole thing out," contradicts Musgrave's mission. In the climactic scene in the square Annie reveals the killing and Attercliffe repeats his phrase. It is Attercliffe who throws himself in front of the Gatling gun that Musgrave orders fired at the townspeople, and who is given the last speech of the play, singing of how "the apple holds a seed will grow / To live and lengthy joy," and asking if, after all, his and Musgrave's hanging will "start an orchard."

Duty is to Arden as repressive a concept as it was to Ibsen, a violence internalized and directed against the free expression of the self. Throughout the play Musgrave is shadowed by the Bargee; he echoes Musgrave's words in one scene, mimicks his gestures in another, even puts the coal-miners through a military drill. "Bargee" chimes alliteratively with Musgrave's nickname Black Jack, and a blackjack is in American usage a bludgeon, the Bargee's name. The hunch-backed Bargee can be seen as Musgrave's doppelgänger, perhaps a visualization of the deforming costs of following duty. He seeks to subvert Musgrave's purposes, and sticks a gun in Musgrave's back in the scene in the square. Together, they illustrate that violence is no answer for violence.

Duty, of course, reflects social imperatives. By making Musgrave a religious man Arden unifies in one image the codification of values in the Law, whether of the Book or of the legal volume, and the means of its enforcement. Musgrave would like to approach the end of the world "in control" with "numbers and order . . . steadiness on parade." The world, however, is a messier place. A military "police action" in Cyprus that resulted in civilian deaths was Arden's starting-point, and within the play such an incident leads Musgrave and his men to desert. Sparky's death is a dramatization of the casual but inherent violence of a society whose structure depends upon enforcement. The class warfare of the colliers against the Mayor and Parson cannot be contained within Musgrave's monolithic vision, but at the end of the play Mrs. Hitchcock, Annie's employer, suggests that the hope for the future is that the colliers will remember Musgrave's message—not the message he preached but the anarchy he demonstrated.

—Anthony Graham-White

THE SHAUGHRAUN.
Play by Dion Boucicault, 1874.

Shortly after his death in 1890, there appeared a posthumous essay by Dion Boucicault in which the protean author-actor-manager recognized that a new drama was emerging. The old, broad, jovial, crowd-pleasing melodrama which he, Douglas Jerrold, and Tom Taylor had produced so prolifically had now seen its day. The future belonged to Ibsen and Zola and their "philosophical school of sociology, for the illustration and argument of ethical problems." It is true that the new drama of his own country, Ireland, initially took a more poetic bent; but when W.B. Yeats, John Synge, and Lady Gregory formed the Abbey Theatre early in the new century, its repertoire was also seen as the antithesis of the patriotic, rollicking, Irish heroics of Boucicault.

Yet time has vindicated the theatre of Boucicault and, curiously, vindicated it more impressively than it has the seldom performed plays of Yeats. In the late 1960's, Yeats's Abbey Theatre revived Boucicault's three major Irish plays, *The Colleen Bawn*, *Arrah-na-Pogue* and *The Shaughraun*; and new audiences found in these old staples of the 19th century charm, wit, theatrical excitement, and fresh delight. Subsequently, some of Boucicault's earlier straight comedies, such as *London Assurance* and *Old Heads and Young Hearts*, have played successfully in London and New York. And in its 1989 season, London's National Theatre found that probably the most attractive draw in the repertoire was its spectacular revival of *The Shaughraun*.

Boucicault said, with some justice, that the economics of the stage in the 1840's turned him from writing classic comedies to churning out facile adaptations from the French or to purveying original potboilers without much originality. "Eh voila! I can spin out these rough-and-tumble dramas as a hen lays eggs. It's a degrading occupation, but more money has been made out of guano than out of poetry." Boucicault is uncharacteristically as well as much too self-deprecatory here. Even though he spent most of his career writing simple commercial entertainments, he treated that profession seriously, and he brought to it an exacting craftsmanship thoroughly tested in the mechanics of what would work on the stage.

The Shaughraun, whose title might be translated from the Irish as "The Wanderer," is probably the most attractive of his Irish plays and shows him in complete command of his craft. First produced on 14 November 1874, at Wallack's Theatre in New York, the play was an immediate success, was constantly revived, and helped form the basis of several fortunes that Boucicault made and lost. Nominally, the play takes a patriotic theme from the Fenian movement and Ireland's desire to break its political ties with England. However, there is a good and noble Englishman as well as a patriotic young Irishman from the Big House, a clever Irish scamp from the bogs, and two dastardly Irish villains from the lumber room of melodrama. In other words, this is not a play about the Irish question, but about the old staples of good and evil and the vicissitudes of true love. In theme, it is no closer to actuality than if it had been produced by a 19th-century Walt Disney.

Its adroit plot is the quintessence of melodrama with lots of ruses, escapes, and cliffhanging moments. These are so neatly structured that their wild implausibility is totally submerged in performance by their compelling theatricality. Further, the plot builds to a succession of brilliant situations such as the wake scene with the keeners wailing over the body of the presumably dead but quite bemused Shaughraun. Undoubtedly this is among the most effective comic scenes ever penned by an Irish dramatist, and some later dramatists, among them J.M. Synge and M.J. Molloy, have paid Boucicault the compliment of borrowing it. But, even in the melodramatic scenes, Boucicault rose to moments of convincing reality. In the last act, for instance, when the enraged peasants turn on the informer, his anguish, as he debates whether to face them or to leap off the cliff, is intensely impressive.

Another Boucicault trait especially notable in *The Shaughraun* is a pervasively playful humour. The dialogue in particular, although hardly rising to wit, is often an eminently playable and genial banter. For instance:

> MOLINEUX: My good girl.
> CLAIRE: So to you (*Aside.*) He takes me for the dairymaid.
> MOLINEUX: Is this place called Swillabeg?
> CLAIRE: No; it is called Shoolabeg.
> MOLINEUX: Beg pardon; your Irish names are so unpronounceable. You see, I'm an Englishman.
> CLAIRE: I remarked your misfortune. Poor creature, you couldn't help it.
> MOLINEUX: I do not regard it as a misfortune.
> CLAIRE: Got accustomed to it, I suppose. Were you born so?

In *The Shaughraun*, Boucicault mingles romance, intrigue, melodrama, humour, and song in eminently craftsmanlike fashion. His accomplishment was not lost on Sean O'Casey who cited Shakespeare and Boucicault as his chief dramatic influences. And, indeed, Boucicault sometimes handles the elements of his craft so well that he brings entertainment about as close as it can come to art.

—Robert Hogan

SHE STOOPS TO CONQUER.
Play by Oliver Goldsmith, 1773.

In essays and in his own practice, Oliver Goldsmith campaigned against the sentimental comedy of his time. In "An Essay on the Theatre" and elsewhere, Goldsmith states his case against sentimental and genteel comedy and in favor of laughing and low comedy; an example of the latter is *She Stoops to Conquer*, which Goldsmith set in opposition to such sentimental comedies as Hugh Kelly's *False Delicacy* and Richard Cumberland's *The West Indian*.

In "An Essay on the Theatre" Goldsmith asks whether exhibiting human distress or human absurdity affords greater entertainment. He argues that the proper subject matter of comedy is "low and middle life" and that universal past practice suggests that "an exhibition of its follies" is preferable to "a detail of its calamities." Nonetheless, recent sentimental comedy depicts the virtues rather than the vices of private life and seeks to evoke tears for mankind's distresses rather than ridiculing its frailties. As amusing as sentimental comedy may be, Goldsmith says, "true comedy" is more amusing. Elsewhere he takes issue with the tendency in genteel comedy to portray only "polite" society and to avoid "low" characters and subjects. He distinguishes between wit and humor; witty characters are admired and emulated, but comedy may properly deal with "humorous" characters whose foibles are to be exposed. This is more easily done with "low" characters because good breeding conceals our absurdities. Hence "high humor" is a contradiction in terms for Goldsmith.

She Stoops to Conquer puts into practice all of the principles outlined above. Goldsmith's play shares sentimental comedy's assumption that man is basically good, but it does not excuse or avoid ridiculing absurd behavior simply because characters are benevolent. Goldsmith's most obvious departures from sentimental comedy lie in his emphasis on laughter rather than tears, his use of farcical situations and "humorous" speech rather than "polite" action and genteel dialogue, and in his avoidance of heavy moralizing.

She Stoops, then, is an attempt to produce an unconventional kind of comedy whose chief purpose is to produce laughter throughout. Such "laughing" comedy is much more difficult to sustain in a full-length play than in a one- or two-act farce. In order to do so, Goldsmith relies chiefly on two sources—situation and character foibles. Perhaps the closest predecessors of *She Stoops* are farce and Farquhar's *The Beaux' Stratagem* insofar as the comedy of *She Stoops* derives largely from situation alone, as in farce, and from situation in conjunction with character, as in *The Beaux' Stratagem*. Characters in Goldsmith's play make humorous mistakes, but not because they should behave differently given their understanding of circumstances. Most of the play's comic effects depend on the initial error of Young Marlow and Hastings mistaking Hardcastle's house for an inn. The inherent improbability of the situation is not bothersome, partly because Goldsmith prepares us for it by such means as having Mrs. Hardcastle refer to the house as an inn and having Kate wear plain clothes in the evening to gratify Hardcastle's whim, and once we accept the initial mistake, we become more willing to accept what follows.

After the situation and the problem of Young Marlow's bashfulness with respectable women are established in Act I, the remainder of the play develops comic effects based on the initial situation. Although the situation remains constant, the various characters' understandings of it do not, and the comedy almost always derives from intentional deception (Tony Lumpkin instigates the deception of Hastings and Young Marlow; Kate adds to the deception; Hastings learns the truth, but further deceives Marlow; Tony further deceives Mrs. Hardcastle; and so on). Aware of the actual state of affairs, the audience is free to laugh at the multiple errors. The effect is similar to dramatic irony, except that Goldsmith pushes it a step farther to a double irony based on multiple levels of understanding (for example, in the deception of Marlow and in the "theft" of Constance Neville's jewels).

Laughter also derives from Goldsmith's ridicule of frailties or foibles. Ridicule in *She Stoops* does not have a moral purpose, nor does it seek reform; in each instance, it is intended simply to evoke good-natured laughter. For example, the country booby, Tony Lumpkin, is coarse and uneducated, but resourceful; he is humorous as a type, and we laugh *with* him as well as *at* him. Similarly, Hardcastle and Mrs. Hardcastle are "humors" characters who are made to look ridiculous, but our laughter is good-natured, partly because both are aware of their foibles. Hardcastle loves everything old, and has told the same jokes for 20 years. Mrs. Hardcastle dotes on Tony even though she is aware of his actual character, and also dotes on London although she has never been there. Both can be made to appear foolish, but there is no moral condemnation of their behavior.

Young Marlow's case is more complicated. His is a social flaw that prevents him from functioning satisfactorily in respectable society. At the end, he is reformed, but he recognizes his fault from the beginning. He is made ridiculous in several ways. One is his pseudo-sentimental conversation with Kate. He is in an embarrassing situation, but his feelings are not in danger of being hurt; hence his distress is comic rather than serious. Another is in his aggressive role with the "disguised" Kate, painting himself as the "adorable rattle of the Ladies Club," which is of course comic in light of his earlier behavior and because Kate already knows his character. He does not fall into the class of comic characters who reform after recognizing their own ridiculousness; instead, he is "reformed" by Kate's deception. That is, the audience is convinced that if he can be intimate with one modest woman, he will thereafter be self-confident, but the change has nothing to do with enhanced self-knowledge.

The least quirky character in the play is also its controlling force as she changes gradually from barmaid to refined young lady. Kate is independent, knows what she wants and how to get it, and possesses considerable self-knowledge. She serves as a stable center, assuring that the harmless foibles of others remain harmless and that the laughter therefore remains good-natured.

—James S. Malek

THE SHEPHEARDES CALENDER.
Poems by Edmund Spenser, 1579.

In 1579, the young Edmund Spenser, mindful of classical precept and practice that the poet who aspires to epic must first serve his apprenticeship in the humbler domains of pastoral, introduced himself to the world of letters with a set of 12 eclogues entitled *The Shepheardes Calender*, the story of Colin Clout, a poet-shepherd torn between unrequited love for Rosalind and the claims of his pastoral duty. It was a tour de force of lyrical virtuosity. Spenser was clearly set to display his command of the most astonishing range of poetic forms and sub-genres: love laments, roundelays, satirical dialogues, the encomium, the funeral elegy, the Theocritean idyll, the animal fable . . . the list could be extended to cover almost all the lyrical kinds available at the time. Equally extensive is the variety of metres and verse forms employed: lyrical iambics in sestets for the love plaints, harsh four-stress couplets for the satires, octosyllables for the "lighter" eclogues, and so on. Spenser also exhibits a new sensitivity to linguistic effects: coinages, dialect words, and archaisms are introduced to enhance stylistic decorum: in the high-flown encomium to Queen Elizabeth in "April," for example, the speaker's remembrance of his own mere shepherd status is signalised by the sudden descent to the rural terms "forswonck and forswatt." Rhetorical devices too are used to elevate and adorn the style of the more lyrical eclogues and to provide decorum of characterisation: for example, the cluster of figures (parison, progressio, traductio, antimetabole) in "Januarye" serves to foreground the poetic pretentions of Colin: "Thou weake, I wanne: thou leane, I quite forlorne: / with mourning pyne I, you with pyning mourne." Further to enhance the work's impact, it appeared with accompanying woodcuts, emblematic conclusions, a lengthy and fascinating preface on the adequacy of the vernacular for poetry, and copious footnotes and glosses to each month, ostensibly by one E.K. (whose identity has never been established).

Superficially the text is given coherence by the seasonal structure and by the modal division of the eclogues (see the "general argument") into "plaintive," "recreative," and "moral"; but the *Calender* achieves poetic unity at a much deeper level by the prevalent theme of frustrated dialogism between Colin and his shepherd peers. Three groups of characters populate the world of the *Calender*. First, forming a kind of choric backdrop, are the old, stoic shepherds of "Februarie," "Maye," and "September" who uphold the claims of duty and the necessity for toil, labour, and endurance in the face of inevitable misery and adversity:

> Must not the world wend in his commun course
> From good to badd, and from badde to worse . . .
>
> And ever my flocke was my chiefe care . . .

Paramount is the imperative always to tend one's flock and refuse the seductive allures of merrymaking or the snares of love. In "Maye," for example, Piers reverses the concept of seasonal decorum proposed by Palinode ("Is not thilke the mery moneth of May?") by warning him that those who go off to the greenwood merrymaking are "shepheards for the Devils stedde, / That playen, while their flockes be unfedde." Since they "tway bene men of elder witt," they should know better than to be envious of the hedonistic youngsters; and to reinforce the moral Piers tells the animal fable of the gullible young kid and the crafty fox. An equally strong ethical note is sounded in "Februarie" as Thenot illustrates his maxim that "Youth is a bubble blown up with breath" by recounting the tale of the old but sturdy oak and the overweening, courtly young briar, whose "Lilly white, and Cremsin redde" cannot long survive deprived of the shelter of his elder and better companion. Diggon Davie, in "September," gives the debate a religious turn: he has been attracted to Rome (literally and metaphorically) and as a result lost all his flock. The moral is again unambiguous:

> For thy with shepheard sittes not playe,
> Or sleepe, as some doen, all the long day:
> But ever liggen in watch and ward,
> From soddein force theyr flocks for to gard.

All these shepherds belong to a very fallen Barclayan world of rough weather, painful toil, and unflinching adherence to duty—a far cry from the erotic, idyllic shepherd of Arcadian pastoral with its crystalline streams, golden-age fecundity, and freedom from the bounds of work and time. Their main thematic function is to foreground the extent to which Colin Clout is alienated from such Puritan mores: to them he is simply in dereliction of duty and no constructive dialogue is possible.

Next come a group of younger shepherds who sympathise with Colin's plight, but, reluctantly adherent to the mores of their elders, are incapable of rendering assistance. Hobbinol can be taken as spokesman for these when he remarks in "June":

> O carefull Colin, I lament thy case,
> Thy teares would make the hardest flint to flowe.
> Ah faithless Rosalind, and voide of grace,
> That art the roote of all this ruthfull woe.

Finally, in the foreground, is the alienated figure of Colin Clout. We first meet him in "Januarye," where, with appropriate seasonal decorum, he compares his tears (over faithless Rosalind) to the icicles that hang on the trees, and admits that unrequited love has made him neglectful of duty. He concludes by breaking his pipe, symbol of pastoral poetry. So Colin is faced with the impossibility of being good shepherd, committed poet, and idealistic lover all at the same time. Colin actually appears in propria persona only in the eclogues of January, June, August, and December; but his plight is kept constantly before the reader by the running commentary provided by his fellow-shepherds in the other eclogues. It appears that 'ere he was "with love so ill bedight" ("October") he had been a laudable shepherd, capable of producing splendid public poetry—witness the superlative hymn of praise to Eliza ("Aprill") and the profoundly moving elegy to Dido ("November"). Now, however, his sheep have become wasted and his poetry self-referential (as in the misanthropic lament in "August"). Is Spenser then presenting love as totally destructive? It would appear so: in "December" Colin reviews his life and his progress from carefree spring to a sad maturity of erotic distress and ethical failure; and, as the year dies, so does Colin.

But nature of course will renew: spring will return. This focuses upon another main theme of the *Calender*—the threefold nature of time. "December" cleverly juxtaposes the linear movement of man from youth to death against the cyclic temporality of the seasons (actualised in the external form of the *Calender* itself) and stresses by implication the theme of the old shepherds, the need to make good use of your life on earth, since it will not regenerate in the new year. Are there, however, no ways of transcending both these natural time-scales? Two hints are given within the *Calender* itself: in "October," Piers makes the Platonic suggestion that love can lift one "up out of the loathesome myre" and "rayse ones mynd above the starry skie"; but this is promptly deflated by Cuddie (who prefers the ephemeral escape of alcohol); and indeed the fate of Colin is sufficient to disprove this whole theory. In "November" Dido *does* achieve eternal life in Heaven, but mortal death can hardly be seen as a solution. It is not until the emblematic epilogue that Spenser gives gives us the answer:

Loe I have made a Calender for every yeare,
That steele in strength, and time in durance shall
outweare . . .

Poetry alone has the ability to transcend the forces of time. Through the art of Spenser, Colin has not lived in vain: he still survives to remind us of the power and the pain of love, of its incompatibility with the grim dictates of duty, and of the plight of poetry caught between the seductions of lyrical self-indulgence and the imperatives of public utterance.

One further thematic layer of the *Calender* must be mentioned. The emphasis has been throughout on the role of the good shepherd, and the archetype of the good shepherd is of course Christ. So it is appropriate that in "Julye" we revert to another Barclayan topic, satirical attack on the Roman Curia, or, in Thomalin's uncompromising terms, on wolves who devour their flock rather than feeding and protecting them. This elaboration of the theological pastoral metaphor has already been adumbrated in the attack on false clergy in "Maye." But the important thing is that these debates on the function of the priesthood are homologously integrated into the Colin story: both articulate the conflict between pastoral duty and self-seeking indulgence.

The Shepheardes Calender, then, is much more than just the virtuoso display of a young poet out to impress the public of his day: it is a profound meditation on the apparently irreconcilable claims of love, duty, and poetry—or erotics, ethics, and aesthetics, themes of profound concern for the writer of the epoch and which appear in various accommodated or displaced modes in almost all the works of the late Elizabethan-early Jacobean period. With its field of reference extended by the religious dimension and its transcendental implications foregrounded by the debate on the power of art over nature, the *Calender* ultimately emerges as a self-sustaining defence of poetry—but a problematic one in which the insistent ground-bass of Puritan doubt is never inaudible. Oh, and the identity of E.K.? My own feeling is that Spenser (as T.S. Eliot was to do many years later) wrote the notes himself as a parody of the pedantic style of his Cambridge tutor, Gabriel Harvey, but that's pure speculation!

—A.W. Lyle

THE SHIELD OF ACHILLES.
Poem by W.H. Auden, 1955.

"The Shield of Achilles" is an extraordinarily evocative poem, beautiful in its design and subtle in its implications. With deceptive simplicity, the work encapsulates many of W. H. Auden's religious and political ideas of the 1940's and early 1950's, presenting them in masterfully controlled, vivid yet understated and nondidactic images. Most impressive is the poem's consummate artistry, which yields a texture intricately woven yet apparently seamless, while at the same time it betrays seemingly contradictory themes that are finally reconciled in the harmonious coexistence of a despairing surface plot and a qualifying counterplot constructed by means of a network of subtle echoes and analogies. Obliquely reflecting its author's Christian existentialism, "The Shield of Achilles" is an inverted expression of Auden's vision of the Just City achieved by and embodying Agape.

Based on the incident in Book XVIII of the *Iliad*, in which Thetis commissions Hephaestos to fashion a new shield for her son Achilles, the poem is structured according to a series of apparent contrasts between the ancient and the modern worlds. These contrasts are reflected in the two distinct stanzaic forms. The parts of the poem that recount classical material employ an eight-line stanza of three stresses per line in which the second and fourth lines and the sixth and eighth lines rhyme. The stanzas that present the chilling visions of contemporary life adapt the "rime royale" form of seven lines rhyming *ababbcc*. The ancient / modern contrasts of the poem mirror the dichotomies between Thetis's naive expectations of what Hephaestos will depict on the shield (as expressed in the eight-line stanzas) and the harsh realities that he actually crafts (as described in the seven-line stanzas).

At first glance, the distinctions between the ancient and modern worlds appear to be the differences between Arcadian peacefulness and urban violence. But the contrasts are more apparent than real, for they dissolve into continuity as the modern realities are revealed as natural consequences of the values embodied by Thetis's "Iron-hearted man-slaying" son and implicit as well in her own request for armor. The poem exposes the disparity between the idyllic appearance of the Homeric world and the ugly realities that the appearance conceals, and it suggests a continuity of those realities into the contemporary world, where

A ragged urchin, aimless and alone,
Loitered about that vacancy: a bird
Flew up to safety from his well-aimed stone:
That girls are raped, that two boys knife a third,
Were axioms to him, who'd never heard
Of any world where promises were kept,
Or one could weep because another wept.

The poem's real subject is not Thetis's reactions to the shield crafted by Hephaestos, but the plight of the individual in the contemporary world reflected on the shield, which is characterized by regimentation, totalitarianism, and violence. By means of a visionary narrative technique that spans enormous gulfs of space and time, by its references to ancient religious ceremonies and its texture of religiously significant terms (congregated, multitude, sign, belief, pieties, sacrifice, etc.), and by the dominating image of the Crucifixion, "The Shield of Achilles" places the contemporary malaise within a historical perspective that encompasses Christianity as well as Homeric Greece.

"The Shield of Achilles" presents contemporary society as an unjust earthly city built on self-love in which order is maintained by coercion and intimidation. It vividly illustrates the force of hate in its ugly pictures of barbed wire and desolate landscapes, of arbitrary persecutions and the alienation of man and nature. What is not obvious, however, is that the poem's portrayal of the force of hate is counterpointed by an implied text—constructed by allusions to the final two books of Paradise Lost and to several biblical passages—that illustrates the power of love.

The most important biblical element of Auden's counterplot is the story of Christ's Crucifixion, which stanzas five and six parody. Even as the poem convicts the contemporary world of rejecting Christ's sacrifice, it also posits the Crucifixion as the historical event against which all human suffering must be viewed and as the supreme symbol of Agape. In the surface plot, the force of the allusion to the Crucifixion is to emphasize the materialism and hopelessness of contemporary society: the modern victims "died as men before their bodies died." In the counterplot, however, the allusion asserts the possibility of love, of meaningful sacrifice, and of redeeming the time. The Crucifixion thus functions in the poem both as a criticism of man's self-love and as a symbol of hope in the midst of despair.

While "The Shield of Achilles" is not an optimistic poem, it nevertheless contains within itself a world of affirmation. Even as it depicts the unjust earthly city, it also testifies to the continuing presence of God's offer of Grace that can create the heavenly city. The suffering Christ, the feast of Agape, the paradise within, the dove of the Holy Spirit: these constitute presences in the poem that are as palpable as the column of soldiers, the barbed wire, the weed-choked field, and the urchin who throws a stone in rejection of God's love. Despite the hostility of the earthly city, the dove of the Holy Spirit "Flew up to safety" and, thus, continues to witness to the covenant of love: it pledges a world where promises are kept and one can weep because another weeps.

—Claude J. Summers

SHIRLEY.
Novel by Charlotte Brontë, 1849.

Until recently, *Shirley* was generally considered an artistic failure, and a shortfall in radical feminism. G.H. Lewes, in the *Edinburgh Review*, called it "a portfolio of sketches." Feminists have been disturbed by the independent heroine's wish to be "mastered" by "a man whose approbation can reward—whose displeasure punish me. A man I shall feel it impossible not to love, and very possible to fear."

Charlotte Brontë disclaimed any power to write about the issues of the day and for this reason, although the novel deals with industrial strife, the setting is not the Chartist unrest of 1848, but put back to the time of the Luddites, at the beginning of the century. Brontë was all her life strongly Tory; she wrote to her old schoolmistress, Miss Wooler, "Mr. Wooler thinks me a much hotter advocate for *change* and what is called political progress than I am . . ." (13 April 1853). Yet she had become interested in politics as a child, in a household which regularly took two newspapers of opposing views, and the novel contrasts the high Tory clergyman, Mr. Helstone, with the Radical dissenting Yorke family, who are in business. Although the author modestly disclaimed any ability to draw male characters, these two men are vital and memorable portraits.

Shirley opens with savage satire on the idle, self-satisfied and self-seeking Church of England clergy. Brontë's publisher, George Smith, begged her to omit this chapter, but it was essential to her purpose. The novel has no real leading male character: the object of Caroline's love, Robert Moore, is less than idealised. A flawed hero, he is compared to Shakespeare's Coriolanus, whose own patrician arrogance led to his downfall, despite his heroic courage and martial virtues. The novel takes an ironic look at marriage and spinsterhood, neither of which offer happiness. Mrs. Yorke is married and the mother of a family, but she is far from happy or fulfilled: her children do not love her. Mr. Helstone's wife has died of neglect. One of the novel's chief triumphs is the characterisation of Robert's sister, Hortense Moore. In it Brontë's astringent wit shows how a woman of sufficient, but limited, intelligence can become a petty tyrant, a victim of her own rigidity. Hortense's chief interests in life are censoriously abusing the British, among whom she lives, and endlessly rearranging, or as Brontë so expressively puts it, "rummaging" her drawers. Her energy is displaced, like that of so many women, into a futile obsession with order, endless tidying up to no real purpose. Hortense acts towards her cousin and pupil Caroline like a repressive mother, though Hortense's quirks have a lot to do with not being married. *Shirley* is a clear-sighted analysis of the place of women in commercial society which offers them no niche.

The writing was less than enjoyable for its author: she lived in an isolated moorland parish, without a single educated family, and her beloved sisters were dead, leaving her the last of six children. In the circumstances, it is unsurprising that a main theme should be loneliness. Although *Shirley* is sometimes considered a "condition of England novel," like those of Disraeli, Dickens, and Gaskell, Brontë's real subject in *Shirley* is hunger: the hunger of working men for bread, the hunger of women for love and satisfying work, a place in the world. It is only superficially about industrial relations: the extended metaphors of bread and stone, egg and scorpion, are about how to cope when starving, physically and emotionally. Caroline Helstone tells her uncle, the Tory clergyman, that she wants to work. He will not hear of it.

Caroline tests the Victorian advice that an unsatisfied woman should do good works, but "these efforts brought her neither health of body nor continued peace of mind . . . her memory kept harping on the name of Robert Moore . . . the mind's soil and its treasures were freezing gradually to barren stagnation."

Shirley is also an elegy: critics have conjectured that Caroline is a retrospective portrait of the author's sister Anne. Caroline, gentle and unhappy, is motherless, until her friend Shirley's governess turns out to be Caroline's mother, who had changed her name after leaving a brutal husband. The rebellious and lively Rose Yorke is a portrait of the author's schoolfriend Mary Taylor, who acknowledged the accuracy of the family portrait, and little Jessie memorialises Mary's sister Martha Taylor, who died suddenly in Belgium. The character of Shirley herself, an independent heiress, strong-willed but benevolent, with a penchant for beautiful silk dresses, is a portrait of Emily Brontë as she mighthave been had she been born to money and not the daughter of a poor parson. Posterity, including Elizabeth Gaskell, the author's biographer, has failed to see any resemblance between the harsh, reserved, eccentric and reclusive Emily and the spirited Shirley, except in the habit of whistling, the possession of a fierce dog, and the fact that Emily, like Shirley, when bitten by a dog she feared to be rabid, cauterised the wound with a household iron.

Shirley, unlike the powerful males in the story, is not so greedy that she ignores suffering. She is determined to defend her property against the mob, but believes it to be her moral responsibility to help the unemployed poor. It is only with a trusted female friend that Shirley can express her feminism. And Shirley ends up like other women, subordinate to her husband. Yet what sets Caroline on the road to recovery is not sexual love, but the recovery of her mother.

Together with her sister Emily, Brontë invented the Yorkshire novel. *Shirley* may be read as a defence of poetry and the romantic imagination, threatened by people like the industrialist Hiram Yorke, who despite his intelligence has no time for them, by a clergy who are spiritually moribund, and by a money-mad society which excludes educated women from the means to acquire money except by the marriages which are impossible unless they have money already.

—Valerie Grosvenor Myer

THE SHOEMAKER'S HOLIDAY.
Play by Thomas Dekker, 1599.

Thomas Dekker's *The Shoemaker's Holiday* is a festival of equivocation. The play rests securely in ambiguity by pledging itself to ritual, first celebrating the disruption of order and process common to the saturnalia and then reconfirming tradition with the announcement of nuptials. Emphasis falls not on character or situation, but on occasion. To admit this is not simply to reconcile ourselves to the contagious vitality indicated in the title, but to respond as well in terms which fully acknowledge the radical oppositions in Dekker's own society: the play evokes the old order of medieval guilds while simultaneously paying homage to the competitive explorer and merchant, admires aristocracy while affirming a new kind of class mobility. The play refuses to take the single point of view either of courtly conduct or of the routine workaday world of shoemaking, despite the strong allegiance to guilds held by Thomas Deloney, a craftsman on whose novel *The Gentle Craft* this play is based. Rather, Dekker's work gathers up antithesis and accommodates contrast: Simon Eyre's repeated exercise in equivocation, "Prince am I none, yet I am princely born," is properly choric.

Acknowledgement of equivocation and ambiguity is demanded throughout the play, which, observed literally, everywhere refuses to square with itself. Dekker praises order and gives us chaos. Sir Roger Otley says of his daughter that she is too low-born to be matched to the Earl of Lincoln's nephew Lacy, yet our sympathies are enlisted for that improbable match and the play aligns our position with that of the lovers. Simon Eyre openly ranks his men—Hodge the foreman, Firke the journeyman, Hans the apprentice—yet we know from the outset that Hans is disguised nobility and that Simon's ordering really inverts that fact. Such occurrences are not misleading. Life, this play repeatedly tells us, is often a yoking together of opposites. What else can we make, after all, of an honest shoemaker when he dons the robes of an alderman and so seizes on treasure through deceit and hypocrisy? How are we to judge a simple girl like Jane who talks in poetry at times indistinguishable from that of her betters, Rose and Lacy? What are we to think of a young gentleman turned draft dodger, of a Lord Mayor who slaps the King on the back as if he were an old college chum?

Dekker's play mirrors such fantastic configurations by choosing to praise both hierarchy and mutability simultaneously, by placing traditional order and obedience alongside social and economic change. A direct confrontation with this play cannot put these juxtapositions aside. Nor need we, for with Dekker such disparate elements are brought to cohere in the singularity of vision afforded by Elizabethan holiday, itself double-edged, advancing folly in order to exorcise it, permitting a Lord of Misrule the better to avow tradition.

To be reminded of the Lord of Misrule and the Christmas festival over which he reigned helps us to understand the role of Simon Eyre. He transforms himself from Lord Mayor to the traditional Lord of Misrule most clearly when he acts as host and ruler with the King himself at the opening of V.5. This makes especially fitting the performance for Elizabeth I on 1 January 1600 (New Style); and explains in part why "the mirth and pleasant matter" of this topsy-turvy world was "by her Highnesse graciously accepted; being indeede no way offensiue," as the title page announces.

In keeping with these revels at court, *The Shoemaker's Holiday* is characterized by an infectious spirit, even a spirit of excess; and it shares with such holidays multiple spectacles, divergent and parallel lines of dramatic plot, the reversal of roles (in the instances of Lacy and Rose, Simon and the King), the songs and morris dance that Simon calls for, and the magnificent banquet toward which the play constantly leads us, and in which it captures most clearly its central and motivating spirit. Prefatory to this, Dekker signals the spirit of holiday in constant allusion: we find references to May Day ("O the month of Maie, the merrie month of Maie, / So frolicke, so gay, and so greene, so greene, so greene") and to midsummer ("Sweete Peg, thou shalt be my Summers Queene") in the first Three-mans Song; to the festival of spring in Simon's request for a morris dance with music ("Some odde crotchets") and a masque ("some deuice") to autumn when Sybil will be "Lady of the Haruest" adorned with fruits and flowers; and to Shrove Tuesday, the day of feasting on pancakes which Simon not unexpectedly chooses as most appropriate for offering his own fine dinner to the craftsmen and apprentices of London. Complementing these allusions to the fact of holiday is a continuum of holiday mood: in Margery's mockery of the aristocracy, in Rose's and Hammon's role-playing in their wooing scene, and in Jane's deliberate ambiguity to Hammon over her future intentions, "If euer I wed man it shall be you." Like Shakespeare's *Twelfth Night*, Dekker's Christmas play insists on acting out life rather than representing it. The play thus becomes indistinguishable from the occasion it advertises and so through its performance accommodates the kaleidoscopic nature of life, culminating finally in the still centre where passion and reason are themselves advanced, but made one and inseparable.

—Arthur F. Kinney

A SHROPSHIRE LAD.
Poems by A.E. Housman, 1896.

This slim volume of 63 short lyrics in the pastoral tradition and predominantly the ballad form, written for the most part during a brief period in 1895, constitutes the main base of A.E. Housman's reputation as a poet. A brilliant classical scholar, he nonetheless denied conscious influence of the classics on his poems, saying that he was aware only of Shakespeare's songs, border ballads, and the poems of Heine as models for his verse. Despite the denials, many of the poems exhibit the classical quality of compression, and not a few reflect Horatian echoes.

The speaker throughout most of the poems is a Shropshire lad. The title was to have been originally *Poems by Terence Hearsay*, and the name Terence appears from time to time. One is addressed to Terence, (stanza VIII); and four others (XXXIV, XLVII, LIII, and LVI) are by other speakers as indicated by the quotation marks. As B.J. Leggett points out in *Housman's Land of Lost Content*, the structure of the work consists of three framing poems (I, LXII, and LXIII), poems set in Shropshire (II–XXXVII), and poems of exile in London (XXXVIII–LXI).

Despite the preponderant play on the theme of death throughout the work—"And the Nile spills his overflow / Beside the Severn's dead" (I, 19–20)—the emphasis in the Shropshire section seems more on the awakening to an awareness of mutability, change, and the transience of life, which alters in the London section to a manful acceptance of life's ills through stoical endurance—"Let us endure an hour and see injustice done" (XLVIII, 12), "Manful like the man of stone" (LI, 26). As a result, many critics have insisted that the key to the poems is philosophical or biographical. Housman abhorred philosophy and called himself, partially in jest, a Cyrenaic pejorist, indicating that he believed conditions on earth were gradually worsening, but that it was not without its possibilities for pleasure, for him mainly intellectual. Also, he explained that the work was not biographical, particularly as he was born in Worcestershire, not Shropshire, and that the geographical details were sometimes wrong. As for his homosexuality, it is as notably absent from his works as is that of Samuel Butler, though stanzas XIII and XIV warn against giving "heart and soul away."

Through the various persona—soldiers, lovers, friends, athletes, murderers, suicides—Housman conveys a wide range of experiences and emotions. Bravery, heroism, seduction, devotion, glory, love, betrayal, and resignation are all there; several poems also dwell on the beauties of nature; some on the work ethic, the necessity to accomplish something while there is yet time; others yearn for places, friends, and times past, all irrevocably lost; and a few recommend a lighter approach like "jesting, dancing, drinking" (XLIX, 7), or making love.

Claiming to be an atheist, Housman nonetheless has several poems with references to God, Christ, and man's soul, though his representation of death is not as a prelude to a hereafter, but merely to eternal peace. Leggett considers parallels in stanzas I, LXII, and LXIII with Milton's *Paradise Lost* and Christ's parable of the sower of seeds. Struck by the similarity between "From either end of Heaven the welkin burns" (*Paradise Lost*, 2, 538) and "From Clee to heaven the beacon burns" (I, 1), between ". . . moping melancholy / And moon-struck madness" (*Paradise Lost*, 11, 485–86) and "Moping melancholy mad" (LXII, 13), and, of course, by the most telling reference of all, "And malt does more than Milton can / To justify God's ways to man" (LXII, 21–22), Leggett goes on to the final stanza of *A Shropshire Lad* where Housman feels that he has sowed a few seeds which may flower in receptive minds as Christ also explained in his parable. Housman, however, is naturalistic, Leggett notes, in keeping with the post-Darwinian period. In fact, the use of "God save the Queen" in stanza I is ironic insofar as bodies of the saviors from the Shropshire Fifty-Third and other regiments are stacked up on the banks of the Nile and other remote areas of the Empire. They, not God, saved the Queen through their bravery, which Housman lauds, while seeming to deplore the prevalence of war. In somewhat the same vein, one can interpret the lines—"A neck God made for other use / Than strangling in a string" (IX, 19–20)—as an ironical statement against the concept of a deity or against capital punishment and man's inhumanity to man. More perplexing is the advice in stanza XLV with regard to removing offending eyes, hands, or feet, but playing the man "stand up and end you, / When your sickness is your soul" (lines 7–8). Suicide is here advocated, but the word "soul" is used generically to indicate the whole being, not in a religious sense. "The Carpenter's Son" (XLVII) is a parallel to Christ's crucifixion, the hanging of a person whose lesson to all is to leave ill alone: "Live, lads, and I will die" (line 28). Finally, in stanza XLVIII, "Be still, my soul, be still"; "Let us endure an hour and see injustice done," the "soul" yearns for sleep and peace again as before it was awakened; but never are there intimations of immortality. In fact, both "high heaven and earth ail from the prime foundation." Enduring the anguish is the only solution offered. Still, as Housman facetiously suggests in stanza LXII, one can prepare oneself to cope with the preponderance of ill in the world by reading his poems, which, by allusion to the story of Mithridates, are only slightly poisonous, but an excellent antidote to deadly doses of life itself.

More memorable, however, by their sparsity, are lyrics extolling the beauties of nature, like the cherry tree in bloom (II), a beauty rendered even more precious by its transience and the finite years of man; or the necessity for meeting the challenge of life, as in "Reveille" (IV); or the "fighting sorrow" of football (XVII); or "To an Athlete Dying Young" (XIX), "the lads that will die in their glory and never be old" (XXIII); or the universal nostalgia for a "land of lost content" (XL); or the sorrow for "golden friends" now laid to rest and sleeping (LIV). Certainly, these "solitary stars" (LXIII, 12) will continue to flower and the striking verse re-echo.

—Wesley D. Sweetser

SILAS MARNER.
Novel by George Eliot, 1861.

George Eliot begins *Silas Marner* with a quotation from Wordsworth's poem "Michael":

> A child, more than all other gifts
> That earth can offer to declining man,
> Brings hope with it, and forward-looking thoughts.

This idea, that a child can bring redemption to an empty or sterile environment, is a recurrent theme in the literature of the romantic period, and is explored further in Eliot's novella.

This opposition of sterility and redemption through a child is inseparably linked in *Silas Marner* to a central structuring symbol which runs as a matrix throughout the book: gold. When Silas comes to the village of Raveloe, he has lost all faith in his religion and in humanity. He turns for solace to his gold, earned through his skill at weaving. Gradually this gold becomes a substitute for the love and friendship he has lost and, as Silas's dependence on the gold increases, so too does his isolation and introspection: "at night came his revelry: at night he closed his shutters and made fast his doors, and drew out his gold." Indeed, so important does his gold become that he thinks of the half-earned guineas as "unborn children"—one of the first phrases in the book to forge the link between the sterile introspection of Silas's life at this point and the redemption through human love that will be effected by Eppie. When Silas's gold is stolen, he feels the "withering desolation of [a] bereavement"—a second link between the two themes.

The symbolic link is forged still further when Silas finds the golden-haired Eppie asleep in his cottage: "Gold—his own gold—brought back to him as mysteriously as it had been taken away." From now on, the redemptive qualities of the child are emphasised. Silas now not only has someone to care for and who loves him but gradually gains the trust and friendship of the other villagers. Dolly Winthrop helps him to care for the young Eppie and he becomes integrated into a community once more. When Eppie is christened, Silas is, too; religious faith has been restored, replacing his prior alienation. Even a sense of humour returns to him: a simple, regenerative humour, based on his involvement with the innocent actions of a young child.

The gold of Eppie's hair is frequently alluded to and direct comparisons are made between this new, metaphorical wealth and the materialistic guineas of Silas's isolation. Eppie is associated with daylight, sunshine, and life. The gold had to be worshipped "in close-locked solitude" and at night. "The gold had kept his thoughts in an ever-repeating circle, leading to nothing beyond itself; but Eppie was an object compacted of changes and hopes that forced his thoughts onwards. . . . " The symbolism is carried through to the end of the novella, where it is specifically associated with another symbol of innocence and purity: at her wedding Eppie's hair "looked like the dash of gold on a lily."

Both the golden guineas and the golden-haired child ramify in their symbolic connotations and reach out to reveal a new association with the theme of dishonesty. If excessive concern for money is inevitably yoked with unhappiness in the book, it is also sometimes linked to dishonesty and the consequences of that dishonesty. In the first place, at the commencement of the story, Silas was unjustly accused of stealing, and the book works out the consequences of this for him. In the second place, Dunstan Cass steals the gold from Silas's cottage and drowns in the quarry as a result. The moral implications of these structural parallels and contrasts are made quite explicit. We also find the reverse of the theme of the redemptive child in Godfrey Cass's marriage. Godfrey and Nancy see their sterile, childless marriage as a punishment for Godfrey's earlier way of life and for his cowardice and dishonesty in not acknowledging that Eppie is his own daughter. Again, the ethical significance is absolutely clear.

A further important symbol in the book is that of the garden which Eppie longs for, emblematic of order, harmony, and fertility. The reader will here make an explicit intertextual set of references to gardens and their iconographic connotations, ranging through Eden, "The Song of Songs," the medieval *Hortus Conclusus*, Renaissance pastoral, and the slightly more ironised but still highly pro-garden visions of Marvell. When we add to this the implications of the Wordsworthian pastoral referred to earlier, there can be no mistaking the force of Eppie's desires. Towards the end of the novella—pushing towards comedic closure—a garden is built around the cottage and a wall erected to keep out the disorder of the wild surroundings. And it is no mere coincidence that Eppie should marry the gardener. Once again, Eliot has invested an intertextual symbol with profound moral significance.

But *Silas Marner* is not purely a symbolic novel. There is also a great deal of realism throughout the book—in the descriptions of the villagers, their habits and their dialect, in the episode at the Rainbow Inn (the conviviality of which forms a vivid contrast to Silas's desolation after the loss of his gold) and in the description of the countryside surrounding Raveloe. The symbolic elements in the characters themselves are also interwoven with a measure of sympathetic (but never sentimental) psychological realism. From the first chapter, we understand why the villagers should feel suspicious of Silas, how it is that whole communities should feed on superstition (even to the detriment of their members) and how it is that Silas should come to rely so completely on his gold. He is never portrayed as a Dickensian miser: Eliot eschews completely the use of flat caricature (at least for her major characters). Rather, through a subtle and gradual building up of our understanding of Silas's situation, the reader cannot help but have every sympathy with him. Note, for example, the incident with the brown earthenware pot in chapter 2.

Even Godfrey, who has done wrong, is patiently portrayed from our first meeting with him in this way, so that we sympathise rather than condemn. Ironically, Eppie brings about his redemption too, as he finally admits to the past, accepts Eppie's refusal to live with him rather than with Silas, and learns to resign himself to his childless marriage. Through Eppie, he comes to accept his wife and what they have together.

The book is subtitled *The Weaver of Raveloe*. The whole text itself represents a gradual weaving together of the threads of symbolism, realism, and the combination of the two. Indeed, the entire novella could be seen as a continued metaphor of the process of weaving as the reader is given significant details, character codes, prolepses, analepses, structural parallels, and mysteries partly solved, all of which force him or her into the position of weaver, amalgamating all the elements into the inseparable fabric and textual unity that is *Silas Marner*.

—Anne Katherine Monaghan

SINISTER STREET.
Novel by Compton Mackenzie, 1913–14.

Introducing a French translation of *Sinister Street* in 1954, André Maurois remarked that it was in the process of becoming a classic, to be ranked alongside *L'Éducation Sentimentale* and, perhaps, *Swann's Way*. Another 40 years later this judgment can be asserted more boldly. Proust's pursuit of times past is secure, while Compton Mackenzie's exploration of childhood, adolescence, and youth continues to achieve greater resonance as the years go by. In Maurois's words, "Le livre a duré."

Sinister Street was conceived as a novel on a generous scale, with consequent effects on its writing and publishing history. Mackenzie set out to portray the moral and emotional growth of the principal character, Michael Fane, from the cossetings and buffetings of earliest childhood, through the closed societies of school and university, to eventual maturity amid the complexities of the world at large, after a vain romantic attempt to save a soul from perdition. The religious theme of spiritual salvation that runs through the book has been little noticed by commentators, who have dwelt more on the manifestations of good and evil.

The Fane household belongs to the comfortably off upper middle-class of Edwardian England, insulated by wealth and privilege from both the respectable poor and the often squalid circumstances, shifts, and stratagems of the destitute and outcast. Michael Fane's growing awareness of that sordid underworld constitutes one of the novel's moral dimensions. Mackenzie enlarged the dramatic possibilities of his theme by drawing a contrast between the Fanes' apparently fortunate circumstances and the emotional deprivation of the two Fane children, felt by Michael in particular, through their mother's frequent sojourns abroad and some mystery about their father. The gradual revelation that the latter, Lord Saxby, was locked into an indissoluble marriage and that the Fane children were born out of wedlock is made only after Saxby's death halfway through the novel.

To portray the complex processes by which a lonely and sensitive child accommodates to such experiences, and acquires emotional and moral self-reliance, requires an ample canvas. As the writing of the novel progressed it became clear that Mackenzie could not contain his theme within a single volume.

Resisting his publisher's advice to replan the novel as a trilogy, he completed for publication the first two parts of a four-part construction, carrying the story from the nursery to the move from public school to Oxford. Volume 1 of *Sinister Street* was published in September 1913; volume 2 written in bursts of sustained effort interrupted by illness, reception into the Roman Catholic church, and the outbreak of war, was completed in October 1914 and published in November. By an odd coincidence Edmund Gosse gave Mackenzie a copy of *Du côté de chez Swann* that October, with the observation that "I seem to discern an expression of the same spirit in your *Sinister Street*, though I am not suggesting any positive resemblance between the two books."

From the outset *Sinister Street* enjoyed a resounding success, boosted by the adventitious fact that the *Daily Mail* not only singled it out for review on the leader page but also took up cudgels against the circulating libraries' censorship of novels considered to be objectionably frank in their treatment of sexual matters. W.H. Smith, who with Boots refused at first to stock *Sinister Street*, was for many years particularly exposed to this criticism. The delicacy with which Michael Fane's sexual initiation is hinted at makes this objection to *Sinister Street* seem incredible today; but the undertones of public school homosexuality in book 2, Brother Aloysius's barely repressed sexual fire, and the steamy excitements of the Seven Sisters Road in the final part of the novel were notably audacious in their time. Weightier critics were also swift to praise *Sinister Street* for more valid literary reasons.

Though the novel may be embellished in a richly romantic tradition—Frank Swinnerton called it lavish, literary, sentimental, and florid, but large, confident, and true—its artistic truth is rigorously controlled by the author's method of projecting events and their significance through Michael Fane's eyes and developing apprehension, from the infant's opening world of daisies as big as moons, through the embarrassments of being a new boy at school, to the posturings of undergraduate life, furtive fascination with the illicit, and the disillusionments of love deromanticised. Compelling one to view everything through Fane's own changing perceptions capitalised on what Henry James called Mackenzie's greatest gift, "the ability to receive the direct impact of life so that you can return it directly to your readers." The brilliance and energy of the whole achievement; the acute ear for the nuances of English speech, from the demotic of cooks and maidservants to the esoteric registers of prep and public school slang; the author's sympathetic imagination and insight; and perhaps above all the vivid and sensuous recreation of the sights, sounds, smells, and atmosphere of pre-World War I London and Oxford, combine to leave an indelible impression.

On reading the first volume Ford Madox Ford wrote prophetically that "Possibly *Sinister Street* is a work of real genius—one of those books that really exist otherwise than as the decorations of a publishing season. . . . " More presciently still, Lascelles Abercrombie noted that in this novel "we seem to be watching that strangest of all modes of evolution, the dissolution of one century's character to make way for the character of another century."

In that sense *Sinister Street*'s potency as the distillation of a past social epoch increases with the years. The book has truly become a classic.

—Stewart F. Sanderson

SIR CHARLES GRANDISON.
(*The History of Sir Charles Grandison.*)
Novel by Samuel Richardson, 1753–54.

In his last novel, *Sir Charles Grandison*, Samuel Richardson justifies his creation of a hero who "approaches too near the faultless character which critics censure as above nature," on the grounds that "Human Nature has often, of late, been shewn in a light too degrading." Sir Charles Grandison is "proposed for an Example," intended to show the interesting variety of goodness compared to the dull sameness of vice. Goodness, however, the reader soon discovers, can have a stultifying effect on plot. When the lovely and vivacious Harriet Byron is abducted from a masquerade in London, her rescue by the calmly all-conquering Grandison quickly puts paid to the suspense of adventure. Instead, Harriet is left to wait for Sir Charles (who is obviously as attracted to her as she is to him) to propose, which he is unable to do for quite some time because of the rival claim of an Italian Catholic, Clementina della Porretta. Family opposition on religious grounds, and the anxieties of her own conscience, drive Clementina temporarily into madness. Sir Charles awaits her recovery and the resolution of his dilemma; finally she leaves him free to marry Harriet, but still turns to him for support when her family recommence their persecution on behalf of another suitor.

There are several subplots: the taming of Sir Charles's saucy sister Charlotte in her initially stormy marriage and eventually happy motherhood; the past history of the wicked father, Sir Thomas Grandison, now safely dead, and of his cruel treatment of Charlotte and her meeker sister Caroline, whose predicament, like that of Clementina, replays Clarissa's struggles with her family; the love of young Emily Jervois for her guardian, Sir Charles, and her attempts to come to terms with his marriage to Harriet; the reform of Sir Charles's dissolute uncle (which, like all the other reforms in the book, is effected by the intervention of Sir Charles); and Sir Charles's performance of his various duties as executor of wills, mediator of family disputes, etc. The reader also witnesses Harriet's continuing rejection of her many other suitors; since Sir Charles hasn't declared his love, conventional morality dictates that her heart should still be free, but she insists that she can't and won't marry any other man while he is still unmarried.

Sir Charles, a great enforcer of rules, is also the allowable exception to them. He won't fight duels, but can always disarm an antagonist by his consummate swordsmanship. When he is challenged by Harriet's abductor, the villainous Sir Hargrave Pollexfen, his coolly correct behaviour leaves Sir Hargrave gnashing his teeth and exclaiming "Curse me, if I can bear my own littleness," while his rakish friend comments "I had rather be Sir Charles Grandison in this one past hour, than the Great Mogul all my life." An 18th-century superhero, Sir Charles always saves the day; but he also resolves all difficulties by converting, befriending and, if necessary, adopting his opponents.

Harriet comments on her good fortune in being thrown out of the London social whirl and into "a family that had no need to look out of itself for entertainments." The Grandisons' habit of renaming everyone they meet as brothers, sisters, cousins, uncles, aunts, and so on, means that by the end of the novel, the Grandison family has not only no need to look out of itself for entertainments, but little chance of doing so, since hardly anyone is left outside it. It's no wonder the Grandisons are so fond of music, with its ritual implying rehearsal, concerted performance, harmony, togetherness. Reading is too private an activity to be viewed without suspicion; conversation is preferable. Individual letters take the form of dialogue, recapitulating parts of previous letters, taking them to task, commenting on them, directing others how to read them. This lengthy epistolary novel grudgingly acknowledges but frequently bewails the need for writing. Letters, after all, signal the limits of the family space to a family which wants to (and finally does) consider itself boundless.

As critics have noted, this familialization is a means of deflecting the threat of sexual desire; Harriet herself first uses it, by insisting on treating a suitor as her brother and his uncle as her father, successfully appealing to the latter's paternal tenderness not to urge her to the marriage. Where all relationships become familial, though, all desires become incestuous; Harriet, initially identified as a "third sister" by Sir Charles, soon finds her love for him anything but sisterly. "He has been more than a father to his *uncle*: Does not that sound strange?" she writes of Sir Charles at one point. It doesn't, in the event, sound much stranger than her own later declaration, "I never forget my relations"; how she can remember them all is a mystery to the reader.

Sir Charles Grandison isn't the novel Richardson wanted it to be; Sir Charles is a repressive and tiresome prig, always in the right, always (reluctantly) prevailed on to act as moral arbiter. All opposition crumbles at his touch; even Charlotte's tearing high spirits are damped at last. Yet the novel was a favourite of Jane Austen's, and one can see why. Richardson's painstaking and subtle characterization, his domestic and emotional concerns, even the (often wearying) minuteness of detail with which he creates his air of reality, are enhanced by a keenly psychological sense of comedy which will keep bubbling up. The scenes between Harriet and Emily, for example, are acutely comic, touching and convincing, as good in their kind as anything that would come after them.

—Caroline Gonda

SIR GAWAIN AND THE GREEN KNIGHT.
Poem by the Gawain Poet, late 14th century

Sir Gawain and the Green Knight, perhaps the most sophisticated alliterative romance in Middle English, appears in a single manuscript (British Library, MS Cotton Nero A.x.)—a small quarto volume that also includes *Patience, Cleanness* (or *Purity*), and *Pearl*. Written near the end of the 14th century and preserved in a scribal hand of the early 15th century, the four Cotton Nero works are often attributed to one anonymous author, an aristocratic contemporary of Chaucer, Langland, and Gower.

While all four Cotton poems signalize the importance of interlaced themes (truth, loyalty, humility, and purity), *Sir Gawain* explores, likewise, both the fusion of and tension between disparate genres. In the opening stanzas of the poem, for example, the "blysse and blunder" of legendary British history, as depicted in the Arthurian chronicles of Geoffrey of Monmouth, Lagamon, and Wace, are traced. The *Gawain*-poet thus focuses on the destruction of Troy, the establishment of ancient city states and realms (Rome, Tuscany, Lombardy, and Britain), and the rise of King Arthur. Despite such echoes of the chronicle tradition, the enchantment of the romance mode gradually permeates the text with the inclusion of Arthurian marvel (*selly*) and wonders (*wonderez*) together with the minstrel-narrator's authoritative appeal to tale-telling convention. Just as the alternation between bliss and turmoil ("blysse and blunder") in the opening lines calls attention to the shifting cyclical movement of *Sir Gawain*, so tension between genres or traditions, alternation, and exchange suggest important structural principles in this romance.

Similarly, after Gawain begins his fateful quest of the Green Knight, elements of a romance topography and of a realistic landscape are charted and juxtaposed by the poet, thereby underscoring the collision between the traditions and values of romance and realism. After traveling through the realm of Logres, the Arthurian kingdom of romance writers, Gawain follows a known medieval route to north

Wales and Cheshire, and the poet thus cites specific place-names, including Anglesey and Wirral Forest. Journeying into the wilderness, the strange regions of a romance nether-world, Gawain then encounters the wondrous creatures who frequently live in the hilly terrain of medieval romances—dragons, forest trolls, ogres, and other wild creatures. Although the primitive dangers of the woodland represent a physical test for Gawain, the chilling blasts of winter loom as a more potent obstacle. This section of *Sir Gawain* thus concludes with a realistic depiction of winter in the north country—freezing sleet, hard icicles, and cresting streams.

A final illustration of the alternation of the romantic and the realistic modes may be found in the delineation of Castle Hautdesert. The detailed workmanship of this castle—ornamental pinnacles, chimneys on tower roofs, turrets, and battlements—reflects late 14th-century architectural fashion, many elements of which are found in the decorative castles portrayed in the Duc de Berry's *Très Riches Heures*. At the same time, however, Castle Hautdesert is linked with whiteness and luminosity, emblematic of the romance imagination (the Otherworld and fairyland). Inasmuch as the castle seems to be cut entirely out of paper, thereby suggesting the decorative paper castles placed over food at medieval feasts, Hautdesert stands forth as a magical romance fortress, apparently unreal yet visually beguiling.

Such an alternation of realistic and romantic modes, mirroring the clash between the audience's everyday observations and the wonders coloring fictional representations of reality, may hint at the carnival spirit of game, play, and exchange suffusing the poem. The opening scene of *Sir Gawain*, for example, pinpoints gleefully the merrymaking of the Yuletide revelry at Camelot. Of particular significance are the "hondeselle" and the "ȝeres-ȝiftes," New Year gifts in an ambiguous exchange game involving hands. As W.R.J. Barron notes so perceptively in his edition-translation of *Sir Gawain*, the tokens hidden in the hand ("hondeselle") may be interpreted as "small gifts offered by the men and given to the ladies who guessed correctly, while those who guessed wrongly paid the forfeit of a kiss." If Barron's interpretation is correct, the New Year game looks forward both to the temptations at Hautdesert, scenes involving Lady Bercilak's offer of gifts and kisses to Gawain, and the third stroke of the Green Knight's axe—Gawain's forfeit of a nick in the neck—at the Green Chapel. Furthermore, the reference to "hondeselle" is crucial because Gawain is forced throughout the poem to examine and to weigh moral alternatives, essentially choices of "hands."

The gamelike structure of *Sir Gawain* is reinforced by the sudden appearance of the mysterious Green Knight at Arthur's court. In the poet's depiction of the Knight, for instance, conventional attributes of the medieval courtier, the Wild Man, and the Green Man are interwoven artfully. Furthermore, the greenness of the Knight is particularly ambiguous and thus unsettling for a medieval audience, especially because green is enriched by conflicting symbolic associations (hope, inconstancy in love, fairyland, life, death, Otherworld creatures, and the devil). Although the Green Knight notes playfully that he wishes to participate in a Christmas game with Arthur and his court, he carries a holly bob, emblematic of good luck in the New Year, in one hand, and a huge battle-axe in the other.

Since the play world in *Sir Gawain* is partially comic entertainment and partially genuine danger, the Green Knight challenges Camelot to a New Year game of exchange of blows. Once a member of Arthur's entourage delivers the first blow, he will receive the Knight's battle-axe as a gift. The play rules of the Knight's game, however, require that the challengee (Gawain) receive an identical blow a year and a day later at the Green Chapel. Resonating throughout the Knight's challenge to Camelot are the voice of authority and the use of legal diction—"year and day," "quitclaim," and "dom." Such legal terms suggest the contractual bonds of the compact which will ensnare Gawain with his acceptance of the Knight's challenge.

The legal coloring of the games in *Sir Gawain* reappears at Castle Hautdesert. Once Gawain tells his host (Bercilak de Hautdesert) that the meeting with the Knight at the Green Chapel is established by solemn agreement, Bercilak persuades Gawain to engage in an "exchange of winnings." The terms of the host's "forwarde" demand that the animals captured by Bercilak on three successive days of hunting be exchanged for Gawain's daily winnings at Hautdesert. So while Bercilak tracks down elusive quarry in the woods (hunting game), his wife engages in a sexual chase of Gawain (courtly love game) within the castle.

This "exchange of winnings" game is solemnized through the construction of three covenants. Each formal agreement reflects and harmonizes with the contractual design of the initial Camelot accord between Gawain and the Green Knight. Although the first two covenants are secured with a handshake or with the consumption of a beverage and are marked by formally sworn oaths before Bercilak's court, the shaping of the third agreement is handled irregularly. Inasmuch as Bercilak and Gawain seal their bargain privately without the use of specific legal terms ("couenaunt" and "forwarde"), the poet's audience may feel that the whole contractual process has been subverted. Furthermore, when Gawain presents Lady Bercilak's gift of three kisses to his host *before* he receives Bercilak's fox pelt and when he conceals the Lady's ornamental green girdle, Gawain is guilty both of breach of contract and of chivalric disloyalty.

While legal covenants and formulations lie at the heart of the games in *Sir Gawain*, particularly the challenge / "beheading game" and the "exchange of winnings," the gamelike structure and the festive spirit of this romance are reflected in the poem's symmetrical design. *Sir Gawain* contains, for example, two "beheadings," two courts (Camelot and Hautdesert), two Yuletide tableaux with two New Year's Days, the Hautdesert indoor games of love juxtaposed with outdoor games of hunting, and two confession scenes (Gawain's confession to the priest at Hautdesert and his acknowledgement of sin to the Knight as lay confessor). Even more significant, perhaps, are the emblematic use of threes, including three signs of the Cross and three prayers on Gawain's arrival at the castle, three temptation scenes, three hunting expeditions, three series of kisses by the Lady, three cockcrows, and three blows of the Knight's axe. Underscoring both the supernatural and gamelike elements in *Sir Gawain*, the number three is linked with magic in folklore and with the Trinity in Christian symbolism. Finally, the number three suggests the devil's three temptations both of Adam (Genesis 3) and of Christ (Matthew 4) as well as Peter's triple repudiation of Christ (Mark 14).

—Robert J. Blanch

SIR ORFEO.
Poem, early 14th century.

Editions

Sir Orfeo, edited by Alan J. Bliss. 1954; revised edition, 1966.
Sir Orfeo and Sir Launfal, edited by Lesley Johnson and Elizabeth Williams. 1984.

Critical Studies: *Orpheus in the Middle Ages* by J.B. Friedman, 1970; *Chivalric Romances* by Lee C. Ramsey, 1983; *English Medieval Romances* by W.R.J. Barron, 1987.

Sir Orfeo is a Middle English poem in octosyllabic couplets. It is based on the classical myth of Orpheus and Eurydice, known to the Middle Ages from Virgil's *Georgics* IV, Ovid's *Metamorphoses* X, and Boethius' *Consolation of Philosophy* III, metre XII. There was probably also a French source, now lost, perhaps based on an earlier Celtic *lai*. The poem combines the themes of magic and love.

The myth of Orpheus, in classical literature a tale of the inevitability of death, has in *Sir Orfeo* the happy ending expected in a lay or romance. Eurydice's death is reinterpreted as her being "taken" by the fairies, and the story shows the triumph of love over the mysterious power of the Otherworld. The story exalts faithful human love of two kinds: that of Orfeo and Heurodis, and that of Orfeo and his loyal steward. The strongest impression given by the poem, however, is that of the terrifying and yet beautiful Otherworld, and the fairies' frightening and inexplicable relationship to humankind.

King Orfeo is married to Heurodis, who puts herself in the fairies' power by falling asleep under a grafted tree. The fairy king tells her that the next day he will come to take her away forever, threatening that the fairies will tear her limb from limb if she resists. When Heurodis awakes, she is temporarily afflicted with a terrifying magically induced madness, in which she wounds and mutilates herself. She then warns Orfeo, who brings a thousand knights to the tree next day to protect her, but Heurodis vanishes from their midst. Orfeo, leaving his kingdom in the care of his steward, roams the wilderness for ten years, sorrowing for her. He then sees her in the fairy hunt, but cannot speak to her. He follows the hunt to Fairyland, where he sees many people thought in this world to be dead. He plays his harp before the fairy king, who promises him whatever he asks as a reward. Thus he wins back Heurodis. He then returns in disguise to his castle to test the faithfulness of his steward by pretending that Orfeo is dead. The steward's grief convinces Orfeo of his loyalty, and he makes the steward his heir. Orfeo and Heurodis reign long and happily together.

Instead of the tragic gloom of the classical story, we have a happy ending. But the brightness is threatening. The Otherworld is a dangerous place, and the fairies frightening people. Their attitude to mortals seems arbitrary: they abduct them and then ignore them. Inside Fairyland, the people stolen by magic lie in the state in which they left the mortal world—some without arms or head, some mad, some drowned or dead in childbirth. We have no inkling of the fairies' motivation. The king does not abduct Heurodis for love; he simply adds her to his collection. Orfeo finds him sharing his throne with the fairy queen while Heurodis lies nearby, still asleep under the grafted tree. This inexplicable attitude is an integral part of fairy lore. The beauties of the Otherworld—the shining crowns, the bright level plain, the crystal palace, the pillars of gold, the precious stones that shine with their own light—are inseparable from the threat of the unknown. Whereas in the classical myth the threat is death, which comes to everyone, in *Sir Orfeo* it is an enchantment more frightening, because less understood: a fate alien to humanity.

In *Sir Orfeo* this heartless Otherworld is strongly contrasted with faithful human love and mutual trust. The most emotional moments in the poem show the unshakeable love of Orfeo and Heurodis. When Heurodis tells Orfeo that she must leave him, her sorrow is compelling:

> Allas, mi lord Sir Orfeo,
> Seththen we first to-gider were
> Ones wroth never we nere,
> Bot ever ich have y-loved the
> As mi liif, and so thou me.

Orfeo's response emphasizes the bond of marriage and his determination to do anything rather than break that bond: "Whider thou gost, ichil with the, / And whider I go, thou shalt with me." Ten years later, when Orfeo encounters his wife in the fairy hunt, we see that this bond has not been broken. Unable to speak, they exchange a long look, and Heurodis weeps as she sees Orfeo reduced to wildness and poverty. This one look enables Orfeo to dare even the dangers of the Otherworld to regain her.

The second instance of mutual love and trust is that of Orfeo and his steward. The steward shows his love for Orfeo by his unfeigned grief at hearing of his "death," even though that death leaves the steward in power. Orfeo keeps faith by honoring the steward beyond his rank, making him his heir. Our respect for Orfeo is increased by his trustworthiness, both as a husband and as a good master. His faithful human love is contrasted with the fairy king's arbitrary exercise of power.

The classical myth has been reworked both in mood and in its ultimate meaning. Instead of gloomy Dis, we have the bright but alien beauty of Fairyland. While Orpheus persuades Pluto and Persephone to pity him, reminding them of their own love, Orfeo addresses a heartless people, not susceptible to human emotion. He does not appeal to the king's sympathies, but tricks him into a rash promise. He wins the bargain with no conditions attached. When he and Heurodis leave Fairyland hand in hand, there is no need to look back. In each story, the look marks the supreme moment. The rash love of Orpheus enables him to reach the Underworld but tempts him to look back. Orfeo's love is steadfast.

After ten years of waiting, he is finally vouchsafed the sight of Heurodis. One look passes between them, and that look draws him to follow her to the Otherworld and regain her without making any mistakes. The two parts of the story, the rescue of his wife and the testing of his steward, are drawn together by Orfeo's character: faithful, dependable, and able to bring about a happy restoration of both his marriage and his kingdom.

—Rosalind Clark

SIR THOMAS MORE.
Play by Anthony Munday, William Shakespeare, and others, written c. 1593–1601.

The *Booke of Sir Thomas More* is the title given to a history play included among the Harleian manuscripts at the British Museum. Edited for the Shakespeare Society by Alexander Dyce in 1844, it received some attention from later scholars, and was reprinted by C.F. Tucker Brooke in his *Shakespeare Apocrypha* (1908). *Sir Thomas More* bears minor resemblances to another drama once attributed to Shakespeare, *Thomas Lord Cromwell* (1602), and is thought to date from the 1590's. Unlike such pseudo-Shakespearean plays as *Edward III* or *Sir John Oldcastle*, however, parts of *Sir Thomas More* exhibit unmistakable signs of Shakespeare's authorship. Furthermore, A.F. Pollard and others have established in *Shakespeare's Hand in the Play of Sir Thomas More* (1923) that the "D" script represented in Harley 7368 is that of Shakespeare himself. But even if the play was a collaborative production, Shakespearean features are too significant to ignore. One key passage in Act II—so designated by modern editors—is of particular interest in this connection. At this juncture More is seen rebuking the London rabble for daring to suggest that ethnic unrest can best be countered by recourse to an orgy of vindictiveness. The animal imagery in this passage ("Would shark on you, and men like ravenous fishes / Would feed on one another") is reminiscent of that used elsewhere by Shakespeare, particularly in *Troilus and Cressida* and *Coriolanus*. Moreover, More's general advice to the rebellious citizens is identical with that tendered in other plays. He attempts to placate the giddy multitude by inveighing against the "innovation" likely to result in civic disturbance, counselling obedience to those in authority. The monarch, he argues, being God's deputy on earth and responsible for implementing the Almighty's will through the agency of law, must be able to count on deference from his subjects; arbitrary revolt against the king's enactments is therefore offensive to God.

More's oratorical style in this scene is essentially Shakespearean in both tone and movement. Act II of the play sounds a note of pathos which pervades the action as a whole, and serves to endear us to the central character after we have ascertained from Act I the causes of the conflict in the body politic which More is called upon to face. The insolence of immigrant craftsmen in early 16th-century London, we discover, has incensed the populace, who resent the tendency which their presence has to reduce the standard of living among true-born English artisans. Hence the clamour for revenge. A petition is drawn up urging the Mayor and aldermen to redress the people's wrong. But the nobles, well aware that they are ill-equipped to prevent trouble from breaking out, rely on Sir Thomas More to persuade the rabble that insurrection will not further their cause. Some of the ringleaders of this incipient rebellion are arrested and brought to justice; but it is More's skilful diplomacy which prevents a mere uprising from developing into a calamitous mutiny; "Master Sheriff More," declares the Mayor, "you have preserved the city / From a most dangerous fierce commotion. . . . " More's arguments are, in fact, sufficiently cogent to convince potential malefactors that militancy is the height of folly: and on the strength of this More gains not only the good will of the citizenry but also the approval of his sovereign, who rewards his sagacity by conferring a knighthood upon him, finally creating him High Chancellor of England. This is the highest point on the ladder of Fortune to which More succeeds in climbing.

From now on More's moral and intellectual calibre becomes abundantly evident; he is represented as a man of high culture, compassion, and sportive good humour, as when a visit from the learned Erasmus is enlivened by a jest of More's devising in which the visitor is gulled into believing that More's servant Randall is More himself—a misconception rectified by the Earl of Surrey when the real Sir Thomas More arrives on the scene. On the occasion of a dinner given to the Lord Mayor of London and his wife at More's Chelsea home, a troupe of strolling players (five in number) appears offering to perform the interlude of *The Marriage of Wit and Wisdom* —a "play within a play" not unlike the "Mousetrap" episode in Hamlet. This interpolation provides a sidelight on More's versatility, since he knows *The Marriage* so well that he can deputise for one of the actors; and Wit is heard to remark: "Did ye mark how extemprically he fell to the matter, and spake Luggins's part almost as it is in the very book set down?" More, obviously, revels in amateur dramatics. But the domestic happiness seemingly assured by his promotion to high office suddenly turns out to be short-lived. He is summoned to court unexpectedly, and as he sets out with his attendants asks "What's the business now, / That all so late his highness sends for me?" His anxiety is ominous. For in the following scene in the Council Chamber at Whitehall, More is presented with an ultimatum which proves in almost no time to be his undoing. Sir Thomas Palmer appears bearing the "articles" which More is required to sign. But he will not be hurried into compliance; like the Bishop of Rochester (John Fisher) he refuses on conscientious grounds to subscribe his name to a document he holds to be of dubious legality.

This turn of events raises some interesting points. Given that playwrights in the 1590's were in the habit of deviating from historical fact, it is perhaps relevant to ask how far an audience at the Globe or the Fortune could be expected to have grasped the true reason for More's arrest and subsequent arraignment. His offence was that as a Catholic he could not allow himself to take the oath of supremacy which Henry VIII—for matrimonial reasons—would have imposed. In the play this crucial issue is not debated, which has the effect of weakening what could have been a powerfully tragic climax. The Earl of Surrey's final remark that "A very learned worthy gentleman / Seals error with his blood" seems a somewhat lame conclusion, though understandable when we remember that *Sir Thomas More* did not escape censure from the vigilant Master of the Revels of the day, Sir Edmund Tilney, who insisted on drastic revisions. This apart, however, there is enough of general interest in this play to give it a unique place among the numerous historical dramas of its time.

—E.D. Mackerness

SIZWE BANSI IS DEAD.
Play by Athol Fugard, 1972.

Sizwe Bansi Is Dead was first performed in 1972 at the Space Theatre in Cape Town, South Africa. Although authorship is generally attributed to Athol Fugard, the play was devised jointly by Fugard and the two actors who featured in the original South African production, John Kani and Winston Ntshona.

The play was conceived as a series of improvisational

sketches allowing its two main characters to rehearse stories that entertain the audience while instructing it on various social and political ills affecting South Africa. The longest and most central of these stories recounts how Sizwe Bansi, a migrant worker without a proper working-permit renounces his name and identity; consequently he can inherit another person's passbook, find legal work, and eventually bring his wife and four children to live with him in Port Elizabeth. But the change of name does not come without a good deal of agonizing and he is haunted by the question: "How do I live as another man's ghost?"

Learning to live as another man's ghost is something that black South Africans, according to the play, endure with a mixture of ironic humor and tragic defiance. In this respect, Sizwe Bansi's anxiety over his name-change is contrasted with the subversive radicalism of Styles, owner of a photographic studio that serves as the setting for the entire play. Styles has set himself a life-mission, as a professional photographer for all occasions, of restoring dignity and hope to "My people. The simple people, who you never find mentioned in the history books." He finds himself in a double role as both a feeder of the system and a subverter of it: after all, he takes the snapshots that help to legitimize the government's passbooks and passports, yet he also takes family snapshots that can linger on as cherished memories in the midst of suffering and oppression.

Styles carries off the double role with artistry and great comical effect. In one of his earliest stories, he explains how, before he set up his own studio, he worked for six years as a manual laborer in the local Ford factory. As one of the few workers who spoke both Xhosa and English he served as a translator for the owner and when, in preparation for a guest visit by Mr. Ford himself, the owner asked that all the workers look happy Styles translated "You must see to it that you are wearing a mask of smiles. Hide your true feelings, brothers." Such irony permeates the play, even its title. "Sizwe" (the nation) and "bansi" (the vast majority) is far from dead; the black majority in South Africa, the play implies, is alive and vigorous even though disenfranchised and therefore politically dead at the ballot box.

Styles's photographic studio, like Fugard's darkened theatre, is a "strong-room of dreams" where the pain and joys of black South African history can be restored and retold. Both Styles's images and Fugard's words are clearly meant to restore and celebrate the memory of black South Africans whose identities, in the eyes of the South African government, are dead as long as there is no photograph or passbook to establish legitimacy. In one of the most powerful stories told in the play, Styles recounts how his father fought bravely for the Allies in World War II only to find that, once returned home, his rights and dignity were once again stripped away. All that remains of him is a photograph. By restoring the photograph, Styles commemorates a part of history that the government has attempted to banish to oblivion. As dream-makers and commemorators, both Fugard and Styles seem to work in similar ways with their respective media.

Like all of Fugard's plays, *Sizwe Bansi* establishes a close and intimate relationship with its audience allowing it to identify powerfully with the characters and to establish emotional ties with them. In order to do this, Fugard deliberately keeps his setting and plot line fairly simple. Unlike other plays such as *"Master Harold" and the Boys* (where he probes the latent hostilities and prejudices in the consciousness of "liberal" white South Africans), *Sizwe Bansi* gives insight into the painful yet joyful and angry consciousness of black South Africans who have learned to live with a vicious system but whose anger is unmistakable.

—Robert S. Burton

SKETCHES BY BOZ.
Fiction by Charles Dickens, 1836.

Published on 8 February 1836, a day after his 24th birthday, *Sketches by Boz, Illustrative of Every-Day Life and Every-Day People* was Charles Dickens's first book. Its success and that of *The Pickwick Papers*, which began serialization on 31 March 1836, led to a "Second Series" being published in December 1836. Almost all the sketches in it had appeared in sundry magazines and newspapers from December 1833 onwards, mostly under the pseudonym Boz, but many were now revised, sometimes substantially, and retitled. The two books, illustrated by George Cruikshank, were re-issued in monthly parts from 1837 to 1839, and the complete collection, now consisting of 56 items re-grouped under the titles "Seven Sketches from Our Parish," "Scenes," "Characters"' and "Tales," re-appeared in book form in 1839.

Though sometimes heavily facetious and uneven in style, *Sketches by Boz* displays many of Dickens's talents and the concerns develped in the novels. As his friend, adviser, and biographer John Forster observed:

> . . . the first sprightly runnings of his genius are undoubtedly here. Mr. Bumble is in the parish sketches, and Mr. Dawkins, the dodger [another *Oliver Twist* character] in the Old-bailey scenes. . . . The observation shown throughout is nothing short of wonderful. Things are painted literally as they are; . . . whatever the picture, whether of every-day vulgar, shabby genteel, or downright low. . . . It was a picture of every-day London at its best and worst, in its humours and enjoyments as well as in its sufferings and sins . . .

Forster also noted and praised (as did many reviewers of this highly successful début) the humour, sentiment, and pathos. The sketches outnumber and generally surpass the stories. Both categories depict "every-day" (middle- and working-class) people, exclusively in London and its environs, which remained Dickens's predominant fictional locale. Many items are concerned with popular amusements ("London Recreations," "Astley's [circus]," "Private Theatres"), always a Dickens preoccupation; two ("A Christmas Dinner," "The New Year,") announce his long association with Christmas sentiment, most richly evident in *A Christmas Carol*.

But if there are much geniality, humour, and high spirits, and a generous appreciation of simple pleasures, the collection includes elements of the grim and macabre ("The Drunkard's Death," "The Black Veil,") and of Dickens's lifelong concern with crime ("The Criminal Courts," "The Prisoners' Van," "A Visit to Newgate"). The latter ends in the condemned cell, and imagines a prisoner awaiting execution, a passage closely anticipating "Fagin's Last Night Alive" written three years later. Many passages in the non-fictional items, indeed, engage Dickens's novelistic skills, such as dialogue, and his "fancy." In "Meditations in Monmouth Street" for instance, looking at the secondhand clothes on sale there, he imagines the characters and careers of their former owners—

> whole rows of coats have started from their pegs, and buttoned up, of their own accord, round the waists of imaginary wearers; lines of trousers have jumped down to meet them; waistcoats have almost burst with anxiety to put themselves on; and half an acre of shoes have suddenly found feet to fit them, and gone stumping down the street . . .

The imaginative exuberance of this is typical, as is the animism (those waistcoats bursting with anxiety). Similarly another stylistic characteristic appears, here in simple form: seeing houses and their inhabitants in terms of one another. Thus in "Seven Dials" (a slummy criminal area which had haunted Dickens's imagination since childhood) he "traverses streets of dirty, straggling houses, with now and then an unexpected court composed of buildings as ill-proportioned and deformed as the half-naked children that wallow in the kennels."

"Our Parish" exhibits some of Dickens's social and political interests, at a time when old ways were being challenged. In "The Election for Beadle," the "great new beadle principles have achieved a proud victory" after "a parochial convulsion" —the beadle is to be elected, not appointed. Other local officials important in future novels are introduced too, such as the workhouse-master ("an admirable specimen of a small tyrant") and the schoolmaster. National politics and institutions appear in "A Parliamentary Sketch" and "Doctors' Commons," where Dickens uses memories of his shorthand reporting days.

"What inexhaustible food for speculation do the streets of London afford!" the essay "Shops and Their Tenants" begins. There are many items about or involving streets—Dickens was eminently and variously street-wise—and shops and other urban facilities or nuisances, and they are characteristically specific: "We had been lounging one evening, down Oxford Street, Holborn, Cheapside, Coleman Street, Finsbury Square . . . " ("The Parlour Orator"). There is much too about the means of locomotion through them ("Hackney-Coach Stands," "Early Coaches," "Omnibuses," "The Last Cab-Driver"). A dynamic—more lately called a kinetic—author, Dickens was always fascinated by movement, travel, and speed, later specializing in stage-coaches and railway transport.

The tales and characters mostly use stock situations—the pomposities of public life and snobbish pretensions of private life, the follies and mishaps of courtship, henpecked husbands, superannuated amorousness, school-marms, mistaken identity, the evils of drink—but there are much vigour and freshness in the writing, both the narration and the dialogue and speechifying. Moreover, as Forster remarks, the most frequent social milieu—"unusually truthful observation of a sort of life between the middle class and the low"—was then "quite unhackneyed ground." Readers were particularly struck by Boz's intimacy with London—"he has minutely observed and most felicitously caught the peculiarities of every class of this great city and its suburbs, from the tradesman down to the cabman or the cad" (*Westminster Review*, July 1837); "Life in London, as revealed in the pages of Boz, opens a new world to thousands born and bred in the same city, whose palaces overshadow their cellars" (*Quarterly Review*, June 1839). Dickens was making a social and moral, not just a picturesque, point in dwelling, here as in later fictions, on the gross disparities so conspicuous in the metropolis: "You turn the corner [from a "filthy and miserable" area]. What a change! All is light and brilliancy" ("Gin-Shops").

—Philip Collins

A SONG TO DAVID.
Poem by Christopher Smart, 1763.

While there is no clear evidence to ascertain a precise date of composition for *A Song to David*, it is very likely that Christopher Smart wrote it during his time of confinement for insanity (1756–63). Notices advertising the publication of a small pilot edition appeared in the *Public Advertiser* of 1763, shortly after Smart's release; and modern critics agree that it belongs to the same creative period as his other major religious poetry (1759–63)—indeed, it is likely that Smart's grand intent was to present the *Song* as the third and climatic part to a tripartite work which would also contain *A Translation of the Psalms of David* and *Hymns and Spiritual Songs for . . . the Church of England*; this work appeared in 1765. Critical reception in 1763 seemed awed by the *Song*'s complexity and uniqueness: the *Monthly Review* describes it as "irregularly great"; the *Critical Review* claims it is "a fine piece of ruins [which] must at once please and affect a sensible mind"; William Mason writes to Thomas Gray that he has seen Smart's *Song* and "must from thence conclude him mad as ever"; and James Boswell calls it "a very curious . . . mixture of dun obscure and glowing genius at times." Reviews of the 1765 version were dismissive, and the work faded from sight until Wordsworth praises Smart's *Song* as an inspired poem, Browning claims that Smart's poem "lit language straight from soul," and Rossetti describes it as "the only great accomplished poem of the last century." Modern scholarship is abundant both in terms of praise for the poetic sublimity of the *Song*, and in terms of the *Song's* extraordinary structural intricacy.

In publishing his *Psalms*, *Hymns*, and *Song* together in this order, Smart essentially takes Christian liturgy—and divine poetry—to a new stage; it is important to view the *Song* in its context. England had sung metrical Psalms from the time of Sternhold and Hopkins (1562) until well into the 18th century, when these were augmented by the hymns of Watts (1707), the Wesleys (1740's and following), and others. Smart pays his debt to these traditional stages of Christian praise in his own *Psalms* and *Hymns*, and then suggests a new possibility—an epiphany—of liturgical and poetic freedom: his *Psalms* are freer lyrically and structurally than most; his *Hymns* engage people in his own (rather than a congregationally shared) vision of the marvels of God's world; and in his *Song* he attempts to portray the religious and sensual excitement of perceiving all the minutiae of creation in praise of their Creator. Everything from "rip'ning canes" to "vinous syrup cedars" to "rich almonds" offer praise by their own beauty and natural function; and as the word "ADORATION" recurs in each stanza (progressing one line lower each stanza and then the movement repeats), the suggestion is that all ranks and orders of being inevitably praise their God by their very existence in a world harmoniously tied together by adoration of a passionately artistic and infinitely caring God. In the *Song* Smart focuses not on the rational or pious traits of the religious consciousness, but rather he wants to revive the emotions, sensations, and imaginative visions of divinity that stimulated the biblical David as poet of the Lord. Elsewhere he writes: "For by the Grace of God I am the Reviver of Adoration among English-men." While reviving the liturgy of adoration, the *Song* also places Smart in a long tradition which saw the Bible itself as sublimely poetic, and "Praise above all" as man's highest calling. While the *Song* praises David's ability to praise, it also praises its own author who asks God to "hail and hear" the "wreath I weave," a new "wreath" of praise surpassing David and characterized by strength and power: "But stronger still, in earth and air, / And in the sea, the man of pray'r."

Yet, paradoxically, this wreath of praise has (true to the Age of Reason) a complex, labyrinthine structure which Smart himself calls an "exact Regularity and Method," a structure which has been the subject of much critical commentary and speculation in the 20th century: some scholars see the 86 stanzas grouped in mystic numbers of "threes or sevens or their multiples," others see them arranged according to musical cadences (a "contrapuntal arrangement," an "elaborate fugue"), and others still see rhetorical patterns of "contrast and comparison," "syntactical parallelism and verbal repetition." Whatever structure one prefers, a high degree of elaborateness was an important feature of the "high ode" or regular "Pindaric Ode" during the classical and Renaissance periods, and certainly in the neoclassical period of the 18th century. The stanzaic form of 8.8.6.8.8.6 with a rhyme scheme of a.a.b.c.c.b (the "romance six") dates back to Chaucer, was popular for 18th-century odes, and, significantly, was a recurrent form in English hymns. But the emotional and visionary power, and the kaleidoscopic whirl of sensuous imagery *within* a highly structured traditional format, make *A Song to David* a unique poetic and religious work in English.

Smart's own prefatory summary of the "contents" of *A Song to David* is concise and illuminating:

> Invocation, ver. 1,2,3,—The Excellence and lustre of David's character in twelve points of view, ver. 4; proved from the history of his life, to ver. 17.—He consecrates his genius for consolation and edification. —The subjects he made choice of—the Supreme Being —angels; men of renown; the works of nature in all directions, either particularly or collectively considered, to ver. 27.—He obtains power over infernal spirits, and the malignity of his enemies; wins the heart of Michael, to ver. 30.—Shews that the pillars of knowledge are the monuments of God's works in the first week, to ver. 38.—An exercise upon the decalogue, from ver. 40 to 49.—The transcendent virtue of praise and adoration, ver. 50 and 51.—An exercise upon the seasons, and the right use of them, from ver. 52 to 64.—An exercise upon the senses, and how to subdue them, from ver. 65 to 71.—An amplification in five degrees, which is wrought up to this conclusion, That the best poet which ever lived was thought worthy of the highest honour which possibly can be conceived, as *the Saviour of the world was ascribed to his house, and called his son in the body*.

Smart's handwritten signature follows: in a gesture in accordance with his supreme belief in this unparalleled work of poetic liturgy, he had personally signed all copies of the first edition.

—Richard Arnold

SONGS OF INNOCENCE AND OF EXPERIENCE.
Poems by William Blake, 1794.

Songs of Innocence and of Experience was not initally conceived as a single collection. The earliest Songs of Innocence were written before 1784, and the collection was completed by 1789. *Songs of Experience* was offered for sale separately in 1793. The two collections appeared together in 1794. Until 1818 William Blake continued to make copies separately, though after that date he consistently printed the two sets together with a common title page which describes them as "showing the two contrary states of the human soul." Since there are also several complementary poems within the two groups the whole collection is best considered as a single unit. This has considerable consequences for our understanding of the poems. Some can be taken straightforwardly, giving central points of reference: "The Divine Image" and "The Voice of the Ancient Bard" in *Songs of Innocence*; "London," "The Garden of Love," and other poems in *Songs of Experience*. But most are dramatic: their speaker is not Blake.

How the speaker's attitudes are placed depends therefore on the context that is invoked, whether of the single collection or of the two together. Taken together Innocence and Experience highlight by contrast each other's strengths and limitations. *Songs of Innocence* articulates through children primitive hopes and fears about life which exist in adults usually only in compromised or suppressed forms. Innocence therefore, as Blake puts it, reproaches us with the errors of acquired folly. Like Wordsworth, Blake instructs adults about their failures by the example of children. The lyrics of Innocence aim to reawaken positive aspects of life lost amid the stultifying constrictions of experience. They are "happy songs / Every child may joy to hear." "Joy" is a key word: the poems celebrate all that promotes it in nature, society, or myths of the supernatural. The Songs of Experience comment in the opposite direction: they exhibit negative forces in life, and so suggest perspectives of which Innocence cannot take account.

The main subjects of the *Songs* are religion, sex, and politics. While in "The Divine Image" Blake asserts his own view of the identity of God and man, *Songs of Innocence* mostly explores the emotional power of a more orthodox Christianity, the belief in a protective, supernatural authority which will finally right all wrongs. This kind of religion can be bad in Blake's terms as a social force since it may reconcile us to inhumane social conditions which properly demand transformation ("The Chimney Sweeper"), but at the individual level it can be positive, real in the comfort it offers for suffering. *Songs of Innocence* accepts what are to Blake the positive aspects of ordinary Christianity, the story of the Incarnation and the idea of Jesus as a child with a child's freshness and vulnerability. The Lamb is a crucial symbol: it points to an aspect of Christian myth and ethics which is a real force against violence, which can bring peace in a way that mutual fear and selfish love never will. In this aspect the radiance of the poems' vision is not a delusion. Their love, joy, and gentleness are not a completely adequate religion because no full account is taken of suffering and evil. But the religion is a genuine and valuable one. Some of the *Songs of Experience* are about religion in this fundamental way: the collection's most famous poem, "The Tyger," is about the awesome and inscrutable Creator. *Songs of Experience* is less concerned, however, with Christianity *per se* and more with the church. The church is the joyless agent of the Old Testament law-giver God whose "Thou shalt not" turns flowers to gravestones ("The Garden of Love"). Jealousy, fear of love, and a perverse pleasure in secrecy are all corruptions endemic to the world of experience which the church institutionalizes, justifies, and reinforces. The church's role in politics is similar: it co-operates with fallen human nature, perverting the egalitarian social message of Jesus into a force defending social injustice. The church is morally blackened by complicity with political power which actively contributes to exploitation and suffering ("London"). The religion which should promote individual freedom and a proper reverence for all life, and should foster, by just social relationships, a sense of the brotherhood of humanity, has become the instrument of repression, oppression, and violence.

As with all Blake's characteristic poetry the *Songs* are a union of poetry and design. Each is printed on one or more engraved plates which were hand-coloured after printing. Some designs are simply illustrations. Some are a form of commentary on or complement to the text, so that the poems are incomplete unless read in their illuminated form. In mode the *Songs* are very varied: some are the direct expression of simple feelings, others the oblique expression of complex ideas; some are symbolic, some narrative; some use myth, others are located in the contemporary social world. Formally, be it in density of language, power or subtlety of rhythm, or lyric beauty in the line or stanza, the lyrics all share an evident verbal craftsmanship which the drafts in Blake's notebook show was often painstakingly achieved. Though the ideas of the *Songs* are continuous with those of Blake's non-lyric poetry of the same period, Blake's stance in his lyrics, particularly in *Songs of Innocence*, is less didactic. In some poems Blake is the Bard whose words are to be, as he puts it in *Milton*, marked well as of our eternal salvation, but the oblique dramatic mode of statement and beauty of form of the *Songs* means that they do not in general demand the assent to or dissent from their ideas with which works written in Blake's prophetic voice challenge the reader.

—David Fuller

SONNETS 33–35 and 71–74.
Poems by William Shakespeare, 1609 (possibly written 1590's).

Their technical excellence and emotional power apart, William Shakespeare's *Sonnets* are unique in the history of love poetry. Appearing at the close of a 200-year tradition, many of the sonnets in the cycle shift the ground of response from that of the "Petrarchan" lover, an idealistic celebrant of an unconsummated relationship to that of a more sophisticated commentator whose love relationships call up such attitudes as boredom, satiety, guilt, neurotic possessiveness, self-loathing, self-pity, anger, and ambivalence, that is, they introduce a number of anxieties evoked by intimate relationships which do not run smoothly. Moreover, the expression of such anxieties involves a speaker whose shifting attitudes and subtle motives are not always known to himself. While many of the sonnets are free from irony and the machinations of a manipulative *persona* (those of praise; those urging the friend to marry), others, in response to highly disturbing situations (such as infidelity in 33–35) or those clearly exhibiting a neurotic state (self-loathing in 71–72) invite close scrutiny of the speaker's motives, especially when progressively revealed in linked sonnets and when they provoke an implied response by the beloved.

Sonnets 33–35 treat the stages of a lover's response to having been deeply hurt by his beloved for some "sensual fault" committed with some "sweet thief." Sonnet 33 reveals the betrayal through an extended simile, establishing a correspondence between imperfect nature and an imperfect beloved. This awareness supposedly enables the speaker to accept his beloved's transgression: "Yet him for this my love no whit disdaineth; / suns of the world may stain when heaven's sun staineth."

That the speaker's effort to rationalize this experience cannot hold against the more powerful need to accuse is evident in the opening to 34: "Why didst thou promise such a beauteous day." The content of the three quatrains show his pain to be irremediable: the repentant beloved's return and admission of shame are inadequate. His pride will not allow forgiveness. The "wound" might be "salved" but the disgrace is not cured. Yet, in the couplet we learn that the beloved has begun to weep, and this act satisfies the speaker: "Ah, but those tears are pearls which thy love sheeds, / And they are rich and ransom all ill deeds." But we know that the beloved's tears have not been prompted by love, as the speaker claims, but by his own verbal assault, ending in line 12 with an allusion to himself as a type of Christ (and by extension, his beloved as a whorish Magdalene whose sorrow and repentance are not enough). When he has emotionally broken his "beloved" adversary, he may become magnanimous in forgiveness.

Sonnet 35 reveals that forgiveness will be a long time in coming, if ever, for after rehearsing the idea that all things in nature are imperfect, including the speaker, it turns out that his "fault" lies in attempting through reason to forgive the beloved: "For to thy sensual fault I bring in sense." He is, therefore, "an accessory" to that third party who "robs" from him. More importantly, in his seemingly objective but self-righteous stance, he is far from self-knowledge. The situational unit remains open-ended. The wound is not healed, the beloved's tears have not been "rich" enough to "ransom all ill deeds." In listening to the speaker's analysis of their situation, we know that the attack goes on.

Sonnets 71–74 are linked by the subject of the speaker's projected death and although the famous sonnet 73 can stand alone as an elegant direct statement of the speaker's confidence in his beloved's commitment to him, it takes on far different significance when viewed as a stage in his psychological movement from open self-abasement in 71–72 to pretended confidence in 73–74. Ostensibly, 71 is a strong statement (unbelievably so?) of the speaker's love. He wishes to be forgotten upon his death if remembrance should bring pain to his beloved and so that his beloved will not have to suffer the mockery of others for having loved one so unworthy. Apart from the contradiction in 71 wherein two references are made to reading the sonnet in the future (lines 5–6 and 9–10), the speaker's attitude to the world (it is "vile") and the description of his death in grotesque terms (he will be dwelling "with vilest worms" and his body will be "compounded. . . . with clay") alert us to the possibility of unconscious motives. Further, 72 develops the theme of his unworthiness to such a degree that it is easier to posit other motives rather than to accept the sonnet as a literal statement of love; that is, we more readily understand that he is calling for reassurance, for a *denial* of his worthlessness, a request for evidence of his value, a plea for loving treatment, and perhaps a plea never to be forgotten (or a statement to that effect).

The application of the repeated thought in the three quatrains of 73 (that the speaker is in the last stage of his life) is not revealed until the couplet in this typically Shakespearean construction. The sonnet is a compliment to the wisdom of the beloved and an assertion of the speaker's awareness that he is well loved:

> This [that I am nearing the end] thou perceivest
> which makes thy love more strong,
> To love that well which thou must leave ere long.

As in 34 where 12 lines of blame evoke tears from the beloved, allowing the speaker to be magnanimous in forgiveness, so between 72 and 73 has occurred an implied response. Reassured of his beloved's commitment after 72, he can now write easily and beautifully about impending death, credit his beloved with the wisdom that he, himself, has so emphatically induced, and even affirm the strength of that love.

The tone of the opening of 74, "But be contented" (remarkably like the opening of 35, "No more be grieved"), is seemingly a continued statement of confidence in his beloved's commitment. Having evoked a positive response, he may write with seeming equanimity about his death, reverse his opinion about the value of his verse (from "I am shamed by that which I bring forth" in 71 to "The very part was consecrate to thee"), and find consolation in equating his spirit (his essential self) with his poetry. Yet just as the speaker in 35 is unable to forgive his unfaithful friend after he has ostensibly done so in 34, the provocation of the beloved continues. Death is still "that fell arrest / Without all bail" and his body will be "the prey of worms," a direct linkage to 71. We may suppose that no response from the beloved can be adequate to the psychological necessity which prompted his motives in the first place.

In these linked sonnets Shakespeare, the conscious artist, presents a speaker who, through rhetorical indirections unconsciously reveals to us more than he knows. Unprecedented in English poetry, these miniature mono-dramas reach a degree of psychological subtlety rivalled only by the characterizations in his own plays.

—Frank Fabry

SONNETS FROM THE PORTUGUESE.
Poems by Elizabeth Barrett Browning, 1850.

During her courtship by Robert Browning in 1845–6 Elizabeth Barrett wrote a sequence of 44 love poems. They were not initially intended for publication and she was reticent even to show them to him, yet when she presented the poems to him in 1849, it was he who insisted on their publication in her *Poems* of 1850, suggesting the title *Sonnets from the Portuguese* partly to disguise their personal nature.

With hindsight, the private character of the *Sonnets* is clearly discernible. Indeed there are moments when the specificity of reference becomes embarrassing, as in the opening line of sonnet XXXIII: "Yes, call me by my pet name!" Despite this, however, the work rewards critical attention, for the poet writes about love from a series of perspectives which subvert the conventional fixities of social and poetic mores. In adopting the form of the Petrarchan sonnet she entered that established tradition of amatory poetry in which, ordinarily, a male speaker addresses a silent and absent female other. Yet Browning's treatment of the relationship between the self and the beloved departs significantly from conventional formulae. The characteristic stasis of courtly love-poetry is replaced by a series of protean shifts as the speaker, and her addressee, are represented in a constantly mobile relation.

Browning's speaker is at times positioned in the standard pose of humble minstrel, a "wandering singer" whose status is lowly beside the "princely" other. This gesture of subordination, however, can collapse into an historically typical self-effacement when the singer appears to lose the will to perform. In sonnet II she locates herself in the feminine position of one who listens rather than expostulates and in the 13th she pleads with her lover to allow the "silence of . . . womanhood" to act as proof of her feeling. If such reticence suggests an adherence to Victorian constructions of femininity, so too does the censoring of physical response that occurs in sonnet XIII.

Juxtaposed with this, however, runs another impulse that articulates and registers emphatically the speaker's right to address. "*I love thee* . . . mark! . . . *I love thee*" (sonnet X). Such exclamatory confidence is complemented on other occasions when the other is unequivocally commanded and instructed. In the 14th sonnet, the speaker refuses to become the simultaneously exalted and subordinate object of patriarchal construction. "Do not say / 'I love her for her smile—her look—her way / Of speaking gently,—for a trick of thought / That falls in well with mine,'." In place of this, she recommends the abstract concept of love "for love's sake only," gesturing towards the possibility of equality in sexual relations—a desire that also emerges in the representation of ungendered souls in sonnet XXII.

The speaker is neither consistently passive nor persistently active and the other is similarly unstable. Although he acts as a muse, he is also a poet, with a poet's need for inspirational aid, and the speaker frequently expresses her willingness to transform herself from writer to muse for his benefit. Such interchangeability upsets the traditional structure of amatory verse, as both parties become lovers and loved ones.

The speaker's unorthodox recognition of the other as an autonomous being alerts her to the dangers of her own narcissistic desire. In sonnet XXIX, she appeals to her lover to "Renew thy presence," keenly sensitive that her fantasised projections potentially overwhelm and obscure him. Such trans-subjective awareness also predisposes the speaker to view *herself* as an object. She describes the effect that the turbulence of emotional commitment has on her physical appearance in sonnet XII, where "this very love . . . when rising up from breast to brow, / Doth crown me with a ruby large enow / To draw men's eyes." If this designates a particularly feminine self-awareness, so too does the portrayal of the self as an ageing woman who does not conform to culturally prescribed standards of beauty (sonnet XVIII). These representations add a further dimension to the poems, as the speaker views herself as the object of another's perceptions. Hence the speaker's attitude is complex. Self-deprecation jostles against proud affirmation, melancholy runs hand in hand with joy.

The opening line of the penultimate and best-known sonnet, "How do I love thee? Let me count the ways" might be seen as central to the sequence as a whole. For it is precisely these "ways," or multiple possibilities, within the love-relationship that constitutes Browning's achievement in *Sonnets from the Portuguese*. The fact that the poems were not originally intended for a public readership allowed her to explore with an unusual honesty "how" she loved and such an enabling freedom incurred the revision of a long-standing poetic tradition. In the best of the Sonnets the poet neither simply conforms to nor straightforwardly resists conventional figurings of subject/object, female/male relations. Rather, she destabilises them, depriving any one amatory structure of absolute or final authority.

—Kathryn Burlinson

SONS AND LOVERS.
Novel by D.H. Lawrence, 1913.

D.H. Lawrence's first and most conventional novel, *Sons and Lovers*, is already the work of an accomplished writer. Grounded in the novelist's autobiography, it is in the fullest sense a sentimental education. Unlike his other works, this novel has a fully integrated plot, relatively little sermonizing, and characters with firm flesh over their analogized bones. If they stand for something, as Lawrence's characters always do, we are not told what. On the other hand, many of the qualities we have learned to associate with this writer are already present: the lavish descriptions of natural phenomena; the use of epic tags as a powerful rhythmic device to establish the resonances of the personae; the erotic thrust of the language; the tendency to refresh images by inverting their conventional charge; the quirky psychology; and the nervous episodic shifts. Add to this the writer's occasionally embarrassing use of naive hyperbole.

Most striking is Lawrence's use of the double or interlace plot so reminiscent of Tolstoy's *Anna Karenina*, though here the pattern is far less mechanical than it is elsewhere. The novel's basic plot line concerns the powerful oedipal attachment developed by Paul Morel's clever, sensitive, frustrated mother, a coal miner's wife tied to a coarse, strong-willed, and occasionally brutal man. A major strand relates to the story of that marriage and her attempts to achieve fulfillment through, first one, and then a second son. Significantly, the novel begins with a full treatment of the pre-Paul experience, her courtship and early disillusionment, the nurturing of her first two children in the dingy miner's house and the devolution of Morel into what is too readily perceived to be a drunken brute. Lawrence is too subtle to indulge in crude typing here. Both the disappointed wife and her husband emerge as complex figures at once internally consistent and capable of surprising shifts in mood and behavior. Her story dominates, however, delineating among other things her efforts to raise her children above the life imposed by the miners' existence.

The mother's life is poised against the well-articulated maturation or *Bildung*, of her physically fragile and sensitive second son, Paul. It is this boy who, after the death of his brother William, captures his mother's imagination and becomes the focus for her affections and ambitions. The novel recounts how the boy gradually extricates himself from his engagement with her. To accomplish this Lawrence resorts to a complex shifting perspective, brief scenes, and frequent bald statements of attitude. This enables him to give appropriate time and the right valence to each of the many protagonists and, more importantly, to phase out the mother as the center of Paul's creative and amorous life.

Anything but reticent, Lawrence combines the flat statement of emotion and attitude with a vividly impressionistic system of reactive prose vignettes. Thus we have the astonishing moments of affinity through nature which characterize some of the more vivid scenes: e.g., Paul's communion with his mother over some flowers and the painful botanical encounters with his first girl, Miriam. Though generally grounded in physical circumstances, the action of this "psychological" fiction is detailed with extraordinary clarity and mood-making precision. It is developed precisely through personal encounters that tend to be highly formulaic, conveyed through the reciprocal awareness of two dueling or communing characters: "[Miriam] suddenly became aware of his keen blue eyes upon her, taking her all in. Instantly her broken boots and her frayed old frock hurt her." If, on occasion, this laying bare of nerve endings grates, in the long run, the novel succeeds because it records not only minute shifts in the mood of its personae but also because, by locating the action on the level of human interactions, it traces the vicissitudes and motivates the development of Paul's spirit. Only Tolstoy has been willing and able to do this on so broad a scale, though Tolstoy is capable of more objectivity than Lawrence.

If at times we may feel that less would be more (as it is in Joyce's *Portrait of the Artist*), we may still find Lawrence's slow accretion of poignant detail and his rhythmic reiteration of personality and physical traits effective. Furthermore, the short scenes enable the writer not only to shift mood and pace, but also to move from emotional intensity to analysis. What makes this tale of a man and three women convincing and engrossing is undoubtedly Lawrence's ability to convince us that shadings of attitude, the minimal signals to which characters respond, are indeed important. Lawrence make us sensitive to the impact of casual remarks, glances, gestures, their capacity to signal turning points in a relationship.

Ultimately it is the anti-oedipal thread wound by Mrs. Morel's two younger rivals that saves Paul, that and his mother's pathetic death. In Miriam, he finds a generous but unsatisfactory surrogate, a young woman willing to sacrifice herself on the altar of his sensibility. This is the rival his mother forcefully rejects. By contrast, the older and more self-reliant Clara Dawes, for whom Paul must battle the brutal Dawes, defines Paul's sexual and emotional freedom without challenging his mother's role. Together, these women set him on the road to the "faintly humming glowing town" of his maturity.

Paul's relationships are all tense and experimental, and though he is clearly the focus of much of the action, neither he nor any of the women is unambiguously admirable or even completely adequate to the moment. It is to this excruciating balance of tensions set against the everyday world of a working-class family that *Sons and Lovers* owes its success, to this and to its meticulously honest and painfully engaging chronicle of Paul's identity crisis.

—David Hayman

THE SPANISH TRAGEDY.
Play by Thomas Kyd, 1589(?).

Published in 1592, *The Spanish Tragedy* was not only one of the most popular Elizabethan plays, appearing in nine editions between 1592 and 1633, but it also was translated and performed widely on the continent. In what is recognized as the first English revenge tragedy, Thomas Kyd established many motifs which became the conventions of later revenge tragedies by Shakespeare, Marston, Tourneur, and Chapman. Kyd's revenge devices include the appearance of a Senecan ghost, interlocking revenge schemes, bloody and violent action, the descent of the revenger-hero into a world of moral darkness and seeming madness, and the accomplishment of revenge within a play-within-a-play.

Kyd creates a playworld informed by four interlocking revenge schemes of the Ghost of Andrea, Horatio, Bel-imperia, and Hieronimo. Andrea, Bel-imperia's secret lover, has been killed dishonorably by Balthazar in the battle with Portugal and now has returned with Revenge from the underworld to watch the earthly play unfold. His friend Horatio, who has captured the Portuguese Prince Balthazar, becomes Bel-imperia's lover, but is murdered by her brother Lorenzo, who wants Balthazar to marry his sister. After his son Horatio's death, Lord Marshal Hieronimo attempts to learn the identities of his son's killers but is prevented from doing so by the power and schemes of the Machiavellian Lorenzo. Nevertheless, through a series of epistolary revelations, he does discover the truth; however, after being unable to obtain legal redress, he becomes a private revenger who kills Balthazar and Lorenzo in the violent play-within-the-play which he creates ostensibly to celebrate the marriage of Bel-imperia and Balthazar.

Generally speaking, *The Spanish Tragedy* has been viewed as a blood revenge tragedy which has little, if any, relationship to the contemporary political situation. However, within the past two decades, critics have argued that *The Spanish Tragedy* contains a political subtext involving the Anglo-Iberian rivalry of the 1580's which culminated in the defeat of the Spanish Armada in 1588. Kyd informs his audience that the play contains a hidden level of meaning by defining it as a mystery in three places. At the outset of the earthly play, Revenge invites Andrea and the audience to "sit . . . down to see the mystery." After Hieronimo's historical masque, the Spanish King asks him to explain its "mystery" of the Hymen dumb show. In these contexts, Kyd refers to plays-within-the-play as mysteries; by analogy *The Spanish Tragedy* is a mystery, that is, a work with secret meanings.

The play's dialogue and action are built on a pattern of secrecy-revelation as Hieronimo, the official justice figure and bereaved father, becomes a quasi-detective searching for the identity of his son's killers, who try to conceal their crime. However, once Hieronimo learns the truth and decides to pursue revenge, he conceals his plans from his intended victims. After he kills them in the "Soliman-Perseda" playlet, he further refuses to reveal everything to his captors in allegiance to "The thing which I have vow'd inviolate." Hieronimo's silence, which he ensures by committing suicide, is a final secret which prompts the audience to go beyond its assertion of concealment to discover the meaning of the mystery.

The title of the play gives one indication of its political subtext. The play concerns the Spanish tragedy, the fall of Catholic Spain, and concomitantly the English comedy, the rise of Protestant England. This subtext is established symbolically in Hieronimo's two plays-within-the-play. At the celebratory banquet, Hieronimo presents an historical masque ostensibly in honor of Spain's recent victory over Portugal, but each of the three scenes presents past battles in which little England defeated the Iberian countries. The onstage Iberian audiences interpret Hieronimo's presentation to suit their current situation, neglecting to realize that England is being celebrated. However, the theater audience is meant to recognize Hieronimo's—and Kyd's—exaltation of England over Iberia.

The political mystery of the historical masque foreshadows Hieronimo's climactic courtly presentation, the revenge playlet in which he kills the Iberian heirs Balthazar and Lorenzo and causes the fall of Babylon-Spain. Hieronimo's final murder of the King of Spain's brother, the Duke of Castile, is not decisive proof that he has descended into homicidal madness but a symbolic strike against the representative of Spain's most powerful province and King Philip II, who was known as the Castilian king. Thus, Hieronimo is not an insane private revenger, as some critics have maintained; rather, he serves as the symbolic representative of the English people, the bearer of the sacred name, *hieros nym*, the hierophantic figure who conducts the mystery ritual of Spain's demise.

Like Aeneas in the sixth book of the *Aeneid*, Andrea rises from his descent into the underworld to witness, along with the theater audience, the historical process leading to the destined defeat of one empire—Spain—and the rise of another—England under Queen Elizabeth, the embodiment of wise rule (Bel-imperia). Recognition of the Anglo-Iberian political subtext helps us to understand that the play's Elizabethan popularity was due not only to its sensationalist qualities but also to its role as the nationalistic celebration of Spain's tragedy and England's comedy.

—Frank Ardolino

THE SPECTATOR. See **THE TATLER.**

SPELT FROM SIBYL'S LEAVES.
Poem by Gerard Manley Hopkins, written 1884.

Gerard Manley Hopkins described this sonnet, in Italian or Petrarchan rhyme with eight stresses to the line (sprung rhythm), as "the longest sonnet ever made," adding that it was intended to be read not with the eye but aloud, "with long rests, long dwells on the rhyme and other marked syllables." The winter of 1884–85 when Hopkins began this sonnet was a period of intense inner turmoil and desolation for him. His poem is bleakly despairing; the oncoming night in the natural world is an emblem of death, both physical and spiritual. All the colors, all the patterns of the world, are merged and terrifyingly reduced to black-white, right-wrong. The reader could appropriately find specific religious imagery of the Last Judgment and Hell in the climactic crisis of the last lines. But because the meanings of the words move in so many directions simultaneously, the sonnet alternatively might describe any neurotically sensitized mind recoiling with horror from incipient madness.

The poem's title suggests the Sibyl at Cumae, a priestess of antiquity who was consulted for advice in worldly or spiritual affairs, as Aeneas did in Book VI of the *Aeneid*. Even in the early Christian church the oracle's status approached that of the biblical prophets; the "Dies Irae" is an ancient hymn in which the Sibyl warns of the Last Judgment. The Cumaean Sibyl usually shuffled palm leaves, on each of which an oracle was written, choosing some at random; alternatively a priestess might write the Sibyl's response to the question on leaves that then were blown out of her cave. Either way, the readings of the leaves could be fearfully ambiguous.

As Hopkins's sonnet begins, the poet has taken the disordered impressions of twilight (the seven initial words that only in the second line are found to modify "evening") and arranged them like palm leaves in order to spell (discover) their significance. Each word acquires from its predecessor and passes onto its successor particular sounds, creating phonetically a sense of gradual change in the evening's progression toward night. "Earnest" should be interpreted as meaning a token of what is to come; "attuneable," meaning to harmonize or blend, also intimates the awesome compression of nature at sundown observed by the poet. As time's womb, home, and hearse of all things, evening is quintessential temporality, encompassing birth, life, and death. It has been observed that Hopkins steers clear of the more obvious word-choice of "tomb," perhaps because the internal rhyme would be a cliché or perhaps because had he used it rather than "hearse," he would have destroyed the special effect of the vowel progression from the open sound of "womb" to the less open "home," to the closed "e" of "hearse"—a tightening vowel order that doubles the day's manifold forms fusing into the single black chariot of death. The near-homophones for the sun ("hornlight," which suggests the horn sides of an old "lanthorn" lantern) and the moon ("hoarlight," frosty white light) together with the gradual appearance of the stars complete the imagery for the encroaching night.

As the distinctions of the dappled day are obliterated, so whole syllables disappear out of words, altering the meaning in significant ways: "earliest stars" becomes "earl stars" (from the Old English, rising-stars); "disremembering" (Irish for "forgetting") becomes the grisly "dismembering"; "reckon but" becomes "reck but." Hopkins uses the dialectical "throughther" (each through the other) to suggest the obliteration of dappled day by the darkening evening. The despair implied by this event is clear to any reader of Hopkins who recalls the opening of "Pied Beauty": "Glory be to God for dappled things," the "dapple-dawn-drawn Falcon" of "The Windhover," and similar joyous celebrations of the multicolored splendor of the daylight world. Hopkins's heart will "round" or whisper to him a warning: night engulfs totally. Only the black on black of dragon-devil leaves that "damask" or ornament the sky remain as light fades.

The cry to the oracle for the tale or prophecy produces the enigmatic image of life as a kind of yarn or thread (recalling the classical Fates spinning, measuring, and cutting the thread of life), once in all its "variety" now being wound off onto only two spools, one black and one white. The oracle has cruelly divined this bipolar alternative to the variety of day and the sameness that night imposes on all things. The imagery segues from the yarn to sheep (from which the yarn may have come) being parted, penned, and packed into two flocks or folds, perhaps calling to mind here the Christian version of the Last Judgment where the sinners are separated from the righteous. "Ware" means to be aware of and to beware of this final division that will tell off—i.e., number and set apart—the manifold diversity of humanity. Or, darker yet, perhaps this is a universe without salvation (at least for the poet) where neither black-white or right-wrong offers relief, but both together become "a rack / Where, selfwrung, selfstrung, sheathe- and shelterless, thóughts agaínst thoughts ín groans grínd." The terror here is that of a mind condemned entirely to its own emotions, nakedly racked upon its own notions of right-wrong. Hopkins's friend and first editor, Robert Bridges, could not understand the presence of the "e" that would have produced "sheatheless" and omitted it, but Hopkins preferred verb to noun and intended the modifier to convey a verbal restlessness. The natural rhythm of the phrase would be "Thóughts a̽gai̽nst thóughts i̽n gróans grínd." But Hopkins wanted the stress to fall on "against," emphasizing the friction. Here Hopkins's imposed rhythm, "Thóughts a̽gaínst tho̽ughts ín gro̽ans grínd," strains against the natural rhythm, creating through utterance an almost physical feeling of tension and anguish that lexical meaning alone could not have produced. Not since John Milton had English literature produced sonnets of such vocal power.

—Gerald Monsman

THE SPOILS OF POYNTON.
Novella by Henry James, 1897.

The Spoils of Poynton began as a short story and turned into a novella as Henry James wrestled with his material. The evolution of the book is extensively documented in the author's *Notebooks* and in the preface he wrote for the New York edition of 1906, and makes a fascinating case-study of the way in which James elaborated his subtlest stories from the detailed working of chance vignettes.

The novella was a favourite form for James, and this is an especially fine example, its limitations compelling him to focus with maximum clarity on the relationship between the four central characters; while plot, character, and settings show a remarkable unity of purpose. Like all James's novellas, the book is a comedy of manners which darkens to near-tragedy without ever losing its light touch or disturbing the glittering witty surface. *The Spoils of Poynton* is also about ideas without in any sense being cerebral; for the ideas are perfectly embodied in the persons and places of the drama.

The apparent core of the story is the struggle between the widowed Mrs. Gereth and her son's fiancée for possession of a country house and its treasures; but as always in James, the real struggle is a moral and spiritual matter which involves each of the characters in their deepest nature. The spoils of the punning title are the occasion for a conflict of values and temperaments hinting at a whole series of Jamesian themes: the relationship of life to art, the battle between the sexes, the clash of cultures, failures of insight and successes of understanding, and the nature of love.

When the stolid, handsome Owen Gereth decides to marry, English laws of inheritance decree that his mother must leave the family home and the magnificent contents she has herself collected. Passionately attached to her treasures, which she cannot bear to abandon to the philistine Mona Brigstocke, she spirits them away to her new house and refuses to give them up. But Mona is equally determined and, although the articles themselves are of no interest to her, she declines to marry Owen until they are restored to the house.

Negotiating to this end with his mother's sensitive and perceptive young friend Fleda Vetch, Owen somewhat improbably falls in love with her, thereby forging the only weak link in the plot chain through the common Jamesian combination of a beautiful, simple, young man and an intelligent woman. But Fleda will not accept Owen until Mona releases him. Anxious to promote the match, Mrs. Gereth returns her spoils to Poynton just too soon, thereby giving Mona the chance to enforce her contract with Owen. Returning for a last visit to Poynton to choose a keepsake offered by the now married Owen, Fleda finds the house burnt to the ground.

As this brief summary makes clear, both the plot and the deeper meaning of the book turn on notions of property and possession. The aptly named Owen *owns* the treasures of Poynton but they really *belong* to his mother who collected them, and to Fleda who understands both the treasures and the spirit which can rightly value them. Indeed, she is finally seen to have an even better claim to Poynton than Mrs. Gereth herself; for Owen's mother, like his fiancée, uses the objects for her own selfish ends. Her lack of aesthetic detachment is a sign of ethical failure. The moral of the story, as so often in James, is that true ownership paradoxically involves renunciation. Only Fleda is able to achieve this. Just as she appreciates the treasures of Poynton without possessing them, so she gives up Owen, whom she truly values more than Mona ever could.

By falling in love with Fleda, Owen shows that he too has some claim not only on the treasures of Poynton but on the far greater prize of human happiness—until Mona devastatingly enforces her own claims, demonstrating that she "owns" Owen by compelling him to honour his promise of marriage. In the end, however, her very triumph is a failure—as the burning of the house signifies, for the things are only a metaphor for the spiritual possession and self-possession which the magnificently physical Mona lacks. To possess something is not to own or to use it but to understand it.

As in three contemporary stories—*In the Cage*, *What Maisie Knew*, and *The Awkward Age*—the action is seen mainly through the eyes of the suffering heroine. From the outset in all three of the stories James emphasises the contrast between the meagreness of the protagonist's material life and her rich inner world, foreshadowing the great dramas of consciousness which appeared in the following decade.

But if these works look forward to *The Golden Bowl*, *The Wings of the Dove*, and *The Ambassadors*, they also look back to James's disastrous recent experiments in the theatre. The sharpness of dialogue, the sense of drama, and—above all—the evolution of his celebrated "scenic method," all point to the experience of writing for the stage. In this respect, *The Spoils of Poynton* is not only a fine work in itself but an important stage in the novelist's development.

—Peter Washington

THE STONES OF VENICE.
Prose by John Ruskin, 1851–53.

The Stones of Venice is essentially a handbook to architecture in general, Venice itself only the excuse. John Ruskin begins with a sketch of Venetian history insisting that this will assist in understanding its architecture. Symptomatic of the growth of historical understanding in the 19th century, Ruskin's insistence is ahead of its time, suggesting the neohistoricist movement of recent years. Most remarkable is his use of the architecture to contribute to the understanding of the history, something modern scholars of the arts are only now learning to do.

There follows an explanation of the basic elements of architecture, from foundation to cornice. Each part is described in its most basic form, that adapted to use. Whatever we may feel about Ruskin's preferences and moral stance, there is still a great deal to be learnt about architecture from this discussion. Ruskin next considers decoration. The point of decoration is to cover and fill the building with all that most delights man; and what most delights man are the works of God. The works of man are almost always inappropriate subjects for decoration. Thus foliation of fenestration (a Gothic decoration) is beautiful both because it is derived from the leaf-shape and is structural in origin, the cusp strengthening the rounded and pointed arches.

Ruskin favours Gothic architecture: if Egyptian is the most sublime and Greek the most pure, Gothic is the most rational because capable of adaptation to all uses without surrendering its essential nature. This is one principle of Ruskin's approach: that architecture is not beautiful, is more or less vulgar or irrational, whose design is not derived from use. *The Stones of Venice* has been not inaccurately described as a defence of the Gothic style.

Examples from Venetian architecture have been constant reference points. But Ruskin next examines some of the great landmarks themselves. (The chapter on St. Mark's is perhaps the best example.) Ruskin's famous word-painting comes into its own in his reading of individual buildings. Its aim is to give in a different medium something resembling the experience of looking at and walking in, for example, St. Mark's.

Chapter 6 of volume 2, "The Nature of the Gothic," gives the best introduction to the whole work. The chapter's aim is precise: to give a definition of Gothic such that the reader may at once recognise Gothic building. The definition is derived from extensive analysis: "*Foliated* Architecture, which uses the pointed arch for the roof proper, and the gable for the roof-mask." But there is more in the nature of the Gothic than technical definitions. As with all architecture it has a moral nature and this affects those who look at (or read, as Ruskin often puts it) the building, as well as the architect, his builders, and craftsmen; it also expresses the moral nature of the builder's culture. Gothic architecture, taking but one facet, expresses the happy freedom of its craftsmen. The Greeks regulated the designs which junior masons could execute; each mason executed those decorations entrusted to him by rote and under close supervision. This led to great purity of work, but it made a slave of the workman. The Gothic craftsman was given great freedom of execution. This lowered the quality of the work, since not all workmen were equally skilled; but it made of the workman an artist, expressing his grief or his joy as best he might: expressing, that is to say, above all his freedom. It is the happy freedom of the builders and craftsmen which is expressed so powerfully in the variety of Gothic architecture (one of its hallmarks), and particularly in its decoration. This happy state of affairs forms a powerful criticism of the 19th century, where a vast proportion of the population stood doing work by rote 10 or more hours a day in appalling conditions. There is a lengthy disquisition on the evils of such an economy, and a suggestion that these evils might be exorcised if a few principles were followed: that physical exercise should always be useful (as opposed to the useless forms pursued by the upper classes) thereby allowing more people more leisure; that except for the absolutely essential, nothing should be manufactured which does not bestow freedom and hence pleasure in the making (the making of glass beads is therefore condemned). Such ideas, developed in other works, have had an important influence on labour movements this century. The moral nature of architecture grows from its design, and Ruskin constantly steps aside from a technical discussion, as here, to elucidate the inner nature of the architecture, or the particular building in question. Not all of the moral ideas are economic. Take this from the conclusion of "St. Mark's": "through century after century of gathering vanity and festering guilt, that white dome of St. Mark's had uttered in the dead ear of Venice, 'Know thou, that for all these things God will bring thee into judgement.' "

The Stones of Venice is incomparably more rich than a summary can indicate; and not the least of its wealth is its poetry. The technical discussions are surrounded by meditations, word pictures, scenes from history and contemporary Venetian life, beautiful images, and perhaps above all always the sea washing the stones of Venice as they rise, fall, and stand neglected:

> Far as the eye can reach, a waste of wild sea moor, of a lurid ashen grey; not like our northern moors with their jet-black pools and purple heath, but lifeless, the colour of sackcloth, with the corrupted sea-water soaking through the roots of its acrid weeds, and gleaming hither and thither through its snaky channels. No gathering of fantastic mists, nor coursing of clouds across it; but melancholy clearness of space in the warm sunset, oppressive . . .
> [To the south] beyond the widening branches of the lagoon, and rising out of the bright lake into which they gather, there are a multitude of towers, dark, and scattered among square-set shapes of clustered palaces, a long and irregular line fretting the southern sky.
> Mother and daughter, you behold them both in their widowhood,—Torcello and Venice.

—J.B. Lethbridge

THE STORY OF AN AFRICAN FARM.
Novel by Olive Schreiner, 1883.

Olive Schreiner's novel *The Story of an African Farm* has attracted the respectful attention of many critics and writers, ranging from Mark Twain to John Berryman. The book is undeniably evocative. In a way the setting on a desolate African farm is crucial to the sense of isolation and to the novel's great emphasis on characterization and on descriptions of nature. Moreover, because several characters grow to reach maturity, and some die relatively early, the reader gains a sense that the farm itself endures and remains as a formative force, ready to stunt or twist whoever lives there next. Schreiner's most famous work can be understood as an example of late 19th-century naturalistic, environmental determinism.

The novel is strong on setting, characterization, irony, imagery, and multiple points of view, though it includes a good deal of adolescent philosophical, poetic, and mystical theorizing. In addition, there is a strong element of feminism in the book, and much attention to women's rights. The characters include a heavy-set Boer woman, Tant' Sannie, a religious, coarse, frequently insensitive woman who married three times and, most importantly, survives. A much more likable character is the naive, equally religious but easily satisfied, kindly widower, Uncle Otto, a German who runs the farm until shortly before his death. His son Waldo, a talented, perceptive, religiously tormented young man, suffers severely from the limited, restrictive environment. Two young girls of opposite character grow to maturity on the farm. Em is practical, non-philosophical, considerate, and thinks of herself as ordinary or mediocre. In contrast, Lyndall is delicate in feature, philosophical, deliberately arch, and willful.

Over time a series of would-be suitors arrive and depart. Bonaparte Blivens, a comical but selfish and deceitful Irishman woos Tant' Sannie and exploits Uncle Otto. In one of the novel's many memorable scenes Bonaparte reveals his vicious nature when he beats Waldo. The children learn their own powerlessness. But later Tant' Sannie catches Bonaparte also wooing her niece. His presence adds some memorable comedy and irony to the novel. Most readers react with great satisfaction when this self-important scoundrel is sent away. Gregory Rose and a mysterious stranger also have complicated courtships as the girls mature.

The characters are sketched so vividly, so concretely, that most readers will remain attentive when the farm's isolation or the descriptions of nature lead a character to some philosophical or mystical musing. Clearly the young children's attempts to think through the demands of conventional religion are touching; the children are stunted and controlled by these restrictions. The novel combines several haunting, evocative descriptions of nature with many explorations of each character's own point of view as the omniscient third-person narrator presents different characters' thoughts. Many of the philosophical musings on religion, life, death, sexual roles, and the purpose of life may have seemed profound to Schreiner, who was only 20 when she began to work on the isolated Fouche farm, Klein Ganna Hoek, in the Cape Colony. She worked on the novel in several locations, from 1875 to 1880, and first published the book under the name Ralph Iron.

The careful modern reader may decide to overlook the pervasive racism and simply appreciate the artful use of bird imagery (hens, chickens, and ostriches) or the strong feminist point of view. Schreiner also uses poetic and thematic juxtapositions of characters and chapters quite skillfully to convey her memorable story of growth, individualization, death, and endurance.

—Victor A. Doyno

STRANGE MEETING.
Poem by Wilfred Owen, written 1918.

When Wilfed Owen's "Strange Meeting" was first published (in the modernist anthology, *Wheels*, 1919), John Middleton Murry described it as "the most magnificent expression of the emotional significance of the war that has yet been achieved by English poetry." Composed at Ripon in the spring of 1918, "Strange Meeting" almost certainly reflects the disaster on the Western Front on 21 March, when an immense German attack smashed through the British line. The onslaught had been foreseen; Owen himself had been sent to the training camp at Ripon earlier in the month to get fit for active service, after over a year in hospital or on home duties recovering from severe shell shock. There seemed no hope now either for peace or for his own survival.

"Strange Meeting" is intensely literary, a poet's testament, cast in the traditional form of a dream-poem. There are echoes of Dante, Spenser, the Bible, mythology, and above all the Romantics. The title comes from Shelley's *The Revolt of Islam*, the phrase "Strange friend" from Tennyson's *In Memoriam*, the cave and meeting from Keats's *Endymion* and *The Fall of Hyperion*, and the idea of killing with a look ("so you frowned / Yesterday through me as you jabbed and killed") from Wilde's "The Ballad of Reading Gaol." The "tunnel" has been cut by the first of all wars, the war of the Titans and the gods, and the image of sleepers in a cave is recurrent in classical and Arthurian myth. Another indication of the poem's literariness is its intricate play on sounds, especially its pararhyme, a device which Owen had been perfecting since the previous summer. The frustrating, melancholy effect of these rhymes is enhanced by the second word in each pair being lower in pitch: "friend / frowned," "killed / cold." But for all its conscious artistry, "Strange Meeting" is based on actual experience. Although Owen probably never killed a man with a bayonet (as an officer, he carried only a revolver), he had seen dying faces and dug-outs full of tormented soldiers; as he recorded in "The Sentry," these sights were the subjects of some of his worst shell shock nightmares.

The "strange meeting" is between two soldiers, the poet and an "other," who have met in battle the day before. Their previous encounter is re-enacted: the other parries the bayonet thrust and grimaces in the agony of death, but this time the raised arms seem like a blessing and the grimace becomes a smile of friendship. Both men recognise the truth by looking at each other: "I knew you in this dark: for so you frowned"; "By his dead smile I knew we stood in Hell." It was the killer's scowl of effort and hate which sent them both to Hell, for the evil of war lies not in weapons but in human impulses. The other reveals himself as another poet, although since he is described in draft work as "a German conscript" the once-current notion that he can be seen as Owen's double is perhaps misleading. Owen is not writing about himself alone but about the pity and truth of war in all ages (hence, too, his suppression of the word "German" and of all contemporary details). In any case, the other's pursuit of eternal Beauty seems less mature than his author's attitude in 1918; only a few weeks earlier Owen had written in his preface: "Above all I am not concerned with Poetry." Perhaps the strange friendship might have been like the one between Owen and his mentor in 1917, Siegfried Sassoon, this time with Owen as the senior partner. His early poetry is full not only of descents into Hell and visions of deathly faces, but also of longings for the perfect friend. Part of the other's speech is based on a Shelleyan exhortation which Owen seems to have written to Sassoon in December 1917, declaring that the two poets "will" stay out of the fighting until they are able to cleanse post-war society with water from the "deep wells" of truth. In "Strange Meeting," "will" becomes "would have"; the poets have killed each other, so the world will either "go content" with the wreckage left by war or "boil bloody" in revolution. This view of the future was derived from Sassoon's adviser, Bertrand Russell, whose wartime books contain similar prophecies. Nevertheless, Sassoon chose to return to the battlefield, and by March Owen knew he would have to follow. There would be no one to draw water from the wells. A great romantic ideal seems to end here, although the ever-growing influence of Owen's poems suggests that his "hopelessness" was not entirely justified.

The closing lines of "Strange Meeting" move from quasi-biblical elaborateness to slow, simple monosyllables. Having met in passionate recognition, the two men prepare to sleep. The poet had seemed to enter Hell alive, but the other's invitation ("Let us sleep now. . . . ") tells him, and us, that both of them are dead. There is no further escape, and their sleep will be "encumbered" with the memories and guilt of war.

—Dominic Hibberd

STRIFE.
Play by John Galsworthy, 1909.

The popular melodrama's treatment of social problems in the mid-19th-century paved the way for much more important attention to these problems in the realistic drama at the turn of the century. Although John Galsworthy's plays have received far fewer stagings in later years than Shaw's witty, more satiric or comic pieces focussing on social ills, they were equally important in their own era, moving their audiences to tears and awareness.

Strife, along with *Justice* and *The Silver Box*, established Galsworthy as a creator of powerful dramas about the sufferings of working-class or lower-middle-class people who somehow broke rules. Yet Galsworthy was not a spokesman for the socialism that so interested Shaw. Nor did he use the simple moral scheme of good versus evil that characterized the melodramas. His thieves and striking mill workers have unpleasant qualities, while his upper classes have one or two representatives who are sympathetic to the sufferings and try to help. Young Edgar Anthony, a director of the works, feels guilt and wants to negotiate a settlement. His father, who had built the company and had a long history of keeping the workers under control, is understandably intransigent. On the other side, the union has deemed the workers' demands too high and withdrawn support, creating a sense that the directors have some grounds for standing firm. David Roberts, the charismatic and single-minded leader of the strikers, is shocking but understandable in his refusal to let his wife accept any food or help from Enid Underwood, the sympathetic wife of the manager. Madge Thomas embodies the ambivalence Galsworthy created, refusing the attentions of one of Roberts's supporters because of the suffering the strike is causing, yet quickly lashing out at Enid in a show of solidarity in refusing any help.

The play builds to a final act heavy with irony. The audience knows the workers have voted against Roberts and given Harness, the union official, power to negotiate. Unaware of this, the directors overrule their chairman and also give Harness power. When Roberts bursts in, insisting on no compromise, he is unaware that neither side remains firm. Harness's "things have travelled past you" applies to both Roberts and old Anthony. The two gain grudging mutual respect from their common situation: "Both broken men." The ultimate irony and indictment of the intransigence that has made the strike drag into February is the realization that the terms are those Harness and the company secretary drew up in October.

Galsworthy achieved concentration and drive by observing the structural unities. During six hours on 7 February, in a Welsh border works town, directors and workers finally reverse stands they had taken four months earlier. Reading of the minutes, explanations, and arguments bring out essential facts and attitudes, and allow a focus on the climactic day. Enid mentions Anne Roberts's physical frailty well before she appears, so Anne's death seems more a catalyst than a melodramatic detail that overburdens the plot merely to cause a few tears. The Board has come from London for the day, and their meeting with the worker delegation provides direct contrast of clothing, manner, and accent.

Galsworthy uses realistic settings to heighten the contrast. Scenes in the cold, bare worker's cottage and muddy tinworks yard are sandwiched between the first and third acts set in the overheated, comfortably furnished manager's home. While directors call for a fire screen to reduce the heat, and enjoy a plentiful lunch, workers' wives keep their children in bed for warmth and to reduce appetites for meagre bread and tea. Anne Roberts dies of a heart condition by a dying fire while one director complains that he may miss a train and be prevented from taking his frail wife to Spain to escape winter.

To some extent Galsworthy uses devices of the well-made play, carefully motivating exits and entrances and tying up most loose ends. The closure is not complete, however, for Roberts and Anthony are left, one without a wife or worker support, the other without his life's work. Although he avoids a strict dualism of mean capitalists grinding down defenseless labour, Galsworthy comes closer to caricaturing the directors, particularly the complaining Wilder, than he does the workers. Concerns for profits and dividends seem less important than the immediate need for food and warmth, as audience sympathy is drawn from the combatants to the wives and children.

Strife is a naturalistic play. The stage directions are meticulous in describing the sets and costumes that create the atmosphere for dialogue and actions. The dialogue is carefully structured, often with fragmentary lines as people interrupt or hunt for words. Although old Thomas has a broad Welsh accent, there are other more subtle details. The valet shows his Cockney roots. Anne Roberts switches suddenly from give-and-take conversation with Madge Thomas to "Yes m'm" when Enid arrives, pointing up class distinctions.

Galsworthy was ahead of his time in dramatizing a strike in 1909, for the first great strike in Britain occurred in 1911. Much as *Justice* made people aware of the horrors of prison, *Strife* made many middle-class London theatre-goers aware of the increasing tensions between labour and capital, the growing role of unions as a negotiating force, and the suffering of families who have never been able to build up savings to tide them over a strike or lack of a job. The profit motive, symbolized by the money the Trenartha Tin Works has made from a process Roberts discovered, the loyalty of workers to their own trades, and the position of the works manager familiar with both sides are all brought out sharply. On a broader scale, the play is also an indictment of pride and intransigence, pointing up the tragedy and lack of gain where there is no compromise.

—Frances A. Shirley

SUBLIME AND BEAUTIFUL.
(*A Philosophical Enquiry into the Origin of Our Ideas of the Sublime and Beautiful.*)
Prose by Edmund Burke, 1757; revised edition, 1759.

In the preface to the first edition of the *Enquiry* (April 1757), Edmund Burke states that "it is four years now since this enquiry was finished," and in a letter to Edmund Malone, Burke states that he "was six or seven years employed on it"; thus the *Enquiry* seems to have been a time-consuming project for Burke, probably taking up the years 1747 to 1753. A major source for Burke's thinking was obviously the recent translation (1739) into English of Longinus's pervasively influential *Peri Hupsous* (*On the Sublime*), a work which reasserts the importance of poetic "inspiration" and emotional power in the creation of, *and* response to, art—these concepts seeming rather refreshingly at odds with the neoclassical emphasis on the "rules" of technical precision, rhetorical mastery, and aesthetic control. In spite of its controversial and innovative nature, however, Burke's *Enquiry* was favourably assessed in the *Literary*, *Critical*, and *Monthly Reviews* of 1757: he had indeed succeeded in troubling the stagnant waters of criticism (an aim he announces in his *Enquiry*); and while he argues in the introductory section, "Of Taste" (1759 edition), that taste is a quality of human artistic perception and understanding that can be developed and refined (*and* that it is a combination of sensation, knowledge, reasoning, and understanding—rather than a single inherent quality), the body of his *Enquiry* is concerned with an innovative treatment of the "sublime" and the "beautiful," their existence and effects in nature and in art.

While Longinus wrote of ways of achieving sublimity in poetry, Burke is more concerned with the aesthetic experience of the reader. In his concern with what can cause a subjective response that is sublime, Burke claims that "Whatever is fitted in any sort to excite the ideas of pain and danger, that is to say, whatever is in any sort terrible, or is conversant about terrible objects, or operates in a manner analogous to terror, is a source of the sublime; that is, it is productive of the strongest emotion which the mind is capable of feeling." Unpleasant stimuli and feelings are much more moving or compelling than pleasurable ones ("pain is stronger in its operation than pleasure"); but then the question arises as to why anyone would seek out these "sublime" sensations. Burke's answer points to the "medium" as well as the "message": what delights a reader or viewer of literature or art is that through artistic form a "certain distance" is interposed between the perceiver and the terrible object or scene being rendered. Even seemingly neutral scenes like huge mountain ranges and powerful rivers convey an impact of sublimity because the reader responds not only to their beauty but to their danger, immensity, and threatening power. Paradoxically, while the reader delights in his or her own actual "safety" he or she can also imaginatively be transposed into the scene with all its terror, power, and immensity.

In defining the "beautiful" Burke first attempts to dispose of major traditional theories: specifically, that beauty is "proportion," that it is reflective of Higher Causes, and that it is linked with moral goodness or perfection. Beauty is, Burke asserts initially, "some quality in bodies, acting mechanically upon the human mind by the intervention of the senses." This "sensationalist" approach shows clearly his epistemological indebtedness to the empirical, positivist theories of Locke, Hartley, and Hume; Burke wants to avoid the "vague and mysterious" deeper theorizing (often moral and / or religious) of other philosophers on the topic of beauty, and wants also to view the phenomenon in a more practical social context. He writes: "I call beauty a social quality; for where women and men [and] other animals give us a sense of joy and pleasure in beholding them . . . they inspire us with sentiments of tenderness and affection . . . ; we like to have them near us, and we enter willingly into a kind of relation with them. . . ." The same is true of natural objects and scenes: it is not so much that they have certain *inherent* qualities which define them as inherently beautiful; it is more that we as readers (or viewers) take certain attitudes toward these things—attitudes which make us strongly attracted to, and desirous of a relationship with, these things. Burke here moves from an ontological toward an existential conception of the quality of beauty: it truly *is* in the eye of the beholder.

Major writers and thinkers in Burke's time and after beheld his *Enquiry* as being of great importance. Samuel Johnson, not known for his patience with erudite philosphical discourse, said (in Boswell's *Life*) that in Burke's essay "we have an example of true criticism." Later, Burke's ideas were seen as looking forward to the Romantics, mainly Wordsworth and Coleridge, in their insistence that before poetry or art can be great it must evoke intense and relevant emotions: the Romantic requisite of "spontaneous overflow of powerful feelings" can be seen in embryo in Burke's *Enquiry*. Influence is discernible in a wide range of later writers as well: Thomas Hardy, Matthew Arnold, and Leslie Stephen in England, and on the continent Burke's impact was, as James T. Boulton has said, "immediate and forceful," particularly in the cases of Diderot, Lessing, and Kant. While discussions of sublimity had been around before the 1750's, Burke was the first to develop such discussions into a system—and this feat alone prompted Kant to say that Burke "deserves to be called the foremost author in this method of treatment." Also important when one reads the *Enquiry*, however, is the style in which it is written. Not only does the prose style have a gripping force and irresistible momentum, but Burke tries at many points to convey something of the aesthetic experience he is analyzing: he vividly illustrates his propositions from the Bible, the epic, and major literary moments, thus enabling the reader's self to *experience* as well as *learn*. As he provocatively states in his preface: "Whatever turns the soul inward on itself, tends to concenter its forces, and to fit it for greater and stronger flights of science."

—Richard Arnold

SUCH IS LIFE.
Fiction by Joseph Furphy, 1903.

Joseph Furphy's *Such Is Life* is a serio-comic work, not strictly speaking a novel, in seven episodes. The episodes were initially planned as a random selection from the compendious diary of the narrator, a Deputy-Assistant Sub-Inspector, whose bureaucratic duties send him to stations in the outback of New South Wales to fill out governmental forms. The episodic structure is calculated to represent a microcosmic view of life as a whole, as emphasized throughout by ending many situations, whether comic or tragic, with the expression "Such is life." The format is later changed from a random diary selection to entries for the ninth day of consecutive months (deviating only in the last chapter for the sake of character continuity).

Long-winded disquisitions on economics, democracy, gentlemen in fiction, and squatters (particularly ridiculing Henry Kingsley's trashy novel *Geoffry Hamlyn*); on the merits of Burke, leader of the ill-fated expedition; on the history of Protestantism and Catholicism in England and Orangeism in Ireland; and on philosophical queries of all sorts are juxtaposed throughout with the yarns and conversations of bullock drivers, squatters, boundary riders, and others, all related in realistic dialects and jargon, with the exception of the perpetual profanity which is only suggested in a self-conscious and affected way by substitute words and parenthetical descriptions to indicate "hell," "bloody," and "bugger." The style is altogether unique and appropriate to the form, for the most part entertaining and racy and only occasionally annoying in its affectations.

The first episode centers around a congregation of five bullock drivers, a down-and-out English younger son, and the narrator, formerly a freighter himself, all assembled for the purpose of "duffing" (stealing) grass from Runnymede's selection by jacking up the fence to let their livestock in. Tom Collins, the narrator, travels with a pack horse, a mare Fancy, and Pup, a ravenous kangaroo dog which never catches a kangaroo, but steals food from people's stores. Tom is tricked into trading his mare for a male called "Clayopathra," which turns out to be a bucker when first saddled each morning, but otherwise is a magnificent specimen which gallops "like *Marching through Georgia*." Much of the night is devoted to telling hard-luck yarns based on curses brought on by immoral acts, and to ridiculing Burke when the Englishman praises his merits. The morning brings frantic activity as the drivers collect their stock before the animals can be impounded.

The next chapter takes place one month later and one hundred miles to the north at Goolumbulla station, where the narrator renews his acquaintance with Dan O'Connell, a Catholic married to an Anglican wife. Dan is a man of unusual intellectual interests and retentiveness inhibited only by lack of opportunity. Tom meets the O'Connells' five-year-old daughter Mary, a perfect bush creature and Young-Australian, and finds a dead swagman under a wilga tree.

The third episode occurs on the Murray River, the border between Victoria and New South Wales. The inspector loses his clothes while attempting to cross the river, and goes away from his camp instead of toward it because of the sinuousness of the river at that point. The situation becomes increasingly hilarious as they recount his desperate efforts to obtain any sort of clothing.

The last four episodes are set once more to the north in New South Wales (the Riverina district) where new characters are introduced: Warrigal Alf (Alf Morris), a sick bullock driver; three boundary riders—an Englishman, a Chinaman, and a Scotsman; Stewart, a rich squatter; another yarn-telling congregation of bullock drivers, whose animals are this time impounded through the treachery of the Chinaman, Paul Sam Young; and the employees at Runnymede station—Mrs. Baudesart, a thrice-widowed housekeeper who has taken a fancy to Tom; Martin and Moriarty, manager and storekeeper respectively; Toby, a cheeky but efficient half-caste station hand; and Nosey Alf (Alf Jones), a cranky boundary rider with a disfigured face and characteristics suggestive of womanhood, and a great musical talent.

The pattern of the work is to reveal more details of characters previously introduced by means of the bush telegraph, word of mouth, snippets of information picked up along the road; the stories are sometimes shocking in their blunt conversational tone and sometimes intriguing in absence of our full knowledge of the facts. For example, in one of the yarning sessions on children lost in the bush, a freighter tells how Dan O'Connell's girl Mary, fearing that her daddy might die like the man under the wilga tree, runs out to seek him and is ultimately found dead in a bilby-hole. Also, Nosey Alf has gone to Queensland where Warrigal Alf had gone after he recovered from his illness, which suggests that Nosey was, in reality, Warrigal's lost wife. This technique is very like the manner in which life itself is revealed to us all by catching glimpses in passing. The generally light-hearted tone is maintained by Tom Collins assuming a different role throughout for each person whom he meets, sometimes to the extreme of using that person's own dialect. This aspect of *Such Is Life* is realistic, since we all "prepare a face for the faces that we meet."

Furphy contributed to the *Bulletin* for ten years before he submitted the voluminous manuscript which was edited into this book and two other works. Although Cecil Hadgraft (*Australian Literature*, 1960) called it "a very odd book" containing "every kind of writing" and with "no recognizable structure," *Such Is Life* has its own charm: its unique style and humor, but especially its authentic detail—local color from a native son—capture forever life in the Riverina in the late 19th century.

—Wesley D. Sweetser

SUMMER LIGHTNING.
(*Fish Preferred* or *Fish-Deferred.*)
Novel by P.G. Wodehouse, 1929.

P.G. Wodehouse wrote two dozen stage shows, and called his novels "musical comedies without the music." It may seem surprising, therefore, that when they are adapted for stage or screen, they flop. It is not that they are badly directed, or use actors inexpert at comedy: in their time both Tom Walls and Ralph Richardson, no less, played Lord Emsworth in *Summer Lightning*. But some other ingredient, crucial to success, seems to be missing—and Wodehouse himself surely suspected this, or he might have taken the dramatic lure more often than he did.

The surprise is greater when one considers the origins of a typical Wodehouse story (and *Summer Lightning* is one of the most typical of all). Those origins are in a kind of literature remote from ordinary English experience in the 1910's, when Wodehouse perfected his formula. They are the stage comedies of ancient Rome, and particularly those of Plautus. In true Plautine style, the story of *Summer Lightning* concerns a young hero (Ronnie Fish) scheming to marry the girl he loves (Sue Brown) despite opposition from foolish or formidable elders (Lord Emsworth; Lady Constance Keeble). Just as in Plautus, the hinges of the plot are impersonation (Sue pretends to be Myra Schoonmaker), blackmail (holding the Empress of Blandings to ransom; threatening to reveal all in Gally's memoirs), and constant cross purposes (starting when Ronnie sees Sue dining and dancing with Hugo Carmody). The cast includes such Plautine stereotypes as the dodderer (Emsworth), the downy old party (Gally), the blusterer (Sir Gregory Parsloe), and not one but two devious hangers-on (Percy Pilbeam; The Efficient Baxter). The scheming slave of Plautus is replaced by Beach the butler, who is in everyone's confidence and is a main participant in hiding the pig and passing Gally's scurrilous manuscript from person to person as the plot proceeds.

Where can Wodehouse have found such Plautine ingredients? Not in English comic novels, whether by such literary grandees as Sterne, Dickens, and Thackeray or by those minor—but just as funny—writers Surtees, the Grossmiths, and Jerome. Not on the stage, where Pinero, music-hall, and Ruritanian musicals ruled, and silly-ass farces (such as those of Ben Travers) were still to come. He might have seen plays by Labiche, Sardou, even Feydeau, but their social snobberies and embarrassments are of an entirely different kind, and their mainsprings uncoil at a most unPlummy pace. Possibly he read or saw Roman comedy at school, and the memory lingered. Or—though this would be astonishing, given the closeness of the similarities—he reinvented Plautine plot-ideas and character-types spontaneously, and the whole thing is no more than benign coincidence.

A third, main element of Wodehouse's art does comes from the English stage, and has no Plautine precedent. That is his dialogue. His characters speak with a kind of dogged ditheriness, a determination to pursue inconsequential thought well past any logical extreme—a classic technique of patter on the English stage, from that of Shakespeare's clowns to the routine of Dan Leno and his foils (who were topping London bills in the 1890's, when Wodehouse was a young banker-about-town). A typical example from *Summer Lightning* comes after Gally gives Lord Emsworth proof that Sir Gregory Parsloe is the pig-napper:

> Lord Emsworth uncoiled himself. Cumulative evidence had done its work. His eyes glittered and he breathed sterterously. "The scoundrel!" "Tough nut, always was." "What shall I do?" "Do? Why, go to him right away and tax him." "Tax him?" "Yes. Look him squarely in the eye and tax him with his crime." "I will! Immediately!" "I'll come with you." "Look him squarely in the eye!" "And tax him!" "And tax him!" "And tax him." Lord Emsworth had reached the hall and was peering agitatedly to right and left. "Where the devil's my hat? I can't find my hat. Somebody's always hiding my hat. I will not have my hats hidden." "You don't need a hat to tax a man with stealing a pig," said the Hon. Galahad, who was well versed in the manners and rules of good society.

Dialogue as good as this, one might imagine, would make *Summer Lightning* entirely stageworthy. It would hardly matter that the plot (like all Wodehouse's plots) was ornate but thin, or that the characters were two-dimensional. The zest of the thing, its pace and zip, would come from what the people say. In fact, no view could be more mistaken. Stage adaptation emphasises not pace but thinness. Two hours of unrelieved conversations like the one quoted would send an audience screaming for the exits. Plautus's vocabulary and metre were subtler and more varied. Leno and his music hall peers kept patter sequences to three or four minutes, moving on fast to eccentric dance or song. In every case, it was variety which made the show.

In *Summer Lightning*, as in all his novels, Wodehouse gives exactly this kind of variety and pace, but by a means not available to the stage dramatist: the ever-present voice of the storyteller. His jokes and his dialogue are jewels, but what makes them shine is the way he strings them. In the quoted passage, for example, the key paragraphs are the first and last. They frame and control the scene. Wodehouse first slows down his narrative, letting us know that he is about to dazzle. Next, he performs his trick. Last, he simultaneously rounds it off and caps it, like a conjurer topping the audience's applause by turning inside out the illusion they have just seen. The placing of that phrase about Gally being "well versed in the manners and rules of good society" is crucial.

All great comic stylists use similar sleight of hand. In Rabelais, Hašek, Heller, the author's commentary refocuses both dialogue and action to make satirical points. In Jane Austen's novels, the ironic, affectionate voice of "Aunt Jane" gives colour to every scene. Wodehouse is in classy company, and the verbal counterpoint he provides (like theirs) can be fully appreciated only as a reader's eye moves across the page. No stage performer, no film actor, can represent for us the way punctuation marks dance in the passage quoted above. Wodehouse's style depends not on original similes (as Waugh claimed), not on dizzy plotting or daft characterisation, but on an accumulation of tiny, perfectly-judged, and one-hundred-per-cent literary effects.

—Kenneth McLeish

SUNSHINE SKETCHES OF A LITTLE TOWN.
Fiction by Stephen Leacock, 1912.

Stephen Leacock's *Sunshine Sketches of a Little Town* presents some characters and events in the life of Mariposa, a small Canadian town, ostensibly circa 1911, and frames them with a preface and envoy. But, though critics agree on the merit of Leacock's book, they argue about whether the humour is gentle, sunny irony or stronger, darker satire, and whether or not the book is a novel. The essential answer is that no sketch is completely self-contained; all benefit from their context, for the book is a linked story sequence which, with its framework, comprises an integrated work of fiction whose purpose and method are process-oriented: helping the audience adjust its perspective towards the values that Leacock seeks to uphold.

These are, as his preface indicates, traditional conservative values: keeping the best of the past while moving into the future. Thus Leacock mentions his membership in the Royal Colonial Institute, the Church of England, and the Conservative Party; thus, in fiction as in life, he chooses the British connection over the new continentalist option in the Reciprocity Election of 1911. Thus too, Leacock's narrator regrets the loss of "the little stone church" which was demolished "though it seemed almost a sacrilege," then, "like so much else in life, was forgotten" in favour of the "New Church" (which becomes a financial albatross until it is burned for the insurance money). And thus there is the nostalgia with which Mariposa is viewed, a nostalgia which is given greater emphasis in "L'Envoi."

Mariposa is not merely a fictionalization of Orillia, or of the Lake Simcoe area where Leacock spent much of his boyhood. Instead, he insists that "Mariposa is not a real town . . . [but] *seventy* or *eighty* of them," a composite Canadian town with composite Canadian characters. As such, it stands for traditional Canada in contrast to the city—not the unnamed Toronto of the fiction's geography or the Montreal of Leacock's professorial life—but the city as symbolic centre of power, money-getting, materialism, alienation, anonymity, and the accompanying decay of community and moral values. Even more pointed is the contrast of the town to the city's Mausoleum Club, which has taken the place of "home" to the narrator's auditor so that he has "half forgotten Mariposa, and long since lost the way to it." The Mausoleum Club represents a kind of emotional and spiritual deadness in comparison with the affection and sense of community that is described in the sketches set in Mariposa. This deadness is what excessive emphasis on city values has led to, and it suggests too a dying of the healthier dreams and values of the auditor's past.

All this is not to deny Leacock's awareness of the absurdities and imperfections of Mariposan life, for of course the foibles, naiveties, poses, and petty hypocrisies of Mariposa are the source of most of the book's humour, and are discussed in successive sketches on business practices, community recreation, religion, romance, and political economy. Accompanying the humorous treatment of institutions and attitudes, however, is a critical comparison of traditional and non-traditional values. Thus, for example, the first two sketches counterpoise two businessmen who incorporate the larger tensions of the city versus community value systems. Josh (a jest) Smith, the outsider from the north country, has built up his wealth through a government food contract and has become the new hotel-keeper and bar-owner; he has an eye for profit and self-advancement, but his non-Mariposan perspective and manipulations suggest danger to some Mariposan values, as is indicated by his constructing a Rats' Cooler (rathskeller) which the town undertaker, Golgotha Gingham, feels to have "the quiet charm of an interment." This suggests an incipient Mausoleum Club. Jefferson (agrarian democracy) Thorpe, the barber located opposite Smith, makes money too—in his case through speculation—but loses it the same way. Unlike Smith, however, Thorpe's intent was to distribute most of his profits among the poor, and after the Cuban land scheme is proved fraudulent he works harder to reimburse Johnson who shared in his unfortunate investment. The contrast in values is clear. Similarly, sketches 4–6 and 7–9, respectively, comment on religion and romance in Mariposa. The former focus on Dean Drone and his New Church, and reveal the error of the assumption that bigger is better; the latter focus on the vicissitudes of the developing romance between Zena Pepperleigh and Peter Pupkin (a bank teller from the Maritimes who shares the value system of Mariposa), and show that love can cast an "enchantment" that can transform life in Mariposa (as does Leacock's book). Smith again plays a role, but where he merely fights a fire (which may jeopardize his hotel), Pupkin responds to "the blood of four generations of Loyalists" and courageously goes to confront an apparent armed robber. The section ends with Pupkin fully entering Mariposan society by marrying Zena and their living in an "enchanted house" with "an enchanted baby": the whole being a triumph for traditional community values.

This makes "L'Envoi" even more poignant, with its emphasis on the auditor's loss of his Mariposa "home" and values. The narrator has tried to reverse the process by taking the auditor back in perspective and memory through his sketches and then by recalling the boyhood joys of hunting and fishing at the lake. The final attempt is in imagination, by a fantasized train journey, not only through space but also through time, back to the way the town was "thirty years ago." The nostalgia of the journey is given added pathos by the fantasy, for as the book ends, the narrator and auditor remain in "the Mausoleum Club, talking of the little Town in the Sunshine that once we knew." The use of "we" in the final sentence reminds us that Leacock too left home 30 years earlier to go to school in Toronto, and the book commemorates his past as well as that of the characters.

John Robert Sorfleet

T

A TALE OF A TUB.
Fiction by Jonathan Swift, 1704.

Jonathan Swift's *A Tale of a Tub*, one of the most sparkling and incisive satires ever written, published anonymously, must be comprehended within the context of the Battle of the Ancients and Moderns. For centuries the so-called "ancients" of Greece and Rome had been exalted and idealized, their sayings recited, their virtues extolled, indeed, such hero-worship at times leading modern writers to despair of ever equalling their grand achievements—particularly in the arts. However, since the time of Bacon in the early 17th century (and even earlier), authors in England and elsewhere had been countering that the new sciences had surpassed the attainments of antiquity, and many a critic proposed that the writings of a Shakespeare, a Jonson, or a Milton had surpassed the creations of a Homer or a Sophocles. After the Restoration of 1660, there was a vast increase in the number of printing presses in England, and the market was increasingly glutted with hack writings and what many considered to be bawdy modern plays and self-serving and self-gratulatory modern essays. If anything, the pendulum had swung to the opposite extreme, and contemporary writers too casually boasted of their own superiority over individuals in every other period of history.

In this environment, Swift's friend and patron, Sir William Temple, had ventured in an elegant and rambling appreciation to praise some of the ancient authors, particularly Aesop and Phalaris (1690). Several moderns, the Rev. William Wotton (1694) and the classical scholar Richard Bentley (1697) took exception to Temple's mild partiality, Bentley even demonstrating that the alleged extreme antiquity of the Epistles of Phalaris was entirely false. As a scholar, Bentley was assuredly correct; but these "modern" authors appeared to be excessively self-confident, arrogant, and pedantic. Swift's indirect response to them, in *A Tale of a Tub*, was initially instigated by this literary dispute.

A Tale of a Tub (the colloquial phrase, "a tale of a tub," denoted a tedious trifle) *was* trifling; it purported throughout to be the contrivance of a "modern" author or hack writer. It consisted, after a clutter of introductory paraphernalia, of a trite and slang-ridden modern allegorical tale, together with extensive explications and dissertations as if by the hand of some modern scholar. Overall, the work gives the impression of a treatise gone haywire: a simple-minded modern story edited and elaborated and explicated by yet another modern. In this way, Swift is able to denigrate what he took to be cheap modern picayune productions as well as the pomp and bombast of so-called "modern" scholarship.

The "tale" itself is a recitation of the history of a modern family, Peter, Martin, and Jack, three brothers. It is a thinly-veiled story of the fragmentation of churches during the Renaissance, the contests and dissensions of Catholics (Peter) with Luther and the Episcopalians (Martin) and with the extreme protestants John Calvin and the Dissenters (Jack). In a sense, it relates religious turmoils that, all in all, become most aggravated in modern times by the violent behavior of Jack, who favors spontaneity and violence; he is presented as essentially mad. This "history" is reported like a fairy tale in chapters 2,4,6, and 11. Supposed scholarly digressions occupy chapters 1,3,5,7,8,9,10, and the Conclusion. These excursions consist primarily of nonsensical puffery: praises of digressions, of moderns, of madness, of the hack author himself. A superficial glance at the chapter numberings will reveal that the "tale" portion of the volume is slowly and inevitably overwhelmed by sections of commentary and digression. Indeed, after the Digression in Praise of Madness (chapter 9), the entire work is overturned, and the empty, rambling, mindless modern mode triumphs and prevails over what little method or purpose had ever seemed to have been initially present.

A number of authors responded to this satire, explaining some of the allusions, and accusing its anonymous author of, among other things, blasphemy. In his Fifth edition (1710), Swift casually incorporated some of his accusers' more naive observations and conjectures verbatim into the footnotes to his text. Thus, at a stroke, Swift added another ring to his circus of pitiful modern "scholarship." What better way to answer one's enemies than to incarcerate them inside your own satiric fiction?

Overall, Swift's satire was never wholly appreciated nor fully understood. It was considered flippant and frequently scandalous, even sacrilegious. Moreover, Swift paid for writing this satire; for decades his reputation undermined chances for his obtaining advancement in the Anglican church. But, as the 20th century has increasingly been coming to recognize, *A Tale of a Tub* constituted a major satire in breadth, complexity, and insight. In a masterstroke of satiric imagining, Swift created a host of *reductio-ad-absurdum* Moderns: they are hugely solipsistic, rebellious against the past, and living only for and in the present moment. Ultimately, they are ignorant of history, lazy, devoid of learning or manners; yet they justify themselves solely on the grounds that they are the Latest, the Most Faddish, the Relevant, the Contemporary. Of necessity, such complete Moderns must be ill-mannered, for decorum or etiquette require the learning of codes of behavior, self-restraint, and the mastery of good breeding; they have no time for such antiquated stuff. As they are presented, all such moderns merely yearn to be momentarily amused, by empty and frivolous jests and news and stories that consist of "Accidents, Turns, and Adventures, both New, Agreeable, and Surprizing." Here is foreshadowed what Ortega y Gasset in 1930 was to designate the "Revolt of the Masses": the rise of mass man in the 20th century—ignorant, transient, bored, restless, concerned with the slang and fads of the present instant.

The implication of Swift's incisive satire is that modern publishers will print any garble or nonsense to bilk their audience and earn some cash; the modern scholar, like his brother, the cheap popular author, will ruthlessly manhandle any text and advance any claims whatsoever to get published. Religious leaders, too, are intent upon inventing the latest sect, just as politicians embrace the latest clique or faction. In the finale of *A Tale of a Tub*, the hack writer confesses to have lost his notes; as a result, he is unable to go on, and brings his volume abruptly (and lamely) to a conclusion. Such moderns must thrive on the likes of Bartlett's *Familiar Quotations* and Roget's *Thesaurus*; they do not have any memory—no knowledge of the past, no storehouse of learning, no discipline, and no inner resources of their own. Such people are both fools *and* knaves (see the debate in chapter 9): they are ignorant predators, know-nothings who would nevertheless hoodwink others to obtain material and monetary enhancement at any cost. Thus, with wit and brilliant humor, Swift indicts modern man and many of his motives just at the gateway to modern times. The satire is richly creative, with a bevy of grim prophecies that 20th-century readers will find to have come all too true.

—John R. Clark

A TALE OF TWO CITIES.
Novel by Charles Dickens, 1859.

As a novelist so much concerned with society and its ills and injustices, it is hardly surprising that Charles Dickens should have written two novels about social disorder in which the corrupt structure that looms up in so many of his books seems in danger of final collapse. The first of these, quite early in his career, was *Barnaby Rudge* (1840–41), in which the anti-Catholic Gordon riots formed the background to a rather conventional love story. The second, towards the end of his career, was *A Tale of Two Cities*, which first appeared during 1859 as eight monthly parts in Dickens's own magazine, *All the Year Round*, and was later published as a novel. It is set in London and Paris at the time of the French Revolution, centering especially on the period of the Terror of 1793.

As a historical novel, *A Tale of Two Cities* has obvious limitations. It is highly derivative, mainly from Thomas Carlyle's extravagant masterpiece, *The French Revolution*, for Dickens did little other research. Moreover, the attention it gives to the Revolution as a historic event is strangely restricted and evasive. Only two of the celebrated episodes of the Revolution are described at any length; the taking of the Bastille and the murder by the crowd of the old tax farmer Foulon, of which Carlyle also makes much. None of the celebrated revolutionary figures appear except for the executioner Samson, and even him we never see. The guillotine thuds away invisible, and though we are told of the great massacres in the prisons and shown a macabre scene of the killers sharpening their bloody weapons in the yard of the Paris branch of Tillson's Bank, we do not see a single aristocrat actually being slaughtered by the people. We get only a limited glimpse of the slums of Paris, in the Faubourg St. Antoine, where the Terror has its birth, and even here our attention is mainly concentrated on the bloodthirsty Defarges who, it turns out in the end, are motivated to play their part in the action through thoughts of family revenge rather than of revolutionary zeal.

The central motif of the novel is in fact that of redemption through love rather than revolution through hate, and the central plot is a love triangle in which one of the two suitors for the heroine dies on the guillotine in the place of his rival. The heroine is Lucie Manette, daughter of a doctor formerly imprisoned in the Bastille, who at the beginning of the book is released, sheltered by Defarge who was his former servant, and brought to a refuge in England. Of the lovers one, Charles Darnay, lives in London as a French tutor, but is really a member of a particularly arrogant aristocratic family, whose pretensions he has already rejected before the Revolution. The other, Sydney Carton, is a brilliant but debauched lawyer. The two men meet dramatically at the Old Bailey, when Darnay stands falsely accused of spying for France, and Carton—who is Darnay's double—stands up to confuse the identificatory evidence of the government spies. Darnay is acquitted—saved for a first time by his darker self—and courts and marries Lucie, whom his double also loved.

Then, when the Revolution starts and the Terror begins, Darnay foolishly returns to France in the hope that he can save the life of a faithful old servant who has been imprisoned. But he is himself arrested under suspicion of being an émigré aristocrat, and condemned when the Defarges reveal that his uncle and father were responsible for Dr. Manette having been sent to the Bastille and for crimes against the family of Madame Defarge for which she has vowed revenge.

It is now that the theme of the double, that gothic device which has been echoing throughout the novel, is completed; Darnay is again rescued by his darker self, Carton, who contrives to take his rival's place in the cells of the Conciergerie and eventually at the guillotine, while Darnay is spirited back to England.

For Darnay it is a return to Lucie and his children and a long happy life. For Carton it means the transcendence of his own unworthiness, and as the book ends we recognize that the real theme is not revolution, though that is what gives the novel its local flavour in time and place, but redemption.

A Tale of Two Cities, in fact, takes its place not in the literature of political conflict, but rather in the literature of the kind of sentimental evangelical Christianity that permeated English life so deeply in the mid-19th century, at the height of the Victorian era. In this sense, it is a heavily didactic book, and to this didacticism we can attribute alike the awkwardness of the implausible and coincidence-ridden plot and the melodramatic stiffness of the characterization. Compared with Dickens at his best, a year later in *Great Expectations*, it gives the impression of an over-contrived but hastily written book, whose grasp on history is tenuous.

—George Woodcock

TAM O' SHANTER.
Poem by Robert Burns, 1791.

Written, like so many of Robert Burns's poems, as the result of an exterior stimulus, "Tam o' Shanter" is one of the greatest narrative poems to have been written in the British Isles. It combines, as is now widely recognised, both Scottish and English poetic traditions: it is the work of a poet who was as intimate with the methods and devices of Augustan neo-classical verse (it can even be seen as a mock-epic imitation of the *Odyssey*) as he was with the folk traditions of rural Scotland. Here Burns is simultaneously the tale-teller of a folk narrative and a formally educated man of letters: he combines the two to forge a major work of literature.

It is the versification of one of three tales associated with the haunted kirk of Alloway which Burns sent to the antiquarian Captain Francis Grose. This anecdote provided the climax of Burns's story, telling how a solitary farmer, travelling past the kirk one midnight, found within it a dance of witches in full swing, accompanied by the bagpipe music of the Devil himself. Among the old women was one whose smock was indecently short, and at the sight of her the farmer could not restrain a crudely ironic compliment. There followed the brief chase to the middle of the river, the escape of the farmer, and the loss of his horse's tail which served as a warning, we are told, to others.

Burns extends this narrative by creating the public house interior (the quintessence of thoughtless pleasure with its warmth, companionship, and dalliance); by imagining a wife, Kate, who while inevitably absent from the scene is nevertheless a potent presence in the poem as a whole; and by describing Tam's ride to the kirk in terms both of the physical oppression of the elements and the mental oppression of a landscape of dreadful associations. He also makes Nannie youthful and attractive, thus focusing the poem's concern with sexuality. Each of these additions is rendered with a concentrated vigour which contributes to the reader's sense that the poem is longer than its 224 lines.

The language of the poem repays the closest attention of practical critics, and every extended account of it dwells on felicities of sound effect, rhythm, and word selection. It is a supreme example of the poetic possibilities of the Scots language. It contains passages in English, however, which critics such as Edwin Muir have pressed into service to illustrate theses about the psychological and aesthetic disadvantages of modern Scotland's linguistic ambivalence. More recent critics, on the other hand, see the contrast between, say,

> She tauld thee weel thou was a skellum,
> A blethering, blustering, drunken blellum

and

> But pleasures are like poppies spread,
> You seize the flower, its bloom is shed . . .

as a sign of Burns's flexible control rather than of cultural impediment. Whether one discusses the poem in terms of a variety of narrators, or whether one hears one multifaceted narrator, the overwhelming sense of the tale being *uttered* is a crucial aspect of its being and success. It is one of the work's many ambiguities that the basic narration, apparently from an outlook very close to that of Tam himself (unrepentantly, thoughtlessly masculine), is interspersed with comments of an ironically thoughtful kind and also with other statements, often in English, which betray a more consciously literary awareness.

This ambiguous utterance reflects an ambiguity of meaning. At first glance a tale of an irresponsible philanderer punished by a moment of terror which just falls short of being eternal, it is concluded by an ironic moral which points up how Tam has actually paid no lasting price for his sinning: it is his horse which is maimed. The poem encourages us—or "ilk man and mother's son" at least—to accept our inclination to drink and to the contemplation of cutty-sarks. Tam is indeed a "poor sinner," but the poem's tone of masculine indulgence (focused and justified, despite the commentator's expressions of sympathy, by the figure of the "sulky sullen dame" of whom the narrator is conscious from the outset) brings out the sympathetic charity in the phrase rather than the condemnation. In a further verbal ambiguity, Tam is indeed "bewitch'd" in the course of his encounter, but this witchery involves the loss of one's heart rather than of one's soul.

Even the satanic centre of the poem, the witches' dance, is ambiguous. Its setting is undeniably hellish—though even at a first reading the accumulation of awful objects on "the haly table" lurches from the hair-raising to the rib-tickling. The nearest these witches get to infernal activity, however, is dancing: they abandon themselves to "mirth and fun" with the same absolute commitment with which Tam had embraced "pleasure" earlier. While "pleasure" may seem hellish to churchgoers and to abandoned wives, its awfulness is far less apparent in the moment of experiencing it—or of reading about it. These witches, at one level of interpretation, stand for "poor sinners" with a love for ordinary social pleasures: their sin, and Tam's, is in giving themselves to the moment, forgetful of spouses, "lang Scots miles," "sage advices," or of an eternal future. One of the functions of the narrator is constantly to remind us of time, and his generalisations from experience, his recollections of the horrors of the landscape, his glance forward to Nannie's future career of destruction, his final admonition to look back in the future, all create the time-steeped context from which pleasure-seekers momentarily escape.

And for a moment, even the piping Satan, generating the mirth and fun in the energetic patterns of "hornpipes, jigs, strathspeys, and reels," is the artist-figure, a force of creative vivacity, stimulated (like Burns himself) by female flesh. What Tam sees in Kirk Alloway is human pleasure and creativity as viewed by those Burns elsewhere calls "the unco' guid."

—David S. Robb

TAMBURLAINE THE GREAT.
Play by Christopher Marlowe, 1587(?).

The hero of *Tamburlaine the Great* is the Tartar Khan Timur (1336–1405), known as Timur-i-Lenk (Timur the Lame), the western form of which is Tamerlane or Tamburlaine. Christopher Marlowe's principal sources are a Latin account of him by Petrus Perondinus (1553) and an English one by George Whetstone (1586). From these he took the chief events of the conqueror's career: the overthrow of the Persian king and of the Turkish emperor, the capture of Damascus, and the defeat of the Sultan of Egypt and the King of Arabia (all in Part 1, Marlowe's original play; in Part 2, written in response to its success in the theatre, he drew upon miscellaneous sources, many unconnected with Tamburlaine's own history, and upon his own invention).

The prologue to Part 1 promises that Tamburlaine shall be seen "Threat'ning the world with high astounding terms / And scourging kingdoms with his conquering sword." In the course of the play he is said to be "Of stature tall, and straightly fashionèd, / Like his desire, lift upwards and divine," and he declares, "I am a lord, for so my deeds shall prove, / And yet a shepherd by my parentage," casting off his shepherd's cloak and appearing in complete armour. His ambition is seen by himself as godlike and by his adversaries as devilish. Generous to his allies, he is ruthless to his enemies: in Part 1 he keeps the conquered Turkish emperor

Bajazeth in a cage, taking him out to serve as his footstool, and in Part 2 he harnesses captive kings to his chariot ("Holla, ye pampered jades of Asia! / What, can ye draw but twenty miles a day . . . ?"). Unconquered by any human opponent, he finally succumbs to a fever and dies lamented by his sons and his generals.

Though Part 2 concludes with his death, Part 1 is a play of triumph concluding in peace as he "takes truce with all the world" and crowns his betrothed, the Sultan's daughter Zenocrate, as queen of all his conquered kingdoms and dominions. Zenocrate is Marlowe's invention. Captured by Tamburlaine at the beginning of the play, she comes to admire and love her captor, and he in turn feels her softening influence: his sole inner conflict is caused by her anxiety for her father's fate in the impending final battle of Part 1. In Part 2 Marlowe dramatizes her death and its effect upon Tamburlaine, whose speeches pass from lyrical pathos ("Now walk the angels on the walls of heaven, / As sentinels to warn th' immortal souls / To entertain divine Zenocrate") to impassioned fury ("Batter the shining palace of the sun / And shiver all the starry firmament, / For amorous Jove hath snatched my love from hence, / Meaning to make her stately queen of heaven"). Also in Part 2 Tamburlaine stabs to death his eldest son for shirking a battle. His two other sons are as warlike as he could desire, and when the elder succeeds him there is no suggestion that the empire he has won will disintegrate, as one of Marlowe's sources insists it did.

In his hero Marlowe has created a figure of undoubted energy and self-confidence, but there has been critical disagreement as to how far he accepts Tamburlaine's self-assessment. Some critics have argued that Marlowe wholeheartedly approves of him, others that he disapproves of him, and others that he is fascinated by his enigmatic mixture of idealism and brutality. The obvious presence of irony in some of Marlowe's other works, notably *The Jew of Malta*, has caused some critics to seek it out here; one episode in Part 2, based on an historical event after the hero's death, does turn upon the duplicity of certain Christians in their dealings with certain pagans, but this seems rather a special instance of Marlowe's scepticism than a key to the interpretation of the whole action and of the character of the protagonist. Various gods are invoked from time to time by various persons, and Tamburlaine once declares (Part 2, V.i. 182–84) that he is the "scourge," that is, the embodied anger, of "a God full of revenging wrath," but there is no clear sign that supernatural powers are either consistently present or consistently absent (the juxtaposition of Christian and pagan heavens in Zenocrate's death-scene is a striking instance of how the emotion of the speaker, not his theology, dictates the images he uses), and it would be unsafe to assume that when the hero falls fatally ill it is because he has just burned the Mahometan scriptures.

The opportunities for theatrical spectacle are many: during the siege of Damascus, Tamburlaine dresses himself and his army on successive days in white, in red, and in black, to symbolize the consequences to the inhabitants if they continue to resist him.

Several other "conqueror plays" were written in imitation of *Tamburlaine the Great*, and it was much quoted and parodied.

—T.W. Craik

THE TAMING OF THE SHREW.
Play by William Shakespeare, 1594.

The Taming of the Shrew follows many of the rules of farce, gaining vitality from disguises, physical action, and numerous plot twists. It is also a play about transformations on several levels, although the others pale by comparison with the story of Petruchio's metamorphosis of hot-tempered, sharp-tongued Katherina into the model Elizabethan wife. Both the taming plot and the more conventional courtship of Bianca are, structurally, entertainments within a frame and part of an elaborate practical joke. The obedience message, however, becomes the final statement of the play because Shakespeare elected not to complete the frame story found in *The Taming of a Shrew*.

The initial transformation, perhaps recalled in reverse by Petruchio's shabby appearance at his wedding, occurs when ragged tinker Christopher Sly, taken from the gutter by a Lord, is bathed, finely dressed, and told he is a lord. Sly is introduced to his "wife," a disguised page instructed to obey "her lord." At the end of this long induction, the theatre audience joins Sly in watching a play supposedly staged for him.

Shakespeare connects the broadly comic yet psychologically interesting taming story with a tale of rival courtships of an apparently ideal young woman. Bianca Minola's marriage is conditional on finding a husband for her shrewish older sister, and Hortensio and Gremio are delighted when Petruchio arrives from Verona to seek a wife and fortune. He is quickly directed to wealthy, beautiful Kate, who is shown abusing her sister and who responds to Hortensio's efforts to give music lessons by breaking a lute over his head.

Physical transformations are essential to the Bianca plot, and Hortensio sets the pattern by having himself presented as a musician. Lucentio arrives in Padua and quickly disguises himself as a tutor for Bianca, while his man, Tranio, becomes "Lucentio" and carries on a successful formal bargaining for her. Eventually a "father" must be found to sign the contract, and an old Pedant is convinced that he must impersonate Vincentio for his own safety. Hortensio has decided to marry a widow by the time the real Vincentio arrives and, after some further confusion, identities are revealed.

The assumption that mild, obedient Bianca is the ideal woman has annoyed some feminists, and the transformation of Kate into a spokesperson for wifely duty has offended many late 20th-century women. The Petruchio-Kate plot seems blatantly male chauvinist. At the same time, however, it is psychologically more interesting than much farce, for it reveals Petruchio's cleverness in bringing out Kate's latent decency as she sees her husband emulate her own displays of temper.

Katherina's early outbursts stem from her disposition and from her jealousy of her sister, which she expresses in physical and verbal abuse. Petruchio, apparently experienced in battle, is not deterred by her reputation. Although he states that she will inherit if he predeceases her, he is interested in her dowry and in having a peaceful marriage. He is often depicted as beating Kate by people only slightly acquainted with the play, but his methods are more varied, subtle, and psychologically oriented. He plays on her insecurity by arriving late and inappropriately dressed for the hastily arranged wedding, making her grateful that he has finally appeared. He deprives her of the wedding banquet and at his lodgings is "more shrew than she." Fatigue, hunger, and sympathy for the Tailor and servants Petruchio is abusing in apparent care of her soon reduce her to the unaccustomed acts of pleading and showing appreciation. Although she still has restive moments and speaks of "the anger of my heart," coached by Grumio she learns to play her role, even accepting Petruchio's declaration that the sun is the moon.

Katherina may have been truly transformed, or she may have learned that she needs to achieve her ends in more subtle ways. There is no soliloquy to reveal her thoughts in the way that Petruchio reveals his strategy. She is motivated to learn correct responses by her desire to return to her father's for the banquet. There she still maintains dominance over the other women, bringing them in when they have refused to heed their husbands' summonses. But there, too, she gives the long speech on the wife's role. Her actions not only win a wager for Petruchio but also earn an increased dowry, the sign of a new paternal approval. For a modern audience, the ending leaves questions. Is it a happy ending because Katherina has a husband and is now appreciated? Is there really a mutual responsibility, with the husband as "Lord . . . king . . . governor," but also protector and risk-taker while she remains "warm at home"? Or is it a happy ending only for the husband who can look forward to "peace, love, and a quiet life" with control of a sizeable dowry?

By Elizabethan standards, where the wealthy Portia gave everything to Bassanio in a speech akin to Kate's (*Merchant of Venice*), the taming plot has a happy end. Kate will achieve a fullness of life that she could not have enjoyed as a conventional shrew. Shakespeare does include the irony of a final transformation, however, in a play where surface and reality are often at odds. Earlier he had hinted at Bianca's wilfulness when she declared she would have her lesson when she pleased. At the end the apparently ideal Bianca and loving widow disobey their new husbands, refusing to come and thereby losing their men's wagers. Unless the women learn from Kate's speech, these apparently good, conventionally entered marriages may be rough. The unconventional, initially oddly matched couple at least have a firm base for their future together, although Katherina may be denied the independence a 20th-century western woman would demand.

—Frances A. Shirley

THE TASK.
Poem by William Cowper, 1785.

By 1783 when William Cowper began to write *The Task*, he was already an accomplished and famous poet, largely due to his *Poems* of 1782. His personal correspondence makes clear that the poem was written between October 1783 and September 1784; it was published in 1785. Cowper's immediate stimulus for writing it is told in the notorious anecdote that his friend Lady Austen challenged him to write a poem on a seemingly insignificant subject, and he did. The Advertisment prefixed to the first edition reads: "The history of the following production is briefly this:—A lady, fond of blank verse, demanded a poem of that kind from the author, and gave him the SOFA for a subject. He obeyed; and, having much leisure, connected another subject with it; and pursuing the train of thought to which his situation and turn of mind led him, brought forth at length, instead of the trifle which he at first intended, a serious affair—a Volume!" Beginning in the tradition of the mock epic with "I sing the SOFA", Cowper proceeds largely by process of association rather than any deliberate plan for a refined, finished product; as he explains: "If the work cannot boast a regular plan . . . it may yet boast, that the reflections are naturally suggested always by the preceding passage, and that the whole has one tendency; to discountenance the modern enthusiasm after a London life, and to recommend rural ease and leisure, as friendly to the cause of piety and virtue."

While anticipating the rather unusual associative movement of the poem, Cowper's statement also makes clear that the poem will have a strong didactic dimension—and this can tend to make it very much a poem of the 18th century, or, more specifically, of the neoclassical school. In a letter to his friend John Newton, in fact, Cowper says that his aim is to teach religion and virtue, and that his poem is primarily didactic. Many critics and readers have commented on the poem's "lessons," among which are the suggestion that rural tranquility is a necessary refreshment from urban frenzy ("God made the country and man made the town"); that nature's beauty and essential harmony remind Cowper of the God who "heal'd, and bade me live"; that nature's myriad appearances can facilitate or even cause emotional changes in the perceiver ("they lull the spirit while they fill the mind"); and that *time* (past, present, and future) all comes together in nature's symbolically cyclical representation of infinity, or God's eternal presence. But the "lessons" are quite unlike those of other 18th-century nature poems: not only are they more *pantheistic* than specifically Christian (and more philosophical than religious), they are, by and large, subtly integrated into the fabric of the poem rather than obtrusively conspicuous. It is probably more accurate to speak of a didactic habit of mind or general mood rather than didactic lessons, episodes, or passages. The main emphasis is less on didactic assertion than it is on the meditative and reflective movement of the narrating consciousness.

Though critics have long recognized the poem's value, its rather unprecedented associative movement has made it difficult to evaluate in conventional neoclassical terms of the 18th century. The *Monthly Review* of 1785 found the poem "always moral, yet never dull," but the reviewer goes on to say that "an imagination like Mr. Cowper's is not to be controlled and confined within the bounds that criticism prescribes." Later critics, such as Robert Burns, claimed: "Is not *The Task* a glorious poem?"; and Wordsworth and Coleridge borrowed from it freely. While Gilbert Thomas alleges that the poem "rambles inconsequently" and presents "a baffling medley of moods and ideas," most modern critics are unanimous in their appreciation of the psychological complexity and perceptual sensitivity of a poem that fascinatingly represents a mind in process of movement between neoclassicism and romanticism—a stage of poetic sensibility sometimes overlooked in literary history. While the main focus of the poem is on nature, in terms of genre *The Task* has been seen as a combination of the English georgic (or even pastoral), the mock-epic, and the epic itself. But it is probably better seen as a precursor to—or even the first example of—the subjective epic; it is very much a prototype for Wordsworth's *Prelude* or Keats's *Endymion* in its portrayal of the state and growth of a poet's mind. Cowper himself writes in the poem that the poet's concern is to follow the "shifts and turns," the "inventions multiform / To which the mind resorts, in chace of terms," in order that he "arrest the fleeting images that fill / The mirror of the mind, and hold them fast . . . 'till he has pencilled off / A faithful likeness of the forms he views."

The focus on nature is much more than just description, however: the poem concerns the effects nature has on the inner self—it is psycho-biographical. Admitting elsewhere that during the time when he wrote the poem he was "often most supremely unhappy" but that he is indebted in good part to that work for having restored his spirits somewhat, Cowper stresses, on his "rambles far and wide," the visual joys of nature and the "rural sights" and "rural sounds" that "exhilarate" and "restore" the contemplative self as it retreats from the "coarser pleasures" of city life to the benign realms of nature. As some modern commentators have said, it is this profound presence of *self* that sets Cowper crucially apart from other 18th-century descriptive nature poets; and one should add that it is the sense of a dynamic intercourse between the perceiving consciousness and the perceived natural world that gives the former sustenance and the latter meaning. The Kantian (and Wordsworthian) concept of the human consciousness and organs of perception "half-creating" the "objective" world being perceived and understood argues for a blurring—or even dissolution—between subject and object, or self and world, which would become a major concern in the literature of later periods, particularly in modern existentialism. Even in terms of literary style, Cowper imitates or animates (through sound devices, rhythm and cadence, internal rhyme, and levels of diction) the twists and turns, moods, and shifting states of his mind in the language of the poem, thus giving the poem its extraordinary appeal to its contemporaries, to the Romantics, and even to modern readers.

—Richard Arnold

THE TATLER.
Periodical edited by Sir Richard Steele, 1709–11.

THE SPECTATOR
Periodical edited by Joseph Addison and Sir Richard Steele, 1711–12.

The *Tatler* and the *Spectator* were the products of an early 18th-century metropolitan coffee house society, the predecessor of Victorian London clubland. Its middle-class readers were educated and literate, interested in books but also commercially minded; the stock exchange was as important to them as the theatre. Addison and Steele found in them an ideal audience and they in turn found in Addison and Steele's periodical writings ideal patterns for their own social behaviour.

Richard Steele was the first to recognise the opportunity. Having lost a comfortable salaried position, he turned to journalism and created the thrice-weekly single-sheet paper the *Tatler*. Each issue was composed of a group of short paragraphs. At the outset it offered, like any other newssheet of the day, a section devoted to foreign and domestic news, but there were also paragraphs on literature, the theatre, and town gossip. To heighten the interest and the cosy illusion that this was a house journal for his chosen clientele, Steele promulgated each paragraph as if from a different coffee house: foreign and domestic news from St. James's coffee-house, "gallantry and entertainment" from White's, poetry from Will's, learning from the Grecian, other subjects "from my own apartment."

As the paper increased in popularity he dropped more and more of the news element and concentrated on writing general essays "from my own apartment," including papers on the engaging Isaac Bickerstaff and his lively half-sister (and allegedly Tatler editor) Jenny Distaff. The beginnings of the modern novel, that middle-class self-viewing mirror, are already apparent in such *Tatler* papers.

Joseph Addison contributed a trial paper to the *Tatler* and thereafter became a regular contributor. When the *Tatler* came to an end in early 1711, he used some of its established formula for opening in March 1711 a new one-sheet daily the *Spectator*. He discarded the news element of its predecessor and concentrated instead on turning out a daily commentary on the life and letters of the day. Each issue offered, not a series of discrete paragraphs, but a complete rounded essay on a single topic. It was a demanding task and Steele contributed many of the papers (he created the character of Sir Roger de Coverley in *Spectator* 6 though it was Addison who was later to develop Sir Roger in depth). Others (like Pope) were occasional contributors. The *Spectator* ran without a break six days a week until December 1712.

Steele and Addison between them created a quiet revolution. Their papers on "minor morals" established a code of civilised behaviour for a new class, feeling its way with increasing confidence into social dominance and power. After reading a paper by Steele on duelling and a paper by Addison on "zeal," they could feel they really belonged to a new age, the excesses of the previous century left well behind. Instead, the *Spectator* with its range of recognisable characters (the merchants, small squires, men-about-town of the *Spectator* Club) held up new patterns of quiet decency. In addition, both Addison and Steele consciously appealed to women; by gentle satire and flattery they included them in their audience. The women in the days of Queen Anne were not to be seen in the coffee houses; but the issues of the *Spectator* were available in many drawing-rooms, ready to provide witty banter on cosmetics and fans and party patches and, for the more serious-minded, reviews of the opera and the theatre and, for the really dedicated, a complete series Saturday after Saturday on Milton's *Paradise Lost*.

When Addison and Steele withdrew from periodical writing, they still remained influential. Others writers (e.g., Johnson in his *Idler* and *Rambler*, Goldsmith in the *Citizen of the World*) continued the periodical essay formula. The *Spectator* in particular was reproduced in provincial newspapers and collected into bound editions in book form. It became the most widely reprinted 18th-century publication. The influence of its informal conversational prose style continues to this day in serious journalism.

The mention of journalism is deliberate. Steele and Addison in the *Tatler* and *Spectator* were journalists, not authors of "books." Readers since their time have become accustomed to encountering their essays in collected form in sets of bound volumes. This was a later—and a secondary—format. The initial issues were daily sheets, read daily and discussed daily. Readers fortunate enough to have access to a major library could well enquire if there are available for inspection even sample copies of a 1711–12 issue of the *Spectator*. Modern book editions obscure the original impact, as they obscure the original spelling and the slower-paced punctuation. The original issues of the *Spectator* have a gravity and an authority that still lies behind good leader-writing and good modern journalism.

—Ian A. Gordon

THE TEMPEST.
Play by William Shakespeare, 1611.

While *The Tempest* takes pride of place as the first play to appear in the First Folio of 1623, it is generally accepted that it was the last play Shakespeare wrote as sole author, though he did go on to write three plays in collaboration with John Fletcher: *Henry VIII*, *The Two Noble Kinsmen*, and the lost *Cardenio*. This fact, together with the presence in the play of Prospero as the artist / magician who controls the narrative and the other characters and who explicitly renounces his art at the end, has encouraged many to interpret *The Tempest* as Shakespeare's "farewell to the stage." Some support for this view has been found in the circumstance that, unusually, there is no known narrative source for the play: Shakespeare seems to have invented the plot himself. Uncharacteristically, he chooses to observe the classical unities of time, place, and action, which necessitates a long narrative speech by Prospero in the second scene telling his daughter Miranda (and the audience) what happened 15 years ago when his brother Antonio usurped the dukedom of Milan and consigned the pair of them to the doubtful fortune of an open boat. While this comes as a dramatic anticlimax after the opening storm scene, *The Tempest* has nevertheless been a popular play on stage, partly because of the opportunities it provides for music and spectacle, and it has inspired a number of adaptations, operas, and films.

The standard post-romantic reading of *The Tempest* tended to focus on the self-consciousness of the artist and on the sophisticated manipulation of ideas about art and nature in the play. It has often been seen as belonging to the newly fashionable genre of pastoral tragicomedy along with the other late comedies—*Pericles*, *The Winter's Tale*, and *Cymbeline*. These four plays form an unusually coherent group in Shakespeare's *oeuvre*, sharing a number of plot elements and themes: they are fairy-tale narratives with family-centred plots beginning in dissension and loss but ending in reconciliation and recovery. They all include quasi-supernatural events and divine interventions, and, perhaps because of this, the psychological realism of the human characters seems diminished when they are compared with the characters in the earlier comedies and tragedies. In *The Tempest*, in particular, while Prospero stands out, Miranda and her lover Ferdinand seem two-dimensional and it is not easy to remember who is who among the ship-wrecked courtiers Alonso, Sebastian, Antonio, Adrian, and Francisco.

Several recent interpretations of *The Tempest* have focused on the politics of the play, in particular its relevance to nascent colonialism. It is known that Shakespeare read and used accounts of contemporary voyages to Bermuda and Virginia, and his ostensibly Mediterranean island has a distinct flavour of the New World. Prospero, having lost his dukedom to his treacherous brother, is accused by Caliban, the "native," of becoming a usurper in his turn: "This island's mine by Sycorax my mother, / Which thou tak'st from me. . . . I am all the subjects that you have, / Which first was mine own king." Caliban, described by Prospero at the end as a "thing of darkness," has sometimes been played by a black actor in modern productions, adding the theme of racism to that of colonialism. Furthermore, a renewed sense of the topical significance of *The Tempest*, which was certainly performed at court on 14 February 1613 during the wedding festivities for James I's daughter Elizabeth to the Elector Palatine, encourages us to see its analysis of the nature of power and authority in terms of the *realpolitik* of dynastic marriages as much as in the individual dominance of the artist or magician.

The ending is in fact rather disturbing and problematic, particularly when compared with the endings of Shakespeare's other late comedies. Where *Pericles*, *The Winter's Tale*, and *Cymbeline* present a whole-hearted celebration of forgiveness, reconciliation, and family reunion, *The Tempest* seems questioning, even cynical. Prospero's speech of forgiveness to Antonio is decidedly grudging: "For you, most wicked sir, whom to call brother / Would even infect my mouth, I do forgive / Thy rankest fault—all of them—and require / My dukedom of thee, which perforce I know / Thou must restore." The stress is at least as much on what he has lost: his art (which he renounces), his daughter (whom he hands over to Ferdinand), and his servant Ariel (whom he frees). He has only death ahead of him. It is moreover difficult for 20th-century readers and audiences to overlook the fact that Prospero's response to Miranda's ecstatic "O brave new world / That has such people in't!" is a chilling "'Tis new to thee." In general, Prospero seems now a more uneasy, puzzling figure than the Olympian artist of earlier interpretations. His moods are somewhat inscrutable, despite his soliloquies, and the motives for his behaviour are not always clear. Ever accommodating to allegorical readings, *The Tempest* seems to change its shape over time, allowing us to interpret it today as a mysterious, enigmatic fable which is richly suggestive but also raises uncomfortable and unanswerable questions about both its personal and its political narratives.

—Ann Thompson

TESS OF THE d'URBERVILLES.
Novel by Thomas Hardy, 1891.

By the time *Tess of the d'Urbervilles* was published in 1891, Thomas Hardy was well established as a popular novelist with 12 novels and a book of short stories to his credit. This book is considered by many to be his finest work, yet it was his first to be met with critical outrage, due largely to the controversial subject matter. In fact, when his next book, *Jude the Obscure*, was also assailed as inflammatory, Hardy became so disillusioned that he retired from novel writing, and spent the last 30 years of his life writing poetry.

Tess of the d'Urbervilles is the story of an innocent young country girl who is seduced by the wealthy Alec d'Urberville. She has an illegitimate child, and, although she knows that she will be ostracized, refuses to ask her seducer for aid. The death of her unfortunate child, Sorrow, is devastating, but Tess bravely goes on, eventually meeting and marrying Angel Clare, a minister's son. Their marriage seems promising, but falls apart when Angel hears about her previous "downfall." Despite revelations of his own sin, the double standard prevails, and he cannot forgive her for hers. Thus she embarks on a life of hardship and travail, until Alec crosses her path again, having now become a preacher. She resists his offers for a while, but, finally is driven to accept his protection. At this point Angel returns from Brazil and finds her with Alec. Her state of mind no longer able to cope, she murders Alec to liberate herself. Tess's tragedy concludes at Stonehenge, where she offers herself up as a sacrifice and is soon taken away to be hanged. " 'Justice' was done," we are told, "and the President of the Immortals, . . . had ended his sport with Tess."

Critics today see *Tess of the d'Urbervilles* as embodying several important themes. The prominence of the countryside in Hardy's works is of major import. Landscape serves not only as a background, but is an inextricable part of the book. So thoroughly is the area of "Wessex" interwoven into the story that it assumes much the same emphasis as its characters. Hardy has constructed a myth of the area, composed of real as well as fictitious places, complete with customs and dialect; all of which lends to his stories a fullness and veracity. This is particularly true in *Tess*, in which the landscape and title character take parallel routes. Tess seems to be one with nature and the paths of her life blend with her surroundings. She grows up in the beautiful Vale of Blakemore, but as her life becomes more and more tragic, so the landscape becomes dark and foreboding. When her husband leaves her, she migrates to the cold north of Flintcomb-Ash, where the harsh land blends with her state of mind to expedite the tragedy of her life. In the final scene at Stonehenge, the antiquity of the setting adds to the significance of her downfall. Throughout the book, the land surrounds, embellishes, and enriches the story and the characters.

The theme of tragedy is often discussed in terms of this book. Fascinated by Greek tragedy, Hardy uses tragic circumstances to enhance the Wessex countryside and its inhabitants. By doing so he not only develops his story, but attains a certain grandeur for his novel. His first attempts at tragedy were *The Return of the Native* and *The Mayor of Casterbridge*, but *Tess of the d'Urbervilles* is the culmination of his efforts. In this work, Hardy projects ancient drama into modern novel form. To accomplish this, he models his book after Aristotle's formula for tragedy, although he focuses on a young country girl instead of a tragic hero. His many classical and Shakespearian allusions add strength to his modern tragedy.

Another theme in *Tess of the d'Urbervilles* is its reflection of the decline of the agricultural community in Victorian England. The forced migration of the Durbeyfields from home to home, and others from farm to farm, is indicative of the ruin of rural society. The erasure of long-standing rural communities was a serious social and spiritual loss, and the homeless despair of Tess's family keeps this problem in the forefront. Their moves around the countryside in search of a home is typical of the dissolving social order, and Tess, who follows the same pattern, can be seen as the symbol of this destruction.

But the most important aspect of this novel is Hardy's concern for the inequitable social conditions of the day. He had always been interested in social issues and had expressed his concerns in his earlier fiction, but in *Tess* he makes "virtue" the dominant theme. The subtitle, *A Pure Woman Faithfully Presented*, makes a strong statement which became the controversial issue of this Victorian book. That Hardy would call a girl "pure" who had been seduced and had an illegitimate child was shocking in his day. In doing so, he attacks Victorian double standards. We see, for instance, that although Angel has himself transgressed, he cannot condone a lesser act in Tess. As a consequence she suffers much, but always retains her belief in herself as a "pure woman." Faced with almost immediate disillusionment and continuing strife, she grows in strength and determination and confronts whatever befalls her. She is deeply aware of her situation and all its implications yet makes conscious choices, not out of desperation, but because of a sense of herself. Hardy sums up his point when he says of Tess that "the beauty or ugliness of a character lays . . . not among things done, but among things willed."

Tess of the d'Urbervilles is one of Hardy's greatest novels, and the development of the character of Tess is one of his greatest achievements. Far from being merely a victim, this simple girl meets the extraordinary challenges of her life and deals with them, making choices that reflect her integrity. Different critics see this book as representative of various literary themes, but there is a clear consensus that in creating Tess, Hardy developed a memorable heroine who is not only the focus of the book but its motivation.

—Ellen Lew Sprechman

THE TESTAMENT OF CRESSEID.
Poem by Robert Henryson, c. 1465–90.

The Testament of Cresseid, Robert Henryson's greatest achievement, purportedly supplies the conclusion the author felt to be missing from Chaucer's *Troilus and Criseyde*. Ironically, by admitting his need to complete the earlier poem, Henryson established the major critical crux of his own work: the question of its primary meaning. It has since been variously viewed as an exemplum of just retribution (for Cressida's betrayal of Troilus), a moralizing commentary on the sins of the flesh, a treatise on the untrustworthiness of a world ruled by fickle Fortune, and a thinly veiled *contemptus mundi* piece. Whatever its underlying design, the poem typifies the medieval period in its images, themes, and instructional nature, despite the author's occasional departures from established convention.

Henryson's tale and professed purpose are simple enough to preclude interpretive difficulty. Although Chaucer saw fit to relate the end of Troilus, he tells us, Cressida's fate is left a mystery, and it is this which *The Testament* illuminates. Cressida, cast off by Diomeid once he has "had all his appetyte / And mair," flees in shame to her father's house. There, she reviles Cupid and Venus as the causes of her misfortune. This blasphemy drives Cupid to summon a parliament of the gods to determine her punishment, an event which Cressida witnesses during a swoon. She is doomed to poverty and disease. Upon waking, Cressida finds herself a leper and, "with cop and clapper," takes her place among like outcasts in the "hospitall at the tounis end." Her vision, however, has brought understanding, and in her famous complaint she laments her inconstancy, her impiety, and the ultimate transience of earthly pleasures. Later, while begging with her fellows, she encounters Troilus. Her former lover does not recognize her but, seeing something in her face which reminds him of "his awen darling," gives her a purse of gold. This gesture causes Cressida to reflect upon the contrasts between his constancy and her own infidelity, and, after making her will, she dies.

Henryson incorporates a myriad of medieval themes and images into his tale, starting with courtly love. He assumes that his readers are familiar with Chaucer's story and are therefore able to understand the charges Cupid levies against the heroine for her breach of the courtly code. Indeed, her transgression, not romantic love itself, brings about her misery. Troilus, on the other hand, upholds the code in remaining true to Cressida despite her betrayal and, in his devotion, generosity, and nobility, exemplifies the chivalric ideal. As Henryson notes, the hero receives his just reward in *Troilus and Criseyde*.

Like Chaucer's work, *The Testament* attempts to reconcile courtly love to the Boethian Christianity embraced by the period. The sentence of the gods is rife with biblical imagery, reflecting the punitive virulence of medieval morality, and its fulfillment confirms the efficacy of self-knowledge through suffering. The image of the lazar house, a recurrent one in medieval literature, symbolizes the terrible nature of God's wrath and is inextricably bound up with Christianity. That Henryson employs it to punish a pagan sinner against courtly love suggests that earthly love is intertwined with that of the divine. The testament proper, however, is even more revealing. In it, Cressida bewails her infidelity to Troilus and her impiety against the gods with equal force. Moreover, her bequests serve as a catalogue of the Christian virtues: charity (the gold left the lazar house), love and repentance (the ring sent to Troilus in memory of herself), chastity (her spirit, commended to Diana), and forgiveness (the tokens left Diomeid).

Although courtly love and Christianity are his dominant themes, Henryson also stresses the concepts of Fortune, on which he places partial blame for Cressida's distress, and the influences of the planets on human character and destiny. His doing so is in part what blurs the import of the poem, for it shifts responsibility from the individual to forces beyond mortal control. Nonetheless, Cressida's testament and the final stanza, exhorting women to learn from her example, return the emphasis to conscious ethical behavior.

As regards poetic convention, *The Testament of Cresseid* is again grounded firmly in medieval tradition. The revelation of the gods' conference to the swooning Cressida represents a doff of the cap to the dream vision genre, and the moral didactic intent was a favourite mode of medieval authors. More interesting, perhaps, are the echoes of the Anglo-Saxon poetic. The concept of *wyrd* finds expression several times, melting into that of Fortune in lines 434–442, and lines 415–433 contain a classic *ubi sunt* lament. Alliteration, too, appears, interwoven with rhyme:

> When he had hard hir greit infirmity,
> Her legacy and lamentatioun,
> And how sho endit in sic poverty,
> He swelt for wo and fell doun in ane swoun;
> For greit sorrow his hart to brist was boun;
> Sihing full sadly, said, "I can no moir;
> Sho was untrew, and wo is me thairfoir."

But Chaucer remains the greatest influence, for his rhyme-royal provides the poem with its shape and its author with the basis for the 9-line variation of the form used for Cressida's complaint.

Despite the obvious debt to Chaucer in both subject and formal aspects, the poem is nonetheless very un-Chaucerian. Little in the way of the original's romance or comic spirit, or even the bitter laughter evinced by the ascended Troilus, characterize its supplement. Rather, darkness and cynicism pervade *The Testament of Cresseid*, qualities sometimes attributed to the Scottish spirit but just as likely a product of Henryson's roots in the middle class, whose pessimistic vision appears in the popular ballads (see, for example, "The Twa Corbies"). The opening of the poem, an obvious adaptation of that of *The Canterbury Tales*, describes spring not as the season of rebirth and love, but as a time of inclement weather and the privations of Lent. The 39-line lament of old age and dampened spirits which immediately follows that opening, and the assertion that the wisdom of years should turn to books rather than to love, prepare the reader for Cressida's dismal fate. The change of Calchas's allegiance from Apollo to Venus and Cupid is similarly sobering, for Henryson has altered the character of the love deities accordingly. Cupid in particular becomes the defender of virtue and constancy and, in pleading his case before the gods, the instrument of retribution. Thus, whether by an impersonal turn of Fortune's wheel or through a fierce divine justice, the deserts of human frailty are ultimately bleak, and the bitterness of transient pleasures lost remains.

—Gwendolyn Morgan

TESTAMENT OF YOUTH.
Prose by Vera Brittain (1893–1970), 1933.

Critical Studies: "On the Battlefield: Vera Brittain's *Testament of Youth*" by Jean Pickering, in *Women's Studies*, 13, 1986; *Brittain* by Hilary Bailey, 1987; *Family Quartet*: *Brittain and Her Family* by John Catlin, 1987; "Brittain's Testament(s)" by Lynne Layton, in *Behind the Lines*: *Gender and the Two World Wars* edited by Margaret R. Higonnet and others, 1987; *Brittain and Winifred Holtby*: *A Working Partnership* by Jean E. Kennard, 1989.

Published in 1933, Vera Brittain's autobiography *Testament of Youth* recounts the author's life up to 1925. Born in 1893, the daughter of a prosperous businessman, Brittain determined at an early age to break away from the conventional patterns of the time and win for herself an education and a career. She went up to Oxford in October 1914 but left the following summer to begin three years of nursing as a VAD nurse in England, Malta, and France. By the end of the war her brother, Edward Brittain; her fiancé, Roland Leighton; and her two closest friends were all dead. Shocked and disillusioned, she returned to Oxford, where, helped by her friendship with Winifred Holtby, she began to build a new life. After taking her degree, she settled in London and embarked on a career as a writer and lecturer. The autobiography ends with her decision to marry the political scientist George Catlin.

Testament of Youth followed a recent proliferation of memoirs and novels about World War I, almost all of them written by men, and it was Brittain's avowed intention to redress the balance by telling the story of the war from a woman's perspective and by emphasising women's contribution to the war effort. Clearly two of her motives were to honour the dead and to effect a personal catharsis by working her way through her painful and enormously vivid memories. To achieve these goals she deliberately attempted what she called a new type of autobiography, a personal story which presents major historical events from the viewpoint of a private individual. But Brittain had other aims too, involving not a commemoration of the past but a challenge to the future. *Testament of Youth* is designed to bear witness to the twin causes of pacifism and feminism which were the themes of her entire life's work. Comparison with the diaries written between 1913 and 1917 reveals the care with which she crafted her material, selecting, arranging, emphasising, and altering so as to shape her story in accordance with her commitment to these two principles.

Although Brittain did not become a committed pacifist until 1936, the pacifist tendency of the autobiography is plain, and its structural and emotional centre is the second part, dealing with the war years. Part I ends with Brittain's account of receiving the news of Leighton's death at the very moment when she was expecting to see him on his return from France for a New Year's leave. The event was the first of her personal tragedies and marks the shift to a grim portrayal of the horrors of war. Writing from the nurse's perspective, she gives the naked reality of war's effects; the waiting beds during a push, the confusion as the wounded are brought in, the colours of the stained dressings, the hideous wounds, the all-encompassing pain and fear are described in graphic detail. Yet Brittain's indictment is not simply emotional, for she also exposes the evil and absurdity of the male-oriented, militaristic culture which she held responsible for the war. Like many of her generation, she felt that the young had been cynically exploited by an older generation which had inculcated a false heroic image of the glory of war and then used that image to further its own selfish interests. Thus she ironically reports the words of the Headmaster of Uppingham School in July 1914: "If a man cannot be useful to his country, he is better off dead." And throughout the narrative she demonstrates, often by direct quotation of her own and Leighton's letters, the dissipation of early idealism in despair and disillusion.

Brittain manipulates the elements of her narrative so as to reinforce this central theme. The structure traces an archetypal pattern of initial optimism, abrupt descent into an underworld, and a slow emergence into a new life. Extracts from diaries and letters add authenticity and the immediacy of actual experience. Two time perspectives are subtly interwoven as past events are presented in the light of subsequent knowledge, thus enhancing the tragedy. The characters assume symbolic stature. Thus Brittain's self-portrait is not just a recreation of an individual life but a representation of an entire generation, for as she describes the deaths of close friends and casual acquaintances, air raids, shipwrecks in Malta, fighting in France, the arrival of the wounded in England, her hallucinations after the Armistice, she incorporates in herself the universal experience of war. Similarly the four soldiers—Leighton, a natural leader; Edward Brittain, a musician; Geoffrey Thurlow, a religious idealist; and Victor Richardson, a devoted friend—come to embody the wasted talents and virtues of all war victims.

Since for Brittain war is the result of men's politics, the theme of pacifism is closely bound up with feminism, the chief subject of the first and third parts. Here Brittain reiterates women's rights to intellectual stimulation, education, and a career. The feminist principle also underlies her celebration of female friendship in the depiction of Holtby's role in her gradual recovery after the war. The narrative ends with a long meditation as she ponders a new concept of marriage, in which the woman retains her freedom and personal identity. Again she uses herself to represent a larger entity, and the account of the restrictions of her early years, her struggle for a university education, her achievement of independence and a career, and her involvement with politics through writing and lecturing reproduces in miniature the course of the women's movement in the past century. As with the pacifist theme, a generational conflict is involved, Leighton and Catlin suggesting a new, enlightened attitude to women, contrasted with the dictatorial, self-centred approach of Brittain's father.

Despite its unflinching depiction of horrors, *Testament of Youth* finally delivers an optimistic message, concluding with the assertion that the misery of the past eventually "led . . . through . . . dark and devious ways to this new beginning." The beginning was not merely for the individual, Vera Brittain, but for an age which she saw as moving forward to establish a better way of life for all men and women.

—Muriel Mellown

THEY FLEE FROM ME.
Poem by Sir Thomas Wyatt, 1557.

"They flee from me" is a poem both common and strange; Sir Thomas Wyatt as usual employs the traditional courtly setting and its language of love as background to a betrayed lover's lament. Yet these elements are forged anew into the original and intense expression of a particular lover.

The lover's struggle to explain and understand the reversal of his fortunes is compelling because it is dramatised as a process. To achieve this the poem is both fluid and, paradoxically, densely focused. This combination is felt most clearly in the poem's resistance to an interpretation; most conspicuously, there is uncertainty over the central lady's identity. She may be simultaneously a real woman, and—allegorically—Fortune and (Courtly) Love, or any one or two of these. This resistance is part of the drama, not a reflection on Wyatt's need for discretion at Henry VIII's court. It is enabled by the widespread use of meaningful ambiguity.

Yet the poem is also the lover's argument. Though formally a ballad in rhyme-royal stanzas, it has a sonnet's involved and developing chain of thought. In presenting his story of betrayal, and his loss of faith in courtly values, the narrator is trying to persuade us to answer his final couplet's half-question, "I would fain know what she hath deserved," on his own terms.

Both drama and argument are sustained through the imagery, and so our interpretations become dependent on it. For Wyatt here goes beyond his Italian models in his determination to subordinate the poem's elements to its dominant poetic ideas or conceits. Through them he gives a rhetorical unity to the poem's fluidity. Yet they are qualified themselves.

"With naked foot *stalking*" begins the traditional metaphor of a hunt as the hunt of love, imagining the women, the "they" in the first line, as predatory birds or beasts. Yet the concretely observed "naked foot"—its juxtaposition exemplifying the poem's verbal subtlety—suggests that the women have an erotic vulnerability. Which is true? The narrator, it seems, is self-deceiving. This sense of an "I," a poetic voice separate from the poet's to this degree, originates with Wyatt. The poem's "continual change" of tone represents the lover's own fickleness while he asserts that of others.

For he alternates between passivity and concealed aggression throughout the poem. "Stalking" was unusual in giving a passive role to the male lover. But then "they" put themselves under his control—"in danger" both means "in danger of scandal" and "in someone's power." By the second stanza the narrator is again passive, which is part of the scene's eroticism, and the pun on "heart" (organ and deer) pictures him again as quarry. He enjoyed pretending to be the prey, but in the final stanza laments that he has become so, presenting his passivity as cruel victimization; he is forsaken for his "gentleness." This quality, important to the courtly lover, he now revalues. He wants us to believe that he has not been unwise, but that trust itself, the values contained in gentleness, are unwise. To us, a tension is apparent between idealized courtliness as against his sexual desire and desire for power.

In all this the simple beauty of the language must not be forgotten; Wyatt's thought is complex, but his words plain and in an order close to speech. In this he is influential, turning English poetry away from the aureate element in medieval lyric. Yet the rhetorical devices he does employ are powerful; the alliterative "strange fashion of forsaking" is haunting and sorrowful. The metre has a rough regularity, varying within narrow restraints. It is basically a five foot and five stress line of ten syllables, though not iambic pentameter. Its irregularity is melodious and expressive; the importance of "stalking," for instance, is emphasized by its reversal of the rhythm of the two preceding iambic feet.

The final stanza, changing time once more, returns us to the sadness of the lover's present from the ecstatic moment of his fulfilled past, and he asks us to consider what "she hath deserved." This balanced politeness is fragile after the bitter irony of: "And I have leave to go of her goodness"; its sense of recrimination builds with the following line's repetition of the initial "And." The lover wants us to answer in the terms of his previous line's summary: "But since that I so kindly am served." "Kindly" is both ironic, in the sense of "pleasantly," and judgemental, suggesting the woman's betrayal of him as an action "according to her nature or kind." But this latter sense forces us to begin considering anew the imagery around "they" and the identity of the woman, remembering how this served the narrator's self-deceit. If the poem has one ending it has many. It has, finally, an aura of strangeness best described by Surrey's epitaph to Wyatt, who had, he says, "A head, where wisdom mysteries did frame."

—John Lee

THINGS FALL APART.
Novel by Chinua Achebe, 1958.

In 1958, when Chinua Achebe's *Things Fall Apart* first appeared, the mindset of hunter-gatherers was a closed book to most fiction readers. We knew plenty about the external details of "primitive" lives: academic studies detailed their myths, languages, and customs, television and film documentaries recorded rituals and ceremonies which had survived, and cemented society, for millennia. But few "civilised" people—how fanged these words are!—bothered to ask how the aboriginal inhabitants of Africa, Australasia, the Americas, thought about each other, the land, the supernatural—attitudes which made them what they were. In 1958 it was rare for anyone in the "first world" even to imagine the possibility that "third world" ideas about life might be just as valid as their own.

Achebe's novel marks the turning-point between this state of mind and the more enlightened understanding which began in the 1960's. He set his book in an unremarkable hunter-gatherer community in Nigeria, but concentrated less on ritual masks or labial clicks than on thought-patterns, emotions, and relationships. When the god-spirits of Umuofia (Achebe's invented community) appear before the people, they are not humans in masks, but superhuman judges whose powers are validated by their hearers' belief in them. The ways Achebe's hero sows yams, or his wives bring him food each evening, are established and ritualised, reinforcing the continuum, the harmony on which existence itself depends. Novelists writing about "civilised" societies do this all the time, unobtrusively burnishing our image of what human life is like each time they describe someone crossing the street, shopping, entering a room, washing, talking, eating. Achebe makes us appreciate that the tapestry of "primitive" everyday life is just as inevitable and just as essential.

Okonkwo, the central character, is the very emblem of such a society. He embodies its values and his existence depends on them. Without a moment's didacticism, Achebe shows us at once what matters to such a man. When one of Okonkwo's wives goes gossiping instead of preparing his evening meal, we understand why Okonkwo feels the need to beat her—not the reaction we might have to identical events in Carson McCullers. When Okonkwo's son challenges his father's opinions, or Okonkwo's daughter falls dangerously ill, we understand Okonkwo's irritation that chattels and possessions are making emotional claims with which he is not equipped to cope. We know in our bones how vital the exact sequence of actions is in the kola-nut ritual; we appreciate that no animal can be killed for food unless it is thought to consent in its own death. Above all, we accept Okonkwo without judging him, as his family does, as a pride of lions accepts the dominant male. One day he will be challenged and defeated; until then, he and only he is allowed to judge his own actions. That is how things have always been, and that is what keeps the community healthy now.

The "pride-male" is a familiar character in western literature, whether he stalks the drawing rooms of Victorian England or the plantations of Louisiana. What is extraordinary about Okonkwo is not his personality—a fictional commonplace—but the parameters of his existence. Everything he does or says, however bizarre it might seem if considered in isolation, is the product of an uncomplicated, systematic growth. Richard Dawkins, in his book *The Blind Watchmaker*, explains how the eye (taken by some Christian fundamentalists to be so complex, and so beautiful, that it could not have appeared spontaneously and is therefore evidence for the existence of God) in fact evolved in millions of tiny steps over billions of years. Achebe shows us similar evolutionary continuity and inevitability in his society, and in Okonkwo its exemplar.

To have produced such a compelling account of something so out of the fictional ordinary would have been achievement enough. But this is just the beginning. Achebe is a political novelist, interested less in the products of change (whether evolutionary or otherwise) than in moments of change themselves. As soon as we know what Okonkwo is, and why, Achebe begins to destroy him. And again, he works within but against the traditional concepts of western fiction. When characters such as Emma Bovary or Raskolnikov are destroyed, their collapse is triggered by some quality inside themselves, or in the society around them. Not so in Okonkwo's case. His character, and the society he lives in, are parts of a continuum which can absorb and cope with shocks. There is no risk of destruction from within: if danger comes (for example when twins are born or the taboo against cannibalism is broken), the transgressor is left to die in the Evil Wood, to return to Mother Earth from which he or she first sprang. Natural selection operates, and its instrument is human choice.

Umuofia society is, however, dangerously vulnerable to shocks from outside, to the unfamiliar. As soon as missionaries come, there is no hope. Until then white people were the stuff of folk tales, as remote from reality as the turtle which tried to fly. Now, suddenly, they are at the village's heart, talking gibberish, too "primitive" to understand the customs and beliefs which are the glue of the people's existence, but sinisterly supported by men with guns. The usual means of dealing with danger are no help at all: when the Christians are offered land to build on, in the Evil Wood, their community flourishes instead of withering. When they ask for followers, and are sent all the sick, lame, and other cast-outs, they turn base humanity to born-again gold. They are a cancer, and as they thrive they kill their host.

Since *Things Fall Apart*, Achebe has written other novels savaging the destructive effects on third-world societies of first-world ideas and life systems. His later books, notably *Arrow of God* and *A Man of the People*, throw spectacular punches in all directions. In *Things Fall Apart* the message is more quietly stated but no less devastating. The book reads like a folk tale for grownups, and its brevity—as in a folk tale—leaves no room for alternative opinion or argument. Not since Swift, in *Gulliver's Travels*, saw off the values of the Age of Enlightenment, has European civilisation had such an unremittingly courteous, silky going-over.

—Kenneth McLeish

THREE MEN IN A BOAT.
Novel by Jerome K. Jerome, 1889.

The first edition of Jerome K. Jerome's *Three Men in a Boat (To say nothing of the Dog)*—to give the work its full title—has a preface beginning

> The chief beauty of this book lies not so much in its literary style, or in the extent and usefulness of the information it conveys, as in its simple truthfulness. Its pages form the record of events that really happened. All that has been done is to colour them; and, for this, no extra charge has been made.

This sets the tone for the 19 chapters which follow, recording an excursion up the Thames from Kingston to Oxford in a double-sculling skiff. A typical chapter-heading suggests the form and content of the record:

> *Our first night–Under canvas–An appeal for help–Contrariness of tea-kettles, how to overcome–Supper–How to feel virtuous–Wanted, a comfortably-appointed, well-drained desert island, neighbourhood of South Pacific Ocean preferred–Funny thing that happened to George's father–A restless night.*

There *is* a narrative, enumerating the places through which the excursionists passed and the adventures that befell them, but it is continually interrupted by anecdotal reminiscences and by reflections both humorous and serious; these interruptions are as essential to the book as is the narrative.

The three men of the title are the narrator (known as J.), William Samuel Harris (known as Harris), and George (known as George). The dog is a fox-terrier of aristocratic name and plebeian tastes. Their interplay is one of the joys of the narrative: when J. packs the bag of clothes and afterwards the others pack the two hampers of food and cooking utensils, both operations have an attentive audience, and Montmorency too takes part, convinced "that, whenever Harris or George reached out their hand for anything, it was his cold damp nose that they wanted." All three men are bachelors, of course, and no women appear except in general reflections: "Of all experiences in connection with towing, the most exciting is being towed by girls. It is a sensation that nobody ought to miss. It takes three girls to tow always; two hold the rope, and the other one runs round and round and giggles." What Harris and J. do for a living is not stated, but "George goes to sleep at a bank from ten to four each day, except Saturdays, when they wake him up and put him outside at two," and there is a notable account of "how George, once upon a time, got up early in the morning," misled by his watch into thinking that it was nearly nine and that he would be late for work, whereas it turned out to be nearly three: he went home, tried to sleep in a chair, tried to play himself at chess, tried to read, and finally went for a walk:

> It was horribly lonesome and dismal, and all the policemen he met regarded him with suspicion, and turned their lanterns on him, and followed him about, and this had such an effect upon him at last that he began to feel as if he really had done something, and he got to slinking down the by-streets and hiding in dark doorways when he heard the regulation flip-flop approaching.

Other digressions describe how J.'s Uncle Podger hangs up a picture, how Harris sings a comic song (this is given in dramatic form, with speech-prefixes and stage-directions), how Harris once went into the maze at Hampton Court and lost his way and that of a large party he collected, and how J. once transported two cheeses from Liverpool to London by train to oblige a friend.

Not all the book is in this humorous key. At Runnymede, Jerome writes a colourful description, in the historic present tense, of King John and his barons assembling for the signing of Magna Carta: the chapter-heading calls it an "historical retrospect, specially inserted for the use of schools," and at the beginning of the next chapter George recalls J. from his reverie to the washing-up, but the description itself, though florid in expression, is not parodic, any more than is the allegorical story of a knight who wandered in the dark forest of Sorrow and had a vision of unspeakable glory (Oscar Wilde's *The Happy Prince and Other Tales* had appeared in the previous year). Three chapters after sighting a drowned dog while making their tea with river water they sight a drowned woman, whose story ("Of course it was the old, old vulgar tragedy") is told briefly and poignantly:

> and then she had gone to see her child—and held it in her arms and kissed it, in a weary, dull sort of way, and without betraying any particular emotion of any kind, and had left it, after putting into its hand a penny box of chocolate she had bought it, and afterwards, with her last few shillings, had taken a ticket and come down to Goring.

In its mingling of seriousness with the prevailing comedy the book recalls Dickens's *Pickwick Papers*. In its reflective passages, often cast in whimsical form, it recalls the essays of Lamb. Its own influence on the English humorous tradition can be seen in Kenneth Grahame's *The Wind in the Willows* and in A.A. Milne's *Winnie-the-Pooh*.

—T.W. Craik

THE TIME MACHINE.
Novel by H.G. Wells, 1895.

By the time it was published in book form H.G. Wells's *The Time Machine*, the best-known of his "scientific romances," had already been serialized three times in very different, usually incomplete forms: as *The Chronic Argonauts* in *Science Schools Journal* (April–June 1888), and under its later title in *National Observer* (March–June 1894) and *New Review* (January–May 1895). It was further revised for Wells's Atlantic Edition (1924), which incorporated changes he marked in a copy some time in 1898 or 1899. Since 1895, Wells's "assault on human self-satisfaction" has never been out of print, and it has considerably influenced most 20th-century time-travel adventures. A contemporary of Wells, Israel Zangwill, said it presented "a vision far more sombre and impressive than the ancient imaginings of the Biblical seers," and the great Argentinian fantasist, Jorge Luis Borges, said that it and Wells's other scientific romances "will be incorporated . . . into the general memory of the species and even transcend the fame of their creator or the extinction of the language in which they were written."

Written in a plain style (Wells once said, "I write as I walk because I want to get somewhere") and in the fantasy traditions of Plato and Swift, *The Time Machine* has a young narrator who greatly admires the older, adventuresome protagonist who is known only as the Time Traveller. The young man tells the story three years after the Time Traveller has disappeared on his quest to document for his audience the realities of the future. He is telling the story as testimony to the powers of the human imagination and as a warning, encouraging his audience to live "as though it were not so" that "the growing pile of civilization [is] only a foolish heaping that must inevitably fall back upon and destroy its makers in the end." Technically, the young man and the Time Traveller resemble the dual protagonists in Joseph Conrad's "Heart of Darkness," except little is done to develop their relationship and their personalities.

The protagonist of this fable of devolution is introduced during his at-home Thursdays in "that luxurious after-dinner atmosphere" of his Richmond home. He entertains his skeptical guests, all of whom are presented as types (Medical Man, Psychologist, Journalist, etc.), with talk of the Fourth Dimension, an idea Wells probably took from a C.H. Hinton essay, and posits that travel in time is indeed possible. He introduces a small model of his time machine, which he makes vanish before their very unbelieving eyes.

The second Thursday features a truly memorable entrance when the Time Traveller, very late in greeting his guests, suddenly enters the dining room "in an amazing plight"—dirty, dusty, dishevelled, limping, and wearing "tattered blood-stained socks." He tells his wondering guests that since their last meeting he has spent eight days [sic] in the future world of 802,701 and witnessed the near extinction of all life some 30 million years into the future. Since their last meeting, he has been in a world where a "too perfect triumph of man" has destroyed civilization and virtually destroyed the human species.

The Time Traveller, committed to Victorian belief in progress, had expected to find "wonderful advances upon our rudimentary civilization." Instead, he found a strangely attenuated world inhabited by the Eloi, who resemble diminutive human beings and strike him as being "consumptive," "indolent," "easily fatigued"—in short, a disillusioning disappointment. Where he expected to find perfected intelligence, he finds beings bereft of intellectual curiosity, productive activity, and basic human feelings such as love, and paralyzed by childlike fear of darkness. Soon the Time Traveller discovers a second species, the subterranean Morlock, a "bleached, obscene, nocturnal Thing" which he variously describes as "little ape-like figures" and "human rats." The Morlocks paradoxically repulse him but also intrigue him because of their obvious intellectual powers and mechanical mastery.

In his adventures, which replicate the archetypal patterns described by Joseph Campbell, the Time Traveller rescues Weena, an Eloi and minor love interest, from drowning, explores the deserted buildings, which become a record of the death of the human intellect, and battles for his life with the Morlocks in fire-engulfed woods. Intellectually, the narrative consists of the Time Traveller attempting to frame a sufficient explanation of the relationship between the Eloi and Morlock, which attempt provides the thematic complexity of the work. At first, he assumes that the Eloi defeated the Morlocks in a class struggle some time in the past, a class struggle he senses is present in the 1890's; he then assumes that the Morlocks won and merely tolerate the Eloi's presence; finally, he learns that the Morlocks are carnivorous and the Eloi are tended as cattle and "harvested" for the Morlock tables during the dark of the moon each month. His adventures are filled with self-authenticating details which explain his physical appearance to his guests, none of which is more memorable than the white mallows he pulls from the pocket in which Weena had hidden them.

As might be expected from a protagonist who is a physical optician, the Time Traveller wishes his generation to *see*. To this end, his tale has all the adventurous features of culture shock in an alien world which ultimately emerges as the contemporary world whose conditions have been extended to their logical conclusions. The Time Traveller warns his audience that the human characteristics of the Eloi and Morlock exist within the individual and are still held together by intellectual curiosity and love. Should these lynchpins be loosened and the present conditions allowed to continue to exist, at some point in the future the human will begin to devolve into the two very different types of creatures.

In any case, entropy will leave Earth a dead planet circling an exhausted Sun, but for the 1890's, Wells intends the dualities of Eloi and Morlock to be interpreted as the oppositions of proletariat and capital, aestheticism and utilitarianism, pastoralism and technology. As the Time Traveller tells his audience, "Take it as a lie—or a prophecy."

—David Leon Higdon

TIMON OF ATHENS.
Play by William Shakespeare, 1607 (?).

Arguably the least effective of his serious plays, *Timon of Athens* offers a bridge between the great tragedies and the subsequent romances (as they have come to be called) that concluded William Shakespeare's career in the theater. Despite so many unsatisfactory aspects, it is a necessary play in any consideration of the full canon, and to ignore it because it is not another *King Lear* is to ignore Shakespeare's clear progression toward deliberately archetypal materials more appropriate to his dramatized fabliaux than to his tragedies. *Timon of Athens* stares in rancor and rants in bile more revolting than anything in Shakespeare's earlier plays; it shares with later ones the sharp shifts in behavior more appropriate to the fairy-tale world of preposterous conflicts and warm reconciliations. More specifically, *Timon of Athens* reflects on the bitterness of betrayal in *Coriolanus* and on the contradictions in time and motivation in *Pericles*, both written in all probability during 1606 to 1608, and in the view of more than one reader, separated in composition by this hybrid study. Some earlier readers placed *Timon of Athens* adjacent to *King Lear*, largely because of parallels in their similar maledictions and cruel shifts from innocence to experience. Recent assessments push it forward for more persuasive reasons. *Timon of Athens*, however, regardless of its place in the canon, has suffered from a paucity of both productions and critical assessments, far less indeed than the modest attention accorded even the two uneasy plays that probably frame it.

The plot is easily summarized: a genial philanthropist turns disillusioned misanthropist when seeming friends desert him after he loses his fortune. In the subplot, a military commander's public behavior and actions reflect Timon's private ones: Alcibiades begins in anger against a corrupt Athens but concludes in restoring order to the city with mercy. His activities offer a mirror image for those of Timon, but more symmetrically than dramatically. In both Timon and Alcibiades, however, human characteristics are subverted by metaphoric ones. Although on occasion Timon's eloquence can suggest earlier protagonists in the passion of his bitterness—even King Lear—it is unlikely that readers or audiences will so easily identify with him or his circumstances. In the first half the play, Timon's largesse is his only charm, so his invective in the second half spews from someone in whom it is difficult to take much human interest. Similarly, Alcibiades is so strongly a military robot during the first half of the play that his largesse in the second half is unengaging. Since the two plots often seem superimposed rather than integrated, their connection is limited to their reflecting human behavior rather than human flesh and blood. Neither evokes any substantial empathy, a rare circumstance in Shakespeare.

The play is unique in another way as well. Timon is no heir-presumptive like Hamlet, or king like Lear, or military giant like Othello or Coriolanus; indeed, in Shakespeare's serious plays he is an alien hero, having neither birthright nor superior ability in his favor. In an Athens corrupted by greed, where even poets and painters fall prey, Timon achieves his prominence only because his wealth crowns him, and his subjects are loyal to his purse rather than to his singular behavior. Until he loses his money, Timon is an uninteresting personality, not a shallow man but a vapid one. There is virtually no poetry in his pontificating about his generosity, and until the end of the third act, he could as easily be spoken of by others rather than speaking for himself. Once bereft of his money, however, Timon becomes painfully human, and the strength of his invective results in some memorable verse. Shakespeare calls upon two familar images through which to convey Timon's plight: the animal kingdom as a human analogy, and the corruptive nature of sexual licentiousness. Both inform Timon's speeches with extravagant power, and they are only less effective in this play than in others, perhaps, because the full play went either unrevised or unfinished.

As commentator, or chorus-figure, Shakespeare supplied Apemantus, "a churlish philosopher" for whom "Friendship's full of dregs." He passes apt judgment on Timon that explains as well some of the difficulty in the play itself: "The middle of humanity thou never knewest, but the extremity of both ends." The play is one of character traits rather than of characters. Even so, at the nadir of his despair, Timon possesses a frightening eloquence, particularly in the curses that open scenes one (1–40) and three (1–24) of Act IV. Removed from their context, they belong in any catalogue to represent Shakespeare's genius. Similarly, Timon's recognition that money corrupts, in that latter scene (25–48, 381–92), is equally strong; moreover, it speaks to the present with disturbing aptness.

—Bruce Kellner

TINTERN ABBEY.
("Lines Composed a Few Miles above Tintern Abbey.")
Poem by William Wordsworth, 1798.

Placed last in the 1798 first edition of Wordsworth and Coleridge's *Lyrical Ballads*, "Lines Composed a Few Miles Above Tintern Abbey, on Revisiting the Banks of the Wye During a Tour, July 13, 1798" offers unusually direct access to the mind and art of Wordsworth as he began the half decade during which his major poetry was written. "Tintern Abbey," as it is always misleadingly called, looks before and after: backward first to the loco-descriptive, 18th-century mode of such poems as "An Evening Walk" and to the ballads of ordinary life in this collection, but forward to the autobiographical, philosophical concerns of the "Intimations Ode" (begun 1802) and the *Prelude* (1805). In its 159 lines the poet expands the act of geographical and chronological location begun in the unusually explicit title to place himself, and this moment of return to the Wye valley having heard the "still, sad music of humanity," on a continuum, sited between a past moment five years before when "first / I came among these hills," and an indefinite future when the validity of *this* moment may rely not on his memory but that of his sister.

Wordsworth's autobiographical model, as Keats recognized so clearly in his "Knowledge is sorrow" letter to Reynolds (3 May 1818), is that of a gradual, inevitable darkening of perception that nevertheless offers a possibility for moral vision:

> . . . sharpening one's vision into the heart and nature of Man, . . . convincing one's nerves that the World is full of Misery and Heartbreak, Pain, Sickness and oppression—whereby the Chamber of Maiden Thought becomes gradually darken'd and at the same time on all sides of it many doors are set open—but all dark—all leading to dark passages—We see not the ballance of good and evil. . . . To this point was Wordsworth come . . . when he wrote "Tintern Abbey," and it seems to me that his Genius is explorative of those dark Passages . . .

The speaker of this exploratory poem opens by modestly insisting on no more than he can easily document: his presence, the scene, the time elapsed since his last visit. The immediacy of details is emphasized, the movement from visual apprehension to speculation is unemphatic, even apologetic. To read the poem is to watch the poet move to a position from which he can claim more: that the sensations (*not* memories) recalled from his earlier visit have in the interim sustained him "in lonely rooms, and 'mid the din / Of towns and cities." The additional benefit, "of aspect more sublime," that he owes to the forms of beauty is something beyond the poet's control: the "blessed mood, / In which the burthen of the mystery, / In which the heavy and the weary weight / Of all this unintelligible world, / Is lightened." Here, as the claims become larger they are made universal, for it is "we" who become a living soul, "see into the life of things"—the poet perhaps recognizing that a reader is less likely to question the validity of an experience he is told he shares.

At the beginning of the third section, the situation is more complex, for the "I" who stands "here" is no longer simply in a place but at a moment in time, conditioned by dim recollections of the past, soothed by a sense of present pleasure, filled with anticipations of this moment's future usefulness. And the "I" who speaks is no more stable than his place: once the glad animal moving unthinking, then a young man following nature, consciously seeking to gratify an appetite immediate and sensual. For either past self, "I cannot paint / What then I was." Yet the present self is no easier to paint, for the ear hears not the pure present sound but blends reflection with apprehension and anticipation. To make this loss of simplicity a gain, a new vocabulary is found—the *presence* that disturbs with the joy of elevated thoughts, the *sense* of something, a *motion*, a *spirit* that inhabits the light of setting sun, round ocean, living air, blue sky, mind of man. The "therefore" that follows seems not an introduction to a truth demonstrated but a gesture of confidence in the face of these assertions. For he has no clearer name for what he is now than he has for the causes of his being it: a well-pleased lover recognizing an anchor, nurse, guide, guardian of the heart, and soul of his moral being.

Perhaps defensively, the poet turns to the previously unmentioned presence of his sister, who in effect becomes the anchor, nurse, guide, guardian—and surrogate for an unbetraying Nature. The language of his poetic heart is in her voice, his former pleasures in her eyes—she is a permanent and *legible* record of what he once was. His prayer for her (more a blessing, in the authority its speaker assumes) builds an alliance of siblings against evil tongues, rash judgments, unkind greetings, and "the dreary intercourse of daily life." He reciprocally acts for her as nurse, anchor, guide. This change of dramatic situation, from metaphysical contemplation in apparent solitude to a scene of dual domestic affection is disarming: consolation for the fear of loss, of mortality, is more easily located in human love than in a "sense" or "presence," and Dorothy is far less likely than Nature to betray the heart that loves her. But a reader may feel that the poet has to an extent begged the question by changing its terms. As in many of Wordsworth's major poems, the power lies in the questions addressed more than in the answers provided.

For rather different reasons, several recent critics have made the poem a test case for a historicist (or anti-historicist) interpretation of Romantic poetry. This poem is full, historicists argue, of hints and traces of a historical world that is being excluded, displaced, or denied: its indirect allusion to other 14ths of July (the fall of the Bastille in 1789, Wordsworth's arrival in France in 1790); to economically displaced cottagers burning charcoal in the woods; to the widely-publicized pollution of the Wye; to the ruin of the Abbey itself. Feminists have argued that Dorothy's gender has enabled the poet to reduce her to an amanuensis rather than an equal participant (he suffers and creates, she merely records). As an evasive gesture, then, the poem is given pride of place among those Romantic works that record a poet's disillusionment with the French Revolution and its aftermath by turning its attention elsewhere, or—especially—inward. Thus the poem's indeterminacy becomes its meaning, and analysis of it, presumably, interminable.

—William W. Heath

'TIS PITY SHE'S A WHORE.
Play by John Ford, 1629–33(?)

In Act I of John Ford's *'Tis Pity She's a Whore*, Annabella's nurse, the ungenerously named Putana, comments to her charge—"Here's threat'ning, challenging, quarreling, and fighting, on every side, and all is for your sake." Parma, where the action takes place, is certainly violent, both in the streets, where gentlemen and their servants battle or wait in ambush, and inside the homes; late in the play, Annabella is dragged on stage by her infuriated husband—"Thus will I pull thy hair, and thus I'll drag / Thy lust-beleper'd body through the dust." Banditti, ready enough for mayhem or murder, are on call. In the lord cardinal's residence, where order should prevail, insolent corruption replaces honesty.

Three violent episodes stand out: the graphic and gruesome death of Hippolita by corrosive poisoning; the messy and bloody stabbing of the innocuous and feeble-minded Bergetto; and the celebrated presentation on stage of Annabella's heart, impaled on her brother's sword. Much of the language, too, is violent in its threats, its rantings, and its explicit description of horrors. Yet the characters seem inured to the violence swirling around them: Donado comments over the corpses on stage in the final moments, "Strange miracle of justice," and "'Tis most just."

The physical violence is consequent on the violent sexual passions that drive the action. Annabella, as Putana observes, is the focus; beautiful, rich, and free-spirited, she enters an incestuous relationship with her brilliant and headstrong brother Giovanni. Meanwhile, Annabella's suitors scheme to destroy each other, while Hippolita, disappointed in her love for Soranzo, rages against mankind as her disguised husband Richardetto looks on and plots revenge. Forced by her pregnancy to marry Soranzo, Annabella reveals her terrible secret and general slaughter follows.

Were the play only a recital of this grisly story, it would be no more than a pornographic curiosity—an example of the characteristic English belief in the villainy of Renaissance Italy. But Ford gives his unsavory tale coherence and direction by identifying four sources of emotional power that drive men and women, and showing how these may struggle against or overwhelm each other.

Religion is one obvious source of power. The Friar who is Giovanni's tutor attempts, futilely, to move him to faith and repentance. Annabella, on the other hand, is less hostile. When she first sees her brother at a distance, she intuitively uses religious imagery to define the beautiful sight: "what blessed shape / Of some celestial creature." She might, in different circumstances, be as happy as Richardetto supposes his niece Philotis will be in a nunnery: "Your home your cloister, your best friends your beads. / Your chaste and single life shall crown your birth." By Act III, the Friar is able to persuade the now distraught Annabella to abandon her lusts and to seek forgiveness—"Heaven is merciful, / And offers grace even now." The power of religion triumphs in her; in her final interview with her brother, she lectures him on Heaven and Hell, and promises that they will meet again in an after-life. At her moment of death she prays for her brother's forgiveness and for mercy for herself.

Giovanni demonstrates the emotional power of reason and logic; he excelled in disputations as a scholar, and in his debates with the Friar he arrogantly appeals to philosophy to justify his behaviour—"What I have done, I'll prove both fit and good." In his final debate with his sister, he speaks of heaven as only a dream, and at the moment of death rejects the plea—"Strive yet to cry to Heaven"—profanely hoping instead for "this grace, / Freely to view my Annabella's face." In his youth he had epitomised the power of learning and knowledge:

> How did the University applaud
> Thy government, behaviour, learning, speech,
> Sweetness, and all that could make up a man!

The incestuous lovers recognise that the powers of religion and reason can be overcome by the power of lust; Giovanni tells his sister that he "Reason'd against the reasons of my love," but was unsuccessful. Like Hippolita, they are driven to despair and madness by their passions.

The fourth power, that can conquer even that of lust, is the power of vengeful rage. This power overwhelms the lovelorn Hippolita, turns Soranzo homicidal, makes Richardetto an agent of revenge, and drives Giovanni to the murder of his beloved sister.

That individual behaviour depends on which power is in control is attested to by the Friar's shrewd question to Giovanni: "hast thou left the schools / Of knowledge to converse with lust and death?" The conflict of powers is suggested by a passage in Act IV, where Vasques attempts to cool Soranzo's rage against Annabella: "Sir, you must be ruled by your reason and not by your fury, that were unhuman and beastly." But Vasques persuades Soranzo only to pretend moderation, the better to learn the truth and rush to a violent revenge: "Delay in vengeance gives a heavier blow."

Ford is presenting a double moral structure; obviously the power of religion is most privileged, with the powers of reason, lust, and rage in a progressive moral descent. However, the lust of Annabella and the murderous passions of Giovanni and Hippolita, while deplorable, are, according to the second moral system, at least forthright and honest. The disguised Richardetto, and the scheming Soranzo and Vasques—by pretending to values they do not hold—are the truly destructive figures.

Imaginative coherence is given to this moral concept by the imagery of the heart, the repository of true feelings, and by the shocking realisation of this image when Annabella's heart is physically displayed. In Act III, when Soranza is courting the still self-assured Annabella, he uses a metaphor of sincerity: "Did you but see my heart, then would you swear—." She, ironically, decodes the metaphor: "That you were dead." When he assaults her in Act IV, he in turn makes the metaphor physical: "I'll rip up thy heart, / And find it [the name of her lover] there." From the opening scene ("Emptied the storehouse of my thoughts and heart," "One soul, one flesh, one love, one heart, one all") the heart, as the image of truth and love, dominates the play. Annabella's "captive heart" is held by her brother, her "heart's delight," at the beginning of their love. When at the end the maddened Giovanni confuses metaphor and reality, literally tearing out her heart—"'tis a heart, / A heart, my lords, in which is mine entomb'd"—he demonstrates how effectively Ford has brought together the affective morality of sincerity, passionate rhetoric, and the power of stagecraft.

—Richard Morton

TITUS ANDRONICUS.
Play by William Shakespeare, 1594.

As a play which presents substantial problems of source, historical context, and textual authenticity, *Titus Andronicus* has generated a diversity of interpretation through its production history, ranging from exercises in Artaudian Theatre of Cruelty to Ovidian lyricism and pastoralism. Like the major Roman plays, it is set at a point of constitutional crisis, with the establishment of a new emperor allowing a context for civic disorder. However, the historical date of the action is vague, to the extent that some elements seem to reflect conditions of Republican society, and there is no consistent articulation of Roman values to make the drama culture-specific. The ethical eclecticism of the work has led one critic to term it "the darkest and most frivolous of Shakespeare's plays."

The tone of the central action is established by the setting of the first scene, where a family tomb is opened to receive the body of yet another of Titus's 25 sons, most of whom have already died in battle. The eldest son of Tamora, the captive queen of the Goths, is sacrificed *ad manes fratrum*, which triggers much of the destructive energy that continues through the play. Tamora, after appealing to numerous virtues which strike no chord in Titus, embarks on a programme of revenge masterminded by her Moorish lover, Aaron. However, the appeal to the *manes* is also significant because they constitute a stronger influence over Titus than principles of mercy and parenthood. The assertion that the human sacrifice occurs "so the shadows be not unappeased, / Nor we disturbed with prodigies on earth" comes from Titus's son Lucius, and has a special authority because it is he who will survive the action to assume the political responsibility for the future, uttering the final speech at the reopening of the tomb. Since the sacrifice is what ostensibly precipitates the rest of the action, it would be consistent with Roman religion to speculate that the *manes* are dissatisfied either with the sacrifice or with the sudden unexpected arrival of yet another brother in an already congested tomb, and that the "prodigies" of the subsequent action are generated by them. However, having emphatically established this numinous dimension, Shakespeare does not extend it substantially; when Tamora's son Demetrius aligns himself with Aaron's stratagem and announces "*Per Stygia, per manes vehor*," his Senecan allusion is loose.

Whereas Tamora's malignant energy is given a valid cause, that of Aaron is closer to the melancholic stereotype, born under Saturn, completely devoid of conscience, and irreligious to the point that he is unable to accept an oath from Lucius. His unmitigated viciousness, which established his stage popularity from the start, reaches a peak when, trapped and proudly terming himself a "black dog," he gleefully lists his crimes and laments his periods of homicidal inertia. Yet even Aaron is given a humanising scene where, after manipulating Titus into amputating his left hand [on stage] to save two of his sons' lives, and sending him in return the sons' heads and the same severed hand, he wanders on the battlefield with the baby he has had with Tamora, who was supposedly the consort of the emperor. Aaron's tenderness to the baby—"Sweet blowse, you are a beauteous blossom, sure"—is ambivalent in terms of audience response, since the child is a catalyst for intense racist attitudes and Aaron's first act on being presented with it is to kill the nurse.

Many critics have observed that the play presents a convergence of two worlds, collating the "civilising" mission of Rome with the anarchy of the barbarians. Certainly, most of the Roman characters at one time or other express such a perspective on the Moor and Goths, but the play does not pivot on cultural polarisation of the kind that constitutes *Antony and Cleopatra*, or even the class oppositions of a play such as *Coriolanus*. Though in the central action barbarism may be seen to triumph over various traditional Roman virtues, generating a vision of Rome as a "wilderness of tigers," those virtues present themselves sporadically, with little ethical coherence, and in any case savagery is by no means a monopoly of the barbarians. Rather, the questioning of human nature is structured by the common Shakespearean device of taking most of the characters through two severely contrasting arenas, the urban environment of the first act and the "natural" rural world of the forest in the second. Ambiance, fields of imagery, and referential energies are radically different in the two locations, but there is a factor of stagecraft which some have seen as pervasive enough to create a total theatrical world view. The stage directions call for an unusually resourceful deployment of extreme stage levels, which have been argued to correspond with the commonplace representation of heaven and hell in medieval drama, and the final act includes a curious metatheatrical scene involving Revenge, Murder, and Rape in the style of the morality plays. In the dialogue, there is certainly no shortage of references to hell, particularly in events around the pit in the second act, but arguing the involvement of heaven is much more difficult, especially as the upper level is initially occupied by Saturninus, the malignant emperor who marries Tamora. In fact, the withdrawal of the gods may be the point of a controversial scene in which the insane Titus announces that Astraea [the goddess Justice] has abandoned the earth and shoots arrows with messages attached to various of the deities: "There's not a god left unsolicited." He specifically tells one son to shoot to Saturn, not to Saturninus: "You were as good to shoot against the wind." Yet the next scene opens with Saturninus entering carrying the arrows: the appeal to heaven has got no further than him. While some critics have found the scene pointless, clumsy, and merely demonstrating Titus's madness, it can also be seen as a graphic and very literal illustration of Titus's *hamartia*, reaching out to a deity with a naivety which is a liability in a world that the gods have deserted.

—Howard McNaughton

TO A SKYLARK.
Poem by Percy Bysshe Shelley, 1820.

"To a Skylark" is a lyric of 21 stanzas, each composed of four lines in trochaic trimeter followed by an alexandrine, each rhyming ababb. The poem expresses two of Percy Bysshe Shelley's most deeply held beliefs about poetry: that it is ideally pure, lyrical, and natural; and that it is effective, a vehicle by which its audience may experience what he calls, in "A Defence of Poetry," "a revolution in thought."

The first six stanzas establish a situation, making clear that the apostrophized skylark is one specific being, an existential source of birdsong to which the speaker, at a moment just past sunset, is listening. The unseen singer is known only by inference from its keen, pervasive song, just as at dawn the moon can be known from its light ("the arrows / Of that silver sphere") although its visible form has faded.

Stanzas 7–12 introduce a series of metaphors, images of things sensed through their effects rather than directly known, which the singer resembles, but surpasses, in effect: "rainbow clouds," an imprisoned maiden whose music "overflows her bower," a glowworm hidden in grass, a rose hidden in foliage, falling spring rain, and "Rain-awakened flowers"—in fact "All that ever was / Joyous, and clear, and fresh." Among the comparisons is a direct inversion (stanza 8) of the poem's larger, implied metaphor (skylark = poet): the speaker compares the singer with "a Poet hidden / In the light of thought" whose "hymns" move the world "To sympathy with hopes and fears it heeded not." This language is very like that of "A Defence of Poetry," where the poet's audience will be compared with "men entranced by the melody of an unseen musician."

Stanzas 13–18 examine the nature of the song and its source, its "fountain," contrasting the skylark's inferred nature with human nature. This song, says the speaker, is more divinely rapturous, more whole and unmixed, than any human song of praise, love, or triumph. It must be inspired by heightened versions of human inspirational "objects" (nature, love, pleasure—stated negatively as "ignorance of pain"), and its quality implies, too, an ignorance of lethargy, annoyance, and "love's sad satiety." Moreover, the singer's knowledge of death must be "more true and deep / Than we mortals dream," implying that the skylark, though knowing death, is *not* mortal. This paradox is resolved in stanza 18 as the speaker declares "We look before and after / And pine for what is not"; the singer, existentially unaware of past and future, lives entirely in the present.

Stanza 19 takes the contrast further: were human beings, like the skylark, free from negative emotions of hate, pride, fear, and sorrow, still human *joy* cannot approach the skylark's apparent joy. This "skill"—for joy is characterized as an intellectual talent, residing in the singer's brain—would be of more value to the poet than books or music. In the final stanza, the speaker (here revealed as Shelley himself) says that, could he learn "half the gladness" the skylark knows, "The world would listen then as [he is] listening now."

Itself a pure, lilting lyric, recalling in meter the unearthly song of invisible Echoes in *Prometheus Unbound*, with which it was published, "To a Skylark" illustrates two bases of Shelley's poetic philosophy that seem at first contradictory. The poet should be unseen, in effect non-existent except as the source of inspired but "unpremeditated" song, an "harmonious madness" that is produced for the singer's pleasure alone but that, in purity and intensity, compels others to listen. But the effect of poetry upon its audience is ultimately practical: it not only commands attention but also, being a distillation of truth, "awakens and enlarges the mind itself by rendering it the receptacle of a thousand unapprehended combinations of thought" ("A Defence of Poetry"). Acting upon the imagination, poetry leads its hearers to "put [themselves] in the place of another and of many others . . . "; it is a moral force, for "the great secret of morals is love; or a going out of our own nature, and an identification of ourselves with the beautiful which exists in thought, action, or person, not our own" ("A Defence of Poetry").

In "To a Skylark" Shelley anticipates the great prose statement of his "A Defence of Poetry" and resolves the apparent conflict between the impracticality of the poet, who like the skylark is a "scorner of the ground," and the practicality of poetry, firmly grounded in social purpose. Imitating the unseen singer, he imaginatively enlarges his existence to include that of the skylark, and concludes by acknowledging the effect of the experience, which has been to refine and amplify the moral power of his own poetic voice.

—Mary K. Patterson Thornburg

TO AUTUMN.
Poem by John Keats, 1820.

Written in September 1819, the ode "To Autumn" is the last of John Keats's odes of that year. It can be dated with precision from a letter Keats wrote to his friend John Hamilton Reynolds on 21 September 1819 in which, commenting on the "temperate sharpness" of the air and on how he preferred the warmth of the "stubble fields" to the "chilly green of the spring," he confides: "this struck me so much in my Sunday's walk (i.e., 19 September) that I composed upon it."

The ode's stanzaic structure approximates in length and rhyme scheme to that of the other odes (with the exception of the first, the irregular "Ode to Psyche") with one notable difference: they are written in 10-line stanzas, whereas the "To Autumn" stanza contains 11 lines, perhaps in structural recognition of the seasonal "o'erbrimming" that is in part the poem's subject.

Although there is virtually unanimous critical acclaim for the poem's supremacy among Keats's works, analyses of its meaning are rather scarce, maybe because it seems to be simply a descriptive piece. As an address to, and description of, Autumn, its meaning seems to derive from and be defined by the preceding odes to which, understood as a sequence, it is quite clearly the conclusion. Specifically, "To Autumn" harks back to "Ode to Psyche," not just through verbal recollection (compare "To Autumn"'s "Then in a wailful choir the small gnats mourn" with "Ode to Psyche"'s "Nor virgin-choir to make delicious moan" and "Let me be thy choir and make a moan") but through thematic association as well: Ian Jack has noted, for example, that Autumn's pose in stanza 2 recalls that in Giulio Romano's *Psyche asleep among the Grain* (*Keats and the Mirror of Art*, 1967). Moreover, in terms of the overall sequence of odes, "To Autumn"'s fullness answers "Ode to Psyche," the first of the odes, once again; for it is a response to the abruptness of "Ode to Psyche"'s opening lines when heard as an allusion to Milton's elegy, *Lycidas* (compare "Hear these tuneless numbers, wrung / By sweet enforcement and remembrance dear" with *Lycidas*, lines 4 and 6: "and with forced fingers rude. . . . Bitter constraint and sad occasion dear"). *Lycidas* begins by commemorating a young man's death through an image of a disrupted seasonal cycle (the poet's "forced fingers" are plucking "berries harsh and crude" because, like Lycidas, they have not yet achieved autumnal ripeness). Keats recalls this in "Psyche" and supplies the ripeness in "To Autumn."

This in turn would suggest that "Psyche" (which means soul in Greek) is itself elegiac, an address to the soul of Keats's recently dead (December 1818) and much loved brother Tom; and that the other odes, too, probably register Keats's grief: the dying youth of "Ode to a Nightingale"; the descents to the underworld in that poem and the "Ode on Melancholy"; the excavated urn of "Ode on a Grecian Urn" and the symbolic funeral urn of "On Indolence" with its three figures so reminiscent of the three Fates are all part of an attempt to confront and comprehend Tom's death and to metamorphose the fact of death into art.

"To Autumn," then, signifies some kind of acceptance of death (note that, in the letter to Reynolds of 21 September quoted above Keats remarks "I always somehow associate Chatterton with autumn," thus forging yet another link between this poem and a youth prematurely dead). Its fulfilled bees (the bee is the emblem of the poet in Plato's *Ion*, as well as being a symbol of the imagination's busy activity, as in Spenser's *Faerie Queene*, II. ix. 51) are the later season's equivalent to the "melodious" singer of the "Ode to a Nightingale"'s first stanza who, in spring, is already trying to force things to their maturity by singing of summer (Greek *melos* = honey), and they are the antidote to the pleasure that turns to death's "poison while the bee-mouth sips" in the "Ode on Melancholy." Furthermore, the "Ode to Autumn"'s image of the gleaner answers, in its otiose fulfilment, the "Ode to a Nightingale"'s sad and exiled Ruth "when, sick for home, / She stood in tears amid the alien corn."

The ode is addressed to Autumn; but it is worth recalling that Keats is not so much addressing the personified season as the goddess of harvest Ceres / Demeter, whose traditional emblem, the sleep-inducing poppy, has already been mentioned, via its derivative opium, in the "Ode to a Nightingale," stanza 1. It is, moreover, mentioned there in an underworld context: the drained opium draught takes one to Lethe, the river of oblivion in Hades. This is significant as a reminder that Ceres was the mother-goddess around whom the main Graeco-Roman mystery religion had formed. Known as the Eleusinian mysteries, the religion's rituals commemorated Ceres's loss of her daughter, Proserpina (Persephone to the Greeks) who was abducted to the underworld by Pluto / Hades, Ceres's ensuing search for her daughter, and Proserpina's cyclical seasonal return to the upper world. In fact, they re-enacted the processes of grievous loss and recovery, and initiates appear to have relived Ceres's experiences by means of opium-induced hallucinations of visits to the underworld. Recently brought to public notice by Thomas Taylor's discourse on them (1790?), but also the subject of Book XI of Apuleius's *Golden Ass*, which Keats had been rereading for the story of Psyche, the mystery religion of Ceres seems to be another clue to the meaning of "To Autumn": after all, even bees are dedicated to Ceres as symbols of her life-giving power, and Keats links bees with their goddess in *Endymion*, III. 38–40.

"To Autumn" thus marks the poet's re-emergence, through Ceres's underworld quest and the grain and fruit which signify the successful completion of her quest, into an emotional landscape of acceptance and completion: autumn's fulness, symbol of Ceres's reunion with Proserpina, is the symbol too of Keats's resignation to the fact of Tom's death and the answer to the premature violation recalled, through *Lycidas*, in "Ode to Psyche."

Yet Ceres's reconciliation is only momentary, a pause in the ongoing cycle of seasons, just as grief, apparently banished, wells up again with all its pristine force. Hence the final stanza, with its reminder of the lost "songs of spring," its gnats lamenting the brevity of life (as well as recalling the singing of the acolytes in "Ode to Psyche") by the sallows (the willows that traditionally signify grief), and its robin redbreast (the bird of sacrifice and mourning). However, its hedge-cricket insists, as perhaps the redbreast's song does also, that grief, when it returns, can find consolation and metamorphosis through poetic utterance; for Keats had, in his earlier work "On the Grasshopper and Cricket," used the cricket as an emblem of the power of the poet's voice even in adversity.

—Douglas Brooks-Davies

TO HIS COY MISTRESS.
Poem by Andrew Marvell, 1681.

To modern readers, "To His Coy Mistress" is undoubtedly the most popular lyric of the 17th century. Yet if this claim were extended to suggest Andrew Marvell as this century's currently most popular poet, it would undoubtedly be challenged by supporters of Donne. How is it, then, that a single lyric can receive that accolade, particularly when its *carpe diem* theme is not only of ancient descent but also makes its appearance in numerous other contemporary lyrics?

The answer seems in part to lie in the many disparate interpretations that were foisted upon or extracted from this 46-line lyric after explication became a familiar critical tool in the 1930's, an approach that was increasingly intensified in the course of the century. Before this development, "To His Coy Mistress" appeared as one among several love poems in the two earliest 18th century editions of the poet following on its initial appearance in the Folio (1681). It was then admired by the romantics though their comments tended to be surprisingly brief ("the sweetness and power" of the verse—Hazlitt). But two of the most popular Victorian anthologies—Palgrave's *The Golden Treasury of Best Songs and Lyrical Poems* (1861) and Archbishop Trench's *Household Book of English Verse* (1868)—excluded it on the grounds of its doubtful propriety. Its status thus developed from being one example of Marvell's love poems (17th and 18th centuries) to being singled out for special admiration by some to its being suppressed by others (19th century) and then to an ever-widening acclaim in the 20th century, with one aberrant critic observing in 1901 that, though it was unique, it could never be the most popular of Marvell's poems.

The poet's contemporaries, familiar as they were with classical tradition, would easily recognize the poem's generic connection with such a popular invitational lyric as Catullus's "Vivamus, mea Lesbia, atque amenus" (*Carmen V*) since the two classical motifs—*carpe diem* (seize the day) and *tempus edax* (devouring time) on which the poet structures his poem were conventional *topoi* in the period. He relies on the first of these motifs to highlight his invitation and counters the force of the second with promise of sexual fulfillment. Contemporaries would also recognize that another contemporary poet, Abraham Cowley, like Catullus before him, had earlier measured his lady's favours to him on the basis of an arithmetical progression, this in a stanza in which the expression "vast eternity" also appears ("My Diet" from his *The Mistress*, 1647) as it does in other 17th-century lyrics. Marvell's neat syllogistic organization—If . . . but . . . therefore—would perhaps also suggest something of Donne's early poetry. Nonetheless, in "To His Coy Mistress" the poet has transmuted the traditional motifs and contemporary analogues into a particular witty and arresting instance of a poem of seduction.

It begins hyperbolically with two broad topographical and temporal references ("world enough and time"); the first of these then narrows to two specific locales—one, the remote banks of the Indian Ganges; the other the relatively nearby banks of the Humber, altogether familiar to a poet who had spent his first 20 years in Yorkshire. The temporal reference, though termed only a "long love's day," is extended, ranging back to 10 years before the flood and forward to the conversion of the Jews. Each of these allusions might suggest a specific date to some religionists in the 17th century though as there was no agreement as to which would be the proper (or most likely) one, both fall under the rhetorical category of unspecifiable and therefore impossible limits (*adúnata*).

Reference to the growth of his "vegetable love" (lines 11–12) accords with the lowest level of the Renaissance doctrine of the three souls (vegetative, sensitive, rational) as well as with the properties of expansion and extension ("vaster than empires and more slow"). The next half-dozen lines in a tenuous blazon specify the length of time to be allotted to praise of his lady's allurements; it is tenuous in that her allurements are enumerated, not described—eyes, forehead, breasts, and heart.

Abruptly the next strophe (or verse paragraph) introduces a sense of urgency, the speaker acknowledging his constant awareness of the quick approach of Time's winged chariot and of nothing more except "deserts of vast eternity" stretching out before the lovers. The next lines refute the earlier hyperbole: Time's ineluctable effect will reduce spatial dimension to a marble vault, his song to silence; her vaunted chastity will be tested by worms and reduced to dust and his lust to ashes.

The solution the poet poses in the last strophe is to reverse the irreversible and specify the means: it is to concentrate on present sexual gratification, which he admits, with ironic candour, will result not in prolonging time but in its speeding up.

As mentioned earlier, in recent years disparate interpretations of the poem have been put forward, some employing rather heavy-handed allegory, one of them, for example, claiming that its theme is "physical virginity is spiritual unchastity." Similarly, its tonal quality has been wrested at times to seem, as one critic put it, as if the Resolved Soul in the combat with Created Pleasure—a very different poem—had taken on the guise of a lover.

The full text of "To His Coy Mistress" appeared in the Folio edition (1681), four years after Marvell's death, though a short version of it which had been copied into a 1672 miscellany was recovered in this century. Few of Marvell's poems were published in his lifetime, and these few were occasional in nature like the commendatory verses on the publication of Lovelace's *Lucasta*. The Folio appeared under the auspices of Marvell's purported wife Mary Marvell, but the three poems on Cromwell were cancelled in almost all copies. A "manuscript volume," now in the Bodleian Library (*Eng. poet. d. 49*), consists of the printed sheets of the Folio and includes the cancelled poems on Cromwell and some corrections of the others. It belonged to William Popple, Marvell's nephew, a personal favorite. Since the poet did not oversee publication of the Folio edition, this corrected "manuscript volume" assumes considerable importance in respect to textual readings.

Two of these relate to lines 33 and 34 of Marvell's most popular lyric where the Popple manuscript reads

Now, therefore, while the youthful glue
Sits on thy skin like morning dew.

The Folio reads " . . . youthful hue / . . . morning glue." The second edition of the poems appeared in 1726 and includes its 18th-century editor's rather cavalier emendation, which has frequently been silently adopted: " . . . youthful hue / . . . morning dew."

Besides the fact of the close family connection between Marvell and the owner of the corrected "manuscript volume," there is external support for its readings; they also appear in the 1672 short version mentioned above and two apt references from Renaissance works illustrate its contextual relevance to the poem: "Life is nothing else but as it were a glue, which in man fastneth the soul and body together" (William Baldwin, 1547) and the 1628 sermon by Archbishop Laud wherein he terms *charity* "the glue of the spirit."

The second textual crux appears in line 44, where the Popple manuscript reads "iron *grates* of life." This is also the reading in the shorter version, whereas the Folio reads iron *gates*.

—Elizabeth Story Donno

TO PENSHURST.
Poem by Ben Jonson, 1616.

"To Penshurst" is a crucial work in Ben Jonson's career; it is one of the most influential poems of the 17th century; and it is an inspired example of the use of classical poetic models to understand and enrich contemporary life.

Penshurst, the seat of the Sidney family, is apostrophized by Jonson as if he had accepted an invitation to visit it and become, temporarily, one of its privileged inhabitants. Jonson's praise begins in the negative—Penshurst is not, like other houses of the rich, built for "envious show"—and recurs throughout to the disparity between Penshurst's ideal values and the false, unnatural world of conventional patrician, and urban, society. He writes, for example, that the fish in its ponds are not predatory, glancing by implication at the contrasting ways of the court: Penshurst's pikes, he fancies, are "weary their own kind to eat." More explicitly Jonson commends Penshurst's hospitality as the opposite of the type offered by ostentatious yet mean society figures whose invitations to their inferiors result only in humiliation: Jonson is "not fain to sit (as some, this day, / At great mens tables) and yet dine away" (that is, on a separate and substandard menu). Yet the poem is not primarily satirical, but descriptive and indeed celebratory. Penshurst is an image of a balanced, self-sufficient, harmonious way of life, and of the ideal cooperation of man with nature. It is not merely an estate, but an abiding and inspiring model of an integrated society and of the conditions under which the full development of human potential can take place.

In conveying this, the poem moves repeatedly from the material facts about the house to their spiritual significance. The description of the park is precise, with an estate agent's eye to its layout and yield: this is no mere flight of fancy. But Jonson sees this wealth as a means to a non-material end: the provision of hospitality, the giving and receiving of the good things of nature (and man's cultivation of nature). The livestock is there to "crowne" Penshurst's "open table," the fruit to be picked by children. No less prosaic is the observation that Penshurst's walls are fashioned from local materials—"of the countrey stone." But Jonson passes from the external fact to an evocation of the house's place as a focus of social harmony: Penshurst was not built by exploiting the surrounding land and its inhabitants but "rear'd with no man's ruin, no man's grone," and all social classes collaborate harmoniously in its economy: "all come in, the farmer and the clowne." Again, however, the rustics are not part of an impossibly selfless paradise: they sometimes send their daughters to the house with their gifts in the hope that this will "commend" them to potential husbands. For all his conceits, Jonson depicts a practical world of mutual collaboration in which good will and faith in the divine order of things intermingle with the operation of the laws of duty, responsibility, and the hierarchical society in general.

A striking feature of the poem is Jonson's use of classical sources, primarily Martial and Horace, to define and elaborate his theme. Jonson does not allude to any particular Horatian poem, but "To Penshurst" is rightly celebrated as the first genuinely successful adaptation into English of the loosely descriptive, discursive style of Horace's epistles. Like Horace's, Jonson's epistle seems structured not by formal logic but by relaxed association. Where Martial is concerned, three Latin epigrams form Jonson's main points of reference: Martial's IX.61, X.30, and III.68. From the first he draws the references to the Roman deities Pan and Bacchus at the beginning of "To Penshurst" which fit less than happily into the quintessentially English setting. In the other Martialian works, however, Jonson finds materials which he is able not only to use but to transcend. Martial's lines in his Epigram III.68 on the offerings the Roman peasantry made to their landlords are transformed into the image of mutual support and harmony at the heart of "To Penshurst" in the description of the villagers "saluting" Penshurst's master and mistress. Martial's idealized description is solidified by Jonson, who draws on actual country life to present a picture firmly rooted in contemporary reality, not a frigid literary imitation.

The last section of the poem is devoted to its lord and lady and their family. Jonson describes how King James visited the house when its mistress was away. She "reap'd / The just reward of her high huswifery," Jonson relates, when Penshurst was found to be admirably prepared for even this level of hospitality despite her absence. Thus, even Penshurst's aristocratic mistress is praised for such mundane matters as the availability of her "linnen" and "plate." Jonson deepens the spiritual note at the close of the poem in referring to the Sidneys' children, who are "taught to pray, / With the whole houshold," and then sums up Penshurst's status as an ideal foster-parent to civilised values by saying that their parents' example teaches the children "the mysteries of manners, armes, and arts"—the social, active, and contemplative powers which were seen in the Renaissance as combining to form the ideal human being.

—Stuart Gillespie

TO THE LIGHTHOUSE.
Novel by Virginia Woolf, 1927.

To the Lighthouse is generally considered to be Virginia Woolf's most accomplished work. It is certainly her most popular one. It was this novel, together with *Mrs. Dalloway* and *The Waves*, that established her reputation as a modernist writer. What makes *To the Lighthouse* a modernist novel is its experimental form. It has no traditional plot structure and no characterisation in the accepted sense. Instead the novel is organised into three parts that are thematically and symbolically connected with each other. Part I ("The Window") covers only a few hours, Part II ("Time Passes") a period of 10 years, and Part III ("The Lighthouse") part of two days. Most of the "action" of the first and final sections of the novel takes place in the minds of the characters and is conveyed through a succession of interior monologues, as the perspective of the novel shifts from character to character. The central section is written in an abstract poetical style and its underlying authorial voice is impersonal. The events of the first part of the novel are evoked through memory in the final section when there is a return to the house in the Hebrides. The first part, which is essentially a celebration of the life generated creatively by Mrs. Ramsay, is shot through with images of light. The second part covers the "dark" years of war and death, and in the final section there is a restoration of the light. This light-dark-light pattern resembles the pattern formed by the beams from the lighthouse, which functions centrally in the novel both as a literal place and as a symbol. The novel begins with a desire to visit the lighthouse and concludes with the journey to it, so the lighthouse is bound up with the journey theme of the novel.

At the centre of the novel are the complementing and contrasting characters of Mr. and Mrs. Ramsay (based on Woolf's parents). Mr. Ramsay, who is a philosopher, searches for intellectual truth with a rigour that makes him difficult to live with. Mrs. Ramsay grasps truth intuitively through her sensitive response to the people she comes in contact with. He needs her warmth to convince him that he lives at the "heart of life"; she relies on his sureness of judgment. Their opposing characteristics are reinforced imagistically, Mr. Ramsay being associated with images of hardness and assertion ("arid scimitar of the male") and Mrs. Ramsay with symbols of softness and warmth ("a column of spray" or a "rosy-flowered tree"). Within this symbolic framework Woolf probes the profound tensions at the core of all relationships between men and women. This is what underlies the verbal exchange at the beginning of the novel, when the youngest child, James, asks to visit the lighthouse: " 'Yes, of course, if it's fine to-morrow,' said Mrs. Ramsay. 'But you'll have to be up with the lark,' she added. . . . 'But,' said his father, stopping in front of the drawing-room window, 'it won't be fine.'" Mrs. Ramsay's words are followed by a long paragraph which reveals the inner feelings of delight in the child. A similar passage of stream of consciousness writing follows his father's words, this time expressing feelings of anger and hatred. The authorial gloss on this situation is: "Such were the extremes of emotion that Mr. Ramsay excited in his children's breasts by his mere presence." The same kind of complex exploration and analysis continues throughout the book as character relates to character and as inner thoughts are revealed in solitude.

The most important of the friends who visit the Ramsay family at their holiday house in the Hebrides (really St. Ives in Cornwall where the Stephen family spent their summer holidays) is Lily Briscoe, who, in the first part of the novel, is painting a picture of Mrs. Ramsay and her son. She is an onlooker figure whose function in the novel is to observe life and recreate its reality in her art. She suddenly grasps the meaning of marriage in a moment of awareness, for instance, when she catches a glimpse of Mr. and Mrs. Ramsay walking across the lawn. In that moment they become for her symbolic figures, as their particularity is transcended to reveal a universal truth. In this way they contribute to her journey in awareness and to her painting which embodies it, both of which are completed at the end of the novel.

The party which is the climax of the first part of *To the Lighthouse* is a symbolic occasion. It will be remembered as a moment of stability in the midst of chaos after Mrs. Ramsay's death. That chaos is conveyed poetically in the central section of the novel. Here there is no coherence in life which seems full of suffering and death, war and anguish: Mrs. Ramsay dies, Andrew Ramsay is killed in the war, and Prue dies in childbirth. The personal anguish and the general sense of disintegration are figured in the decline of the house, which is finally rescued from its dereliction and restored.

The vision of the book is, then, an optimistic one. Out of the multiple oscillations between life and death, joy and sorrow, light and dark, the ebb and flow of the sea, there is an expressed belief in the survival of the human spirit: Mr. Ramsay springs like a young man onto the rock of the lighthouse, and Lily Briscoe draws a line in the centre of her canvas thus unifying, as Mrs. Ramsay did at the dinner party, the separate forms that had been resistant to her attempts to unify them. She has learned from Mrs. Ramsay that life "from being made up of little separate incidents which one lived one by one, became curled and whole like a wave."

—Stella McNichol

TOM BROWN'S SCHOOL DAYS.
Novel by Thomas Hughes, 1857.

Tom Brown's School Days is the most famous of all public school stories and the progenitor of a genre of school books, popular for nearly a hundred years, celebrating loyalty to the institution and one's peers. It was written for Thomas Hughes's eight-year old son, as an introduction to public school life, and many subsequent fictitious boys, such as Lycidas Marsh in Desmond Coke's *The Bending of a Twig* (1906), read it in preparation for school life and were duly horrified. It is set in Rugby just after the arrival of Dr. Arnold in 1828 (a little before Hughes's own time). The atmosphere generally is brutal and disorderly, and Arnold is seen introducing the reforms that were to make him famous, "for he had found School, and School-house, in a state of monstrous licence and misrule." By the end of the book his rule is firmly established and unquestioned, and it is his personality, as Hughes sees it, that pervades the narrative although Hughes never fully understood his aims.

The first quarter of *Tom Brown's School Days* is set not at Rugby, but in the Berkshire village of Uffington, in the Vale of the White Horse, where Hughes himself lived. Here we see the small Tom, the squire's son, getting his first schooling, and get a foretaste of the message—mens sana in corpore sano—which is to run through so much of the rest. No education is any good, says Hughes, referring here to the working man, without "something to try the muscles of men's bodies, and the endurance of their hearts, and to make them rejoice in their strength." This was not part of Arnold's ethic. He was no games worshipper, and indeed it is worthy of note that in the chapter "Tom Brown's Last Match" where Rugby plays an MCC team—a fixture which must have been the highpoint of the school cricket season—"the Doctor" and his family have already departed for the holidays.

Tom Brown, for his first two years at Rugby, is the ordinary unreflective boy. He venerates the Doctor—"the tall gallant form, the kindling eye, the voice, now soft as the low notes of a flute, now clear and stirring as the call of the light infantry bugle"—but this does not stop him tumbling into scrapes, fighting, trying to outwit the masters, and avoiding work as craftily as he knows how. The turning point comes when, at the Doctor's instigation (though he does not know this until the end of his school career), he is given charge of George Arthur, a delicate new boy, and is obliged to shed his old careless ways and look after him. In the end it is Arthur, the stronger character of the two, who persuades him to give up using cribs to prepare his Latin and Greek, and to read his Bible. But his ambitions are still simple: "I want to be A1 at cricket and football, and all the other games, and to make my hands keep my head against any fellow, lout or gentleman. I want to get into the Sixth before I leave, and to please the Doctor, and I want to carry away just as much Latin and Greek as will take me through Oxford respectably. . . . "

At this stage he is still totally ignorant of Arnold's aims, and unaware of how he has influenced the school. The real Arnold wanted pupils who would of their own free will behave in an honourable manner without threat of punishment. He detested the "moral childishness" he found in communities of boys, the deference to public opinion, the herd instinct. It was in his efforts to counteract this evil, to teach boys to stand by themselves, consulting their own consciences alone, that he used his sixth form to govern and to set a good example, thus promoting the prefect system which was to become a feature of the reformed public schools. Some of the more impressionable of his sixth form—Clough is the most famous example—developed into over-scrupulous and diffident adults as a result of Arnold's teaching, but it washed over Tom Brown, as one infers it did over Hughes and most of his contemporaries. Tom had given up the use of cribs, not because he felt it was morally wrong, but because he reckoned that the Doctor would not like it, and because he wanted to please Arthur. We catch an oblique glimpse, however, of the Clough type of Rugbeian and of Hughes's total incomprehension of this, in the preface. Hughes refers to remarks by several reviewers: "They have stated that the Rugby undergraduates they remember at the Universities were 'a solemn array,' 'boys turned into men before their time,' a 'semi-political, semi-sacerdotal fraternity' &c." Hughes will have none of it; it is "genial and hearty freshness and youthfulness" that characterized his schoolfellows, he insists.

Just as Tom is about to leave, a conversation with one of the masters suddenly reveals to him something of Arnold's greatness. "He gave way at all points, and the enemy marched right over him . . . It had taken eight long years to do it, but now it was done thoroughly, and there wasn't a corner of him which didn't believe in the Doctor." He departs "a hero-worshipper, who would have satisfied the soul of Thomas Carlyle himself." And a hero-worshipper he remains. The reader's last glimpse of Hughes is in 1842, just after Arnold's death, mourning by the grave beneath the altar of the man who had opened his eyes to "the glory of his birthright." Hughes represented the sturdy, straightforward boy of spirit who stood by his comrades and would defend the institution to which he belonged to the death. And this was the torch that was to be handed on to the writers of school books who followed him.

—Gillian Avery

TOM JONES.
(*The History of Tom Jones, A Foundling.*)
Novel by Henry Fielding, 1749.

The History of Tom Jones, A Foundling is generally acclaimed as Henry Fielding's masterpiece in its combination of dazzlingly virtuoso plot (Coleridge described it as one of "the three most perfect ever planned"), comic range, irony, variety of moods, and emotional and psychological intensity. It was Fielding's third major novel, born of mature reconsideration of the formula of the "comic epic poem in prose" which he had pioneered in *Joseph Andrews* and of deeply disturbing experiences, both public and domestic. The public experience was the threat to the Hanoverian monarchy and the constitution that it represented by the Jacobite rebellion of 1745; the domestic one was the death of his wife, Charlotte, whom he remembers explicitly in the opening chapter of Book 13 and upon whom the character of the novel's heroine, Sophia Western, is loosely based.

Brilliant intricacy of plot is matched in *Tom Jones* by corresponding intricacy of formal structure, for Fielding still believed, along with such conservative contemporaries as Pope, in the symbolic value of literary structure as a model of providential order (a notion inherited from Renaissance neo-Platonism). Its 18 books—the total alludes to the number of books in the first edition of Archbishop Fénelon's influential prose epic *Télémaque* (1699), a moralised "continuation" of Homer's *Odyssey*, and thus marks Fielding's novel, too, as a journey novel in the Odysseyan tradition—are arranged in a system of complex symmetries in accordance with ancient epic practice: three sets of six books deal respectively with Tom's upbringing in the country and expulsion by his Uncle Allworthy; his journey to London; and his experiences in London and return home. Within this broad symmetrical array the reader is led to detect further symmetries: the first and last books both have 13 chapters, and there are explicit cross-references between them; the most complicated (and celebrated) episode in the novel in which all the travellers' paths cross, that at the Upton inn, occupies the centre of the novel (Books 9 and 10); interpolated stories correspond to each other exactly: the Man of the Hill's long tale in Book 8 (the second book of the central section of six books) is answered by Mrs. Fitzpatrick's in Book 11 (second from the end of the central block); this block opens with the Quaker's tale of his daughter (Book 7, chapter 10) and concludes with the thematically relevant puppet show (Book 12, chapter 5).

Such elaborateness marks a refinement on the structural complexities of *Joseph Andrews* and *Jonathan Wild*; but whereas in *Joseph Andrews* especially structure had obviously reinforced the work's comic affirmation of an essentially benevolent universe, in *Tom Jones* it seems, in its hectic over-determinateness, to be almost as mocking as the symmetries and coincidences of a late Hardy novel. For it is a curiously dark and anxious work. Unlike any other novel of its century which claims to be about lost, foundling, or wandering heroes, it explores loss and displacement in an almost existential way. Tom's foundling status isn't just a plot *motif* but, rather, the *meaning* of the novel; and it isn't merely a device for exploring human benevolence (or lack of it) in relation to the underprivileged (something Fielding was deeply committed to): it is, instead, a way into areas of considerable psychological complexity. For one thing, the novel generates a double for Tom in the form of the legitimate child Blifil, whose father soon dies and who is, in fact, Tom's half-brother. He is born in Book 2 and spends the rest of the novel blighting Tom's life. The question the novel raises is, who (or what), exactly, *is* Blifil? Is he metaphysical evil? Is he a psychological double for Tom? For it is clear that he is no mere rogue, and the prefatory essays to each of the novel's books in which Fielding discusses his theory and practice of writing are designed to implicate us as readers in the varieties of the novel's self-questioning.

Then again, Tom is offered various reputed and symbolic fathers and mothers (Allworthy himself, Partridge, Jenny Jones, Lady Bellaston), so that the question the novel raises seems to be not so much who are (or were) Tom's parents? but, rather, what is the significance of parents for the child's sense of identity? The incest motif—Tom jumps into bed at Upton with Jenny Jones (now known as Jenny Waters) and is later told that he has made love to his own mother—suggests, as do several plot parallels, that we are in the territory of Sophocles's *Oedipus*: like Sophocles, Fielding suggests that there is some necessary relationship between paternal absence and the discovery of maternal identity through sexual knowledge.

The profundity of the novel's questioning of the foundling's status (its working title had been simply *The Foundling*) is evident even from names. Blifil is known by his father's surname: he has nominal legitimacy but is morally illegitimate. Tom is always known by his supposed mother's surname, Jones. But in fact his mother was Bridget Allworthy, and his father was a passing visitor called Will Summer. His is a haunting name, but he, described in a couple of sentences only, turns out to be the non-discovery of the book. For it is the psychological journey to the parent (or so this text tells us) that is more important than parental identity itself. And why should Tom retain his mother's name? At the very least, this fact questions the status of inherited patronymics.

And it is here that the psychological plot implicates political discourse. For while Tom quests for his parents, Bonny Prince Charlie has invaded and the constitutional monarchy is threatened. Tom enlists on the side of the Hanoverians; his companion Partridge is a Jacobite, believing firmly in the divine right of the ejected Stuarts. The constitutional monarch is a benevolent father; the Stuarts, accused of tyranny by their opponents, regarded themselves as the fathers of their country. Tom's quest for his father raises questions about our perception and acceptance of kingship in the realm. The Man of the Hill irrupts into the action in Books 8 and 9 to tell of the expulsion of James II in 1688 and to draw the parallel with the invasion of 1745.

Tom's persecution and quest are paralleled by Sophia Western's. She, daughter of Allworthy's Jacobite neighbour Squire Western, is intended for Blifil but loves Tom. Imprisoned by her father (Fielding is influenced here by Richardson's monumental text of female persecution, *Clarissa*, 1747–48), she escapes, and their journeys shadow each other until, finally, misunderstandings cleared away, they marry. The significance of her name (Sophia = Wisdom in Greek) is relevant but not primary; for as her cousin and travelling companion Harriet Fitzpatrick reveals in her autobiographical tale in Book 11, woman's (and women's) history is to a large extent a story of domestic persecution, oppression, violence, and loneliness. Its message is, do not marry if you wish to remain in control of your destiny. Her tale, too, reveals parallels between domestic and constitutional politics. Sophia's part of *Tom Jones* conveys clear signals of female freedom: Tom cannot marry her until he recognises the woman's right to freedom from male hegemony; the Stuarts cannot reinherit the realm because they refused to negotiate their absolutist hegemony. It is in its working out of such perceptions that *Tom Jones*'s brilliance lies.

—Douglas Brooks-Davies

TONO-BUNGAY.
Novel by H.G. Wells, 1908.

H.G. Wells wrote *Tono-Bungay* as one might pack a carpetbag, ramming in ideas, preoccupations, and instances which a tidier author might have kept in separate packages. The novel is, first and foremost, a social comedy about the rise and rise of an ordinary, likeable man who has zip, zest, and marketable ideas, who makes a fortune and—this being Edwardian England—does his best to learn how to live like a "proper gent." Second, it is a caustic study of changing society, of the bonfire of Victorian certainties, and the phoenix-like birth of 20th-century moral and intellectual attitudes. And third, it is a hymn to Wells's view that science and technology are keys to the future, that innovation, not adherence to precedents, will lead triumphantly to the health, wealth, and happiness of humankind.

Thus, from the start, this book is *sui generis*, an amalgam (so to speak) of *Mr. Polly*, *The First Men in the Moon*, and *A Modern Utopia*. It is bound together and controlled by humour, and by a view of human bustle and a darkness reminiscent (and worthy) of Wells's great master, Dickens. In fact, the only Dickensian quality missing is verisimilitude in the dialogue. Dickens, an amateur actor, knew how to write as people actually speak, and how to reveal character in speech patterns; Wells had no such experience, and his characters utter Ideas or speak in clichés which lack inner life, representing rather than revealing both personality and emotion. (This is one reason why Dickens can readily be adapted for radio, film, or television, and Wells—except by Orson Welles—cannot.)

At heart, *Tono-Bungay* is a fairy tale, reworking themes from the Arabian Nights. Tono-Bungay itself is a patent medicine, advertised (by the book's narrator, George Ponderevo) as "health, wealth, and happiness in a bottle." It is a version both of the elixir of immortality and of the lodestone which, it was believed, would turn base materials to gold. It brings its inventor, George's uncle Teddy, previously unimagined riches, and propels him to the pinnacle of society. His tragedy, the book's comedy, is that the lodestone never quite transforms base humanity itself: Teddy never becomes a toff, never—to use a Wellsian phrase—transmogrifies himself. The genie in the bottle grants every wish, so long as you never question it—but as soon as belief wavers, catastrophe begins. One can even see, in George Ponderevo's passion for powered flight (an all-but-fantastical notion in 1909), an allusion to the great birds which carry Sindbad and others to realms far beyond earthbound reach—an idea brought to splendid fruition towards the end of the book, when the heavier-than-air machine rescues Teddy and George from all their creditors.

The novel's heart of darkness comes from the fact that Tono-Bungay is a fraud. It is 99% distilled water, and its success owes more to the credulity of those who buy it than to pharmacy. George Ponderevo knows this, and is racked by doubts. His is the hype which sells the stuff, his fortune comes from it, and he can bring himself neither to like what he does nor stop it. He tries, and rejects, the justification that those who buy Tono-Bungay need it, that it works because they think it works. He seeks to use his wealth to buy happiness, social-climbing into a marriage which proves one of the most sterile and miserable in all English literature. Addicted to wealth and hooked on deceit, he finally retreats from his uncle's world, devoting himself to flying experiments and becoming a Scythropian recluse. He sails to Africa on a ludicrous, characteristically romantic and self-deluding expedition to fetch a shipload of magic material ("quap"), only to have the cargo sink the boat (because its radioactivity destroys the timbers) and drown the Ponderevo fortune with it. In the end he abandons all ambition to benefit the human race, and turns to designing warships.

The blend of fairy tale and social bitterness makes for a powerful, energetic story. But Wells has several other, equally urgent, things to say. He begins the novel with an account of George's boyhood (son of a housekeeper to the gentry; apprentice baker; eager student ambushed by sex from intellectual activity), and he fills his characters' mouths with scientific and social moralising in the style of Fabian Society pamphlets. A thriftier literary hand (Somerset Maugham, say) might have held such items back, as material for other books. To Wells, they must have seemed essential. The early chapters set up the atmosphere of change, of elision between old ways and new, which was vital to the story. The moralising served to highlight messages about the Way We Live Now which might otherwise have been be lost in a mass of comic incident.

Viewed by the strictest literary standards, *Tono-Bungay* is a failure: sprawling, unruly, an untrimmed hedge. But as you read it, all such carping is swept away by the gusto and geniality of Wells's invention. He loves his characters, and revels especially in the sparkle of Teddy Ponderevo's mind. Tono-Bungay, for Teddy, is merely that one of his ideas which catches public attention. The air is ablaze with schemes, and he grabs them as eagerly as a child reaches out for stars. He is dazzle personified; he makes the novel hum. Who would not buy Tono-Bungay—or indeed, *Tono-Bungay*—from such a man?

—Kenneth McLeish

TOTTEL'S MISCELLANY.
(*Songs and Sonnets.*)
Collection of poems, 1557.

Edition

Tottel's Miscellany, edited by H.E. Rollins. 2 vols., 1928–29; revised edition, 1965.

Critical Study: "The Sonnets in *Tottel's Miscellany*" by W.R. Parker, in *Publications of the Modern Language Association*, 54, 1939.

Published initially on 5 June 1557 as *Songes and Sonettes, written by the ryght honorable Lorde Henry Haward late Earle of Surrey, and other*, *Tottel's Miscellany*, as it has come to be known, is the most significant of all the poetry anthologies of the 16th century. Within a month of its initial publication it was reset and reissued in the form of its eight subsequent editions over the next 30 years. In their combined forms the enterprising printer, Richard Tottel, presented to an eager readership 310 poems by various courtly writers. Despite its original title, which gives precedence to Surrey's pieces, the anthology is most notable for its printing of a substantial portion of Sir Thomas Wyatt's poems (97, 18 of which are preserved *only* here). Surrey and Nicholas Grimald's poems, some 40 of each, complete the number of named contributors, but also represented are John Heywood, Thomas Norton, Lord Vaux, Sir John Cheke, Thomas Churchyard, and even one by Chaucer from an early printed edition of his works. With the exception of Nicholas Grimald's contribution (he may have been the editor of the first edition) the *Miscellany*, as Hyder Rollins has put it, comprises "poems unauthorized by their writers, most of whom were dead." What did its readers discover in it?

If they expected a large proportion of "edifying" verses, they may have been surprised by the overwhelming majority of love poems within the first third of the anthology (the contributions of Surrey and Wyatt in that order) and somewhat puzzled by the intricacies of the sonnet form. Among their other poems, nine sonnets appear consecutively by Surrey; 15 by Wyatt. Recognizing as we must that the sonnet form did not come into its own until the decade of the 1590's with the posthumous publication of Sidney's *Astrophel and Stella*, did Tottel's readers appreciate the formal difficulties and ingenuity of this new kind of poetry? That Tottel may have believed his readers to need some coaching may be inferred from his practice of providing titles which point to the nature of the "invention" in each and from the opening sentences of his dedication, "To the Reader":

> That to have to have well written in verse, yea and in small parcels, deserveth great praise, the works of divers Latins, Italians, and other, do prove sufficiently. That our tongue is able in that kind to do us praiseworthily as the rest, the honorable style of the noble Earl of Surrey, and the weightiness of the deep witted Sir Thomas Wyatt the elder's verse . . . do show abundantly.

Tottel seems to have realized that if his readers did not recognize "deep-wittedness" in these love poems they would be disappointed and critical, and even as late as 1576 we find George Gascoigne urging those who would write poetry to avoid the "perpetual oration" and ground their pieces in "some fine and good invention." At any rate by introducing short poems intricately constructed, the *Miscellany* stands as a document of first importance.

With Nicholas Grimald's contribution and the rest of the unacknowledged poems, the *Miscellany* takes on a distinctly humanistic cast. Nearly half of the remainder are philosophical or mythological in content, and here and there throughout are adaptations and paraphrases from Ovid, Horace, Seneca, and Lucretius.

Stylistically, the anthology is remarkable for its metrical smoothness throughout. Apparently this characteristic is attributable to the editor—be he Grimald, Churchill, or Tottel himself—for which he has been sufficiently condemned, especially for tampering with Wyatt's meters. Yet, as Rollins points out, the net effect upon readers of that day and for the future of English poetry must be regarded as salubrious. Some time ago Paul Fussell noted that the incessant metrical regularity of mid-century poetry provided a sure base upon which the later Elizabethan poets were to work their meaningful rhythmic variations.

Another stylistic feature of the whole is its use of nonfunctional alliteration. Because the poetry of this time is grounded in the late medieval alliterative revival, one cannot expect and one does not find relief from the incessant searching after the letter. Yet in the contributions of Wyatt and Surrey the use of alliteration is far less obvious than everywhere else in the anthology.

Finally, Tottel's is a compendium of verse forms. In it the contemporary reader found *ottava rima*, *terza rima*, *douzains*, quatrains, rhyme-royal, blank verse, nine sonnets (in addition to those by Wyatt and Surrey), and everywhere poulter's measure. Surrey, himself, wrote nine in this meter, and because of the prestige of his name, he must be assigned the blame for the reams of it written after its publication.

Apart from the immediate influence of the *Miscellany* upon subsequent anthologies such as *A Handful of Pleasant Delights* (1566) and *A Gorgeous Gallery of Gallant Inventions* (1578) and several others in the 1590's, it is most important for carrying the large number of poems by its two most talented courtly makers, Wyatt and Surrey. They are acknowledged again and again by their Elizabethan successors, for an example of which let Ben Jonson speak for the opinion of his contemporaries: "for their times admirable: and the more, because they began Eloquence with us."

—Frank Fabry

TRACTS FOR THE TIMES.
Prose by John Henry Newman and others, 1833–41.

On 14 July 1833, in the University Church of Oxford, John Keble preached the Assize Sermon on National Apostasy, which according to John Henry Newman marked the beginning of the Oxford Movement. This movement, which was to change the history of the Church of England, arose in reaction to the liberalising reforms of the 1830's and the rationalist thought on which these reforms were based. Keble, Newman, and many others were profoundly disturbed by these developments; when the church itself was directly threatened by rationalism and secularism, they were outraged. Their love for the church, and their anger with the forces that threatened it drove them into battle, and one of their first weapons was the tract.

"Speak I must," writes Newman at the beginning of the first tract (dated 9 September 1833), "for the times are very evil, yet no one speaks against them." This sense of compulsion and urgency pervades all the early tracts. They are brief, direct, and powerful. Their sentences are short, their diction unpretentious. They insist on the authority of the church, deriving that authority from its origins, preaching the Apostolic Succession and the consequent importance of the priest's office. Although such teaching inevitably led to accusations of "Romanism," it is carefully based on the Book of Common Prayer and on the writings of the great Anglican divines of the 16th and 17th centuries.

The *Tracts for the Times* were "the expression of individual minds," as Newman explained in his *Apologia pro Vita Sua*, rather than the expression of a party line (consensus was in any case difficult to achieve). Newman himself wrote most of the earlier tracts; other contributors included Arthur Perceval, Isaac Williams, William Palmer, and the brothers John and Thomas Keble. They were largely distributed by the authors and their sympathisers, who would ride or tramp about from parsonage to parsonage distributing bundles of them.

The character of the tracts and of the Oxford Movement changed with the advent of Edward Bouverie Pusey. Pusey, although still comparatively young, already had a position of some power within Oxford as the Regius Professor of Divinity and a canon of Christ Church. When late in 1834 he aligned himself with the Tractarians, he provided them with a natural and respected leader (Newman considered himself lacking in the qualities of leadership). The tracts gained "more sobriety, more gravity, more careful pains, more sense of responsibility"; they also literally gained weight. Pusey's first tract (Tract 18, "On the Benefits of The System of Fasting") was not only the first to be signed (with the initials E.B.P.), it was also the longest of the tracts so far, while Pusey's three combined tracts (67, 68, and 69) on Baptism together covered more than 300 pages. This change is significant: if the tracts lost their earlier stringency, they gained in the capacity to discuss in depth matters of spiritual and theological importance.

Pusey's tracts on Baptism, with their insistence on the importance of the sacrament and their severe treatment of post-baptismal sin, provided a focus for the increasing animosity against the Oxford Movement. Another kind of suspicion became articulate in the hostile reaction to John Keble's Tract 89, "On the Mysticism attributed to the Early Fathers of the Church"; the very word mysticism was enough to condemn in certain quarters this lengthy and scholarly justification of allegorization of the scriptures and the natural world. A similar but more intense fury was provoked by Isaac Williams's Tract 87, "On Reserve in Communicating Religious Knowledge." Although this tract was directed at the perennially offensive distortions and simplifications of popular preachers, it was seen by those who read not much further than the title as a revelation of the secretive, disingenuous, and conspiratorial nature of Tractarianism.

The tract which finally let loose "a universal storm of indignation" against the Tractarians was Newman's Tract 90, "Remarks on Certain Passages in the Thirty-Nine Articles." The acknowledged aim of this tract was "to show that while our Prayer Book is acknowledged on all hands to be of Catholic origin, our Articles also, the offspring of an uncatholic age, are, through God's good providence, to say the least, not uncatholic, and may be subscribed by those who aim at being catholic in heart and doctrine." Years after, in the *Apologia pro Vita Sua*, Newman wrote bitterly of the general outcry against him and his beliefs: "In every part of the country and every class of society, through every organ and occasion of opinion, in newspapers and periodicals, at meetings, in pulpits, at dinner-tables, in coffee-rooms, in railway carriages, I was denounced as a traitor who had laid his train and was detected in the very act of firing it against the time-honoured Establishment." Newman refused to withdraw the tract but acknowledged the disapproval of the Bishop of Oxford and resigned his place in the movement: "I have acted," he wrote, "because others did not act, and have sacrificed a quiet which I prized. May God be with me in time to come as He has been hitherto!" Tract 90 was to be the last of the tracts.

In 1845 when Newman was finally accepted into the Roman Catholic church, it seemed for a time as if the Oxford Movement was dead. Soon, however, it became apparent, as new churches were built and old churches became more insistent on the sacraments, as Anglican orders were set up for both women and for men, that in fact the movement was very much alive. Indeed it would continue as a living force within the Anglican church throughout the 20th century.

—June Sturrock

TRADITION AND THE INDIVIDUAL TALENT.
Prose by T.S. Eliot, 1919.

T.S. Eliot's "Tradition and the Individual Talent" is an essay that is both interesting in itself and also a turning-point in literary criticism in the English-speaking world. As any reader will note, the essay takes issue with many of the assumptions about the writing of poetry that were current at the time the essay appeared. Eliot tried to modify and correct these assumptions.

Some of the errors—errors from Eliot's point of view, of course—were venerable, and Eliot modifies these theories rather than cancels them. Other errors—particularly the view that the poet seeks above all else self-expression—were more recent, and Eliot flatly discredits them. But some older notions, such as Matthew Arnold's that the study of literature should be the study of the best that has been thought and said, find a subordinate place in Eliot's effort to set right the relation between tradition (the best that has been thought and said) and the ability, the "talent," of the individual poet.

Perhaps it is the more recent error that stirred Eliot to lecture his generation; poets and critics alike often saw the composition of poems as a way in which the poet drew aside from conventional society and conventional modes of thought and was faithful to the particular reality he knew best: his own self, his own stable of passions. These, in much poetry and poetic theory of the time, were what the poet should be faithful to; he could safely ignore the more distant past. Instead, the current poet (the "individual talent") had the duty of fixing his attention on his own contemporary and often quite fleeting passions.

To such service many "individual talents" were, in Eliot's day, devoted. Eliot wished to see these talents diverted to the service of the complex traditions that make up western literature—traditions which, in the early 20th century (and later) were often dismissed as irrelevant to the expressions of "modern" and "personal" emotions. The first part of Eliot's essay is an argument to the contrary: that without some knowledge of what literature has been and has accomplished, the contemporary poet is at sea. That is, without the compass-findings provided by tradition, the modern poet—and by implication, the modern novelist and the modern dramatist—cannot write. Further, the compass-indications can be understood as pointing to something of great value, and this "something" is nothing less than the accumulation of western literary expression. It is an accumulation that begins with Homer and takes us (and the modern poet) through Dante and writers in other literatures and, of course, through the rich body of literary expression in English.

Eliot is quite clear about what is set up by this conscious relation of the modern writer to the literary past. The relation is not (at least primarily) an apprenticeship to the moral values that all men should practice in their lives. (This is the mistaken theme of Arnold and others; "tradition" is more than a moral school where one studies questions of moral and political behavior.) The modern poet, when he masters the literary past and uses it, has benefits that are chiefly esthetic. In many later essays, Eliot as the conscious Christian makes quite clear that moral benefits also accrue from thoughtful immersion in what is called the Christian tradition. But this is not Eliot's theme in "Tradition and the Individual Talent." For in this early essay, Eliot is not concerned with the ethical rectitude or the religious salvation of the writer. Instead, he focuses on a narrower concern: the esthetic deliverance of the writer from damaging isolation from the literary past, from damaging trust in the inate value of the writer's own "individual talent," a talent that, some modern persons suppose, contains within its own limits all the artistic skill that a writer needs.

Such a faith, Eliot believes, is misplaced. The modern writer, if only for esthetic reasons, needs to know as much as possible, of the "all" that artists from Homer onwards have created. And the current writer's knowledge of the past must be omnivorous rather than selective; he must try to be at home in all the worlds of letters that have existed. He must, for the sake of his writing, lose his petty self and walk through the halls of tradition in order to be instructed there.

Such is the act of faith that Eliot advises: a pursuit of the excellent by means of submission to all that has been excellent. It is a pursuit that puts aside a contrary act of faith: a poet's belief that excellence begins with his own talent and may very likely perish when he is gone.

The second part of Eliot's essay turns to the practical problem: what shape do the actual labors of the poet (and of other writers) take? What happens as the sheets of paper covered by the writer accumulate, the products of the writer who has immersed his individual talent in talents (the modern writer should admit this) that are greater than his? There should be in such work an interplay of passion and feeling. Passion and feeling, to the careless judgment, may seem to be closely related to each other. Eliot judges the matter otherwise and does so on the basis of evidence he finds in various areas where "tradition" has accumulated. Passion and feeling are sharply opposed to each other, and the modern poet, like all past writers of verse, must set up an interplay between the two. Passion is the emotion that causes a poet to set forth on a particular journey (the expression of love, of devotion to one's country, etc.). But the poet needs assistance as the path of his journey winds here and there. This assistance comes from the feelings that happen to be his particular endowment. The poet's feelings compose a disorderly congeries of memories of physical sensations and literary recollections ("traditions") that is in his possession. The collection of feelings cannot help but be "personal," "individual." Thus, the writer cannot avoid being "himself" as he expresses a certain passion. But he needs to press forward in his particular account of some strong passion fully aware of how some of his peers—a few of them still alive but most of them dead—have performed their similar tasks. In short, the 20th-century poet needs to widen his awareness of his particular passion if he is to make a wise use of the disorderly feeling his special being encloses.

Such is the essence of Eliot's widely influential argument. It is an argument that has given shape to large portions of subsequent literary-critical awareness. Many more recent students of literature have taken their cues from this essay and other essays by Eliot. And Eliot's presence can be felt even in works that travel in other directions. For example, the basic tension between the individual writer and traditions, between the poet and his forebears, is read quite differently in Harold Bloom's *The Anxiety of Influence: A Theory of Poetry*. Yet one suspects that if Eliot had not written so decisively, Bloom's conception of the on-going battle between the poet and the past masters who threaten to overshadow and even overpower his imagination would not have been so clearly seen.

In short, Eliot's essay has been, in a current critical term, a seminal essay. That is, much has grown from the terrain cultivated by Eliot's spade in this work.

—Harold H. Watts

TRAVELS IN ARABIA DESERTA.
Prose by Charles Montagu Doughty (1843–1926), 1888.

Critical Studies: introduction by T.E. Lawrence to *Travels in Arabia Deserta*, 1921; *Doughty: A Critical Study* by Barker Fairley, 1927; *The Life of Doughty* by David Hogarth, 1928; *Doughty: A Study of His Prose and Verse* by Anne Treneer, 1935; *Doughty's English* by Walt Taylor, 1939; *English Travellers in the Near East* by Robin Fedden, 1958; *Three Victorian Travellers* by Thomas Assad, 1964; *Doughty* by Stephen E. Tabachnick, 1981, and *Explorations in Doughty's Arabia Deserta* edited by Tabachnick, 1987.

"It is not comfortable," observed T.E. Lawrence, "to have to write about *Arabia Deserta* . . . a book not like other books . . . a bible of its kind." Lawrence's analogy may be taken quite literally. *Arabia Deserta*, like the Bible, contains many kinds of writing, has epic sweep, and is seldom read through, yet its devotees cannot read or write or speak about it without emotion. Wilfrid Scawen Blunt, himself an Eastern traveller, thought Charles Montagu Doughty's re-creation of his 21 months of wandering with the Bedouin (1876–78) the best prose of the century, and several pre-Raphaelite and fin de siècle poets—Burne-Jones, William Morris, and Robert Bridges—were admirers. Robin Fedden calls it "One of the most impressive books in the English language," and compares it to *Paradise Lost*. Tabachnick's centennial commemoration had to deploy scholars from university departments of history, geology, geography, anthropology, English, and Near Eastern studies to cover its various facets.

The book's geography follows Doughty's itinerary. The early chapters recounting his passage to Medain Salih with the Muslim *haj* (pilgrim caravan to Mecca) to view ancient rock inscriptions form a kind of prologue, after which he follows the Bedouin. Visits to a few towns mark the phases of the action thereafter. The first, centering on Teyma, is a relatively happy interval with Fukara and later Moahib tribesmen. Journeying to Hayil with the Bishr and meeting Prince Ibn Rashid, he encounters increasing hostility. Hellish times follow in and around Kheybar as Doughty seeks protection against prejudice and even violence, returns to Hayil, but is expelled and sent to other towns. Finally he makes his way to Tayif and thence to Jidda and safety.

Doughty's considerable sufferings, and his reticence about his motives, have always piqued readers' curiosity, and theorists have rushed to fill this vacuum at the centre of the narrative. He had studied natural science, and while his travel notebooks preserve few emotional reactions and even less dialogue, they are full of geological remarks on Arabian landforms. "Of surpassing interest to the many minds, which seek after philosophical knowledge and instruction," he once wrote, "is the Story of the Earth": i.e., *geo-logos*. And not only to their minds: Doughty was an ardent disciple of the new evolutionary geology who *felt* landscapes deeply and spiritually as expressing the Creator. A devout man, though not an orthodox Christian, he reverenced the Bedouin as descendants of the biblical patriarchs, preserving something of their way of life. He was also a patriot who thought of the British "race" as of vaguely Near Eastern origin, so the Arabs represent "roots" in that respect too. The common denominator of these various motives is the primitivist's impulse to simplify, to get back to pure origins, to bare essentials. It should be noted, however, that he first planned a much shorter excursion, that he tried to leave after the first six months but could not maintain the pace and so had to stay for another year.

One of the many remarkable aspects of the book is the way it confirms the development in aesthetics described by Hardy (in *Return of the Native*) as the shift from "the vale of Tempe" to "a gaunt waste in Thule" as the standard of Beauty. Doughty's "gaunt waste" is farther south, but "the immense mountain blackness, terrible and lowering, of the Harra" shares the titanic associations and "chastened sublimity" of Egdon Heath, and appealed powerfully to the austere young Englishman, fascinated by whatever was bare and empty, even barren and desolate, in Arabia. Even after a year of tribulations, he praised the nomad existence as the best; its pain and hunger were essential to the spiritual life. Doughty hoped, like Vergil, to purify and renew his culture through his art, though his sensibility was more modern than that comparison implies. There is a stunning moment when he is shown a well-watered mountain ravine with some greenery; suddenly he asks his guide to give him a camel and abandon him there: it is enough. In Doughty we feel the beginnings of a minimalist outlook, finding more in less.

Technically, the book is more demanding than most travel literature. Doughty uses "Khalil" (his name in Arabia) as a character who plays the role of a *saiehh* or "wandering anchorite in the fable of human life," and whose adventures are recounted by a narrator (sometimes distinguishable from Doughty). More problematical is the style that put off publishers but delights aficionados: a varied, densely textured, and often poetic compound of Arabisms, Latinisms, and English archaisms. "My main intention," wrote Doughty in 1902, "was . . . to continue the older tradition of Chaucer and Spenser, resisting to my power the decadence of the English language."

No resistance could have been stouter: to read Doughty is to rediscover English. "The sun's great rundle" turns out to be a variant of the mediaeval "roundel," a circle. The spirit "waver[ing] her eyas wings" is behaving like a nestling ready to fly. Doughty was more than an etymologist, though: he created neologisms and portmanteau words. "Rimples" are wrinkles and dimples; the nomads "dazing" in their hot afternoon tents are dazed, dozing, and lazing. He moves qualities of the environment into the human perceiver ("desolate Arabs") and vice versa ("sickly climate") with the freedom of a poet. Arabic words, syntax, and idioms ("drink smoke") impart the regional flavour. Combining all these qualities gives the essential Doughty: "There is a startled conscience within a man of his *mesquin* being, and profane, in presence of the divine stature of the elemental world!" *Mesquin* is Arabic for "weak"; profane is Latin *pro-fanus*, "outside the temple," here placed outside of its normal word order and clause. Nature, "the elemental world," is the temple. Sentences this rich are not uncommon in Doughty, who toiled over the book for years—rather like Vergil, polishing ten lines a day—and would not change a word to gain a publisher. The integrity of the man and the artistic integrity of the book are one, and total.

—Richard Bevis

TRAVESTIES.
Play by Tom Stoppard, 1974.

Many of Tom Stoppard's plays, especially earlier in his career, take shape as spin-offs from other famous dramas. *Rosencrantz and Guildenstern Are Dead* is the best-known of this unique dramatic species, though *Dogg's Hamlet* and *Cahoot's Macbeth* also enjoy popularity among some scholars. *Travesties* fits into a similar mould in that Oscar Wilde's glistening comedy *The Importance of Being Earnest* partially serves as springboard. In *Travesties*, however, an even more dominant inspiration springs from historical events laden with political significance—such as are found in *Every Good Boy Deserves Favour*, *Professional Foul*, and *Night and Day*. Stoppard is struck by the historical paradox that Lenin, James Joyce, and Tristan Tzara (father of Dadaism) all happened to reside in Zurich at the same time during World War I. From that ironic circumstance the dramatist weaves together their lives in a wild, comical concoction, farcically stretching audience credulity as well as limits of the English language.

Given the free-flow scene settings, Stoppard prudently restricts his formal stage sets to two, one being the main reading room of the Zurich library and the other the home of Henry Carr, a minor British government official assigned to Zurich at the time. Henry Carr serves as unifying element among the three historical protagonists as well as the connecting link to Oscar Wilde's play. Stoppard provides much of the needed background information in an introduction called "Henry Wilfred Carr, 1894–1962" which precedes the published text of *Travesties*. From that commentary we learn that Henry Carr, as an English functionary in Zurich, was approached in 1918 by James Joyce to take an acting role in an English-speaking performance of *The Importance of Being Earnest*. Authoritative biographies explain that Joyce agreed to become business manager of the English Players, a group of English expatriates who wished to keep their native culture vital while living in Zurich. Carr was asked to participate primarily because he had admitted to having acted before. An unfortunate falling out occurred after the first performance when a misunderstanding over money led Joyce and Carr to sue one another. From that starting point, Stoppard structures a string of zany scenes which begin as Carr's reminiscings as an old man and include hefty portions of Dadaist art aesthetics, Joyce's rationalisations (personal and artistic) for evading the war, and Lenin's beliefs concerning "bohemian intellectuals" and the place of art in his political paradigms.

The initial scene opens in the Zurich library where parodic versions of Lenin, Tzara, and Joyce sit at the same table. Each pursues his own objective: Joyce dictates his soon-to-be classic *Ulysses* to Gwendolen, Tristan Tzara "creates" poetry by drawing individual words from a hat, and Lenin (Vladimir Ilyich Ulyanov) works intently on his book on imperialism. Once the audience has identified the characters and their mannerisms, the scene shifts to the chambers of Henry Carr, portrayed mostly through his voice as old and lost in reminiscences. He tries to focus on how he had first met the famed James Joyce through the Oscar Wilde play enterprise, and it is evident throughout the play that "Old Carr" possesses a slippery memory that is not entirely reliable. As though writing his memoirs in his head, Carr begins in several ways to codify his experiences with Joyce 40 years earlier: "My memories, is it, then? Life and times, friend of the famous. Memories of James Joyce. James Joyce As I Knew Him." His initial statements about Joyce are formal, objective, and generally praising. But as he draws nearer to memories of his legal battles with the author, Carr loses control, describing Joyce as "a liar and a hypocrite, a tight-fisted, sponging, fornicating drunk not worth the paper."

The same process follows regarding the other historical figures whom Carr may—or may not—have actually known: "What was he like, Lenin, I am often asked" and "*Dada*!—down with reason, logic, causality, coherence, tradition, proportion, sense and consequence, my art belongs to Dada 'cos Dada 'e treats me so—well then, *Memories of Dada by a Consular Friend of the Famous in Old Zurich: A Sketch*." Several times throughout *Travesties* the celebrities go to Carr's residence in flashbacks to engage an appropriately "youthified" Carr figure in witty discussions on art, politics, and society. By the end of Act I, because it has observed Carr's impatient arguments with Joyce, Tzara, and Lenin, the audience not only knows the crotchets of Carr but also the fundamental tenets underlying the aspirations of his famous acquaintances.

Stoppard is able to rummage around so varied, complex personages with the help of fluid time and space shifts. What he calls "time-slips" are particularly useful for furnishing vital background information to the audience. In such "time-slips" a scene will commence with certain material expressed through dialogue interchange. But soon the conversation slips back to the beginning point of the interchange to start anew, the next time to offer another set of background data. Seven such "time-slips" occur in Act I, helping to inform the audience about a wide range of historical and theoretical issues concerning the characters and times. Act II may strike some viewers as less vital, because much of it is given over to conveying long sections of Lenin's political tracts.

Yet even when deluged with challenging and contradictory concepts, the audience is continuously amused by virtue of Stoppard's dazzling verbal arsenal. No playwright today can transcend his brilliant diction and incredibly intricate syntax which leads to such lines as "no, Tzara—yes!—wrote his name in the snow with a walking stick and said: There! I think I'll call it The Alps. Oh the yes-no's of yesteryear." *Travesties* may not excel as total theatre, but it has few rivals as an exhibition of hilarious verbal gymnastics.

—C. J. Gianakaris

TREASURE ISLAND.
Novel by Robert Louis Stevenson, 1883.

In 1881, Robert Louis Stevenson wrote to W.E. Henley of a book he had just begun, soon to become his first published novel. The manuscript title was *The Sea Cook; or, Treasure Island: A Story for Boys*; in Stevenson's words,

> it is about Buccaneers, . . . begins in the "Admiral Benbow" public-house on the Devon coast, . . . is all about a map, and a treasure, and a mutiny, and a derelict ship, and a current, and a fine old Squire Trelawney . . . , and a doctor, . . . and a sea-cook with one leg, and a sea song . . .

Especially important as imaginative genesis for the novel was a detailed map drawn in play with his stepson:

> as I pored upon my map of *Treasure Island*, the future characters of the book began to appear there visibly among imaginary woods; . . . fighting and hunting treasure, . . . The next thing I knew I was writing out a list of chapters . . . It was to be a story for boys ("My First Book").

As children's literature, *Treasure Island* reveals many characteristics in common with other boys' books: there is an adolescent protagonist who, soon freed of parental restraints (his sickly father dies, and he leaves his mother behind), goes on a successful quest for treasure; there is an emphasis on fast-paced adventure, during which the semi-orphaned hero makes a long journey to an unknown land, uncovers treachery his elders have overlooked, gains allies, learns skills, is tested, and wins both respect and praise for his bravery and sense of honour; and there is the boy's fantasy fulfilment of saving the lives of adult authority figures, first his mother and then his shipmates, in part as a result of rising above the limitations they tend to put upon him. In short, Jim's quest is a metaphor for his journey from youth to manhood, from ignorant innocence to learned (and earned) experience, a journey that is symbolically compressed into the actual voyage, the island, and the tests he encounters there.

But the book is more than this. Jim is not only the boy-hero, he is also the novel's narrator, writing the tale some years after the main events. In this regard the novel is not only a *Bildungsroman*, it is also a *Kunstlerroman*, a partial portrayal of Jim's development as an artist: from a naive and passive observer in the first 11 chapters—ending with the disillusioning shock of revelation in the apple barrel—to an increasingly active, creative role, initially as participant-hero on the island, then, after returning to England, as the one who tells the story. It is Jim who re-creates the rush of events by the power and immediacy of his writing; it is Jim who maintains the integrity of his first-person narration by having Dr. Livesey briefly recount the events which Jim did not experience; and it is Jim who learns and tries to communicate not only the adventure but also its human costs: thus the bleak reminder in chapter 33 of the "blood and sorrow" and "shame and lies and cruelty" the treasure has cost, thus Jim's reluctance to go back to the island for the remaining treasure, and thus the final sentence wherein Jim's childhood dream-phantoms are replaced by actual nightmare recollections of "that accursed island." Indeed, Stevenson's success as an author lies partly in the extent to which he is able to remove himself from the reader's consciousness and let Jim, his proxy, with his mix of both adolescent and adult perspectives, narrate the novel.

The use of Jim as a proxy also justifies Stevenson's ambivalent portrayal of Long John Silver. For Jim, the ambivalence derives from his changing relationship to the pirate. He is drawn to the positive force of Silver's personality yet repelled by his ruthless amorality. For Stevenson, the ambivalence derives from Silver's genesis in his friend Henley; though without "all his finer qualities," Silver still has Henley's "strength, his courage, his quickness, and his magnificent geniality"—characteristics which Stevenson hoped to reveal "in terms of the culture of a raw tarpaulin" ("My First Book"). Stevenson's admiration mitigates some negative aspects of the pirate's personality; though Silver is a treacherous liar and ruthless murderer, he is also a rugged individualist, like Henley "unconquered," a man whose talents call him to rise above the limitations of his condition, whose desire is not for immediate gratification and wealth per se (unlike the other pirates) but for what he thinks wealth can bring—a change in class-status from seaman to gentleman, epitomized by his thought of being "in Parlyment, and riding in my coach."

Of course, things are not so simple; Silver is mistaken in thinking the mere possession of wealth will make him a gentleman. As even Ben Gunn knows, a gentleman's word of honour is reliable; Silver's is not. The Squire, the Captain, and the Doctor—upper-middle-class symbols of order, restraint, and decency as opposed to the near chaos, impulse to instant self-gratification, and immorality of the pirate world—are the real gentlemen, and of these it is the Doctor who best models the civilized values of his class. He is the adult Jim most closely resembles, and he serves as Jim's surrogate father. Indeed, the Doctor, like Jim, combines the talent of authorship with readiness to act, with humanity even towards injured enemies, and with integrity. These characteristics have their counterparts in Jim's many-faceted actions, in his help to Hands and Silver, and in his decision to keep his word to Silver when in the stockade. As Long John admits, the Doctor is "a good man and a true; I never seen a better man!"; as the Doctor's emulator, Jim evidences his eligibility for a gentleman's status. This first novel, then, reinforces the values of Stevenson's class, but there is also some hint of the ambiguity that is more evident in his later works.

—John Robert Sorfleet

TRILBY.
Novel by George du Maurier, 1894.

Trilby, George du Maurier's second novel, was serialized in *Harper's Magazine* in 1894 and published in book form in the same year. In the following year it was dramatized (not by du Maurier). Its great popularity no doubt sprang both from its affectionate, humorous, and detailed portrayal of the *vie de Bohème* of Paris in the 1850's and from its climax, in which the tone-deaf heroine, hypnotized by the musical genius Svengali into becoming a phenomenal singer, loses her powers when his influence is withdrawn by his sudden death. The name Svengali has become proverbial; the naming of a style of felt hat after the heroine has no connection with anything in the novel.

Three young artists—Taffy, the Laird of Cockpen, and Little Billee (nicknamed after the hero of Thackeray's ballad)—are visited in their studio by the black-bearded pianist Svengali, half-German, half-Pole, "of Jewish aspect, well-featured but sinister," and his protégé, the violinist Gecko, with whom he makes divine music. Attracted by their playing, an artist's model, who has been sitting for a sculptor in the same building, enters and introduces herself as Trilby O'Ferrall. Trilby is a tall girl about 18 years old, the orphaned daughter of an alcoholic Irish classical scholar and a Scottish barmaid, and has a little brother, Jeannot; she has been a laundress before becoming a model, and has since had several lovers. All five men, in their various ways, adore her. Svengali's courtship is humorously malign—he visualizes her ending up in the Morgue, and her fine skeleton in a glass case at the medical school, if she refuses to share his expected prosperity—and though he once cures her of an attack of neuralgia by hypnosis she views him as "a big hungry spider." Little Billee's passion is idealistic; he is so horrified by finding her publicly posing naked in a life class that he flees to Barbizon for a month; on his return she has reverted from a model to a laundress, continues to visit him and his friends, and at last consents to marry him. His mother and clergyman uncle arrive, scandalized at Trilby's social situation and history, but Trilby's act of renunciation greatly moves Mrs. Bagot. Trilby now leaves Paris, and Little Billee suffers a serious illness and is taken back to England; meanwhile news arrives at the studio that Trilby's little brother has died and that she has disappeared.

Little Billee becomes a famous artist but feels that his emotions are atrophied; a romance with his sister's friend Alice comes to an end because his reading of Darwin shocks her clergyman father. Some five years later he and his two friends revisit Paris, and attend a concert where Svengali conducts the orchestra, Gecko leads it, and Trilby (now known as La Svengali) sings, among other pieces, a Chopin impromptu which Svengali had played at their first meeting; Little Billee's frozen heart is thawed. During the visit Trilby, in a carriage with Svengali, refuses to recognize Little Billee, and Svengali insults him in an hotel, Taffy revenging the insult by pulling Svengali's nose and cuffing him. Trilby now sings at one of Jullien's London concerts, with Svengali seated in a box facing the stage. The sight of the three friends in the audience gives him a fatal heart attack, Trilby's voice reverts to its primitive tunelessness, and disorder breaks out. She goes into a decline, tended by the three friends and Little Billee's mother; she relates how Svengali saved her from suicidal despair, but she utterly disbelieves that she ever appeared in public as a singer before the fatal night; then one day a large photograph of Svengali arrives, dressed as for the Paris concert, and as she gazes at it she sings the Chopin impromptu for the last time and falls into her last sleep. Little Billee does not long outlive her. Twenty years later Taffy, now married to Little Billee's sister, meets Gecko in Paris and is told how "there were two Trilbys," the second—a mere image—being Svengali's creation through his hypnotic skill.

In 1892 a committee of the British Medical Association had reported favourably upon hypnosis after a searching investigation, so it was a topical theme. Du Maurier's account of Svengali's achievement is fanciful, but carries sufficient conviction in the context of the story: the curing of Trilby's neuralgia is artfully introduced at an early stage. The whole novel is carefully planned, though its style is deliberately easy-going, with plenty of allusive authorial reflections rather in the manner of du Maurier's admired Thackeray. The mixture of fact and invention is Thackerayan too: La Svengali is praised by Berlioz in 12 articles ("now out of print") and by Gautier ("I forget in which journal this eloquent tribute appeared"), while Herr Blagner writes a diatribe against "Svengalismus." Several of du Maurier's friends are pictured within the novel, as another friend, Alfred Ainger, records in the *Dictionary of National Biography*: when William Bagot and Frederick Walker, "those two singularly gifted boys," are compared, the hidden point lies in the fact that Walker (1840–75) was none other than the model for Little Billee, though he was never a member of the young du Maurier's artist circle in Paris.

In his moral attitude towards Trilby's sexual past, du Maurier is broad-minded, taking the view that the only sins of which one should repent are those that hurt others: Trilby's dialogue with Mrs. Bagot on the subject, in the last section of the novel, is worth attention. He goes to some unobtrusive trouble to counteract any suspicion that Svengali may have taken sexual advantage of Trilby: he told her, she relates, that he could not marry her because he had a wife living, in Prussia, "and three children, which he declared were not his," but in settling Svengali's affairs it turns out that all these were pure invention, and later Gecko attributes Svengali's spiteful behaviour towards Little Billee to envy. Svengali himself, with all his faults, including a streak of cruelty, is not inhuman or beyond the reach of du Maurier's generous spirit.

—T.W. Craik

TRINKET'S COLT.
Story by Somerville and Ross, 1899.

Much 19th century Irish fiction used the convention of the traveller's tale as the basis for a portrait of life in Ireland, that country which was said to be more foreign to the English than even Timbuctoo. In the convention a visitor, usually a young Englishman, arrives in Ireland and is gradually educated in the conflicting and ambiguous realities of Irish life.

In Somerville and Ross's series of short stories relating the experiences of the Resident Magistrate of the fictional west Cork town of Skebawn, this convention is employed. Major Yeates, the young, Oxford-educated, potential dispenser of English law and order, arrives in Ireland only to find that he has come to a country where nothing is quite as it seems or as it ought to be. He is forced into a series of comic conflicts with the native Irish and with the Anglo-Irish ascendancy class, primarily represented by Skebawn's Master of Hounds, Flurry Knox. Generally speaking, it is the Irish who emerge victorious from these conflicts leaving Major Yeates at a considerable disadvantage, often on the wrong side of the very law which he is supposed to uphold.

"Trinket's Colt" is typical of the R.M. stories. As it opens we are in Skebawn on petty sessions day and Major Yeates encounters Flurry Knox and asks him to get a four-year-old colt for a friend. The story simply tells of the hilarious fix this leads to as Flurry steals a colt from his grandmother accompanied by the unwitting Major Yeates who eventually ends up hiding, along with the colt which has been buried in a sandpit, in a clump of furze bushes. At the climax of the story the Major abandons his honour and his dignity and, tortured with furze prickles, has to listen to Mrs. Knox tell her grandson that she will appeal to Major Yeates for the truth as she believes him to be a gentleman. Both Major Yeates and the colt are ignominiously exposed by Mrs. Knox's yapping dog, and the story ends in an explosion of laughter as Mrs. Knox acquits the Major since he seems to have fallen among thieves and forgives Flurry for his theft in appreciation of his cleverness. "Upon my conscience . . . I'd give a guinea to have thought of it myself!"

Although writing at the time of the Irish literary revival, Somerville and Ross seem curiously untouched by the revival's reinterpretation of the Irish past, instead they confine their interest to the ranks of the Anglo-Irish ascendancy in their "big houses" and to their relations with their tenants and servants. In their portrayal of Irish life the Anglo-Irish are seen to be primarily interested in horses and dogs, in hunting, fishing, and shooting. Flurry is typical of this class, but he is also resourceful and cunning, lawless when there is something more important at stake, and he has the "Irish" characteristics of deceit, exaggeration, and always being able to talk himself colourfully out of any scrape. His grandmother is untypical in that she is a woman of learning, well able to discourse on Virgil, but she and her surroundings are described in terms which, with remarkable economy of detail, evoke a whole way of life in its decline. She is arrogant, imperious, refined, and has a strong hand on her once noble estate which is allowed to run to rack and ruin. She appears dressed like a scarecrow, dirty but wearing a "magnificent diamond." Everything in her house speaks of past luxury and present poverty. There is superb port, terrible sherry. Bad soup is served in a magnificent, but dirty, tureen. Superb salmon appears on a cracked kitchen plate. Major Yeates notes the incongruity of it all but his view is generally benign and his first-person narrative tone is amused.

Not so when the native Irish are described. Throughout the R.M. stories, there is constant reference to the dirt and smell of the people who appear before Major Yeates. At the beginning of "Trinket's Colt" he feels the need to escape from "the bellowing of the attorneys, and the smell of their clients." Servants generally are unkempt, surly, drunk, and disorganised. The streets of Skebawn are full of "soddenly screwed people," a maid servant has "the head of a being whose matted head rose suddenly into view . . . as I have seen the head of a Zulu woman peer over a bush." The only saving graces of the native Irish are their ability to circumvent the law and, closely related to this, their speech. Slipper, who assists in the theft of the colt, is represented using a broad dialect. "Oh murdher, oh murdher, Misther Flurry! What kept ye at all? 'Twould perish the crows to be waiting here the way I am these two hours—" Flurry's speech, while being distinctively Hiberno-English in its syntactical structure, is less marked by non-standard pronunciation, "Oh, is it that filly? . . . she's gone these three weeks from me." Mrs. Knox and Major Yeates use standard English. These variations in speech patterns add to the comic conflict but it is the character of Major Yeates as the classic, innocent "fall-guy" forever caught in the plots of those who know this world better than he and who are not burdened by principles, the demands of job, or social status, or a belief in "justice," which is essential to the comedy. Since these are comic tales, the Major is always saved but his predicament allows for an analysis of cultures in conflict and the narrator's dual role as purveyor of standard values and victim of Irish duplicity provides a medium for that sense of authorial ambiguity (very prevalent in Anglo-Irish literature) towards the material portrayed which is perhaps, more even than the comedy or the representation of the Anglo-Irish in decline, the most striking feature of this story.

—Anne Clune

TRISTRAM SHANDY.
(*The Life and Opinions of Tristram Shandy, Gentleman.*)
Novel by Laurence Sterne, 1759–67.

Laurence Sterne's novel was published in nine volumes between 1759 and 1767. He was 47 when he published the first two volumes, and virtually unknown. By 1768, when he died, he was a literary celebrity.

Sterne wrote to a correspondent that *Tristram Shandy* "was made and formed to baffle all criticism . . . it is either above the power or beneath the attention of any critic or hypercritic whatsoever."

Certainly it has not proved to be beneath the attention of critics, for almost from the moment of first publication Sterne's novel has provoked strong reactions. It has been condemned roundly on "moral" grounds by critics from Richardson to Leavis—the former thought it "execrable," characterised by "mean, dirty Wit," while the latter referred to Sterne's "irresponsible (and nasty) trifling." Sterne's religious vocation fuelled many of the complaints directed against the alleged obscenity of the work. The scandal of a cleric writing "a bawdy book" was confirmed and compounded by biographical gossip centring on Sterne's alleged philandering, or his tempestuous relationship with his wife, or his supposed neglect of his indigent mother. Charges of plagiarism confirmed his dubious character for those of a censorious inclination—his use of Rabelais, Cervantes, Swift, Burton, or Locke justifying their condemnations. Questions as to his honesty and integrity, and the sincerity of his celebrated sentimentalism are what lie behind Thackeray's virulent attacks upon him. "He is always looking in my face, watching his effect, uncertain whether I think him an imposter or not; posture-making, coaxing, and imploring me," the Victorian wrote.

Not that the formal eccentricity of the book itself has escaped censure. Samuel Johnson delivered an Olympian judgement: "Nothing odd will do long. *Tristram Shandy* did not last." Odd it may have been, but last it did. E.M. Forster said, "There is a god in *Tristram Shandy*, and his name is Muddle," and many before and after Forster have deplored the eclectic disorder (as it seems) of the book.

The source of the book's comic anarchy is of course the narrator, Tristram, who stands self-consciously between the reader and the promised story of his life and misfortunes. "Story" is sacrificed to narrative "discourse." It is a device that balks and frustrates the reader's expectations. The very conventional role of the first-person narrator is given an unconventional twist by Tristram's character as storyteller for he is thoroughly whimsical in his judgement of what requires to be told and in what order he will tell it. Moreover, a reader appears from time to time in the person of some kind of surrogate for the implied reader, who is lectured, teased, bullied, and interrogated by the narrator. In this way, Sterne ensures that the whole process of the production and consumption of the text (involving participation from Sterne himself, the "author," the narrator, the fictional reader, the implied reader, and the "real" reader!) is displayed and debated. In this nexus of negotiations that constitute "the novel" few tacit assumptions or conventions pass unchallenged. We are taken up at every stage with the problems of what constitutes "the story" and of *how* to tell it, with its coherence and its construction, ultimately with the question of artifice. Which is why Viktor Shklovsky (for whom art was technique) called *Tristram Shandy* the most plotted and least storied novel—and in that respect therefore "the most typical novel"—in world literature.

Just as the novel incorporates the mutual relationships between narrator, "story," and reader into the fiction itself, so they each bring different concepts of Time into the discussion. The time of the action is a matter, as Tristram notes, of "the train and succession" of ideas and in fiction it is well respected—"the true scholastic pendulum"—whereas the narrator's time (the time it takes to give an account of events that have their own time-scheme) and the reader's time (the time it takes to read the narrator's account of these events) are generally neglected. Sterne ensures that there will be an ironic exposure of the conventional allowances and modes for the representation of Time. He relishes the paradoxes that Tristram brings to our attention, defying temporal linearity in the narrative, or playing it off against the measure of the narrator's or the narratee's time. Having begun with the misfortune that befell his "little gentleman," the homunculus, even before the moment of conception, jinxed by Time indeed, by the association between sex and the monthly winding of the clocks, by a mechanical servitude to Time, Tristram labours as a narrator to do justice to the task, only to find himself obliged to go backwards, exploring causes and associations, hobbyhorsical or otherwise, in order that the full implication of an event or an action should not be missed or misrepresented. Giving a truthful and coherent account of oneself is an all but impossible task, so interwoven into the fabric of our lives are diverse and apparently irreconcilable elements. "In short there is no end of it;—for my own part I own that I have been at it these six weeks, making all the speed I possibly could,—and am not yet born." One can never *simply* tell the story, even as a first-person narrator. Sterne makes fun of the reductive implications of such novelistic conventions in order to present us instead with a world irreducibly complex. His is a form that declares the limitations of form.

Not only the mechanisms of causality but issues of coherence and the authority of the narrating voice are fundamentally undermined by the device of Tristram's narration. The digressive tendencies, the admission of non-literary materials, the use of foreign languages, the borrowing and plagiarism, the blank pages, the black pages, the missing pages, the squiggle, and so on, all ensure that the question of integrity, order, coherence is never far from the reader's mind. What is implied of course is something about the eclectic and disorderly character of human thought.

At the root of this issue is also the question of language. For language is far from being simply a social means of denoting things and states. It is subject to personalisation to a considerable degree—to the influence of an individual's hobbyhorse. Confusions arise precisely for this reason. Sterne is fond of occasions in which language proves a source of misunderstanding rather than a means of communicating. And he seeks occasions to breed the slippery and (by one standard) imperfect character of language. Not only do his characters themselves respond to language in ways that are quite specific to their own preoccupations (i.e., hobbyhorsically), but Sterne encourages his readers to look with great attention not only at what he says, but at the possible implications and innuendos his words might carry. The whole negotiated character of the novel involves just that—from the interruption at the end of the first chapter onwards. "*Did ever woman, since the creation of the world, interrupt a man with such a silly question?* Pray, what was your father saying?" The fictional reader interrupts Tristram precisely because he has innocently misunderstood (through a naivety in itself understandable) the word "interrupt." He must be schooled (and the implied reader with him) to read with greater awareness—must take account of, for example, *since the creation of the world*—for the novel is to be a highly collaborative exercise. Moreover, language can require an exacting interpretation or it can incorporate silence or gesture—like Trim's gesture in dropping his hat—for this reason much in Sterne's novel resides in the punctuation. This fuller sense of language is consistent with Sterne's strategies in the novel as a whole.

The essence of the collaboration is often the exploitation of a bawdy sense. But having set his reader to read in a way that is alerted to the *double entendre* or innuendo (as, for example, in the business of Noses), Sterne is of course not above rebuking them for what he characterises as a tendency to take his words in a "bad sense"! ("I declare that by that word I mean a Nose, and nothing more, or less," he says, but the punctuation of that final phrase is itself suggestive!) Yet in Sterne even the referential character of language is troublesome. This it is that threatens the health of Uncle Toby:—"his life was put in jeopardy by words!" That is, by the "unsteady uses of words which have perplexed the clearest understandings." What Tristram has in mind at this point is the relentless technical jargon of siege warfare, the clutch of whose complexities are in some sense evaded by Trim's suggestion that they reconstruct the battlefield itself in miniature. Uncle Toby is himself of course rendered naive by his monomania, as on the famous occasion of the Widow Wadman's pointed enquiry, anxious as she is about the exact character and extent of Uncle Toby's groin wound, her glance towards the waistband of his breeches ineffectual, her words unfortunately ambiguous: "And whereabouts did you receive this sad blow?" Toby of course replies, not by putting *his* finger where she had anticipated, but instead placing *her* finger on the very spot—on the large map of the town of Namur!

—Brian W.M. Scobie

TRIVIA.
Poem by John Gay, 1716.

Published in January 1716, John Gay's *Trivia; or, The Art of Walking the Streets of London* is an urban georgic teaching the science of safely navigating the streets of the great metropolis. The couplet poem is divided into three Books offering instructions respectively on: (I) "Of the Implements for walking the Streets, and Signs of the Weather"; (II) "Of Walking the Streets by Day"; and (III) "Of Walking the Streets by Night." Gay establishes a mock-heroic mood from his initiatory invocation of his Trivia, "the Goddess of Streets and High-Ways," as his muse:

> Through Winter Streets to steer your Course aright,
> How to walk clean by Day, and safe by Night,
> How jostling Crouds, with Prudence, to decline,
> When to assert the Wall, and when resign,
> I sing: Thou *Trivia*, Goddess, aid my Song,
> Thro' spacious Streets conduct thy Bard along.

Offering sage advice on a wide variety of relevant topics from appropriate shoes, coats, and canes to where to find delicious oysters and how to avoid diseased whores, Gay's Walker puts his acuity of observation at the disposal of like-minded "honest Men." Guided by the Walker's wary eye, every description is an exercise in code-breaking. We avoid "jostling Crouds," he instructs, because of the ingenuity of pickpockets:

> Nor is thy Flaxen Wigg with Safety worn;
> High on the Shoulder, in a Basket born,
> Lurks the sly Boy; whose Hand to Rapine bred,
> Plucks off the curling Honours of thy Head.

Gay's Walker grandly announces his intention "To tread in Paths to ancient Bards unknown"; but, in one sense, nothing could be further from the truth. Gay's genius in *Trivia* lies in the appropriation and transformation of existing genres. His "Advertisement" acknowledges that he owes "several Hints of it to Dr. Swift"; and, in fact, there is scarcely a syllable of Swift's "Description" poems that Gay does not imbed somewhere in his much more ambitious work. Unsophisticated descriptions of London "rambles," like Thomas D'Urfey's *Collin's Walk Through London and Westminster* (1690), were popular; and *Trivia* is, first and foremost, an alternately affectionate and satiric description of the city to which Gay appends an extensive "Index." Gay elevates the humble genre of the "ramble" to the heights of art by adapting various Virgilian touches and making the *Georgics* his model. Gay's first mock poem, *Wine*, was stimulated by John Philips's georgic *Cyder* (1708); but *Trivia* more imaginatively uses the manner of Virgil's depiction of the rural ideal together with the matter of London "rambles" to produce an urban georgic that is at once celebratory and implicitly critical.

Critics are divided on the question of Gay's ideology and moral earnestness in *Trivia*. Succinctly put, they disagree whether Gay is praising London or condemning it. The dark interpretation contends that Gay's poem is a deliberate "counterblast against Whig ideals of grandeur," a "Juvenalian georgic" suffused with "Tory gloom." Dark interpreters emphasize Gay's depictions of whores, cripples, beggars, and the whole baggage of urban poverty and disease, finding the moral center of the poem in the pathetic description of the orphan bootblack and his patron: "*Cloacina* (Goddess of the Tide/Whose sable Streams beneath the City glide)." Critics urging lighter interpretations discover "something energetic and life-giving [even] in the currents of filth that course beneath the streets of London" and find in the Goddess of Ordure an incarnation of charity and industry.

Both the celebratory and the satiric schools are too horny-handed in their interpretations; and while recent critics who react to both by identifying a "pattern of contradictions and ironic deferments" which bespeak Gay's deliberate aversion to any ideological pronouncements in "light verse" can be accused of trivializing *Trivia*, they are certainly right in denying that the primary focus of the poem is the modern degeneration of the city from the ancient rural ideal. Gay's Walker is a modern Spectator and he does make moral pronouncements; but the London that he describes is an invigorating spectacle and his moral earnestness never exceeds polite Horatian bounds, as when he contrasts the laudable lot of those afoot with the degenerate race that ride in coaches:

[There] the brib'd Lawyer, sunk in Velvet, sleeps;
The starving Orphan, as he passes, weeps;
There flames a Fool, begirt with tinselled Slaves,
Who wastes the Wealth of a whole Race of Knaves. . . .
May the proud Chariot never be my Fate,
If purchas'd at so mean, so dear a Rate;
O rather give me sweet Content on Foot,
Wrapt in my Vertue, and a good *Surtout*!

Wrapped in Virgil's rhetoric and animated alternately by Gay's sentimentality and irony, *Trivia* recreates a realistic 18th-century London into something that seems as rich and strange today as it must have to his contemporaries.

—Harry M. Solomon

TROILUS AND CRESSIDA.
Play by William Shakespeare, 1602 (?).

"Lechery, lechery, still war and lechery," Thersites observes in this bewildering play, "nothing else holds fashion." *Troilus and Cressida* is as well one of William Shakespeare's most powerful plays, apparently unproduced after its own time, if even then, until the turn of the 20th century. Recently, however, it has been often revived. Its bleak views of political opportunism masquerading as honor, and sexual licentiousness masquerading as love, have proven "amazing and modern," as the Polish critic Jan Kott rightly observed. Thersites is only one of Shakespeare's chorus-figures in *Troilus and Cressida*, a foul-mouthed enlisted man in the Greek army who reminds the audience insistently of the powerful bond between sexual lust and military aggression. The other chorus-figure, equally repellent, is Pandarus, a Trojan pimp who sings the most vulgar song Shakespeare ever wrote, and who in the epilogue to the play bequeaths his venereal diseases to the audience. Further, Pandarus and Thersites do double-duty in the play by serving as its clown figures, although their humor offers scant salubrious ballast for the play's essential nihilism. Not only through these two but through nearly every other character, Shakespeare seems to have gone out of his way to populate a world stewing in its own corruption.

In the first act of the play, Ulysses observes that political disorder makes of everything "an universal prey" and will eventually "eat up himself"; in the last act, Thersites say that "lechery eats himself." Between these parallel observations about war and love, the actions in the two plots of *Troilus and Cressida* reflect each other disturbingly. In this cruel juxtaposition of events from Homer's *Iliad* and Chaucer's *Troilus and Criseyde* Shakespeare reduces everything to hollow politics and besotted sexuality, eventually and inevitably fused into a single vision of a world committing suicide through violence, stupidity, greed, and physical passion.

In the controlling action of the play—the stalemated Trojan War—Shakespeare debases his Greek chieftains with an almost resolute regularity: Nestor is an ageing drone; Ulysses is more devious than wise; Ajax is a muscle-bound dunce; Menelaus is widely mocked as a cuckold; Agamemnon is a pompous windbag; Achilles is a preening homosexual who sits out the war in his tent with his "male-whore" Patroclus. The Trojans come off no better: none of them pays the slightest attention to an insane Cassandra's alarming prophesies; Hector knowingly saves face at the expense of common sense; Troilus is an inexperienced teenager swaggering boastfully about honor; Paris lounges around the palace with Helen while his brothers fight the Greeks over her. As if his irony needed any further honing, Shakespeare turns Helen herself into a bawdy, well-seasoned voluptuary instead of mythology's most beautiful woman in the world. Similarly, in Shakespeare's version of Homer's noble single combat, Achilles has his henchmen slaughter an unarmed Hector.

Meanwhile, the eponymous Troilus and Cressida are protagonists in what is essentially a subplot that follows the chronology of events in Chaucer's narrative poem. Shakespeare's young lovers, however, bear no resemblance to Chaucer's medieval couple. Troilus is more ardent adolescent, confusing his glands with his heart, than he is knightly scourge of the Greeks in battle. Alternately mooning over and lusting after Cressida, he is too imperceptive to arouse much sympathy. When late in the play he turns impotent voyeur, spying on Cressida in the arms of Diomedes, audiences are more likely to be disgusted than surprised. Shakespeare's Cressida shares little more than her name with the widow in Chaucer's poem. Physically at least, she is a virgin, but having come of age during what Thersites describes as an "argument" over "a whore and a cuckold" she is well aware of the value of her only commodity, her body. When eventually she sleeps with Troilus, the off-stage love-making has been preceded immediately by two telling scenes. In the first, Pandarus sings his song—in which a woman's initial pain during sex turns to pleasure—to Paris and Helen whose own erotic activities have brought about the war. In the second, Troilus and Cressida engage in a richly erotic verbal seduction, pitting a man's sexual prowess and limitations against a woman's expectations and sexual pleasure. Subsequently, when an apparently aroused but unsatisfied Cressida is taken hostage and responds to the kisses from a chorus line of Greek commanders—there is no indication that these are polite exchanges—audiences are again more likely to be disgusted than surprised.

During the time that Troilus and Cressida have consummated their liaison off-stage, one of the great speeches in the play occurs, ironically about the inconstancy of human nature and perseverance keeping "honor bright" (III. iii. 145–80). The other speech comes much earlier in the play, an elaborate series of extended metaphors on the necessity of an orderly chain of command (I. iii. 78–124), but by the end of the play everything has fallen into disorder. It cannot be by accident that Shakespeare assigned both speeches to the skeptical Ulysses.

Although the gods never appear on-stage, they are invoked throughout *Troilus and Cressida*; similarly then, it cannot be by accident—as this extraordinary play insists—that the offspring of Ares (Mars, god of war) and Aphrodite (Venus, goddess of love) is Eros.

—Bruce Kellner

TROILUS AND CRISEYDE.
Poem by Geoffrey Chaucer, c. 1385.

Troilus and Criseyde represents Geoffrey Chaucer's principal contribution to the romance and, along with *The Canterbury Tales*, his major achievement. More than a love story, the work exhibits a medley of late medieval philosophical and ideological concerns, which Chaucer interweaves with the complexities of human psychology and motivation. The resultant tension accounts for its enduring influence on British writers: in the late 15th century, Henryson felt compelled to reconcile the two in his *Testament of Cresseid*; Shakespeare's bitter play, written more than 100 years later, asserts the inefficacy of behavioral paradigms in the face of human passions; and Dryden's 1679 version reconfirms the value of ideals in accordance with the author's theories of decorum and moral purpose. Nonetheless, despite its eclectic nature, the medieval poem remains in essence a romance, set in a well-established tradition of recasting, within the constraints of contemporary conventions, the matter of classical Greece and Rome.

The Trojan War provided a particularly appropriate context for Chaucer's love story for, according to English pseudohistory, Britain was first settled by Brute, descendent of the sole Trojan survivor (see Laȝamon's *Brut* and Geoffrey of Monmouth's *Historia Regum Britanniae*). The tale itself, however, has no basis in classical legend or native tradition. Both characters receive but brief mention in Homer's *Iliad*, Troilus as one of Priam's many sons and Cressida (Chryseis) as a Theban captive over whom Achilles and Agamemnon quarrel. They surface again in 3rd-century Latin histories of the war, purportedly translations of eyewitness accounts by Dares Phygius and Dictys Cretensis, which served as major sources for medieval authors. Neither significantly develops the characters or posits any relationship between them. Such first occurs in Benoit de Sainte-Maure's *Roman de Troie* (c. 1160), which contains a recurring motif of Briseida's infidelity to Troilus. Here, the lovers—wronged-but-faithful suitor and scornful courtly mistress—are cast in the *fin amor* tradition. Their story, however, remains vague and incomplete, a minor interlude in the greater Trojan epic. Two centuries passed before it developed as an independent history of love and betrayal.

Boccaccio's *Il Filostrato* (1336) relates the tale much as we find it in Chaucer and is believed to have been his immediate source. The work exemplifies the courtly tradition not only in plot details and characterization but in form: an autobiographical allegory of the author's affair with Maria d'Aquino, it is, as the final canto reveals, an offering to her. On both levels, it reflects the diminishing seriousness of courtly love in Renaissance art. Chaucer, on the other hand, wrote within a solidly medieval context. In adapting *Il Filostrato*, he elevated idealized love to its former status and transformed a personal epistle into a poem of broad concerns which embodies much of the world view of 14th-century England.

Written in rhyme-royal, *Troilus and Criseyde* employs the standard motifs of courtly romance—love at first sight, prolonged secret courtship, pining suitor, coy but merciful mistress—which require little comment. More perplexing are the conflicts arising between secular and religious ideologies. These, along with a pervasive comic strain, lead to the poem's main critical crux: the question of whether it is primarily a Christian tragedy or one of courtly love. Certainly, the narrator's interpolations, the reflections and actions of the characters themselves, suggest that love stands as the highest earthly good, not only bringing happiness but improving the moral being of the lover. Indeed, love so ennobles Troilus,

> That swich a vois was of hym and a stevene,
> Thorughout the world, of honour and largesse,
> That it up rong unto the yate of hevene . . .
> He was, and ay, the first in armes dyght,
> And certeynly, but if that bokes erre,
> Save Ector most ydred of any wight;
> And this encrees of hardynesse and myght
> Com hym of love, his ladies thank to wynne
> That altered his spirit so withinne.

His just reward is a place in heaven. Pandarus, despite his comic qualities, poses as a priest in the religion of love whose "conversion" of Troilus saves the latter from despair. Cressida's faithlessness, on the other hand, brings about his fall.

Nonetheless, certain elements strain against the glorification of romantic love. Pandarus might be viewed as a scheming pragmatist and a bawd; Troilus as foolish and remiss in duty when he languishes in love-sickness, weak and base in plotting with his friend; and Diomed's courtship of Cressida a parody of that by Troilus, exposing courtly love as a self-serving and destructive game. Furthermore, love rides Fortune's wheel (a recurrent image in the poem) and is therefore untrustworthy. Finally, Troilus' epiphany, echoing in his ironic laughter as he gazes down upon "this litel spot of erthe," supports the narrator's admonition to reject love in favor of divine considerations and seems to confirm the *contemptus mundi* vision peeking through at several points in the text.

Chaucer may be accused, perhaps, of trying to have it both ways, for he neither rejects any of the ideologies presented nor resolves the debate (most obvious in Troilus' Book 4 reflections upon Cressida's imminent departure) between determinism and free will. Moreover, romantic love may be viewed in Boethian terms as the imperfect earthly equivalent of divine love, of lesser value but nonetheless a virtuous pursuit for weak humanity. In this case, the tragedy lies in Troilus' inability to moderate his passions according to either the courtly code (he is not deterred by Cressida's inconstancy) or Boethian concepts.

The complexity of theme allows for considerable debate over character. Troilus may be hero or fool, his cohort priest or panderer. The most perplexing personage, however, is the heroine, who constitutes an intricate study in fear. While other characters, driven by friendship, lust, honor, or despair, act forcefully, Cressida continually weighs the dangers facing her: the precarious freedom of widowhood against bondage to a powerfully protective lover, threats to her person or reputation against a loss of chastity, survival in an enemy camp against betrayal of true love. She forever teeters between awareness and naivety, at once a pragmatic survivor, a puppet to the manipulations of others, and a plaything of Fate. Even Chaucer's attitude toward her is ambiguous, for he overtly forgives her while repeatedly drawing attention to her condemnation by others.

The greatest strength of *Troilus and Criseyde*, perhaps, lies in its very failure to answer the questions it raises and in its suspension of the characters between contradictory ideals and impulses. For, given other equally ambiguous works such as *Sir Gawain and the Green Knight*, this may be the psychological and ideological paradox in which the author and his audience were caught.

—Gwendolyn Morgan

THE TURN OF THE SCREW.
Story by Henry James, 1898.

Henry James was fascinated by the ghost story. He felt that to be truly effective tales of the supernatural should not simply recount otherwordly "events" but instead should portray the effects of those events upon a sensitive observer. James acted upon this theory in writing *The Turn of the Screw*, and created a tale which has horrified, and mystified, generations of readers. Few works of art have elicited such acerbic, polemical, and often fanciful critical debate.

The debate grows out of the ambiguities imposed by the way James limits point of view. From the moment that the governess's narrative takes over the story, our knowledge is strictly limited: all that we learn of the events at Bly, we learn through her. There is no omniscient narrator who can tell us directly what "really" happened or read the other characters' minds; all we have is the record of what the governess sees, or thinks she sees, and what she determines that others think and feel.

The governess tells a disturbing story. She, an inexperienced young woman, accepts a position as governess to two orphaned children who live on a remote country estate. Their uncle in London demands an unusual condition: she is never to report to him nor communicate with him in any way. She is to be head of the household and manage everything herself. The governness is charmed with her two small charges, eight-year-old Flora and 10-year-old Miles, although she is disturbed to find that Miles has been dismissed from school on mysterious grounds. All apparently goes well until the governess sees an unknown and quite horrifying man in one of the towers of the house and later at a window. She learns that the man she saw was surely Peter Quint, the master's former valet, but that Quint is dead!

It soon becomes clear to her that Quint and the previous governess, Miss Jessel (who is also dead), were "infamous" when alive, corrupted the children, and have now returned for them from beyond the grave; the seemingly innocent children welcome the demonic visitors. The frightened young woman struggles against this apparently invincible evil with no help but that of the unimaginative housekeeper, the aptly-named Mrs. Grose, who cannot see the ghosts herself. The governess repeatedly doubts her own sanity and becomes nearly as eager to vindicate herself as to save the children. She does apparently save little Flora, but she saves Miles only in the most equivocal way: when she wrenches the boy's spirit away from Peter Quint, the "white face of damnation" at the window, he dies of the shock, "dispossessed."

But many readers have claimed that there is a second, hidden story beneath the governess's narrative: the governess is mad, the ghosts are hallucinations, and the true horror of the story is that two innocent children are placed in the sole care of a madwoman, who literally frightens one of them to death.

These readers find support in the governess's nervous anxiety and insomnia, her romantic dreams about her employer, her father's reported "eccentricities," her confessed aptitude for sensing ghostly phenomena, and most of all in the fact that nobody else ever sees (or admits seeing?) the ghosts. These readers explain the children's growing uneasiness as a normal reaction to the peculiar behavior of their governess. And they point to the indisputable fact that the governess draws sweeping and horrifying inferences from very small and ambiguous pieces of evidence.

But, finally, any reader who claims that the evil spirits are merely the governess's hallucinations is left with an inexplicable kernel of "fact": how could the governess decribe Peter Quint exactly, point by point, when she had never seen him nor heard of him, unless she really did see his "spirit?" Quint's is an unusual face, with attributes traditionally ascribed to the devil; the governess describes him minutely and Mrs. Grose recognizes the portrait at once. Furthermore, James himself wrote about the tale as a well-crafted ghost story, not simply a case study of madness.

James wrote that he wanted to "give the impression of the communication to the children of the most infernal imaginable evil and danger," and he wisely determined to leave the specifics of that evil to the imagination of each reader, only supplying hints that it was somehow sexual. "Only make the reader's general vision of evil intense enough, I said to myself . . . and his own experience, his own imagination, his own sympathy (with the children) and horror (of their false friends) will supply him quite sufficiently with all the particulars. Make him *think* the evil, make him think it for himself, and you are released from weak specifications." The question of the governess's sanity can be seen in this light: ambiguity is much more disturbing than specificity. The lingering ambiguities give yet another turn of the screw to the disquieting effect of this disturbing story.

—Mollie Sandock

THE TWA CORBIES.
Ballad, possibly 15th century.

This remarkable poem, artistically one of the greatest of the Scottish ballads that have come down to us, is closely related to the English version called "The Three Ravens." Francis Child, in fact, considers the two works versions of basically the same ballad, and in his monumental collection of *The English and Scottish Popular Ballads* (1882–98) he groups them together as No. 26, under the title of "The Three Ravens." Child uses this title presumably because his text of the English ballad dates from a printing in 1611, whereas the earliest printed text of "The Twa Corbies" came nearly two centuries later. It first appeared in Sir Walter Scott's *Minstrelsy of the Scottish Border* (1802), communicated to Scott through Charles Kirkpatrick Sharpe from a Miss Erskine of Alva (near Stirling), who in turn copied it down from the recitation of an "old woman." Unaccountably, Child gives the Scots version first, though he clearly believes it to be the later of the two since he calls it "a cynical variation of the tender little English ballad." "The Twa Corbies" may in fact be the older version in oral tradition; at some point it may even have passed through a French metamorphosis as "Les Trois Corbeaux" (with Scots "Twa" mistranslated as French "Trois"), and then back into English as "The Three Ravens." Or it may have happened the other way around. In the final analysis, it is impossible to know which is really the older, the Scots story of a young knight murdered by his lover so that she may take "anither mate," or the English account of a faithful, pregnant lady lovingly burying the body of her slain knight and then dying herself of a broken heart. The latter version crossed the Atlantic and is still current in Iowa and Texas, and probably elsewhere in the U.S., involving the corpse of a horse rather than a knight, and using the refrain of "oh Billy Magee Magar."

One thing is certain: the Scots form of this ballad is by far the greater in terms of poetic art and sheer dramatic power. Its structure is simple but overwhelmingly effective: stanza 1 poses the question by one of these predatory birds ("Where sall we gang and dine to-day?"); the rest of this brief poem (stanzas 2–5) gives us the answer by the other "corbie." In stanzas 2 and 3 the situation is gradually revealed, not directly but by hints and inferences ("And naebody kens that he lies there,/But his hawk, his hound, and lady fair"), building powerful suspense and tension. In stanzas 4 and 5 the full horror of the murder is developed with gruesome detail ("And I'll pike out his bonny blue een"), culminating in stanza 5 on a note of mystery and terror.

This spare outline is fleshed out in a style that is chillingly effective throughout. Child and others have characterized the general tone as cynical, but the corbies are not really cynical —their attitude rather is one of grim, matter-of-fact acceptance of the horror. This ballad, incidentally, is unusual in having a first-person human narrator who overhears the ghastly dialogue of the corbies. There is a gradual buildup through skillful shifts in style; from the suggestion of ruthless hunger among these obscene birds of prey in the opening stanza, to flat statement of the circumstances of the murder in stanzas 2 and 3, to the appalling anatomical detail of stanza 4, and finally to the overwhelming sense of desolation in the terse closing lines of stanza 5—"Oer his white banes when they are bare, / The wind shall blaw for evermair." This image, it should be noted, surely provided Edgar Allan Poe with the refrain of "Nevermore" for his poem "The Raven," and possibly also the line "Tis the wind and nothing more." The birds are given some human qualities, but are at the same time distanced from normal human feelings in this situation. They tell their story with matter-of-fact realism, with understated acceptance of horrible murder and treachery as though these deeds were part of the *natural* scene; they simply observe what has happened and record the evidence from a neutral point of view—the "lady" is not condemned. The corbies in the end are only birds with a practical predatory interest in where their next meal is coming from—"So we may mak our dinner sweet."

Altogether, "The Twa Corbies" has a stark, compelling power. Like all genuine folk ballads it has an impersonal quality, despite the first-person narrator (who never intrudes or comments). The bird speakers, as we have seen, are themselves totally neutral, taking no moral or even aesthetic stance in relation to the slaughter of the knight. And this aloofness is part of the secret of the poem's success: what is *not* said enhances the effect enormously, as the reader's imagination is forced to fill in the awful details, to create the full human context of the crime. The few graphic facts given by the birds are aptly chosen for this purpose.

In style this is an extraordinarily taut, concise ballad; there is not a superfluous word in it. The result is a small miracle of verbal magic—the reader feels that the slightest change in wording would ruin the total impact, as he can in fact see by considering the several minor variations recorded by Child. "The Twa Corbies" has unforgettable phrasing, the feeling of inevitability that is a sign of the highest art.

—Allan H. MacLaine

TWELFTH NIGHT.
Play by William Shakespeare, 1601–02(?).

Twelfth Night; or, What You Will is one of William Shakespeare's two comedies which introduce twins who are mistaken for each other. In the earlier *The Comedy of Errors* this device had been the mainspring of the plot, but in *Twelfth Night* it is secondary to the situation of the heroine Viola who, shipwrecked on Illyria's coast and then serving Duke Orsino in the disguise of a page, is made the messenger of his love-suit to the Countess Olivia; Olivia falls in love with the messenger, who is herself in love with the Duke. This situation is resolved by the arrival of Viola's identical twin Sebastian (who was separated from her in the shipwreck), to whom Olivia proposes marriage and is immediately united; when Viola's identity is finally revealed the Duke recognizes that it is she whom he loves and must marry. Another suitor to Olivia is Sir Andrew Aguecheek, a foolish poltroon whom her drunken kinsman Sir Toby Belch encourages and exploits. Her sour and presumptuous steward Malvolio becomes her third suitor when Sir Toby and her waiting-woman Maria place an anonymous love-letter in his path, urging him to cast his humble slough and appear fresh in cross-garters and yellow stockings; when he accosts Olivia in this costume, persistently smiling as the letter has also instructed him, he is treated as a madman.

Shakespeare based his comedy on "Apolonius and Silla" in Barnaby Rich's prose collection *Farewell to Military Profession* (1581), a romantic story derived from an Italian play of mistaken identity on the Plautine model, *Gl'Ingannati* (The Deceived Ones, 1531), but he omitted the heroine's previous love for the duke, her adventures before her shipwreck, and her committal to prison for making the duke's beloved pregnant (which has been done by her twin brother). All the Malvolio and Aguecheek material is his invention. At one point Sir Andrew's jealousy of the favour shown by Olivia to the Duke's page results in a challenge and a duel, which is interrupted by Antonio, Sebastian's rescuer and friend; Antonio, who has been the Duke's wartime enemy, is now arrested, and is indignant at the supposed Sebastian's treating him as a stranger; later Sir Andrew, believing that the Duke's page is a coward, meets Sebastian and strikes him, getting well beaten himself, and it is this brawl that brings Olivia and Sebastian together. This mingling of the serious with the light-hearted is very characteristic of *Twelfth Night*, which has a vein of melancholy running through it. Olivia is in mourning for a dead brother. Viola's scene with the Duke (II. iv), in which they listen to the song "Come away, death," contains her tale of woman's constancy beginning "My father had a daughter loved a man, / As it might be, perhaps, were I a woman, / I should your lordship." Antonio faces the danger of death. The reunion of Viola with her brother in the final scene, even though she has never lost hope of his survival, is touched with wonder.

Malvolio has sometimes been viewed as a near-tragic figure, particularly in the scene (IV. ii) in which he has been shut in a darkened room, from which he protests that though treated as a madman he is in his right wits, and in the final scene, in which he learns how he has been made a fool of, and flings out with the line "I'll be revenged on the whole pack of you." But it has to be remembered that his treatment is the revenge of others on his churlishness (which he has shown not only to Sir Toby, Maria, and Olivia's fool Feste, but to Viola herself), that in the dark-room scene his interlocutor is Feste who is giving a lively performance of two roles, his own and that of "Sir Topas the curate," that his self-esteem has not suffered from his treatment, and that Orsino takes steps to have his rage pacified.

The genial irony with which Shakespeare, in this comedy as in his others, treats the delusions of lovers has sometimes led to Orsino's and Olivia's being regarded as culpably absurd in their actions and sentiments: they have been charged with narcissism and affectation, and their presentation has been called satirical. But both are respectfully spoken of (by the sea captain who has rescued Viola from the shipwreck, for instance), and it is reasonable to take their marriages to Viola and Sebastian as embodiments of the harmony in which Shakespearean comedy always issues (some critical opinion to the contrary notwithstanding).

Olivia has said, of the smiling Malvolio, "I am as mad as he, / If sad and merry madness equal be," Orsino has accused Antonio of "madness" in insisting that the young man in their presence has been in his company for three months, and Feste has many comments on wisdom and folly. The play's title perhaps reflects the theme of confusion, topsy-turveydom, and (particularly in Sir Toby) Saturnalian licence associated with the last day of the Christmas holiday season, while at the same time being inconsequential in the manner of the titles of Shakespeare's two previous comedies, *Much Ado About Nothing* and *As You Like It*.

—T.W. Craik

THE TWO GENTLEMEN OF VERONA.
Play by William Shakespeare, 1594(?).

The Two Gentlemen of Verona is one of William Shakespeare's earliest comedies and possibly his very first play. The text, which survives only in the First Folio of 1623, printed some 30 years after it was first written and performed, contains some striking inconsistencies in references to times, places, and even the names and titles of characters, giving rise to speculation that the play was cut and/or revised at some point. The subject matter derives ultimately from medieval courtly romance transmitted through the Italianate novella and, more specifically, through the highly stylized dramas of John Lyly fashionable in the 1580's—plays such as *Campaspe* and *Endymion*.

The Two Gentlemen is in general less widely admired and less frequently performed than Shakespeare's other earliest comedies, *The Taming of the Shrew* and *The Comedy of Errors,* both of which are more farcical in tone. On the other hand, as Shakespeare's first full-blown attempt at romantic comedy, it is more readily identified and discussed as the direct precursor of his more famous works in that genre such as *A Midsummer Night's Dream*, *As You Like It*, and *Twelfth Night*. Like these better-known plays, *The Two Gentlemen* focuses on the ways in which romantic love transforms the lives of young men and women, causing them to defy their parents, run away from home, forget their former lovers, betray their friends, and totally subordinate themselves to its influence. As in the later plays, the extravagances and absurdities of the lovers are parodied by minor characters and mocked by witty servants. It is interesting, however, that Shakespeare is already treating the female characters more seriously and sympathetically than the male characters here.

The young friends from Verona who are the heroes in this play, Valentine and Proteus, travel to Milan where they both fall in love with the same woman, Silvia, daughter of the Duke. For Proteus, this means betraying Julia whom he imagines he has left behind in Verona, but who has in fact disguised herself as a male page and followed him to Milan where she becomes his servant and reluctant go-between, discovering honour and generosity in her "rival" Silvia. Valentine's suit is not favoured by Silvia's father and, after a failed attempt to elope with her, he is banished to the forest where he falls in with some friendly outlaws and becomes their leader. Silvia, threatened with an enforced marriage to the man of her father's choice, manages to escape to the forest pursued by Proteus who is in turn pursued by Julia. In a somewhat surprising climax, Proteus, after rescuing Silvia from some of the outlaws, tries to rape her, but is prevented by the fortunate appearance of Valentine. Proteus apologizes to Valentine who, in order to prove that he has forgiven him, offers to give up Silvia to his friend. At this point Julia (still in disguise) faints, precipitating a more sensible ending.

Critics have found fault with the dramatic structure of the play, with its tone, and in particular with its ending. All have been accused of showing the marks of immature apprentice work. It is often remarked that Shakespeare's theatrical technique seems uncertain here: group scenes are inclined to be awkward and most of the speeches are monologues, duologues, or asides. It has been questioned whether the rather stilted tone is serious or whether the author might be satirising or burlesquing the conventions of romance in this play, especially in some aspects of his presentation of Valentine who cuts rather a comic and unbelievable figure. The reverses of the ending, with the silent Silvia passed from one man to another like a parcel, seem problematic and even offensive to modern audiences and readers.

Yet *The Two Gentlemen of Verona* also has considerable strengths. Julia for example is a spirited and interesting heroine whose role and disguise look forward to Viola in *Twelfth Night*. The complicated scene in which she overhears Proteus betraying her by wooing Silvia is an assured example of

Shakespeare's ability to manipulate a number of levels of knowledge or awareness and a worthy forerunner of the similar scene in *Troilus and Cressida* in which Troilus witnesses Cressida betraying him with Diomedes. Despite some artificiality, there is also lyric grace in the romantic rhetoric, and the comic prose of the servants is often highly effective. In a good production the partnership of Proteus's servant Launce and his recalcitrant dog Crab can steal the show, though the need for a competent canine performer may also have contributed to the theatre's neglect of the play. And while the theme of "love *versus* friendship" seems awkwardly handled here, especially at the end, *The Two Gentlemen of Verona* remains a seminal source for later uses of similar material in *A Midsummer Night's Dream* and *The Two Noble Kinsmen*.

—Ann Thompson

THE TWO NOBLE KINSMEN.
Play by William Shakespeare and John Fletcher, 1613.

The Two Noble Kinsmen was probably the last play with which William Shakespeare was associated; the title page of the first quarto edition of 1634 attributes it to him jointly with John Fletcher, Shakespeare's successor as playwright to the King's Men. Though the play was not included in the authoritative First Folio collection of Shakespeare's works, this may have been for copyright reasons. The argument that it reflects major participation by Shakespeare at several points has gained general acceptance, and the text has recently been much re-edited from this point of view. It is now often included in complete collections of Shakespeare's works, and has been performed with success after being ignored for most of the 18th and 19th centuries.

Though the story follows lost Tudor plays derived from Chaucer's *Knight's Tale*, the script is designed in the fanciful spirit of Shakespeare's other "late romances" as a more tragical sequel to *A Midsummer Night's Dream*. The later play's plot begins just before the marriage of Theseus to his Amazonian captive Hippolyta, a marriage which in this version of the story is interrupted by the demand of three widows that he wreak revenge for their dead husbands on Creon, King of Thebes. In successfully discharging this duty Theseus captures Palamon and Arcite, the two nephews of Creon in the play's title, whose amatory vicissitudes it chronicles in a spirit of wry amusement finally modulating to pathos. Indeed, the play generally explores the confusions and frustrations occasioned by the human reproductive drive's dislocation of individual choices, whether those of the widows, of Theseus, or of the two unmarried pairs of youthful lovers. The plot creates a similar permutation of crossed loves to *A Midsummer Night's Dream* when the two imprisoned kinsmen quarrel over who shall be the lover of Emilia, sister to Hippolyta, whom they glimpse moments after they have sworn eternal friendship.

The play is full of such calculated reversals of human decisions and expectations, mostly to the disadvantage of Emilia, who is not firmly committed to either of her suitors, and also of their jailer's daughter, who goes mad with frustrated love for Palamon. This drama of courtship is interlaced with quaint preparations for a rustic celebration of May Day focussed on an elaborate morris dance (borrowed from a masque by Francis Beaumont) which serves a function akin to *Pyramus and Thisbe* in ritually celebrating the triumph of the sexual drive over human will. After obtaining their freedom, the kinsmen on their own make several ambivalent and frustrated attempts to settle their claims to Emilia, only to be obliged to determine the issue in a climactic combat to the death at the orders of Theseus. Arcite wins through his devotion to Mars, though he forfeits his victory by a fatal accident which ensures the success of Palamon, devotee of Venus, on the verge of execution—an outcome which Emilia, a follower of Diana, must reluctantly accept. Meanwhile, the fugitive and disoriented Jailer's Daughter is finally tricked into accepting a more appropriate suitor. After all these reversals of expectation the play leaves audiences ruefully aware of the great discrepancy between human plans and the divine determination of their outcomes.

Critical opinion has mostly been quite hostile to the play's seeming discontinuities and its artificial character, usually blamed on Fletcher, but in performance the script has proved surprisingly successful both in the 17th century and in the 20th century since its first modern revival by the Old Vic in 1928. The role of the Jailer's Daughter, which blends the pathos of Ophelia with the humour of Helena, has always won actresses great approval: Mary Davis, its performer in Sir William Davenant's revival at the Restoration, gained thereby the affections of Charles II, and it has won less intimate accolades for modern actresses. The part effectively establishes the unique tone of the play as a blend of pathos and humour which audiences quickly learn to savour but which critics have barely begun to define, let alone sanction. The play's somewhat wordy and mannered texture requires a highly stylized, unrealistic performance suiting the courtly audiences for which it was probably first written. However, there is general agreement on the substantial gain to the canon in the modern recovery of this text as a performable reflection of the ultimate phase of Shakespeare's career.

—Hugh M. Richmond

U

ULYSSES.
Poem by Robert Graves, 1933.

"Ulysses," according to Martin Seymour-Smith, and other poems from *Poems 1930–1933* such as "The Bards," "Down, Wanton, Down!" and "On Dwelling," are "now much anthologized and firmly entrenched in the Robert Graves canon as standard examples of his best work" (*Graves: His Life and Work*, 1982).

In many ways, however, the poem, written in the early 1930's, represents a strand in Graves's writing which has been underestimated in the wake of the pseudo-theology he adumbrated in *The White Goddess*, a system of belief which was to dominate the poetry of his later years until his death in 1985. This book and subsequent works of scholarship such as *The Greek Myths* deployed, in the manner of Sir James Frazer's *The Golden Bough*, a vast repertoire of mythological, historical, and anthropological reference to argue for an ancient proto-religion of a variously named Mother Goddess, subsequently displaced by male divinities of war and "civilisation," but which for Graves still lay at the origins of the poetic impulse, and was worshipped by "genuine" poets in the figure of the Muse.

Graves wrote in the poem "Darien" that "It is a poet's privilege and fate / To fall enamoured" of the White Goddess. For all its anthropologizing bent, his mythology drew to a considerable extent on the spilt religiosity and mystical masochism of the medieval *amour courtois* tradition. In many fine poems of love, death, and fate, it gave Graves "metaphors for poetry" in much the same way as Yeat's philosophy of history in *A Vision*, and it rationalised to his own satisfaction Graves's many years of spiritual submission to his domineering muse and "mistress," the American poet Laura Riding. Whatever her effects on the poet's life, however, Riding, who shared his household but rarely his bed for most of these years, brought great gains to his poetry, purging it of its vapid Georgianism and wistful cadences, modernising his style in keeping with her own stringent and elliptical verse. Graves's friend and fellow war poet, Siegfried Sassoon, wrote complainingly in his own copy of *Poems 1930–1933* of what he saw as her negative influence, under which Graves "makes his meaning difficult by oddity, and forbids himself to allow emotion a hearing & an outlet." But her influence is a positive one in this poem, to be detected in the tough-minded attitudes and the worldly, modern idioms of the verse, while the robust cynicism suggests a poet who in his best work learnt as much by resistance and stubbornness as by emulation and discipleship.

Clearly in reaction against the elegiac plangencies of Tennyson's "Ulysses," this poem is more in keeping with the modernist, jeering spirit of James Joyce's *Ulysses*, still, in the 1930's a live item of scandal and legal dispute. But the reworking of the Homeric myth also owes much to Graves's interest in Samuel Butler's thesis that the *Odyssey* was written by a woman, a theory that later found expression in Graves's novel *Homer's Daughter*, which rewrote the encounter between Odysseus and Nausicaa as the autobiographical romance fiction of a teenage princess with a crush and literary pretensions.

It is instructive to compare the poem's cynical, "sophisticated" view of promiscuity with the much later poem written under the aegis of the Goddess, "Woman and Tree":

> To love one woman, or to sit
> Always beneath the same tall tree,
> Argues a certain lack of wit
> Two steps from imbecility.

The poet here is no wide-eyed innocent confronting the incomprehensible values of "Don Juan Tenorio." On the contrary, there is a dry wit in acknowledging that such a lifestyle is one for which the poet, "sworn to feed / On every food the senses know," might well claim an "inexorable need." Rather its romantic impulse is underwritten by the knowing rejection of these temptations, in tribute to the one woman sufficient "Wholly to glamour his wild heart," affirming, in spite of the poet's dedication "To change and chance," faith in "a sole woman's fatefulness."

Despite the apparent difference between this wilful lyric ingenuousness and the tone of "Ulysses," both poems share a central tenet. For the worldly Ulysses too there is really only one woman: "Penelope and Circe seemed as one." In his White Goddess phase Graves seems to have resolved the dilemma of "Tree and Woman" (and of his actual life) by casting the series of young women with whom he fell in love as all manifestations of what "Darien" calls "the one Muse / Who variously haunts this island earth." The worldly-wisdom of "Ulysses" thus provides a proleptic deconstruction of the improbable fidelities proclaimed in the later poems. If, for the senescent Graves, all lovers are really avatars of the one Goddess, the "much-tossed Ulysses" knows in middle age that this is a canny self-exculpation—knows, with wry sophistication, that at night all cats are grey.

Promiscuity is the very pattern of the poem's development. The antitheses and inversions of such formulae as "She like a whore . . . and wifely she" enact the emotional tergiversations of a situation where transient function usurps original identity. The wife Penelope is inverted to a whore, as the whorish Circe bears him a son, in a syntax which parallels Ulysses's brutal and capricious way with his women. Penelope's role is to make "his lewd fancies run." The real woman becomes merely the pretext for an open-ended proliferation of fantasies, the signifier of an endless flight from closure. In the same way, the series of antitheses on which the poem is constructed multiplies alternatives: wife / whore, Penelope / Circe, lewd fancies / paternity, Scylla and Charybdis, sea storms / lotus island, all symbolised by the clashing rocks of the Symplegades between which Ulysses has to sail. But this system of apparently simple binaries also multiplies complication. In the first instance, these opposites are not seen as alternatives, for Ulysses seeks, like Tennyson's avid hero, to experience both. Counter-changings suggests a turn and turn about, eddying out from one to other, but the process is actually more polymorphous than this. Binaries proliferate in the third stanza into the Sirens' *throng*, a movement confirmed in stanza four in the exponential "One, two and many." The overriding antithesis of the poem is that of mind and body. But the repetition of the word "flesh," reproducing this spawning proliferation (five instances in the one stanza), upsets the symmetry of antithesis by overwhelming the one instance of "mind," which is totally subjected to flesh: "Flesh set one purpose only in the mind."

The vulnerable body, bound hand and foot, tormented by lewd fancies, terrors, fear, groaning and sweating, metonymically depicted by unstopped ears and blind eyes, overwhelms the wiles and wit of the controlling cerebral self. There is only "one pleasure," "one purpose" in the imagining and the act, but plural "terrors." If Ulysses is a "he," third person singular, the women are "they," plural and collectivised by contrast, "One, two and many," while flesh lacks an article, generalised, omnipresent, a dominant principle rather than a particular body. The crescendo of the last sentence of stanza four has a direct sexual rhythm, obsessive, urgent, the dash itself the moment at which that urgency issues in a climax which is also loss of power, in a post-orgasmic decline across the enjambement which leads him to "find / Still those same terrors wherewith flesh was racked." "Racked" (with its possible pun on "wracked," ship-wrecked), despite its momentary pause, leads on to the renewal of urgency, for finding here is only the confirmation and repetition of an old and unsatisfying knowledge. Flesh, that is, is not absolute ruler. At the end of the sentence it in turn becomes, in the passive voice, the terrorized victim of something greater, which is both familiar ("those same terrors") and all the more powerful for not being specified.

In this poem, opposites merge in a shared menace, where angry seas and lotus islands alike threaten the lonely autonomy of the male principle, which fears solitude yet finds in that condition the ground of its independence. The ambiguous relation to desire, that which *can't* be assuaged yet constantly demands assuaging, is the paradox at the heart of the whole poem, with which antithesis is a classic linguistic strategy for coming to terms. Antitheses seem to restore decorum in the last, almost Augustan stanza. But this is not really the case. The skilful alliteration gives an illusion of order, counterposing witty wiles and far-known fame, though this is not a proper antithesis. "Won or lost" is; but it is dissolved by the negative of "he was nothing," which ironically recalls that in order to escape from the Cyclops's wrath Ulysses proclaimed himself a "Nobody." Heterogeneity is invoked again by an allusion which also suppresses identity in the phrase "Every king's daughter." Unlike Penelope and Circe, Nausicaa is not named here, but is swamped in a plurality where she loses her uniqueness, becoming stereotypical, generic. Similarly the named Ithaca of Ulysses's homing becomes an everywhere: "all lands to him were Ithaca." Ulysses too is "much-tossed," without specific detail. The final antithesis, in which Ulysses both loathes the fraud and puts up with it so as not to bed alone, establishes him as the biggest fraud of all, wily and witty, deceiving others with his tall tales and, undeceived himself, cynically putting his principles to bed with his conquests.

The *Odyssey* is a poem of the *nostos*, or return home. In the last stanza of "Ulysses" the hero comes home only to find that Ithaca is everywhere, and hence nowhere, that in fact he has never been away but also that he can't ever in that case go home again. "Home" is, in one sense, the transitory resting-place of each new woman's body. In its closure the poem also returns home rhetorically in the rhyme-word "love-tossed," which in echoing the opening "much-tossed" translates the rough seas of actual voyaging into a sexual turbulence, and brings out the indelicate innuendo of the word (cf. "done"), suggesting that for Ulysses all sex was a form of masturbation. This might be seen in retrospect as a powerful auto-criticism of the way Graves himself ruthlessly exploited his own successive "muses" as a series of pretexts for a self-regarding poetry.

"Terrified," repeated in "those same terrors," adds a further twist to the poem. In a sense, this perpetual moving-on is not a search for home but a flight from fear. Behind love and lust, carnal and spiritual eroticism alike lies this deeper motive. Ulysses's unassuaged sexual itch expresses a deeper male anxiety, of being mastered, of losing control to a more powerful force, that female sexuality identified with death in the figure of the Sirens. Fear is a protective mechanism; it "forewarns" and thus enables him to devise a strategy for survival. Ulysses will not give up the pleasures that threaten terrifying loss of control, but he experiences them through an elaborate mimickry of that loss, tied to the mast, his sailors with their ears stopped to prevent them hearing both the Sirens' song and his countermanding orders, while he can enjoy the ecstatic abandon of their singing. Since he is powerless to give in to the Sirens' blandishments, he remains perversely in control. In the process, though, he never really experiences that liberating loss of self he craves, and remains thus haunted by his fear, confronting it again in each new situation of seduction and escape. He lives, that is, in a sickness-unto-death, not the gay blade of insouciant phallic authority, but a nightmare-ridden sensualist (see "The Succubus" and "To Sleep") whose wiles and wit are all desperate attempts to elude ecstatic surrender. The last word of the poem reveals his real terror, that of being "alone" with himself, recognising the nullity that issues from evading possession ("Yet he was nothing to be won or lost").

For Graves, in many of his poems, apparent vulnerability becomes a way of retaining mastery: "bound fast / Hand and foot helpless to the vessel's mast, / Yet would not stop his ears." The reversal of traditional sexual roles is almost parodic here as, tied to the phallic mast, incapacitated but erect, as if bound helpless to his own sexuality ("stood" is deliberate innuendo), his unstopped ears are open like the female sex to the penetration of the Sirens' song. If his daring is what makes him a hero, mastering his fears, the groaning and sweating are clearly those of a sexual encounter. Hungry for experience, like Tennyson's Ulysses, for whom "all experience is an arch wherethrough / Gleams that untravelled world," Graves's Ulysses seeks, not the elusive horizon of a desired fulfilment, but to elude the enclosing straits of the act which fascinates and terrifies him.

This is a well-made poem, wittily containing its terrors with a skilful play of alliteration, assonance, and rhyme to forge a coherent, masterful form. The waggish, libertine tone, recalling Rochester, is reinforced by this verbal control. Syntax is deployed with consummate skill. Each stanza comprises one sentence, until the last, where the final two lines, making one sentence, reach conclusion by reweaving the preceding rhymes. Stanzas 1, 2, and 4 share the same rhyme scheme, abaab. Stanza 3 rhymes abbab, and the last stanza rhymes aabba. This irregularity within the appearance of order relates to the dominant theme. Each stanza of this poem about couplings contains at least one couplet, while the last has two couplets which derive an extra sense of closure by the return of the first couplet's rhyme-word at the end of the last line. The eccentric couplet in stanza 3 makes "bound fast" appear bound fast in the middle of the stanza, and the return of the rhyme at the close of the stanza reinforces the sense of both completion and escape, the word "past," as past passive, bringing closure after the participial present continuous of "daring."

The two couplets of the last stanza are particularly effective. The first couplet expresses the teenage girl's romantic ideal of monogamy, its pace breathless in the speeded-up second line, with its internal rhyme of "daughter sought," ending on the closure of imaginary possession in "her own." This is immediately unsettled by a new couplet which, beginning with "Yet," is in direct antithesis to the dream of capture it enshrines. These "yets" constitute an act of resistance and of qualification that refuses simple conclusions. The new sentence which completes the couplet half-way through its own momentum enacts this sense of passing through. The enjambement rhyme, stressing the loathing as much as the love, prepares for the second worldly-wise "yet," as the return of the rhyme-word from the first couplet enacts widowing and return simultaneously, giving a sense of unsatisfactory closure as the hero comes home to a negative aloneness. Capably containing its own terrors within the reassurances of rhyme and stanza, "Ulysses" testifies to the craftsmanship as much as the witchery of Graves's poetry at its best.

—Stan Smith

ULYSSES.
Novel by James Joyce, 1922.

It is generally accepted that *Ulysses* is the novel that changed the direction of 20th-century fiction written in English. In James Joyce's depiction of the events that unfold on 16 June 1904 in Dublin, and more specifically in the life of Leopold Bloom, the basic attributes of what has come to be called modernism constitute an artistic assault upon conventional fiction. Describing Joyce's technique in the *Dial* in 1923, T.S. Eliot said: "It is simply a way of controlling, of ordering, of giving a shape and a significance to the immense panorama of futility and anarchy which is contemporary history. . . . Instead of narrative method, we may now use the mythical method. It is, I seriously believe, a step toward making the modern world possible for art." Whether or not the common reader was ready for this new way of telling a story might be another question.

In this regard, it is important to ascertain just what it is Joyce meant by "myth," and this is no easy problem to solve with certainty. Thanks to Joyce's own comments and hints, we know that the structure of *Ulysses* is to a large extent based upon that of Homer's *Odyssey*. Yet Joyce utilizes conventional mythology in a way that is different from most of his contemporaries. While writers like Eliot, Pound, and even D.H. Lawrence evoke glorious figures from their Western cultural heritage to highlight and to undercut the reduced stature of their present day protagonists, Joyce is intent upon discovering a nobility and humanity inherent in a bourgeois existence that allows Leopold Bloom, his wife Molly, and their Dublin acquaintance Stephen Dedalus to maintain an equal footing with Odysseus, Penelope, and Telemachus. Joyce's "mythical method" allows these Dubliners to coexist with their Hellenic counterparts because both groups represent a paradigm of the attributes and qualities that their respective societies hold up as essential for the attainment of a meaningful, a significant existence. Myth is a living thing that functions as a superstructure for any viable culture, and any one mythic figure is just as valid as any other, as *Ulysses* itself will demonstrate.

Viewed on its surface, the world of Bloom's Dublin is indeed a riotous and chaotic concatenation of seemingly unrelated characters and events that often make little sense on a first reading. Yet Joyce marshals the trivia and minutiae of everyday occurrences into a controlled scenario that reveals the inner lives of the characters. Thus, Bloom's chance sighting of a midwife will cause him to recall and reflect upon the untimely death of his infant son Rudy and the speedy maturation of his teenage daughter Milly, along with the deterioration of his relationship with Molly. The midwife serves as a touchstone that evokes the deeper levels of Bloom's inner consciousness, and her brief appearance provides a focal point for the organization of Bloom's random thoughts, thus functioning as a centering device. Stephen Dedalus has come upon the same midwife earlier in the day, and his train of thought has followed along the same lines of sexuality, birth, and death, with his typically pessimistic emphasis on sterility in sharp contrast to Bloom's optimism on the same subjects. Often Joyce will organize the reflections of several seemingly unrelated characters around their reactions to minute occurrences, such as a cloud passing before the sun, a wadded up advertisement floating down the Liffey River, or the promenade of the Lord Lieutenant's cavalcade along the streets of Dublin.

Coincidence is another device that Joyce manipulates to draw his characters together, since in his view there is no chance meeting that is not fraught with purpose and possibility. Bloom and Stephen, archetypal father and son surrogates, observe and bump into each other several times throughout the day before their ultimate coming together at 7 Eccles Street. The fortune-telling cards that Molly lays out on the bedclothes that morning seem to indicate a successful ending to her adulterous tryst with Blazes Boylan, and it seems that virtually every one of the major characters has had some sort of dream or vision the night before that foreshadows what is to occur that day. In the approximately 18 years that Joyce took to ponder and to write his novel, he made sure that each of the seemingly random strands of narrative could finally be seen as coming together to form a coherent whole. Accidental encounters and topics of speculation that are reflected from one character's mind to another's serve to underline one of the novel's basic premises—there is a shape and a form to day-to-day existence, if only we can look deeply enough to perceive it.

In order to peel away the layers of self-protection and repression in which the characters have swathed themselves, the narrative switches or changes its point of view incessantly as we move through the novel. *Ulysses* has been credited as the work that refines and even perfects the technique of stream of consciousness, in which the reader becomes privy to the innermost thoughts of the characters, in the direct and immediate way that fragments and snippets of perception file across the screen of the mind. The final monologue of Molly Bloom in the Penelope chapter is probably the salient example of Joyce's taking a consciousness and turning it inside out, but this is only one of a myriad of techniques that manage to turn point of view into something resembling a kaleidoscope. Since there are no spatial or temporal transitions necessarily laid out between individual chapters, a reader must become immediately acclimatized to a wide array of voices that tell the story from one different point of view after another. Style itself becomes a virtual character in the novel.

Thus, the fairly stable and recognizable consciousnesses of Bloom and Dedalus are supplemented by the bold headlines of the newspaper chapter, the Shakespearian language and cadence of the library chapter, and the musical lilts and experimentation of the voice that describes the events in the Ormond Hotel Bar. A nameless Dublin lounger recounts Bloom's adventures in Barney Kiernan's pub, counterpointed by stylistic parodies from yet another unknown source, Gerty MacDowell describes Bloom with the purple prose of turn of the century romantic fiction, and the chapter at the lying-in hospital laboriously parodies the growth and development of English prose from its beginnings to contemporary Dublin street slang. In what is arguably the premier stylistic tour de force of *Ulysses*, Joyce casts the Circe chapter in Bella Cohen's brothel in dramatic dialogue to lay bare the subconscious fears and desires of the characters in ways that would be impossible in conventional prose. The reader is given sensitive information that would never surface in the mind, even in an ego-controlled stream of consciousness. The multiplicity of perspectives renders a Leopold Bloom with psychological dimensions that cannot be encompassed in realistic fiction, a figure both basic and complex who combines the cuckoldry of Menelaus with the cunning of Odysseus.

Perhaps Bloom's most admirable quality is that he is a truly sentient being, constantly and consistently questioning the nature of his environment and his relationship to the people within it. Though he is viewed by many of his fellows as an outsider, a Jew in Catholic Ireland and a cuckold in a society of male chauvinists, Bloom himself, surprisingly enough, is thoroughly involved with his place in the larger community. It is in his essential archetypal roles as husband, lover, son, and father that Bloom comes to personify the mythic hero that Joyce creates for the 20th century. In Joyce's redefinition of the concept of hero that the modern age requires, Bloom is notable for his openness, his ability to look inwardly with a clear eye, and the simple human love that his behavior exemplifies. By the end of the novel, Bloom is able to perceive and admit his own share of the responsibility for Molly's adultery, and it is clear that the preservation of their marriage is his central concern. Actually, however, most of the questions raised by the narrative will not be answered by the time Molly utters her ultimate "Yes." It is unclear whether or not Bloom will receive his breakfast in bed the next morning (or whether or not he has actually asked for it), signalling a possible renewal of their relationship, or whether or not his nocturnal adventures with Stephen Dedalus will have any effect on the future of the young poet. For Joyce, there is no need for formal closure, since what is of overwhelming concern in *Ulysses* is the interactions of the characters in which they demonstrate their innate humanity. In his usual mixture of simplicity and profundity, Leopold Bloom has earlier named the concept that lies behind the complicated perambulations of Joyce's latter-day Odysseus: "Love, says Bloom. I mean the opposite of hatred."

—Michael H. Begnal

UNCLE SILAS.
Novel by Sheridan Le Fanu, 1864.

Irish fiction in the 19th century, particularly from the late 1840's to the onset of George Moore's career in the 1880's, has suffered from a degree of critical neglect which has been less than benign, and which has had a distorting effect on both the history of the Irish novel and Irish literary history more generally considered. The inadequacy of this state of critical affairs is ably demonstrated by Sheridan Le Fanu's *Uncle Silas*. Commonly regarded as the author's most powerful novel, it is both an artistic success and a typically oblique treatment of the claustrophobia, tensions, and threats which beset the Anglo-Irish gentry as the long day of their political and social ascendancy began to wane.

Unlike many of his literary contemporaries in Ireland, Le Fanu has a secure if not very prominent place in the history of 19th-century English fiction. His reputation is based on the exemplifications of the gothic mode in literature provided by such widely-anthologised short stories as "Carmilla" and "Green Tea." This view of Le Fanu's output is necessarily restricted. While much of Le Fanu's work satisfies the generic expectations invoked by the term gothic, this author uses the genre with a full awareness of its wider cultural and socio-political implications, as *Uncle Silas* reveals. The fate of houses and their families, often enshrined by exponents of gothic in the history of their female protagonists, has in the best of Le Fanu's work a range and resonance which is at once more terrifying and more humanely embodied than similar material at the hands of Edgar Allan Poe.

The story of the protagonist of *Uncle Silas*, Maud Ruthyn, is a persuasive case in point. Set in rural Derbyshire—ostensibly a decisive distance from Ireland—the plot has all the involuted compulsiveness associated both with the Victorian three-decker novel in general and with the inward character of gothic fiction in particular. Suffice to say that Maud is at the mercy of her scheming uncle Silas. The cumulative effect of the plot against her and of the increasing horror and helplessness which accompany Maud's discovery of evil generate a considerable degree of tension, all the more palpable and plausible for the manner in which it steadily and irresistibly emerges from the protagonist's own even narrative tempo. In terms of canonical literary history, *Uncle Silas* is noteworthy both for its masterly rendering of the gothic novel's inverted picturesqueness, and for its anticipation of the psychological and moral explorations of gothic which contribute significantly to the evolution of fictional form in the late 19th century, as is illustrated in the fiction of Henry James, to cite perhaps the most striking instance.

Locating *Uncle Silas* in the context of Irish literary culture reveals in bolder relief the work's historical importance. Its treatment of a Derbyshire shadowland, aesthetically intact but morally problematical, is a tacit invitation to see the novel not merely as a sufficient enactment of the generic potentiality of its storyline but as a parable in which abstractions such as inheritance, property, innocence, and probity are dramatised. It is not too difficult to infer from the essential neutrality of the social dimension of "Derbyshire" that what the author has in mind is not a familiar treatment of men and manners. On the contrary, the unwitting and unwonted vulnerability which characterises Maud's attachment to what is hers by right articulates a fear so profound that only the collapse of a world can plausibly warrant it.

The world in question is that of the Anglo-Irish establishment to which Le Fanu belonged by birth. Subsequent historical events bringing about this land-owning class's eclipse may seem to lend a spuriously prophetic air to *Uncle Silas*. More relevant, and less fortuitous, is its proleptic relationship to the preoccupation with ghostly provenances and the spirit world which constitute one of the narrative mainstays of Anglo-Irish fiction since Le Fanu. Le Fanu's introduction of a religious dimension to the drama of exploitation and survival in *Uncle Silas*, revealed in the work's Swedenborgian overtones and undertow, is one of the means by which the novel can be linked with both the visionary aspect of the most important Anglo-Irish writer in the generation immediately following Le Fanu's, W.B. Yeats, and of that aspect's recuperative cultural implications. The religious dimension also facilitates the perception of Maud Ruthyn as a recognisable Victorian protagonist, the integrity of whose personality and the uncertainty of whose world offers an intense reading of the age's conflict of faith and doubt. Noteworthy for its craftsmanship, *Uncle Silas* is also a strikingly revealing cultural document.

—George O'Brien

UNDER MILK WOOD.
Radio play by Dylan Thomas, 1954.

Under Milk Wood is the most celebrated full-length play for radio, or "play for voices" as Dylan Thomas designated it, that the BBC has produced in 70 years of broadcasting. For many people, it is the outstanding example of the genre, an unsurpassed and virtually unsurpassable achievement. It is important to stress the *radio* provenance of *Under Milk Wood* because Thomas conceived it specifically for a medium he knew well as writer, actor, and reader. He did not write it for the stage, although it has often been staged, usually with a considerable degree of awkwardness, and he therefore did not set out to satisfy conventional dramatic expectations. Neither did he write it as a purely literary work, in the way that he did his poems and stories.

Under Milk Wood was first broadcast on 25 January 1954, only a couple of months after the drama surrounding Thomas's early death while on a literary tour of the U.S., which included stage-readings of the new work. It soon became a cult text, contributing to the Dylanmania of the mid-1950's. At that time, *Under Milk Wood* was often treated as a fresh start for Thomas as a dramatist, one that he tragically did not live to fulfil. However, it makes much more sense to see the play as the culmination of his career as a scriptwriter of radio features and talks during the 1940's. The BBC Features Department, which produced *Under Milk Wood*, was distinct from its Drama Department, and concentrated on dramatized documentaries that made full imaginative use of the enormous flexibility of radio, unrestricted by any visual representation. The Features Department also produced fictional works that were radiogenic and feature-like in form rather than conventionally dramatic, plays of the latter sort being the province of the Drama Department.

Thomas's original conception for a play for voices about an imaginary Welsh village, provisionally entitled *The Town Was Mad*, did have a plot structure, but he abandoned this for the freewheeling style of the feature, which he had mastered, notably in *Return Journey*. Nevertheless the most obvious precursor of *Under Milk Wood* in Thomas's *oeuvre* is a radio talk he broadcast in 1944, *Early One Morning* (revised as *Quite Early One Morning*), a verbal sketch of a Welsh seaside town containing episodes, characters, and phrases that also appear in the play. In writing this and other highly individual talks for the medium, Thomas developed his exuberant and witty "radio prose," intended for aural impact. These are words for the air and the ear, not for the page or the eye. It was this playful, alliterative, and assonantal style that Thomas brought to its apogee in *Under Milk Wood*.

Just as the play's content exists in outline in *Early One Morning*, its form and technique owe something to three feature scripts Thomas wrote not long after the war: *The Londoner*, "Margate—Past and Present," and *Return Journey*. With a good deal of comic observation, *The Londoner* depicts a typical day in the life of a representative working-class family in Shepherd's Bush, just as *Under Milk Wood* surveys in a broad comic way the inhabitants of Llareggub during a 24-hour period. Like *The Londoner, Under Milk Wood* is episodic in form, introduces many characters, includes dreams and fantasies as well as everyday reality, and shifts rapidly in time and space, and between dialogue and interior monologue. To provide continuity and overall coherence, the use of a narrator is almost indispensable in radio features, and *The Londoner* is no exception. For the considerably longer *Under Milk Wood*, Thomas made the unusual decision to employ two narrators in the interest of aural variety, but he had already tried a similar technique in a modest way in "Margate." Although this lacks a pervasive omniscient narrator, the central narrative, which provides more factual information than *The Londoner* even though it possesses greater dramatic potential, is framed by unconventional episodes involving two anonymous voices, which at times sound like an internal dialogue within the writer himself.

Apart from *Under Milk Wood, Return Journey* is probably Thomas's finest radio script, a deeply personal feature about his quest for his younger, pre-war self during a visit to his home town of Swansea, still in ruins after its devastation by German bombing. By combining for the first time the verbal style of his radio talks with the form of the feature, Thomas showed how his idiosyncratic "radio prose" could be used to great advantage in something other than a talk, and therefore prepared the way for *Under Milk Wood*. The highly developed role of the Narrator in *Return Journey* as a central consciousness rather than a technical device also points forward to *Under Milk Wood*, both works being more profitably interpreted in terms of "narrative" than of "drama"—or of other categories imposed by critics, including "poetry" and "epic." Indeed it is only by putting *Under Milk Wood* into its radio context that it can be appreciated for what it is and for what Thomas intended to be when, in a letter to Marguerite Caetani, he called it "an impression for voices, an entertainment out of the darkness, of the town I live in," written "simply and warmly and comically with lots of movement and varieties of moods, so that, at many levels, through sight and speech, description and dialogue, evocation and parody, you came to know the town as an inhabitant of it."

Thomas's adoption and adaptation of the feature form solved his problem of how to present an entire community on radio, encompassing the living and the dead, voices from the present and the past, about 40 adult villagers and their memories, not to mention a number of schoolchildren. Only a writer with a very sure grasp of radio could have orchestrated the voices with such extraordinary flexibility, handling them with total disregard of orthodox theatrical assumptions and varying the method of presentation so as to avoid monotony in an extended work without normal dramatic momentum. The village of Llareggub comes alive as a whole, and most of the characters are extremely vivid even though each of them occupies only a small part of the play and has little psychological depth. This is because Thomas draws them with broad strokes as universal comic types, but in doing so he does not exclude the possibility of deep emotion and pathos. Such moments do occur, especially in the presentation of the old, blind sailor, Captain Cat, and the promiscuous, fertile earth-mother, Polly Garter.

Kenneth Tynan's view of the work as "a true comedy of humours" is helpful, but it needs to be balanced by Laurence Lerner's suggestion that *Under Milk Wood* is a version of pastoral. This totally repudiates realistic interpretations, based on the hopelessly misguided assumption that Llareggub corresponds to one of the small towns on the Welsh coast where Thomas lived—Laugharne or Newquay. Yet there is nothing transparent about his treatment of Welsh village life, which he transforms imaginatively to the level of myth by employing a blend of conventions and modes that Polonius would designate "comic-pastoral-romance." If *Under Milk Wood* could be considered realistically, the characters would be "a nasty lot" and Llareggub would be a grotesque falsification of country life in Wales. But Thomas's comic incongruities, zany flights of fantasy, and surreal humour contribute to his amused yet sympathetic and warm-hearted survey of human behaviour, delighting in the sheer variety of life rather than intent on moral criticism. The bizarre gallery of characters Thomas creates are far from exemplary, but they are redeemed by the pervasive tolerance and benevolence of what he calls "a place of love," seen by Mary Ann Sailors as an amalgam of the Garden of Eden, the Peaceable Kingdom, the Promised Land, and Paradise Regained. For all its oddities, Llareggub is paradoxically a place of innocence. Like some of Thomas's best poems, *Under Milk Wood* is a celebratory work, almost religious in its open-armed inclusiveness, and Thomas's letter to Marguerite Caetani makes it clear that he knew exactly what he was doing: "all the eccentrics . . . , by their own rights, are ordinary and good; and the First Voice, and the poet preacher, never judge nor condemn but explain and make strangely simple and simply strange."

—Peter Lewis

UNDER THE VOLCANO.
Novel by Malcolm Lowry, 1947.

Under the Volcano, the greatest of Malcolm Lowry's works, represents the culmination of his thematic and technical experiments. Lowry was never able again to achieve the success of this book. Based in part on Lowry's own misadventures in Mexico, the book ultimately presents a cautionary vision of the fascist world into which civilization in the second half of the 20th century seemed to be sliding. The book is mainly in the form of interior monologues, with a modified stream of consciousness technique.

The events of the novel focus primarily on the last 12 hours of Geoffrey Firmin, a British ex-consul in southern Mexico. In and around Quauhnahuac (the ancient Indian name for the modern Mexican city of Cuernavaca) on the Day of the Dead celebration (2 November) in 1938, Firmin is reunited with his ex-wife Yvonne (whom he has not seen for nearly a year) and his younger half-brother Hugh—a kind of revolutionary with serious self-doubts—who has had a brief affair with Yvonne in the past. Firmin is deep within the abyss of alcoholism, but his drinking only serves to accentuate his anxiety about these two, who are at one point joined by Jacques Laruelle, a vain French film director who, too, has enjoyed a brief sexual episode with Yvonne. Drawn to these people, who obviously respect him, yet repulsed by "the weight of [their] past" transgressions against him, Firmin eventually erupts in a frantic burst of confused emotion and rushes away from them to his favorite cantina, a dingy "Fascist joint" ironically called El Farolito (The Little Lighthouse, "which lights the storm and invites it"). There, without satisfaction, he engages in sex with a prostitute and is accosted by a sadistic trio of local officials headed, strangely enough, by one called the Chief of Gardeners. Accused of obscure crimes, Firmin is pushed outside, shot, and thrown into a deep ravine. A dead dog is thrown in after him.

The novel's first chapter begins exactly one year after these events and centers on Laruelle as he recalls the tragedy. Not only did Firmin die, but Yvonne, too, perished at the same time in a different manner, and Hugh is probably dead after volunteering for a suicide mission for the the Loyalists in the Spanish Civil War. Within the last year, the Nazis have invaded Poland, and World War II has begun; in other words, the deaths of these three related characters paralleled the fall of Europe into the hands of the fascists. From this point, the rest of the novel's 12 chapters represent a flashback to 2 November 1938, from 7 a.m. to 7 p.m., with each chapter—alternating from within the consciousnesses of the three main characters—dealing with approximately one hour.

Lowry shows the breakup of order in the lives of his characters by developing a multi-layered, highly allusive and symbolic structure. The book is packed with biblical, mythological, historical, and literary allusions. It is not unusual, for example, to find references made to Genesis, Augustine, Dante, Milton, Thomas Burnet, Poe, Henry James, the Cabbala, Coleridge, Marston, Shelley, Calderon, Julian Green, and Ignatius Donnelly in one brief passage. This almost unfathomable number of allusions threatens to distort any sensible reading of the book. However, Lowry groups certain kinds of allusions together, suggesting various levels upon which the story can be interpreted: realistic, political, religious, occult, and mythic. Lowry does not make all five levels parallel; he interweaves them with cross-references and symbols. For instance, the barranca that yawns through the landscape of the book represents the abyss of fascism, Dante's Malebolge, the Cabbala's pit of destruction, the psychological hole of existential despair, and a feminine sexual symbol, as well as being an actual ravine in Quauhnahuac. Lowry makes his landscape his inscape.

Lowry also makes potential technical problems assets. Like any stream of consciousness writer, he must impose order upon the arbitrary and erratic flow of thoughts he is representing. The use of indirect as opposed to direct interior monologues gives him more control over his work because the third-person voice allows him to choose between a wider range of descriptive and expository material. The interior dialogues help to delineate that fine line between hallucination and mystical insight which is crucial to various themes of the story. Lowry controls the stream of consciousness through syntactic manipulation, montage, and other ordering devices. Figures of speech, especially those emphasizing analogy and contrast, the distorted English of his Spanish-speaking characters, and epigraphs contribute to the overall effect.

But these technical aspects figure more in the construction of the text, not the overall design of the story. In order to establish coherence, Lowry exploits the classical unities of place, character, action, and—most important to the themes of the novel—time. Motifs and recurring words or phrases run throughout the book (often in parodic form), and these, too, help associate unrelated ideas. All of these "design-governing postures" work together to make *Under the Volcano* Lowry's one fully-realized success.

—Dana A. Grove

THE UNFORTUNATE TRAVELLER.
Fiction by Thomas Nashe, 1594.

The Unfortunate Traveller, Thomas Nashe's major fiction and one of the most significant latter-day works of a humanist-oriented poetics, is like other humanist works before it in the form of an exegesis. It takes its text from Nashe's earlier work *Christs Teares*: "Trauel & care for wealth, riches, and honor, is but care & trauel for trauel and care," But this fictive survey of the values of humanism stretches over a far broader terrain than the works of others that preceded it—Thérouanne, Hampton Court, Marignano, Münster, Middleborough, Rotterdam, Wittenberg, Venice, Florence, Rome, Bologna, and Ardres and Guines—and it purposely scrambles the chronology of real events—the battles of Thérouanne (1513) and Marignano (1515), the Anabaptist uprising at Münster (1534) conflated with the battle of Frankenhausen (1525), the sweating sickness in London (1517), Luther's debate with Carlstadt at Wittenberg (1519), the publications of the *Encomium Moriae* of Erasmus (1509) and the *Utopia* of Sir Thomas More (1516), and the meeting at the Field of the Cloth of Gold (1520)—to see if by such hermeneutics some deeper humanist pattern of learning might emerge.

What emerges in fact, however, is a new humanist *encomium moriae*, or praise of folly, for the putative narrator-hero, Jack Wilton, learns how little, in fact, he really knows and how little knowledge may help him in the disturbing world in which he finds himself. Nashe begins with praising folly himself, in his dedicatory epistle to Wriothesley, Earl of Southampton, as his "Ingenuous honorable Lord"—that is, variously *ingenious* or *ingenuous*, a new wise fool like himself, and like Jack. To this paradoxical patron, Nashe offers a paradoxical work, a "phantasticall Treatise" in which he nevertheless promises "some reasonable coneuyance of historie." It is a letter following a custom known to "methodicall antiquity," which introduces a work of "a cleane different vaine." Such statements are not antithetical; but they are not congruent either: the wit comes in seeing how, as coupling ideas, they just miss firm jointure. The tone here is also distinctively Rabelaisian, drawing on one of Nashe's own most admired predecessors. Like Rabelais, Nashe spoofs the preliminary matter to his book; like Rabelais, Jack Wilton resembles the earlier Panurge (Greek *panourgos*, or knave) whose journey across Europe will also, in its course, test his cunning, challenge his ideas, and transform his confidence and self-reliance into doubt, terror, and despair before confronting him with the ultimate mysteries of existence. As if to point directly to this similarity, Jack Wilson, like Rabelais's characters, tells us his story, poxy boozers that we are, from an alehouse: "soft let me drinke before I go anie further."

Jack's account actually begins with a nearly harmless rogue's progress. Jack joyfully portrays himself as a cutpurse turned confidence man who relies solely on his ingenuity—on the inventiveness and the exuberance of his humanist rhetoric to create out of nothing a local habitation and a name which he can extort. He swindles others not out of need but out of indulgent exploitation. Without pause or embarrassment he moves from one trick to another in a dazzling display of rhetorical creativity. The foolish and the proud fall easy victims to him, as he undermines order from within. But as he continues on his journey, it is Jack who becomes increasingly proud and foolish as he finds the larger world becoming more chaotic, and more alien. Even the humanists who taught him his classical rhetoric are denied him now: when he visits Erasmus and More in Rotterdam he finds that they have become corrupted; these brightest hopes of learning and self-reliance are calling on the magic of Agrippa and summoning the ghost of Cicero.

This key visit to Erasmus and More is bounded by two significant passages—the murderous rebellion at Münster and the self-indulgent scholasticism at Wittenberg—and it has no effect on either of them. With this placement of episodes, Nashe seems to be suggesting that even the best of the humanists could not save the modern world run mad with its own selfish and schismatic causes. But as Jack continues his travels, things only seem to get worse: death and decay emerge everywhere. Even the "banished earl" who befriends Jack becomes outmoded. "Get thee home, my young lad," he tells Jack, having preserved him from hanging, "lay thy bones peaceably in the sepulcher of thy fathers, waxe olde in ouerlooking thy grounds, be at hand to close the eyes of thy kinred"; but he saves Jack from one death only to allow him to confront more. And such an open analogy indicates those more implicit. Jack's self-proclaimed scouring of evil reminds us of the motives that, earlier in Jack's fiction, so drive the Anabaptists, whose beliefs are also corrupted by baser motives of personal revenge. John of Leyden's narrow escape, in fact, anticipates Jack Wilton's. Jack's "life," as Nashe's subtitle clearly announces, is the chief, the *only*, subject of this work because each event to which he is witness or in which he participates not only affects him but reflects him—and helps us to define that life, from his spiritual condition to his mental condition to his physical vulnerability as the novel proceeds. At the conclusion, in the holy city of Rome, Jack finds only the wicked greed of Zacharie, the wicked lust of Juliana, and the corruption of the papacy itself. Jack has moved, in turn, from victimizing others to becoming the chief victim himself—forced onto a table to be sliced up for a lesson in anatomy—and all the intelligence of humanist philosophy, of art (in Surrey or in the pleasure garden) or in science will not save him.

Travel in this work is thus likened to *travail*—to labor and to suffering, and the lessons of life are the lessons of primal sin. As Jack's world turns wholly upside-down, Jack learns that inversion is itself the truest wisdom: that learning is a matter of humility, not pride; of accepting, not searching; indeed, our destinies, we are told at the work's end—as this hero in life races back to a battlefield in order to survive—are pronouncedly *un*searchable. Learning carries its own risks, and its own costs, while the antithesis—constant travel, constant travail, constant *exposure*—only bring about, from the blood of Thérouanne and the sickness in London onward, a sense of contingency and tragedy that show the fall inherent in human pride and human learning, and that presage the Last Judgment itself.

—Arthur F. Kinney

UTOPIA.
Prose by Sir Thomas More, 1516 (in Latin; translated into English, 1551).

Before *Utopia* became an English book in 1551, in a translation by Ralph Robinson, it had run through half a dozen Latin editions in the major publishing centres of continental Europe, with translations into German, Italian, and French. Sir Thomas More continues to have an international rather than insular audience; the journal *Moreana* of the Amici Thomae Mori is published in France.

Literally translated, the title page of the Latin edition, seen through the press by Erasmus, reads *The Best State of a Commonwealth and the New Island of Utopia, A Truly Golden Handbook, No Less Beneficial than Entertaining, by the Distinguished and Eloquent Author, Thomas More, Citizen and Sheriff of the famous City of London*. The balanced phrases suggest polarities in More's perennially fascinating playful work or serious game. Is the general theory of the best state of a commonwealth identical with the specific description of an island whose institutions are dismissed very near the end of the work as "absurdly established"? The name of the island is part of the ambiguity and the playfulness or sombreness; as "Utopia" or noplace and "Eutopia" or goodplace, it puns on opposing views.

In part, *Utopia* is a traveller's tale, told by a Portuguese mariner named Raphael Hythloday, said to have sailed with Amerigo Vespucci. This traveller, whose monologue describing the island Utopia occupies practically all of the long Book II (almost three-quarters of the whole), has a name which underlines the ambiguities of More's view. Is he a messenger bringing good tidings, as his first name suggests? His surname, in contrast, can be translated as "expert in trifles" or "speaker of nonsense." Raphael's description of the island plays off both against Book I and against More's prefatory letter to his friend Peter Giles. These early sections of *Utopia* are full of proper names, lovingly celebrated individuals including Giles himself and More's old master Cardinal Morton. The scene is precisely set: a real diplomatic mission to Flanders in 1515, a visit with Giles in Antwerp during a recess of the mission, his cordial and respectful introduction of Raphael Hythloday after a church service at Notre Dame, and conversation in the garden of More's lodging. The lively interchange of ideas here contrasts with Book II; in brief, there is a shift from dialogue to monologue, from individuals to institutions, and from the religious framework quietly invoked when More placed his speakers in a garden, after a church service, to the rational principles of an island whose government and economy were formed outside Christianity.

Cordial as the conversation is, there is a great deal of conflict between views expressed by the fictional character Raphael Hythloday and by the character More. The difference between More-the-author and More-the-character is as great as the better known contrast between Chaucer-the-poet and Chaucer-the-pilgrim in the *Canterbury Tales*, and as ironic. Is it a quarrel he is having with himself, when More's narrator tries to convince Hythloday that it is his duty to become adviser to a prince, prompting the traveller to argue forcefully the futility and frustration of such a position? In opposed epigrammatic phrases, one argues that "What you cannot turn to good you must make as little bad as you can," while the other, with a freedom from compromise any diplomat must envy, responds that accommodation means only "that men may be bad in greater comfort."

With radical simplicity the Utopians avoid the ills of Europe: all private property is abolished. Pungent descriptions of crime, poverty, unemployment, ostentatious luxury, and idleness in Book I give way in Book II to Hythloday's eulogy of a country which is literally a "commonwealth," where there are no beggars, no gentlemen, no money. Satire does not absolutely disappear into simple praise, but the exact balance between the "beneficial" and the "entertaining" is sometimes problematical. On a scale ranging from the ideal through the practical to the amusing or the bizarre, one might try to place some details that Raphael Hythloday reports as simple facts: a six-hour working day for all citizens, the abolition of lawyers, the use of gold for chamberpots, the admission of women to the priesthood, and the ways in which the whole society resembles a college or monastic community, with marriage and children added.

In the final pages, Hythloday celebrates Utopian justice with moral fervour and castigates "so-called" commonwealths elsewhere as he considers the miserable labour and small reward of "the common labourer, the carter, the carpenter and the farmer"; he piles up catalogues of evils caused by greed for money and of anxieties caused by want. More, the character, objects that Utopian abolition of private property "utterly overthrows all the nobility, magnificence, splendor, and majesty which are, in the estimation of the common people, the true glories and ornaments of the commonwealth." The author More juxtaposes sympathy for the common worker with ironic respect for common opinion, and the book ends wistfully: "there are very many features in the Utopian commonwealth which it is easier for me to wish for in our countries than to have any hope of seeing realised."

—Kay Gilliland Stevenson

V

A VALEDICTION: FORBIDDING MOURNING.
Poem by John Donne, 1633 (written 1612).

"A Valediction: Forbidding Mourning" is one of the poems in which John Donne, the profane lover, and John Donne, the academic Divine, are most happily at one. The lover's passion is apparent, but so is tranquillity of spirit. The poem bears most of the familiar hallmarks of Donne's work: it is an expression of intense feeling carried by a series of clever and witty comparisons; the speaking voice of the poem addresses an imagined listener directly; and generally that voice employs a fairly natural syntax, frequently settling for half-rhymes.

This lover's tranquillity is evident in the opening lines of the poem. Frequently Donne's poems begin dramatically and explosively—"Busy old fool, unruly sun . . . " or "Batter my heart, three-personed God . . . ," but this one takes measured steps with a four-line simile introducing the main clause of the sentence which occupies the next verse of the poem. The simile itself invokes "virtuous men" who "passe mildly away," men who are far removed from the passionate, impetuous, cynical, and amoral lover of poems like "The Flea" or "Womans Constancy." These imagined virtuous men are also far removed from the Dean of St. Paul's, tortured by visions of death and sin, in lines such as these which open Holy Sonnet 11:

Spit in my face you Jewes, and pierce my side,
Buffet, and scoff, scourge, and crucifie mee,
For I have sinn'd, and sinn'd, and onely hee,
Who could do no iniquitie, hath dyed: . . .

However, the comparison of lovers with a dying man carries, in addition to the suggestion that their parting will be a type of death, the suggestion of the lover's climax, for which dying is, of course, a common euphemism. Again, typical of Donne's love poetry is the sexual *double entendre*. And similar *double entendres* exist in the third verse which mentions earthquakes and the swaying of the spheres (which in Ptolemaic astronomy surround the earth); in the sixth verse which talks of the expansion of the lovers' souls; and in the famous compass simile of the final three verses. Thus, under the surface where the departing lover speaks movingly of the depth and spiritual strength of their love, there is a constant undercurrent of physical passion. This lover may "Care lesse, eyes, lips, and hands to misse" but, nevertheless, the line lingers softly over the thought of the partner's physical presence.

There is also, with the depth of feeling, a slightly detached intellect very much apparent in the construction of this poem. Donne constantly demonstrated his omnivorous learning in the imagery of his poetry. One set of recurring images is based on Ptolemaic astronomy which placed the earth at the centre of a series of spheres on which moved the sun and stars; the ninth was a crystalline sphere, the swaying motion of which caused the equinoxes. This is the trepidation of the spheres referred to in the third verse of "A Valediction: Forbidding Mourning." The intellect processing the emotion is also apparent in the concluding simile. Although absorbed in the thoughts of a painful separation, the lover's valediction includes a simile based on an instrument of mathematics and, appropriately, navigation. The partner who remains behind is the fixed leg of the compass around whom in a perfect circle moves the other; the larger the radius of the circle, the more the "fixt foot" leans after its companion. The stability of the one at home perfects the journey of the one abroad and finally draws the partner back to the starting point. The circle, of course, being perfectly symmetrical and endless, is the ideal image for this perfect physical and spiritual love.

Finally, it is interesting to observe how frequently Donne links a verse to what has gone before, or otherwise promotes the cohesion of thoughts, so that the overall effect is similar in its rhythms to that of people reluctantly saying goodbye. In the first two verses, there is the carefully conceived opening argument against tears and visible grief; this is followed by two more verses presenting similar arguments, each contained within its respective verse. Up to this stage the lover seems to have prepared for the parting and to be in control. However, with the conjunction "But" at the beginning of the fifth verse, the impersonal arguments give way to personal statements of how it will feel to be apart. The planned reasoning gives way to thoughts which seem to come more spontaneously: "Our two soules . . . which are one"—"If they be two." And the initial word of each of the last two verses stresses the continuity of the thought, which seemed to have been concluded with the stop at the end of the previous verse; the lover seems each time to turn back once more to sustain the contact.

So, as is typical of the best of Donne's work, art conceals its artifice, and intellect combines with poetic instinct to produce a poem which is both emotionally and critically satisfying.

—Peggy Nightingale

VALMOUTH.
Novel by Ronald Firbank, 1919.

Admirers of Ronald Firbank's novels—admittedly a modest number for a modest list—will vary widely in their choices for his best book. *Valmouth*, coming at mid-career, however, may be quintessential, since it balances better than any of the others the strange elements through which his work is always identified: disembodied and fleeting dialogue, by turns bewildering and hilarious; an inventive if blasphemous hagiography; set-pieces built to link several vague narrative threads woven from several interlocking stories; extravagant characters with preposterous names; arias and duets without music for fantastic exchanges with the reader. Firbank's sexual and religious innuendo, which sometimes fails to compensate for taste with humor, is mostly under control in *Valmouth*, even on occasion inspired.

The novel is not unique in Firbank's little canon, however; nearly any other volume would serve as a fair enough introduction to the work of this peculiar writer. In *Valmouth*, however, Firbank escapes some of his irritating precocity in the novels that preceded it, *Vainglory*, *Inclinations*, and *Caprice*. Similarly, his deliriously silly surfaces often seem at odds with the cruelty in the books that followed *Valmouth*, each tragic in its independent way: the religious agony in *The Flower Beneath the Foot*, the destruction of innocence in *Prancing Nigger*, the ridiculous and pathetic pederasty in *Concerning the Eccentricities of Cardinal Pirelli*. Further, *Valmouth* is an excellent place to begin because the other novels may make more sense in its aftermath.

It has received perhaps the greatest exposure. Published first, like all of the others, at Firbank's expense, 500 copies were issued in November 1919; it was reprinted with the others in 1928 and 1929, reprinted in paperback and in an omnibus in the 1950's, included, of course, in *The Complete Firbank* in 1961, issued with illustrations by Phillippe Julian, and turned into a musical comedy by Sandy Wilson.

Originally called "The Centenarians of Glennyfurry," *Valmouth* is the name of a English seaside spa where the qualities of the waters insure astonishing longevity, not only in years but in sexual urges too. A number of amorous alliances—or aspirations to them—suggest that age is no deterrent, although other matters sometimes intrude.

Lady Parvula de Panzoust, well past the last bloom of her youth, develops a passion for David Tooke, a handsome young dairyman whose sister Thetis Tooke longs for Captain Dick Thoroughfare. He has just returned from a sea voyage to Hare-Hatch House in Valmouth (of which he is son and heir) to join his black bride-to-be, Niri-Esther, although his tastes extend to include Jack Whorwood, his "middy-chum" who at sea has proven to Dick "what Patroclus was to Achilles, and even more." Granny Tooke, meanwhile, is enamoured of her black masseuse, Mrs. Yajnavalkya. Arguably Firbank's most inspired creation, "Mrs. Yaj" is a combination of Hattie McDaniel as "Mammy" in *Gone with the Wind* and the Dragon Lady in *Terry and the Pirates*: "Dat is a speciality ob de house—de cultivation ob de toes. Vot is dair so important? O wen I consider de foot . . . de precious precious foot! For de foot support de body; it bear de burden ob ten thousand treasures! . . . *Kra*. And dat's vot I alvays say." She is equally loquacious about Niri-Esther, passed off as her niece: "Niri-Esther's clothes, I sometimes venture to tink, are a little too vainglorious!!! At her age . . . and until I was past eighteen, I nebber had more in de course ob a year dan a bit ob cotton loincloth. You may wear it how you please, my poor mother would say, but dat is all you'll get! And so, dear me, I generally used to put it on my head." Niri-Esther becomes the object of Mrs. Hurstpierpoint's affections, although that ageing dowager is more often preoccupied with her collection of religious relics. Fondling "the toe of the Madonna's married sister," she listens to her maid read to her of one of Firbank's more astonishing saints: "One day St. Automona de Meris, seeing a young novice yawning, suddenly spat into her mouth, and *that* without malice or thought of mischief. Some 90 hours afterwards the said young novice brought into the world the Blessed St. Elizabeth Bathilde, who, by dint of skipping, changed her sex at the age of forty and became a man."

Valmouth concludes with a wedding, although none of the attempted liaisons has come to fruition. In the final sentence, the bride is chasing a butterfly in the garden, a moment that anticipates a small scene in *Prancing Nigger* that might stand for all of Firbank's work, when a little boy attempts to enter the gates of the city: "Have you nothing, young man, to declare?" asks the guard. " . . . Butterflies!" "Exempt of duty. Pass."

—Bruce Kellner

VANITY FAIR.
Novel by William Makepeace Thackeray, 1848.

The story of William Makepeace Thackeray's *Vanity Fair* is set in the period of the Battle of Waterloo and later. The title reverberates with associations, and should alert us to the fact that the book is a morality. Vanity Fair, in John Bunyan's allegory *The Pilgrim's Progress* (1678), is where poor Faithful was stoned to death by a worldly and wicked populace. It recalls, too, Ecclesiastes 1:2: "Vanity of vanities, saith the preacher; vanity of vanities, all is vanity." The novel's closing words quote from the Latin of the Vulgate: "Ah! *Vanitas vanitatum*! which of us is happy in this world? Which of us has his desire? Or, having it, is satisfied?—come children, let us shut up the box and the puppets. . . . " *Vanity Fair* is based on the medieval concept of the world as stage. Like Jonathan Swift, Thackeray is a master of irony, and none of his explicit statements should be taken at face value. The words of D.H. Lawrence are relevant: "Never trust the teller, trust the tale." The tension between tale and teller is a major component of Thackeray's art. His pretence at detachment, derived from his beloved Fielding, has misled readers into thinking that he despised his own tale, along with his characters. Yet he tells us clearly enough, for example in chapter 8, what he is about:

> . . . my kind reader will please to remember that this history has *Vanity Fair* for a title, and that Vanity Fair is a very vain, wicked, foolish place, full of all sorts of humbugs and falsenesses and pretensions . . .

While Christian, in Bunyan's fable, completes his journey, Faithful is the hero martyred at Vanity Fair. In the novel, Dobbin plays the role of Faithful: he does not die, but his reward is too petty for his deserts.

The novel opens at a demure girls' school in Chiswick, where rich, pampered Amelia Sedley is leaving for home, accompanied by the French instructor, Rebecca Sharp, on her way to become a governess. Amelia is sweet-natured, but insipid and foolish. Critics have tried to argue that Becky is "good-humoured" because Thackeray calls her so, but we are warned early that she is a "dangerous bird." Rebecca's background is not respectable: her father was a drunken artist, and her mother a French opera girl (Victorian shorthand for "loose woman"). "The humble calling of her female parent Miss Sharp never alluded to . . . " Rebecca is consumed by envy of the privileged boarders, but latches on to Amelia, and sets her cap at Amelia's rich bachelor brother, the gross Joseph Sedley, Collector of Boggley Wallah in India, but he escapes her clutches. She then goes to work for the family of Sir Pitt Crawley, an uncouth baronet who derives in part from Squire Western in Fielding's *Tom Jones*, and secretly marries Sir Pitt's younger son, Rawdon. The couple are forced to live on their wits, not paying bills. Rawdon becomes a professional gambler. He and Becky climb higher and higher in society, with no visible means of support. Becky is even presented to George IV, " . . . there too was Vanity." Throughout the novel, there is a play on the two meanings of the word vanity: futility and vain conceit.

Rawdon is arrested for debt, and when his kind sister-in-law, Lady Jane, gets him out of debtor's prison, he comes home to find Rebecca with the rich, dissolute Marquis of Steyne (read "Stain"). The novelist asks us slyly, "Was she guilty or not? She said not, but who could tell . . . if that corrupt heart was in this case pure?"

The innuendo about Becky's "virtue" is resumed in chapter 64, where she is imaged as a mermaid, attractive above the waist, but with a hideous tail under the waterline. She has degenerated from kept woman to common prostitute. Like Swift's Yahoos and Milton's Satan, Becky, though evil, has all the life, while loving plodders like Dobbin represent patient merit spurned by the unworthy. Dobbin marries Amelia, and is disappointed. Just as Dobbin is the true hero, Lady Jane Crawley, principled and loving, is the true heroine. The imagery throughout is of brilliance and sparkle, true and false lights.

Thackeray has been accused of cynicism on the one hand and sentimentality on the other. Gordon Ray, Thackeray's biographer, has argued that Thackeray's marriage was less happy than Thackeray admitted, and that Amelia is a portrait of the weak-minded Mrs. Thackeray. As evidence, he believes that Thackeray idealises Amelia at the start of the story and patronises her at the end. But the novel establishes at once that Amelia is good but too trusting, while Rebecca is hard and vindictive. As to the cynicism, his audience recognized that Thackeray was writing about a demi-mondaine. Thackeray's string of apparently innocent questions as to what "really" happened is a strategy for coping with Victorian prudery. He hints expertly at unpleasant facts: we learn that old Sir Pitt became helpless and had to be "fed and cleaned like a baby"—that Sir Pitt became incontinent. Thackeray regretted the loss of the previous century's frankness. In the preface to *Pendennis*, dated 26 November 1850, he wrote: "Since the author of *Tom Jones* was buried, no writer of fiction among us has been permitted to depict to his utmost power a MAN." The overcoming of this difficulty has led to much misreading, but in *Vanity Fair* Thackeray shows a fine moral poise and a masterly, playful, control of tone.

—Valerie Grosvenor Myer

THE VANITY OF HUMAN WISHES.
Poem by Samuel Johnson, 1749.

Samuel Johnson's most famous poem, *The Vanity of Human Wishes*, can serve as an ideal example of the aesthetics and values of 18th-century neoclassical poetry. Johnson's poem is a re-creation of Juvenal's tenth satire, with a similarity of focus but with a collection of more recent, usually British, examples to develop the philosophical theme. Although Johnson modified Juvenal's stoic ending to adapt it to his own Christian faith, the later poet assimilated his knowledge of the classics so thoroughly, so smoothly, that the attentive reader will find it useful to keep thinking of the Latin meanings of the English poem's vocabulary.

Like many Augustan poems, *The Vanity of Human Wishes* uses balance, parallelism, repetition, chiasmus, irony, and allusion in the formation of the end-stopped couplets. Johnson's poem also has a strong caesura and frequently displays the verbal economy associated with *sententiae*. In addition the poem creates great tonal variety and vitality, ranging from a grand authoritative mood, "Let observation with extensive view / Survey mankind . . . ," to a quiet, deeply personal note, and to a slashing, biting, satiric tone, concluding with a moderate measured mood of religious acceptance. Johnson gains universality and vigor for the poem by characteristically combining abstract or generalized nouns with active, concrete verbs. The poet repeatedly uses imagery depicting rising or falling action as well as confusion and change.

The poem convincingly demonstrates Johnson's astonishingly retentive memory. He once claimed, in conversation, that he needed to write down only the first half of the lines, relying on his mnemonic powers—and the memorial convenience of his couplet rhymes—to recreate the unwritten parts of the lines. The discovery of a notebook (now in the Hyde collection) verified this unusual method of retention. Moreover, the discovery also revealed that Johnson could revise the poem in light of changing circumstances and personal disappointment. For example, the 1749 first printing catalogued some difficulties that beset the scholar's life: "Toil, want, the garret, and the jail." But after he was the victim of a financial disappointment, and expressed his attitude in a letter (7 February 1755) to Lord Chesterfield, Johnson revised the line by dropping "the garret" and instead warned against "the patron." (Volume 6 of the Yale Edition includes the manuscript revisions of the poems.)

The poem's explicit theme is the foolishness, uselessness, and egotistical short-sightedness of human desires. The word "Vanity" also carries religious allusive meaning, as in "Vanity, Vanity, all is Vanity." The poem can be read as an 18th-century duplication of a medieval "Wheel of Fortune" poem: that is, all who rise by committing themselves to the deceptive goods of the world are ultimately cast down. The truly devout, Johnson suggests, do not pray for a particular personal goal (which will be temporary or deceptive), but instead pray that God's will be done.

The 368-line poem begins with a 98-line general introduction which invokes Observation and History to comment upon human folly. The ancient philosopher Democritus is asked to rise again to ridicule, and the sage or wise person's mind focuses on England. As an exemplification of a foolish desire held by humanity lines 99–128 retell the glory and fall of Cardinal Wolsey, followed by a six-line generalizing catalogue of other famous men who ultimately fall. In a section with autobiographical origins Johnson traces chronologically, in lines 135–174, the rise and difficulties in a scholar's career, with three additional cautionary examples. It is said that later in Johnson's life, when he heard the lines about the scholar's life and obstacles read aloud, he wept. Lines 175–254 provide examples of military or political men who gained their wishes and suffered final defeat.

The closing portion of the poem turns to a more personal, yet more universal level, recommending the philosophical *via media* as against the ravages of time and aging. Sorrows can mount as relatives or friends sicken. The standard *topos* of fading Beauty leads to the final advice to hope and pray, "But leave to Heaven the measure and the choice." The range, polish, specificity, and verbal sting of Johnson's poem place it in the top rank of 18th-century wisdom poetry.

—Victor A. Doyno

VATHEK.
(*An Arabian Tale.*)
Novel by William Beckford, 1786.

William Beckford's *Vathek* tends to be discussed along with other early examples of gothic fiction, but though it shares many of the gothic's tendencies in the dramatisation of potentially disruptive and self-destructive psychic energies it is, in other respects, quite distinctive. It represents the first attempt to absorb into English fiction the materials and the narrative features of Eastern storytelling, including the then fairly recently available fables of *The Arabian Nights*. It allows fantasy and magic to form the basis of narrative. And above all it makes the language of extravagance and excess not the high point but the norm in its mode of narration.

The Caliph Vathek has possessed absolute power from childhood. His subjects rush to obey him and his displeasure can result in a glare from his terrible eye which causes convulsions and instant death. He reigns by fear as well as a residual affection which the story shows him steadily destroying by his cruel acts. However the human imagination can starve in the midst of absolute earthly power and Vathek is drawn into a double quest: for earthly love, and for power over the very heavens. The former search will lead him to disturb and destroy the innocent childish love of the idealised Nouronihar and Gulchenrouz. The latter causes him to build his own equivalent of the Tower of Babel, a structure to which he can retire to be safe from the envy and wrath of his subjects and to threaten the heavens with the consequences of his displeasure. In this tower his mother, the sorceress Carathis, also has her apartments, in which she performs odious sacrifices and weaves her evil spells.

The story develops with the arrival of a Giaour who promises Vathek entry into the secret vaults in which lie concealed the treasures and talismans of the pre-Adamite Sultans. Lured on by the prospect of infinite wealth and power, Vathek sets forth. On his way he is persuaded to perform acts of wickedness (including an attempt at mass child slaughter) which effectively ensure the damnation of his soul: for the Giaour has, in fact, been sent to tempt Vathek by Eblis the Prince of Hell. Progressing from wickedness to wickedness, and forever in the grip of his own urges and appetites, Vathek reaches the Halls of Eblis. He and Carathis enter, at the highest point of their self confidence and spiritual pride, the gates close and they are trapped in an infinity of everlasting torment.

The characters of Vathek and Carathis are what chiefly link Beckford's story with the gothic tradition in English fiction. Unlike Horace Walpole's Manfred, Vathek lives untroubled by conscience and (until the moment when Hell encloses him) he defies custom and the laws of Heaven by indulging his appetites and seeking self-gratification without remorse. After *Vathek* the gothic villain gained a new energy. Lewis's Ambrosio and Radcliffe's Montoni owe much to him, and once melancholy and a sense of sin have been reintegrated with the type he can be found again among the gloomy autocrats of Byron's Eastern tales. Carathis, a spirited study in unsexed feminine energy (owing something at least to Lady Macbeth, as seen in her first act appearance with the letter) represents a pioneering study of female aggressiveness at the opposite pole from Walpole's heroines. She proved too disturbing in her implications to be developed again (except to some extent by Lewis with his psychotic Mother Superior in *The Monk*) until the time of Wilkie Collins and Victorian gothic fiction.

Like most 18th-century experimental writers, Beckford had read Milton with attention. In *Paradise Lost* he found a quarry for his imaginative experiments. The scenes in Hell in Books 1 and 2 of Milton's poem offered him a mode for suggesting vistas of endless horror, and the Halls of Eblis in the last section of *Vathek* possess a Miltonic sense of space and dread. The character of Milton's Satan is divided between the Giaour, Vathek's tempter, and the infernal monarch Eblis, a fallen angel rather than a pantomime demon, whose combination of youthful beauty and everlasting anguish once again point forward towards Byron's early heroes and, in particular, Childe Harold, thus feeding into a whole convention of later romantic and early Victorian writing.

Beckford originally wrote *Vathek* in French, leaving the work of translation to his protégé Rev. Samuel Henley. Though Beckford partly supervised Henley's work, the translation was issued without his final approval. Henley lost or destroyed Beckford's original manuscript and when the novel was eventually published in French it was in a translation from Henley's text which, once again, Beckford had prepared by another hand and only partly supervised. It is, therefore, impossible to be sure how closely the apparently humourless tone of the English version with its Latinate polysyllables and solemn parading of hyperbolical language actually represents what Beckford intended. For, as critics point out, *Vathek* is a tale rooted in Beckford's own situation: arising out of his sense of the dangers attendant upon his wealth, his self-willed, undisciplined impulsiveness, and his sexual ambivalence. In many of its episodes the book suggests the possibility of self satire, or of burlesquing its own extravagant mode. But the uncertain status of the text means that the point cannot be satisfactorily established, and criticism has traditionally interpreted the work as if devoid of satirical or burlesque intent.

—William Ruddick

VENICE PRESERVED.
Play by Thomas Otway, 1682.

Thomas Otway's most distinguished and popular play, *Venice Preserved; or, A Plot Discovered* (produced 9 February 1682) inserts acid comedy and political satire into a blank-verse historical tragedy loaded with pathos. It responds to the Exclusion Crisis of 1678–81, in which a group led by the Earl of Shaftesbury engineered political benefit from an alleged Catholic plot to murder high officials: Shaftesbury sought to weaken the king, Charles II, and put an oligarchy in effective control of the country, just as a weak, elected doge and strong senate governed Venice. Writing when Shaftesbury's ambitions had just been thwarted, Otway in turn put the political case that even if one postulates an evil plot, Venetian oligarchy is just as evil. He takes dramatic advantage of having two equally unsavory groups, the senate and the rebels, by trapping between them a married couple, Belvidera and Jaffeir, who are the emotional foci of the play. Their torments and the dubious character of every Venetian shown, save Belvidera, make one question what is "preserved" in such a Venice.

Working loosely from the Abbé de Saint-Réal's account of an actual conspiracy in 1618, *La conjuration des espagnols contre la république de Venise* (1674), Otway develops the rebels and the senators in parallel. (The rebels are somewhat more bloodthirsty but also more manly.) Each group has a chief representative close to the central couple: Belvidera's father, the senator Priuli, damns his child to loathsome destitution because three years earlier she married without his consent, and Jaffeir's friend Pierre embroils the couple in violent revolution because the Venetian property system has let his love, the whore Aquilina, yield to the rich old senator Antonio. Antonio himself employs Aquilina to engage with him in sadomasochistic foot fetishism, thus balancing in lechery a chief plotter, the old Renault, who tries to rape Belvidera.

In such a setting, love, honor, and manliness fail as guides to action, and mere self-justification gives base acts a false legitimacy. Before the play begins, Jaffeir has squandered his small fortune to show public opinion that he has married Belvidera for love, not money. During the play, he remains the weak, distracted prey of others' opinion. Poor, evicted, and rebuffed by Priuli, he turns to Pierre, shifting loyalty from Venice to the conspiracy. He even offers the conspiratorial ruffians his wife, a suffering ingénue, as hostage for his faith. At her pleading, though, and appalled by the rebels' plans to burn and butcher all Venice, he reveals the plot to the Senate in exchange for their vow, later equivocated away, to spare his erstwhile comrades' lives. Finally disgraced as a turncoat, Jaffeir readies himself to stab Belvidera, does stab Pierre (to save him from death on the wheel), and commits suicide. Belvidera, once more deserted, dies mad.

With their deaths, the conspirators' execution, and Priuli's withdrawal into perpetual mourning, only the depraved Antonio and the whore Aquilina are left of the chief characters. Although at the end of the play they are offstage and for the moment hostile, one has every reason to suppose that their connection will resume. It is based on self-interested paradoxes of domination and submission which are central to the themes of *Venice Preserved*. Perhaps Otway's final political comment is in sustaining this perverse liaison of old and young, rich and poor, employer and employee, beast and mistress in the midst of disaster: Aquilina may represent Venice itself, a republic that Pierre calls an "*Adriatique* Whore," and the figure of Antonio was widely taken to allude to Shaftesbury, whose Christian name was Anthony and who in 1682 was, like Antonio, 61 years of age.

In keeping with the rancid Venice he portrays, Otway fills *Venice Preserved* with images of nature gone bad, which he sets against imagery of bucolic nature, ideal and unrealized, in the private dialogue of Belvidera and Jaffeir. While they speak of turtle doves and the wings of a pitying angel, the real world of the play labels people, for example, "lazy vermin," "a haggard owl, a worthless kite of prey," a "filthy cuckoo," "a dog, that comes to howl," an "unnecessary, useless, giddy-brained ass," a "toad," or an "old hideous animal." Squirming before Aquilina, Antonio makes these metaphors literal, as he barks, howls, and begs her to kick and spit on him. More generally, so do the "unnatural" acts, all defended as "natural," of those who betray their country, renounce a child, pawn a tormented wife for social credit, or break their vows. It is no wonder that the crazed Belvidera glimpses innocent nature in broken images: "Murmuring streams, soft shades, and springing flowers, / Lutes, laurels, seas of milk, and ships of amber."

The pathos of *Venice Preserved*, its stirring and cynical political rhetoric, the black comedy of the scenes between Antonio and Aquilina (when the stage tolerated such scandalous material), and its encompassing, dark view of life made it the most successful tragedy of its time. It long remained in the repertory after the Exclusion Crisis had become a casual memory, and is one of the very rare non-Shakespearean tragedies of the 17th century to enjoy occasional revivals today.

—Eric Rothstein

VENUS AND ADONIS.
Poem by William Shakespeare, 1593.

Venus and Adonis, generally troubling to learned commentators and traditionally rated low on the scale of William Shakespeare's own achievements, gave no trouble at all to his contemporaries, providing delight to "the younger sort" and the revenue of some ten editions to its publisher. Despite its high stylization (it is a compendium of rhetorical schemes) and the fact that it was licensed by the Archbishop of Canterbury, this Ovidian piece, formally classified as "erotic narrative" has even been called "pornographic." To those who believe that significant literature must please and instruct, it has been found wanting in the latter and to the new critics it has no center, its tonal unity destroyed by the "tragedy" of the death of Adonis and Venus' subsequent lament.

Traditionally, Ovid's own writings have been a problem for the sober sort. Augustus banished him, citing the *Amores* as part cause; the late Middle Ages moralized the *Metamorphoses* into acceptability; and Arthur Golding felt the need to provide a lengthy introductory defense of his translation of it (1567), arguing its content to be compatible with the Bible, if not as worthy. But both Marlowe and Shakespeare understood the efficacy of Ovid, and each in his own way attempted to recreate his temper for their time. Like Ovid they retell an ancient myth, irrelevant to their present culture, in an elegant style together with invented matter of their own, presented by a playfully ironic narrator. Along the way they create received "wisdom" with *pseudo-sententiae*, offered in narrative asides, and by applying their myths to an explanation of some natural phenomenon. They recognized that the beautiful and grotesque, the humorous and sorrowful, could exist side by side, and that their new myths stood in parodic relationship to Homer and the epic tradition (and in *Venus and Adonis* to Petrarchanism, pastoralism, and complaint literature).

That Marlowe's poem, even in its unfinished state, is more successfully Ovidian and more accomplished than Shakespeare's is beyond dispute. Yet the first part of *Venus and Adonis* is a masterpiece of comic wit based on the inversion of male and female sexual roles, and the so-called "tragic" second part aptly moves toward its primary Ovidian function of explaining why "sorrow on love hereafter shall attend," this just prior to Adonis' metamorphosis into an anemone and the poem's closing lines.

We are alerted early to the essentially comic nature of the poem's first 800 lines. In what must be the most abrupt opening of any narrative, Shakespeare sets the scene and action with characteristic imagery in one stanza:

Even as the sun with purple-colored face
Had ta'en his last leave of the weeping morn,
Rose-cheeked Adonis hied him to the chase;
Hunting he loved, but love he laughed to scorn.
Sick-thoughted Venus makes amain unto him,
And like a bold-faced suitor 'gins to woo him.

In the next three stanzas Venus invites Adonis to sit with her, and, without waiting for an answer, plucks him from his horse and has him on the ground by force in a wink (including the tying of the horse) at which the narrator, admiring her manual dexterity ironically observes, "Oh, how quick is love." In short order we are supplied with an epic simile (a hungry eagle devouring its prey, but applied to Venus' kissing) and others calculated to Anglicize the narrative: "Look how a bird lies tangled in a net, / So fastened in her arms Adonis lies." Later, as Adonis smiles in disdain when Venus compares herself to a park where he might graze on "sweet bottom-grass and high delightful plain" his dimples, the hyperbolizing narrator observes, are "lovely caves . . . round enchanting pits," which open "their mouths to swallow Venus' liking."

Among other comic delights are Adonis' first words, withheld until stanza 31, "Fie, no more of love! / The sun doth burn my face—I must remove" and Venus' punning reply, "What bare excuses mak'st thou to be gone"; Adonis depicted conventionally in a "bonnet," which Shakespeare puts to good comic use:

Now was she just before him as he sat,
And like a lowly lover down she kneels;
With one fair hand she heaveth up his hat,
Her other tender hand his fair cheek feels;

a Petrarchan cliché applied literally to Venus as love personified, providing a slapstick image and an elegant chiastic line:

And at his look she flatly falleth down,
For looks kill love, and love by looks reviveth;

anti-climax formed by dialogue alternating with the narrator's disappointed voice:

"Tell me, love's master, shall we meet tomorrow?
Say, shall we? shall we? wilt thou make the match?"
He tells her no;

witty casuistry and word-play: "Thou wast begot; to get it is thy duty;" and even within the boar-hunting episode the comic images persist: a wounded hound is "a flap-mouthed mourner," and "she meets another sadly scowling, / To whom she speaks and he replies with howling."

When Adonis finally speaks at length, it turns out that he is a severe moralist possessed of an unlikely wisdom far beyond his years. Ironically, his seven stanzas of reproof might just have qualified the poem for publication, giving it enough redeeming social importance to escape official censure.

The so-called "tragic" ending, from Venus' discovery of the dead Adonis to her departure for Paphos, where she "Means to immure herself and not be seen," is typically Ovidian in its mixture of beautiful and grotesque images. Adonis' "soft flank" is "drenched with purple tears" and Venus in falling on his body "stains her face with his congealed blood," but this literary pathos is undercut by Venus' lengthy prophecy of the ways in which love shall always bring sorrow with it, the poem's mythic point, and by Adonis' metamorphosis, the poem's anticipated ending.

In his dedication of the poem to the Earl of Southampton, Shakespeare states that his intention is to please and that he will later turn his efforts to "some graver labor." We may be sure that his contemporary readers (like Ovid's in Rome under Augustus) so used to serious works expressing the institutionalized morality of their time, appreciated the merely delightful.

—Frank Fabry

THE VICAR OF WAKEFIELD.
Novel by Oliver Goldsmith, 1766.

Often seen by his contemporaries as an outrageous, even at times ludicrous, character, Oliver Goldsmith was a prolific, though uneven, writer. Certainly the poem *The Deserted Village*, the play *She Stoops to Conquer*, and the novel *The Vicar of Wakefield* are all testament to the versatility of his creative talents.

Supposedly sold by Samuel Johnson to help settle rent owed by Goldsmith, *The Vicar of Wakefield* was published in 1766, though it was no doubt written some years before that. The *Monthly Review* of May 1766, described the novel as a "singular tale" that was "difficult to characterize." And surely it still is. "A book," Goldsmith wrote in the Advertisement, "may be amusing with numerous errors, or it may be very dull without a single absurdity." That the plot of the novel rests on the improbable and the coincidental and perhaps at times even on the absurd is obvious early on. At the same time, however, the book reflects the universal conflict between the real and the ideal—the what is and the what ought to be. In that sense *The Vicar of Wakefield* is remarkable for the period of rationalism in which it was published.

Reminiscent of *The Deserted Village*, the opening scene of the novel is a quiet rural community in which the good Dr. Primrose, surrounded by his wife and six children, carries out his duties as Vicar, with only a few "little rubs which Providence sends to enhance the value of its other favours." It is not long, however, before these "little rubs" become abrasive indeed, and Dr. Primrose and his family find themselves caught in a kind of whirlpool of injustice and misfortune that draws them ever deeper into the pit of mortification and calamity.

Beginning with a disagreement about divorce between Dr. Primrose and the father of the girl his son George hopes to marry, fate contrives to test the moral fortitude of the Vicar and his family. Like Job, Dr. Primrose sees his family and his life suffer one blow after another: his broker runs off with the family money; son George's wedding plans are aborted; the family is forced to move to the estate of wealthy and villainous Squire Thornhill; daughters Olivia and Sophia are slandered; Olivia is lured into eloping with Squire Thornhill; the Primrose house burns to the ground; Dr. Primrose himself is thrown into debtor's prison by Squire Thornhill; daughter

Sophia is kidnapped. These tribulations, among others, would seem enough to cast doubt on the Psalmist's statement that the righteous man is never deserted. But not for the good Dr. Primrose. For 185 pages of the novel his misfortunes accumulate, and he accepts them steadfastly, until at last happier prospects begin to appear. In only 23 pages all is set right again: George marries; Olivia finds that her forced marriage to Squire Thornhill was not legal; Sophia marries Sir William Thornhill, the squire's uncle; Squire Thornhill is undone for his machinations; and Dr. Primrose settles down to enjoy the felicities of his declining years, once again a wealthy man.

To grasp the essential significance of *The Vicar of Wakefield* one must go beyond the romantic sentimentality and occasional silliness of the plot. Prior to writing the novel, Goldsmith had castigated novels and romances for teaching "the youthful mind to sigh after beauty and happiness which never existed, to despise the little good which fortune has mixed in our cup, by expecting more than she ever gave." If Goldsmith believed his own words, then *The Vicar of Wakefield* may be viewed as a satire on the whole concept of virtue rewarded and the guileless and unworldly Dr. Primrose as nothing more than a kind of Theophrastian caricature, a man of platitudes without substance, without passion—actually a man who could not really suffer and for whom the real and the ideal are both mere abstractions cancelling each other out. Not a Job nor a Lear nor a Captain Ahab, Dr. Primrose does not seek an answer to the question of why man must suffer. Indeed, in his sermon in the prison he admits that such an answer has not been found and that even if it were, it might well be useless. In another sense, Dr. Primrose may be seen as a symbol of human endurance in the face of such unanswerable questions. Through a deft blending of laughter and tears, Goldsmith succeeds in presenting the often gullible Vicar as not only a laughable innocent, but also as one who uses that innocence to mask a more somber life view—indeed one of the memorable characters of English fiction.

Whatever else it is, *The Vicar of Wakefield* is a novel replete with scenes ranging from the comic to the poetic that, taken collectively, have brought a keen delight to readers over the years—a delight that stems not so much from probability as from improbability.

—Wilton Eckley

THE VILLAGE.
Poem by George Crabbe, 1783.

George Crabbe's career falls into two clear phases. Between 1775 and 1785 he wrote genre studies—*Inebriety*, *The Library*, *The Village*, and *The Newspaper*. With the exception of *The Village* they show no signs of that extraordinary originality which developed when he began publishing again in 1806, and when his true forte—the analysis of character through the medium of the verse tale—was developed. Yet *The Village*, which Samuel Johnson, Edmund Burke, and Charles James Fox all admired, does make a unique contribution to English poetry.

In starkly realistic terms the poem describes Aldeburgh, Crabbe's Suffolk birthplace: at the time of writing a desolate, neglected, and impoverished seaport from which the river Alde had deviated, leaving the place unnavigable. The sense of loneliness, bitter poverty, and sterility which the poem brilliantly captures looks forward to the mordant observation of Crabbe's post-1806 oeuvre, and stamps him as a writer of genuine originality, even though the couplet form itself and the descriptive subject are characteristic of much post-Augustan writing.

The Village is animated by another sense of grievance as well. Goldsmith's *The Deserted Village* (1770) had caught the popular imagination, and its slightly sentimental / nostalgic tone rather softened the impact of rural depopulation and poverty which followed the enclosure acts, with the break-up of old-established patterns of social interdependency which had sustained British agriculture for over a hundred years. Crabbe believed that this sentimental sub-Virgilian pastoralism was intellectually and politically dishonest, and represented untruth both in nature and in art. "I paint the cot, As Truth will have it, and as bards will not," he exclaims, and attempts to carry through his bifurcated attack on the sentimental eclogue—"mechanic echoes of the Mantuan song"—and upon dishonest social history—"what form[s] the real picture of the poor."

The opening "literary" section of part one of the poem makes valid points regarding some contemporary nature writing. But in itself it would not make Crabbe's poem live. The real strength of the work lies in the section where Crabbe turns from his attack on a meretricious poetic kind and looks at Aldeburgh itself. He describes the scenery, the occupants, the labours, and the trials of those who dwell on this harsh and unfruitful soil. The flat, dull, arid countryside evokes his most powerful writing:

> Lo! where the heath, with withering brake grown o'er,
> Lends the light turf that warms the neighbouring poor;
> . . . Rank weeds, that every art and care defy,
> Reign o'er the land, and rob the blighted rye:
> There thistles stretch their prickly arms afar,
> And to the ragged infant threaten war;
> There poppies nodding, mock the hope of toil;
> There the blue bugloss paints the sterile soil;
> Hardy and high, above the slender sheaf,
> The slimy mallow waves her silky leaf;
> O'er the young shoot the charlock throws a shade,
> And clasping tares cling round the sickly blade,

The subterranean sympathy which informs this superficial bleakness is remarkable but characteristic. Crabbe was an informed amateur of both botany and geology, but he evinced a preference for hedgerow weeds and for geologically dull rocks. Coupled to a strong sense of pessimism in his nature this creates in his work a uniquely trenchant and sardonic view of the minutiae of nature—and later of human nature too.

Part one of *The Village* then concentrates upon the hitherto sentimentalised lot of the village poor, including Crabbe's famous description of the workhouse and its inmates, which stirred so many contemporary consciences. Both priest and doctor are vehemently criticised as venal and uncaring, underpinning the radical socialism of Crabbe's stance.

Part two lacks this sustained power. It begins by trying to show the counteracting pleasures of rural life, but these, characteristically, degenerate into drunkenness, seduction, scandalmongering, and poaching. Then follows the contentious conclusion in which Crabbe argues that all these ills of the poor are meliorated if we consider the misfortunes which may afflict their social betters. He instances the death of Lord Robert Manners (younger brother of his then patron, the

Duke of Rutland), who had been killed in a naval engagement against the French in 1782. The process of argument seems entirely spurious, the fulsome diatribe intellectually dislocated from the brilliant detailed observation and the legitimate anger with which the poet contemplated the miseries of Suffolk seaboard life.

The Village embodies qualities which were later confirmed in *The Borough* and in *Tales in Verse*; mordant wit, originality of observation, freshness of subject matter, social concern, concentration upon the minute and the apparently "unpoetical." Its technique is patchy—Crabbe never quite knew whether to imitate the chiselled elegance of Pope or the more powerful iambics of Dryden, and its argument is flawed by the multiplicity of themes. But it made his name, and has justly lasted as a work of real originality and force.

—T. Bareham

VILLETTE.
Novel by Charlotte Brontë, 1853.

When Charlotte Brontë wrote *Villette*, her last novel, she had recently watched the lingering deaths of her three remaining siblings, who were not only the people closest to her on earth, but those with whom she had developed her imaginative life. Her bereavement must have brought back the desolation she had felt when forced to recognize the end of her only romance, her hopeless love for Constantin Heger. Passionate by nature, yet facing a life without love, she struggled against crippling depression; her only possible escape was through writing. In *Villette*, with brave resolution, she came to terms with emotional deprivation. The book is autobiographical insofar as Lucy Snowe, the protagonist and narrator, goes to teach in a school in Brussels ("Villette") and falls in love with her literature professor. Characteristically curbing wish-fulfilling fantasy by her need to face reality, Brontë lets her heroine win the love of Professor Paul Emanuel, but emphasizes his unromantic qualities and does not let them marry. The possibility of marriage does not even come up with regard to Lucy's first love, the typical romantic hero John Graham Bretton, because he is "a 'curled darling' of Nature and of Fortune" (letter to her publisher).

Brontë, convinced that some people are providentially ordained for happiness and others for sorrow and disappointment, portrays her heroine as a woman made lonely and unhappy first by circumstance and then by the effects of deprivation on her character. Lucy presents herself as an outsider: no one warmly cares for her, and she maintains her self-esteem by emulating their coolness (Snowe) and privately depreciating them. Lacking beauty, sweetness, and a cheerful disposition, she fears rejection; consequently, she conceals her need and capacity for love under an apathetic manner that repels love and attention. Because she is not loved, Lucy is depressed and insecure; she makes her situation worse by her pervasively negative attitude. She represses every hope because she is convinced it must be inconsistent with a rational assessment of reality. She clings to the safety of a drab, narrow existence and has to be forced into taking advantage of opportunities that will lead her toward growth and fulfillment. Yet Lucy's self-imposed restrictions cannot solve her problems, for her insistent reiteration that she lacks passion, emotion, and energy betrays her unusually intense need to live and love. Her psychological strain appears in her ill-concealed envy of those she professes to disdain and resentment at those who accept her self-effacing manner as genuine, as well as the violent images she uses to describe her repression of hope. Finally, when she is left alone during the school vacation, the strain brings her close to psychotic breakdown.

Because Lucy conceals her personality so successfully, it must be revealed indirectly through other characters. Paulina, who elicits intense interest from Lucy as well as gratuitously waspish criticism, displays the capacity for unconditional devotion that Lucy feels and fears in herself. The headmistress, Madame Beck, attracts Lucy by demonstrating the total rational control that she aims for, but also disgusts her by lacking the warm feeling that Lucy tries unsuccessfully to repress in herself. John Bretton, the school doctor, illustrates Lucy's character by contrast, since he has been favored by nature and fortune. Handsome, self-confident, optimistic, resilient, instinctively well-disposed toward everyone, he is everything that Lucy is not. She cannot help falling in love with him, although she sees the gulf between them. She desperately cherishes his letters, even as she recognizes that he wrote them merely from a good-natured wish to cheer her up.

Yet this healthy nature has its limitations: Bretton is perceptibly shallow and insensitive. Not only is he unaware of Lucy's love, but he persists in seeing her as placid and inoffensive. Paul Emanuel, on the other hand, quickly perceives her strong will, passion, and ambition; indeed, he sees them more clearly than she does herself. Both characters have feelings too intense to be easily controlled, demonstrated in his case by outbursts of temper and in hers by the force required to keep calm. Because they are alike, he alone can see what she is and value her for it. His unconventional courtship, teasing and bullying redeemed by obvious interest and caring, jars her out of her icy reserve and liberates her to respond emotionally. Because he is as far from the conventional romantic hero as she is from the heroine—he is small and ugly, childishly vain and testy, sometimes even ridiculous—she can hope for his love without being castigated by her reason. However, their love cannot be consummated: Brontë implies that he is drowned in a terrible storm at sea. This is appropriate, since storm is Lucy's natural element, as sunshine is Bretton's. Although she attains independence and professional satisfaction in running the school Paul has set up for her—for the self-confidence she has gained from their love enables her to make her school a success—the happiness of emotional fulfillment is not for her.

Brontë's greatest achievement in *Villette* is her gripping creation of a reticent and morbid character who habitually disguises her feelings not only from the world, but from herself. The presentation teases us into involvement because we must understand Lucy by means of her own distorted and evasive narration and interpret her through indirect means, such as her horrifying dreams or her seemingly inexplicable bond with the shallow coquette Ginevra. Even though Lucy's repellent personality makes her hard to like, Brontë compels us to care deeply about her.

—Katharine M. Rogers

A VINDICATION OF THE RIGHTS OF WOMAN.
Prose by Mary Wollstonecraft, 1792.

A Vindication of the Rights of Woman is generally considered to be the founding text of Anglo-American feminism. But Mary Wollstonecraft's engagement with Enlightenment constructions of "woman," particularly Rousseau's Sophy in *Émile* (1792), requires feminists' critical attention.

The salient characteristic of "woman" in Rousseau's novel is the fluency with which her body speaks. Woman's powerful physical presence not only overrides linguistic messages, but also speaks when "woman" herself is silent. *Émile*'s narrator tells the wife-seeking Émile, "Why do you consult their [women's] words when it is not their mouths that speak? Consult their eyes, their colour, their breathing, . . . that is the language nature gave them for your answer." Rousseau's views on women's education are structured by the construction of "woman" as physical presence. Accordingly, he states in Book 5 of *Émile* that women should be educated solely to be obedient and attractive to men.

Wollstonecraft criticises Rousseau's views on the education of women at some length in the *Vindication*. For Wollstonecraft, education is the first step in forming an individual who is capable of moving gradually towards that "perfection" which she felt was attainable by all individuals through the exercise of reason. Because the education of women had hitherto been in the hands of men who view education as "preparation for life" rather than progress towards perfection, women's education has been particularly limited, and their understanding in consequence has been denied. Educated to be the companions of men, to be sexually enticing and attractive, women are, for Wollstonecraft, the fanciful capricious beings that men complain they are. Wollstonecraft's alternative view of education for women is one which allows them to lead rational lives, and to be the rational beings she believes them to be.

The rhetorical strategies which structure this argument are particularly significant. Wollstonecraft presents her text as asking "plain questions" and "establishing" "unequivocal answers." In other words, Wollstonecraft's text presents itself as "scientific," as the articulation of what she calls "truths that appear . . . incontrovertible." If women are educated in a manner which Wollstonecraft calls "rational," then she is positive that their current "capricious" behaviour will disappear. This seems an unproblematic assertion; but if we explore the metaphor of the scientific method implied in "prove," we come across interesting contradictions.

The *Vindication* accepts the validity of the parallel between repetition—proof—and Truth which the inductive method establishes. "Surveying the history of woman, . . . ," Wollstonecraft says, "[w]hat does history disclose but marks of inferiority, and how few women have emancipated themselves from the galling yoke of sovereign man?" History clearly shows the *repeated* marks of inferiority in women—it shows that there is some *truth* in what male satirists say about women.

Clearly, this is not the conclusion that the *Vindication* strives for, and Wollstonecraft must deconstruct the correlation between what is "repeatable," or is called "proof" by the inductive method, and what can be called *truth*. She does this through the example of a young girl, educated at home, who is "condemned to sit for hours together listening to the idle chat of weak nurses, or to attend to her mother's toilet." As a result of these conditions, that a young girl "will imitate her mother or aunts, and amuse herself by adorning her lifeless doll, as they do in dressing her . . . is undoubtedly a most natural consequence." Wollstonecraft asserts that the repeated phenomenon of young girls' interest in fashion and dolls is not the TRUTH about women, but the result of specific material conditions. She makes a distinction between what she calls "natural" (the inevitable consequence of certain conditions—what we term material conditions) and TRUTH. Though the process by which young girls become "feminised" is repeatable, there is no immutable eternal truth to be gleaned from it.

It is a point which Wollstonecraft makes over and over again in her attempt to deconstruct the correlation of repetition and truth, and replace it with the parallelism of repetition and material conditions. It is "daily example," the insistent repetition of specific material conditions, not an innate or essential quality in women, which Wollstonecraft wants to stress as conditioning influences on female behaviour. Having thus interrupted the movement from repetition to proof to truth, Wollstonecraft is able to reject the "truth about women" that the parallelism articulates. That definition is one which, like Rousseau's, privileges women's bodies as a "site" or locus of their "truth." She rejects the traditional notion that woman's "perfection" is her BODY because to site woman's "perfection" in her body is to suggest that her very TRUTH is sited there also.

Having disturbed the progression from repetition to truth Wollstonecraft employs a tactic which renders problematic the rest of the *Vindication*. She outlines an alternative education system which educates boys and girls together, and which uses what she terms the "habitual propriety of behaviour." The term "habitual" here is important; it suggests that it is in the repeatable that we will find "truth." It is in the daily schooling of girls with boys, the "habitual" propriety of behaviour, that the "true" nature of women will be revealed. Wollstonecraft argues throughout her chapter on the education of women that there is some "natural" rational essence of woman that has been repressed by inferior education, and that will be released by a reformed, rational education.

Having deconstructed the equation of repetition with truth, Wollstonecraft utilises that equation to redefine women's character. It is a recourse to a "scientific method" which her argument dictates, but is already labelled unsuitable for the pursuit of "truth." Having altered the material conditions of female education, Wollstonecraft wants also to declare the end product of that rational system "true." Consequently Wollstonecraft, like Rousseau, articulates a definition of woman which also constructs the body, not intellectual reason, as the site of female meaning. The maternal body (note the "scene" of breastfeeding in Book 5) becomes the body in which, noting the "habitual exercise of mutual sympathy" that structures the mother / child relation for Wollstonecraft, she inscribes woman's meaning. In place of the female body which Rousseau defined in terms of male sexual access, Wollstonecraft's rational woman, her "maternal body," is still defined in terms of sexual presence and the "impressions" she makes on men.

—Susan Hamilton

A VISION.
Prose by William Butler Yeats, 1925.

It has been said, with justice, that "*A Vision*, with its doubtful origins, its bizarre terminology, and the unfashionable drift of its philosophy, is an awkward book to swallow"

(*Yeats: His Poetry and Thought* by A.G. Stock). Certainly, it is difficult, within a narrow compass, to give an adequate account of a book which, in its two editions, took almost 20 years to assemble and which was intended to be a systematic exposition of William Butler Yeats's ideas on history and metaphysics. That the writing of *A Vision* was crucially important to Yeats is attested to by his own comments. It was, he said, "a last act of defence against the chaos of the world, and I hope for ten years to write out of my renewed security." The book represented, then, another of Yeats's attempts to organize all the disparate elements of his thought, speculation, and eclectic reading into an organic unity, to create a metaphor for the correlation of all things, a system that would unite the antinomies or oppositions between which he believed all existence constantly moved. It was not intended to be a reflection of actuality, but rather "a vision," a "lunar parable," a "stylistic arrangement of experience," which would allow him "to hold in a single thought reality and justice" and to frame his sense of "the soul's history."

The spirit communicators who gave him, initially through his wife's automatic writing, the outline of the system, told him that they had come to give him "metaphors for poetry." Consequently, even if *A Vision* were not to be regarded as significant in itself, or important as part of Yeats's lifelong attempt to make clear the indivisible pattern of his life and his work and bring both to that "completion" he was still striving for a few weeks before his death, it would demand attention because of the increased power and mastery of the poetry written out of it or against its background and as an explication of the ideas that gave rise to such poems as "The Second Coming," "Leda and the Swan," the Byzantium poems and "All Souls' Night."

The system enunciated in *A Vision* depends crucially on Yeats's view that all human life and human history depend on a mingling of fundamental opposites. The theme of *A Vision* was to be "the way of the soul between the sun and the moon." The explication of the theme relies heavily on two crucial diagrams. The first diagram is that of a pair of interpenetrating cones which Yeats called gyres. These gyres are the solar, or Primary gyre which is essentially physical and objective, and the lunar, or Antithetical gyre which is essentially spiritual and subjective. Because the gyres interpenetrate, one always contains elements of the other. The concept of gyres, expanding and contracting as the centuries proceed, allowed Yeats to expound his theory of history.

Yeats wrote *A Vision* during a period of violence at home and abroad. Thoughts of apocalypse obsessed him and were reinforced by his reading of writers like Nietzsche who proposed a cyclical or apocalyptic view of history. His own view was that "our civilization was about to reverse itself, or some new civilization about to be born from all that our age had rejected." What was happening in his own time would happen again in the future and had happened many times in the past. In Yeats's system the coming of a new gyre is ushered in by an annunciation, (the rape of Leda by the Swan, Mary and the dove), is born amid violence and chaos, and will be dominated by characteristics totally opposite to those which have prevailed in the previous gyre. At certain stages when the antithetical tincture is in the ascendant, great ages occur when it is possible to develop human excellence and social harmony; "unity of Being" becomes possible in a civilization where politics, art, and a high sense of human excellence combine. Such ages (each separated by a period of a thousand years) are Athens in the time of the sculptor Phidias, the Byzantine Empire and the Italian Renaissance. Yeats's own age, however, is dominated by the Primary gyre in which the individual creative spirit is asked to obey the "levelling spirit" of mass democracy and of various "systems." Signs of the violence and fragmentation which would culminate in a bloody armageddon are all around. The new Antithetical gyre which will be ushered in amid this violence will reach its climax around the year 2500.

A more complex diagram is that of the Great Wheel, which, based on the lunar month of 28 phases, represents everything, including the 28 basic phases of each cycle of world history, the 28 phases of any single life, and the 28 incarnations a man must live through. However, Yeats used the phases of the moon primarily to outline a theory of personality, and to elaborate those theories of the Mask he had been proposing for many years. In the system, 26 different types of personality are defined. Phase 1, the dark of the moon, corresponds to the extreme of the Primary gyre and phase 15, the full moon, corresponds to the extreme of the Antithetical gyre. Since there is no intermingling of opposites at these phases, no human life is possible. The phase on the opposite side of the wheel represents the Mask. Personality types on the solar, objective, side of the diagram are scientists, businessmen, and athletes, scholars, saints, and fools, and can be happy only by clinging to the physical and rejecting the Mask, the opposite, subjective type. On the Lunar side, which Yeats favoured, are the artists and men of passion who must choose to wear a Mask but are faced with a choice between a true and false Mask. It seems clear enough that Yeats would have placed himself at phase 17, with Dante and Shelley, men capable of Unity of Being if they choose the True Mask of "Simplification through Intensity" by using their synthetic power to achieve simplicity—as Yeats was doing in *A Vision*.

—Anne Clune

THE VISION OF JUDGEMENT.
Poem by Lord Byron, 1822.

In May 1821, the Poet Laureate Robert Southey published *A Vision of Judgement*, celebrating the reception of the late George III into Heaven, literally damning the king's political opponents, and in his preface denouncing what he called "the Satanic school" of poetry, "men of diseased hearts and depraved imaginations." Lord Byron objected not only to this last attack, clearly directed at him; but to what he saw as a virtual whitewash of George's reign, to the arrogance of picturing a God with Southey's exact political views, to the brutality of the theology, and to the fact that Southey was betraying his own earlier republican idealism. The poem which takes up all these topics, *The Vision of Judgement* of 1822, therefore needs to be very flexible, varying in tone from direct mockery through irony to the deeply serious. The one thing it must not be is vicious. Byron had to hand the ideal satirical tool: the *ottava rima* stanza (eight lines of pentameter rhyming abababcc), which could be employed to produce satire basically light and witty, but with great potential for variance of tone.

Much of this is seen in the opening of the poem. Byron's version of Heaven at first seems just amusing, with St. Peter's rusty keys and the angels singing out of tune; but this is a deliberate contrast to the grimness of Southey's Heaven, and furthermore there is a shift of perception as we realize the keys are rusty because most people have gone to Hell since the French Revolution broke out, and are introduced to the recording angels, hard at work on the death-count, until forced to give up by "the crowning carnage, Waterloo." It is an indication of the balanced position he is trying to achieve, that in the next stanza, Byron apportions the blame for Waterloo equally between Napoleon and Wellington. This is soon evident again as he indicates his own attitude to George III, "although no tyrant one / Who shielded tyrants," a good farmer but a bad king. We have to be careful here, however: paying an enemy compliments amidst major accusations in order to appear fair is an old satirical technique.

The central section of the poem is the discussion between Satan and St. Michael as to George III's ultimate destination. Byron thus undermines Southey's assumptions on this score, particularly as when the king arrives at the pearly gates nobody knows who he is. He has already (stanzas 13–15) undermined Southey's basic theological assumptions about the Church of England being best and damnation being the most important Christian doctrine. Byron has no time for a religious outlook which rejoices in the prospect of "that immortal fry / Of almost every body born to die." He now produces a Satan very different from Southey's primitive monster. His introduction in stanza 24 is packed with Miltonic references, but as stanzas 33–34 tell us, the basic model is from the Book of Job, a Satan who can talk on equal terms with God Himself. Thus when he meets St. Michael, "between his Darkness and his Brightness / There passed a mutual glance of great politeness." This Satan is in fact pretty Byronic; which is a neat answer to the "Satanic school" accusation. Satan's views are Byron's views, with the same (apparent) fairness and balance. He grants George III his "household abstinence" and "neutral virtues"; but "He ever warred with freedom and the free." When St. Michael asks for witnesses against George III, and to his embarrassment millions start to turn up, Satan is pleased to compromise and have only two actually speak. Here again there is balance: the speakers are two great Whig heroes, Wilkes and Junius, but their status is soon diminished, the former seen as a turncoat and the latter as a coward for writing under a pseudonym.

The climax of the poem is the arrival of Southey himself, hauled up from a (raining) Lake District by a devil who has spotted him writing his *A Vision of Judgement*, "a libel— / No less on History—than the Holy Bible," a summary of Byron's objections to its political distortions and ugly theology. The scene becomes one of high comedy (stanzas 90–92), with a conclusion of pure farce at the mass exit when Southey starts to recite his own poetry; but in between (stanzas 97–98) has come the inevitable serious statement, on Southey's apostasy: "He had written praises of a Regicide; / He had written praises of all kings whatever."

The final problem is, what to do with poor old George. Byron cannot do a Southey, and send him to Hell; but the opposite would imply approval. So the king slips into Heaven while nobody is looking. This witty compromise encapsulates the whole achievement of the poem.

—P.E. Hewison

THE VIVISECTOR.
Novel by Patrick White, 1970.

Patrick White's eighth novel, *The Vivisector*, published in 1970, is a novel of the big city: Sydney, Australia. The creation of the dominant central character, the painter Hurtle Duffield, brings together several crucial concerns of the writer: a continued exploration of the mental and physical landscapes that underpin his work, a fascination with the intangible process by which a personal vision is transformed into canvas and paint, and, ultimately, a consideration of the role of the artist in contemporary society.

White's much-admired earlier novels, *The Tree of Man* and *Voss* deal with the archetypal struggle of the early pioneers in Australia to subdue the land by exploration and by settlement, his heroes searching at the same time for some kind of spiritual significance in these unforgiving landscapes of desert and scrub. In turning to the city of his childhood, Sydney, White is evoking an urban landscape that he both loves and despises. In his self-portrait, *Flaws in the Glass*, White stated that "setting out to portray a convincing artist, I wanted at the same time to paint a portrait of my city: wet, boiling, superficial, brash, beautiful, ugly Sydney, developing during my lifetime from a sunlit village into this present-day parvenu bastard, compound of San Francisco and Chicago."

White's affinity with the fine arts, and with painting in particular, can be seen in all his novels. The figure of the artist is invariably isolated and often rejected by society. An intensely visual writer, White uses language in such a way that his descriptions become almost painterly in quality. As a young writer he felt himself to be a painter manqué, struggling with the "rocks and sticks of words." He admits in his self-portrait that "whether Hurtle Duffield is or is not a painter, I see him as a composite of several I have known, welded together by the one I have in me but never became."

The duality of the artist, involved in life and yet necessarily detached; creator and destroyer; is given shape in the novel through the two lives that young Hurtle Duffield has to live. Born into the warm muddle of a large and improvident family, Hurtle is sold as a young boy for 500 pounds to a wealthy family who live in a splendid house in the best part of Sydney. He learns a new language, but memories cause him to straddle two worlds, and later when he buys his own house in Sydney he purchases one with a similar split personality: one side of the house looks over a tree-lined road which "must have had pretentions." But the back of the house looks over Chubb's Lane, a very different area, full of noise, smells, and cheerful dereliction. For the painter, "the two faces of the house complemented each other; one taken away might have upset the balance: together they made what was necessary for his fulfillment and happiness."

Hurtle's artistic sensibility is enhanced by his relationship with the well-to-do Courtney family and the beautiful objects with which they surround themselves. He is particularly drawn to a vivid seascape by the French 19th-century painter Boudin, which creates in him a physical longing to touch and even lick the paint. Increasingly the desire to paint becomes uncontrollable and is frequently linked to sexual desire and satisfaction. When Hurtle returns to Australia after serving in World War I and spending some time in Paris, he establishes a relationship with a cheerful prostitute, Nance Lightfoot. Her body brings back childhood memories of dawn light on folded pastures and the rounded shapes of sheep, yet these are moulded into a nervous, physical energy that drives his painting so that it becomes a quasi-sexual experience: "he began fiddling, rubbing, masturbating in nervous paint on a narrow board." In portraying his fellow-artist Kathy Volkov at the piano "he thrust against the virgin board." With brush in hand, he sweats, his tongue laps, he possesses the girl he paints.

The ability of the painter to create brilliant and disturbing images is to some extent associated with the romantic role of the artist as seer, but this role is usually thrust upon Hurtle by the wealthy women collectors who are drawn to him. The inherently destructive features of the artist become more and more dominant; he understands with greater percipience than others, but he can also inflict deeper wounds. Duffield is gifted; he is a seer; yet he is also a destroyer. The image of the vivisector, dissecting and observing living tissue, is a brutally sustained image. The artist is several times accused of this kind of dispassionate cruelty, forcing others to suffer while he stays aloof, observing and noting the palpitating flesh before transforming suffering into art. A pattern emerges which demonstrates the way in which the artist feeds on life; chance encounters on park benches or on ferry trips around the harbour are enough to send him rushing desperately back to his studio to transform quivering emotions into paint.

Increasing public recognition of Hurtle Duffield as an artist allows White to indulge in a little pungent satire directed at the Sydney bourgeoisie, a target that he seldom misses. Duffield is given a major retrospective exhibition at the end of his life (he has already declined a knighthood) but nothing interests him apart from the completion of his final visionary paintings, the so-called "God Paintings." Like the explorer Voss in the middle of the Australian desert, Duffield is reduced to a ramshackle ruin of a man who finally accepts the need to be humble to reach God. White breaks down language to reflect Duffield's mental impairment after his stroke; his last few months are compressed into a vivid stream of impressions that flows without punctuation, thickly-textured experience that is given added tension by the knowledge that his hold on life is precarious.

Poet Derek Mahon finds in *The Vivisector* "the psychopathy of artistic creation" and sees the novel as a major achievement. Other critics have compared it to the great Russian novels of the 19th century. For White, it is the artist, whether a musician, a painter, or a writer, who will teach us how to look at our lives, our relationships with others, and our relationship to the land. *The Vivisector* measures the achievement and the sacrifice of such a figure.

—Margaret B. Lewis

VOLPONE.
Play by Ben Jonson, 1605–06.

At first sight, *Volpone* might seem primarily a scathing assault on emergent capitalism. A tradition of interpretation fostered by L.C. Knights (*Drama and Society in the Age of Jonson*) encourages the view that the main target of Ben Jonson's satire is acquisitiveness. All the human-animals of this corrupt Venice are besotted with lust for gold: the very opening soliloquy in which Volpone idolises money in blasphemous terms ("Open the shrine, that I may see my saint") is taken as a cutting attack on commodity fetishism. While no doubt partly true, this reading of the text tends to minimise the essential differences between Volpone and the gulls on whom he preys. Moreover, it ignores the structure of the play.

Volpone is clearly based on a conflict between two "worlds"—the artful domain of the main protagonist's bedchamber and the "real" world of Venice outside. In the former Volpone reigns supreme, like a monarch, aided and abetted by his unnatural trio of courtiers, Nano, Androgyno, and Castrone, and given practical assistance by his chief councillor, Mosca. This is above all a world of art: Volpone's consummate skill in disguise is enough to turn the vultures who enter, hoping to be made his heirs, into drivelling imbeciles. It is worth noting that Volpone himself is proud of the accolades he received when he "acted young Antinous, and attracted / The eyes and ears of all the ladies present"; furthermore he admits to Mosca that he isn't interested so much in the money itself (miserliness in Volpone is never foregrounded) as "in the cunning purchase" thereof—in other words, the artful cunning and acting ability he displays is its own reward. The effect of this is to neutralise our ethical responses. Volpone's tricks are indeed criminal, but the dupes are so irredeemably foolish and Volpone himself so consummately skilful and intelligent that the bedchamber is converted from a "den / Of villany" into an amoral world of art. Jonson, by depicting a universe where nearly all the main characters are wicked, forces us into a position of ethical relativism, and naturally our impulse is to sympathise with wit, verbal mastery, even quaintness, rather than with doting senile acquisitiveness: our criteria become aesthetic.

Our admiration for Volpone's cleverness is enhanced by his virtuoso performance in the mountebank scene—an advertising scenario that could teach Saatchi and Saatchi a thing or two—but, despite the total mastery over the crowd that his rhetorical expertise ensures, this scene sows the seeds of Volpone's eventual undoing by introducing Celia as an object of desire. In Act I we saw Voltore, Corbaccio, and Corvino utterly fooled by Volpone's art; and there seems no reason why this state of affairs shouldn't go on indefinitely. What introduces the element of dramatic conflict is the central rape scene where Volpone attempts to extend his territorial domain by taking over illegitimate prey, the virtuous Celia, and moreover doing so by force. This scene problematises further the audience's ethical responses: until now, Volpone has been deceiving basically wicked characters, and our moral judgement has been suspended because they deserve all they get. Here, however, a more rigorously critical evaluation is called for. Rape cannot be condoned, and Volpone should not succeed. But in fact he engineers the seduction attempt with such style, panache, and rhetorical flair that Celia's coldly stilted responses seem almost like a refusal to play the game and alienate the sympathies of the audience even further. Volpone, on the contrary, dazzles us with his art: any moral objection of Celia's is easily demolished with wit and logic: "Thou hast in place of a base husband found / A worthy lover." Very true! He touches more emotional chords in the carpe diem song whose intertextual plangencies cogently plead the need for love in a universe of time and decay. The seduction speeches themselves are full of sensuous and colourful imagery ranging from the exotic ("tongues of nightingales") to the mythical ("The milk of unicorns") as he contrives to tempt Celia with delights that are not in nature.

This is indeed a world of art where Jonson uses all the powers of poetry to seduce his audience into an aesthetic response towards what, if Volpone had his way, would actually be a hideous crime. As a result, when Bonario rushes in with "Forbear, foul ravisher! Libidinous swine!" we feel abruptly shifted to a world of moral judgement and even perhaps irritated that he has spoilt the fun. Such a colourless character, however virtuous, cannot hold the audience in his sway as Volpone has. We must be glad that the latter's evil design has been thwarted, but the allure of his rhetorical performance remains.

Nevertheless, this failure points the way to Volpone's doom: by moving from the realm of his bedchamber where gulls are willingly duped to an external world where he attempts to force virtue to his desires, Volpone has overreached. Yet despite the fact that he must now know that this is asking for trouble, he seems driven by some almost perverse urge to continue his forays outside. He even admits of his redoutable disguise that "Here, 'twas good, in private, / But in your public—*Cavè*, whilst I breathe", but persists in donning yet another habit (that of a Commandadore) in order further to plague Corbaccio and Corvino. Nemesis is nigh, and Volpone soon finds himself "caught / In [his] own noose," and shortly after sentenced to an indefinite term in prison "cramped with irons."

Yet such has been the appeal of his wiliness, his verbal and histrionic skills, his sheer impudence, nearly all directed against characters even worse than himself, that the "mortifying of a Fox" comes as a disappointment to many readers: suddenly jolted into an ethical world of crime and punishment, we resist the severity of the sentence (especially when meted out by a corrupt court) and agree with Volpone's declaration in the crucial epilogue that, despite the necessity of being "punished by the laws" in the *moral* dimension, he has done no crime against us—delighted us rather, in *aesthetic* terms, and fully deserved the final applause he craves (and receives). By thus flinging art and nature, disguise and reality, aesthetics and ethics into conflict, Jonson has problematised a sensitive area of early 17th-century thought—something he will return to with rather different conclusions a few years later in *The Alchemist*.

—A.W. Lyle

VOSS.
Novel by Patrick White, 1957.

In the "Prologue in Heaven" which precedes part 1 of Goethe's *Faust*, the Lord grants Mephistopheles's plea for permission to bedevil Faust and remarks that in this undertaking, evil will be pressed into His service. Paradoxically, Mephistopheles's attentions will serve to deepen the "divine discontent" with which Faust knows himself blessed and afflicted. Faust's spirit, already "restless and profound," will now wander farther and look even deeper, but in the process, it will be "[led] into clarity." Faust will never stop sinning until he stops striving, but such a sinking into sloth or satisfaction is here viewed as the only really mortal sin. Since life both is and mandates process, stasis reflects a succumbing to death.

A similar paradox and a similar paradigm of spiritual growth inform Patrick White's novel *Voss*. The fifth of his 12 novels, it is central to his *oeuvre* in this and in several other ways. Not only is it a work of White's mid-career, but like most of his major fictions, it is structured as a quest of the spirit. Again like these, it defines that quest in ambiguous and inconclusive terms. The holy grail is nothing less than the meaning of life, but it is always to be sought, never found. In fact, the failure to reach it is precisely what fuels the ongoing search. Thus, in the words of Frank Le Mesurier, one of the novel's characters and in many ways a double for Voss, "The mystery of life is not solved by success, which is an end in itself, but in failure, in perpetual struggle, in becoming."

Voss's expedition into the heart of Australia is therefore, as Walter Slatoff has said in another context, a "quest for failure." The protagonist, however, must learn how to name this goal before he can seek it. He starts with a very different programme in mind, one which projects success on a very grand scale.

The novel is set in mid-19th-century Australia and opens in Sydney where Voss is collecting supplies and reluctantly enlisting men to accompany him into central Australia. Subsequent plot incidents are drawn in part from the journals of Ludwig Leichhardt, Edward Eyre, and other actual explorers of the period, but the novel uses these in the service of allegory rather than history. In other words, Voss's penetration of a continent quickly becomes a metaphor for his real project: to locate the centre and true ground of his being. At the outset, however, he has confused ideas of what and where these might be.

Voss would prefer to enter the desert of self alone and on foot, in the posture of a suppliant pilgrim, but what he ultimately intends to adore there is himself. He confidently expects apotheosis: he will be deified by posterity which will honor him; by history which will vindicate him; by his men; by the natives; by the land itself which will respond to him like a willing and worshipful lover. White warns us early on that events will disabuse Voss of these notions.

The fact that Mr. Bonner, a prosperous Sydney businessman, is underwriting his mission prevents Voss from going it alone and also forces him into contact with the Bonner family and with Laura Trevelyan, the orphan niece they have raised. The novel's opening scene bring Voss and Laura together in a meeting which reveals to us, if not yet to them, that they mirror each other in prideful isolation and fancied self-sufficiency. Against their respective wills, they find themselves fascinated with each other, drawn together by the instinctive perception that each represents the true quest upon which the other must embark. Laura will demonstrate for Voss the gentle, meek, and self-effacing "dog-eyed love" which he thinks he detests and can do without; Voss will show Laura the monstrous dimensions to which pride can hypertrophy. Both will need to own and conquer in themselves what the other enacts.

By the time he leaves Sydney, Voss is in love with Laura, but still dismissing love as a pathological and passing obsession. However, under the healing influence of Rhine Towers (one of the last outposts at which the party pauses before tackling the desert) and of its owners the Sandersons, whose lives hypostatize Christian love and service, Voss writes to Laura to ask for her hand. She accepts, but demands that he adopt the humility and engaged "human status" she has lately set as her own spiritual agenda. He plots, instead, to raise her to the level of spiritual distance from life at which she can share the "throne" he intends to mount.

By this point, the novel has already split, focusing alternately on Laura in Sydney and Voss in his increasingly purgatorial wilderness, thereby allowing us to gauge and compare the spiritual distances each has covered. As their complementary journeys proceed, we learn that Laura's discipline of humility will be accomplished through her dealings with her maid and the maid's illegitimate daughter, characters who bear the allegorically suggestive names of Rose Portion and Mercy. Rose's pregnancy, delivery, and death shortly after childbirth allow Laura to understand life as a process leading to death, a state which itself is nullified in reciprocal surrender to new life. Mercy's gestation and birth also give Laura the chance to experience and express her love for Voss as sensual, sexual, procreative, protective, nurturing, and finally, sacrificial in the Christian sense. In the crisis of Voss's execution—an event she shares with him in a state partaking of fevered delirium, hallucination, and telepathy—Laura comes to know the centrality of Mercy to her salvation and accepts both the child and the spiritual agency she stands for as mitigating the awful suffering which life exacts.

Although Laura seems to languish in emotional coma for years after Voss's death, she is eventually tortured back into life by her memories and ends the novel able to affirm all facets of experience. Hers is the final word on Voss, of whom she says: "I am convinced that [he] had in him a little of Christ, like other men. If he was composed of evil along with the good, he struggled with that evil. And failed." Earlier, she has alerted us to the imperative nature of that failure, deciding that "When man is truly humbled, when he has learned that he is not God, then he is nearest to becoming so. In the end, he may ascend."

Thus it is Laura who provides a coherent perspective in which to place Voss's journey. Is hers, then, the evaluation of Voss which White wants the reader to adopt? There is much evidence to support this interpretation. Clearly, his party's hardships, the defection or death of his men, and his own final helplessness as a captive of the natives he was to rule teach Voss that he is "the man who was not God." It is equally clear that as Voss accepts his own mortality, he reconciles himself to the human love Laura offers him and the human weakness she has surprised in him. But the validity of her account of Voss has also been rendered problematic.

One source of difficulty is White's rich, densely metaphorical language, whose blossoming meanings refuse to be anatomized. It was perhaps this aspect of the prose which led Ted Hughes to remark that in *Voss*, White had proved himself "the most exciting poet Australia has yet produced." Further complications of meaning arise because the stations of Voss's spiritual journey are not as clearly marked as Laura's were. Nor are we given access to Voss's thoughts in his final moments; he is permitted no summation of his experience or speculation on its significance. Instead, White focuses attention on Jackie, the Aboriginal boy who accompanied the expedition as guide, served as faithful disciple, and at last attempts to exorcise the white demon by hacking off its head. The exorcism fails, of course, and he spends the rest of his life haunted by Voss, as Laura does and as readers are challenged to do.

In the novel's closing scene, Laura hopes that Voss's "legend will be written down . . . by those who have been troubled by it." Her charge suggests that in important ways, the legend remains opaque, even to her. If we adopt a metafictional perspective for a moment, we can hypothesize that this opacity has already "troubled" White into speech. In addition, it seems to go on troubling his critics who, more than 30 years after the novel's appearance, still occupy it as a battleground. The legend of Voss has lodged itself in the Australian psyche to the extent that an opera has been made of it (libretto by David Malouf), and the notion of filming the tale periodically resurfaces, despite past disappointments in the attempt. Perhaps the hope is that, transposed into another medium, the legend will at last grow transparent.

But White's intention seems instead to have been that the story should forever force readers off into their own deserts after Voss, to search him out as Colonel Hebden in the novel tries to do. In the end, then, *Voss* works to exacerbate our own spiritual restlessness. In the Faustian sense, it sends us all about the Lord's business.

—Carolyn Bliss

W

WAITING FOR GODOT.
Play by Samuel Beckett, 1954
(in French, as *En Attendant Godot*, 1952).

Waiting for Godot is seen by many critics as a parable of man's hope and persistence in the face of disappointment, and by some as an absurd, repetitive study in futility. The latter take their cue from the reiteration of the idea of the opening line and closing stage direction: "Nothing to be done," and "They do not move." The former put more emphasis on the fact that two homeless men return day after day to the appointed place, where they wait for Godot and show each other tenderness and affection in spite of pain and the sight of physical cruelty.

The audience watches Vladimir and Estragon pass two in an apparent series of days by the side of the road, in a landscape distinguished only by a mound and a tree which sprouts a few leaves for the second act. Each day domineering Pozzo and his human beast of burden, Lucky, come through, divert the tramps for a while, then go out on some journey that is never explained. While Vladimir and Estragon are tied to each other by need for company, and tied to the spot by the expectation that Godot will come and save them, Pozzo and Lucky are physically linked by a rope that serves as leash for Lucky in the first act and guide for the now blind Pozzo in the second act. Near the end of each act, a boy who cannot remember ever seeing the tramps before brings a message that Mr. Godot will not come this evening, but surely will be there tomorrow. The repetition of events and even words in the two acts, with no change or progression for Vladimir and Estragon, puzzled or disappointed many audiences in the 1950's, when plays that had conventional plots, more respectable central figures, and some resolution were the norm.

Those more open-minded about what could constitute great drama realized that *Godot* was a complex play, tantalizing in its employment of cultural and biblical references, interesting in its use of language, and carefully constructed to show hope in a world where hopes are routinely dashed and man is reduced to barest necessities. The most positive element is the relationship of the tramps, which seems to be more than a selfish need for human company. Though one might say they lack the energy to part company, we twice see them coming together after a night apart. At one of the moments when they contemplate suicide, Estragon struggles to explain why Vladimir should hang himself first. "Gogo light—bough no break—Gogo dead. Didi heavy—bough break—Didi alone." Their talking, even when apparently pointless, is calculated to require responses and keep up contact. They argue, toss out phrases that combine to make a statement, struggle to remember things, occasionally lose patience, but continually affirm their mutual existence in a world lacking any absolute truths.

The days of waiting that would be intolerable to most of us are a positive element in their lives, giving them purpose. "In this immense confusion one thing alone is clear. We are waiting for Godot. . . . we have kept our appointment." At one point, they say they hope for salvation when he comes. Although we can question the truth of any of the statements in the play, Godot seems to be a figure of power, perhaps with a white beard. Many critics state absolutely that he is God, although in the original French the name would not have had the suggestiveness it does in English. If Beckett is writing a parable of the human condition, however, Godot is certainly a metaphor for the principle that gives meaning and hope to daily existence. Vladimir and Estragon are not concerned with an afterlife so much as a meeting on earth that will somehow affect their lives.

The tramps have more mundane concerns, too. Estragon hopes someday to have socks to cushion his ill-fitting boots. Vladimir produces turnips, a carrot, and finally a radish for the hungry Estragon. Beckett has distinguished between these two elderly men with their faint memories of a more respectable youth in the 1890's. Vladimir is the leader, reminding Estragon that they are waiting, often leading the conversation, chiding Gogo for not taking his boots off daily, scolding him for asking Pozzo for bones. When they reunite, he is solicitous, aware that Gogo will never go far without him.

Memory is unreliable. Thinking reaches its lowest level when Lucky, reacting to a command and the outside stimulus of a hat, "thinks" in a long nonsense speech. The self-centered Pozzo admits he cannot remember. The young boy seems very unsure of his information. Lucky, ironically named, is at the bottom of the hierarchy, subject to the commands of his master and physical stimuli that regulate every movement. By contrast, Vladimir and Estragon can make some choices. Physical pain suffuses the play: beatings are referred to, kicks are delivered, Didi voids with difficulty, Estragon's feet hurt. Suicide is a leitmotif, and an alternative that the tramps consider repeatedly, but lack the means or will to effect.

Beckett makes grotesque use of vaudeville turns that add a grim comedy. All four men wear bowler hats, and there is business switching them. Lucky attempts a dance routine and holds the stage with his "thinking," people crash to the ground in heaps amid picnic supplies, Vladimir and Estragon start stories and songs. For the audience, there is nervous laughter and pain, as the actions of Charlie Chaplin's wistful tramp are taken a rung down the ladder of life. Toward the end of the play, Vladimir sums up the uncertainties and the shocking juxtapositions of life and death and something in between: "Tomorrow, when I wake, or think I do, what shall I say of today? That with Estragon my friend, . . . I waited for Godot? That Pozzo passed, . . . But in all that what truth will there be? . . . Astride of a grave and a difficult birth. Down in the hole, lingeringly, the grave-digger puts on the forceps."

—Frances A. Shirley

THE WASTE LAND.
Poem by T.S. Eliot, 1922.

When *The Waste Land* first appeared, in 1922, it was widely rejected as arid and incomprehensible, even as a tasteless joke at the expense of its readers. A more perceptive response shows it to be neither. T.S. Eliot's poem works through "a heap of broken images," the reflection of a world of fragments; but the aim is to weave these fragments into a harmony, which however is not to be imposed upon them, but must emerge—if at all—at the end of the creative process.

The first of the poem's five sections—*The Burial of the Dead*—opens with an evocation of springtime memories, in which the month of rebirth becomes the month of deception, "breeding lilacs out of the dead land," tenuous intimations of life in "a heap of stony rubbish." In such a world certainty is sought in the ambiguous revelations of the medium Madame Sosostris, "known to be the wisest woman in Europe, / With a wicked pack of cards." She brings a series of sinister images—"the drowned Phoenician sailor," "Belladonna . . . The lady of situations," the Hanged Man—which will reappear in the course of the poem and which have in common a preoccupation with death under a variety of forms. This opening "movement" ends with a vision of the "Unreal City," where the crowds streaming each morning across London Bridge are seen as so many souls moving into Dante's Hell.

In the second section, *A Game of Chess*, the vision narrows to two sketches of vacancy and boredom in different "situations" of life. Both concern loveless "desire." A woman of leisure alternately addresses herself and her lover in tense staccato rhythms which answer to the emptiness and isolation stressed in an obsessive reiteration of the key word of the episode: "You know *nothing*? Do you see *nothing*? Do you remember / *Nothing*?" At this moment of rising tension a contrasting motif emerges in the form of an evocative echo from *The Tempest*: "Those are pearls that were his eyes." Two possible attitudes to death balance the sordid reality of "rat's alley" against the delicate beauty of Shakespeare's marine symbolism. A possible relationship between them may emerge by the end of the poem; but for the moment the sense of vacancy prevails in the return of the question "Are you alive or not? Is there nothing in your head?" and is underlined in a parallel episode by the gossip of two women in a working-class pub at the expense of a third who lives in fear of old age, unwanted children, and betrayal by her husband in search of "a good time" after demobilization. At the end of the "movement" the obsessive time-theme emerges in the final call of the barman—"Hurry up, please, it's time"—both as an urgent call to responsible choice and as an indication of the bleak reality which threatens to render it meaningless.

The third section, *The Fire Sermon*, is central to the entire conception. Against a background of the Thames, seen both in its commerce-stained modern aspect and in the more romantic light projected by the poets of the past, the pursuit of "desire" is embodied in the loveless seduction of a bored typist by "a small house agent's clerk." Seen through the eyes of a spectator, the blind seer Tiresias whose vision constitutes, as Eliot himself said, the substance of the poem, the episode marks the point at which its separate fragments begin to come together in a possible pattern. The Buddha and St. Augustine, representing ascetic tradition in East and West, are found to agree in presenting fire—the symbol of "desire"—as both consuming and purifying: "Burning burning burning burning / O Lord, thou pluckest me out." The first broken intimation of prayer prepares the way for as much positive resolution as the poem is prepared to offer.

After the short lyrical interlude *Death by Water*, which takes up a theme equivocally announced by Madame Sosostris and confirmed in the Shakespearean echo of *A Game of Chess*, the final "movement," *What the Thunder Said*, proposes a tentative ordering and recapitulation. Once more we are in the desert, the Waste Land; but the arid landscape is now associated with the Passion of Christ—the silence in the orchard, the red light on sweaty faces, the agony in stony places—and from it there emerges the vision (reality or illusion?) of the risen Saviour on the road to Emmaus. The dryness of the desert leads to a descent into delirium as the absent water—symbol of life and restoration—becomes an obsessive presence in the imagination of the suffering pilgrim.

The hoped for relief, however, does not come. The moment of vision is replaced by an impression, equally conceived in delirium, of general ruin. The "falling towers" of the great cities of the past—London, Rome, Athens, Jerusalem—are, like the city of *The Burial of the Dead*, "unreal," and the voices evocative of past beliefs which emerge from them sing "out of empty cisterns and exhausted wells." Yet once again, and at the culminating moment of delirium, the vision changes. The voice of the cock is heard, heralding the long-awaited break in the drought. As a "damp gust" promises rain for the parched soil, the thunder affirms as much positive vision as can be available to those who dwell in the Waste Land.

"Thus spoke the Thunder." Its message is conveyed in a triple Sanskrit exhortation: "Give, Sympathize, Control." The three words answer to a logical progression. What must be "given" is "The awful daring of a moment's surrender": acceptance of the risk involved in the commitment by which alone our lives may become more than empty memories preserved in blank obituaries. To "give," in turn, is to aspire to "sympathize," to relate our isolation to that of our fellow human beings imprisoned in the private worlds of their own experience. Those who have accepted the risk of commitment and projected it into sympathy may, according to the third and final admonition, aspire to exercise "control" over their lives. The "boat" which they steer may be expected to respond "gladly," in joyful affirmation, to the hand now—and only now—"expert with sail and oar."

We note, however, that this sketch of a possible release remains tentative. The "boat" *would have responded*: the statement remains conditional rather than directly affirmative. As the poem ends its shadowy protagonist sits on the shore, with the "arid plain" still in sight, though now behind him, tentatively surpassed. The picture of human endeavour is still dominated by collapse and ruin, but the hope has emerged that the lives of individuals may be redeemed by the effort to achieve such personal order as may be within our reach. "Shall I at least set my lands in order?" To this end the speaker has "shored" certain fragments of tradition against his "ruin": fragments which have been present through the poem in the form of "broken," disconnected images and which he may now aspire to relate positively to his developed experience. Though *The Waste Land* is not to be read as a poem of religious affirmation, it bears within itself implications of further progress.

—Derek A. Traversi

WATER THEM GERANIUMS.
Story by Henry Lawson, 1901.

Henry Lawson's Joe Wilson stories fit what is sometimes known as the "whole book" pattern, in that the same characters recur in them though the linking structure is loose. Joe Wilson, the protagonist in most of the stories, is also the narrator; his view of the bush differs radically from the familiar one in the art of the period, the 1890's. The painters of the Heidelberg School, sometimes known as the Australian Impressionists, portray a golden landscape, often with heroic solitary male figures silhouetted against an azure sky, and other writers for the *Bulletin* bestow a glamour and excitement on bush life which are significantly absent from Lawson's writing. His version of heroism is endurance, in a bleak and hostile landscape:

> It was a dreary, hopeless track. There was no horizon, nothing but the rough ashen trunks of the gnarled and stunted trees in all directions, little or no undergrowth, and the ground, save for the coarse, brownish tufts of dead grass, as bare as the road, for it was a dry season.

It is a setting defined by negatives, and this reflects its inhabitants, who are preoccupied by what it lacks: beauty, fertility, distinctive features. Many of the adjectives used for it could equally apply to humans ("hopeless," "gnarled and stunted," "dead") with the implication, borne out in the narrative, that the bush cripples those who try to make a living out of it.

Lawson's distinctive style echoes the sparseness of the setting; his advice to other writers was: "Cut out every word from your copy that you can possibly do without." "Water Them Geraniums" concerns the only neighbours Joe Wilson and his wife Mary have when they move to a new selection (piece of land) at Lahey's Creek. Mrs. Spicer works on her land with virtually no help from her husband and grown-up children, who are mostly absent; she struggles to bring up a large brood of small children, and dies, indirectly as a result of the humiliation of one of her sons being publicly charged with theft. Joe Wilson tells the story as if he were "yarning" with a mate; it opens with an incomplete sentence that sounds like part of an ongoing conversation: "The time Mary and I shifted out into the Bush from Gulgong to 'settle on the land' at Lahey's Creek." There is a persuasive authenticity about the narrator's voice, specifically a laconic understatement and an evasiveness about expressing human disasters directly; he does not describe Mrs. Spicer's corpse but comments: "she was past carin' right enough." After a day of terrible marital rows, backbreaking labour, and blighted prospects Joe remarks: "Somehow I didn't feel satisfied with the way things had gone." The apparently flat realism of the story is justified by the importance of domestic equipment in the bush; Joe's preoccupation with material objects is explicable in his circumstances and provides a stark picture of bush life for the uninitiated reader:

> Geraniums were the only flowers I saw grow in the drought out there. I remembered this woman had a few dirty grey-green leaves behind some sticks against the bark wall near the door . . . ashes were thrown there—with an idea of helping the flowers, I suppose; and greasy dish-water, when fresh water was scarce—till you might as well try to water a dish of fat.

The symbolic significance of this passage links Mrs. Spicer with other bushwomen in the story; her words in the title reveal an aspiration towards the impossible which kills her. The wife of the previous selector at Lahey's Creek had died, and Joe refers to the fact that, not long after Mrs. Spicer's death, "Mary lay, white and still." The framing for Mrs. Spicer's story is the Wilsons' arrival, and the reader is aware of how one story reflects the other. Mary makes Joe put on a collar and go for a Sunday walk in the bush, just as Mrs. Spicer clings to the fiction of having a garden. Mrs. Spicer comments that her husband used to be different, just as Joe thinks that he and Mary had once been sweethearts but had become strangers. Joe's comment, "What women some men are!" is profoundly ironic, in that the story reveals the volatility and selfishness of the men, and the sense and tenacity of the women, whose aspirations to maintaining a civilised life seem to be attempts to retain self-respect and to protect their children. They, unlike the men, are only "past carin'" when they are dead; it is the men in the story who drink to become oblivious to their situation, or steal, or disappear, while their womenfolk remain at home. The title of the first part, "A Lonely Track," is a comment on the lives of the bushwomen.

—Angela Smith

THE WATER-BABIES.
Novel by Charles Kingsley, 1863.

The survival of *The Water-Babies*, when so many other children's books have sunk into oblivion, is hard to explain. This rambling, inchoate allegory, apparently about purgatory (though Charles Kingsley as a staunch Protestant would not have relished this term) and salvation through water and natural history is one of the handful of Victorian children's classics whose title is known to the general reader. But after the opening chapters much of the text is incomprehensible to children. There are splenetic outbursts against objects of the author's dislike—"Measles, Monks, Scarlatina, Idols, Whooping-coughs, Popes, Wars, Peacemongers, Famines, Quacks, Unpaid bills, Tight stays, Potatoes, Bad wine, Despots, Demagogues" runs one list of "all the ills which flesh is heir to." There are allusions to scientific controversies of the moment, and private jokes such as the catalogues of words and objects (many of them archaic or obscure), presumably imitated from the Urquhart translation of Rabelais, so that even for a well-informed adult a gloss is necessary for full understanding. There is also much moralizing aimed at parents and teachers. Kingsley rides many hobby-horses up a complex maze of avenues, and such narrative as there is in the latter half of the book is constantly interrupted by digressions.

The opening chapter is however memorable. "Once upon a time there was a little chimney-sweep, and his name was Tom." One midsummer morning Tom and his master, Grimes, set out to sweep chimneys at Harthover Place. Tom loses his way in the tangle of flues and comes down in the bedroom of Ellie, the little daughter of the house, and is astounded by the white cleanliness of his surroundings. Then he catches sight of his own reflection, "a little ugly, black, ragged figure, with bleared eyes and grinning white teeth" and finds out for the first time that he is dirty. He flees in panic, pursued by the whole household, and runs 10 miles over the moors, until, exhausted and tormented by thirst, he scrambles down a thousand feet of rock face to a valley where he can see water. Though a kindly woman has pity on him and takes him in, he wanders in delirium to the stream, and there, to the ordinary eye, he drowns. But Kingsley tells us that though his body is buried in Vendale churchyard, he has really become a water-baby, cleansed of all his sooty former shell.

The second part of the book shows Tom among the water creatures. Kingsley, who felt passionately that "the great fairy Science, who is likely to be queen of all the fairies for many a year to come, can only do you good" (and indeed that a knowledge of the natural world was a way to salvation), describes underwater life with a scientist's accuracy, at the same time insisting that "no one has a right to say that no water-babies exist" and that it is only "children who read Aunt Agitate's Arguments, or Cousin Cramchild's Conversations; or lads who go to popular lectures" who would have such doubts. The learned professor who tells Ellie that there are no water-babies is punished by "a very terrible old fairy" who forces him to believe in all manner of fabulous creatures. Kingsley's message here is presumably that scientific knowledge should not exclude a sense of wonder, nor religious belief.

Tom at this stage, though outwardly clean, has not yet cast off the old Adam. He teases and torments the water-things, and has to be taken in hand by Mrs. Bedonebyasyoudid who achieves her ends by punishment (punishment being a theme which features largely in Victorian writing for the young), and by the milder Mrs. Doasyouwouldbedoneby whose method is love. Neither of these can make him wholly good, however, and he is handed over to Ellie, who after a fall on the rocks has been carried away by the fairies to be a water-baby herself. She teaches him much, but spiritual perfection and the complete union with Ellie (described as going home with Ellie on Sundays) which he desires can only apparently come from a quest to the Other-end-of-Nowhere. This final section of the book is the most disorganized of all, and memorable only for Kingsley's fable of the Tomtoddies, children who have been kept at their lessons by ambitious parents "till their brains grew big, and their bodies grew small, and they were all changed into turnips, with little but water inside." Tom reaches his destination, helps to rescue his old and now repentant master, Grimes, and is judged to have "won his spurs in the great battle" and to be fit for Ellie. At this point Kingsley has forgotten that he is dealing with the afterworld and that Tom's body lies in Vendale churchyard, for we are told that he becomes "a great man of science, and can plan railroads and steam-engines, and electric telegraphs and rifled guns."

"And what shall we learn from this parable?" Kingsley says, supposedly to his small son Grenville for whom it was written. The lengthy moral is hardly more clear than the narrative. It seems that one should be kind to newts who are really those water-babies who are stupid and dirty. "Meanwhile, do you learn your lessons, and thank God that you have plenty of cold water to wash in; and wash in it too, like a true Englishman. And then, if my story is not true, something better is; and if I am not quite right, still you will be, as long as you stick to hard work and cold water." Though it is a fairy tale it carries the same message as many a sermon in a public school chapel. *The Water-Babies* undeniably has some fine moments, but it lacks organization and is marred by self-indulgent ramblings. For those who are interested in the character of Kingsley, it is perhaps the novel in which he most clearly reveals himself.

—Gillian Avery

THE WAVES.
Novel by Virginia Woolf, 1931.

In her diary Virginia Woolf described *The Waves* as "my first work in my own style" although at the time of its publication in 1931 she was 49 and the widely acclaimed author of several novels, short stories, and essays. The most overtly experimental of Woolf's novels, its critical reception was initially mixed and today *The Waves* continues to inspire strong reaction, both positive and negative; the near total absence of plot in the novel led Ralph Freedman to describe it as "radically lyrical," Frank Kermode as "an intolerable bore." Recent criticism has begun to recognize a shift, not amounting to a breach, that in the 1930's moved Woolf toward more adventurous literary experimentation; *The Waves* may be seen as inaugerating the period of "late Woolf."

In style and format *The Waves* breaks with the conventions of novelistic verisimilitude more conspicuously than Woolf's previous fiction, being presented as a series of dramatic soliloquies spoken by six protagonists—three male (Louis, Bernard, Neville), three female (Jinny, Susan, Rhoda)—which in turn are separated into groups by several poetic, imagistic interludes tracking, from morning until night, the appearance and effects of the sun across an interior, a garden, and a seascape. As the interludes follow the progress and decline of a day, with the suggestion of cyclical time embodied in the sun's course, the soliloquies track their speakers from early childhood to middle age, suggesting a linear temporality; these larger narrative movements are echoed by recurring images of linearity and circularity scattered throughout the text, and both are related to its implicit and explicit preoccupation with narrativity as such. The problem of time is also related to the most important unifying theme of the soliloquies, their preoccupation with the premature death of the silent figure of Percival, a school friend beloved by all six soliloquists whose loss seems to cement their association as much as his presence had done.

Despite the emphatic and even stereotypical differentiation of the six voices, their common focus on Percival, as well as various imagistic and musical elements that play throughout the soliloquies, insinuate a deeper underlying identity, just as individual waves in the ocean emerge only to return again to a common oneness. Indeed, the contrast of articulation and merging, difference and identity, plays throughout the text at every level. To the extent that the narrative has any structured action, it consists in the periodic dispersal and reunion of the six friends at different stages of their lives, which is accompanied by the speakers' explicit reflection on their feelings of separation and identity. The interludes, meanwhile, emphasize alternately the differentiating effect of sunlight as it disperses shadow, and its power to fuse appearances in a dazzling glow; phonically, Woolf's text plays obsessively with sound effects that elide the difference between words. The play of antinomies is related, finally, to the structure of gender opposition that is at once advanced and undermined by the text, both in the symmetrical distribution of male and female speakers, the pointed asymmetry or inequality of the education received by males and females respectively, and the stereotypical terms in which their gender identity is sometimes lived. For this reason, as a study in intersubjectivity that contests the boundaries not only of the ego but also of gender itself, *The Waves* merges the radical experimentation of late Woolf with the more radical feminism explicitly embraced by Woolf in the text of *Three Guineas*.

The Waves has been described as Woolf's collective fictional biography of the Bloomsbury group, and specific parallels to members of that circle have been proposed: Neville, the homosexual aesthete, is likened to Lytton Strachey; Louis, the fastidious Australian, to T.S. Eliot (another "outlander," though more a satellite than a member of Bloomsbury); Susan, the archtypal earth mother, to Woolf's sister Vanessa Bell; and Percival to her much-beloved brother Thoby Stephen, an important catalyst of Bloomsbury who, like Percival, died in India at a tender age. As her diary attests, Woolf was interested in fictional and experimental biography, and an attempt to write the biography of a collective subject might reasonably follow from the more playful experiment of *Orlando*, the biography of a subject whose identity resides in its sexual instability. But the tie-in between Bloomsbury and *The Waves* is probably best made in more general and theoretical terms: like G.E. Moore's *Principia Ethica*, an important text for many "Bloomsberries," *The Waves* focuses on the importance of friendship rather than marriage or romance; its exploration of aesthetic principles, largely through the figures of Neville and the androgynous-minded writer Bernard (who is often taken as Woolf's privileged representative in the text) is informed by the theories of Roger Fry and Clive Bell, and the visual style of the interludes by the art of Vanessa Bell; while the complex, ambiguous intimacy and unconventional eroticism that characterizes relations between the six speakers is distinctly reminiscent of Bloomsbury.

—Elizabeth Hirsh

THE WAY OF ALL FLESH.
Novel by Samuel Butler, 1903.

When Samuel "Erewhon" Butler died in 1902, he left behind a novel he had begun in 1873 and fretted over until 1884. The disheveled manuscript bore the title *Ernest Pontifex; or, The Way of All Flesh. A Story of English Domestic Life*. Butler's literary executor tidied up the work and published it in 1903 as *The Way of All Flesh*. Sardonically autobiographical concerning the protagonist's relation to his parents, the novel meant to its first readers all that Butler could have hoped for—a genealogical narrative that knocked the stuffing out of Victorian morality. The satire pretends, through irony, to a disinterested realism from an ingenuous narrator, who gives in full letters from successive parents that are transparently hypocritical or obtuse. Except for the several levels of irony and the sayings of a leering Dickensian landlady, Mrs. Jupp, the style is as flat as a millstone.

Butler had published several books that rejected Darwinian "luck" in favour of evolutionary "cunning." Every creature, he argued, by unconscious memory does best what it learned to do within the bodies of its ancestors. Although Christianity is repeatedly thrashed in the novel, Butler's evolutionary theories are only passively present.

Old Mr. Pontifex improved the family's genes; successive generations alternately strengthened and impaired the line. Old Pontifex, a carpenter, was a self-taught artist and musician. He lived up to the meaning in Latin of his surname, bridge-builder. Later Pontifexes justified instead the connotation of pomposity. George, son of old Pontifex and his obstinate wife, was educated too rapidly by London relatives into an empty sophistication as a self-assured publisher of religious books. When his son Theobald expressed scruples against ordination as a clergyman, George threatened to cut him off until Theobald acquiesced. Theobald would have conceded when George again "shook his will" against marriage to Christina Allaby, but the Allabys had trapped the dull-witted Theobald.

Their son Ernest was baptized in water from the Jordan sponged up, after an accident, from the cellar floor. From birth to college, Ernest suffers parental oppression without reserve. Whenever Theobald's temper clouded, a rain of blows, verbal and physical, fell on little Ernest. The headmaster of Roughborough School, Dr. Skinner, a combination of Arnold of Rugby and Dickens's Pecksniff, continues the skinning of Ernest. When the servant Ellen is dismissed for pregnancy, Ernest gives her a watch bestowed by his aunt Alethaea; he is caught in a lie when Ellen pawns the watch locally, but he cannot even guess what his mother means by a suspected loss of purity.

Ernest, who was born as Butler was in 1835, went to Cambridge when Butler did. There, learning the dogmas needed to make a clergyman of him and reading "literary garbage" by Kingsley, Dickens, and others who taught respect for poverty, he encountered distasteful Evangelicals, post-Tractarian thieves who invest his money (from Alethaea) in a college of Spiritual Pathology, and, a true revelation to Ernest, the handsome, smoothly accomplished, irreligious, and amoral Townley. Ordained and eager to regenerate the Church, Ernest takes lodgings in Ashpit Place near Drury Lane. There he quickly discovers that Cambridge did not teach him how to counter the scepticism of a tinker who had read Robert Chambers's *Vestiges of the Natural History of Creation* and has not taught him how to tell a respectable young lady from a prostitute. His consequent error, when he determines to free himself from purity, results in his being sentenced, by a magistrate shocked that blameless parents and every effort to shield the boy from impurity have failed, to six months at hard labour.

Realism, subverted mostly by satiric irony in the early chapters, turns to parable in the encounters with the doubting tinker, the demure prostitute Miss Snow, and, when Miss Snow was busy with Townley, Miss Maitland, who flees flushed and trembling from Ernest into, by chance, a policeman. The later chapters, retaining realism of tone, pursue didactic fantasy. In a reversal of Victorian autobiography and fiction, Ernest undergoes a conversion from Christianity and determines never to see his parents again and to take no money from them. Butler himself had suffered the Prufrockian paralysis of detesting his father but not daring to abandon his inheritance. Ernest has the better fortune of being assured by his godfather, Edward Overton (our narrator), that Alethaea has left an allowance for him. By coincidence Ernest encounters Ellen; against the bachelor Overton's advice, he marries her. They open a shop and prosper until her drunkenness undoes them. By a coincidental discovery that she has been married before, Ernest at 26 is again free. There are two children, whom Ernest pays a bargeman at Gravesend one pound a week to raise lest they be miseducated as he was. When Ernest receives from Overton the full inheritance from Alethaea, he first experiences anew the insincerities of his family, then travels for a few years, and finally, with several Victorian illusions still to be deflated, he begins to write "semi-theological, semi-social" books and essays of the kind Butler had written.

—Carl Woodring

THE WAY OF THE WORLD.
Play by William Congreve, 1700.

When Thomas Betterton spoke the prologue to *The Way of the World* in March 1700, expressing the author's intention above all to please with this play written "with toil," he was surely fully aware of the hopes which had been placed in William Congreve's new play to revive his company's flagging fortunes. The play did not come up to expectations, however, contemporaries offering problems with the plot or the satire as reasons. When the play was later published for posterity, Congreve expressed astonishment at its success "for but little of it was prepared for . . . general taste." He thus neither admitted that he had tried to please, nor acknowledged the play's poor reception, although he implied that the play has the graces of those by Terence, where the "artful solution of the fable" was not, however, always appreciated by the "multitude."

Over the years the fable itself has come to be regarded as "famously incomprehensible"; certainly familial, emotional, and legal relationships, as well as motives and actions are withheld as much from the audience as from other characters. Additionally, modern critics have been disconcerted that the "artful solution" depends on a prior legal transaction, rather than being generated by the play's action or even being particularly consistent with the hero's personality. On the other hand, however, one might regard this legal transaction as consistently one among the many ploys which characters undertake to protect themselves or to gain advantage over others. For some a ploy's power fails when it is discovered, for others the ploy itself is the blackmail of threatened revelation; finally, for Mirabell, public knowledge is crucial to the ploy's efficacy.

Mirabell's early attempts to deceive Lady Wishfort and gain access to her niece Millamant come into the first category and, like all the characters, he perceives their dramatic nature. His sham addresses to the old lady have failed before the play begins because he is not much of an actor, despite her account in Act IV of his trances and tremblings, ardours and ecstasies, kneelings and risings. The new ploy, whereby Waitwell is to court her as "Sir Rowland" is "a matter of some mirth" in which Mirabell, now the actor / manager, can pretend to be injured while gaining a hold over his prospective aunt-in-law. The ploy fails when the acting stops and Mrs. Fainall (Lady Wishfort's daughter) speaks plainly to the maid Foible while the "audience," Mrs. Marwood (Fainall's current mistress), is still present, hidden in the closet. It is slowly and necessarily revealed, however, that Mirabell had "written" his play earlier, by marrying his former mistress to Fainall for whom she had then a "partial opinion and fondness," while himself retaining her estate in trust to ensure her liberty.

Almost Mirabell's equal in his power to devise, manage, and act in his own drama is this Fainall, but his plans are consistently undercut. In his affair with Mrs. Marwood he thinks he is in control while ignoring his wife's "advances" to Mirabell; but he is to discover that she has indeed been this rival's mistress. Equally, Mrs. Marwood's malice unintentionally foils his wish to benefit financially from his cousin-in-law, Millamant, making a disobedient match with Mirabell. His stratagems failing, he makes a crude attempt to blackmail Lady Wishfort with her daughter's earlier affair and then becomes a player in Mirabell's own drama by trying to make Sir Wilfull drunk and thus forestall the apparent engagement to Millamant. His strategic fallibility might render him ridiculous and pathetic, were it not for his savage language and the raw exposure of his scorn, jealousy, resentment, rage, and guilt concerning Mrs. Marwood.

Others are also players in Mirabell's drama. Lady Wishfort, with her varnished face, affected language, pious surroundings, and planned movements is an actress without a plot. Unwittingly, though, she plays in Mirabell's: as an earlier object of his feigned addresses and then of "Sir Rowland's" and finally as an abject petitioner of Mirabell to save herself from apparent ruin. Others knowingly act parts for Mirabell: Waitwell and Foible for a farm as their reward, Sir Wilfull (not a stupid bumpkin after all) with "compassion upon lovers" for "the gentleman loves her and she loves him, and they deserve one another."

Earlier manners comedy had also made use of the witty strategist's power to manipulate others, although Etherege, for instance, exposes Dorimant to embarrassing scenes he has not planned. By contrast Congreve does not manipulate the plot against the hero. Possibly this is because Mirabell is a more wholly admirable figure than Dorimant, and Congreve allows this more generous spirit to be endorsed by the play's action. This attractiveness is best seen in Mirabell's exchanges with Millamant and particularly in their famous "proviso" scene. Each has privately already admitted interest in the other; now, wary and vulnerable, each is anxious to provide against sources of matrimonial dislike. Millamant's concern is with her personal identity in marriage, Mirabell's with maintaining her naturalness. The optimism thus generated is prepared at the end to extend its spirit even to the guilty Fainall, whose restrictive and blackmailing provisos have been totally thwarted.

For the shameless Fainall his actions are but "the way of the world," although he would willingly retire to "another world" to live adulterously with Marwood on the spoils of robbery. If the world's moral sanctions are a hindrance to Fainall, the machinations of lovers are evidence of the "bad world" to Lady Wishfort. She has brought up her daughter in ignorance of this world, and herself wishes to retire as a shepherdess of fiction. For Mirabell and Millamant, however, the world is manageable, not by escaping or ignoring it, but by a clear-sighted, tolerant, and generous participation. In this respect therefore, even if not immediately popular, the play ought nevertheless to have been perceived as a more cogent answer to Collier's attack on the immorality of the stage than the explicit defence Congreve had written two years earlier.

—Barbara A. Murray

THE WEALTH OF NATIONS.
(*An Inquiry into the Nature and Causes of the Wealth of Nations.*)
Prose by Adam Smith (1723–90), 1776.

Edition

The Wealth of Nations, edited by R.H. Campbell and others. 2 vols., 1976.

Bibliography: *Smith: A Bibliographical Checklist of Critical Writings 1876–1950* by B. Franklin and F. Cordasco, 1950; *A Selected Bibliography of Significant Works about Smith* by Martha Bolar Lightwood, 1984.

Critical Studies: *Life of Smith* by John Rae, 1895; *Smith: Founder of the Science of Economics* by E.R. Pike, 1965; *The Individual in Society: Papers on Smith* by A.L. Macfie, 1967; *Essays on Smith* edited by Andrew S. Skinner and Thomas Wilson, 1975; *Smith* by R.H. Campbell, 1982; *Smith* by D. Raphael, 1985.

Adam Smith's *The Wealth of Nations* was not only the first systematic treatise on political economy, but it was also among the most influential. Smith addressed questions of political economy from an historical standpoint, attempting to trace the development of economic systems and uncover fundamental laws governing economic activity.

On his account, human societies pass through four discernible stages of development: hunting, nomadic pasturing, farming of fixed plots, and commercial exchange. At each stage in this development, societies devise institutions and practices suited to their needs. Smith thus treats laws of property, the magistracy, and forms of political organization as conditioned by the underlying economic conditions of the society; in this respect, he anticipated the Marxist conception of history and its typical base-superstructure model of society.

The principal task in *The Wealth of Nations* is to depict the workings of the economy in the commercial stage of society and thereby to show how wealth is created and distributed. Smith identified the division of labour as the key to the creation of wealth, noting that more can be produced per capita if the labour of production is divided among many. The hallmark of the commercial economy is the phenomenon of exchange; *The Wealth of Nations* proceeds with a two-sector model of the commercial economy in which agriculture and manufacture are the sources of wealth, and exchange of agricultural for manufactured goods (either by direct barter or through the medium of money) is the fundamental economic transaction.

In analyzing the exchanges in a commercial economy, Smith made recourse to a theory of human nature which he had developed in his 1759 work *The Theory of the Moral Sentiments*. There, he had depicted human actions as controlled by two contrary sets of basic motivations: selfish interests on the one side and "fellow feeling" or natural sympathy on the other. In *The Wealth of Nations*, exchanges are seen as motivated entirely by selfish interests, so that the desire for gain underlies all exchanges of goods. As Smith sums it up in a famous passage: "It is not from the benevolence of the butcher, the brewer, or the baker, that we expect our dinner, but from their regard to their own interest."

Although self-interested exchange is the foundation of the commercial economy, Smith argued that in the pursuit of their own interests, individuals would be led "as if by a hidden hand" to outcomes which they had not originally foreseen. Thus, a free exchange of commodities for money will lead to the establishment of a mutually agreeable rate of exchange which none of the agents could necessarily have predicted, and other aspects of a well-functioning market economy (such as production levels and the distribution of goods) will arise as unintended outcomes.

A large part of *The Wealth of Nations* is given over to Smith's critique of policies which would restrict the operation of the free market and diverge from pure *laissez faire* capitalism. In making his case, Smith considers the commercial society as composed of three "orders" or classes: landowners, manufacturers, and wage labourers. Each gains a specific kind of return from the exchanges in the economy (rent to the landholder, profit to the manufacturer, and wages to the labourer), and the question arises how to ensure that each gets his due. Smith insisted that any government regulation on the exchanges between the orders would institute a form of special privilege for one group against the others. On Smith's model, unrestrained competition among self-interested individuals will ensure that goods are priced at their "natural" levels, and *laissez faire* policies will result in the maximal production of wealth and its optimal distribution. Of course, Smith was aware that inequalities will arise from such a system, but he held that these were unavoidable and would be moderated by the force of our natural sympathy for the poverty of individuals.

The influence of Smith's *The Wealth of Nations* over the last two centuries can hardly be overstated. Such diverse figures as Karl Marx and Margaret Thatcher have borrowed from it, and its conception of economic activity as the outcome of rational agents concerned with maximizing their own gain remains fundamental to political economy. This is all the more remarkable in view of the fact that *The Wealth of Nations* was written before the advent of the large-scale industrial manufacture so characteristic of modern economies.

—Douglas M. Jesseph

THE WEDDING.
Story by V.S. Pritchett, 1975.

"The Wedding" is representative of V.S. Pritchett's best short stories. It displays the deft characterization, the incisively succinct storytelling, and the aptly quirky diction for which he is justly celebrated. As in most of his work, Pritchett's focus in "The Wedding" is on character development. His protagonists here are Tom Fletcher, 40, a wealthy, widowed, cattle farmer from a county family of 200 years standing, and Chris Tilly Jackson, 30 plus, a local girl of undistinguished background who, rebelling, had eloped with an aristocratic intellectual, then divorced, and has now returned to teach at a nearby college. Also typically, the plot is scant. All that really happens is that the two protagonists are somehow drawn together despite notably clashing personalities.

The key to Pritchett's characters, he writes elsewhere, is that they "live for projecting the fantasies of their inner, imaginative life." The protagonists of "The Wedding" are just such fantasy projectors. They conflict because their projected fantasies are antithetical. Fletcher adopts the persona, with which he characterizes his lifelong friend and neighbor, Ted: "nobbut a rough farmer's boy," and Mrs. Jackson assumes the role of a cool sophisticate and scholar, a role caricatured by her foil, her effetely intellectual fellow-teacher, Messel. Fletcher finds his entertainment in televised boxing; Mrs. Jackson hers in "looking for howlers" in the Latin inscriptions on ancient church walls.

Pritchett choreographs an alternating revulsion-attraction between these protagonists until, stimulated by the sensual excitement of the rites of a country wedding, they are inexorably attracted to each other. As comfortable as their fantasy selves have become, these must yield to their elementally human desire for personal and sexual intimacy. The story thus culminates ironically, but inevitably, in the joining—the wedding—of the characters' lives. Thematically, Pritchett casts a seriocomic eye on human pretensions in "The

Wedding" and shows that even the most dearly held cannot compete with the needs of the human animal.

In a strikingly economic opening dialogue between Fletcher and Ted, which at once characterizes and sets the plot in motion, Pritchett introduces Fletcher. We see him projecting the image of an outspoken anti-intellectual, a male chauvinist wallowing in the untrammeled masculinity of his country culture: "That's Mrs. Jackson, the little bitch from the College, Mary's teacher. I'd give ten pounds to anyone who'd take her up [Mt.] Scor on a Sunday afternoon and pull her tights down. Filling my girl with a lot of parlez-vous. What's the good of French? Bugger, you can't talk French to your Herefords, Ted." Fletcher's fantasy role also accommodates a deep-core selfishness: "She's putting ideas into my Mary's head. It was all poor Doris's doing, sending the girl to a snobby college like that and now they want to send her to Oxford. . . . I'll be alone in that house now, Ted, if I let Mary go. . . . I want my girl at home talking English. And doing the wages."

In Fletcher, however, Pritchett is not simply depicting a 20th-century Squire Western. Fletcher is an intelligent man who values intelligence. When Ted says, "I can't stand so much forehead in a woman," he replies: "It's the best part. . . . But you wouldn't know that." Sometimes the incongruity leads to a comic muddle of ideas: " 'She ran through twenty thousand pounds of her husband's money.' He swelled with satisfaction at the size of the sum and at the thought that a local girl could do that. 'She's got a brain.'" Fletcher seems a rough man who enjoys the local custom of lassoing women after weddings and even takes delight in their discomfort: "Us country lads like a bit of sport." Yet Pritchett also reveals Fletcher's authentic gentleness. He writes offhandedly: "on the way . . . he picked up a child that had fallen."

Chris Jackson is more open about her fantasy projection. She informs Messel that she "invented herself," as all girls do. Despite—or perhaps because—her roots, as the daughter of a drunken seedsman-taverner, are planted almost as deeply as Fletcher's in the crude local soil, she chooses to create for herself a role nearly the reverse of Fletcher's rough-hewn country boy. As Pritchett describes her, she projects a cool, intellectual, self-contained image: "Her fair hair was drawn straight back from her forehead into a bun at the back. . . . Her pretty voice was cooled by all the knowledge in her head. . . . She was pale as a bone and her humor was dry."

As a rebellious girl, Chris Tilly had "always wanted to be a duchess." When she eloped, she became that duchess imaginatively, descendant of a putative Comte de Tillet. Vandenesse painted an impressionistic portrait of her in that role and substantiated the fantasy.

Thus Pritchett sets up his antagonists. The battleground for their combat is Mary, Fletcher's daughter and Mrs. Jackson's student. She encourages Mary to pursue an academic career; he wants her to take care of his home and keep his books. But Mary also serves as the catalyst that brings the antagonists together, or rather the solvent that begins to cut through the habitual, though outgrown, fantasies that keep them at odds. Fletcher has an important insight when he thinks about Mary and his trophy cups: " 'My daughter's my business. . . . ' He looked around the room. 'Look at the state those cups are in. Old Mrs. Prosser comes in, but now Flo's [married and] gone, who will clean them?' Fletcher was himself startled by his own turn of mind." And Mrs. Jackson experiences a similar revelation during her conversation with the runaway Mary. Mary had broken with her father after watching him lasso her respected teacher at her sister's wedding. But though Mrs. Jackson did not react to the lassoing with laughter as the other women had, she found her response to Fletcher's rope on her body inexplicably ambiguous. And listening to the rebellious Mary, she suddenly withdraws her identification with her protégée and asks herself: "why have I got to relive my life?" This thought somehow releases her from the "years of self accusation." She makes a crucial decision and returns Mary to her father. Her concession deeply touches Fletcher. He keeps repeating: "You brought Mary home."

Still, projected fantasies die hard—even when no longer useful or appropriate. When Fletcher comes to claim her, Mrs. Jackson still "put on a prudish busy face . . . harsh and prim." Yet working on her underneath is an irresistible attraction: when she thought of him, she felt "all the strength running coldly out of her legs and then rushing back up her body and tossing in her heart."

In the end what Shaw terms the life force triumphs. Fletcher says: "You and me have got to do a deal. I want you over at the farm." His decision to court Mrs. Jackson is not based on Mary: "We'll do what you like about Mary." And it's not based on housekeeping: "I did [the trophy cups] myself this morning." It is rooted in Fletcher's primeval human need and desire to which Chris Jackson's own sensual humanity responds.

Pritchett says he was attracted to writing short stories especially because of their "intricacy of design." He completes the symmetry of "The Wedding," by giving the last word to the foils, Ted and Messel—the embodiments, perhaps the caricatures, of Tom and Chris's respective invented selves. Ted, "the simple country lad," just couldn't believe the match. He "denied it all until Tom had his house repainted and Mrs. Jackson left the college." But Messel is a more insightful character. Pritchett concludes the tale with Messel's interpretation of it. In his fey manner Messel underlines the symbolism of the Vandenesse portrait to express Pritchett's final statement about outgrowing projected fantasies: "Messel went about saying Vandenesse was a third-rate painter with a knack for catching girls inventing themselves but no good when they had turned thirty."

—Beth S. Neman

WHAT THE BUTLER SAW.
Play by Joe Orton, 1969.

Joe Orton's biographer, John Lahr, has described Orton as "the master farceur of his age" and there is little doubt that *What the Butler Saw* is the culmination of Orton's brief, meteoric career as a master of "serious farce." Unlike the clever commercial farce of such playwrights as Ray Cooney or Neil Simon, Orton's farce achieves a challenging intellectual dimension, and in *What the Butler Saw* Orton penned his masterpiece, tying his outrageous and zany humor to a compellingly satiric vision of human society in the 20th century.

The epigraph for *What the Butler Saw* comes from Cyril Tourneur's (or Thomas Middleton's) early 17th-century play, *The Revenger's Tragedy*, and provides a framework for Orton's fictive world: "Surely we're all mad people, and they / Whom we think are, are not." Orton's play takes place on a single day in the consulting room of Dr. Prentice's private psychiatric clinic, and the hospital serves as a metaphor for the world as Orton saw it. Dr. Rance, another psychiatrist, proclaims that "you can't be a rationalist in an irrational world. It isn't rational . . . "; later he consoles a patient by saying, "your mind has given way. You'll find the experience invaluable in your efforts to come to terms with 20th-century living." Orton's vision of the world is darkly pessimistic and critical, a product most likely of his own personal disfranchisement. His Leicester working-class roots, the consistent social rejection he felt until his literary success, and his homosexual lifestyle led Orton to feel that he was on the outside looking in at a world where all was not as it pretended to be. Orton's authority figures, like Drs. Prentice and Rank, are raging but shallow and incompetent megalomaniacs who capriciously tyrannize everyone they can, habitually abusing logic and language to satisfy their self-aggrandizing personal ends. Institutions fare no better, as they simply reflect short-sighted, illogical, and self-serving behavior on a larger scale. The constabulary, for example, is portrayed in *What the Butler Saw*, as in *Loot*, as ineffectual, if not counterproductive:

> Prentice: You imagine you'll be safe from acts of indecency in a police station?
> Geraldine: Of course.
> Prentice: I wish I shared your optimism.

There are few heroes in Orton's plays but plenty of incompetent and even vicious people who live to exploit others. In *What the Butler Saw*, Dr. Prentice's asylum becomes a symbolic maelstrom that engulfs and attempts to victimize the play's most sympathetic character, Geraldine Barclay.

The play begins with Geraldine coming from the Friendly Faces Employment Bureau to apply for her first job, a secretarial position with Dr. Prentice. Prentice tries immediately to seduce her, is interrupted by his equally lascivious wife, and then that interruption sets off a series of complications that pulls Geraldine deeper and deeper into Prentice's mad world. In order to hide his attempted seduction, Prentice allows Geraldine to be identified as a patient, undressed, certified as insane, and committed. Her head is shaved, she is dressed as a boy, and then she can't convince anyone of either her gender or her identity, finally being accused of complicity in murder.

Of course, as serious and potentially tragic as all of this sounds, it is carried out in the marvelously high spirits that typify the farcical genre. Mrs. Prentice's ill-timed entrance in the opening seduction scene galvanizes the play into other extravagant and bizarre plot complications that are driven by a breathlessly frenetic pace, innumerable surprises, and outrageous sight gags. But perhaps above all, with Orton, this farcical skill means extravagant and Wildean epigrammatic wit. The measure of Orton's genius lies predominantly in the way clever language can shock, even outrage, and at the same time suggest serious commentary: "Have you taken up transvestism? I'd no idea our marriage teetered on the edge of fashion." "Our marriage is like the peace of God—it passeth all understanding."

The apotheosis of this Ortonesque wit comes in a mock Euripedian / Wildean resolution, a reconciliation scene that brings together long-lost brothers, sisters, fathers, mothers, husbands, and wives as they all climb a rope ladder into a resplendent skylight. In this inflated image of transcendence, Orton satirizes the complacent and perhaps desperate modern illusions that would sweep serious conflict away and would find all well that can be construed as ending well. Dr. Prentice characterizes the day's events as a series of "peccadilloes" that can be overlooked by "keeping them out of the papers." But it was clear to Orton "how disturbing the questions of the mad can be. . . . No madman ever accepts madness. Only the sane do that."

Under the imprimatur of traditionally farcical character and action, the audience of *What the Butler Saw* is comically assaulted with what Maurice Charney calls "polymorphous perversity." Audiences are challenged to find humor in nearly all possibilities of deviant sexual behavior and even in the consistent allusiveness to the private parts of Winston Churchill. But behind Orton's deliberately shocking, grotesque, and even crude and vulgar humor lurks a keen social consciousness. The world seems mad? It is only a literary exaggeration. The proximity of the fictional to the real world is meant to be frightening.

—Terry Nienhuis

THE WHITE DEVIL.
Play by John Webster, 1612.

John Webster's *The White Devil* is, with his *The Duchess of Malfi*, one of the half-dozen outstanding Jacobean revenge tragedies. The genre, initiated by Thomas Kyd's *The Spanish Tragedy* (c. 1589), is best known from Shakespeare's *Hamlet* which, in Horatio's penultimate speech, concludes with a summary account of its characteristic elements: "carnal, bloody, and unnatural acts, / . . . accidental judgements, casual slaughters, / . . . deaths put on by cunning and forced cause, / . . . purposes mistook / Fall'n on th'inventors' heads." Gruesome they undoubtedly are, but in the best of these tragedies the grotesqueries are not an end in themselves. Since private revenge threatens so directly the foundations of civil society and poses inescapable moral questions (see Matthew 6 and 18 and Romans 13), its use as a plot motif leads inevitably to the interrogation of legal, political, and religious codes. Revenge tragedy hence frequently develops into a critique of society's constitutional and religious institutions, and can be radical in its implications. A note of alienated outrage at the way social hierarchies behave is struck immediately in *The White Devil* as Ludovico fulminates against the partisan exercise of political power by "men of princely rank": "Great men sell sheep, thus to be cut in pieces, / When first they have shorn them bare and sold their fleeces." The exchanges in this first scene leave no doubt that courts are places of profligacy, cupidity, and perversity. The ensuing horrors are representations of moral and social anarchy, of a pervasive cultural corruption.

The tendency of Jacobean dramas like *The White Devil* to be located in Italy may be understood as an expedient to gain for the dramatist the freedom to canvass disturbing and subversive ideas in his presentation of courts and their culture. Suggestions which would never have been tolerated if applied directly to the English court might legitimately be made of Roman Catholic Italy which Protestant and patriotic England regarded as the seat of the Great Whore, the Antichrist. It was, besides, the land of Machiavelli, whose thought, imperfectly understood, gave to English drama a distinct figure, the Machiavellian villain, master of ingenious and secretive plots, prepared to do anything to secure his ends. Flamineo in *The White Devil*, who rejoices in "the rare tricks of a Machiavillian," and who believes that "who knows policy and her true aspect / Shall find her ways winding and indirect," is an unusually complex example of the type. He clear-sightedly sees that "Knaves do grow great by being great men's apes"; he has a mordant, sometimes stoical, wit, and, though a plotter, is never a hypocrite. His amoral rejection of all obligations ("I am i'th' way to study a long silence— / To prate were idle. I remember nothing" is his parody of a dying confession) has a kind of impressive integrity about it.

And yet it would be absurd to talk of a character who prostitutes his sister, murders his brother, and drives his mother to madness as admirable. If revenge tragedy frequently develops into a critique of social institutions, equally often it is disorientating in its effect and import: how far is sympathy due to a character who, cruelly treated, perpetrates cruelties? The problematic nature of revenge tragedy in general, and of Webster in particular, provokes ambivalent, even contradictory, responses. This ambivalence most disturbingly surrounds the protagonist, Vittoria Corombona; witness the oxymoron of the title, which is repeated in different terms in the play: "Excellent devil"; "glorious strumpet." Vittoria, like the Duchess of Malfi (it is a singularity of Webster that he centres each of his great tragedies on a woman), finds herself the victim of a conspiracy perpetrated by the most influential agents of the state, representatives of the civil (Francisco de' Medici, Duke of Florence) and religious power (Cardinal Monticelso, afterwards Pope Paul IV). It is not possible to claim, as it is with the Duchess of Malfi, that Vittoria is guilty of no more than flouting social conventions: she is certainly an adulteress and seems to suggest and connive at, if not actually to be complicit in, the murder of her husband (I.ii.261–2). Justice and injustice become, however, confused categories in the great trial scene (III.ii). Far from being disinterested and impartial observers of the case, both Francisco and Monticelso act from self-interest and will in the very next scene (IV.i) themselves plot the murder of Vittoria's lover, Brachiano. Vittoria rightly admonishes the Cardinal, "If you be my accuser, / Pray cease to be my judge." Furthermore, the charges against Vittoria are presented with such misogynistic venom that their validity is called into question ("the cardinal's too bitter," observes an English onlooker). For her part, Vittoria refuses the submissive role of overawed suppliant or defenceless woman. She shows herself well able to turn the court's proceedings to her advantage and, with her "brave spirit," is both intellectually adroit and wittily acute in her retorts. From a feminist perspective, the trial scene tellingly presents the forces of patriarchy ranged to silence a woman whose exceptional ability threatens their hegemony. The effect is rather to vindicate Vittoria and to condemn her accusers than to confirm the verdict of guilty which is brought in: "your names / Of 'whore' and 'murderess,' they proceed from you, / As if a man should spit against the wind, / The filth returns in's face." When, at the conclusion of her trial, Vittoria cries out "A rape, a rape! / . . . you have ravished justice, / Forced her to do your pleasure," Monticelso exclaims, "Fie, she's mad," but there remains a disturbing sense in which Vittoria's defiant "Know . . . / Through darkness diamonds spread their richest light" answers to our experience of the play; hers is by far the brightest human spirit in it.

—N.H. Keeble

THE WHITSUN WEDDINGS.
Poem by Philip Larkin, 1964.

As the title poem of the book which many regard as Philip Larkin's best, "The Whitsun Weddings" is one of that handful of spacious, ambitious pieces—along with such poems as "Church Going," "The Building," or "Aubade"—on which his claim to major stature partly rests. Yet it has received less in the way of serious critical attention than one might expect, perhaps because of its apparent bias towards the descriptive and evocative. Larkin himself, in keeping with his Hardyesque principles, encouraged that illusion, saying anyone reading it aloud should go for "a level, even a plodding, descriptive note, until the mysterious last lines, when the poem should suddenly lift off the ground." In fact the supposedly neutral descriptive approach rapidly involves the poem in all kinds of issues from the social and political to the abstract and philosophical.

Larkin here is the semi-detached observer, trying to reach some sense of oneness with the objects of the world and with other people, but also aware of the ways in which that attempt doesn't fully succeed. The poem's totalizing impulse begins with images which stress space, amplitude, and distance, perceived literally at first from the train window but later apprehended in the imagination. "All" is a powerful word here as in much post-romantic poetry, charting the poet's attempt to break free from his isolated sensibility and grasp some sense of wholeness in an apparently fragmentary experience. But there is also a collectivising impulse, seeing things in categories: not only objects (houses, building-plots, poplars, shadows) but people too (porters, girls, fathers, mothers, couples). It is by contrast with these undifferentiated collective plurals that the poem's images of uniqueness and the unexpected make their impact. The shared experience of the train journey is not recognised as shared, except by the speaker, with his twin privileges of middle-class freedoms and the poet's detachment. And he is uneasy about the sharing: there may be some measure of affection in the almost painterly precision of his observation of others, such as the girls dressed in "lemons, mauves, and olive-ochres," but these and other phrases also emphasise a gulf in tastes and manners. And so the poem records the ambivalences of its attempts at social solidarity. Likewise in dealing with the repeated contrast between town and country the poem carefully subverts stock responses. This is most striking in the description of London's "postal districts packed like squares of wheat," an image which might suggest the city re-imagined to resemble the conventionally beautiful patchwork-quilt English landscape, but which might equally well summon up suggestions of manufactured breakfast food packed in a box, something processed rather than supposedly natural.

As in many a Hardy poem which appears merely to be "seeing" and "noticing" things, there turns out to be a sustained unobtrusive emphasis on the perceiving mind as partly constituting the reality which it thinks it sees. In talking of "a street / Of blinding windscreens," or calling the horizon the place "Where sky and Lincolnshire and water meet," the poem reveals how ordinary sensory experience is dependent on the location of the perceiving eye. Soon this relativism extends to the human and emotional world too, and as the poet sees "it all again in different terms," and "each face" in the wedding groups "seemed to define / Just what it saw departing," we come close to a solipsist vision. As the relatives watch the newly married couples depart on the train, what they see depends on who they are: "children frowned / At something dull; fathers had never known / Success so huge and wholly farcical." Always sceptical about weddings, Larkin stresses that a shared experience can also isolate. These distortions and contingencies are set within another distorting frame, for the poem announces itself with its opening words—"That Whitsun"—as an act of memory, and elsewhere emphasises the tunnel visions of the memory, as the objectivity of "Some fifty minutes" shrinks to "Just long enough to settle hats and say / *I nearly died*." Any naive confidence in the unproblematic nature of description or observation has long since been undermined. Doubts of a similar kind affect language itself. The high formal elaboration of the poem, with its perfect control of a very ambitious stanza form, is at odds with a tone which mostly tries to pass itself off as a self-effacing piece of ordinary speech. Larkin is hedging his bets: are we being offered something embarrassingly grand called "art," or something much more modest?

In all these ways, the poem registers characteristically 20th-century dilemmas and strains. But if it is modern in its problems, it turns to the past for its remedies. For the "lift" at the end of the poem, magnificently achieved through the mysterious images of the "sense of falling" and the "arrow-shower / Sent out of sight, somewhere becoming rain," finally emphasises the ability of the imagination to transcend the unreliable particularities and awkward encounters of the present, and to deal instead with what is not here and now. As the poet vests himself in the power of the romantic imagination, the journey of exploration is at an an end.

—R.J.C. Watt

WIDE SARGASSO SEA.
Novel by Jean Rhys, 1966.

Jean Rhys's *Wide Sargasso Sea*, a retelling of the story of *Jane Eyre* in order to supply the untold, silenced story of the first Mrs. Rochester, has become a classic of both feminist and postcolonial revisionings. Infuriated by Charlotte Brontë's racist portrayal of the Creole madwoman in the attic, Rhys emphasises her role as the legacy of imperialism concealed in the heart of every English gentleman's castle. Rechristening her "Antoinette," Rhys arranges her story in three parts, the first narrated by Antoinette, describing her childhood in Jamaica, the second by Rochester, describing their honeymoon, the third at Thornfield, narrated by Antoinette herself. The narrative method highlights the fact that Antoinette loses control of her story once married. Entry into the patriarchal order entails the silencing of woman, so that Rochester's becomes the master narrative, and Antoinette is subject to the tales and inventions of others. It is only at the very end, in rebellion, that she regains her voice.

In Part One, which provides Antoinette with a history, Rhys revises Brontë's tactics. Where Brontë makes Bertha and Jane antithetical, the one a barrier to the other's happiness, a dark alter ego of subconscious passion, Rhys gives Antoinette a background similar to Jane's: orphanhood, poverty, social humiliation, repressive religious schooling, and lack of love. The only real difference between the two women is their cultural position—one on the margins of Empire, one at the centre. Antoinette's personal history is also firmly politicised. As the offspring of a slave-owner in post-Emancipation Jamaica, she is detested by blacks as well as by more prosperous whites. She is also rejected by her mother. Imagistically, Rhys emphasises the weakness of the mother-daughter bond as not only fatal to Antoinette's sense of self (a view confirmed by modern psychoanalytic theory) but also as symbolic of the lack of sustenance and definition offered by the "Mother country" to its dependencies. *Wide Sargasso Sea*, a text born from *Jane Eyre*, is deliberately situated before most of the events of *Jane Eyre* occur, in order to reconstitute itself as the mother text or point of origin of the European novel. Reproduction and textual production are linked, so that *Wide Sargasso Sea*, a "prequel" to *Jane Eyre*, becomes its necessary precursor. By converting *Jane Eyre* into sequel, Rhys enjoins future readers to envisage Victorian Britain as dependent upon her colonies, just as Brontë's heroine depends upon a colonial inheritance and the obliteration of its colonial source.

Antoinette's history also becomes representative of West Indian history. In a society founded on the buying and selling of human beings, her marriage to Rochester is also envisaged as an economic transaction. Possessed for profit, given a more "English" name, transported overseas to become a captive, and treated as an animal and degenerate, Antoinette experiences slavery in her own person, and reacts, just as her father's former slaves did, by setting a torch to the Great House. Rochester's motivations reflect his engrained racial and sexual prejudices. In Part Two, honeymooning on a magic island, Rochester resents Antoinette's independent knowledge of her female-identified world and, like Prospero with Caliban, accuses her of sexual guilt and enslaves her. For Rochester, who espouses proto-Victorian views on the proper forms of female sexuality, only madwomen and prostitutes can enjoy sexual pleasure. Antoinette's failure to "lie back and think of England"—still less the Empire—is fatal to her. Rochester re-names her, silences her, and incarcerates her as a madwoman.

The ending of the novel has been much debated. For some readers Antoinette cannot escape the fate which Brontë has prepared for her and thus the novel is in essence an exercise in cultural determinism, "revising" Antoinette from malevolent lunatic only as far as passive, if innocent, victim. The novel ends, however, before the fire, which is presented only in internalised fashion, through Antoinette's dream. As readers we may choose to "finish her off" in Brontë's terms, or not. We may know, in intertextual terms, that her death lies just beyond the ending, but *Jane Eyre* "knew" many things which *Wide Sargasso Sea* questions. In her dream Antoinette sees herself jumping from the battlements back in time and space towards her black friend Tia, and her childhood home, also burned by former slaves. Her final action therefore aligns her with a female and West Indian world, and with a revolt against slavery. West Indian commentators have also noted the relation of the ending to the story of the Tribe Boys (suicide as defiance) and to the burning tree of life in pre-Columbian myth, by climbing which a defeated Caribbean people escaped from their enemies and were transmuted into sparks, and thence, as stars, into the sky. Antoinette's dream is therefore both a retaliation and a re-entry into a lost paradise and a lost West Indian point of origin. Phoenix-like she takes flight into the heaven of another culture.

—Judie Newman

WILD OATS.
Play by John O'Keeffe, 1791.

William Hazlitt may have called John O'Keeffe "the English Molière," but this Irish dramatist included more plot complexities and farce in his plays than 17th-century France would have accepted. *Wild Oats* characteristically mixes sentiment and good humour so that the audience is buoyed through the moralistic speeches and social comment by physical action, tricks, and comic ironies.

Like many of the melodramatists who followed him, O'Keeffe sympathized with the good-hearted poor. The cottager or soldier, threatened with loss of house or fiancée to the wealthy money lender or officer, was finally justly rewarded. Like the melodramatists, too, O'Keeffe was often topical. Peter the Great learned western ways in *The Czar Peter*, while a poor veteran of the American Revolution returned to claim his love in *The Poor Soldier*. The British navy and patriotism, Quakers, travelling actors, loss of contacts in the East Indies, and inheritance law are subjects in *Wild Oats*. Sir George Thunder has retired, but wants to see his old ship well crewed and pursues three deserters. His son, Harry, threatens to disgrace the family by disappearing from the academy at Portsmouth. Rover, trained as an actor in the Indies, has returned to England to seek his lost family. Sir George's niece, Lady Amaranth, has become a Quaker to secure an inheritance under terms of her cousin's will. All these characters meet on Lady Amaranth's Hampshire estate, where the villain, Farmer Gammon, is spitefully trying to dispossess poor Banks and his sister for debt because she has refused to marry him.

O'Keeffe manoeuvres his characters into intricately worked combinations, sometimes apparently by chance and sometimes by their careful design. Although we can see the basis for Hazlitt's comparison to Molière in O'Keeffe's treatment of the hypocritical Quaker steward, Ephraim Smooth, in the way evil is its own undoing, and in the morally earnest stance against self-seeking, we are also aware of a sentimental strain that is much closer to Steele and other 18th-century writers. In fact, the return after years in the East, the discovery of a long-lost child and sibling, and even the change of the father's name occurred earlier in Steele's *The Conscious Lovers*.

Much of O'Keeffe's popularity came from his numerous farces and afterpieces, and farce techniques are often combined with sentiment in the full-length comedies. In *Wild Oats* there are speedy plot twists, especially in mid-play, where Harry masterminds a fiction that Rover is Harry and Sir George is really an actor participating in a scheme to secure Lady Amaranth's fortune. Success at first turns on keeping people apart, then on keeping them off balance when they do meet.

There is speed in the last act, too, but it seems to stem more from the need to create tension and then resolve everything, than from a desire to create a farcical situation. The deserters appear, giving Rover a chance to protect Sir George and win his affection. These rogues then try to turn in Rover for a reward offered for robbers, thinking no one will defend the strolling player. Of course, in O'Keeffe's world the Banks family, whom Rover had helped earlier, and Sir George both attest Rover's innocence and the deserters are captured. The accusations are brought at Lady Amaranth's, where everyone comes together in the final reunion scene. There is little time for reflection as people rush about, and the deserter plot seems a needless luxuriance. There are enough evil forces in Gammon, Smooth, and various Sheriff's men to give Rover a chance to prove himself. Another way could have been found to bring Sir George to his niece's, or to let him demonstrate his patriotism. The rogues do place Rover in real danger and heighten tension, and also demonstrate a social problem that was probably quite common near any port.

A close examination of the plot reveal careful attention to details. An audience familiar with reunion plays would recognize that John Dory, the old boatswain, is preparing the denouement as he confides in the first act that he had provided a real chaplain years ago when Sir George wanted to pretend a wedding and take advantage of a young woman. Thunder's own repentance makes him worthy of the last-act reunion with Banks's sister, Amelia, and his affection for Rover and desire to adopt him is the last in a series of hints that Rover is the lost son. The travelling players and their production of *As You Like It* with local talent helps draw people together and reveal the flexibility of Lady Amaranth in contrast to the caricature Quaker, Smooth. Legality is also an important thread that brings people into contact in different combinations. Gammon uses the law against Banks. Smooth oversteps himself in administering the law. Amelia was legally married. As the oldest son, Rover will inherit, but he and Lady Amaranth have it in their power to settle money on Harry, the younger half-brother.

Even the choice of *As You Like It* adds resonance, for Orlando also was dispossessed but had a native nobility, and Rosalind fell in love with him as easily as Lady Amaranth does with Rover. Some of the casting for this ill-rehearsed performance provides additional humour, while Amaranth and Rover are suitable for the leads.

O'Keeffe often created speech patterns that reflected a person's background. The Quakers "thee's" and "thou's" are used consistently by Smooth and frequently by Lady Amaranth. John Dory and, to a lesser degree, Sir George speak a nautical jargon. Rover habitually and sometimes absurdly quotes from plays rather than speaking his own words. These quotations are a tour de force and suggest what plays O'Keeffe's audience were familiar with, from Shakespeare to Goldsmith. *Wild Oats* is often ebullient, and much of the spirit of the play comes from Rover's vigour and good heartedness, whether spouting lines as himself or pretending to be another. Although sentiment shapes the ending, humour suffuses much of the play.

—Frances A. Shirley

THE WIND IN THE WILLOWS.
Fiction by Kenneth Grahame, 1908.

"It matters very little whether or not Mr. Grahame writes any more," declared the *Academy* periodical in an 1897 profile of the author. "He has given us a book, a four-square piece of literature complete in itself." Which was the book? Not *The Wind in the Willows*, still in the unplanned future, but *The Golden Age*, a linked collection of semi-autobiographical childhood sketches, elegantly written, and for years, with its sequel *Dream Days*, a runaway bestseller.

When *The Wind in the Willows*, the long-awaited new Kenneth Grahame work, appeared at last in 1908, readers were baffled and disappointed. Several publishers, indeed, had (to their later sorrow) turned it down. Reviewers, with a very few exceptions, were not polite. The *Times Literary*

Supplement fretfully wrote it off as "a book with hardly a smile in it, through which we wander in a haze of perplexity, uninterested in the story itself and at a loss to understand the deeper purpose. . . . As a contribution to natural history the work is negligible." This was the tone of most of the critical notices. But Arnold Bennett voiced a different view. "The author may call his chief characters the Rat, the Mole, the Toad—they are human beings, and they are meant to be nothing but human beings. . . . The book is an urbane exercise at the expense of the English character and of mankind. . . . It is entirely successful."

Bennett may have been deliberately teasing, but his main points strike the truth. What perplexed the early critics was, quite simply, the animal cast. In fables, folk tales, nursery rhymes, verse satire, the age-old animal / human formula had its place. But a work of fiction, for adult as well as child reading, with contemporary references too (railways, motor cars)—that was another matter. It was certainly not a familiar device in the early century. (*The Jungle Book*, by contrast, has a human at its centre and the animals are essentially themselves.) But the doubts soon passed. *The Wind in the Willows* was, as Bennett had said, a human story—more close to Grahame himself than readers could have known. In any case the animal mask was essential, solving many practical problems. How else—especially if children were to read the tale—could it have been told? Transformed into humans, Rat and Mole would not have been children, out on holiday adventures, but leisured bachelor solitaries. As little woodland riverside creatures (which, for all their human concerns, they recognisably are) their time is their own; the age question vanishes. (Tolkien would later solve this problem by inventing his own creatures.)

The actual making of the book has been clearly charted. The first seeds were in the form of bedtime stories told by Grahame to his small son Alistair ("Mouse") who demanded tales "about moles, giraffes and water rats." Childlike himself, Grahame was later to prove a disastrous father to this boy. But he could readily make rapport with an eagerly listening four-year-old. Soon, the central place in the saga passed to another character "He's with Master Mouse, Madam, he's telling him some ditty or other about a Toad," the young Wiltshire maid explained to Mrs. Grahame. Immortal words! When the boy went with his governess to the seaside, Grahame sent further episodes by post. These documents the admirable Miss Stott preserved and presently returned. There the matter might have stayed had not a determined journalist, Constance Smedley, used flattery, energy, guile, and help to overcome Grahame's indolence. But as the writer in him rose to the surface, so did his interest in Rat and Mole, two aspects you could say, of himself. It is Rat and Mole who eventually dominate the book, and remain in the adult mind.

So much for the outward facts. But—however quickly written—most works of imagination have a deep inward history. Grahame did not write an autobiography, but no direct account could reveal more of his inward life than this curious fantasy. What is it about? Mole, creature of the sheltering earth, leaves his underground home on a fine spring morning, meets riverside Rat, creature of light and water, and they have adventures together, delightful, strange (in one visionary episode they glimpse the mighty Pan), briefly frightening (when lost in the Wild Wood), but ending in rescue and comfort. Feasting is frequent, often replacing plot. They unite to save the vain, preposterous Toad from his manic obsessions (notably the new invention the motor car)—and Toad's misadventures provide action-comedy for very young extroverts. But look again; there are undercurrents of fear and doubt, of visionary longings, failed ambitions, private nightmares, nostalgia for a pre-industrial past. Wild Wood and Wide World tempt, but are best avoided.

The Wind in the Willows remains in vigorous print. Indeed, if a single book were to be chosen to represent the English myth (prose fiction section)—in other words, Englishness—*The Wind in the Willows* has a strong chance of being that one. Yet how can this be? It is a badly shaped book for a start. The style is far from simple; it abounds in absorbed quotation, parody (Homer, *Lavengro*), and ornate descriptive passages. Its values are not merely "middle class" (a term of current opprobrium) but almost feudal: Badger is squire, hedgehogs are low indeed. Not a single female animal can be found, whether in Wild Wood or on river bank. There are, to be sure, two or three human females in the Toad story; they would be unthinkable, though, in any of the Rat / Mole episodes.

Yet the book has a persistent life of its own. Even the enigmatic undercurrents have a part in this: you return for a second or third reading. As for the pleasures, the freedom, the camaraderie, the loyalties, the wonders of discovery, the cosiness of a home in winter, the radiant summer—these are lasting in their appeal. There is something more. For a nation of obstinate dreamers, finding sustenance even in travel brochure and garden catalogue, the pastoral daydream lives on, through every social change. The river that runs reassuringly through the tale is no prop of fiction, nor is the woodland, nor the tunnelled earth. And in the animals themselves, fact and fantasy are brilliantly fused. Note that Grahame calls each by its generic name: Rat, Mole, Badger; that no other of its kind exists in the tale. Thus Rat, you would say, is the spirit of ratness; Mole, the spirit of moleness. For all their human tastes, they *have* this quality.

Animal Farm, *The Insect Play*, *Watership Down*, and legions of lesser works have given the animal / human genre an accepted place in literature. Is it farfetched to trace this back to Grahame? He did not see himself as an innovator and an original; it was not his intention to be either—but he could be accounted both.

—Naomi Lewis

THE WINDHOVER.
Poem by Gerard Manley Hopkins, written 1877.

In preparing for the Jesuit priesthood, Gerard Manley Hopkins was sent to St. Beuno's College in North Wales. During this period of his life he wrote some of his most lyrical poems under the inspiration of his religious training and experience and his study of the multiple alliterative patterns of the Welsh language called *cynghanedd* (note the word chimes and stresses). His poem "The Windhover" is the most famous; Hopkins himself thought it the best poem he had written which may be why in a later transcription he dedicated it "to Christ our Lord." Readers have confirmed his estimation, for hundreds of readings of the poem have been written.

The sonnet was written in the Italian eight / six mode. In the octet the speaker narrates his observation of the majestic flight of a kestrel (small falcon-hawk), called a "windhover" because in hunting its prey it can stop its flight by hovering into the wind to scan the ground. Finding nothing it will bank against the wind in smooth swoops or side-slip downwind again and then suddenly "stride" up against the wind to hover once more. The poet "caught" this bird's magnificent flight one morning; that is, in Hopkins's poetics, saw its essential being-energy enacted in its unique flight pattern. He was moved to characterize the falcon in terms of French medieval chivalry, a "dauphin" or crown prince of the "kingdom of daylight" hence "drawn" by the dappled dawning of the sun's rise. The poet fashions the bird as a marvelous rider controlling his horse as it bestrides the air beneath him, controlling its movement in the air as it hovers, swoops, pivots, and strides higher to hover in the wind again. The poet describes the falcon's flight in words such as "riding," "rolling," "striding," "rein," "swing," "sweeps," "hurl," "gliding," "rebuff." So majestic is the bird's flight to the poet "catcher," so revealing of its distinct "being-identity," he was moved ("heart / stirred") to feel the call to utter his own unique human selfness with a parallel sense of self-revelation, a masterly self-declaring achievement.

But the poet was about to become a priest-follower of Christ, an act that would alter his personality expressed through his human nature. How could he possess the bird's mastery in his actions as a Christian poet-priest? The poet saw the answer instantly through the primal consciousness of his epiphanic imagination: Christ's Incarnation was a divine act in which Christ co-inheres in all created things, and thus this little firey prince-falcon had "buckled" into its being the creative energy of Christ which it displayed in its magnificent flight. How could the poet utter a parallel "buckle" of Christ in himself?

In the first tercet of the sestet the poet calls for a charge of energy to be circuited from the chivalric Christ-bird into himself, "Brute beauty and valour and act, oh, air pride, plume, here / Buckle." Commentators have explored many meanings for "Buckle," the gist of all of them is connect, bind, transform (in the sense of "buckle under"). The verb can be read as both indicative and imperative. As a follower of Christ, the poet-priest's "mastery" is to offer his unique selfness to the greater glory of God in imitation of Christ's life—humility, obedience, and sacrifice. The poet says that if he lives in Christ's spirit this way, then it follows ("AND" which the poet capitalized to stress the hugeness of the consequence of such a "buckle") that the energy ("fire" as divine beauty and love) that will utterly "break from" his priestly self (flight) will be ever so much brighter, more beautiful, greatly powerful ("more dangerous"). In the joy of this understanding he exclaims Christ, "O my chevalier!" This is to say that Christ (figured in the falcon) is the true Dauphin-Knight of the universe "striding / High there."

In the last tercet, the poet explains his assertion by noting a deep mystery about living the Incarnation so faithfully: just as an old rusty plow shines itself and the earth it cuts in the plod of plowing ("sillion / Shine"), or when some embers in a dying fire fall from the grate revealing a small but bright effusion of heat and light ("Fall," "gall," and "gash"), so was the poverty, labor, and bitterness of the life of Jesus a terrible humbling "buckle," and yet the majesty of his nature and the brilliant light emanating from his sacrifice have shone regally in the world ever since ("gash gold-vermilion")—the divine minion of eternal morning.

This great religious sonnet is considered by many readers as the richest Christian poem written in the last 200 years. But it should be remarked that this poem is but one of a canon estimated by critics as the most significant religious poetry written since that of John Donne in the 17th century.

—David Anthony Downes

THE WINGS OF THE DOVE.
Novel by Henry James, 1902.

In *The Wings of the Dove* we are already in Henry James's last and most difficult phase, after *The Awkward Age* and *The Sacred Fount* and immediately before *The Ambassadors* and *The Golden Bowl*. The obscurity, elaboration, and subtlety of all these works are likely to leave permanent critical disagreement between those who find his greatest achievement in the simpler works of the 1880's and those who find the last phase the richest and the best. Some features of the earlier work remain, however. The international theme, the broad contrast between America and Europe, about which James had brooded for so long, takes here a form of surprisingly simple contrast. Milly Theale is at least as innocent and generous as any earlier American heroine, while Kate Croy, her father, Merton Densher, and Lord Mark are all in different ways corrupt representatives of England. On the other hand, Milly is entirely free from the ignorant brashness and Puritan-materialist crudity which the author had found in some of his earlier American groups. The difference is signalled by associating her closely with a picture in the National Gallery by Bronzino, a product and a type of the old, rich, aesthetic Europe to which one side of James responded so eagerly. If James may be thought naive in supposing that original sin had less grip on one side of the Atlantic than the other, it may be that the over-simplification is artistically justified by the dramatic interest it creates.

The complexities are woven into a stark and simple plot-fabric. Kate Croy supposes that the only way she can merge her incompatible aims, to be rich and to marry the poor man she loves, is to allow Merton Densher to marry the dying Milly and inherit her wealth. He weakly agrees, and, when the plot appears to succeed beyond expectation, since he obtains the money in Milly's will without marrying her, it is found after all to fail, because the cynicism required for its success has been undermined by Milly's generosity. The scene in which the diabolic pact is made, as Kate agrees to give herself sexually in return for his spiritual surrender to the plan to make use of Milly in loveless marriage, is characteristic of James in many ways. There is the shameful secret lurking under a civilized surface. The words used are so ordinary that they might have been overheard without giving the listener an inkling of their meaning:

> And if I do understand?
> I'll do everything.
> Well, I understand.
> On your honour?
> On my honour.
> You'll come?
> I'll come.

The words are spoken while an acquaintance is approaching across a crowded room to speak to them. The word "honour" has a fine and pervasive irony, yet cannot be called implausible as a word that might actually have been used. Most characteristic of all is the evasive language by which the sexual secret is given.

The book is not, however, told in clear tones of black and white. Milly may be wholly white, but the villainous pair are found to fall short of the villainy their scheme requires. They become more interesting as they find they have over-rated their own single-mindedness. Densher, confronted in his last Venetian interview with the dying Milly by the fact that she has been told by Lord Mark of the plot against her, finds himself unable to deny it; and, as he tells Kate later, if he had brought himself to deny it, he would have felt impelled to turn his false denial into a true one by refusing to marry Kate. Kate who felt, or imagined she would feel, no jealousy of the man she loved in the arms of another, is surprised to find herself jealous of the dead. It is a jealousy that strangely combines the sexual and the spiritual. Sexually Densher has not touched Milly, but Kate resents and fears the influence of her goodness, the power of Christian forgiveness that could repay such an injury with her money, and her implied blessing on the marriage which would make use of it.

So the book ends with what Oliver Elton finely called "a deep, resonant discord." Densher will marry Kate if she agrees to give up the money. The parting which follows includes a shared understanding that Milly's forgiveness has defeated and disarmed them.

The fine texture of James's late prose may be as well illustrated by the book's first sentence as by the last: "She waited, Kate Croy . . . " (in this case for the repellent father, who helps to prevent sympathy being altogether withdrawn from the daughter). This waiting is the symbolic attitude in which she remains throughout, until on the last page we see that she has been waiting for something that will never come.

Complaints that Milly herself is not fully realized in the reader's experience are perhaps beside the mark. The first part of the story is told mainly through Kate's consciousness, the second through Densher's. We are to know Milly indirectly through her gradually changing influence on each. The more barren, morally, the soil on which the seed of her generosity is sown, the more arresting is the crop. Moreover, James wrote in his preface that he had long thought of a certain sort of young American "as more the 'heir of all the ages' than any other young person." Her symbolic force may be increased by a certain degree of abstraction. Her wealth, her generosity, and her early death are the salient features which require little supporting detail. Her partial victory over greed and moral obtuseness is best shown in the feelings of the others.

—A.O.J. Cockshut

WINNIE-THE-POOH and **THE HOUSE AT POOH CORNER.**
Fiction by A.A. Milne, 1926 and 1928.

Any close criticism of A.A. Milne's children's stories is written under the shadow of Frederick Crews's *The Pooh Perplex*, that entertaining parody of a student casebook with its essays on such topics as "The Hierarchy of Heroism in *Winnie-the-Pooh*" and "A.A. Milne's Honey—Balloon—Pit —Gun—Tail—Bathtub complex"—the bath*tub* giving away their transatlantic origins. As Alison Lurie once put it, Crews managed "to stifle almost all critical comment on *Winnie-the-Pooh* for a decade."

The books are among the most famous of all children's stories, along with the *Alice* books, the Peter Rabbit stories, and *The Wind in the Willows*. The characters are not only instantly recognisable in Ernest Shepard's illustrations but can be used as a quick way of describing someone. A recent caption to a review in the New Zealand *Listener* called Philip Larkin "the Eeyore of English poetry." We all know people like Tigger, like Eeyore, like Kanga. We recognise them in ourselves. Critics disagree in reading them. John Rowe Townsend in *Written for Children* (1974), while realising "how very good they are," considered the stories "as totally without hidden significance as anything ever written," while Peter Hunt in *Writers for Children* (1988) decided they are "still the complex work of a complex man, and they include a fascinating series of subtexts that can tell us a lot about the relationships of child, adult, story, and book."

The first Winnie-the-Pooh story was written in December 1925 in response to a request to Milne from the *Evening News* to write a story for their Christmas number. Milne was asked as the famous author of the bestselling book of poems *When We Were Very Young*. He found it difficult to comply with the request. His wife suggested he should write down one of the bedtime stories he told his son—but Milne said they were "a completely contemptible mix-up." Nameless knights and indistinguishable princesses did the usual sort of things. There was just one story that was a bit different—a story about the child's own toy bear, who already possessed the odd name of Winnie-the-Pooh, though he would also go under the name, not only of Sanders, but of Edward Bear. (It was as Edward Bear or Teddy that he had made his first appearance in *When We Were Very Young*.) Milne's story about the bear and a balloon and some bees duly appeared in the *Evening News* and eventually became the first chapter of the book.

Winnie-the-Pooh and *The House at Pooh Corner* are episodic, with each chapter standing on its own. Milne started with a supporting, rather awkward, commentary with the author and his son intruding and commenting, but this is very soon abandoned. Unity is given by the fact that all the adventures take place in the forest, and, of course, by the central role played by Pooh himself. The other animals—Piglet, Eeyore, Rabbit, and Owl (the latter two both invented and not based on the boy's toys)—are all seen in relation to Pooh. They are joined by Kanga and Roo, and later, in the second book, by Tigger—toys specially purchased for the roles they could play in stories.

The small adventures, involving expeditions and birthdays, homes, food, and the weather, are well within the understanding of small pre-school listeners; but there is enough in the telling for the adult reader to enjoy the reading and to feel particularly the resonance of the ending of the second book, when the boy Christopher is beginning to grow up, to put away childish things, to be educated.

The books have always had their passionate devotees but also their detractors—one of the earliest of these being Dorothy Parker in the *New Yorker*. Milne came to hate the books and the word "whimsical" which was so often applied to them. The four children's books were written over a period of only five years, but they hung round Milne's neck like the proverbial albatross. It was only at the very end of his life that he could accept that it was Pooh who was immortal.

—Ann Thwaite

THE WINTER'S TALE.
Play by William Shakespeare, 1610(?).

The Winter's Tale, one of William Shakespeare's last plays, presents an intriguing challenge to traditional notions of drama. Written by early 1611, the play was first published in the 1623 First Folio in which it appears at the end of the comedies. It has been conjectured that the compositors of the First Folio were confused about whether the play was a comedy or a tragedy, as they were unsure about the genre of Shakespeare's other romances, dividing them between tragedy (*Cymbeline*), comedy (*The Tempest* first and *The Winter's Tale* last), and leaving *Pericles* out altogether. There is certainly a blend of comedy, even farce, with tragedy in *The Winter's Tale* along with a gorgeous pastiche of pastoralism and realism.

Shakespeare's chief source was Robert Greene's *Pandosto*, a popular novella that contained many elements of Greek romance. Along with the pastoral scenes, romances characteristically involve princesses of wondrous beauty and goodness, the disruption of royal life which is subsequently repaired, often through the revealing of true identities, and marvels of nature and the supernatural. Shakespeare appears to have purposely moved *The Winter's Tale* closer to Greek romance than his source, not only through the creation of a happy ending but by the addition of more romance motifs, especially those involving the infamous and non-existent sea coast of Bohemia at the center and turning point of the play (III. 3), and through his choice of Greek character names. Shakespeare's comic rogues usually carry English names regardless of their location; Autolycus in *The Winter's Tale* is an exception.

Yet tragedy occurs early in the play with the death of the innocent son, Mamillius, whose death coldly brings into question the possibilities of poetic justice. At the same time the play presents a formulaic comedy of young lovers, Perdita and Florizel, being thwarted by an older generation. *The Winter's Tale* offers an interesting twist to *Romeo and Juliet*, and unlike *Love's Labour's Lost*, which ends with a note of death and a song of winter, *The Winter's Tale* ends as a comedy should with spring and the restoration of life and family.

The play's title offers its own challenge. It is a comedy title like *A Midsummer Night's Dream*, *Measure for Measure*, and *Twelfth Night*, but rather than *A Winter's Tale* the title insists that it is *The Winter's Tale*. The concluding events of the play are "like an old tale" we are told three times, yet just before Hermione is accused of adultery by Leontes, she asks Mamillius for a merry tale. "A sad tale's best for winter," the boy replies; "I have one / of sprites and goblins. . . . There was a man . . . Dwelt by a churchyard." The tale is interrupted here, but this introduction foreshadows Leontes's fate and may suggest the winter's tale within the larger scope of the entire play.

The structure of *The Winter's Tale* has been called unorthodox, which Shakespeare seems to delight in. At several points he calls our attention to the nature of drama and, with some parallels to Prospero in *The Tempest*, Paulina acts as a director of the drama within the play. *The Winter's Tale* contains one of Shakespeare's most famous and fantastic stage directions, "Exit pursued by a bear," and the statue scene at the end of the play is perhaps the most spectacular in the Shakespearean canon.

The figure of Time appears as a chorus at the beginning of Act IV to introduce the scene in Bohemia 16 years after the events that open the play, and Time can be seen here as another director, similar to Paulina. Time claims the "power / To o'erthrow law, and in one self-born hour / To plant and o'erwhelm custom." This is in reference to the lack of adherence to the classical unity of time in drama, of having "dramatic" time closely follow "actual" time. Shakespeare was to conform to the unities of time, action, and place in his next play—and last solo work—*The Tempest*, but here he seems intentionally to refuse to conform.

In any case, this wide gap of time in *The Winter's Tale* has prompted critics to see the play as a two-part structure that hinges on the famous line of the old shepherd who finds the baby Perdita abandoned on the "beach" of Bohemia: "Now bless thyself: thou met'st with things dying, I with things new born" (III. iii. 109–110). The first part of the play, then, contains Leontes's jealous tyranny and innocent deaths; the second part consists of the reformation of Leontes and the restoration of Perdita and Hermione, along with the reconciliation and union of Sicily and Bohemia. The second part of the play reverses or even transforms the first part. Others have found a triptych structure, seeing the play as a kind of divine comedy or, as Louis Martz has observed, "a trilogy of redemption on the Aeschylean model," the parts following the literary modes of tragedy, pastoral, and miracle.

The play continues to challenge expectations. Paulina is rewarded with a husband at the end, a clear reversal of the usual pattern of old tales. Shakespeare downplays the recognition of Perdita—it happens offstage—in order to concentrate on the restoration of Hermione, and *The Winter's Tale* is Shakespeare's only play in which he does not take the audience into his confidence but uses surprise instead with the living statue of Hermione.

The Winter's Tale has generated numerous and conflicting critical views. It has been seen as a religious allegory or infused with religious symbolism; as following the myth of Proserpina or that of Pygmalion; as a political-historical allegory, a dialectic or struggle between court and country; a dialectic between art and nature; and the play has attracted psychoanalytic and feminist readings.

In the end, however, all critical views, all rational views at least, are overtly challenged. In disobedience to his father, Florizel proclaims that he is advised by his "fancy." "If my reason / Will thereto be obedient, I have reason; / If not, my senses, better pleased with madness, / Do bid it welcome." Later, when Paulina teases Leontes about the life-like "statue" of Hermione that "He'll think anon it lives," the transported Leontes gasps, "No settled senses of the world can match / The pleasure of that madness." We are left with visions of madness reminiscent of Theseus's lunatic, lover, and poet from *A Midsummer Night's Dream*, yet by the end of this romance, these kinds of madness offer more creativity, vitality, and love than the world of reason that opened the play.

Perhaps Shakespeare's greatest departure from Greene is through his different use of time. In *Pandosto*, which is subtitled "The Triumph of Time," time is a revealer. But in *The Winter's Tale*, time both destroys and restores. Indeed, the play deliberately defies time. This is the challenge of *The Winter's Tale*.

—James M. Dutcher

WODWO.
Poem by Ted Hughes, 1961.

"Wodwo," which first appeared in the 15 September 1961 issue of the *New Statesman* and subsequently became the title poem of a pivotal 1967 collection of Ted Hughes's work, figures forth a theme crucial to his entire oeuvre, namely, the nature of the self and its relation to the world. Hughes derives the name "wodwo" from the 14th-century alliterative romance *Sir Gawain and the Green Knight*, lines 720–724 of which serve as an epigraph to the *Wodwo* volume. The creatures with which Sir Gawain does battle in that passage include serpents, wolves, boars, giants, and "wodwos, that lived in the rocks." Just what status to impute to these wodwos remains a source of perplexity: where do they fall on the scale of existence? someplace between the animals and the giants? Hughes further complicates matters by having *his* wodwo partake of this confusion.

"What am I?" asks the wodwo, both speaker and protagonist in Hughes's poem. Not "who," but "what": identity is evidently being sought here on a plane more fundamental than that of personality. It is, in any case, difficult to define oneself as a person except in relation to an other, and the issue of where self leaves off and other begins is very much a puzzle for the wodwo:

> What am I to split
> The glassy grain of water looking upward I see the bed
> Of the river above me upside down very clear
> What am I doing here in mid-air?

Much of the time the world's axis appears seated on the speaker's shoulders—"I suppose I am the exact centre"—and selfhood co-terminous with his intentional horizon. Running through a forest till exhaustion halts him, he remarks: "that's touching one wall of me / for the moment." At other times a Cartesian gap opens between subject and object and the opaqueness of things troubles him: "Do these weeds / know me," he wonders, "do I fit in their world?" The wodwo's self-discovery and his exploration of otherness constitute, at bottom, a single process wherein he distinguishes himself from the environment to which he remains, all the same, connected. In lines 6–8, for instance, he simultaneously examines both himself and a curious object:

> Why do I find
> this frog so interesting as I inspect its most secret
> interior and make it my own?

As with all living things, the wodwo nourishes himself—quite literally here, it appears—on that which is alien to him. But his appropriations are, unlike those of lesser beings, acts of reflexive consciousness; in everything he experiences, he experiences himself.

The poet's description of his wodwo as "some sort of satyr or half-man or half-animal, . . . just a little larval being" seems unnecessarily denigrative. Admittedly, compared with the hawks, otters, and jaguars one finds elsewhere in Hughes's poetry, the wodwo cuts a rather poor figure. Neither is he prepossessing from the human standpoint—and yet the line of his development lies in that direction. Whatever their degree of splendor, the beasts are bound by instinct, whereas the wodwo is not. He presents himself as a being at once ruminative and restless, but in no wise belligerent like his namesake in *Sir Gawain* nor churlish in the manner of a Caliban. Incipient the wodwo may be, knowing very little, but already he possesses as a free gift—"I've no threads / fastening me to anything"—the sort of reflective intelligence that renders autonomy possible. Does existence precede essence in the case of this wodwo, seemingly "dropped / out of nothing casually," or has he "an owner" whose fingerprints one might somewhere detect on his creature? The poem offers no decisive answer to this question, although if one takes the last part of it to refer to a deity, then one has to say that there is no trace of the God of Jewish and Christian tradition. If, on the other hand, the wodwo's artistic creator is meant, then there are fingerprints enough.

The wodwo has sprung into being, like Adam, with verbal powers full-blown. Initially his interior monologue has the look of traditional verse: the first letters of lines and sentences are capitalized and syntactical units for the most part conventionally punctuated. As the poem progresses, however, punctuation marks grow increasingly sparse and capitals, except for an insistent "I," drop out altogether, the fluid language serving as a transparent medium for the speaker's quickening consciousness. It is, of course, the author who miraculously grants his wodwo the words that enable him to reflect and that confer upon him his freedom. In a companion poem to "Wodwo," "Full Moon and Little Frieda," Hughes's infant daughter, in one of her first utterances, names the moon, at which that orb recoils "like an artist gazing amazed at a work / That points at him amazed." The question is, finally, who has given the poet, himself every inch the awed seeker, *his* words.

—Richard K. Cross

THE WOMAN IN WHITE.
Novel by Wilkie Collins, 1860.

In its general outline and many of its details, Wilkie Collins's *The Woman in White* is a conventional melodramatic thriller. It has a midnight meeting with a mysterious woman, a prophetic dream, a Secret with a capital S, an assassin from a dreaded Italian brotherhood, and an "unseen Design" leading to "the unknown Retribution and the inevitable End." It has, in Laura Fairlie, beautiful prospective heiress of a handsome country estate, the appropriate suffering heroine, who is deprived of her identity and fortune by the combined villainy of Count Fosco and Sir Percival Glyde, and restored by the resolution and courage of the young drawing-master who loves her, Walter Hartright. The novel dramatizes the archetypal conflict between good and evil and ends, as especially its middle-class readers would wish, with the absolute triumph of the morally pure and socially responsible and productive. With little money and few friends, with no motive other than love and the desire for justice, Hartright perseveres in his seemingly "hopeless struggle against Rank and Power," the embodiment of heroic self-help, and is rewarded, paradoxically but satisfyingly, with a new life in the gentry class and a son who is, as the last page emphasizes, "the Heir of Limmeridge."

What distinguishes *The Woman in White* from most other examples of its type, making its weekly installments a social event when it first appeared and giving it classic status today, is the consummate skill with which Collins handles traditional materials and some significant innovations. The plot is original, complex, gripping, setting a new standard for Collins's contemporaries, several of whom borrowed its central device. Also original, as Collins asserts in his 1860 preface, is the mode of narration, a collection of manuscript narratives by individual characters, no one of whom knows the whole story. This device enabled Collins to create the excitement and apparent reality of courtroom testimony of first-hand experience, and to vary the novel's tone by employing an idiosyncratic style and perspective for each narrator. In moving from the earnestness of Hartright and Marian Halcombe to the ludicrous self-absorption and hypochondria of Frederick Fairlie, to the social correctness of Mrs. Michelson (who, in accordance with Christian principles, has "always cultivated a feeling of humane indulgence for foreigners"), to the witty, self-approving description by Count Fosco of his audacious crimes, Collins presents a rich and entertaining cast of characters and caricatures, two of whom are especially noteworthy. Masculine in appearance, critical of conventional feminine qualities and with the intelligence, courage, and directness her society usually ascribed to men, Marian Halcombe is an early version of the New Woman who is an important development in the literature of the 1860's. Far more than her relatively colorless half-sister, Laura Fairlie, Marian engages the reader's interest and admiration, just as she engages the affection of the perceptive Count Fosco. However, it is Fosco himself who, as the *Times* reviewer and others realized, is "the great character of the novel." A mass of contradictions and eccentricities, at once corpulent and dainty, sensitive and ruthless, lover of pet mice and destroyer of identities, Fosco simultaneously amuses us and challenges the foundations of morality and social order. Unlike the more conventionally villainous Sir Percival, limited in outlook and brutal in his methods, Fosco is a Napoleon of crime, an individual who, liberated by his superiority to the "narrow scruples" of ordinary men, "snaps his big fingers" at laws and conventions and effectively anatomizes the hypocrisies and failures of English society and its vaunted liberalism. Fosco is exciting and dangerous because combined with his intelligence and charm is the ability to articulate the reader's own social misgivings and impulses toward rebellion.

In the midst of their admiration for *The Woman in White*, some contemporary reviewers found its special features disturbing. In emphasizing plot rather than character development, the novel reversed the balance preferred by the prevailing aesthetic. In combining the traditional materials of melodrama with an emphasis on contemporaneity and circumstantiality, the novel blurred the conventional distinction between realistic fiction and romance. And in making Count Fosco so appealing, the novel blurred conventional moral responses as well. Collins had in fact created a controversial new form, the sensation novel, which was to dominate the popular fiction of the 1860's, with himself and Mary Elizabeth Braddon its acknowledged masters. When subsequent novels confirmed and developed the subversive qualities of *The Woman in White*, reviewers became increasingly hostile, attributing the popularity of the sensation novel to the tastelessness of an ill-educated middle-class readership. Modern commentators, with a taste for subversion but no higher opinion of Victorian readers, often criticize the ultimate conventionality of these novels as Collins's capitulation to middle-class morality. However, the audience for Collins's fiction in the 1860's was neither ill-informed nor wholly orthodox. Readers found in *The Woman in White* and its successors melodrama imbued with a new energy and sophistication, capable of expressing their own conflicting impulses by combining subversive techniques and ideas—about the nature of woman, about the hypocrisies and restrictions of propriety, about the instability of social identity—with the traditional satisfactions of a familiar form.

—Randolph Ivy

A WOMAN KILLED WITH KINDNESS.
Play by Thomas Heywood, 1603.

Thomas Heywood's *A Woman Killed with Kindness* is set in Yorkshire, far from the centre of political power; the main character, Master Frankford, is an unambitious country gentleman, and the melancholy events leading to the death of his wife, Anne, are personal matters. The play has regularly been classified as a domestic tragedy—the first English play to deal unsensationally with the private life of the family.

But although the plot may lack heroic stature, Heywood's characters are not of humble status. Frankford is "by my birth / Companion with a king." His wife's "birth / Is noble, and her education such / As might become the daughter of a prince." In the subplot, Sir Charles Mountford is proud of his family's 300-year-old gentility and property. Moreover, Frankford and Anne describe their plight in high scriptural terms ("I am as far from hoping such sweet grace / As Lucifer from Heaven"), giving theological dimension to what might otherwise seem no more than a sordid incident:

> As freely from the low depth of my soul
> As my Redeemer hath forgiven His death,
> I pardon thee.

The lively and bawdy by-play of the servants, together with sheriff's men, huntsmen, falconers, coachmen, carters, country wenches, and bumpkins, is a counterpoint to the tragedy and assures the audience that the central action has repercussions beyond the family life of the protagonists. The novel aspects of the play are in this way framed by traditional elements, including a highly conventional subplot.

Master Frankford and his wife Anne seem an ideal, loving couple, until his trusted friend Wendoll, despite his guilt-feelings and self-hatred, seduces her. Their adultery revealed, she expects—indeed would welcome—a barbarous revenge, but Frankford restrains his violent impulses and exiles her to his country house. She will have all the comforts she is used to, but no access to her husband and children. Unable to bear this lonely divorce, her remorse and regret lead to her death, after a last-minute reconciliation with her husband. In the subplot, Sir Francis Acton, Anne's brother, hounds his former friend, the unfortunate Sir Charles, into bankruptcy and imprisonment. Sir Charles and his sister Susan are universally scorned. After Sir Francis is smitten with lustful desires towards Susan and tempts her with renewed wealth, he is converted by her probity, legitimising his lusts and offering marriage. All friends again, they hasten to Anne's death-bed.

The potency of *A Woman Killed with Kindness* comes from the tension between its general conventionality and the vital moral issue that it seems almost to stumble across. The cheerfully festive wedding that opens the play, the racy escapades of the servants, the impassioned (if second-hand) rhetoric of the poverty-stricken Sir Charles all show Heywood as a consummate man of the theatre. The discovery scene, in which Frankford and his servant sneak into their own house, is an exciting and skilful piece of staging. A game of cards between Wendoll, Anne, and Frankford, replete with *double-entendres* and with the dynamics of the game matching the dynamics of the human triangle, is a masterly piece of writing. But nothing prepares the audience for the issue posed by Frankford's extraordinary decision. When he tells Anne of her exile, her first comment is, "A mild sentence." When he adds the proviso— "I charge thee never after this sad day / To see me . . . / Nor challenge any part in my two children" —she is speechless. A 20th-century audience, tutored by a different literary tradition and social environment, will notice the force of "*my* two children." Heywood's contemporaries may have realised more slowly how fatal this "kindness" is. The brilliant use of a stage property provides a key insight: Frankford, determined to rid himself of all signs of Anne, sends her lute after her. She plays a sad tune on it and then orders it destroyed (it is broken off-stage, no doubt because of theatrical frugality). The broken lute symbolises the broken marriage, the lost children, and the lack of order and meaning in her new life. In an existence defined by absence, Anne refuses to take food until she can regain presence—that of Christ:

> I never will nor smile, nor sleep, nor rest,
> But when my tears have wash'd my black soul white,
> Sweet Saviour, to Thy hands I yield my sprite.

But Anne's religious penance cannot restore her past content, and Frankford's "kindness" similarly destroys his own happiness—"in mere pity / Of thy weak state I'll wish to die with thee."

Frankford's cool decision, apparently undertaken as an act of mildness and humanity, is ultimately more destructive than any hot-tempered revenge.

Anne's betrayal of her husband—so sudden as to seem implausible to some critics—is ironically prepared for in the opening scene by a comparison with her impetuous brother:

> Your sister takes not after you, Sir Francis . . .
> [She] Hath to her dower her mother's modesty.

Her submissive behaviour is much praised. But events show that the same passionate nature drives brother and sister. Sir Francis's story follows the conventions of tragicomedy—his reformation wipes out his sins and his victims forget their sufferings; the woman he had tried to prostitute happily becomes his wife. Anne's story cannot be so neatly packaged. The dramatic conventions of adultery permit murderous wives (Alice Arden of Faversham), victims (Desdemona), or cheerful and unrepentant free-spirits (the merry wives of Windsor). The conventions have no way of showing the emptiness of lost love and the stumbles of human decency; Heywood's alternative must be worked out with original, painful, and moving realism.

—Richard Morton

WOMEN BEWARE WOMEN.
Play by Thomas Middleton, 1625–27(?).

The title of Thomas Middleton's *Women Beware Women* (the first noun is vocative, and the verb imperative) applies principally to the part played by Livia, a rich Florentine widow aged 39, in corrupting two younger women, Bianca and Isabella. Bianca, the daughter of a rich Venetian, has eloped with Leantio, a young man employed in Venice as a merchant's clerk, who has brought her to live secretly at his mother's house. While he is away at work the two women see the Duke of Florence pass by, and the Duke is taken with Bianca's beauty. One of his courtiers incites Livia, for their mutual benefit, to procure Bianca for the Duke, and, as Leantio's mother is on visiting terms with her, she easily has Bianca brought to her house, shown over it by the courtier, and presently seduced by the Duke in an upper room. Bianca, as the Duke's mistress, scorns her husband and his mother, while Livia, who now sees Leantio for the first time, persuades him to become her lover and share her wealth.

Meanwhile Livia's brother Hippolito is sexually attracted to their niece Isabella, who is innocently fond of him. When he reveals his passion she is horrified, but Livia makes her believe that she is illegitimate and not his blood-relation at all, and they thereupon become lovers. Isabella is to be married to a clownish young man, the ward of the Duke's courtier: she accepts him in order to screen her continuing affair with Hippolito.

Matters come to a crisis when the Duke's brother, a Cardinal, denounces his adultery and puts the fear of damnation into him; instead of giving up Bianca he resolves to have Leantio killed so that he can marry her, and therefore he tells Hippolito of Leantio's affair with Livia, with the result that Hippolito fights a duel with the young man and kills him. Livia, in her grief and rage, reveals to Isabella that the story of her illegitimacy was a lie, and to the Duke's courtier that his ward's new bride has been living in incest with her uncle. Revengeful feelings on all sides lead to a scene of general destruction at a wedding-masque for Bianca and the Duke, under cover of which Isabella, Hippolito, the Duke's courtier, and Livia are all killed. Bianca, likewise using the masque as an opportunity to give her enemy the Cardinal a poisoned cup, finds that the Duke has drunk from it instead, and in despair drains it herself. The Cardinal draws the moral: "Sin, what thou art these ruins show too piteously."

Middleton has contrived this sensational plot by combining two stories. The first is from Italian history. Bianca Cappello, like Webster's Vittoria Corombona, really existed: she became the mistress of Francesco de' Medici in 1564, in circumstances like those of the play, she and her husband having eloped from Venice in the previous year. Their story was told in fictional form by Celio Malespini in 1609, though it did not include the poisoning of the Duke in mistake for the Cardinal, which came from another source. The second story, of Isabella and Hippolito, closely follows an anonymous short novel of that name in French, published in 1597. In combining these stories Middleton made many changes to concentrate and unify the material, and the tragic wedding-masque—which Swinburne called "preposterous beyond extenuation"—is wholly his invention. Isabella, playing a nymph, poisons Livia, playing Juno, with incense, but not before Livia has thrown flaming gold upon her; the Duke's courtier falls through a trap-door on to spikes, and Hippolito is shot full of poisoned arrows by pages playing Cupids. The fact that the Duke repeatedly puzzles over the masque's deviations from its synopsis suggests that Middleton expected this denouement to provoke some laughter as well as horror: similar mingling can be found in his other plays, and in *The Revenger's Tragedy*, which may be his.

Theatrical irony of a subtler kind is found in the scene at Livia's house where she and Leantio's mother play at chess while Bianca is being delivered up to the Duke, Livia's comments on the game bearing a covert reference to the Duke's conquest, and in the scene where Hippolito dances with Isabella in order to show her off to her prospective husband.

The social world of the play is strongly presented, particularly in the scenes at Livia's house and at that of Leantio's mother, to whom Livia genially condescends; Bianca's radical change from an affectionate and grateful wife and daughter-in-law to a dissatisfied social upstart is also emphasised, and there is a sharp encounter between her and her husband when he too has changed, into a prosperous gigolo. Moral criticism is powerfully voiced in Middleton's characteristic generalizations: "Methinks it should strike earthquakes in adulterers, / When e'en the very sheets they commit sin in / May prove, for aught they know, all their last garments."

—T.W. Craik

WOMEN IN LOVE.
Novel by D.H. Lawrence, 1920.

Women in Love is generally considered to be D.H. Lawrence's masterpiece. It is an apocalyptic work that embodies the spirit of a civilization in decline. It covers a wider canvas than his earlier works, reflecting the social mobility that came about in England through education. The Brangwen girls Ursula and Gudrun connect different worlds ranging from Hermione's elegant country house to bohemian London, and finally they move beyond England to Europe. Lawrence's earlier novel on the Brangwens, *The Rainbow* (1915), was first conceived of as *The Sisters*, and material left over from it was developed into *Women in Love*. *The Rainbow*, which traces chronologically the history of three generations of the Brangwen family, ends with the emergence of Ursula Brangwen as an independent young woman confronting the modern world and believing that in it she will find fulfilment. Though Ursula's story links the two novels, *Women in Love* differs from *The Rainbow* in both the vision of the world that it presents and the way in which it is constructed. What had profoundly altered Lawrence's vision of the world was the the trauma of World War I.

The world of *Women in Love* is a world in dissolution. Lawrence does not actually refer to the war but the novel is imbued with the sense of anguish and unreality that the war had produced. The way in which it moved industrial society towards the abyss is expressed in the lives of the four central characters. Gudrun and Ursula, Gerald and Birkin, live in a fragmented world of the present, detached from their roots and constantly on the move. The structure of the novel expresses this. Instead of a series of relationships following on from each other, as in *The Rainbow*, there are two pairs of interlocked relationships round which the novel revolves. That of Birkin and Ursula ends in hope with a certain measure of promised fulfilment after a long and laborious discussion of the nature of love and of the problems inherent in human relationships. The movement of this pair is towards life and is essentially life-affirming. In contrast to this Gerald and Gudrun's relationship tends towards dissolution and death. The polarities of life and death are embodied in these two relationships, as the novel explores the complexity of the journey towards salvation or destruction.

At the beginning of the novel the Brangwen sisters talk about love and marriage. Their questions and uncertainties suggest at once that the world of the novel is an unsettled one, something borne out by the vast amount of argument and discussion that goes on throughout the book. Birkin, who is the most articulate of the characters, is a mouth-piece for Lawrence's ideas. He fears that the world has become too corrupt to be saved. One manifestation of this is that man has set his sights too exclusively on material gain. Industrialisation has produced a mechanised man dissociated from his roots and hollow at the core. His friend Gerald Crich is one such man. Gerald has mechanised his father's mine so that it runs with total, almost automatic, efficiency. His management delights the workers: "They were exalted by belonging to this great and superhuman system which was beyond feeling or reason, something really godlike." Gerald is the god of the machine. He is a hollow man like Conrad's Mr. Kurtz, his life embodying the process of dissolution.

Birkin, on the other hand, works out within his own consciousness and through discussions with Ursula and Gerald a position that will enable him to survive. He dissociates himself from what society has become in order to find a new way of living. One symbolic indication of this is that after he and Ursula have bought an attractive old chair in a street market they give it away because it would come to represent for them a continuity with the past. They detach themselves from the English social structure when they resign from their jobs.

In his essay "The Crown," which expressed his deepest feelings in the early years of the war, Lawrence explored the state of western civilization in a variety of images and concepts stemming from the basic opposition of the lion and the unicorn. In the conclusion he affirms that man's salvation is in relatedness and, correspondingly, that art is the revelation of such relatedness. The essay is interesting because of the way in which Lawrence built his thoughts about war into the essential dualistic framework underpinning his vision of life: "our great civilized form is broken," but there is "a whole new universe to grow up into" because "Destruction and Creation are the two relative opposites between opposing infinities." Restoration and salvation will come, he argues, from the tension between those "opposing infinities." Lawrence gave flesh to these ideas in *Women in Love*.

—Stella McNichol

THE WORLD.
Poem by Henry Vaughan, 1650.

"The World," first published in *Silex Scintillans; or, Sacred Poems and Private Ejaculations*, is one of Henry Vaughan's best-known poems. Striking in its imagery and rich in its allusive texture, it is both a "private ejaculation" and a subtle, publicly directed outcry against the triumphant Parliamentarians, who by 1650 had destroyed Vaughan's beloved Church of England.

Cast as a vision, it opens with one of Vaughan's most beautiful and evocative images: "I saw Eternity the other night / Like a great *Ring* of pure and endless light, / All calm, as it was bright." It then quickly proceeds to a lengthy consideration of "the world / And all her train," concentrating in turn on "The doting Lover," "The darksome States-man," "The fearfull miser," and "The down-right Epicure." It concludes with the speaker's denunciation of "fools" who "prefer dark night / Before true light" and a revelation, whispered by some unnamed but obviously divine or angelic exegete, that turns again to the opening image: "*This Ring the Bride-groome did for none provide / But for his Bride*."

Although its opening image has been much admired, some critics have seen "The World" as a failed poem, a work whose allegedly pedestrian middle does not live up to the inspired heights of its beginning and conclusion. But both directly and indirectly, Vaughan indicates that the poem exists not for the image of the ring of light alone. It contrasts the timebound and the eternal, darkness and light, the world of the here and now and the New Jerusalem to come. Thus, the mundane centre of the poem is functional and deliberate, providing the earthly perspective against which to measure the heavenly.

As with many of the poems in *Silex Scintillans*, "The World" is accompanied by a biblical epigraph that provides both a context for and a key to its interpretation, two verses from the Gospel of John that read: *All that is in the world, the lust of the flesh, the lust of the Eys, and the pride of life, is not of the father, but is of the world. And the world passeth away, and the lusts thereof, but he that doth the will of god abideth for ever.* As its title indicates, Vaughan's poem seeks, through its portraits of the worldly lover, statesman, miser, and epicure, to document concretely specific manifestations of the two varieties of lust and the pride condemned in the gospel passage. Like John's Gospel, "The World" contrasts these all too prevalent earth-centred failures with the unworldliness of the comparative few who, following the will of God, "weep and sing" and are thus allowed to soar "into the *Ring*" of eternity.

Added to the epigraph's direct statement of context and intent is the telling allusion, in the whispered final sentence of the poem, to another biblical passage: the wedding of the Lamb in the Book of Revelation. That marriage is conventionally interpreted as the union of Christ with the body of his true believers, who will constitute the inhabitants of the New Jerusalem. The allusion to Revelation underscores the perspective of the speaker in "The World." Like John of Patmos, he is vouchsafed a vision; and, like John, is provided with a supernatural teacher to explain the meaning of the symbolic image that he sees: only the faithful may expect to inherit eternity. The ring of eternity is the wedding ring of Christ and his church.

A key metaphor in the poem's conclusion is flight. The few "soar'd up into the *Ring*," while "most would use no wing." Although this passage has been interpreted as suggesting Predestination, it may also be interpreted in a less sectarian way: because they are in love with the world, most refuse to soar above it. The figure of the "wing" recalls the conclusion of "Easter Wings" by Vaughan's mentor, George Herbert. There, the speaker begs of Christ, "With thee / Let me combine, / And feel this day thy victorie: / For, if I imp my wing on thine, / Affliction shall advance the flight in me."

The vision expressed in "The World" may also be interpreted as a publicly directed outcry against the Parliamentary desecration of the Church of England in the 1640's. Like John of Patmos, Vaughan believed that the wicked had gained control of his world, and that they were persecuting those truly faithful to God. In *The Mount of Olives* of 1652 he enjoins his readers to exercise their religion privately "in these times of persecution and triall"; and he offers "A Prayer in time of persecution and Heresie" in which he indignantly and sorrowfully rehearses the disfigurement of the church by the Parliamentarians. Hence it is that in "The World," the faithful "weep" as well as sing. And hence it is that the "darksome States-man" is fed with "Churches and altars." "The World," like the Book of Revelation to which it alludes, is apocalyptic. Set in times and circumstances that their authors believe to be unregenerately wicked, both envision as the only possible solution to that prevalent wickedness a cataclysmic end to time and the world as mankind has experienced them and a shift—for the faithful few—into the eternity of the New Jerusalem.

—Ted-Larry Pebworth

THE WRECK OF THE DEUTSCHLAND.
Poem by Gerard Manley Hopkins, written 1875–76.

On 4 December 1875 a transatlantic steamship left Bremen in Germany carrying emigrants for New York. Driven off course by bad weather, the *Deutschland* foundered in the treacherous shoals of the outermost reaches of the Thames estuary. Rescue did not come for 30 hours, by which time many had drowned. "Five German nuns . . . Clasped hands and were drowned together, the chief sister, a gaunt woman 6 ft. high, calling out loudly and often 'O Christ, come quickly!' till the end came," as the *Times* reported.

These events occasioned the most ambitious of Gerard Manley Hopkins's completed poems and the first composition of his poetic maturity, written to break a self-imposed abstention which had lasted since he had joined the Jesuits seven years earlier. But they are not the poem's whole subject, for as Hopkins wrote, "The 'Deutschland' would be more generally interesting if there were more wreck and less discourse, I know, but still it is an ode and not primarily a narrative." The poem's business, in the true tradition of the ode, is that of lyrical meditation or reflection on a large issue.

Part the First of the poem says nothing of the shipwreck, instead dealing autobiographically with Hopkins's own relations with God and describing an unspecified spiritual experience which, though harrowing, was ultimately comforting. In emphasising that God is both destructive and merciful—"Thou art lightning and love, I found it, a winter and warm"—Hopkins sets forth the attitude which is to govern his response to the shipwreck too. Likewise the difficult passage from stanzas 6 to 8 though open to much theological debate about Duns Scotus's theory of the Incarnation, finally seems to stress God's perpetual presence in the world, something which the drowning nun will also call upon. In these respects the poem is a theodicy, attempting to justify God's ways. The attempt was pressing for Hopkins as a fervid patriot, for his co-religionists had been left to die by the people of his own country.

Death speaks the first words of Part the Second, for Hopkins does not intend it to have the last. The description of the shipwreck which follows offers scope for some of Hopkins's most exuberant linguistic effects. From stanza 17 the entire second half of the poem concerns itself either with the meaning of the tall nun's words and actions, or with the thoughts which they provoke in the poet. From him in turn "words break" forth, suggesting that both nun and poet are faintly echoing in their own way the all-creating Word of God. Just as the tall nun is praised for her power to "read" and "word" correctly the meaning concealed in the "unshapeable shock night" so too Hopkins reads and interprets, using words which denote signs, such as "cipher," "mark," "stigma," "signal," "token," "lettering." The poem is concerned with the construction of meaning; its subject is not so much the wreck as the meaning of the wreck; and that meaning is not waiting, fixed and unproblematic, within the story of the wreck, but has to be sought, and produced by interpretation.

Some controversy in recent years has centred on stanza 28, following Elisabeth W. Schneider's suggestion that Hopkins is here claiming a miracle, that Christ actually appeared on earth in response to the nun's cry. Rather it seems the latter part of the poem deals with fervent hopes and wishes, not with facts nor with claims about any particular actions of Christ. The significant verbs near the end are in the imperative, not the indicative: "Let him ride . . . in his triumph"; "Let him easter in us," expressing Hopkins's wish to see Christ reborn in people's hearts and actively ruling his kingdom there. But this and much else remains open to debate.

This was the poem in which Hopkins first put into practice his theories on Sprung Rhythm, the essence of which is to break free from the tyranny of "alternating" rhythm by counting stresses only and permitting any number of unstressed syllables in a line—as he put it, quoting from stanza 2, "why, if it is forcible in prose to say 'lashed: rod,' am I obliged to weaken this in verse, which ought to be stronger, not weaker, into 'lashed birch-rod' or something?" But the poem also deploys as many other radical techniques as he could cram in, such as *cynghanedd* (consonant-chime, following strict rules from Welsh models); an elaborate stanzaic pattern; rhymes which wrap across line-breaks; and syntax which is often muscle-bound. All of this leads to a verbal texture which is as intense, energetic, and rich as he could make it, even if the plain sense sometimes gets the worst of it.

"The Wreck of the Deutschland" is a decadent work in the sense that form and language, at least at first sight, seem to outweigh content and meaning. In the end, though, particularly in the more theological passages, the poem's meanings are far from simple, single, or easy. The paradox is that such an acutely aesthetic sensibility as Hopkins's was also wedded to the idea that there were indeed absolute meanings and supreme truths crying out to be expressed. Needless to say, it was all too much for contemporary taste. The poem was rejected for publication; like much of Hopkins's work it did not appear until 1918; and it did not attract wide attention until the rise of the New Critics, to whom it seemed modern rather than Victorian, and to whose moral and analytical assumptions it proved particularly apt.

—R.J.C. Watt

WULF AND EADWACER.
Poem, possibly mid-10th century.

Edition

The Anglo-Saxon Poetic Records, vol. 3, edited by G.P. Krapp and E. van K. Dobbie. 1936.

Critical Studies: *The Old English Elegies* edited by Martin Green, 1983; "*Wulf and Eadwacer*: The Adulterous Woman Reconsidered" by Dolores Warwick Frese, in *Religion and Literature*, Winter 1983; "*Wulf and Eadwacer*: A Passion Pent" by Stanley B. Greenfield, in *Anglo-Saxon England*, 15, 1986; "*Wulf and Eadwacer*: A Reinterpretation and Some Conjectures" by Seiichi Suzuki, in *Neuphilologische Mitteilungen*, vol. 88, no. 2, 1987; "*Wulf and Eadwacer*, *The Wife's Lament*, and Women's Love Lyrics in the Middle Ages" by Lois Bragg, in *Germanisch-Romanische Monatsschrift Grundzüge*, vol. 39, no. 3, 1989.

Wulf and Eadwacer stands with *The Wife's Lament* as the only surviving Anglo-Saxon poetry in the female voice. While the author is unknown, the passionate and personal tone, along with the rejection of social exigency in favor of emotional need, betrays a sensibility very different from that usually at work in secular writings of the period. Certain evidence suggests this sensibility might indeed be a woman's. Even so, the poem's significance rests upon more than the gender of the narrator, for its imagery and craftsmanship are among the finest in Old English literature.

The situation in *Wulf* is sufficiently vague for the poem once to have been considered the first of the riddles (which it directly precedes in the Exeter Book manuscript) and later a mere fragment. Now believed complete in itself, it might have existed within the context of one of the great heroic cycles, although which, if any, has never been satisfactorily established. To consider only what is related thus seems the safest approach. We know the speaker is unhappily married or otherwise attached to the brave warrior Eadwacer, but that she yearns for Wulf, a leader of men on another island toward whom her people bear murderous animosity. She has, in her despair, found some qualified comfort in Eadwacer's arms but has also found her connection to him "loath." Finally fallen ill from pining, she openly defies her husband and glories in her infidelity. Her closing comment casts her song in the elegiac mode as she mourns the impossibility of her love:

> þæt mon eaþe tosliteð   þaet nafre gesomnad waes,
> uncer giedd geador.
> (That man easily rends   which was never strongly joined,
> our song together.)

Linguistic difficulties permit disagreement even with this basic reading. Some critics, for example, see Wulf as the speaker's rightful husband and Eadwacer as her captor, but this strains against the image of Wulf as a lone, secretive wanderer. Occasionally, the repeated observation "willaþ hy hine aþecgan gif he on þreat cymed" is interpreted as her people's willingness to accept in times of danger a man otherwise exiled. This, too, seems unlikely as *aþecgan* means "to consume" or "to kill." The most interesting ambiguity lies in the final two lines, which describe equally well the woman's illicit passion not condoned by her tribe and her match to a man she does not love. But no point of contention affects the lyric import of the piece: anger at being denied emotional satisfaction by tribal taboos, desperation in grasping for a substitute, anguish in realizing the inefficacy of that course of action. Equations between the speaker's environment and her emotional state—the situation of herself and Wulf on different islands and her weeping alone in the rain—underscore her sense of isolation and grief.

The emphasis on personal emotion to the denegation of communal opinion, unusual in Anglo-Saxon poetry, led Kemp Malone to posit a relationship between *Wulf and Eadwacer* (and its sister elegy) and the European *frauenlieder*, "songs put in the mouths of women who gave free utterance to the feelings of their hearts" ("Two Old English

Frauenlieder," *Old English Literature*, 1963). More recently, Jane Chance observed that the speakers of both poems "ironically" cast themselves as *scopa* (the archetype eminently social and heroic) to sing their failures as "peace-weavers" for their people (*Woman as Hero in Old English Literature*, 1986). Both theories are revealing, yet Malone's ignores the cultural significance of these verses and Chance's the anger and defiance which seemingly preclude a sense of shame. The speaker of *Wulf* consciously detaches herself from her tribe with the refrain "ungelic is us," "it is different with us," an assertion enhanced by the island imagery and Wulf's far roaming. Further, it foreshadows her antisocial denial of the significance of her attachment to Eadwacer:

> Gehyrest þu Eadwacer? Uncearne earne hwelp
> bireþ Wulf to wuda.
> þæt mon eaþe tosliteð þaet nafre gesomnad waes
> (Do you hear, Eadwacer? Our wretched whelp Wulf
> bears to the woods.
> That man easily rends which was never strongly joined)

What seems to underlie the poem, then, is a challenge to social paradigms subordinating the individual to the community and a rejection of the arranged matches spawned thereby. The persona of *scop* is thus doubly ironic, for the singer of truth offers a song of wisdom (*giedd*) which denies the validity of the cultural constructs which gave him (her) being.

Due perhaps to its ambiguity, perhaps to its departures from mainstream poetry in tone and formal matters, the elegy's artistry is much underrated. Lyrical and introspective, *Wulf* contains some intricate imagery. Its finest metaphor comes in the equation of *Wulf* the lover to Wulf (*wulf*) the predator. While Eadwacer, the approved mate, is firmly entrenched with the tribe, Wulf "wanders wide"; he visits "seldom," secretly; and he carries the "whelp" conceived with his lover "to the woods," recalling his namesake's rapacious behavior. Yet, typical of the poem's ironic reversals, the wolf becomes the prey. The choice of *aþecgan*, with its connotation of devouring, to describe his enemies' intentions extends the conceit and is, moreover, echoed in the narrator's assertion that her sickness results from Wulf's absence, "not lack of food."

Wulf's formal sophistication is striking. It not only fulfills alliterative and stress requirements but evinces a sensitivity to prosodic density, which reflects emotional movements and, together with the unusual refrains and the unpaired half-lines so troubling to earlier critics, imparts a stanzaic organization clearer than that usually conceded the work. The opening establishes social animosity toward Wulf in two long, smooth lines and the "otherness" of the lovers in the abrupt partial line "ungelic is us." Lines 4–8 define the lovers' unwanted separation and link it to that animosity, ending with the same short refrain. The speaker's emotional history follows, moving into a declaration of present love with the brief "Wulf, my Wulf!" The hard, vowel-alliterated line 16 begins her defiant scream at Eadwacer, concluded in the next (unmatched) half-line. The final one-and-a-half lines contain a gnomic generalization and its application to the lovers' predicament.

This peculiar elegy—compact, elusive, intricate—suggests that the individual's desires were not always subordinated to the common consensus in the Anglo-Saxon shame culture. Since *The Wife's Lament* mirrors *Wulf and Eadwacer*'s thematic structure and embodies similarly raw emotion, it may well be that the two feminine elegies represent an Old English tradition of woman's poetry, akin to *frauenlieder* but with a powerful cultural relevance missing from the continental genre. For, these sister elegies contain not so much laments of failed peace-weavers but protests against that social role, which made emotional satisfaction unattainable.

—Gwendolyn Morgan

WUTHERING HEIGHTS.
Novel by Emily Brontë, 1847.

Mr. Lockwood, a conventional young gentleman who has retired to rural Yorkshire because he feels disgusted with society, calls on his nearest neighbor at Wuthering Heights. He is appalled by the naked hatred and violence he finds in the household, which includes Heathcliff, the morose owner; Hareton Earnshaw, a boor who appears like a servant but does not act like one; and Catherine Linton Heathcliff, whose beauty and gentility do not accord with her sour, intimidated manner. Lockwood gets their history from Nelly Dean, who has served the family from childhood. Thus opens Emily Brontë's *Wuthering Heights*.

The story concerns the passionate relationships among the Earnshaws of windswept Wuthering Heights, the Lintons of sheltered Thrushcross Grange, and Heathcliff, an adopted child whom old Mr. Earnshaw picked up in the slums of Liverpool. By telling it through Lockwood and Nelly, who are normal, everyday people, Brontë gains credibility for the extravagant emotions of her major actors. Secondly, the continuity of the two narrators holds together a story that involves two generations. Most important, filtering the events through these narrators' minds conditions the reader's responses. Lockwood's comically inept attempts to make sense of the situation at the Heights suggests the inadequacy of conventional attitudes to deal with extraordinary experience. Nelly Dean, who knows the setting and the people, interprets them with more understanding and thus predisposes the reader to sympathize with, if not accept, their extreme passions.

The story centers on the love of Heathcliff and Catherine Earnshaw, whose devotion creates a childish Eden for them even in the harsh environment of Wuthering Heights. But when her elder brother, Hindley, degrades Heathcliff into a boor, and Catherine sees the attractive cultivated life at Thrushcross Grange, she makes the fatal mistake of marrying Edgar Linton—fatal because she is rejecting the man with whom she can be herself for one who will, gently but inexorably, require her to suppress herself. When Heathcliff reappears, having acquired money and a gentleman's education, and Edgar insists that she choose between them, she falls into a brain fever and, shortly after, dies giving birth to a daughter, Cathy. Heathcliff revenges himself by marrying Edgar's sister, Isabella, whom he despises, by encouraging Hindley to destroy himself through drink, and by raising Hindley's son, Hareton, as a farm hand. When the book opens, Heathcliff controls both the Grange and the Heights and has reduced the proper heirs to a cowed vixen and an illiterate boor. Ten months later, however, when Lockwood revisits the area, the evil has worked its way out: Heathcliff has rejoined Catherine in death, freeing Hareton and the younger Cathy to reclaim their good qualities and fall in love.

In the beginning of *Wuthering Heights*, Lockwood is trapped by a life-threatening snowstorm; at the end, he watches moths fluttering among the hare-bells under a benign sky. The repeating cycle of Nature confirms the restoration of harmony in the social world and the ability of gentle things to endure as well as harsh ones. For there are no sharp distinctions in this novel between human and non-human nature. The "gaunt" thorn trees by Wuthering Heights are bent by the wind so they seem to be stretching their limbs "as if craving alms of the sun"; and Heathcliff, planning to brutalize Hareton as he had been brutalized, gloats: "We'll see if one tree won't grow as crooked as another, with the same wind to twist it!" Catherine cannot breathe at the Grange and cries for the bracing air of the Heights; her gentler daughter's idea of paradise is a world animated by the west wind, all rustling leaves and "great swells of grass undulating in waves to the breeze." Brontë's vision of the unity of Nature generates evocative metaphors that mark *Wuthering Heights* as a poet's book; so does her superbly lyrical language at emotional high points, such as Nelly's description of the dead Catherine (chapter 16).

According to David Cecil's brilliant interpretation (*Early Victorian Novelists*, 1934), Brontë saw the entire universe—animate and inanimate, mental and physical—as the expression of two spiritual principles: storm and calm. Storm is strong and dynamic, harsh and ruthless; calm is gentle and merciful, timid and passive. Heathcliff and the Earnshaws are forceful, realistic, capable of intense love and hate; the Lintons are non-violent, sentimental, mild, law-abiding, and considerate. Ideally, the two principles work in harmony; but if they are blocked, they become destructive. When Catherine and Heathcliff are separated by class distinction—that is, are prevented from following the course that their nature dictates—she dies and he wrecks everyone around him. Cecil compares him to a river that normally brings life-giving water, but floods the countryside if its natural course is blocked. Hareton and the younger Cathy, each the child of one stormy and one calm parent, are better balanced than the older generation and can form a stable union. In the two generations, Brontë displays the grandeur of Romantic passion—single-minded, uncompromising, capable of unlimited empathy, impervious to worldly considerations—and at the same time criticizes it. The love of Hareton and Cathy is domestic rather than sublime, and it is not expressed with overwhelming imaginative force like the earlier love; but it is kind and considerate, it reflects a mature capacity to adjust to circumstances, and it will be able to survive in civilized adult society.

Catherine's marriage to Edgar Linton was a conventional romantic match, based on his good looks, pleasantness, and infatuation with her. It is superficial and inadequate because the two do not share the same feelings or understand each other. Since Edgar does not truly know Catherine, he cannot meet her needs; and she assumes a false self to meet his expectations. Heathcliff, in contrast, knows and loves what she is; and their union figures an undivided personality, true to itself. Sandra Gilbert and Susan Gubar interpret Catherine's self-betrayal in social terms (*The Madwoman in the Attic*, 1979). With Heathcliff, she had been "half-savage and hardy, and free" (chapter 12); married to Edgar, she must dwindle into the lady of Thrushcross Grange—decorous, delicate, and restricted. The joyous energy of her girlhood yields to periods of depression after her marriage and finally, when she fully recognizes what she has done to herself, to alienation and death.

However, Brontë did not so much rebel against the traditional feminine role as she ignored conventional gender definitions. Her distinction between strong, stormy characters and passive, mild ones cuts right across sex lines: the older Catherine's fearlessness is not unfeminine, nor is Edgar's gentleness unmasculine. Conventional definitions of right and wrong are similarly ignored. Strong natures turn destructive when they are twisted from their proper development, and so do mild ones: after a few weeks of marriage to Heathcliff, sweet, refined Isabella Linton greedily eyes a deadly weapon. The Lintons are models of conventional goodness, yet this does not give them higher moral value than the passionate characters. Isabella is incapable of sadism, but she is attracted to it, as we see when she elopes with Heathcliff after he has hanged her dog. Edgar's attitude toward Heathcliff proves Nelly's claim that, "We *must* be for ourselves in the long run; the mild and generous are only more justly selfish than the domineering" (chapter 10). People have different natures and must be accepted for what they are—as, in general, Nelly accepts them. Brontë's poetic vision includes on equal terms all manifestations of Nature—storm and calm, violence and orderliness, female and male, human and non-human, dream and external reality, life and death.

—Katharine M. Rogers

Z

ZULEIKA DOBSON.
Novel by Max Beerbohm, 1911.

Zuleika Dobson, subtitled *An Oxford Love Story*, is the only full-length work by a writer mainly associated with shorter forms such as the essay, the short story, the parody, and the review. Max Beerbohm is also, of course, a brilliant caricaturist, and many of the scenes in this novel, which conveys a strong sense of specific locations, reveal the artist's as well as the writer's eye.

Its publication within a year of Edward VII's death is significant. Edward's short reign was in some respects a kind of postscript to the Victorian era in which Beerbohm had been born and received his own Oxford education, and *Zuleika Dobson* is one of those texts that embody the ethos of a world that vanished with the outbreak of war in 1914. Though he lived until 1956, Beerbohm had begun his literary career in the 1890's and as an undergraduate had come under the influence of Oscar Wilde. Throughout his long life he continued to represent, in his person as well as his writings, the convictions of the Aesthetic Movement and of dandyism. In a note written for a new edition of the novel just after World War II, he recognized that "any young readers of the book" might find his presentation of Oxford life wildly unrealistic, but hastened to assure them that "my fantasy was far more like to the old Oxford than was the old Oxford like to the place now besieged and invaded by Lord Nuffield's armies" (the reference is to the transformation of Oxford into a centre of the automobile manufacturing industry).

The same note of 1946 states that, whereas some readers of 1911 appeared to regard the book as a satire, "I myself had supposed it was just a fantasy." Beerbohm is hardly a satirist in the fullest sense of the word: while he finds pleasure in exposing human folly, he is not interested in reform and shows nothing of the Swiftian anger and disgust at the spectacle of human wickedness. But it will not quite do to label the novel a "fantasy" and leave it at that: though there are certainly elements of fantasy—for example, in the opening chapter, when the "high grim busts of the Roman Emperors" outside the Sheldonian Theatre break out into "great beads of perspiration" as the heroine passes by—much of the book gives an affectionately detailed picture of Oxford as Beerbohm knew and loved it. The Oxford depicted is that of the author's own undergraduate days 20 years earlier, not far in time from the "city of dreaming spires" of Matthew Arnold's famous description, and even closer to the Oxford on which Wilde's calculated exploitation of his own flamboyant personality had made such an impression. The book was therefore nostalgic not only from the vantage-point of 1946 but even from that of 1911, and Beerbohm himself lived to see the disappearance of the university he had known: aristocratic, leisured, and for all practical purposes all-male, like the public schools from which most of its members came and the London clubs that many of them in due course joined.

The slight narrative relates the impact upon this society of a young woman who perhaps represents Beerbohm's light-hearted version of the "New Woman" presented by serious novelists of the period. Her arrival in Oxford causes a sensation that reaches its climax when—with the single exception of the plebeian Noaks, who clumsily trips in the rush—all the undergraduates dash to the river and drown themselves from unrequited love for Zuleika. (Their fate perhaps owes something to Browning's well-known poem "The Pied Piper of Hamelin.") The epilogue ends with the heroine about to move on to Cambridge, presumably to repeat her exploits.

The strength of the work lies in its comic inventiveness and in the wit and elegance of Beerbohm's prose. Psychological realism is limited and moral purpose non-existent: indeed it neatly illustrates Wilde's aphorism, in the preface to *The Picture of Dorian Gray*, that "There is no such thing as a moral or an immoral book. Books are well written or badly written." As Beerbohm's biographer David Cecil said, "*Zuleika Dobson* is an extreme if light-hearted expression of the aesthetic point of view." The same critic aptly comments that its characters "have the same relation to the characters in a serious novel as the figures in Max's cartoons have to serious portraits." Although, in what may be intended as a parody of the manner of serious fiction, the story opens in the prosaic setting of a railway station, what follows is unconstrained by the conventions normally operating within the tradition of fictional realism.

At the same time Beerbohm does not strain his fantasy by allowing it to get out of hand. As he explained in a letter to his friend Reginald Turner, he wanted the characters "to *behave like* real people, within the limits of the absurdity conditioned. I wanted to forge the links of logic correctly *from my premises*; because it seemed to me that thereby—that is, by taking the characters solemnly—the fun of the absurdity would be by contrast the greater."

Zuleika Dobson, which was favourably reviewed on its publication, quickly established itself as a minor classic and has been many times reprinted. David Cecil described it as "the most ambitious of all [Beerbohm's] literary works, the most elaborate and highly wrought in style."

—Norman Page

TITLE INDEX

The following index includes the titles of all books listed in the Fiction, Verse, and Plays sections of the Publications lists in volumes 1 and 2. These abbreviations are used:

f	fiction
v	verse
p	play
scr	screenplay
radio	radio play
tv	television play

A few titles from other sections (Collections, Other, Prose, etc.) are listed; in these cases no abbreviation appears before the author's name. Titles appearing in **bold** are subjects of individual essays in volume 3.

Dark Night (v Sinclair), 1924
Dark Night's Work (f Gaskell), 1863
Dark Night's Work (p Boucicault), 1870
Dark of Summer (f Linklater), 1956
Dark Places of the Heart (f Christina Stead), 1966
Dark Room (f Narayan), 1938
Dark Sisters (f Kavan), 1930
Dark Testament (f Abrahams), 1942
Dark Tower (f C. Lewis), 1977
Dark Tower (radio MacNeice), 1946
Dark Valley (radio Auden), 1940
Dark Weeping (v Russell), 1929
Darkening Ecliptic (v McAuley), 1944
Darkening Fire (v Layton), 1975
Darkening Green (f C. Mackenzie), 1934
Dark-Eyed Lady (f Coppard), 1947
Darkness (f Hanley), 1973
Darkness (p O'Flaherty), 1926
Darkness and Day (f Compton-Burnett), 1951
Darkness at Noon (f Koestler), 1940
Darkness at Pemberley (f T. White), 1932
Darkness Visible (f Golding), 1979
Darkness Visible (p Hook), 1811
Darkwater Hall Mystery (f Amis), 1978
Darling Buds of May (f Bates), 1958
Darling Tom (f Strong), 1952
Darlinghurst Nights and Morning Glories (v Slessor), 1933
Dartmoor (v Hemans), 1821
Dartmoor Idylls (f Baring-Gould), 1896
Dash for Khartoum (f Henty), 1891
Dashwoods (f Rudd), 1911
Dauber (v Masefield), 1913
Daughter (p Knowles), 1836
Daughter Buffalo (f Frame), 1972
Daughter of the Hawk (f Forester), 1928
Daughter to Marry (p Planché), 1828
Daughter-in-Law (p Lawrence), 1965
Daughter's a Daughter (f Christie), 1952
Daughters and Sons (f Compton-Burnett), 1937
Daughters of Dawn (p Carman), 1913
Daughters of the Night (f Wallace), 1925
Dave (p Gregory), 1927
Davenport Dunn (f Lever), 1859
David (v Birney), 1942
David (p Lawrence), 1926
David (radio Purdy), 1961
David and Broccoli (tv Mortimer), 1960
David and Golia (v Drayton), 1630
David and Goliath (p H. More), 1782
David Balfour (f Stevenson), 1893
David Blaize (f E. Benson), 1916
David Copperfield (f Dickens), 1850
David Copperfield (scr Hugh Walpole), 1934
David Elginbrod (f MacDonald), 1863
David Garrick (p Robertson), 1864
David Garrick (f Robertson), 1865
David Grieve (f M. Ward), 1892
David of King's (f E. Benson), 1924
David Simple (f S. Fielding), 1744
Davideis (v A. Cowley), 1656
Dawn (f Haggard), 1884
Dawn (p Symons), 1915
Dawn Island (f Martineau), 1845
Dawn of a To-morrow (f Burnett), 1906
Dawn of a Tomorrow (p Burnett), 1909
Dawn's Left Hand (f D. Richardson), 1931
Dawson Pedigree (f Sayers), 1928
Day (v Armstrong), 1761
Day (v Cunningham), 1761
Day, A Night, and a Morrow (p Bax), 1948
Day and Night (v Bethell), 1939
Day and Night (v Livesay), 1944
Day and Night Songs (v Allingham), 1854
Day at an Inn (p Hook), 1823
Day by the Sea (p Hunter), 1953
Day Dreams (f O'Connor), 1973
Day in the Dark (f Bowen), 1965
Day in Turkey (p H. Cowley), 1791
Day of Creation (f Ballard), 1987
Day of Forever (f Ballard), 1967
Day of Glory (p Bates), 1945
Day of Reckoning (p Houghton), 1912
Day of Reckoning (p Planché), 1850
Day of the Scorpion (f P. Scott), 1968
Day of the Tortoise (f Bates), 1961
Day of Trial (f Griffin), 1853
Day of Uniting (f Wallace), 1926
Day Out for Lucy (tv Hanley), 1965
Day That Flanagan Died (p Baxter), 1969
Day We Got Drunk on Cake (f Trevor), 1967
Day Will Come (f Braddon), 1889
Day Will Dawn (scr Rattigan), 1942
Daybreak (f Palmer), 1932
Day-Dream Communiqué (v Sillitoe), 1977
Daydreams (scr Wells), 1928
Daylight and Nightmare (f Chesterton), 1986
Daylight Moon (v Murray), 1987
Daylight on Saturday (f Priestley), 1943
Days and Nights (v Brathwaite), 1975
Days and Nights (v Symons), 1889
Days Departed (v Bowles), 1828
Day's End (f Bates), 1928
Days of My Life (f Oliphant), 1857
Days of the Year (v Austin), 1886
Days of Yore (p Cumberland), 1796
Day's Ride (f Lever), 1863
Day's Work (f Kipling), 1898
De Cive (Hobbes), 1642
De Corpore (Hobbes), 1655
De Foelici et Semper Augusto Jacobi (v Ayton), 1603
De Homine (Hobbes), 1655
De Literis Antiquae Britanniae (v G. Fletcher the Elder), 1633
De Mirabilibus Pecci Carmen (v Hobbes), 1666
De Monfort (p Baillie), 1798
De Profundis (Wilde), 1905
De Regimine Principum (v Hoccleve)
De Sapienta Veterum (Bacon), 1609
Deacon (p H. Jones), 1890
Deacon Brodie (p Henley, Stevenson), 1880
Dead Alive (p O'Keeffe), 1781
Dead Boxer (f Carleton), 1850
Dead City (p Symons), 1898
Dead Kingdom (v Montague), 1984
Dead Letters (f Baring), 1910
Dead Letters (v Blunden), 1922
Dead Love Has Chains (f Braddon), 1907
Dead Man Leading (f Pritchett), 1937
Dead Man's Folly (f Christie), 1956
Dead Man's Mirror (f Christie), 1937
Dead Man's Plack (f Hudson), 1920
Dead Man's Rock (f Quiller-Couch), 1887
Dead Men Rising (f K. Mackenzie), 1951
Dead Men's Shoes (f Braddon), 1876

Half a Minute's Silence (f Baring), 1925
Half an Eye (f Hanley), 1937
Half an Hour (p Barrie), 1913
Half an Hour's Courtship (p Planché), 1821
Half Moon (f F. Ford), 1909
Half Sir (f Griffin), 1857
Half-Caste (f Mulock), 1851
Half-Caste (p Robertson), 1856
Half-Crown Bob (f Warung), 1898
Half-Hearted (f Buchan), 1900
Half-Way (v Auden), 1965
Halfway House (v Blunden), 1932
Halfway House (radio MacNeice), 1942
Halidon Hill (p Walter Scott), 1822
Hall of Healing (p O'Casey), 1951
Hall Porter (p Lover), 1839
Halleluiah (v Wither), 1641
Hallmarked (p Galsworthy), 1921
Halloran's Little Boat (p Keneally), 1966
Hallowed Ground (p Brighouse), 1942
Hallowe'en Party (f Christie), 1969
Halton Boys (f Crawford), 1979
Halves (p Doyle), 1899
Ham and the Porcupine (f Kipling), 1935
Ham Funeral (p P. White), 1961
Hamiltons (f Gore), 1834
Hamlet (p Davenant), 1661
Hamlet (p Garrick), 1772
Hamlet (p Shakespeare), 1601
Hamlet (v T. Warton), 1859
Hamlet Travestie (p Poole), 1810
Hamlet, with Alterations (p Murphy), 1811
Hampdens (f Martineau), 1880
Hand and Soul (v D. Rossetti), 1869
Hand in Glove (f Marsh), 1962
Hand of Ethelberta (f Hardy), 1876
Hand of Power (f Wallace), 1927
Hand on the Rail (p B. Mason), 1965
Handcuffs (p Reaney), 1975
Handful of Dust (f Waugh), 1934
Handful of Earth (v Purdy), 1977
Handful of Gladsome Verses Given to the Queen's Majesty at Woodstock (v Churchyard), 1592
Handful of Pennies (f Porter), 1958
Handful of Watercress (p Arden), 1976
Handley Cross (f Surtees), 1843
Handmaid's Tale (f Atwood), 1985
Handmaid's Tale (scr Pinter), 1990
Hands (tv Weldon), 1972
Hands Across the Sea (p Coward), 1936
Hands All Round (v Tennyson), 1882
Handsome Hernani (p H. Byron), 1879
Handsome Is That Handsome Does (p T. Taylor), 1870
Handy Andy (f Lover), 1842
Hanging and Marriage (p Carey), 1722
Hanging In (v Souster), 1979
Hanging Judge (p Stevenson), 1887
Hangman Ties the Holly (v Wilkinson), 1955
Hangman's Holiday (f Sayers), 1933
Hangover (f Sargeson), 1967
Hanky Park (p Greenwood), 1971
Hannah (f Mulock), 1872
Hannah (p Smart), 1764
Hannah Hewit (f Dibdin), 1792
Hannah Hewit (p Dibdin), 1798
Hannibal and Scipio (p Nabbes), 1635
Hannibal Takes a Hand (f J. Lindsay), 1941
Hanrahan's Oath (p Gregory), 1918
Hans Feet in Love (f Sansom), 1971
Hans Frost (f Hugh Walpole), 1929
Hans of Iceland (p Fitzball), 1825
Hans von Stein (p Fitzball), 1851
Hapgood (p Stoppard), 1988
Happiest Day of My Life (p Buckstone), 1829
Happiness (f Lavin), 1969
Happiness (f Prichard), 1967
Happy and Glorious (p L. Housman), 1945
Happy Arcadia (p Gilbert), 1872
Happy Autumn Fields (tv Trevor), 1980
Happy Christmas (f D. du Maurier), 1940
Happy Days (p Beckett), 1961
Happy Days (p Greenwood), 1958
Happy Family (p Palmer), 1921
Happy Foreigner (f Bagnold), 1920
Happy Hangman (p Brighouse), 1922
Happy Haven (p Arden), 1960
Happy Hypocrite (f Beerbohm), 1897
Happy Hypocrite (p Beerbohm), 1900
Happy Hypocrite (p Dane), 1936
Happy Land (p Gilbert), 1873
Happy Land (p M. Clarke), 1880
Happy Man (p Lover), 1839
Happy New Year (v Rickword), 1928
Happy Nuptials (p Carey), 1733
Happy Pair (v Sedley), 1702
Happy Prince (f Wilde), 1888
Happy Return (f Forester), 1937
Happy Return (f Thirkell), 1952
Happy Returns (f Thirkell), 1952
Happy Stories (f Leacock), 1943
Happy Valley (f P. White), 1939
Happy-Go-Lucky Morgans (f E. Thomas), 1913
Harbingers (v Blunden), 1916
Harbour Watch (p Kipling), 1913
Hard Cash (f Reade), 1863
Hard Hit (p H. Jones), 1887
Hard Life (f F. O'Brien), 1961
Hard of Hearing (v Nicholson), 1974
Hard Struggle (p John Westland Marston), 1858
Hard Times (f Dickens), 1854
Harding's Luck (f Nesbit), 1909
Hare and Hornbill (v p'Bitek), 1978
Hark, Hark, the Lark! (f Bates), 1961
Harlequin and Georgy Barnwell (p Buckstone), 1836
Harlequin and Humpty Dumpty (p Fitzball), 1850
Harlequin and Jack of Newberry (p Moncrieff), 1840
Harlequin and My Lady Lee (p Moncrieff), 1840
Harlequin and Poor Richard (p Buckstone), 1840
Harlequin and the Giant Helmet (p Planché), 1840
Harlequin and the Sleeping Beauty (p Buckstone), 1843
Harlequin and the Three Bears (p Buckstone), 1853
Harlequin Beauty and the Beast (p H. Byron), 1862
Harlequin Bluebeard (p H. Byron), 1866
Harlequin Cock-Robin (p Gilbert), 1867
Harlequin Columbus (p T. Taylor), 1853
Harlequin Freemason (p Dibdin), 1780
Harlequin in Derry (p O'Keeffe), 1770
Harlequin in Waterford (p O'Keeffe), 1767
Harlequin King Nutcracker (p Planché), 1853
Harlequin Phantom of a Day (p Dibdin), 1783
Harlequin Prince Graceful (p Planché), 1868
Harlequin Rambler (p O'Keeffe), 1784
Harlequin St. George and the Dragon (p H. Byron), 1863
Harlequin Teague (p Colman the Elder, O'Keeffe), 1782

Hero Rises Up (p Arden), 1968
Herod (p Phillips), 1901
Herod and Mariamne (p Dane), 1938
Herod the Great (p Boyle), 1694
Heroes and Kings (v C. Williams), 1930
Heroic Epistle to Sir James Wright (v Combe), 1779
Heroic Epistle to Sir William Chambers (v W. Mason), 1773
Heroic Epistle to the Noble Author of The Duchess of Devonshire's Cow (v Combe), 1777
Heroic Idyls (v Landor), 1863
Heroic Postscript to the Public (v W. Mason), 1774
Heroic Stanzas to the Memory of Oliver, Late Lord Protector (v Dryden), 1659
Heroic Stubbs (p H. Jones), 1906
Herr Paulus (f Besant), 1888
Herries Chronicle (f Hugh Walpole), from 1930
Herself Surprised (f Cary), 1941
Hershel of Ostropol (p Klein), 1939
He's Much to Blame (p Holcroft), 1798
Hesperides (v Herrick), 1648
Hessian Prisoner (f Bates), 1930
Hester (f Oliphant), 1883
Hester Lilly (f E. Taylor), 1954
Hester's Mystery (p Pinero), 1880
Hetty (f H. Kingsley), 1871
Hetty Dorval (f E. Wilson), 1947
Hetty Wesley (f Quiller-Couch), 1903
Heu-Heu (f Haggard), 1924
Hexagon (v Porter), 1956
Hey for Honesty, Down with Knavery (p Randolph), 1651
Hibernian Nights' Entertainments (v Ferguson), 1887
Hickory, Dickory, Death (f Christie), 1955
Hickory, Dickory, Dock (f Christie), 1955
Hidden Doors (f N. Gunn), 1929
Hidden Foe (f Henty), 1890
Hidden Hand (p T. Taylor), 1864
Hidden Laughter (p S. Gray), 1990
Hidden Life (v MacDonald), 1864
Hidden Player (f Noyes), 1924
Hidden Treasure (p Poole), 1820
Hide and Seek (f Wilkie Collins), 1854
Hierarchy of the Blessed Angels (v T. Heywood), 1635
Hieroglyphic Tales (f Horace Walpole), 1785
Hieroglyphics of the Life of Man (v Quarles), 1638
High and Low (v Betjeman), 1966
High Bid (p H. James), 1908
High Germany (v F. Ford), 1912
High Jinks (p Lonsdale), 1916
High, Low, Jack, and the Game (p Planché), 1833
High Rising (f Thirkell), 1933
High Road (p Lonsdale), 1927
High Spirits (f R. Davies), 1982
High Summer (tv Rattigan), 1972
High Toby (p Priestley), 1948
High Wind in Jamaica (f R. Hughes), 1929
High Windows (v Larkin), 1974
Highland Fling (f N. Mitford), 1931
Highland Night (f N. Gunn), 1935
Highland Officer (f Defoe), 1718
Highland Reel (p O'Keeffe), 1788
Highland River (f N. Gunn), 1937
Highland Widow (f Walter Scott), 1827
Highlander (v Macpherson), 1758
Highly Improbable (p Gilbert), 1867
High-Rise (f Ballard), 1975
Highway in the Sun (radio Selvon), 1967
Hilary St. Ives (f Ainsworth), 1870
Hilda Lessways (f A. Bennett), 1911
Hilda Wade (f Doyle), 1900
Hildesheim (v Baring), 1899
Hill of Dreams (f Machen), 1907
Hill of Howth (f Strong), 1953
Hill of Vision (v Stephens), 1912
Hill Station (f Farrell), 1981
Hillarys (p Brighouse, Houghton), 1915
Hilliad (v Smart), 1753
Hillingdon Hall (f Surtees), 1845
Hills Were Joyful Together (f Mais), 1953
Hillyars and the Burtons (f H. Kingsley), 1865
Himatia-Poleos (p Munday), 1614
Hind and the Panther (v Dryden), 1687
Hind and the Panther Transversed to the Story of the Country Mouse and the City Mouse (v Prior), 1687
Hindle Wakes (f Brighouse), 1927
Hindle Wakes (p Houghton), 1912
Hindoo Robber (p Fitzball), 1836
Hint to Husbands (p Cumberland), 1806
Hippy Hippy Who Cares (tv Weldon), 1968
Hips and Haws (v Coppard), 1922
Hired Baby (f Corelli), 1891
Hireling (f Hartley), 1957
Hiroshima Poems (v Purdy), 1972
His Darling Sin (f Braddon), 1899
His Excellency (p Gilbert), 1894
His Excellency – The Governor (p P. Carroll), 1939
His Favourite Flower (p L. Housman), 1921
His Fellow Men (f Dunsany), 1952
His First Campaign (p Planché), 1832
His Grace of Osmonde (f Burnett), 1897
His House in Order (p Pinero), 1906
His Last Bow (f Doyle), 1917
His Little Mother (f Mulock), 1881
His Majesty (p H. Barker), 1928
His Majesty's Embassy (p Baring), 1923
His Natural Life (f M. Clarke), 1874
His People (f R. Graham), 1906
His Sainted Grandmother (p Dunsany), 1926
His Wife (p H. Jones), 1881
His Worship the Mayor (f Greenwood), 1934
Historical Dramas (p T. Taylor), 1877
Historical Dramas (p Yonge), 1864
Historical Odes (v Dixon), 1864
Historical Register for the Year 1736 (p H. Fielding), 1737
Historical Romances (f Doyle), 1931
History and Adventures of an Atom (f Smollett), 1769
History of Anthony Waring (f Sinclair), 1927
History of Charles the Eighth of France (p Crowne), 1671
History of England (T. Macaulay), 1848
History of England (v Kipling), 1911
History of John Gilpin (v Cowper), 1785
History of Johnny Quae Genus (v Combe), 1822
History of King Richard III (T. More), 1543
History of Laetitia Atkins (f Defoe), 1776
History of Little Davy's New Hat (v Bloomfield), 1815
History of Mr. Polly (f Wells), 1910
History of Our Own Times (F. Ford), 1988
History of Queen Mab (v Drayton), 1751
History of Samson (v Quarles), 1631
History of Sir Francis Drake (p Davenant), 1658
History of Sir Thomas Thumb (f Yonge), 1855
History of the Decline and Fall of the Roman Empire (E. Gibbon), 1761
History of the Grand Rebellion (v N. Ward), 1713
History of the Grande Amour (v Hawes), 1554

It Was a Lover and His Lass (f Oliphant), 1883
It Was the Calm and Silent Night (v Domett), 1884
It Was the Nightingale (f Williamson), 1962
It Wasn't Me (tv Hanley), 1969
Italian (f Radcliffe), 1797
Italian Girl (f Murdoch), 1964
Italian Girl (p Murdoch), 1967
Italian Husband (p Ravenscroft), 1697
Italian Letters (f Godwin), 1783
Italian Madrigals Englished (v T. Watson), 1590
Italian Mother (v Swinburne), 1918
Italian Table (tv Trevor), 1970
Italian Visit (v Day Lewis), 1953
Italics (v Landor), 1848
Italy (v Rogers), 1822
It's a Battlefield (f G. Greene), 1934
It's a Gamble (p Brighouse), 1928
It's about Cinderella (p Shaffer), 1969
It's an Old Country (f Priestley), 1967
It's Harder to Be Anybody (radio Richler), 1961
It's Never Over (f Callaghan), 1930
It's Never Too Late to Mend (p Reade), 1864
It's Not Very Nice (p Strong), 1954
It's Only round the Corner (p H. Jones), 1878
It's Time Something Happened (p Doyle), 1925
Ivanhoe (f Walter Scott), 1819
Ivanhoe (p H. Byron), 1862
Ivanhoe (p Moncrieff), 1820
Ivory Child (f Haggard), 1916
Ivory Door (p Milne), 1927
Ivory Gate (f Besant), 1892
Ivory Tower (f H. James), 1917
Ivy Gripped the Steps (f Bowen), 1946
Iwan (p Fitzball), 1823
Ixion in Heaven (f Disraeli), 1853
Ixion's Wheel (v Gustafson), 1969

Jacaranda Tree (f Bates), 1949
Jack Archer (f Henty), 1883
Jack Brag (f Hook), 1837
Jack Drum's Entertainment (p John Marston), 1600
Jack Frost's Little Prisoners (f Baring-Gould), 1887
Jack Hinton (f Lever), 1843
Jack Juggler (p Udall), 1563
Jack o' Judgment (f Wallace), 1920
Jack of Newbery (f Deloney), 1619
Jack Sheppard (f Ainsworth), 1839
Jack Sheppard (f Defoe), 1933
Jack Sheppard (p Boucicault, Buckstone), 1839
Jack Sheppard the Housebreaker (p Moncrieff), 1825
Jack Straw (p Maugham), 1908
Jack Straw's Castle (v T. Gunn), 1975
Jack the Giant Killer (p H. Byron), 1859
Jack the Giant Queller (p H. Brooke), 1749
Jack Winter's Dream (radio Baxter), 1958
Jack Without Magic (v Curnow), 1946
Jackdaw (p Gregory), 1907
Jackdaw (v Colum), 1939
Jackets (p Bond), 1989
Jacob (p L. Housman), 1942
Jacob and Esau (p Udall), 1568
Jacob Faithful (f Marryat), 1834
Jacob Two-Two series (Richler), from 1975
Jacobite (p Planché), 1847
Jacobite Exile (f Henty), 1893
Jacob's Room (f Woolf), 1922
Jacopo the Bravo (p Buckstone), 1887
Jacqueline (scr O'Flaherty), 1956
Jacqueline (v Rogers), 1814
Jacquetta (f Baring-Gould), 1890
Jagua Nana (f Ekwensi), 1961
Jagua Nana's Daughter (f Ekwensi), 1986
Jake's Thing (f Amis), 1978
Jalna series (de la Roche), from 1927
Jamaica Inn (f D. du Maurier), 1936
Jamaica Inn (scr Priestley), 1939
Jamaica Labrish (v L. Bennett), 1966
Jamaican Dialect Verses (v L. Bennett), 1942
Jamaican Humour in Dialect (v L. Bennett), 1943
Jamaicans (f V. Reid), 1976
James the Fogey (p H. Jones), 1900
James the Second (f Ainsworth), 1848
James Wallace (f Bage), 1788
Jan Van Hunks (v D. Rossetti), 1912
Jane (f Corelli), 1897
Jane and Prudence (f Pym), 1953
Jane Annie (p Barrie, Doyle), 1893
Jane Austen in Manhattan (tv Jhabvala), 1980
Jane Clegg (p Ervine), 1913
Jane Eyre (f C. Brontë), 1847
Jane Eyre (scr Huxley), 1944
Jane Eyre (p Weldon), 1986
Jane of Lantern Hill (f Montgomery), 1937
Jane Paul (p Fitzball), 1842
Jane Shore (p Rowe), 1714
Jane Sinclair (f Carleton), 1843
Janet (f Oliphant), 1891
Janet Pride (p Boucicault), 1854
Janitor (tv Duncan), 1955
Janus (f G. Barker), 1935
Japanese Garland (v Blunden), 1928
Japanese Impromptus (v Bax), 1914
Japhet in Search of a Father (f Marryat), 1835
Jarl's Daughter (f Burnett), 1879
Jarwin and Cuffy (f Ballantyne), 1878
Jazz and Jasper (f Gerhardie), 1928
Je ne parle pas français (f Mansfield), 1918
Jealous Ghost (f Strong), 1930
Jealous God (f Braine), 1964
Jealous Lovers (p Randolph), 1632
Jealous Wife (p Colman the Elder), 1761
Jealousy (p Reade), 1878
Jeames's Diary (f Thackeray), 1846
Jeanie Deans (p Boucicault), 1860
Jeeves (f Wodehouse), 1923
Jeeves (p Ayckbourn), 1975
Jeeves and the Feudal Spirit (f Wodehouse), 1954
Jeeves and the Tie That Binds (f Wodehouse), 1971
Jeeves in the Offing (f Wodehouse), 1960
Jekyll and Hyde (f Stevenson), 1886
Jemmy and Jenny Jessamy (f Haywood), 1753
Jenkinses (p Planché), 1830
Jenny and Meggy (v Ramsay), 1723
Jenny Villiers (f Priestley), 1947
Jenny Villiers (p Priestley), 1946
Jenny Wren (p Gilbert), 1867
Jeremy (f Hugh Walpole), 1919
Jeremy and Hamlet (f Hugh Walpole), 1923
Jeremy at Crale (f Hugh Walpole), 1927
Jericho's Red Brick Battlements (radio Purdy), 1969
Jero Plays (p Soyinka), 1973
Jero's Metamorphosis (p Soyinka), 1973
Jerusalem (v Blake), 1804
Jerusalem Blues (2) (v Baxter), 1971

Love in Several Masques (p H. Fielding), 1728
Love in the City (p Bickerstaff), 1767
Love in the Desert (p Binyon), 1928
Love in the Environs of Voronezh (v Sillitoe), 1968
Love in Youth (f F. Harris), 1916
Love Is Enough (v Morris), 1872
Love Laughs at Locksmiths (p Colman the Younger), 1803
Love Letters Between a Nobleman and His Sister (f Behn), 1683
Love Letters on Blue Paper (f Wesker), 1974
Love Letters on Blue Paper (tv Wesker), 1976
Love Lies Dreaming (f Forester), 1927
Love Lyrics (v Blunt), 1892
Love Makes a Man (p Cibber), 1700
Love Match (p A. Bennett), 1922
Love Me Little, Love Me Long (f Reade), 1859
Love of a Good Woman (tv Trevor), 1976
Love of Fame (v E. Young), 1728
Love of Gain (v M. Lewis), 1799
Love of King David and Fair Bethsabe (p Peele), 1594
Love of Long Ago (f Corelli), 1920
Love of Myrrhine and Konallis (v Aldington), 1926
Love of Order (v Richard Graves), 1773
Love on the Dole (f Greenwood), 1933
Love on the Dole (p Greenwood), 1934
Love on the Dole (scr Greenwood), 1941
Love One Another (f Rickword), 1929
Love Passage (p Jacobs), 1913
Love Passes By (p H. Barker), 1932
Love Pavilion (f P. Scott), 1960
Love Poems (v Austin), 1912
Love Poems (v G. Barker), 1947
Love Poems (v Blunt), 1902
Love Poems (v Lawrence), 1913
Love Poems (v Layton), 1978
Love Poems of Myrrhine and Konallis (v Aldington), 1917
Love Respelt (v Robert Graves), 1965
Love Respelt Again (v Robert Graves), 1969
Love Restored (p Jonson), 1612
Love Sonnets of Proteus (v Blunt), 1881
Love the Conqueror Worm (v Layton), 1953
Love Tricks (p Shirley), 1667
Love Triumphant (p Dryden), 1694
Love Will Find Out the Way (p Shirley), 1661
Love-Adept (f Hartley), 1969
Love—and the Philosopher (f Corelli), 1923
Love-Chase (p Knowles), 1837
Loved and Envied (f Bagnold), 1951
Loved and the Lost (f Callaghan), 1951
Loved Helen (v T. White), 1929
Loved One (f Waugh), 1948
Loved One (scr Isherwood), 1965
Lovel the Widower (f Thackeray), 1860
Love-Letters on All Occasions Lately Passed Between Persons of Distinction (f Haywood), 1730
Lovelock Version (f Shadbolt), 1980
Lovels of Arden (f Braddon), 1871
Lovely Lady (f Lawrence), 1933
Lover (f Dane), 1924
Lover (f D. du Maurier), 1961
Lover (tv Pinter), 1963
Lover by Proxy (p Boucicault), 1842
Lovers (p Friel), 1967
Lovers and Friends (f E. Benson), 1921
Lovers and Lesser Men (v Layton), 1973
Lovers Courageous (scr Lonsdale), 1932
Lover's Fate (f Anthony Hope), 1894
Lover's Gift (v Tagore), 1918
Lovers in Acadie (f Roberts), 1924
Lovers in London (f Milne), 1905
Lovers Made Men (p Jonson), 1617
Lover's Melancholy (p J. Ford), 1628
Lover's Melancholy (p Macklin), 1748
Lovers of Their Time (f Trevor), 1978
Lovers' Progress (p J. Fletcher), 1623
Lovers' Progress (p Massinger), 1647
Lovers' Resolutions (p Cumberland), 1802
Lovers' Song-Book (v W. Davies), 1933
Lover's Tale (v Tennyson), 1832
Lovers' Vows (p Inchbald), 1798
Love's Adventures (p Cavendish), 1662
Love's Alarum (p Planché), 1821
Love's Contrivance (p Centlivre), 1703
Love's Cross-Currents (f Swinburne), 1901
Love's Cruelty (p Shirley), 1631
Love's Cruelty (v Symons), 1923
Love's Cure (p F. Beaumont, J. Fletcher, Massinger), 1647
Love's Frailties (p Holcroft), 1794
Love's Harvest (f M. Ward), 1929
Love's Labour's Lost (p Auden), 1972
Love's Labour's Lost (p Shakespeare), 1594
Love's Last Shift (p Cibber), 1696
Love's Logic (f Anthony Hope), 1908
Love's Metamorphosis (p Lyly), 1589
Love's Mistress (p T. Heywood), 1634
Loves of Arcadia (p Braddon), 1860
Loves of Cass McGuire (radio Friel), 1966
Loves of Joanna Godden (scr Bates), 1947
Loves of the Angels (v Thomas Moore), 1823
Loves of the Plants (v Darwin), 1789
Love's Old Sweet Song (radio Whiting), 1950
Love's Pilgrimage (p F. Beaumont, J. Fletcher), 1616
Love's Riddle (p A. Cowley), 1638
Love's Sacrifice (p J. Ford), 1632
Love's Shadow (f Leverson), 1908
Love's Song (p Anthony Hope), 1916
Love's Triumph (p Planché), 1862
Love's Triumph Through Callipolis (p Jonson), 1631
Love's Welcome at Bolsover (p Jonson), 1634
Love's Widowhood (v Austin), 1889
Lovesick (radio Caryl Churchill), 1967
Love-Sick Court (p Brome), 1633
Love-Songs and Elegies (v Ghose), 1898
Loving (f H. Green), 1945
Loving Ballad of Lord Bateman (v Thackeray), 1839
Loving Ballad to Brother Jonathan (v Tupper), 1848
Loving Eye (f Sansom), 1956
Loving Memory (tv Harrison), 1987
Loving Spirit (f D. du Maurier), 1931
Low Back Car (v Lover), 1855
Low Life (p de la Roche), 1925
Low Notes on a High Level (f Priestley), 1954
Low Tide on Grand-Pré (v Carman), 1889
Low Water (p Pinero), 1884
Lowery Road (v Strong), 1923
Low-Flying Aircraft (f Ballard), 1976
Low's Company (v Strong), 1952
Loyal Brother (p Southerne), 1682
Loyal Effusion (p Dibdin), 1794
Loyal General (p Tate), 1679
Loyal Subject (p J. Fletcher), 1618
Loyalties (v Drinkwater), 1918
Loyalties (p Galsworthy), 1922
Loyalties (f R. Williams), 1985

Mr. Bolfry (p Bridie), 1943
Mister Bosphorus and the Muses (p F. Ford), 1923
Mr. Brandywine Chooses a Gravestone (radio Baxter), 1967
Mr. Britling Sees It Through (f Wells), 1916
Mr. Buckstone's Ascent of Mount Parnassus (p Planché), 1853
Mr. Buckstone's Voyage round the Globe (in Leicester Square) (p Planché), 1854
Mr. Bumps and His Monkey (f de la Mare), 1942
Mr. Butterfry (f Porter), 1970
Mr. Byculla (f Linklater), 1950
Mr. Chairman (p Fitzball), 1829
Mr. Clutterbuck's Election (f Belloc), 1908
Mr. Commissioner Sanders (f Wallace), 1930
Mr. Director (p Weldon), 1978
Mr. Dollinger (p Lessing), 1958
Mr. Facey Romford's Hounds (f Surtees), 1865
Mr. Faithful (p Dunsany), 1927
Mr. Fleight (f F. Ford), 1913
Mr. Fortune's Maggot (f S. Warner), 1927
Mister Fox (f Ballantyne), 1857
Mr. Fox (p Dane), 1927
Mr. Fox and Mr. First (radio Weldon), 1974
Mr. Gilhooley (f O'Flaherty), 1926
Mr. Gillie (p Bridie), 1950
Mr. Gladstone's Comforter (p L. Housman), 1929
Mr. Guffin's Elopement (p Grossmith), 1882
Mr. H— (p Lamb), 1806
Mr. Hampden's Speech (v Denham), 1643
Mr. Huckster of 1958 (v Curnow), 1958
Mr. Huffam (f Hugh Walpole), 1948
Mister Johnson (f Cary), 1939
Mr. Jorkens Remembers Africa (f Dunsany), 1934
Mr. Justice Maxell (f Wallace), 1922
Mr. Know-All (scr Sherriff), 1950
Mr. Limberham (p Dryden), 1678
Mr. Livermore's Dream (p Pinero), 1917
Mr. Love and Justice (f MacInnes), 1960
Mr. Loveday's Little Outing (f Waugh), 1936
Mr. Luby's Fear of Heaven (radio Mortimer), 1976
Mr. Meeson's Will (f Haggard), 1888
Mr. Midshipman Easy (f Marryat), 1836
Mr. Midshipman Hornblower (f Forester), 1950
Mr. Mulliner Speaking (f Wodehouse), 1929
Mr. Nightingale's Diary (p Dickens), 1851
Mr. Noon (f Lawrence), 1984
Mr. Norris Changes Trains (f Isherwood), 1935
Mr. O'Dwyer's Dancing Party (p Baxter), 1968
Mr. Parker Pyne, Detective (f Christie), 1934
Mr. Pepys (p Bax), 1926
Mr. Perrin and Mr. Traill (f Hugh Walpole), 1911
Mr. Perrin and Mr. Traill (scr Strong), 1948
Mr. Peter Piper (p Boucicault), 1846
Mr. Petre (f Belloc), 1925
Mr. Petunia (f Gogarty), 1945
Mr. Pim (f Milne), 1921
Mr. Pim Passes By (f Milne), 1929
Mr. Pim Passes By (p Milne), 1919
Mr. Polly (f Wells), 1910
Mr. Ponge (tv Hanley), 1965
Mr. Prohack (f A. Bennett), 1922
Mr. Prohack (p A. Bennett), 1927
Mr. Punch's Dramatic Sequels (p Hankin), 1901
Mr. Pye (f Peake), 1953
Mr. Reeder Returns (f Wallace), 1932
Mr. Sampath (f Narayan), 1949
Mr. Scarborough's Family (f Trollope), 1883
Mr. Sims (p Hood), 1829
Mr. Sliggen's Hour (p Dunsany), 1937
Mr. Somebody (p Brighouse), 1936
Mr. Sponge's Sporting Tour (f Surtees), 1853
Mr. Standfast (f Buchan), 1919
Mr. Steinmann's Corner (p Sutro), 1902
Mr. Stone and the Knights Companion (f Naipaul), 1963
Mr. Tasker's Gods (f T. Powys), 1925
Mr. Teddy (f E. Benson), 1917
Mr. Waddington of Wyck (f Sinclair), 1921
Mr. Weston's Good Wine (f T. Powys), 1927
Mr. Whatnot (p Ayckbourn), 1963
Mr. Williams of Hamburg (radio Bax), 1943
Mr. Witt's Window (f Anthony Hope), 1892
Mr. Wray's Cash-Box (f Wilkie Collins), 1852
Mr. Zouch, Superman (f Powell), 1934
Mistress (v A. Cowley), 1647
Mistress (p Wesker), 1989
Mrs. Acland's Ghosts (tv Trevor), 1975
Mrs. Ames (f E. Benson), 1912
Mistress and Maid (f Mulock), 1863
Mrs. Armytage (f Gore), 1836
Mrs. Arthur (f Oliphant), 1877
Mrs. Carteret Receives (f Hartley), 1971
Mrs. Caudle's Curtain Lecture (p Jerrold), 1845
Mrs. Craddock (f Maugham), 1902
Mrs. Curgenven of Curgenven (f Baring-Gould), 1893
Mrs. Dalloway (f Woolf), 1925
Mrs. Dane's Defence (p H. Jones), 1900
Mrs. Dot (p Maugham), 1908
Mrs. Dukes' Million (f W. Lewis), 1977
Mrs. Eckdorf in O'Neill's Hotel (f Trevor), 1969
Mrs. Esmond's Life (f Bates), 1930
Mrs. Golightly (f E. Wilson), 1961
Mrs. Harrison (p Masefield), 1909
Mrs. Kimber (v O. Sitwell), 1937
Mrs. Martin's Man (f Ervine), 1914
Mrs. Martin's Man (p Ervine), 1954
Mistress Masham's Repose (T. White), 1946
Mrs. Maxon Protests (f Anthony Hope), 1911
Mrs. McGinty's Dead (f Christie), 1952
Mrs. Midnight's Orations (v Smart), 1763
Mrs. Miniver (scr Sherriff), 1942
Mistress of Jalna (p de la Roche), 1951
Mistress of Phil'arete (v Wither), 1622
Mistress of the Mill (p Moncrieff), 1849
Mistress of Vision (v Thompson), 1918
Mrs. Palfrey at the Claremont (f E. Taylor), 1971
Mrs. Palfrey at the Claremont (tv Lawler), 1973
Mistress Pat (f Montgomery), 1935
Mrs. Perkins's Ball (f Thackeray), 1847
Mrs. Silly (tv Trevor), 1983
Mrs. Temperly (f H. James), 1889
Mrs. Warren's Profession (p Shaw), 1898
Mrs. Waterbury's Millennium (p Bridie), 1935
Mrs. William Jones and Bill (f Wallace), 1926
Mithraic Emblems (v R. Campbell), 1936
Mithridates (p N. Lee), 1678
Mixed Doubles (p Ayckbourn, Pinter, Weldon), 1969
Mixed Life (Hilton)
Mixed Marriage (p Ervine), 1911
Mixer (f Wallace), 1927
Mixture as Before (f Maugham), 1940
Mixture of Frailties (f R. Davies), 1958
M'Lady (p Wallace), 1921
Mnemosyne Lay in Dust (v A. Clarke), 1966
Mob (p Galsworthy), 1914

No Other Man (f Noyes), 1940
No Other Road (radio MacNeice), 1948
No Other Tiger (f A. Mason), 1927
No Other Tiger (p A. Mason), 1928
No Other Way (f Besant), 1902
No Painted Plumage (f T. Powys), 1934
No Place Like (f Gordimer), 1978
No Prelude! (p Colman the Younger), 1803
No Remittance (f Davin), 1959
No Room at the Inn (p Arden), 1976
No Room at the Inn (scr D. Thomas), 1948
No Second Spring (v Purdy), 1977
No Star on the Way Back (tv Nicholson), 1963
No Star on the Way Back (v Nicholson), 1967
No Surrender (f Henty), 1899
No Thoroughfare (p Wilkie Collins, Dickens), 1867
No Thoroughfare (f Wilkie Collins, Dickens), 1890
No Thoroughfare (p Grossmith), 1869
No Whipping nor Ripping (v Breton), 1601
No Why (p Whiting), 1961
No Wit, No Help Like a Woman's (p Middleton), 1613
No Witchcraft for Sale (f Lessing), 1956
Noah and the Waters (v Day Lewis), 1936
Noah's Flood (v Drayton), 1630
Noah's Flood (p Lawrence), 1965
Nobby (f Wallace), 1916
Noble Gentleman (p F. Beaumont, J. Fletcher), 1625
Noble Jilt (p Trollope), 1923
Noble Life (f Mulock), 1866
Noble Peasant (p Holcroft), 1784
Noble Soldier (Dekker), 1634
Noble Spaniard (p Maugham), 1909
Noble Spanish Soldier (p Dekker), 1622
Noble Vagabond (p H. Jones), 1886
Nocturnae Silvani Potenti For a Floral Inebriation (v S. Sitwell), 1972
Nocturne in Palermo (p Bax), 1924
Noémi (f Baring-Gould), 1895
Noémie (p Robertson), 1855
No-Good Friday (p Fugard), 1958
Nohow On (f Beckett), 1989
Nomads (p Whiting), 1965
Non-Combatants (f R. Macaulay), 1916
None So Blind as Those Who Won't See (p Dibdin), 1782
Nones (v Auden), 1951
Nongogo (p Fugard), 1959
Non-Juror (p Cibber), 1717
Nonsense Novels (f Leacock), 1911
Nonsense Songs (v Lear), 1870
Non-Stop Connolly Show (p Arden), 1975
Nor the Years Condemn (f Hyde), 1938
Norma (p Planché), 1837
Norman Church (v Milne), 1948
Norman Conquests (p Ayckbourn), 1973
Normandy Pippins (p H. Byron), 1874
Norsemen in the West (f Ballantyne), 1872
North (f Beckett), 1972
North (v Heaney), 1975
North and South (f Gaskell), 1855
North Briton (Charles Churchill), 1763
North Face (f Renault), 1948
North of Summer (v Purdy), 1967
North Ship (v Larkin), 1945
North Star (v Binyon), 1941
North Wall (f Davidson), 1885
North Wind of Love (f C. Mackenzie), 1944
Northanger Abbey (f Austen), 1817
Northbridge Rectory (f Thirkell), 1941
Northern Aspect (p J. Gray), 1895
Northern Cuckold (v N. Ward), 1721
Northern Lass (p Brome), 1629
Northern Light (v Strong), 1930
Northern Star (v A. Hill), 1718
Northern Star (p Robertson), 1855
Northerners (p Brighouse), 1914
Northing Tramp (f Wallace), 1926
Northward Ho (p Dekker, Webster), 1605
Norwegian Ghost Story (f Gosse), 1967
No's Knife (f Beckett), 1967
Nosce Teipsum (v J. Davies), 1599
Nosebag (radio MacNeice), 1944
Nosegay of Weeds (p O'Keeffe), 1798
Nostromo (f Conrad), 1904
Not a Bad Judge (p Planché), 1848
Not after Midnight (f D. du Maurier), 1971
Not All the Dead Are Buried (tv Duncan), 1960
Not at All Jealous (p Robertson), 1871
Not Christmas, But Guy Fawkes (p B. Mason), 1976
Not Counting the Savages (tv B. Johnson), 1972
Not for Publication (f Gordimer), 1965
Not Here, Not Now (f Davin), 1970
Not Honour More (f Cary), 1955
Not I (p Beckett), 1972
Not I (tv Beckett), 1977
Not If I Know It (p H. Byron), 1871
Not If I Know It (f Trollope), 1883
Not in Narrow Seas (v Curnow), 1939
Not, Not, Not, Not, Not Enough Oxygen (radio Caryl Churchill), 1971
Not One Returns to Tell (radio Johnston), 1946
Not So Bad as We Seem (p Bulwer-Lytton), 1851
Not Such a Fool as He Looks (p H. Byron), 1868
Not That He Brought Flowers (v R. Thomas), 1968
Not to Disturb (f Spark), 1971
Not Waving But Drowning (v Stevie Smith), 1957
Not Yet the Dodo (v Coward), 1967
Note for Bibliophiles (v S. Sitwell), 1972
Note Forger (p Fitzball), 1835
Note in Music (f Lehmann), 1930
Note of Hand (p Cumberland), 1774
Notebook on My New Poems (v S. Sitwell), 1972
Notebook on Twenty Canons of Giant Art (v S. Sitwell), 1972
Notes for Poems (v Plomer), 1927
Notes from the Land of the Dead (v Kinsella), 1972
Notes of a Son and Brother (H. James), 1914
Notes Towards a Poem That Can Never Be Written (v Atwood), 1981
Nothing (f H. Green), 1950
Nothing Hurts for Long (f D. du Maurier), 1943
Nothing like Leather (f Pritchett), 1935
Nothing like the Sun (f Burgess), 1964
Nothing New (f Mulock), 1857
Nothing Serious (f Wodehouse), 1950
Nothing Serious (p Wodehouse), 1950
Nothing Too Much (v MacCaig), 1976
Nothing up My Sleeve (p Duncan), 1950
Nothing Will Be the Same Again (tv Hanley), 1968
Notorious Impostor (f Settle), 1692
Notorious Impostor Wili Morrell (f Settle), 1694
Notorious Mrs. Ebbsmith (p Pinero), 1895
Nottingham Captain (p Wesker), 1962
Nottingham Castle (v Bailey), 1878
Noughts and Crosses (f Quiller-Couch), 1891

Old and Young (p Poole), 1822
Old Bachelor (p Congreve), 1693
Old Bank House (f Thirkell), 1949
Old Blastus of Bandicoot (f Franklin), 1931
Old Blood (f Mittelholzer), 1958
Old Booty (v Moncrieff), 1830
Old Boys (f Trevor), 1964
Old Boys (p Trevor), 1971
Old Chums (p H. Byron), 1876
Old City Manners (p Lennox), 1775
Old Clothesman (p Holcroft), 1799
Old Couple (p May), 1636
Old Court (f Ainsworth), 1867
Old Curiosity Shop (f Dickens), 1841
Old Curiosity Shop (tv Trevor), 1979
Old Dark House (f Priestley), 1928
Old Dark House (scr Sherriff), 1932
Old Debauchees (p H. Fielding), 1732
Old Devils (f Amis), 1986
Old Dovecote (f Garnett), 1928
Old English (p Galsworthy), 1924
Old English Baron (f Reeve), 1778
Old Fires and Profitable Ghosts (f Quiller-Couch), 1900
Old Flames (p S. Gray), 1990
Old Folks of the Centuries (p Dunsany), 1930
Old Foolishness (p P. Carroll), 1940
Old Fortunatus (p Dekker), 1599
Old Friends (p Barrie), 1910
Old Guard (p Boucicault), 1840
Old Heads and Young Hearts (p Boucicault), 1844
Old Heads on Young Shoulders (p Moncrieff), 1830
Old Homestead (f Rudd), 1917
Old Huntsman (v Sassoon), 1917
Old Iron (scr Travers), 1938
Old Joe (f de la Mare), 1927
Old Judge (f Haliburton), 1849
Old King Cole (p Bax), 1921
Old King Cole (v Chesterton), 1920
Old King's Tale (p Dunsany), 1925
Old Ladies (f Hugh Walpole), 1924
Old Lady Mary (f Oliphant), 1885
Old Lady Says "No!" (p Johnston), 1929
Old Lady Shows Her Medals (p Barrie), 1917
Old Landmarks and Old Laws (f Martineau), 1852
Old Law (p Middleton, Rowley), 1618
Old Lights for New Chancels (v Betjeman), 1940
Old Lion (f de la Mare), 1942
Old London (f E. Benson), 1937
Old Mad-Cap's New Gallimaufry (v Breton), 1602
Old Madhouse (f De Morgan), 1919
Old Maid (p Murphy), 1761
Old Maids (p Knowles), 1841
Old Maids' Club (f Zangwill), 1892
Old Man (p Wallace), 1931
Old Man (scr Wallace), 1931
Old Man of the Mountains (p Nicholson), 1945
Old Man Sleeps Alone (radio Arden), 1982
Old Man Taught Wisdom (p H. Fielding), 1735
Old Manor House (f C. Smith), 1793
Old Man's Hat (tv Weldon), 1972
Old Man's Love (f Trollope), 1884
Old Man's Road (v Auden), 1956
Old Man's Youth (f De Morgan), 1921
Old Maps and New (v MacCaig), 1978
Old Margaret (f H. Kingsley), 1871
Old Master (f Garnett), 1967
Old Master (p H. Jones), 1880
Old Men (v de la Mare), 1913
Old Men at the Zoo (f A. Wilson), 1961
Old Men of the Sea (f C. Mackenzie), 1924
Old Mr. Tredgold (f Oliphant), 1895
Old Mode and the New (p D'Urfey), 1703
Old Mortality (f Walter Scott), 1816
Old Music (p N. Gunn), 1939
Old Mythologies (v Montague), 1965
Old Offender (p Planché), 1859
Old Ones (p Wesker), 1972
Old Order Changes (f Mallock), 1886
Old Pastures (v Colum), 1930
Old People (v Montague), 1960
Old Possum's Book of Practical Cats (v T. Eliot), 1939
Old Raiger (v Masefield), 1964
Old Reliable (f Wodehouse), 1951
Old Sailors (p H. Byron), 1874
Old Saint Paul's (f Ainsworth), 1841
Old School (p Boucicault), 1846
Old Score (p Gilbert), 1869
Old Ships (v Flecker), 1915
Old Soldiers (p H. Byron), 1873
Old Song (f Stevenson), 1982
Old Spookses' Pass (v Crawford), 1884
Old Stag (f Williamson), 1926
Old Story (p H. Byron), 1861
Old Strife at Plant's (f Cary), 1956
Old Testament and the New (p Houghton), 1914
Old Testament Plays (p L. Housman), 1950
Old Thorn (f Hudson), 1920
Old Times (p Pinter), 1971
Old Tune (radio Beckett), 1960
Old War (v Fuller), 1974
Old Wives Tale (p Peele), 1591
Old Wives' Tale (f A. Bennett), 1908
Old Woman and the Cow (f Anand), 1960
Old Woman and the Mayflowers (v Purdy), 1962
Old Woman of Eighty (p Dibdin)
Old Woman Remembers (p Gregory), 1923
Old World Idylls (v A. Dobson), 1883
Old-Fashioned Love (v T. Watson), 1594
Old-Fashioned Pilgrimage (v A. Clarke), 1967
Ole George Comes to Tea (p Ervine), 1927
O'Leary's Orchard (f M. Duggan), 1970
Olive (f Mulock), 1850
Oliver Cromwell (p Drinkwater), 1921
Oliver Newman (v Southey), 1845
Oliver Twist (f Dickens), 1838
Oliver's Bride (f Oliphant), 1885
Oliver's Island (p Milne), 1918
Olla Podrida (f Marryat), 1840
Olney Hymns (v Cowper), 1779
Olor Iscanus (v Vaughan), 1651
Olton Pools (v Drinkwater), 1916
Olympians (p Priestley), 1949
Olympic Devils (p Planché), 1831
Olympic Pic-Nic (p Lover), 1835
Olympic Revels (p Planché), 1831
Olympus in an Uproar (p O'Keeffe), 1796
Omai (p O'Keeffe), 1785
Omala (p Fitzball), 1825
Ombra (p Fitzball), 1842
Ombra (f Oliphant), 1872
Omen (f Galt), 1826
Omens (v Sydney Goodsir Smith), 1955
Omeros (v Walcott), 1989
Omniana (Coleridge, Southey), 1812

One Wonderful Week (f Forester), 1927
One Year's Time (f Milne), 1942
O'Neill (v Bulwer-Lytton), 1827
One-Man Masque (p Reaney), 1960
One-Way Song (v W. Lewis), 1933
One-Woman Plays (p Wesker), 1989
Only a Clod (f Braddon), 1865
Only Jealousy of Emer (p Yeats), 1919
Only Legend (p Drinkwater), 1913
Only Mugs Work (f Greenwood), 1938
Only Penitent (f T. Powys), 1931
Only Problem (f Spark), 1984
Open Air Plays (p Brighouse), 1926
Open Boat (radio Hanley), 1941
Open Door (p Fry), 1936
Open Door (f Oliphant), 1885
Open Door (f Sillitoe), 1989
Open Door (p Sutro), 1906
Open House (p Buckstone), 1833
Open House (p H. Byron), 1885
Open Letter (v Heaney), 1983
Open Sky (f Strong), 1939
Open the Door (f O. Sitwell), 1941
Open Verdict (f Braddon), 1878
Open Windows (p A. Mason), 1913
Opening Day (f Gascoyne), 1933
Opening Night (f Marsh), 1951
Opera (f Gore), 1832
Opera of Operas (p Haywood), 1733
Opera Wonyosi (p Soyinka), 1977
Operette (p Coward), 1938
Ophelia (f S. Fielding), 1760
Opportunity (p Shirley), 1634
Op. cit., et cetera (v S. Sitwell), 1972
Op. 1 (v Sayers), 1916
Opus 7 (v S. Warner), 1931
Or Hawk or Basilisk (v Glover), 1978
Ora pro nobis (p Duncan), 1940
Oracle in the Heart (v Raine), 1980
Oracles of Apollo (p Brighouse), 1926
Oral History (tv Gordimer), 1985
Orange and Green (f Henty), 1888
Orange Tree and the Humble Bee (p H. Byron), 1871
Orange-Girl (f Besant), 1899
Orangeman (p Ervine), 1913
Orara (v Kendall), 1881
Orator (f Wallace), 1928
Oratorio for Sasquatch, Man and Two Androids (v Atwood), 1970
Orators (p Foote), 1762
Orators (v Auden), 1932
Orchestra (v J. Davies), 1596
Ordeal by Innocence (f Christie), 1958
Ordeal by Marriage (f Buchan), 1915
Ordeal of Gilbert Pinfold (f Waugh), 1957
Ordeal of Richard Feverel (f Meredith), 1859
Ordinary (p Cartwright), 1651
Oresteia (p Harrison), 1981
Orestes (p de Tabley), 1867
Orestes (p Fugard), 1971
Orestes (p J. Hughes), 1717
Orestes (p J. Lindsay), 1967
Orestes (v Phillips), 1884
Organist (p H. Jones), 1892
Orghast (p Ted Hughes), 1971
O'Riada's Farewell (v Montague), 1974
Oriel O'Hanlon (radio G. Barker), 1957
Orient Express (f G. Greene), 1933
Oriental Eclogues (v William Collins), 1757
Orientations (f Maugham), 1899
Origin of the Veil (v Langhorne), 1773
Original Love-Letters Between a Lady of Quality and a Person of Inferior Station (f Combe), 1784
Original Poems on Several Occasions (v Reeve), 1769
Original Poetry by Victor and Cazire (v P. Shelley), 1810
Original Songs for the Rifle Volunteers (v Lover), 1861
Original Stories from Real Life (Wollstonecraft), 1788
Orion (v Roberts), 1880
Orissers (f Myers), 1922
Orkney (tv G. Brown), 1971
Orlando (f Woolf), 1928
Orlando Furioso (p R. Greene), 1591
Orley Farm (f Trollope), 1862
Ormington (f Gore), 1842
Ormond (f Edgeworth), 1817
Ornaments in Jade (f Machen), 1924
Oroonoko (f Behn), 1688
Oroonoko (p Southerne), 1695
Orphan (p Otway), 1680
Orphan Island (f R. Macaulay), 1924
Orphan of China (p Murphy), 1759
Orphans (f Oliphant), 1858
Orpharion (f R. Greene), 1599
Orpheus (ballet Bond), 1979
Orpheus (v Davie), 1974
Orpheus (p Galt), 1814
Orpheus (radio Ted Hughes), 1971
Orpheus and Eurydice (p H. Byron), 1863
Orpheus and Eurydice (p J. Dennis), 1707
Orpheus and Euridice (v Sydney Goodsir Smith), 1955
Orpheus in Diloeryum (p Sassoon), 1908
Orpheus in Mayfair (f Baring), 1909
Orpheus in the Haymarket (p Planché), 1865
Orpheus in the Underworld (p Noyes), 1911
Orpheus in Thrace (v de Tabley), 1901
Orphide (v A. Clarke), 1970
Orra (p Baillie), 1798
Orra (v W. Barnes), 1822
Orts (v Ted Hughes), 1978
Osbornes (f E. Benson), 1910
Osmyn the Renegade (p Maturin), 1830
Osorio (p Coleridge), 1873
Ossian (v Macpherson), 1765
Ossian's Address to the Sun (v Lord Byron), 1898
Ostella (v Tatham), 1650
Oswald Bastable (f Nesbit), 1905
O'Thello (p Dickens), 1833
Othello (p Shakespeare), 1604
Othello's Daughter (f MacNamara), 1942
Othello's Occupation (f Strong), 1945
Other Days (p Robertson), 1883
Other Exiles (v Brathwaite), 1975
Other Half (v Wright), 1966
Other House (f H. James), 1896
Other Landscape (f N. Gunn), 1954
Other Lovers (f Finlayson), 1976
Other Man (f Wallace), 1911
Other Paris (f Gallant), 1956
Other People's Lives (p Milne), 1932
Other People's Worlds (f Trevor), 1980
Other Place (f Priestley), 1953
Other Places (p Pinter), 1982
Other Poems (v Meynell), 1896
Other Side (tv Mortimer), 1967

Poems of Conformity (v C. Williams), 1917
Poems of Dedication (v Spender), 1946
Poems of Felicity (v Traherne), 1910
Poems of Love and Earth (v Drinkwater), 1912
Poems of Many Years (v Blunden), 1957
Poems of Men and Hours (v Drinkwater), 1911
Poems of Monarchy and Religion (v Greville), 1670
Poems of Places and People (v G. Barker), 1971
Poems of Rural Life in Common English (v W. Barnes), 1868
Poems of Rural Life in the Dorset Dialect (v W. Barnes), 1844
Poems of the East-West Synthesis (v MacDiarmid), 1946
Poems of the English Roadside (v Meredith), 1862
Poems of the New World (v Noyes), 1942
Poems of the Past and Present (v R. Hall), 1910
Poems of the Past and the Present (v Hardy), 1901
Poems of the Wanderer (v Masefield), 1930
Poems of Thirty Years (v Bottomley), 1925
Poems on Japan (v Blunden), 1967
Poems on Most of the Festivals of the Church (v Boyle), 1681
Poems on the Loss and Re-Building of St. Mary's Church, Cardiff (v Wordsworth), 1842
Poems on the War (v Meynell), 1916
Poems on Various Occasions (v Lord Byron), 1807
Poems on Various Subjects (v Coleridge), 1796
Poems Partly of Rural Life (v W. Barnes), 1846
Poems Soft and Loud (v Dutton), 1967
Poems to Paintings by William Johnstone 1933 (v MacDiarmid), 1963
Poems Unpleasant (v Baxter), 1952
Poems, Written Chiefly at Bremhill (v Bowles), 1809
Poems Written in Discouragement (v Yeats), 1913
Poems Written in Early Youth (v T. Eliot), 1950
Poems Written in the Year MCMXIII (v Bridges), 1914
Poet (v John Westland Marston), 1838
Poet and the Lunatic (f Chesterton), 1929
Poet at Play (v MacDiarmid), 1965
Poetaster (p Jonson), 1601
Poetasters of Ispahan (p Bax), 1912
Poetic Sermon (v Ramsay), 1724
Poetica Stromata (v Corbett), 1648
Poetical Address to Edmund Burke (v Bowles), 1791
Poetical Blossoms (v A. Cowley), 1633
Poetical Entertainer (v N. Ward), 1712
Poetical Epistle to Samuel Johnson (v Murphy), 1760
Poetical Epistle to Sir Joshua Reynolds (v Combe), 1777
Poetical Essay in Manner of Elegy on the Death of His Majesty (v Cunningham), 1760
Poetical Essays (v Daniel), 1599
Poetical Pieces (v W. Barnes), 1820
Poetical Rhapsody (v J. Davies), 1602
Poetical Sketches (v Blake), 1783
Poetical Vagaries (v Colman the Younger), 1812
Poetical Version of Certain Psalms of David (v Cumberland), 1801
Poetical Works of the Late Thomas Little, Esq (v Thomas Moore), 1801
Poetry as an Universal Nature (v John Westland Marston), 1838
Poetry for Supper (v R. Thomas), 1958
Poetry Harbinger (v Fairburn, Glover), 1958
Poetry of Anna Matilda (v H. Cowley), 1788
Poetry of Pathos and Delight (v Patmore), 1896
Poetry Promenade (radio MacNeice), 1946
Poetry Recital (v Stephens), 1925
Poet's Alphabet (v W. Davies), 1925
Poet's Calendar (v W. Davies), 1927
Poet's Circuits (v Colum), 1960
Poet's Complaint of His Muse (v Otway), 1680
Poet's Enchiridion (v E. Browning), 1914
Poet's Harvest Home (v William Bell Scott), 1882
Poet's Home (v Harpur), 1862
Poet's Meeting (v R. Thomas), 1983
Poet's Pilgrimage to Waterloo (v Southey), 1816
Poet's Pub (f Linklater), 1929
Poet's Ramble after Riches (v N. Ward), 1691
Poets Remembered (v Hodgson), 1967
Pohutukawa Tree (p B. Mason), 1957
Point Counter Point (f Huxley), 1928
Point of Transfer (tv Purdy), 1961
Point of View (f H. James), 1883
Point Valaine (p Coward), 1935
Pointed Roofs (f D. Richardson), 1915
Poirot, Hercule series (f Christie), from 1920
Poison Belt (f Doyle), 1913
Poison Island (f Quiller-Couch), 1906
Poison Ladies (f Bates), 1976
Poison Pen (scr Hunter), 1939
Poisoned Lands (v Montague), 1961
Poisoned Paradise (f Service), 1922
Poland (v T. Campbell), 1831
Polaris (radio Weldon), 1978
Polaris (f Weldon), 1985
Polemo-Medinia inter Vitarvam et Nebernam (v Drummond), 1645
Pole-Vaulter (v Layton), 1974
Policeman and the Rose (f Rao), 1978
Policy (p Robertson), 1871
Polish Tales (f Gore), 1833
Polite Farces for the Drawing-Room (p A. Bennett), 1900
Polite Satires (p Bax), 1922
Politesse (p Barrie), 1918
Political Justice (Godwin), 1793
Political Ode (v Lord Byron), 1880
Political Poems (v Praed), 1835
Political Romance (f Sterne), 1759
Politician (p Shirley), 1639
Pollio (v Mickle), 1766
Polly (p Bax), 1922
Polly (p Colman the Elder), 1777
Polly (p Gay), 1729
Polly Honeycombe (p Colman the Elder), 1760
Polly Oliver (f Coppard), 1935
Polyglots (f Gerhardie), 1925
Polyglots (radio Manning), 1977
Polygon (p Brighouse), 1911
Polyhymnia (v Peele), 1590
Polyolbion (v Drayton), 1612
Polypheme (p Cibber), 1734
Polyphemus (v Austin), 1901
Pom Pom (p Wodehouse), 1916
Pomander of Verse (v Nesbit), 1895
Pomegranates (v R. Campbell), 1932
Pomes Penyeach (v Joyce), 1927
Pomfret Towers (f Thirkell), 1938
Pomona Lactodorum (v S. Sitwell), 1972
Pomp and Circumstance (f Coward), 1960
Pompeii (v Hawker), 1827
Pompeii (v T. Macaulay), 1819
Pompey (p K. Philips), 1663
Pompey the Great (p Dorset, Godolphin, Sedley, Waller), 1664

Pompey the Great His Fair Cornelia's Tragedy (p Kyd), 1595
Pongo and the Bull (f Belloc), 1910
Pontiac and the Green Man (p R. Davies), 1977
Poobie (v Linklater), 1925
Pool of Vishnu (f Myers), 1940
Poor Baby (tv Weldon), 1975
Poor Caroline (f Holtby), 1931
Poor Clare (f Hartley), 1968
Poor Fellow, My Country (f X. Herbert), 1975
Poor Gentleman (p Colman the Younger), 1801
Poor Gentleman (f Oliphant), 1886
Poor Jack (p Buckstone), 1840
Poor Jack (f Marryat), 1840
Poor Judas (p Bagnold), 1946
Poor Laws and Paupers Illustrated (f Martineau), 1833
Poor Little Thing (p Jerome), 1914
Poor Man (f S. Benson), 1922
Poor Man and His Parish Church (v Hawker), 1843
Poor Men's Music (v E. Sitwell), 1950
Poor Miss Finch (f Wilkie Collins), 1872
Poor Mother (tv Weldon), 1970
Poor Mouth (f F. O'Brien), 1973
Poor of Liverpool (p Boucicault), 1864
Poor of New York (p Boucicault), 1857
Poor Old Haymarket (p Colman the Younger), 1792
Poor Parson (f Rudd), 1907
Poor Relations (f C. Mackenzie), 1919
Poor Scholar (f Carleton), 1869
Poor Shepherd (v Gay), 1720
Poor Soldier (p O'Keeffe), 1783
Poor Tom (f Muir), 1932
Poor Vulcan (p Dibdin), 1778
Poor Young People (v E. Sitwell, O. Sitwell, S. Sitwell), 1925
Poorhouse (p Gregory), 1904
Popanilla (f Disraeli), 1853
Pope Joan (p Settle), 1680
Pope of Rome (Boucicault), 1850
Pope's Wedding (p Bond), 1962
Popping the Question (p Buckstone), 1830
Popular Felons (p Jerrold), 1825
Popular Member (f Gore), 1844
Popular Verses (v Lawson), 1924
Popularity (p Moncrieff), 1839
Porcupine, Peter series (Cobbett), from 1795
Porius (f J. Powys), 1951
Porphyrion (v Binyon), 1898
Porta Pietatis (p T. Heywood), 1638
Portent (f MacDonald), 1864
Portrait (p Colman the Elder), 1770
Portrait (tv Duncan), 1954
Portrait (f F. Ford), 1910
Portrait (p Robinson), 1925
Portrait in a Mirror (f Morgan), 1929
Portrait of a Gentleman in Slippers (p Milne), 1926
Portrait of a Lady (f H. James), 1881
Portrait of a Man with Red Hair (f Hugh Walpole), 1925
Portrait of Mr. W.H (f Wilde), 1901
Portrait of the Artist as a Young Dog (f D. Thomas), 1940
Portrait of the Artist as a Young Man (f Joyce), 1916
Portrait-Royal (v Tate), 1703
Portraits of Places (H. James), 1883
Posies (v Gascoigne), 1575
Position at Noon (f Linklater), 1958
Positive Man (p O'Keeffe), 1782
Positives (v T. Gunn), 1966
Possession (f de la Roche), 1923
Possession (p L. Housman), 1922
Post Haste (f Ballantyne), 1880
Post Office (p Tagore), 1913
Postcard (v R. Thomas), 1968
Postcards to Pulcinella (v Duncan), 1941
Postern of Fate (f Christie), 1973
Posthumous Bartas (v Sylvester), 1606
Posthumous Fragments of Margaret Nicholson (v P. Shelley), 1810
Posthumous Papers of the Pickwick Club (f Dickens), 1837
Postmaster-General (f Belloc), 1932
Post-Mortem (p Coward), 1931
Post-Operative Instructions (v Livesay), 1968
Postscripts (Priestley), 1940
Postures (f Rhys), 1928
Pot Geranium (v Nicholson), 1954
Pot Luck (scr Travers), 1936
Pot of Broth (p Yeats), 1902
Pot of Caviare (p Doyle), 1910
Potch and Colour (f Prichard), 1944
Pothunters (f Wodehouse), 1902
Potter (tv Travers), 1948
Potterism (f R. Macaulay), 1920
Potting Shed (p G. Greene), 1957
Pound on Demand (p O'Casey), 1934
Poverty and Pride (p Reade), 1856
Powassan's Drum (D. Scott), 1985
Power and the Glory (f G. Greene), 1940
Power of Darkness (f Anand), 1958
Power of Love (f Manley), 1720
Power of the Dead (f Williamson), 1963
Power Politics (v Atwood), 1971
Power-House (f Buchan), 1916
Powers of the Air (p T. Sturge Moore), 1920
Practical Criticism (Richards), 1929
Practical Possum (v T. Eliot), 1947
Praeludium (p Randolph), 1630
Praeterita (v de Tabley), 1863
Praeterita (Ruskin), 1886
Prairie Chief (f Ballantyne), 1886
Praise (tv Gordimer), 1985
Praise of Life (v Binyon), 1896
Praise of Poetry Out of Sir Philip Sidney (p Churchyard), 1595
Praise of Private Life (Harington),
Praise of Wine (v Belloc), 1931
Praise Singer (f Renault), 1978
Prancing Nigger (f Firbank), 1924
Prater Violet (f Isherwood), 1945
Praxis (f Weldon), 1978
Pray for the Wanderer (f K. O'Brien), 1938
Prayer for My Son (f Hugh Walpole), 1936
Prayer for Peace (v Noyes), 1911
Precepts and Practice (f Hook), 1840
Precepts of Conjugal Happiness (v Langhorne), 1767
Precious Bane (f M. Webb), 1924
Precipice (f MacLennan), 1948
Precisely (p Pinter), 1983
Preface to America (tv Duncan), 1959
Prefaces, Biographical and Critical, to the Works of the English Poets (S. Johnson), 1779
Prefaces to Shakespeare (H.Barker), 1927
Prefect's Uncle (f Wodehouse), 1903
Preferment (f Gore), 1840
Preghiere (v G. Hill), 1964
Prehistoric Burials (v Sassoon), 1932

Prisoner of Chillon (v Lord Byron), 1816
Prisoner of Grace (f Cary), 1952
Prisoner of Mademoiselle (f Roberts), 1904
Prisoner of War (p Jerrold), 1842
Prisoner of Zenda (f Anthony Hope), 1894
Prisoners (p Killigrew), 1632
Prisoner's Progress (radio MacNeice), 1954
Private Angelo (f Linklater), 1946
Private Country (v Durrell), 1943
Private Devotions (Andrewes)
Private Drafts (v Durrell), 1955
Private Ear (p Shaffer), 1962
Private Enterprise (p Ervine), 1947
Private Enterprise (f Thirkell), 1947
Private Entertainment of the King and Queen at Highgate (p Jonson), 1604
Private History (p Courage), 1938
Private Life (f H. James), 1893
Private Life of an Indian Prince (f Anand), 1953
Private Life of Don Juan (scr Lonsdale), 1934
Private Lives (p Coward), 1930
Private Memoirs and Confessions of a Justified Sinner (f Hogg), 1824
Private Papers of Henry Ryecroft (f Gissing), 1903
Private Room (p Pinero), 1928
Private Rooms (p Priestley), 1953
Private Selby (f Wallace), 1912
Private Wound (f Day Lewis, as Blake), 1968
Privateer's-Man One Hundred Years Ago (f Marryat), 1846
Privilege of Place (p Martyn), 1915
Privy Seal (f F. Ford), 1907
Pro Patria Australia (v Gilmore), 1945
Pro Vere Autumni Lachrymae (v Chapman), 1622
Problem at Pollensa Bay (f Christie), 1943
Procedures for Underground (v Atwood), 1970
Proceed, Sergeant Lamb (f Robert Graves), 1941
Procession (v Steele), 1695
Prodigal Child (f Storey), 1982
Prodigal Father (radio Shaffer), 1957
Prodigal Son (p Plomer), 1968
Prodigals and Their Inheritance (f Oliphant), 1885
Product (v R. FitzGerald), 1977
Proems (v Durrell), 1938
Professional Foul (tv Stoppard), 1977
Professor (f C. Brontë), 1857
Professor (p Porter), 1965
Professor (f R. Warner), 1938
Professor Challenger Stories (f Doyle), 1952
Professor's Love Story (p Barrie), 1892
Profit and Loss (p Sherriff), 1923
Profit of Imprisonment (v Sylvester), 1594
Profitable Meditations Fitted to Man's Different Condition (v Bunyan), 1661
Profligate (p Pinero), 1889
Progress (p Ervine), 1922
Progress (f R. Graham), 1905
Progress (p Robertson), 1869
Progress and Prejudice (f Gore), 1854
Progress of a Divine (v Savage), 1735
Progress of Gallantry (v Richard Graves), 1774
Progress of Honesty (v D'Urfey), 1681
Progress of Julius (f D. du Maurier), 1933
Progress of Love (v Lyttelton), 1732
Progress of Love (f Munro), 1986
Progress of Mind (v William Bell Scott), 1838
Progress of Wit (v A. Hill), 1730
Projectors (p J. Wilson), 1665
Prologue (p D. Scott), 1923
Prometheus Bound (v E. Browning), 1833
Prometheus on His Crag (v Ted Hughes), 1973
Prometheus the Firegiver (p Bridges), 1883
Prometheus Unbound (p P. Shelley), 1820
Promise of Love (f Renault), 1939
Promise of May (p Tennyson), 1882
Promos and Cassandra (p Whetstone), 1578
Promotion (p Planché), 1833
Prompter's Box (p H. Byron), 1870
Proper Marriage (f Lessing), 1954
Prophecy of Famine (v Charles Churchill), 1763
Prophecy of Queen Emma (v Mickle), 1782
Prophesy to the Wind (p Nicholson), 1949
Prophet (p Fitzball), 1849
Prophetess (p J. Fletcher, Massinger), 1622
Prophetess (p Galt), 1814
Prophet's Mantle (f Nesbit), 1885
Proposal (p Bridie), 1932
Propria Quae Maribus (f Reade), 1857
Proprietor (radio A. Campbell), 1964
Proserpine (p Baring), 1908
Proserpine and Midas (p M. Shelley), 1922
Prosopopoeia Britannica (v Wither), 1648
Prospect (v James Thomson), 1735
Prospect of Death (v Pomfret), 1700
Prospect of Plenty (v Ramsay), 1720
Prospect of the Sea (f D. Thomas), 1955
Prospero's Cell (Durrell), 1945
Protective Custody (radio Koestler), 1942
Protector (v Wither), 1655
Prothalamion (v Spenser), 1596
Proust Recaptured (radio P. Johnson), 1948
Proust Reconstructions (radio P. Johnson), 1948
Proust Screenplay (p Pinter), 1977
Proverbial Philosophy (v Tupper), 1838
Proverbs (v Lydgate)
Proverbs in Porcelain (v A. Dobson), 1877
Providence (scr Mercer), 1978
Providence (v Mickle), 1762
Providence (p Smart), 1777
Provoked Husband (p Cibber, Vanbrugh), 1728
Provoked Wife (p Vanbrugh), 1697
Provost (f Galt), 1822
Prudence Corner (p Brighouse), 1927
Prude's Progress (p Jerome), 1895
Prufrock and Other Observations (v T. Eliot), 1917
Prunella (p H. Barker, L. Housman), 1904
Prurient Prude (p Reade), 1866
Prussian Officer (f Lawrence), 1914
P's and Q's (f Yonge), 1872
Psalms (v Frere), 1839
Psalms and Songs (v Lowry), 1975
Psalms of David (v Sidney), 1823
Psalms of David (v Smart), 1765
Psalms of David (v Wither), 1632
Psalms of David Imitated (v Watts), 1719
Psalms of David Turned into Meter (v H. King), 1651
Psalter or Psalms of David (v Keble), 1839
Psalterium Carolinum (v Stanley), 1657
Pseudodoxia Epidemica (T. Browne), 1646
Pseudo-Martyr (Donne), 1610
Psmith in the City (f Wodehouse), 1910
Psmith, Journalist (f Wodehouse), 1915
Psyche (v Joseph Beaumont), 1648
Psyche (p Shadwell), 1675
Psyche Apocalypte (v E. Browning), 1876

Quest of the Sangraal (v Hawker), 1864
Question about Hell (tv Amis), 1964
Question of Geography (p Berger), 1984
Question of Poetry (v Raine), 1969
Question of Proof (f Day Lewis, as Blake), 1935
Question of Sex (p A. Bennett), 1900
Question of Upbringing (f Powell), 1951
Question Time (p R. Davies), 1975
Questions at the Well (v F. Ford), 1893
Quetzalcoatl (f Lawrence), 1926
Quick Service (f Wodehouse), 1940
Quick Work (p Pinero), 1919
Quid pro Quo (p Gore), 1844
Quiet American (f G. Greene), 1955
Quiet as Moss (v A. Young), 1959
Quiet Heart (f Oliphant), 1854
Quiet Life (f Burnett), 1878
Quiet Wedding (scr Rattigan), 1941
Quiller Memorandum (scr Pinter), 1966
Quintessence of Ibsenism (Shaw), 1891
Quintus Servinton (f Savery), 1831
Quinx (f Durrell), 1985
Quisanté (f Anthony Hope), 1900
Quite Early One Morning (radio D. Thomas), 1944
Quite the Reverse (p Poole), 1839

Rabbit and a Leg (p R. Hughes), 1924
Rabbit at the Well (p Brathwaite), 1961
Rabbit Race (p Duncan), 1963
Race (f Ross), 1982
Rachel (v Pratt), 1917
Rachel Is Coming (p Boucicault), 1855
Rachel, Rachel (f Laurence), 1968
Rachel Ray (f Trollope), 1863
Rachel the Reaper (p Reade), 1871
Rack (tv Priestley), 1958
Racketty-Packetty House (f Burnett), 1906
Racketty-Packetty House (p Burnett), 1912
Rackety Colt (f G. Butler), 1989
Rada (p Noyes), 1914
Radcliffe (f Storey), 1963
Radiant Way (f Drabble), 1987
Radical (f Galt), 1832
Radical Cure (p Boucicault), 1850
Radio II (p Beckett), 1976
Raffle (p Dunsany), 1928
Raft (radio Clark), 1964
Rag and Bone Shop (v Birney), 1971
Ragazza (tv Mercer), 1978
Rage in Heaven (scr Isherwood), 1941
Ragged Trousered Philanthropists (f Tressell), 1914
Ragged Trousered Philanthropists (p Tressell), 1928
Ragman's Daughter (f Sillitoe), 1963
Ragman's Daughter (p Sillitoe), 1966
Ragman's Daughter (scr Sillitoe), 1972
Ragnhild (p J. Lindsay), 1927
Raid from Beauséjour (f Roberts), 1894
Raiders' Dawn (v A. Lewis), 1942
Railroad Children (f Yonge), 1855
Railway Accident (f Upward), 1969
Railway Children (f Nesbit), 1906
Railway Man and His Children (f Oliphant), 1891
Rain (f Maugham), 1933
Rain Forest (f Manning), 1974
Rain Stop Play (radio Selvon), 1967
Rainbirds (f Frame), 1968
Rainbow (f Lawrence), 1915
Rainbow (v S. Warner), 1932
Rainbow and the Rose (v Nesbit), 1905
Rainbow Bird (f Palmer), 1957
Rainbow Queen (f Nesbit), 1903
Rainbow Valley (f Montgomery), 1919
Rain-Check (v Souster), 1975
Rainy June (f Ouida), 1885
Raj Quartet (f P. Scott), 1976
Rajah Amar (f Myers), 1935
Rake and His Pupil (p Buckstone), 1833
Rakehelly Man (v Fairburn), 1946
Rake's Progress (p Auden), 1951
Raleigh (p Tupper), 1866
Ralph Roister Doister (p Udall), 1553
Ralph the Bailiff (f Braddon), 1862
Ralph the Heir (f Trollope), 1871
Rambler (S. Johnson), 1750
Rambling Fuddle-Caps (v N. Ward), 1706
Rambling Rakes (f N. Ward), 1700
Rambling Sailor (v Mew), 1929
Rampolli (v MacDonald), 1897
Ranald Bannerman's Boyhood (f MacDonald), 1871
Ranche in the Valley (f Henty), 1892
Randall and the River of Time (f Forester), 1950
Randall's Thumb (p Gilbert), 1871
Randolph (v Austin), 1854
Ranger's Daughter (p Fitzball), 1843
Rank and Riches (p Wilkie Collins), 1883
Ranolf and Amohia (v Domett), 1872
Ranter (v Elliott), 1830
Rape of Lucrece (p T. Heywood), 1603
Rape of Lucrece (v Shakespeare), 1594
Rape of Lucretia (p Duncan), 1946
Rape of the Lock (v Pope), 1714
Rape upon Rape (p H. Fielding), 1730
Rapid Thaw (p Robertson), 1867
Rapparee (p Boucicault), 1870
Raptures (v W. Davies), 1918
Rapunzel (v Baxter), 1952
Rare Device (radio Mortimer), 1965
Rash Act (f F. Ford), 1933
Rash Resolve (f Haywood), 1724
Rasputin (p Bax), 1929
Rasputin (p Gerhardie), 1960
Rasputin's End (p Spender), 1963
Rasselas (f S. Johnson), 1768
Rat Trap (p Coward), 1924
Rational Princess (p Brighouse), 1926
Rats (p Christie), 1962
Rats (v Sillitoe), 1960
Rauberbraut (p Fitzball), 1829
Ravenna (v Wilde), 1878
Raven's Almanac (f Dekker), 1609
Ravens' Brood (f E. Benson), 1934
Ravens of Orleans (p Moncrieff), 1820
Ravenshoe (f H. Kingsley), 1862
Ravished Soul and the Blessed Weeper (v Breton), 1601
Raw Edges (v Livesay), 1981
Raw Material (f Sillitoe), 1972
Rawdon's Roof (f Lawrence), 1928
Raymond and Agnes (p Fitzball), 1855
Raymond and Agnes (p M. Lewis), 1809
Rayner (p Baillie), 1804
Razor Grinder (p Dibdin)
Razor's Edge (f Maugham), 1944
Reader, Here You'll Plainly See Judgement Perverted by These Three (v T. Heywood), 1641

Sard Harker (f Masefield), 1924
Sardanapalus (p Lord Byron), 1821
Sartor Resartus (f Carlyle), 1836
Satan Absolved (p Blunt), 1899
Satan in Search of His Wife (v Lamb), 1831
Satanic Verses (f Rushdie), 1988
Satire Against Reason and Mankind (v Rochester), 1679
Satire Against Virtue (v Oldham), 1679
Satire Against Wine (v N. Ward), 1705
Satire Against Wit (v Richard Blackmore), 1700
Satire, Dedicated to His Most Excellent Majesty (v Wither), 1614
Satire of the Three Estates (p D. Lindsay), 1540
Satire on Satirists and Admonition to Detractors (v Landor), 1836
Satire's Comic Project (v Ramsay), 1720
Satires of Circumstance (v Hardy), 1914
Satires upon the Jesuits (v Oldham), 1681
Satirical Poems (v Sassoon), 1926
Satiromastix (p Dekker), 1601
Saturday Life (f R. Hall), 1925
Saturday Market (v Mew), 1921
Saturday Night and Sunday Morning (f Sillitoe), 1958
Saturday Night and Sunday Morning (scr Sillitoe), 1960
Saturday Night at the Crown (f Greenwood), 1959
Saturday Night at the Crown (p Greenwood), 1954
Saturn over the Water (f Priestley), 1961
Saucer of Larks (f Friel), 1962
Saul (p A. Hill), 1760
Sauve Qui Peut (f Durrell), 1966
Saved (p Bond), 1965
Saved by the Lifeboat (f Ballantyne), 1869
Saville (f Storey), 1976
Saviors (radio Dane), 1940
Savonarola (p Austin), 1881
Savonarola e il Priore di San Marco (v Landor), 1860
Sawbones Memorial (f Ross), 1974
Saxon Shillin' (p Colum), 1903
Say Nothing (radio Hanley), 1961
Sayings and Doings (f Hook), 1824
Says the Muse to Me, Says She (v Strong), 1922
Scale of Perfection (Hilton)
Scales of Justice (f Marsh), 1955
Scamps of London (p Moncrieff), 1843
Scan Mag (p Poole), 1840
Scandal at Coventry (radio Dane), 1958
Scandal of Father Brown (f Chesterton), 1935
Scandal of Spring (f Boyd), 1934
Scandalous Affair of Mr. Kettle and Mrs. Moon (p Priestley), 1955
Scandalum Magnatum (v D'Urfey), 1682
Scandaroon (f Williamson), 1972
Scapegoat (f D. du Maurier), 1957
Scape-Goat (p Poole), 1825
Scapegoat (f T. Powys), 1966
Scapegoats and Rabies (v Ted Hughes), 1967
Scaramouch in Naxos (p Davidson), 1889
Scaramouche a Philosopher (p Ravenscroft), 1677
Scaramuccia (p Fitzball), 1839
Scarcity of Love (f Kavan), 1956
Scarecrow (f de la Mare), 1945
Scaring Off of Teddy Dawson (p Brighouse), 1911
Scarlet and Hyssop (f E. Benson), 1902
Scarlet Shawl (f Jefferies), 1874
Scarlet Sword (f Bates), 1950
Scarperer (f Behan), 1964
Scarronides (v Cotton), 1664
Scene at Abbotsford (f Walter Scott), 1829
Scenes and Characters (f Yonge), 1847
Scenes and Hymns of Life (v Hemans), 1834
Scenes from an Album (radio Trevor), 1975
Scenes from Kenneth (f Yonge), 1899
Scenes of Childhood (f S. Warner), 1981
Scenes of Clerical Life (f G. Eliot), 1858
Scented Gardens for the Blind (f Frame), 1963
Sceptic (v Hemans), 1820
Sceptic (v Thomas Moore), 1809
Sceptical Muse (v Pomfret), 1699
Sceptred Flute (v Naidu), 1928
Scherzo di Capriccio (v S. Sitwell), 1972
Scherzo di Fantasia (v S. Sitwell), 1972
Schiffbrüchig (p Maugham), 1902
Schindler's Ark (f Keneally), 1982
Schindler's List (f Keneally), 1982
Scholar (p Buckstone), 1835
School (p Robertson), 1869
School for Arrogance (p Holcroft), 1791
School for Coquettes (p Gore), 1831
School for Fathers (p Bickerstaff), 1770
School for Friends (p P. White), 1935
School for Greybeards (p H. Cowley), 1786
School for Grown Children (p Morton), 1827
School for Guardians (p Murphy), 1767
School for Husbands (p Macklin), 1968
School for Love (f Manning), 1951
School for Lovers (p Whitehead), 1762
School for Scandal (p Boucicault), 1878
School for Scandal (p Sheridan), 1777
School for Scheming (p Boucicault), 1847
School for Widows (p Cumberland), 1789
School for Widows (f Reeve), 1791
School for Wives (p Kelly), 1773
School of Compliment (p Shirley), 1625
School of Eloquence (p H. Cowley), 1780
School of Politics (f N. Ward), 1690
School of Reform (p Morton), 1805
Schoolboy (p Cibber), 1702
Schoolboy Lyrics (v Kipling), 1881
Schooldays at Rugby (f Thomas Hughes), 1857
Schoolfellows (p Jerrold), 1835
Schoolmaster (Ascham), 1570
Schoolmistress (p Pinero), 1886
School-Mistress (v Shenstone), 1742
Schoolroom (tv Trevor), 1972
Schoolroom Window (p K. O'Brien), 1937
Schooner Came to Atia (f Finlayson), 1953
Schreber's Nervous Illness (radio Caryl Churchill), 1972
Schubert (p Duncan), 1980
Scilla's Metamorphosis (v Lodge), 1589
Scoop (radio Christie, Dane, Sayers), 1931
Scoop (f Christie, Dane, Sayers), 1983
Scoop (f Waugh), 1938
Scornful Lady (p F. Beaumont, J. Fletcher), 1613
Scorpion (v Stevie Smith), 1972
Scorpion God (f Golding), 1971
Scotch Nationality (v Elliott), 1824
Scotland's Lament (v Barrie), 1895
Scots' Apostacy (v Cleveland), 1646
Scots Figgaries (p Tatham), 1652
Scots Hairst (f L. Gibbon), 1967
Scots Musical Museum (v Burns), 1787
Scots Ode to the British Antiquarians (v Ramsay), 1726
Scots Quair (f L. Gibbon), 1946
Scots Songs (v Ramsay), 1718

Secret Memoirs of the Late Mr. Duncan Campbel (f Haywood), 1732
Secret of Chimneys (f Christie), 1925
Secret of Father Brown (f Chesterton), 1927
Secret of Narcisse (f Gosse), 1892
Secret of the Kyriels (f Nesbit), 1899
Secret of the Tower (f Anthony Hope), 1919
Secret Orchards (tv Trevor), 1980
Secret Pass (p Fitzball), 1852
Secret People (scr Cary), 1952
Secret Pilgrim (f le Carré), 1991
Secret Places of the Heart (f Wells), 1922
Secret Power (f Corelli), 1921
Secret River (f R. Macaulay), 1909
Secret Rose (f Yeats), 1897
Secret Service (p Planché), 1834
Secret Trails (f Roberts), 1916
Secretary (p Knowles), 1843
Secrets (v W. Davies), 1924
Secrets Worth Knowing (p Morton), 1798
Secular Masque (p Dryden), 1700
Secular Ode in Commemoration of the Glorious Revolution (v W. Mason), 1788
Sedan Chair (p Fitzball), 1832
Seduction (p Holcroft), 1787
See the Old Lady Decently (f B. Johnson), 1975
See What You've Done (tv Amis), 1974
See You Later (p Wodehouse), 1918
Seed and the Sower (f van der Post), 1963
Seed of Adam (p C. Williams), 1948
Seeds of Time (v Drinkwater), 1921
Seedtime (f Palmer), 1957
Seekers (f Bates), 1926
Seeking the Bubbles (tv Lawler), 1975
Sejanus His Fall (p Jonson), 1603
Séjour (f Beckett), 1970
Select Conversations with an Uncle (f Wells), 1895
Selected Life (v Kinsella), 1972
Selected Profane Verse and Sacred Poetry (v A. Smith), 1946
Selective Affinities (v Dutton), 1985
Self (f Gore), 1845
Self Condemned (f W. Lewis), 1954
Self to Self (v de la Mare), 1928
Self-Completing Tree (v Livesay), 1986
Self-Control (f Brunton), 1811
Self's the Man (p Davidson), 1901
Semele (p Congreve), 1710
Semi-Monde (p Coward), 1977
Send Round the Hat (f Lawson), 1907
Seneca's Oedipus (p Ted Hughes), 1968
Sensation Dramas for the Back Drawing Room (p H. Byron), 1864
Sensation Novel (p Gilbert), 1871
Sensational Tales (f M. Clarke), 1886
Sense and Sensation (p T. Taylor), 1864
Sense and Sensibility (f Austen), 1811
Sense of Detachment (p Osborne), 1972
Sense of Humour (f Pritchett), 1956
Sense of Movement (v T. Gunn), 1957
Sense of Reality (f G. Greene), 1963
Sense of the Past (f H. James), 1917
Sensibility (v H. More), 1782
Sentimental Agents (f Lessing), 1983
Sentimental Journey Through France and Italy (f Sterne), 1768
Sentimental Tommy (f Barrie), 1896
Sentimentalists (p Meridith), 1910
Sentinel (p Boucicault), 1853
Sentinel of the Alma (p Lover), 1854
Senza Alcun Sospetto (radio Walcott), 1950
Separate Lives (f Palmer), 1931
Separate Maintenance (p Colman the Elder), 1779
Separate Peace (tv Stoppard), 1966
Separate Tables (p Rattigan), 1954
Separate Tables (scr Rattigan), 1958
Separation (p Baillie), 1836
Separation and Reparation (p Morton), 1830
September (p Bond), 1990
September Tide (p D. du Maurier), 1948
Sequence for Francis Parkman (v Davie), 1961
Sequence of Sonnets on the Death of Browning (v Swinburne), 1890
Sequences (v Gustafson), 1979
Sequences (v Sassoon), 1956
Ser Taldo's Bride (p Drinkwater), 1911
Seraglio (p Dibdin), 1776
Seraphim (v E. Browning), 1838
Seraphina (radio G. Barker), 1956
Seraphine (p Boucicault), 1869
Serena Blandish (f Bagnold), 1924
Serena of Oakwood (v Fitzball), 1815
Serenade to a Sister (v S. Sitwell), 1972
Serf (p T. Taylor), 1865
Sergeant Dunn, CID (f Wallace), 1962
Sergeant Lamb of the Ninth (f Robert Graves), 1940
Sergeant Lamb's America (f Robert Graves), 1940
Sergeant Sir Peter (f Wallace), 1932
Sergeant's Wife (p Banim), 1827
Serio-Comic Governess (p Zangwill), 1904
Serious Money (p Caryl Churchill), 1987
Serious Thing (p Gogarty), 1919
Serjeant Musgrave's Dance (p Arden), 1959
Sermon on Swift (v A. Clarke), 1968
Sermons of Mr. Yorick (Sterne), 1760
Serpent (f N. Gunn), 1943
Serpent and the Rope (f Rao), 1960
Serpent of Division (v Lydgate),
Servant (scr Pinter), 1963
Servant Boy (v Heaney), 1971
Servant Girl (tv Atwood), 1974
Servant of the Public (f Anthony Hope), 1905
Servants (p Murdoch), 1980
Servants and the Snow (p Murdoch), 1970
Service Not Included (tv Ayckbourn), 1974
Service with a Smile (f Wodehouse), 1961
Servitors (f Hunter), 1934
Servitude (v Dodsley), 1729
Sesame and Lilies (Ruskin), 1865
Set of Six (f Conrad), 1908
Set of Variations (f O'Connor), 1969
Set to Music (p Coward), 1939
Setting the World on Fire (f A. Wilson), 1980
Settler and the Savage (f Ballantyne), 1876
Settlers at Home (f Martineau), 1841
Settlers in Canada (f Marryat), 1844
Settlers of the Marsh (f Grove), 1925
Settling Day (p T. Taylor), 1865
Seven Against Reeves (f Aldington), 1938
Seven Ages of Woman (f C. Mackenzie), 1923
Seven Arms (f Strong), 1935
Seven Champions of Christendom (p Planché), 1849
Seven Days in New Crete (f Robert Graves), 1949
Seven Deadly Sins of London (f Dekker), 1606

Spare the Rod (p P. Johnson, Snow), 1951
Sparkenbroke (f Morgan), 1936
Sparkling Cyanide (f Christie), 1945
Sparrow (p Ayckbourn), 1967
Spartacus (f L. Gibbon), 1933
Spartan Dame (p Southerne), 1719
Speak of the Mearns (f L. Gibbon), 1982
Speak, Parrot (v Skelton), 1521
Speak to the Earth (v A. Young), 1939
Speaking for Scotland (v MacDiarmid), 1939
Special Duties (tv Mortimer), 1975
Specimens of Modern Poets (v Swinburne), 1880
Speckled Band (p Doyle), 1910
Spectator (Addison, Steele), 1712
Spectre Bridegroom (p Moncrieff), 1821
Speculation (v Anstey), 1780
Speculum Speculativum (v Wither), 1660
Speeches at Prince Henry's Barriers (p Jonson), 1610
Speeches for Doctor Frankenstein (v Atwood), 1966
Speed the Plough (p Morton), 1800
Spell (f C. Brontë), 1931
Spell for Green Corn (radio G. Brown), 1967
Spell for Old Bones (f Linklater), 1949
Spell of the Yukon (v Service), 1907
Spella Ho (f Bates), 1938
Spell-Bound (p Boucicault), 1879
Spendthrift (f Ainsworth), 1857
Spendthrift (p Jerrold), 1850
Sphinx (v Wilde), 1894
Sphinx at Gizeh (p Dunsany), 1912
Sphinx of Eaglehawk (f Boldrewood), 1895
Sphinx Theologica (v Benlowes), 1636
Spider (radio Weldon), 1973
Spider and the Fly (v J. Heywood), 1556
Spider Danced a Cozy Jig (v Layton), 1984
Spider's Palace (f R. Hughes), 1931
Spider's Web (p Christie), 1954
Spiel (p Beckett), 1963
Spikenard (v L. Housman), 1898
Spinsters in Jeopardy (f Marsh), 1953
Spiral Ascent (f Upward), 1977
Spire (f Golding), 1964
Spires and Gantries (radio MacNeice), 1956
Spirit of Bambatse (f Haggard), 1906
Spirit of Discovery (v Bowles), 1804
Spirit of the Age (Hazlitt), 1825
Spirit Rises (f S. Warner), 1962
Spirits in Bondage (v C. Lewis), 1919
Spiritual Exercises (v Spender), 1943
Spiritual Poems (v J. Gray), 1896
Spiritual Quixote (f Richard Graves), 1773
Spleen (p Colman the Elder), 1776
Spleen (v M. Green), 1737
Spleen (v Winchilsea), 1709
Splendid Shilling (v J. Philips), 1701
Splendid Spur (f Quiller-Couch), 1889
Splendid Village (v Elliott), 1833
Splinter in the Heart (f Purdy), 1990
Splinter of Ice (tv Weldon), 1972
Spoiled (tv S. Gray), 1968
Spoiled Child (p Bickerstaff), 1790
Spoils (v Bunting), 1965
Spoils of Poynton (f H. James), 1897
Spoilt City (f Manning), 1962
Sponono (p Paton), 1962
Sponsalia Polyxenae (v Landor), 1819
Spook Stories (f E. Benson), 1928
Sport of Chance (f Sharp), 1888
Sport of Nature (f Gordimer), 1987
Sport Royal (f Anthony Hope), 1893
Sporting Rights (p Brighouse), 1943
Spots of the Leopard (p Baxter), 1963
Spotted Dick (p Travers), 1939
Spouter (p Murphy), 1756
Spreading the News (p Gregory), 1904
Sprigs of Laurel (p O'Keeffe), 1793
Spring (v James Thomson), 1728
Spring Awakening (p Bond), 1974
Spring Cleaning (f Burnett), 1908
Spring Cleaning (p Lonsdale), 1923
Spring Days (f G. Moore), 1888
Spring Fever (f Wodehouse), 1948
Spring Gardens (p Planché), 1846
Spring in Bloomsbury (p Brighouse), 1911
Spring of a Lion (f Haggard), 1899
Spring of Joy (v M. Webb), 1917
Spring Picture (f D. du Maurier), 1944
Spring Song (f Bates), 1927
Spring Song (f Cary), 1960
Spring Song (v Purdy), 1968
Spring Song (f F. Reid), 1916
Spring Sowing (f O'Flaherty), 1924
Spring, Summer, Autumn, Winter (v Ted Hughes), 1974
Spring Tide (p Priestley), 1936
Springboard (v MacNeice), 1944
Springboard to Nowhere (f Wodehouse), 1950
Springhaven (f R.D. Blackmore), 1887
Spring's Glory (p Nabbes), 1638
Spur of the Moment (p H. Byron), 1872
Spy upon the Conjurer (f Haywood), 1724
Spy Who Came In from the Cold (f le Carré), 1963
Spy Who Loved Me (f Fleming), 1962
Squanders of Castle Squander (f Carleton), 1852
Square Cat (p Ayckbourn), 1959
Square Egg (f Saki), 1924
Square Emerald (f Wallace), 1926
Square Peg (f Masefield), 1937
Square Pegs (p Bax), 1919
Squaring the Circle (tv Stoppard), 1984
Squatter's Dream (f Boldrewood), 1890
Squeaker (f Wallace), 1927
Squeaker (p Wallace), 1928
Squeaker (scr Wallace), 1930
Squealer (f Wallace), 1928
Squire (f Bagnold), 1938
Squire (p Pinero), 1881
Squire Arden (f Oliphant), 1871
Squire Brainless (p A. Hill), 1710
Squire of Alsatia (p Shadwell), 1688
Squire Oldsapp (p D'Urfey), 1678
Squire Speaks (p R. Mason), 1938
Squire Trelooby (p Congreve, Vanbrugh, Walsh), 1704
'Squire Turned Ferret (v Pope), 1727
Squire's Last Shilling (p H. Byron), 1870
Squire's Return (p Cumberland), 1773
S.S. Elizabethan (radio Hanley), 1941
Stable Boy (v Peacock), 1820
Stage Coach (p Farquhar), 1701
Stage Fright (scr Bridie), 1950
Stage Play (p Gilbert), 1890
Stage Struck (p S. Gray), 1979
Stage-Beaux Tossed in a Blanket (p T. Brown), 1704
Stage-Coach Journey to Exeter (f Manley), 1725
Stained Radiance (f L. Gibbon), 1930

Tower of the Dream (v Harpur), 1865
Towers of Silence (f P. Scott), 1971
Towers of Trebizond (f R. Macaulay), 1956
Towie Castle (p Bottomley), 1929
Town and Country (p Morton), 1807
Town and Country Lovers (f Gordimer), 1980
Town Before You (p H. Cowley), 1794
Town Fop (p Behn), 1676
Town Major of Miraucourt (f Priestley), 1930
Town Traveller (f Gissing), 1898
Toxin (f Ouida), 1895
Toxophilus (Ascham), 1545
Toy (p O'Keeffe), 1789
Toy Cart (p Symons), 1916
Toys of Peace (f Saki), 1919
Toy-Shop (p Dodsley), 1735
Trackers of Oxyrhynchus (p Harrison), 1988
Tractor and the Corn Goddess (f Anand), 1947
Tracts for the Times (Keble, Newman), from 1833
Tracy's Ambition (f Griffin), 1830
Trafalgar Day 1940 (v Dane), 1940
Trafalgar Medal (p Buckstone), 1863
Traffics and Discoveries (f Kipling), 1904
Tragedy a la Mode (p Foote), 1760
Tragedy in Green (f Firbank), 1980
Tragedy of Count Alarcos (p Disraeli), 1839
Tragedy of Donohoe (p Harpur), 1987
Tragedy of Korosko (f Doyle), 1898
Tragedy of Nan (p Masefield), 1908
Tragedy of Ovid (p Cokayne), 1662
Tragedy of Pompey the Great (p Masefield), 1910
Tragedy of Sophonisba (p James Thomson), 1730
Tragedy of Tragedies (p H. Fielding), 1731
Tragedy of Zara (p A. Hill), 1735
Tragic Comedians (f Meredith), 1880
Tragic Mothers (p T. Sturge Moore), 1920
Tragic Muse (f H. James), 1890
Tragic Muse (p Bridie), 1935
Tragic Nesta (p Bax), 1934
Tragical Complaint of Elstred (v Lodge), 1593
Trail of '98 (f Service), 1910
Trail of the Serpent (f Braddon), 1861
Train to Banbury (radio O'Faolain), 1947
Train to Pakistan (f Singh), 1956
Traitor (p Shirley), 1631
Traitor (v Combe), 1781
Traitor's Gate (f Wallace), 1927
Traitors in Our Way (p MacNeice), 1957
Traits and Stories of the Irish Peasantry (f Carleton), 1830
Tramp (f Wallace), 1965
Transatlantic Tunnel (scr Dane), 1935
Transcripts from Nature (v Sharp), 1884
Transformed Metamorphosis (v Tourneur), 1600
Transition (v Durrell), 1934
Transitional Poem (v Day Lewis), 1929
Translations (p Friel), 1980
Translations and Tomfooleries (p Shaw), 1926
Translations from Camoens (v Hemans), 1818
Transmutation (f Gore), 1854
Trap (f D. Richardson), 1925
Trap (p Sutro), 1918
Trappolin Creduto Principe (p Cokayne), 1658
Trappolin Supposed a Prince (p Cokayne), 1658
Traps (p Caryl Churchill), 1977
Trash Dedicated Without Respect to J. Halse, Esq., M.P. (v Praed), 1833
Travail of Gold (f E. Benson), 1933
Travel Tales of Mr. Joseph Jorkens (f Dunsany), 1931
Travelers (f Jhabvala), 1973
Traveller (v de la Mare), 1945
Traveller (v Goldsmith), 1764
Traveller in Time (v A. Young), 1958
Traveller Returns (p Dane), 1927
Traveller Without Luggage (p Whiting), 1959
Travellers (p Palmer), 1923
Travellers (f Strong), 1945
Travellers (radio Trevor), 1982
Traveller's Litany (v Baxter), 1955
Traveller's Room (p Fitzball), 1847
Traveller's Samples (f O'Connor), 1951
Traveller's Tale (v Bax), 1921
Travelling Carriage (p Planché), 1835
Travelling Companions (f H. James), 1919
Travelling Grave (f Hartley), 1948
Travelling Man (p Gregory, Yeats), 1909
Travelling Musicians (p Page), 1984
Travelling People (f B. Johnson), 1963
Travels in Nihilon (f Sillitoe), 1971
Travels into Several Remote Nations of the World, by Captain Lemuel Gulliver (f Swift), 1726
Travels of Three English Brothers (p Day, Rowley), 1607
Travels with a Donkey in the Cévennes (Stevenson), 1879
Travels with My Aunt (f G. Greene), 1969
Travesties (p Stoppard), 1974
Trawl (f B. Johnson), 1966
Treason in the Egg (f Strong), 1958
Treasure Box (v Robert Graves), 1919
Treasure Island (f Stevenson), 1883
Treasure of Heaven (f Corelli), 1906
Treasure of the Incas (f Henty), 1902
Treasure of the Lake (f Haggard), 1926
Treasure on Pelican (p Priestley), 1952
Treasure on Pelican Island (tv Priestley), 1951
Treasure Seekers (f Nesbit), 1899
Treasure Trove (f Lover), 1844
Treasures in the Marshes (f Yonge), 1893
Tree (f Bates), 1930
Tree Clock (v Heaney), 1990
Tree for Strings (v MacCaig), 1977
Tree House (v Baxter), 1974
Tree of Heaven (f Sinclair), 1917
Tree of Idleness (v Durrell), 1955
Tree of Man (f P. White), 1955
Tree of the Sun (f W. Harris), 1978
Tree on Fire (f Sillitoe), 1967
Trees (v Monro), 1916
Trees, Effigies, Moving Objects (v Curnow), 1972
Trelawny of the "Wells" (p Pinero), 1898
Trembling of the Earth (v Churchyard), 1602
Trembling of the Leaf (f Maugham), 1921
Tremendous Adventures of Major Brown (f Chesterton), 1903
Tremor of Intent (f Burgess), 1966
Trespasser (f Lawrence), 1912
Trevanion (p John Westland Marston), 1849
Trevannion (f Strong), 1948
Trial (p Baillie), 1798
Trial (f Yonge), 1864
Trial and Error (p Strong), 1939
Trial by Jury (p Gilbert), 1875
Trial by Jury (p Hook), 1811
Trial of a City (v Birney), 1952
Trial of a Judge (p Spender), 1938
Trial of Dedan Kimathi (p Ngugi), 1976

NOTES
ON
CONTRIBUTORS

ALCOCK, Peter. Former Senior Lecturer in English, Massey University, Palmerston North, New Zealand; associate editor, *World Literature Written in English*. Honorary life member of the South Pacific Association for Commonwealth Literature and Language Studies. **Essays:** Blanche Baughan; Denis Glover; Edith Searle Grossman; *Pig Island Letters*.

ALEXANDER, M.J. Berry Professor of English Literature, University of St. Andrews, Scotland. Author of *The Earliest English Poems*, 1966, *Beowulf: A Verse Translation*, 1973, *Twelve Poems*, 1978, *The Poetic Achievement of Ezra Pound*, 1979, *Old English Riddles from the Exeter Book*, 1980, and *History of Old English Literature*, 1983. Editor, with A.N. Jeffares, of the *Macmillan Anthologies of English Literature*, 5 vols., 1989. **Essays:** Hilaire Belloc; Laurence Binyon; Rupert Brooke; *Beowulf*.

ALLEN, Walter. Novelist and literary critic. Author of eight novels (the most recent being *Get Out Early*, 1986, and *Accosting Profiles*, 1989); several critical works, including *Arnold Bennett*, 1948, *Reading a Novel*, 1949 (revised 1956, 1963), *Joyce Cary*, 1953 (revised 1963, 1971), *The English Novel*, 1954, *Six Great Novelists*, 1955, *The Novel Today*, 1955 (revised 1960), *George Eliot*, 1964, *The Modern Novel in Britain and the United States* (British edition: *Tradition and Dream*), 1964, *Some Aspects of the American Short Story*, 1973, and *The Short Story in English*, 1981; social history, including *The Urgent West: The American Dream and Modern Man*, 1969; and memoirs (*As I Walked Down New Grub Street*, 1981). Has taught at several universities in Britain, the U.S., and Canada. **Essays:** George Eliot; Richard Hughes; Rudyard Kipling; Arthur Morrison; Dorothy Richardson; H.G. Wells.

ALWES, Derek B. Doctoral candidate, University of Massachusetts, Amherst. Author of "Who knowes not Colin Clout? Spenser's Self-Advertisement in *The Faerie Queene*, Book VI," in *Modern Philology*, August 1990. **Essays:** *Amoretti*; *The Defence of Poesy*.

AMORE, Adelaide P. Professor of English, Southern Connecticut State University, New Haven. Editor of *A Woman's Inner World: Selected Poetry and Prose of Anne Bradstreet*, 1983, and *Oroonoko; or, The History of a Slave* by Aphra Behn, 1987. **Essays:** Mary Wollstonecraft; *Oroonoko*.

ANDERSON, W.E.K. Head Master, Eton College, Berkshire. Editor of *The Journal of Sir Walter Scott*, 1972, and *The Percy Letters*, vol. 9, 1989. **Essay:** Sir Walter Scott.

ARDOLINO, Frank. Associate Professor of English, University of Hawaii, Manoa. Author of *Thomas Kyd's Mystery Play: Myth and Ritual in The Spanish Tragedy*, 1985, and articles on Kyd and Robert Greene. **Essays:** *Friar Bacon and Friar Bungay*; *The Spanish Tragedy*.

ARNOLD, Richard. Associate Professor of English, University of Lethbridge, Alberta. Author of articles on English hymns, Chaucer, Cowper, Samuel Johnson, Lampman, Smart, and other topics. **Essays:** *A Journal of the Plague Year*; *A Song to David*; *Sublime and Beautiful*; *The Task*.

ARVIDSON, K.O. Associate Professor of English, University of Waikato, Hamilton, New Zealand; member of the editorial board, *Journal of New Zealand Literature*. Author of *Riding the Pendulum: Poems 1961–1969*, 1973, and articles on Polynesian and New Zealand literature. **Essay:** Allen Curnow.

ASHLEY, Leonard R. N. Professor of English, Brooklyn College, City University of New York. Author of *Colley Cibber*, 1965, *Nineteenth-Century British Drama*, 1967, *Authorship and Evidence: A Study of Attribution and the Renaissance Drama*, 1968, *History of the Short Story*, 1968, *George Peele*, 1970, *The Wonderful World of Superstition, Prophecy, and Luck*, 1984, *The Wonderful World of Magic and Witchcraft*, 1986, *The Dictionary of Sex Slang*, 1987, and *Elizabethan Popular Culture*, 1988. Editor of the *Enriched Classics* series, several anthologies of fiction and drama, and a number of facsimile editions. **Essays:** Henry Brooke; John Baldwin Buckstone; Henry Chettle; Anthony Munday; Terence Rattigan; Elkanah Settle.

ASTLE, David. Former Principal Lecturer in Communication Studies, Sheffield City Polytechnic; now retired. **Essays:** Lascelles Abercrombie; Roy Fuller; "Sailing to Byzantium."

AVERY, Gillian. Author 20 books for children (the most recent being *Huck and Her Time Machine*, 1977, *Mouldy's Orphan*, 1978, and *Sixpence!*, 1979), and books for adults, including two novels—*The Lost Railway*, 1980, and *Onlookers*, 1983—and *Mrs. Ewing*, 1961, *Nineteenth Century Children: Heroes and Heroines in English Children's Stories 1780–1900* (with Angela Bull), 1965, *Childhood's Pattern: A Study of the Heroes and Heroines of Children's Fiction 1770–1950*, 1975, and *The Best Type of Girl: A History of Girls' Independent Schools*, 1991. Editor of several anthologies for children and of works by Juliana Horatia Ewing, Andrew Lang, Charlotte Yonge, Frances Hodgson Burnett, Mary Louisa Molesworth, E.V. Lucas, and other writers. **Essays:** George Grossmith; Thomas Hughes; Francis Kilvert; Charlotte Yonge; *Tom Brown's School Days*; *The Water-Babies*.

BACHELDER, Frances H. Freelance writer. Author of an essay in *The Life and Work of Barbara Pym* edited by Dale Salwak, 1987, and of *Mary Roberts Rinehart* (forthcoming). **Essay:** Barbara Pym.

BACKSCHEIDER, Paula R. Professor of English, University of Rochester, New York. Author of *A Being More Intense: A Study of the Prose Works of Bunyan, Swift, and Defoe*, 1984, *Daniel Defoe: Ambition and Innovation*, 1986, *Daniel Defoe: His Life*, 1989, and *Moll Flanders: The Making of a Criminal Mind*, 1990. Editor of the Garland *Eighteenth-Century Drama* series (69 vols.) and *Restoration* *and Eighteenth-Century Dramatists* (Dictionary of Literary Biography), 3 vols., 1989. **Essay:** John Crowne.

BAKER, Denise N. Associate Professor of English, University of North Carolina, Greensboro. Author of articles on medieval literature in *Speculum* and *Viator*. **Essay:** *Confessio Amantis*.

BAKER, Lee C.R. Associate Professor of English, High Point College, North Carolina. Author of articles on Carlyle, Browning, and other writers in *Victorians Institute Journal*, *Victorian Poetry*, *Studies in Philology*, and *Victorian Newsletter*. **Essay:** *Sartor Resartus*.

BAREHAM, T. Senior Lecturer in English, University of Ulster, Coleraine, County Londonderry. Author of *George Crabbe: A Critical Study*, 1977, *A Bibliography of Crabbe* (with S. Gattrell), 1978, and *Malcolm Lowry*, 1989. Editor of *Anthony Trollope*, 1980, *Trollope: The Barsetshire Novels: A Casebook*, 1983, and *Stoppard: Rosencrantz and Guildenstern Are Dead, Jumpers, Travesties: A Casebook*, 1990. **Essays:** Sir Richard Blackmore; Robert Bloomfield; William Lisle Bowles; George Crabbe; Stephen Duck; Sir Samuel Garth; Samuel Rogers; Tom Stoppard; *Amelia*; *Barnaby Rudge*; *Coriolanus*; *Rosencrantz and Guildenstern Are Dead*; *The Village*.

BARKER, Debra Stoner. Assistant Professor of English, Butler University, Indianapolis. Author of articles and reviews in *American Notes and Queries*, *Balcones Review*, and other journals. **Essay:** Alan Sillitoe.

BARKER, Jonathan. Literature officer, British Council, London. Author of articles and reviews in *Agenda, PN Review*, *Poetry Wales*, *Times Literary Supplement*, and other journals. Editor of *The Arts Council Poetry Library Catalogue*, 6th edition, 1981, *Selected Poems of W.H. Davies*, 1985, *Poetry Book Society Anthology 1986–1987*, 1986, *The Art of Edward Thomas*, 1987, *Thirty Years of the Poetry Book Society, 1956–1986*, 1988, and *Collected Poems of Norman Cameron* (with Warren Hope), 1990. Librarian, Arts Council Poetry Library, 1973–88. **Essay:** Norman Cameron.

BARNES, John. Reader in English, La Trobe University, Bundoora, Victoria. Author of *Henry Kingsley and Colonial Fiction*, 1971, and articles on Peter Cowan, Hal Porter, and Patrick White. **Essays:** Henry Kingsley; Vance Palmer.

BATTESTIN, Martin C. William R. Kenan, Jr., Professor of English, University of Virginia, Charlottesville. Author of *The Moral Basis of Fielding's Art*, 1959, *The Providence of Wit: Aspects of Form in Augustan Literature and the Arts*, 1974, and *Henry Fielding: A Life*, 1989. Editor of *Joseph Andrews*, *Tom Jones*, and *Amelia* for the Wesleyan Edition of Fielding's works, and of *British Novelists 1660–1800* (Dictionary of Literary Biography), 2 vols., 1985. **Essay:** Henry Fielding.

BEGNAL, Michael H. Professor of English and Comparative Literature, Pennsylvania State University, University Park. Author of *Joseph Sheridan Le Fanu*, 1971, *A Conceptual Guide to Finnegans Wake* (with Fritz Senn), 1974, *Narrator and Character in Finnegans Wake* (with Grace Eckley), 1975, and *Dreamscheme: Narrative and Voice in Finnegans Wake*, 1988. Editor of *On Miracle Ground: Essays on the Fiction of Lawrence Durrell*, 1990. **Essays:** *Molloy*, *Malone Dies*, and *The Unnamable*; *Ulysses* (by James Joyce).

BENKOVITZ, Miriam J. Late Professor of English, Skidmore College, Saratoga Springs, New York. Author of *Ronald Firbank: A Bibliography*, 1963 (and supplement), *Firbank: A Biography*, 1969, and *Aubrey Beardsley*, 1980. Editor of *Edwy and Elgiva* by Fanny Burney, 1957, and *A Passionate Prodigality* by Richard Aldington, 1976. Died 1986. **Essays:** Ronald Firbank; Frederick Rolfe.

BENSEN, Alice R. Professor Emerita of English, Eastern Michigan University, Ypsilanti. Author of *Rose Macaulay*, 1969. **Essay:** Charlotte Mew.

BERGONZI, Bernard. Professor of English, University of Warwick, Coventry. Author of *Descartes and the Animals*, 1954, *The Early H.G. Wells*, 1961, *Anthony Powell*, 1962 (revised 1971), *Heroes' Twilight: A Study of the Literature of the Great War*, 1965 (2nd edition 1980), *The Situation of the Novel*, 1970 (2nd edition 1979), *T.S. Eliot*, 1971 (2nd edition 1978), *Gerard Manley Hopkins*, 1977, *Reading the Thirties*, 1978, *Years: Sixteen Poems*, 1979, *The Roman Persuasion* (novel), 1981, *The Myth of Modernism and Twentieth-Century Literature*, 1986, and *Exploding English*, 1990. Editor of *Poetry 1870 to 1914*, 1980. **Essays:** Roy Campbell; Philip Larkin.

BERGONZI, Gabriel. Freelance writer and lecturer. Died 1984. **Essays:** Ada Leverson; Alice Meynell.

BERRY, Francis. Professor of English, Royal Holloway College, University of London; now emeritus. Author of several books of poetry (the most recent being *From the Red Fort*, 1984), a novel (*I Tell of Greenland*, 1977), radio plays, critical works including *Poets' Grammar*, 1958, and *Poetry and the Physical Voice*, 1962, and studies of Herbert Read, Shakespeare, and John Masefield. **Essays:** Matthew Arnold; Lord Byron; Arthur Hugh Clough; Sir John Denham; John Masefield.

BEVIS, Richard. Professor of English, University of British Columbia, Vancouver. Author of *The Laughing Tradition: Stage Comedy in Garrick's Day*, 1980, and *English Drama: Restoration and Eighteenth Century 1660–1789*, 1988. Editor of *Eighteenth Century Drama: Afterpieces*, 1970. **Essays:** George Colman the Elder; John Dennis; Samuel Foote; Charles Macklin; William Whitehead; *The Ascent of F6*; *The Double-Dealer*; *An Essay on Man*; *The Man of Feeling*; *Robinson Crusoe*; *Travels in Arabia Deserta*.

BISIGNANO, Dominic J. Associate Professor of English, Indiana University–Purdue University, Indianapolis. **Essays:** Stella Benson; Sylvia Townsend Warner.

BLACKALL, Jean Frantz. Professor of English, Cornell University, Ithaca, New York; member of the board of editors, *Henry James Review*. Author of *Jamesian Ambiguity and the Sacred Fount*, 1966, and articles on Harold Frederic, Henry James, Charlotte Brontë, and Edith Wharton. **Essays:** *The Ambassadors*; *The Portrait of a Lady*.

BLAMIRES, David. Reader in German, University of Manchester; editor of the David Jones Society *Newsletter*. Author of *An Echoing Death* (poetry), 1965, *Characterization and Individuality in Wolfram's Parzifal*, 1966, *The Bible Half Hour*, 1968, *David Jones, Artist and Writer*, 1971 (revised 1978), *Homosexuality from the Inside*, 1973, *Towards a Theology of Gay Liberation* (with others), 1977, *Herzog Ernst and the Otherworld Voyage*, 1979, and a study of

Quakerism. Co-editor of *Studies in Medieval Literature and Languages*, 1973, and co-translator of *Medieval Comic Tales*, 1973. **Essays:** David Jones; Vernon Watkins.

BLANCH, Robert J. Professor of English, Northeastern University, Boston. Author of *Sir Gawain and the Green Knight: A Reference Guide*, 1983, and numerous articles on medieval literature. Editor of *Sir Gawain and Pearl: Critical Essays*, 1966, *Style and Symbolism in Piers Plowman*, 1969, *Chaucer in the Eighties* (with Julian Wasserman), 1986, and *Text and Matter: New Critical Perspectives of the Pearl Poet* (with Miriam Miller and Julian Wasserman), 1990. **Essay:** *Sir Gawain and the Green Knight.*

BLISS, Carolyn. Member of the Department of English, University of Utah, Salt Lake City; editor, American Association of Australian Literary Studies *Newsletter*. Author of *Patrick White's Fiction: The Paradox of Fortunate Failure*, 1986, and the chapter on White in *International Literature in English* edited by Robert L. Ross, 1991. **Essay:** *Voss*.

BLOOM, Edward A. Professor of English, Brown University, Providence, Rhode Island. Author of *Samuel Johnson in Grub Street*, 1957; *The Order of Poetry* (with C. H. Philbrick and E. M. Blistein), 1961; *Willa Cather's Gift of Sympathy* (with Lillian D. Bloom), 1962; *The Order of Fiction*, 1964; *Joseph Addison's Sociable Animal* (with Lillian D. Bloom), 1971. Editor of *The Journals and Letters of Frances Burney*, vol. 8 (with Lillian D. Bloom), 1978, *Addison and Steele: The Critical Heritage* (with Lillian D. Bloom), 1980, and *Educating the Audience* (with others), 1984. **Essay:** Fanny Burney.

BOGDANOR, Vernon. Lecturer in Politics, Brasenose College, Oxford. Author of *Devolution*, 1979, *The People and the Party System*, 1981, *Multi-Party Politics and the Constitution*, 1983, and *What Is Proportional Representation?*, 1984. Editor of *Lothair* by Benjamin Disraeli, 1975, and *The Blackwell Encyclopaedia of Political Institutions*, 1987. **Essay:** Benjamin Disraeli.

BOLL, Theophilus E. M. Emeritus Professor of English, University of Pennsylvania, Philadelphia; research consultant, *English Literature in Transition*. Author of *The Works of Edwin Pugh: A Chapter in the Novel of Humble London Life*, 1934, *Miss May Sinclair, Novelist: A Biographical and Critical Introduction*, 1973, and an essay on Stephen Hudson in *Richard, Myrtle and I*, edited by Violet Schiff, 1962. **Essay:** May Sinclair.

BOOTH, Roy. Lecturer in English, Royal Holloway and Bedford New College, University of London, Egham, Surrey. Author of articles on Donne and Webster in *English*. **Essay:** *Measure for Measure*.

BOTTRALL, Margaret. Biographer and critic; former University Lecturer, Department of Education, and Senior Tutor, Hughes Hall, University of Cambridge. Author of *George Herbert*, 1954, *Izaak Walton*, 1956, and *Every Man a Phoenix: Studies in Seventeenth-Century Autobiography*, 1958. Editor of *Personal Records*, 1961, *Blake's Songs of Innocence and Experience*, 1970, and *Gerard Manley Hopkins: Poems: A Casebook*, 1975. **Essays:** Richard Crashaw; John Hookham Frere; Lord Herbert of Cherbury; John Keble; Edith Sitwell; Izaak Walton; Anne Finch, Countess of Winchilsea; *The Compleat Angler*; *The Country Parson*; "The Pearl"; *Religio Medici*.

BOTTRALL, Ronald. Poet and travel writer; teacher and member of the British Council or UN staffs in Finland, Singapore, Italy, Sweden, Brazil, Greece, and Japan. Author of several books of poetry, including *The Collected Poems*, 1961, *Poems 1955–1973*, 1974, and *Against a Setting Sun: Poems 1974–1983*, 1984, and of *Rome*, 1968. Co-editor of works by T.S. Eliot and of poetry anthologies. Died 1989. **Essay:** L.H. Myers.

BOVE, Cheryl K. Assistant Professor of English, Ball State University, Muncie, Indiana. Author of *A Character Index and Guide to the Fiction of Iris Murdoch*, 1986, "America and Americans in the Novels of Iris Murdoch," in *Encounters with Iris Murdoch* edited by Richard Todd, 1988, and other essays and reviews. **Essay:** Iris Murdoch.

BRAKE, Laurel. Lecturer in Literature, Centre for Extra-Mural Studies, Birkbeck College, University of London; co-editor, *Pater Newsletter*. Editor of *The Year's Work in English Studies*, from 1981, and *Investigating Victorian Journalism*, 1990. **Essays:** John Arden; William Morris; Alfred, Lord Tennyson; *Marius the Epicurean*; *The Renaissance*.

BRATTON, J.S. Reader in Theatre and Cultural Studies, Royal Holloway and Bedford New College, University of London, Egham, Surrey. Author of *The Victorian Popular Ballad*, 1975, *The Impact of Victorian Children's Fiction*, 1981, and *Music Hall: Performance and Style*, 1986. Editor of *The Coral Island* by R.M. Ballantyne, 1990. **Essays:** Lewis Carroll; G.A. Henty; Thomas Hood; George MacDonald; Frederick Marryat; T.H. White.

BREWER, Derek. Emeritus Professor, Cambridge University, and Life Fellow of Emmanuel College. Author of *Chaucer*, 1953 (revised 1973), *Chaucer and His World*, 1978, *Symbolic Stories*, 1980, *Tradition and Innovation in Chaucer*, 1982, *English Gothic Literature*, 1983, *Chaucer: The Poet as Storyteller*, 1984, and *An Introduction to Chaucer*, 1984. Editor of *Chaucer and Chaucerians*, 1966, and *Chaucer: The Critical Heritage*, 2 vols., 1978. **Essays:** *The Canterbury Tales*; *Cleanness*; "The Monkey's Paw."

BRISSENDEN, Alan. Reader in English, University of Adelaide, Australia; joint general editor, Tudor and Stuart Text series. Author of *Rolf Boldrewood*, 1972, and *Shakespeare and the Dance*, 1981. Editor of *A Chaste Maid in Cheapside* by Thomas Middleton, 1968, *Shakespeare and Some Others*, 1976, and *The Portable Boldrewood*, 1979 (revised 1989). **Essays:** Rolf Boldrewood; Barnaby Rich; William Rowley; *As You Like It*.

BROOKS-DAVIES, Douglas. Senior Lecturer in English, University of Manchester. Author of *Spenser's Faerie Queene: A Commentary on Books I and II*, 1977, *Pope's Dunciad and the Queen of the Night: A Study in Emotional Jacobitism*, 1985, and *Fielding, Dickens, Gosse, Iris Murdoch and Oedipal Hamlet*, 1989. **Essays:** Fay Weldon; *Fanny Hill; Father and Son*; *Lycidas*; *Orchestra*; *The Sea, The Sea*; "To Autumn"; *Tom Jones*.

BROWN, Cedric C. Senior Lecturer in English, University of Reading, Berkshire. Author of *Milton's Aristocratic Entertainments*, 1985. Editor of *The Poems and Masques of Aurelian Townshend*, 1983. **Essay:** Aurelian Townshend.

BROWN, Lloyd W. Member of the Department of Comparative Literature, University of Southern California, Los Angeles. Author of *West Indian Poetry*, 1978 (revised 1984), *Amiri Baraka*, 1980, and *Women Writers in Black Africa*, 1981. Editor of *The Black Writer in Africa and the Americas*, 1973. **Essays:** Louise Bennett; Roger Mais.

BROWN, Mary. Former Lecturer in English Studies, University of Ulster, Coleraine, County Londonderry. **Essay:** I. Compton-Burnett.

BROWN, Phyllis Rugg. Lecturer in English, Santa Clara University, California. Editor (with Georgia Ronan Crampton and Fred C. Robinson) of *Modes of Interpretation in Old English Literature*, 1986. **Essays:** *The Anglo-Saxon Chronicle*; *The Exeter Book*.

BROWN, Terence. Associate Professor of English, Trinity College, Dublin. Author of *Louis MacNeice: Sceptical Vision*, 1975, *Northern Voices: Poets from Ulster*, 1975, *Ireland: A Social and Cultural History 1922–1979*, 1981, and *Impressions of Dublin*, 1986. Editor of *Time Was Away: The World of Louis MacNeice* (with Alec Reid), 1974, *Sir Samuel Ferguson* (with Barbara Hayley), 1987, and *Tradition and Influence in Anglo-Irish Poetry* (with Nicholas Grene), 1989. **Essays:** Padraic Colum; Aubrey De Vere; W.R. Rodgers.

BRUMMER, Ross. Member of the Department of English, St. John's University, Jamaica, New York. **Essay:** Edward FitzGerald.

BURLINSON, Kathryn. Lecturer in English, University of Southampton, Hampshire. Author of "What Language Can Utter the Feeling: Identity in the Poetry of Emily Brontë," in *Creating the Self: Subjectivity in Literature from the Romantics to the Present Day* edited by P. Stockwell and P. Shaw, 1991. **Essays:** Elizabeth Barrett Browning; *Aurora Leigh*; *Sonnets from the Portuguese*.

BURTON, Robert S. Assistant Professor of English, California State University, Chico. **Essays:** John Fowles; Raymond Williams; *Lucky Jim*; *Sizwe Bansi Is Dead*.

BUTLER, Lance St. John. Lecturer in English, University of Stirling, Scotland. Author of *Thomas Hardy*, 1978, *Beckett and the Meaning of Being: A Study in Ontological Parable*, 1984, *Victorian Doubt: Literary and Cultural Discourses*, 1990, and *Modern Approaches to Literary Criticism: The Freedom of the Text*, 1990. Editor of *Alternative Hardy*, 1989, and *Rethinking Beckett* (with Robin J. Davies), 1990. **Essays:** *Atalanta in Calydon*; "Dover Beach"; *Handley Cross*; "The Hound of Heaven"; *In Memoriam*; "My Last Duchess"; *The Pickwick Papers*; *Rubáiyát of Omar Khayyám*.

BUTTER, P.H. Emeritus Regius Professor of English, University of Glasgow. Author of *Shelley's Idols of the Cave*, 1954, *Francis Thompson*, 1961, *Edwin Muir*, 1962, and *Edwin Muir: Man and Poet*, 1966. Editor of *Alastor, Prometheus Unbound, and Other Poems*, by Shelley, 1971, *Selected Letters of Edwin Muir*, 1974, *Selected Poems of William Blake*, 1982, and *The Truth of Imagination: Some Uncollected Reviews and Essays by Edwin Muir*, 1988. **Essays:** George Mackay Brown; Edwin Muir; Percy Bysshe Shelley; Francis Thompson; *The Marriage of Heaven and Hell*; *Milton*.

BYER, James E. Associate Professor of English, Western Carolina University, Cullowhee, North Carolina. Author of several articles on American and African literature. **Essays:** *Lorna Doone*; *The Ordeal of Richard Feverel*.

CADOGAN, Mary. Secretary of an educational trust, governor of an international school, and freelance writer. Author of three books on popular literature with Patricia Craig—*You're a Brick, Angela!*, 1976, *Women and Children First*, 1978, *The Lady Investigates*, 1981—three volumes of *The Charles Hamilton Companion* (with John Wernham), 1976–82, *The Morcove Companion* (with Tommy Keen), 1981, *From Wharton Lodge to Linton Hall: The Charles Hamilton Christmas Companion* (with Tommy Keen), 1984, *Richmal Crompton: The Woman Behind William*, 1986, *Frank Richards: The Chap Behind the Chums*, 1988, and *The William Companion*, 1990. **Essay:** *Alice's Adventures in Wonderland* and *Through the Looking-Glass*.

CALDER, Angus. Reader in Arts, Open University in Scotland, Edinburgh. Author of *The People's War: Britain 1939–1945*, 1969, *Russia Discovered: Nineteenth-Century Fiction from Pushkin to Chekhov*, 1976, *Revolutionary Empire*, 1982, *T.S. Eliot*, 1987, and *Byron*, 1987. Editor, *Writers in East Africa* (with Andrew Gurr), 1974, *Old Mortality* by Scott, 1975, and *Speak for Yourself* (with others), 1984. **Essay:** *The Prime of Miss Jean Brodie*.

CALDER, Charles. Assistant in English, University of Aberdeen. Author of articles on Shakespeare. **Essays:** Alexander Hume; Mary Renault; *Henry V*; *Henry VI*, parts 1–3.

CALDER, Robert L. Professor of English, University of Saskatchewan, Saskatoon. Author of *W. Somerset Maugham and the Quest for Freedom*, 1972, and *Willie: The Life of W. Somerset Maugham*, 1989. **Essay:** "Rain."

CAMPBELL, Ian. Reader in English Literature, University of Edinburgh. Author of *Thomas Carlyle*, 1974, *Lewis Grassic Gibbon*, 1985, and other books and articles on Victorian literature and Scottish literature. Associate editor of the Duke-Edinburgh *Carlyle Letters*, and editor of Carlyle's *Reminiscences* and *Selected Essays*. **Essays:** James Bridie; John Buchan; Thomas Carlyle; George Douglas; Allan Ramsay; *The French Revolution*.

CARNALL, Geoffrey. Reader in English Literature, University of Edinburgh. Author of *Robert Southey and His Age*, 1960, *Robert Southey*, 1964, and *The Mid-Eighteenth Century* (with John Butt), a volume in the Oxford History of English Literature, 1979. Editor of *Pope, Dickens and Others: Essays and Addresses by John Butt*, 1969, and *The Impeachment of Warren Hastings* (with Colin Nicholson), 1989. **Essays:** Charlotte Lennox; Robert Southey.

CAUWELS, Janice M. Freelance writer; formerly taught at Emory University, Atlanta, and University of Minnesota, Minneapolis. Author of *Bulimia*, 1983, *The Body Shop*, 1986, and articles on Elizabeth Inchbald and other writers. **Essay:** Catherine Gore.

CEVASCO, G.A. Associate Professor of English, St. John's University, Jamaica, New York. Author of numerous books, including *Salvador Dali*, 1971, *Oscar Wilde*, 1972, *J.-K. Huysmans: A Reference Guide*, 1980, *John Gray*, 1982, *The Sitwells*, 1987, and *Three Decadent Poets: Ernest*

Dowson, John Gray, and Lionel Johnson: An Annotated Bibliography, 1990. **Essays:** John Gray; Sacheverell Sitwell.

CHITHAM, Edward. Tutor and Counsellor, Open University, Milton Keynes, Buckinghamshire. Author of *The Black Country*, 1972, *Ghost in the Water*, 1973, *Brontë Facts and Brontë Problems* (with T.J. Winnifrith), 1983, *The Brontës' Irish Background*, 1986, and *A Life of Emily Brontë*, 1987. Editor of *The Poems of Anne Brontë*, 1979. **Essays:** Mary Webb; *Jane Eyre*.

CLARK, Axel. Lecturer in English, Australian National University, Canberra. Author of *Christopher Brennan: A Critical Biography*, 1980, and *Henry Handel Richardson: Fiction in the Making* (vol. 1 of biography), 1990. **Essay:** *The Fortunes of Richard Mahony*.

CLARK, David R. Professor Emeritus of English, University of Massachusetts, Amherst. Author of *W.B. Yeats and the Theatre of Desolate Reality*, 1965, *Lyric Resonance: Glosses on Some Poems by Yeats, Frost, Crane, Cummings, and Others*, 1972, and *Yeats at Songs and Choruses*, 1983. Editor or co-editor of *Reading Poetry*, 1968, *Druid Craft: The Writing of The Shadowy Waters*, 1972, *Critical Essays on Hart Crane*, 1982, and *W.B. Yeats: The Writing of Sophocles' King Oedipus*, 1989. **Essays:** *Adonais*; *Epithalamion*; "Ode to a Nightingale."

CLARK, John R. Professor of English, University of South Florida, Tampa. Author of *Form and Frenzy in Swift's Tale of a Tub*, 1970, *Senecan Tragedy*, 1988, *Seneca: A Critical Bibliography 1900–1980*, 1989, and of many articles, reviews, and translations in periodicals. Editor of *Satire—That Blasted Art* (anthology), 1973, and of satire issues of *Seventeenth-Century News*, Spring-Summer 1975 and *Thalia*, Spring-Summer 1982. **Essays:** Tom Brown; Earl of Dorset; John Oldham; Samuel Pepys; Matthew Prior; *A Tale of a Tub*.

CLARK, Leonard. Author and editor of many books of poetry, fiction, and nonfiction for children and adults, including *Collected Poems and Verses for Children*, 1975, *Winter to Winter and Other Poems*, 1977, and studies of Alfred Williams, Walter de la Mare, and Andrew Young; inspector of schools in Devon, Yorkshire, and London: *The Inspector Remembers: A Diary of One of Her Majesty's Inspectors of Schools 1936–1970*, 1976. Died 1981. **Essay:** Andrew Young.

CLARK, Rosalind. Assistant Professor of English, Saint Mary's College, Notre Dame, Indiana. Author of *The Great Queens: Irish Goddesses from the Morrigan to Cathleen Ni Houlihan*, 1990. **Essay:** *Sir Orfeo*.

CLUCAS, Garth. Freelance writer. **Essay:** Geoffrey Dutton.

CLUNE, Anne. Senior Lecturer in English, Trinity College, Dublin. Author of *Flann O'Brien: A Critical Introduction to His Writings* (as Anne Clissman), 1975. **Essays:** Anthony Burgess; Lennox Robinson; *At Swim-Two-Birds*; *Brideshead Revisited*; *Northanger Abbey*; *Riders to the Sea*; "Trinket's Colt"; *A Vision*.

COCKSHUT, A.O.J. G.M. Young Lecturer in Nineteenth Century Literature, Oxford University, and Fellow of Hertford College. Author of *Anthony Trollope: A Critical Study*, 1955, *Anglican Attitudes: A Study of Victorian Religious Controversies*, 1959, *The Imagination of Charles Dickens*, 1961, *The Unbelievers: English Agnostic Thought 1840–1890*, 1964, *The Achievement of Walter Scott*, 1969, *Truth to Life: The Art of Biography in the Nineteenth Century*, 1974, *Man and Woman: Love in the Novel*, 1977, and *The Art of Autobiography in 19th and 20th Century England*, 1984. Editor of *Religious Controversies of the Nineteenth Century: Selected Documents*, 1966, and *Miss Mackenzie* by Trollope, 1988. **Essays:** Introduction: The Novel to 1900; Jane Austen; Elizabeth Bowen; Charles Dickens; George Gissing; Coventry Patmore; Angus Wilson; *Apologia pro Vita Sua*; *Culture and Anarchy*; *Dombey and Son*; *Felix Holt*; *Idylls of the King*; *The Mayor of Casterbridge*; *Middlemarch*; *Murder in the Cathedral*; *Nightmare Abbey*; *Our Mutual Friend*; *The Wings of the Dove*.

COHEN, Morton N. Professor Emeritus of English, City University of New York. Author of *Rider Haggard: His Life and Work*, 1960 (revised 1968). Editor of *Kipling to Haggard: The Record of a Friendship*, 1965, *The Letters of Lewis Carroll*, 2 vols., 1979 (*Selected Letters*, 1982), and *Lewis Carroll: Interviews and Recollections*, 1989. **Essay:** H. Rider Haggard.

COHN, Ruby. Professor of Comparative Drama, University of California, Davis; co-editor, *Modern Drama*, *Theatre Journal*, and *Cambridge Guide to World Drama*. Author of *Samuel Beckett: The Comic Gamut*, 1962, *Currents in Contemporary Drama*, 1969, *Edward Albee*, 1969, *Dialogue in American Drama*, 1971, *Back to Beckett*, 1971, *Modern Shakespeare Offshoots*, 1976, *Just Play: Beckett's Theatre*, 1980, *New American Dramatists 1960–1980*, 1982, and *From Desire to Godot*, 1987. **Essay:** Samuel Beckett.

COLLINS, Philip. Professor of English, University of Leicester; now retired. Author of *James Boswell*, 1956, *Dickens and Crime*, 1962 (revised 1963), *Dickens and Education*, 1963 (revised 1964), *The Impress of the Moving Age*, 1965, and *Reading Aloud: A Victorian Métier*, 1972. Editor of *Dickens: The Critical Heritage*, 1971, *Dickens: Interviews and Recollections*, 2 vols., 1981, *Thackeray: Interviews and Recollections*, 1983, and *The Annotated Dickens* (with Edward Giuliano), 1986. **Essays:** *Adam Bede*; *North and South*; *Oliver Twist*; *Scenes of Clerical Life*; *Sketches by Boz*.

COLMER, John. Emeritus Professor of English, University of Adelaide, Australia. Author of *Coleridge: Critic of Society*, 1959, *Approaches to the Novel*, 1967, *E.M. Forster: A Passage to India*, 1967, *Forster: The Personal Voice*, 1975, *Patrick White: Riders in the Chariot*, 1977, *Coleridge to Catch-22: Images of Society*, 1978, *Patrick White*, 1984, and *Australian Autobiography: The Personal Quest*, 1989. Editor of works by Coleridge and of *The Penguin Book of Australian Autobiography*, 1987. **Essay:** E.M. Forster.

COOK, Philip S. Lecturer in Drama, University of Manchester. **Essay:** *The Castle of Perseverance*.

COPLAND, R.A. Former member of the Department of English, University of Canterbury, Christchurch, New Zealand. **Essays:** James Courage; Robert Paltock; Denton Welch.

COWASJEE, Saros. Professor of English, University of Regina, Saskatchewan. Author of *Sean O'Casey: The Man Behind the Plays*, 1963 (revised 1965), *O'Casey*, 1966, *Stories* *and Sketches*, 1970, *Goodbye to Elsa*, 1974, *Coolie: An Assessment*, 1976, *So Many Freedoms: A Study of the Major Fiction of Mulk Raj Anand*, 1978, *The Last of the Maharajas*, 1978, and *Suffer Little Children*, 1982. Editor of fiction and letters by Anand, and of several anthologies of fiction, including *Stories from the Raj*, 1983, *More Stories from the Raj and After*, 1986, and *Women Writers of the Raj*, 1990. **Essay:** Sean O'Casey.

COX, Don Richard. Professor of English, University of Tennessee, Knoxville. Author of *Sexuality and Victorian Literature*, 1984, *Arthur Conan Doyle*, 1985, and *The Mystery of Edwin Drood: An Annotated Bibliography*, 1991. **Essays:** *The Hound of the Baskervilles*; *The Mystery of Edwin Drood*.

CRADDOCK, Patricia B. Professor of English, University of Florida, Gainesville. Author of *Young Gibbon, Gentleman of Letters*, 1982, and *Gibbon, Luminous Historian 1772–1794*, 1989, and of *Gibbon: A Reference Guide* (with Margaret Craddock Huff), 1987. Editor of *The English Essays* by Gibbon, 1972. **Essay:** Edward Gibbon.

CRAIG, Patricia. Freelance writer. Author of three books on popular literature with Mary Cadogan—*You're a Brick, Angela!*, 1976, *Women and Children First*, 1978, and *The Lady Investigates*, 1981—and of *Elizabeth Bowen*, 1986. **Essay:** Rosamond Lehmann.

CRAIK, T.W. Emeritus Professor of English, University of Durham. Author of *The Tudor Interlude*, 1958, and *The Comic Tales of Chaucer*, 1964. Joint general editor of *The Revels History of Drama in the English Language*, editor of plays by Massinger, Marlowe, Beaumont and Fletcher, and Shakespeare, and co-editor of *Selected Poetry and Prose of Donne*, 1986. **Essays:** Henry Medwall; George Peele; Thomas Sackville and Thomas Norton; Nicholas Udall; Robert Wilson; *Eastward Ho*; *Hero and Leander*; *The Maid's Tragedy*; *The Merry Wives of Windsor*; *The Plain-Dealer*; *Tamburlaine the Great*; *Three Men in a Boat*; *Trilby*; *Twelfth Night*; *Women Beware Women*.

CROSS, Richard K. Professor of English, University of Maryland, College Park. Author of *Flaubert and Joyce: The Rite of Fiction*, 1971, *Malcolm Lowry: A Preface to His Fiction*, 1980, and articles on Shakespeare, Lowry, Richard Eberhart, and Randall Jarrell. **Essays:** *The Good Soldier*; "Wodwo."

CROSSAN, Greg. Senior Lecturer in English, Massey University, Palmerston North, New Zealand. Author of *A Relish for Eternity: The Process of Divinization in the Poetry of John Clare*, 1976. New Zealand contributor to *Annual Bibliography of English Language and Literature*. **Essay:** Felicia Hemans.

CUSICK, Edmund. Lecturer in English, St. David's University College, Lampeter, Wales. Author of "MacDonald and Jung," in *The Gold Thread: Essays on George MacDonald* edited by William Raeper, 1990. **Essays:** *King Solomon's Mines*; "Lamia"; *Macbeth*; *Maud*; *The Mysteries of Udolpho*.

DACE, Tish. Professor of English, Southeastern Massachusetts University, North Dartmouth; contributor to *Plays International, Plays and Players, Theater Week, Theatre Crafts, Other Stages, Village Voice*, New York *Times*, *American Theatre, Playbill*, and other periodicals. Author of *LeRoi Jones (Imamu Amiri Baraka): A Checklist of Works by and about Him*, 1971, *The Theatre Student: Modern Theatre and Drama*, 1973, and *Langston Hughes: Early Critical Responses*, 1991. **Essays:** David Mercer; John Mortimer; Harold Pinter.

DAHL, Curtis. Samuel Valentine Cole Professor of English, Wheaton College, Norton, Massachusetts. Author of *Robert Montgomery Bird*, and articles on William Cullen Bryant, Edward Bulwer-Lytton, and Benjamin Disraeli. Editor of *There She Blows: A Narrative of a Whaling Voyage*, 1971. **Essays:** Edward Bulwer-Lytton; Algernon Charles Swinburne.

DANIELS, William. Professor of English, Rhodes College, Memphis, Tennessee; now retired. Author of articles on George William Russell and Yeats in *Dublin University Review*, *Irish University Review*, and *Eire-Ireland*. **Essay:** George William Russell.

DARLING, Robert. Assistant Professor of English, Keuka College, Keuka Park, New York. Author of poetry, reviews, and criticism in more than 30 periodicals. **Essay:** A.D. Hope.

DAVIDSON, Peter. Lecturer in English, University of Leiden, Netherlands. **Essays:** "Corinna's Going a-Maying"; "An Horatian Ode upon Cromwell's Return from Ireland."

DAVIS, Walter R. Professor of English, Brown University, Providence, Rhode Island. Author of *A Map of Arcadia*, 1965, and of articles on Surrey, Lodge, Spenser, Drayton, Bacon, and Browne. Editor of *The Works of Thomas Campion*, 1967, *Idea and Act in Elizabethan Fiction*, 1969, and *Twentieth-Century Interpretations of Much Ado about Nothing*, 1969. **Essays:** Francis Bacon; John Cleveland; Richard Lovelace; Sir Philip Sidney.

DAVISON, Dennis. Senior Lecturer in English, Monash University, Clayton, Victoria. Author of *Andrew Marvell's Poems*, 1963, *Dryden*, 1968, *W.H. Auden*, 1970, and numerous plays (the most recent being *Come Live with Me*, 1987, and *Maid in Australia*, 1988). Editor of *Andrew Marvell: Selected Poetry and Prose*, 1952, *Restoration Comedies*, 1970, *The Penguin Book of Eighteenth-Century English Verse*, 1973, and works by Marcus Clarke; translator of plays by Becque, Turgenev, Scribe, Ibsen, and Strindberg. **Essay:** Guy Butler.

DeMATTEIS, Daniel. Freelance writer; former teacher at Scarborough College, University of Toronto. **Essays:** Henry Glapthorne; Thomas Nabbes.

DePORTE, Michael. Professor of English, University of New Hampshire, Durham. Author of *Nightmares and Hobbyhorses: Swift, Sterne, and Augustan Ideas of Madness*, 1974, and essays on Byron, Davenant, Godwin, Otway, Pope, and Swift. Editor of *Enthusiasmus Triumphatus* by Henry More, 1966, *Discourse on Madness* by Thomas Tryon, 1973, *Lucida Intervalla* by James Carkesse, 1979, and *The Art of Memory* by Marius D'Assigny, 1985. **Essay:** Laurence Sterne.

DONNELLY, Hugo. Lecturer in English, University of Leeds. **Essays:** John Braine; Thom Gunn; Frank Harris; Kathleen Raine.

DONNO, Elizabeth Story. Senior Research Associate, Huntington Library, San Marino, California; member of the advisory board, *Huntington Quarterly*. Editor of *Metamorphosis of Ajax* by Sir John Harington, 1962, *Elizabethan Minor Epics*, 1963, *The Complete Poetry of Andrew Marvell*, 1972, *An Elizabethan in 1582: The Diary of Richard Madox*, 1976, *Marvell: The Critical Heritage*, 1978, and *Twelfth Night* by Shakespeare, 1985 (New Cambridge Shakespeare). **Essays:** Introduction: Renaissance Prose and Poetry; Michael Drayton; Thomas Nashe; John Stow; *Antony and Cleopatra*; *The Chronicles of England, Scotland, and Ireland*; *Rosalynde*; "To His Coy Mistress."

DONOVAN, Dennis G. Late Professor of English, University of North Carolina, Chapel Hill. Author of bibliographies and checklists on Sir Thomas Browne, Robert Burton, John Evelyn, Thomas Middleton, Samuel Pepys, and other 17th-century writers. **Essay:** Robert Burton.

DOWDEN, Wilfred S. Professor of English, Rice University, Houston; now retired. Author of *Joseph Conrad: The Imaged Style*, 1970. Editor of *The Letters of Thomas Moore*, 2 vols., 1964. **Essay:** Thomas Moore.

DOWNES, David Anthony. Senior Professor of English, California State University, Chico. Author of *Hopkins: A Study of His Ignatian Spirit*, 1959 (revised as *The Ignatian Personality of Hopkins*, 1990), *The Temper of Victorian Belief: Religious Novels of Pater, Kingsley, and Newman*, 1972, *The Great Sacrifice: Studies in Hopkins*, 1983, *Ruskin's Landscape of Beatitude*, 1984, and *Hopkins's Sanctifying Imagination*, 1985. **Essay:** "The Windhover."

DOWNIE, J.A. Senior Lecturer in English, Goldsmiths' College, University of London. Author of *Robert Harley and the Press: Propaganda and Public Opinion in the Age of Swift and Defoe*, 1979, and *Swift, Political Writer*, 1984. **Essay:** Thomas Hobbes.

DOYLE, Charles. Professor of English, University of Victoria, British Columbia. Author of *Small Prophets and Quick Returns: Reflections on New Zealand Poetry*, 1966, *R.A.K. Mason*, 1970, *James K. Baxter*, 1976, *William Carlos Williams and the American Poem*, 1982, and *Richard Aldington: A Biography*, 1989, and (as Mike Doyle) of several books of poetry, including *A Steady Hand*, 1982, and *The Urge to Raise Hats*, 1989. Editor of critical collections on Wallace Stevens and William Carlos Williams. **Essays:** Richard Aldington; James K. Baxter; R.A.K. Mason.

DOYNO, Victor A. Professor of English, State University of New York, Buffalo. Editor of *Parthenophil and Parthenophe* by Barnabe Barnes, 1971. **Essays:** Barnabe Barnes; Tom Robertson; *The Story of an African Farm*; *The Vanity of Human Wishes*.

DRAKAKIS, John. Lecturer in English, University of Stirling, Scotland. **Essay:** Shakerley Marmion.

DRAPER, R.P. Regius Chalmers Professor of English, University of Aberdeen, Scotland. Author of *D.H. Lawrence*, 1964, and *An Annotated Critical Bibliography of Thomas Hardy* (with Martin Ray), 1989. Editor of *Lawrence: The Critical Heritage*, 1970, *Hardy: The Tragic Novels: A Casebook*, 1975, *The Literature of Region and Nation*, 1989, and *The Epic: Developments in Criticism*, 1990. **Essay:** D.H. Lawrence.

DUNLAP, Rhodes. Professor Emeritus of English, University of Iowa, Iowa City. Editor of *The Poems of Thomas Carew*, 1949. **Essays:** Thomas Carew; William Cartwright; William Habington; Thomas Killigrew; Thomas May; James Shirley; "Air and Angels"; "The Altar"; *Epicoene*.

DUTCHER, James M. Assistant Professor of English and director of the honors program, Holyoke Community College, Massachusetts. **Essay:** *The Winter's Tale*.

DUTTON, Geoffrey. See his own entry. **Essay:** Patrick White.

EASINGWOOD, Peter. Lecturer in English, University of Dundee, Scotland. **Essay:** John Cowper Powys.

ECKLEY, Grace. Emeritus Professor, Drake University, Des Moines, Iowa. Author of *Benedict Kiely*, 1972, *Edna O'Brien*, 1974, *Narrator and Character in Finnegans Wake* (with Michael H. Begnal), 1975, *Finley Peter Dunne*, 1981, and *Children's Lore in Finnegans Wake*, 1985. **Essays:** *De Profundis*; *Finnegans Wake*; *The Man Who Died*.

ECKLEY, Wilton. Head of Humanities and Social Sciences, and director of the honors program, Colorado School of Mines, Golden. Author of *E.E. Cummings*, 1968, *Harriette Arnow*, 1974, *T.S. Stribling*, 1975, *Herbert Hoover*, 1980, and *The American Circus*, 1984. **Essays:** *An Essay on the Principle of Population*; *Henry Esmond*; *Leviathan*; *The Rights of Man*; *The Vicar of Wakefield*.

EDMONDS, Joanne H. Instructor in English, Ball State University, Muncie, Indiana. **Essay:** *A Dance to the Music of Time*.

EHRENPREIS, Anne Henry. Private scholar. Editor of *The Literary Ballad*, 1966; *The Old Manor House*, 1969, and *Emmeline*, 1971, both by Charlotte Smith; and *Northanger Abbey* by Jane Austen, 1972. **Essay:** Charlotte Smith.

ELLIOTT, Brian. Former Reader in Australian Literary Studies, University of Adelaide. Author of *Leviathan's Inch* (novel), 1946, *Singing to the Cattle and Other Australian Essays*, 1947, *Marcus Clarke*, 1958, *The Landscape of Australian Poetry*, 1967, and *Adam Lindsay Gordon*, 1973. Editor of *Coast to Coast: Australian Stories 1948*, 1949, *Bards in the Wilderness: Australian Poetry to 1920* (with Adrian Mitchell), 1970, and *The Jindyworobaks*, 1979. **Essays:** Martin Boyd; Charles Harpur; Xavier Herbert; Andrew Barton Paterson; Steele Rudd.

EVANS, Patrick. Senior Lecturer in English, University of Canterbury, Christchurch, New Zealand. Author of *An Inward Sun: The Novels of Janet Frame*, 1971, *Janet Frame*, 1977, *The Penguin History of New Zealand Literature*, 1990, and of fiction (*Being Eaten Alive*, 1980, and *Making It*, 1989) and plays (*The Meeting*, 1985, and *Stuff*, 1990). **Essay:** Janet Frame.

FABRY, Frank. Professor of English, University of South Florida, Tampa. Author of articles on Sidney, Shakespeare, Crashaw, and on satire in *Renaissance Quarterly, English Literary Renaissance, Shakespeare Quarterly*, and *Seventeenth-Century News*. **Essays:** Roger Ascham; Richard Barnfield; Nicholas Breton; Sir Thomas Elyot; William Warner; Thomas Watson; *Delia*; "On the Wounds of Our

Crucified Lord"; *Sonnets* 33–35 and 71–74; *Tottel's Miscellany*; *Venus and Adonis*.

FARWELL, Harold. Associate Professor of English, Western Carolina University, Cullowhee, North Carolina; reporter for *Opera News*; prose editor of the *Arts Journal*. **Essays:** Chinua Achebe; *A Bend in the River*; *Pygmalion*.

FAULKNER, Peter. Reader in English, University of Exeter, Devon. Author of *William Morris and W.B. Yeats*, 1962, *Yeats and the Irish Eighteenth Century*, 1965, *Humanism and the English Novel*, 1976, *Modernism*, 1977, *Robert Bage*, 1979, *Angus Wilson: Mimic and Moralist*, 1980, *Against the Age: An Introduction to William Morris*, 1980, and *Yeats*, 1987. Editor of *William Morris: The Critical Heritage*, 1973, works by Morris, *The Picture of Dorian Gray* by Wilde, 1976, *Hermsprong* by Bage, 1985, *Jane Morris to Wilfrid Scawen Blunt*, 1986, *A Modernist Reader*, 1986, and *A Victorian Reader*, 1989. **Essays:** R.D. Blackmore; Samuel Butler (b. 1835); Thomas Holcroft; Walter Savage Landor; Charles Robert Maturin; John Stuart Mill; John Moore; Hannah More; Thomas Love Peacock; *Barrack-Room Ballads*; *The Egoist*; "The Haystack in the Floods."

FERRIER, Carole. Reader in English, University of Queensland, Brisbane; editor, *Hecate: A Women's Interdisciplinary Journal*. Editor of *Gender, Politics, and Fiction: Twentieth-Century Australian Women's Novels*, 1985. **Essays:** Miles Franklin; *Owls Do Cry*.

FIELDING, Penelope. Lecturer in English, University of Bristol. **Essays:** *Moll Flanders*; *Redgauntlet*.

FITZGERALD-HOYT, Mary. Associate Professor of English, Siena College, Loudonville, New York. Author of "Neither Apes Nor Angels: The Irish in *The Damnation of Theron Ware*," in *Greyfriar*, 19, 1988. **Essays:** Brian Friel; *Children of the Ghetto*; *A Christmas Carol*; *Dream on Monkey Mountain*.

FLETCHER, Ian. Late Professor of English, University of Reading, Berkshire. Author of poetry and plays, and of *Walter Pater*, 1959 (revised 1971), *A Catalogue of Imagist Poets* (with Wallace Martin), 1966, *Beaumont and Fletcher*, 1967, and *Swinburne*, 1973. Editor of anthologies of poetry and drama, and of works by Lionel Johnson, Victor Plarr, John Gray, and George Gissing. Died 1988. **Essays:** Max Beerbohm; Oliver St. John Gogarty; Henry Arthur Jones; T. Sturge Moore; Shaw Neilson; Walter Pater.

FOLTINEK, Herbert. Professor of English and American Literature, University of Vienna. Author of *Vorstufen zum Viktorianischen Realismus*, 1968, *Fieldings Tom Jones und das österreichische Drama*, 1976, *George Eliot*, 1982, *Dramatische Ansätze in der englischen Romanliteratur des achtzehnten Jahrhunderts*, 1983, and *Charles Dickens und der Zwang des Systems*, 1987. Editor of *Arthur Schnitzler: Grosse Szene*, 1959, and *Marriage* by Susan Ferrier, 1971. **Essays:** Susan Ferrier; Theodore Hook; *Martin Chuzzlewit*.

FOREY, Margaret. Director of Drama, Durham School; former lecturer at the University of Durham. Author of "Cleveland's 'Square Cap': Some Questions of Structure and Date," in *Durham University Journal*, 1974. **Essays:** Edward Benlowes; Richard Corbett; Jasper Mayne; Thomas Randolph; Thomas Stanley; William Strode; Edmund Waller; *The Go-Between*; *Journey's End*; "Kinship"; "L'Allegro" and "Il Penseroso."

FRASER, G.S. Late Reader in Modern English Literature, University of Leicester. Author of several books of poetry (collected as *Poems*, 1981); travel books; critical studies of Yeats, Dylan Thomas, Pound, Durrell, P.H. Newby, and Pope; and *The Modern Writer and His World*, 1953, *Vision and Rhetoric*, 1959, *Metre, Rhythm and Free Verse*, 1970, *Essays on Twentieth-Century Poets*, 1977, and *A Stranger and Afraid: The Autobiography of an Intellectual*, 1983. Editor of works by Keith Douglas and Robert Burns, and of verse anthologies. Died 1980. **Essays:** Frederick Locker-Lampson; Osbert Sitwell.

FRENCH, R.B.D. Late Senior Lecturer in English Literature, Trinity College, Dublin; correspondent for the *Times*, London, and contributor to other newspapers and periodicals. Author of *P.G. Wodehouse*, 1966, and of screenplays and revues. **Essay:** P.G. Wodehouse.

FRENCH, Warren. Professor of English and director of the Center for American Studies, Indiana University-Purdue University, Indianapolis, retired 1986; member of the editorial board, *American Literature* and *Twentieth-Century Literature*; editor of the American Authors series for Twayne publishers. Author of *John Steinbeck*, 1961 (revised 1975), *Frank Norris*, 1962, *J.D. Salinger*, 1963 (revised 1976), *A Companion to the Grapes of Wrath*, 1963, *The Social Novel at the End of an Era*, 1966, *A Season of Promise*, 1968, *The South in Film*, 1981, and *Jack Kerouac*, 1986. Editor of a series on American literature, *The Thirties*, 1967, *The Forties*, 1968, *The Fifties*, 1971, and *The Twenties*, 1975. **Essays:** Edgar Mittelholzer; Khushwant Singh.

FULLER, David. Lecturer in English, University of Durham. Author of *Blake's Heroic Argument*, 1988. **Essays:** *A Portrait of the Artist as a Young Man*; *Songs of Innocence and of Experience*.

GÉRIN, Winifred. Biographer and critic. Author of *Anne Brontë*, 1959, *Branwell Brontë*, 1961, *Charlotte Brontë*, 1967, *Horatia Nelson*, 1970, *Emily Brontë*, 1971, *The Brontës*, 2 vols., 1973, and *Elizabeth Gaskell: A Biography*, 1976. Editor of *Five Novelettes* by Charlotte Brontë, 1971. Died 1981. **Essays:** Anne Brontë; Charlotte Brontë; Emily Brontë.

GIANAKARIS, C.J. Professor of English and Theatre, Western Michigan University, Kalamazoo; founding co-editor, *Comparative Drama*. Author of *Plutarch*, 1970, and *Foundations of Drama*, 1975. Editor or co-editor of *Antony and Cleopatra* by Shakespeare, 1969, *Drama and the Middle Ages*, 1984, *Drama in the Twentieth Century*, 1985, *The Drama of the Renaissance*, 1986. **Essays:** *Every Man in His Humour*; *A Midsummer Night's Dream*; *Travesties*.

GIBBS, A.M. Professor of English, Macquarie University, New South Wales, Australia. Author of *Shaw*, 1969, and *The Art and Mind of Shaw*, 1983. Editor of *The Shorter Poems, and Songs from the Plays and Masques* by Sir William Davenant, 1972. **Essay:** Sir William Davenant.

GILL, Roma. Former member of the Department of English, University of Sheffield, Yorkshire. Editor of *The Plays of Christopher Marlowe*, 1971, *William Empson: The Man and His Work*, 1974, *Complete Works* by Marlowe, 1987–, and works by Middleton and Tourneur. **Essays:** John

Bale; Aston Cokayne; Giles Fletcher the Elder; Thomas Lodge; Christopher Marlowe; Thomas Middleton; Cyril Tourneur.

GILLESPIE, Stuart. Lecturer in English Literature, University of Glasgow. Editor of *Poets on the Classics: An Anthology*, 1988, and general editor of *Translation and Literature*. **Essays:** *An Essay on Criticism*; *Henry IV*, part 1; *Henry IV*, part 2; *Mac Flecknoe*; "To Penshurst."

GLASRUD, Clarence A. Professor of English Emeritus, Moorhead State University, Minnesota; advisory editor, *Studies in American Fiction*; member of the Board of Publications, Norwegian-American Historical Association. Author of *Hjalmar Hjorth Boyesen: A Biographical and Critical Study*, 1963, *The Moorhead Normal School*, 1987, and *Moorhead State Teachers College*, 1990. Editor of *The Age of Anxiety*, 1960, *A Heritage Deferred*, 1981, *Roy Johnson's Red River Valley*, 1982, *A Special Relationship*, 1983, *A Heritage Fulfilled*, 1983, and *L'Heritage Tranquile*, 1987. **Essay:** Mazo de la Roche.

GLEN, Duncan. Emeritus Professor, Nottingham Polytechnic; publisher, Akros Publications, and former editor of *Akros*; partner, Galliard Publications; editor of the Scottish Poetry Library Newsletter (*SPLA*). Author of more than 30 books of poetry, and of numerous critical books, including *Hugh MacDiarmid and the Scottish Renaissance*, 1964, *Scottish Poetry Now*, 1966, *A Bibliography of Scottish Poets from Stevenson to 1974*, 1974, *The Autobiography of a Poet*, 1986, and other studies of Scottish literature. Editor of several anthologies, including *Selected Essays of Hugh MacDiarmid*, 1969, *Hugh MacDiarmid: A Critical Survey*, 1972, and *European Poetry in Scotland: An Anthology of Translations* (with Peter France), 1989. **Essay:** Hugh MacDiarmid.

GONDA, Caroline. Lecturer in English, University of Dundee, Scotland. **Essays:** Mary Brunton; Mary Hays; Angela Thirkell; *Evelina*; *The Monk*; *Sir Charles Grandison*.

GONZALEZ, Alexander G. Assistant Professor of English, State University of New York, Cortland; member of the editorial board of *Mid-Hudson Language Studies* and the advisory panel of *Notes on Modern Irish Literature*. Author of articles on George Moore, Seaumas O'Kelly, James Joyce, Liam O'Flaherty, Brinsley MacNamara, and other Irish writers. **Essays:** Brinsley MacNamara; *The Hostage*; *Juno and the Paycock*; *The Playboy of the Western World*.

GORDON, Ian A. Emeritus Professor of English, Victoria University, Wellington, New Zealand. Author of numerous books, including *John Skelton, Poet Laureate*, 1943, *Katherine Mansfield*, 1954 (revised 1971), *The Movement of English Prose*, 1966, and *John Galt*, 1972. Editor of dictionaries and a thesaurus, and of works by Galt, Mansfield, and William Shenstone. **Essays:** Ælfric; Lancelot Andrewes; John Galt; Robert Greene; Thomas Heywood; John Lyly; George Lyttelton; Katherine Mansfield; Sir Thomas More; William Shenstone; *The Advancement of Learning*; *Capricornia*; *Essays*; *Gitanjali*; Martin Marprelate pamphlets; *Of Dramatic Poesy*; *Pilgrimage*; *The Tatler* and *The Spectator*.

GRAHAM, Colin. Research student, Department of English, University of Bristol. Author of an essay on Flann O'Brien in *Massacre*, February 1990. **Essays:** Walter Greenwood; Stephen Spender; *Autumn Journal*.

GRAHAM, Desmond. Senior Lecturer in English, University of Newcastle upon Tyne. Author of *Introduction to Poetry*, 1968, *Keith Douglas: A Biography*, 1974, and *The Truth of War: Owen, Blunden, and Rosenberg*, 1984. Editor of *The Complete Poems of Keith Douglas*, 1978, and *Alamein to Zem Zem*, 1979, and *A Prose Miscellany*, 1985, both by Douglas. **Essays:** Keith Douglas; Sidney Keyes.

GRAHAM-WHITE, Anthony. Professor, Department of Communication and Theater, University of Illinois, Chicago. Author of *The Drama of Black Africa*, 1974, and articles in *Yale/Theatre*, *Das Englische Drama nach 1945*, 1980, and *Journal of Drama Theory and Criticism*, 1990. Former editor of *Educational Theatre Journal* (now *Theatre Journal*). **Essays:** John Pepper Clark; *Mucedorus*; *Serjeant Musgrave's Dance*.

GRAY, Douglas. J.R.R. Tolkien Professor of English, Oxford University, and Professorial Fellow, Lady Margaret Hall. Author of *Themes and Images in the Medieval English Religious Lyric*, 1972, *A Chaucer Glossary* (with others), 1979, and *Robert Henryson*, 1979. Editor of *A Selection of Religious Lyrics*, 1975, and *The Oxford Book of Late Medieval Verse and Prose*, 1985. **Essays:** *Ancrene Riwle* (or *Ancrene Wisse*); *Brut*.

GREEN, Dorothy. Honorary Visiting Fellow, Royal Military College, Canberra. Author of *Ulysses Bound*, 1973 (revised as *Henry Handel Richardson and Her Fiction*, 1986), a revised edition of *The History of Australian Literature* by H.M. Green, 1984, and *The Music of Love* (essays), 1985; also author (as Dorothy Auchterlonie) of several books of poetry, including *The Dolphin*, 1967, and *Something to Someone*, 1984. Editor of *Australian Poetry*, 1968. **Essays:** C.J. Brennan; Rosemary Dobson; Robert D. FitzGerald; Mary Gilmore; Henry Kendall; Kenneth Mackenzie; Henry Handel Richardson; Kenneth Slessor; Christina Stead; Douglas Stewart; Francis Webb.

GREEN, Roger Lancelyn. Author of more than 50 books including fiction and verse for children and adults, retellings of folk and fairy tales, and critical studies of Andrew Lang, A.E.W. Mason, Lewis Carroll, J.M. Barrie, Mary Louisa Molesworth, C.S. Lewis, and Rudyard Kipling; also editor of works by these authors and others, and translator of plays by Sophocles. Died 1987. **Essays:** J.M. Barrie; Arthur Conan Doyle; Kenneth Grahame; Andrew Lang; A.E.W. Mason.

GREENLEES, Ian. Former Director of the British Institute, Florence. Author of *Norman Douglas*, 1957. **Essays:** Norman Douglas; Ouida.

GRIFFIN, Ernest. Former Professor of English, York University, Downsview, Ontario. Author of *Manual of English Prose Composition*, 1958, *The Dramatic Chorus in English Literary Theory and Practice*, 1959, *Bibliography of Literature and Religion*, 1967, and *John Middleton Murry*, 1969. Editor of *Eugene O'Neill: A Collection of Criticism*, 1976. **Essay:** Rex Warner.

GROVE, Dana A. Professor of English, Indian Hills Community College, Ottumwa, Iowa. Author of *A Rhetorical Analysis of Under the Volcano*, 1989. **Essay:** *Under the Volcano*.

GRUNDY, Joan. Professor Emeritus of English, Royal Holloway College, University of London. Author of *The*

Spenserian Poets, 1969, and *Hardy and the Sister Arts*, 1979. Editor of *The Poems of Henry Constable*, 1960. **Essays:** Henry Constable; Giles Fletcher the Younger; Phineas Fletcher; Ivor Gurney; Norman Nicholson; George Wither.

GRYLLS, David. University Lecturer in Literature, Department for External Studies, Oxford University. **Essays:** *Jude the Obscure*; *New Grub Street*.

GURR, Andrew. Professor of English, University of Reading, Berskshire. Author of *The Shakespearean Stage 1574–1642*, 1970 (revised 1980), *Hamlet and the Distracted Globe*, 1978, *Writers in Exile*, 1981, *Katherine Mansfield* (with Clare Hanson), 1981, *Playgoing in Shakespeare's London*, 1987, and *Rebuilding Shakespeare's Globe*, with John Orrell, 1989. Editor of several plays by Beaumont and Fletcher, and of *Black Aesthetics* (with Pio Zirimu), 1973, *Writers in East Africa* (with Angus Calder), 1974, and *Richard II* by Shakespeare, 1984. **Essay:** Francis Beaumont.

HABER, Richard. Associate Professor of English and Coordinator of Freshman Composition, Western New England College, Springfield, Massachusetts. **Essay:** *Endymion*.

HALLORAN, William F. Dean of the College of Letters and Science, University of Wisconsin, Milwaukee. **Essay:** William Sharp.

HAMILTON, Harlan W. Professor Emeritus of English, Case Western Reserve University, Cleveland. Author of *Doctor Syntax: A Silhouette of William Combe*, 1969, and articles on Johnson and Combe in *English Studies Today*, *Western Humanities Review*, and *PMLA*. **Essays:** William Combe; John Pomfret.

HAMILTON, Susan. Assistant Professor of English, University of Alberta, Edmonton. Author of *Still Lives: Gender and the Literature of the Victorian Vivisection Controversy* (forthcoming). **Essays:** *Cranford*; *East Lynne*; "The Function of Criticism at the Present Time"; *A Vindication of the Rights of Woman*.

HARMON, Maurice. Associate Professor of Anglo-Irish Literature and Drama, University College, Dublin; editor, *Irish University Review*. Author of *Sean O'Faolain: A Critical Introduction*, 1966 (revised 1985), *Modern Irish Literature*, 1967, *The Poetry of Thomas Kinsella*, 1974, *Select Bibliography for the Study of Anglo-Irish Literature and Its Background*, 1976, *A Short History of Anglo-Irish Literature from the Origins to the Present* (with Roger McHugh), 1982, and *Austin Clarke: A Critical Introduction*, 1989. Editor of works by or about Shakespeare, Synge, Richard Murphy, and Anglo-Irish poetry and fiction. **Essays:** Austin Clarke; Seamus Heaney.

HART, Clive. Professor of Literature, University of Essex, Colchester. Author of *Structure and Motif in Finnegans Wake*, 1962, *A Concordance to Finnegans Wake*, 1963, *Joyce's Ulysses*, 1968, *A Topographical Guide to Joyce's Ulysses* (with Leo Knuth), 1975, and *Ulysses: A Review of the Three Texts* (with Philip Gaskell), 1989. Editor of *Joyce's Dubliners: Critical Essays*, 1969, *Joyce's Ulysses* (with David Hayman), 1974, and *Assessing the 1984 Ulysses* (with C. George Sandulescu), 1986. **Essays:** Henry Green; James Joyce.

HASSLER, Donald M. Professor of English, Kent State University, Kent, Ohio; editor, *Extrapolation*. Author of *Erasmus Darwin*, 1973, *The Comedian as the Letter D: Erasmus Darwin's Comic Materialism*, 1973, *Comic Tones in Science Fiction*, 1982, *Hal Clement*, 1982, *Patterns of the Fantastic*, 2 vols., 1983–84, and *Isaac Asimov*, 1987. Co-editor of *Death and the Serpent! Immortality in Science Fiction and Fantasy*, 1985. **Essays:** Erasmus Darwin; John Locke; Anna Seward; *The Castle of Otranto*; *The Origin of Species*; *Ossian*.

HATTON, Gwynneth. Former teacher and freelance editor. **Essay:** William De Morgan.

HAYMAN, David. Professor of the Humanities, University of Wisconsin, Madison. Author of *Louis Ferdinand Céline*, 1965, *Ulysses: The Mechanics of Meaning*, 1970, *Re-Forming the Narrative: Toward a Mechanics of Modernist Fiction*, 1987, and *The Wake in Transit*, 1990. Editor of *A First-Draft Version of Finnegans Wake*, 1963, and *Joyce's Ulysses* (with Clive Hart), 1974. **Essays:** *Endgame*; *The Horse's Mouth*; *Lavengro*; *Sons and Lovers*.

HEATH, William W. Professor of English, Amherst College, Massachusetts. Author of *Elizabeth Bowen: An Introduction to Her Novels*, 1961, and *Wordsworth and Coleridge: A Study of Their Literary Relations 1801–1802*, 1972. Editor of *Discussions of Jane Austen*, 1960, and *Major British Poets of the Romantic Period*, 1973. **Essays:** *The Death of the Heart*; *The End of the Affair*; *Sense and Sensibility*; "Tintern Abbey."

HEATH-STUBBS, John. Writer and lecturer. Author of more than 30 books of poetry (*Collected Poems 1943–1987*, 1988), a book of plays, and of *The Darkling Plain: A Study of the Later Fortunes of Romanticism*, 1950, *Charles Williams*, 1955, and studies of the verse satire, the ode, and the pastoral. Editor of anthologies and works by Shelley, Tennyson, Swift, Pope, and Gray; translator of works by Leopardi, de Vigny, and others. **Essays:** Mark Akenside; Alfred Austin; William Barnes; Wilfrid Scawen Blunt; Charles Churchill; Samuel Taylor Coleridge; Ernest Dowson; William Drummond; William Mickle; Ambrose Philips; Christina Rossetti; Dante Gabriel Rossetti; Thomas Tickell.

HENNESSY, Brendan. Freelance writer and lecturer, and consultant in journalism. Author of *The Gothic Novel*, 1978, *Writing Feature Articles*, 1989, and several volumes in the Writers and Their Work series. **Essays:** Frederick Lonsdale; R.C. Sherriff; Ben Travers; *Imaginary Conversations*.

HEWISON, P.E. Lecturer in English, University of Aberdeen, Scotland. Author of articles and reviews on Restoration and Augustan literature. **Essays:** Sir Charles Sedley; *Absalom and Achitophel*; *A Satire Against Reason and Mankind*; *The Vision of Judgement*.

HIBBERD, Dominic. Freelance writer. Author of *Owen the Poet*, 1986, and *The First World War*, 1990. Editor of *War Poems and Others* by Owen, 1973, *Poetry of the First World War: A Casebook*, 1981, and *Poetry of the Great War: An Anthology* (with John Onions), 1986. **Essays:** Saki; "Strange Meeting."

HIGDON, David Leon. Paul Whitefield Horn Professor of English, Texas Tech University, Lubbock; editor, *Conradiana*. Author of *Shadows of the Past in Contemporary*

British Fiction, 1985. **Essays:** John Berger; B.S. Johnson; *The Time Machine*.

HILSON, J. C. Late Lecturer in English, University of Leicester. Editor of *Augustan Worlds* (with M. M. B. Jones and J. R. Watson), 1978, and *An Essay on Historical Composition* by James Moor, 1978. Author of articles on Hume, Richardson, Smollett, and Conrad. Died 1980. **Essays:** Roger Boyle; John Cleland; Graham Greene; Tobias Smollett.

HIRSH, Elizabeth. Honorary Fellow in Women's Studies, University of Wisconsin, Madison. Author of "No Record of Reply: *In Memoriam* and Victorian Language Theory," in *English Literary History*, Spring 1988, and "Imaginary Images: H.D., Modernism, and the Psychoanalysis of Seeing," in *Discontented Discourses* edited by Marlene Baur and Richard Feldstein, 1988. **Essays:** Radclyffe Hall; *The Waves*.

HOFFMAN, Daniel. Poet-in-Residence and Felix E. Schelling Professor of English, University of Pennsylvania, Philadelphia. Author of several books of poetry, the most recent being *Hang-Gliding from Helicon: New and Selected Poems 1948–1988*, 1988, and of critical works including *The Poetry of Stephen Crane*, 1957, *Form and Fable in American Fiction*, 1961, *Barbarous Knowledge: Myth in the Poetry of Yeats, Graves, and Muir*, 1967, *Poe Poe Poe Poe Poe Poe Poe*, 1972, and *Faulkner's Country Matters*, 1989. Editor of the *Harvard Guide to Contemporary American Writing*, 1979, and of anthologies and works by Crane. **Essay:** Robert Graves.

HOGAN, Robert. Freelance writer; Professor of English, University of Delaware, Newark. Author or co-author of *The Experiments of Sean O'Casey*, 1960, *Arthur Miller*, 1964, *The Independence of Elmer Rice*, 1965, *The Plain Style*, 1967, *After the Irish Renaissance*, 1967, *Dion Boucicault*, 1969, *The Fan Club*, 1969, *Lost Plays of the Irish Renaissance*, 1970, *Eimar O'Duffy*, 1972, *Mervyn Wall*, 1972, *Conor Cruise O'Brien*, 1974, and *"Since O'Casey" and Other Essays on Irish Drama*, 1983. Editor of *The Modern Irish Drama: A Documentary History* (with others), from 1975, and *The Dictionary of Irish Literature*, 1979. **Essays:** Dion Boucicault; Paul Vincent Carroll; George Fitzmaurice; Denis Johnston; *Heartbreak House*; *The Madras House*; *The Man of Mode*; *The School for Scandal*; *The Shaughraun*.

HOKENSON, Jan. Professor and Chair of Languages and Linguistics, Florida Atlantic University, Boca Raton. Author of several articles on modern European and American writers of fiction. Editor of *Forms of the Fantastic*. **Essay:** Robert Tressell.

HOLM, Janis Butler. Associate Professor of English, Ohio University, Athens. Author of articles on early modern literature and culture. Editor of *The Mirrhor of Modestie* by Thomas Salter, 1987. **Essay:** *The Mirror for Magistrates*.

HUDSON, Derek. Freelance writer and editor. Author of books on Winthrop Mackworth Praed, Thomas Barnes, Norman O'Neill, Charles Keene, Martin Tupper, James Pryde, Lewis Carroll, Sir Joshua Reynolds, Arthur Rackham, A.J. Munby, and Sir Gerald Kelly, and on journalism and topography. Editor of anthologies and of the diary of Henry Crabb Robinson. **Essays:** L.A.G. Strong; Martin Tupper.

HUGHES, Leo. Former Professor of English, University of Texas, Austin. Author of *A Century of English Farce*, 1956, and *The Drama's Patrons*, 1971. Editor of *Ten English Farces* (with Arthur H. Scouten), 1948, and *The Plain-Dealer* by William Wycherley, 1967. **Essay:** Edward Ravenscroft.

HUGHEY, Ruth. Late Professor of English, Ohio State University, Columbus. Author of *John Harington of Stepney, Tudor Gentleman*, 1971, and of articles on Harington, Elizabeth Grymeston, and Elizabeth I. Editor of *The Correspondence of Lady Katherine Paston*, 1941, and *The Arundel Harington Manuscript of Tudor Poetry*, 2 vols., 1960. Died 1980. **Essay:** Sir John Harington.

HUSSEY, S.S. Professor of English, University of Lancaster. Author of *Chaucer: An Introduction*, 1971 (revised 1981), *The Literary Language of Shakespeare*, 1982, and articles on Walter Hilton, medieval mystics, Chaucer, Langland, and Shakespeare. Editor of *Piers Plowman: Critical Approaches*, 1969. **Essay:** Walter Hilton.

HUTCHINGS, W.B. Lecturer in English Literature, University of Manchester; co-editor, *Proceedings of the English Association North*; British correspondent, *World Shakespeare Bibliography*. Author of *The Poetry of William Cowper*, 1983, and co-author of *Literary Criticism: A Practical Guide for Students*, 1989. **Essays:** *Cooper's Hill*; *The Dunciad*; "The Garden"; *Night-Thoughts*; *The Pleasures of Imagination*.

HYDE, William J. Professor of English, University of Wisconsin, La Crosse. Author of articles on George Eliot, Hardy, Richard Jefferies, and Sabine Baring-Gould in *PMLA*, *Victorian Studies*, *Victorian Newsletter*, and other periodicals. **Essays:** Sabine Baring-Gould; Richard Jefferies.

IVY, Randolph. Associate Professor of English, Randolph-Macon Woman's College at the University of Reading, Berkshire. **Essays:** Mary Elizabeth Braddon; Wilkie Collins; *Lady Audley's Secret*; *The Woman in White*.

JEFFARES, A. Norman. Professor Emeritus of English Studies, University of Stirling, Scotland; general editor of the Writers and Critics series and the New Oxford English series; past editor of *A Review of English Studies* and *Ariel*. Author of *Yeats: Man and Poet*, 1949 (revised 1962), *Seven Centuries of Poetry*, 1956, *Oliver Goldsmith*, 1959, *Gogarty*, 1961, *George Moore*, 1965, *A Critical Commentary on She Stoops to Conquer*, 1966, *A Commentary on the Collected Poems* (1968) and *Collected Plays* (1975, with A.S. Knowland) *of Yeats*, *Anglo-Irish Literature*, 1982, *A New Commentary on the Poems of W.B. Yeats*, 1984, and *W.B. Yeats: A New Biography*, 1988. Editor of *Scott's Mind and Art*, 1969, *Restoration Comedy*, 1974, *Yeats: The Critical Heritage*, 1977, *Poems of W.B. Yeats: A New Selecton*, 1984, *Yeats's Poems*, 1989, and *Yeats's Vision*, 1990. Formerly chairman of the Literature Section of the Scottish Arts Council; life president, International Association for the Study of Anglo-Irish Literature. **Essays:** Joyce Cary; William Congreve; William Cowper; Charles Lever; Richard Brinsley Sheridan; William Butler Yeats.

JEFFREY, David Lyle. Professor of English, University of Ottawa. Author of *The Early English Lyric and Franciscan Spirituality*, 1975, *By Things Seen: Reference and Recognition in Medieval Thought*, 1979, and *Toward a Perfect Love: The Spiritual Counsel of Walter Hilton*, 1986. Editor of *Chaucer* *and Scriptural Tradition*, 1984, *The Law of Love: English Spirituality in the Age of Wyclif*, 1988, and *The Anglo-Norman Lyric* (with Brian J. Levy), 1990, and general editor of *A Dictionary of Biblical Tradition in English Literature*, 1991. **Essays:** Richard Rolle; *The Cloud of Unknowing*.

JENNINGS, Wade. Director of Undergraduate Programs in English, Ball State University, Muncie, Indiana. Author of articles on Hardy, Browning, and other Victoran writers. Editor, with Joseph Trimmer, *Fictions*, 2nd edition, 1989. **Essay:** "Poems of 1912–13."

JERNIGAN, Jay. Professor of English, Eastern Michigan University, Ypsilanti. Author of *Henry Demarest Lloyd*, 1976, *William Allen White*, 1983, and articles on George Moore and Yeats in *Kansas Quarterly*, *English Literature in Transition*, *Bulletin of Bibliography*, and other journals. **Essay:** George Moore.

JESSEPH, Douglas M. Assistant Professor of Philosophy, Illinois Institute of Technology, Chicago. **Essay:** *The Wealth of Nations*.

JONES, Lawrence. Associate Professor of English, University of Otago, Dunedin, New Zealand. Author of *Barbed Wire and Mirrors: Essays on New Zealand Prose*, 1987, and of the section on the novel in *The Oxford History of New Zealand Literature* (forthcoming). **Essays:** Dan Davin; Maurice Duggan; Maurice Shadbolt; "Old Man's Story."

JOSEPH, M.K. Late Professor of English, University of Auckland, New Zealand. Author of three books of poetry, five novels, and of *Byron the Poet*, 1964. Editor of *Frankenstein* by Mary Shelley, 1969. Died 1981. **Essays:** William Falconer; Mary Shelley.

JOYNER, Nancy Carol. Member of the Department of English, Western Carolina University, Cullowhee, North Carolina. Author of *Edwin Arlington Robinson: A Reference Guide*, 1978, and of articles on modern fiction, including "Cin cin nat i: Postmodern Appalachian Fiction," in *Apaalachian Heritage*, 1988. **Essay:** Ngaio Marsh.

KALLICH, Martin. Professor of English, Northern Illinois University, DeKalb; now retired. Author of *The Psychological Milieu of Lytton Strachey*, 1961, *The American Revolution Through British Eyes* (with others), 1962, *Heav'n's First Law: Rhetoric and Order in Pope's Essay on Man*, 1967, *Oedipus: Myth and Drama* (with others), 1968, *The Other End of the Egg: Religious Satire in Gulliver's Travels*, 1970, *The Association of Ideas and Critical Theory in Eighteenth-Century England*, 1970, *Horace Walpole*, 1971, *A Book of the Sonnet* (with others), 1972, and *British Poetry and the American Revolution: A Bibliographical Survey of Pamphlets, Journals, Newspapers, Prints*, 1988. **Essays:** Edmund Burke; John Scott; Horace Walpole.

KEEBLE, N.H. Reader in English, University of Stirling, Scotland. Author of *Richard Baxter: Puritan Man of Letters*, 1982, and *The Literary Culture of Nonconformity in Later Seventeenth-Century England*, 1987. Editor of *The Autobiography of Richard Baxter*, 1974, *The Pilgrim's Progress*, 1984, and *John Bunyan: Conventicle and Parnassus: Tercentenary Essays*, 1988. **Essays:** *Astrophel and Stella*; *The Changeling*; *Doctor Faustus*; *The Pilgrim's Progress*; *Samson Agonistes*; *The White Devil*.

KELLNER, Bruce. Professor of English, Millersville University, Pennsylvania. Author of *Carl Van Vechten and the Irreverent Decades*, 1968, *A Bibliography of the Work of Carl Van Vechten*, 1980, *A Gertrude Stein Companion Content with The Example*, 1988, and *Last Dandy: Ralph Barton*, 1991. Editor of *Keep a-Inchin' Along: Selected Writings about Black Art and Letters*, 1979, and *The Harlem Renaissance: A Historical Dictionary*, 1984 (revised 1987). **Essays:** Robert Service; "The force that through the green fuse drives the flower"; *The Man Who Loved Children*; *Timon of Athens*; *Troilus and Cressida*; *Valmouth*.

KELLY, Gary. Professor of English, University of Alberta, Edmonton. Author of *The English Jacobin Novel 1780–1805*, 1976. Editor of *Mary, and The Wrongs of Woman* by Mary Wollstonecraft, 1976. **Essays:** Robert Bage; William Godwin; Elizabeth Inchbald; Amelia Opie; Ann Radcliffe.

KELLY, Richard. Professor of English, University of Tennessee, Knoxville. Author of *Douglas William Jerrold*, 1972, *Lewis Carroll*, 1977, *Great Cartoonists of Nineteenth-Century Punch*, 1978, *George du Maurier*, 1983, *Graham Greene*, 1984, *Daphne du Maurier*, 1987, and *V.S. Naipaul*, 1989. Editor of *The Best of Mr. Punch: The Humorous Writings of Douglas William Jerrold*, 1970. **Essays:** Daphne du Maurier; George du Maurier; Douglas William Jerrold; Edward Lear.

KELSALL, Malcolm. Professor of English, University of Wales, College of Cardiff; advisory editor, *Byron Journal*. Author of *Christopher Marlowe*, 1981, and *Byron's Politics*, 1987. Editor of *The Adventures of David Simple* by Sarah Fielding, 1969, *Venice Preserved* by Thomas Otway, 1969, *Love for Love* by William Congreve, 1969, and *The Playboy of the Western World* by J.M. Synge, 1975. **Essays:** Joseph Addison; Sarah Fielding; Edward Martyn.

KEMP, Peter. Freelance writer; regular fiction reviewer for the *Sunday Times* and theatre reviewer for the *Independent*, both London. Author of *Muriel Spark*, 1974, *H.G. Wells and the Culminating Ape*, 1982, and *The Thorns of Memory*, 1990. **Essay:** Siegfried Sassoon.

KENDLE, Burton. Professor of English, Roosevelt University, Chicago. Author of articles on D.H. Lawrence, John Cheever, William March, Tennessee Williams, and other writers, and on screenwriting. **Essays:** Sir John Davies; Thomas Deloney; Simon Gray; John Skelton.

KER, I.T. Former Lecturer in English, University of York. Author of *John Henry Newman: A Biography*, 1988, and *The Achievement of John Henry Newman*, 1990. Editor of *The Idea of a University*, 1976, and *An Essay in Aid of a Grammar of Assent*, 1985, both by Newman, and co-editor of *Letters of Diaries of Newman*, vols. 1–4, 1978–80. **Essay:** John Henry Newman.

KERRIDGE, Richard. Teacher of English and Drama, Haywards Heath Sixth Form College, Sussex. Author of literary criticism in *Cambridge Quarterly*, *Swansea Review*, and *English*, nature writing, and a forthcoming study of J.H. Prynne. **Essay:** Thomas Keneally.

KIERNAN, Brian. Associate Professor of English, University of Sydney. Author of *Images of Society and Nature* (on the Australian novel), 1971, and *Patrick White*, 1980. Editor of collections of short stories, criticism, and the work of Henry Lawson. **Essays:** Joseph Furphy; Henry Lawson.

KING, Jeannette. Senior Lecturer in Communication and Media Studies, Aberdeen College of Commerce, Scotland. Author of *Tragedy in the Victorian Novel: Theory and Practice in the Novels of George Eliot, Thomas Hardy, and Henry James*, 1978, *An Open Guide to Jane Eyre*, 1986, and *Doris Lessing*, 1989. **Essay:** Doris Lessing.

KINNEY, Arthur F. Thomas W. Copeland Professor of Literary History, University of Massachusetts, Amherst; founding editor, *English Literary Renaissance*; series editor for Twayne publishers. Author of numerous books, including *On Seven Shakespearean Tragedies* and *Comedies*, 2 vols., 1968–69, *Rogues, Vagabonds, and Sturdy Beggars*, 1974, *Elizabethan Backgrounds*, 1974, *Faulkner's Narrative Poetics*, 1978, *Dorothy Parker*, 1978, *Rhetoric and Poetic in Thomas More's Utopia*, 1979, *Flannery O'Connor's Library*, 1985, *Humanist Poetics: Thought, Rhetoric, and Fiction in Sixteenth-Century England*, 1986, *John Skelton: Priest as Poet*, 1987, *Renaissance Historicism* (with Dan Collins), 1988, and *Continental Humanist Poetics*, 1989. Editor of *Sir Philip Sidney: 1586 and the Creation of a Legend* (with others), 1986, *Sidney in Retrospect*, 1988, *Sidney's Achievements* (with others), 1990, and other collections on English and American writers. **Essays:** Richard Hakluyt; *Euphues*; *The Shoemaker's Holiday*; *The Unfortunate Traveller*.

KLEIN, Holger. Professor of English, University of Poitiers, France; co-editor, *New Comparison*. Author of *Das weibliche Porträt in der Versdichtung der englischen Renaissance*, 2 vols., 1970, and *J. B. Priestley's Plays*, 1988. Editor of *The First World War in Fiction*, 1976, *The Second World War in Fiction*, 1984, and *English and Scottish Sonnet Sequences of the Renaissance*, 2 vols., 1984; editor and translator of *The Country Wife/Die Unschuld vom Lande*, 1972, and *Hamlet*, 2 vols., 1984. **Essays:** J.B. Priestley; *The Good Companions*; *Hamlet*; *Much Ado about Nothing*.

KOON, Helene Wickham. Professor of English, California State University, San Bernardino; member of the editorial board of *Restoration*. Author of *The Female Spectator*, 1976, *Eugène Scribe*, 1979, *Colley Cibber*, 1986, and *How Shakespeare Won the West*, 1988. **Essays:** Colley Cibber; John Evelyn; Aaron Hill; *The Clandestine Marriage*; *The Conscious Lovers*; *The Provoked Wife*; *The Recruiting Officer*; *The Rivals*.

KORG, Jacob. Professor of English, University of Washington, Seattle. Author of *George Gissing: A Critical Biography*, 1963, *Dylan Thomas*, 1965, *Language in Modern Literature*, 1979, and *Browning and Italy*, 1983. Editor of *Commonplace Book* by Gissing, 1962, and *Gissing on Fiction* (with Cynthia Korg), 1978. **Essays:** "As kingfishers catch fire"; "Childe Roland to the Dark Tower Came"; "Fra Lippo Lippi"; *Lord Jim*; *Modern Love*; *The Private Papers of Henry Ryecroft*.

KUGLER, B.T. Director, Harper House Children's Service, Hertfordshire. Author of articles in *British Journal of Psychiatry*, *Psychiatry Research*, and other journals and collections. **Essay:** W.S. Graham.

KUNZ, Don. Professor of English, University of Rhode Island, Kingston. Author of *The Drama of Thomas Shadwell*, 1972, and of articles on Shadwell in *Restoration and Eighteenth Century Theatre Research*. **Essay:** Thomas Shadwell.

LANE, Jamie. Senior Lecturer, Wandsworth Youth and Community Apprenticeship Scheme, London; former co-ordinator, City Roads residential project for drug users. **Essay:** *Confessions of an English Opium Eater*.

LEE, John. Ph.D. research student, Department of English, University of Bristol. **Essays:** Tony Harrison; "They flee from me."

LESTER, G.A. Senior Lecturer in English Language and Medieval Literature, University of Sheffield, Yorkshire. Author of *The Anglo-Saxons*, 1976, *Three Late Medieval Morality Plays*, 1981, *Sir John Paston's Grete Boke*, 1984, *Index of Middle English Prose, Handlist II*, 1985, *Chaucer's Pardoner's Prologue and Tale*, 1987. Editor of *De Re Militari* by Vegetius, 1988. **Essays:** Cynewulf; John Heywood; Wakefield Master; *The Dream of the Rood*; *Everyman*; *The Second Shepherds' Play*.

LETHBRIDGE, J.B. Postgraduate student, Magdalene College, Cambridge; former lecturer at Union College, Lincoln, Nebraska, and Newbold College, Bracknell, Berkshire. **Essays:** Agatha Christie; R.S. Thomas; Edgar Wallace; *The History of England*; *Modern Painters*; *The Stones of Venice*.

LEVERNIER, James A. Associate Professor of English and Director of American Studies, University of Arkansas, Little Rock. Co-author of *Structuring Paragraphs: A Guide to Effective Writing*, 2nd edition 1986, and articles in *ESQ: A Journal of the American Renaissance, Research Studies, Markham Review, Explicator*, and other periodicals. Editor or co-editor of *An Essay for the Recording of Illustrious Providences* by Increase Mather, 1977, *The Indians and Their Captives*, 1977, *Souldiery Spiritualized: Seven Sermons Preached Before the Artillery Companies of New England 1674–1774*, 1979, *Sermons and Cannonballs*, 1982, and *American Writers Before 1800: A Biographical and Critical Reference Guide*, 3 vols., 1984. **Essay:** Thomas Paine.

LEWIS, Margaret B. Biographer. Author of *Ngaio Marsh: A Life Divided*, 1991. **Essay:** *The Vivisector*.

LEWIS, Naomi. Writer, critic, and broadcaster. Author of *A Visit to Mrs. Wilcox*, 1957, *Fantasy Books for Children*, 1975 (revised 1977), books for children, including *Once Upon a Rainbow*, 1981, *Come with Us*, 1982, *A Mouse's Tail*, 1983, *Wedding Birds*, 1986, and *The Stepsister*, 1987, several retellings of fairytales, including, most recently, *The Flying Trunk and Other Stories from Andersen*, 1986, *Stories from the Arabian Nights*, 1987, and *Cry Wolf and Other Aesop Fables*, 1988, *Proud Knight, Fair Lady: The Twelve Lais of Marie de France*, 1989, and of introductory essays to works on or by Hans Christian Andersen, E. Nesbit, Christina Rossetti, Arthur Waley, and others; contributor to the *Observer*, *New Statesman*, *Times Literary Supplement*, *Listener*, and other periodicals. Editor of *A Peculiar Music: Poems for Young Readers* by Emily Brontë, 1971, *The Silent Playmate: A Collection of Doll Stories*, 1979, and the anthologies *A Footprint on the Air*, 1983, and *Messages*, 1985. **Essays:** *The Angel in the House*; *The Cloister and the Hearth*; "I Hid My Love"; *Peter Pan*; "R. Alcona to J. Brenzaida"; *The Wind in the Willows*.

LEWIS, Peter. Reader in English, University of Durham. Author of *John Gay: The Beggar's Opera*, 1976, *Orwell: The Road to 1984*, 1981, *John le Carré*, 1984, *Fielding's Burlesque Drama*, 1987, *Eric Ambler*, 1990, and *The National: A Dream Made Concrete*, 1990. Editor of *The Beggar's Opera* by Gay, 1973, *Poems '74* (anthology of Anglo-Welsh poetry), 1974, *Papers of the Radio Literature Conference 1977*, 1978, *Radio Drama*, 1981, and *John Gay and the Scriblerians* (with Nigel Wood), 1988. **Essays:** Basil Bunting; George Farquhar; John Gay; John le Carré; George Lillo; Sir John Vanbrugh; John Wilson; *Under Milk Wood*.

LINDSAY, Maurice. Consultant, Scottish Civic Trust, Glasgow; co-editor, *Scottish Review*. Author of more than 20 books of poetry, including *Collected Poems*, 1979, and *The Scottish Dog*, 1989; plays; travel and historical works; and critical studies, including *Robert Burns: The Man, His Work, The Legend*, 1954 (revised 1968, 1978), *The Burns Encyclopaedia*, 1959 (revised 1970, 1980), *History of Scottish Literature*, 1977, and *Francis George Scott and the Scottish Renaissance*, 1980; and an autobiography, *Thank You for Having Me*, 1983. **Essays:** John Armstrong; Joanna Baillie; James Beattie; Robert Burns; Thomas Campbell; John Davidson; Thomas De Quincey; William Dunbar; R.B. Cunninghame Graham; Neil M. Gunn; Sir David Lindsay; Norman MacCaig; Harold Monro; Sydney Goodsir Smith; Robert Louis Stevenson; *The Castle of Indolence*; *A Drunk Man Looks at the Thistle*; *English Bards and Scotch Reviewers*; *The Heart of Mid-Lothian*; *The Provost*.

LINK, Frederick M. Professor of English, University of Nebraska, Lincoln. Author of *Aphra Behn*, 1968, *English Drama 1660–1800: A Guide to Information Sources*, 1976, and *John O'Keeffe: A Bibliography*, 1983. Editor of *The Rover* by Behn, 1967, *Aureng-Zebe* by Dryden, 1971, and facsimile editions of *The Plays of Hannah Cowley*, 2 vols., 1979, and *The Plays of John O'Keeffe*, 4 vols., 1981. **Essays:** Aphra Behn; Henry Carey; Hannah Cowley.

LIVESAY, Dorothy. See her own entry. **Essay:** Isabella Valancy Crawford.

LOE, Thomas. Professor of English, State University of New York, Oswego. Author of articles on Katherine Anne Porter, Conrad, le Carré, Bellow, Dickens, Charlotte Brontë, Joyce, and Waugh in *Notes on Contemporary Literature*, *Conradiana*, *James Joyce Quarterly*, and other journals. **Essays:** "The Dead"; "Heart of Darkness."

LUCAS, John. Professor and Head of the Department of English and Drama, Loughborough University, Leicestershire; advisory editor, *Victorian Studies, Literature and History*, and *Journal of European Studies*. Author of *Tradition and Tolerance in 19th-Century Fiction*, 1966, *The Melancholy Man: A Study of Dickens*, 1970, *Arnold Bennett*, 1975, *Egilssaga: The Poems*, 1975, *The Literature of Change: Studies in the Nineteenth-Century Provincial Novel*, 1977, *The 1930's: Challenge to Orthodoxy*, 1978, *Romantic to Modern*, 1982, *Moderns and Contemporaries*, 1985, *Modern English Poetry from Hardy to Hughes*, 1986, and *England and Englishness*, 1990. Editor of *Literature and Politics in the Nineteenth Century*, 1971, and works by Crabbe, Austen, and Goldsmith. **Essays:** Philip James Bailey; Arnold Bennett; Walter Besant; Marie Corelli; Matthew Green; Ebenezer Jones; Charles Kingsley; William Hurrell Mallock; John Westland Marston; William Mason; V.S. Pritchett; John Wilmot, Earl of Rochester; John Whiting.

LYLE, A.W. Lecturer in English, University of Sheffield, Yorkshire. **Essays:** Alexander Barclay; William Browne; George Gascoigne; Joseph Hall; I.A. Richards; *Bartholomew Fair*; "Ode on Melancholy" (with Anne Katherine Monaghan); *The Shepheardes Calender*; *Volpone*.

LYON, John M. Lecturer in English, University of Bristol. Author of *The Merchant of Venice* (Harvester New Critical Introductions to Shakespeare), 1988, introductions to *The Light That Failed* by Kipling, 1988, and *Lady Chatterley's Lover* by Lawrence, 1990, and articles on Shakespeare, Jonson, Kipling, Conrad, and contemporary poetry. **Essays:** *Lady Chatterley's Lover*; *Romeo and Juliet*.

MACK, Douglas S. Lecturer in English, University of Stirling, Scotland; editor, *Bibliotheck*. Author of *James Hogg's Prose: An Annotated Listing*, 1985. Editor of works by Hogg. **Essay:** James Hogg.

MACKERNESS, E.D. Former Reader in English Literature, University of Sheffield, Yorkshire. Author of *The Heeded Voice: Studies in the Literary Status of the Anglican Sermon 1830–1900*, 1959, *A Social History of English Music*, 1964, and *Somewhere Further North: A History of Music in Sheffield*, 1974. Editor of *The Journals of George Sturt 1890–1927*, 1967, and *The Spirit of the Age* by William Hazlitt, 1969. **Essays:** Thomas Campion; John Hughes; *Areopagitica*; *Gorboduc*; *The Lives of the English Poets*; *Sir Thomas More*.

MacLAINE, Allan H. Professor of English, University of Rhode Island, Kingston. Author of *The Student's Comprehensive Guide to the Canterbury Tales*, 1964, *Robert Fergusson*, 1965, *Allan Ramsay*, 1985, and articles on Burns. **Essays:** Introduction: The Beginnings to 1558; Gavin Douglas; Robert Fergusson; Thomas Gray; "Holy Willie's Prayer"; *Ode on a Distant Prospect of Eton College*; "The Twa Corbies."

MACLEOD, Norman. Senior Lecturer in English Language, University of Edinburgh. Author of articles on literary and linguistic topics, and particularly the language of modern novelists. **Essays:** Kingsley Amis; *The Battle of Maldon*.

MacNIVEN, Ian S. Member of the Department of Humanities, State University of New York Maritime College, Fort Schuyler. Editor of *Literary Lifelines: The Richard Aldington–Lawrence Durrell Correspondence* (with Harry T. Moore), 1981, *The Modernists: Studies in a Literary Phenomenon* (with Lawrence B. Gamache), 1987, *The Durrell–Miller Letters 1935–1980*, 1988, and two "Lawrence Durrell Issues" of *Twentieth Century Literature* (with Carol Peirce), 1987. **Essay:** Lawrence Durrell.

MACRAE, Alasdair D.F. Lecturer in English Studies, University of Stirling, Scotland. Author of *Macbeth*, 1979, *The Waste Land*, 1980, *Shelley*, 1983, and articles on Seamus Heaney, Les Murray, and W.B. Yeats. **Essay:** Les Murray.

MacSHANE, Frank. Professor, School of the Arts, and Director of the Translation Center, Columbia University, New York. Author of *Many Golden Ages*, 1963, *The Life and Work of Ford Madox Ford*, 1965, *The Life of Raymond Chandler*, 1976, *The Life of John O'Hara*, 1980, and *Into Eternity: James Jones: The Life of an American Writer*, 1985. Editor of works by Chandler, Ford, O'Hara, and Jorge Luis

Borges; translator of several books by Miguel Serrano. **Essay:** Ford Madox Ford.

MAES-JELINEK, Hena. Professor of English and Commonwealth Literature, University of Liège, Belgium; general editor, with others, *Cross/Cultures: Readings in Post-Colonial Literatures in English* series. Author of *Criticism of Society in the English Novel Between the Wars*, 1970, *The Naked Design*, 1976, *Wilson Harris*, 1982, and *Heart of Darkness: A Critical Commentary*, 1982. Editor of *Commonwealth Literature and the Modern World*, 1975, *Multiple Worlds, Multiple Words* (with P. Michel and P. Michel-Michot), 1987, *A Shaping of Connections: Commonwealth Literature Then and Now* (with Kirsten Holst Petersen and Anna Rutherford), 1989, and *Crisis and Creativity in the New Literatures in English* (with Geoffrey Davis), 1990. **Essay:** Wilson Harris.

MALEK, James S. Professor of English and Dean of the College of Liberal Arts, University of Nevada, Las Vegas. Author of *The Arts Compared: An Aspect of Eighteenth-Century British Aesthetics*, 1974, and of articles in *Modern Philology*, *The Journal of Aesthetics and Art Criticism*, *Neuphilologische Mitteilungen*, *Texas Studies in Literature and Language*, and other periodicals. Editor of a facsimile edition of *The Plays of John Home*, 1980. **Essays:** Sir George Etherege; John Home; Arthur Murphy; *The Beaux' Stratagem*; *Douglas*; *She Stoops to Conquer*.

MARRS, Suzanne. Professor of English, Millsaps College, Jackson, Mississippi. Author of articles in *American Literature*, *Southern Review*, *Mississippi Quarterly*, and other journals. **Essay:** Thomas Chandler Haliburton.

McCALLUM, John. Senior Lecturer in Theatre Studies and director of the Australian Theatre Studies Centre, University of New South Wales, Kensington. Author of many articles on recent Australian drama. **Essay:** Ray Lawler.

McCORMACK, W.J. University teacher. Editor of *A Festschrift for Francis Stuart on His Seventieth Birthday*, 1972, *The Eustace Diamonds* by Trollope, 1983, and co-editor of *The Absentee* by Maria Edgeworth, 1988. **Essays:** Brendan Behan; Maria Edgeworth; Sheridan Le Fanu; Samuel Lover; Bram Stoker.

McCRACKEN, David. Professor of English, University of Washington, Seattle. Author of *Junius and Philip Francis*, 1979, *Wordsworth and the Lake District*, 1984, and articles on Wordsworth, Johnson, Godwin, Burke, and other writers. Editor of *Caleb Williams* by Godwin, 1970. **Essays:** William Beckford; Matthew Gregory Lewis.

McDIARMID, Matthew P. Reader in English, University of Aberdeen, Scotland; now retired. Author of *Robert Henryson*, 1981, *Not in My Own Land* (poems), 1984, and of numerous essays on Scots writers. Editor of works by John Barbour, Robert Fergusson, Hary, Sir David Lindsay, and James I. **Essays:** John Barbour; Hary; Sir Richard Holland.

McDOUGALL, Russell. Senior Lecturer in English, University of New England, Armidale, New South Wales. Editor of *Australian/Canadian Literatures in English: Comparative Perspectives*, 1987, *(Un)Common Ground: Essays in the New Literatures* (with Andrew Taylor), 1990, and *South of Capricornia 1924–1935: Stories by Xavier Herbert*, 1990. **Essay:** Randolph Stow.

McGLYNN, Paul D. Member of the Department of English, Eastern Michigan University, Ypsilanti. **Essay:** Henry Mackenzie.

McGOWAN, Ian. Lecturer in English Studies and Director of the Centre for Publishing Studies, University of Stirling, Scotland. Author of *Charles Dickens: Little Dorrit*, 1984, and *The Restoration and Eighteenth Century*, 1989. **Essays:** *Emma*; *Little Dorrit*; *Persuasion*; *A Sentimental Journey Through France and Italy*.

McKAY, F.M. Former Reader in English, Victoria University, Wellington, New Zealand; founding editor, *Poetry New Zealand* and *Journal of New Zealand Literature*. Author of *The Life of James K. Baxter*, 1990. Editor of *James K. Baxter as Critic*, 1978. **Essays:** Alistair Campbell; Eileen Duggan; C.K. Stead.

McLEISH, Kenneth. Author and translator; regular reviewer for the *Sunday Times*, London. Author of many books for adults and children, including *Shakespeare's People A-Z*, 1985, *The Penguin Companion to the Arts in the Twentieth Century*, 1985, and *The Good Reading Guide*, 2nd edition 1990. Translator of works by Catullus, Aeschylus, Sophocles, Aristophanes, Ibsen, Feydeau, Labiche, and Lope de Vega. **Essays:** *I, Claudius* and *Claudius the God*; *The Painter of Signs*; *Summer Lightning*; *Things Fall Apart*; *Tono-Bungay*.

McNAUGHTON, Howard. Reader in English, University of Canterbury, Christchurch, New Zealand. Author of *Bruce Mason*, 1976, *New Zealand Drama*, 1981, and the section on the novel in *The Oxford History of New Zealand Literature* (forthcoming). Editor of *Contemporary New Zealand Plays*, 1976, and *James K. Baxter: Collected Plays*, 1982. **Essays:** Introduction: 20th-Century Drama; Alan Ayckbourn; Enid Bagnold; Edward Bond; Caryl Churchill; Jane Mander; Bruce Mason; *The Road*; *The Second Mrs. Tanqueray*; *Titus Andronicus*.

McNICHOL, Stella. Lecturer in English, University of Lancaster. Author of *Virginia Woolf and the Poetry of Fiction*, 1990, and *The Early Twentieth-Century English Novel: A Modern Introduction*, 1991. Editor of *Mrs. Dalloway's Party: A Short Story Sequence*, 1973. **Essays:** Virginia Woolf; *The Forsyte Saga*; *The Golden Bowl*; *The Old Wives' Tale*; *To the Lighthouse*; *Women in Love*.

MEDCALF, Stephen. Reader in English, University of Sussex, Brighton. Author of *William Golding*, 1975, and articles on Chesterton, Wodehouse, and other writers. Editor of *The Vanity of Dogmatizing: The Three Versions* by Joseph Glanvill. **Essays:** M.R. James; Jerome K. Jerome; C.S. Lewis; J.R.R. Tolkien; Charles Williams.

MEGAW, Moira. Lecturer in English, University of Bristol. Author of "An Empson Bibliography," in *William Empson: The Man and His Work* edited by Roma Gill, 1974. **Essay:** *Julius Caesar*.

MELLOWN, Muriel. Professor of English, North Carolina Central University, Durham. Author of "Francis Jeffrey, Lord Byron, and *English Bards and Scotch Reviewers*," in *Studies in Scottish Literature*, 1981, the introduction to *British Literary Magazines 4: The Modern Age*, 1986, and "Lady Rhondda and the Changing Faces of British Feminism," in *Frontiers*, 1987. **Essays:** *Biographia Literaria*; *Childe Harold's*

Pilgrimage; *Don Juan*; "The Lady of Shalott"; *Testament of Youth*.

MILLER, Gayle H. Assistant Professor and Director of Freshman English, Western Carolina University, Cullowhee, North Carolina. **Essay:** *Revelations of Divine Love*.

MILLER, Timothy C. Assistant Professor of English, Millersville University, Pennsylvania. Author of articles on Milton in the *Explicator*, *Restoration*, and *American Notes and Queries*. **Essay:** *Paradise Lost*.

MINER, Earl. Townsend Martin Professor of English and Comparative Literature, Princeton University, New Jersey. Author of *Dryden's Poetry*, 1967, *An Introduction to Japanese Court Poetry*, 1968, *The Metaphysical Mode from Donne to Cowley*, 1969, *The Cavalier Mode from Jonson to Cotton*, 1971, *The Restoration Mode from Milton to Dryden*, 1974, *Literary Uses of Typology*, 1977, *Principles of Classical Japanese Literature*, 1985, and *The Princeton Companion to Classical Japanese Literature* (with others), 1985. Editor of *Restoration Dramatists*, 1966, *Seventeenth-Century Imagery*, 1971, *Dryden*, 1972, *Illustrious Evidence: Approaches to English Literature of the Early Seventeenth Century*, 1975, and *A History of Japanese Literature*, 2 vols., 1984–86; translator of *Japanese Linked Poetry*, 1978, and *The Monkey's Straw Raincoat and Other Poetry of the Basho School*, 1982. **Essays:** Samuel Butler (b. 1613); Charles Cotton; John Dryden.

MINER, Madonne M. Associate Professor of English, University of Wyoming, Laramie. Author of *Insatiable Appetites: Twentieth-Century American Women's Bestsellers*, 1984. **Essays:** *The Handmaid's Tale*; *Mrs. Warren's Profession*.

MIRZA, Gail. Freelance writer and translator; joint editor, *Journal of Humanistic and Interdisciplinary Studies*. Author of a work on Juan Ramón Jiménez, Tagore, and Yeats. **Essay** (with H.A. Mirza): Rabindranath Tagore.

MIRZA, H.A. Former teacher of literature and interdisciplinary studies. University of Connecticut, Storrs; joint editor, *Journal of Humanistic and Interdisciplinary Studies*. Author of articles on literature, philosophy, psychology, and East-West studies. **Essay** (with Gail Mirza): Rabindranath Tagore.

MITCHELL, Jerome. Professor of English, University of Georgia, Athens. Author of *Thomas Hoccleve: A Study in Early 15th-Century English Poetic*, 1968, *The Walter Scott Operas*, 1977, and *Scott, Chaucer, and Medieval Romance*, 1987. **Essay:** Thomas Hoccleve.

MITCHELL, Judith N. Associate Professor of English, Rhode Island College, Providence. Author of articles in *English Journal*, *Journal of Popular Culture*, and other periodicals. **Essays:** Kate O'Brien; *Anne of Green Gables*; *The Jungle Books*.

MONAGHAN, Anne Katherine. Member of the Department of English, University of Sheffield, Yorkshire. Founding editor, *Kingfisher* magazine. **Essays:** *An Elegy Written in a Country Churchyard*; "Ode on Melancholy" (with A.W. Lyle); *Silas Marner*.

MONSMAN, Gerald. Professor of English, University of Arizona, Tucson. Author of *Pater's Portraits: Mythic Pattern in the Fiction of Pater*, 1967, *Pater*, 1977, *Pater's Art of Autobiography*, 1980, and *Confessions of a Prosaic Dreamer: Lamb's Art of Autobiography*, 1984. **Essays:** *The Essays of Elia*; "Spelt from Sibyl's Leaves."

MOORE, Catherine E. Associate Professor of English, North Carolina State University, Raleigh. **Essay:** Anna Barbauld.

MORGAN, Gwendolyn. Assistant Professor of English, Montana State University, Bozeman. Author of "The Unsung Heroine: May Welland in Wharton's *The Age of Innocence*," in *Heroines of Popular Culture* edited by Pat Browne, 1986, "Chaucer's *Anelida and Arcite*: The Conclusion of the Complaint," in *Explicator*, Winter 1989, and "Christianity and Alienation: The Anglo-Saxon Elegies," in *In Geardagum*, 11, 1990. **Essays:** Caedmon's *Hymn*; *The Testament of Cresseid*; *Troilus and Criseyde*; *Wulf and Eadwacer*.

MORGAN, Margery. Emeritus Reader in English and Theatre Studies, University of Lancaster. Author of *A Drama of Political Man: A Study in the Plays of Harley Granville Barker*, 1961, *The Shavian Playground: An Exploration of the Art of G.B. Shaw*, 1972, *Shaw* (Writers and Their Works series), 2 vols., 1982, *August Strindberg*, 1985, and *York Handbook on Drama: Plays, Theatre and Performance*, 1987. Editor of *File on Shaw*, 1989, and *File on Wilde*, 1990. **Essays:** Harley Granville Barker; Laurence Housman; James Robinson Planché; Peter Shaffer; Bernard Shaw; David Storey; Alfred Sutro; *Man and Superman*; *Nostromo*; *Purgatory*.

MORPURGO, J.E. Emeritus Professor of American Literature, University of Leeds. Author of *The Birth of the USA* and *The Growth of the USA* (both with Russel B. Nye), 2 vols., 1955 (revised 1970 and 1976), *Barnes Wallis: A Biography*, 1972, *Allen Lane: King Penguin*, 1979, *Master of None: An Autobiography*, 1990, and books on Athens and Venice. Editor of *Charles Lamb and Elia*, 1949, *Autobiography* by Leigh Hunt, 1949, *Last Days of Shelley and Byron* by E.J. Trelawny, 1952, *Poems of John Keats*, 1953 (revised 1985), *The Spy* by James Fenimore Cooper, 1968, *Cobbett's America*, 1985, and an anthology on rugby football. **Essays:** Edmund Blunden; John Burgoyne; Charles Lamb; Hugh MacLennan; *The Autobiography of Leigh Hunt*.

MORRISON, Kristin. Professor of English, Boston College. Author of *Canters and Chronicles: The Use of Narrative in the Plays of Samuel Beckett and Harold Pinter*, 1983, and articles on William Trevor and Beckett. **Essays:** William Trevor; *The Birthday Party*; "Guests of the Nation."

MORRISSEY, L.J. Late member of the Department of English, University of Saskatchewan, Saskatoon. Author of *Gulliver's Travels*, 1978, *Fielding: A Reference Guide*, 1980, and of articles on English street theatre and the theatrical records of the London guilds. Editor of *The Plays of Fielding*, 1979. Died 1988. **Essay:** John Tatham.

MORTON, Richard. Professor of English, McMaster University, Hamilton, Ontario; associate editor, *Eighteenth-Century Fiction*. Author of *An Outline of the Works of Dylan Thomas*, 1970, *An Outline of the Works of W.B. Yeats*, 1971, *The Poetry of Anne Sexton: The Chronology of a Pilgrimage*, 1989, and numerous articles on medieval and Renaissance drama. Editor of John Gay's *Three*

Hours after Marriage (with William Peterson), 1961, and *The Poems of Sir Aston Cokayne*, 1977. **Essays:** Nathan Field; *A Chaste Maid in Cheapside*; *The Duchess of Malfi*; *The Fair Maid of the West*; *The Honest Whore*; *Hyde Park*; *A New Way to Pay Old Debts*; *'Tis Pity She's a Whore*; *A Woman Killed with Kindness*.

MUIR, Kenneth. Professor Emeritus of English Literature, University of Liverpool; editor, *Shakespeare Survey*, and vice-president, International Shakespeare Association. Author of many books, including *King Lear*, 1952, *Elizabethan Lyrics*, 1953, *John Milton*, 1955, *Shakespeare and the Tragic Pattern*, 1958, *Shakespeare the Collaborator*, 1960, *Sidney*, 1960, *Shakespeare's Sources*, 2 vols., 1961, *Life and Letters of Sir Thomas Wyatt*, 1963, *Introduction to Elizabethan Literature*, 1967, *The Comedy of Manners*, 1970, *Shakespeare's Tragic Sequence*, 1972, *The Singularity of Shakespeare*, 1977, *Shakespeare's Comic Sequence*, 1979, and *Negative Capability and the Art of the Dramatist*, 1987. Editor of several plays by and collections about Shakespeare, and of works by Wyatt and Middleton; translator of five plays by Racine and seven plays by Calderón. **Essays:** Introduction: The Romantic Period; William Blake; Andrew Marvell; Henry Howard, Earl of Surrey.

MUIRHEAD, John. Senior Lecturer in English, Massey University, Palmerston North, New Zealand. **Essay:** Roderick Finlayson.

MUNRO, John M. Director of Outreach Services, American University in Cairo, Egypt. Author of *English Poetry in Transition*, 1968, *Arthur Symons*, 1969, *Decadent Poetry in the 1890's*, 1970, *The Royal Aquarium: Failure of a Victorian Compromise*, 1971, *James Elroy Flecker*, 1976, *A Mutual Concern*, 1977, and other books. Editor of *Selected Poems of Theo. Marzials*, 1973, and *Arthur Symons: Selected Letters 1880–1935* (with Karl Beckson), 1989. **Essays:** Lord de Tabley; James Elroy Flecker; Anthony Hope; William Watson; *Kim*; "Kubla Khan"; "The Lake Isle of Innisfree"; *The Prisoner of Zenda*.

MURRAY, Barbara A. Lecturer in English, University of St. Andrews, Scotland. Author of *Thomas Hardy: Far from the Madding Crowd*, 1980, and articles on Shakespeare and Otway. **Essays:** *The Country-Wife*; *The Way of the World*.

MURRAY, Isobel. Senior Lecturer in English, University of Aberdeen, Scotland. Author of *Ten Modern Scottish Novels* (with Bob Tait), 1974. Editor of *The Picture of Dorian Gray*, 1974, *Complete Shorter Fiction*, 1979, *Writings*, 1989, and *The Soul of Man and Prison Writings*, 1990, all by Oscar Wilde, and *Beyond This Limit: Selected Shorter Fiction*, 1986, and *A Girl Must Live: Stories and Poems*, 1990, both by Naomi Mitchison. **Essays:** Oscar Wilde; *Salome*.

MYER, Michael Grosvenor. Freelance critic and feature writer. Theatre critic for the *Guardian*, book reviewer for the *Times*, and regular contributor to many other journals and books. **Essays:** Noël Coward; *Cider with Rosie*; *Hobson's Choice*; *Lays of Ancient Rome*.

MYER, Valerie Grosvenor. Freelance writer and lecturer. Author of *Margaret Drabble: Puritanism and Permissiveness*, 1974, *Jane Austen*, 1980, *Charlotte Brontë: Truculent Spirit*, 1988, *Culture Shock* (novel), 1988, *A Victorian Lady in Africa: The Story of Mary Kingsley*, 1989, and *Ten Great English Novelists*, 1990. Editor of *Laurence Sterne: Riddles and Mysteries*, 1984, and *Samuel Richardson: Passion and Prudence*, 1986. **Essays:** Margaret Drabble; Nancy Mitford; *The Browning Version*; *A Handful of Dust*; *The Mill on the Floss*; *Private Lives*; *Shirley*; *Vanity Fair*.

NADEL, I.B. Professor of English, University of British Columbia, Vancouver. Author of *Biography: Fiction, Fact and Form*, 1984, *Joyce and the Jews*, 1988, and articles on Victorian writing and Jewish fiction. Editor, with William E. Fredeman, *Victorian Novelists after 1885*, 1983, *Victorian Novelists Before 1885*, 1983, *Victorian Poets Before 1850*, 1984, and *Victorian Poets after 1850*, 1985 (all in Dictionary of Literary Biography). **Essay:** Harriet Martineau.

NEMAN, Beth S. Associate Professor of English, Wilmington College, Ohio. Author of *Teaching Students to Write*, 1980, *Writing Effectively*, 1983 (revised 1989), and articles on Defoe, Swift, and Crowne. **Essay:** "The Wedding."

NESBITT, Bruce. Freelance editor and speechwriter; former member of the Department of English, Simon Fraser University, Burnaby, British Columbia. Editor of *Earle Birney*, 1974. **Essays:** Archibald Lampman; Margaret Laurence; Dorothy Livesay; E.J. Pratt; F.R. Scott.

NEWMAN, Judie. Lecturer in English, University of Newcastle upon Tyne. Author of *Saul Bellow and History*, 1984, *John Updike*, 1988, and *Nadine Gordimer*, 1988. Co-editor of the British Association for American Studies pamphlets series. **Essays:** J.G. Farrell; Ruth Prawer Jhabvala; V.S. Naipaul; Paul Scott; *The Conservationist*; *Rebecca*; *Wide Sargasso Sea*.

NEWTON, K.M. Senior Lecturer in English, University of Dundee, Scotland. Author of *George Eliot: Romantic Humanist*, 1981, *In Defence of Literary Interpretation: Theory and Practice*, 1986, and *Interpreting the Text: A Critical Introduction to the Theory and Practice of Literary Interpretation*, 1990. Editor of *Twentieth-Century Literary Theory: A Reader*, 1988. **Essays:** *Daniel Deronda*; *Great Expectations*; *The Homecoming*; *Othello*.

NIENHUIS, Terry. Member of the Department of English, Western Carolina University, Cullowhee, North Carolina. **Essays:** Athol Fugard; Edward Moore; *Look Back in Anger*; *What the Butler Saw*.

NIGHTINGALE, Peggy. Senior Lecturer, Professional Development Centre, University of New South Wales. Author of *Improving Student Writing*, 1986, *Journey Through Darkness: The Writing of V.S. Naipaul*, 1987, and *Literacy by Degrees* (with others), 1988. Editor, *A Sense of Place in the New Literatures in English*, 1986. **Essay:** "A Valediction: Forbidding Mourning."

NIVEN, Alastair. Literature Director, Arts Council of Great Britain; editor, *Journal of Commonwealth Literature*. Author of *D.H. Lawrence: The Novels*, 1978, *The Yoke of Pity: A Study of the Fictional Writings of Mulk Raj Anand*, 1978, and *The Commonwealth of Universities* (with Hugh W. Springer), 1987. Editor of *The Commonwealth Writer Overseas*, 1976, *Under Another Sky: The Commonwealth Poetry Prize Anthology*, 1987, and *Truth Within Fiction: A Study of Raja Rao's The Serpent and the Rope*, 1989. **Essays:** Gabriel Okara; Raja Rao; Mordecai Richler.

NORDLAND, Brady. Freelance writer. **Essays:** S.T. Dobell; John Ruskin.

NORTON-SMITH, J. Late Reader in English Language and Literature, University of Dundee, Scotland; former editor of *Reading Medieval Studies* and general editor of Brill's Medieval and Renaissance Authors series. Author of *Six Poems and Six Drawings* (with Fritz Janschka), 1972, *Geoffrey Chaucer*, 1974, and *William Langland*, 1983. Editor of *Poems* by John Lydgate, 1966, *The Kingis Quair* by James I, 1971, and *The Quare of Jelusy*, 1975. Died 1988. **Essays:** James I, King of Scotland; John Lydgate.

NYE, Robert. Poet, novelist, and critic; poetry editor, the *Scotsman*, and poetry critic for the *Times*. Author of several books of poetry (most recently *A Collection of Poems 1955–1988*, 1989), six novels (including *Falstaff*, 1976, *Faust*, 1980, and *The Voyage of the Destiny*, 1982), short stories (*The Facts of Life and Other Fictions*, 1983), plays for stage and radio, and books for children. Editor of selections of poetry by Ralegh, Barnes, and Swinburne, and translator of *Beowulf*. **Essay:** Anna Kavan.

O'BRIEN, George. Associate Professor of English, Georgetown University, Washington, D.C. Author of *Brian Friel*, 1990. **Essays:** John Banim; Denis Devlin; Gerald Griffin; Patrick Kavanagh; Thomas Kinsella; Mary Lavin; John Montague; Flann O'Brien; Frank O'Connor; Sean O'Faolain; Liam O'Flaherty; Sydney Owenson; "Easter 1916"; "Lovers of the Lake"; *Uncle Silas*.

OLDSEY, Bernard. Freelance writer. Author of *The Art of William Golding* (with Stanley Weintraub), 1965, *The Spanish Season* (novel), 1970, *Hemingway's Hidden Craft*, 1979, and *Ernest Hemingway: The Papers of a Writer*, 1981. Editor of *British Novelists 1930–1959* (Dictionary of Literary Biography), 2 vols., 1983, and *Critical Essays on George Orwell*, 1986. **Essay:** William Golding.

OLIVER-MORDEN, B.C. Teacher and editor. **Essays:** William Collins; Oliver Goldsmith; Laurie Lee; James Macpherson; Mervyn Peake; William Bell Scott.

ORR, Leonard. Assistant Professor of English, Washington State University, Richland. Author of *Research in Critical Theory since 1965: A Classified Bibliography*, 1989, and *Problems and Poetics of the Nonaristotelian Novel*, 1990. Editor of *Yeats and Postmodernism*, 1990. **Essays:** J.G. Ballard; *Mrs. Dalloway*; *The Secret Agent*.

OSBERG, Richard H. Associate Professor of English, Santa Clara University, California. Author of *Sir Gawain and the Green Knight: A New Edition and Verse Translation*, 1990, and articles on medieval and Renaissance literature. **Essays:** *The Owl and the Nightingale*; *Pearl*.

O'TOOLE, Bridget. Teacher and freelance writer. Contributor to *Across a Roaring Hill* edited by Gerald Dawe and Edna Longley, 1985. **Essays:** Ebenezer Elliott; James Thomson (B.V.).

PAGE, Malcolm. Professor of English, Simon Fraser University, Burnaby, British Columbia. Author of *John Arden*, 1984, and *Richard II*, 1987. Editor of volumes in the Writers on File series on John Arden, Alan Ayckbourn, David Hare, John Osborne, Peter Shaffer, and Tom Stoppard. **Essays:** Colin MacInnes; John Osborne; Arnold Wesker; *Howards End*.

PAGE, Norman. Professor of Modern English Literature, University of Nottingham; general editor, Macmillan Modern Novelists and Macmillian Author Chronologies series. Author of *The Language of Jane Austen*, 1972, *Speech in the English Novel*, 1973 (revised 1987), *Thomas Hardy*, 1977, *E.M. Forster's Posthumous Fiction*, 1977, *A.E. Housman: A Critical Biography*, 1983, *A Dickens Companion*, 1984, *A Kipling Companion*, 1984, *A Conrad Companion*, 1986, *E.M. Forster*, 1987, *A Dickens Chronology*, 1988, *A Byron Chronology*, 1988, *Bleak House: A Novel of Connections*, 1990, *A Dr. Johnson Chronology*, 1990, and *Muriel Spark*, 1990. Editor of *Wilkie Collins: The Critical Heritage*, 1974, *Thomas Hardy: The Writer and His Background*, 1980, *D.H. Lawrence: Interviews and Recollections*, 2 vols., 1981, *Nabokov: The Critical Heritage*, 1982, *Tennyson: Interviews and Recollections*, 1983, *Henry James: Interviews and Recollections*, 1984, *William Golding Novels 1954–1967: A Casebook*, 1985, *Byron: Interviews and Recollections*, 1985, and *Dr. Johnson: Interviews and Recollections*, 1987. **Essays:** Muriel Spark; *Bleak House*; *David Copperfield*; *Mr. Perrin and Mr. Traill*; "Mountain Lion"; *The Old Curiosity Shop; The Return of the Native*; *Zuleika Dobson*.

PARKER, Andrew. Freelance writer. **Essay:** *Fair Stood the Wind for France*.

PATRIDES, C.A. Late Professor of English, University of Michigan, Ann Arbor. Author of *Milton and the Christian Tradition*, 1966, *The Grand Design of God: The Literary Form of the Christian View of History*, 1972, *The Language of Renaissance Poetry*, 1972, *Premises and Motifs in Renaissance Thought and Literature*, 1984, and *An Annotated Critical Bibliography of Milton*, 1987. Editor of *Milton's Lycidas: The Tradition and the Poem*, 1961 (revised 1963), *Milton's Epic Poetry: Essays on Paradise Lost and Paradise Regained*, 1967, *Approaches to Paradise Lost*, 1968, *The Cambridge Platonists*, 1969, *Approaches to Marvell*, 1978, *The Age of Milton* (with Raymond B. Waddington), 1980, *Approaches to Sir Thomas Browne*, 1982, *George Herbert: The Critical Heritage*, 1983, and works by Ralegh, Milton, Herbert, Browne, and Donne. Died 1986. **Essays:** Sir Thomas Browne; Sir Walter Ralegh.

PAUL, Jay S. Professor of English, Christopher Newport College, Newport News, Virginia. Author of poetry, fiction, essays, and reviews in periodicals. **Essay:** Dom Moraes.

PEARCY, Roy J. Professor of English, University of Oklahoma, Norman. Author of articles on Chaucer, Dunbar, and the Alliterative *Morte Arthure*. **Essays:** *Havelok*; *Lament for the Makaris*; *Morte Arthure* (Alliterative).

PEARSALL, Derek. Gurney Professor of English, Harvard University, Cambridge, Massachusetts; Honorary Professor of English, University of York. Author of *John Lydgate*, 1970, *Landscapes and Seasons of the Medieval World* (with Elizabeth Salter), 1973, *Old English and Middle English Poetry*, 1977, and *The Canterbury Tales: A Critical Study*, 1985. Editor of *The Floure and the Leafe*, 1962, *Piers Plowman: The C Text* by William Langland, 1978, *The Nun's Priest's Tale* (Variorum Chaucer), 1983, *Manuscripts and Readers in Fifteenth-Century England*, 1983, and *Manuscripts and Texts: Editorial Problems in Later Middle English*

Literature, 1987. **Essays:** Gawain Poet; John Gower; William Langland; Laȝamon.

PEBWORTH, Ted-Larry. William E. Stirton Professor in the Humanities and Professor of English, University of Michigan, Dearborn. Author of *Ben Jonson* (with Claude J. Summers), 1979. Editor (with Summers), of *The Eagle and the Dove: Reassessing Donne*, 1986, and *The Muses Common-weale: Poetry and Politics in the Seventeenth Century*, 1988. **Essay:** "The World."

PEDEN, William. Professor Emeritus of English, University of Missouri, Columbia; general editor, Twayne Critical History of the Modern Short Story series. Author of *Some Aspects of Jefferson Bibliography*, 1940, *Night in Funland and Other Stories*, 1968, *Short Fiction: Shape and Substance*, 1971, and *Twilight at Monticello* (novel), 1973. Editor or co-editor of *The American Short Story: Continuity and Change*, 1964 (revised 1975), *New Writing from South Carolina*, 1971, and works by Jefferson, John Adams, John Quincy Adams, and Hubert Crackanthorpe. **Essay:** William Sansom.

PEIRCE, Carol. Professor of English and Communications Design, University of Baltimore; associate editor, *Deus Loci: The Lawrence Durrell Journal*. Author of essays in *Poe and Our Times* edited by Benjamin Fisher IV, 1986, *Critical Essays on Lawrence Durrell* edited by Alan Warren Friedman, 1987, *Into the Labyrinth: Essays on the Art of Lawrence Durrell* edited by Frank Kersnowski, 1989, and *On Miracle Ground: Essays on the Fiction of Lawrence Durrell* edited by Michael H. Begnal, 1990. Editor of two "Lawrence Durrell Issues" of *Twentieth Century Literature* (with Ian S. MacNiven), 1987. **Essay:** *The Alexandria Quartet*.

PERKINS, Barbara M. Managing editor, *Journal of Narrative Technique*, Eastern Michigan University, Ypsilanti. Author or editor of *The Practical Imagination* (with others), 1987, *Contemporary American Literature* (with George Perkins), 1988, and of articles in *Harper Handbook to Literature*, *American Literary Magazines: The Eighteenth and Nineteenth Centuries*, *The World Book Encyclopedia*, and other books and journals. **Essay:** Sir Thomas Malory.

PERKINS, George. Professor of English, Eastern Michigan University, Ypsilanti. Author or editor of *Writing Clear Prose*, 1964, *Varieties of Prose*, 1966, *The Theory of the American Novel*, 1970, *Realistic American Short Fiction*, 1972, *American Poetic Theory*, 1972, *The Harper Handbook to Literature* (with others), 1985, *The Practical Imagination* (with others), 1987, *Contemporary American Literature* (with Barbara M. Perkins), 1988, and *The American Tradition in Literature* (with others), 7th edition, 1990. **Essay:** Henry James.

PETERSEN, Kirsten Holst. Member of the Commonwealth Literature Division, University of Aarhus, Denmark; reviewer for *Danida*. Author of *A Critical View of John Pepper Clark's Selected Poems*, 1981. Editor of *Enigma of Values* (with Anna Rutherford), 1975, *Cowries and Kobos: The West African Oral Tale and Short Story* (with Rutherford), 1981, *A Double Colonization* (with Rutherford), 1985, *Displaced Persons* (with Rutherford), 1988, and *A Shaping of Connections: Commonwealth Literature Then and Now* (with Rutherford and Hena Maes-Jelinek), 1989. **Essays:** George Lamming; Alan Paton; Laurens van der Post.

PINION, F.B. Former Sub-Dean and Reader in English Studies, University of Sheffield, Yorkshire; former editor, *Thomas Hardy Society Review*. Author of *A Hardy Companion*, 1968 (revised 1976), *A Jane Austen Companion*, 1975 (revised 1976), *A Brontë Companion*, 1975, *A Commentary on the Poems of Thomas Hardy*, 1976, *Thomas Hardy: Art and Thought*, 1977, *A D.H. Lawrence Companion*, 1978, *A George Eliot Companion*, 1981, *A Wordsworth Companion*, 1984, *A Tennyson Companion*, 1984, *A T.S. Eliot Companion*, 1986, *A Wordsworth Chronology*, 1988, *A Thomas Hardy Dictionary*, 1989, *Hardy the Writer*, 1990, and *A Tennyson Chronology*, 1990. Editor of *Men and Women* by Robert Browning, 1963, *A Charles Lamb Selection*, 1965, *A George Eliot Miscellany*, 1982, and works by and collections about Hardy. **Essay:** Thomas Hardy.

PITMAN, Ruth. Lecturer in English, University of Bristol. Editor of *Edward Lear's Tennyson*, 1988. **Essay:** "The Owl and the Pussy-Cat."

PITTOCK, Joan. Senior Lecturer in English, University of Aberdeen, Scotland; founding editor, *British Journal for Eighteenth Century Studies*. Author of *The Ascendancy of Taste: The Achievement of Joseph and Thomas Warton*, 1973. Editor of *Odes on Various Subjects 1746* by Joseph Warton, 1977, *George Hardinge: Rowley and Chatterton in the Shades 1782*, 1979, and *Aberdeen and the Enlightenment* (with J.J. Carter), 1987. **Essays:** Joseph Warton; Thomas Warton.

PITTOCK, Murray G.H. Lecturer in English, University of Edinburgh. Author of articles in *Aberdeen and the Enlightenment* edited by Joan Pittock and J.J. Carter, 1987, and *Culture and Revolution*, 1990. Editor of *Selected Letters of Lionel Johnson*, 1988, and *New Jacobite Songs of the Forty-Five*, 1989. **Essay:** *Prometheus Unbound*.

POLLARD, Arthur. Emeritus Professor of English, University of Hull. Author of *Mrs. Gaskell, Novelist and Biographer*, 1965, *Trollope's Political Novels*, 1968, *Anthony Trollope*, 1978, and *The Landscape of the Brontës*, 1988. Editor of *The Letters of Mrs. Gaskell* (with J.A.V. Chapple), 1966, *The Victorians* (Sphere History of Literature in English), 1969 (revised 1987), *Crabbe: The Critical Heritage*, 1972, *Thackeray: Vanity Fair: A Casebook*, 1978, *Marvell Poems: A Casebook*, 1980, and *The Complete Poetical Works of George Crabbe* (with Norma Dalrymple-Champneys), 1988. **Essays:** Introduction: The Victorian Period; John Byrom; Richard Hooker; John Langhorne; James McAuley; R.S. Surtees; Judith Wright; Edward Young; *The Book of Common Prayer*; *Mary Barton*.

POLLARD, Phyllis M. Senior Lecturer in English, Humberside Polytechnic, Hull. Contributor on African literature to *The Year's Work in English Studies*. **Essays:** Wole Soyinka; *Cry, The Beloved Country*.

PRESS, John. British Council Officer; now retired. Author of four books of poetry (*Uncertainties*, 1965, *Guy Fawkes Night*, 1959, *Troika*, 1977, and *A Girl with Beehive Hair*, 1986), and several critical books, including *The Fire and the Fountain*, 1955, *The Chequer'd Shade*, 1958, *Rule and Energy*, 1963, *Louis MacNeice*, 1965, *A Map of Modern English Verse*, 1969, *The Lengthening Shadows*, 1971, *John Betjeman*, 1974, *Poets of World War I*, 1983, and *Poets of World War II*, 1984. **Essays:** John Betjeman; Robert Bridges; Donald Davie; W.H. Davies; David Gascoyne; Robert

Herrick; Louis MacNeice; William Plomer; Charles Hamilton Sorley; Bernard Spencer.

PRINCE, Gilbert P., Jr. Professor of English, California State University, Chico. **Essays:** *All for Love*; "A Beautiful Young Nymph Going to Bed."

PUNTER, David. Professor of English Studies, University of Stirling, Scotland. Author of *The Literature of Terror: A History of Gothic Fictions from 1765 to the Present Day*, 1980, *Romanticism and Ideology* (with David Aers and Jonathan Cook), 1981, *Blake, Hegel and Dialectic*, 1982, *The Hidden Script*, 1985, and *The Romantic Unconscious*, 1989. **Essays:** George Barker; Lord Dunsany; Salman Rushdie; *The Heart of the Matter*; *Melmoth the Wanderer*; "The Rime of the Ancient Mariner."

PYLE, Hilary. Freelance writer. Author of *James Stephens: His Work and an Account of His Life*, 1965, and *Jack B. Yeats: A Biography*, 1970 (revised 1989). **Essay:** James Stephens.

QUAYLE, Eric. Freelance writer. Author of *Ballantyne the Brave*, 1967, and a bibliography of Ballantyne, *The Ruin of Sir Walter Scott*, 1968, *The Collector's Book* series, 4 vols., 1971–73, *Old Cook Books: An Illustrated History*, 1978, *Early Children's Books: A Collector's Guide*, 1983, *The Magic Ointment and Other Cornish Legends*, 1986, and *The Shining Princess and Other Japanese Legends*, 1989. **Essay:** R.M. Ballantyne.

RAWLINSON, Gloria. Freelance writer. Author of two books of poetry, *The Island Where I Was Born*, 1955, and *Of Clouds and Pebbles*, 1963. Editor of *Houses by the Sea*, 1952, and *The Godwits Fly*, 1970, both by Robin Hyde. **Essay:** Robin Hyde.

RAWSON, C.J. Professor of English, Yale University, New Haven, Connecticut; general editor, Unwin Critical Library. Author of *Henry Fielding and the Augustan Ideal under Stress*, 1972, *Gulliver and the Gentle Reader*, 1973, and *Order from Confusion Sprung: Studies in Eighteenth-Century Literature from Swift to Cooper*, 1985. Editor of *Swift*, 1971, *Fielding: A Critical Anthology*, 1973, *Yeats and Anglo-Irish Literature*, 1973, *The Character of Swift's Satire: A Revised Focus*, 1983, *English Satire and the Satiric Tradition*, 1984, and *The Collected Poems of Thomas Parnell* (with F.P. Lock), 1989. **Essays:** Thomas Parnell; Jonathan Swift.

RAYMOND, Meredith B. Professor of English, University of Massachusetts, Amherst. Author of *Swinburne's Poetics: Theory and Practice*, 1971. Editor, with Mary Rose Sullivan, *The Letters of Elizabeth Barrett Browning to Mary Russell Mitford 1836–1854*, 3 vols., 1983, and *Women of Letters: Selected Letters of Elizabeth Barrett Browning and Mary Russell Mitford*, 1987. **Essay:** *The Ring and the Book*.

REDEKOP, E.H. Associate Professor of English, University of Western Ontario, London. Author of *Margaret Avison*, 1970. **Essay:** Margaret Avison.

REES, Joan. Emeritus Professor of English, University of Birmingham. Author of *Samuel Daniel*, 1964, *Fulke Greville: A Critical Biography*, 1971, *Jane Austen: Woman and Writer*, 1976, *Shakespeare and the Story*, 1978, and *The Poetry of D.G. Rossetti: Modes of Self-Expression*, 1981. Editor of *Selected Writings* by Greville, 1973. **Essays:** Samuel Daniel; Sir Fulke Greville.

REEVE, N.H. Lecturer in English, University College, Swansea; editor, *Swansea Review*. Author of *Rex Warner: An Introduction*, 1989, and articles on contemporary poetry in *English, Poetry Wales, The Many Review*, and other journals. **Essays:** Maurice Baring; Forrest Reid; *Green Mansions*.

REEVES, James. Author of more than 50 books, including poetry (*Collected Poems,* 1974), plays, and books for children; critical works include *The Critical Sense*, 1956, *Understanding Poetry*, 1965, *Commitment to Poetry*, 1969, *Inside Poetry* (with Martin Seymour-Smith), 1970, and *The Reputation and Writings of Alexander Pope*, 1976. Editor of many collections and anthologies, and of works by D. H. Lawrence, Donne, Clare, Hopkins, Robert Browning, Dickinson, Coleridge, Graves, Swift, Johnson, Marvell, Gray, Whitman, Hardy, and others; translator of fairy tales. Died 1978. **Essays:** Thomas Lovell Beddoes; George Darley; Sir Thomas Wyatt.

REID, Ian. Professor of Literature, Deakin University, Geelong, Victoria. Author of *The Short Story*, 1977, *Fiction and the Depression in Australia and New Zealand*, 1978, and *Narrative Exchanges*, 1991. **Essays:** John Mulgan; Frank Sargeson; Kylie Tennant; "At the Bay"; *The Prelude*.

REYNOLDS, William D. Professor of English, Hope College, Holland, Michigan. Author of articles on medieval literature, Dorothy L. Sayers, and J.R.R. Tolkien. **Essays:** Dorothy L. Sayers; *The Parliament of Fowls*; *The Seafarer*.

RIACH, Alan. Senior Tutor in English, University of Waikato, Hamilton, New Zealand. Author of *The Folding Map: Poems 1978–1988*, 1990, *Hugh MacDiarmid's Epic Poetry* (forthcoming), and essays and poetry in journals in Scotland and New Zealand. **Essay:** Edward Kamau Brathwaite.

RICHARDS, Robert F. Associate Professor of English, University of Denver, Colorado. Author of articles on esthetics, politics and literature, Ernest Hemingway, F. Scott Fitzgerald, Ralph Hodgson and Thomas Hornsby Ferril, and the introduction to Ferril's *Words for Denver and Other Poems*, 1966. Editor of *Concise Dictionary of American Literature*, 1969. **Essay:** A.A. Milne.

RICHETTI, John. Professor of English, University of Pennsylvania, Philadelphia. Author of *Popular Fiction Before Richardson: Narrative Patterns 1700–1739*, 1969, *Defoe's Narratives: Situations and Structures*, 1975, *Philosophical Writing: Locke, Berkeley, Hume*, 1983, and *Defoe*, 1987. **Essays:** Eliza Haywood; Delariviere Manley; Samuel Richardson.

RICHMOND, Hugh M. Professor of English, University of California, Berkeley. Author of *The School of Love: The Evolution of the Stuart Love Lyric*, 1964, *Shakespeare's Political Plays*, 1967, *Shakespeare's Sexual Comedy*, 1971, *Renaissance Landscapes: English Lyrics in a European Tradition*, 1973, *The Christian Revolutionary: John Milton*, 1974, *Puritans and Libertines: Anglo-French Literary Relations in the Reformation*, 1981, and *Shakespeare in Performance: Richard III*, 1990. Editor of *Henry IV* part 1, 1971, and *Henry VIII*, 1971, both by Shakespeare. **Essays:**

"Bermudas"; *Comus*; *Henry VIII*; *Love's Labour's Lost*; *The Two Noble Kinsman*.

RICHMOND, Velma Bourgeois. Professor of English, Holy Names College, Oakland, California. Author of *Laments for the Dead in Medieval Narrative*, 1966, *The Popularity of Middle English Romance*, 1975, and *Muriel Spark*, 1984. **Essay:** G.K. Chesterton.

RIPPY, Frances Mayhew. Professor of English, Ball State University, Muncie, Indiana. Author of *Matthew Prior*, 1986, and articles on Prior, Pope, and American literary documents. **Essays:** Christopher Fry; *Arden of Faversham*; *Pamela*; *The Rape of the Lock*.

ROARK, Chris. Assistant Professor of English, John Carroll University, University Heights, Ohio. Author of "Lavatch and Service in *All's Well That Ends Well*," in *Studies in English Literature*, Spring 1988, and a forthcoming study of Shakespeare's wise fools. **Essays:** *All's Well That Ends Well*; *The Anniversaries*.

ROBB, David S. Lecturer in English, University of Dundee, Scotland. Author of *George MacDonald*, 1987. **Essays:** *Old Mortality*; *The Private Memoirs and Confessions of a Justified Sinner*; "Tam o' Shanter."

ROBB, Paul H. Freelance writer. **Essays:** *Animal Farm*; *Brighton Rock*.

ROBERTSON, Karen. Visiting Assistant Professor of English, Vassar College, Poughkeepsie, New York. Author of articles on Renaissance revenge tragedy. Editor of the forthcoming books *Sexuality and Politics in Renaissance Drama* (with Carole Levin) and John Pikeryng's *Horestes* (with Jodi George). **Essays:** *Edward II*; *The Revenger's Tragedy*.

ROBERTSON, R.M. Assistant Professor of English, Rhode Island College, Providence. Author of articles on Ford Madox Ford and Willa Cather. **Essays:** Peter Abrahams; Cyprian Ekwensi.

ROGAL, Samuel J. Member of the Department of Humanities, Illinois Valley Community College, Oglesby. Author of articles on hymns and sacred music, John Wesley, George Eliot, Pope, and Milton, in the *Serif, Eighteenth-Century Life, Nineteenth-Century Fiction, Milton*, and other journals. **Essay:** Charles Wesley.

ROGERS, Katharine M. Research Professor of Literature, American University, Washington, D.C. Author of *The Troublesome Helpmate: A History of Misogyny in Literature*, 1966, *William Wycherley*, 1972, *Feminism in Eighteenth-Century England*, 1982, and *Frances Burney: The World of "Female Difficulties"*, 1990. Editor of *Before Their Time: Six Women Writers of the Eighteenth Century*, 1979, *Selected Poems* by Anne Finch, Countess of Winchilsea, 1979, and co-editor of *The Meridian Anthology of Early Women Writers*, 1987. **Essays:** *Villette*; *Wuthering Heights*.

ROGERS, Pat. Professor in Liberal Arts, University of South Florida, Tampa. Author of *Grub Street: Studies in a Subculture*, 1972 (revised as *Hacks and Dunces*, 1980), *The Augustan Vision*, 1974, *An Introduction to Pope*, 1975, *Henry Fielding: A Biography*, 1979, *Robinson Crusoe*, 1979, *Literature and Popular Culture in the Eighteenth Century*, 1985, and *Eighteenth-Century Encounters*, 1985. Editor of *A Tour Through Great Britain* by Defoe, 1971 (new abridgement 1989), *Defoe: The Critical Heritage*, 1972, *The Eighteenth Century*, 1978, *The Complete Poems of Jonathan Swift*, 1983, *The Oxford Illustrated History of English Literture*, 1987, and *The Enduring Legacy: Pope Tercentenary Essays* (with G.S. Rousseau), 1988. **Essays:** Introduction: Restoration and 18th-Century Prose and Poetry; Susanna Centlivre; Daniel Defoe; William Diaper; John Philips; Alexander Pope; *The Beggar's Opera*.

ROSE, Jean. Doctoral student in English, University of Exeter, Devon. **Essay:** Geoffrey Hill.

ROTHSTEIN, Eric. Edgar W. Lacy Professor of English, University of Wisconsin, Madison. Author of *George Farquhar*, 1967, *Restoration Tragedy: Form and the Process of Change*, 1967, *Systems of Order and Inquiry in Later Eighteenth-Century Fiction*, 1975, *Restoration and Eighteenth-Century Poetry 1660–1780*, 1981, and *The Designs of Carolean Comedy* (with F.M. Kavenik), 1988. Co-editor of *The Augustan Milieu*, 1970. **Essays:** Christopher Anstey; *The Relapse*; *The Seasons*; *Venice Preserved*.

ROWLAND, S.A. Freelance writer. **Essay:** Robertson Davies.

RUDDICK, William. Lecturer in English Literature, University of Manchester; editor, *Charles Lamb Bulletin*. Author of articles on Coleridge, Byron, Scott, and other writers of the Romantic period, and on modern poetry. **Essays:** E.F. Benson; Edward Fitzball; Leigh Hunt; Rose Macaulay; Mary Russell Mitford; Arthur Quiller-Couch; *The London Merchant*; "My First Acquaintance with Poets"; *Vathek*.

RUOFF, James E. Former Associate Professor of English, City College, City University of New York. Author of *Elizabethan Poetry and Prose*, 1972, *Crowell Handbook of Elizabethan and Stuart Literature*, 1973, and *Major Shakespearean Tragedies* (with Edward G. Quinn), 1973. **Essays:** John Bunyan; Thomas Churchyard; Abraham Cowley; Thomas Dekker; John Fletcher; Sir John Suckling; Thomas Tusser; George Whetstone.

RUTENBERG, Daniel. Member of the Department of Humanities, University of South Florida, Tampa. **Essays:** Austin Dobson; Barsetshire series.

RUTHERFORD, Anna. Head of the Commonwealth Literature Division, University of Aarhus, Denmark; editor, *Kunapipi*, and chair of the European branch of the Commonwealth Literature and Language Association. Editor of *Commonwealth Short Stories* (with Donald Hannah), 1971, *Commonwealth* (essays), 1972, *Enigma of Values* (with Kirsten Holst Petersen), 1975, *Cowries and Kobos: The West African Oral Tale and Short Story* (with Petersen), 1981, *A Double Colonization* (with Petersen), 1985, *Displaced Persons* (with Petersen), 1988, *Aboriginal Culture Today*, 1988, and *A Shaping of Connections: Commonwealth Literature Then and Now* (with Petersen and Hena Maes-Jelinek), 1989. **Essays:** Mulk Raj Anand; John A. Lee; Hal Porter; Katharine Susannah Prichard; Vic Reid; Henry Savery; Price Warung.

SADDLEMYER, Ann. Master of Massey College and Professor of English and Drama, University of Toronto.

Author of *The World of W.B. Yeats* (with Robin Skelton), 1965, *In Defence of Lady Gregory, Playwright*, 1966, *Synge and Modern Comedy*, 1968, and *Wisdom, Magic, Sensation: W.B. Yeats in the 1930's*, 1988. Editor of *The Plays of J.M. Synge*, 1968, *The Plays of Lady Gregory*, 1971, *Theatre Business: The Correspondence of the First Abbey Theatre Directors: William Butler Yeats, Lady Gregory, and J.M. Synge*, 1982, *The Collected Letters of J.M. Synge*, 2 vols., 1983–84, *Lady Gregory: Fifty Years After* (with Colin Smythe), 1987, and *Early Stages: Essays on the Theatre in Ontario 1800–1914*, 1990. **Essays:** Lady Gregory; J.M. Synge.

SADLER, Geoff. Acting Librarian, Local Studies, Chesterfield, Derbyshire. Author of 17 western novels as Jeff Sadler and Wes Calhoun, a trilogy of plantation novels (as Geoffrey Sadler), a 5-volume history of Chesterfield librarians 1879–1944, and *Journey to Freedom* (with Antoni Snarski), 1990. Editor of the reference book *Twentieth-Century Western Writers*, 2nd edition, 1991. **Essays:** Amos Tutuola; Derek Walcott.

SALGĀDO, Gāmini. Late Professor of English, University of Exeter, Devon. Author of *Eyewitnesses of Shakespeare: Firsthand Accounts of Performances 1590–1890*, 1975, *The Elizabethan Underworld*, 1977, and *The Everyman Companion to the Theatre* (with Peter Thomson), 1985. Editor of *Sons and Lovers: A Collection of Critical Essays*, 1969, *Cony Catchers and Bawdy Baskets*, 1973, works by D. H. Lawrence and Shakespeare, and collections of Jacobean and Restoration plays. **Essays:** Richard Brome; John Ford; Ben Jonson; Thomas Kyd; Philip Massinger; John Webster.

SAMBROOK, A.J. Professor of English, University of Southampton, Hampshire. Author of *A Poet Hidden: The Life of Richard Watson Dixon*, 1962, *Cobbett*, 1973, *English Pastoral Poetry*, 1983, and *The Eighteenth Century: The Intellectual and Cultural Context of English Literature 1700–1789*, 1986. Editor of *The Scribleriad*, 1967, *Pre-Raphaelitism: Patterns of Literary Criticism*, 1974, and *The Seasons*, 1981, and *The Castle of Indolence and Other Poems*, 1986, both by James Thomson. **Essays:** Robert Blair; William Cobbett; John Cunningham; Richard Watson Dixon; James Grainger; David Mallet; Lady Mary Wortley Montagu; Richard Savage; William Somerville; James Thomson; William Walsh; "The City of Dreadful Night"; *The Deserted Village*; *An Essay Concerning Human Understanding*; *The House of Life*.

SAMSON, Anne. Part-time member of the faculty, University of Warwick. Author of *The Knight's Tale* (Master Guide), 1987. **Essays:** F.R. Leavis; *The Book of Margery Kempe*; *Patience*.

SANDERSON, Stewart F. Honorary Harold Orton Fellow, University of Leeds, now retired; former chairman of the Literature Committee, Scottish Arts Council. Author of *Ernest Hemingway*, 1961 (revised 1970), and of many articles on British and comparative folklore and ethnology, and on modern literature. Editor of *The Secret Common-Wealth* by Robert Kirk, 1970, *The Linguistic Atlas of England* (with others), 1978, *Studies in Linguistic Geography*, 1985, and *Word Maps*, 1987. **Essays:** George Borrow; Ian Fleming; Eric Linklater; Compton Mackenzie; Brian Moore; Anthony Powell; *Dr. Jekyll and Mr. Hyde*; *Sinister Street*.

SANDOCK, Mollie. Assistant Professor of English, Valparaiso University, Indiana. Author of articles on 19th-century literature and on librarianship in *Modern Philology, Library Quarterly, Nineteenth-Century Literature*, and other periodicals. **Essay:** *The Turn of the Screw*.

SAUL, George Brandon. Late Professor of English, University of Connecticut, Storrs. Author of fiction (*The Wild Queen*, 1967), poetry (*Hound and Unicorn*, 1969, and *Adam Unregenerate*, 1977), and of critical works, including *Prolegomena to the Study of Yeats's Poems* (1957) and *Plays* (1958), *Traditional Irish Literature and Its Backgrounds*, 1970, *Withdrawn in Gold*, 1970, and *In Praise of the Half-Forgotten: Essays*, 1976. Also a composer. Died 1986. **Essay:** A.E. Coppard.

SCHRANK, Bernice. Professor of English, Memorial University of Newfoundland, St. John's. Author of articles on O'Casey in *Twentieth Century Literature, Irish University Review*, and *Literature in Wissenschaft und Unterricht*. **Essays:** Mavis Gallant; Olivia Manning; *Castle Rackrent*; *The Plough and the Stars*.

SCHWARZ, Daniel R. Professor of English, Cornell University, Ithaca, New York. Author of *Disraeli's Fiction*, 1979, *Conrad: Almayer's Folly to Under Western Eyes*, 1980, *Conrad: The Later Fiction*, 1982, *The Humanistic Heritage: Critical Theories of the English Novel from James to Hillis Miller*, 1986, *Reading Joyce's Ulysses*, 1986, *The Transformation of the English Novel 1890–1930*, 1989, and *The Case for a Humanist Poetics*, 1991. **Essays:** Joseph Conrad; Dylan Thomas; *The Rainbow*; "The Secret Sharer."

SCOBIE, Brian W.M. Lecturer in English, University of Leeds. Editor of *A Woman Killed with Kindness* by Thomas Heywood, 1985. **Essays:** Lewis Grassic Gibbon; Robert Henryson; *Krapp's Last Tape*; "The Love Song of J. Alfred Prufrock"; *Tristram Shandy*.

SCOUTEN, Arthur H. Former Professor of English, University of Pennsylvania, Philadelphia. Author of *The Revels History of Drama in English: Volume 5: 1660–1750* (with others), 1976, *The Poetry of Jonathan Swift* (with Robert C. Elliot), 1981, and articles on Swift, Defoe, and the London theatre. Editor of *Ten English Farces* (with Leo Hughes), 1948, *The London Stage 1660–1800*, part 3, 2 vols., 1961, and part 1, 1965, *A Bibliography of the Writings of Jonathan Swift* by Herman Teerink, 1963, and *The Country Gentleman* (with Robert D. Hume) by Buckingham and Sir Robert Howard, 1976. **Essays:** Introduction: Restoration and 18th-Century Drama; John Banks; Thomas D'Urfey; Sir Robert Howard; Nathaniel Lee.

SELL, Roger D. Professor of English Language and Literature, Åbo Akademi University, Finland. Author of *Trespassing Ghost: A Critical Study of Andrew Young*, 1978, and *The Reluctant Naturalism of Amelia*, 1983. Editor of *The Shorter Poems of Sir John Beaumont*, 1974. **Essay:** Sir John Beaumont.

SELLICK, Robert. Senior Lecturer in English, University of Adelaide, Australia. **Essay:** C.J. Dennis.

SEWELL, Brocard. Priest of the Carmelite Order (English Province); former Lecturer in English, Mount Carmel College, Niagara Falls, Ontario; former editor of *Aylesford Review*. Author of *Montague Summers: A Memoir*, 1966, *Footnote to the Nineties: A Memoir of John Gray and André Raffalovich*, 1968, *The Vatican Oracle*, 1970, *Olive Custance*,

1975, *Cecil Chesterton*, 1978, *Like Black Swans: Some People and Themes*, 1982, *In the Dorian Mode: A Life of John Gray*, 1983, *Cancel All Our Vows*, 1988, and *G.K.'s Weekly: An Appraisal*, 1990. Editor of *Arthur Machen: Essays by Various Hands*, 1960, *Baron Corvo: A Collection of Essays by Various Hands* (with Cecil Woolf), 1961 (as *New Quests for Corvo*, 1965), *Two Friends: John Gray and André Raffalovich*, 1963, *Theodore: Essays on T.F. Powys*, 1964, *Henry Williamson: The Man, The Writings*, 1980, and *Frances Horovitz, Poet*, 1987. **Essays:** Robert Stephen Hawker; Henry Williamson.

SHADY, Raymond C. Former member of the Department of English, St. John Fisher College, Rochester, New York. Editor of *Love's Mistress* by Thomas Heywood, 1977. **Essays:** John Day; John Marston.

SHATTOCK, Joanne. Lecturer in English, and bibliographer for the Victorian Studies Centre, University of Leicester. Author of articles on Victorian periodicals and reviewing, and the public readings of Dickens and Thackeray; contributor to *The Wellesley Index to Victorian Periodicals*. **Essays:** Dinah Maria Mulock; Margaret Oliphant; Joseph Henry Shorthouse.

SHATZKY, Joel. Member of the Department of English, State University of New York, Cortland. **Essay:** *Saint Joan*.

SHAW, Marion. Senior Lecturer in English, University of Hull. **Essay:** Winifred Holtby.

SHEIDLEY, William E. Professor of English, University of Connecticut, Storrs. Author of *Barnabe Googe*, 1981, and articles on Marlowe, Shakespeare, and mid-Tudor poetry in *Concerning Poetry*, *Studies in English Literature*, *Journal of English and Germanic Philology*, *Studies in Philology*, *Modern Language Quarterly*, and *Hamlet Studies*.**Essays:** Barnabe Googe; George Turbervile; Thomas, Lord Vaux.

SHIRE, Helena Mennie. Fellow of Robinson College, Cambridge; former Senior Research Fellow in the Arts, Carnegie Trust for the Universities of Scotland. Author of *Song, Dance and Poetry of the Court of Scotland under King James VI*, 1969, and *A Preface to Spenser*, 1978. Editor of *The Wrong Music: The Collected Poems of Olive Fraser*, 1989. **Essays:** Sir Robert Ayton; Alexander Montgomerie; Edmund Spenser.

SHIRLEY, Frances A. Professor of English, Wheaton College, Norton, Massachusetts. **Essays:** *The Devils*; *King John*; *The Lady's Not for Burning*; *Major Barbara*; *Saved*; *Strife*; *The Taming of the Shrew*; *Waiting for Godot*; *Wild Oats*.

SHRIMPTON, J.S. Assistant Master, Blundell's School, Tiverton, Devon. **Essay:** *Hard Times*.

SILKIN, Jon. Founding co-editor, *Stand* magazine, and co-founding editor, Northern House publishers, Newcastle upon Tyne. Author of more than 20 books of poetry (the most recent being *The Ship's Pasture*, 1986, and *Selected Poems*, 1988), and of *Out of Battle: The Poetry of the Great War*, 1972 (revised 1987). Editor of several anthologies of poetry, fiction, and prose, and of *Wilfred Owen: Poems*, 1985; translator of *Against Parting* by Nathan Zach. **Essays:** Herbert Read; Isaac Rosenberg.

SIMPSON, Peter. Former member of the Department of English, University of Canterbury, Christchurch, New Zealand. Author of *Ronald Hugh Morrieson*, 1982. Editor of *Look Back Harder: Critical Writings 1935–1984* by Allen Curnow, 1987. **Essays:** Mary Ursula Bethell; A. R. D. Fairburn; William Pember Reeves.

SIVARAMAKRISHNA, M. Former Reader in English, Osmania University, Hyderabad; editor *Tenor* magazine. Author of many articles on English and American literature. **Essay:** Sarojini Naidu.

SKRETKOWICZ, Victor. Lecturer in English, University of Dundee, Scotland. Editor of *The Countess of Pembroke's Arcadia (The New Arcadia)* by Sir Philip Sidney, 1987. **Essay:** *Arcadia*.

SMALL, Ian C. Senior Lecturer in English, University of Birmingham. **Essay:** Lionel Johnson.

SMITH, A.J.M. See his own entry. **Essay:** Ralph Gustafson.

SMITH, Angela. Director, Centre of Commonwealth Studies, University of Stirling, Scotland. Author of *East African Writing in English*, 1989. **Essays:** Introduction: Commonwealth Literature; Ngugi wa Thiong'o; "The Daughters of the Late Colonel"; "Water Them Geraniums."

SMITH, David J. Senior Lecturer in English, University of Adelaide, Australia. **Essay:** Jack Lindsay.

SMITH, Elton E. Professor of Victorian Literature, University of South Florida, Tampa. Author of *The Two Voices: A Tennyson Study*, 1964, *William Godwin* (with Esther Marian Greenwell Smith), 1965, *Louis MacNeice*, 1970, *The Angry Young Men of the Thirties*, 1975, and *Charles Reade*, 1976. **Essays:** C. Day Lewis; Charles Reade.

SMITH, Paul J. British Council representative, most recently based in Berlin and Burma. **Essays:** Preface to *Lyrical Ballads*; *The Rape of Lucrece*.

SMITH, Rowland. Professor of English and Dean of Arts and Social Sciences, Dalhousie University, Halifax, Nova Scotia. Author of *Lyric and Polemic: The Literary Personality of Roy Campbell*, 1972. Editor of *Exile and Tradition: Studies in African and Caribbean Literature*, 1976, and *Critical Essays on Nadine Gordimer*, 1990. **Essays:** Nadine Gordimer; Edward Upward.

SMITH, Stan. Professor and Head of English, University of Dundee, Scotland; director, with R.J.C. Watt, Auden Concordance Project; general editor, with Raman Selden, Longman Critical Reader series. Author of *A Sadly Contracted Hero: The Comic Self in Post-War American Fiction*, 1981, *Inviolable Voice: History and Twentieth-Century Poetry*, 1982, *W.H. Auden*, 1985, *Edward Thomas*, 1986, *W.B. Yeats: A Critical Introduction*, 1990, and *The Origins of Modernism*, 1991. **Essays:** Introduction: 20th-Century Poetry; W.H. Auden; W.E. Henley; Ted Hughes (with James C.Q. Stewart); Alfred Noyes; Edward Thomas; *The Age of Anxiety*; "On the Move"; "The Second Coming"; "Ulysses" (by Robert Graves).

SOLOMON, Harry M. Hollifield Professor of English Literature, Auburn University, Alabama. Author of *Sir*

Richard Blackmore, 1980, and a forthcoming biography of Robert Dodsley. Editor of a facsimile edition of two plays by Dodsley. **Essays:** Robert Dodsley; William King; Katherine Philips; *The Rival Queens*; *Trivia*.

SORFLEET, John Robert. Associate Professor of English and Canadian Studies, Concordia University, Montreal; editor, *Journal of Canadian Fiction*. Editor of *Raymond Knister: Poems, Stories, and Essays* (with David Arnason and John G. Moss), 1975, *The Poems of Bliss Carman*, 1976, *L.M. Montgomery: An Assessment*, 1976, *Canadian Children's Drama and Theatre*, 1978, and *The Manor House of De Villerai* by Leprohon, 1985. **Essays:** Raymond Knister; *Sunshine Sketches of a Little Town*; *Treasure Island*.

SPEAR, Hilda D. Senior Lecturer in English, University of Dundee, Scotland. Author of *Remembering, We Forget* (on the poetry of World War I), 1978, books on works by Emily Brontë, Conrad, Forster, Fowles, Golding, Hardy, and Lawrence, and the biographical and bibliographical sections of *The Pelican Guide to English Literature 5*, 1957. Editor of *The English Poems of Calverley*, 1974, *Poems and Selected Letters* by Charles Hamilton Sorley, 1978, and *Sword and Pen: Poems of 1915 from Dundee and Tayside* (with Bruce Pandrich), 1989. **Essays:** Richard Harris Barham; Charles Stuart Calverley; Winthrop Mackworth Praed; Sam Selvon; *A Passage to India*.

SPECTOR, Robert D. Coordinator of Humanities, Long Island University, Brooklyn, New York. Author of *English Literary Periodicals and the Climate of Opinion During the Seven Years' War*, 1966, *Tobias George Smollett*, 1968 (revised 1989), *Pär Lagerkvist*, 1973, *Arthur Murphy*, 1979, *Tobias Smollett: A Reference Guide*, 1980, *The English Gothic*, 1984, and *Backgrounds to Restoration and Eighteenth-Century English Literature*, 1989. Editor of *Essays on the 18th-Century Novel*, 1964. **Essays:** *Pride and Prejudice*; *Roderick Random*.

SPENCER, Christopher. Professor of English, University of North Carolina, Greensboro. Author of *Nahum Tate*, 1972. Editor of *Davenant's Macbeth from the Yale Manuscript*, 1961, and *Five Restoration Adaptations of Shakespeare*, 1965. **Essay:** Nahum Tate.

SPENCER, Jane. Lecturer in English Literature, University of Exeter, Devon. Author of *The Rise of the Woman Novelist: From Aphra Behn to Jane Austen*, 1986. **Essays:** *The Female Quixote*; *The Rover*.

SPETTIGUE, Douglas O. Professor of English, Queen's University, Kingston, Ontario. Author of *Frederick Philip Grove*, 1969, *FPG: The European Years*, 1973, and articles on Ernest Buckler, Robertson Davies, Grove, and other writers. Translator (with Christine Helmers and A.W. Riley) of *Fanny Essler* by Grove, 2 vols., 1984. **Essay:** Frederick Philip Grove.

SPIVACK, Charlotte. Professor of English, University of Massachusetts, Amherst. Author of *Early English Drama*, 1966, *George Chapman*, 1967, *The Comedy of Evil on Shakespeare's Stage*, 1978, *Ursula K. Le Guin*, 1984, and *Merlin's Daughters: Contemporary Women Fantasy Writers*, 1987. **Essays:** E. Nesbit; *Bussy D'Ambois*; *The Lord of the Rings*; *The Malcontent*.

SPRECHMAN, Ellen Lew. Instructor in English, Florida International University, North Miami. Has given conference papers on Hardy. **Essay:** *Tess of the d'Urbervilles*.

STAGG, Louis Charles. Professor of English and director of Graduate Studies, Memphis State University, Tennessee. Author or co-author of *Index to Poe's Critical Vocabulary*, 1966, *The Figurative Language of Shakespeare's Chief 17th-Century Contemporaries: An Index*, revised 3rd edition, 1982, *The Figurative Language of the Tragedies of Shakespeare's Chief 16th-Century Contemporaries: An Index*, 1984, and numerous articles and reviews. **Essay:** Nicholas Rowe.

STALLWORTHY, Jon. Reader in English Literature, Oxford University. Author of several books of verse (the most recent collection being *The Anzac Sonata*, 1986), *Between the Lines: Yeats's Poetry in the Making*, 1963, *Vision and Revision in Yeats's Last Poems*, 1969, *Wilfred Owen*, 1974, and *Poets of the First World War*, 1974. Editor of *The Complete Poems and Fragments of Wilfred Owen*, 1983, *The Oxford Book of War Poetry*, 1984, other anthologies of poetry, and a casebook on Yeats; translator of *The Twelve and Other Poems* by Alexander Blok, 1970, *Selected Poems* by Boris Pasternak, 1983, and an anthology of Polish poetry. **Essay:** Wilfred Owen.

STANNARD, Martin. Lecturer in English, University of Leicester. Author of *Evelyn Waugh: The Early Years 1903–1939*, 1986. Editor of *Waugh: The Critical Heritage*, 1984. **Essays:** Michael Arlen; David Garnett; William Gerhardie; Christopher Isherwood; Evelyn Waugh.

STEDMAN, Jane W. Professor Emeritus of English, Roosevelt University, Chicago. Author of articles and reviews in anthologies of Victorian studies, scholarly journals, and *Opera News*. Editor of *Gilbert Before Sullivan: Six Comic Plays*, 1967. **Essays:** W.S. Gilbert; Tom Taylor; *Iolanthe*; *Lalla Rookh*.

STERNLICHT, Sanford. Adjunct Professor of English, Syracuse University, New York. Author of *John Webster's Imagery and the Webster Canon*, 1972, *John Masefield*, 1977, *C. S. Forester*, 1981, *Padraic Colum*, 1985, *John Galsworthy*, 1987, *R. F. Delderfield*, 1988, and *Stevie Smith*, 1990. Editor of *Selected Short Stories*, 1985, *Selected Plays*, 1986, and *Selected Poems*, 1989, all by Padraic Colum. **Essays:** C.S. Forester; John Galsworthy.

STEVENSON, Christine. Assistant editor, *Medical History*, Wellcome Institute for the History of Medicine, London. Author of articles on the history of Scandinavian art and design, and on the history of lunatic asylums. **Essay:** *The Deptford Trilogy*.

STEVENSON, Kay Gilliland. Lecturer in Literature, University of Essex, Colchester. **Essays:** William Alabaster; Francis Quarles; Robert Southwell; Joshua Sylvester; Sir Henry Wotton; *The Book of the Duchess*; *The House of Fame*; *Utopia*.

STEWART, James C.Q. Tutorial assistant for the Department of English, University of Dundee, Scotland; research assistant for the Auden Concordance Project. Author of articles on Auden and Marvell, and of poetry in various anthologies. **Essay:** Ted Hughes (with Stan Smith).

STOKES, Edward. Former Reader in English, University of Tasmania, Hobart. Author of *The Novels of Henry Green*, 1959, *James Hanley*, 1964, and *Hawthorne's Influence on Dickens and George Eliot*, 1985. **Essay:** James Hanley.

STOREY, Graham. University Reader (retired) and Fellow Emeritus of Trinity Hall, Cambridge. Author of *A Preface to Hopkins*, 1981, and *Bleak House: A Critical Study*, 1987. Editor of *The Journals and Papers of Gerard Manley Hopkins*, 2 vols., 1959, *Letters of Charles Dickens* (Pilgrim Edition, with Madeline House and Kathleen Tillotson), vols. 1–3, 5–6, 1965–88, *Hopkins: Selections*, 1967, and *Revolutionary Prose of the English Civil War* (with Howard Erskine-Hill), 1983. **Essay:** Gerard Manley Hopkins.

STOTT, Rebecca. Lecturer in English, University of York. **Essay:** *Dracula*.

STOUCK, David. Professor of English, Simon Fraser University, Burnaby, British Columbia. Author of *Willa Cather's Imagination*, 1975, *Major Canadian Authors*, 1984, and *The Wardells and Vosburghs: Records of a Loyalist Family*, 1986. **Essays:** Sinclair Ross; Ethel Wilson.

STOVEL, Bruce. Associate Professor of English, University of Alberta, Edmonton. **Essays:** *Clarissa*; *Humphry Clinker*; *Joseph Andrews*; *Mansfield Park*; *A Modest Proposal*.

STROUP, Thomas B. Professor Emeritus, University of Kentucky, Lexington. Author of a book on composition, and of *Microcosmos: The Shape of the Elizabethan Play*, 1965, and *Religious Rite and Ceremony in Milton's Poetry*, 1968. Editor or joint editor of *Humanistic Scholarship in the South*, 1948, *South Atlantic Studies for Sturgis E. Leavitt*, 1953, *The Works of Nathaniel Lee*, 2 vols., 1954–55, *The Selected Poems of George Daniel of Beswick*, 1959, *The Cestus: A Mask*, 1962, *The University and the American Future*, 1965, and *The Humanities and the Understanding of Reality*, 1966. **Essay:** Thomas Otway.

STURROCK, June. Associate Professor of English, Simon Fraser University, Burnaby, British Columbia; editor, *Journal of Distance Education*. Author of articles on Wordsworth, Charlotte Yonge, Samuel Richardson, Stanley Middleton, and other writers, and on distance education. **Essays:** "A Defence of Poetry"; *Goblin Market*; *Tracts for the Times*.

SUMMERS, Claude J. William E. Stirton Professor in the Humanities and Professor of English Literature, University of Michigan, Dearborn. Author of *Christopher Marlowe and the Politics of Power*, 1973, *Ben Jonson* (with Ted-Larry Pebworth), 1979, *Christopher Isherwood*, 1980, *E.M. Forster*, 1983, and *Gay Fictions: Wilde to Stonewall*, 1990. Editor (with Pebworth) of *The Eagle and the Dove: Reassessing Donne*, 1986, and *The Muses Common-weale: Poetry and Politics in the Seventeenth Century*, 1988. **Essays:** *The Berlin Stories*; "The Shield of Achilles."

SUMMERS, David A. Assistant Professor of English, Seattle Pacific University. Has given conference papers on Malory, Spenser, Shakespeare, T.S. Eliot, and Tolkien. **Essay:** *Richard II*.

SUMMERS, Joseph H. Roswell S. Burrows Professor Emeritus of English, University of Rochester, Rochester, New York. Author of *George Herbert: Religion and Art*, 1954, *The Muse's Method: An Introduction to Paradise Lost*, 1962, *The Heirs of Donne and Jonson*, 1970, and *Dreams of Love and Power*, 1984. Editor of *Selected Poems* by Andrew Marvell, 1961, *The Lyric and Dramatic Milton*, 1965, and *Selected Poetry* by George Herbert, 1967. **Essays:** George Herbert; Henry King.

SUTHERLAND, John. Professor of English, California Institute of Technology, Pasadena. Author of *Thackeray at Work*, 1974, *Victorian Novelists and Publishers*, 1976, *Fiction and the Fiction Industry*, 1978, *Bestsellers: Popular Fiction of the 1970's*, 1980, *Offensive Literature: Decensorship in Britain*, 1982, *The Longman Companion to Victorian Fiction*, 1988 (as *The Stanford Companion to Victorian Fiction*, 1989), and *Mrs. Humphry Ward: Eminent Victorian, Pre-eminent Edwardian*, 1990. Editor of works by Thackerary, Trollope, and Jack London. **Essay:** William Makepeace Thackeray.

SWEETSER, Wesley D. Professor Emeritus of English, State University of New York, Oswego. Author of *Arthur Machen*, 1964, *A Bibliography of Machen* (with Adrian Goldstone), 1965, and *Ralph Hodgson: A Bibliography*, 1974 (revised 1980). **Essays:** Marcus Clarke; Alfred Domett; Ralph Hodgson; Arthur Machen; George Meredith; *Erewhon*; *For the Term of His Nature Life*; "Ode on a Grecian Urn"; *A Shropshire Lad*; *Such Is Life*.

TASCH, Peter A. Professor of English, Temple University, Philadelphia; editor, *Scriblerian*. Author of *The Dramatic Cobbler: The Life and Works of Isaac Bickerstaff*, 1971. Editor of *Fables by the Late Mr. Gay*, 1970, and facsimile editions of plays by Bickerstaff and George Colman the Younger. **Essays:** Isaac Bickerstaff; Charles Dibdin; David Garrick; Hugh Kelly.

TAYLOR, Donald S. Member of the Department of English, University of Oregon, Eugene. Author of *Thomas Chatterton's Art: Experiments in Imagined History*, 1978, and *R.G. Collingwood: A Bibliography*, 1988. Editor of *The Complete Works of Thomas Chatterton*, 2 vols., 1971. **Essay:** Thomas Chatterton.

TAYLOR, Myron. Late Associate Professor of English, State University of New York, Albany. Author of articles on Shakespeare in *Christian Scholar*, *Studies in English*, and *Shakespeare Quarterly*. Died 1989. **Essay:** John Milton.

THOMAS, Ned. Senior Lecturer in English, University College of Wales, Aberystwyth; founding editor, *Planet* magazine. Author of *George Orwell*, 1965, *The Welsh Extremist: Essays on Modern Welsh Literature and Society*, 1971, and *Derek Walcott: Poet of the Islands*, 1980. **Essay:** Jean Rhys.

THOMPSON, Ann. Reader in English, University of Liverpool. Author of *Shakespeare's Chaucer*, 1978, *Shakespeare: Meaning and Metaphor* (with John O. Thompson), 1978, and *The Critics' Debate*, 1988. Editor of *William Shakespeare: The Taming of the Shrew*, 1984, and *Teaching Women: Feminism and English Studies* (with Helen Wilcox), 1989. **Essays:** *Cymbeline*; *The Tempest*; *The Two Gentlemen of Verona*.

THOMSON, Peter. Professor of Drama, University of Exeter, Devon. Author of *Brecht* (with Jan Needle), 1981, *Shakespeare's Theatre*, 1983, and *The Everyman Companion* *to the Theatre* (with Gāmini Salgādo), 1985. Editor of *Julius Caesar* by Shakespeare, 1970, *Essays on Nineteenth-Century British Theatre* (with Kenneth Richards), 1971, *The Eighteenth-Century English Stage* (with Richards), 1973, *Lord Byron's Family* by Malcolm Elwin, 1975, and *Plays* by Dion Boucicault, 1984. **Essays:** H.J. Byron; George Colman the Younger; Pierce Egan; James Sheridan Knowles; Stephen Leacock; William Thomas Moncrieff; Thomas Morton; John O'Keeffe; Joe Orton; Arthur Wing Pinero; John Poole; *The Admirable Crichton*; *Hindle Wakes*.

THORNBURG, Mary K. Patterson. Freelance writer. Author of *The Monster in the Mirror: Gender and the Sentimental/Gothic Myth in Frankenstein*, 1987. **Essays:** *Frankenstein*; "To a Skylark."

THORNTON, Ralph R. Former Associate Professor of English, La Salle College, Philadelphia. Editor of *The Wive's Excuse*, 1973, and *The Maid's Last Prayer*, 1978, both by Thomas Southerne. **Essay:** Thomas Southerne.

THWAITE, Ann. Freelance writer. Author of 20 books for children and of three biographies, *Waiting for the Party: The Life of Frances Hodgson Burnett*, 1974, *Edmund Gosse: A Literary Landscape*, 1984, and *A.A. Milne: His Life*, 1989. Editor of the *Allsorts* series for children, 1969–75, and *My Oxford*, 1977. **Essays:** Frances Hodgson Burnett; Edmund Gosse; *Winnie-the-Pooh* and *The House at Pooh Corner*.

THWAITE, Anthony. Freelance writer; editorial director, André Deutsch publishers, London. Author of several books of poetry (*Collected Poems*, 1988), travel books, a history book for children, and critical works, including *Essays on Contemporary English Poetry*, 1957 (revised as *Contemporary English Poetry: An Introduction*, 1959), *Poetry Today*, 1973 (revised 1985), *Twentieth-Century English Poetry*, 1978, and *Six Centuries of Verse*, 1984. Editor of *Larkin at Sixty*, 1982, *Collected Poems* by Philip Larkin, 1988, and several anthologies of poetry. **Essays:** A.E. Housman; Stevie Smith; Arthur Symons.

TIBBLE, Anne. Freelance writer. Author of *African Literature*, 1964, *The Story of English Literature*, 1970, *The God Spigo* (novel), 1976, two volumes of autobiography, and books on Helen Keller, Gertrude Bell, Gordon, and John Clare. Editor of works by Clare. Died 1980. **Essays:** John Clare; Christopher Okigbo; Okot p'Bitek.

TIGER, Virginia. Professor of English, Rutgers University, Newark, New Jersey. Author of *William Golding: The Dark Fields of Discovery*, 1974, and *Everywoman*, 1976. Editor of *Critical Essays on Doris Lessing* (with Claire Sprague), 1986. **Essays:** *The Golden Notebook*; *Lord of the Flies*.

TOMLIN, E.W.F. Freelance writer, broadcaster, and lecturer. Author of *The Approach to Metaphysics*, 1947, *The Western Philosophers*, 1950, *The Eastern Philosophers*, 1952, *Simone Weil*, 1954, *Living and Knowing*, 1955, *Wyndham Lewis*, 1955, *R.G. Collingwood*, 1956, *Tokyo Essays*, 1967, *T.S. Eliot: A Friendship*, 1988, and books on Turkey and Japan. Editor of *Wyndham Lewis: An Anthology of His Prose*, 1969, *Dickens: A Centenary Volume*, 1970, and *Arnold Toynbee: A Selection from His Works*, 1979. Died 1988. **Essays:** Ronald Duncan; Wyndham Lewis.

TRACY, Clarence. Visiting Professor of English, University of Toronto. Author of *The Artificial Bastard: The Life of Richard Savage*, 1953, and *A Portrait of Richard Graves*, 1987. Editor of *Poetical Works of Richard Savage*, 1962, *The Spiritual Quixote* by Richard Graves, 1968, *Browning's Mind and Art: Essays*, 1968, *Johnson's Life of Savage*, 1971, and *The Rape Observed* by Pope, 1974. **Essay:** Richard Graves.

TRAINER, James. Professor of German, University of Stirling, Scotland. Editor of *The Old English Baron* by Clara Reeve, 1967. **Essay:** Clara Reeve.

TRAVERSI, Derek A. Emeritus Professor of English Literature, Swarthmore College, Pennsylvania. Author of *An Approach to Shakespeare*, 1938 (revised 1968), *Shakespeare: The Last Phase*, 1954, *Shakespeare: From Richard II to Henry V*, 1957, *Shakespeare: The Roman Plays*, 1963, *T. S. Eliot: The Longer Poems*, 1976, *The Literary Imagination: Studies in Dante, Chaucer, and Shakespeare*, 1982, *The Canterbury Tales: A Reading*, 1983, and *Chaucer: The Earlier Poetry*, 1987. **Essays:** Introduction: Renaissance Drama; Geoffrey Chaucer; T.S. Eliot; William Shakespeare; *The Faerie Queene*; *Four Quartets*; *Richard III*; *The Waste Land*.

TRUSSLER, Simon. Senior Lecturer in Drama, Goldsmiths' College, University of London; editor, *New Theatre Quarterly*, Cambridge. Author of several books on theatre and drama, including *Shakespearean Concepts*, 1989, and studies of Osborne, Wesker, Whiting, Pinter, and Edward Bond, and of articles on theatre bibliography and classification. Editor of two collections of 18th-century plays, *Royal Shakespeare Company Yearbook*, annually since 1978, *New Theatre Voices of the Seventies* (interviews), 1982, and the Swan Theatre Plays and Writers on File series. **Essays:** George Villiers, Duke of Buckingham; Richard Cumberland; N.F. Simpson; Sir Richard Steele.

TYDEMAN, William M. Professor of English, University College of North Wales, Bangor. Author of *The Theatre in the Middle Ages*, 1978, and *English Medieval Theatre 1400–1500*, 1986. Editor of *English Poetry 1400–1580*, 1970, *Plays by Tom Robertson*, 1982, *Four Tudor Comedies*, 1984, and *Marlowe: A Guide Through the Critical Maze*, 1989. **Essays:** Clifford Bax; Gordon Bottomley; Harold Brighouse; Clemence Dane; John Drinkwater; St. John Ervine; St. John Hankin; Stephen Hawes; Stanley Houghton; N.C. Hunter; W.W. Jacobs; Stephen Phillips; John Rastell.

UPCHURCH, David A. Member of the Department of English, Indiana University East, Richmond. **Essay:** *The Picture of Dorian Gray*.

VARHUS, Sara B. Associate Professor of English and Associate Dean, State University of New York, Oswego; editor, *Forum for Honors*. Author of "Lively Examples: Gilbert Burnet's Use of Biography," in *Restoration*, Spring 1987, and a forthcoming article on *The Rambler*. **Essays:** Margaret Cavendish; *A Dictionary of the English Language*; *The History of the World*; *The Life of Samuel Johnson*; *The Rambler* and *The Idler*.

VENTURO, David F. Assistant Professor of English, Clark University, Worcester, Massachusetts. Author of *Johnson the Poet* (forthcoming), and articles on Johnson in *Studies in Philology*, Winter 1988, and in *The Age of Johnson* edited by Paul J. Korshin, 1990. **Essays:** *Gulliver's Travels*; *Rasselas*.

VIGUERS, Susan T. Associate Professor, University of the Arts, Philadelphia. Author of *With Child: One Couple's Journey to Their Adopted Children*, 1986, and articles on Peele, Jonson, and other writers. **Essays:** *The Alchemist*; *King Lear*; *The Knight of the Burning Pestle*.

WADDINGTON, Raymond B. Professor of English, University of California, Davis; editor, Garland Studies in the Renaissance; member of the editorial board, *Sixteenth Century Journal*. Author of *The Mind's Empire: Myth and Form in George Chapman's Narrative Poems*, 1974, and of articles on Shakespeare, Chapman, Milton, and other writers. Editor, *The Rhetoric of Renaissance Poetry from Wyatt to Milton* (with Thomas O. Sloan), 1974, and *The Age of Milton* (with C.A. Patrides), 1980. **Essays:** George Chapman; *Paradise Regained*.

WALL, Stephen. Fellow of Keble College, Oxford; co-editor, *Essays in Criticism*. Author of *Trollope and Character*, 1988 (as *Trollope: Living with Character*, 1989). Editor of *Charles Dickens: A Critical Anthology*, 1970. **Essay:** Anthony Trollope.

WALLACH, Mark I. Partner, Calfee Halter and Griswold, Cleveland, Ohio. Author of *Christopher Morley* (with Jon Bracker), 1976, articles on Morley in *Markham Review* and *Dictionary of Literary Biography*, and articles in *Case Western Reserve Law Review* and other periodicals. **Essay:** C.P. Snow.

WALSH, George. Publisher and freelance writer. **Essay:** Manmohan Ghose.

WALSH, Marcus. Lecturer in English, University of Birmingham. Author of articles on Swift, Bentley, Smart, and on issues in the history of editorial and interpretative theory. Editor of *Selected Poems of John Gay*, 1979, and with Karina Williamson, of *Complete Poetical Works of Christopher Smart*, from 1980, and of *Selected Poems* by Smart, 1990. **Essays:** James Boswell; John Dyer; Samuel Johnson; Christopher Smart; Isaac Watts.

WALSH, William. Emeritus Professor of Commonwealth Literature, University of Leeds. Author of *The Use of Imagination: Educational Thought and the Literary Mind*, 1959, *A Human Idiom: Literature and Humanity*, 1964, *Coleridge: The Work and the Relevance*, 1967, *A Manifold Voice: Studies in Commonwealth Literature*, 1970, *R.K. Narayan*, 1971, *Commonwealth Literature*, 1973, *V.S. Naipaul*, 1973, *D.J. Enright: Poet of Humanism*, 1974, *Patrick White's Fiction*, 1977, *F.R. Leavis*, 1980, *Introduction to Keats*, 1981, *R.K. Narayan: A Critical Appreciation*, 1982, and *Indian Literature in English*, 1990. Editor of *Readings in Commonwealth Literature*, 1973. **Essays:** Earle Birney; John Keats; A.M. Klein; Anne Wilkinson.

WALTON, Priscilla L. Assistant Professor of English, University of Lethbridge, Alberta. Author of articles on Henry James and Alice Walker in *Scripta Mediterranea*, *Ariel*, and *North Dakota Quarterly*. **Essay:** Palliser series.

WARNER, Alan. Professor Emeritus, University of Ulster, Coleraine, County Londonderry. Author of *A Short Guide to English Style*, 1961, *Clay Is the Word: Patrick Kavanagh 1904–1967*, 1973, *William Allingham*, 1975, *A Guide to Anglo-Irish Literature*, 1981, and *On Foot in Ulster*, 1983. Editor of *The Selected John Hewitt*, 1981. **Essays:** William Allingham; William Carleton; Mark Rutherford; Somerville and Ross.

WASHINGTON, Peter. Freelance writer. Author of *Fraud: Literary Theory and the End of English*, 1990. **Essay:** *The Spoils of Poynton*.

WATSON, J.R. Professor of English, University of Durham. Author of *Picturesque Landscape and English Romantic Poetry*, 1970, *A Leicester Calendar*, 1976, *Wordsworth's Vital Soul: The Sacred and Profane in Wordsworth's Poetry*, 1982, *English Poetry of the Romantic Period 1789–1830*, 1985, and *The Poetry of Gerard Manley Hopkins*, 1987. Editor of *Victorian Poetry* (with N.P. Messenger), 1974, *Browning: Men and Women: A Casebook*, 1974, *Everyman Book of Victorian Verse*, 1982, and *Companion to Hymns and Psalms* (with others), 1988. **Essay:** William Wordsworth.

WATT, R.J.C. Lecturer in English and Dean of Students in the Faculty of Arts and Social Sciences, University of Dundee, Scotland; director, with Stan Smith, Auden Concordance Project. Author of an introductory study of Hopkins and of articles on modern poetry, textual problems in Shakespeare, and literary computing. Editor of a forthcoming edition of Hopkins. **Essays:** "The Whitsun Weddings"; "The Wreck of the Deutschland."

WATTS, Harold H. Professor Emeritus of English, Purdue University, West Lafayette, Indiana. Author of *The Modern Reader's Guide to the Bible*, 1949, *Ezra Pound and the Cantos*, 1952, *Hound and Quarry*, 1953, *The Modern Reader's Guide to Religions*, 1964, and *Aldous Huxley*, 1969. **Essays:** L.P. Hartley; Arthur Koestler; P.H. Newby; "Tradition and the Individual Talent."

WEALES, Gerald. Emeritus Professor of English, University of Pennsylvania, Philadelphia; drama critic for the *Reporter* and *Commonweal*. Author of *Religion in Modern English Drama*, 1961, *American Drama since World War II*, 1962, *A Play and Its Parts*, 1964, *Tennessee Williams*, 1965, *The Jumping-Off Place: American Drama in the 1960's*, 1969, *Clifford Odets*, 1971 (revised 1985), and *Canned Goods as Caviar: American Film Comedy in the 1930's*, 1985. Editor of several collections of plays and essays and of *The Complete Plays of William Wycherley*, 1966. **Essay:** William Wycherley.

WELCH, Robert. Professor of English, University of Ulster, Coleraine, County Londonderry. Author of *A Guide to Animal Farm*, 1978, *Anglo-Irish Poetry 1800–1900*, 1978, *Irish Poetry from Moore to Yeats*, 1980, and *A History of Verse Translation from the Irish*, 1988. Editor of *The Way Back: George Moore's The Untilled Field and The Lake*, 1982, and *Literature and the Art of Creation*, 1988. **Essays:** Sir Samuel Ferguson; James Clarence Mangan.

WHEELER, Thomas. Professor of English, University of Tennessee, Knoxville. Author of *Paradise Lost and the Modern Reader*, 1974, of annotated bibliographies of *Macbeth* and *The Merchant of Venice*, and of articles on Bacon, Milton, Machiavelli, and Sir Thomas More. **Essays:** John Aubrey; Joseph Beaumont; Sidney Godolphin; *The Merchant of Venice*.

WHITWORTH, Charles W. Lecturer in English, and Associate Fellow of the Shakespeare Institute, University of Birmingham; U.K. editor, *Cahiers Elisabéthains*. Author of articles in *The Spenser Encyclopedia* and in journals. Editor of *Three Sixteenth-Century Comedies*, 1984, and *Prose Fiction of Shakespeare's Time*, in *Shakespeariana*, 1989. **Essays:** *The Comedy of Errors*; *Gammer Gurton's Needle*; *The Old Wives Tale*; *Pericles*; *Ralph Roister Doister*.

WILLIAMS, John Stuart. Former Head of the Department of Communications, South Glamorgan Institute of Higher Education, Cardiff. Author of four books of poetry, including *Dic Penderyn and Other Poems*, 1970, and *Banna Strand*, 1974. Editor of three anthologies of poetry. **Essay:** Alun Lewis.

WILLY, Margaret. Lecturer for the British Council, and at the City Literary Institute, and Morley College, London. Author of two books of poetry (*The Invisible Sun*, 1946, and *Every Star a Tongue*, 1951), and several critical books, including studies of Chaucer, Traherne, Fielding, Browning, Crashaw, Vaughan, Emily Brontë, and English diarists. Editor of two anthologies and of plays by Goldsmith. **Essays:** H. E. Bates; Robert Browning; Walter de la Mare; John Donne; Pamela Hansford Johnson; W. Somerset Maugham; Charles Morgan; Elizabeth Taylor; Thomas Traherne; Henry Vaughan.

WINNIFRITH, T.J. Freelance writer; former Senior Lecturer in English, University of Warwick. Author of *The Brontës and Their Background: Romance and Reality*, 1973 (revised 1988), *The Brontës*, 1977, *Brontë Facts and Brontë Problems* (with Edward Chitham), 1983, *A New Life of Charlotte Brontë*, 1987, and *Charlotte and Emily Brontë: Literary Lives*, 1989. Editor of *The Poems of Branwell Brontë*, 1983, *The Poems of Charlotte Brontë*, 1984, and *The Philosophy of Leisure* (with others), 1989. **Essays:** Elizabeth Gaskell; Olive Schreiner; Mrs. Humphry Ward.

WOHLGELERNTER, Maurice. Professor of English, Baruch College, City University of New York. Author of *Israel Zangwill: A Study*, 1964, and *Frank O'Connor: An Introduction*, 1977. Editor of *History, Philosophy, and Spiritual Democracy: Essays in Honor of Joseph Leon Blau*, 1980, and *The Great Hatred* by Maurice Samuel, 1988. **Essay:** Israel Zangwill.

WOLFE, Peter. Professor of English, University of Missouri, St. Louis. Author of *The Disciplined Heart: Iris Murdoch and Her Novels*, 1966, *Mary Renault*, 1969, *Rebecca West: Artist and Thinker*, 1971, *Graham Greene the Entertainer*, 1972, *John Fowles: Magus and Moralist*, 1976 (revised 1979), *Dreamers Who Live Their Dreams: The World of Ross Macdonald*, 1977, *Jean Rhys*, 1980, *Beams Falling: The Art of Dashiell Hammett*, 1980, *Laden Choirs: The Fiction of Patrick White*, 1983, *Something More than Night: The Case of Raymond Chandler*, 1985, *Corridors of Deceit: The World of John le Carré*, 1987, and *Yukio Mishima*, 1989. Editor of *Essays in Graham Greene*, 1987, and *Critical Essays on Patrick White*, 1990. **Essay:** Rebecca West.

WOOD, Michael. Professor of English, University of Exeter, Devon. Author of *Stendhal*, 1971, *America in the Movies*, 1975 (2nd edition 1989), and *García Márquez: One Hundred Years of Solitude*, 1990. **Essay:** William Empson.

WOODCOCK, George. Free-lance writer, lecturer, and editor. Author of poetry (*Collected Poems*, 1983), plays, travel books, biographies, and autobiography (*Letter to the Past*, 1983), and works on history and politics; critical works include *William Godwin*, 1946, *The Incomparable Aphra*, 1948, *The Paradox of Oscar Wilde*, 1949, *The Crystal Spirit* (on Orwell), 1966, *Hugh MacLennan*, 1969, *Odysseus Ever Returning*: *Canadian Writers and Writing*, 1970, *Mordecai Richler*, 1970, *Dawn and the Darkest Hour* (on Aldous Huxley), 1972, *Herbert Read*, 1972, *Thomas Merton*, 1978, *The World of Canadian Writing*, 1980, *Orwell's Message*, 1984, and *Northern Spring*, 1987. Editor of anthologies and of works by Charles Lamb, Malcolm Lowry, Wyndham Lewis, Margaret Laurence, Hardy, Meredith, and others. **Essays:** Introduction: 20th-Century Fiction; Morley Callaghan; Bliss Carman; Cyril Connolly; William Hazlitt; W.H. Hudson; Aldous Huxley; Irving Layton; Malcolm Lowry; Charles Mair; Alice Munro; R.K. Narayan; George Orwell; P.K. Page; Al Purdy; Charles G.D. Roberts; Duncan Campbell Scott; A.J.M. Smith; Raymond Souster; Ned Ward; *Brave New World*; *Caleb Williams*; *News from Nowhere*; *Nineteen Eighty-Four*; *Rural Rides*; *A Tale of Two Cities*.

WOODRING, Carl. Woodberry Professor of Literature Emeritus, Columbia University, New York. Author of *Victorian Samplers*, 1952, *Politics in the Poetry of Coleridge*, 1961, *Wordsworth*, 1965, *Virginia Woolf*, 1966, *Politics in English Romantic Poetry*, 1970, and *Nature into Art: Cultural Transformations in Nineteenth-Century Britain*, 1989. Editor of *Prose of the Romantic Period*, 1961. **Essays:** "Christabel"; "The Eve of St. Agnes"; *The Importance of Being Earnest*; "Intimations of Immortality from Recollections of Early Childhood"; "Ode to the West Wind"; *On Liberty*; *The Way of All Flesh*.

WORTH, George J. Professor of English, University of Kansas, Lawrence. Author of *James Hannay: His Life and Works*, 1964, *William Harrison Ainsworth*, 1972, *Dickensian Melodrama*, 1978, *Thomas Hughes*, 1984, and *Great Expectations: An Annotated Bibliography*, 1986. **Essay:** William Harrison Ainsworth.

YORK, Lorraine M. Assistant Professor of English, McMaster University, Hamilton, Ontario. Author of *The Other Side of Dailiness: Photography in the Works of Alice Munro, Timothy Findley, Michael Ondaatje, and Margaret Laurence*, 1988, and articles on Canadian writers, photography, and postmodernism. **Essays:** Margaret Atwood; L.M. Montgomery; James Reaney.

YOUNG, Alan. Honorary Lecturer in English, University of Manchester. Author of *Dada and After: Extremist Modernism and English Literature*, 1981, and *A Bibliography of Seven Writers of the English Literary Left* (with Alan Munton), 1981. Editor of *Essays and Opinions 1921–1931*, 1974, and *Literature in Society: Essays and Opinions 2, 1931–1978*, 1978, both by Edgell Rickword, and *The Collected Poems of Christopher Caudwell*, 1986. **Essay:** Edgell Rickword.

YOUNG, Kenneth. Former literary and political adviser, Beaverbrook Newspapers. Author of *John Dryden*, 1954, *A.J. Balfour*, 1963, *Churchill and Beaverbrook*, 1966, *Compton Mackenzie*, 1968, *The Greek Passion*, 1969, *Stanley Baldwin*, 1976, *A Neighbourhood of Writers*, 1980, and other biographies and works on political and social history. Editor of *The Diaries of Sir Robert Bruce Lockhart*, 1980. Died 1985.

Essays: Thomas Babington Macaulay; T.F. Powys; Hugh Walpole.

ZUNDER, William. Lecturer in English, University of Hull. Author of *The Poetry of John Donne*, 1982, *Jacobean Poetry and Prose*, 1988, and an article in *Elizabethan Marlowe*, 1990. **Essay:** "Batter my heart."